The Qur'ān

Comparative Islamic Studies

Series Editor: Brannon Wheeler, US Naval Academy

This series, like its companion journal of the same title, publishes work that integrates Islamic studies into the contemporary study of religion, thus providing an opportunity for expert scholars of Islam to demonstrate the more general significance of their research both to comparatavists and to specialists working in other areas. Attention to Islamic materials from outside the central Arabic lands is of special interest, as are comparisons which stress the diversity of Islam as it interacts with changing human conditions.

Published:

Notes from the Fortune-Telling Parrot
Islam and the Struggle for Religious Pluralism in Pakistan
David Pinault

Earth, Empire and Sacred Text
Muslims and Christians as Trustees of Creation
David L. Johnston

Ibn Arabi and the Contemporary West
Beshara and the Ibn Arabi Society
Isobel Jeffery-Street

Prolegomena to a History of Islamic Manichaeism
John C. Reeves

Orientalists, Islamists and the Global Public Sphere
A Genealogy of the Modern Essentialist Image of Islam
Dietrich Jung

Prophecy and Power
Muhammad and the Qur'an in the Light of Comparison
Marilyn Robinson Waldman
Edited by Bruce B. Lawrence, with Lindsay Jones and Robert M. Baum

East by Mid-East
Studies in Cultural, Historical and Strategic Connectivities
Edited by Brannon Wheeler and Anchi Hoh

The Qur'ān

A NEW ANNOTATED TRANSLATION

A. J. Droge

equinox

SHEFFIELD UK BRISTOL CT

Published by Equinox Publishing Ltd.

UK: Unit S3, Kelham House, 3 Lancaster Street, Sheffied S3 8AF

USA: ISD, 70 Enterprise Drive, Bristol, CT 06010

www.equinoxpub.com

First published 2013

Reprinted with corrections April 2014

British Library Cataloguing-in-Publication Data

A catalogue record for this book is available from the British Library.

ISBN 978-1-84553-944-3 (hardback)
ISBN 978-1-84553-945-0 (paperback)

Library of Congress Cataloging-in-Publication Data

Koran. English. 2013.
The Qur'ān : a new annotated translation / translation and annotations by A.J. Droge.
p. cm. -- (Comparative Islamic studies)
Includes bibliographical references and index.
ISBN 978-1-84553-944-3 (hb) -- ISBN 978-1-84553-945-0 (pb)
I. Droge, Arthur J., 1953- II. Title.
BP109.D76 2013
297.1'22521--dc23

2012045139

Typeset and edited by Queenston Publishing, Hamilton, Ontario, Canada

Printed by Lightning Source, Inc., La Vergne, TN and Lighting Source UK Ltd., Milton Keynes, UK.

FOR JONATHAN Z. SMITH

AND THE ONE WHO KNOWS

καὶ πῦρ ἀπλήστῳ τύφετ᾽ ἐνὶ κραδίῃ

Contents

Preface

This annotated translation of the Qur'ān is designed for students of religion by a fellow student of religion. It endeavors to provide in one volume a resource comparable to what is available for most other ancient religious texts, including the Jewish and Christian Bibles. While there is certainly no shortage of English translations of the Qur'ān currently on the market, there has been a longstanding need for an edition of the text suitable for use in an academic setting. I speak from the experience of twenty-five years of teaching university students in North America. There simply is no Qur'ān for the classroom.

One might have expected that by now someone would have undertaken such a project, but I finally grew impatient and decided to do it myself. In designing this edition I have drawn on my experience of teaching about the Qur'ān, but I have also had to resist the temptation of idiosyncrasy. So I have attempted to steer a course between the Scylla of 'traditionalist' and Charybdis of 'revisionist' approaches to the Qur'ān. (Readers of the following Introduction will soon discover where my sympathies lie.) The choice of a middle course, I realize, risks inviting the wrath of both monsters, but my calculation has been to try to make this edition as useful as possible for as wide an academic audience as possible. Utility, not conviction, has been my watchword.

In keeping with this utilitarian goal my translation aims not at elegance but strives for as literal a rendering of the Arabic as English will allow. In this way, it is hoped, readers will gain access to the Qur'ān's distinctive idiom – its 'voice,' as it were – in a rendition that seeks to remain close to the way it was originally expressed. As is well known, however, we do not as yet (and alas may never) possess a critical edition of the Arabic text of the Qur'ān. The text translated here is known as the 'Egyptian standard' or 'Cairo edition,' first published in 1924 CE/1342 AH by a committee of Muslim scholars. Though not a critical edition, it has achieved a kind of *de facto* canonical status in both the religious *and* secular academic worlds. My use of the Cairo edition therefore is simply a matter of convenience.

The annotations accompanying the translation are not intended to be a commentary, but seek to provide further information on some of the technicalities of the text and to explicate the meaning of obscure passages. They also contain ample references to parallel passages both within the Qur'ān itself, as well as comparatively among the 'scriptures' of Judaism and Christianity, and sometimes beyond. The annotations draw heavily on a range of scholarship to which the Guide to Further Reading records my debt.

Readers should feel free to skip the Introduction, if they wish, and proceed directly to the text. Before doing so I would only recommend perusing the short final section of the Introduction ('About this edition') and glancing at the Glossary of Key Names, Terms, and Abbreviations. Readers will find a comprehensive Index at the back, as well as a Guide to Further Reading, Timeline, Map, and Synopsis following the Introduction.

Acknowledgments

My interest in the Qur'ān began some three decades ago and quite by accident. While a student at Chicago I was smuggled incognito into Professor Jonathan Z. Smith's lectures on 'The Bible in Western Civilization.' There we read 'the books' – *ta biblia* – of Jews, Christians, and Muslims comparatively, as well as in light of comparable materials from the civilizations of the ancient Mediterranean and Near East. That was my first glimpse of the excitement and potential such a comparative agenda held for reconfiguring the traditionally segregated studies of Judaism, Christianity, and Islam. I have since taught my own versions of that course at Chicago, San Diego, and now Toronto, but have never escaped its formative influence. For all that I owe him, the dedication betokens only a fraction of my gratitude and admiration.

This book could not have appeared without the support of many people. I must thank my publisher Janet Joyce for her wisdom, creativity, and unfailing encouragement, especially at several crucial points when all seemed lost. I am grateful as well to Brannon Wheeler for including this book in his series on Comparative Islamic Studies. Five expert reviewers have deeply obliged me by their generous and careful reading of earlier drafts of the manuscript. But for their vigilance the number of errors would have been much more numerous than it will in any case turn out to be. A special word of thanks is due to Russell Adams of Queenston Publishing for the truly heroic feat of taming so wild a beast as the manuscript originally delivered to him. Finally I have enjoyed the advice and benefit of many colleagues, students, friends, and family while I worked on this project – too many to thank individually here – but without Penelope Jones and Umair Khan, I would still be stuck at page one wondering where the last three years had gone. *Sine quibus non.*

Sidi Bou Said
April 2013

A.J.D.

Introduction: The Myth of the Book

Text and context

It is often said that the Qur'ān is unintelligible without some prior knowledge of Muḥammad's life. Indeed the habit of reading the Qur'ān *through* the life of the Prophet – that is, contextualizing individual passages of the Qur'ān within the framework of the Prophet's 'biography' (Ar. *sīra*) – is not just the customary practice of religious readers. It is, with few exceptions, the conventional method for understanding the Qur'ān among secular scholars. Custom and convention *per se* have a 'taken-for-granted' or 'common-sense' air about them; they are, in a word, 'obvious.' That is why it is so difficult, and at times risky, to see things otherwise. In the case of the Qur'ān, secular scholars may differ from Muslim scholars over how they parcel out individual *sūras*, or units of the Qur'ān, as 'Meccan' or 'Medinan,' but there is near universal agreement among them that this is how the *sūras* are to be divided. In other words both religious *and* secular scholars are committed to the view that the Qur'ān corresponds to the career of Muḥammad, which began sometime about 610 CE in the city of Mecca (located in modern-day Saudi Arabia), and then recommenced in 622 CE/1 AH when Muḥammad fled to the city of Yathrib, some 250 miles to the north, which came to be known as 'al-Madīna,' or 'the City,' short for the 'City of the Prophet.' On this and other fundamental points there is little that separates most contemporary secular scholars of the Qur'ān from their medieval Muslim confreres. The difference is really one of degree. While all scholars recognize that the biographical tradition is problematic, and that traditional reports about the 'occasions of revelation' (Ar. *asbāb al-nuzūl*) cannot be accepted uncritically, they nevertheless hold that the life of Muḥammad provides the only reliable basis for understanding the Qur'ān.

Now, the curious thing is that the Qur'ān nowhere demands to be read in light of any one individual's life. Certainly it has little to say about the biography of a seventh-century prophet named 'Muḥammad.' The closest we get to one (at least so it is claimed) is the following sketch in *sūra* 93 of Muḥammad's life before his call to be God's messenger:

> Did He not find you an orphan and give (you) refuge? Did He not find you astray and guide (you)? Did He not find you poor and enrich (you)?[1]

These three questions are traditionally understood as addressed by God to Muḥammad, though nothing in Q93 makes this explicit. These lines could equally be understood as spoken by the Prophet and intended for believers generally, especially the second one – 'Did He not find you astray and guide (you)?' – which implies a participation in the worship of other gods or 'paganism.' However that may be, notice that the Prophet's name is not mentioned in Q93. In fact the name 'Muḥammad' occurs in only four verses of the Qur'ān and is never used when the Prophet is addressed directly.[2] Without knowing from the traditional *sīra* that the Qur'ān was 'dictated' by God (via the angel Gabriel) to Muḥammad, who was merely reciting the words he had heard, we would be at a loss in many cases to discern who is speaking to whom.

1. Q93.6-8 (references to the Qur'ān will be cited as follows: Q *sūra* # . verse #).
2. See Q3.144; 33.40; 47.2; 48.29. The name also occurs as the title of Q47. A few modern scholars have wondered whether 'Muḥammad' is not an epithet ('the praised one') rather than a proper name. According to Q61.6, Jesus predicted that the coming prophet would be named 'Aḥmad.' The vocative 'Prophet!' is used thirteen times as a form of address, 'Messenger!' twice. There are about two hundred references to 'the Messenger' (Ar. *al-rasūl*) and about thirty to 'the Prophet' (*al-nabī*).

Nor does the Qur'ān even hint that its *sūras* are to be divided between 'Meccan' and 'Medinan' periods, or any other geographical or chronological division.[3] Mecca is mentioned only once, Medina not at all,[4] and only a handful of other places are referred to by name – 'Arafāt (Q2.198), Badr (Q3.123), Becca (Q3.96), al-Ḥijr (Q15.80), Ḥunayn (Q9.25), Yathrib (Q33.13), Umm al-Qurā (Q6.92; 42.7) – but without any indication of their location. There are only two references to the Ka'ba, which is also called the 'Sacred House' (Q5.95, 97), but we are not told where it is located. If it is identical with the 'House' built by Abraham and Ishmael (Q2.125-127; 22.26), it would be in the vicinity of 'al-Ṣafā and al-Marwa' (Q2.158), but again we are not given their location. If we only had the Qur'ān, we might never guess that its story unfolded in the 'Ḥijāz' or (southwestern) 'Arabia,' neither of which is ever mentioned.[5]

Of the two great empires of the day, the Byzantine (Christian) Greeks and the Sassanid (Zoroastrian) Persians, only the former receives a mention.[6] At the level of people, 'Jews' and 'Christians' are referred frequently, yet the 'Quraysh,' said to be the paramount tribe of Mecca, are mentioned only once,[7] and tellingly none of the individuals who figure so prominently in the biographical tradition is ever referred to by name.[8] In fact only two contemporary individuals are named in the entire Qur'ān: a certain Zayd (Q33.37) and Abū Lahab (Q111.1). Since the latter means 'Father of the Flame,' it is probably a nickname and does not necessarily designate a historical figure. In sum it appears that the Qur'ān is not directly interested in its historical context at all. 'It is,' in the words of F.E. Peters, 'a text without context.'[9]

So what explains the persistence among secular academics of the traditional way of reading the Qur'ān though the life of Muḥammad? Why does their approach differ so little from that of medieval Muslim scholars? One answer is that it has been institutionalized over the course of a century and a half, and has become its own kind of academic orthodoxy. Institutions are notoriously slow to change, because like any organism they have a vested interest in reproducing themselves in the future. Generations of graduate students have been, and continue to be, 'disciplined' on the basis of this method of studying the Qur'ān. Another answer is that however secular the academic study of religion may claim to be, it continues to be a bastion of conservatism within the academy, and has generally resisted engaging the critical discourses associated with other areas of academic study. As Bruce Lincoln recently described the state of the field:

> Although critical inquiry has become commonplace in other disciplines, it still offends many students of religion, who denounce it as 'reductionism.' This charge is meant to silence critique. The failure to treat religion 'as religion' – that is, the refusal to ratify its claim of transcendent nature and sacrosanct status – may be regarded as heresy and sacrilege by those who construct themselves as religious, but it is the

3. The 114 *sūras* of the Qur'ān are not arranged in chronological order but roughly in order of descending length. Prior to printing, books were made and written by hand. It was therefore crucial to know in advance how many pages a book would need to accommodate the text(s) to be copied into it. The longest-to-shortest arrangement, though not foolproof, made it less likely that a scribe would run out of space at the end. The same organizational scheme was used, for example, with the letters of the apostle Paul in the earliest manuscript we have of them, and this is also how they are arranged in the present New Testament.
4. 'Mecca' (Ar. *Makka*) is referred to at Q48.24, though it is not identified as a city. Ar. *al-madīna* ('the city') is too general to be taken as a proper name (see e.g. Q18.19). The 'people of Yathrib' are addressed at Q33.13, but it is tradition which identifies 'Yathrib' with 'Medina' or the 'City of the Prophet' (Ar. *Madīnat al-Nabī*).
5. There are at least as many clues which point (north by northwest from present-day Mecca) in the direction of Syria-Palestine (see e.g. Q11.83, 89; 30.3; 37.137; 46.27). In late antiquity 'Arabia' could refer to a very wide geographical area, from the northwest corner of the Syrian desert to the southwest coast of the Arabian peninsula.
6. See Q30.2, though the event referred to is not clear, and the reference is further complicated by a variant reading.
7. See Q106.1. They are commanded to 'serve the Lord of this House' (Q106.3), but no further details are given. Tradition identifies them as the leading tribe of Mecca.
8. For example, there is no mention of Muḥammad's uncle Abū Ṭālib or cousin 'Alī, none of his wives Khadīja and 'Ā'isha or daughter Fāṭima, and none of his companions Abū Bakr, 'Umar, and 'Uthmān.
9. F.E. Peters, *Muhammad and the Origins of Islam* (Albany: SUNY Press, 1994) 259.

starting point for those who construct themselves as historians.[10]

To put that another way, reverence may be a religious virtue, but it should not be a scholarly one.[11]

Some perspective on the state of Qur'ānic studies may be gained by looking across disciplinary boundaries to an analogous situation in the study of the New Testament and the origins of Christianity. Until fairly recently the dominant academic version of Christian origins differed little from the traditional theological one. Both focused on a very small set of persons and events, and told a similar story with a singular beginning and linear plot. Simply put, the Christian story was 'foretold' by the prophets of the 'Old Testament,' fulfilled in the life of 'Jesus of Nazareth,' and carried out into the Roman world by the 'apostle Paul.' Yet as some scholars have only recently begun to argue, the writings that comprise the New Testament do not reflect or even acknowledge this traditional story or 'myth of beginnings.' Instead it is the myth itself which makes this claim upon the New Testament and provides the context for its interpretation.[12] The New Testament, it turns out, does not tell one story. But this is not at all surprising, for the New Testament is more an *archive* of texts rather than a *single* book. Only after the conventional picture has been set aside can these individual texts be recontextualized, and a genuinely historical project of reconstructing Christian origins proceed.[13]

Perhaps it is time to take a similar approach with the Qur'ān. What would result if we set the traditional story of Islamic origins aside and tried to understand the Qur'ān on its own terms, so to speak, apart from the life of Muḥammad? Let me pose that question another way: If no critical reader of the New Testament should presume that the gospel of 'Matthew' or 'John' (say) is best understood in light of the third-century CE commentary of Origen, why should a critical reader of the Qur'ān presume that the *sūra* of 'Abraham' or 'Noah' (say) is best understood in light of the third-century AH commentary of al-Ṭabarī? In a sense this is just what Muḥammad Shaḥrūr has urged by suggesting that the Qur'ān be read 'as if the Prophet had just died' – that is, quite apart from the elaborate superstructure of medieval commentary and tradition.[14]

To approach the Qur'ān apart from the tradition about it is no small challenge, since it flies in the face of both religious and academic orthodoxies. For one thing, such an approach might require a willingness to read the Qur'ān as if it, too, is an *archive* of texts rather than a *single* book. If the Qur'ān turns out to be less

10. Bruce Lincoln, 'Theses on Method,' *Method & Theory in the Study of Religion* 8 (1996) 225-227, quotation from p. 227 (thesis '12'). Lest anyone suppose that Lincoln thinks critical inquiry should be directed only toward religion, see thesis '9': 'Critical inquiry...ought [to] probe scholarly discourse and practice as much as any other' (p. 226).

11. Only a slight paraphrase of Lincoln's thesis '5' ('Theses on Method,' 226).

12. See e.g. Burton L. Mack, *Who Wrote the New Testament? The Making of the Christian Myth* (New York: HarperCollins, 1995) 6-9.

13. Of course, this is not to say that success is a foregone conclusion in such a project. For one thing it is no easy task to set *any* conventional picture aside. (Revisionists remain as much a minority in the field of biblical studies as they do within Qur'ānic studies.) Another is that the evidence, once disambiguated, may be opaque or prove inadequate to the task of historical reconstruction. Still, this would not disqualify the project *as* historical. To render a verdict of 'not proved' or to admit that 'we do not know' is not tantamount to failure. Each is a legitimate historical conclusion, and moreover potentially salutary, for it can be important to know *that* we do not know. (Ideally speaking, this is what distinguishes the historian's discourse from the religionist's: whereas the former's talk is self-consciously corrigible, the latter's is self-confidently incorrigible. In practice, however, both discourses evince a curious mixture of dogma and uncertainty.)

14. See Muḥammad Shaḥrūr, *Al-Kitāb wa-l-Qur'ān: qirā'a mu'āṣira* [*The Book and the Qur'ān: A Contemporary Reading*] (Damascus: Ahālī, 1990) 41. I owe this reference to Gabriel Said Reynolds, who contends that the '*tafsīr* [exegetical] traditions do not preserve the Qur'ān's ancient meaning, and to insist otherwise does a disservice both to *tafsīr* and to the Qur'ān' (*The Qur'ān and Its Biblical Subtext* [London: Routledge, 2010] 19, and 253-254 for the reference to Shaḥrūr). Reynolds' point holds true not just of the '*tafsīr* traditions,' but of 'Tradition' as a whole (and for that matter of Origen and the gospels of Matthew and John as well).

like a 'book' and more like a 'library,' then consistency ought not to be purchased at too high a price. Readers should not be surprised to discover within its pages a variety of viewpoints and perspectives, as well as unresolved tensions and contradictions. For another, such an approach will entail finding an alternative (or alternatives) to the traditional context for reading the Qur'ān. In other words it will oblige the interpreter to attend to the human and contingent aspects of a text which is otherwise held to be transcendent and eternal. Such a project may strike the religionist as disorienting or perhaps even disrespectful, but it is the historian's modus operandi, and in fact springs from a profound respect for evidence.

So let us set aside the guidebooks of tradition – for the moment anyway, we shall return to them soon enough – and take some tentative steps on our own into Qur'ānic territory. Allow me to begin by reformulating my opening sentence as a question: Is the Qur'ān really unintelligible without some prior knowledge of Muḥammad's life? The answer would appear to be 'no,' for even if the Qur'ān displays little direct interest in its own context – that is, in *historical* persons, places, and events – it devotes plenty of attention to a host of *storied* persons, places, and events. To put that another way, we might say that the Qur'ān is interested in *historic* figures rather than *historical* ones. It abounds in the stories of prophets – Noah, Abraham, Moses, and Jesus, to name only the most frequently recurring ones – who had been sent by God before the coming of the final Prophet. Moses is mentioned by name 136 times in the Qur'ān, more often than any other prophet, indeed more than any other *character*, save God himself. Abraham enjoys a similar stature.[15] But they are only two in a long line of prophets and messengers, beginning with Noah, who had been sent to every age and people. The frequency with which their stories are told and retold strongly suggests that the Qur'ān wants to situate its own Prophet distinctly within – if not contemporary *history* – something which the Qur'ān considers far more important: the *story* of religion.

But there is more. Quite unexpectedly, the Qur'ān places itself within this story as much as its Prophet. I would wager that no other ancient text is more conscious of itself *as a text* than the Qur'ān. Certainly few if any religious books are as self-referential. Just the name alone – 'al-Qur'ān' or 'the Recitation' – occurs some seventy times in a text about the length of the New Testament. Alongside references to 'the Qur'ān' are far more numerous instances of 'the Book' (Ar. *al-kitāb*). The word occurs more than 250 times in the Qur'ān, and not only as a term of self-reference. It is also used of a veritable 'library' of books, including the 'Torah' of Moses and 'Gospel' of Jesus, as well as the heavenly Book from which all the others were thought to be derived. But the Qur'ān is 'the clear Book' or 'the Book that makes (things) clear' (Ar. *al-kitāb al-mubīn*).[16] It is 'the wise Book,'[17] a 'blessed' and 'cherished Book.'[18] The Qur'ān is also called 'the wise Reminder,' which has been 'sent down' for this very purpose: to be a 'reminder to the mindful,' 'to the believers,' indeed 'to the worlds.'[19] And there are many more titles and epithets. One looks in vain for such a pronounced 'scriptural self-consciousness' in the Bibles of either Judaism or Christianity, whose practitioners the Qur'ān refers to variously as the 'People of the Book' or the 'People of the Reminder' or the 'People of the Gospel.' For all the emphasis, then, on the Qur'ān as an 'oral text,' it appears to be, well, rather bookish.[20] Yet there is more than mere self-reference in the Qur'ān. What we soon discover is a complex mythology of the Book.

---

15. Though even Abraham (mentioned 69 times by name) runs a distant second to Moses. They are followed by Noah (43 times), Lot (27 times), Joseph (27 times, though only twice outside of Q12), and Jesus (25 times).
16. See Q5.15; 12.1; 26.2; 27.1; 28.2; 43.2; 44.2; cf. Q15.1; 36.69 ('clear Qur'ān'). The 'Torah' of Moses is also referred to as 'the clear Book' or 'the Book that makes (things) clear' (Q37.117).
17. 'The wise Book' (Q10.1; 31.2); cf. 'the wise Qur'ān' (Q36.2); 'the wise Reminder' (Q3.58).
18. 'Blessed Book' (Q38.29); 'cherished' or 'hidden Book' (Q56.78).
19. 'The wise Reminder' (Q3.58); 'a reminder to the mindful' (Q11.114); 'a reminder to believers' (Q7.2; 11.120); 'a reminder to the worlds' (Q6.90; 12.104; 38.87; 68.52; 81.27). The 'Torah' of Moses is also referred to as 'the Reminder' (Q21.105).
20. Notice especially Q96.4: God teaches humanity 'by the pen' (Ar. *bil-qalami*).

If we consider the Qur'ān with an eye for the story it tells about itself, we can discern two intertwining narratives, each with its own distinctive vocabulary, but which only rarely intersect. One part of the story revolves around the 'inspiration' of the Prophet; the other concerns the 'revelation' of the Qur'ān as a book 'from heaven.' As we turn our attention to each, let us keep in mind an important distinction Jonathan Z. Smith has made regarding the terms 'revelation' and 'inspiration.' Although they are often confused in popular imagination, they are quite different categories in the history of religions. Inspiration means, literally, having one's 'breath' taken over by the 'breath' (Lat. *spiritus*) of God (or a god). It is thus the positive counterpart to, and can sometimes be mistaken for, demonic 'possession.' Revelation, on the other hand, is the transmission of knowledge from the divine to the human, and often in written form. So construed, inspiration is a 'person-category,' revelation a 'book-category.' Or another way of putting the distinction is that whereas books are revealed, individuals are inspired. Although at times these categories may overlap – that is, a book is revealed to an inspired person – this is a relatively rare phenomenon in the history of religions. What do we find in the case of the Prophet and his Book?[21]

An 'inspired' Prophet

The Qur'ānic accounts which focus on the inspiration of the Prophet occur in two forms: *visions* and *auditions*, or reports of what the Prophet saw and what he heard. There are only two 'vision-texts' in the entire Qur'ān, and perhaps for that reason they have been the subject of intense scrutiny and debate. They are found at Q53.1-18 and Q81.15-25, which almost all scholars consider early 'Meccan' *sūras*.[22] In fact they may be variant recensions of each other. The former passage actually describes two separate visions, the first of which is introduced by an unidentified speaker who swears an oath to the truthfulness of the Prophet:

> **1** By the star when it falls![23] **2** Your companion [the Prophet] has not gone astray, nor has he erred, **3** nor
> does he speak on a whim. **4** It is nothing but an inspiration inspired. **5** One harsh in power has taught him
> **6** – One full of strength! He stood poised, **7** while He was at the highest horizon, **8** then He drew near and
> came down. **9** He was two bow-lengths tall, or nearly.[24] **10** And so He inspired His servant (with) what He
> inspired. **11** His heart did not lie about *what it saw*. **12** Will you dispute with him about *what he sees*?

Tradition would eventually come to understand this account as a vision of the angel Gabriel. He was the 'one harsh in power...full of strength' who appeared to Muḥammad and 'taught him' the Qur'ān. Even so, tradition is not unanimous on this score, for some of the companions of the Prophet are said to have believed that it was God himself whom the Prophet saw.[25] And indeed similar epithets are applied to God elsewhere in the Qur'ān.[26] But it is really the reference to 'His servant' or 'slave' (Ar. *'abdihi*) which makes this conclusion unavoidable, since such a designation is better understood of a human's relationship to God rather than to an angel, even Gabriel. In other words this vision describes a 'theophany' or appearance of God.

Then Q53 proceeds to report another appearance:

> **13** Certainly he [the Prophet] *saw* Him at a second descent, **14** by the Lote Tree of the Boundary, **15** near
> which is the Garden of the Refuge, **16** when (there) covered the Lote Tree what covered (it). **17** His *sight*

21. For more on these categories, see [Jonathan Z. Smith], arts. 'inspiration,' 'revelation,' in *idem* (ed.), *The HarperCollins Dictionary of Religion* (San Francisco: HarperSanFrancisco, 1995) 492 and 926-927. Generally speaking, inspiration is a Graeco-Roman phenomenon, revelation an ancient Near Eastern one, though by late antiquity the distinction is largely moot.
22. Though many place Q81 before Q53, chronologically.
23. 'By the star...,' i.e. '*I swear* by the star...' (cf. the oath introducing the vision at Q81.15-18 below).
24. Or 'two bow-lengths away, or nearer.'
25. Both Ibn 'Abbās and Anas ibn Mālik believed it was a vision of God. The singular word 'tradition' can be a misleading term, since it does not always speak with a single voice.
26. See e.g. Q4.84; 8.52; 40.22; 51.58.

did not turn aside, nor did it transgress. **18** Certainly he *saw* one of the greatest signs of his Lord.

The 'Lote Tree of the Boundary' and 'Garden of the Refuge' are mentioned only here in the Qur'ān. Tradition would come to identify the latter as heaven and the former as a celestial tree marking the boundary between heaven and earth. Yet both probably refer to terrestrial places rather than heavenly ones, in keeping with this vision as another 'descent' of God. The theophany to Moses likewise occurred at a 'tree' (Q28.30) in 'the holy wādi of Ṭuwā' (Q20.12; 79.16), and was described almost identically as 'one of Our greatest signs' (Q20.23). And just as that theophany served as the occasion for Moses' call to be a prophet, so the theophany reported here may have a similar purpose. Like Moses, the Prophet too was called through a direct appearance of God.

I have italicized the words for 'seeing' in both accounts in order to make clear that the focus in each passage is on what the Prophet saw. While the transmission of content is implied in the first vision (e.g. by the line '[God] inspired...what He inspired'), what is stressed is that the Prophet was not mistaken or deceived in his vision: 'His heart did not lie about *what it saw*' (Q53.10-11).[27] Curiously, then, neither theophany reports any words being spoken. Each is without explicit content. By sharp contrast, as we soon shall see, the biographical tradition would emphasize what Muḥammad *heard* (from Gabriel) rather than, as here, what the Prophet *saw* (God).

The second 'vision-text' is found at Q81.15-25. It too begins with an oath, but this time an elaborate one:

15 I swear by the slinking (stars), **16** the runners, the hiders, **17** by the night when it departs, **18** by the dawn when it breathes![28] **19** Surely it is indeed the word[29] of an honorable messenger **20** – one full of power, secure with the Holder of the throne, **21** one (to be) obeyed, (and) furthermore trustworthy. **22** Your companion [the Prophet] is not possessed.[30] **23** Certainly he did see Him on the clear horizon. **24** He is not grudging of the unseen. **25** It is not the word of an accursed satan.

The reader will be struck immediately by the way in which this passage echoes or alludes to the first theophany.[31] In fact it may be a new recension of it.[32] The solemnity of the introductory oaths – this time in the first person singular – implies a more highly charged polemical context. The voice, again unidentified, testifies to the truthfulness of the 'honorable messenger' in the strongest possible terms: he is neither lying nor demon possessed. Once again tradition would come to identify the messenger as Gabriel, and name him as the one whom the Prophet saw 'on the clear horizon.' But 'honorable messenger' is more likely a reference to the Prophet himself, who saw God, not Gabriel, high in the sky.[33] Quite apart from the fact that 'Gabriel' (Ar. *Jibrīl*) is named only three times in the entire Qur'ān,[34] the pronouncement, 'It is indeed the word of an honorable messenger,' occurs also at Q69.40, where it clearly refers to the Prophet. And, not surprisingly, Moses too is called an 'honorable messenger' at Q44.17. In other words this designation is typically predicated of *human* messengers, not angelic ones. Some modern scholars contend that vv. 20-21 were later added to Q81 to make Gabriel the 'honorable messenger,' and to turn what was originally a theophany into an 'angelophany' (or vision of Gabriel). That may well

27. Here as elsewhere the Prophet's 'heart' is spoken of as synonymous with his 'mind.'
28. The scene describes the break of day, when the stars 'retreat' and 'hide,' and night 'departs.'
29. Or 'speech' (i.e. way of speaking).
30. Literally, 'jinn-struck' (Ar. *majnūn*).
31. Cf. Q81.20-23 and Q53.1-3, 7, 11-12.
32. By that I mean that Q81.15-25 may be more than an 'allusion' to Q53.1-12; it may be a rewriting of it. In the ancient world texts were always subject to revision, alteration, and adaptation. 'Fixity' would not become a feature of textual transmission until the invention of printing. In any case it appears that Q81 follows Q53 chronologically, just the reverse of what many scholars claim.
33. Cf. Q53.7, 'He [God] was at the highest horizon.'
34. See Q2.97-98; 66.4. Only the former passage mentions his role as mediator of revelation.

be correct, yet the fact remains that the angels are only rarely spoken of as agents of revelation in the Qur'ān.[35] The biographical tradition, however, would eventually harmonize the 'vision-texts' of Q53 and Q81, and understand them both as appearances of Gabriel, the mediator of revelation to Muḥammad. It is all the more striking, therefore, that neither Q53 nor Q81 reports any words being spoken.

When content is transmitted in the Qur'ān, it is not in the context of a vision but rather assumes the form of verbal commands. For example, we encounter the imperative 'Recite!' at Q96.1-5, considered by many scholars to be the *first* revelation:

> **1** *Recite* in the name of your Lord[36] who creates, **2** creates the human from a clot. **3** *Recite*, for your Lord[37] is the Most Generous, **4** who teaches by the pen, **5** teaches the human what he does not know.

The command 'Recite!' or 'Read aloud!' (Ar. *iqra'*, from the verb *qara'a*), gives the title to 'The Recitation' (*al-Qur'ān*), a word which is not attested prior to the Qur'ān itself.[38] The reference to God's instruction 'by the pen,' along with the injunction to 'read aloud' or 'recite,' would seem to imply the existence of a *physical* book, however much the *oral* nature of the Qur'ān has been stressed by scholars. What humankind did not know has now been revealed in *written* form.[39]

There is almost no information in the Qur'ān itself about how the 'mechanics' of inspiration works. In fact the Qur'ān does not even identify the speaker of the words 'Recite...' in Q96, any more than it did the speaker in the two 'vision-texts' of Q53 and Q81. Later tradition, however, provides detailed accounts of the first revelation to 'Muḥammad,' as well as of the revelatory process itself. In so doing it creatively weaves together into a single story what was discrete in the Qur'ān. Perhaps the best known example is found in *The Life of the Messenger of God* (*Sīrat Rasūl Allāh*), composed by Ibn Hishām (d. 833 CE/218 AH), but relying on the (now lost) history of Ibn Isḥāq (d. 767 CE/150 AH). The *Life* relates the following report about the first revelation to Muḥammad and his call to be God's messenger:

> In the month of Ramaḍān in which God willed concerning [Muḥammad] what He willed of His grace, the Messenger set forth to [Mount] Ḥirā' as was his wont, and his family with him. When it was the night on which God honored [Muḥammad] with his mission...Gabriel brought him the command of God. 'He came to me,' said the Messenger of God, '*while I was asleep*, with a coverlet of brocade *on which there was some writing*, and said, "Recite!"[40] I said, "What shall I recite?" He pressed me with it so tightly that I thought it was death. Then he let me go and said, "Recite!" I said, "What shall I recite?" He pressed me with it again so that I thought it was death. Then he let me go and said, "Recite!" I said, "What shall I recite?" He pressed me with it a third time, so that I thought it was death, and said, "Recite!" I said, "What shall I recite" – and this I said only to deliver myself from him, lest he should do the same again. [Gabriel] said,
>
> "Recite in the name of your Lord who creates, creates the human from a clot.
>
> Recite, for Your Lord is the Most Generous, who teaches by the pen, teaches the human what he does not know." [Q 96.1-5]

35. Exceptional are: Q16.2; 37.3; 77.5; 97.1-4. Of course, if the 'We passages' refer to (or include) the angels, then these would provide other instances. More about this below.
36. Or 'Recite: In the name of your Lord....'
37. Or 'Recite: And your Lord....'
38. In the Syrian Christian tradition, 'Recitation' (Syr. *qeryānā*) denoted both 'scripture reading' and the 'scripture read aloud' (i.e. in a liturgical setting).
39. See further Q2.151; 4.113; 6.91; cf. Q2.239; 21.105; 55.1-4; 68.1. Many scholars hold that Q96.1-5 were the words which Muḥammad received in the visions referred to above in Q53 and Q81, and are therefore the very first lines of the Qur'ān to be revealed. But this may only be an inference on their part, based on the logical priority of the command to 'recite' (*iqra'*), since this word is from the same root as 'Qur'ān.' In any case it goes beyond what the Qur'ān itself asserts. Other scholars have claimed that Q1 or Q74.1-5 was revealed first, and still others that it was the *basmala* ('In the name of God, the Merciful, the Compassionate'). Once again 'tradition' turns out not to be uniform or to speak with only one voice.
40. Or 'Read aloud!' Notice the reference to the 'coverlet' with writing on it.

> So I recited it, and he departed from me. And *I awoke from my sleep*, and it was as though these words were written on my heart. When I was midway on the mountain [of Ḥirā'], I heard a voice saying, "Muḥammad! You are the Messenger of God and I am Gabriel." I raised my head toward heaven to see, and suddenly there was Gabriel in the form of man with his feet astride the horizon, saying, "Muḥammad! You are the Messenger of God and I am Gabriel." I stood gazing at him.... Then he parted from me and I from him, returning to my family.'[41]

In the story told by Ibn Hishām, the 'audition' reported anonymously at Q96.1-5 has become part of a 'dream-vision' recounted in the first person by Muḥammad himself, who 'saw' and 'heard' Gabriel (not God) while he was asleep, for after Gabriel's departure Muḥammad 'woke up.' The dream thus becomes the occasion for the revelation of Q96.1-5, which Gabriel delivers both in written *and* oral form when he utters the command 'Recite!' Yet the story does not end there. The dream is immediately followed by a 'waking vision' of Gabriel (again, not God), in language recalling the 'vision-texts' of Q53 and Q81. In other words the *Life* has harmonized the theophanies of Q53 and Q81, combined them with Q96, and turned them into visions *and* auditions of the angel Gabriel. What appeared to be three separate episodes in the Qur'ān, has become a single story of the inaugural revelation according to the *Life*.

Tradition understands the entire Qur'ān to be 'divine discourse,' with Muḥammad the recipient and Gabriel the mediator of revelation. But an analysis of the Qur'ān itself indicates that the question of who is speaking, who is addressed, and how, is more complicated than the traditional view has it.[42] In some passages, in fact, it is not even clear that God is the one who is speaking, and that it may be the Prophet himself who speaks, as it were, in his own person.[43] In other passages, where it seems clear that God is the speaker, he delivers his words *directly* – occasionally in the first-person singular – without any mediator, angelic or human.[44] Much more common, however, is the occurrence of the first-person plural, implying that it is God and/or the angels who are speaking.

When content is transmitted, the imperative 'Say!' (Ar. *qul*) is far more common than the order 'Recite!' Although 'Say!' is a distinctive feature of Qur'ānic discourse, it is not unique. We find a similar form of address in the 'messenger-formula' of many prophetic texts in the Bible, especially the Book of Ezekiel:

> Then the spirit of Yahweh fell upon me, and he [or, it] said to me, 'Say: "Thus says Yahweh, 'So have you said, House of Israel! [etc. etc.]'"'[45]

This is precisely what we think of when we use the term 'inspiration,' a word whose root (from Latin *inspirare*) means 'to breathe into.' To be 'inspired' is to be 'in-spirited;' it is to have one's own breath replaced by divine 'breath' or 'spirit.' In fact this is just how Ezekiel describes it: 'A spirit [Hebr. *rūaḥ*] entered into me.'[46] (This is also why 'inspiration' is always potentially open to the charge of demonic

41. Translation by A. Guillaume, *The Life of Muhammad: A Translation of Ibn Isḥāq's* Sīrat Rasūl Allāh (Oxford/Karachi: Oxford Univ. Press, 1955) 105-106 (§§153-154), slightly altered.

42. It would be more accurate to say that the Qur'ān 'belongs to the genre of anonymous religious literature' (so Matthias Radscheit, art. 'Provocation,' *Encyclopaedia of the Qur'ān*, 5 vols. [Leiden: Brill, 2001-2006] 4.310). The title 'The Recitation' bears no attribution to its recipient or 'author.' It is not 'The Recitation of (or to) so and so.' In its anonymity the Qur'ān is like much of biblical literature. Consider the famous opening lines of the Jewish Bible and Christian Old Testament: 'When God began to create the sky and the earth...' and so on (Genesis 1.1). The question of whose 'voice' we hear is likewise enigmatic. Nowhere are we told who is speaking or to whom, or who the text's author is. Only centuries later would tradition attribute authorship of the 'Torah' to Moses, just as each of the 'Gospels' would eventually be assigned an author, title, and audience. All of these are *secondary* claims about texts which were originally anonymous. The Qur'ān presents an analogous case.

43. See e.g. Q6.104, 114a; 26.221; 27.91; 91.1-10; 92.14-21; 101.1-11; 102.1-8; 103.1-3.

44. See e.g. Q2.40-41, 47, 186; 13.32; 22.48; 32.13; 51.56-57; 67.18; 74.11-15.

45. Ezekiel 11.5; cf. 11.16, 17; 12.23, 28; 13.18; 14.6; 17.1-3, 9; 19.1-2; 20.1-3 etc.

46. Ezekiel 2.2; cf. 3.24. The prophet Jeremiah offers a more graphic description: 'Then Yahweh put out his hand and

'possession.') In such cases of ecstatic speech there is a temporary suspension of the prophet's own agency; he is reduced to being merely the deity's mouthpiece, which delivers divine discourse verbatim. Simply put, the messenger is utterly subordinated to the message.

Yet there is almost no information in the Qur'ān about how inspiration is perceived. In what is said to be one of the later texts of the Qur'ān, we find an exceedingly brief but precise description:

> Say: 'Whoever is an enemy to Gabriel – surely he has brought it down on your heart by the permission of God, confirming what was before it, and as a guidance and good news to the believers.'[47]

Here, as often in ancient literature, the Prophet's 'heart' is spoken of as synonymous with his 'mind.' But what is it exactly that Gabriel has 'brought down' (Ar. *nazzala*)? Whatever 'it' may refer to, the appearance of Gabriel as the agent of God's revelation will not come as any surprise to readers attuned to biblical tradition, for this is the role he plays in both Jewish and Christian scriptures as well.[48] Here, however, it is said that Gabriel 'brought down' something which 'confirms what was before it.' 'It' must therefore be a reference to the descent of a *book* – that is, not inspiration in general, but the very Qur'ān itself – which validates the *books* which had been 'sent down' before it: namely, the 'Torah' of Moses and 'Gospel' of Jesus.[49]

This scant description of how the Qur'ān, as a book, was revealed to the Prophet recasts the 'mechanics' of inspiration, and sheds an entirely new light on 'how' the Prophet perceived it. The crucial line might be paraphrased as follows: 'Gabriel brought the Qur'ān down and put it into the Prophet's mind.'[50] The perfect tense, moreover, implies that Gabriel brought it down *all at once*. In the digital age we might liken it to the instant downloading of an 'e-book' from a website to a computer's hard drive. Understood in this sense, Q2.97 stretches the idea of the Prophet's 'inspiration.' What entered into him was not a spirit but a book! The Prophet's literal 'incorporation' of a heavenly book may thus explain why not only the Qur'ān but also the Prophet himself can be called a 'reminder.'[51]

It is, however, the *suddenness* of Gabriel's appearance which occasions the greatest surprise, for he appears out of nowhere, and then vanishes just as quickly. This is the only such reference to Gabriel in the entire Qur'ān, and it stands in unresolved tension with hundreds of other passages in which both revelation and inspiration are characterized as *unmediated*.[52]

---

touched my mouth, and Yahweh said to me, "Now I have put my words in your mouth"' (Jeremiah 1.9; cf. Exodus 4.12 [Moses]; Deuteronomy 18.18 [the 'prophet like Moses' yet to come]). The formula 'the word of Yahweh came to so and so' occurs more than 100 times in the Hebrew Bible. The phenomenon of 'inspiration' is also found in the New Testament (see Luke 1.15, 41, 67; Acts 2.4; 4.8, 31; 13.9; cf. 1 Corinthians 12.3; Revelation 1.10; 4.2).

47. Q2.97.

48. Among many examples, see Daniel 8.15-26; 9.20-27; Luke 1.10-20, 26-37. In the verse immediately following (Q2.98) Gabriel is paired with Michael, as he is, for example, at 1 Enoch 9.1; 10.9-12; 40.9-10; 54.6; 71.8-9, 13; cf. Daniel 10.13, 21; 12.1; Jude 1.9; and Revelation 12.7-9. Unnamed angels play similar roles in the biblical books of Ezekiel and Zechariah.

49. See e.g. Q3.3; 5.48; 35.31; 46.30.

50. According to Q16.102, 'the holy spirit brought it down;' the same is said of 'the trustworthy spirit' at Q26.193. This led some interpreters to identify 'the spirit' with Gabriel. More about this below.

51. See Q65.10-11; cf. Q88.21. There are biblical parallels for this idea of 'incorporation' in the 'eating' or 'swallowing' of a heavenly book presented to a prophet, either by an angel or God himself (see e.g. Ezekiel 3.1-3; Revelation 10.8-11; cf. Jeremiah 15.16).

52. Gabriel is only mentioned again at Q66.4, as one of the Prophet's 'protectors.' It should be noted, however, that Gabriel's role as the mediator of revelation in the *Life* of Ibn Hishām is not as pervasive as one might suppose, or expect, especially in light of the story cited above of the 'first' revelation. Instead we find God often speaking directly to Muḥammad in the *Life*, just as he does to the Prophet in the Qur'ān. See e.g. Ibn Hishām, *Life* §§235-237 (Guillaume, pp. 162-164), where the formulas 'So God revealed concerning...,' 'And He revealed concerning...,' 'He mentions...,' and 'He says...' occur again and again without any reference to Gabriel.

The Qur'ān is most specific about the 'mechanics' of inspiration at Q42.51-52:

> **51** It is not (fitting) for any human being that God should speak to him, except (by) inspiration, or from behind a veil, or (that) He should send a messenger and he [the messenger] inspire by His permission whatever He pleases. Surely He is most high, wise. **52** In this way We have inspired you [the Prophet] (with) a spirit of Our command. You did not know what the Book was, nor (what) belief (was), but We have made it a light by means of which We guide whomever We please of Our servants.

According to the first verse (51) God can choose to communicate in any of three ways: by 'inspiration' (Ar. *waḥy*), 'from behind a veil' (*ḥijāb*), or through the 'sending of a messenger' (*rasūl*). On the face of it these appear to be three different *modes* of inspiration which might be glossed as: directly, obliquely, and through an intermediary.[53] In any case the following verse (52) implies that God's inspiration of the Prophet was by this third mode – via a 'messenger' – despite the far more numerous instances of direct address in the Qur'ān (including actual theophanies!). The messenger, however, does not appear to be an angel, but is further described as a 'spirit of Our command' or a 'spirit from Our command' (Ar. *rūḥ min amrinā*). Later interpreters identified this 'spirit' with the angel Gabriel, and while it is tempting to follow them, the connection is never made explicit in the Qur'ān.

Let us linger for a moment over the meaning of two key words derived from the Arabic root *w-ḥ-y*. The noun 'inspiration' (Ar. *waḥy*) occurs only six times in the Qur'ān, but the verb 'to inspire' (*awḥā*) is found some seventy-two times in a variety of contexts. Both the verbal and nominal forms of the root *w-ḥ-y* became technical terms in Islamic tradition, and were understood to mean the 'dictation' of the words of the Qur'ān to Muḥammad by the angel Gabriel. Qur'ānic usage, however, is not nearly so precise or limited. In fact the verb *awḥā* displays a fairly wide semantic range, extending from 'prompt' or 'suggest,' to 'instruct' or 'order,' to 'inspire.' Surprisingly, the word is not confined exclusively to *prophetic* revelation, for God can 'inspire' each of the seven heavens with its special task (Q41.12), or 'inspire' the earth to tell its story at the Last Day (Q99.4-5), or even 'inspire' the bees to build hives in trees and mountains (Q16.68).[54] Yet even when *awḥā* is addressed to prophets, it does not always imply the transmission, much less dictation, of verbal content. For example, God 'inspired' Noah to build the ark (Q23.27; cf. Q11.37), just as he 'inspired' Moses to set out with his people from Egypt (Q20.77) and to strike the sea with his staff (Q26.63), and as he likewise 'inspired' the Prophet to follow the 'creed of Abraham' (Q16.123).

Richard Bell has argued that the fundamental sense of *waḥy* is '*the communication of an idea by some quick suggestion or prompting*, or as we might say, by the flash of inspiration. (...) [B]ut it was left to Muḥammad himself to find the precise words in which to speak.'[55] That is a far cry from the traditional idea of divine dictation. Would Bell's understanding of *waḥy* imply that the Prophet was something like an 'inspired' poet? The Qur'ānic answer is an emphatic 'no.' 'Poet' was one of the words the Prophet's opponents used in dismissing him as a canting arriviste: 'Are we to abandon our gods for a jinn-struck poet?' (Q37.36). The Qur'ān is acutely sensitive to the fine line between divine inspiration and both poetic imagination and demonic possession. If God could 'inspire,' so could the 'satans' and the 'jinn' (Q6.112, 121).[56]

---

53. Admittedly it is not very clear what 'from behind a veil' means. At Q33.53 believers are enjoined to address the Prophet's wives 'from behind a veil.' The expression may thus suggest an 'audition,' but without seeing anything for reasons of etiquette. If so, then the preceding '(by) inspiration' may refer not only to God's direct speech but also to his 'self-presentation' in a theophany (as at Q53.4-10).

54. Furthermore 'inspirational agency' is not reserved exclusively for God. In one instance a human being is the subject of the verb *awḥā* (Zachariah at Q19.11).

55. See W. Montgomery Watt and Richard Bell, *Bell's Introduction to the Qur'ān* (Edinburgh: Edinburgh Univ. Press, 1970), 20-25, quotation from pp. 21-22 (emphasis in the original; the second part of the quotation is Watt's elaboration of Bell's point). Bell consistently rendered Ar. *waḥy* and *awḥā* as 'suggestion' and 'suggested' in *The Qur'ān: Translated, with a Critical Re-arrangement of the Surahs*, 2 vols. (Edinburgh: T. & T. Clark, 1937-1939).

56. Cf. Q7.20; 20.120 (Satan 'whispered' to Adam).

Once again we see that 'inspiration' is inherently controversial. The Qur'ān even shares the prejudice against 'poets' insofar as it too criticizes them (Q26.224-226). In fact the word for 'poet' (Ar. *shā'ir*) may originally have been closer to 'diviner' or 'soothsayer,' and in one passage there seems to be very little difference between 'oracle-giver,' 'madman,' and 'poet' (Q52.29-30). In any case the Qur'ān is emphatic in denying that the Prophet was either a poet (Q69.41; cf. Q36.69; 52.30) or possessed (Q81.22; cf. Q68.2). On the latter charge, at least, he was in good company, for the same accusation had been leveled against Noah (Q23.25; 54.9) and Moses (Q26.27; 51.39) – indeed against *every* previous prophet (Q51.52).

There is one passage in the Qur'ān which insists that all prophets had experienced the same kind of 'inspiration' (Ar. *waḥy*). The only exception was Moses, to whom God had spoken *directly*:

> Surely We have inspired you [Ar. *awḥaynā ilayka*] as We inspired Noah and the prophets after him, and as We inspired Abraham, and Ishmael, and Isaac, and Jacob, and the tribes, and Jesus, and Job, and Jonah, and Aaron, and Solomon, and We gave David (the) Psalms, and messengers We have already recounted to you before, and messengers We have not recounted to you – but God spoke to Moses directly.[57]

There are a few other passages which also attest to Moses' uniqueness in having spoken directly with God, but they may be nothing more than an acknowledgement of the special privilege accorded Moses in the Bible and tradition, namely that Moses spoke with God 'face to face,'[58] for in all these cases inspiration comes from God *directly*. Gabriel's presumptive role as mediator is – with one notable exception (Q2.97) – as much a secondary tradition as the widespread notion of a mechanical 'dictation' of the Qur'ān – again with one notable exception. The Prophet receives the following instructions at Q75.16-19:

> **16** Do not move your tongue with it to hurry it. **17** Surely on Us (depends) its collection and its recitation.
> **18** When We recite it, follow its recitation. **19** Then surely on Us (depends) its explanation.

Unless 'We' refers to the angels, this passage implies that the Prophet actually heard the Qur'ān recited or dictated by God himself.[59]

A Book 'from heaven'

So far we have considered how the Qur'ān describes the inspiration of its Prophet. We now turn to the other part of story the Qur'ān tells about itself – the dominant one, as it turns out – which has to do with the 'sending down' or 'descent' of the Qur'ān as a 'book from heaven.' As we have seen, the Arabic words *waḥy* and *awḥā* are two important terms for 'inspiration,' but they are overshadowed by the words derived from the Arabic root *n-z-l*, especially the verbal forms *nazzala* and *anzala* ('to send down'), which occur some 250 times in the Qur'ān. Indeed the nominal form *tanzīl* ('a sending down') can even be employed as a shorthand designation for the Qur'ān itself: 'Surely it is a sending down from the Lord of the worlds' (Q26.192).[60]

We have already encountered the verb *nazzala* at Q2.97, where Gabriel was credited with having 'brought down' the Qur'ān on the Prophet's heart. This is attributed to 'the trustworthy spirit' (Ar. *rūḥ al-amīn*) at Q26.193 and to the 'holy spirit' (*rūḥ al-qudus*) at Q16.102. This coincidence led most interpreters to identify the spirit with Gabriel, and thereby they were able to bring these passages into alignment. Typically, however, it is God himself who 'sends down' the Qur'ān, just as he is the agent of inspiration in general. On one occasion this is expressed in the first-person singular, when God speaks directly to the

57. Q4.163-164.

58. See Exodus 33.11; Numbers 12.8; Deuteronomy 34.10.

59. Cf. Q87.6: 'We shall make you recite, and you will not forget – except whatever God pleases;' and Q20.114: 'Do not be in a hurry with the Qur'ān, before its inspiration [Ar. *waḥy*] is completed to you, but say: "My Lord, increase me in knowledge."'

60. See also Q20.4; 41.2, 42; 56.80; 69.43; cf. Q17.106.

'Sons of Israel' about the Qur'ān: 'Believe in what I have sent down' (Q2.41), but more often it is found in either the first-person plural or third-person singular. Here are a few key examples:

> By the clear Book! Surely We sent it down on a blessed night. (Q44.2-3)
>
> Surely We sent it down on the Night of the Decree. (Q97.1)
>
> He has sent down on you [the Prophet] the Book with the truth,[61] confirming what was before it, and He sent down the Torah and the Gospel before (this) as guidance for the people. (Q3.3-4)

In all these passages the perfect tense of the verb ('sent down' or 'has sent down') implies an act which occurred 'all at once' – indeed on a *single* night – despite the traditional claim that the Qur'ān was revealed to Muḥammad at intervals over a period of approximately twenty years, beginning in 610 CE and ending shortly before his death in 632 CE/11 AH. However Q2.185 refers to 'the month of Ramaḍān in which the Qur'ān was sent down.' Later interpreters harmonized all three passages by identifying the 'blessed night' (Ar. *laylat mubārak*) and the 'Night of the Decree' (*laylat al-qadr*) as a single night, which they also claimed was one of the last ten nights in 'the month of Ramaḍān.' In so doing they took the perfective tense of the verb in these verses to refer to the descent of the Qur'ān from the highest to the lowest of the seven heavens, whence it was revealed to Muḥammad by Gabriel as occasion required. There are other passages, however, like the ones cited above, which indicate that the Qur'ān was 'sent down' or revealed to the Prophet all at once.[62] In fact there is one passage which seems to insist upon it:

> Surely We – We have sent down on you [the Prophet] the Qur'ān *once and for all.* (Q76.23)

A more literal rendering of this verse would be: 'We have sent down on you the Qur'ān (with) a sending down.' In this instance, however, tradition understands the verbal noun 'a sending down' (Ar. *tanzīl*) to mean 'gradually' or 'in stages,' consistent with the view that the Qur'ān was revealed over a period of some twenty years. And, not surprisingly, this is how most modern translators render *tanzīl* at Q76.23. Here are a few representative examples from widely used English translations, with the crucial word or words placed in italics:

> It is We Who have sent down the Qur'ān to thee *by stages.*[63]
> We have revealed the Qur'an to you *gradually.*[64]
> We Ourself have sent down this Qur'an to you [Prophet] *in gradual revelation.*[65]

All three translators construe *tanzīl* ('a sending down') adverbially; that is, as modifying the action of the main verb. By contrast Arthur J. Arberry preferred to render it more literally:

> Surely We have sent down the Koran on thee, *a sending down.*[66]

Arberry takes *tanzīl* in apposition with 'the Koran,' though he leaves this for the reader to discern by not introducing 'as' before 'a sending down.' But what could 'We have sent down the Koran as a sending down' possibly mean? The three previous translations are preferable precisely because they do not leave the reader guessing about the meaning of the passage. In my opinion, however, they are mistaken in taking *tanzīl* adverbially, when it would be better construed as a cognate accusative, one of the most common uses of the verbal noun in Arabic, as well as in other Semitic languages. As such *tanzīl*

61. Or 'in truth,' 'truly.'
62. See Q2.89; 3.3, 7; 4.105; 5.48; 6.92; 8.41; 16.64; 17.106; 26.193-194; 28.86; 46.12, 30.
63. Abdullah Yusuf Ali, *The Holy Qur'an* (Lahore: Shaikh Muḥammad Ashraf, 1934).
64. Ahmed Ali, *Al-Qur'ān: A Contemporary Translation* (Princeton: Princeton Univ. Press, 1988).
65. M.A.S. Abdel Haleem, *The Qur'an* (Oxford: Oxford Univ. Press, 2004).
66. Arthur J. Arberry, *The Koran Interpreted*, 2 vols. (London: Allen & Unwin, 1955) 2.316; cf. Marmaduke Pickthall, *The Meaning of the Glorious Koran* (London: Knopf, 1930): 'Lo! We, even We, have revealed unto thee the Qur'ān, *a revelation.*'

('a sending down') serves the purpose of emphasizing the action of the main verb *nazzalnā* ('We have sent down'), but the translator must find the right word(s) in English to describe just how the action of the main verb has been rendered emphatic. In my judgment the Arabic wants to say that the act of 'sending down' the Qur'ān has taken place 'all at once' or 'once and for all' – and not from the highest to the lowest heaven, but to the Prophet himself. Hence my translation: 'We have sent down on you the Qur'ān *once and for all*.'[67]

We find the same construction used again at Q17.105-106:

> **105** With the truth[68] We have sent it down, and with the truth it has come down. We have sent you only as a bringer of good news and a warner. **106** (It is) a Qur'ān – We have divided it, so that you may recite it to the people at intervals, and *We have sent it down once and for all.*

The tenor of the entire passage, not just the final statement, suggests an action which is complete. The declaration 'We have sent it down once and for all' is yet another emphatic response to the Prophets' skeptics, who only a few lines earlier had challenged him to 'bring down' (Ar. *tunazzila*) a book from heaven (Q17.93). The preceding 'We have divided it' (Ar. *faraqnāhu*) does not appear to be a reference to a 'gradual' or 'serial' mode of revelation; it seems instead to refer to some division or partition of the text of the Qur'ān for the purpose of the Prophet's recitation or reading aloud to the people 'at intervals.'[69]

More than a few passages attest that the Qur'ān was 'sent down' by God in the same way as the 'Torah' and 'Gospel' – that is, 'all at once' – as Q3.3 seems to take for granted: 'He has sent down on you the Book with the truth, confirming what was before it, and He sent down the Torah and the Gospel' (Q3.3).[70] What would be so surprising about the fact that each of these three 'Books' had been revealed similarly, especially given the references in the Qur'ān to the idea of three 'parallel' scriptures?[71] Once again the traditional view of a 'gradual' revelation begins to look like another secondary claim about the text, rather than something firmly established in the text. Yet we have already seen this was the case with the traditional understanding of Gabriel's role as the agent of revelation, as well as the widespread notion of a mechanical 'dictation' of the Qur'ān. The belief in a 'gradual' revelation of the Qur'ān appears to be a creation of tradition too – with one possible exception:

> Do not be in a hurry with the Qur'ān, before its inspiration [Ar. *waḥy*] is completed to you, but say: 'My Lord, increase me in knowledge.'[72]

Later interpreters claimed that it was the Qur'ān's 'serial' mode of revelation which distinguished it from the revelation of the 'Torah' to Moses. Here we should consider for a moment the potential advantages *for an exegete* of a claim that the Qur'ān had been revealed over the course of some twenty years rather than having been sent down all at once. For one thing it would set the Qur'ān apart from all other scriptures as unique in this regard, to say nothing of its Prophet. More importantly, however, it would offer an exegete a way to negotiate 'inconsistencies' and 'contradictions' in the text by being able to arrange them according to a scenario of an unfolding revelation at different times and places. The 'occasional' nature of revelation would also allow the exegete the possibility of prioritizing or ranking some passages over others – indeed of asserting that some 'earlier' passages had been 'abrogated' or

67. Richard Bell, *The Qur'ān*, offers a similar (albeit awkward) translation of the Arabic: 'Verily it is We who have sent down to thee the Qur'ān *actually*;' cf. Alan Jones, *The Qur'ān* (Exeter: Short Run Press, 2007): 'Truly We have sent down to you the Recitation.' In any case it is hard to justify a 'serial' mode of revelation on the basis of Q76.23.

68. Or 'In truth,' 'Truly.'

69. Or perhaps 'slowly' (cf. Q20.114; 25.32).

70. Cf. Q29.47. For the idea that Moses was given the Torah all at once, see e.g. Q2.53, 87; 5.44; 17.2, 4; for Jesus and the Gospel, see e.g. Q3.48; 5.46; 19.30; 57.27.

71. Articulated most explicitly at Q9.111, but see also Q2.136; 3.84; 29.46-47; cf. Q5.48; 6.92; 46.12.

72. Q20.114; cf. Q75.16-19 (cited above, p. xxi).

'replaced' by 'later' ones. Finally, if the Qur'ān had been delivered piece by piece *as occasion required*, the exegete could then remove individual passages from their Qur'ānic contexts and recontextualize them within stories about the 'occasions of revelation' (Ar. *asbāb al-nuzūl*). These new contexts would in turn furnish the exegete with new opportunities to play with the meaning of the text.[73]

Such interpretive strategies were not unique to Muslim exegetes but can also be found in the repertoires – 'the toolkits,' as it were – of Jewish and Christian interpreters of the Bible. For there were similarly conflicting views within Judaism and Christianity about the revelation of the Torah. Some thought the Torah had been given to Moses directly by God, others held that it was not God but an angel (or angels) who had delivered it to Moses. Some went so far as to claim that 'rebel angels' had handed down the Torah as part of a cosmic plot to enslave humanity. Christian exegetes likewise utilized the idea of an unfolding revelation whereby their 'New Testament' was considered to have 'abrogated' parts of the 'Old.' There were even some Jewish interpreters who, like their Muslim counterparts on the Qur'ān, claimed that the Torah had been transmitted in 'serial' fashion – that is, 'scroll by scroll' – while others claimed that it had been transmitted 'all at once.'[74] We shall pursue some of these issues further in a moment, but now let us return once more to the 'descent' of the Qur'ān as a book 'from heaven.'

The celestial origin of the Qur'ān is expressed in a number of different ways, perhaps none more famously than at Q43.2-4:

> **2** By the clear Book! **3** Surely We have made it an Arabic Qur'ān, so that you [plur.] may understand. **4** And surely it is in the mother of the Book, with Us, most high indeed, wise.

Here the Qur'ān declares itself to be a translation into Arabic – that is, the reproduction in history – of the contents of a heavenly archetype. The specification 'Arabic Qur'ān' (Ar. *qur'ān 'arabiyya*) may imply the existence of 'other Qur'āns,' as it were, in other languages, but it may well be an answer to some objection, perhaps that Hebrew was considered to be the *lingua sacra*.[75] Notice in particular that the epithets 'most high' and 'wise,' usually reserved for God, are here heaped upon the heavenly 'mother of the Book' (Ar. *umm al-kitāb*).[76] It is the 'mother' presumably because it represents the original from which not just the Qur'ān was derived, but other sacred books as well. Even so, it is hard to be sure just what is meant by this designation, since it occurs only here and at Q3.7 and Q13.39. In the former passage *umm al-kitāb* refers to the 'clearly composed verses' of the Qur'ān, not to a heavenly archetype. Yet where the Qur'ān appears to be a patchwork, tradition strives once again to weave together a seamless garment.

The notion of a heavenly book is how many interpreters explain the 'guarded Tablet' mentioned at Q85.22:

> **21** Yes! It is a glorious Qur'ān, **22** in a guarded Tablet.

The phrase 'in a guarded Tablet' (Ar. *fī lawḥin maḥfūẓin*) could be translated 'preserved on a tablet,' which would change the meaning considerably. Wooden tablets coated with stucco or wax were well-known writing surfaces in the ancient world. The same word is used in the plural for the 'Tablets' of Moses, as well as the wooden 'boards' of Noah's ark.[77] Nevertheless the 'guarded Tablet' (Ar. *lawḥ maḥfūẓ*) is traditionally understood to refer to a heavenly archetype, which is also linked with the 'hidden Book' referred to at Q56.77-80:

> **77** Surely it is an honorable Qur'ān indeed, **78** in a hidden Book! **79** No one touches it but the purified.
> **80** (It is) a sending down from the Lord of the worlds.

---

73. On this, see especially Andrew Rippin, 'The Function of *asbāb al-nuzūl* in Qur'ānic Exegesis,' *Bulletin of the School of Oriental and African Studies* 51 (1988) 1-20.
74. See Babylonian Talmud, Gittin 60a.
75. See also Q12.2; 13.37; 16.103; 20.113; 39.28; 41.3; 42.7; 46.12.
76. Cf. 'the wise Qur'ān' (Q36.2), 'the wise Book' (Q31.2), 'the wise Reminder' (Q3.58).
77. The 'planks' of Noah's ark (Q54.13), the 'Tablets' of Moses (Q7.145, 150, 154).

Here again the phrase 'in a hidden Book' could be understood to refer to a physical 'cherished Book' (Ar. *kitāb maknūn*) which contained the written Qur'ān. Notice what appears to be a reference to its ritual handling in the following line: 'No one touches it but the purified.' This may be how another passage should be construed at Q80.11-16:

> **11** Surely it is a reminder **12** – and whoever pleases (may) take heed of it – **13** (written) in honored pages, **14** exalted (and) purified, **15** by the hands of scribes, **16** (who are) honorable (and) dutiful.

Are the scribes referred to here the angels, who composed a *heavenly* Book, or are they human scribes who produced an *actual* book? The word translated 'pages' is literally 'leaves' or 'sheets' (Ar. *ṣuḥuf*) and seems to designate the written Qur'ān itself, rather than a heavenly archetype, as is traditionally claimed. The same applies to yet another passage at Q98.2-3, which refers to the Prophet as

> **2** a messenger from God, reciting purified pages, **3** in which (there are) true books.

Again, does this refer to the Prophet's 'recitation' of a heavenly book or to his 'reading aloud' from an actual one? It is hard to be sure, but elsewhere the word 'pages' (*ṣuḥuf*) occurs in connection with existing texts, above all those associated with Abraham and Moses. The two references to 'the *ṣuḥuf* of Abraham and Moses' imply something like 'scriptures' (whether in the form of a scroll or a codex), and perhaps that the 'Torah of Moses' was thought to be separate from the 'Book of Abraham.'[78] Since Abraham was a prophet,[79] it would not be surprising that he too was thought to have received a written revelation or 'book.' Taken together these passages make it likely that Q98.2 refers to the written Qur'ān rather than to its celestial archetype. Nevertheless many scholars read this passage too as a reference to the 'mother of the Book,' which not only contained the Qur'ān, but the other 'true books' derived from it: namely, the 'Torah' of Moses, the 'Psalms' of David, and the 'Gospel' of Jesus. These are the only books which are identified by title and linked with specific individuals.

There is debate among scholars about whether there was only one heavenly Book or several, for numerous passages in the Qur'ān appear to refer to other celestial 'Books.' Some of these passages indicate the existence of a separate 'Book of Destiny,' or cosmic script, by which all things have been determined by God,[80] while others mention a heavenly 'Record' of the deeds of humans kept by the 'recording angels,' which will be opened or unrolled on the Last Day.[81] One traditional view has it that these are only parts of a single, all-encompassing celestial Book, from which the Qur'ān, like the Torah and Gospel before it, had been 'sent down.' Thus none of the individual Books – Torah, Gospel, *or* Qur'ān – exhausts the contents of the heavenly archetype; each is in some sense a partial reproduction of it.[82] Perhaps for this very reason all of them are to be believed. This is expressed most clearly (and ecumenically) at Q2.136, when the believers are commanded:

> Say: 'We believe in God, and what has been sent down to us, and what has been sent down to Abraham, and Ishmael, and Isaac, and Jacob, and the tribes, and what was given to Moses and Jesus, and what was given to the prophets from their Lord. We make no distinction between any of them.'[83]

Just as the Prophet himself affirms at Q42.15:

> Say: 'I believe in whatever Book God has sent down.'

---

78. See Q53.36-37; 87.18-19; cf. Q20.133, 'the former pages' or 'the first scriptures' (Ar. *al-ṣuḥuf al-ūlā*).
79. See already Genesis 20.7.
80. See e.g. Q6.59; 10.61; 22.70; 57.22.
81. See e.g. Q18.49; 81.10; 82.10-12; cf. Q17.71; 69.19, 25; 84.7, 10.
82. See e.g. Q3.23; 4.41, 51
83. See also Q2.4; 3.84; 4.136; 29.46.

Islam thus shares with Judaism a belief in a heavenly prototype of scripture. Moreover the notion of the 'sending down' of the Qur'ān from heaven is structurally comparable to the 'sending down' of the heavenly Son in Christianity. Just as God's *Logos* is held to be 'embodied' in a historical person, so here it is 'embodied' in a historical text: 'The Word became Book!'

Who wrote the Qur'ān?

That question may strike some readers as obvious and others as irreverent. Yet the answer may not be as evident or impious as the question first appears. While the Qur'ān asserts its derivation from heaven, it says nothing directly about how it came to be a physical book. There are some hints in the Qur'ān, as we have just seen, which may point to the existence of an actual book,[84] and some scholars have attributed the initiative for this to Muḥammad himself. On five occasions in Q19 the Prophet is instructed to 'mention' or 'remember in the Book' Mary (16), Abraham (41), Moses (51), Ishmael (54), and Idrīs (56), which may indicate that the composition of a book was underway at some point.[85] The famous opening of Q2, 'That is the Book – (there is) no doubt about it' (Q2.2), implies that such a book may have actually appeared.[86] These passages led Richard Bell to the view 'that the Qur'ān was in written form when the redactors [i.e. those who are said to have compiled the first edition] started their work, whether actually written by Muḥammad himself, as [Bell] personally believe[d], or by others at his dictation.'[87]

If something like the *present* Qur'ān existed already in the lifetime of Muḥammad, how different its composition and transmission would be in comparison to the rather messy composition and textual histories of the Bibles of Judaism and Christianity! Here would be a single book, by a single 'author,' which, apart from a few controversial verses, had been transmitted intact down to the present. Its chain of transmission – God → Gabriel → Muḥammad → written Qur'ān → reader/hearer – would not just guarantee that the content of revelation had been transmitted intact and without interference, it would also make the revelatory event of the distant past utterly and immediately present to the contemporary hearer or reader. That is why it is so surprising to discover that the earliest traditions concerning the history of the Qur'ān *as a text* cast doubt upon it and consider it to be 'flawed' and 'incomplete.' According to an oft-cited 'report' (Ar. *ḥadīth*), the pious son of the second caliph 'Umar said,

> Let none of you say, 'I have got the whole of the Qur'ān.' How does he know what all of it is? *Much of the Qur'ān has gone*. Let him say instead, 'I have got what has survived.'[88]

Traditional stories about the 'first collection' of the Qur'ān vary widely and defy easy summary.[89] According to the (now) dominant account of the Persian *ḥadīth*-scholar, al-Bukhārī (d. 870 CE/256 AH), there was a debate as to whether such a collection was even appropriate – that is, whether the Prophet's

84. See also Q25.4-5 (and notice the reference to the Prophet's literacy).

85. On the other hand, the formula may simply be intended to 'remind' the audience of a particular story 'in the Book' (i.e. in the 'Torah' or 'Gospel'); cf. the repeated formula 'And remember...' in Q38, used to introduce the stories of David (17), Job (41), Abraham, Isaac, and Jacob (45), and Ishmael, Elisha, and Dhū-l-Kifl (48).

86. See also Q6.92, 155; 46.12: 'This is a Book;' Q11.1: 'A Book – its verses have been clearly composed;' Q41.3: 'A Book – its verses made distinct – an Arabic Qur'ān;' Q52.2-3: 'a Book written on parchment unrolled.'

87. Bell, *The Qur'ān* 1.vi. There are certainly many signs of editorial activity in the Qur'ān, evidenced by sudden alterations in rhyme scheme, abrupt changes of subject, and breaks in syntax. But when this activity occurred and who was responsible for it is not clear. Traditional scholars explain (and prize) these features of the Qur'ān as its unique, daring style, rather than seeing it as evidence of hasty composition or redaction and revision.

88. Al-Suyūṭī, *Al-Itqān fī 'ulūm al-Qur'ān*, 2 vols. in 1 (Cairo: Ḥalabī, 1935) 2.25 (translation from John Burton, *The Collection of the Qur'ān* [Cambridge: Cambridge Univ. Press, 1977] 117).

89. The standard technical analysis remains that of John Burton, *Collection of the Qur'ān* 117-137 (see previous n.). There is a remarkably clear and succinct account of this staggeringly complex subject by Aliza Shnizer, 'Sacrality and Collection,' in Andrew Rippin (ed.), *The Blackwell Companion to the Qur'ān* (Oxford: Blackwell, 2006) 165-171.

companions should undertake what the Prophet himself *did not do*:

> Zayd ibn Thābit said: 'Abū Bakr [caliph 632-634 CE/11-13 AH] sent for me at the time of the battle of al-Yamāma, and 'Umar ibn al-Khaṭṭāb [caliph 634-644 CE/13-23 AH] was with him. Abū Bakr said: 'Umar has come to me and said: 'Death was rampant at the battle of al-Yamāma and took with it many reciters of the Qur'ān. I fear lest death in battle overtake the reciters of the Qur'ān in the provinces and so a large part of the Qur'ān be lost. I think you should give orders to collect the Qur'ān.'
>
> 'What,' I asked 'Umar, '*do you wish to do something which the Messenger of God himself did not do*?' 'By God,' replied 'Umar, 'it would be a good deed.' Umar did not leave off urging me until at length God opened my heart to this and I thought as 'Umar did.
>
> Zayd continued: Abū Bakr said to me: 'You are a young man, intelligent, and we see no fault in you. Moreover, *you have already written down the revelation for the Messenger of God*, may God bless and save him. Therefore go and seek the Qur'ān and collect it.'
>
> By God, *if he had ordered me to move a mountain, it would not have been harder for me than his order to collect the Qur'ān*. 'What,' I asked, '*will you do something which the Messenger of God himself, may God bless and save him, did not do*?' 'By God,' replied Abū Bakr, 'it would be a good deed.'
>
> 'Umar did not leave off urging me until at length God opened my heart to this as He had opened the hearts of Abū Bakr and 'Umar.
>
> Then I searched out and collected the parts of the Qur'ān, whether they were written on palm leaves or flat stones or in the hearts of men. Thus I found the end of *sūrat al-Tawba* [Q9.128-129], which I had not been able to find anywhere else, in the possession of Abū Khuzayma al-Anṣārī, having found it with no one else.... The pages [Ar. *ṣuḥuf*] remained in the possession of Abū Bakr until his death, then in 'Umar's for as long as he lived, and then with Ḥafṣa, the daughter of 'Umar.[90]

If we accept the reliability of this account, several conclusions follow: (1) that Muḥammad did not leave behind a complete written text of the Qur'ān; (2) that the Qur'ān was preserved only in fragments and primarily in oral form; and (3) that within two years of the Prophet's death an 'official written collection' of the Qur'ān had been made. But there are serious problems with this account, both on internal and external grounds.[91] Each of its basic points is contradicted by alternative *ḥadīths*, which variously attribute a 'collection' of the Qur'ān to each of the first four caliphs (Abū Bakr, 'Umar, 'Uthmān, and 'Alī). As well, there are reports which maintain that no official collection of the Qur'ān existed prior to the third caliph, 'Uthmān. Moreover 'Umar's command to Zayd, Muḥammad's young secretary, to 'go and seek the Qur'ān and collect it' makes little sense if Zayd had 'already written down the revelation for the Messenger of God,' as Abū Bakr is explicitly reported to have said.

The next stage in the collection of the Qur'ān, again according to the standard account, was the reconciliation of various written *codices*. This is usually attributed to 'Uthmān, though the impetus for it is said to have come from 'Uthmān's general, Ḥudhayfa, when he happened to notice that his Syrian and Iraqi armies read different Qur'āns. Ḥudhayfa therefore urged 'Uthmān to establish a standard edition, before the Muslims found themselves in the same situation as the Jews and Christians – adrift on a sea of textual confusion. According to this account, there were multiple versions of the Qur'ān in circulation in a variety of Arabic dialects. The 'editorial committee' appointed by 'Uthmān was charged with the task of reducing all these dialects to one, that of the Quraysh (held to be Muḥammad's own dialect), and all other codices were allegedly destroyed.

> Anas ibn Malik said: Ḥudhayfa ibn al-Yamān accompanied 'Uthmān [caliph 644-656 CE/23-35 AH] when he was preparing the army of Syria together with the army of Iraq to conquer Armenia and Azharbayjān.

---

90. Al-Bukhārī, *Ṣaḥīḥ* 3.392-393 (translation from F.E. Peters, *A Reader on Classical Islam* [Princeton: Princeton Univ. Press, 1994] 179-180, slightly altered).

91. See Burton, *Collection of the Qur'ān* 120-128.

> Ḥudhayfa was astonished by the differences in the (two armies') reading of the Qur'ān, and said to 'Uthmān, 'Commander of the Faithful! Catch hold of this community before they begin to differ about their Book as do the Jews and Christians.'
>
> 'Uthmān sent to Ḥafṣa to say, 'Send us the pages [Ar. *ṣuḥuf*]. We shall copy them into codices [*maṣāḥif*] and return them to you.'
>
> Ḥafṣa sent them to 'Uthmān, who ordered Zayd ibn Thābit, Abdullāh ibn al-Zubayr, Sa'īd ibn al-'Āṣ, and 'Abd al-Raḥmān ibn al-Ḥārith ibn Hishām to copy them into codices. 'Uthmān said to the three of them who were of the tribe of the Quraysh, 'If you differ from Zayd ibn Thābit on anything in the Qur'ān, write it down according to the language of the Quraysh, for it is in their language that the Qur'ān was sent down.'
>
> They did as he ordered, and when they had copied the pages into codices, 'Uthmān returned the pages to Ḥafṣa. He sent copies of the codex [Ar. *muṣḥaf*] which they made in all directions and gave orders to burn every page and codex which differed from it.[92]

This account inspires as little confidence as the previous collection story, with which it exists in uneasy tension. For it was not simply a matter of 'Uthmān reproducing the 'pages' previously collected by Abū Bakr between two covers – that is, in the form of a book – which would follow seamlessly on the first account. Rather 'Uthmān is said to have produced a single text (or *textus receptus*) out of a welter of 'rival Qur'āns.' Now, quite apart from the questions of whether a caliph would actually burn copies of the Qur'ān, or whether the present Qur'ān is actually in the Quraysh dialect, 'Uthmān's undertaking makes little sense in light of the earlier account, which offered not a hint of the existence of any rival Qur'āns.

John Burton has argued that all the collection stories are fictions, not only the ones recounted above, and he further contends that they were fabricated by later exegetes to conceal the fact that the Qur'ān was not produced by 'Uthmān, or by any other caliph, but was collected and edited by Muḥammad himself. Subjecting the mass of traditions about the collection of the Qur'ān to painstaking analysis, Burton reaches four fundamental conclusions: (1) The 'Uthmānic collection 'need never have occurred.' The so-called 'Companion codices' (or 'rival Qur'āns') are only cited with respect to single verses, and this 'exegetical device' uniformly 'aim[s] at countering, elucidating, or even evading the 'Uthmān text.' Thus the 'Companion codices' must be posterior to that text and not prior to it.[93] (2) The tradition of the 'Uthmanic collection (cited above) represents a late attempt to harmonize the conflicting attributions of such a collection to Muḥammad's four immediate successors. 'The circumstances in which the task was first taken up were such in which the loss of [Qur'ānic texts was] very easily conceivable, yet the task [was] presented as having been executed with such supererogatory care that the ['Uthmanic] text was projected as having been beyond doubt complete. The two motifs concretise the forces pulling in opposite directions in the minds of the Muslims on the question of the completeness/incompleteness of the Qur'ān, according as they were engaging in internal or in external polemic.'[94] (3) Despite the hotchpotch of traditions concerning the collection of the Qur'ān, 'the *one common motif shared by every single Muslim account*..., uniting all the *ḥadīth*s, ...is precisely this allegation that, whoever it may have been who for the first time...had brought together the Qur'ān texts, *it was certainly not the Prophet*.'[95] In order to invest 'Tradition' (*Sunna*, with a capital 'S'), which Muslim scholars controlled, with a status equal to 'Scripture,' these same scholars 'simply could not afford to be seen in possession of a text [of the Qur'ān] that had come down to them in writing from the Prophet. This explains why the classical *ḥadīth*s had to place the

92. Al-Bukhārī, *Ṣaḥīḥ* 3.394 (translation from Peters, *Reader on Classical Islam* 180, slightly altered).
93. Burton, *Collection of the Qur'ān* 228-229.
94. Burton, *Collection of the Qur'ān* 230-231 ('Further, the question arises internally from the implications of the exegesis of certain verses apparently referring to the Prophet's forgetting/being caused to forget certain unspecified parts of the revelation').
95. Burton, *Collection of the Qur'ān* 231 (my emphasis).

collection of the Qur'ān texts into the time following the death of Muḥammad. *The connection between the Qur'ān document and the Prophet to whom it had been revealed had at all costs to be broken.*'[96] Thus the traditions about a 'flawed' or 'incomplete' transmission of the Qur'ān were the creation of later Muslim scholars attempting to create space for their own interpretive labors. In this way, for example, they could 'discover' elements of Islamic law, which were nowhere referred to in the 'Uthmānic text, in allegedly still-surviving Qur'ān texts.[97] (4) Hence Burton's momentous conclusion: 'What we have today in our hands is the *muṣḥaf* of Muḥammad.'[98] The Qur'ān was written down by none other than Muḥammad himself!

Burton's analysis of the traditional stories of the 'collection' of the Qur'ān is built upon the foundations laid by two pioneer studies of classical *ḥadīths*: Joseph Schacht's *The Origins of Muhammadan Jurisprudence* (1950), which in turn had developed the earlier insights of Ignaz Goldziher's *Muhammedanische Studien* (1889-1890).[99] Goldziher had concluded that

> [c]loser acquaintance with the vast stock of *ḥadīths* induces skeptical caution rather than optimistic trust regarding the material brought together in the carefully compiled collections. We...will probably consider by far the greater part of it as the result of the religious, historical and social development of Islam during the first two centuries [AH]. The *ḥadīth* will not serve as a document for the infancy of Islam, but rather as a reflection of the tendencies which appeared in the community during the maturer stages of its development. (...) This makes the proper appreciation and study of the *ḥadīth* so important for an understanding of Islam, in the evolution of which the most notable phases are accompanied by successive stages in the creation of *ḥadīth*.[100]

This was Goldziher's 'brilliant discovery,' according to Burton, his 'magnificent insight,' which most modern scholars accept in principle but fail to put into practice.[101] Goldziher contended that the classical *ḥadīths* were not memorized traditions about Muḥammad, but were 'invented' to justify competing viewpoints, beliefs, and practices of later Muslims. This explains why, for example, there are so many different and contradictory *ḥadīths* on one and the same question.[102]

Joseph Schacht developed Goldziher's insight further through an analysis of the legal *ḥadīths*.[103] For this material Schacht was able to demonstrate that, rather than spreading out from the centers of Islam (especially Medina), the legal *ḥadīths* were exemplary of local 'customary practice' (*sunna*, with a small 's'), and were originally formulated without reference either to Muḥammad or the Qur'ān. 'Attribution' (Ar. *isnād*) of individual *ḥadīths* was itself an innovation which came into being in the arguments waged by legal scholars in the Islamic communities of Iraq and the Ḥijāz to provide accreditation for their conflicting doctrines. Indeed at first these doctrines were not even connected with the 'Companions of the Prophet' or their successors. Attribution was to the immediately preceding generation, then to the generation before that, and so on. The references to Muḥammad, as well as the insertion of Qur'ānic 'proof texts,' reflected a later stage in the development of a process which Schacht could trace back no farther than the end of the Umayyad period (c. 750 CE/132 AH), which had furnished much of

96. Burton, *Collection of the Qur'ān* 136 (my emphasis).
97. Burton, *Collection of the Qur'ān* 232.
98. Burton, *Collection of the Qur'ān* 239-240.
99. Joseph Schacht, *The Origins of Muhammadan Jurisprudence* (Oxford: Clarendon Press, 1950); Ignaz Goldziher, *Muslim Studies*, tr. C.R. Barber and S.M. Stern, 2 vols. (London: Allen & Unwin, 1966, 1971 [1889, 1890]); see Burton's summary of their contribution in *idem*, *An Introduction to the Ḥadīth* (Edinburgh: Edinburgh Univ. Press, 1994) ix-xxvi.
100. Goldziher, *Muslim Studies* 2.19 (cited in Burton, *Introduction to the Ḥadīth* xvi-xvii).
101. Burton, *Introduction to the Ḥadīth* xvii.
102. See e.g. Goldziher, *Muslim Studies* 2.78, 81, 85.
103. That is, Schacht concentrated on *fiqh*, Islamic 'sacred law' or 'jurisprudence,' which comprises cultic and ritual matters as well as political and legal rules.

the raw materials for Muslim legal specialists. According to Schacht, Islamic law did not derive from the Qur'ān but developed out of Umayyad administrative practice, and this practice often diverged from the intentions and explicit wordings of the Qur'ān. '[L]egal norms based on the Koran,' concluded Schacht, 'were introduced into [Islamic] law almost invariably at a secondary stage.'[104]

The contributions of Goldziher and Schacht informed John Burton's skeptical stance toward Islamic tradition in his important study of *The Collection of the Qur'ān* (1977). Even before that book, however, Burton had issued the following programmatic statement about the value of Islamic tradition for a historical understanding of the Qur'ān:

> Here is the key to the understanding of the Qur'ān in the position it held in the historical perspective which separated Muḥammadanism from Islam. *So long as we continue to approach the Qur'ān by means of the literature of Islam we must inevitably travel in a circle.* Have we already forgotten the warning of Zarkashī ("'the occasions of revelation' are of the nature of justification of the doctrine from the verse, not of the nature of a report concerning something which historically occurred nor that the occurrence in fact occasioned the revelation")? Have we so soon forgotten Goldziher's marvellous discoveries on the nature and function of the traditions? *If we daily apply these to one type of tradition ought we not in consistency to apply them to all types, most of all to any traditions relating to the Qur'ān, to the reading of its texts, to the circumstances of its revelation, to its collection, to its interpretation?* In the Qur'ān field results as fundamental and revolutionary as those achieved by Professor Schacht in the field of the *fiqh* remain to be won. The complacency of Orientalists *vis-à-vis* the Islamic traditions on the Qur'ān has prevented not merely the solution but the very identification of the central Qur'ān problem.[105]

I have quoted this passage at length because it so clearly articulates a set of fundamental questions which every reader of the Qur'ān must face and try to answer. What importance does tradition have for a historical understanding of the Qur'ān? Does it provide the indispensable lens which focuses our vision or must it be dispensed with because it occludes our vision? Does tradition carry us back to the origins of Islam in the early seventh century CE (first century AH), or will it take us back no farther than c. 800 CE/180 AH? Are there reasons for regarding parts of the tradition as reliable but other parts as unreliable? And, if so, what are the criteria that will allow us to make this distinction? Finally, if we reject (some) tradition as 'mere invention,' have we thereby failed *as historians* to recognize tradition's own creativity as well as the importance of studying tradition in its own right? My concern here is not to answer these questions directly, but only to insist that the very act of entertaining them is what constitutes a critical reading of the Qur'ān.[106]

For the moment let us return once more to 1977, which turned out to be a very good year for Qur'ānic studies. If Joseph Schacht was correct, that Qur'ānic 'proof texts' were only inserted into *ḥadīth*s at a

104. Schacht, *Origins of Muhammadan Jurisprudence* 191, see also 224-227); cf. *idem*, *An Introduction to Islamic Law* (Oxford: Clarendon Press, 1964) 18: '[A]ny but the most perfunctory attention given to the Koranic norms, and any but the most elementary conclusions, belong almost invariably to a secondary stage of development of doctrine,' and: 'there are several cases in which the early doctrine of Islamic law diverged from the explicit wording of the Koran.'

105. Burton, review of William Montgomery Watt, *Companion to the Qur'ān* (London: Allen & Unwin, 1967), in *Bulletin of the School of Oriental and African Studies* 32 (1969) 387-389, quotation from p. 388 (my emphasis).

106. Most scholars of the Qur'ān continue to regard *ḥadīth*s as reasonably trustworthy (especially the 'historical' as opposed to the 'legal' *ḥadīth*s). For those who wish to pursue these questions further, I recommend the following studies as a good place to begin: Herbert Berg, *The Development of Exegesis in Early Islam: The Authenticity of Muslim Literature from the Formative Period* (Richmond: Curzon, 2000); Harald Motski, 'The Collection of the Qur'ān: A Reconsideration of Western Views in Light of Recent Methodological Developments,' *Der Islam* 78 (2001) 1-34; *idem*, 'The Question of the Authenticity of Muslim Traditions Reconsidered: A Review Article,' in Herbert Berg (ed.), *Method and Theory in the Study of Islamic Origins*, Islamic History and Civilization, Studies and Texts 49 (Leiden: Brill, 2003) 211-257; and Herbert Berg, 'Competing Paradigms in the Study of Islamic Origins: Qur'ān 15:89-91 and the Value of *Isnād*s,' in *idem* (ed.), *Method and Theory in the Study of Islamic Origins* 259-290.

later stage in their transmission, an alternative possibility presents itself: *No Qur'ān was cited because no Qur'ān existed.* This was the conclusion reached in another momentous book published in the very same year as Burton's *Collection of the Qur'ān*. I am referring to John Wansbrough's controversial and often misunderstood *Quranic Studies: Sources and Methods of Scriptural Interpretation.*[107] For Wansbrough, no Qur'ān was cited because there was no Qur'ān until some three centuries after Muḥammad. He reached this conclusion on the basis of three kinds of evidence: (1) Schacht's work, which established that there was no reference to the Qur'ān in the legal *ḥadīths* of the first two centuries after Muḥammad's death; (2) the important creedal formulation, the *Fiqh Akbar I* (mid-eighth century CE/mid-second century AH), makes no mention of the Qur'ān; and (3) *tafsīr*, or exegetical literature, which presumes a text of the Qur'ān, does not begin to appear until the third century after Muḥammad's death.[108]

Simply put, Wansbrough had cut the link between Muḥammad and the Qur'ān, when no one before this had seriously questioned its antiquity. Whereas the biographical tradition presented the Qur'ān as rooted firmly in the life of Muḥammad, and only truly comprehensible in that setting, for Wansbrough the 'Arabian prophet' had no historical connection with the contents of the Qur'ān. In fact it was through the composition of the *sīra*, he contended, that later Muslim scholars attempted to connect the essentially anonymous content of the Qur'ān with an ostensibly historical figure in Arabia.

Like Burton, Wansbrough too regarded as fictions the various collection stories and accounts of 'Companion codices,' but he understood their purpose differently from Burton. Wansbrough argued that they were created in order to give ancient authority to a text that was not 'canonized' until centuries later, and not in Arabia in the seventh century CE, but in the eighth to ninth centuries CE in 'Abbāssid Iraq. There in its capital city of Baghdad were skilled professional scribes, not to mention books and booksellers. Furthermore, Wansbrough contended that the actual compilation of the Qur'ān was a much more fluid process than the traditional accounts presented. On the basis of its composite structure – that is, the Qur'ān's apparently random and seemingly arbitrary sense of organization – Wansbrough conceived of its compilation as 'an organic development' rather than as 'a carefully executed project.'

> Particularly in the *exempla* of salvation history, characterized by variant traditions, but also in passages of exclusively paraenetic or eschatological content, ellipses and repetitions are such as to suggest not the carefully executed project of one or many men, but rather the product of an organic development from originally independent traditions during a long period of transmission.[109]

This process, moreover, entailed the 'gradual juxtaposition of originally separate collections of *logia*,' or independent sayings-complexes, which later came to be seen as direct utterances of God through Gabriel and Muḥammad. That is, the essentially anonymous material of the Qur'ān was only later linked to an 'Arabian prophet.' Wansbrough argued that the traditional *sīra* represents a historicization of these *logia* in the 'life of Muḥammad,' which is just the reverse of the relationship posited by tradition. He refers to the 'life' as the 'Muhammadan *evangelium*,' doubtless on the analogy of the way in which free-floating sayings (*logia*) came to be attached to a 'Galilean prophet,' and then were later 'historicized' in the Christian 'gospels' (*evangelia*). 'The failure to eliminate repetition in the canon[ical Qur'ān],' Wansbrough speculated, 'might be attributed to the status these *logia* had already achieved in the several (!) communities within which they originated and by whose members they were transmitted.' Thus despite the traditional emphasis on single centers of activity – Mecca and Medina – these prophetic

107. Originally published in 1977, it has been reissued by Prometheus Books under the supervision of Andrew Rippin, who provides a foreword, translation of key terms and passages, and expanded notes – all of it invaluable to the first-time reader. See now John Wansbrough, *Quranic Studies: Sources and Methods of Scriptural Interpretation* (Amherst, NY: Prometheus Books, 2004). The pagination remains unchanged from the first printing.

108. See Wansbrough, *Quranic Studies* 44-46, 202-207, 226-227 *et passim*.

109. Wansbrough, *Quranic Studies* 44.

logia originated in different communities at different times 'in environments [which were] essentially sectarian but within the mainstream of oriental monotheism.' In other words, for Wansbrough, the composite nature of the sayings material suggests polygenesis rather than a single point of origin or 'big bang.'[110]

It is not possible here to do justice to the richness and subtlety of the works of Wansbrough and Burton, or to the vigorous debate which has ensued since their original publication in 1977. Nor is it necessary here to take sides. Though these two scholars could not differ more on the question of when and how the Qur'ān came to be, they do serve to return us to the question with which we began: Can the Qur'ān be understood apart from centuries of later tradition about it? Their answer is not only 'yes,' but that it must be so understood if it is to be read historically. To give John Burton the final word: 'So long as we continue to approach the Qur'ān by means of the literature of Islam we must inevitably travel in a circle.'

A Qur'ān from Cairo

Thus far we have explored the story the Qur'ān tells about itself, and interrogated some of the stories tradition relates about the Qur'ān, but we have yet to ask the most basic question of all: What do we mean by 'the Qur'ān'? Although it declares itself to be a Book which has 'come down' from heaven, how has the Qur'ān 'come down' to us through history?

The history of the *written* Qur'ān is quite complex and only imperfectly understood. As is well known, though rarely acknowledged (especially by translators!), there is no 'critical edition' of the Qur'ān. A critical edition is one in which all extant manuscripts (as well as citations) of a text are catalogued, collated, and their variants noted, in the hope of establishing the original wording of a text, or getting as close to its original wording as the surviving manuscripts allow. 'Manuscript' is the key word here. It comes from Latin and means 'written by hand.' That is just what books were before printing: handwritten, and also handmade. Apart from documentary papyri and some inscriptions on stone, no ancient text survives in the form in which it was originally written. Scholars refer to this original as an 'autograph,' from a Greek word meaning 'the writing itself.' This bears repeating: no autograph survives of any ancient literary text – none of the *Epic of Gilgamesh* or Herodotus' *Histories*, none of any texts in the Bible, and none of the Qur'ān. In some cases only a single copy of a text survives, and on occasion that one copy may be badly damaged, either from the destructive forces of history or climate, and so exist only in fragmentary form. In fact the vast majority of ancient literature has simply not survived at all. But what has come down to us has done so because of the extraordinary human labor of scribes who copied out texts by hand. This applies even to the chance discoveries of texts like the Nag Hammadi codices in 1945, the Qumran scrolls in 1946, and the cache of Qur'ān manuscripts uncovered in the Great Mosque of Ṣan'ā' in 1972. None of these three 'finds' contains any autographs; all of the texts are handwritten scribal copies of earlier handwritten copies and so on. In cases where multiple copies of a single work exist, the manuscripts do not agree. In fact no two copies of any ancient manuscript agree entirely. There are always discrepancies, however slight.[111]

110. Wansbrough, *Quranic Studies* 47, 49, 50, 56 (quotations from p. 50), cf. 77-84. Wansbrough refused to identify a specific source for what was, only later, to become Islam. His reference to 'environments essentially sectarian but within the mainstream of oriental monotheism' designates a broad spectrum of separatist religious communities of the Middle East in Late Antiquity, which he sometimes calls 'Judaeo-Christian' or 'Ebionite,' but by this he does not mean to identify a particular group or sect, and certainly not one which 'influenced' Muḥammad or from which Islam 'emerged.' See further John Wansbrough, *The Sectarian Milieu: Content and Composition of Islamic Salvation History* (Oxford: Oxford University Press, 1978).

111. For example, more than 5,000 manuscripts exist of the New Testament in Greek, ranging from tiny scraps of papyrus, containing a line or two, to massive parchment tomes, containing the entire Bible (and more). No two of these manuscripts agree, nor has anyone yet been able to count all the differences and disagreements among them. Scholars estimate the number of variants to be somewhere between 200,000 and 300,000.

Modern textual criticism is therefore faced with a daunting challenge. Its goal is to reconstruct, as far as possible, the original form of an ancient text by (1) carefully comparing all surviving copies of a text (as well as citations of it by later writers), (2) correcting the mistakes and/or deliberate changes made by scribes who copied the texts, and (3) trying to fill in the *lacunae* ('gaps') in a damaged text. The first procedure is called 'collation;' the second is referred to as 'emendation;' and the third is designated 'restoration.' There may be instances, however, in which it is clear that no surviving manuscript preserves the original wording. In such cases a textual critic may make a 'conjectural emendation.' In the published critical edition of a text, the editor will defend his or her decisions through a system of notations, called a 'critical apparatus,' at the bottom of the page (listing, for example, the important variants for a particular word or phrase), and through the use of various symbols in the text (to indicate, for example, a doubtful word or a *lacuna*). Textual criticism is a tedious, often messy, and sometimes inconclusive affair. It is no easy task, then, to determine the 'original' wording of an ancient text. This is also true of some texts composed only a relatively short time ago. None of Shakespeare's plays survives as an autograph, and for most of them there are two or more printed (!) versions with differences among them. Like all work in the human sciences, then, the results of textual criticism are always tentative, provisional, and above all corrigible, especially as new evidence comes to light.

But what does a student or translator do when there is no critical edition of a text? In the case of the Qur'ān there are really only two choices at present. S/he must use either of two standard printed editions: Gustav Flügel's *Corani textus arabicus*, first published in Leipzig in 1834 CE (1252 AH), or *al-Qur'ān al-karīm*, first published in Cairo in 1342 AH (1924 CE) under the auspices of the Egyptian government. Neither is a critical edition. The Flügel edition, which employs a different system of versification, served for a time as the standard text for European scholars, and Richard Bell used it for his English translation of 1937-1939,[112] but it was never an edition that met with approval by Muslim scholars. It gradually became obsolete, when it was replaced by the Cairo edition, which is now widely seen as the 'official' or 'standard text' of the Qur'ān. Yet this edition did not impose itself from heaven; quite the contrary. From the first, the Cairo Qur'ān was a parochial affair. It was commissioned in response to complaints the Egyptian government had received about variations in the texts of Qur'āns the government had been importing for use in secondary schools. In other words, the appointed committee of scholars was not charged with the task of establishing a uniform text of the Qur'ān for the Muslim world at large, but for the purposes of religious education in Egypt. Nevertheless, the Cairo Qur'ān has achieved a kind of *de facto* canonical status in both the religious *and* secular academic worlds.[113]

It should be pointed out that the scholars who labored on the Cairo edition did not attempt to reconstruct the most original form of the text of the Qur'ān; on occasion in fact the Cairo edition is at odds with the evidence of existing manuscripts. Instead these scholars sought to preserve one of the accepted 'readings' or 'recitations' (Ar. *qirā'āt*) of the Qur'ān which is said to have originated in the eighth century CE (second century AH) in the Iraqi city of Kufa. It is known technically as the version of Ḥafṣ (d. 796 CE/180 AH) from the reading of 'Āṣim (d. 744 CE/127 AH). But here we must pause for a moment and give some attention to just what is meant by different 'readings' of the Qur'ān.

The idea of 'readings' or *qirā'āt* has a specialized meaning in Islamic tradition, and does not refer to what modern text critics call 'textual variants.' Even if one accepts the reliability of the traditional stories about

---

112. To the best of my knowledge Bell is the only English translator who indicates which edition of the Arabic text he is translating *and* acknowledges that 'there is as yet no critical edition of the text available' (*The Qur'ān* 1.v). In a footnote Bell reports that 'such an edition, with full apparatus criticus, is in course of preparation, by Dr. [Arthur] Jeffrey of Cairo.' Jeffrey's edition never appeared.

113. For more about the Cairo edition, see Gotthelf Bergsträsser, 'Koranlesung in Kairo,' *Der Islam* 20 (1932) 1-42; Michael W. Albin, art. 'Printing of the Qur'ān,' *Encyclopaedia of the Qur'ān* 4.264-276, esp. 269-272; and François Déroche, 'Written Transmission,' in Rippin (ed.), *Blackwell Companion to the Qur'ān* 183-185.

the creation of the 'Uthmānic text of the Qur'ān, the process by which that text came to prevail over its rivals is far from clear, and tradition reports that there were even discrepancies among the 'official' copies sent out by 'Uthmān. In other words, even the traditional collection stories do not account for the establishment of a 'fixed' text. As Andrew Rippin has well observed, 'Elements such as the fixing of the Arabic script, the establishment of written formats of manuscripts, and the codification of variant readings are all spoken of in [traditional] accounts as *subsequent* to the initial collection stories by a significant time period.'[114]

Originally Arabic was written only in consonants, and in a few cases the same letter form was used for two or more different consonants. With the use of a consonantal script, vocalization (or 'voweling') is left up to the reader. In such a situation the possibility exists that even when there is agreement about the consonants, there can be different vocalizations, and hence different meanings can be construed from the same consonants. Some scholars have speculated that the 'Uthmānic text, written only in a consonantal script and with poor word division, may have been more a 'mnemonic device' or 'prompt text' designed for public recital, rather than a proper edition of the text for private reading and study. However that may be, the process of the establishment of the text of the Qur'ān would prove to be a long one, just as it would be in the case of the Bible. It took Jewish scholars (the 'Masoretes') until the eighth or ninth century CE to fix the text of the Hebrew scriptures.[115] The textual history of the Christian Bible was an even longer and more chaotic affair, compounded by the proliferation of translations of the Greek text into other languages (e.g. Latin, Syriac, Coptic, and eventually even Arabic). Its text has never been fixed. The notion of 'the Bible' existing, say, at the Jewish Council of Yavneh (135 CE) or Christian Council of Nicea (325 CE) is therefore as anachronistic as 'the Qur'ān' existing under 'Uthmān.[116]

In the ninth and tenth centuries CE (third and fourth centuries AH), there were debates over improving the script in which the text of the Qur'ān was written. These improvements are chiefly associated with Ibn Mujāhid (d. 936 CE/324 AH), a Baghdadi scholar, who undertook the difficult task of restricting the number of acceptable 'readings,' while at the same time denying those scholars who insisted that there should only be one uniform reading. Ibn Mujāhid came up with seven accepted systems of vocalizing the consonantal text of the Qur'ān, based on the readings which prevailed in five metropolitan centers: one each from Medina, Mecca, Bosra, and Damascus, and three from Kufa. For each of these 'readings' there were also two slightly different 'versions' or 'recensions.' This system was made official in 934 CE/322 AH, and, as might be expected, traditions were invented to secure its antiquity. One of these has God reciting the Qur'ān to Muḥammad in one *qirā'a*, and, when Muḥammad asked for more, God gave him an additional six *qirā'āt*. Other readings beyond the seven, however, continued to be used in commentaries on the Qur'ān, as well as in other philological and grammatical works.[117] Of the seven readings only two versions are now in general use: the previously mentioned version of Ḥafṣ from the reading of 'Āṣim, and a somewhat more conservative reading which is said to have originated in Medina, namely, the version of Warsh (d. 812 CE/197 AH) from the reading of Nāfi' (d. 785 CE/169 AH), which is

114. Andrew Rippin, 'Foreword' to Wansbrough, *Quranic Studies* (2004) xv (my emphasis).

115. There were a number of different attempts to fix the pronunciation of the Hebrew text of scripture. (The impetus for this may have come from Christian translations of the Bible into Syriac.) Three systems of vocalization are known: they are called the Palestinian, the Babylonian supralinear, and the Tiberian. Only the third one achieved lasting success.

116. Most scholars now doubt whether there ever was a rabbinic 'Council of Yavneh' which decided the 'canon' of the Hebrew Bible. I use it merely by way of example. My reference to the 'Council of Nicea' is likewise only an example. In fact there was no ecumenical council declaration establishing the canon of the Christian Bible until the Council of Trent in 1546 CE. The ruling of that body pertained only to the status of the 'Apocrypha,' in the wake of the Protestant reformers' rejection of certain books of the Old Testament. At best one can speak of 'local canons.'

117. This simplifies a much more complex story; see further Christopher Melchert, 'Ibn Mujāhid and the Establishment of Seven Qur'ānic Readings,' *Studia Islamica* 91 (2000) 5-22.

in use mainly in the Maghrib or northwestern Africa. The Cairo edition of 1924 reproduced the former version, and as much for political reasons as scholarly ones.

A critical edition of the Qur'ān, therefore, remains a desideratum, though some secular scholars have questioned whether such an edition is even possible, and most religious scholars dismiss it as unnecessary. Shortly after the publication of the Cairo edition, a number of European scholars began the task of assembling a critical edition, but the project was ultimately abandoned as a result of a series of mysterious events which read like something straight out of an Agatha Christie novel. The project has now been taken up again by a research team at the Free University of Berlin, though the prospects of the 'Corpus Coranicum' remain uncertain. Nevertheless there has been a renewal of interest in the text of the Qur'ān of late. Facsimile editions of early Qur'ān manuscripts are beginning to be published, while we await further news about the now famous Qur'ān manuscripts discovered in Ṣan'ā', which some scholars think will lead to significant changes being made in the standard text of the Cairo edition. Time will tell.

I recount the history of the Cairo edition simply because most translators do not identify the edition of the text with which they are working. In a sense that silence is justifiable, since there are only two choices a translator has anyway. (It might be more accurate to say that s/he has none, now that the Flügel edition is little more than a historical footnote.) But a first-time reader of the Qur'ān in translation is likely not to know on what textual basis it rests. The failure to name the edition of the Arabic text being translated contributes to a tacit assumption that the Qur'ān, even in translation, is above or outside of history. That can be a reflex of religious belief as well as an aesthetic judgment. Every true 'classic' or work of 'genius,' it is often said, transcends its own time. At least so it is claimed. I feel no need here to question such a belief or challenge such a judgment. I only want to make clear to the reader of this translation that it is based upon a text with a history, and a history that did not end in 1924. Changes, albeit minor, were made in subsequent editions of the Cairo text: one published later in 1924, another in 1936, and yet another in 1960. There will be changes in the text of the Qur'ān still to come, but probably from different quarters. My use of the Cairo edition therefore is simply a matter of convenience. Except in a very few cases I have followed its readings as well as its system of versification.

About this edition

No one style of translation fits all texts, and some texts admit of a variety of different styles of translation. Mine aims not at elegance but strives for as literal a rendering of the Arabic as English will allow. The poet and philosopher Rudolf Pannwitz has written that 'the basic error of the translator is that he preserves the state in which his own language happens to be instead of allowing his language to be powerfully affected by the foreign tongue.'[118] One of the many challenges of the Qur'ān is that it is unpredictably complex, evocatively associative, and polysemous. For these reasons, as well as more demanding theological ones, most translations cut, compress, paraphrase, and invent freely. I have taken a different approach. My goal has been to make the translation literal to the point of transparency, as well as to maintain consistency in the rendering of words and phrases, and even to mimic word order wherever possible. The result is a kind of Arabicized (or Qur'ānicized) English which strives to capture in translation something of the power and pervasive strangeness of the original. Some may find the translation overly literal, even a bit awkward in places, but my hope is that more will gain access to the Qur'ān's distinctive idiom in a rendition that strives to remain as close as possible to the way it is expressed in Arabic, with only a minimum of smoothing and polishing.

This is what I have reached for anyway, even if ultimately it may have been beyond my grasp. I readily acknowledge that there are more than a few words, phrases, and occasionally whole sentences whose meaning has simply escaped me. At those moments I felt acutely the exasperation voiced by the histo-

118. Cited by Walter Benjamin, 'The Task of the Translator,' in his *Illuminations*, tr. Harry Zohn (New York: Schocken Books, 1968) 69-82, quotation from p. 81.

rian Ernst Badian over another ancient text: 'It survives only to taunt us with our ignorance.'[119] There is some solace in knowing that I am not entirely alone in my uncertainty and ignorance. In the case of some words I transliterated (conservatively), in other instances I followed my predecessors (sheepishly), in a few places I conjectured (tentatively), but in each case this is registered in the annotations for the reader to see. Finally, the reader should be on alert for words and phrases not in the original Arabic, but which have been added for the sake of clarity. These are enclosed within parentheses. In this way, it is hoped, the reader will be able to distinguish the bones from the plaster of paris.

As the reader opens this edition and turns to a particular *sūra*, s/he will find that it is provided with its own introduction and its relative dating in the opinion of scholars. Here I follow in the footsteps of the Cairo editors. They introduce each *sūra* by giving its name, followed by the marker 'Meccan' or 'Medinan' to indicate its place of revelation, and finally the name of the *sūra* which was revealed immediately before it. For example, this is how they introduce Q19:

> *Sūra* of Mary – Meccan – except verses 58 and 71, which are Medinan – it was revealed after 'the Creator' [i.e. Q35].[120]

In parceling out *sūras* between Mecca and Medina, the Cairo editors drew eclectically on several traditional sources, so the chronology of the *sūras* in their edition does not correspond exactly with any one traditional list. The same eclecticism applies to the editors' identification of Medinan verses 'inserted' into Meccan *sūras* and of Meccan verses 'inserted' into Medinan *sūras*. Because what I am presenting is a translation of the Cairo edition, I thought it worthwhile to provide the reader with this information. In addition I also indicate how (some) secular scholars come down on the issue of dating *sūras*. (The reader will soon discover that in most cases there is very little difference between modern and traditional systems of dating.) It is my hope that readers will find this information useful, but I should point out that I do not subscribe to secular scholars' attempts to place the *sūras* in chronological order, any more than I do to the Cairo edition's chronology of the *sūras*. In any case readers should know that this information is not part of the Qur'ān itself, but a product of tradition. Merely as an aside, it appears that none of the *sūras* of the Qur'ān manuscripts discovered in the Great Mosque of Ṣan'ā' is identified as 'Meccan' or 'Medinan.'

If the translation is the heart of this edition, the annotations are its body. Readers will find them keyed to the text and divided according to their boldface topical headings at the bottom of each page. The topical headings are designed to provide readers with guideposts to help them find their way through what can seem, at times, a labyrinthine text. (This is especially so for the first-time reader.) The annotations are not intended to be a commentary, but seek to provide further information on some of the technicalities of the text and to explicate the meaning of obscure passages. On many occasions alternative renderings are offered in the annotations. In general, annotations to key terms are supplied on the first occurrence of the term in a particular *sūra*, so only in very long *sūras* has it been necessary to repeat them. The annotations draw heavily on a range of critical scholarship to which the 'Guide to Further Reading' records my debt. I have, however, deliberately resisted the temptation of letting tradition (*sīra* and *tafsīr*) fill in the gaps or predetermine the meaning of the text. In other words I make an effort not to conflate text and tradition. When I do make concessions to traditional interpretations, it is clearly marked by 'according to tradition' or 'this is said to refer to' etc. Even in the annotations, then, I try as much as possible to let the Qur'ān speak for itself. This is accomplished through a system of numerous cross-references to parallel (or at least relevant) passages within the Qur'ān, so that wherever possible

119. Ernst Badian, *Roman Imperialism in the Late Republic* (Ithaca: Cornell Univ. Press, 1968) 104 n. 26, in reference to a famous inscription (the so-called 'Pirate Law') found at Delphi.

120. By systematically working through these headings one can produce a chronological list of the Cairo edition's 114 *sūras*. Neal Robinson has done us a favor by doing just that, and the reader may find the list in his *Discovering the Qur'an: A Contemporary Approach to a Veiled Text*, 2nd ed. (Washington, DC: Georgetown Univ. Press, 2003) 72-73.

the Qur'ān is able to elucidate the Qur'ān. But there is more. The annotations also offer an abundance of comparative references to the 'scriptures' of Judaism and Christianity, and sometimes beyond them (even Homer and the Roman poet Ovid get a mention). These comparative references will show the extent to which the Qur'ān is part of a much wider conversation than might initially be supposed. Utility has been the watchword throughout. Recognizing that few will read the Qur'ān from beginning to end, this edition has been designed to facilitate ready reference. Most of the annotations are cross-referenced, and important ones repeated, so that readers may jump into the text at almost any point and still find their way around. A comprehensive index at the back further enhances the volume's usefulness.[121]

Traduttore, traditore. So goes the old Italian pun. Every translation is an act of betrayal, even one devoted to the principle of literal fidelity. Allow me to be the first, then, to acknowledge that the book now in the reader's hand (or electronic device) is not the Qur'ān. My reason for doing so, however, is not based on a notion (for some, doctrine) that the Qur'ān is, in its essence, uniquely untranslatable – which is to say, incommensurable. Quite the contrary. It derives from the much less grand recognition that no translation is ever fully adequate, that there will always be discrepancy, and that the adequacy of any translation can and should be debated. Yet by this ordinary, indeed homely admission, I also wish to register my commitment to the possibility of 'translation' as such – that is, to a project broader still, of which this book, as well as the series in which it appears, is a part, and to which I hope it will contribute.

'Language *entails* translatability,' as Hans Penner has forcefully argued.[122] To insist otherwise – to reject the possibility of translation – is to adopt a model of unintelligibility. Such a premise, as Jonathan Z. Smith has repeatedly cautioned,

> denies the work of culture and the study of culture. It sets aside the reason that most of the human sciences are, first and foremost, linguistic enterprises. For it is the issue of translation, that 'this' is never quite 'that,' and, therefore, that acts of interpretation are required that marks the human sciences. It is thought about translation, an affair of the in between that is always relative and never fully adequate; it is thought about translation across languages, and times, between text and reader, speaker and hearer, that energizes the human sciences as disciplines and suggests the intellectual contributions they make.[123]

So no, the book in your hand is not the Qur'ān, but then what is? What do we mean by *the* Qur'ān, a text which is *in itself* held to be a translation? That is the really interesting and important question. To play just a little with Smith's rendition of the Korzybski aphorism about maps: Translation is not text – but translations are all we possess.[124]

121. My recommendation is that users of this edition begin by reading the first short *sūra* (Q1.1-7) and roughly the first half of the second (Q2.1-167), but that is only a suggestion.

122. Hans H. Penner, 'Interpretation,' in Willi Braun and Russell T. McCutcheon (eds.), *Guide to the Study of Religion* (London/New York: Cassell, 2000) 57-71, quotation from p. 69 (emphasis in original). Penner goes on to urge: 'What we must grasp, and grasp firmly, is the premise that there is no such thing as "religious language" in need of a special grammar, semantics or code book' (p. 70).

123. Jonathan Z. Smith, 'Differential Equations: On Constructing the Other,' in *idem, Relating Religion: Essays in the History of Religions* (Chicago/London: Univ. of Chicago Press, 2004) 230-250, quotation from pp. 246-247. Elsewhere Smith has argued that 'explanation is, at heart, an act of translation, of redescription' ('The Topography of the Sacred,' in *Relating Religion* 101-116, quotation from pp. 105-106). I much appreciate his analysis in 'A Twice-told Tale: The History of the History of Religions' History,' in *Relating Religion* 362-374 (originally published in *Numen* 48 [2001] 131-146), especially its peroration: To deny the legitimacy of translation 'condemns the field [of the history of religions] to live in the world of Borges' Pierre Menard, in which a tale must always be identically "twice-told," where a word can only be translated by itself' (p. 372).

124. See Jonathan Z. Smith, *Map is Not Territory: Studies in the History of Religions* (Leiden: Brill, 1978) 309.

Guide to Further Reading

The following selective bibliography focuses exclusively on the Qur'ān, rather than including works about Muḥammad and the origins and early history of Islam. It has been compiled to reflect a spectrum of critical viewpoints and approaches, ranging from 'traditionalist' to 'revisionist.'[1] Aside from a few notable exceptions, it is limited to recent works in English, and to books rather than articles in journals, encyclopedias, and essay collections (though references to the latter are included). Additional bibliography (literally tons of it) will be found in the footnotes and bibliographies of the works listed here, as well as in the new exhaustive bibliography compiled by Morteza Karimi-Nia, listed under 'General reference works' below. Readers may also wish to consult the following journals for new publications on a wide variety of texts and topics relevant to Qur'ānic studies, as well as for reviews of recently published books in the field: *Arabica, Bulletin of the School of Oriental and African Studies, Comparative Islamic Studies, International Journal of Middle East Studies, Jerusalem Studies in Arabic and Islam, Journal of the American Oriental Society, Journal of Near Eastern Studies, Journal of Qur'anic Studies, Journal of Semitic Studies, Studia Islamica,* and *The Muslim World.* Finally, the *Index Islamicus* is a database which indexes literature on Islam, the Middle East, and the Muslim world.

(On) English translations of the Qur'ān

Abdel Haleem, M.A.S. *The Qur'an.* Oxford: Oxford University Press, 2004.

Ali, A. *Al-Qur'ān: A Contemporary Translation.* Princeton: Princeton University Press, 1988.

Arberry, A.J. *The Koran Interpreted.* 2 vols. London: Allen & Unwin, 1955.

Bell, R. *The Qur'ān: Translated, with a Critical Re-arrangement of the Surahs.* 2 vols. Edinburgh: T. & T. Clark, 1937-1939.

Elmarsafy, Z. *The Enlightenment Qur'an: The Politics of Translation and the Construction of Islam.* Oxford: Oneworld, 2009.

Fakhry, M. *An Interpretation of the Qur'an: English Translation of the Meanings.* New York: New York University Press, 2002.

Jones, A. *The Qur'ān.* Exeter: Short Run Press, 2007.

Khalidi, T. *The Qur'an: A New Translation.* London: Penguin, 2008.

Mohammed, K. 'Assessing English Translations of the Qur'an.' *The Middle East Quarterly* 12 (2005) 58-71.

Pickthall, M. *The Meaning of the Glorious Koran.* London: Knopf, 1930.

Yusuf Ali, A. *The Holy Qur'an: Text, Translation and Commentary.* Lahore: Shaikh Muḥammad Ashraf, 1934.

1. Lest there be any misunderstanding, by 'traditionalist' and 'revisionist' I do not mean 'uncritical' and 'critical.' When it comes to dividing the field of Qur'ānic studies (and religious studies generally), I prefer the terms employed by Herbert Berg – 'sanguine' and 'skeptical' – insofar as they focus attention on method (which raises a more interesting set of questions) rather than results. The distinction is, of course, artificial, but not arbitrary. It may be better to think in terms of a spectrum or continuum, rather than a clear-cut division, but that in turn raises the question of whether there really is a 'middle ground.' See further Herbert Berg, 'Competing Paradigms in the Study of Islamic Origins,' in *idem* (ed.), *Method and Theory in the Study of Islamic Origins*, Islamic History and Civilization, Studies and Texts 49 (Leiden: Brill, 2003) 261 n. 4; and Herbert Berg and Sarah Rollens, 'The historical Muḥammad and the historical Jesus: A comparison of scholarly reinventions and reinterpretations,' *Studies in Religion/Sciences Religieuses* 37 (2008) 271-292.

General reference works

Karimi-Nia, M. *Bibliography of Qur'anic Studies in European Languages.* Qum: Center for Translation of the Holy Quran, 2013.

Kassis, H.E. *A Concordance of the Qur'an.* Berkeley: University of California Press, 1983.

Leaman, O. (ed.) *The Qur'an: An Encyclopedia.* London: Routledge, 2006.

McAuliffe, J.D. (ed.) *The Encyclopaedia of the Qur'ān.* 5 vols. Leiden: Brill, 2001-2006.

Mir, M. *Dictionary of Qur'ānic Terms and Concepts.* New York: Garland, 1987.

Paret, R. *Der Koran: Kommentar und Konkordanz.* Stuttgart: Kohlhammer, 1971.

Peters, F.E. *A Reader on Classical Islam.* Princeton: Princeton University Press, 1994.

Watt, W.M. *Companion to the Qur'ān.* Oxford: Oneworld, 1994 [1967].

Introductions to the Qur'ān

Abdel Haleem, M.A.S. *Understanding the Qur'an: Themes and Style.* London: Tauris, 2000.

Cook, M. *The Koran: A Very Short Introduction.* Oxford: Oxford University Press, 2000.

Ernst, C.F. *How to Read the Qur'an: A New Guide, with Select Translations.* Chapel Hill: University of North Carolina Press, 2011.

Esack, F. *The Qur'an: A User's Guide.* Oxford: Oneworld, 2005.

Gade, A.M. *The Qur'ān: An Introduction.* Oxford: Oneworld, 2010.

Lawrence, B. *The Qur'an: A Biography.* New York: Atlantic Monthly Press, 2006.

Mattson, I. *The Story of the Qur'an: Its History and Place in Muslim Life.* Oxford: Blackwell, 2008.

McAuliffe, J.D. (ed.) *The Cambridge Companion to the Qur'ān.* Cambridge: Cambridge University Press, 2006.

Rahman, F. *Major Themes of the Qur'ān.* 2nd ed. Chicago: University of Chicago Press, 2009 [1980].

Rippin, A. (ed.) *The Blackwell Companion to the Qur'ān.* Oxford: Blackwell, 2006.

Robinson, N. *Discovering the Qur'an: A Contemporary Approach to a Veiled Text,* 2nd ed. Washington, DC: Georgetown University Press, 2003.

Sells, M. *Approaching the Qur'án: The Early Revelations.* Ashland: White Cloud Press, 1999.

Watt, W.M. and R. Bell. *Bell's Introduction to the Qur'ān.* Edinburgh: Edinburgh University Press, 1970.

Welch, A.T. art. 'al-Ḳur'ān.' *Encyclopaedia of Islam.* 2nd ed. 12 vols. Leiden: Brill, 1954-2004 [1981]. 5.400-429.

Special studies

As-Said, L. *The Recited Koran: A History of the First Recorded Version.* Ed. and tr. B. Weiss, M.A. Rauf, and M. Berger. Princeton: Darwin Press, 1975.

Ayoub, M. *The Qur'an and Its Interpreters.* 2 vols. Albany: SUNY Press, 1984-1992.

Boullata, I.J. (ed.) *Literary Structures of Religious Meaning in the Qur'ān.* Richmond: Curzon, 2000.

Burton, J. 'Those are the High-flying Cranes.' *Journal of Semitic Studies* 15 (1970) 246-265.

Burton, J. *The Collection of the Qur'ān.* Cambridge: Cambridge University Press, 1977.

El-Awa, S.M.S. *Textual Relations in the Qur'ān: Relevance, Coherence and Structure.* London: Routledge, 2005.

Hawting, G.R. and A.-K. Shareef. (eds.) *Approaches to the Qur'an.* London: Routledge, 1993.

Gätje, H. *The Qur'ān and its Exegesis: Selected Texts with Classical and Modern Muslim Interpretations.* Ed. and tr. A.T. Welch. Oxford: Oneworld, 1996 [1971].

Gwyne, R.W. *Logic, Rhetoric, and Legal Reasoning in the Qur'ān: God's Arguments.* London: RoutledgeCurzon, 2004.

Izutsu,T. *God and Man in the Koran: Semantics of the Koranic Weltanschauung*. Tokyo: The Keio Institute of Cultural and Linguistic Studies, 1964.

Izutsu, T. *Ethico-Religious Concepts in the Qur'ān*. Montreal: McGill University Press, 2002 [1966].

Jeffrey, A. *The Foreign Vocabulary of the Qur'ān*. Baroda: Oriental Institute, 1938.

Jeffrey, A. *The Qur'ān as Scripture*. New York: Russell F. Moore, 1952.

Jomier, J. *The Great Themes of the Qur'an*. London: SCM Press, 1997.

Madigan, D.A. *The Qur'ān's Self-Image: Writing and Authority in Islam's Scripture*. Princeton: Princeton University Press, 2001.

Mir, M. *Coherence in the Qur'ān*. Indianapolis: American Trust Publications, 1986.

Neuwirth, A. *Studien zur Komposition der mekkanischen Suren*. 2., erweiterte Auflage. Berlin: Walter de Gruyter, 2007.

Neuwirth, A. *et al.* (eds.) *The Qur'ān in Context: Historical and Literary Investigations into the Qur'anic Milieu*. Leiden: Brill, 2010.

O'Shaughnessy, T.J. *Eschatological Themes in the Qur'ān*. Manila: Loyola School of Theology, 1986.

Reeves, J.C. (ed.) *Bible and Qur'ān: Essays in Scriptural Intertextuality*. Atlanta: Society of Biblical Literature, 2003.

Reynolds, G.S. *The Qur'ān and Its Biblical Subtext*. London: Routledge, 2010.

Reynolds, G.S. (ed.) *The Qur'ān in Its Historical Context*. London: Routledge, 2008.

Reynolds, G.S. (ed.) *New Perspectives on the Qur'ān: The Qur'ān in Its Historical Context 2*. London: Routledge, 2011.

Rippin, A. *The Qur'an and its Interpretive Tradition*. Aldershot: Variorum/Ashgate, 2001.

Rippin, A. (ed.) *The Qur'an: Formative Interpretation*. Aldershot: Ashgate, 1999.

Rippin, A. (ed.) *The Qurán: Style and Contents*. Aldershot: Ashgate, 2001.

Rubin, U. *Between Bible and Qur'ān: The Children of Israel and the Islamic Self-Image*. Princeton: Darwin Press, 1999.

Saleh, W. 'In Search of a Comprehensible Qur'ān: A Survey of Some Recent Scholarly Works.' *Bulletin of the Royal Institute for Inter-Faith Studies* 5 (2003) 143-162.

Smith, J.Z. 'Religion and Bible.' *Journal of Biblical Literature* 128 (2009) 5-27.

Stowasser, B.F. *Women in the Qur'an, Traditions, and Interpretation*. New York: Oxford University Press, 1994.

Tlili, S. *Animals in the Qur'an*. Cambridge: Cambridge University Press, 2012.

Tottoli, R. *Biblical Prophets in the Qur'ān and Muslim Literature*. Richmond: Curzon, 2002.

Wadud, A. *Qur'an and Woman: Rereading the Sacred Text from a Woman's Perspective*. Oxford: Oxford University Press, 1999.

Wansbrough, J. *Quranic Studies: Sources and Methods of Scriptural Interpretation*. Foreword, Translations, and Expanded Notes by Andrew Rippin. Amherst: Prometheus Books, 2004 [1977].

Wheeler, B. *Prophets in the Quran: An Introduction to the Quran and Muslim Exegesis*. London: Continuum, 2002.

Wheeler, B. *Moses in the Quran and Islamic Exegesis*. London: RoutledgeCurzon, 2002.

Widengren, G. *Muḥammad, the Apostle of God, and his Ascension*. Uppsala: A.B. Lundequistska Bokhandeln, 1955.

Wild, S. (ed.) *The Qur'an as Text*. Leiden: Brill, 1996.

Wild, S. (ed.) *Self-Referentiality in the Qur'ān*. Wiesbaden: Harrassowitz, 2006.

Glossary of Key Names, Terms, and Abbreviations

The following explanations are intended to clarify important names, terms, and abbreviations which occur in the annotations accompanying the translation.

AH: indicates dates according to the Islamic calendar (from Lat. *anno Hegirae*, or 'in the year of the Hijra'), also called the 'Hijrī calendar' (Ar. *al-taqwīm al-hijrī*). Year 1 AH = 622 CE.

Ar.: Arabic; part of a large and widespread Semitic language family, but one of the latest of these to be attested in literature. Scattered inscriptions have been found in Arabic from the 4th century CE. The Qur'ān is the first great work written in Arabic, though the precise kind of Arabic is debated by scholars. With the spread of Islam, spoken dialects of Arabic took root throughout the Middle East, north Africa, and Spain, and many Arabic words have found their way into other languages, including even English. Although Arabic is closely associated with Islam, it is not the native language of a majority of the world's Muslims. Arabic is, however, the native language of some Christians and Jews, who address God as 'Allāh' as do Muslims. Today Arabic is the official language of twenty-five countries.

Aram.: Aramaic; a Semitic language closely related to Hebrew and Arabic, attested from the 9th century BCE to the present. Aramaic was the *lingua franca* of the Achaemenid Persian empire, and by the 6th century BCE had replaced Hebrew as the language of Palestine. Some portions of the Hebrew Bible were written in Aramaic, and eventually much of the Bible was translated into Aramaic. In late antiquity Aramaic flourished in the Middle East, resulting in the development of a number of dialects. A vast literature was produced or preserved in Aramaic, including the Palestinian Talmud and Samaritan Pentateuch.

BCE: indicates dates before the Common Era, equivalent to BC ('before Christ') in the Christian Gregorian calendar.

c.: circa.

Cairo edition: an edition of the Arabic text of the Qur'ān, first published in 1924 CE/1342 AH (and then in subsequent editions), prepared by a committee of Muslim scholars at the behest of the Egyptian government. Although not a 'critical edition,' it has become the standard text of the Qur'ān in both the religious and secular academic worlds.

CE: indicates dates according to the Common Era, equivalent to AD (from Lat. *anno Domini*, or 'in the year of the Lord') of the Christian Gregorian calendar.

cf.: compare.

codex: a Latin word for a type of book made from sheets of parchment, papyrus, and finally paper, folded in half and assembled in one or several quires, which were then stitched along the length of the fold. By the 4th century CE, the codex had become the predominant form in which texts were produced, replacing the earlier 'scroll' or 'roll.' Muslims and Christians chose to transmit their sacred texts in the form of the codex; by contrast Jews preferred to use the scroll for copies of the Torah.

codices: (plur. of 'codex') often used as a translation for Ar. *maṣāḥif* (sing. *muṣḥaf*) referring to the early 'codices' (i.e. 'versions' of the Qur'ān) produced by the Prophets 'companions' (e.g. Ibn 'Abbās and Ibn Mas'ūd). None of these has survived but they are referred to by later writers.

d.: died.

e.g.: for example.

Eng.: English.

epexegetical: a grammatical construction providing additional or explanatory material.

Ethiop.: Ethiopic; refers to Ge'ez, a Semitic language of northern Ethiopia, which became the official language of the kingdom of Axum. When Axum converted to Christianity in the 4th century CE, Ge'ez also acquired the status of the liturgical language of the Abyssinian church. The Bible was translated into Ge'ez, including the books of Enoch and Jubilees. Ge'ez remains the liturgical language of Ethiopian Christians and Jews.

fem.: feminine.

Gk.: Greek; part of a widespread Indo-European language family, and its longest documented member. It existed originally in many dialects native to the southern Balkan peninsula, western Asia Minor, and the Aegean. These were reduced to one ('Attic') following the conquests of Alexander III of Macedon (d. 323 BCE). A later form of this dialect, called *koinē*, became the *lingua franca* of the Roman empire in the eastern Mediterranean and parts of the Middle East. Many Greek words found their way into the provincial languages of these regions. The Jewish Bible was eventually translated into Greek (called the 'Septuagint'). Greek is also the language in which the Christian New Testament was written. Late antiquity saw the rise of medieval or Byzantine Greek, which was the official language of the Byzantine empire as well as the liturgical language of Byzantine Christianity. Modern Greek is the official language of Greece and Cyprus.

Hebr.: Hebrew; a local Semitic language of Palestine, closely related to Aramaic, and attested from the 10th century BCE. By late antiquity it had become almost exclusively a literary language. Most of the Bible is written in Hebrew, as are many of the texts discovered at Qumran, and the rabbinic legal compilation known as the Mishnah (c. 250 CE). However, only in the 9th century CE were Jewish scholars (called 'Masoretes') able to fix the 'transmission' (*masora*) of the text of the Hebrew Bible, by creating a system for 'voweling' or vocalizing what had been before merely a consonantal text. While Hebrew remains the liturgical language of Jews, the 20th century saw the creation of 'Israeli Hebrew.'

Ibn 'Abbās: a cousin and celebrated 'companion' of the Prophet; considered an expert in *tafsīr*, or the interpretation of the Qur'ān. Many traditions about the Prophet go back to him (d. 686 CE/68 AH).

Ibn Mas'ūd: a celebrated 'companion' of the Prophet; said to have compiled a pre-'Uthmānic version (or *muṣḥaf*) of the Qur'ān (d. 652/3 CE/32 AH).

i.e.: that is.

lacuna: a missing section of a text. In this edition a lacuna in the text is marked by [...].

Lat.: Latin; an Indo-European language, originally spoken only in the area of central western Italy ('Latium'). This local language became the administrative language of the Roman empire, especially in the West, until the empire's dissolution in the late 5th century CE and the development of 'Romance' languages derived from Latin. Many Latin words found their way into the provincial languages of Rome's empire. Latin was the spoken and liturgical language of Christianity in the West. The Christian Bible was translated into Latin by Jerome (c. 400 CE) and is known as the 'Vulgate.'

lex talionis: law of retaliation ('an eye for an eye' etc.).

lit.: literally

masc.: masculine.

n.: note.

nn.: notes.

par.: parallel.

partitive: a grammatical construction referring to only part of a whole.

plur.: plural.

Q: Qur'ān; references to the Qur'ān are cited as follows: Q sūra # . verse # (versification is according to the Cairo edition).

scroll: or 'roll' (Lat. *volumen*), made from sheets of papyrus or parchment, joined end to end to form a long strip of writing surface, attached at either end by rollers that allowed horizontal scrolling. The dominant form in which texts were produced until the advent of the 'codex.'

Septuagint: from Latin *septuaginta* ('seventy'), refers to the Greek translation of the Jewish scriptures. It was so named because of a legendary story in which the translation was carried out by seventy (or seventy-two) Jewish scholars brought from Palestine to Egypt by Ptolemy II Philadelphus (reigned 285-246 BCE). The Septuagint was the 'Bible' for Greek-speaking Jews and early Christians.

sing.: singular.

Syr.: Syriac; originally a dialect of Aramaic, classical Syriac became a major literary language throughout the Middle East from the 4th to 8th centuries CE, and had a strong influence on the development of Arabic. It remains the liturgical language of Syriac Christianity.

Ubayy ibn Ka'b: a scribe and 'companion' of the Prophet; said to have compiled a pre-'Uthmānic version (or *muṣḥaf*) of the Qur'ān (d. 649 CE/29 AH).

v.: verse.

vv.: verses.

Timeline

The following dates are all CE ('Common Era'). Many dates are approximate, and some open to doubt.

527-565	reign of Byzantine emperor Justinian
530-579	reign of Sassanid Persian emperor Khusro I
537	dedication of the church of Hagia Sophia
540	Khusro I takes Antioch
540-561	period of Persian/Byzantine warfare
554	Byzantine conquest of southern Spain
c. 570-632	dates for Muḥammad
572-591	period of Persian/Byzantine warfare
582-602	reign of Byzantine emperor Maurice
591-628	reign of Sassanid Persian emperor Khusro II
c. 600	compilation of the Babylonian Talmud
602-629	period of Persian/Byzantine warfare
610-641	reign of Byzantine emperor Heraclius
610	Muḥammad's first 'vision'
613	Persians take Antioch
614	Persians take Jerusalem
619	Persians take Alexandria
622	Muḥammad's flight from Mecca to Medina, beginning of the Muslim era (16 July)
627	final campaign of Heraclius in Persia
629	Muslims take Mecca
632-661	rule of Muḥammad's successors ('caliphs'), Abū Bakr (632-634), 'Umar (634-644), 'Uthmān (644-656), and 'Alī (656-661)
635	Muslims take Damascus
636	Muslim victory over the Byzantines at the battle of Yarmuk (end of Byzantine control of Syria), Muslim victory over the Persians at the battle of al-Qādisiyya (Sassanid empire declines)
637	Muslims take Antioch
638	Muslims take Jerusalem

642	Muslims take Alexandria
644-656	caliphate of 'Uthmān, during which the text of the Qur'ān was definitively fixed, according to Muslim tradition
661-750	Umayyad caliphate, rules from Damascus
677	Muslim siege of Constantinople
691	completion of Dome of the Rock
692-724	Al-Hajjaj, Ummayad governor of Iraq
695	first Muslim coins minted
698	Muslims take Carthage
699	Arabic replaces Greek in administration
711	Muslims invade Spain
715	completion of Great Mosque of Damascus
717	defeat of Muslims at Constantinople
732	Franks defeat Muslims at the battle of Tours/Poitiers
750	revolt of the Abbasids, beginning of the Abbasid caliphate
750-1258	Abbasid caliphate, rules from Baghdad
c. 755-1031	independent Umayyad dynasty in Spain
762	foundation of Baghdad as Abbasid capital
786-809	reign of Abbasid caliph Hārūn al-Rashīd
800	coronation of Charlemagne as 'emperor of the Romans' by Pope Leo III
c. 870	possible Greek translation of the Qur'ān, by Nicetas Byzantius, at Constantinople
884	first reported translation of the Qur'ān, in Alwar (Sindh, India, now Pakistan), at the request of the Hindu Raja Mehruk (but it is not known whether this was into Hindi, Sanskrit, or the local Sindhi language)
c. 973	foundation of al-Azhar university in Cairo
1096	first Crusade launched
1099	Christian crusaders capture Jerusalem
1143	first Latin translation of the Qur'ān, by a committee under the direction of Robert of Ketton, at the behest of Peter the Venerable, abbot of Cluny
1146	second Crusade launched
1169-1193	Salah al-Dīn ('Saladin') rules Egypt, recaptures Jerusalem in 1187
1190	third Crusade launched
1204	fourth Crusade, capture and sack of Constantinople
1299-1922	Ottoman empire

c. 1450	invention in Europe of printing with movable type
1537-1538	first, unsuccessful attempt to print the complete Arabic text of the Qur'ān, in Venice (all but one copy was destroyed)
1543	first printed edition of the Qur'ān in translation (based on an 'improved' version of Robert of Ketton's Latin translation) published at Basel, by Theodor Bibliander of Zurich, with prefaces by Martin Luther and Philip Melancthon (the city council of Basel had initially banned publication, but relented at Luther's insistence)
1547	first modern language translation of the Qur'ān into Italian, by Andrea Arrivabene (based on the Latin translation)
1647	first French translation of the Qur'ān, by André du Ryer (based on the Latin translation)
1649	first English translation of the Qur'ān, by Alexander Ross (based on du Ryer's French translation)
1695	first successful attempt to print the complete Arabic text of the Qur'ān, by Abraham Hinckelmann, a German theologian and pastor, in Hamburg
1698	second successful attempt to print the complete Arabic text of the Qur'ān, along with a new Latin translation and commentary, by Ludovico Maracci, an Italian priest and confessor to Pope Innocent XII, in Padua
1734	first English translation based on the Arabic text of the Qur'ān, by George Sale, an early member of the (Anglican) Society for Promoting Christian Knowledge
1787	publication of the first Qur'ān printed by a Muslim, Mullāh Osmān Ismā'īl, in Saint Petersburg
1834	publication of Gustav Flügel's *Corani arabicus textus* at Leipzig (became the standard text for European scholars)
1860	publication of Theodor Nöldeke's *Geschichte des Qorāns* at Göttingen (a landmark work)
1924	publication of the 'Egyptian standard' or 'Cairo edition' of the Qur'ān, by a committee under the direction of Muḥammad ibn 'Alī al-Ḥusaynī al-Ḥaddād (has become the *de facto* canonical text of the Qur'ān)
1972	accidental discovery of fragments of 'early' Qur'ān manuscripts in the Great Mosque of Ṣan'ā', Yemen

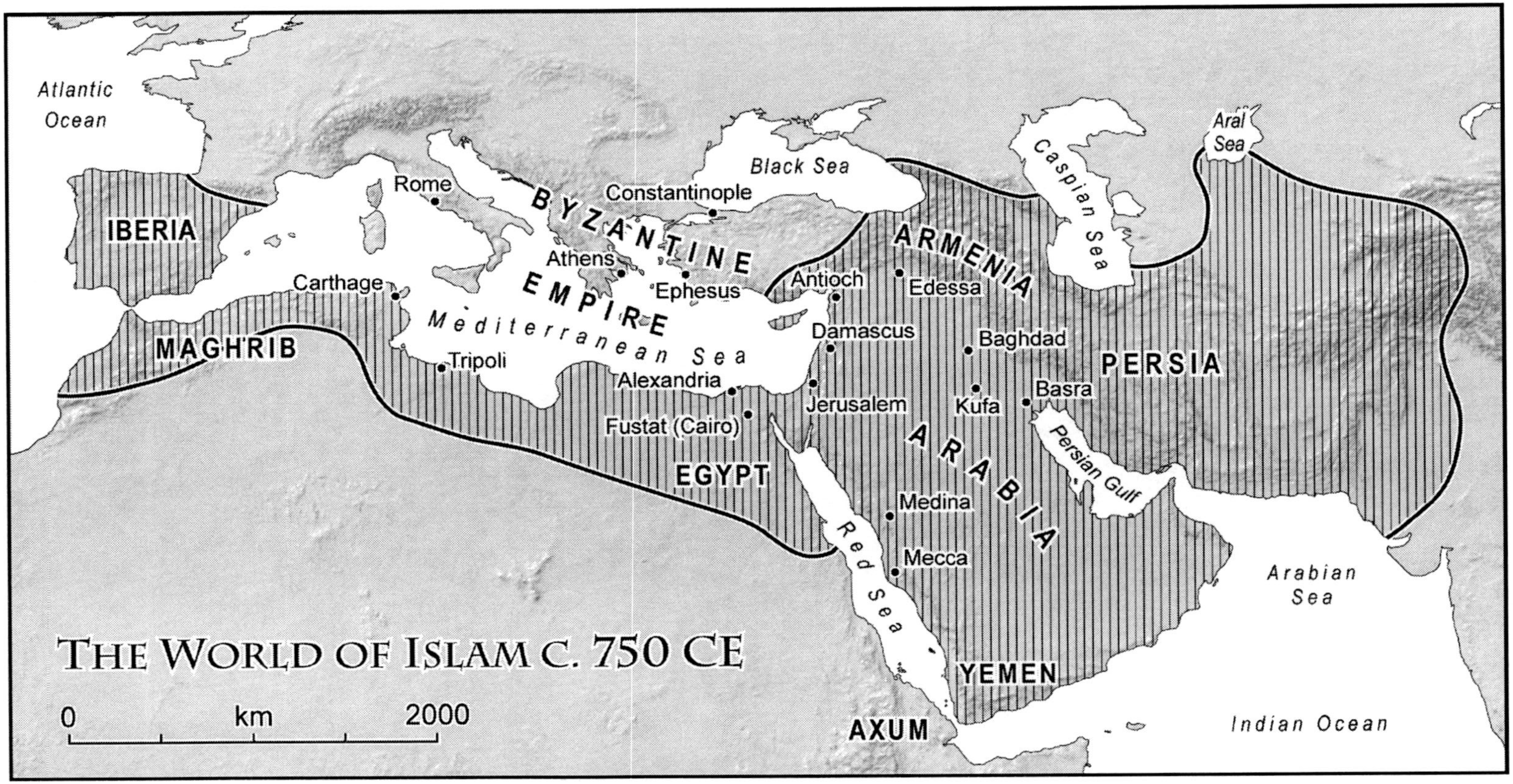
THE WORLD OF ISLAM C. 750 CE
0
km
2000
Atlantic Ocean
IBERIA
MAGHRIB
Rome
Carthage
Tripoli
BYZANTINE EMPIRE
Athens
Ephesus
Constantinople
Black Sea
Mediterranean Sea
Alexandria
Fustat (Cairo)
EGYPT
Antioch
Damascus
Jerusalem
Edessa
ARMENIA
Caspian Sea
Aral Sea
Baghdad
Kufa
Basra
PERSIA
Persian Gulf
ARABIA
Medina
Mecca
Red Sea
YEMEN
AXUM
Arabian Sea
Indian Ocean

Synopsis: The Qur'ān at a Glance

1 The Opening
This short prayer serves as the introduction to the Qur'ān. It is sometimes referred to as the 'essence of the Qur'ān' and is an important part of worship, both public and private.

2 The Cow
By far the longest sūra, it includes accounts of Adam's fall, Moses and Pharaoh, Israel's disobedience, and the religion of Abraham and his building of God's 'House,' toward which prayer is now directed. Instruction on a variety of topics occupies most of its second half (on food, retaliation, wills, fasting, fighting, pilgrimage, marriage, divorce, usury, almsgiving, and prayer).

3 House of 'Imrān
This sūra opens with a pronouncement about the divine origin of the Qur'ān, including its relationship to the prior scriptures of Jews and Christians. After this come stories of Zachariah, Mary, Jesus and his disciples, and Abraham as a Muslim. Criticism of Jewish disbelief, exhortation to the believers, and encouragement in the aftermath of defeat occupy most of the remainder of the sūra.

4 Women
This sūra takes its name from the many instructions regarding women, but it also offers guidance on a variety of other topics, including the treatment of orphans, marriage, property, inheritance, and fighting. The Prophet is put forward as God's representative and the supreme arbiter of all disputes. There are also polemical passages against the 'hypocrites' and the 'People of the Book,' including the claim that Jesus was not crucified.

5 The Table
This sūra offers instruction on a variety of topics (e.g. prayer, pilgrimage, and food), and prescribes punishment for certain offenses (e.g. murder and theft). Several passages condemn various 'pagan' practices, but many more are critical of Jewish disobedience and Christian doctrine, and believers are warned against entering into alliance with the 'People of the Book.' Its title refers to the miraculous 'table' of food sent down to Jesus and his disciples.

6 Livestock
This sūra emphasizes the creative power of one God, especially as manifested in the signs of an ordered natural world, and on that basis attacks the folly of idolatry, charging that other so-called gods are really 'jinn.' The story of Abraham's rejection of idols is repeated, and a parallel is drawn between the 'religion' of Abraham and the Prophet, as well as between the Torah of Moses and the Prophet's Qur'ān.

7 The Heights
Following an introductory reference to 'the Book' and a warning about judgment, this sūra falls into three main parts: the story of Iblīs and Adam's fall, a series of stories about the destruction of disobedient generations of the past, and the story of Moses, Pharaoh, and the Sons of Israel.

8 The Spoils
Most of this sūra is connected with victory in battle.

9 Repentance

This sūra deals with various matters connected with struggling for the cause of God. It opens with a renunciation of all treaty obligations with the 'idolaters.' This is followed by a short exhortation to fight against the 'People of the Book.' Then comes a sustained diatribe against the 'hypocrites' and others for their refusal to fight alongside the Prophet. It concludes by emphasizing again the duty to struggle for the cause.

10 Jonah

This sūra opens with a declaration of God's creative power which eventually leads into a condemnation of idolatry. The certainty of judgment and the authenticity of the Qur'ān are also stressed. A final section contains stories about Noah and Moses.

11 Hūd

This sūra is made up almost entirely of stories about the messengers Noah, Hūd, Ṣāliḥ, Abraham, Lot, Shu'ayb, and Moses.

12 Joseph

This sūra is devoted almost entirely to the story of Joseph, beloved son of Jacob.

13 The Thunder

This sūra is an assemblage of short passages touching on a variety of topics, including God's power and providence, rewards and punishments, and encouragement to the Prophet.

14 Abraham

This sūra, like the previous one, is an assemblage of short passages touching on a variety of topics, including a brief recounting of the stories of Moses and other messengers, human ingratitude for God's blessings, and the prayer of Abraham.

15 Al-Ḥijr

This sūra contains accounts of the rebellion of Iblīs and the angels' visits to Abraham and Lot. Two short stories of judgment follow: the punishment of the inhabitants of 'the Grove' and 'al-Ḥijr.'

16 The Bee

This sūra treats a variety of topics. In general it extols God's creative power and condemns the foolishness of idolatry. A final section sheds important light on the revelation of the Qur'ān.

17 The Journey

This sūra opens with the famous report of a 'night journey.' A variety of topics follow, including a series of commandments resembling the decalogue, as well as passages dealing with the nature and purpose of the Qur'ān. The Prophet's role as the 'messenger' is emphasized, and disbelievers are chastised for their objection that he is merely a human being who performs no miracles.

18 The Cave

This sūra is composed almost entirely of stories. The three main ones are: the 'Men of the Cave,' Moses and the servant, and Dhū-l-Qarnayn, a figure usually identified with Alexander the Great.

19 Mary

This sūra begins with a series of stories about earlier prophets. The longest of these is the story of Mary and Jesus, from which it receives its title. The remainder of the sūra explains the role of angels, responds to objections about the resurrection, and pronounces judgment on disbelievers.

20 Ṭā' Hā'

This sūra is devoted almost entirely to the story of Moses. It features accounts of his early life, call to be a messenger, struggles with Pharaoh, exodus from Egypt, and finally the episode of 'the calf.' It concludes with sections on the Last Day and the 'covenant with Adam.'

21 The Prophets

This sūra begins with a warning of approaching judgment and condemns idolatry in the face of God's power and providence. The second half is comprised of a series of stories about earlier prophets.

22 The Pilgrimage

This sūra takes its title from the reference to the Ḥajj, the pilgrimage originally established by Abraham. In addition to dealing with matters connected with the pilgrimage, it condemns those who deny believers access to the 'Sacred Mosque,' and concludes by urging believers to remain steadfast to the religion of Abraham.

23 The Believers

This sūra opens with an enumeration of the virtues of believers. It then extols the signs of God's power and providence, relates accounts of earlier messengers, and emphasizes the certainty of resurrection and judgment.

24 The Light

This sūra takes its title from the reference to God as 'the light of the heavens and the earth.' It is made up mostly of regulations governing the household, including appropriate dress, conduct, and sexual behavior.

25 The Deliverance

This sūra begins by responding to the disbelievers' rejection of the Prophet and his message, and then warns them by way of examples of earlier generations who were punished for similar disbelief. The second half of the sūra is largely devoted to the signs of God's power and providence discernible in the natural world. It concludes with a description of the characteristic qualities of God's servants.

26 The Poets

This sūra is made up almost entirely of stories about the messengers Moses, Abraham, Noah, Hūd, Ṣāliḥ, Lot, and Shu'ayb.

27 The Ant

This sūra opens with a reference to the Qur'ān as 'guidance and good news' and closes with a description of the Day of Judgment. It recounts the stories of earlier messengers, including one about Solomon and the Queen of Sheba. God's power and uniqueness are also emphasized.

28 The Story

This sūra is devoted almost entirely to the story of Moses, featuring accounts of his childhood and early life, his call to be a messenger, and finally his struggles with Pharaoh. It concludes with three scenes of judgment and a final word of encouragement to the Prophet.

29 The Spider

This sūra begins by exhorting believers to remain steadfast in the face of opposition, and then recounts the stories of seven previous messengers. It also describes the nature of 'the Book' revealed to the Prophet, as well as its relationship to the prior scriptures of the 'People of the Book.'

30 The Romans

This sūra opens with a reference to a military defeat of the Byzantine empire, which is followed by a prophecy of their ultimate victory over the Sassanid Persians. It then extols the signs of God's power in nature as evidence of his benevolence and ability to raise the dead.

31 Luqmān

This sūra takes its title from the story of Luqmān, a sage who presents his son with a succinct version of his wisdom. Among its diverse themes, it extols the signs of God's power and providence, and warns disbelievers of the certainty of judgment.

32 The Prostration

This sūra opens with a pronouncement about the truth of the Qur'ān. It then extols God's power as creator and defends the resurrection against the objection of disbelievers, whose fate is contrasted with the ultimate vindication of believers.

33 The Factions

This sūra is said to refer to the siege of Medina (627 CE/5 AH) by 'factions' of Meccans and their allies. The rest of the sūra deals with the Prophet's marriage to a woman formerly married to his adopted son, as well as with other matters concerning his wives.

34 Sheba

The main subject of this sūra is the certainty of judgment and resurrection. It also relates story of the people of Sheba.

35 Creator

The first part of this sūra is in the form of an address to the people, setting forth the claims of God. It then shifts to address the Prophet, consoling him with the reminder that previous messengers also faced rejection. It concludes with the different fates awaiting believers and disbelievers.

36 Yā' Sīn

This sūra begins with an affirmation of the Prophet's mission. It then relates a parable about a 'disbelieving city,' enumerates the signs of God's power and providence, and describes the different fates awaiting believers and disbelievers.

37 The Ones Who Line Up

This sūra opens with an emphatic declaration of the unity and creative power of God. Next come sections on the resurrection and the different fates awaiting believers and disbelievers, followed by stories of earlier messengers from Noah to Jonah. It concludes with a refutation of the worship of angels as 'daughters of God.'

38 Ṣād

The first part of this sūra describes the defiance of the Prophet's contemporaries. Next come stories of David, Solomon, Job, and several others. It then describes the different fates awaiting believers and disbelievers, before concluding with the story of Iblīs.

39 The Companies

This sūra opens with a statement of the unity and creative power of God. The contrasting fates of believers and disbelievers occupy much of the remainder of the sūra. It concludes with a vivid description of the Day of Judgment.

40 Forgiver

This sūra consists mainly of the story of Moses, with a number of features which set it apart from other versions.

41 Made Distinct

This sūra opens with a declaration of the 'sending down' of the Qur'ān. It extols God as creator and pronounces judgment on those who refuse to recognize the signs of his power and providence.

42 Consultation

This sūra opens by extolling the power and majesty of God and stresses the purpose of the Qur'ān as a warning. Next comes a declaration of the unity of religion in the face of religious differences. The contrasting fates of believers and disbelievers occupy much of the remainder of the sūra. The conclusion is noteworthy for the light it sheds on different modes of revelation.

43 Decoration

This sūra condemns the folly of idolatry (especially the idea that God has 'daughters'), and warns of the dangers of persistent disbelief. It goes on to recount the stories of Moses and Jesus, and concludes with a vivid scene of judgment.

44 The Smoke

This sūra opens with a declaration of the 'sending down' of the Qur'ān, followed by a warning that punishment is coming. It recounts the story of Pharaoh and the Sons of Israel, defends the idea of resurrection, and concludes with a description of the rewards and punishments awaiting the righteous and wicked.

45 The Kneeling

This sūra opens with a declaration of the 'sending down' of the Qur'ān and an enumeration of the signs of God's power and providence in nature. The Prophet is urged to follow God's path independently of the Sons of Israel. The sūra concludes with a judgment scene at which each community will be found 'kneeling.'

46 The Sand Dunes

This sūra opens with a declaration of the 'sending down' of the Qur'ān, and then condemns the folly of idolatry in the face of God's power and providence. The Prophet is set forth as a typical messenger whose 'Book' confirms the Torah of Moses. Next comes the story of the punishment of the people of 'Ād, followed by one about a band of jinn who came to believe after listening to the Qur'ān. A conclusion stresses the certainty of resurrection and judgment.

47 Muḥammad

Much of this sūra is concerned with matters of war.

48 The Victory

This sūra offers encouragement to the Prophet and his followers after conflict with Mecca.

49 The Private Rooms

This sūra is deals with the conduct of the Prophet's followers in their interactions with him and each other.

50 Qāf

This sūra opens by defending the resurrection through an appeal to the signs of God's power and providence in nature. It stresses the certainty of death and judgment, and concludes with words of advice for the Prophet.

51 The Scatterers

This sūra opens with a series of vivid affirmations of the certainty and imminence of the Day of Judgment. Next comes the story of Abraham and his guests, followed by briefer reports of the punishment of Pharaoh and the peoples of 'Ād, Thamūd, and Noah. A final section extols God's power and providence.

52 The Mountain

This sūra opens with a series of affirmations of the certainty and imminence of the Day of Judgment. This is followed by a description of the delights awaiting the righteous in Paradise. The latter half of the sūra is an unrelenting diatribe against the disbelievers.

53 The Star

This sūra opens with the reports of two 'visions.' These are followed by a section rejecting the idea that angels are the 'daughters of God.' It concludes with a summary of the contents of 'the scrolls of Moses and Abraham.'

54 The Moon

This sūra consists almost entirely of the stories of earlier generations which were destroyed for their disobedience. Both the beginning and end warn that judgment is near.

55 The Merciful

The first half of this sūra recounts God's blessings, the second describes the punishments of the wicked and rewards of the righteous. One of its distinctive features is that it addresses both people and jinn.

56 The Falling

This sūra opens with a vivid description of the Last Day, when people will be divided into three classes – 'the foremost' and 'the companions on the right and left' – whose rewards and punishments are then described. The second half of the sūra extols God's power and providence, and praises the Qur'ān.

57 Iron

This sūra opens by extolling the glory of God, and then appeals for belief and contributions in support of the cause. It describes the different fates awaiting the 'hypocrites' and believers, and concludes with a reference to the previous messengers Abraham, Noah, and Jesus.

58 The Disputer

This sūra deals with the case of a woman who disputed her husband's attempt to end their marriage. The remainder is a warning that those who oppose the Prophet will suffer defeat both in this world and the next.

59 The Gathering

Most of this sūra is said to refer to the expulsion of the Banū Naḍīr (a Jewish tribe) from Medina.

60 The Examined Woman

This sūra warns believers about secret alliances with the enemy. It also gives instructions on how to treat women who leave their husbands to join the believers, as well as what to do about the wives of believers who run off.

61 The Lines

This sūra consists of several short passages. Notable among them is a section on the Sons of Israel's opposition to Moses, Jesus, and finally the Prophet, whose coming (under the name of 'Aḥmad') Jesus is said to have predicted.

62 The Assembly

This sūra consists of several short passages. The Prophet is identified as a 'native' messenger, Jewish exceptionalism is criticized, and prayer is established on Friday.

63 The Hypocrites

This sūra is comprised of two passages, one describing the 'hypocrites' and the other admonishing the believers.

64 Mutual Defrauding

This sūra extols the glory, power, and knowledge of God, and then describes the different fates awaiting believers and disbelievers.

65 Divorce

This sūra is mostly comprised of regulations concerning divorce.

66 The Forbidding

The first half of this sūra deals with an incident between the Prophet and his wives. It concludes by giving famous examples from the past of believing and disbelieving women.

67 The Kingdom

This sūra consists mostly of short passages, many of which revolve around the theme of God's power.

68 The Pen

This sūra opens with a denial that the Prophet is 'possessed,' before turning to denounce one of his opponents directly. Next comes a parable warning against arrogant self-satisfaction, followed by a section on eschatological rewards and punishments, and a concluding exhortation to the Prophet.

69 The Payment Due

This sūra begins with a reference to earlier generations who dismissed the threat of punishment and were destroyed. It then describes the terror of the Last Day and Judgment, and concludes with an affirmation the truth of the Qur'ān.

70 The Stairways

This sūra begins by responding to a question about the coming punishment. A description of those who will enter the Garden follows. It then concludes by assuring the Prophet that his opponents are doomed.

71 Noah

This sūra is devoted entirely to Noah, including details not found in other iterations of his story.

72 The Jinn

This sūra begins with a report of a band of jinn who heard the Prophet reciting the Qur'ān. Their affirmation of belief makes up the first half of the sūra; the latter half contains a series of pronouncements by the Prophet.

73 The Enwrapped One

This sūra opens with the Prophet being urged to spend the night attending to the Qur'ān. This is followed by a warning to the people and an appeal for belief.

74 The Cloaked One

This sūra is a collection of diverse passages. It opens with a command to the Prophet to 'arise and warn.' This is followed by sections dealing with an opponent, the number of angels guarding Hell, and the fate awaiting those who disregard the message.

75 The Resurrection

This sūra is a collection of short passages, most of which revolve around the Last Day and God's power to raise the dead. Noteworthy among them is a section dealing with the Prophet's method of reciting the Qur'ān.

76 The Human

This sūra opens with a reference to the generation of humans, describes the rewards awaiting the righteous, and closes with an exhortation to the Prophet to remain steadfast.

77 The Ones Sent Forth

This sūra, unified by the theme of coming punishment, opens with a series of vivid affirmations of the certainty of judgment, and then describes the signs of the Last Day. The remainder of the sūra is a series of eschatological 'woes' directed against those who deny the Judgment.

78 The News

This sūra, which begins with 'the news' of impending judgment, extols the power and providence of God, and describes the events of the Last Day, including the different fates awaiting believers and disbelievers.

79 The Snatchers

This sūra opens with a dramatic description of sinners at the resurrection. This is followed by an abridged version of the story of Moses, as well as passages on God's providential power and the different fates awaiting the righteous and wicked. It concludes with the question: when will the Hour strike?

80 He Frowned

This sūra begins by admonishing the Prophet not to be concerned exclusively with the rich. Next come sections on the authority of the written message and human ingratitude for God's providential care. It concludes with a vivid scene of the Last Day.

81 The Shrouding

This sūra consists of two distinct passages. The first is a description of events of the Last Day; the latter relates a 'vision' on the part of the Prophet.

82 The Rending

This sūra falls into three related parts: events of the Last Day, the certainty of Judgment, and an explanation of Judgment Day.

83 The Defrauders

This sūra opens with a denunciation of those who cheat others by giving 'short measure.' Their punishment is contrasted with the fate the righteous.

84 The Splitting

This sūra opens with a description of events of the Last Day which culminate in resurrection and judgment. It concludes with a warning to those who reject the Qur'ān.

85 The Constellations

This sūra promises punishment for disbelievers and reward for believers.

86 The Night Visitor

This sūra stresses God's power to raise the dead and the accountability of each individual before him.

87 The Most High

This sūra promises the Prophet God's support in reciting the Qur'ān, and commends those who accept its message. It concludes by emphasizing the superiority of the future life over the present one.

88 The Covering

This sūra contrasts the fates of the righteous and the wicked on the Day of Judgment. It concludes with an exhortation to the Prophet to continue in his role as a 'warner.'

89 The Dawn

This sūra describes the punishment of earlier generations and concludes with a scene of judgment.

90 The Land

This sūra criticizes people who take the easy path and neglect the hard climb to virtue. Only the latter leads to reward, while the former ends in punishment.

91 The Sun

This sūra consists of two passages. The first is a series of oaths which culminate in the contrast between true success and failure. The second passage recounts the story of the people of Thamūd, who were destroyed for their evildoing.

92 The Night

This sūra, like the previous one, begins with a series of oaths which culminate in the contrast between two ways in life. It concludes with the contrasting fates awaiting the righteous and wicked.

93 The Morning Light

This sūra offers the Prophet reassurance and encouragement.

94 The Expanding

This sūra, like the previous one, offers the Prophet reassurance by recounting God's past favor.

95 The Fig

This sūra is concerned to alleviate any doubt or hesitancy the Prophet may have had about proclaiming the coming Judgment.

96 The Clot

This sūra, regarded by some as the first revelation, opens with an exhortation to the Prophet to 'recite' in the name of God the creator. The second part is a warning to one of the Prophet's opponents.

97 The Decree

This sūra describes the night on which the Qur'ān was sent down.

98 The Clear Sign

This sūra explains the cause of religious divisions, and then describes the fate awaiting believers and disbelievers.

99 The Earthquake

This sūra describes one of the events which will accompany the Day of Resurrection.

100 The Runners

This sūra decries people's ingratitude to God and their lust for wealth.

101 The Striking

This sūra vividly describes one of the events of the Last Day.

102 Rivalry

This sūra condemns competition for wealth and status.

103 The Afternoon

This sūra declares the impoverished state of human existence.

104 The Slanderer
This sūra attacks wealthy critics of the Prophet and his followers.

105 The Elephant
This sūra is said to refer to an attack on Mecca by Abraha, the Christian Abyssinian ruler of Yemen.

106 Quraysh
This sūra is an appeal to the Quraysh to worship God in gratitude for his benefits.

107 Assistance
The sūra links neglect of the poor to denial of Judgment, before turning to condemn false piety.

108 Abundance
This sūra offers the Prophet encouragement after insult.

109 The Disbelievers
This sūra declares the Prophet's complete break with the disbelievers.

110 Help
This sūra foresees the coming triumph.

111 The Fiber
This sūra is said to be a curse upon the Prophet's uncle, who opposed him at Mecca.

112 Devotion
This sūra emphasizes the oneness and uniqueness of God.

113 The Daybreak
The sūra is an apotropaic prayer to ward off magic.

114 The People
This sūra is an apotropaic prayer to ward off evil suggestions.

The Qur'ān

1 The Opening ✿ Al-Fātiḥa

1 In the Name of God, the Merciful, the Compassionate.[1]

2 Praise (be)[2] to God, Lord of the worlds,[3] 3 the Merciful, the Compassionate, 4 Master[4] of the Day of Judgment.[5] 5 You we serve[6] and You we seek for help. 6 Guide us to the straight path:[7] 7 the path of those whom You have blessed,[8] not (the path) of those on whom (Your) anger falls, nor of those who go astray.

Q1: As its title suggests, this short prayer serves as the introduction to the Qur'ān, though it has also had several other names (e.g. 'The Praise'). It is sometimes referred to as the 'mother' or 'essence of the Qur'ān' (Ar. *umm al-Qur'ān*), and is an important part of worship, both public and private. Whether it was originally part of the Qur'ān is uncertain. The early codices (Ar. *maṣāḥif*) of Ibn 'Abbās and Ibn Mas'ūd are said to have omitted it.

1 Invocation

1. *In the Name of God...*: or 'By the name of God...' (Ar. *bi-smi llāhi...*). This invocation, called the *basmala* (a word formed from the first four consonants, *b-s-m-l*), or *bismillāh* (a combination of the first three words), is recited before every sūra except the ninth, but only here is it counted as a verse by the Cairo edition. Scholars disagree about the origin of the *basmala* and its placement at the head of the sūras. The formula occurs one other time in the Qur'ān, as the opening of Solomon's letter to the queen of Sheba (Q27.30; cf. Q2.163; 41.2; 59.22). Behind the rendering 'God' stands the Arabic word 'Allāh,' the name of God employed by Muslims as well as Arabic-speaking Jews and Christians. It is the predominant name for God in the Qur'ān (occurring well over 2500 times), though it is completely absent from thirty-three sūras in which the deity is referred to simply as 'Lord' (Ar. *rabb*). 'Allāh' is not a proper name but probably a contraction of *al-ilāh* (lit. 'the god'). In Arabic the word *ilāh* (plur. *ālihat*) is used as a generic term for 'god' (plur. 'gods'). Some scholars, however, contend that 'Allāh' was derived from the word for 'God' in Aramaic or Syriac (*alāhā*). The cult of Allāh predates Islam and was known throughout southern Syria and northern Arabia, as well as at Mecca, where a stone-built shrine called the Ka'ba was said to be his 'House.' There is no great difference in meaning between 'merciful' (Ar. *raḥmān*) and 'compassionate' (*raḥīm*); cf. Exodus 34.6, 'a God merciful and compassionate' (see also 2 Chronicles 30.9; Nehemiah 9.17, 31; Joel 2.13; Jonah 4.2; James 5.11).

2–7 Prayer

2. *(be)*: or '(belongs);' cf. Q6.1; 10.10; 17.111; 18.1; 27.15; 34.1; 35.1; 37.182; 39.75; 40.65.
3. *Lord of the worlds*: this title (Ar. *rabb al-'ālamīn*) may mean 'Lord of the heavens and the earth' (see Q26.23-28; 45.36), but elsewhere 'the worlds' suggests something like 'the inhabitants of the world' or 'all peoples' (e.g. Q2.47; 6.90; 25.1; 29.10). So perhaps a better rendering would be 'Lord of all peoples.' It is traditionally understood to refer to all realms of being (e.g. humans, angels, jinn etc.), as well as to this world and the next. Cf. the Jewish liturgical form of addressing God as 'Lord of the worlds' (Hebr. *ribbōn ha'ōlāmīm*) and the Christian designation of God as 'Lord of heaven and earth' (e.g. Matthew 11.25; Acts 17.24; cf. Revelation 15.3). Roman emperors often styled themselves as 'Lord of the whole world' or 'Lord of all peoples' (Lat. *dominus orbis terrarum*).
4. *Master*: or 'King,' depending on how the word is vocalized (cf. Q7.187; 82.19).
5. *Day of Judgment*: Ar. *yawm al-dīn*, also called the 'Day of Resurrection,' the 'Last Day,' or simply the 'Day' or the 'Hour' (see e.g. Q39.67-74; 81.1-14; 89.21-30; cf. Matthew 25.31-46; Revelation 20.11-12). In the Qur'ān 'eschatological' judgment falls mostly on individuals, who receive their rewards and punishments at the end of days, but there are also frequently recurring stories of 'temporal' judgment, in which various communities of the past were punished in history for their sins.
6. *serve*: or 'worship;' use of the first-person plur. shows Q1 was intended for liturgical repetition as a prayer.
7. *the straight path*: Ar. *al-ṣirāṭ al-mustaqīm* occurs 32 times in the Qur'ān, but only here and Q37.118 with the article. It refers to the revealed 'path' of religious truth and right conduct. The Arabic word *ṣirāṭ* has its origins in Latin *strata* (cf. Eng. 'street'), the word for the kind of 'paved road' (*via strata*) the Romans were famous for building so straight throughout their empire.
8. *whom You have blessed*: or 'on whom You have conferred prosperity' (cf. Q4.69-70; 19.58).

2 The Cow ۞ Al-Baqara

In the Name of God, the Merciful, the Compassionate

1 Alif Lām Mīm.[1]

2 That is the Book[2] – (there is) no doubt about it[3] – a guidance[4] for the ones who guard (themselves),[5]
3 who believe in the unseen,[6] and observe the prayer,[7] and contribute[8] from what We have provided
them, **4** and who believe in what has been sent down to you,[9] and what was sent down before you,[10] and
they are certain of the Hereafter.[11] **5** Those (stand) on guidance from their Lord, and those – they are the
ones who prosper. **6** Surely[12] those who disbelieve – (it is) the same for them whether you warn them or

---

Q2: By far the longest sūra, Q2 defies easy summary. It includes accounts of Adam's fall, Moses and Pharaoh, Israel's disobedience, and the religion of Abraham and his building of God's 'House,' toward which prayer is now directed. Instruction on a wide variety of topics occupies most of the second half of the sūra (on food, retaliation, wills, fasting, fighting, pilgrimage, marriage, divorce, usury, almsgiving, and prayer). Its title comes from the story of 'the cow' which the Israelites were commanded to sacrifice (Q2.67-71). Most scholars, traditional and modern, assign Q2 to the 'Medinan' period; indeed many consider it the first of the 'Medinan' sūras (including the Cairo edition).

1 Letters

1. *Alif Lām Mīm*: the names of Arabic letters ', *l*, and *m*. The same letter combination occurs at the beginning of Q3, Q7 (with an additional 'ṣād'), and in a block of sūras from Q29 to Q32. Twenty-nine sūras begin with letters like these, ranging from one to five. No satisfactory explanation has been given for their occurrence. The Cairo edition varies in counting these letters as a separate verse (as here), or as the beginning of the first verse. The *Song of Roland* (11th cent. CE, but based on much earlier sources) contains an analogous phenomenon. The letters AOI, which appear in certain places throughout the text, are equally mysterious and have likewise never been adequately explained.

2–7 The Book, believers and disbelievers

2. *the Book*: Ar. *al-kitāb* occurs frequently and with several different meanings, but its most common use is in reference to God's revelation to the Prophet and to certain religious communities, especially Jews and Christians, who are called the 'People of the Book' (see e.g. Q2.105, 109 below). Here it may signal a transition from 'recited scripture' to 'written scripture' (i.e. the Qur'ān in written form).
3. *no doubt about it*: or 'no doubt in it' (cf. e.g. Q10.37; 32.2).
4. *guidance*: one of the most frequent terms (Ar. *hudā*) for revelation in general, and the Qur'ān in particular (see e.g. Q2.185 below).
5. *guard (themselves)*: against evil, or God (a very common phrase).
6. *the unseen*: lit. 'that which is absent' or 'hidden' (Ar. *al-ghayb*); it can refer to the 'divine realm' in general, as well as to 'the future' or 'the distant past,' or all that is beyond human ken. The 'unseen' is known only to God, except what he chooses to reveal (see e.g. Q2.33 below; 3.179; 6.59, 73; 19.78; 72.26-27; cf. Hebrews 11.1; Romans 8.24-25; 2 Corinthians 4.18; 5.7).
7. *the prayer*: the ritual prayer (or *ṣalāt*).
8. *contribute*: lit. 'spend' (for those in need or for the cause).
9. *what has been sent down to you*: the revelation of the Qur'ān to the Prophet.
10. *what was sent down before you*: the 'Torah' of Moses and 'Gospel' of Jesus.
11. *the Hereafter*: lit. 'the last' or 'the end' (Ar. *al-ākhira*); the standard picture of Qur'ānic eschatology is described in terms of the joys of a heavenly Garden and the agonies of Hell (see e.g. Q7.38-51; 41.19-24; 55.33-78; 56.11-44; 69.19-36; 76.4-22; 83.15-28).
12. *Surely*: some translations ignore the sentence-head particle *inna* (and its satellite, the emphatic particle *la-*); others render it inconsistently. Cf. the use of *hinnē* ('lo!' 'behold!' 'see!'), the demonstrative particle in biblical Hebrew.

do not warn them. They will not believe. **7** God has set a seal on their hearts[13] and on their hearing, and on their sight (there is) a covering.[14] For them (there is) a great punishment.[15]

8 (There are) some people who say, 'We believe in God and in the Last Day,' but they are not believers. **9** They try to deceive God and the believers, but they only deceive themselves, though they do not realize (it). **10** In their hearts is a sickness, so God has increased their sickness, and for them (there is) a painful punishment because they have lied. **11** When it is said to them, 'Do not foment corruption on the earth,'[16] they say, 'We are setting (things) right.'[17] **12** Is it not a fact that they – they are the ones who foment corruption, though they do not realize (it)? **13** When it is said to them, 'Believe as the people believe,'[18] they say, 'Shall we believe as the fools believe?' Is it not a fact that they – they are the fools, but they do not know (it)? **14** When they meet those who believe, they say, 'We believe,' but when they go privately to their satans,[19] they say, 'Surely we are with you. We were only mocking.' **15** God will mock them, and increase them in their insolent transgression, wandering blindly. **16** Those are the ones who have purchased error[20] with the (price of) guidance. Their transaction has not profited (them), and they have not been (rightly) guided. **17** Their parable is like the parable of the one who kindled a fire. When it lit up what was around him, God took away their light, and left them in darkness – they do not see. **18** Without hearing or speech or sight – so they do not return. **19** Or (it is) like a cloudburst from the sky, with darkness and thunder and lightning. They put their fingers in their ears because of the thunderbolts, afraid of death – God surrounds the disbelievers. **20** The lightning almost takes away their sight. Whenever it flashes for them, they walk in it, but when it becomes dark over them, they stand (still). If God (so) pleased, He could indeed take away their hearing and their sight. Surely God is powerful over everything.

21 People![21] Serve your Lord, who created you and those who were before you, so that you may guard (yourselves). **22** (He it is) who made the earth as a couch for you, and the sky a dome,[22] and sent down water from the sky, by means of which He produced fruits as a provision for you. So do not set up[23] rivals[24] to God, when you know (better). **23** If you are in doubt about what We have sent down to Our servant,[25] then bring a sūra like it,[26] and call your witnesses, other than God, if you are truthful. **24** If you

13. *hearts*: here, as often, the heart is spoken of as synonymous with mind or understanding.
14. *set a seal...a covering*: cf. the similar idea at Isaiah 6.9-10; Mark 4.11-12.
15. *punishment*: or 'torment,' 'torture' (Ar. *'adhāb*), the first of more than 300 occurrences of this word in the Qur'ān.

8–20 False believers

16. *Do not foment corruption on the earth*: a common phrase which refers to acting wickedly or in a way that harms the community (see e.g. Q2.30, 60, 205 below), but what is meant is never specified exactly.
17. *setting (things) right*: or 'acting uprightly.'
18. *as the people believe*: usually understood as referring to the community of believers in Medina.
19. *satans*: or 'demons' (Ar. *shayāṭīn*); they are counterparts to the 'angels,' and are individually assigned to people to incite them to evil (see Q19.83; 43.36; cf. Q7.27; 23.97; 41.25). Their leader is 'Satan' (see n. on Q2.36 below). Here 'satans' is used as a derogatory reference to the 'gods' of the disbelievers or perhaps their leaders (cf. Q2.102 below; 6.112, 121).
20. *error*: lit. 'straying.'

21–25 Exhortation to believers

21. *People!*: this vocative is usually understood as a 'Meccan' form of address, since the common form of address in Medina was 'You who believe!' (cf. Q2.168 below).
22. *dome*: lit. 'something erected (overhead);' cf. Q40.64.
23. *set up*: lit. 'make.'
24. *rivals*: or 'equals' (Ar. *andād*), i.e. other gods alleged to be equal with God.
25. *Our servant*: the Prophet; the word 'servant' (Ar. *'abd*) also means 'slave.'
26. *bring a sūra like it*: or 'bring a scripture like it.' The failure of the Prophet's contemporaries to take up this challenge (cf. Q10.38; 11.13; 28.49; 52.34) was later seen as proof that it was impossible, and the Qur'ān's 'inimita-

do not (do this), and you will not (do it), then guard (yourselves) against the Fire[27] – its fuel is people and stones[28] – which is prepared for the disbelievers.

25 Give good news to those who believe and do righteous deeds, that for them (there are) Gardens[29] through which rivers flow. Whenever they are provided with fruit from there as provision, they will say, 'This is what we were provided with before,' (for) they will be given similar things (to eat).[30] There they will also have pure spouses, and there they will remain.

26 Surely God is not ashamed to strike a parable even of a gnat or anything above it. As for those who believe, they know that it is the truth from their Lord, but as for those who disbelieve, they will say, 'What does God intend by this parable?' He leads many astray by it and guides many by it,[31] but He does not lead any astray by it except the wicked, **27** who break the covenant of God,[32] after its ratification, and sever what God has commanded to be joined, and foment corruption on the earth. Those – they are the losers. **28** How can you disbelieve in God, when you were (once) dead and He gave you life?[33] Then He causes you to die, then He gives you life (again), (and) then to Him you are returned?[34] **29** He (it is) who created for you what is on the earth – all (of it). Then He mounted (upward) to the sky and fashioned them (as) seven heavens. He has knowledge of everything.

30 (Remember) when[35] your Lord said to the angels,[36] 'Surely I am placing[37] on the earth a ruler.'[38] They said, 'Will You place on it someone who will foment corruption on it, and shed blood,[39] while we glorify (You) with Your praise and call You holy?' He said, 'Surely I know what you do not know.' **31** And He taught

---

bility' (referred to as the *i'jāz al-qur'ān*) would be taken as proof of its miraculous nature and divine origin. The word 'sūra,' which may be related to Hebr. *shūrāh* ('row') or to Syr. *ṣurṭā* ('writing' or 'text of scripture'), refers here to a 'unit' of revelation, and not to present sūras, though there is no indication how long these 'units' were. Some verses mention a sūra being 'sent down' (e.g. Q9.64; 24.1; 47.20) in a way similar to terms like 'sign' or 'verse' (Ar. *āya*), 'book' (*kitāb*), and 'recitation' (*qur'ān*).

27. *the Fire*: Ar. *al-nār* is the most common of the various designations for Hell (cf. Q2.119, 206 below).

28. *stones*: reference obscure; perhaps 'brimstone' or 'stone idols' is meant (cf. Q66.6).

29. *Gardens*: the Qur'ān's eschatological imagery is sometimes of 'Gardens' (e.g. Q4.57; cf. Q9.72; 13.23 [of Eden]; 10.9; 56.12 [of Bliss]), or of a singular 'Garden' (e.g. Q2.34, 82 below; 3.133; 11.108; 43.70-73; 47.15). In two passages the word 'Paradise' is used (see n. on Q23.11; cf. Q18.107, 'Gardens of Paradise').

30. *similar things (to eat)*: meaning obscure; the idea may be that the food of heaven will resemble earthly food.

26–29 Appeal to disbelievers

31. *He leads many astray...guides many by it*: cf. the similar rationale for Jesus' use of parables at Mark 4.11-12.

32. *covenant of God*: a reference to the covenant at Sinai, and thus to the 'Sons of Israel' (see Q2.40-48 below).

33. *gave you life*: i.e. at birth, contrasted with the prior state of non-existence or 'death.'

34. *returned*: for judgment.

30–39 The story of Adam, Iblīs, and the Fall from Paradise

35. *(Remember) when...*: a stock narrative formula; the Arabic particle *idh* often marks the beginning of a story, and means something like 'Once...,' or 'There was a time when...,' or 'Remember when....' For the story that follows, cf. the versions at Q7.10-25; 15.28-48; 20.115-123; and Genesis 2.4-3.24.

36. *angels*: celestial beings who act as God's agents (Q15.8) and 'messengers' (Q22.75; 35.1, with two, three, or four wings). They watch over humans and record their deeds (Q13.11; 82.10-12), call them in at death (Q6.61; 16.28, 32), and will be present at the Judgment (Q2.210; 39.75; 69.17). They also surround the throne of God, where they sing his praises (Q40.7; 42.5). Since the angels are clearly the speakers in a few passages (e.g. Q19.64-65; 37.161-166), it may be that some of the numerous 'We' passages that refer to God in the third person are spoken by them. Otherwise the angels are seldom referred to as agents of revelation (see Q16.2; 37.3; 77.5; 97.1-4).

37. *placing*: or 'making.'

38. *ruler*: the basic meaning of Ar. *khalīfa* is 'successor' (see e.g. Q6.133; 7.69, 74; 24.55), but 'ruler' is better here (cf. Genesis 1.28, where God gives humans 'sovereignty' over his creation).

39. *blood*: lit. 'the bloods.'

Adam[40] the names – all of them.[41] Then He presented them to the angels, and said, 'Inform Me of the names of these, if you are truthful.' **32** They said, 'Glory to You! We have no knowledge except for what You have taught us. Surely You – You are the Knowing, the Wise.'[42] **33** He said, 'Adam! Inform them of their names.' And when he had informed them of their names, He said, 'Did I not say to you, "Surely I know the unseen (things) of the heavens and the earth"? I know what you reveal and what you have concealed.'

34 (Remember) when We said to the angels, 'Prostrate yourselves before Adam,'[43] and they prostrated themselves, except Iblīs.[44] He refused and became arrogant, and was one of the disbelievers. **35** And We said, 'Adam! Inhabit the Garden, you and your wife,[45] and eat freely of it wherever you please, but do not go near this tree,[46] or you will both be among the evildoers.' **36** Then Satan[47] caused them both to slip from there, and to go out from where they were. And We said, 'Go down,[48] some of you an enemy to others![49] The earth is a dwelling place for you, and enjoyment (of life) for a time.' **37** Then Adam received certain words from his Lord, and He turned to him (in forgiveness).[50] Surely He – He is the One who turns (in forgiveness), the Compassionate. **38** We said, 'Go down from it – all (of you)! If any guidance comes to you from Me, whoever follows My guidance – (there will be) no fear on them, nor will they sorrow. **39** But those who disbelieve and call Our signs[51] a lie – those are the companions of the Fire. There they will remain.'

40 Sons of Israel! Remember My blessing which I bestowed on you. Fulfill My covenant (and) I shall fulfill your covenant, and Me – fear Me (alone). **41** Believe in what I have sent down,[52] confirming what is with you,[53] and do not be the first to disbelieve in it. Do not sell My signs[54] for a small price, and guard

---

40. *Adam*: always used as a personal name in the Qur'ān.
41. *all of them*: lit. 'all of it;' said to refer to 'the names of all things;' but cf. Genesis 2.20, where Adam is allowed to name all the animals.
42. *the Knowing, the Wise*: a common feature of Qur'ānic style is to have a verse end with two names of God.
43. *Prostrate yourselves before Adam*: the prostration of the angels before Adam is not a part of the Genesis account, but was a prominent theme in Christian tradition (see e.g. Hebrews 1.6; Life of Adam and Eve 12.1-16.1; Cave of Treasures 2.22-25).
44. *except Iblīs*: related to the Greek word *diabolos* ('accuser,' cf. Eng. 'devil'), through Syriac (*dīblūs* or *diyābūlūs*). In the Septuagint *diabolos* is sometimes used to translate 'Satan' (Hebr. *sāṭān*, 'accuser'), and in the New Testament the word is used to designate the chief of the forces of evil (e.g. Matthew 4.1). The passage above implies that Iblīs was originally one of the angels; cf. Q18.50, where he is said to be one of the jinn.
45. *your wife*: Adam's wife 'Eve' (Ar. *Ḥawwā'*) is not referred to by name in the Qur'ān.
46. *this tree*: see also Q7.19; 20.120 ('Tree of Immortality'); cf. Genesis 2.15-17; 3.1-2 ('Tree of Knowledge').
47. *Satan*: lit. 'the Satan' (Ar. *al-shayṭān*; cf. Hebr. *ha-sāṭān*, 'the accuser'), presumably identical with Iblīs. Satan is described as provoking humans to evil (Q2.168; 8.48; 16.63; 17.61-64), whispering in their hearts (Q7.20; 20.120; 114.4-6), and even tampering with the messages revealed to prophets (Q22.52).
48. *Go down*: i.e. from the heavenly Garden to earth.
49. *some of you an enemy to others*: 'you' is plur. here, and probably refers to humanity in general, whereas in the previous line 'you' was dual (referring to Adam and his wife).
50. *He turned to him (in forgiveness)*: Adam's sin is forgiven; the Christian doctrine of 'original sin' is as foreign to the Qur'ān as it is to the Jewish Bible.
51. *signs*: Ar. *āyāt* (sing. *āya*; cf. Syr. *āthā*; Hebr. *'ōth*) here refer to the basic 'units' of revelation (or 'verses,' in that sense), though the Qur'ān gives no indication of the length of these 'units,' and they are not to be identified with present verses. Depending on the context, however, 'signs' can also refer to 'natural phenomena' (as 'signs' of God's power and providence), to 'miracles' and other extraordinary events (associated with the work of God's messengers), or to 'revelation' in general.

40–48 Appeal to the Sons of Israel

52. *what I have sent down*: the Qur'ān.
53. *what is with you*: the Torah of Moses.
54. *signs*: or 'verses.'

(yourselves) against Me. **42** Do not mix the truth with falsehood, and do not conceal the truth when you know (better). **43** Observe the prayer and give the alms,[55] and bow with the ones who bow. **44** Do you command the people to piety and forget yourselves, though you recite the Book?[56] Will you not understand? **45** Seek help in patience and the prayer. Surely it[57] is hard[58] indeed, except for the humble, **46** who think that they will meet their Lord, and that they will return to Him. **47** Sons of Israel! Remember My blessing which I bestowed on you, and that I have favored you over the worlds.[59] **48** Guard (yourselves) against a Day when no one will intercede for another at all, and no intercession will be accepted from him, and no compensation taken from him, nor will they be helped.[60]

49 (Remember) when We rescued you from the house of Pharaoh.[61] They were inflicting on you the evil punishment, slaughtering your sons and sparing your women.[62] In that was a great test from your Lord. **50** And when We parted the sea for you, We rescued you, and We drowned the house of Pharaoh while you were looking on.

51 (Remember) when We appointed for Moses[63] forty nights. Then you took the calf[64] after he (was gone), and you were evildoers. **52** Then We pardoned you after that, so that you might be thankful. **53** And (remember) when We gave Moses the Book[65] and the Deliverance,[66] so that you might be (rightly) guided. **54** And when Moses said to his people, 'My people! Surely you have done yourselves evil by taking the calf. So turn to your Creator (in repentance), and kill one another.[67] That will be better for you in

55. *observe the prayer and give the alms*: i.e. *ṣalāt*, the ritual prayer, and *zakāt*, a kind of tithe required for the benefit of the poor, as well as other purposes. This is a recurring phrase in the Qur'ān, though the precise requirements for each are not specified.
56. *recite the Book*: or 'read the Book' (i.e. the Torah).
57. *it*: antecedent unclear; perhaps 'true righteousness.'
58. *hard*: lit. 'great.'
59. *favored you over the worlds*: or 'preferred you over all peoples;' the distinctiveness of Israel's election is recognized (see Q2.122 below; 3.33; 6.86; 7.140; 44.32; 45.16).
60. *no intercession...no compensation...*: judgment falls on individuals, whom neither family nor friends can help (an implicit rejection of the Christian ideas of 'vicarious atonement' and 'intercession' by the saints); cf. Q2.123 below.

49–50 Israel's deliverance from Pharaoh

61. *Pharaoh*: Ar. *Fir'awn* is used as the proper name for the ruler of Egypt in the Qur'ān. The Bible nowhere mentions the name of the pharaoh of the exodus.
62. *slaughtering your sons and sparing your women*: cf. Pharaoh's order to kill all Hebrew boys but spare the girls (Exodus 1.15-16, 22).

51–74 Examples of Israel's disobedience

63. *Moses*: Ar. *Mūsā* is mentioned by name 136 times in the Qur'ān, more frequently than any other prophet. Only Abraham enjoys a similar stature, though even he runs a distant second (69 times). The name 'Muḥammad' occurs only four times, though there about two hundred references to 'the messenger' (Ar. *al-rasūl*) and about thirty to 'the prophet' (*al-nabī*).
64. *took the calf*: i.e. as a god; for the story, see Q7.148-153; 20.83-98; cf. the 'golden calf' of Exodus 32.1-35.
65. *the Book*: the Torah.
66. *the Deliverance*: Ar. *al-furqān* is a difficult term to translate. It may be related to Syr. *purqānā* ('salvation'), but influenced in meaning by Ar. *faraqa* ('to separate, distinguish'). The term occurs at six other places in the Qur'ān (Q2.185; 3.4; 8.29, 41; 21.48; 25.1). In all but one it is a designation either for the Book 'sent down' to Moses or to the Prophet (once it is 'given' to the believers). However, Q8.41 refers to the 'Day of al-Furqān, the day the two forces met.' It is uncertain whether this refers to the day on which the Qur'ān was 'delivered,' or to 'deliverance' in battle, or indeed to both. Many scholars take the 'Day of al-Furqān' as referring to the Muslim victory at the battle of Badr (624 CE/2 AH).
67. *kill one another*: lit. 'kill yourselves' (i.e. the transgressors); cf. Exodus 32.27, '...each of you kill your brother, your friend, and your neighbor.'

the sight of your Creator.' Then He turned to you (in forgiveness). Surely He – He is the One who turns (in forgiveness), the Compassionate.

55 (Remember) when you said, 'Moses! We shall not believe you until we see God openly,'[68] and the thunderbolt took you while you were looking on. **56** Then We raised you up after your death, so that you might be thankful. **57** And We overshadowed you (with) the cloud, and We sent down on you the manna and the quails:[69] 'Eat from the good things which We have provided you.' They did not do Us evil, but they did themselves evil.

58 (Remember) when We said, 'Enter this town and eat freely of it wherever you please, and enter the gate in prostration and say: "Ḥiṭṭa."[70] We shall forgive you your sins and increase the doers of good.'
59 But those who did evil exchanged a word other than that which had been spoken to them. So We sent down on those who did evil wrath from the sky, because they were acting wickedly.

60 (Remember) when Moses asked for water for his people, and We said, 'Strike the rock with your staff,' and (there) gushed forth from it twelve springs.[71] All the people already knew their drinking place: 'Eat and drink from the provision of God, and do not act wickedly on the earth, fomenting corruption.'

61 (Remember) when you said, 'Moses! We cannot endure just one kind of food. Call on your Lord for us, that He may bring forth for us some of what the earth grows: its green herbs, its cucumbers, its corn, its lentils, and its onions.'[72] He said, 'Would you exchange what is worse for what is better? Go (back) down to Egypt! Surely you will have what you ask for.' Humiliation and poverty were stamped upon them, and they incurred the anger of God. That was because they had disbelieved in the signs of God, and killed the prophets without any right.[73] That was because they disobeyed and went on transgressing.
62 Surely those who believe, and those who are Jews,[74] and the Christians,[75] and the Sabians[76] – whoever believes in God and the Last Day, and does righteousness – they have their reward with their Lord. (There will be) no fear on them, nor will they sorrow.

63 (Remember) when We took a covenant with you, and raised the mountain above you:[77] 'Hold fast

---

68. *see God openly*: see Q4.153; cf. Exodus 19.21.

69. *the cloud...the manna and the quails*: referring to God's appearance to the Israelites in the 'pillar of cloud' (see e.g. Exodus 13.21; 33.9-10; 40.38; Numbers 9.15; 14.14; Psalm 105.39; 1 Corinthians 10.1; cf. Q2.210 below); and to their provision of food from heaven (see Exodus 16.1-36; Numbers 11.1-35; John 6.31; 1 Corinthians 10.3).

70. *Ḥiṭṭa*: meaning uncertain, as is the identity of the town (Jerusalem?); cf. Q7.161.

71. *twelve springs*: one for each tribe; see Q7.160; cf. Exodus 17.1-7; Numbers 20.2-13.

72. *green herbs, etc....*: cf. Numbers 11.4-5.

73. *killed the prophets without any right*: a common accusation against the Sons of Israel in both the Qur'ān (e.g. Q2.87, 91; 3.21, 112, 181, 183; 4.155; 5.70) and the New Testament (e.g. Luke 11.39-52; 13.34-35; 1 Thessalonians 2.14-16; Hebrews 11.37-38), though there is no evidence for this in the Jewish Bible itself. It is a tradition which emerges later in Christian anti-Jewish polemic. For the important designation 'prophet,' see n. on Q2.87 below.

74. *those who are Jews*: lit. 'those who have judaized,' or follow Jewish law, punning on the name Yahūd.

75. *Christians*: Ar. *al-Naṣārā* is the Qur'ānic designation for 'the Christians.' The term occurs some fourteen times, seven in this sūra alone (see Q2.111, 113, 120, 135, 140 below). The town of 'Nazareth' in northern Palestine was considered the home of Jesus (Matthew 4.13; Luke 4.16), and so he was called 'the Nazarene' by some (e.g. Mark 1.24; Matthew 2.23; Luke 18.37; John 18.5). According to Acts 24.5 the early Christians were also called 'Nazarenes.' The Babylonian Talmud uses the related word 'Notzerim' contemptuously of the Christians.

76. *Sabians*: perhaps 'baptizers' (Ar. *Ṣābi'ūn*), but it is not certain who they were. They are mentioned again at Q5.69 and 22.17, where they are grouped with Jews, Christians, and Zoroastrians. Some scholars think the name refers to the Mandaeans of southern Iraq, who revere John the Baptist as the messiah.

77. *raised the mountain above you*: i.e. Mount Sinai (Q23.20; 95.2); see Q2.93 (below); 4.154; and 7.171 ('shook the mountain above them'); cf. the description of the theophany at Sinai at Exodus 19.16-20.

what We have given you,[78] and remember what is in it, so that you may guard (yourselves).' **64** Then
you turned away after that, and if (it were) not (for the) favor of God on you, and His mercy, you would
indeed have been among the losers. **65** Certainly you know those of you who transgressed in (the matter
of) the sabbath, and (that) We said to them, 'Become apes, skulking away!'[79] **66** We made it a punishment
for their own time and what followed, and an admonition for the ones who guard (themselves).

67 (Remember) when Moses said to his people, 'Surely God commands you to slaughter a cow.'[80] They
said, 'Do you take us in mockery?' He said, 'I take refuge with God from being one of the ignorant.'
68 They said, 'Call on your Lord for us, so that He may make clear to us what it (should be).' He said,
'Surely He says, "Surely it is to be a cow, not old and not young, (but) an age between that." Do what
you are commanded!' **69** They said, 'Call on your Lord for us, so that He may make clear to us what color
it (should be).' He said, 'Surely He says, "Surely it is to be a yellow cow, its color bright, delighting to
the onlookers."' **70** They said, 'Call on your Lord for us, so that He may make clear to us what (kind) it
(should be). Surely cows are all alike to us. And surely (then), if God pleases, we shall indeed be (rightly)
guided.' **71** He said, 'Surely He says, "Surely it is to be a cow, not broken in[81] to plough the earth or to
water the field, (but one that is) sound, without any blemish on it."' They said, 'Now you have brought
the truth.' So they slaughtered it, though they nearly did not.

72 (Remember) when you[82] killed a man, and you argued about it, but God brought forth what you were
concealing. **73** So We said, 'Strike him with part of it.'[83] In this way God brings the dead to life, and shows
you His signs[84] so that you may understand. **74** Then your hearts became hardened after that, and they
(became) like stones or even harder. Surely (there are) some stones indeed from which rivers gush forth,
and surely (there are) some indeed which have been split open, so that water comes out of them, and
surely (there are) some indeed which fall down from fear of God. God is not oblivious of what you do.

75 Are you[85] eager that they should believe you , even though a group of them has already heard the
word of God, (and) then altered it[86] after they had understood it – and they know (they have done this)?
76 When they meet those who believe, they say, 'We believe,' but when some of them meet with others, they say, 'Do you report to them what God has disclosed to you,[87] so that they may dispute with you
by means of it in the presence of your Lord?[88] Will you not understand?' **77** Do they not know that God
knows what they keep secret and what they speak aloud? **78** Some of them are common people[89] – they

---

78. *what We have given you*: the Torah (cf. Q2.93 below; 7.171).
79. *Become apes, skulking away*: for the story, see Q7.163-167 (cf. Q5.60).
80. *God commands you to slaughter a cow*: reference obscure; cf. Numbers 19.1-9; Deuteronomy 21.1-9.
81. *not broken in*: lit. 'not subservient.'
82. *you*: plur.
83. *part of it*: i.e. part of the cow they had slaughtered.
84. *signs*: here 'miracles.'

75–82 Jewish alteration and forging of scripture

85. *you*: plur.; the Prophet is here addressing the believers; the following 'they' refers to the Jews.
86. *altered it*: later interpreted as 'corrupted it,' but the Qur'ān itself speaks only of punning with words (Q4.46) and concealing certain verses (e.g. those alleged to be predictions of the coming of the Prophet), rather than wholesale 'corruption' (Ar. *taḥrīf*); cf. Q2.79 below; 5.13, 41.
87. *disclosed to you*: lit. 'opened to you.'
88. *so that they may dispute...*: the concern on the part of the Jews is that the believers will be able to dispute successfully with them, if they (the believers) learn 'too much' about the Torah from them (the Jews).
89. *common people*: or 'native people;' the word (Ar. *ummiyyūn*) is sometimes taken to mean 'unlettered,' and thus may reflect the pejorative Jewish conception of the 'people of the land' (Hebr. *'am hā-'āretz*) as 'uneducated' or 'ignorant.' This sense would fit the present verse with the words 'who do not know the Book.' But the word probably means something like 'gentiles' (cf. Hebr. *gōyīm*) in the sense of a people without a written scripture, and thus refers

do not know the Book, only wishful thinking, and they only conjecture. **79** So woe to those who write the Book with their (own) hands,[90] (and) then say, 'This is from God,' in order to sell it for a small price.[91] Woe to them for what their hands have written, and woe to them for what they earn. **80** And they say, 'The Fire will only touch us for a number of days.' Say:[92] 'Have you taken a covenant with God? God will not break His covenant. Or do you say about God what you do not know? **81** Yes indeed! Whoever commits[93] evil and is encompassed by his sin – those are the companions of the Fire. There they will remain. **82** But those who believe and do righteous deeds – those are the companions of the Garden. There they will remain.'

83 (Remember) when We took a covenant with the Sons of Israel:[94] 'Do not serve (anyone) but God, and (do) good to parents and family, and the orphans, and the poor, and speak well to the people, and observe the prayer and give the alms.' Then you turned away in aversion, except for a few of you. **84** And when We took a covenant with you: 'Do not shed your (own) blood, and do not expel your (own people) from your homes,' then you agreed (to it) and bore witness. **85** Then you became those who were killing yourselves, and expelling some of you from their homes, supporting each other against them in sin and enmity. And if they come to you as captives, you ransom (them), though their expulsion was forbidden to you. Do you believe in part of the Book and disbelieve in part?[95] What is the payment for the one among you who does that, except disgrace in this present life, and on the Day of Resurrection they will be returned to the harshest punishment? God is not oblivious of what you do. **86** Those are the ones who have purchased this present life with (the price of) the Hereafter. The punishment will not be lightened for them, nor will they be helped.

87 Certainly We gave Moses the Book, and followed up after him with the messengers,[96] and We gave

---

to the 'gentile Arabs' (cf. Q3.20, 75; 62.2). This would also fit the references to the Prophet as 'the *ummī* (or 'gentile') prophet' (Ar. *al-nabī al-ummī*; see Q7.157-158). Traditional scholars interpret *ummī* as 'illiterate,' and claim that Muḥammad could not read or write (thereby further emphasizing the miraculous character of the Qur'ān).

90. *who write the Book with their (own) hands*: i.e. forge false scriptures.

91. *to sell it for a small price*: this may imply that they tried to sell spurious scriptures to the Prophet (cf. Q5.41).

92. *Say*: the sing. imperative *qul* ('Say!' or 'Speak!') introduces more than 300 sayings scattered throughout the Qur'ān. Sometimes these sayings stand alone, at other times they are grouped together (e.g. Q6.56-66), at still others they are an integral part of the context of the passage in which they are found (as here). On five occasions, 'say' introduces a sūra (Q72, 109, 112, 113, 114). In almost all cases, 'say' is understood as addressing only the Prophet, but see Q2.136 (below) and 29.46, where the believers are thus addressed (cf. Q3.84; 112.1). Cf. e.g. the similar form of address to the prophet Ezekiel: 'Then the spirit of Yahweh fell upon me, and he said to me, "Say: 'Thus says Yahweh, etc.'"' (Ezekiel 11.5; see also 11.16, 17; 12.23, 28; 13.18; 14.6; 17.1-3, 9; 19.1-2; 20.1-3 etc.).

93. *commits*: lit. 'earns.'

83–103 Examples of Israel's disobedience (continued)

94. *covenant with the Sons of Israel*: cf. Exodus 20.1-17.

95. *believe in part...and disbelieve in part*: i.e. obey some commands of the Torah while ignoring others (cf. James 2.10-11).

96. *messengers*: the Qur'ān uses the title 'messenger' (Ar. *rasūl*), as well as 'prophet' (Ar. *nabī*), to designate those individuals specially sent by God. Although distinctions in rank and function are sometimes made between the two titles, there is no sharp difference between them. The main difference is their application. Aside from the Prophet, the title 'prophet' is only used of those who appear in biblical tradition (though none of the 'writing prophets' is mentioned), and not of any in Arabic tradition. In some instances the same individual can be designated both a 'messenger' and a 'prophet' (e.g. Ishmael [Q19.54] and Moses [Q19.51]). This is certainly the case with the Prophet (Q7.157), who is also called the 'seal of the prophets' (Q33.40), probably meaning that he is the final one. Those sent as 'messengers' and 'prophets' are also called 'bringers of good news' and 'warners' (see n. on Q2.119 below). Contrary to popular opinion, a prophet generally does not predict the future. Cf. the biblical understanding of a 'prophet' (Hebr. *nabī'*) as a 'warner' against idolatry (e.g. 2 Kings 17.13-18), and the idea of an 'apostle' (Gk. *apostolos*) as a 'messenger' sent to proclaim 'good news' (e.g. Galatians 1.1), and sometimes linked with the title 'prophet' (e.g. Luke 11.49; Revelation 18.20).

Jesus, son of Mary,[97] the clear signs,[98] and supported him with the holy spirit.[99] (But) whenever a messenger brought you what you yourselves did not desire, did you became arrogant, and some you called liars and some you killed?[100] **88** And they say, 'Our hearts are covered.'[101] No! God has cursed them for their disbelief, and so little will they believe. **89** When (there) came to them a Book from God, confirming what was with them[102] – though before (this) they had asked for victory[103] against those who disbelieved – when what they recognized came to them, they disbelieved in it. So the curse of God is on the disbelievers. **90** Evil is what they have sold themselves for: they disbelieve in what God has sent down, (because of) envy that God should send down some of His favor on whomever He pleases of His servants. So they have incurred anger upon anger, and for the disbelievers (there is) a humiliating punishment.

91 When it is said to them, 'Believe in what God has sent down,' they say, 'We believe in what has been sent down on us,' but they disbelieve in anything after that, when it is the truth confirming what is with them. Say: 'Why did you kill the prophets of God before,[104] if you were believers?' **92** Certainly Moses brought you the clear signs,[105] (but) then you took the calf after he (was gone), and you were evildoers. **93** And when We took a covenant with you, and raised the mountain above you:[106] 'Hold fast what We have given you,[107] and hear,' they said, 'We hear and disobey.'[108] And they were made to drink the calf in their hearts because of their disbelief.[109] Say: 'Evil is what your belief commands you, if you are believers.'

94 Say: 'If the Home of the Hereafter with God is yours alone, to the exclusion of the people,[110] and not for (the rest of) the people, wish for death, if you are truthful.'[111] **95** But they will never wish for it because of what their (own) hands have sent forward.[112] God knows the evildoers. **96** Indeed you[113] will find them the most desirous of people for life – even more so than the idolaters.[114] One of them wishes to live for a thousand years, but (even) such a long life will not spare him from the punishment. God sees what they do.

97. *son of Mary*: there is no mention in the Qur'ān of Joseph, Jesus' putative father (cf. Mark 6.3).
98. *the clear signs*: or 'the clear proofs,' 'the indisputable evidence' (Ar. *al-bayyināt*), referring to Jesus' miracles (see Q5.110; cf. e.g. Q2.92, of Moses; Q6.57; 11.17, of the Prophet).
99. *holy spirit*: or 'spirit of holiness' (Ar. *rūḥ al-qudus*); cf. Q2.253 below; 5.110.
100. *some you killed*: see n. on Q2.61 above; cf. Q5.70.
101. *covered*: or 'uncircumcised;' i.e. unable to receive the message or understand it; also a biblical metaphor (cf. Leviticus 26.41; Deuteronomy 10.16; 30.6; Jeremiah 4.4; 9.26; Ezekiel 44.7, 9; Acts 7.51; Romans 2.28-29).
102. *confirming what was with them*: the Qur'ān 'confirms' the Torah (cf. Q2.41 above).
103. *asked for victory*: or 'sought an opening.'
104. *before*: i.e. in former times, presumably referring to the ancestors of the Jews.
105. *the clear signs*: or 'the clear proofs,' 'the indisputable evidence.'
106. *raised the mountain above you*: see n. on Q2.63 above.
107. *what we have given you*: the Torah.
108. *We hear and disobey*: instead of 'We hear and obey,' perhaps punning on the resemblance between Ar. *sami'nā wa-'aṣaynā* and Hebr. *shāma'nū wə-'asīnū* ('we will hear and do [it];' Deuteronomy 5.27).
109. *made to drink the calf...*: cf. Exodus 32.20, Moses took the calf, burned it and ground it into dust, and then scattered it on the water and made the Israelites drink it.
110. *yours alone, to the exclusion of the people*: a sarcastic allusion to the idea of Israel as God's 'chosen people' (cf. Q62.6).
111. *wish for death...*: i.e. if they are certain of heaven, they should long for death, since heaven is better than life (cf. Q62.6-7).
112. *because of what their (own) hands have sent forward*: i.e. their misdeeds, which will be awaiting them at the Judgment.
113. *you*: the Prophet, or perhaps intended generally ('one').
114. *the idolaters*: or 'those who associate (other gods with God).'

97 Say: 'Whoever is an enemy to Gabriel[115] – surely he has brought it down[116] on your heart[117] by the permission of God, confirming what was before it,[118] and as a guidance and good news[119] to the believers. **98** Whoever is an enemy to God, and His angels, and His messengers, and Gabriel and Michael – surely God is an enemy to the disbelievers.' **99** Certainly We have sent down to you[120] clear signs,[121] and no one disbelieves them except the wicked. **100** Whenever they have made a covenant, did a group of them toss it away? No! Most of them do not believe. **101** When a messenger came to them from God, confirming what was with them, a group of those who were given the Book tossed the Book of God[122] behind their backs, as if they did not know (about it). **102** And they followed what the satans used to recite over the kingdom of Solomon.[123] Solomon did not disbelieve, but the satans disbelieved. They taught the people magic, and what had been sent down to the two angels (in) Babylon, Hārūt and Mārūt.[124] Neither of them taught anyone, unless they both (first) said, 'We are only a temptation,[125] so do not disbelieve.' And they learned from both of them how to separate a husband from his wife.[126] Yet they did not harm anyone in this way, except by the permission of God. What they learned (only) harmed them and did not benefit them. Certainly they knew that whoever buys it has no share in the Hereafter. Evil indeed is what they have sold themselves for, if (only) they knew. **103** If they had believed and guarded (themselves), a reward from God (would) indeed (have been) better, if (only) they knew.

104 You who believe! Do not say, 'Observe us,' but say, 'Regard us,'[127] and hear. For the disbelievers (there is) a painful punishment. **105** Those who disbelieve among the People of the Book,[128] and the idolaters, do not like (it) that anything good should be sent down on you[129] from your Lord. But God chooses whomever He pleases for His mercy, and God is full of great favor. **106** Whatever verse We cancel or cause to be forgotten,[130] We bring a better (one) than it, or (one) similar to it. Do you not

---

115. *Gabriel*: Jibrīl is mentioned three times by name in the Qur'ān (cf. Q2.98 below; 66.4). He also appears as God's agent of revelation in Jewish and Christian tradition (e.g. Daniel 8.15-26; 9.20-27; Luke 1.10-20, 26-37), along with Michael (e.g. Daniel 10.13, 21; 12.1; Jude 1.9; Revelation 12.7-9; cf. Q2.98 below). Contrary to popular opinion, Gabriel is never identified in the Qur'ān as one of the angels (see following n.).
116. *he [Gabriel] has brought it down*: in other passages this is attributed to 'the spirit' (see e.g. Q16.102, 'the holy spirit;' 26.193, 'the trustworthy spirit;' cf. 40.15, 'the spirit of His command'). On this and other modes of revelation, see Q42.51-52.
117. *your heart*: the Prophet's heart (here, as often, the heart is spoken of as synonymous with mind).
118. *confirming what was before it*: the Qur'ān 'confirms' the Torah of Moses and Gospel of Jesus (see e.g. Q3.3; 5.48; 35.31; 46.30).
119. *good news*: Ar. *bushra* is related to the Christian Arabic word for 'good news' or 'gospel' (*bishāra*). It is generally used in this positive sense, but can also refer to punishment (e.g. Q3.21; 4.138; 9.3, 34; 31.7; 45.8; 84.24; see also n. on Q2.119 below).
120. *you*: the Prophet.
121. *clear signs*: or 'signs as proof' (here 'signs' probably means 'verses').
122. *Book of God*: refers to the Torah (as does the preceding 'Book'); cf. Q3.23, 187.
123. *what the satans used to recite...*: books containing magical spells or charms; Solomon was a renowned figure in Jewish magic.
124. *Hārūt and Mārūt*: reference obscure.
125. *temptation*: or 'trial,' 'test.'
126. *how to separate a husband from his wife*: by means of magical love spells.

104–110 Warning about the People of the Book

127. *Observe us... Regard us*: meaning obscure; see also Q4.46.
128. *People of the Book*: Jews and perhaps Christians.
129. *you*: plur.
130. *Whatever verse We cancel or cause to be forgotten*: this passage, along with a few others (Q13.39; 16.101; 22.52),

know[131] that God is powerful over everything? **107** Do you not know that God – to Him (belongs) the kingdom of the heavens and the earth, and you have no ally[132] and no helper other than God. **108** Or do you wish to question your messenger, as Moses was questioned before?[133] Whoever exchanges belief for disbelief has indeed gone astray from the right way. **109** Many of the People of the Book would like (it) if you turned back into disbelievers, after your believing, (because of) jealousy on their part, after the truth has become clear to them. So pardon and excuse (them),[134] until God brings His command.[135] Surely God is powerful over everything. **110** Observe the prayer and give the alms. Whatever good you send forward for yourselves, you will find it with God. Surely God sees what you do.

111 They say, 'No one will enter the Garden unless they are Jews or Christians.' That is their wishful thinking. Say: 'Bring your proof, if you are truthful.' **112** Yes indeed! Whoever submits his face to God, and he is a doer of good, has his reward with his Lord. (There will be) no fear on them, nor will they sorrow. **113** The Jews say, 'The Christians have no ground to stand on;' and the Christians say, 'The Jews have no ground to stand on,' though they (both) recite the Book. In this way those who have no knowledge say something similar to their saying. God will judge between them on the Day of Resurrection concerning their differences.

114 And who is more evil than the one who prevents the mosques of God[136] from having His name remembered in them, and strives for their destruction? Those – it was not for them to enter them except in fear. For them (there is) disgrace in this world, and a great punishment for them in the Hereafter. **115** The East and the West (belong) to God, so wherever you turn, there is the face of God.[137] Surely God is embracing, knowing.

116 They say,[138] 'God has taken a son.'[139] Glory to Him! No! Whatever is in the heavens and the earth (belongs) to Him. All are obedient before Him **117** – Originator of the heavens and the earth. When He decrees something, He simply says to it, 'Be!'[140] and it is.

118 Those who have no knowledge say, 'If only God would speak to us, or a sign would come to us.' In this way those who were before them said something similar to their saying. Their hearts are alike. We have

---

provides the basis for the later, and much more elaborate, theory of 'abrogation' (*naskh*), according to which certain commands in the Qur'ān had been canceled and replaced by others. The words 'or cause to be forgotten' (i.e. by the Prophet) imply that some 'verses' have not been retained in the present Qur'ān (see Q22.52n.; 87.6-7). The Qur'ān gives no indication of the length of these 'verses' (or 'units' of revelation) which were forgotten or canceled and replaced. The phenomenon of 'abrogation' is not unique to the Qur'ān; cf. e.g. the sayings attributed to Jesus at Matthew 5.21-48; 15.10-20, which 'alter' various commandments of the Torah, and the remark at Mark 7.19b, which declares all foods 'clean' despite the Torah's explicit dietary restrictions.

131. *Do you not know...*: addressed to the Prophet, or perhaps more generally ('Does one not know...').

132. *ally*: or 'guardian;' Ar. *walī* implies the obligation of mutual protection, almost in the sense of 'friend' or 'brother.'

133. *as Moses was questioned before*: see Q2.67-71 above.

134. *pardon and excuse (them)*: plur. imperative.

135. *command*: some kind of divine intervention is meant, probably judgment (cf. Q4.47; 5.52; 7.150; 10.24; 16.1, 33; 54.50).

111–121 Diatribe against Jews and Christians

136. *mosques of God*: the use of the plur. 'mosques' (Ar. *masājid*) is unusual and difficult to understand; perhaps it refers to Christian churches (cf. Q7.29; 18.21; 22.40).

137. *the face of God*: i.e. God's favor.

138. *They say*: the Christians, though this claim always remains anonymous.

139. *son*: or 'child' (Ar. *walad*), but referring to Christian claims about Jesus as God's son (cf. Q4.171; 10.68; 19.88-92; 21.26; 25.2).

140. *Be!*: God's creative word (Ar. *kun*); cf. Q3.47 (to Mary), 59 (of Jesus and Adam); 6.73; 16.40; 19.35; 36.82; 40.68.

already made the signs clear to a people (who) are certain (in their belief). **119** Surely We have sent you[141] with the truth, as a bringer of good news and a warner.[142] You will not be questioned[143] about the companions of the Furnace.[144]

120 Neither the Jews nor the Christians will ever be pleased with you[145] until you follow their creed.[146] Say: 'Surely the guidance of God – it is the (true) guidance.' If indeed you follow their (vain) desires, after the knowledge which has come to you, you will have no ally and no helper against God. **121** Those to whom We have given the Book recite it as it should be recited. Those (people) believe in it. But whoever disbelieves in it – those (people) – they are the losers.

122 Sons of Israel! Remember My blessing which I bestowed on you, and that I have favored you over the worlds. **123** Guard (yourselves) against a Day when no one will intercede for another at all, and no compensation will be accepted from him, and no intercession will benefit him, nor will they be helped.

124 (Remember) when his Lord tested Abraham with (certain) words,[147] and he fulfilled them. He said, 'Surely I am going to make you a leader[148] for the people.' He said, 'And of my descendants?' He said, 'My covenant does not extend to the evildoers.'[149] **125** And when We made the House[150] a place of meeting and security for the people, and (said), 'Take the standing place of Abraham as a place of prayer,' and We made a covenant with Abraham and Ishmael: 'Both of you purify My House for the ones who go around (it),[151] and the ones who are devoted to it, and the ones who bow, (and) the ones who prostrate themselves.' **126** And when Abraham said, 'My Lord, make this land secure,[152] and provide its people with fruits – whoever of them who believes in God and the Last Day,' He said, 'And whoever disbelieves – I shall give him enjoyment (of life) for a little (while), (and) then I shall force him to the punishment of the Fire – and it is an evil destination!' **127** And when Abraham raised up the foundations of the House,[153] and Ishmael (with him): 'Our Lord, accept (this) from us. Surely You – You are the Hearing, the Knowing. **128** Our Lord, make us both submitted to You, and (make) from our descendants a community submitted[154] to You. And show us our rituals, and turn to us (in forgiveness). Surely You – You are the One who turns (in forgiveness), the Compassionate. **129** Our Lord, raise up among them a messenger from among

---

141. *you*: the Prophet.
142. *bringer of good news...warner*: in general the titles 'bringer of good news'(Ar. *bashīr*) and 'warner' (*nadhīr*) designate two contrasting functions of messengers and prophets: to 'give good news' about rewards for the righteous and to 'warn' of punishments for the wicked (see e.g. Q2.213; 6.48; 11.2; 33.45; 35.24; 48.8).
143. *You will not be questioned*: i.e. at the Judgment.
144. *the Furnace*: next to 'the Fire' and 'Gehenna,' the third most common name for Hell (Ar. *al-jaḥīm*), occurring twenty-six times (cf. Q2.24, 206).
145. *you*: the Prophet.
146. *creed*: or 'form of religion' (Ar. *milla*); also used of Abraham (e.g. Q2.130, 135 below).

122–123 Appeal to the Sons of Israel

124–129 Abraham at Mecca

147. *with (certain) words*: referring to God's command that Abraham sacrifice his son (for the story, see Q37.102-113).
148. *leader*: or 'model' (Ar. *imām*), a term later used for the leader of a religious community; see also Q21.73 (Isaac and Jacob); 28.5; 32.24 (people of Israel); cf. Q11.17 (the Book of Moses).
149. *My covenant does not extend to the evildoers*: religion, not genealogy, determines who are the 'children of Abraham.'
150. *the House*: Ar. *al-bayt*; traditionally identified with the Ka'ba or sanctuary of Mecca (see n. on Q5.95).
151. *the ones who go around (it)*: i.e. who circumambulate the Ka'ba (cf. Q22.26, 29).
152. *make this land secure*: said to refer to the sacred area (or *ḥaram*) of Mecca, where bloodshed was forbidden.
153. *raised up the foundations of the House*: cf. Q14.37, where it appears that it was already in existence before Abraham.
154. *make us both submitted...a community submitted*: i.e. Muslims (Ar. *muslimayn...umma muslima*).

them, to recite Your signs to them, and to teach them the Book and the wisdom,[155] and to purify them.[156] Surely You – You are the Mighty, the Wise.'

130 Who prefers (another creed) to the creed of Abraham[157] except the one who makes a fool of himself? Certainly We have chosen him in this world, and surely in the Hereafter he will indeed be among the righteous. **131** When his Lord said to him, 'Submit!,'[158] he said, 'I have submitted to the Lord of the worlds.'[159] **132** And Abraham charged his sons with this, and Jacob (did too):[160] 'My sons! Surely God has chosen the (true) religion[161] for you, so do not die without submitting.'[162] **133** Or were you witnesses[163] when death approached Jacob, when he said to his sons, 'What will you serve after me?' They said, 'We will serve your God, and the God of your fathers, Abraham, and Ishmael, and Isaac: one God – to Him we submit.'[164] **134** That community has passed away.[165] To it what it has earned, and to you what you have earned.[166] You will not be questioned about what they have done.

135 They say, 'Be Jews or Christians, (and then) you will be (rightly) guided.' Say: 'No! The creed of Abraham the Ḥanīf.[167] He was not one of the idolaters.' **136** Say:[168] 'We believe in God, and what has been sent down to us, and what has been sent down to Abraham, and Ishmael, and Isaac, and Jacob, and the tribes, and what was given to Moses and Jesus, and what was given to the prophets from their Lord. We make

---

155. *the wisdom*: Ar. *al-ḥikma* is another designation for the revelation, or a part of it (cf. Hebr. *ḥokhma*). God sends down 'the Book and the wisdom' (e.g. Q2.231 below). 'The signs' and 'the wisdom' were recited in believers' homes according to Q33.34; cf. Q4.105, where it is said that the Prophet is to 'judge' (*taḥkum*) among the people on the basis of the Book sent down to him (see also Q3.79n; 4.55; 5.42-43; 6.89; 13.37).

156. *purify them*: or perhaps 'appoint *zakāt* for them' (Ar. *yuzakkīhim*); cf. Q2.151 below.

130–141 The religion of Abraham

157. *creed of Abraham*: or 'religion of Abraham' (Ar. *millat Ibrāhīm*), a pure monotheism identical with the revelation to the Prophet. Islam is thus a restoration of the religion of Abraham, and in this sense superior to the 'later' religions of Judaism and Christianity (see below Q2.135n.).

158. *Submit*: or 'Surrender' (Ar. *aslim*), the imperative corresponding to the noun *islām*.

159. *Lord of the worlds*: for this title, see n. on Q1.2.

160. *and Jacob (did too)*: it is not clear whether 'Jacob' is the object or subject of the verb (probably the latter).

161. *the (true) religion*: the word for 'religion' is a homonym of 'judgment' (Ar. *dīn*).

162. *without submitting*: or 'without becoming Muslims.'

163. *were you witnesses*: addressing Jews and Christians, whose religions were 'later' than Abraham's.

164. *submit*: or 'are Muslims.'

165. *That community has passed away*: referring to the *umma* of Abraham and his immediate descendants as a distinct community, both prior to and separate from Jews and Christians (see Q2.141 below; cf. Q16.120).

166. *To it what it has earned, and to you what you have earned*: or 'It (the community of Abraham) will have what it has earned, and you (Jews and Christians) will have what you have earned' (i.e. rewards or punishments for what each community has done); see Q2.139-141 below; 28.55; 42.15; cf. Q109.6.

167. *Abraham the Ḥanīf*: the meaning of the epithet *ḥanīf* is uncertain. The word occurs ten times in the Qur'ān (twice in the plur. *ḥunafā'*), mostly in connection with Abraham. It is usually taken to mean something like 'pristine' or 'original monotheist' (see e.g. Q3.67, 95; 6.79, 161; 16.120; cf. Q10.105; 16.123; 30.30). While it is claimed that there were 'seekers after God' in pre-Islamic Arabia, there is no reliable evidence that any of them called himself a *ḥanīf*. The word may be related to Syr. *ḥanpā*, the term applied by pre-Islamic Christian writers to designate a 'gentile' or 'pagan,' and so in the opposite sense from what it is usually said to mean in the Qur'ān. Accordingly it may mean something like 'Abraham the Gentile' (similar in meaning to Ar. *ummī*, see nn. on Q2.78 above; 7.157), and thus the following sentence would be a qualification: i.e. '*Yet* he [Abraham] was not one of the idolaters.' Most scholars, however, take this sentence as a definition of *ḥanīf*.

168. *Say*: plur. imperative, addressed to the believers (see Q29.46; cf. Q3.84).

no distinction[169] between any of them, and to Him we submit.'[170] **137** If they believe in something like what you believe in, they have been (rightly) guided, but if they turn away, they are only in defiance.[171] God will be sufficient for you[172] against them. He is the Hearing, the Knowing.

138 The dye(ing)[173] of God, and who is better than God at dye(ing)? We serve Him. **139** Say: 'Do you[174] dispute with us about God, when He is our Lord and your Lord? To us our deeds and to you your deeds.[175] We are devoted to Him. **140** Or do you say, "Abraham, and Ishmael, and Isaac, and Jacob, and the tribes were Jews or Christians"?'[176] Say: 'Do you know better, or God? Who is more evil than the one who conceals a testimony[177] which he has from God? God is not oblivious of what you do.' **141** That community has passed away.[178] To it what it has earned, and to you what you have earned. You will not be questioned about what they have done.

142 The fools among the people will say, 'What has turned them from the direction (of prayer) which they were (facing) toward?'[179] Say: 'The East and the West (belong) to God. He guides whomever He pleases to a straight path.' **143** In this way We have made you a community (in the) middle, so that you may be witnesses over the people,[180] and that the messenger may be a witness over you. And We established the direction (of prayer) which you[181] were (facing) toward only so that We might know the one who would follow the messenger from the one who would turn back on his heels.[182] Surely it was hard[183] indeed, except for those whom God guided. But God was not one to let your[184] belief go to waste. Surely God is indeed kind (and) compassionate with the people.

---

169. *no distinction*: or 'no division,' implying that all those listed received in essence the same revelation (see Q3.84; 4.136; 29.46-47; cf. Q9.111).
170. *submit*: or 'are Muslims.'
171. *defiance*: or 'disobedience,' 'schism.'
172. *you*: the Prophet.
173. *dye(ing)*: Ar. *ṣibgha* usually refers to 'color' or 'dye,' but the exact meaning is uncertain. A number of translators render the word as 'baptism,' but it is not clear how it came to be so construed. In any case it is doubtful that there is a reference to Christian baptism here. Some commentators take *ṣibgha* as a synonym for 'creed' (*milla*) which occurs three verses earlier at Q2.135.
174. *you*: addressing Jews and Christians.
175. *To us our deeds and to you your deeds*: or 'We have our deeds and you have your deeds' (cf. Q2.134 above).
176. *...were Jews or Christians*: the point is that Judaism and Christianity are later than, and hence inferior to, the religion of Abraham and the patriarchs (cf. the apostle Paul's similar privileging of Abraham in Galatians 3 and Romans 4).
177. *testimony*: or 'witness;' in this case, scriptural evidence 'testifying' to the priority of Abraham over both Moses and Jesus (and hence over Judaism and Christianity).
178. *That community has passed away*: i.e. the community of Abraham and his descendants (see n. on Q2.134 above).

142–152 Change in the direction of prayer

179. *the direction (of prayer)...*: Ar. *qibla* signifies the 'direction' a worshipper faces in prayer. While most Christians faced east (toward the rising sun), the first Muslims are said to have faced Jerusalem, apparently following Jewish practice.
180. *over the people*: or 'against the people.'
181. *you*: the Prophet.
182. *so that We might know...*: this gives the reason for the change, but no verse exists mandating Jerusalem (or any other place) as the former direction of prayer.
183. *hard*: lit. 'great.'
184. *your*: plur.

144 We do see you[185] turning your face about in the sky,[186] and We shall indeed turn you in a direction which you will be pleased with. Turn your face in the direction of the Sacred Mosque,[187] and wherever you are, turn your faces in its direction.[188] Surely those who have been given the Book know indeed that it is the truth from their Lord. God is not oblivious of what they do. **145** Yet even if you[189] bring every sign to those who have been given the Book, they will not follow your direction. You are not a follower of their direction, nor are they followers of each other's direction.[190] If indeed you follow their (vain) desires, after the knowledge which has come to you, surely then you will indeed be among the evildoers. **146** Those to whom We have given the Book recognize it,[191] as they recognize their (own) sons, yet surely a group of them indeed conceals the truth[192] – and they know (it). **147** The truth is from your Lord, so do not be one of the doubters. **148** Each has a direction to which he turns. So race[193] (toward doing) good deeds. Wherever you may be, God will bring you all together. Surely God is powerful over everything.

149 From wherever you[194] go forth, turn your face toward the Sacred Mosque. Surely it is the truth indeed from your Lord. God is not oblivious of what you do. **150** From wherever you go forth, turn your face toward the Sacred Mosque. And wherever you[195] are, turn your faces toward it, so that the people will not have any argument against you[196] – except for the evildoers among them; do not fear them, but fear Me – and so that I may complete My blessing on you, and that you may be (rightly) guided, **151** even as We have sent among you a messenger from among you. He recites to you Our signs,[197] and purifies you, and teaches you the Book and the wisdom, and teaches you what you did not know. **152** So remember Me (and) I shall remember you. Be thankful to Me and do not be ungrateful to Me.[198]

153 You who believe! Seek help in patience and prayer. Surely God is with the patient. **154** Do not say of anyone who is killed in the way of God,[199] '(They are) dead.' No! (They are) alive,[200] but you do not realize (it). **155** We shall indeed test you with some (experience) of fear and hunger, and loss of wealth and lives and fruits. But give good news[201] to the patient, **156** who say, when a smiting smites them, 'Surely we (belong) to God, and surely to Him we return.' **157** Those – on them (there are) blessings from their Lord, and mercy. Those – they are the (rightly) guided ones.

---

185. *you*: the Prophet.
186. *turning your face about in the sky*: looking for the (or a different) *qibla*.
187. *Sacred Mosque*: traditionally identified with the Ka'ba at Mecca (see n. on Q5.95); the same command recurs at Q2.149, 150 below.
188. *turn your faces in its direction*: what was first a command to the Prophet is now enjoined on all believers (repeated at Q2.150 below).
189. *you*: the Prophet.
190. *...each other's direction*: the different directions of prayer distinguish Muslims, Jews, and Christians.
191. *recognize it*: the antecedent is missing, but 'it' probably refers to the Qur'ān (cf. Q6.20).
192. *conceals the truth*: probably referring to the predictions in the Torah and Gospel of the coming of the Prophet.
193. *So race...*: plur. imperative.
194. *you*: the Prophet.
195. *you*: plur.
196. *argument against you*: plur.; apparently some had objected to the former direction of prayer (Jerusalem?).
197. *signs*: or 'verses.'
198. *do not be ungrateful to Me*: or 'do not be disbelievers in Me' (perhaps a pun).

153–157 Those who die fighting for the cause

199. *killed in the way of God*: i.e. while fighting for the cause.
200. *(They are) alive*: those killed while fighting for the cause of God go straight to Paradise, and do not have to wait for the general resurrection (see Q3.169).
201. *give good news*: addressed to the Prophet.

158 Surely al-Ṣafā and al-Marwa[202] are among the symbols[203] of God. Whoever performs pilgrimage to the House[204] or performs visitation[205] – (there is) no blame on him if he goes around both of them.[206] And whoever does good voluntarily – surely God is thankful, knowing.

159 Surely those[207] who conceal what We have sent down of the clear signs and the guidance, after We have made it clear to the people in the Book, those – God will curse them, and the cursers[208] will curse them, **160** except for those who turn (in repentance), and set (things) right, and make (it) clear.[209] Those – I shall turn to them (in forgiveness). I am the One who turns (in forgiveness), the Compassionate.
161 Surely those who disbelieve, and die while they are disbelievers, those – on them is the curse of God, and the angels, and the people all together. **162** There[210] (they will) remain – the punishment will not be lightened for them, nor will they be spared.

163 Your God is one God – (there is) no god but Him, the Merciful, the Compassionate. **164** Surely in the creation of the heavens and the earth, and the alternation of the night and the day, and the ship which runs on the sea with what benefits the people, and the water which God sends down from the sky, and by means of it gives the earth life after its death, and He scatters[211] on it all (kinds of) creatures, and (in the) changing of the winds, and the clouds controlled between the sky and the earth – (all these are) signs[212] indeed for a people who understand. **165** But (there are) some of the people who set up[213] rivals[214] to God. They love them with a love like (that given to) God. Yet those who believe are stronger in love for God. If (only) those who do evil could see (the Day), when they will see the punishment, that the power (belongs) to God altogether, and that God is harsh in punishment. **166** When those who were followed[215] disown those who followed them, and they see the punishment, and the ties[216] with them are cut,
167 and those who followed say, 'If (only) we had (another) turn, so that we might disown them as they have disowned us.' In this way God will show them their deeds as regrets for them. They will never escape from the Fire.

168 People! Eat from what is permitted[217] (and) good on the earth, and do not follow the footsteps of

---

158 Ṣafā and Marwa

202 *al-Ṣafā and al-Marwa*: two hills near the Ka'ba in present-day Mecca.

203. *symbols*: meaning uncertain (Ar. *sha'ā'ir*); cf. Q5.2.

204. *performs pilgrimage to the House*: i.e. to the Ka'ba (for the pilgrimage or Ḥajj, see Q2.196-203 below).

205. *performs visitation*: i.e. the 'Umra or 'lesser pilgrimage' (mentioned only here and Q2.196 below).

206. *goes around both of them*: 'circumambulation' is now used only of going around the Ka'ba; the ritual at Ṣafā and Marwa is known as 'running' (*sa'y*), in commemoration of Hagar's search for water.

159–162 Warning to those who conceal the Book

207. *those*: Jews and perhaps Christians (cf. Q2.174 below; 3.187).

208. *the cursers*: the angels, as the following verse makes clear (cf. Q3.87).

209. *and make (it) clear*: i.e. what they had previously concealed.

210. *There*: lit. 'In it,' i.e. under the curse, or perhaps in Hell (cf. Q3.88).

163–167 Warning to idolaters

211. *scatters*: as a sower scatters seed.

212. *signs*: i.e. the order and goodness of nature indicate the existence of a powerful and providential creator.

213. *set up*: lit. 'make.'

214. *rivals*: or 'equals' (Ar. *andād*), i.e. other gods alleged to be equal with God.

215. *those who were followed*: referring to the other gods (cf. Q6.94).

216. *the ties*: lit. 'the ropes.'

168–173 Instruction about food

217. *permitted*: Ar. *ḥalāl*.

Satan. Surely he is clear enemy to you. **169** He only commands you to evil and immorality,[218] and that you should say about God what you do not know. **170** When it is said to them, 'Follow what God has sent down,' they say, 'No! We shall follow what we found our fathers doing' – even though their fathers did not understand anything and were not (rightly) guided? **171** The parable of those who disbelieve is like the parable of the one who calls out to what hears nothing but a shout and a cry. Without hearing or speech or sight – they do not understand.

172 You who believe! Eat from the good things which We have provided you, and be thankful to God, if it is Him you serve. **173** He has only forbidden[219] to you: the dead (animal),[220] and the blood,[221] and swine's flesh,[222] and what has been dedicated to (a god) other than God.[223] But whoever is forced (by necessity),[224] not desiring or (deliberately) transgressing – no sin (rests) on him. Surely God is forgiving, compassionate.

174 Surely those[225] who conceal what God has sent down of the Book, and sell it for a small price, those – they will not eat (anything) but the Fire in their bellies. God will not speak to them on the Day of Resurrection, nor will He purify them. For them (there is) a painful punishment. **175** Those are the ones who have purchased error[226] with the (price of) guidance, and punishment with the price of forgiveness. How determined they are to (reach) the Fire! **176** That is because God has sent down the Book with the truth.[227] Surely those who differ about the Book are indeed in extreme defiance.[228]

177 Piety is not turning your faces toward the East and the West, but (true) piety (belongs to) the one who believes in God and the Last Day, and the angels, and the Book, and the prophets, and (who) gives his wealth, despite his love for it,[229] to family, and the orphans, and the poor, and the traveler,[230] and beggars, and for the (freeing of) slaves,[231] and (who) observes the prayer and gives the alms, and those who fulfill their covenant when they have made it, and those who are patient under violence and hardship, and in times of peril. Those are the ones who are truthful, and those – they are the ones who guard (themselves).

178 You who believe! The (law of) retaliation[232] is prescribed[233] for you in (the case of) those who have been killed: the free man for the free man, the slave for the slave, and the female for the female. But

218. *immorality*: i.e. sexual immorality (cf. Q2.268 below; 7.28, 30; 24.21).
219. *forbidden*: lit. 'made sacred' (Ar. *ḥarrama*), i.e. taboo.
220. *the dead (animal)*: i.e. 'carrion;' cf. Leviticus 17.15.
221. *the blood*: cf. Genesis 9.4; Leviticus 17.10-12; Acts 15.29.
222. *swine's flesh*: cf. Leviticus 11.7; Deuteronomy 14.8.
223. *dedicated to (a god) other than God*: i.e. what has been sacrificed or dedicated to 'other gods' (for this list of forbidden foods, see also Q5.3; 6.145; 16.115; cf. Acts 15.29; 1 Corinthians 8.1-13; 10.23-30).
224. *forced (by necessity)*: i.e. compelled to eat something forbidden.

174–176 Warning to those who conceal the Book

225. *those*: Jews and perhaps Christians (cf. Q2.159 above).
226. *error*: lit. 'straying.'
227. *with the truth*: or 'in truth,' 'truly.'
228. *extreme defiance*: or 'wide schism.'

177 True righteousness

229. *despite his love for it*: or 'for love of Him.'
230. *traveler*: lit. 'son of the way.'
231. *(freeing of) slaves*: or '(ransoming of) captives.'

178–179 Retaliation

232. *retaliation*: cf. the biblical prescription of 'an eye for an eye...' (Exodus 21.23-35; see also Genesis 9.5; Leviticus 24.17-2; Numbers 35.31).
233. *prescribed*: lit. 'written;' i.e. implying scriptural authority.

whoever is granted any pardon for it by his brother,[234] it should be (done) rightfully, and payment should be rendered with kindness. That is a concession from your Lord, and a mercy. Whoever transgresses after that – for him (there is) a painful punishment. **179** In the (law of) retaliation (there is) life for you – those (of you) with understanding! – so that you may guard (yourselves).

180 It is prescribed for you, when death approaches one of you, if he leaves behind any goods, (to make) bequests for parents and family rightfully. (It is) an obligation on the ones who guard (themselves). **181** And whoever changes it after hearing (it) – the sin (rests) only on those who change it. Surely God is hearing, knowing. **182** But whoever suspects any injustice or sin from the one making the bequest, and resolves (the matter) between them[235] – no sin (rests) on him. Surely God is forgiving, compassionate.

183 You who believe! Fasting is prescribed for you, as it was prescribed for those who were before you,[236] so that you may guard (yourselves). **184** (Fast for) a number of days.[237] Whoever of you is sick or on a journey, (let him fast) a certain number of other days. And for those who can afford it, (there is) a ransom:[238] feeding a poor person. Whoever does good voluntarily[239] – it is better for him. But to fast is better for you, if (only) you knew.

185 The month of Ramaḍān, in which the Qur'ān[240] was sent down[241] as a guidance for the people, and as clear signs of the guidance and the Deliverance:[242] so whoever of you is present during the month, let him fast in it, but whoever of you is sick or on a journey, (let him fast) a certain number of other days. God wishes to make it easy for you, and does not wish any hardship for you. And (He wishes) that you should fulfill the number (of days), and that you should magnify God for having guided you, and that you should be thankful. **186** When My servants ask you[243] about Me, surely I am near. I respond to the call of the caller when he calls on Me. So let them respond to Me, and believe in Me, so that they may be led aright.

---

234. *granted any pardon for it by his brother*: i.e. if some other form of compensation is accepted by the victim's brother or next of kin.

180–182 Wills

235. *resolves (the matter) between them*: i.e. resolves the matter about which the testator had been in error or unfair.

183–187 Fasting

236. *those who were before you*: the Jews.
237. *a number of days*: unspecified, but perhaps the thirty days of the month of Ramaḍān, mentioned in the next verse.
238. *ransom*: i.e. as a compensation for not observing the fast (cf. Q2.196 below).
239. *does good voluntarily*: perhaps by doing more than the bare minimum of feeding the poor.
240. *Qur'ān*: this word (lit. 'recitation' or 'reading') occurs some seventy times and has several distinct meanings. Here 'the Qur'ān' (with the definite article) comes close to its present meaning as the name of the Muslim scripture (cf. Q9.111), but the word *qur'ān* can also denote a single passage or 'unit' of revelation (like *āya* and *sūra*), of unspecified length (e.g. Q10.61; 13.31; 72.1). In most cases it describes the revelation 'sent down' to the Prophet (e.g. Q20.2; 76.23), but it can also refer to something in God's possession, larger than what was revealed (e.g. Q17.82; 43.2-4). In still other passages 'the Qur'ān' refers to a collection of revelations in the Prophet's possession, which he is commanded to recite or read aloud (e.g. Q16.98; 17.45; 27.91-92).
241. *The month of Ramaḍān, in which the Qur'ān was sent down*: this reflects a different understanding than the traditional one, according to which the Qur'ān was 'sent down' or revealed at intervals over a period of some twenty years. Some interpreters understand this verse as referring to the descent of the Qur'ān from the highest to the lowest of the seven heavens, whence it was revealed to Muḥammad as occasion required. But there are other passages like this one, which indicate that the Qur'ān was 'sent down' or revealed all at once (see Q44.3; 97.1; cf. Q2.89; 3.3, 7; 4.105; 5.48; 6.92; 8.41; 16.64; 17.106; 26.193-194; 28.86; 46.12, 30; 76.23). There were similarly conflicting views within Judaism about the revelation of the Torah. According to the Babylonian Talmud (Gittin 60a), some thought the Torah had been 'transmitted scroll by scroll,' others that it had been 'transmitted entire.'
242. *the Deliverance*: another name for the Qur'ān; see n. on Q2.53 above.
243. *you*: the Prophet.

187 It is permitted to you on the night of the fast to have sexual relations with your wives. They are a covering for you, and you are a covering for them. God knows that you have been betraying yourselves (in this regard), and has turned to you (in forgiveness) and pardoned you. So now have relations with them, and seek what God has prescribed for you.[244] And eat and drink, until a white thread may be discerned from a black thread at the dawn. Then keep the fast completely until night, and do not have relations with them while you are devoted to the mosques. Those are the limits (set by) God, so do not go near them. In this way God makes clear His signs[245] to the people, so that they may guard (themselves).

188 Do not consume your wealth among yourselves by means of falsehood,[246] nor offer it to the judges,[247] so that you may consume some of the property of the people sinfully, when you know (better).

189 They ask you[248] about the new moons.[249] Say: 'They are appointed times for the people, and for the pilgrimage.'

It is not piety to come to (your) houses from their backs,[250] but (true) piety (belongs to) the one who guards (himself). Come to (your) houses by their doors, and guard (yourselves) against God, so that you may prosper.

190 Fight in the way of God against those who fight against you, but do not commit aggression. Surely
God does not love the aggressors.[251] **191** And kill them wherever you come upon them, and expel them
from where they expelled you.[252] Persecution[253] is worse than killing. But do not fight them near the
Sacred Mosque[254] until they fight you there. If they fight you, kill them – such is the payment for the disbelievers. **192** But if they stop (fighting) – surely God is forgiving, compassionate. **193** Fight them until
(there) is no persecution and the religion is God's.[255] But if they stop, (let there be) no aggression, except
against the evildoers. **194** The sacred month for the sacred month; sacred things are (subject to the law
of) retaliation.[256] Whoever commits aggression against you, commit aggression against him in the same manner (as) he committed aggression against you. Guard (yourselves) against God, and know that God is with the ones who guard (themselves).

195 Contribute in the way of God.[257] Do not cast (yourselves) to destruction with your own hands, but do good. Surely God loves the doers of good.

---

244. *what God has prescribed for you*: probably children.

245. *signs*: or 'verses.'

188 Misuse of wealth

246. *by means of falsehood*: perhaps through unscrupulous business practices or usury (cf. Q4.29, 161).

247. *nor offer it to the judges*: as a bribe.

189a New moons

248. *you*: the Prophet.

249. *new moons*: lunar time-reckoning was retained by Islam, but the point of the question is not clear.

189b Entering through the front door

250. *come to (your) houses from their backs*: meaning obscure.

190–194 Fighting for the cause of God

251. *aggression...aggressors*: or 'transgression...transgressors' (cf. Q5.87).

252. *from where they expelled you*: said to be Mecca.

253. *Persecution*: lit. 'the persecution' or 'the oppression' (Ar. *al-fitna*); the word varies widely in meaning, but here it refers to the persecution of believers (cf. Q2.217 below).

254. *near the Sacred Mosque*: said to refer to the precinct of the Ka'ba, which was considered sacred.

255. *Fight them...*: plur. imperative; cf. Q8.39; contrast Q2.256; 10.99; 12.103; 16.37.

256. *sacred things are (subject to the law of) retaliation*: the idea seems to be that the *lex talionis* (Q2.178-179 above) applies in the realm of the sacred as well as the profane.

195 Contributing to the cause of God

257. *Contribute...*: lit. 'Spend...;' i.e. make contributions of money or goods for the cause.

196 Complete the pilgrimage[258] and the visitation[259] for God. But if you are prevented, (make) whatever offering[260] is easy to obtain. Do not shave your heads until the offering has reached its lawful place.[261] Whoever of you is sick or has an injury to his head, (there is) a ransom[262] of fasting or a freewill offering[263] or a sacrifice. When you are secure, whoever makes use of (the time from) the visitation until the pilgrimage,[264] (let him make) whatever offering is easy to obtain. Whoever cannot find (an offering), (let him perform) a fast of three days during the pilgrimage, and seven (days) when you return. That is ten (days) in all. That is for the one whose family is not present at the Sacred Mosque. Guard (yourselves) against God, and know that God is harsh in retribution.

197 The pilgrimage (falls in certain) specified months. Whoever undertakes the pilgrimage in them – (there should be) no sexual relations or wickedness or quarreling during the pilgrimage. Whatever good you do, God knows it. And take provision (for the journey), but surely the best provision is the guarding (of oneself). So guard (yourselves) against Me, those (of you) with understanding!

198 (There is) no blame on you in seeking favor from your Lord.[265] When you press on from 'Arafāt,[266]
remember God at the Sacred Monument,[267] and remember Him as He has guided you, though before you
were indeed among those who had gone astray. **199** Then press on from where the people press on, and
ask forgiveness from God. Surely God is forgiving, compassionate. **200** When you have performed your
rituals, remember God, as you remember your fathers, or (even with) greater remembrance. (There are)
some of the people who say, 'Our Lord, give us (good) in this world.' For them (there will be) no share in
the Hereafter. **201** But (there are others) of them who say, 'Our Lord, give us good in this world and good
in the Hereafter, and guard us against the punishment of the Fire.' **202** Those – for them (there will be)
a portion of what they have earned, and God is quick at the reckoning.

203 Remember God during a (certain) number of days. Whoever hurries (through it) in two days – no sin (rests) on him, and whoever delays – no sin (rests) on him,[268] (at least) for the one who guards (himself). Guard (yourselves) against God, and know that you will be gathered to Him.

204 Among the people (there is) one who impresses you[269] (with) his speech in this present life, and
who calls God to witness about what is in his heart, though he is the most contentious of opponents.
205 And when he turns away, he strives to foment corruption on the earth, and to destroy the crops and

---

196–203 Regulations concerning the pilgrimage

258. *the pilgrimage*: or 'the Ḥajj;' see also Q3.97; 22.27-36; and cf. Exodus 23.14-17; 34.18-24, for Israel's three annual pilgrimages (Hebr. *ḥag*) to God's sanctuary. The detailed regulations pertaining to the Ḥajj are not recorded in the Qur'ān.
259. *the visitation*: the 'Umra or 'lesser pilgrimage' to Mecca (see Q2.158 above).
260. *offering*: i.e. an animal for sacrifice.
261. *lawful place*: for sacrifice (cf. Q22.33; 48.25)
262. *ransom*: i.e. as a compensation for not shaving the head.
263. *freewill offering*: or 'voluntary contribution' (Ar. *ṣadaqa*) to benefit the community (cf. Q9.60).
264. *(the time from) the visitation until the pilgrimage*: meaning obscure.
265. *seeking favor from your Lord*: i.e. seeking to make a livelihood.
266. *press on from 'Arafāt*: a hill some 22 km. from Mecca, visited on the second day of the pilgrimage. After the ritual of 'standing at 'Arafāt' from midday to sunset, the pilgrim moves on to Muzdalifa (8 km. away).
267. *the Sacred Monument*: reference obscure; said to be a place on the eastern side of Muzdalifa, and now identified with 'the Mosque of the Sacred Grove.'
268. *Whoever hurries...delays ...no sin (rests) on him*: though the pilgrimage proper usually occupies three days, it is 'no sin' to complete it in two days, or to take a longer time.

204–207 False and true servants

269. *you*: the Prophet.

livestock. God does not love the (fomenting of) corruption. **206** When it is said to him, 'Guard (yourself) against God,' false pride carries him away to more sin. Gehenna[270] will be enough for him – it is an evil bed indeed! **207** But among the people (there is) one who sells himself,[271] seeking the approval of God. God is kind with (His) servants.

208 You who believe! Enter into the unity[272] all together, and do not follow the footsteps of Satan. Surely he is a clear enemy to you. **209** But if you slip, after the clear signs have come to you, know that God is mighty, wise.

210 Do they expect (anything) but God to come to them in the shadow of the cloud with the angels? The affair has been decided, and to God (all) affairs return. **211** Ask the Sons of Israel how many of the clear signs We gave them. Whoever changes the blessing of God after it has come to him – surely God is harsh in retribution. **212** This present life is made to appear enticing to those who disbelieve, and they ridicule those who believe. But the ones who guard (themselves) will be above them on the Day of Resurrection. God provides for whomever He pleases without reckoning.

213 The people were (once) one community.[273] Then God raised up the prophets as bringers of good news and warners,[274] and with them He sent down the Book[275] with the truth to judge among the people concerning their differences. Only those who had been given it differed concerning it, after the clear signs had come to them, (because of) envy among themselves.[276] And God guided those who believed to the truth concerning which they differed, by His permission. God guides whomever He pleases to a straight path.

214 Or did you think that you would enter the Garden before you had experienced what those who passed away before you experienced? Violence and hardship touched them, and they were (so) shaken that the messenger,[277] and those who believed with him, said, 'When will the help of God come?' Is it not a fact that the help of God is near?

215 They ask you[278] (about) what they should contribute.[279] Say: 'Whatever good you have contributed is for parents and family, and the orphans, and the poor, and the traveler. Whatever good you do, surely God knows about it.'

---

270. *Gehenna*: next to 'the Fire,' the second-most common name for Hell (Ar. *Jahannam*), occurring seventy-eight times. The 'Valley of Hinnom' (Hebr. *Gehinnom*) was a ravine southwest of Jerusalem, where the Judeans made offerings to Baal and conducted child sacrifice by fire (e.g. 2 Kings 23.10; 2 Chronicles 28.3; Jeremiah 7.32; 19.3-6). In later Jewish and Christian belief, 'Gehenna' became the eschatological destination of the wicked, where they would be burned (see e.g. Matthew 5.22, 29, 30; 18.9; 23.33; James 3.6).

271. *sells himself*: into 'slavery;' used here metaphorically of 'service' to God.

208–214 Appeal for unity

272. *unity*: the meaning of Ar. *al-silm* is uncertain; it is usually interpreted in the sense of 'submission' (*islām*) to God (a variant reading has *al-salm*, 'state of peace'), but it may be just an appeal for unity among the believers.

273. *people were (once) one community*: the idea seems to be that the original unity of humanity became divided as the result of God's sending of prophets with their messages (cf. Q5.48; 6.35, 149; 10.19; 11.118; 13.31; 16.9, 93; 32.13; 42.8, 14). The diversity of religions, elsewhere deplored as 'the factions' or 'sectarians' (Ar. *al-aḥzāb*), is here said to have its origin in God. Cf. Genesis 11.1-9 for the story of how humanity's original unity became divided as a result of God's confusing the language of the builders of the 'Tower of Babel.'

274. *bringers of good news...warners*: for these roles, see n. on Q2.119 above.

275. *the Book*: the sing. is used here, though the reference may be to the Torah and the Gospel.

276. *envy among themselves*: referring to Jews and Christians, and their disputes (cf. Q2.253 below; 3.19; 5.14; 42.14; 45.17).

277. *the messenger*: not the Prophet, but some unnamed messenger to an unidentified people of the past.

215 Contributions

278. *you*: the Prophet, here and in the following repetitions of this introductory formula.

279. *contribute*: lit. 'spend.'

216 Fighting is prescribed for you, though it is hateful to you. You may happen to hate a thing though it is good for you, and you may happen to love a thing though it is bad for you. God knows and you do not know. **217** They ask you about the sacred month[280] – (about) fighting during it. Say: 'Fighting during it is a serious (matter), but keeping (people) from the way of God – and disbelief in Him – and the Sacred Mosque, and expelling its people from it, (are even) more serious in the sight of God. Persecution is more serious than killing.' They will not stop fighting you until they turn you back from your religion, if they can. Whoever of you turns away from his religion and dies while he is a disbeliever, those – their deeds have come to nothing in this world and the Hereafter. Those are the companions of the Fire. There they will remain. **218** Surely those who believe, and those who have emigrated[281] and struggled[282] in the way of God, those – they hope for the mercy of God. God is forgiving, compassionate.

219 They ask you about wine[283] and games of chance.[284] Say: 'In both of them (there is) great sin, but (also some) benefits for the people, yet their sin is greater than their benefit.'

They ask you about what they should contribute. Say: 'The excess.'[285] In this way God makes clear to you the signs,[286] so that you may reflect **220** in this world and the Hereafter.

They ask you about the orphans. Say: 'Setting right (their affairs) for them is good. And if you become partners with them,[287] (they are) your brothers. God knows the one who foments corruption from the one who sets (things) right. If God (so) pleased, He could indeed cause you to suffer. Surely God is mighty, wise.'

221 Do not marry idolatrous women[288] until they believe. A believing slave girl is better than a (free) idolatrous woman, even if she pleases you. And do not marry idolatrous men until they believe. A believing slave is better than a (free) idolatrous man, even if he pleases you. Those (people) – they call (you) to the Fire, but God calls (you) to the Garden and forgiveness, by His permission. He makes clear His signs[289] to the people, so that they may take heed.[290]

222 They ask you about menstruation. Say: 'It is harmful.[291] Withdraw from women in menstruation, and do not go near them until they are clean.[292] When they have cleansed themselves, come to them as God has commanded you.' Surely God loves those who turn (in repentance), and He loves those who purify themselves. **223** Your women are (like) a field for you, so come to your field when you wish, and

---

216–218 Fighting for the cause of God

280. *the sacred month*: cf. Q2.194 above; for the 'four sacred months,' see Q9.36.
281. *those who have emigrated*: said to be from Mecca to Medina, though this is not explicitly stated in the Qur'ān.
282. *struggled*: or 'fought.'

219a Wine and gambling

283. *wine*: Ar. *khamr* is to be avoided, despite its 'usefulness' (cf. Q4.43; 5.90); according to Q16.67, wine (Ar. *sakar*) is to be enjoyed as one of many 'signs' of God's providence (cf. Q47.15, where *khamr* is one of the delights of heaven).
284. *games of chance*: Ar. *maysir* is said to have been a form of gambling (cf. Q5.90).

219b–220a Contributions

285. *excess*: or 'abundance,' perhaps meaning what one can spare above one's needs (cf. Q7.199), but the meaning is obscure.
286. *signs*: or 'verses.'

220b Orphans

287. *become partners with them*: lit. 'associate with them;' perhaps in business or in their affairs generally.

221–237 Marriage, divorce, and laws concerning family affairs

288. *idolatrous women*: lit. women who 'associate (other gods with God);' followed by their male counterparts.
289. *signs*: or 'verses.'
290. *take heed*: or 'be reminded,' 'remember.'
291. *harmful*: i.e. ritually defiling.
292. *clean*: i.e. restored to a state of ritual purity.

send forward (something) for yourselves.[293] Guard (yourselves) against God, and know that you will meet Him. And give good news to the believers.[294]

224 Do not, on account of your oaths, make God an obstacle to doing good, and guarding (yourselves), and setting (things) right among the people.[295] Surely God is hearing, knowing. **225** God will not take you to task for a slip in your oaths, but He will take you to task for what your hearts have earned. God is forgiving, forbearing.

226 For those who renounce their wives, (there is) a waiting period of four months. If they return – surely God is forgiving, compassionate. **227** But if they are determined to divorce – surely God is hearing, knowing. **228** (Let) the divorced women wait by themselves for three periods.[296] It is not permitted to them to conceal what God has created in their wombs, if they believe in God and the Last Day. Their husbands have a better right to take them back in that (period), if they wish to set (things) right. Women rightfully have the same privilege (as is exercised) over them, but men have a rank above them. God is mighty, wise.

229 Divorce (may take place) twice,[297] (with the option of) retaining (them) rightfully, or sending (them) away with kindness. It is not permitted to you to take (back) anything of what you have given them, unless the two of them fear that they cannot maintain the limits (set by) God. But if you fear that they cannot maintain the limits (set by) God, (there is) no blame on either of them in what she ransoms (herself) with.[298] Those are the limits (set by) God, so do not transgress them. Whoever transgresses the limits (set by) God, those – they are the evildoers. **230** If he divorces her,[299] she is not permitted to him (to marry) after that, until she marries another husband. And then if he[300] divorces her, (there is) no blame on (either of) them to return to each other, if they think that they can maintain the limits (set by) God. Those are the limits (set by) God. He makes them clear to a people who know.

231 When you divorce women, and they have reached (the end of) their term, either retain them rightfully, or send them away rightfully. Do not retain them harmfully, so that you transgress. Whoever does that has done himself evil. Do not take the signs[301] of God in mockery, but remember the blessing of God on you, and what he has sent down to you of the Book[302] and the wisdom. He admonishes you by means of it. Guard (yourselves) against God, and know that God has knowledge of everything. **232** When you divorce women, and they have reached (the end of) their term, do not prevent them from marrying their (new) husbands, when they make an agreement together rightfully. That is what anyone who believes in

293. *send forward (something) for yourselves*: probably children are meant, though it is usually interpreted as doing or saying something pious before sexual intercourse.

294. *give good news...*: addressed to the Prophet.

295. *Do not, on account of your oaths, make God an obstacle...*: i.e. by taking such oaths as would hinder the fulfillment of one's obligations (cf. Mark 7.9-13).

296. *for three periods*: i.e. a divorced woman may not remarry until after a 'waiting period' (Ar. *'idda*) of 'three menstrual cycles;' the following sentence states that it is unlawful to hide a pregnancy.

297. *Divorce (may take place) twice*: usually taken to mean that a husband may divorce his wife twice and remarry her; but if he divorces her a third time, it is not lawful for them to remarry, until she has been married to another man and been divorced by him (see Q2.230 below).

298. *what she ransoms (herself) with*: the meaning seems to be that if there is a financial obstacle to the dissolution of the marriage, the woman may gain her freedom by paying back to the man what would otherwise rightfully belong to her.

299. *If he divorces her*: usually taken to mean a 'third time' (see Q2.228), but it may simply refer to 'after the three-month waiting period.'

300. *he*: the second husband.

301. *signs*: or 'verses.'

302. *of the Book*: either the Qur'ān or the heavenly archetype, depending on whether 'of" has a partitive or an epexegetical meaning (elucidating the preceding 'what').

God and the Last Day is admonished. That is purer for you, and cleaner. God knows and you do not know.

233 Mothers shall nurse their children for two full years,[303] for those who wish to complete the nursing (period). (It is an obligation) on the father for him (to supply) their provision and their clothing rightfully. No one is to be burdened beyond their capacity. A mother is not to suffer on account of her child, nor a father on account of his child. The (father's) heir has a similar (obligation) to that. If the two of them wish, by mutual consent and consultation, to wean (the child earlier), (there is) no blame on (either of) them. And if you wish to seek nursing[304] for your children, (there is) no blame on you, provided you pay what you have rightfully promised. Guard (yourselves) against God, and know that God sees what you do.

234 Those of you who are taken,[305] and leave behind wives – (let the widows) wait by themselves for four months and ten (days).[306] When they have reached (the end) of their waiting period, (there is) no blame on you[307] for what they may rightfully do with themselves. God is aware of what you do. **235** (There is) no blame on you concerning the proposals[308] you offer to women, or (the proposals) you conceal within yourselves. God knows that you will be thinking about them. But do not make a proposal to them in secret, unless you speak rightful words. And do not tie the knot of marriage until the prescribed (term)[309] has reached its end. Know that God knows what is within you. So beware of Him, and know that God is forgiving, forbearing.

236 (There is) no blame on you if you divorce women whom you have not touched, nor promised any bridal gift to them. Yet provide for them rightfully – the wealthy according to his means, and the poor according to his means – (it is) an obligation on the doers of good. **237** If you divorce them before you have touched them, but you have already promised them a bridal gift, (give them) half of what you have promised, unless they relinquish (it), or he relinquishes (it) in whose hand is the knot of marriage. To relinquish (it) is nearer to the guarding (of oneself), and do not forget generosity among you. Surely God sees what you do.

238 Watch over[310] the prayers, and the middle prayer.[311] And stand before God obedient. **239** If you fear (danger), (pray) on foot or (while) riding. But when you are secure, remember God, since He has taught you what you did not know.

240 Those of you who (are about to be) taken,[312] and (are going to) leave behind wives, (let them make) a bequest for their wives: provision for the year[313] without evicting (them from their homes). But if they do leave, (there is) no blame on you for what they may rightfully do with themselves. God is mighty, wise. **241** For divorced women (there is) a rightful provision – (it is) an obligation on the ones who guard (themselves). **242** In this way God makes clear to you His signs,[314] so that you may understand.

---

303. *for two full years*: i.e. after the divorce.
304. *seek nursing*: i.e. employ a wet-nurse.
305. *taken*: in death.
306. *four months and ten (days)*: the text reads 'four months and ten' ('days' is usually supplied after 'ten'), but the stipulated waiting period could be fourteen months ('four months and ten'); cf. Q2.240 (below), where a year is prescribed. In either case, the waiting period ensures that the widow is not pregnant.
307. *you*: plur.
308. *proposals*: i.e. proposals of marriage to widows during the waiting period.
309. *the prescribed (term)*: lit. 'the book;' i.e. the period of time prescribed at Q2.234 above.

238–239 Prayer

310. *Watch over*: plur. imperative.
311. *the middle prayer*: usually taken as a reference to the afternoon prayer (Ar. *'aṣr*), but the five times of prayer are not explicitly mentioned in the Qur'ān.

240–242 Provision for widows

312. *taken*: in death.
313. *for the year*: following death.
314. *signs*: or 'verses.'

243 Have you[315] not considered[316] those who went forth from their homes – and they were thousands – afraid of death? And God said to them, 'Die!' (But) then He brought them to life.[317] Surely God is indeed full of favor to the people, but most of the people are not thankful (for it). **244** So fight in the way of God, and know that God is hearing, knowing. **245** Who is the one who will lend to God a good loan,[318] and He will double it for him many times? God withdraws and extends,[319] and to Him you will be returned.

246 Have you[320] not considered the assembly of the Sons of Israel after (the time of) Moses? They said to a prophet of theirs,[321] 'Raise up a king for us, (and) we shall fight in the way of God.' He said, 'Is it possible that, if fighting is prescribed for you, you will not fight?' They said, 'Why should we not fight in the way of God, when we have been expelled from our homes and our children?' Yet when fighting was prescribed for them, they (all) turned away, except for a few of them. God has knowledge of the evildoers.

247 And their prophet said to them, 'Surely God has raised up for you Ṭālūt[322] as king.' They said, 'How can he possess the kingship over us, when we are more deserving of the kingship than him, and he has not been given abundant wealth?' He said, 'Surely God has chosen him (to be) over you, and has increased him abundantly in knowledge and stature. God gives His kingdom to whomever He pleases. God is embracing, knowing.'

248 And their prophet said to them, 'Surely the sign of his kingship is that the ark[323] will come to you. In it is a Sakīna[324] from your Lord, and a remnant of what the house of Moses and the house of Aaron left behind.[325] The angels (will) carry it. Surely in that is a sign indeed for you, if you are believers.'

249 When Ṭālūt set out with his forces, he said, 'Surely God is going to test you by means of a river. Whoever drinks from it is not on my side,[326] but whoever does not taste it is surely on my side, except for whoever scoops (it) up with his hand.'[327] But they (all) drank from it, except for a few. So when he crossed it, he and those who believed with him, they said, 'We have no strength today against Jālūt[328] and his forces.' But those who thought that they would meet God said, 'How many a small cohort has overcome a large cohort by the permission of God? God is with the patient.' **250** So when they went forth to (battle) Jālūt and his forces, they said, 'Our Lord, pour out on us patience, and make firm our feet, and

243–245 Fighting for the cause of God

315. *you*: the Prophet, or perhaps intended generally ('one').
316. *considered*: lit. 'seen.'
317. *...then He brought them to life*: the story referred to here is unknown.
318. *lend to God a good loan*: by contributing to or 'investing in' God's cause (cf. Q5.12; 30.39; 57.11; 64.17; 73.20).
319. *withdraws and extends*: his provision.

246–251 The story of Saul, Goliath, and David

320. *you*: the Prophet, or perhaps intended generally.
321. *a prophet of theirs*: Samuel, according to the story in 1 Samuel 8.
322. *Ṭālūt*: or Saul, according to 1 Samuel 9.1-10.16; the form of the name resembles Jālūt, the name for Goliath at Q2.249 (below).
323. *the ark*: cf. the 'ark of God' at 1 Samuel 3.3.
324. *Sakīna*: generally has the meaning of 'assurance' (Q9.26, 40; 48.4, 18, 26), but here it seems to refer to some visible, though mysterious, object (cf. Hebr. *shekīnā*, referring to the visible manifestation of God's 'glory').
325. *a remnant...left behind*: according to one biblical tradition, the ark contained only the stone tablets of Moses (Exodus 25.10-22; 1 Kings 8.9), but according to another it held the tablets as well as the rod of Aaron and a jar of manna (Hebrews 9.4; cf. Exodus 16.33-34; Numbers 17.25-26).
326. *on my side*: lit. 'of me.'
327. *whoever scoops (it) up with his hand*: here an aspect of the story of Gideon (Judges 7.4-7) has found its way into the story of Saul.
328. *Jālūt*: Goliath (cf. the story at 1 Samuel 17.1-58).

help us against the people who are disbelievers.' **251** And they routed them by the permission of God, and David[329] killed Jālūt, and God gave him the kingdom and the wisdom, and taught him about whatever He pleased. If God had not repelled some of the people by means of others, the earth would indeed have been corrupted. But God is full of favor to the worlds.

252 Those are the signs[330] of God. We recite them to you[331] in truth. Surely you are indeed one of the
envoys.[332] **253** Those are the messengers – We have favored some of them over others.[333] (There were) some of them to whom God spoke,[334] and some of them He raised in rank. And We gave Jesus, son of Mary, the clear signs, and supported him with the holy spirit.[335] If God had (so) pleased, those who (came) after them would not have fought each other, after the clear signs had come to them. But they differed, and (there were) some of them who believed and some of them who disbelieved. If God had (so) pleased, they would not have fought each other. But God does whatever He wills.

254 You who believe! Contribute from what We have provided you, before a Day comes when (there will be) no bargaining, and no friendship, and no intercession. The disbelievers – they are the evildoers.

255 God – (there is) no god but Him, the Living, the Everlasting. Slumber does not overtake Him, nor sleep. To Him (belongs) whatever is in the heavens and whatever is on the earth. Who is the one who will intercede with Him, except by His permission? He knows whatever is before them and whatever is behind them, but they cannot encompass any of His knowledge, except whatever He pleases. His throne[336] comprehends the heavens and the earth. Watching over both of them does not weary him. He is the Most High,[337] the Almighty.

256 (There is) no compulsion in religion. The right (course) has become clearly distinguished from error. Whoever disbelieves in al-Ṭāghūt,[338] and believes in God, has grasped the firmest handle, (which)
does not break. God is hearing, knowing. **257** God is the ally of those who believe. He brings them out of the darkness into the light. But those who disbelieve – their allies are al-Ṭāghūt, who bring them out of the light into the darkness. Those are the companions of the Fire. There they will remain.

258 Have you[339] not considered the one who disputed (with) Abraham[340] concerning his Lord, because God had

329. *David*: a 'prophet' (see Q4.163n.).

252–253 The Prophet among the messengers

330. *signs*: or 'verses.'
331. *you*: the Prophet.
332. *the envoys*: lit. 'the ones who are sent' (Ar. *al-mursalūn*), a designation roughly equivalent to 'messengers' (*rusul*).
333. *favored some of them over others*: or 'preferred some of them over others.' Not all messengers are equal (nor all 'prophets,' Q17.55; cf. Q27.15). The most celebrated are presumably those whose stories are recounted most often in the Qur'ān: Moses, Abraham, Noah, Lot, Jesus, Hūd, Ṣāliḥ, Shu'ayb, and of course the Prophet himself.
334. *to whom God spoke*: or 'who spoke to God,' notably Moses (see Q4.164; 7.143; 19.52; cf. Q42.51n.).
335. *holy spirit*: or 'spirit of holiness.'

254 Contributions

255 The 'Throne Verse'

336. *throne*: from which the universe is controlled (cf. Q7.54; 10.3; 25.59; 32.4); the word for 'throne' (Ar. *kursī*) is used only here and of Solomon (Q38.34).
337. *the Most High*: Ar. *al-'aliyu*; cf. 'God Most High (Hebr. *Ēl 'Elyōn*) maker of heaven and earth' (Genesis 14.19, 22).

256–257 No compulsion in religion

338. *al-Ṭāghūt*: perhaps '(other) gods' or 'idols' (cf. Q16.36; 39.17), but sometimes taken as a proper name (see Q4.60, 76, where it appears to be another name for Satan). It may be related to the word for 'gods' in Ethiop. (*ṭā'ōt*).

258–260 God gives life to the dead

339. *you*: the Prophet, or perhaps intended generally.
340. *the one who disputed (with) Abraham*: reference obscure.

given him the kingdom? When Abraham said, 'My Lord is the One who gives life and causes death,' he said, 'I give life and cause death.' Abraham said, 'Surely God brings the sun from the East, so you bring it from the West.' And then the one who disbelieved was confounded. God does not guide the people who are evildoers.

259 Or (have you not considered) the example of the one who passed by a town that had collapsed in ruins?[341] He said, 'How will God give this (town) life after its death?' So God caused him to die for a hundred years, (and) then raised him up. He said, 'How long have you remained (dead)?' He said, 'I have remained (dead) for a day or part of a day.' He said, 'No! You have remained (dead) for a hundred years. Look at your food and drink, it has not spoiled, and look at your donkey – and (this happened) so that We might make you a sign to the people – and look at the bones, how We raise them up, (and) then clothe them with flesh.' So when it became clear to him, he said, 'I know that God is powerful over everything.'

260 (Remember) when Abraham said, 'My Lord, show me how You give the dead life.' He said, 'Have you not believed?' He said, 'Yes indeed! But (show me) to satisfy my heart.'[342] He said, 'Take four birds,[343] and take them close to you,[344] then place a piece of them on each hill, (and) then call them. They will come rushing to you. Know that God is mighty, wise.'

261 The parable of those who contribute their wealth in the way of God is like the parable of a grain of corn that grows seven ears: in each ear (there are) a hundred grains. (So) God doubles for whomever He pleases. God is embracing, knowing. **262** Those who contribute their wealth in the way of God, (and) then do not follow up what they have contributed (with) insult and injury, for them – their reward is with their Lord. (There will be) no fear on them, nor will they sorrow. **263** Rightful words and forgiveness are better than a freewill offering[345] followed by injury. God is wealthy, forbearing.

264 You who believe! Do not invalidate your freewill offerings by insult and injury, like the one who contributes his wealth in order to be seen by the people, but who does not believe in God and the Last Day. His parable is like the parable of a smooth rock with dirt on top of it. A heavy rain smites it (and) leaves it bare. They have no power over anything they have earned. God does not guide the people who are disbelievers. **265** But the parable of those who contribute their wealth, seeking the approval of God and confirmation for themselves, is like the parable of a garden on a hill. A heavy rain smites it, and it yields its produce twofold. And if a heavy rain does not smite it, a shower (does). God sees what you do.

266 Would any of you like to have a garden of date palms and grapes, (with) rivers flowing through it, and in it (there is) every (kind of) fruit for him? (Then) old age smites him, and he has (only) weak children. Then a whirlwind, with a fire in it, smites it. Then it was burned. In this way God makes clear to you the signs, so that you will reflect.[346]

267 You who believe! Contribute from the good things you have earned, and from what We have produced for you from the earth. And do not designate for contributions bad things, when you would never take them (yourselves), except with disdain. Know that God is wealthy, praiseworthy.

268 Satan promises you poverty, and commands you to immorality, but God promises you forgiveness from Him, and favor. God is embracing, knowing. **269** He gives wisdom to whomever He pleases, and whoever is given wisdom has been given much good. Yet no one takes heed except those with understanding.

---

341. *the example of the one who passed by a town...*: reference obscure; if the town is Jerusalem, then it may refer to Ezekiel, especially since the following passage seems to allude to Ezekiel's 'vision' (Ezekiel 37.1-14).

342. *satisfy my heart*: or 'put my mind at rest.'

343. *Take four birds...*: cf. the ritual performed by Abraham at Genesis 15.7-21.

344. *take them close to you*: meaning obscure.

261–274 Contributing to the cause of God

345. *freewill offering*: or 'voluntary contribution.'

346. *...so that you will reflect*: with these preceding parables, cf. Matthew 7.24-27; Mark 4.1-20.

270 Whatever contribution you make, and whatever vow you vow, surely God knows it. But the evildoers have no helper.

271 If you make freewill offerings publicly, that is excellent, but if you hide it and give it to the poor, that is better for you, and will absolve you of some of your evil deeds. God is aware of what you do.

272 Their guidance is not (dependent) on you,[347] but God guides whomever He pleases. Whatever good you contribute is for yourselves,[348] even though you contribute (as a result of) seeking the face of God.[349] And whatever good you contribute will be repaid to you in full, and you will not be done evil. **273** (Free-will offerings are) for the poor who are constrained[350] in the way of God, and are unable to strike forth on the earth. The ignorant suppose them to be rich because of (their) self-restraint,[351] but you know them by their mark – they do not constantly beg from people. Whatever good you contribute, surely God knows it. **274** Those who contribute their wealth in the night and in the day, in secret and in open, for them – their reward is with their Lord. (There will be) no fear on them, nor will they sorrow.

275 Those who devour usury[352] will not stand, except as one stands whom Satan has overthrown by (his) touch.[353] That is because they have said, 'Trade is just like usury,' though God has permitted trade and forbidden usury. Whoever receives an admonition from his Lord, and stops (practicing usury), will have whatever is past,[354] and his case is in the hands of God, but whoever returns (to usury) – those are the companions of the Fire. There they will remain. **276** God destroys usury but causes freewill offerings to bear interest. God does not love any ungrateful one[355] (or) sinner. **277** Surely those who believe and do righteous deeds, and observe the prayer and give the alms, for them – their reward is with their Lord. (There will be) no fear on them, nor will they sorrow.

278 You who believe! Guard (yourselves) against God, and give up the usury that is (still) outstanding, if you are believers. **279** If you do not, be on notice of war from God and His messenger. But if you turn (in repentance), you will have your principal. You will not have committed evil or been done evil. **280** If he[356] should be in hardship, (let there be) a postponement until (there is) some relief (of his situation). But that you remit (it as) a freewill offering[357] is better for you, if (only) you knew. **281** Guard (yourselves) against a Day on which you will be returned to God. Then everyone will be paid in full what they have earned – and they will not be done evil.

282 You who believe! When you contract a debt with one another for a fixed term, write it down. Let a scribe write it down fairly between you, and let the scribe not refuse to write it down, seeing that God has taught him.[358] So let him write, and let the one who owes the debt dictate, and let him guard

---

347. *you*: the Prophet.
348. *for yourselves*: i.e. to your own benefit.
349. *seeking the face of God*: i.e. desiring God's favor.
350. *constrained*: i.e. 'limited' or 'restricted' by their poverty.
351. *self-restraint*: i.e. in not asking for alms.

275–284 Usury, debts, and contracts

352. *usury*: lit. 'increase' or 'gain' (Ar. *ribā*), usually taken to refer to the lending of money at interest.
353. *Satan has overthrown by (his) touch*: the image is of a person in the throes of raving madness, or convulsions accompanying possession.
354. *will have whatever is past*: i.e. will able to retain his past gains.
355. *ungrateful one*: or 'disbeliever' (a pun).
356. *he*: i.e. the debtor, who is obligated to return the principal.
357. *remit (it as) a freewill offering*: i.e. make the loan an outright gift.
358. *...seeing that God has taught him*: notice that the 'art' of writing is presupposed, and considered to be a skill taught to humans by God (cf. e.g. Q68.1; 96.4-5).

(himself) against God his Lord, and not diminish anything from it. If the one who owes the debt is weak of mind or body, or unable to dictate himself, let his ally[359] dictate fairly. And call in two of your men as witnesses, or, if there are not two men, then one man and two women, from those present whom you approve of as witnesses, so that if one of the two women goes astray, the other will remind her. And let the witnesses not refuse when they are called on. Do not disdain to write it down, (however) small or large, with its due date. That is more upright in the sight of God, more reliable for witnessing (it), and (makes it) more likely that you will not be in doubt (afterwards) – unless it is an actual transaction you exchange among yourselves, and then (there is) no blame on you if you do not write it down. But take witnesses when you do business with each other. Only let the scribe or the witness not injure either party, or, if you do, that is wickedness on your part. So guard (yourselves) against God. God teaches you, and God has knowledge of everything.

283 And if you are on a journey, and do not find a scribe, (let) a security be taken. But if one of you trusts another, let him who is trusted pay back what is entrusted, and let him guard (himself) against God his Lord. Do not conceal the testimony. Whoever conceals it, surely he is sinful – (that is) his heart. God knows what you do.

284 To God (belongs) whatever is in the heavens and whatever is on the earth. Whether you reveal what is within you or hide it, God will call you to account for it. He forgives whomever He pleases and He punishes whomever He pleases. God is powerful over everything.

285 The messenger believes in what has been sent down to him from his Lord, and (so do) the believers. Each one believes in God, and His angels, and His Books,[360] and His messengers. We make no distinction[361] between any of His messengers. And they say, 'We hear and obey. (Grant us) Your forgiveness, our Lord. To You is the (final) destination.'

286 God does not burden any person beyond his capacity.[362] What they have earned is either to their credit or against their account.[363]

'Our Lord, do not take us to task if we forget or make a mistake. Our Lord, do not lay on us a burden such as You laid on those before us.[364] Our Lord, do not burden us beyond what we have the strength (to bear). Pardon us, and forgive us, and have compassion on us. You are our Protector. Help us against the people who are disbelievers.'

---

359. *ally*: or 'guardian;' Ar. *walī* implies the obligation of mutual protection, almost in the sense of 'friend' or 'brother.'

285–286 Profession of belief and a final prayer

360. *Books*: the plur. (Ar. *kutub*) recognizes the individual scriptures of Jews, Christians, and Muslims (see Q4.136; 46.12; 98.3; cf. Q9.111).

361. *no distinction*: or 'no division,' implying that all messengers received in essence the same revelation.

362. *beyond his capacity*: God does not impose any duty on humans which they are not able to perform (cf. 1 Corinthians 10.13).

363. *to their credit or against their account*: as the result of good or bad deeds.

364. *on those before us*: a reference to the many commandments and prohibitions imposed on the Sons of Israel.

3 House of 'Imrān ✿ Āl-'Imrān

In the Name of God, the Merciful, the Compassionate

1 Alif Lām Mīm.[1]

2 God – (there is) no god but Him, the Living, the Everlasting. **3** He has sent down on you[2] the Book[3] with the truth,[4] confirming what was before it, and He sent down the Torah and the Gospel[5] **4** before (this) as guidance[6] for the people, and (now) He has sent down the Deliverance.[7] Surely those who disbelieve in the signs[8] of God – for them (there is) a harsh punishment. God is mighty, a taker of vengeance.

5 Surely God – nothing is hidden from Him on the earth or in the sky. **6** He (it is) who fashions you in the wombs as He pleases. (There is) no god but Him, the Mighty, the Wise.

7 He (it is) who has sent down on you the Book, of which some verses are clearly composed[9] – they are the mother of the Book[10] – but others are ambiguous.[11] As for those in whose hearts (there is) a turning aside, they follow the ambiguous part of it, seeking (to cause) trouble[12] and seeking its interpretation. No one knows its interpretation except God. And (as for) the ones firmly grounded in knowledge, they say, 'We believe in it. All (of it) is from our Lord.' Yet no one takes heed[13] except those with understanding.

Q3: This sūra opens with a pronouncement about the divine origin of the Qur'ān, including its relationship to the previous scriptures of Jews and Christians. After this come stories of Zachariah, Mary, Jesus and his disciples, and Abraham as a Muslim. Criticism of Jewish disbelief, exhortation to the believers, and encouragement in the aftermath of defeat occupy most of the remainder of the sūra. Its title derives from the reference to the 'house of 'Imrān' at Q3.33. Most scholars, traditional and modern, assign Q3 to the 'Medinan' period.

1 Letters

1. *Alif Lām Mīm*: the names of the Arabic letters ', *l*, and *m*. The same letter combination occurs at the beginning of Q2, Q7 (with an additional 'ṣād'), and in a block of sūras from Q29 to Q32. Twenty-nine sūras begin with letters like these, ranging from one to five. No satisfactory explanation has been given for their occurrence. The Cairo edition varies in counting these letters as a separate verse (as here), or as the beginning of the first verse.

2–9 The Book

2. *you*: the Prophet, repeated at Q3.7 below.
3. *the Book*: here referring to the Qur'ān not only as a 'recited' but also 'written' scripture (see n. on Q2.2).
4. *with the truth*: or 'in truth,' 'truly.'
5. *...the Torah and the Gospel*: the Qur'ān 'confirms' the revelation to Moses in 'the Torah' (Ar. *al-Tawrāt*) and the revelation to Jesus in 'the Gospel' (Ar. *al-Injīl*); cf. e.g. Q2.97; 5.48; 35.31; 46.30.
6. *guidance*: one of the most frequent terms (Ar. *hudā*) for revelation in general.
7. *the Deliverance*: here another name for the Qur'ān (see n. on Q2.53).
8. *signs*: or 'verses' (see n. on Q2.39).
9. *clearly composed*: Ar. *muḥkamāt*; for this idea, cf. Q11.1; 22.52; 47.20.
10. *mother of the Book*: Ar. *umm al-kitāb* is usually taken as a reference to the heavenly original or archetype of all revelation. According to this view, the Qur'ān, like the Torah and the Gospel, is only a portion of this all encompassing 'Book' (see Q13.39; 43.4; cf. Q56.78, 'hidden Book;' 85.22, 'guarded Tablet'). Here, however, the 'mother of the Book' appears to refer to the 'clearly composed verses' of the Qur'ān (i.e. its 'essence').
11. *ambiguous*: or 'resembling (one another),' lit. 'alike' (Ar. *mutashābihāt*); cf. Q39.23.
12. *trouble*: or 'discord' (Ar. *fitna* has a range of meanings).
13. *takes heed*: or 'remembers.'

8 'Our Lord, do not cause our hearts to turn aside after You have guided us, and grant us mercy from Yourself. Surely You – You are the Giver. **9** Our Lord, surely You will gather the people for a Day[14] – (there is) no doubt about it. Surely God will not break the appointment.'

10 Surely those who disbelieve – neither their wealth nor their children will be of any use against God. And those – they will be fuel for the Fire,[15] **11** like the case of the house of Pharaoh, and those who were before them, who called Our signs a lie. God seized them because of their sins, and God is harsh in retribution. **12** Say[16] to those who disbelieve: 'You will be conquered and gathered into Gehenna[17] – it is an evil bed!' **13** There was a sign for you in the two cohorts which met:[18] one cohort fighting in the way of God, and another disbelieving. They saw them twice as many (as themselves) with (their own) eyesight.[19] God supports with His help whomever He pleases. Surely in that is a lesson indeed for those have sight.

14 Enticing to the people is love of desires: women and sons, qinṭārs upon qinṭārs of gold and silver,[20] and the finest horses, cattle, and fields. That is the provision of this present life. But God – with Him is the best place of return. **15** Say: 'Shall I inform you of (something) better than that? For the ones who guard (themselves),[21] (there are) Gardens[22] with their Lord, through which rivers flow, there to remain, and (there are) pure spouses and approval from God.' God sees (His) servants[23] **16** who say, 'Our Lord, surely we believe. Forgive us our sins and guard us against the punishment of the Fire.' **17** (They are) the patient, the truthful, the obedient, those who contribute,[24] the askers of forgiveness in the mornings.

18 God has borne witness that (there is) no god but Him – and (so have) the angels,[25] and the people of knowledge, (who) uphold justice. (There is) no god but Him, the Mighty, the Wise. **19** Surely the religion with God is Islam.[26] Those who were given the Book did not differ until after the knowledge had come to them,[27] (because of) envy among themselves.[28] Whoever disbelieves in the signs[29] of God – surely God is quick at the reckoning. **20** If they dispute with you,[30] say: 'I have submitted to God, and (so have) those

---

14. *Day*: of judgment.

10–17 Fate of believers and disbelievers

15. *the Fire*: Ar. *al-nār* is the most common of the various designations for Hell.
16. *Say*: on this form of address, see n. on Q2.80.
17. *Gehenna*: a name for Hell (see n. on Q2.206).
18. *the two cohorts which met*: said to refer to the victory of the Muslim forces over the Meccans at the battle of Badr (624 CE/2 AH); see Q3.123 below.
19. *twice as many (as themselves)...*: God is said to have frightened the Meccans by causing them to see the Muslim forces as twice the size of their own.
20. *qinṭārs upon qinṭārs of gold and silver*: i.e. hoarding large amounts of gold and silver (coins?); cf. Q3.75 below. A *centenarius* was a Roman official drawing a salary of 100,000 sesterces (cf. Gk. *kentenarion*, 'weighing 100 lbs.').
21. *guard (themselves)*: against evil, or God.
22. *Gardens*: in heaven (for this imagery, see n. on Q2.25).
23. *servants*: the word 'servant' (Ar. *'abd*) also means 'slave.'
24. *contribute*: lit. 'spend' (i.e. for those in need or for the cause).

18–20 Islam the religion

25. *angels*: for these beings and their various roles, see n. on Q2.30.
26. *Islam*: lit. 'the submission' or 'the surrender' (to God); cf. Q5.3. The early codex (Ar. *muṣḥaf*) of Ibn Mas'ūd is reported to have read *ḥanīfiyya* instead of *islām* here, so this may mean that before the religion was called 'Islam' it was called by some 'Ḥanīfiyya' or 'Ḥanīfite religion' (see n. on Ḥanīf at Q2.135).
27. *until after the knowledge had come to them*: i.e. differences arose only after the revelation had been given.
28. *envy among themselves*: referring to Jews and Christians, and their disputes (cf. Q2.213, 253; 5.14; 42.14; 45.17).
29. *signs*: or 'verses.'
30. *you*: the Prophet.

who follow me.' And say to those who have been given the Book, and to the common people:[31] 'Have you submitted?' If they submit, they have been (rightly) guided, but if they turn away – only (dependent) on you is the delivery (of the message). God sees (His) servants.

21 Surely those who disbelieve in the signs of God, and kill the prophets without any right,[32] and kill those of the people who command justice – give them news of a painful punishment. **22** Those are the ones whose deeds come to nothing in this world and the Hereafter.[33] They will have no helpers.

23 Have you[34] not seen those who were given a portion of the Book?[35] They were called to the Book of God in order that it might judge between them.[36] Then a group of them turned away in aversion. **24** That is because they said, 'The Fire will only touch us for a number of days.' What they forged[37] has deceived them in their religion. **25** How (will it be) when We gather them for a Day – (there is) no doubt about it – and everyone will be paid in full what he has earned,[38] and they will not be done evil? **26** Say: 'God! Master[39] of the kingdom, You give the kingdom to whomever You please and You take away the kingdom from whomever You please. You exalt whomever You please and You humble whomever You please. In Your hand is the good. Surely You are powerful over everything. **27** You cause the night to pass into the day, and cause the day to pass into the night. You bring forth the living from the dead, and bring forth the dead from the living. You provide for whomever You please without reckoning.'

28 Let not the believers take the disbelievers as allies,[40] rather than the believers – whoever does that, he has nothing from God – unless you guard (yourselves) against them as a precaution. God warns you to beware of Him. To God is the (final) destination. **29** Say: 'Whether you hide what is in your hearts[41] or reveal it, God knows it. He knows whatever is in the heavens and whatever is on the earth. God is powerful over everything.' **30** On the Day when everyone will find the good he has done brought forward, and (also) the evil he has done, he will wish that there were a great distance between himself and it.[42] God warns you to beware of Him. God is kind with (His) servants. **31** Say: 'If you love God, follow me. God will love you and will forgive you your sins. God is forgiving, compassionate.' **32** Say: 'Obey God and the messenger.'[43] If they turn away – surely God does not love the disbelievers.

---

31. *common people*: or 'native people;' i.e. the Arabs, or 'those who have not been given the Book' (cf. Q3.75 below; see n. on Q2.78).

21–27 Diatribe against the Jews

32. *kill the prophets without any right*: a common accusation (cf. Q3.112, 181 below; see n. on Q2.61).
33. *the Hereafter*: see n. on Q2.4.
34. *you*: the Prophet, or perhaps intended generally ('one').
35. *those who were given a portion of the Book*: here referring to the Jews. This differs from the expressions 'those who were given the Book' (Q2.101, 144, 145; 3.19, 20; 4.131 etc.) and 'those to whom We have given the Book' (Q2.121; 6.20, 114; 13.36 etc.). The reference to 'a portion (Ar. *naṣīb*) of the Book' (cf. Q4.44, 51) may imply that no Book (Torah, Gospel, or Qur'ān) represents the heavenly archetype (or 'mother of the Book') in its entirety; each is in some sense partial (cf. Q2.285; 4.136; 5.44; 46.12; 98.3).
36. *Book of God...might judge between them*: 'Book of God' refers to the Torah (see Q3.93, 187 below; cf. Q2.101).
37. *what they forged*: perhaps false scriptures (cf. Q2.79; 3.94 below).
38. *what he has earned*: i.e. rewards or punishments for what each has done.
39. *Master*: or 'King,' depending on how the word is vocalized.

28–32 Warning about alliance with disbelievers

40. *allies*: Ar. *awliyā'* implies the obligation of mutual protection, almost in the sense of 'friends' or 'brothers.'
41. *hearts*: lit. 'chests,' considered the seat of knowledge and understanding.
42. *it*: the evil.
43. *the messenger*: for this important title, see n. on Q2.87.

33 Surely God has chosen Adam and Noah, and the house of Abraham and the house of 'Imrān[44] over the worlds,[45] **34** some of them descendents of others. God is hearing, knowing.

35 (Remember) when[46] the wife of 'Imrān said, 'My Lord, surely I vow to You what is in my belly,[47] (to be) dedicated (to Your service). Accept (it) from me. Surely You – You are the Hearing, the Knowing.' **36** And when she had delivered her, she said, 'My Lord, surely I have delivered her, a female' – God knew very well what she had delivered, (since) the male is not like the female[48] – 'and I have named her Mary,[49] and I seek refuge for her with You, and for her descendants, from the accursed Satan.'[50] **37** So her Lord accepted her fully and caused her to grow up well, and Zachariah took charge of her. Whenever Zachariah entered upon her (in) the place of prayer,[51] he found a provision (of food) with her. He said, 'Mary! Where does this (food) come to you from?' She said, 'It is from God.[52] Surely God provides for whomever He pleases without reckoning.' **38** There Zachariah called on his Lord.[53] He said, 'My Lord, grant me a good descendant from Yourself. Surely You are the Hearer of the call.'[54] **39** And the angels called him while he was standing, praying in the place of prayer: 'God gives you good news of John, confirming a word from God.[55] (He will be) a man of honor,[56] and an ascetic, and a prophet from among the righteous.' **40** He said, 'My Lord, how shall I have a boy, when old age has already come upon me and my wife cannot conceive?'[57] He said, 'So (it will be)! God does whatever He pleases.' **41** He said, 'My Lord, make a sign for me.' He said, 'Your sign is that you will not speak to the people for three days, except by gestures. Remember your Lord often, and glorify (Him) in the evening and the morning.'

42 And (remember) when the angels said,[58] 'Mary! Surely God has chosen you and purified you, and He has chosen you over all other women.[59] **43** Mary! Be obedient to your Lord, and prostrate yourself and

---

33–34 God's chosen people

44. *'Imrān*: the father of Mary, according to what follows (Q3.35-36 below; 66.12); cf. Amram, the father of Moses, Aaron, and their sister Miriam (according to Exodus 6.20; 15.20-21; Numbers 26.59; 1 Chronicles 6.3).
45. *over the worlds*: or 'over all peoples;' for God's election, see e.g. Q2.47, 122; 6.86; 7.140.

35–41 The story of Mary, Zachariah, and John the Baptist

46. *(Remember) when...*: a stock narrative formula; the Arabic particle *idh* often marks the beginning of a story, and means something like 'Once...,' or 'There was a time when...,' or 'Remember when....'
47. *belly*: i.e. womb.
48. *God knew...*: this phrase looks like a later insertion.
49. *Mary*: the only woman referred to by name in the Qur'ān. Though she is not considered a 'prophet,' she is listed among them at Q21.91, and God addresses her as a 'messenger' at Q23.51.
50. *the accursed Satan*: or 'Satan the stoned' (Ar. *al-shayṭān al-rajīm*); for this figure, see n. on Q2.36.
51. *the place of prayer*: or 'the prayer niche' (Ar. *al-miḥrāb*) of a mosque, but here it refers to the temple in Jerusalem (cf. Q19.11), where Zachariah served as a priest, according to Luke 1.21-23; cf. the Proto-Gospel of James 8.1, 'Mary was in the temple of the Lord.'
52. *It is from God*: cf. the Proto-Gospel of James 8.1, 'Mary was in the temple of the Lord, ...receiving her food from the hand of an angel.'
53. *Zachariah called on his Lord*: for the story that follows, cf. the version at Q19.2-11.
54. *call*: or 'petition,' 'plea' (cf. Q2.186).
55. *confirming a word from God*: referring to Jesus (cf. Q3.45 below).
56. *man of honor*: Ar. *sayyid*.
57. *my wife cannot conceive*: not a reference to Mary, who was only under Zachariah's guardianship; Zachariah's wife was Elizabeth, according to Luke 1.5.

42–47 The announcement of Jesus' birth

58. *And (remember) when the angels said...*: for the story that follows, cf. the version at Q19.16-21; and Matthew 1.18-25; Luke 1.26-38; and the Proto-Gospel of James 11.1-3; 12.2 (where the angel Gabriel is specifically mentioned).
59. *over all other women*: lit. 'over the women of the worlds' (cf. Luke 1.28-30).

bow with the ones who bow.' **44** – That is one of the stories[60] of the unseen.[61] We inspired you[62] (with) it. You were not with them when they cast their pens[63] (as lots to see) which of them would take charge of Mary. Nor were you with them when they were disputing. – **45** When the angels said, 'Mary! Surely God gives you good news of a word from Him:[64] his name is the Messiah,[65] Jesus, son of Mary,[66] eminent in this world and the Hereafter, and one of those brought near.[67] **46** He will speak to the people (while he is still) in the cradle[68] and in adulthood, and (he will be) one of the righteous.' **47** She said, 'My Lord, how shall I have a child, when no man has touched me?' He said, 'So (it will be)! God creates whatever He pleases. When He decrees something, He simply says to it, "Be!"[69] and it is.'

48 And He will teach him the Book and the wisdom,[70] and the Torah and the Gospel. **49** And (He will make him) a messenger to the Sons of Israel.[71] 'Surely I have brought you a sign[72] from your Lord: I shall create for you the form of a bird from clay.[73] Then I will breathe into it and it will become a bird by the permission of God. And I shall heal the blind and the leper, and give the dead life by the permission of God. And I shall inform you of what you may eat, and what you may store up in your houses. Surely in that is a sign indeed for you, if you are believers. **50** And (I come) confirming what was before me of the Torah,[74] and to make permitted to you some things which were forbidden to you (before). I have brought you a sign from your Lord, so guard (yourselves) against God, and obey me. **51** Surely God is my Lord and your Lord, so serve Him! This is a straight path.'

52 When Jesus perceived disbelief from them, he said, 'Who will be my helpers[75] to God?' The disciples[76] said, 'We will be the helpers of God. We believe in God. Bear witness that we submit.[77] **53** Our Lord, we

---

60. *stories*: or 'news.'
61. *the unseen*: here referring to 'the distant past' (see n. on Q2.3; cf. Q11.49 [Noah]; 12.102 [Joseph]).
62. *you*: the Prophet.
63. *when they cast their pens*: these may be the angelic 'scribes' who compose the 'Book of God' or the 'recording angels' who write the 'Record' of all things; but cf. the Proto-Gospel of James 8.2-9.3, where Mary's widower-suitors are commanded to bring 'rods' with them to the temple to determine whose wife she would be. Eventually Joseph was chosen.
64. *a word from Him*: see also Q4.171; cf. John 1.1, where Jesus is called God's 'word' (Gk. *logos*).
65. *the Messiah*: the Qur'ān uses this title (Ar. *al-Masīḥ*) almost as a proper name, without any discussion of the ideas associated with it.
66. *son of Mary*: there is no mention in the Qur'ān of Joseph, Jesus' putative father (cf. Mark 6.3).
67. *those brought near*: to God's throne; 'the ones brought near' (Ar. *al-muqarrabūn*, cognate with Hebr. *kerūbīm*) is a designation of special privilege in God's 'court,' also used of the angels (Q4.172) and certain believers (Q56.10-12).
68. *in the cradle*: see Q19.29-33.
69. *Be!*: God's creative word (Ar. *kun*); cf. Q2.117; 3.59 (of Jesus and Adam); 6.73; 16.40; 19.35; 36.82; 40.68.

48–58 The mission and miracles of Jesus

70. *the wisdom*: see n. on Q2.129.
71. *And (He will make him) a messenger to the Sons of Israel*: this phrase seems out of place here, and may have originally been part of what the angels said to Mary at Q3.45-46.
72. *sign*: or 'miracle;' Jesus is now speaking.
73. *...the form of a bird from clay*: see Q5.110; cf. the Infancy Gospel of Thomas 2.2-4, where the child Jesus fashioned twelve birds out of clay, and then made them come to life and fly off by clapping his hands and shouting, 'Be gone!'
74. *of the Torah*: has either a partitive or an epexegetical meaning (elucidating the preceding 'what').
75. *helpers*: Ar. *anṣār* is a pun on the name for 'Christians' (Ar. *Naṣārā*); 'helpers' was also the title given to the believers among the people of Medina (as distinguished from the 'emigrants' from Mecca).
76. *The disciples*: or 'The apostles' (Ar. *al-ḥawārīyūn*), a word used only of Jesus' followers (cf. Q5.111, 112; 61.14).
77. *that we submit*: or 'that we are Muslims' (cf. Q5.111).

believe in what You have sent down, and we follow the messenger. So write us down among the witnesses.'

54 They schemed,[78] but God schemed (too), and God is the best of schemers. **55** (Remember) when God said, 'Jesus! Surely I am going to take you[79] and raise you to Myself, and purify you from those who disbelieve. And I am going to place those who follow you above[80] those who disbelieve until the Day of Resurrection. Then to Me is your[81] return, and I shall judge between you concerning your differences. **56** As for those who disbelieve, I shall punish them (with) a harsh punishment in this world and the Hereafter. They will have no helpers.' **57** As for those who believe and do righteous deeds, He[82] will pay them their rewards in full. God does not love the evildoers. **58** That – We recite it to you[83] from the signs[84] and the wise Reminder.[85]

59 Surely the likeness of Jesus is, with God, as the likeness of Adam.[86] He created him from dust,[87] (and) then He said to him, 'Be!'[88] and he was. **60** The truth (is) from your Lord, so do not be one of the doubters. **61** Whoever disputes with you[89] about him, after what has come to you of the knowledge,[90] say: 'Come, let us call our sons and your sons, our wives and your wives, ourselves and yourselves. Then let us pray earnestly and place the curse of God upon the liars.' **62** Surely this – it indeed is the true account. (There is) nothing of (the nature of) a god but God. Surely God – He indeed is the Mighty, the Wise. **63** If they turn away – surely God knows the fomenters of corruption.

64 Say: 'People of the Book! Come to a word (which is) common between us and you:[91] "We do not serve

---

78. *They schemed*: i.e. the opponents of Jesus who plotted against him. What God devised or 'schemed' in return was the substitution of a phantasm or some other person for Jesus at the crucifixion (see Q4.157).
79. *take you*: in death; there are conflicting views of Jesus' fate in the Qur'ān (cf. Q4.157-158; 5.117; and what Jesus says of himself at Q19.33).
80. *place...above*: or 'make...superior to.'
81. *your*: plur.
82. *He*: notice the sudden shift from first- to third-person sing., and then to first-person plur. in the following verse.
83. *you*: the Prophet.
84. *signs*: or 'verses.'
85. *Reminder*: or 'Remembrance' (Ar. *dhikr*), referring to the revelation in general, or (as here) to the Qur'ān in particular (see e.g. Q6.90; 7.63, 69; cf. Q16.43; 21.7, 'People of the Reminder'). The meaning is not simply the remembering of something forgotten, but rather keeping something before the mind by repeatedly calling it to attention, with the sense of 'admonition,' 'exhortation,' and even 'warning' (e.g. Q73.19; 76.29). The Prophet is the 'one who reminds' (*mudhakkir*, Q88.21). Thus at Q50.45 he is instructed to 'admonish (lit. 'remind') by the Qur'ān' (cf. Q6.70; 51.55; 52.29; 87.9; 88.21). Once the Prophet himself is referred to as the 'reminder' (Q88.21; Q65.10-11).

59–63 Jesus is human, not divine

86. *the likeness of Jesus is...as the likeness of Adam*: both Jesus and Adam were created by God's word ('Be!'). Similarly, God 'breathed his spirit into' Adam (Q15.29; 32.9; 38.72) and 'strengthened' Jesus with the 'holy spirit' (Q2.87, 253; 5.110). Mary was also impregnated by 'Our spirit' (Q19.17; 21.91; 66.12). Nevertheless both Adam and Jesus were human beings according to the Qur'ān. Cf. Paul's Adam-Christ typology at Romans 5.12-21; 1 Corinthians 15.21-23, 45-49; Colossians 1.15-16.
87. *from dust*: see Q18.37; 22.5; 30.20; 35.11; 40.67 (cf. Genesis 2.7, 'from the dust of the ground'); 'from clay,' according to Q6.2; 7.12; 15.26; 17.61; 23.12; 32.7; 38.71, 76; 55.14; 'from water,' according to Q21.30; 24.45; 25.54.
88. *Be!*: see n. on Q3.47 above.
89. *you*: the Prophet.
90. *of the knowledge*: has either a partitive or an epexegetical meaning (elucidating the preceding 'what').

64–68 Appeal to the People of the Book: Abraham was a Muslim

91. *a word...common between us and you*: i.e. doctrines held in common by Jews, Christians, and Muslims.

(anyone) but God, and do not associate (anything) with Him,[92] and do not take each other as Lords instead of God."' If they turn away, say:[93] 'Bear witness that we are Muslims.'

65 People of the Book! Why do you dispute about Abraham, when the Torah and the Gospel were not sent down until after him.[94] Will you not understand? **66** There you are! Those who have disputed about what you know. Why do you dispute about what you do not know? God knows, but you do not know. **67** Abraham was not a Jew, nor a Christian, but he was a Ḥanīf,[95] a Muslim. He was not one of the idolaters.[96] **68** Surely the people nearest to Abraham are those indeed who followed him, and this prophet, and those who believe. God is the ally of the believers.

69 A contingent of the People of the Book would like to lead you astray, but they only lead themselves astray, though they do not realize (it). **70** People of the Book! Why do you disbelieve in the signs[97] of God, when you are witnesses (to them)? **71** People of the Book! Why do you mix the truth with falsehood, and conceal the truth,[98] when you know (better)? **72** A contingent of the People of the Book has said, 'Believe in what has been sent down on those who believe at the beginning of the day, and disbelieve at the end of it, perhaps (then) they may return.'[99] **73** And: 'Do not believe (anyone) except the one who follows your religion.' Say: 'Surely the (true) guidance is the guidance of God – that anyone should be given what you have been given, or (that) they should dispute with you before your Lord!'[100] Say: 'Surely favor is in the hand of God. He gives it to whomever He pleases. God is embracing, knowing. **74** He chooses whomever He pleases for His mercy, and God is full of great favor.'

75 Among the People of the Book (there is) one who, if you[101] entrust him with a qinṭār,[102] will pay it back to you, but among them (there is) one who, if you entrust him with a dīnār,[103] will not pay it back to you unless you stand over him. That is because they say, '(There is) no way (of obligation) on us concerning the common people.'[104] They speak lies against God, and they know (it). **76** Yes indeed! Whoever fulfills his covenant and guards (himself) – surely God loves the ones who guard (themselves). **77** Surely those who sell the covenant of God and their oaths for a small price will have no share in the Hereafter. God will not speak to them or look at them on the Day of Resurrection, nor will He purify them. For them (there is) a painful punishment.

78 Surely (there is) indeed a group of them who twist their tongues with the Book,[105] so that you will think

---

92. *do not associate (anything) with Him*: i.e. ascribe divinity to some other being alongside God (*shirk*).
93. *say*: plur. imperative.
94. *until after him*: the point is that the Torah of Moses and Gospel of Jesus are later than the religion of Abraham. Paul makes a similar point about the superiority of Abraham to Moses in Galatians 3 and Romans 4.
95. *Ḥanīf*: or perhaps 'Gentile' (see n. on Q2.135; cf. Q3.95 below).
96. *the idolaters*: or 'the ones who associate (other gods with God).'

69–85 Diatribe against the People of the Book

97. *signs*: or 'verses.'
98. *conceal the truth*: a reference to their concealing the prophecies about the Prophet in the Torah.
99. *...perhaps (then) they may return*: i.e. by first saying that they believed, and then that they did not believe, they hoped that they would cause others to abandon their belief.
100. *or (that) they should dispute with you...*: i.e. dispute the fact that the Muslims are now the people favored by God.
101. *you*: sing.
102. *qinṭār*: a 'large sum' of money (see n. on Q3.14 above; cf. Q4.20); the contrast is with the following reference to a single coin.
103. *dīnār*: a unit of currency (cf. the Roman *denarius*), greater than a dirham (Q12.20). These are the only references to coinage in the Qur'ān (Q18.19 may refer to 'paper money').
104. *common people*: or 'native people;' i.e. the Arabs (see n. on Q2.78).
105. *twist their tongues with the Book*: i.e. in reciting the Torah they play with words in order to distort the meaning

it is from the Book, when it is not from the Book. And they say, 'It is from God,' when it is not from God. They speak lies against God, and they know (it). **79** It is not (possible) for a human being that God should give him the Book, and the judgment,[106] and the prophetic office, (and) then he should say to the people, 'Be my servants instead of God's.'[107] Rather (he would say), 'Be rabbis by what you have been teaching of the Book[108] and by what you have been studying (of it).' **80** He would not command you to take the angels and the prophets as Lords. Would he command you to disbelief after you have submitted?[109]

81 (Remember) when God took a covenant with the prophets:[110] 'Whatever indeed I have given you of the Book and wisdom,[111] when a messenger comes to you confirming what is with you, you are to believe in him and you are to help him.' He said, 'Do you agree and accept My burden on that (condition)?' They said, 'We agree.' He said, 'Bear witness, and I shall be with you among the witnesses.' **82** Whoever turns away after that, those – they are the wicked.

83 Do they desire a religion other than God's, when whoever is in the heavens and the earth has submitted to Him, willingly or unwillingly, and to Him they will be returned? **84** Say: 'We believe in God,[112] and what has been sent down on us, and what has been sent down on Abraham, and Ishmael, and Isaac, and Jacob, and the tribes, and what was given to Moses, and Jesus, and the prophets from their Lord. We make no distinction[113] between any of them, and to Him we submit.'[114] **85** Whoever desires a religion other than Islam, it will not be accepted from him, and in the Hereafter he will be one of the losers.

86 How will God guide a people who have disbelieved after having believed,[115] and (after) they have borne witness that the messenger is true, and the clear signs[116] have come to them? God does not guide the people who are evildoers. **87** Those – their payment is that on them (rests) the curse of God, and the angels, and the people all together. **88** There[117] (they will) remain – the punishment will not be lightened for them, nor will they be spared **89** – except for those who turn (in repentance) after that and set (things) right. Surely God is forgiving, compassionate. **90** Surely those who disbelieve after their believing, (and) then increase in disbelief – their repentance will not be accepted. And those – they are the ones who go astray. **91** Surely those who disbelieve, and die while they are disbelievers – not all the world's gold would be accepted from (any) one of them, even if he (tried to) ransom (himself) with it. Those – for them (there is) a painful punishment. They will have no helpers.

---

of the text (see e.g. Q2.75-79).

106. *judgment*: or 'wisdom,' depending on how the word is vocalized (Ar. *ḥukm* or *ḥikma*); cf. Q2.129n.; 4.105; 5.42-43; 6.89; 13.37 etc.

107. *Be my servants instead of God's*: this passage rejects the notion that any prophet (and especially Jesus) was other than a human being.

108. *what you have been teaching of the Book*: another reading is 'what you know of the Book' ('of the Book' has either a partitive or an epexegetical meaning, elucidating the preceding 'what').

109. *after you have submitted*: or 'after you have become Muslims.'

110. *covenant with the prophets*: cf. Q33.7 for a list of these prophets.

111. *wisdom*: see n. on Q2.129.

112. *Say: 'We believe in God...'*: though the imperative 'Say!' is sing., it must here be construed as addressing the believers generally (see Q2.136; 29.46; cf. Q112.1).

113. *no distinction*: or 'no division,' implying that all those listed here received in essence the same revelation (see Q2.136; 29.46-47; cf. Q9.111).

114. *submit*: or 'are Muslims.'

86–91 Warning against apostasy

115. *disbelieved after having believed*: i.e. committed apostasy, though repentance is still possible (see Q3.89 below).

116. *the clear signs*: or 'the clear proofs,' 'the indisputable evidence.'

117. *There*: lit. 'In it,' i.e. under the curse, or perhaps in Hell (cf. Q2.162).

92 You will not attain piety until you contribute from what you love, and whatever you contribute, surely God knows it.

93 All food was permitted to the Sons of Israel, except for what Israel[118] forbade himself before the Torah was sent down.[119] Say: 'Bring the Torah and read it, if you are truthful.' **94** Whoever forges lies against God after that, those – they are the evildoers. **95** Say: 'God has spoken the truth, so follow the creed of Abraham the Ḥanīf.[120] He was not one of the idolaters.'

96 Surely the first House laid down for the people was indeed that at Becca,[121] a blessed (House) and a guidance for the worlds.[122] **97** In it are clear signs: the standing place of Abraham. Whoever enters it is secure.[123] Pilgrimage to the House is (an obligation) on the people to God – (for) anyone who is able (to make) a way to it. Whoever disbelieves – surely God is wealthy beyond the worlds.[124]

98 Say: 'People of the Book! Why do you disbelieve in the signs[125] of God, when God is a witness of what you do?' **99** Say: 'People of the Book! Why do you keep those who believe from the way of God, desiring (to make) it crooked, when you are witnesses? God is not oblivious of what you do.'

100 You who believe! If you obey a group of those who have been given the Book, they will turn you back (into) disbelievers after having believed. **101** Yet how can you disbelieve, when the signs of God are recited to you, and His messenger is among you? Whoever holds fast to God has been guided to a straight path.

102 You who believe! Guard (yourselves) against God – guarding (yourselves) against Him is an obligation – and (see to it that) you do not die unless you have submitted.[126] **103** And hold fast to the rope of God – all (of you) – and do not become divided. Remember the blessing of God on you: when you were enemies and He united your hearts, so that by His blessing you became brothers. You were on the brink of a pit of the Fire, and He saved you from it. In this way God makes clear to you His signs, so that you may be (rightly) guided.

104 Let there be (one) community of you, calling (people) to good, and commanding right and forbidding wrong. Those – they are the ones who prosper. **105** Do not be like those who became divided and differed,[127] after the clear signs had come to them. Those – for them (there is) a great punishment, **106** on the Day when (some) faces will become white and (other) faces will become black. As for those whose faces are blackened: 'Did you disbelieve after having believed? Taste the punishment for what you were disbelieving!' **107** As for those whose faces are whitened, (they will be) in the mercy of God. There they will remain.

---

92 Contributions

93–95 Jewish food laws

118. *Israel*: here referring to the patriarch Jacob/Israel (cf. Q19.58).
119. *before the Torah was sent down*: cf. the 'pre-Sinaitic' food laws of Genesis 9.3-4 (Noah); 32.32 (Jacob/Israel).
120. *Abraham the Ḥanīf*: or perhaps 'Abraham the Gentile' (see n. on Q2.135; cf. Q3.67 above).

96–97 Pilgrimage a duty

121. *Becca*: Ar. *Bakka* occurs only here; tradition identifies it with 'Mecca' (Q48.24), in which case the 'House' would be the Ka'ba (see Q5.95n.). Some modern scholars dispute this identification.
122. *for the worlds*: or 'for all peoples.'
123. *Whoever enters it is secure*: because bloodshed was forbidden in the sacred area (or *ḥaram*) of Mecca.
124. *wealthy beyond the worlds*: i.e. God has no need of anyone or anything.

98–99 Warning to the People of the Book

125. *signs*: or 'verses.'

100–109 Warning to believers

126. *unless you have submitted*: or 'except as Muslims.'
127. *those who became divided and differed*: referring to Jews and Christians.

108 Those are the signs of God. We recite them to you[128] in truth. God does not intend any evil to the worlds.
109 To God (belongs) whatever is in the heavens and whatever is on the earth. To God all affairs are
returned.

110 You are the best community (ever) brought forth for humankind, commanding right and forbidding
wrong, and believing in God. If the People of the Book had believed, it would indeed have been better for
them. Some of them are believers, but most of them are wicked. **111** They will not cause you any harm,
except for a (little) hurt. And if they fight you, they will turn their backs to you, (and) then they will not
be helped. **112** Humiliation will be stamped upon them wherever they are found, unless (they grasp) a
rope from God and a rope from the people.[129] They have incurred the anger of God, and poverty will be
stamped upon them. That is because they have disbelieved in the signs of God and killed the prophets
without any right.[130] That is because they have disobeyed and transgressed.

113 (Yet) they are not (all) alike. Among the People of the Book (there is) a community[131] (which is)
upstanding. They recite the signs[132] of God during the hours of the night and prostrate themselves.
114 They believe in God and the Last Day, and command right and forbid wrong, and are quick in the
(doing of) good deeds. Those are among the righteous. **115** Whatever good they do, they will not be
denied (the reward of) it. God knows the ones who guard (themselves). **116** Surely those who disbelieve
– neither their wealth nor their children will be of any use against God – those are the companions of the
Fire. There they will remain. **117** The parable of what they contribute in this present life is like the parable of a freezing wind, which smites the field of a people who have done themselves evil, and destroys it.
God did not do them evil, but they did themselves evil.

118 You who believe! Do not take outsiders as intimate friends. They will not fail to cause you ruin. They
desire what you are distressed at. (Their) hatred is already apparent from their mouths, but what their
hearts[133] hide is (even) greater. We have already made clear to you the signs, if you are understanding.
119 There you are! You are those who love them, but they do not love you. You believe in the Book – all
of it.[134] And when they meet you they say, 'We believe,' but when they are alone, they bite their fingers at
you out of rage. Say: 'Die in your rage! Surely God knows what is in the hearts.' **120** If some good touches
you, it distresses them, but if some evil smites you, they gloat over it. Yet if you are patient and guard
(yourselves), their plot will not harm you at all. Surely God encompasses what they do.

121 (Remember) when you[135] went out early from your family to post the believers (in their) positions
for the battle[136] – God is hearing, knowing – **122** when two contingents of you were inclined to lose

---

128. *you*: the Prophet.

110–112 Muslims are the best community

129. *a rope from God...from the people*: i.e. unless they enter into some form of 'bond' or alliance with the Muslims.

130. *killed the prophets without any right*: a common accusation (cf. Q3.21, 181; see n. on Q2.61).

113–117 Believers among the People of the Book

131. *a community*: probably a reference to the Christians.

132. *recite the signs*: or 'read the verses aloud.'

118–120 Breaking off relations with outsiders

133. *hearts*: lit. 'chests,' considered the seat of knowledge and understanding (also in the following verse).

134. *all of it*: i.e. not only what was revealed to the Prophet, but also what was revealed to Moses and Jesus, in contrast to those Jews and Christians who did not acknowledge the Prophet's revelation.

121–129 Address after defeat in battle

135. *you*: the Prophet.

136. *for the battle*: reference uncertain; said to be the battle near Mount Uḥud (about 8 km from Medina), where in 625 CE/3 AH Meccan forces are reported to have defeated the Muslims.

courage, though God was their ally – in God let the believers put their trust. **123** Certainly God helped you[137] at Badr,[138] when you were an utterly insignificant (force). So guard (yourselves) against God, that you may be thankful.

124 (Remember) when you[139] said to the believers, 'Is it not sufficient for you that your Lord increases you with three thousand angels (specially) sent down?[140] **125** Yes indeed! If you are patient and guard (yourselves), and they[141] come against you suddenly, your Lord will increase you with five thousand angels (specially) designated.' **126** God only intended that as good news for you, and to satisfy your hearts by means of it. Help (comes) only from God, the Mighty, the Wise, **127** so that He might cut off a part of those who disbelieve, or disgrace them, so that they would turn back disappointed. **128** You[142] have nothing to do with the matter, whether He turns to them (in forgiveness) or punishes them. Surely they are evildoers. **129** To God (belongs) whatever is in the heavens and whatever is on the earth. He forgives whomever He pleases and He punishes whomever He pleases. God is forgiving, compassionate.

130 You who believe! Do not devour usury,[143] (making it) double and redouble, but guard (yourselves) against God, so that you may prosper. **131** And guard (yourselves) against the Fire which is prepared for the disbelievers.

132 Obey God and the messenger, so that you may receive compassion. **133** And be quick to (obtain) forgiveness from your Lord, and a Garden – its width (is like) the heavens and the earth – prepared for the ones who guard (themselves), **134** who contribute (alms) in prosperity and adversity,[144] and who choke back their anger and pardon the people. God loves the doers of good, **135** and those who, when they commit immorality[145] or do themselves evil, remember God and ask forgiveness for their sins – and who forgives sins but God? – and do not persist in (doing) what they did, when they know (better). **136** Those – their payment is forgiveness from their Lord, and Gardens through which rivers flow, there to remain. Excellent is the reward of the doers![146]

137 Customary practices have passed away before you.[147] Travel the earth and see how the end was for the ones who called (it) a lie.[148] **138** This[149] is an explanation for the people, and a guidance and admonition for the ones who guard (themselves).

---

137. *you*: plur.
138. *Badr*: only mentioned here explicitly; cf. Q3.13 above.
139. *you*: the Prophet.
140. *three thousand angels…sent down*: cf. Q8.9 ('a thousand angels').
141. *they*: the enemy.
142. *You*: the Prophet.

130–131 Prohibition of usury

143. *usury*: lit. 'increase' or 'gain' (Ar. *ribā*), but exactly what is prohibited remains unclear; it is usually taken to refer to the lending of money at interest.

132–136 Promise of heavenly rewards

144. *who contribute...*: the opposite of those who lend money at interest.
145. *immorality*: or 'indecency' (Ar. *fāḥisha*), of a sexual nature.
146. *the doers*: of righteous deeds.

137–138 Threat of punishment

147. *Customary practices have passed away before you*: plur.; a reference to previous peoples who followed their own 'customary practice' (Ar. *sunna*) instead of God's, and were punished for their disbelief (see n. on Q7.59).
148. *...who called (it) a lie*: i.e. who rejected the warning of imminent judgment; the remains of their destroyed cities were believed to be still visible (cf. Q6.11, 148; 16.36; 43.25).
149. *This*: the Qur'ān.

139 Do not grow weak[150] and do not sorrow, when you are the prevailing (force), if you are believers. **140** If a wound has touched you, a similar wound has already touched the enemy.[151] We cause days like this to alternate among the people, so that God may know those who believe, and that He may take martyrs from you – God does not love the evildoers – **141** and so that God may purge those who believe, and destroy the disbelievers.[152] **142** Or did you think that you would enter the Garden, when God did not yet know those of you who would struggle,[153] and know the (ones who would be) patient? **143** Certainly you were desiring death before you met it. Now you have seen it, and you are staring (at it).[154]

144 Muḥammad[155] is only a messenger.[156] Messengers have already passed away before him. If he dies or is killed, will you turn back on your heels? Whoever turns back on his heels will not harm God at all. God will repay the thankful. **145** It is not (given) to anyone to die, except by the permission of God – (it is) determined (in) writing.[157] Whoever desires the reward of this world, We shall give him (a share) of it, and whoever desires the reward of the Hereafter, We shall give him (a share) of it. We shall repay the thankful.

146 How many a prophet has fought, (and) with him (fought) many masters?[158] Yet they did not weaken at what smote them in the way of God. They were not weak nor did they humiliate themselves. God loves the patient. **147** All that they said was, 'Our Lord, forgive us our sins and our wantonness in our affair, and make firm our feet, and give us victory over the people who are disbelievers.' **148** So God gave them the reward of this world and the good reward of the Hereafter. God loves the doers of good.

149 You who believe! If you obey those who disbelieve, they will turn you back on your heels, and you will return as losers. **150** No! God is your Protector. He is the best of helpers. **151** We shall cast dread into the hearts of those who disbelieve, because they have associated with God[159] what He has not sent down any authority for. Their refuge is the Fire. Evil is the dwelling place of the evildoers!

152 Certainly God fulfilled His promise to you when you were killing them by His permission, until you lost courage and argued about the matter, and disobeyed after He had shown you what you love.[160] (There are) some of you who desire this world, and some of you who desire the Hereafter. Then He turned you away from them, so that He might test you. Certainly He has pardoned you. God is full of favor to the believers.

139–151 Address after defeat in battle (continued)

150. *Do not grow weak...*: a continuation of the previous section (Q3.121-129).
151. *the enemy*: lit. 'the people.'
152. *...and destroy the disbelievers*: i.e. the purpose of defeat was to weed out disbelievers from the ranks of the believers.
153. *struggle*: or 'fight.'
154. *desiring death...staring (at it)*: i.e. they longed for the honor of martyrdom, only to be dismayed in the face of actual death.
155. *Muḥammad*: the first of four occurrences of this name (see also Q33.40; 47.2 [and title]; 48.29; cf. Q61.6, 'Aḥmad'). Some modern scholars question whether it was an actual name originally. It could be read as an adjective and taken as an epithet ('the praised one').
156. *only a messenger*: exactly what is said of Jesus, see Q4.171; 5.75; cf. Q19.19 (the 'spirit' sent to Mary).
157. *determined (in) writing*: or 'determined (in) a book;' i.e. the date of a person's death is written by God in a 'Book' (see n. on Q6.59; cf. Q3.154 below).
158. *masters*: or 'rabbis' (Ar. *rabbaniyyūn*).
159. *associated with God*: i.e. ascribed divinity to other beings alongside God (Ar. *shirk*).

152–155 Explanation for the defeat

160. *what you love*: perhaps the spoils of the enemy or victory. Tradition reports that there was quarrelling over spoils after an initial victory, with some fighters leaving their positions against the command of Muḥammad.

153 (Remember) when you were going up,[161] and not turning aside for anyone, and the messenger was calling to you from behind: He repaid you (with) distress upon distress, so that you might not sorrow over what eluded you[162] or what smote you. God is aware of what you do. **154** Then, after the distress, He sent down on you security: a slumber covering a contingent of you, but (another) contingent (of you) was obsessed about themselves, thinking about God (something) other than the truth – thought(s) of the (time of) ignorance.[163] They were saying, 'Do we have any part at all in the affair?' Say: 'Surely the affair – all of it – (belongs) to God.' They hide within themselves what they do not reveal to you.[164] They were saying, 'If we had any part in the affair, we would not have been killed here.' Say: '(Even) if you had been in your houses, those for whom death was written[165] would (still) indeed have gone forth to the places where they lie (dead).' (That happened) in order that God might test what was in your hearts,[166] and that He might purge what was in your hearts. God knows what is in the hearts. **155** Surely those of you who turned back on the day the two forces met – (it was) only Satan (who) caused them to slip because of something they had earned.[167] Certainly God has pardoned them. Surely God is forgiving, forbearing.

156 You who believe! Do not be like those who disbelieve, and say of their brothers when they strike forth on the earth or are on a raid, 'If they had been with us, they would not have died or been killed' – so that God may make that a (cause of) regret in their hearts. (It is) God (who) gives life and causes death. God sees what you do. **157** If indeed you are killed in the way of God, or die – forgiveness from God, and mercy, are indeed better than what they accumulate.[168] **158** If indeed you die or are killed, you will indeed be gathered to God. **159** (It was) by a mercy from God (that) you have been soft on them.[169] If you had been harsh (and) stern of heart, they would indeed have deserted from your ranks. So pardon them, and ask forgiveness for them, and consult with them about the affair. When you have made up your mind, put your trust in God. Surely God loves the ones who put their trust (in Him). **160** If God helps you, (there is) no one to overcome you, but if He forsakes you, who (is there) who (will) help you after Him? In God let the believers put their trust.

161 It is not for a prophet to defraud.[170] Whoever defrauds will bring what he has defrauded on the Day of Resurrection. Then everyone will be paid in full what they have earned – and they will not be done evil. **162** Is the one who follows after the approval of God like the one who incurs the anger of God? His refuge will be Gehenna – and it is an evil destination! **163** They (have different) ranks[171] with God, and God sees what they do. **164** Certainly God bestowed favor on the believers when He raised up among

---

161. *(Remember) when you were going up*: reference uncertain; said to refer to Muslim fighters climbing the hill of Uḥud.
162. *what eluded you*: probably the spoils they failed to take, or the victory that escaped them.
163. *the (time of) ignorance*: i.e. the pre-Islamic period of ignorance about God (Ar. *al-jāhiliyya*).
164. *you*: the Prophet.
165. *written*: see n. on Q3.145 above.
166. *hearts*: lit. 'chests,' considered the seat of knowledge and understanding.
167. *because of something they had earned*: i.e. for some sin they had committed.

156–160 Comfort for the mourners

168. *what they accumulate*: i.e. wealth or worldly goods.
169. *you have been soft on them*: addressed to the Prophet; it is said to refer to those fighters who faltered at the battle of Uḥud.

161–165 Appeal for loyalty

170. *defraud*: said to refer to the Prophet's handling of the spoils taken at the battle of Badr.
171. *ranks*: or 'degrees,' of honor and dishonour, or rewards and punishments.

them a messenger from among them, to recite His signs[172] to them, and to purify them,[173] and to teach them the Book and the wisdom, though before (this) they were indeed clearly astray.[174] **165** Why, when a smiting smote you – you had already smitten twice (as many in comparison to) it[175] – did you say, 'How is this?' Say: 'You yourselves are to blame.[176] Surely God is powerful over everything.'

166 What smote you on the day when the two forces met (happened) by the permission of God, so that He might know the (true) believers, **167** and that He might know those who played the hypocrite.[177] It was said to them, 'Come, fight in the way of God, or defend!' But they said, 'If we knew (how) to fight,[178] we would indeed follow you.' They were nearer to disbelief that day than to belief. They were saying with their mouths what was not in their hearts. But God knows what they were concealing – **168** those who said of their brothers, when they (themselves) sat (at home), 'If they had obeyed us, they would not have been killed.' Say: 'Avert death from yourselves, if you are truthful.'

169 Do not think of those who have been killed in the way of God as dead. No! (They are) alive with their Lord[179] (and) provided for, **170** gloating over what God has given them of his favor, and welcoming the good news about those who have not (yet) joined them of those who stayed behind – that (there will be) no fear on them, nor will they sorrow. **171** They welcome the good news of blessing from God, and favor, and that God does not let the reward of the believers go to waste. **172** Those who responded (to the call of) God and the messenger after the wound had smitten them – for those of them who have done good and guarded (themselves), (there is) a great reward. **173** (They are) those to whom the people said, 'Surely the enemy[180] has gathered against you, so fear them!' But it increased them in belief, and they said, 'God is enough for us. Excellent is the Guardian.' **174** So they turned back by the blessing and favor of God, without any evil touching them. They followed after the approval of God, and God is full of great favor. **175** That is only Satan (who) frightens his allies.[181] Do not fear them, but fear Me, if you are believers.

176 Do not let those who are quick to disbelieve cause you[182] sorrow. Surely they will not harm God at all. God does not wish to assign to them[183] any share in the Hereafter. For them (there is) a great punishment. **177** Surely those who have purchased disbelief with the (price of) belief will not harm God at all. For them (there is) a painful punishment. **178** And let not those who disbelieve think that We spare them for their own good. We only spare them so that they will increase in sin! For them (there is) a humiliating

---

172. *recite His signs*: or 'read His verses aloud.'

173. *purify them*: or perhaps 'appoint *zakāt* for them' (cf. Q2.129, 151; 62.2).

174. *clearly astray*: lit. 'in clear straying.'

175. *smitten twice (as many in comparison to) it*: traditionally taken to mean that the believers had killed twice as many fighters at Badr as they lost at Uḥud.

176. *You yourselves are to blame*: lit. 'It is from yourselves.'

166–175 Explanation for the defeat (continued)

177. *those who played the hypocrite*: i.e. the reason for the defeat was to distinguish between true and false believers (cf. Q3.140-141, 154 above). Some scholars consider the verb used here (Ar. *nāfaqa*) to be the origin of the epithet 'hypocrites' (Ar. *munāfiqūn*).

178. *If we knew (how) to fight*: the next sentence makes clear that this was merely an excuse.

179. *(They are) alive with their Lord*: those killed fighting for the cause of God go straight to Paradise, and do not have to wait for the general resurrection (cf. Q2.154).

180. *the enemy*: lit. 'the people.'

181. *allies*: Ar. *awliyā'* implies the obligation of mutual protection, almost in the sense of 'friends' or 'brothers.'

176–180 Disbelievers warned, believers encouraged

182. *you*: the Prophet.

183. *assign to them*: lit. 'make for them.'

punishment. **179** God is not one to leave the believers in (the situation) you are in[184] until He separates the bad from the good.[185] Nor is God one to inform you of the unseen,[186] but God chooses from His messengers whomever He pleases.[187] So believe in God and His messengers. If you believe and guard (yourselves), for you (there is) a great reward. **180** And let not those who are stingy with what God has given them of His favor think that it is good for them. No! It is bad for them. What they are stingy with will be hung about their necks on the Day of Resurrection. To God (belongs) the inheritance of the heavens and the earth. God is aware of what you do.

181 Certainly God has heard the words of those who said, 'Surely God is poor and we are rich.'[188] We shall write down what they have said, along with their killing the prophets without any right,[189] and We shall say, 'Taste the punishment of the burning (Fire)! **182** That is for what your (own) hands have sent forward,[190] and (know) that God is not an evildoer to (His) servants.'

183 Those (are the same people) who said, 'Surely God has made us promise not to believe in any messenger until he brings a sacrifice which fire devours.'[191] Say: 'Messengers have come to you before me with the clear signs, and with that which you spoke of. So why did you kill them, if you are truthful?' **184** If they call you a liar, (know that) messengers have been called liars before you, who brought the clear signs, and the scriptures,[192] and the illuminating Book.[193]

185 Every person will taste death, and you[194] will only be paid your rewards in full on the Day of Resurrection. Whoever is removed from the Fire and admitted to the Garden has triumphed. This present life is nothing but a deceptive enjoyment. **186** You will indeed be tested concerning your wealth and your own lives, and you will indeed hear from those who were given the Book before you, and from those who are idolaters, much hurt. But if you are patient and guard (yourselves) – surely that is one of the determining factors in (all) affairs.

187 (Remember) when God took a covenant with those who had been given the Book: 'You shall indeed make it clear to the people, and shall not conceal it.' But they tossed it behind their backs, and sold it for a small price. Evil is what they purchased! **188** Do not think[195] (that) those who gloat over what they have brought, and like to be praised for what they have not done – do not think that they are in (a place of) safety from the punishment. For them (there is) a painful punishment. **189** To God (belongs) the kingdom of the heavens and the earth. God is powerful over everything.

---

184. *(the situation) you are in*: i.e. of believers living mixed up with disbelievers.
185. *until He separates the bad from the good*: at the Judgment (cf. Q8.37).
186. *the unseen*: here referring to the future (see n. on Q2.3).
187. *chooses from His messengers whomever He pleases*: or 'chooses whomever He pleases to be among his messengers.'

181–189 Diatribe against the Jews

188. *God is poor and we are rich*: probably a derisive reference to the appeals to 'lend to God a good loan' (Q2.245; 3.12; 57.11; 64.17; 73.20).
189. *their killing the prophets without any right*: an indication that the Jews are being addressed (cf. Q3.21 above; see n. on Q2.61).
190. *what your (own) hands have sent forward*: i.e. their deeds, which are 'sent forward' to the Judgment.
191. *a sacrifice which fire devours*: an allusion to the story of the contest between the prophet Elijah and the prophets of Baal (1 Kings 18.17-46).
192. *the scriptures*: Ar. *al-zubur*; see Q16.44; 23.53; 26.196; 35.25; cf. Q54.43, 52 (where it seems to refer to the 'Book of Destiny').
193. *the illuminating Book*: it is not clear what this 'Book' refers to (the same sequence occurs at Q35.25; cf. Q22.8; 31.20).
194. *you*: plur.
195. *Do not think*: sing. imperative.

190 Surely in the creation of the heavens and earth, and (in) the alternation of the night and the day, (there are) signs indeed for those with understanding, **191** who remember God, whether standing or sitting or (lying) on their sides,[196] and reflect on the creation of the heavens and the earth: 'Our Lord, You have not created this in vain. Glory to You! Guard us against the punishment of the Fire. **192** Our Lord, surely You – whomever You cause to enter the Fire, You have disgraced him. The evildoers will have no helpers. **193** Our Lord, surely we have heard a caller calling (us) to belief (saying): "Believe in your Lord!" So we have believed. Our Lord, forgive us our sins, and absolve us of our evil deeds, and take us[197] with the pious. **194** Our Lord, give us what You have promised us on (the assurance of) Your messengers, and do not disgrace us on the Day of Resurrection. Surely You will not break the appointment.' **195** And their Lord responded to them: 'Surely I do not let a deed of anyone of you go to waste – whether male or female – you are all alike. Those who have emigrated,[198] and were expelled from their homes, and suffered harm in My way, and have fought and been killed – I shall indeed absolve them of their evil deeds, and I shall indeed cause them to enter Gardens through which rivers flow. A reward from God! God – with Him is the best reward.'

196 Do not let the disbelievers' comings and goings in the lands deceive you. **197** A little enjoyment (of life), then their refuge is Gehenna – it is an evil resting place! **198** But the ones who guard (themselves) against their Lord – for them (there are) Gardens through which rivers flow, there to remain. A reception from God! And what is with God is better for the pious.

199 Surely (there are) some of the People of the Book who indeed believe in God,[199] and what has been sent down to you, and what has been sent down to them, humbling themselves before God. They do not sell the signs of God for a small price. Those – for them their reward is with their Lord. Surely God is quick at the reckoning.

200 You who believe! Be patient and strive in patience, and be steadfast, and guard (yourselves) against God, so that you may prosper.

190–195 Believers' prayers answered

196. *standing or sitting or (lying) on their sides*: i.e. continually.

197. *take us*: in death.

198. *those who have emigrated*: from Mecca to Medina, though this is not explicitly stated in the Qur'ān.

196–198 Encouragement to the Prophet

199 Believers among the People of the Book

199. *some of the People of the Book...*: cf. Q3.113 above.

200 Final exhortation

4 Women ❁ Al-Nisā’

In the Name of God, the Merciful, the Compassionate

1 People! Guard (yourselves) against your Lord, who created you from one person,[1] and from him created his wife, and scattered[2] from the two of them many men and women. And guard (yourselves) against God, whom you ask each other questions about,[3] and (guard yourselves against) the wombs.[4] Surely God is watching over you.[5]

2 Give the orphans their property, and do not exchange the bad for the good,[6] and do not consume their property along with your own. Surely it is a great crime. **3** If you fear that you will not act fairly toward the orphan girls, marry what seems good to you of the women: two, or three, or four.[7] But if you fear that you will not be fair, (marry only) one, or what your right (hands) own.[8] That (will make it) more likely that you will not be biased.[9] **4** Give the women their dowries as a gift. If they remit to you any part of it on their own, consume it with satisfaction (and) pleasure. **5** Do not give the foolish your property which God has assigned to you[10] to maintain, but provide for them by means of it and clothe them, and speak to them rightful words. **6** Test the orphan girls until they reach (the age of) marriage. If you perceive right judgment in them, hand over their property to them. Do not consume it wantonly or hastily before they are grown up. Whoever is wealthy should refrain (from using it), and whoever is poor should use (it) rightfully. And when you do hand over their property to them, take witnesses over them. God is sufficient as a reckoner.

7 To the men (belongs) a portion of what parents and family leave, and to the women (belongs) a portion of what parents and family leave, (whether there is) a little of it or a lot, an obligatory portion. **8** When the family, the orphans, and the poor are present at the distribution (of the estate), provide for them from it, and speak to them rightful words. **9** Let those fear who, if they left behind them weak descendants, would fear for them. Let them guard (themselves) against God, and speak a direct word. **10** Surely those who consume the property of the orphans in an evil manner, they only consume fire in their bellies, and they will burn in a blazing (Fire).

Q4: This sūra takes its name from the many instructions regarding women, but it also offers guidance on a variety of other topics, including the treatment of orphans, marriage, property, inheritance, and fighting. The Prophet is put forward as God’s representative and the supreme arbiter of all disputes. There are also polemical passages against the ‘hypocrites’ and the ‘People of the Book,’ including the claim that Jesus was not crucified. Most scholars, traditional and modern, assign Q4 to the ‘Medinan’ period.

1 Introduction

1. *one person*: Adam.
2. *scattered*: as a sower scatters seed.
3. *whom you ask each other questions about*: meaning obscure; perhaps questioning God’s regulations.
4. *(guard yourselves against) the wombs*: meaning obscure; perhaps ‘respect family ties’ (cf. Q47.22).
5. *is watching over you*: lit. ‘has been a watcher over you’ (cf. Q5.117; 33.52).

2–6 Treatment of orphans and instructions on marriage

6. *do not exchange the bad for the good*: i.e. do not swindle or defraud them.
7. *two, or three, or four*: permission to have up to four wives is based on this verse.
8. *what your right (hands) own*: i.e. female slaves.
9. *biased*: meaning uncertain.
10. *assigned to you*: lit. ‘made for you.’

11 God charges you concerning your children: to the male, a share equal to two females. But if they be (only) women,[11] more than two, then to them two-thirds of what he leaves. But if there be (only) one, then to her a half. And to his parents, to each of them, a sixth of what he leaves, if he has children. But if he has no children, and his heirs are his parents, then to his mother a third. And if he has brothers, then to his mother the sixth, after any bequest he may have made or any debt (has been paid). Whether your fathers or your sons are of most benefit to you,[12] you do not know. (This is) an obligation from God. Surely God is knowing, wise.

12 And to you a half of what your wives leave, if they have no children. But if they have children, then to you the fourth of what they leave, after any bequest they may have made or any debt (has been paid). And to them the fourth of what you leave, if you have no children. But if you have children, then to them the eighth of what you leave, after any bequest you may have made or any debt (has been paid). If a man or a woman has no direct heir, but has a brother or a sister, then to each of them the sixth. But if they are more (numerous) than that, then they share in the third, after any bequest he may have made or any debt (has been paid), without prejudice (to anyone). (This is) a directive[13] from God. God is knowing, forbearing.

13 Those are the limits (set by) God. Whoever obeys God and His messenger[14] – He will cause him to enter Gardens[15] through which rivers flow, there to remain. That is the great triumph! **14** But whoever disobeys God and His messenger, and transgresses His limits – He will cause him to enter the Fire,[16] there to remain. For him (there is) a humiliating punishment.

15 (As for) those of your women who commit immorality,[17] call witnesses against them, four of you. If they bear witness (to the truth of the allegation), confine them in their houses until death takes them,[18] or God makes a way for (dealing with) them. **16** And (if) two of you commit it,[19] harm both of them. But if they turn (in repentance) and set (things) right, let them be. Surely God turns (in forgiveness), compassionate. **17** But God only turns (in forgiveness) to those who do evil in ignorance, (and) then turn (in repentance) soon after. Then God will turn to them (in forgiveness). God is knowing, wise. **18** But (His) turning (in forgiveness) is not for those who continue to do evil deeds, and only when death approaches say, 'Surely I turn (in repentance) now.' Nor (does He turn in forgiveness) to those who die while they are still disbelievers. Those – for them We have prepared a painful punishment.

19 You who believe! It is not permitted to you to inherit women against their will.[20] And do not prevent them,[21] so that you may take part of what you have given them, unless they commit clear immorality.

7–14 Laws of inheritance

11. *if they be (only) women*: i.e. if there are no male children.
12. *of most benefit to you*: or 'most entitled to benefit from you.'
13. *directive*: lit. 'bequest.'
14. *His messenger*: for this important title, see n. on Q2.87.
15. *Gardens*: in heaven (for this imagery, see n. on Q2.25).
16. *the Fire*: Ar. *al-nār* is the most common of the various designations for Hell.

15–28 Regulations concerning women and marriage

17. *immorality*: or 'indecency' (Ar. *fāḥisha*), of a sexual nature.
18. *confine them in their houses...*: cf. the punishment for adultery at Q24.2-3.
19. *it*: i.e. sexual immorality; traditionally taken to refer to two men, but it could also refer to illicit sex between a man and woman.
20. *to inherit women against their will*: usually taken to refer to the custom for a woman, on the death of her husband, to become the wife of his eldest son (by another woman, cf. Q4.22 below), or of some other close relative (cf. the instructions for 'levirate marriage' at Deuteronomy 25.5-10; Ruth 3.12; Mark 12.18-25).
21. *prevent them*: i.e. from divorce and remarriage.

Associate with them rightfully. If you dislike them, it may be that you dislike something in which God has placed much good. **20** And if you wish to exchange a wife for (another) wife,[22] and you have given one of them a qinṭār,[23] take (back) none of it. Would you take it (back by) slander and clear sin? **21** How can you take it (back), seeing that one of you has gone into the other, and they have taken a firm pledge from you?

22 Do not marry women whom your fathers have married, unless it is a thing of the past. Surely it is an immorality, an abhorrent thing, and an evil way. **23** Forbidden to you are:[24] your mothers, your daughters, your sisters, your paternal aunts, your maternal aunts, (your) brothers' daughters, (your) sisters' daughters, the mothers who have nursed you, (those who are) your sisters by nursing,[25] your wives' mothers, and your stepdaughters who are in your care, (born) of wives you have gone into – but if you have not gone into them, (there is) no blame on you – and wives of your sons, those of your own loins, and that you should have two sisters at the same time, unless it is a thing of the past. Surely God is forgiving, compassionate. **24** And (also forbidden to you are) married women, except what your right (hands) own.[26] (This is) a written decree[27] of God for you. (All women) beyond that are permitted to you to seek (to obtain) by means of your wealth, taking (them) in marriage, not in immorality. So (because of) what you enjoy from them in this way, give them their marriage gifts[28] as an obligation. (There is) no blame on you in anything you may give them by mutual agreement beyond this obligation. Surely God is knowing, wise.

25 Whoever among you cannot wait to marry believing, free women, (let them take) believing young women from what your right (hands) own. God knows your belief, (for) you are all alike. Marry them with the permission of their families, and give them their rightful marriage gifts, (as) married women, not (as) women who commit immorality or take secret lovers. But if they commit immorality after they are married, they will be liable to half the punishment (inflicted) on free women. That (provision) is for those of you who fear sin. Yet to be patient (would be) better for you. God is forgiving, compassionate. **26** God wishes to make (things) clear to you, and to guide you in the customary ways of those who were before you, and to turn toward you (in forgiveness). God is knowing, wise. **27** God wishes to turn toward you (in forgiveness), but those who follow (their) lusts wish you to swerve far away. **28** God wishes to lighten (your burdens) for you, (for) the human was created weak.

29 You who believe! Do not consume your property among yourselves by means of falsehood,[29] but (let there) be a transaction among you by mutual agreement. And do not kill one another.[30] Surely God is compassionate with you. **30** Whoever does that in enmity and evil – We shall burn him in a Fire. That is easy for God. **31** If you avoid the gross (sins) of what you are forbidden (to commit), We shall absolve you of your (other) evil deeds, and We shall cause you to enter (through) an entrance of honor.

32 Do not long for what God has bestowed in favor on some of you over others. To the men (belongs) a portion of what they have earned, and to the women (belongs) a portion of what they have earned.

---

22. *exchange a wife for (another) wife*: through divorce and remarriage.
23. *a qinṭār*: i.e. a large sum of money as a marriage gift (see Q3.14, 75).
24. *Forbidden to you are ...*: i.e. 'You are forbidden from marrying....'
25. *the mothers who have nursed you, (those who are) your sisters by nursing*: the so-called 'milk-relationship' creates a connection as close as blood-relationship.
26. *what your right (hands) own*: i.e. female slaves, even if married.
27. *a written decree*: lit. 'a book.'
28. *their marriage gifts*: lit. 'their rewards,' probably referring to the payment of a 'dower' for support in the event a wife should survive her husband.

29–31 Gambling and murder

29. *by means of falsehood*: perhaps through gambling or unscrupulous business practices.
30. *do not kill one another*: lit. 'do not kill yourselves.'

32–33 Do not covet

Ask God for some of His favor. Surely God has knowledge of everything. **33** To everyone We have appointed[31] heirs of what parents and family leave; and those with whom your right (hands) have made a pledge, give them their portion. Surely God is a witness over everything.

34 Men are supervisors of women because God has favored some of them over others, and because they have contributed from their wealth.[32] Righteous women are obedient,[33] watching over (affairs) in the absence (of their husbands)[34] because God has watched over (them). (As for) those women whom you fear may be rebellious: admonish them, avoid them in bed,[35] and (finally) strike them. If they obey you, do not seek (any further) way[36] against them. Surely God is most high, great. **35** If you fear a breach between the two,[37] send an arbiter from his family and an arbiter from her family. If they both wish to set (things) right, God will effect a reconciliation between the two. Surely God is knowing, aware.

36 Serve[38] God, and do not associate anything with Him, and (do) good to parents and to family, and the orphans and the poor, and the neighbor who is related and the neighbor who is a stranger, and the companion at your side, and the traveler,[39] and what your right (hands) own.

Surely God does not love anyone who is arrogant (and) boastful, **37** (nor) those who are stingy, and (who) command the people to be stingy, and conceal what God has given them of his favor. We have prepared for the disbelievers a humiliating punishment. **38** (Nor does God love) those who contribute their wealth to show off (before) the people, and who do not believe in God and the Last Day. Whoever has Satan[40] for his comrade – he is an evil comrade! **39** What (harm would it do) them if they believed in God and the Last Day, and contributed from what God has provided them? But God knows about them. **40** Surely God does not do (even) a speck's weight of evil. If it is a good (deed), He doubles it, and gives from Himself a great reward. **41** How (will it be) when We bring from each community a witness, and bring you[41] as a witness against them (all)? **42** On that Day those who have disbelieved and disobeyed the messenger will wish that the earth were leveled with them.[42] But they will not (be able to) conceal (any) account[43] from God.

43 You who believe! Do not go near the prayer[44] when you are drunk, until you know what you are saying,[45]

---

31. *appointed*: lit. 'made.'

34–35 Men's responsibilities for women

32. *they have contributed from their wealth*: probably referring to material support in general.
33. *obedient*: for this idea, cf. Genesis 3.6; 1 Timothy 2.11.
34. *watching over (affairs) in the absence (of their husbands)*: meaning obscure (lit. 'watching over the unseen').
35. *avoid them...*: or 'flee from them...;' i.e. have no sexual relations with them (from the same root as Hijra).
36. *(any further) way*: of punishment.
37. *the two*: husband and wife.

36a Serve God

38. *Serve*: or 'Worship' (plur. imperative).
39. *traveler*: lit. 'son of the way.'

36b–42 Warning about withholding contributions

40. *Satan*: for this figure, see n. on Q2.36.
41. *you*: the Prophet.
42. *leveled with them*: or 'made equal with them,' i.e. taken in ransom for them.
43. *account*: or 'report' (Ar. *ḥadīth*).

43 Preparation for prayer

44. *the prayer*: the ritual prayer (or *ṣalāt*).
45. *until you know what you are saying*: such a proviso presumes that the consumption of alcohol is permitted.

or (when you are) defiled,[46] unless (you are) travelers (on the) way, until you wash yourselves. If you are sick or on a journey, or if one of you has come from the toilet, or if you have touched women, and you do not find any water, take clean soil and wipe your faces and your hands. Surely God is pardoning, forgiving.

44 Do you[47] not see those who have been given a portion of the Book?[48] They purchase error[49] and wish that you[50] would go astray from the way. **45** God knows about your enemies. God is sufficient as an ally, and God is sufficient as a helper. **46** Some of those who are Jews[51] alter words from their positions,[52] and they say, 'We hear and disobey,' and 'Hear, and do not hear,' and 'Observe us,' twisting with their tongues[53] and vilifying the religion. If they had said, 'We hear and obey,' and 'Hear,' and 'Regard us,' it would indeed have been better for them, and more just. But God has cursed them for their disbelief, and so they do not believe, except for a few.[54]

47 You who have been given the Book! Believe in what We have sent down, confirming what is with you,[55] before We obliterate faces, and turn them on their backs, or curse them as We cursed the men of the sabbath,[56] and God's command is done.[57] **48** Surely God does not forgive (anything) being associated with Him, but He forgives what is other than that for whomever He pleases. Whoever associates (anything) with God has forged a great sin. **49** Do you not see those who claim purity for themselves? No! (It is) God (who) purifies whomever He pleases – and they will not be done evil in the slightest.[58] **50** See how they forge lies against God. That suffices as a clear sin.

51 Do you not see those who have been given a portion of the Book? They believe in al-Jibt and al-Ṭāghūt,[59] and they say to those who disbelieve, 'These are better guided (as to the) way than those who believe.' **52** Those are the ones whom God has cursed, and whomever God has cursed – for him you will not find any helper. **53** Or do they have a portion of the kingdom?[60] If that were so, they do not give the people the slightest thing.[61] **54** Or are they jealous of the people for what God has given them

---

46. *defiled*: i.e. in a state of ritual impurity.

44–57 Diatribe against the People of the Book

47. *you*: the Prophet, or perhaps intended generally (throughout this section).
48. *those who have been given a portion of the Book*: here referring to the Jews. This differs from the expressions 'those who have been given the Book' (Q2.101, 144, 145; 3.19, 20; 4.131 etc.) and 'those to whom We have given the Book' (Q2.121; 6.20, 114; 13.36 etc.). The reference to 'a portion (Ar. *naṣīb*) of the Book' (cf. Q3.23; 4.51 below) may imply that no Book (Torah, Gospel, or Qur'ān) represents the heavenly archetype (or 'mother of the Book') in its entirety; each is in some sense partial (cf. Q2.285; 4.136; 5.44; 46.12; 98.3).
49. *error*: lit. 'straying' (cf. Q2.16, 175, 'They have purchased error with the [price of] guidance').
50. *you*: plur.
51. *those who are Jews*: lit. 'those who have judaized,' or follow Jewish law, punning on the name Yahūd.
52. *alter words from their positions*: or 'change the meanings of words' (cf. Q2.75; 5.13, 41); some examples are given in the following lines.
53. *twisting with their tongues*: i.e. playing with words in order to distort their meanings (cf. Q2.93, 104).
54. *except for a few*: or 'except a little' (cf. Q2.88).
55. *confirming what is with you*: the Qur'ān 'confirms' the Torah.
56. *men of the sabbath*: for the story, see Q7.163-167 (cf. Q2.65-66; 5.60; 23.108).
57. *God's command is done*: here referring to judgment (cf. Q2.109; 5.52; 7.150; 10.24; 16.1, 33).
58. *in the slightest*: lit. 'a fiber on a date seed.'
59. *al-Jibt and al-Ṭāghūt*: possibly '(other) gods and idols' (al-Jibt occurs only here; for al-Ṭāghūt, see n. on Q2.256; cf. Q4.60, 76 below). Notice the charge of idolatry here laid against the 'People of the Book' (see also Q9.30-33; 30.30-33; 42.13-14; and cf. the idolatrous episode of 'the calf' at Q7.148-153; 20.83-98).
60. *do they have a portion of the kingdom*: since the Jews had no political power at this time, this may refer to their claim to have a share in God's kingdom.
61. *the slightest thing*: lit. 'a speck of a date seed.'

of His favor? Yet We gave the house of Abraham[62] the Book and the wisdom,[63] and We gave them a great kingdom. **55** (There are) some of them who believe in it, and some of them who keep (people) from it.[64] Gehenna[65] is sufficient as a blazing (Fire). **56** Surely those who disbelieve in Our signs[66] – We shall burn them in a Fire. Whenever their skins are completely burned, We shall exchange their skins for others, so that they may (continue to) feel the punishment. Surely God is mighty, wise. **57** But those who believe and do righteous deeds – We shall cause them to enter Gardens through which rivers flow, there to remain forever. There they will have pure spouses, and We shall cause them to enter sheltering shade.

58 Surely God commands you[67] to pay back deposits to their (rightful) owners, and when you judge between the people, to judge with justice. Surely God gives you admonition which is excellent. Surely God is hearing, seeing.

59 You who believe! Obey God, and obey the messenger and those (who have) the command among you. If you argue about anything, refer it to God and the messenger, if you believe in God and the Last Day. That is better and fairer in interpretation. **60** Do you[68] not see those who claim that they believe in what has been sent down to you, and what was sent down before you? They wish to go (with their disputes) to al-Ṭāghūt[69] for judgment. Yet they have been commanded to disbelieve in him. Satan wishes to lead them very far astray.[70] **61** When it is said to them, 'Come to what God has sent down,[71] and to the messenger,' you see the hypocrites keeping (people) from you.[72] **62** How (will it be) when a smiting smites them for what their (own) hands have sent forward?[73] Then they will come to you swearing, 'By God! We wanted nothing but good and reconciliation.' **63** Those are the ones who – God knows what is in their hearts.[74] So turn away from them, and admonish them, and speak to them effective words about themselves.

64 We have not sent any messenger, except that he should be obeyed, by the permission of God. If, when they did themselves evil, they had come to you and asked forgiveness from God, and the messenger had asked forgiveness for them, they would indeed have found God turning (in forgiveness), compassionate. **65** But no! By your Lord![75] They will not believe until they make you[76] judge concerning their disputes. Then they would have no difficulty with what you decided, and would submit (in full) submission.

---

62. *house of Abraham*: here probably referring to Israel.
63. *the Book and the wisdom*: probably a reference to the Torah; but see Q53.36-37; 87.18-19, for the 'scrolls of Abraham.'
64. *in it...from it*: antecedent unclear; 'it' could refer to 'the Book' (i.e. the Torah) or more likely the Qur'ān (i.e. 'what We have sent down,' Q4.47 above).
65. *Gehenna*: a name for Hell (see n. on Q2.206).
66. *signs*: or 'verses.'

58 Return of deposits

67. *you*: plur.

59–70 Disputes referred to the Prophet

68. *you*: the Prophet, or perhaps intended generally.
69. *al-Ṭāghūt*: here perhaps another name for Satan (cf. Q4.76 below).
70. *lead them very far astray*: lit. 'lead them astray (with) a far straying.'
71. *what God has sent down*: the Qur'ān.
72. *you*: the Prophet.
73. *what their (own) hands have sent forward*: i.e. their deeds, which are 'sent forward' to the Judgment.
74. *hearts*: here, as often, the heart is spoken of as synonymous with mind.
75. *By your Lord*: for God's unusual 'swearing by himself,' cf. Q15.92; 16.56, 63; 19.68; 70.40; and Hebrews 6.13 (Genesis 22.16); but perhaps it is the angels who are speaking here.
76. *you*: the Prophet.

66 If We had prescribed[77] for them: 'Kill one another'[78] or 'Go forth from your homes,' they would not have done it, except for a few of them. Yet if they had done what they were admonished (to do), it would indeed have been better for them, and a firmer foundation (for them). **67** And then We would indeed have given them a great reward from Us, **68** and indeed guided them to a straight path. **69** Whoever obeys God and the messenger are with those whom God has blessed: the prophets, and the truthful, and the martyrs, and the righteous. Those are good companions! **70** That is the favor of God. God is sufficient as a knower.

71 You who believe! Take your precautions.[79] Go forth in detachments or go forth all together. **72** Surely among you (there is) the one indeed who lags behind, and if a smiting smites you, he says, 'God has blessed me because I was not a martyr with them.' **73** But if indeed some favor from God smites you, he will indeed say – as if there had not been any friendship between you and him – 'Would that I had been with them and attained a great triumph!' **74** So let those who sell this present life for (the price of) the Hereafter[80] fight in the way of God. Whoever fights in the way of God – whether he is killed or conquers – We shall give him a great reward. **75** What is with you (that) you do you not fight in the way of God, and (on behalf of) the weak among the men, women, and children, who say, 'Our Lord, bring us out of this town of the evildoers,[81] and make for us an ally from Yourself, and make for us a helper from Yourself'? **76** Those who believe fight in the way of God, and those who disbelieve fight in the way of al-Ṭāghūt. So fight the allies[82] of Satan![83] Surely the plot of Satan is weak.

77 Do you[84] not see those to whom it was said, 'Restrain your hands,[85] and observe the prayer and give the alms'?[86] Then, when fighting is prescribed for them, suddenly (there is) a group of them who fear the people as (much as) they fear God, or even more. And they say, 'Our Lord, why have you prescribed fighting for us? Why not spare us for a time near (at hand)?'[87] Say:[88] 'The enjoyment of this world is a small thing, but the Hereafter is better for the one who guards (himself).[89] You will not be done evil in the slightest.'[90] **78** Wherever you are, death will overtake you, even though you are in well-built towers. And if some good smites them, they say, 'This is from God,' but if some evil smites them, they say, 'This is from you.'[91] Say: 'Everything is from God.' What is (the matter) with these people? They hardly understand any report.[92]

---

77. *prescribed*: lit. 'written.'
78. *Kill one another*: lit. 'Kill yourselves;' cf. Q2.54, the punishment of the Israelites after their worship of 'the calf.'

71–78 Fighting for the cause of God

79. *Take your precautions*: or possibly 'Make your preparations' (for battle).
80. *the Hereafter*: see n. on Q2.4.
81. *town of the evildoers*: said to refer to Mecca.
82. *allies*: Ar. *awliyā'* implies the obligation of mutual protection, almost in the sense of 'friends' or 'brothers.'
83. *Satan*: implying that 'al-Ṭāghūt' is merely another name for Satan (cf. Q4.60 above).
84. *you*: the Prophet.
85. *Restrain your hands*: from violence or fighting.
86. *observe the prayer and give the alms*: i.e. *ṣalāt*, the ritual prayer, and *zakāt*, a kind of tithe required for the benefit of the poor, as well as other purposes.
87. *for a time near (at hand)*: i.e. until death comes in its natural course.
88. *Say*: on this form of address, see n. on Q2.80.
89. *guards (himself)*: against evil, or God.
90. *in the slightest*: lit. 'a fiber on a date seed.'
91. *you*: the Prophet.
92. *report*: or 'account' (Ar. *ḥadīth*).

79 Whatever good smites you[93] is from God, and whatever evil smites you is from yourself. We have sent you[94] as a messenger to the people. God is sufficient as a witness. **80** Whoever obeys the messenger has obeyed God, but whoever turns away – We have not sent you as a watcher[95] over them. **81** They say, '(We pledge) obedience (to you).' But when they go forth from your presence, a contingent of them plans by night (to do) other than what you say. God is writing down what they plan. So turn away from them and put your trust in God. God is sufficient as a guardian.

82 Do they not contemplate the Qur'ān?[96] If it were from any other than God, they would indeed have found in it much contradiction.

83 When any matter comes to them concerning security or fear, they divulge it.[97] But if they were to refer it to the messenger and to those (who have) the command among them, those who investigate (such things) would indeed have known (about) it. If (it were) not (for the) favor of God on you,[98] and His mercy, you would indeed have followed Satan, except for a few (of you).

84 Fight in the way of God![99] You are only responsible[100] for yourself, but urge on the believers. It may be that God will restrain the violence of those who disbelieve. God is harsher in violence, and harsher in punishing.

85 Whoever intercedes with a good intercession will have a portion of it for himself, but whoever intercedes with an evil intercession will have a portion of it for himself. God is powerful over everything.

86 When you receive a greeting, reply with a better greeting, or return it.[101] Surely God is a reckoner of everything.

87 God – (there is) no god but Him. He will indeed gather you to the Day of Resurrection – (there is) no doubt about it. Who is more truthful than God in report?[102]

88 What is (the matter) with you? (Are there) two cohorts (of you) concerning the hypocrites, when God has overthrown them for what they have earned?[103] Do you wish to guide the one whom God has led astray? Whomever God has led astray – you[104] will not find a way for him. **89** They want you[105] to disbelieve as they have disbelieved, and then you would be alike. Do not take any allies[106] from them, until they emigrate in the way of God. If they turn back, seize them and kill them wherever you find

---

79–84 Encouragement to the Prophet

93. *you*: the Prophet.
94. *you*: the Prophet.
95. *watcher*: or 'overseer,' 'keeper.'
96. *the Qur'ān*: here 'the Qur'ān' comes close to its present meaning as the name of the Muslim scripture (cf. Q9.111; see n. on Q2.185).
97. *they divulge it*: perhaps betraying secrets to the enemy, or just spreading rumors.
98. *you*: plur.
99. *Fight in the way of God*: addressed to the Prophet, as is the following sentence.
100. *responsible*: lit. 'burdened.

85 Intercession

86 Returning greetings

101. *...a better greeting, or return it*: see Q4.94 below.

87 Resurrection certain

102. *report*: or 'account' (Ar. *ḥadīth*).

88–91 Treatment of hypocrites

103. *for what they have earned*: i.e. for the sins they have committed.
104. *you*: or 'one.'
105. *you*: plur.
106. *allies*: Ar. *awliyā'* implies the obligation of mutual protection, almost in the sense of 'friends' or 'brothers.'

them. Do not take any ally or helper from them, **90** except those who join a people with whom you have a treaty, or who come to you with their hearts[107] restrained from fighting you or fighting their own people. If God had (so) pleased, He would indeed have given them power over you, and they would indeed have fought you. If they withdraw from you, and do not fight you but offer you peace,[108] God has not made a way for you against them. **91** You will find others wishing that they were safe from you, and safe from their (own) people. Whenever they are returned to temptation, they are overwhelmed by it. If they do not withdraw from you alone, and offer you peace, and restrain their hands, seize them and kill them wherever you come upon them. Those (people) – We give you clear authority against them.

92 It is not for a believer to kill a believer, except by mistake. Whoever kills a believer by mistake, (the penalty is) the setting free of a believing slave, and compensation (is to be) paid to his family,[109] unless they remit (it as) a freewill offering.[110] If he[111] is from a people (who are) an enemy to you, and he is a believer, (the penalty is) the setting free of a believing slave. If he is from a people with whom you have a treaty, compensation (is to be) paid to his family and the setting free of a believing slave. Whoever does not find (the means to do that), (the penalty is) a fast for two months consecutively – a repentance (prescribed) by God. God is knowing, wise. **93** Whoever kills a believer intentionally, his payment is Gehenna – there to remain. God will be angry with him, and curse him, and prepare a great punishment for him.

94 You who believe! When you strike forth in the way of God,[112] be discerning, and do not say to the one who offers you peace,[113] 'You are not a believer,' seeking (the fleeting) goods of this present life. For (there are) many spoils with God. You (too) were like that before, but God bestowed favor on you. So be discerning. Surely God is aware of what you do.

95 Those of the believers who sit (at home) – other than the injured – are not equal with the ones who struggle[114] in the way of God with their wealth and their lives. God favors in rank the ones who struggle with their wealth and their lives over the ones who sit (at home). To each God has promised the good (reward),[115] but God favors (with) a great reward the ones who struggle over the ones who sit (at home):
96 (higher) ranks from Him, and forgiveness and mercy. Surely God is forgiving, compassionate.

97 Surely those who – (when) the angels take them[116] (while they are doing) themselves evil – they[117] will say, 'What (condition) were you in?' They[118] will say, 'We were weak on the earth.'[119] They[120] will say,

---

107. *hearts*: lit. 'chests,' considered the seat of knowledge and understanding.

108. *offer you peace*: lit. 'cast before you the peace' (Ar. *al-salām*, a distinctive Muslim greeting), with the implication of submission (*islām*) to God.

92–93 Believers not to kill believers

109. *his family*: i.e. the family of the believer who was killed.

110. *freewill offering*: or 'voluntary contribution' (Ar. *ṣadaqa*) to benefit the community (cf. Q9.60).

111. *he*: i.e. the victim.

94 Believers not to seek spoils aggressively

112. *strike forth in the way of God*: i.e. on campaign.

113. *offers you peace*: see n. on Q4.90 above.

95–96 Fighting and staying behind

114. *the ones who struggle*: or 'the ones who fight' (Ar. *al-mujāhidūn*).

115. *the good (reward)*: the future life.

97–100 Emigrating

116. *take them*: in death (cf. Q6.61; for the angels and their various roles, see n. on Q2.30).

117. *they*: the angels.

118. *They*: those the angels take away.

119. *We were weak on the earth*: cf. Q4.75 above.

120. *They*: the angels.

'Was God's earth not wide (enough),[121] so that you might have emigrated in it?' And those – their refuge is Gehenna – and it is an evil destination! – **98** except for the (truly) weak among the men, women, and hildren, (who) were not able (to devise) a plan and were not guided to a way (of escape). **99** Those – God may pardon them, (for) God is pardoning, forgiving. **100** Whoever emigrates in the way of God will find on the earth many places of refuge and abundance (of provisions). And whoever goes forth from his house, emigrating to God and His messenger, (and) then death overtakes him – his reward falls on God (to pay). Surely God is forgiving, compassionate.

101 When you strike forth on the earth, (there is) no blame on you to shorten the prayer,[122] if you fear that those who disbelieve may attack you. Surely the disbelievers are your clear enemies. **102** When you[123] are among them, and establish the prayer for them, let a contingent of them stand with you, and let them take their weapons. When they have prostrated themselves, let them be behind you, and let another contingent (which has) not prayed come (forward) and pray with you. Let them take their precautions and their weapons. Those who disbelieve want you to be oblivious of your weapons and your baggage. Then they would launch an attack on you (all at) once. (There is) no blame on you if you lay down your weapons because of the harmful effect of rain on you or (because) you are sick. But take your precautions. Surely God has prepared for the disbelievers a humiliating punishment. **103** When you[124] have finished the prayer, remember God, whether standing or sitting or (lying) on your sides.[125] Then, when you are secure, observe the prayer. Surely the prayer is a written decree[126] for the believers at appointed times.[127] **104** But do not grow weak in seeking out the enemy. If you are suffering, surely they (too) are suffering as you are suffering, while what you hope for from God they do not hope for. God is knowing, wise.

105 Surely We have sent down to you the Book with the truth,[128] so that you may judge between the people by what God has shown you.[129] Do not be an advocate on behalf of the treacherous. **106** Ask forgiveness from God. Surely God is forgiving, compassionate. **107** Do not dispute on behalf of those who betray themselves. Surely God does not love anyone who is a traitor (or) sinner. **108** They hide themselves from the people, but they do not hide themselves from God. For He is with them when they plan by night (with) the words He finds displeasing. God encompasses what they do. **109** There you are! Those who have disputed on their behalf in this present life, but who will dispute with God on their behalf on the Day of Resurrection? Or who will be a guardian over them? **110** Whoever does evil or does himself evil, (and) then asks forgiveness from God, he will find God is forgiving, compassionate. **111** Whoever earns sin,[130] only earns it against himself. God is knowing, wise. **112** Whoever earns a mistake or sin, (and) then hurls it against an innocent person,[131] will bear (the burden of) slander and clear sin.

121. *Was God's earth not wide (enough)*: for this idea, cf. Q29.56; 39.10.

101–104 Prayer in times of danger

122. *the prayer*: the ritual prayer (or *ṣalāt*).

123. *you*: the Prophet.

124. *you*: plur.

125. *standing or sitting or (lying) on your sides*: i.e. continually.

126. *a written decree*: lit. 'a book.'

127. *appointed times*: these times are not precisely specified in the Qur'ān, but see Q11.114; 17.78; 20.130; 30.17; 50.39; 62.9.

105–115 No leniency for traitors

128. *with the truth*: or 'in truth,' 'truly.'

129. *so that you may judge...*: i.e. the Prophet is to use the Qur'ān as the basis for judgment.

130. *earns sin*: i.e. commits a sin.

131. *hurls it against an innocent person*: i.e. falsely accuses someone.

113 If (it were) not (for the) favor of God on you,[132] and His mercy, a contingent of them was indeed determined to lead you astray. But they only lead themselves astray; they will not harm you at all. God has sent down on you the Book and the wisdom, and He has taught you what you did not know. The favor of God on you is great. **114** (There is) no good in much of their secret talk, except for the one who commands voluntary giving, or what is right, or setting (things) right among the people. Whoever does that, seeking the approval of God – We shall give him a great reward. **115** But whoever breaks with the messenger after the guidance[133] has become clear to him, and follows a way other (than that) of the believers – We shall turn him (over) to what he has turned to, and burn him in Gehenna – and it is an evil destination!

116 Surely God does not forgive (anything) being associated with Him, but He forgives what is other than that for whomever He pleases. Whoever associates (anything) with God has gone very far astray. **117** They only call on females[134] instead of Him. They only call on a rebellious Satan.[135] **118** God cursed him, and he[136] said, 'I shall indeed take an obligatory portion of Your servants, **119** and I shall indeed lead them astray and fill them with longings, and I shall indeed command them and they will cut off the ears of the cattle.[137] I shall indeed command them and they will alter the creation of God.' Whoever takes Satan as an ally, instead of God, has lost utterly (and) clearly.[138] **120** He makes promises to them and fills them with longings. Yet Satan does not promise them (anything) but deception. **121** Those – their refuge is Gehenna, and they will not find any place of escape from it. **122** But those who have believed and done righteous deeds, We shall cause them to enter Gardens through which rivers flow, there to remain forever – the promise of God in truth! Who is more truthful than God in speaking?

123 (This) is not[139] (in accord) with your[140] wishful thinking, nor (in accord with the) wishful thinking of the People of the Book. Whoever does evil will be repaid with it, and he will not find for himself any ally or helper other than God. **124** But whoever does righteous deeds – whether male or female – and he is a believer, those will enter the Garden – and they will not be done evil in the slightest.

125 Who is better in religion than one who submits his face to God, and is a doer of good, and follows the creed of Abraham the Ḥanīf?[141] God took Abraham as a friend.[142] **126** To God (belongs) whatever is in the heavens and whatever is on the earth. God encompasses everything.

127 They ask you for a pronouncement about women.[143] Say: 'God makes a pronouncement to you about

---

132. *you*: the Prophet.

133. *the guidance*: one of the most frequent terms (Ar. *al-hudā*) for revelation in general, and the Qur'ān in particular.

116–122 Idolatry and true religion

134. *females*: the so-called 'daughters of God' (Q16.57; cf. Q53.19-21); elsewhere identified as angels (Q17.40; 37.150; 43.19-20; 53.26-27).

135. *a rebellious Satan*: the claim is that they actually worship Satan, instead of the 'female gods' they claim.

136. *he*: Satan.

137. *cut off the ears of the cattle*: apparently a 'pagan' practice (cf. Q5.103).

138. *has lost utterly (and) clearly*: lit. 'has lost a clear loss.'

123–124 Evil punished, righteousness rewarded

139. *(This) is not...*: the meaning of this sentence is obscure.

140. *your*: sing.

125–126 The religion of Abraham

141. *Abraham the Ḥanīf*: or perhaps 'Abraham the Gentile' (see n. on Q2.135).

142. *as a friend*: Ar. *khalīl*; for this idea, cf. Isaiah 41.8; 2 Chronicles 20.7; James 2.23.

127–130 Instructions concerning women

143. *They ask you...*: the Prophet; cf. what has already been said at Q4.15-28, 34-42 above.

them, and what is recited[144] to you in the Book (gives instruction) about female orphans to whom you do not give what is prescribed for them, though you wish to marry them, and (about) the weak among the children, and that you secure justice for the orphans. Whatever good you do, surely God knows about it.'

128 If a woman fears mistreatment from her husband, or desertion, (there is) no blame on the two of them if they set (things) right between themselves. Setting (things) right is better, but people are prone to greed. If you do good and guard (yourselves) – surely God is aware of what you do.

129 You[145] will not be able to act fairly among the women,[146] even though you are eager (to do so). But do not turn completely away (from one of them) so that you leave her, as it were, in suspense. If you set (things) right and guard (yourselves) – surely God is forgiving, compassionate. **130** But if the two of them separate, God will enrich each (of them) from His abundance. God is embracing, wise.

131 To God (belongs) whatever is in the heavens and whatever is on the earth. Certainly We have charged those who were given the Book before you, and you (as well), 'Guard (yourselves) against God!' But if you disbelieve – surely to God (belongs) whatever is in the heavens and whatever is on the earth. God is wealthy, praiseworthy.

132 To God (belongs) whatever is in the heavens and whatever is on the earth. God is sufficient as a guardian. **133** If He (so) pleases, He will do away with you, people, and bring others (in your place). God is powerful over that.

134 Whoever desires the reward of this world – with God is the reward of this world and the Hereafter. God is hearing, seeing.

135 You who believe! Be supervisors in justice, witnesses for God, even if it is against yourselves or your parents and family. Whether he be rich or poor, God (stands) closer to both of them.[147] Do not follow (your vain) desire or you will (not) act fairly. If you turn aside or turn away – surely God is aware of what you do.

136 You who believe! Believe in God and His messenger, and the Book He has sent down on His messenger, and the Book which He sent down before (this).[148] Whoever disbelieves in God and His angels, and His Books and His messengers, and the Last Day, has gone very far astray. **137** Surely those who have believed, then disbelieved, then believed (again), then disbelieved (again), (and) then increased in disbelief – God will not forgive them or guide them (to the) way.

138 Give the hypocrites the news[149] that for them (there is) a painful punishment **139** – those who take the disbelievers as allies[150] instead of the believers. Do they seek honor with them? Surely honor (belongs) to God altogether. **140** He has already sent down on you[151] in the Book: 'When you hear[152] the signs[153] of God being disbelieved and mocked, do not sit with them until they banter about some other topic.[154] Otherwise you will surely be like them.' Surely God is going to gather the hypocrites and the disbelievers into Gehenna

144. *recited*: or 'read aloud.'

145. *You*: plur.

146. *the women*: i.e. your wives.

131–137 Consequences of belief and disbelief

147. *God (stands) closer to both of them*: meaning obscure.

148. *the Book which He sent down before (this)*: the Torah.

138–152 Diatribe against the hypocrites and disbelievers

149. *Give the hypocrites the news*: lit. 'the good news,' perhaps meant sarcastically (see n. on Q2.119).

150. *allies*: Ar. *awliyā'* implies the obligation of mutual protection, almost in the sense of 'friends' or 'brothers.'

151. *you*: plur.

152. *When you hear …*: apparently referring to Q6.68.

153. *signs*: or 'verses.'

154. *topic*: Ar. *ḥadīth*.

– all (of them). **141** (The hypocrites are) those who wait (to see what happens) with you.[155] If a victory[156] comes to you from God, they say, 'Were we not with you?' But if a portion (of good fortune) falls to the disbelievers, they say, 'Did we not prevail over you, and protect you from the believers?'[157] God will judge between you on the Day of Resurrection. God will not make a way for the disbelievers over the believers.

142 The hypocrites (try to) deceive God, but He deceives them. When they stand up for the prayer, they stand up in a lazy fashion, showing off (before) the people, but they do not remember God, except a little, **143** wavering between (this and) that, (belonging) neither to these nor to those. Whomever God leads astray – you[158] will not find a way for him.

144 You who believe! Do not take disbelievers as allies instead of the believers. Do you wish to give God clear authority against you?

145 Surely the hypocrites will be in the lowest level of the Fire, and you[159] will not find for them any helper, **146** except those who turn (in repentance), and set (things) right, and hold fast to God, and devote their religion to God.[160] Those are with the believers, and God will give the believers a great reward. **147** Why would God punish you, if you are thankful and believe? God is thankful, knowing.

148 God does not love the public utterance of evil words, except (by one) who has suffered evil. God is hearing, knowing. **149** If you do good openly or you hide it, or you pardon an evil – surely God is pardoning, powerful.

150 Surely those who disbelieve in God and His messengers, and wish to make a distinction[161] between God and His messengers, and say, 'We believe in part, but disbelieve in part,' and wish to take a way between (this and) that, **151** those – they in truth are the disbelievers. And We have prepared for the disbelievers a humiliating punishment. **152** But those who believe in God and His messengers, and make no distinction between any of them, those – He will give them their rewards. God is forgiving, compassionate.

153 The People of the Book[162] ask you to bring down on them a Book from the sky.[163] They had already asked Moses for (something) greater than that, for they said, 'Show us God openly!'[164] So the thunderbolt took them for their evildoing. Then they took the calf,[165] after the clear signs[166] had come to them. But We pardoned them for that, and We gave Moses clear authority. **154** And We raised the mountain above them,[167] with their covenant, and We said to them, 'Enter the gate in prostration.'[168] And We said

155. *you*: plur.
156. *victory*: lit. 'opening.'
157. *Did we not prevail...and protect you from the believers*: addressed by the hypocrites to the disbelievers, claiming that without their help the disbelievers could not have defended themselves against the believers.
158. *you*: or 'one.'
159. *you*: or 'one.'
160. *devote their religion to God*: i.e. serve God alone to the exclusion of all others.
161. *distinction*: or 'division;' since all messengers brought in essence the same message, all should be believed without distinction (see e.g. Q2.135-136; 3.84-85 etc.). Jews and Christians who refused to recognize the Prophet are thus 'disbelievers.'

153–162 Diatribe against the People of the Book

162. *People of the Book*: here referring to the Jews.
163. *from the sky*: or 'from heaven;' i.e. the Jews demand that the Prophet bring them something comparable to what Moses brought down from Mount Sinai.
164. *Show us God openly*: see Q.2.55; cf. Exodus 19.21.
165. *took the calf*: i.e. as a god; see Q7.148-153; 20.83-98 (cf. the story of the 'golden calf' at Exodus 32.1-35).
166. *the clear signs*: or 'the clear proofs,' 'the indisputable evidence.'
167. *raised the mountain above them*: Mount Sinai; see n. on Q2.63 (cf. the description of the theophany at Sinai at Exodus 19.16-20).
168. *Enter the gate...*: see Q2.58; 7.161.

to them, 'Do not transgress the sabbath.' And We made a firm covenant with them. **155** So for their breaking their covenant, and their disbelief in the signs of God, and their killing the prophets without any right,[169] and their saying, 'Our hearts are covered'[170] – No! God set a seal on them for their disbelief, so they do not believe,[171] except for a few – **156** and for their disbelief, and their saying against Mary a great slander,[172] **157** and for their saying, 'Surely we killed the Messiah,[173] Jesus, son of Mary,[174] the messenger of God' – yet they did not kill him, nor did they crucify him,[175] but it (only) seemed like (that) to them.[176] Surely those who differ about him[177] are indeed in doubt about him.[178] They have no knowledge about him,[179] only the following of conjecture.[180] Certainly they did not kill him. **158** No! God raised him to Himself.[181] God is mighty, wise.

159 (There is) not one of the People of the Book who will indeed believe in him before his death, and on the Day of Resurrection he will be a witness against them.[182] **160** So for the evildoing of those who are Jews,[183] We have made (certain) good things forbidden to them which were permitted to them (before),[184] and (also) for their keeping many (people) from the way of God. **161** And (for) their taking usury, when they were forbidden (to take) it, and (for) their consuming the wealth of the people by means of falsehood, We have prepared for the disbelievers among them a painful punishment. **162** But the ones who are firm in knowledge among them – and the believers – believe in what has been sent down to

---

169. *killing the prophets without any right*: for this idea, see n. on Q2.61.
170. *covered*: or 'uncircumcised;' i.e. unable to receive the message or understand it; also a biblical metaphor (cf. Leviticus 26.41; Deuteronomy 10.16; 30.6; Jeremiah 4.4; 9.26; Ezekiel 44.7, 9; Acts 7.51; Romans 2.28-29).
171. *so they do not believe*: or 'cannot believe' (cf. Q2.6-7; and the similar idea at Isaiah 6.9-10; Mark 4.11-12).
172. *slander*: i.e. an accusation of fornication, and thus implying that Jesus was 'illegitimate,' rather than having been born miraculously (see Q19.16-36).
173. *the Messiah*: the Qur'ān uses this title (Ar. *al-Masīḥ*) almost as a proper name, without any discussion of the ideas associated with it.
174. *son of Mary*: there is no mention in the Qur'ān of Joseph, Jesus' putative father (cf. Mark 6.3).
175. *did not kill him, nor...crucify him*: a clear denial of Jesus' death, and surprising in light of the Qur'ān's repeated accusation that the People of the Book typically 'killed the prophets' (but there are conflicting reports about the fate of Jesus in the Qur'ān, cf. Q3.55; 5.117; and what Jesus says of himself at Q19.33).
176. *it (only) seemed like (that) to them*: the Ar. phrase *shubbiha lahum* is ambiguous, and could mean that the Jews only supposed they had killed Jesus, but God raised him, or that 'a likeness (of him) was made to appear to them,' and was crucified in his place. Even in the latter case the Qur'ān's claim that Jesus did not die is in accord with certain early Christian accounts. According to Basilides, a 2nd-century CE Syrian Christian: '[Jesus] did not suffer, but a certain Simon of Cyrene was compelled to carry his cross for him, and this [Simon] was transformed by him [Jesus], so that he was thought to be Jesus himself, and was crucified through ignorance and error. Jesus, however, took on the form of Simon, and stood by laughing at them. For since he was the incorporeal power and the Mind of the unborn Father, he was transformed in whatever way he pleased, and in this way he ascended to him who sent him, laughing at them, since he could not be held and was invisible to all' (from Irenaeus, *Against Heresies* 1.24.4). For similar stories, see the Second Treatise of the Great Seth 56; Apocalypse of Peter 81; Acts of John 97-99.
177. *him*: or 'it.'
178. *him*: or 'it.'
179. *him*: or 'it.'
180. *conjecture*: or 'opinion,' as opposed to 'revealed (i.e. certain) knowledge.'
181. *raised him to Himself*: referring to Jesus' resurrection/ascension into heaven.
182. *a witness against them*: referrring to Jesus' role at the Judgment, when he will bear witness against his would-be murderers (cf. e.g. John 5.25-29).
183. *those who are Jews*: lit. 'those who have judaized,' or follow Jewish law, punning on the name Yahūd.
184. *forbidden...which were permitted to them (before)*: a reference to and explanation for Jewish dietary restrictions.

you,[185] and what has been sent down before you. And the ones who observe the prayer, and who give the alms, and who believe in God and the Last Day, those – We shall give them a great reward.

163 Surely We have inspired you[186] as We inspired Noah and the prophets after him, and as We inspired Abraham, and Ishmael, and Isaac, and Jacob, and the tribes, and Jesus, and Job, and Jonah, and Aaron, and Solomon, and We gave David (the) Psalms,[187] **164** and messengers We have already recounted to you before, and messengers We have not recounted to you – but God spoke to Moses directly[188] – **165** (and) messengers bringing good news and warning, so that the people might have no argument against God after (the coming of) the messengers. God is mighty, wise.

166 But God bears witness to what He has sent down to you[189] – He sent it down with His knowledge – and the angels (also) bear witness. Yet God is sufficient as a witness. **167** Surely those who disbelieve and keep (people) from the way of God – they have gone very far astray. **168** Surely those who disbelieve and do evil – God will not forgive them, nor will He guide them (to any) road, **169** except the road to Gehenna, there to remain forever. That is easy for God. **170** People! The messenger has brought you the truth from your Lord, so believe! (It will be) better for you. But if you disbelieve – surely to God (belongs) whatever is in the heavens and the earth. God is knowing, wise.

171 People of the Book![190] Do not go beyond the limits in your religion, and do not say about God (anything) but the truth. The Messiah, Jesus, son of Mary, was only a messenger[191] of God, and His word,[192] which He cast into Mary, and a spirit from Him.[193] So believe in God and His messengers, but do not say, 'Three.'[194] Stop! (It will be) better for you. God is only one God. Glory to Him! (Far be it) that He should have a son! To Him (belongs) whatever is in the heavens and whatever is on the earth. God is sufficient as a guardian. **172** The Messiah does not disdain to be a servant of God,[195] nor will the angels, the ones brought near.[196] Whoever disdains His service and becomes arrogant – He will gather them to Himself – all (of them). **173** As for those who believe and do righteous deeds, He will pay them their rewards in full and increase them from His favor. But as for those who have become disdainful and arrogant, He will punish them with a painful punishment. They will not find for themselves any ally or helper other than God.

---

185. *you*: the Prophet.

163–170 The inspired Prophet and his predecessors

186. *you*: the Prophet.
187. *Psalms*: or perhaps simply a 'scripture' or 'book' (Ar. *zabūr* [sing.]); cf. Q17.55; 21.105 (quoting Psalm 37.29); for the plur. *al-zubur*, see n. on Q3.184.
188. *God spoke to Moses directly*: see Q7.143; 19.52; cf. Q2.253; 42.51n.; Moses spoke with God 'face to face,' according to Exodus 33.11; Numbers 12.8; Deuteronomy 34.10.
189. *you*: the Prophet.

171–173 Diatribe against the People of the Book

190. *People of the Book*: here referring to the Christians.
191. *only a messenger*: see also Q5.75; cf. Q3.144 (Muḥammad); 19.19 (the 'spirit' sent to Mary).
192. *His word*: see also Q3.39, 45; cf. John 1.1, where Jesus is called God's 'word' (Gk. *logos*).
193. *a spirit from Him*: presumably because Mary was impregnated by the spirit (Q19.17n.; 21.91; 66.12); elsewhere it is said that Jesus was strengthened by the 'holy spirit' (Q2.87, 253; 5.110).
194. *Three*: a reference to the Christian doctrine of the trinity.
195. *servant of God*: the word 'servant' (Ar. *'abd*) also means 'slave.'
196. *the ones brought near*: to God's throne (cf. Q40.7). Ar. *al-muqarrabūn* (cognate with Hebr. *kerūbīm*) is a designation of special privilege in the royal court (cf. Q7.114; 26.42); here it is applied to the angels in God's heavenly 'court.' The same expression is used of Jesus (Q3.45) and of certain believers (Q56.10-12).

174 People! A proof has come to you from your Lord: We have sent down to you a clear light. **175** As for those who believe in God and hold fast to Him, He will cause them to enter into mercy from Himself, and favor, and He will guide them to Himself (on) a straight path.

176 They ask you for a pronouncement.[197] Say: 'God makes a pronouncement to you about the person who leaves no direct heirs. If a man perishes without children, but has a sister, then to her a half of what he leaves, and he is her heir if she has no children. If there are two (sisters), then to them two-thirds of what he leaves. If there are brothers and sisters, then to the male a share equal to two females. God makes (this) clear to you, so that you do not go astray. God has knowledge of everything.

174–175 Appeal for belief

176 Indirect heirs and their inheritance

197. *They ask you...*: the Prophet; cf. what has already been said about inheritance at Q4.12 above.

5 The Table ❁ Al-Mā'ida

In the Name of God, the Merciful, the Compassionate

1 You who believe! Fulfill (your) pledges.[1]

Permitted to you (to eat) is (any) animal of the livestock,[2] except for what is recited to you.[3] The hunting (of wild game) is not permitted when you are (in a state of) sanctity.[4] Surely God decrees whatever He wills.

2 You who believe! Do not profane the symbols[5] of God, nor the sacred month,[6] nor the offering,[7] nor the ornaments,[8] nor (those) going to the Sacred House[9] seeking favor from their Lord and approval. But when you are free (from your state of sanctity), hunt (wild game).[10] Do not let hatred of the people who kept you from (going to) the Sacred Mosque provoke you to commit aggression. Help one another to piety and the guarding (of yourselves), and do not help each other to sin and enmity. Guard (yourselves) against God. Surely God is harsh in retribution.

3 Forbidden to you (to eat) are: the dead (animal),[11] and the blood,[12] and swine's flesh,[13] and what has been dedicated to (a god) other than God,[14] and the strangled (to death), and the beaten (to death), and the fallen (to death), and the gored (to death), and what a wild animal has devoured – except what you have slaughtered[15] – and what has been sacrificed on stones.[16] And (it is forbidden) that you should

---

Q5: This sūra offers instruction on a variety of topics (e.g. prayer, pilgrimage, and food), and prescribes punishment for certain offenses (e.g. murder and theft). Several passages condemn various 'pagan' practices, but many more are critical of Jewish disobedience and Christian doctrine, and believers are warned against entering into alliance with the 'People of the Book.' Q5 receives its title from the miraculous 'table' of food sent down to Jesus and his disciples (Q5.111-115). Most scholars, traditional and modern, assign Q5 to the 'Medinan' period.

1–5 Various regulations concerning pledges, food, pilgrimage, and marriage

1. *pledges*: or 'contracts;' lit. 'the knots' (cf. Q4.33; 5.89 below).
2. *livestock*: lit. 'cattle.'
3. *except for what is recited to you*: i.e. except what is forbidden in passages of the Qur'ān already 'recited' (cf. Q2.173; 5.3; 16.115).
4. *(in a state of) sanctity*: said to mean while wearing the special garb (or *iḥrām*) on pilgrimage.
5. *symbols*: meaning uncertain (Ar. *sha'ā'ir*); it may refer to Ṣafā and Marwa, two hills near the Ka'ba in Mecca (cf. Q2.158), or to cult-symbols or rituals in general.
6. *sacred month*: this may refer to the period of pilgrimage (cf. Q5.97 below) or to any of the 'four sacred months' (cf. Q9.36).
7. *the offering*: i.e. an animal for sacrifice.
8. *ornaments*: possibly garlands placed around the necks of sacrificial animals.
9. *Sacred House*: the Ka'ba (see n. on Q5.95 below); cf. the 'Sacred Mosque' in the following sentence.
10. *hunt (wild game)*: this clause seems misplaced, and would fit better in v. 1.
11. *the dead (animal)*: i.e. 'carrion;' cf. Leviticus 17.15.
12. *the blood*: cf. Genesis 9.4; Leviticus 17.10-12; Acts 15.29.
13. *swine's flesh*: cf. Leviticus 11.7; Deuteronomy 14.8.
14. *dedicated to (a god) other than God*: i.e. what has been sacrificed or dedicated to 'other gods' (see Q2.173; 6.145; 16.115; cf. Acts 15.29; 1 Corinthians 8.1-13; 10.23-30).
15. *except what you have slaughtered*: i.e. a wounded animal properly killed (by bleeding it) may be eaten.
16. *on stones:* or 'stone altars,' dedicated to other gods.

divide by divination arrows[17] – that is wickedness for you.

Today[18] those who disbelieve have no hope of (ever destroying) your religion. So do not fear them, but fear Me. Today I have perfected your religion for you, and I have completed My blessing on you, and I have approved Islam[19] for you as a religion.

But if anyone is forced by hunger,[20] without intending to sin – surely God is forgiving, compassionate.

4 They ask you[21] what is permitted to them (to eat). Say:[22] 'The good things are permitted to you, and what you have taught some of (your) hunting animals (to catch), training (them), (and) teaching them some of what God has taught you. So eat from what they catch for you, and mention[23] the name of God over it, and guard (yourselves) against God. Surely God is quick at the reckoning.' **5** Today the good things are permitted to you, and the food of those who have been given the Book is permitted to you, and your food is permitted to them.

(Permitted to you are) the chaste women among the believers, and the chaste women among those who have been given the Book before you, once you have given them their marriage gifts,[24] taking (them) in marriage, not in immorality, nor taking (them) as secret lovers.[25] Whoever disbelieves in the faith, his deed has come to nothing, and in the Hereafter[26] he will be one of the losers.

6 You who believe! When you stand up for the prayer,[27] wash your faces and your hands up to the elbows, and wipe your heads and your feet up to the ankles. If you are defiled,[28] purify yourselves. If you are sick or on a journey, or if one of you has come from the toilet, or if you have touched women, and you do not find any water, take clean earth and wipe your faces and your hands with it.[29] God does not wish to place any difficulty on you, but He wishes to purify you and to complete His blessing on you, so that you may be thankful.

7 Remember the blessing of God on you, and His covenant with which He bound you, when you said, 'We hear and obey.'[30] Guard (yourselves) against God. Surely God knows what is in the hearts.[31]

8 You who believe! Be supervisors for God, witnesses in justice, and do not let hatred of a people provoke you to act unfairly. Act fairly! It is nearer to guarding (yourselves). Guard (yourselves) against God. Surely God is aware of what you do. **9** God has promised those who believe and do righteous deeds (that

17. *divide by divinination arrows*: i.e. drawing lots by means of a special set of arrows (see Q5.90 below).
18. *Today...Today...*: the following two sentences, which interrupt the regulations on food, are out of place in their present location.
19. *Islam*: lit. 'the submission' or 'the surrender' to God (Ar. *al-Islām*).
20. *if anyone is forced by hunger*: i.e. compelled to eat something forbidden.
21. *you*: the Prophet.
22. *Say*: on this form of address, see n. on Q2.80.
23. *mention*: or 'remember.'
24. *their marriage gifts*: lit. 'their rewards,' probably referring to the payment of a 'dower' for support in the event a wife should survive her husband.
25. *not in immorality, nor taking (them) as secret lovers*: cf. Q4.24-25
26. *the Hereafter*: see n. on Q2.4.

6–7 Preparation for the prayer

27. *the prayer*: the ritual prayer (or *ṣalāt*).
28. *defiled*: i.e. in a state of ritual impurity.
29. *wipe your faces and your hands with it*: cf. Q4.43.
30. *We hear and obey*: this verse may refer to the Jews (cf. Q4.46).
31. *hearts*: lit. 'chests,' considered the seat of knowledge and understanding.

8–10 Just witnesses

there is) forgiveness for them and a great reward. **10** But those who disbelieve and call Our signs[32] a lie – those are the companions of the Furnace.[33]

11 You who believe! Remember the blessing of God on you. When a people were determined to stretch out their hands against you, He restrained their hands from you. Guard (yourselves) against God, and in God let the believers put their trust.

12 Certainly God took a covenant with the Sons of Israel, and We raised up among them twelve chieftains,[34] and God said, 'Surely I am with you. If indeed you observe the prayer and give the alms,[35] and believe in My messengers[36] and support them, and lend to God a good loan,[37] I shall indeed absolve you of your evil deeds, and cause you to enter Gardens[38] through which rivers flow. But whoever of you disbelieves after that has gone astray from the right way.'

13 For their breaking their covenant, We cursed them and made their hearts hard. They alter words from their positions,[39] and have forgotten part of what they were reminded of. You[40] will continue to see treachery from them, except for a few of them. Yet pardon them and excuse (them). Surely God loves the doers of good.

14 And with those who say, 'Surely we are Christians,'[41] We took a covenant, but they have forgotten part of what they were reminded of. So We stirred up enmity and hatred among them,[42] until the Day of Resurrection, and (then) God will inform them about what they have done.

15 People of the Book! Our messenger has come to you, making clear to you much of what you have been hiding of the Book,[43] and overlooking much.[44] Now a light and a clear Book from God[45] has come to you.
16 By means of it God guides those who follow after His approval (in the) ways of peace,[46] and He brings them out of the darkness to the light, by His permission, and guides them to a straight path.

17 Certainly they disbelieve who say, 'Surely God – He is the Messiah,[47] son of Mary.'[48] Say: 'Who could

---

32. *signs*: or 'verses' (see n. on Q2.39).
33. *the Furnace*: a name for Hell (Ar. *al-jaḥīm*).

11 A threat averted

12–19 Diatribe against the People of the Book

34. *twelve chieftains*: presumably 'heads' the twelve tribes; cf. Moses' appointment of 'judges' (Exodus 18.13-26) and 'elders' (Numbers 11.16-17), though neither was twelve in number.
35. *observe the prayer and give the alms*: i.e. *ṣalāt*, the ritual prayer, and *zakāt*, a kind of tithe required for the benefit of the poor, as well as other purposes.
36. *messengers*: for this important title, see n. on Q2.87.
37. *lend to God a good loan*: by contributing to or 'investing in' God's cause (cf. Q2.245; 30.39; 57.18; 64.17; 73.20).
38. *Gardens*: in heaven (for this imagery, see n. on Q2.25).
39. *alter words from their positions*: or 'change the meanings of words' (cf. Q2.75, 93, 104; 4.46; 5.41 below).
40. *You*: the Prophet.
41. *Christians*: Ar. *Naṣārā*; see n. on Q2.62 (cf. Q5.18, 51, 69, 82 below).
42. *enmity and hatred among them*: probably a reference to the bitter 'sectarian divisions' among the Christians.
43. *what you have been hiding of the Book*: notably predictions concerning the coming of the Prophet (cf. e.g. Q2.146, 159, 174; 3.71, 187).
44. *and overlooking much*: perhaps a reference to Christians 'overlooking' what they considered no longer relevant (i.e. many of the ritual commandments and prohibitions of the 'Old Testament').
45. *a light and a clear Book from God*: the Qur'ān.
46. *peace*: lit. 'the peace' (Ar. *al-salām*), with the implication of submission (*islām*) to God (cf. Q6.127; 10.25).
47. *the Messiah*: the Qur'ān uses this title (Ar. *al-Masīḥ*) almost as a proper name, without any discussion of the ideas associated with it.
48. *son of Mary*: there is no mention in the Qur'ān of Joseph, Jesus' putative father (cf. Mark 6.3).

do anything against God if He wished to destroy the Messiah, son of Mary, and his mother, and whoever is on the earth – all (of them) together? To God (belongs) the kingdom of the heavens and the earth, and whatever is between them. He creates whatever He pleases. God is powerful over everything.'

18 The Jews and the Christians say, 'We are the sons of God, and His beloved.' Say: 'Then why does He punish you for your sins? No! You are human beings, (part) of what He created. He forgives whomever He pleases and He punishes whomever He pleases. To God (belongs) the kingdom of the heavens and the earth, and whatever is between them. To Him is the (final) destination.'

19 People of the Book! Our messenger has come to you, making (things) clear to you after an interval[49] between the messengers, in case you should say, 'No bringer of good news has come to us, nor any warner.' Now a bringer of good news and a warner[50] has come to you. God is powerful over everything.

20 (Remember) when[51] Moses said to his people, 'My people! Remember the blessing of God on you, when He made prophets[52] among you, and made you kings, and gave you what He had not given to anyone of the worlds.[53] **21** My people! Enter the Holy Land which God has prescribed[54] for you, and do not turn your backs, or you will turn out (to be) losers.' **22** They said, 'Moses! Surely (there is) an oppressive people in it,[55] and we shall not (be able to) enter it until they depart from it. If they depart from it, we shall enter (it).' **23** Two men[56] among those who feared (God), whom God had blessed, said, 'Enter (through) the gate against them. When you have entered it, you will be victorious. Put your trust in God, if you are believers.' **24** They said, 'Moses! Surely we shall never enter it as long as they remain in it. So you and your Lord go, and both of you fight. Surely we shall be sitting here.' **25** He[57] said, 'My Lord, surely I have no control over (anyone) but myself and my brother.[58] Make a separation between us and this wicked people.' **26** He[59] said, 'Surely it[60] is forbidden to them for forty years, while they wander on the earth. So do not grieve over this wicked people.'

27 Recite[61] to them the story[62] of Adam's two sons[63] in truth: when they both offered a sacrifice, and it was accepted from one of them, but was not accepted from the other. (One) said, 'I shall indeed kill you.' (The other) said, 'God only accepts (offerings) from the ones who guard (themselves). **28** If indeed you stretch out your hand against me, to kill me, (still) I shall not stretch out my hand against you, to kill you.

---

49. *an interval*: this 'interval' (Ar. *fatra*) is traditionally understood as the period of time between Jesus and the Prophet, during which there were no messengers.
50. *bringer of good news...warner*: for these roles, see n. on Q2.119.

20–26 Israel refuses to enter the Holy Land

51. *(Remember) when...*: a stock narrative formula; the Arabic particle *idh* often marks the beginning of a story, and means something like 'Once...,' or 'There was a time when...,' or 'Remember when....'
52. *prophets*: for this important title, see n. on Q2.87.
53. *of the worlds*: or 'of all peoples' (cf. Q2.47n.).
54. *prescribed*: lit. 'written.'
55. *an oppressive people in it*: i.e. 'in the land' (cf. Numbers 13.28).
56. *Two men*: Joshua and Caleb, according to Numbers 14.6.
57. *He*: Moses.
58. *my brother*: Aaron.
59. *He*: God.
60. *it*: the Holy Land.

27–31 The story of Adam's two sons

61. *Recite...*: or 'Read aloud...' (addressed to the Prophet).
62. *story*: or 'news.'
63. *Adam's two sons*: Cain and Abel (Ar. *Qābil* and *Hābil*), though they are not named in the Qur'ān (cf. Genesis 4.3-12).

Surely I fear God, Lord of the worlds.[64] **29** Surely I wish that you would incur my sin and your sin, so that you may be one of the companions of the Fire.[65] That is the reward of the evildoers.' **30** Then his (own) self[66] compelled him to the killing of his brother. So he killed him and became one of the losers. **31** Then God raised up a raven,[67] scratching in the earth, to show him how to hide the shame of his brother.[68] He said, 'Woe is me! Am I unable to be like this raven, and hide the shame of my brother?' And then he became one of the regretful.

32 From that time We prescribed for the Sons of Israel that whoever kills a person, except (in retaliation) for another, or (for) fomenting corruption on the earth, (it is) as if he had killed all the people. And whoever gives (a person) life, (it is) as if he had given all the people life.[69] Certainly Our messengers have brought them the clear signs,[70] yet even after that many of them act wantonly on the earth.

33 The penalty[71] (for) those who wage war (against) God and His messenger, and who strive in fomenting corruption on the earth, is that they be killed or crucified, or their hands and feet on opposite sides be cut off, or they be banished from the earth. That is a disgrace for them in this world, and in the Hereafter (there will be) a great punishment for them, **34** except those who turn (in repentance) before you have them in your power. Know that God is forgiving, compassionate.

35 You who believe! Guard (yourselves) against God, and seek access to Him, and struggle in His way, so that you may prosper. **36** Surely those who disbelieve, even if they had whatever is on the earth – all (of it) and as much again – to ransom (themselves) with it from punishment on the Day of Resurrection, it would not be accepted from them. For them (there is) a painful punishment. **37** They will wish to get out of the Fire, but they will not get out of it. For them (there is) a lasting punishment.

38 (As for) the male thief and the female thief: cut off their hands as a penalty for what they have done[72] – a punishment from God. God is mighty, wise. **39** Whoever turns (in repentance) after his evildoing and sets (things) right – surely God will turn to him (in forgiveness). Surely God is forgiving, compassionate. **40** Do you not know[73] that God – to Him (belongs) the kingdom of the heavens and the earth – He punishes whomever He pleases and He forgives whomever He pleases. God is powerful over everything.

41 Messenger! Do not let those who are quick to disbelief cause you sorrow. (They are) among those who say with their mouths, 'We believe,' but their hearts do not believe. Among those who are Jews[74] (there are) those who listen to lies, (and who) listen to (other) people who have not come to you. They alter

---

64. *Lord of the worlds*: for this title, see n. on Q1.2.
65. *the Fire*: Ar. *al-nār* is the most common of the various designations for Hell.
66. *his (own) self*: cf. Q12.53, 'the self is indeed an instigator of evil.'
67. *a raven*: in Jewish lore a raven indicated to Adam the form of burial for Abel (see Jerusalem Targum on Genesis 4.8).
68. *shame of his brother*: probably the nakedness of the corpse, not the murder.

32 Punishment for murder

69. *whoever kills a person..., whoever gives (a person) life...*: prescribed in the 'oral Torah' or Mishnah (Sanhedrin 4.5).
70. *the clear signs*: or 'the clear proofs,' 'the indisputable evidence.'

33–34 Punishment for fighting against God and the Messenger

71. *penalty*: lit. 'payment.'

35–37 Fighting for the cause of God

38–40 Punishment for theft

72. *penalty for what they have done*: lit. 'payment for what they have earned.'
73. *Do you not know*: addressed to the Prophet, or perhaps intended generally ('Does one not know...').

41–43 Encouragement in the face of disbelief

74. *those who are Jews*: lit. 'those who have judaized,' or follow Jewish law, punning on the name Yahūd.

words from their positions,[75] (and) say, 'If you are given this, take it, but if you are not given it, beware.'[76] If God wishes to test[77] anyone, you[78] will not have any power for him against God. Those are the ones whose hearts God does not wish to purify. For them (there is) disgrace in this world, and in the Hereafter (there will be) a great punishment for them. **42** (They are) listeners to lies (and) consumers of what is forbidden.[79] If they come to you, judge between them or turn away from them. If you turn away from them, they will not harm you at all. But if you judge, judge between them in justice. Surely God loves the ones who act fairly. **43** Yet how will they make you (their) judge, when they have the Torah, containing the judgment of God, (and) then turn away after that? Those (people) are not with the believers.

44 Surely We sent down the Torah, containing guidance and light. By means of it the prophets who had submitted[80] rendered judgment for those who were Jews,[81] and (so did) the rabbis and the teachers, with what they were entrusted of the Book of God,[82] and they were witnesses to it. So do not fear the people, but fear Me, and do not sell[83] My signs[84] for a small price. Whoever does not judge by what God has sent down, those – they are the disbelievers. **45** We prescribed[85] for them in it:[86] 'The life for the life, and the eye for the eye, and the nose for the nose, and the ear for the ear, and the tooth for the tooth, and (for) the wounds retaliation.'[87] But whoever remits it as a freewill offering,[88] it will be an atonement for him.[89] Whoever does not judge by what God has sent down, those – they are the evildoers.

46 And in their footsteps We followed up with Jesus, son of Mary, confirming what was with him of the Torah,[90] and We gave him the Gospel, containing guidance and light, and confirming what was with him of the Torah, and as guidance and admonition to the ones who guard (themselves). **47** So let the People of the Gospel judge by what God has sent down in it. Whoever does not judge by what God has sent down, those – they are the wicked.

48 And We have sent down to you[91] the Book with the truth,[92] confirming what was with him[93] of the

75. *alter words from their positions*: or 'change the meanings of words' (see Q5.13n. above).
76. *If you are given this, take it, but if you are not given it, beware*: meaning obscure; it may refer to their attempt to pass off forged 'scriptures' (cf. Q2.79).
77. *test*: or 'tempt.'
78. *you*: the Prophet.
79. *consumers of what is forbidden*: probably a reference to 'usury,' rather than a violation of food laws (cf. Q5.62 below).

44–47 Torah and Gospel

80. *had submitted*: or 'surrendered' (to God), with the suggestion 'were Muslims.'
81. *those who were Jews*: lit. 'those who had judaized.'
82. *Book of God*: this probably refers to the Torah (cf. Q2.101; 3.23), but it may be a reference to the heavenly archetype or source of all scripture. According to this view, the Torah is only a portion of this all encompassing Book (cf. Q13.39; 43.4, 'mother of the Book; 56.78, 'hidden Book;' 85.22, 'guarded Tablet').
83. *do not fear..., do not sell*: plur. imperatives.
84. *signs*: or 'verses.'
85. *prescribed*: or 'wrote.'
86. *it*: the Torah.
87. *The life for the life, etc....*: a nearly verbatim quotation of the *lex talionis* of Exodus 21.23-25; cf. Q2.178.
88. *freewill offering*: or 'voluntary contribution' (Ar. *ṣadaqa*) to benefit the community (cf. Q9.60).
89. *atonement for him*: i.e. for his sins.
90. *of the Torah*: has either a partitive or an epexegetical meaning (elucidating the preceding 'what').

48–50 The Prophet's Book

91. *you*: the Prophet.
92. *with the truth*: or 'in truth,' 'truly.'
93. *what was with him*: lit. 'what was between his (i.e. Jesus') hands;' i.e. the Qur'ān 'confirms' the Gospel, as the

Book,[94] and as a preserver of it.[95] So judge between them by what God has sent down, and do not follow their (vain) desires (away) from what has come to you of the truth. For each of you[96] We have made a pathway[97] and an open road. If God had (so) pleased, He would indeed have made you one community,[98] but (He did not do so) in order to test you by what He has given you. So race (toward doing) good deeds. To God is your return – all (of you) – and then He will inform you about your differences.[99] **49** (So) judge between them by what God has sent down, and do not follow their (vain) desires, and beware of them in case they tempt you (to turn away) from any part of what God has sent down to you. If they turn away, know that God intends to smite them for some of their sins. Surely many of the people are wicked indeed. **50** Is it the judgment of the (time of) ignorance[100] they seek? Yet who is better in judgment than God, for a people who are certain (in their belief)?

51 You who believe! Do not take the Jews and the Christians as allies.[101] They are allies of each other. Whoever of you takes them as allies is already one of them. Surely God does not guide the people who are evildoers. **52** Yet you[102] see those in whose hearts is a sickness[103] – they are quick (to turn) to them, (and) they say, 'We fear that disaster may smite us.' But it may be that God will bring the victory,[104] or some command from Himself,[105] and they will be full of regret for what they kept secret within themselves. **53** But those who believe will say, 'Are these those who swore by God the most solemn of their oaths: (that) surely they were indeed with you? Their deeds have come to nothing, and they are the losers.'

54 You who believe! Whoever of you turns back from his religion, God will bring (another) people whom He loves, and who love Him, (who are) humble toward the believers, mighty toward the disbelievers, (who) struggle in the way of God, and do not fear the blame of anyone.[106] That is the favor of God. He gives it to whomever He pleases. God is embracing, knowing. **55** Your only ally is God, and His messenger, and the believers who observe the prayer and give the alms, and who bow. **56** Whoever takes God as an ally, and His messenger, and those who believe – surely the faction of God, they are the victors.

57 You who believe! Do not take those who take your religion in mockery and jest as allies, (either) from those who were given the Book before you, or (from) the disbelievers. Guard (yourselves) against

---

Gospel had 'confirmed' the Torah (cf. e.g. Q2.97; 3.3; 35.31; 46.30).

94. *of the Book*: has either a partitive or an epexegetical meaning (elucidating the preceding 'what').
95. *preserver of it*: meaning obscure (cf. Q59.23).
96. *For each of you...*: i.e. Jews, Christians, and Muslims have their own 'paths' assigned by God.
97. *pathway*: Ar. *sharīʿa*, but its later meaning as 'law' is not entirely appropriate here; instead the sense is that God has revealed an independent 'pathway' to truth for each religion (cf. Q45.18).
98. *one community*: for this idea, see n. on Q2.213.
99. *...about your differences*: i.e. Judaism, Christianity, and Islam are to continue, each to be judged according to its own revelation (Torah, Gospel, Qur'ān). Only at the Judgment will God make clear the truth regarding those issues about which the three religions differed.
100. *the (time of) ignorance*: i.e. the pre-Islamic period of ignorance about God (Ar. *al-jāhiliyya*).

51–53 Warning against alliance with Jews and Christians

101. *allies*: Ar. *awliyāʾ* implies the obligation of mutual protection, almost in the sense of 'friends' or 'brothers.'
102. *you*: the Prophet.
103. *those in whose hearts (there is) a sickness*: usually taken as a reference to the 'hypocrites.'
104. *victory*: lit. 'opening.'
105. *command from Himself*: i.e. some direct intervention, probably judgment (cf. Q2.109; 4.47; 7.150; 10.24; 16.1, 33; 54.50).

54–56 Warning against apostasy

106. *the blame of anyone*: lit. 'the blame of the blamer.'

57–66 Warning against those who ridicule religion

God, if you are believers. **58** When you make the call to prayer, they take it in mockery and jest. That is because they are a people who do not understand. **59** Say: 'People of the Book! Do you take vengeance on us (for any other reason) than that we believe in God and what has been sent down to us, and what was sent down before (this), and because most of you are wicked?' **60** Say: 'Shall I inform you of (something) worse than that? Retribution with God! Whomever God has cursed, and whomever He is angry with – some of whom He made apes,[107] and pigs, and slaves of al-Ṭāghūt[108] – those are in a worse situation and farther astray from the right way.'

61 When they come to you,[109] they say, 'We believe,' but they have already entered in disbelief and will depart in it. God knows what they are concealing. **62** You see many of them being quick to sin and enmity, and consuming what is forbidden.[110] Evil indeed is what they have done! **63** Why do the rabbis and the teachers not forbid them from their saying what is a sin and (from) their consuming what is forbidden? Evil indeed is what they have done!

64 The Jews say, 'The hand of God is chained.' (May) their hands (be) chained, and (may) they (be) cursed for what they say! No! Both His hands are outstretched: He gives[111] as He pleases. What has been sent down to you[112] from your Lord will indeed increase many of them in insolent transgression and disbelief. We have cast enmity and hatred among them until the Day of Resurrection. Whenever they light the fire of war, God extinguishes it. But they strive (at) fomenting corruption on the earth, and God does not love the fomenters of corruption. **65** Had the People of the Book believed and guarded (themselves), We would indeed have absolved them of their evil deeds, and caused them to enter Gardens of Bliss.[113]
66 Had they observed the Torah and the Gospel, and what was sent down to them from their Lord, they would indeed have eaten from (what was) above them and from (what was) beneath their feet.[114] Some of them are a moderate community,[115] but most of them – evil is what they do.

67 Messenger! Deliver what has been sent down to you from your Lord. If you do not, you have not delivered His message. God will protect you from the people. Surely God does not guide the people who are disbelievers. **68** Say: 'People of the Book! You are (standing) on nothing until you observe the Torah and the Gospel, and what has been sent down to you from your Lord.' But what has been sent down to you[116] from your Lord will indeed increase many of them in insolent transgression and disbelief. So do not grieve over the people who are disbelievers. **69** Surely those who believe, and those who are Jews,[117] and the Sabians,[118] and the Christians – whoever believes in God and the Last Day, and does righteousness – (there will be) no fear on them, nor will they sorrow.

70 Certainly We took a covenant with the Sons of Israel, and We sent messengers to them. Whenever

107. *some of whom He made apes*: for the story, see Q7.163-167 (cf. Q2.65).
108. *slaves of al-Ṭāghūt*: or 'worshippers of (other) gods' or 'idols,' or perhaps 'of Satan' (see n. on Q2.256).
109. *you*: plur.
110. *consuming what is forbidden*: lit. 'consuming the forbidden;' probably a reference to 'usury,' rather than a violation of food laws (cf. Q5.42 above).
111. *gives*: lit. 'spends.'
112. *you*: the Prophet.
113. *Gardens of Bliss*: in heaven (for this imagery, see n. on Q2.25).
114. *(what was) above...(what was) beneath their feet*: meaning obscure; perhaps 'what is in the sky and on earth.'
115. *a moderate community*: it is not clear whether this *umma* is comprised of Jews or Christians, or both.

67–69 Appeal to the People of the Book

116. *what has been sent down to you*: the Prophet, referring to the Qur'ān.
117. *those who are Jews*: lit. 'those have who judaized,' or follow Jewish law, punning on the name Yahūd.
118. *Sabians*: see n. on Q2.62; here they are referred to out of usual order.

70–71 Diatribe against the Sons of Israel

a messenger brought them what they themselves did not desire, some they called liars and some they killed. **71** They thought that there would be no trouble[119] (for them), so they became blind and deaf. Then God turned to them (in forgiveness), (and) then many of them became blind and deaf (again). Yet God sees what they do.

72 Certainly they have disbelieved who say, 'Surely God – He is the Messiah, son of Mary,' when the Messiah said, 'Sons of Israel! Serve God, my Lord and your Lord. Surely he who associates (anything) with God, God has forbidden him (from) the Garden, and his refuge is the Fire. The evildoers have no helpers.' **73** Certainly they have disbelieved who say, 'Surely God is the third of three,'[120] when (there is) no god but one God. If they do not stop what they are saying, a painful punishment will indeed strike those of them who disbelieve. **74** Will they not turn to God (in repentance) and ask forgiveness from Him? God is forgiving, compassionate. **75** The Messiah, son of Mary, was only a messenger.[121] Messengers have passed away before him. His mother was a truthful woman.[122] They both ate food.[123] See how We make clear the signs to them, then see how deluded they are. **76** Say: 'Do you serve what has no power to (cause) you harm or benefit, instead of God (alone)? God – He is the Hearing, the Knowing.' **77** Say: 'People of the Book! Do not go beyond the limits in your religion, (saying anything) other than the truth, and do not follow (the vain) desires of a people who went astray before (you).[124] They have led many astray, and they have gone astray from the right way.'

78 Those of the Sons of Israel who disbelieved were cursed by the tongue of David and Jesus, son of Mary – that was because they disobeyed and were transgressing. **79** They did not forbid each other any evildoing. Evil indeed is what they have done! **80** You[125] see many of them taking those who disbelieve as allies. Evil indeed is what they have sent forward[126] for themselves! That (is why) God became angry with them, and in the punishment they will remain. **81** If they had believed in God and the prophet, and what has been sent down to him, they would not have taken them as friends. But many of them are wicked.

82 Certainly you[127] will find that the most violent of people in enmity to the believers are the Jews and the idolaters.[128] Certainly you will find that the closest of them in affection to the believers are those who say, 'We are Christians.'[129] That is because (there are) priests and monks among them, and because they are not arrogant. **83** When they hear what has been sent down to the messenger, you[130] see their eyes overflowing with tears because of what they recognize of the truth. They say, 'Our Lord, we

---

119. *trouble*: or 'trial,' 'tribulation' (Ar. *fitna* has a range of meanings).

72–77 Diatribe against the Christian doctrine of the trinity

120. *God is the third of three*: referring to the Christian doctrine of the trinity, though the Qur'ān has in mind God, Jesus, and Mary (see Q5.75, 116 below).
121. *only a messenger*: see also Q4.171; cf. Q3.144 (Muḥammad); 19.19 (the 'spirit' sent to Mary)
122. *a truthful woman*: perhaps meaning that Mary did not claim her son was divine, or a rejoinder to the Jewish 'slander' that she conceived an illegitimate child (cf. Q4.156n.).
123. *They both ate food*: i.e. as proof of their mortality (cf. Q21.8; 23.33; 25.7 [the Prophet], 20); only God and the angels do not require food (see Q6.14; 11.70).
124. *a people who went astray before (you)*: referring to the Jews.

78–81 Sons of Israel cursed by David and Jesus

125. *you*: the Prophet.
126. *sent forward*: to the Judgment.

82–86 Christians more favorable than the Jews and idolaters

127. *you*: the Prophet.
128. *the idolaters*: or 'those who associate (other gods with God).'
129. *We are Christians*: the attitude expressed here toward the Christians is unparalleled (cf. Q57.27).
130. *you*: the Prophet, or perhaps intended generally ('one').

believe, so write us down among those who bear witness. **84** Why should we not believe in God and (in) what has come to us of the truth, when we are eager for our Lord to cause us to enter with the people who are righteous?' **85** So God has rewarded them for what they said (with) Gardens through which rivers flow, there to remain. That is the reward for the doers of good. **86** But those who disbelieve and call Our signs a lie, those are the companions of the Furnace.

87 You who believe! Do not forbid the good things which God has permitted to you, and do not transgress. Surely God does not love the transgressors. **88** Eat from what God has provided you as permitted[131] (and) good, and guard (yourselves) against God – the One in whom you are believers.

89 God will not take you to task for a slip in your oaths, but He will take you to task for what you have pledged by oath. Atonement for it[132] is the feeding of ten poor persons with the average (amount of food) which you feed your households, or clothing them, or the setting free of a slave. Whoever does not find (the means to do that), (the penalty is) a fast for three days. That is the atonement for your oaths when you have sworn (them, and broken them). But guard your oaths! In this way God makes clear to you His signs,[133] so that you may be thankful.

90 You who believe! Wine,[134] games of chance,[135] stones,[136] and divination arrows are an abomination, part of the work of Satan.[137] So avoid it in order that you may prosper. **91** Satan only wishes to cause enmity and hatred among you with wine and games of chance, and to keep you from the remembrance of God and from the prayer. Will you refrain? **92** Obey God, and obey the messenger, and beware! If you do turn away, know that only (dependent) on Our messenger is the clear delivery (of the message).

93 (There is) no blame on those who believe and do righteous deeds for what they may have eaten,[138] so long as they guard (themselves) and believe and do righteous deeds, (and) then (again) guard (themselves) and believe, (and) then (again) guard (themselves) and do good. God loves the doers of good.

94 You who believe! God will indeed test[139] you with some of the wild game which your hands and spears obtain, so that God may know who fears Him in the unseen.[140] Whoever transgresses after that, for him (there is) a painful punishment.

95 You who believe! Do not kill wild game when you are (in a state of) sanctity.[141] Whoever of you kills it intentionally, (there is) a penalty equivalent (to) what he has killed from the livestock – as two just men among you will determine it – as an offering to reach the Ka'ba.[142] Or (there is) a penalty of the feeding

---

87–96 Regulations concerning food, oaths, wine, and gambling

131. *permitted*: Ar. *ḥalāl*.
132. *Atonement for it*: i.e. for breaking an oath.
133. *signs*: or 'verses.'
134. *Wine*: Ar. *khamr* is to be avoided here and at Q2.219 (cf. Q4.43), but permitted at Q16.67 (Ar. *sakar*); cf. Q47.15, where *khamr* is one of the delights of heaven.
135. *games of chance*: a game in which lots are drawn (Ar. *maysir*); cf. Q2.219.
136. *stones*: possibly 'stone altars' or 'stone images' (cf. Q5.3 above).
137. *Satan*: for this figure, see n. on Q2.36.
138. *(There is) no blame...for what they may have eaten*: this appears to make eating or drinking something forbidden not a very serious matter for believers.
139. *test*: or 'tempt.'
140. *in the unseen*: or 'in secret' (see n. on Q2.3).
141. *(in a state of) sanctity*: presumably on pilgrimage (cf. Q5.1 above).
142. *Ka'ba*: a word derived from the root meaning 'cube,' and said to refer to the ancient sanctuary of Mecca. It occurs in only two verses (Q5.95, 97), the latter of which makes clear that the 'Ka'ba' and the 'Sacred House' are synonymous. God twice refers to it as 'My House' (Q2.125; 22.26; cf. Q14.37; 106.3), the foundations of which Abraham and Ishmael built (Q2.127).

of poor persons, or the equivalent of that in fasting, so that he may taste the consequence of his action. God pardons whatever is past, but whoever returns (to repeat his offense) – God will take vengeance on him. God is mighty, a taker of vengeance.

96 Permitted to you is the wild game of the sea and its food, as a provision for you and for the travelers. But forbidden to you is the wild game on the shore, as long as you are (in a state of) sanctity. Guard (yourselves) against God, the One to whom you will be gathered.

97 God has made the Ka'ba – the Sacred House – an establishment for the people, and (also) the sacred month, the offering, and the ornaments.[143] That is so that you may know that God knows whatever is in the heavens and whatever is on the earth, and that God has knowledge of everything. **98** Know that God is harsh in retribution, and that God is forgiving, compassionate. **99** Nothing (depends) on the messenger except the delivery (of the message). God knows what you[144] reveal and what you conceal.

100 Say: 'The bad and the good are not equal, even though the abundance of bad may cause you[145] to wonder.' Guard (yourselves) against God – those (of you) with understanding! – so that you may prosper.

101 You who believe! Do not ask about anything which, if it were disclosed to you, would distress you. But if you do ask about it, when the Qur'ān[146] is being sent down, it will be disclosed to you. God pardons it, (for) God is forgiving, forbearing. **102** A people before you asked about it, (and) then became disbelievers in it.

103 God has not appointed any baḥīra or sā'iba or waṣīla or ḥāmi,[147] but those who disbelieve forge lies against God. Most of them do not understand. **104** When it is said to them, 'Come to what God has sent down, and to the messenger,' they say, 'What we found our fathers doing is (good) enough for us.' Even if their fathers had no knowledge and were not (rightly) guided? **105** You who believe! Look to yourselves. No one who goes astray can harm you, if you are (rightly) guided. To God is your return – all (of you) – and then He will inform you about what you have done.

106 You who believe! When death approaches one of you, the testimony[148] among you at the time (of making) bequests will be (that of) two just men of you, or two others of (a people) other than you, if you strike forth on the earth and the smiting of death smites you. Detain them both after the prayer, and let them both swear by God, if you have your doubts (about them): 'We will not sell it[149] for a price, even if he happens to be a family member, and we will not conceal the testimony of God.[150] Surely then we would indeed be among the sinners.' **107** If it is discovered that they both (were guilty of) sin,[151] let two others take their place, from those who have a rightful claim against the two former (false witnesses),

---

97–99 The Ka'ba established by God

143. *the sacred month, the offering, and the ornaments*: see nn. on Q5.2 above.

144. *you*: plur.

100 Evil and good not equal

145. *you*: or 'one.'

101–102 Questions discouraged

146. *the Qur'ān*: here used in a general way to refer to the 'revelation' sent down to the Prophet (cf. Q20.2; 76.23; see n. on Q2.185).

103–105 Diatribe against the pagans

147. *baḥīra or sā'iba or waṣīla or ḥāmi*: meaning uncertain; perhaps a reference to different kinds of animals (cattle?) dedicated to other gods (cf. Q6.136-139).

106–108 Instructions for the witnessing of wills

148. *testimony*: or 'witnessing.'

149. *it*: their testimony.

150. *the testimony of God*: i.e. the testimony prescribed by God.

151. *sin*: i.e. of giving false testimony.

and let them both swear by God: 'Certainly our testimony is truer than the testimony of the other two, and we have not transgressed. Surely then we would indeed be among the evildoers.' **108** That will make it more likely that they will give testimony directly,[152] or (else) they will be afraid that (their) oaths will be turned back after they have sworn them. Guard (yourselves) against God and hear! God does not guide the people who are wicked.

109 On the Day when God gathers the messengers, He will say, 'What response were you given?'[153] They will say, 'We have no knowledge. Surely You – You are the Knower of the unseen.'[154]

110 (Remember) when God said, 'Jesus, son of Mary! Remember My blessing on you and on your mother, when I supported you with the holy spirit,[155] (and) you spoke to the people (while you were still) in the cradle,[156] and in adulthood. And when I taught you the Book and the wisdom,[157] and the Torah and the Gospel. And when you created the form of a bird from clay by My permission, and you breathed into it, and it became a bird by My permission,[158] and you healed the blind and the leper by My permission. And when you brought forth the dead by My permission, and when I restrained the Sons of Israel from (violence against) you.[159] When you brought them the clear signs,[160] those among them who had disbelieved said, "This is nothing but clear magic."'

111 (Remember) when I inspired the disciples:[161] 'Believe in Me and in My messenger.' They said, 'We believe. Bear witness that we submit.'[162] **112** And when the disciples said, 'Jesus, son of Mary! Is your Lord able to send down on us a table from the sky?,'[163] he said, 'Guard (yourselves) against God, if you are believers.' **113** They said, 'We wish to eat from it and satisfy our hearts,[164] so that we may know with certainty that you have spoken truthfully to us, and that we may be among the witnesses to it.' **114** Jesus, son of Mary, said, 'God! Our Lord, send down on us a table from the sky, to be a festival for us – for the first of us and last of us[165] – and a sign[166] from You. Provide for us, (for) You are the best of providers.' **115** God said, 'Surely I am going to send it down on you. Whoever of you disbelieves after that – surely I shall punish him (with) a punishment (as) I have not punished anyone among the worlds.'

---

152. *directly*: lit. 'on its face.'

109 Messengers will be judged

153. *What response were you given?*: i.e. what response did you receive to your proclamation of the message?
154. *the unseen*: see n. on Q2.3.

110 The miracles of Jesus

155. *holy spirit*: or 'spirit of holiness' (Ar. *rūḥ al-qudus*); cf. Q2.87, 253.
156. *in the cradle*: for the story, see Q19.27-33.
157. *the wisdom*: see n. on Q2.129.
158. *became a bird by My permission*: see Q3.49; cf. the Infancy Gospel of Thomas 2.2-4, where the child Jesus fashioned twelve birds out of clay, and then made them come to life and fly away.
159. *from (violence against) you*: i.e. by not allowing them to crucify Jesus (see Q4.157-158).
160. *the clear signs*: or 'the clear proofs,' 'the indisputable evidence;' here referring to the miracles of Jesus (cf. Q2.87, 253; 43.63; 61.6).

111–115 The miracle of the table

161. *the disciples*: the word 'disciples' or 'apostles' (Ar. *al-ḥawārīyūn*) is only used of Jesus' followers (cf. Q3.52; 61.14).
162. *that we submit*: or 'that we are Muslims' (cf. Q3.52).
163. *a table from the sky*: or 'from heaven;' probably a reference to the Christian eucharist or 'Lord's table,' but it may also allude to the feeding miracles in the Gospels (e.g. Mark 6.30-44; 8.1-9). The word 'table' (Ar. *mā'ida*) occurs only here, and gives this sūra its title.
164. *satisfy our hearts*: or 'put our minds at rest.'
165. *for the first of us and last of us*: or 'for all generations of us.'
166. *sign*: or 'miracle.'

116 (Remember) when God said, 'Jesus, son of Mary! Did you say to the people, "Take me and my mother
as two gods instead of God (alone)"?' He said, 'Glory to You! It is not for me to say what I have no right
(to say). If I had said it, You would have known it. You know what is within me, but I do not know
what is within You. Surely You – You are the Knower of the unseen. **117** I only said to them what You
commanded me: "Serve God, my Lord and your Lord!" And I was a witness over them as long as I was
among them. But when You took me,[167] You became the Watcher over them. You are a Witness over
everything. **118** If You punish them – surely they are Your servants. If You forgive them – surely You are
the Mighty, the Wise.' **119** God said, 'This is the Day[168] when their truthfulness will benefit the truthful.
For them (there are) Gardens through which rivers flow, there to remain forever. God is pleased with
them, and they are pleased with Him. That is the great triumph!' **120** To God (belongs) the kingdom of
the heavens and the earth, and whatever is in them. He is powerful over everything.

116–120 Jesus rejects worship of himself and his mother

167. *took me*: in death; there are conflicting views of Jesus' fate in the Qur'ān (cf. Q3.55; 4.157-158; and what Jesus says of himself at Q19.33).

168. *This is the Day*: may indicate that the preceding is presented as a scene of what will occur at the Judgment.

6 Livestock ☸ Al-An'ām

In the Name of God, the Merciful, the Compassionate

1 Praise (be)[1] to God, who created the heavens and the earth, and made the darkness and the light![2] Then (despite that) those who disbelieve equate (others) with their Lord. **2** He (it is) who created you from clay,[3] then decreed a time – and a time appointed by Him[4] – then (despite that) you are in doubt. **3** He is God in the heavens and on the earth. He knows your secret and your public utterance, and He knows what you earn.[5] **4** Yet not a sign[6] comes to them from the signs of their Lord without their turning away from it. **5** They called the truth a lie when it came to them, but the story[7] of what they were mocking[8] will come to them.[9]

6 Do they not see how many a generation We have destroyed before them?[10] We established them on the earth in a way in which We have not established you, and We sent the sky (down) on them in abundance (of rain), and made rivers to flow beneath them, and then We destroyed them because of their sins, and produced another generation after them. **7** Even if We had sent down on you[11] a Book (written) on papyrus,[12] and they touched it with their hands, those who disbelieve would indeed have said, 'This is nothing but clear magic.' **8** They say, 'If only an angel were sent down on him.'[13] Even if We had

---

Q6: This sūra emphasizes the creative power of one God, especially as manifested in the 'signs' of an ordered natural world, and on that basis attacks the folly of idolatry, charging that other so-called gods are really 'jinn.' The story of Abraham's rejection of idols is repeated, and a parallel is drawn between the 'religion' of Abraham and the Prophet, as well as between the 'Books' given to Moses and the Prophet. Q6 is traditionally assigned to the 'Meccan' period, except for a few verses which are said to have been revealed at Medina. While most modern scholars accept this dating, some contend that Q6 is an amalgam of materials from various periods. Its title refers to the practice of dedicating 'livestock' to other gods besides God (Q6.136-139).

1–5 God the creator

1. *(be)*: or '(belongs).'
2. *created the heavens and the earth, and made the darkness and the light*: cf. e.g. Isaiah 45.7, 12.
3. *from clay*: see Q7.12; 15.26; 17.61; 23.12; 32.7; 38.71, 76; 55.14; 'from dust,' according to Q3.59; 18.37; 22.5; 30.20; 35.11; 40.67; 'from water,' according to Q21.30; 24.45; 25.54.
4. *decreed a time – and a time appointed by Him*: God determines the 'time' or 'term' (Ar. *ajal*) of a person's death (see Q6.60 below).
5. *what you earn*: i.e. rewards and punishments for good and bad deeds.
6. *sign*: of God's creative power (for the various meanings of this term, see n. on Q2.39).
7. *story*: or 'news' (cf. Q6.34 below).
8. *what they were mocking*: the threat of judgment and punishment.
9. *will come to them*: it appears that their end is near (cf. Q6.67 below).

6–11 Punishment of earlier generations a warning

10. *how many a generation We have destroyed before them*: a reference to previous peoples who were punished for their sins (cf. Q6.11 below; see n. on Q7.59). The remains of their destroyed cities were believed to be still visible (cf. Q3.137; 6.11 below).
11. *you*: the Prophet.
12. *papyrus*: Ar. *qirṭās* (cf. Gk. *chartēs*); the word occurs only here and at Q6.91 (below), where it is used in reference to the Torah of Moses (cf. Q52.2-3, 'a Book written on parchment').
13. *him*: the Prophet; their request may reflect contemporary expectations that a (true) prophet would be

sent down an angel, the matter would indeed have been decided, (and) then they would not be spared. **9** Even if We had made him[14] an angel, We would indeed have made him[15] a man, and have confused for them what they are confusing. **10** Certainly messengers[16] have been mocked before you, but those of them who ridiculed (were) overwhelmed (by) what they were mocking.[17] **11** Say:[18] 'Travel the earth and see how the end was for the ones who called (it) a lie.'[19]

12 Say: 'To whom (belongs) whatever is in the heavens and the earth?' Say: 'To God. He has prescribed[20] mercy for Himself. He will indeed gather you to the Day of Resurrection – (there is) no doubt about it. Those who have lost their (own) selves, they do not believe. **13** To Him (belongs) whatever dwells in the night and the day. He is the Hearing, the Knowing.'

14 Say: 'Shall I take any other ally than God, Creator of the heavens and the earth, when He feeds (others) and is not fed?'[21] Say: 'Surely I have been commanded to be the first of those who have submitted,' and: 'Do not be one of the idolaters!'[22] **15** Say: 'Surely I fear, if I disobey my Lord, the punishment of a great Day.' **16** Whoever is turned from it[23] on that Day – He has had compassion on him. That is the clear triumph! **17** If God touches you[24] with any harm, (there is) no one to remove it but Him, and if He touches you with any good – He is powerful over everything. **18** He is the Supreme One above His servants.[25] He is the Wise, the Aware.

19 Say: 'What thing (is) greater as a witness?' Say: 'God is witness between me and you, and I have been inspired (with) this Qur'ān[26] so that I may warn you by means of it, and whomever it reaches. Do you indeed bear witness that (there are) other gods with God?' Say: 'I do not bear witness.' Say: 'He is only one God. Surely I am free of what you associate.'[27] **20** Those to whom We have given the Book[28] recognize it,[29] as they recognize their own sons. Those who have lost their (own) selves, they do not believe.

---

accompanied by supernatural manifestations, or that he would be more than an ordinary human (see Q6.37, 50 below; cf. Q11.12; 25.7).

14. *him*: the messenger.
15. *him*: the angel sent as a messenger.
16. *messengers*: for this important title, see n. on Q2.87.
17. *what they were mocking*: the threat of judgment and punishment (cf. Q21.41).
18. *Say*: on this form of address, see n. on Q2.80.
19. *who called (it) a lie*: i.e. who rejected the warning of imminent judgment; the remains of their destroyed cities were believed to be still visible (cf. Q3.137; 6.148; 16.36; 43.25; see n. on Q7.59).

12–18 The power of God

20. *prescribed*: lit. 'written' (cf. Q6.54 below).
21. *is not fed*: i.e. God does not require sacrifices 'for food,' as other gods do (cf. Q20.132; 22.37; 51.57).
22. *the idolaters*: or 'the ones who associate (other gods with God).'
23. *turned from it*: i.e. spared punishment.
24. *you*: sing., but intended generally ('one').
25. *servants*: the word 'servants,' which also means 'slaves,' is used here in the sense of 'all people.'

19–24 God is witness

26. *this Qur'ān*: or perhaps 'this recitation,' since the expression (Ar. *hādhā al-qur'ān*) is sometimes used only in reference to a part of the Qur'ān (cf. Q10.61; 13.31; 72.1; see n. on Q2.185). Otherwise, 'this Qur'ān' may come close to its present meaning as the name of the Muslim scripture (cf. Q9.111), and perhaps imply the existence of 'other Qur'āns' (cf. Q39.27-28).
27. *I am free of what you associate*: i.e. other gods with God; exactly what Abraham says at Q6.78 below.
28. *Those to whom we have given the Book*: i.e. Jews and Christians. The Cairo edition, reflecting the views of traditional scholars, attributes this verse (and v. 23 below) to the 'Medinan' period.
29. *recognize it*: the Qur'ān; but 'him' (i.e. the Prophet) is also possible grammatically (cf. Q2.146).

21 Who is more evil than the one who forges a lie against God, or calls His signs[30] a lie? Surely the evildoers will not prosper. **22** On the Day when We shall gather them – all (of them) – We shall say to those who associated, 'Where are your associates whom you used to claim (as gods)?' **23** Then their only excuse will be to claim, 'By God, our Lord! We have not been idolaters.' **24** See how they lie against themselves, and (how) what they forged has abandoned them![31]

25 (There are) some of them who listen to you,[32] but We have made coverings over their hearts, so that they do not understand it,[33] and a heaviness in their ears. If they see any sign,[34] they do not believe in it, so that when they come to dispute with you, those who disbelieve say, 'This is nothing but old tales.'[35] **26** They keep (others) from it, and keep (themselves) from it, but they only destroy themselves, though they do not realize (it). **27** If (only) you[36] could see when they are made to stand before the Fire:[37] they will say, 'Would that we (could) be returned, and had not called the signs of our Lord a lie, but were among the believers.' **28** No! What they were hiding before has (now) become apparent to them. Even if they were returned, they would indeed return to what they were forbidden. Surely they are liars indeed!

29 They say, 'There is nothing but our present life. We are not going to be raised up.' **30** If (only) you could see when they are made to stand before their Lord: He will say, 'Is this not the truth?' They will say, 'Yes indeed! By our Lord!' He will say, 'Taste the punishment for what you were disbelieving.' **31** Lost (are) those who call the meeting with God[38] a lie – until, when the Hour[39] comes upon them unexpectedly, they say, 'Alas for us, because of what we neglected concerning it!' They bear their burdens[40] on their backs. Is it not a fact that evil is what they bear? **32** This present life is nothing but jest and diversion.[41] Yet the Home of the Hereafter[42] is indeed better for the ones who guard (themselves).[43] Will you not understand?

33 We know that what they say causes you[44] sorrow. Yet surely they do not call you a liar, but the evildoers are denying the signs of God. **34** Certainly messengers have been called liars before you, yet they patiently endured being called liars, and suffered harm, until Our help came to them. No one can change the words of God. Certainly some of the story has (already) come to you about the envoys (before you).[45]

---

30. *signs*: or 'verses.'
31. *abandoned them*: lit. 'gone astray from them;' i.e. their gods have deserted them (cf. Q6.94 below; 10.28-30).

25–32 Diatribe against the disbelievers

32. *you*: the Prophet.
33. *it*: the warning about judgment and punishment.
34. *sign*: of impending judgment.
35. *old tales*: or 'tales of the ancients' (Ar. *asāṭīr al-awwalīn*); the expression occurs nines times as a contemptuous reference to the stories of earlier generations who were punished for disobeying their prophets (see n. on Q7.59; cf. Q25.5, where it accompanies an accusation of fraud).
36. *you*: the Prophet, or perhaps intended generally (and at v. 30 below).
37. *the Fire*: Ar. *al-nār* is the most common of the various designations for Hell.
38. *the meeting with God*: on the Day of Judgment.
39. *the Hour*: of judgment.
40. *their burdens*: probably their sins.
41. *jest and diversion*: i.e. trivial in comparison with the Hereafter.
42. *Home of the Hereafter*: see n. on Q2.4.
43. *guard (themselves)*: against evil, or God.

33–36 Encouragement to the Prophet

44. *you*: the Prophet.
45. *the envoys (before you)*: lit. 'the ones who are sent' (Ar. *al-mursalūn*), a designation roughly equivalent to 'messengers' (*rusul*); the 'story' is a reference to the reports of previous messengers who were likewise rejected by

35 But if their aversion is hard on you, (even) if you were able to seek out an opening in the earth, or a ladder into the sky, to bring them a sign [...].[46] If God had (so) pleased, He would indeed have gathered them to the guidance.[47] Do not be one of the ignorant. **36** Only those who hear[48] respond, but the dead – God will raise them up. Then to Him they will be returned.

37 They (also) say, 'If only a sign were sent down on him from his Lord.'[49] Say: 'Surely God is able to send down a sign,' but most of them do not know (it). **38** (There is) no creature on the earth, nor (any) bird flying with both its wings, but (they are) communities like you. We have not neglected anything in the Book.[50] Then to their Lord they will be gathered. **39** Those who call Our signs a lie are deaf and speechless in the darkness. Whomever God pleases, He leads astray, and whomever He pleases, He places him on a straight path. **40** Say: 'Do you see yourselves?[51] If the punishment of God comes upon you, or the Hour comes upon you, will you call on (any god) other than God, if you are truthful?' **41** No! You will call on Him, and He will remove what you call on Him for, if He pleases, and you will forget what you associate.[52]

42 Certainly We have sent to communities before you,[53] and We seized them with violence and hardship, so that they might humble themselves. **43** If only they had humbled themselves when Our violence came upon them! But their hearts were hard, and Satan[54] made what they were doing appear enticing to them. **44** So when they forgot what they were reminded of, We opened on them the gates of everything,[55] until they gloated over what they were given, when (once again) We seized them unexpectedly, and suddenly they were in despair. **45** So the last remnant of the people who did evil was cut off. Praise (be)[56] to God, Lord of the worlds![57]

46 Say: 'Do you see? If God takes away your hearing and your sight, and sets a seal on your hearts, who is a god other than God to bring it (back) to you?' See how We vary the signs? Then they (still) turn away. **47** Say: 'Do you see yourselves?[58] If the punishment of God comes upon you, unexpectedly or openly,[59] will any be destroyed but the people who are evildoers?' **48** We send the envoys only as bringers of good news and warners.[60] Whoever believes and sets (things) right – (there will be) no fear on them, nor will

---

their own people (see n. on Q7.59).

46. *to bring them a sign [...]*: there may be a lacuna here, but the meaning is that even if the Prophet could miraculously descend into the earth or ascend into heaven, the disbelievers would still not be convinced.

47. *the guidance*: one of the most frequent terms (Ar. *al-hudā*) for revelation in general, and the Qur'ān in particular.

48. *hear*: i.e. understand (cf. Q6.25 above).

37–41 Demand for a sign

49. *If only a sign were sent down...*: i.e. they demand a miracle from the Prophet before they will believe him (cf. Q17.90-95; 25.7-8, 20-21, 32; and the similar demand for a 'sign' from the opponents of Jesus at John 2.18; 6.30).

50. *the Book*: see n. on Q6.59 below.

51. *Do you see yourselves*: although the verb is sing., the object pronoun is plur.

52. *what you associate*: other gods with God.

42–45 Punishment of earlier generations a warning

53. *communities before you*: i.e. communities to whom messengers were sent before the Prophet's time (see e.g. Q7.59-102; 11.25-109; 15.87n.).

54. *Satan*: for this figure, see n. on Q2.36.

55. *We opened on them the gates of everything*: i.e. restored them to their former prosperity.

56. *(be)*: or '(belongs).'

57. *Lord of the worlds*: for this title, see n. on Q1.2.

46–55 Warning to disbelievers

58. *Do you see yourselves*: although the verb is sing., the object pronoun is plur.

59. *openly*: i.e. after you have been warned.

60. *bringers of good news...warners*: for these roles, see n. on Q2.119.

they sorrow. **49** But those who call Our signs a lie – the punishment will touch them because they were acting wickedly.

50 Say: 'I do not say to you, "The storehouses of God are with me."[61] I do not know the unseen,[62] nor do I say to you, "I am an angel." I only follow what I am inspired (with).' Say: 'Are the blind and the sighted equal? Will you not reflect?'

51 Warn by means of it[63] those who fear that they will be gathered to their Lord – they have no ally and no intercessor other than Him – so that they may guard (themselves). **52** And do not drive away those who call on their Lord in the morning and the evening, desiring His face.[64] Nothing of their account (falls) on you,[65] and nothing of your account (falls) on them, (that) you should drive them away and so become one of the evildoers. **53** In this way We have tested some of them by means of others,[66] so that they will say, 'Are these (the ones) on whom God has bestowed favor among us?' Is it not God (who) knows the thankful? **54** When those who believe in Our signs[67] come to you, say: 'Peace (be) upon you! Your Lord has prescribed mercy for Himself. Whoever of you does evil in ignorance, (and) then turns (in repentance) after that and sets (things) right – surely He is forgiving, compassionate.' **55** In this way We make the signs distinct,[68] and (We do this) so that the way of the sinners may become clear.

56 Say: 'Surely I am forbidden to serve those whom you call on instead of God.' Say: 'I do not follow your (vain) desires, (for) then I would indeed have gone astray, and not be one of the (rightly) guided.' **57** Say: 'I (stand) on a clear sign[69] from my Lord, but you have called it[70] a lie. What you seek to hurry[71] is not in my power. Judgment (belongs) only to God. He recounts[72] the truth, and He is the best of judges.'[73] **58** Say: 'If what you seek to hurry were in my power, the matter would indeed have been decided between you and me. God knows about the evildoers.'

59 With Him are the keys[74] of the unseen.[75] No one knows them but Him. He knows whatever is on the shore and the sea. Not a leaf falls but He knows of it. (There is) not a grain in the darkness of the earth, and nothing ripe or withered, but (it is recorded) in a clear Book.[76] **60** He (it is) who takes you

---

61. *The storehouses of God are with me*: i.e. the Prophet denies that he can enrich his followers.
62. *the unseen*: here referring to 'the future' (see n. on Q2.3), and a reminder that prophets do not predict the future.
63. *it*: the antecedent is 'what I am inspired (with),' so 'it' may refer to the Qur'ān (cf. Q6.70 below).
64. *desiring His face*: i.e. seeking God's favor; cf. Psalms 24.3-6; 27.7-9; 105.4; 2 Chronicles 7.14.
65. *you*: the Prophet.
66. *tested some of them by means of others*: i.e. by differences in wealth and status.
67. *signs*: or 'verses.'
68. *make the signs distinct*: or 'expound the verses' (cf. below Q6.97, 98, 114, 119, 126, 154).

56–58 The Prophet serves God alone

69. *clear sign*: or 'clear proof,' 'indisputable evidence.'
70. *it*: the antecedent is not 'a clear sign' but the threatened punishment (as what follows makes clear).
71. *what you seek to hurry*: i.e. the threatened judgment, which the disbelievers have scoffed at.
72. *recounts*: a variant reading is 'decides;' but cf. Q3.62; 7.7; 11.120; 18.13.
73. *judges*: lit. 'deciders' or 'distinguishers;' i.e. between the righteous and the wicked (cf. Q37.21; 44.40; 77.13; 78.17).

59–67 God is powerful over all

74. *keys*: or 'openings' (cf. Q72.26).
75. *the unseen*: see n. on Q2.3.
76. *a clear Book*: not the Qur'ān, but the 'Book of God' or 'Book of Destiny' by which everything is ordained, or a heavenly 'Record' of all things (see Q6.38 above; 9.36; 10.61; 11.6; 13.38; 22.70; 57.22 etc.; cf. e.g. Psalm 56.8; Isaiah 65.6; Malachi 3.16; Daniel 7.10; 1 Enoch 90.20).

in the night,[77] and He knows what you have earned in the day. Then He raises you up in it,[78] so that an appointed time[79] may be completed. Then to Him is your return, (and) then He will inform you about what you have done. **61** He is the Supreme One over His servants. He sends watchers over you,[80] until, when death comes to one of you, Our messengers take him[81] – and they do not neglect (their duty). **62** Then they are returned to God, their true Protector. Is it not a fact that judgment (belongs) to Him? He is the quickest of reckoners.

63 Say: 'Who rescues you from the dangers[82] of the shore and the sea? You call on Him in humility and in secret: "If indeed He rescues us from this, we shall indeed be among the thankful."' **64** Say: 'God rescues you from it, and from every distress, (but) then you associate.'[83] **65** Say: 'He is the One able to raise up punishment against you, from above you or from beneath your feet, or to confuse you (into different) parties, and make some of you taste violence from others.' See how We vary the signs, so that they may understand. **66** But your people have called it[84] a lie, when it is the truth. Say: 'I am not a guardian over you. **67** Every prophecy will come true.[85] Soon you will know!'

68 When you[86] see those who banter about Our signs, turn away from them until they banter about some other topic.[87] If Satan makes you forget (this), do not sit, after (you give) the Reminder,[88] with the people who are evildoers. **69** Nothing of their account (falls) on the ones who guard (themselves), but (it is) a reminder, so that they (too) may guard (themselves). **70** Leave those who take their religion as jest and diversion. This present life has deceived them. Remind (them) by means of it,[89] in case a person be given up to destruction for what he has earned.[90] He has no ally and no intercessor other than God. Even if he were to offer any equal compensation,[91] it would not be accepted from him. Those are the ones who are given up to destruction for what they have earned. For them (there will be) a drink of boiling (water) and a painful punishment, because they were disbelieving.

71 Say: 'Shall we call on what does not benefit us or harm us, instead of God (alone), and turn back on

77. *takes you in the night*: this expression usually means 'takes away in death' (see the following v.), but here it seems to mean that an individual's 'self' or 'soul' goes to God during sleep, and then returns to normal 'waking' life until its appointed time to die (cf. Q39.42). In other words, falling asleep and waking up is a daily reminder of the certainty of death and resurrection.
78. *it*: the day.
79. *an appointed time*: or 'term' (Ar. *ajal*), i.e. the precise date of a person's death is predetermined (cf. Q6.2 above).
80. *watchers over you*: angels who record the deeds of humans (see Q10.21; 82.10-12; 86.4).
81. *Our messengers take him*: here referring to the angels who take away humans in death (see Q4.97; 6.93; 7.37; 8.50; 16.28, 32; 47.27; 50.17-19; cf. Q32.11, where there is only one 'angel of death').
82. *dangers*: lit. 'darknesses.'
83. *then you associate*: other gods with God.
84. *it*: either judgment or the Qur'ān.
85. *Every prophecy will come true*: lit. 'For every (piece of) news (there is) a dwelling place' (cf. Q6.5 above).

68–70 Avoid foolish discussions

86. *you*: the Prophet.
87. *topic*: Ar. *ḥadīth*.
88. *the Reminder*: here referring to the Qur'ān (cf. Q6.70, 90 below; see n. on Q3.58).
89. *Remind (them) by means of it*: i.e. the Prophet is to admonish or warn them by the Qur'ān (cf. Q50.45; 51.55; 52.29; 87.9; 88.21).
90. *for what he has earned*: i.e. for the sins he has committed.
91. *equal compensation*: as ransom.

71–73 God alone guides

our heels after God has guided us? – Like the one whom the satans[92] have lured on the earth, (and he is) confused, though he has companions who call him to the guidance (saying): "Come to us"?' Say: 'Surely the guidance of God – it is the (true) guidance, and we have been commanded to submit to the Lord of the worlds,[93] **72** and (to say), "Observe the prayer[94] and guard (yourselves) against Him, (for) He is the One to whom you will be gathered."' **73** He (it is) who created the heavens and the earth in truth.[95] On the day when He says 'Be!'[96] it is. His word is the truth, and the kingdom (will belong) to Him on the Day when there will be a blast on the trumpet.[97] (He is) the Knower of the unseen and the seen.[98] He is the Wise, the Aware.

74 (Remember) when[99] Abraham said to his father Āzar:[100] 'Do you take idols as gods? Surely I see you and your people are clearly astray.'[101] **75** In this way We were showing Abraham the kingdom of the heavens and the earth, and (this took place) so that he might be one of those who are certain. **76** When night descended on him, he saw a star.[102] He said, 'This is my Lord.' But when it set, he said, 'I do not love what vanishes.'[103] **77** When he saw the moon rising, he said, 'This is my Lord.' But when it set, he said, 'Surely if my Lord does not guide me, I shall indeed be one of the people who go astray.' **78** When he saw the sun rising, he said, 'This is my Lord – this is greater!' But when it set he said, 'My people! Surely I am free of what you associate.[104] **79** Surely I have turned my face to Him who created the heavens and the earth – (being) a Ḥanīf.[105] Yet I am not one of the idolaters.' **80** But his people disputed with him. He said, 'Do you dispute with me about God, when He has indeed guided me? I do not fear what you associate with Him, unless (it be) that my Lord wills something (against me). My Lord comprehends everything in knowledge. Will you not take heed?[106] **81** How should I fear what you have associated, when you are not afraid to associate with God what He has not sent down on you any authority for?' Which of the two groups has (more) right to security, if you know? **82** Those who have believed, and have not confused their belief with evildoing, those – for them (there is) the (true) security, and they are (rightly) guided. **83** That (was) Our argument. We gave it to Abraham against his people. We raise in rank whomever We please. Surely your Lord is wise, knowing.

---

92. *satans*: or 'demons' (Ar. *shayāṭīn*); individually assigned to incite people to evil (see Q19.83; 43.36; cf. Q23.97; 41.25).
93. *Lord of the worlds*: for this title, see n. on Q1.2.
94. *the prayer*: the ritual prayer (or *ṣalāt*).
95. *in truth*: or 'with the truth.'
96. *Be!*: God's creative word (Ar. *kun*); cf. Q2.117; 3.47 (to Mary), 59 (of Jesus and Adam); 16.40; 19.35; 36.82; 40.68.
97. *a blast on the trumpet*: the Last Day will be announced by the blast of a trumpet (e.g. Q18.99; 20.102; 39.68 [a double blast]; 69.13; 74.8; 78.18; cf. Matthew 24.31; 1 Corinthians 15.52; 1 Thessalonians 4.16).
98. *the seen*: lit. 'the witnessed.'

74–90 The story of Abraham and his descendants

99. *(Remember) when...*: a stock narrative formula; the Arabic particle *idh* often marks the beginning of a story, and means something like 'Once...,' or 'There was a time when...,' or 'Remember when....' For the story that follows, cf. the version at Q21.51-71.
100. *Āzar*: not named elsewhere; Abraham's father was Terah, according to Genesis 11.27, 31 (though a certain 'Eleazar' was Abraham's servant, according to Genesis 15.2).
101. *clearly astray*: lit. 'in clear straying.'
102. *he saw a star*: see Q37.88-89; cf. Genesis 15.5; Jubilees 12.16-17; Apocalypse of Abraham 7.8-10.
103. *what vanishes*: lit. 'the setters.'
104. *I am free of what you associate*: exactly what the Prophet was commanded to say at Q6.19 (above).
105. *(being) a Ḥanīf*: or perhaps '(though I am) a Gentile' (see n. on Q2.135; cf. Q6.161 below).
106. *take heed*: or 'be reminded,' 'remember.'

84 And We granted him Isaac and Jacob[107] – each one We guided, and Noah We guided before (them) – and of his descendants (were) David, and Solomon, and Job, and Joseph, and Moses, and Aaron – in this way We repay the doers of good – **85** and Zachariah, and John, and Jesus, and Elijah[108] – each one was of the righteous – **86** and Ishmael, and Elisha,[109] and Jonah, and Lot – each one We favored over the worlds[110] **87** – and some of their fathers, and their descendants, and their brothers. We chose them and guided them to a straight path. **88** That is the guidance of God. He guides by means of it whomever He pleases of His servants. If they had associated, what they did would indeed have come to nothing for them. **89** Those are the ones to whom We gave the Book,[111] and the judgment,[112] and the prophetic office. If these (people)[113] disbelieve in it,[114] We have already entrusted it to a people who do not disbelieve in it.[115] **90** Those are the ones whom God has guided. Follow their guidance.[116] Say: 'I do not ask you for any reward for it. It is nothing but a reminder to the worlds.'[117]

91 They[118] have not measured God (with) due measure, when they said, 'God has not sent down anything on a human being.' Say: 'Who sent down the Book which Moses brought as a light and a guidance for the people? You make it (into) sheets of papyrus[119] – you reveal (some of) it, but you hide much (of it).[120] And you were taught what you did not know – neither you nor your fathers.' Say: 'God,'[121] and leave them in their banter (while) they jest.

92 This is a Book: We have sent it down, blessed, confirming that which was before it.[122] And (We sent it down) so that you[123] may warn the Mother of Towns[124] and those around it. Those who believe in the Hereafter believe in it, and they keep guard over their prayers. **93** Who is more evil than the one who

107. *Isaac and Jacob*: Ishmael is mentioned later (Q6.86), but without any apparent connection to Abraham (cf. Q11.71; 19.49-55; 21.72-85; 38.45-48). In other passages, however, emphasis is placed on Ishmael as Abraham's son (see e.g. Q2.125, 127; 3.84; 4.163; 14.39).

108. *Elijah*: mentioned only here and at Q37.123-132. The form of the name (Ar. *Ilyās*) is in accord with Christian usage (Gk. *Elias*) rather than Jewish (Hebr. *Elijah*).

109. *Elisha*: Ar. *Alyasaʿ* or *al-Yasaʿ* (he is mentioned only here and at Q38.48).

110. *favored over the worlds*: or 'preferred over all peoples;' the distinctiveness of Israel's election is recognized (see Q2.47, 122; 3.33; 7.140; 44.32; 45.16).

111. *the Book*: the Torah (cf. Q3.79; 29.27; 45.16; 57.26).

112. *the judgment*: or 'the wisdom' (see n. on Q3.79).

113. *these (people)*: refers to the Jews.

114. *it*: 'it' (fem.) would strictly refer to 'the prophetic office' (fem.), or else 'it' may refer to 'the Book, the judgment, and the prophetic office' altogether, which have now been given to the believers as God's new chosen people.

115. *a people who do not disbelieve in it*: refers to the believers or Muslims.

116. *Follow their guidance*: i.e. the guidance of Abraham and his descendants named above (either addressed to the Prophet, or intended for the Jews).

117. *to the worlds*: or 'to all peoples,' emphasizing the universality of the message.

91 Revelation to a human being?

118. *They*: reference uncertain, but probably the Jews in light of what follows. The Cairo edition attributes this verse (and v. 93 below) to the 'Medinan' period.

119. *make it (into) sheets of papyrus*: or perhaps 'copied it onto sheets of papyrus' (see n. on Q6.7 above).

120. *hide much (of it)*: e.g. the predictions of the coming of the Prophet.

121. *'God'*: i.e. God sent it down to Moses, thus answering the preceding question, 'Who sent down the Book...?'

92–93a The Book sent to the Prophet

122. *This is a Book...confirming that which was before it*: the Qur'ān 'confirms' the Torah of Moses and Gospel of Jesus (cf. Q6.154-155 below).

123. *you*: the Prophet, or perhaps intended generally.

124. *Mother of Towns*: Ar. *umm al-qurā* is said to refer to Mecca (cf. Q42.7).

forges a lie against God, or says, 'I am inspired,' when he is not inspired at all, or the one who says, 'I will send down the equivalent of what God has sent down'?

If (only) you[125] could see when the evildoers are in the throes of death, and the angels are stretching out their hands (saying):[126] 'Out with yourselves! Today you are repaid (with) the punishment of humiliation because you spoke about God (something) other than the truth, and (because) you behaved arrogantly toward His signs.' **94** 'Certainly[127] you have come to Us individually, as We created you the first time,[128] and you have left what We bestowed on you[129] behind your backs. Nor do We see with you your intercessors, whom you claimed to be associates (with God) on your behalf.[130] Certainly (the bond) between you has been cut, and what you used to claim (as gods) has abandoned you.'[131]

95 Surely God is the splitter of the grain and the date seed.[132] He brings forth the living from the dead, and brings forth the dead from the living. That is God. How are you (so) deluded? **96** (He is) the splitter of the dawn,[133] and has made the night for rest, and the sun and moon for reckoning.[134] That is the decree of the Mighty, the Knowing. **97** He (it is) who has made the stars for you, so that you might be guided by them in the darkness of the shore and the sea. We have made the signs distinct for a people who know. **98** And He (it is) who produced you from one person,[135] and (gave you) a dwelling place and a place of deposit.[136] We have made the signs distinct for a people who understand. **99** He (it is) who has sent down water from the sky, and We have brought forth by means of it vegetation of every (kind), and brought forth green (leaves). We bring forth from it thick-clustered grain, and from the date palm, from its sheath, (We bring forth) bunches of dates near (at hand), and gardens of grapes, and olives, and pomegranates, alike and different. Look at its fruit, when it bears fruit, and its ripening. Surely in that are signs indeed for a people who believe.

100 They make the jinn[137] associates with God, when He created them, and they assign to Him[138] sons and

---

93b–94 A judgment scene

125. *you*: the Prophet, or perhaps intended generally ('one').
126. *the angels are stretching out their hands...*: i.e. the 'angels of death,' as they come to take humans away.
127. *Certainly...*: the scene now switches to the Judgment, and God is the speaker.
128. *the first time*: i.e. at birth.
129. *what We bestowed on you*: wealth and possessions.
130. *on your behalf*: lit. 'in you' (cf. Q6.22 above)
131. *has abandoned you*: lit. 'has gone astray from you' (a pun).

95–99 Signs of God's power and providence

132. *splitter of the grain and the date seed*: i.e. God is the one who causes them to sprout.
133. *splitter of the dawn*: from the darkness.
134. *reckoning*: of time and the calendar, based on the movements of the sun and moon.
135. *one person*: Adam.
136. *a dwelling place...a place of deposit*: probably a reference to life (on earth) and death (in the earth).

100–108 The folly of idolatry

137. *the jinn*: Ar. *jinn* (sing. *jinnī*) are created from 'fire' (Q15.27; 55.15), and not from 'clay' like humans. Some of them are said to be believers (Q46.29; 72.14), though most will end up in Gehenna (Q11.119). Like the demons and 'unclean spirits' of the New Testament (see e.g. Mark 5.13), they can take possession of a person and lead him astray (Q6.128; 41.29), and this is true even of prophets (Q6.112). Iblīs is said to be one of them (Q18.50). In the passage above, the claim is made that those who worship idols are really worshipping 'jinn' (cf. Q34.40-42; 37.158-159; contrast Q53.23n.). Cf. the apostle Paul's similar charge that the gods worshipped by 'pagans' are in fact demons (1 Corinthians 10.19-22). Some scholars contend that in the 'Meccan' sūras the existence of the 'jinn' is taken for granted, but that the term disappears from the 'Medinan' sūras (i.e. shortly after the Hijra). The same may be true of the related term 'satans.'
138. *assign to Him*: lit. 'make for Him.'

daughters without any knowledge. Glory to Him! He is exalted above what they allege. **101** Originator of the heavens and the earth – how can He have a son[139] when He has no consort,[140] (and) when He created everything and has knowledge of everything? **102** That is God, your Lord. (There is) no god but Him, Creator of everything. So serve Him![141] He is guardian over everything. **103** Sight does not reach Him, but He reaches sight. He is the Gentle, the Aware.

104 Now evidence has come to you from your Lord: whoever sees – it is to his advantage,[142] and whoever is blind – it is to his disadvantage.[143] I am not a watcher[144] over you. **105** In this way We vary the signs, so that they will say, 'You have studied,'[145] and that We may make it clear to a people who know. **106** Follow what you[146] are inspired (with) from your Lord – (there is) no god but Him – and turn away from the idolaters. **107** If God had (so) pleased, they would not have been idolaters. We have not made you a watcher over them, nor are you a guardian over them. **108** Do not revile[147] those (gods) on whom they call instead of God, or they will revile God in enmity without any knowledge. In this way We make their deed(s) appear enticing to every community. Then to their Lord is their return, and He will inform them about what they have done.

109 They have sworn by God the most solemn of their oaths: if a sign comes to them, they will indeed believe in it. Say: 'The signs (are) only with God.'[148] What will make you realize that, when it does come, they will not believe? **110** We shall turn their hearts and their sight away (from the sign), just as (We did when) they did not believe in it the first time, and We shall leave them in their insolent transgression, wandering blindly. **111** Even if We had sent down the angels to them, and the dead had spoken to them,[149] and (even if) We had gathered together everything against them head on, they would (still) not believe, unless God (so) pleased. But most of them are ignorant.

112 In this way We have assigned[150] to every prophet an enemy – satans of the humans and jinn[151] – some of them inspiring[152] others (with) decorative speech as a deception. If your Lord had (so) pleased, they would not have done it. So leave them and what they forge. **113** And (it is) so that the hearts of those who do not believe in the Hereafter may incline to it,[153] and that they may be delighted by it, and that they

---

139. *son*: or 'child' (Ar. *walad*).
140. *no consort*: i.e. no female companion or wife (cf. Q72.3).
141. *serve Him*: or 'worship Him' (plur. imperative).
142. *to his advantage*: lit. 'for his self' or 'soul.'
143. *to his disadvantage*: lit. 'against it' (i.e. his self).
144. *watcher*: or 'overseer,' 'keeper,' referring to the Prophet (cf. Q6.107 below).
145. *You have studied*: implying that the Prophet derived his knowledge from books, not from revelation.
146. *you*: the Prophet.
147. *Do not revile*: plur. imperative; the word occurs only here.

109–111 Demand for a sign

148. *The signs (are) only with God*: meaning that miracles are only in God's power to perform or grant.
149. *the dead had spoken to them*: cf. Luke 16.31.

112–117 Opposition to the Prophet

150. *assigned*: lit. 'made.'
151. *satans of the humans and jinn*: referring to the 'gods' of the disbelievers or perhaps their leaders (cf. Q2.14 , 102; for the 'jinn,' see n. on Q6.100 above).
152. *inspiring*: the technical term 'inspire' (Ar. *yūḥī*) is used here, implying that 'satans' and 'jinn' can induce 'counterfeit inspiration' or 'demonic possession' (see Q6.121 below; cf. Q22.52).
153. *may incline to it*: i.e. to the satans' deception or 'what they forge' (cf. Q19.83)

may acquire what they are acquiring.[154] **114** Shall I[155] seek (anyone) other than God as a judge? He (it is) who has sent down to you[156] the Book,[157] set forth distinctly.[158] Those to whom We have (already) given the Book[159] know that it[160] is sent down from your[161] Lord with the truth.[162] Do not be one of the doubters.

115 Perfect is the word of your Lord in truth and justice. No one can change His words. He is the Hearing, the Knowing. **116** If you[163] obey the majority of those on the earth, they will lead you astray from the way of God. They only follow conjecture[164] and they only guess. **117** Surely your Lord – He knows who goes astray from His way and He knows the ones who are (rightly) guided.

118 Eat from that over which the name of God has been mentioned,[165] if you are believers in His signs.[166] **119** What is (the matter) with you that you do not eat from that over which the name of God has been mentioned, when He has already made distinct[167] for you what He has forbidden you (to eat), unless you are forced to (eat) it?[168] Surely many are indeed led astray by their (vain) desires without realizing (it). Surely your Lord – He knows about the transgressors. **120** Forsake (both) obvious and hidden sin.[169] Surely those who earn sin will be repaid for what they have earned. **121** Do not eat that over which the name of God has not been mentioned. Surely it is wickedness indeed! Surely the satans inspire their allies, so that they may dispute with you. If you obey them, surely you will be idolaters indeed! **122** Is the one who was dead, and We gave him life (again), and made for him a light to walk by among the people, like the one who is to be compared to (a person) in the darkness from which he never emerges? In this way what they have done was made to appear enticing to the disbelievers.

123 In this way We have placed in every town great ones among its sinners,[170] so that they might scheme there. Yet they do not scheme against (anyone) but themselves, though they do not realize (it). **124** When a sign comes to them, they say, 'We will not believe until we are given (something) similar to what was given to the messengers of God.' God knows where He places His message. Disgrace in God's sight will smite those who have sinned, and (also) a harsh punishment, for what they were scheming.

---

154. *acquire what they are acquiring*: punishment for their sins.
155. *Shall I...*: since it is the Prophet who must be speaking here, an introductory 'say' may have fallen out. The Cairo edition attributes this verse to the 'Medinan' period.
156. *you*: plur.
157. *the Book*: here referring to the Qur'ān.
158. *set forth distinctly*: or 'expounded' (like the 'Book' of Moses, see Q6.154 below; cf. Q7.52, 145; 10.37; 11.1; 12.111; 41.3, 44).
159. *the Book*: here referring to the Torah.
160. *it*: the Qur'ān.
161. *your*: sing. (and in the next v.)
162. *with the truth*: or 'in truth,' 'truly.'
163. *you*: the Prophet.
164. *conjecture*: or 'opinion,' as opposed to 'revealed (i.e. certain) knowledge' (cf. Q6.148 below).

118–122 Regulations concerning food

165. *mentioned*: or 'remembered.'
166. *signs*: or 'verses.'
167. *made distinct*: or 'expounded.'
168. *unless you are forced to (eat) it*: see Q6.145 below.
169. *obvious and hidden sin*: see Q6.151 below; 7.33.

123–127 Paragons of sin

170. *great ones among its sinners*: i.e. leaders or paragons of wickedness.

125 Whomever God intends to guide, He expands his heart[171] to Islam,[172] and whomever He intends to lead astray, He makes his heart narrow (and) constricted, as if he were climbing up into the sky. In this way God places the abomination on those who do not believe. **126** This is the path of your Lord – straight. We have made the signs distinct for a people who take heed.[173] **127** For them (there is) the Home of peace[174] with their Lord. He is their ally for what they have done.

128 On the Day when He will gather them all together: 'Assembly of the jinn! You have acquired many of humankind.'[175] And their allies among humankind will say, 'Our Lord, some of us have profited by others, but (now) we have reached our time which You appointed for us.'[176] He will say, 'The Fire is your dwelling place, there to remain' – except for whomever[177] God pleases. Surely your Lord is wise, knowing.
129 In this way We make some of the evildoers allies of others for what they have earned.

130 'Assembly of the jinn and humans! Did messengers not come to you from among you, recounting to you My signs and warning you of the meeting of this Day of yours?' They will say, 'We bear witness against ourselves.' This present life deceived them, and they bear witness against themselves that they were disbelievers. **131** That (is because) your Lord was not one to destroy the towns in an evil manner, while their people were oblivious.[178] **132** And for each (there are) ranks[179] according to what they have done, and your Lord is not oblivious of what they do. **133** Your Lord is the wealthy One,[180] the One full of mercy. If He (so) pleases, He will do away with you,[181] and appoint as a successor after you whomever[182] He pleases, just as He produced you from the descendants of another people.[183] **134** Surely what you are promised will indeed come, and you cannot escape (it).[184] **135** Say: 'My people! Do as you are able. Surely I am going to do (what I can). Soon you will know to whom the final Home (belongs).[185] Surely he – the evildoers will not prosper.'

136 They assign to God[186] a portion of the crops and the livestock[187] which He created,[188] and they say, 'This is for God' – so they claim – 'and this is for our associates.'[189] But what is for their associates does

171. *expands his heart*: or 'opens his mind' (lit. 'expands his chest'); cf. Q20.25 (of Moses); 94.1 (of the Prophet).
172. *Islam*: lit. 'the submission' or 'the surrender' to God (Ar. *al-Islām*).
173. *take heed*: or 'are reminded,' 'remember.'
174. *peace*: Ar. *salām* connotes 'submission' (*islām*) to God (cf. Q10.25).

128–135 A judgment scene: jinn and humans

175. *acquired many of humankind*: as adherents (lit. 'made much of humankind').
176. *time...appointed for us*: see Q6.60 above.
177. *whomever*: lit. 'whatever.'
178. *while their people were oblivious*: i.e. before the inhabitants were warned and had an opportunity to repent (cf. Q11.117; 26.208-209; 28.59).
179. *ranks*: or 'degrees,' of honor and dishonour, or rewards and punishments.
180. *the wealthy One*: i.e. God has no need of anyone or anything.
181. *you*: plur.
182. *whomever*: lit. 'whatever.'
183. *from the descendants of another people*: reference uncertain; it may mean that the Prophet's contemporaries were thought to be the descendants of another, previously destroyed people.
184. *what you are promised...cannot escape (it)*: judgment.
185. *Soon you will know...*: this makes it appear that the end is near.

136–140 Idolatry and infanticide condemned

186. *assign to God*: lit. 'make for God.'
187. *livestock*: lit. 'cattle' (cf. Q5.103; 16.56).
188. *created*: lit. 'sown.'
189. *our associates*: the other gods.

not reach God, and what is for God reaches their associates. Evil is what they judge! **137** In this way their associates made the killing of their children[190] appear enticing to many of the idolaters, in order that they might bring them to ruin and confuse their religion for them. If God had (so) pleased, they would not have done it. So leave them and what they forge.[191] **138** They say, 'These livestock and crops are forbidden. No one may eat them, except for whomever we please' – so they claim – 'and livestock whose backs have been forbidden, and livestock over which the name of God is not to be mentioned' – forging (lies) against Him.[192] He will repay them for what they have forged. **139** They say, 'What is in the bellies[193] of these livestock is exclusively for our males and forbidden to our wives. But if it is (born) dead, they will (all) be partakers in it.' He will repay them for their attributing (these things to Him). Surely He is wise, knowing. **140** Lost (are) those who kill their children in foolishness, without any knowledge, and forbid what God has provided them, forging (lies) against God. They have gone astray and are not (rightly) guided.

141 He (it is) who produces gardens, trellised and untrellised,[194] and date palms and crops of diverse produce, and olives and pomegranates, alike and different. Eat from its fruits when it bears fruit, and give its due (portion) on the day of its harvest. But do not act wantonly. Surely He does not love the wanton. **142** And of the livestock (there are some for) burden and (some for) slaughter. Eat from what God has provided you, and do not follow the footsteps of Satan. Surely he is clear enemy to you.

143 Eight pairs: two of the sheep, and two of the goats. Say: 'Has He forbidden the two males or the two females? Or what the wombs of the two females contain? Inform me with knowledge, if you are truthful.'

144 And two of the camels,[195] and two of the cows. Say: 'Has He forbidden the two males or the two females? Or what the wombs of the two females contain? Or were you witnesses when God charged you with this (command)? Who is more evil than the one who forges a lie against God, in order to lead the people astray without (their) realizing (it)? Surely God does not guide the people who are evildoers.'

145 Say: 'I do not find in what I have been inspired (with[196] anything) forbidden to one who eats of it, unless it is (already) dead, or blood (which is) shed, or swine's flesh – surely it is an abomination – or – something wicked – it has been dedicated to (a god) other than God.'[197] But whoever is forced (by necessity),[198] not desiring or (deliberately) transgressing – surely your Lord is forgiving, compassionate.

146 To those who are Jews[199] We have forbidden every (animal) with claws,[200] and of the cows and the sheep and goats We have forbidden to them their fat, except what their backs carry, or their entrails,

---

190. *the killing of their children*: i.e. child sacrifice (see Q6.140 below), but perhaps infanticide is also meant (see Q6.151 below).

191. *So leave them...*: addressed to the Prophet.

192. *forging (lies) against Him*: i.e. claiming that God had sanctioned their ritual practices (cf. Q10.59-60).

193. *bellies*: i.e. wombs.

141–150 Regulations concerning food

194. *trellised and untrellised*: or 'terraced and unterraced.' The Cairo edition attributes this verse to the 'Medinan' period.

195. *camels*: may be eaten (forbidden according to Leviticus 11.4; Deuteronomy 14.7)

196. *what I have been inspired (with)...*: this passage summarizes the regulations concerning meat (cf. Q2.173), and also explains why additional restrictions were placed upon the Jews.

197. *dedicated to (a god) other than God*: see Q2.173; 5.3; 16.115; cf. Acts 15.29; 1 Corinthians 8.1-13; 10.23-30.

198. *forced (by necessity)*: i.e. compelled to eat something forbidden.

199. *those who are Jews*: lit. 'those who have judaized,' or follow Jewish law, punning on the name Yahūd.

200. *with claws*: the literal meaning of the word. Some scholars take it to refer to the prohibition against eating the meat of land animals with 'divided hooves' (cf. Leviticus 11.4-8; Deuteronomy 14.7-8), but this seems unlikely. Perhaps it refers to certain kinds of shellfish (cf. Leviticus 11.9-12).

or what is mixed with the bone. We repaid them that for their envy.[201] Surely We are truthful indeed. **147** If they call you a liar, say: 'Your Lord is full of abundant mercy, but His violence will not be turned back from the people who are sinners.'

148 The idolaters will say, 'If God had (so) pleased, we would not have been idolaters, nor our fathers, nor would we have forbidden anything.' In this way the people before them called (it) a lie, until they tasted Our violence. Say: 'Do you have any knowledge? Bring it forth for us! You only follow conjecture and you only guess.' **149** Say: 'To God (belongs) the conclusive argument. If He had (so) pleased, He would indeed have guided you all.'[202] **150** Say: 'Produce your witnesses who (will) bear witness that God has forbidden this.' If they do bear witness, do not bear witness with them.[203] Do not follow the desires of those who call Our signs a lie, and who do not believe in the Hereafter, and (who) equate (others) with their Lord.

151 Say: 'Come! I will recite[204] what your Lord has forbidden to you: Do not associate anything with Him, and (do) good to parents, and do not kill your children because of poverty – We shall provide for you and them – and do not go near (any) immoral deeds,[205] neither what is obvious of them nor what is hidden, and do not kill the person whom God has forbidden (to be killed),[206] except by right.[207] That is what He has charged you with, so that you may understand. **152** Do not go near the property of the orphan, except to improve it,[208] until he reaches his maturity. Fill up the measure and the scale in justice. We do not burden anyone beyond their capacity. When you speak, be fair, even if he is a family member.[209] Fulfill the covenant of God. That is what He has charged you with, so that you may take heed. **153** And (know) that this is My straight path. So follow it, and do not follow the ways (of others), or it will diverge with you from His way. That is what He has charged you with, so that you may guard (yourselves).'

154 Then We gave Moses the Book,[210] complete[211] for the one who does good, and a distinct setting forth of everything,[212] and a guidance and mercy, so that they[213] might believe in the meeting with their Lord.[214] **155** And this is a Book:[215] We have sent it down, blessed. Follow it and guard (yourselves), so that you may receive compassion. **156** Otherwise you would say, 'The Book has only been sent down on two contingents (of people) before us,[216] and we were indeed oblivious of their studies.'[217] **157** Or you would say, 'If (only) the Book had been sent down to us, we would indeed have been better guided than them.'

---

201. *for their envy*: i.e. out of jealousy that God had now chosen others to receive his revelation (see Q2.90).

202. *guided you all*: for this idea, see n. on Q2.213.

203. *do not bear witness with them*: addressed to the Prophet, as is the following sentence.

151–153 Summary of religious obligations

204. *recite*: or 'read aloud.' The Cairo edition attributes the following three verses to the 'Medinan' period.

205. *immoral deeds*: lit. 'the immoralities' (Ar. *al-fawāḥisha*), usually of a sexual nature.

206. *forbidden (to be killed)*: i.e. made sacrosanct or inviolable.

207. *except by right*: i.e. for just cause.

208. *except to improve it*: lit. 'except with what is better' (cf. Q4.2, 10; 17.34).

209. *even if he is a family member*: i.e. fairness requires showing no favoritism, even to family members.

154–158 The Books given to Moses and the Prophet

210. *the Book*: the Torah.

211. *complete*: lit. 'a completion' or 'perfection;' but the meaning of this phrase is obscure.

212. *a distinct setting forth of everything*: see Q7.52, 145; cf. Q6.114 above; 10.37; 11.1; 12.111; 41.3, 44.

213. *they*: the Sons of Israel.

214. *the meeting with their Lord*: on the Day of Judgment.

215. *this is a Book*: here referring to the Qur'ān (see n. on Q2.2; cf. Q6.92 above).

216. *two contingents...before us*: Jews and Christians.

217. *their studies*: or perhaps 'their teachings.'

Yet a clear sign[218] has come to you from your Lord, and a guidance and mercy. Who is more evil than the one who calls the signs of God a lie, and turns away from them? We shall repay those who turn away from Our signs (with) an evil punishment for their turning away. **158** Do they expect (anything) but the angels to come to them,[219] or your Lord to come,[220] or one of the signs of your Lord to come?[221] On the Day when one of the signs of your Lord comes, belief will not benefit anyone who did not believe before, or (who did not) earn some good through his belief. Say: '(Just) wait! Surely We (too) are waiting.'

159 Surely those who have divided up their religion[222] and become (different) parties – you are no part of them.[223] Their affair (belongs) only to God, and He will inform them about what they have done. **160** Whoever brings a good deed will have ten equal to it, but whoever brings an evil deed will only be paid the equal of it – and they will not be done evil. **161** Say: 'Surely my Lord has guided me to a straight path, a right religion, the creed of Abraham the Ḥanīf.[224] He was not one of the idolaters.'

162 Say: 'Surely my prayer and my sacrifice,[225] and my living and my dying, are for God, Lord of the worlds. **163** He has no associate.[226] With that I have been commanded, and I am the first of those who submit.'[227]

164 Say: 'Shall I seek a Lord other than God, when He is the Lord of everything? No one earns (anything) except against himself, and no one bearing a burden bears the burden of another.[228] Then to your Lord is your return, (and) then He will inform you about your differences.'[229] **165** He (it is) who has made you successors on the earth,[230] and raised some of you above others in rank, so that He might test you by what He has given you. Surely your Lord is quick in retribution, yet surely He is indeed forgiving, compassionate.

---

218. *clear sign*: or 'clear proof,' 'indisputable evidence' (referring to the Qur'ān).
219. *angels to come to them*: i.e. to take them away at death.
220. *your Lord to come*: on the Day of Judgment.
221. *one of the signs of your Lord to come*: referring to some eschatological sign accompanying the arrival of the Last Day.

159–161 The Prophet's religion is Abraham's religion

222. *those who have divided up their religion*: Jews and Christians (cf. Q30.32).
223. *you are no part of them*: i.e. the Prophet is not to be concerned with them.
224. *Abraham the Ḥanīf*: or perhaps 'Abraham the Gentile' (see n. on Q2.135; cf. Q6.79 above).

162–165 Submission to God

225. *sacrifice*: a word (Ar. *nusuk*) which connotes other forms of worship as well (see Q2.196; cf. Q2.128, 200; 22.34, 67).
226. *no associate*: 'no partner' or 'no equal.'
227. *those who submit*: or 'the Muslims.'
228. *no one...bears the burden of another*: i.e. judgment falls on individuals, whom neither family nor friends can help (an implicit rejection of the Christian doctrine of 'vicarious atonement' and 'intercession' by the saints); cf. Q17.15; 35.18; 39.7; 53.38.
229. *...about your differences*: it is not clear where the quotation introduced by 'say' concludes.
230. *successors on the earth*: or 'rulers on the earth' (Ar. *khalā'if*, plur. of *khalīfa*). Adam was appointed God's 'ruler' on earth (Q2.30), but here the word may mean 'successors' of previous generations (see e.g. Q6.133 above; 7.69, 74; 24.55; 27.62).

7 The Heights ✽ Al-Aʿrāf

In the Name of God, the Merciful, the Compassionate

1 Alif Lām Mīm Ṣād.[1]

2 A Book[2] sent down to you[3] – so let there be no heaviness in your heart[4] because of it – in order that you
may warn by means of it, and as a reminder[5] to the believers. **3** Follow[6] what has been sent down to you
from your Lord, and do not follow any allies other than Him. Little do you take heed![7]

4 How many a town have We destroyed! Our violence came upon it at night, or (while) they were
relaxing at midday. **5** Their only cry, when Our violence came upon them, was that they said, 'Surely We
were evildoers!' **6** We shall indeed question those to whom (a messenger) was sent, and We shall indeed
question the envoys.[8] **7** We shall indeed recount to them with knowledge, (for) We were not absent.[9]
8 The weighing[10] on that Day (will be) the true (weighing). Whoever's scales are heavy,[11] those – they
are the ones who prosper, **9** but whoever's scales are light, those are the ones who have lost their (own)
selves, because of the evil they have done to Our signs.[12]

10 Certainly We have established you on the earth, and provided for you a means of living on it – little

---

Q7: Following an introductory reference to 'the Book' and a warning about judgment, Q7 falls into three main parts: the story of Iblīs and Adam's fall (Q7.10-25), a series of stories about the destruction of disobedient peoples of the past (Q7.59-102), and the story of Moses, Pharaoh, and the Sons of Israel (Q7.103-174). This sūra, like the previous one, is assigned by most scholars to the 'Meccan' period, though a few verses are considered to be 'Medinan.' Q7 receives its title from the enigmatic reference to 'the heights' at Q7.46.

1 Letters

1. *Alif Lām Mīm Ṣād*: the names of the Arabic letters ', *l*, *m*, and *ṣ*. Apart from an additional 'ṣād,' the same letter combination introduces sūras Q2-3 and Q29-32.Twenty-nine sūras begin with letters like these, ranging from one to five. No satisfactory explanation has been given for their occurrence. The Cairo edition varies in counting these letters as a separate verse (as here), or as the beginning of the first verse.

2–3 The Book

2. *A Book*: here referring to the Qur'ān not only as a 'recited' but also 'written' scripture (see n. on Q2.2).
3. *you*: the Prophet.
4. *heaviness in your heart*: lit. 'tightening' or 'constriction in your chest' (considered the seat of knowledge and understanding); perhaps this means 'doubt,' because of the poor response to the revelation (cf. Q11.12; 15.97).
5. *reminder*: or 'remembrance' (cf. Q7.63, 69 below; see n. on Q3.58).
6. *Follow*: plur. imperative.
7. *take heed*: or 'remember.'

4–9 Judgment

8. *the envoys*: lit. 'the ones who are sent' (Ar. *al-mursalūn*), a designation roughly equivalent to 'messengers' (*rusul*); cf. Q7.75, 77 below.
9. *...We were not absent*: i.e. at the Judgment all will be revealed about what the messengers have said and done.
10. *The weighing*: of good and bad deeds.
11. *scales are heavy*: good deeds are 'heavier' than evil deeds (see Q18.105).
12. *signs*: or 'verses' (see n. on Q2.39).

10–25 The story of Adam, Iblīs, and the Fall from Paradise

thanks you show! **11** Certainly We created you, (and) then fashioned you. Then We said to the angels,[13] 'Prostrate yourselves before Adam,'[14] and they prostrated themselves, except Iblīs.[15] He was not one of those who prostrated themselves. **12** He[16] said, 'What kept you from prostrating yourself when I commanded you?' He[17] said, 'I am better than him.[18] You created me from fire, but You created him from clay.'[19] **13** He said, 'Go down from here![20] It is not for you to be arrogant here. Get out! Surely you are one of the disgraced.' **14** He said, 'Spare me until the Day when they are raised up.' **15** He said, 'Surely you are one of the spared.' **16** He said, 'Because you have made me err, I shall indeed sit (in wait) for them (on) Your straight path. **17** Then I shall indeed come upon them, from before them and from behind them, and from their right and from their left, and You will not find most of them thankful.' **18** He said, 'Get out of here, detested (and) rejected! Whoever of them follows you – I shall indeed fill Gehenna[21] with you – all (of you)!'[22]

19 'Adam! Inhabit the Garden, you and your wife,[23] and eat freely of it wherever you please, but do not go near this tree,[24] or you will both be among the evildoers.' **20** Then Satan whispered to them both,[25] to reveal to them both what was hidden from them of their shameful parts.[26] He said, 'Your Lord has only forbidden you both from this tree to keep you both from becoming two angels, or from becoming two of the immortals.'[27] **21** And he swore to them both, 'Surely I am indeed one of your trusty advisers.' **22** So he caused them both to fall by means of deception. And when they both had tasted the tree, their shameful parts became apparent to them,[28] and they both began fastening on themselves some leaves of the Garden. But their Lord called to them both, 'Did I not forbid you both from that tree, and say to you both, "Surely Satan is a clear enemy to you"?' **23** They both said, 'Our Lord, we have done ourselves evil. If You do not forgive us, and have compassion on us, we shall indeed be among the losers.' **24** He said, 'Go down, some of you an enemy to others![29] The earth is a dwelling place for you, and enjoyment (of life) for a time.' **25** He said, 'On it you will live and on it you will die, and from it you will be brought forth.'[30]

13. *angels*: for these beings and their various roles, see n. on Q2.30.
14. *Prostrate yourselves before Adam*: the prostration of the angels before Adam is not a part of the Genesis account, but was a prominent theme in Christian tradition (see e.g. Hebrews 1.6; Life of Adam and Eve 12.1-16.1; Cave of Treasures 2.22-25).
15. *except Iblīs*: see n. on Q2.34; for the story that follows, cf. the versions at Q2.34-39; 15.28-48; 20.115-123; and Genesis 2.4-3.24.
16. *He*: God.
17. *He*: Iblīs.
18. *him*: Adam.
19. *from clay*: see Q6.2; 15.26; 17.61; 23.12; 32.7; 38.71, 76; 55.14; 'from dust,' according to Q3.59; 18.37; 22.5; 30.20; 35.11; 40.67; 'from water,' according to Q21.30; 24.45; 25.54.
20. *from here*: lit. 'from it,' i.e. from the heavenly Garden or Paradise (cf. Q7.19 below; see n. on Q2.25).
21. *Gehenna*: a name for Hell (see n. on Q2.206).
22. *...all (of you)*: cf. Q38.85; elsewhere God swears to 'fill Gehenna with jinn and people' (Q11.119; 32.13).
23. *your wife*: 'Eve' is not referred to by name in the Qur'ān.
24. *this tree*: see also Q2.35; 20.120 ('Tree of Immortality'); cf. Genesis 2.15-17; 3.1-2 ('Tree of Knowledge').
25. *Satan whispered to them both*: Satan 'whispers' to Adam alone at Q20.120; cf. Q2.36; and Genesis 3.1-24, for the story of the temptation of Eve.
26. *their shameful parts*: their genitalia.
27. *becoming two of the immortals*: cf. Genesis 3.5, 'You will be like gods, knowing good and evil.'
28. *their shameful parts became apparent to them*: i.e. they realized that they were naked.
29. *some of you an enemy to others*: 'you' is plur. here, and probably refers to humanity in general, whereas in the previous lines 'you' was dual (referring to Adam and his wife).
30. *brought forth*: at the resurrection.

26 Sons of Adam![31] We sent down on you clothing – it covers your shameful parts – and feathers.[32] Yet the clothing of guarding (yourselves)[33] – that is better. That is one of the signs of God, so that they may take heed.[34]

27 Sons of Adam! Do not let Satan tempt you, as he drove your parents out of the Garden, stripping both of them of their clothing in order to show both of them their shameful parts. Surely he sees you – he and his ilk – from where you do not see them. Surely We have made the satans[35] allies of those who do not believe.

28 When they commit immorality,[36] they say, 'We found our fathers doing it, and God has commanded us (to do) it.' Say:[37] 'Surely God does not command immorality. Do you say about God what you do not know?' **29** Say: 'My Lord has commanded justice. Set your faces in every mosque, and call on Him, devoting (your) religion to Him.[38] As He brought you about, (so) will you return. **30** (One) group He has guided, and (another) group – their going astray was deserved.[39] Surely they have taken the satans as allies instead of God, and they think that they are (rightly) guided.'

31 Sons of Adam! Take your adornment[40] in every mosque, and eat and drink, but do not act wantonly. Surely He does not love the wanton. **32** Say: 'Who has forbidden the adornment of God which He has brought forth for His servants,[41] and the good things of (His) provision?' Say: 'It[42] is exclusively for those who have believed in[43] this present life on the Day of Resurrection.' In this way We make the signs distinct[44] for a people who know.

33 Say: 'My Lord has only forbidden immoral deeds[45] – (both) what is obvious of them and what is hidden – and all sin and envy – without any right – and that you associate[46] with God what He has not sent down any authority for, and that you say about God what you do not know.' **34** For every community (there is) a time.[47] When their time comes, they will not delay (it) by an hour, nor will they advance (it by an hour).

35 Sons of Adam! If messengers[48] from among you should come to you, recounting to you My signs, whoever guards (himself)[49] and sets (things) right – (there will be) no fear on them, nor will they sorrow.

26–37 Address to the Sons of Adam

31. *Sons of Adam*: this address occurs only six times, five of them in this sūra alone (Q7.26, 27, 31, 35, 172; 36.60).
32. *We sent down on you clothing...and feathers*: most translators take the latter word (Ar. *rīsh*) as a metaphor for 'adornment' or 'finery' (as in the Eng. expression, 'fine feathers'); cf. the special 'garments of skin' created by God himself to clothe Adam and Eve prior to their departure from Eden (Genesis 3.21).
33. *the clothing of guarding (yourselves)*: i.e. against evil; for this idea, cf. Ephesians 6.10-18; Romans 13.12-14.
34. *take heed*: or 'be reminded,' 'remember.'
35. *satans*: or 'demons' (Satan's 'ilk'); individually assigned to incite people to evil (see Q19.83; 43.36; cf. Q23.97; 41.25).
36. *immorality*: or 'indecency' (Ar. *fāḥisha*), probably of a sexual nature (cf. Q7.33, 80 below).
37. *Say*: on this form of address, see n. on Q2.80.
38. *devoting (your) religion to Him*: i.e. serving God alone.
39. *their going astray was deserved*: or 'they were rightly destined to go astray' (cf. Q16.36)
40. *Take your adornment*: reference uncertain (cf. Q7.26 above); usually interpreted as 'finest clothes.'
41. *servants*: the word 'servant' (Ar. *'abd*) also means 'slave.'
42. *It*: antecedent unclear; perhaps the 'adornments' and 'good things' in the first half of the verse.
43. *in*: i.e. 'during.'
44. *make the signs distinct*: or 'expound the verses' (cf. Q7.52, 145, 174 below).
45. *immoral deeds*: lit. 'the immoralities' (Ar. *al-fawāḥisha*), usually of a sexual nature.
46. *associate*: other gods with God.
47. *time*: or 'term' (Ar. *ajal*), which is predetermined and cannot be changed (cf. Q10.48-49; 16.61; 34.29-30).
48. *messengers*: for this important title, see n. on Q2.87.
49. *guards (himself)*: against evil, or God.

36 But those who call Our signs a lie, and become arrogant about it – those are the companions of the Fire.[50] There they will remain. **37** Who is more evil than the one who forges a lie against God, or calls His signs a lie? Those – their portion of the Book will reach them,[51] until, when Our messengers[52] come to them, to take them,[53] they say, 'Where is what you used to call on (as gods) instead of God?' They will say, 'They have abandoned us,'[54] and they will bear witness against themselves that they were disbelievers.

38 He will say, 'Enter into the Fire, among the communities of jinn[55] and humans who have passed away before you.' Whenever a (new) community enters, it curses its sister (community), until, when they have all followed each other into it, the last of them will say to the first of them, 'Our Lord, these led us astray, so give them a double punishment of the Fire.' He will say, 'To each a double, but you do not know.'
39 And the first of them will say to the last of them, 'You have no advantage over us, so taste the punishment for what you have earned.'

40 Surely those who call Our signs a lie, and are arrogant about it – the gates of the sky will not be opened for them, nor will they enter the Garden, until the camel passes through the eye of the needle.[56] In this way We repay the sinners. **41** They have a bed in Gehenna, and coverings above them.[57] In this way
We repay the evildoers. **42** But those who believe and do righteous deeds – We do not burden anyone beyond their capacity – those are the companions of the Garden. There they will remain. **43** We shall strip away whatever rancor is in their hearts.[58] Beneath them rivers will flow, and they will say, 'Praise (be)[59] to God, who has guided us to this! We would not have been guided if God had not guided us. Certainly the messengers of our Lord have brought the truth.' And they will be called out to: 'That is the Garden! You have inherited it for what you have done.' **44** The companions of the Garden will call out to the companions of the Fire: 'We have found what our Lord promised us (to be) true. So have you found what your Lord promised (to be) true?' They will say, 'Yes!' And then a caller will call out among them: 'The curse of God is on the evildoers, **45** who keep (people) from the way of God and desire (to make) it crooked, and they are disbelievers in the Hereafter.'[60]

46 Between both (groups) of them (there is) a partition,[61] and on the heights[62] (there are) men who recognize each (of them) by their marks, and they call out to the companions of the Garden: 'Peace (be) upon you! They have not entered it, as much as they were eager (to do so).' **47** And when their sight is turned toward the companions of the Fire, they say, 'Our Lord, do not place us among the people who

---

50. *the Fire*: Ar. *al-nār* is the most common of the various designations for Hell.
51. *their portion of the Book will reach them*: i.e. they will receive their due 'portion' (Ar. *naṣīb*) of what is written in the heavenly 'Book' or 'Record' of their deeds (cf. Q11.109).
52. *Our messengers*: here referring to the 'angels of death' (see n. on Q6.61).
53. *take them*: in death.
54. *abandoned us*: lit. 'gone astray from us;' i.e. their gods have deserted them.

38–51 A JUDGMENT SCENE

55. *jinn*: for these beings, see n. on Q6.100.
56. *until the camel passes through the eye of the needle*: the same phrase is used by Jesus of the impossibility of the rich ever entering God's kingdom (Mark 10.25 par.); for the imagery of the heavenly 'Garden,' see n. on Q2.25.
57. *coverings above them*: perhaps of fire (cf. Q39.16), but the imagery is obscure (cf. Q12.107; 88.1).
58. *hearts*: lit. 'chests,' considered the seat of knowledge and understanding.
59. *(be)*: or '(belongs).'
60. *the Hereafter*: see n. on Q2.4.
61. *partition*: lit. a 'veil' (Ar. *ḥijāb*), between heaven and hell (cf. Q57.13, a 'wall').
62. *heights*: meaning uncertain (Ar. *a'rāf*), though it is said to refer to the 'heights of the partition;' the 'men on the *a'rāf*' appear to be overseers of the final separation of the righteous and the wicked (cf. a similar scene at Matthew 25.31-46).

are evildoers.' **48** The men of the heights will call out to men whom they recognize by their marks, (and) say, 'Your hoarding[63] is of no use to you, nor what you were arrogant (about). **49** Are these[64] the ones whom you swore God would not reach with (His) mercy? Enter the Garden![65] (There will be) no fear on you, nor will you sorrow.'

50 And the companions of the Fire will call out to the companions of the Garden: 'Pour some water on us,[66] or some of what God has provided you!' They will say, 'Surely God has forbidden both to the disbelievers, **51** who have taken their religion as diversion and jest. This present life has deceived them.' So today We forget them as they forgot the meeting of this Day of theirs, and because they have denied Our signs.

52 Certainly We have brought them a Book[67] – We have made it distinct[68] on (the basis of) knowledge – as a guidance[69] and mercy for a people who believe. **53** Do they expect anything but its interpretation?[70] On the Day when its interpretation comes, those who forgot it before will say, 'The messengers of our Lord have brought the truth. Have we any intercessors to intercede for us? Or (may) we return so that we might do other than what we have done?' They have lost their (own) selves, and what they forged[71] has abandoned them.

54 Surely your Lord is God, who created the heavens and the earth in six days.[72] Then He mounted the throne. The night covers the day, which it pursues urgently,[73] and the sun, and the moon, and the stars are subjected, (all) by His command. Is it not (a fact) that to Him (belong) the creation and the command?[74] Blessed (be) God, Lord of the worlds![75]

55 Call on your Lord in humility and in secret. Surely He does not love the transgressors. **56** Do not foment corruption on the earth after it has been set right, and call on Him in fear and in eagerness. Surely the mercy of God is near to the doers of good. **57** He (it is) who sends the winds as good news before His mercy,[76] until, when it brings a cloud heavy (with rain), We drive it to some barren[77] land, and send down water by means of it, and bring forth by means of it every (kind of) fruit. In this way We bring forth the dead, so that you may take heed.[78] **58** (As for) the good land, its vegetation comes forth by the

63. *hoarding*: of wealth.
64. *these*: i.e. the group in heaven.
65. *Enter the Garden*: an abrupt switch of address from one group to the other (it is not clear whether the 'men on the heights' utter this final command, or God).
66. *Pour some water on us*: cf. the similar request of the rich man (in Hades) to Abraham at Luke 16.24.

52–53 The Book and its fulfillment

67. *a Book*: the Qur'ān (see n. on Q2.2).
68. *made it distinct*: or 'expounded it' (like the 'Tablets' of Moses, see Q7.145 below; cf. Q6.114; 10.37; 11.1; 12.111; 41.3, 44).
69. *guidance*: one of the most frequent terms (Ar. *hudā*) for revelation in general, and the Qur'ān in particular.
70. *its interpretation*: i.e. the fulfillment of its promises and threats.
71. *what they forged*: i.e. their invented gods.

54–58 Signs of God's power and providence

72. *in six days*: cf. Q10.3; 11.7; 25.59; 32.4; 41.9-12; 50.38; 57.4; and Genesis 1.1-31.
73. *which it pursues urgently*: referring to the night as it rapidly follows upon the day.
74. *to Him (belong) the creation and the command*: i.e. God creates and then controls the universe from his throne (see Q2.255; 10.3; 25.59; 32.4).
75. *Lord of the worlds*: for this title, see n. on Q1.2.
76. *before His mercy*: i.e. before the coming rain.
77. *barren*: lit. 'dead' (notice the sudden shift from third- to first-person discourse).
78. *take heed*: or 'be reminded,' 'remember.'

permission of its Lord, but (as for) the bad, (its vegetation) comes forth only poorly. In this way We vary the signs for a people who are thankful.

59 Certainly We sent Noah to his people,[79] and he said, 'My people! Serve God! You have no god other than Him. Surely I fear for you the punishment of a great Day.' **60** The assembly[80] of his people said, 'Surely We see you are indeed clearly astray.'[81] **61** He said, 'My people! (There is) nothing astray in me, but I am a messenger from the Lord of the worlds. **62** I deliver to you the messages of my Lord and I offer advice to you. I know from God what you do not know. **63** Are you amazed that a reminder has come to you from your Lord by means of[82] a (mere) man[83] from among you, so that he may warn you, and that you may guard (yourselves), and that you may receive compassion?' **64** But they called him a liar, so We rescued him and those with him in the ship,[84] and We drowned those who called Our signs a lie. Surely they were a blind people.

65 And to 'Ād (We sent) their brother Hūd.[85] He said, 'My people! Serve God! You have no god other than Him. Will you not guard (yourselves)?' **66** The assembly of those who disbelieved among his people said, 'Surely we see you are indeed in foolishness, and surely we think you are indeed one of the liars.' **67** He said, 'My people! (There is) no foolishness in me, but I am a messenger from the Lord of the worlds. **68** I deliver to you the messages of my Lord and I am a trustworthy adviser for you. **69** Are you amazed that a reminder has come to you from your Lord by means of a (mere) man from among you, so that he may warn you? (Remember) when He made you successors after the people of Noah, and increased you in size abundantly. Remember the blessings of God, so that you may prosper.' **70** They said, 'Have you come to us (with the message) that we should serve God alone, and forsake what our fathers have served? Bring us what you promise us,[86] if you are one of the truthful.' **71** He said, 'Abomination and anger from your Lord have fallen upon you. Will you dispute with me about names which you have named,[87] you and your fathers? God has not sent down any authority for it. (Just) wait! Surely I shall be one of those waiting with you.' **72** So We rescued him and those with him by a mercy from Us, and We cut off the last remnant of those who called Our signs a lie and were not believers.

59–64 The story of Noah and his people

79. *We sent Noah to his people*: this begins a series of 'punishment stories' (Q7.59-102) in which the emphasis is on temporal rather than eschatological judgment: i.e. punishment falls on communities in history rather than at the final judgment. The plot is usually the same: (1) a messenger is sent to a particular people; (2) he delivers his message but is rejected; (3) then God destroys the people for their disbelief. Although the peoples vary, the seven main ones are: the peoples of Hūd (the 'Ād), Ṣāliḥ (the Thamūd), and Shu'ayb (the Midianites), and the peoples of Noah, Abraham, Lot, and Moses (see e.g. Q11.25-109; 22.42-51; 23.23-48; 26.10-191; 29.14-40; 37.69-148; 51.24-46; 54.9-42; cf. 15.87). Compare the similar 'prophetic' understanding of history at 2 Kings 17.7-20. Scholars of the Bible refer to this as the 'Deuteronomic principle.' For the story of Noah that follows, cf. the versions at Q10.71-73; 11.25-34; 23.23-30; 26.105-120; and Genesis 6.5-10.1.

80. *assembly*: the word (Ar. *mala'*) is the same one used in traditional accounts of the 'assembly' of leaders at Mecca. This may indicate how the description of previous messengers and their peoples has been shaped by conditions in Mecca (or vice versa). In any case, the preaching of the Prophet and Noah are mirror images, as is the response of their respective peoples.

81. *clearly astray*: lit. 'in clear straying.'

82. *by means of*: lit. 'on.'

83. *a (mere) man*: this reflects an expectation that the messenger would be an angel or 'divine man' (cf. Q7.69 below).

84. *the ship*: Noah's 'ark' (cf. Q10.73; 11.37; and Genesis 7.11-16); according to Q66.10, Noah's wife perished.

65–72 The story of Hūd and the people of 'Ād

85. *Hūd*: for the story that follows, cf. the versions at Q11.50-60; 26.123-140.

86. *what you promise us*: what you threaten us with (i.e. punishment).

87. *names which you have named*: referring to their false gods (cf. Q12.40; 53.23).

73 And to Thamūd (We sent) their brother Ṣāliḥ.[88] He said, 'My people! Serve God! You have no god other than Him. A clear sign[89] has come to you from your Lord: this is the she-camel of God,[90] a sign for you. Let her graze on God's earth, and do not touch her with evil, or a painful punishment will seize you. **74** Remember when He made you successors after 'Ād and settled you on the earth: you took palaces from its plains, and carved houses out of the mountains. Remember the blessings of God, and do not act wickedly on the earth, fomenting corruption.' **75** The assembly of those who were arrogant among his people said to those who were weak, to those of them who believed, 'Do you (really) know that Ṣāliḥ is an envoy from his Lord?' They said, 'Surely We are believers in what he has been sent with.' **76** Those who were arrogant said, 'Surely we are disbelievers in what you have believed.' **77** So they wounded[91] the she-camel, and disdained the command of their Lord, and said, 'Ṣāliḥ! Bring us what you promise us, if you are one of the envoys.' **78** And then the earthquake[92] seized them, and morning found them leveled in their home(s). **79** So he turned away from them, and said, 'My people! Certainly I have delivered to you the message of my Lord and I offered advice to you, but you do not like advisers.'

80 And Lot,[93] when he said to his people, 'Do you commit (such) immorality[94] (as) no one in all the worlds has committed before you? **81** Surely you approach men with lust instead of women. Yes! You are a wanton people.' **82** But the only response of his people was that they said, 'Expel them from your town, (for) surely they are men who keep themselves clean.'[95] **83** So We rescued him and his family, except his wife – she was one of those who stayed behind. **84** And We rained down on them a rain.[96] See how the end was for the sinners!

85 And to Midian (We sent) their brother Shu'ayb.[97] He said, 'My people! Serve God! You have no god other than Him. A clear sign has come to you from your Lord.[98] Fill up the measure and the scale, and do not shortchange the people of their wealth,[99] and do not foment corruption on the earth after it has been set right. That is better for you, if you are believers. **86** And do not sit in every path making threats,[100] and keeping from the way of God those who believe in Him, and desiring (to make) it crooked. Remember when you were few (in number) and He multiplied you. And see how the end was for the fomenters

---

73–79 The story of Ṣāliḥ and the people of Thamūd

88. *Ṣāliḥ*: the name means 'righteous;' for the story that follows, cf. the versions at Q11.61-68; 26.141-158; 27.45-53. The people of Thamūd were inhabitants of ancient Arabia, and are mentioned in an inscription of the Assyrian king Sargon II (c. 715 BCE), as well as in the writings of Ariston of Chios, Ptolemy, and Pliny the Elder.
89. *clear sign*: or 'clear proof,' 'indisputable evidence.'
90. *the she-camel of God*: the commentators relate a story of how the people of Thamūd demanded a sign, and agreed that both they and Ṣāliḥ should call on their gods, and that all should accept as true the god who answered. The gods of the Thamūd were silent, but when Ṣāliḥ prayed, a rock brought forth a camel which immediately gave birth to a foal. Still the Thamūd refused to acknowledge God and eventually killed the she-camel. None of this, however, is mentioned in the Qur'ān.
91. *wounded*: or perhaps 'killed.'
92. *earthquake*: cf. Q11.67; 54.31 ('a cry'); 41.17; 51.44 ('a thunderbolt').

80–84 The story of Lot and his people

93. *Lot*: for the story that follows, cf. the longer versions at Q11.77-83; 15.57-74; 26.160-173; and Genesis 19.1-29.
94. *immorality*: lit. 'the immorality;' here referring to 'sodomy' (cf. Genesis 19.4-5).
95. *who keep themselves clean*: or 'who hold themselves to be clean' (said in derision).
96. *A rain*: of stones of baked clay, according to Q11.82; 15.74.

85–93 The story of Shu'ayb and the people of Midian

97. *Shu'ayb*: for the story that follows, cf. the versions at Q11.84-95; 26.176-189 (sent to the people of 'the Grove').
98. *A clear sign has come...*: reference obscure.
99. *Fill up..., and do not shortchange...*: a distinctive feature of the story of Midian (cf. Q11.85; cf. Q26.181-183).
100. *making threats*: lit. 'making promises' (cf. Q7.70 above).

of corruption! **87** If (there is) a contingent of you who believe in that with which I have been sent, and a contingent who do not believe, be patient until God judges between us, (for) He is the best of judges.' **88** The assembly of those who were arrogant among his people said, 'We shall indeed expel you, Shu'ayb, and those who believe with you, from our town, or else you will indeed return to our creed.' He said, 'Even if we are unwilling? **89** We would have forged a lie against God, if we returned to your creed after God rescued us from it. It is not for us to return to it, unless God our Lord (so) pleases. Our Lord comprehends everything in knowledge. In God we have put our trust. Our Lord, disclose[101] the truth between us and our people, (for) You are the best of disclosers.'[102] **90** The assembly of those who disbelieved among his people said, 'If indeed you follow Shu'ayb, surely then you will be losers indeed.' **91** And then the earthquake[103] seized them, and morning found them leveled in their home(s). **92** Those who called Shu'ayb a liar – (it was) as if they had not lived in prosperity there. Those who called Shu'ayb a liar – they were the losers. **93** So he turned away from them, and said, 'My people! Certainly I have delivered to you the messages of my Lord and I offered advice to you. How shall I grieve over a disbelieving people?'

94 We have not sent any prophet[104] to a town, except that We seized its people with violence and hardship, so that they might humble themselves. **95** Then We exchanged good for evil, until they forgot (about it), and said, 'Hardship and prosperity have touched our fathers.'[105] So we seized them unexpectedly, when they did not realize (it). **96** Yet if the people of the towns had believed and guarded (themselves), We would indeed have opened on them blessings from the sky and the earth. But they called (it) a lie,[106] so We seized them for what they had earned.

97 Do the people of the towns[107] feel secure that Our violence will not come upon them at night, while they are sleeping? **98** Or do the people of the towns feel secure that Our violence will not come upon them in the daylight, while they jest? **99** Do they feel secure against the scheme of God? No one feels secure against the scheme of God except the people who are losers. **100** Or is it not a guide for those who inherit the earth after its (former) people that, if We (so) please, We could smite them because of their sins, and We could set a seal on their hearts so that they do not hear?

101 Those were the towns – We recount to you[108] some of their stories.[109] Certainly their messengers brought them the clear signs,[110] but they were not (able) to believe what they had called a lie before. In this way God sets a seal on the hearts of the disbelievers. **102** We did not find any covenant with most of them, but We found most of them wicked.

103 Then, after them, We raised up Moses with Our signs to Pharaoh and his assembly, but they did evil to them.[111] See how the end was for the fomenters of corruption! **104** Moses said, 'Pharaoh! Surely I am

---

101. *disclose*: lit. 'open.'

102. *...best of disclosers*: lit. 'openers;' cf. Q26.118 (Noah); 34.26; 48.1 (the Prophet).

103. *the earthquake*: cf. Q11.94 ('the cry'); 29.37.

94–102 Conclusion to the stories of previous messengers

104. *prophet*: for this important title, see n. on Q2.87.

105. *Hardship and prosperity have touched our fathers*: i.e. they supposed that life's ups and downs were part of the natural course of affairs, and not contingent on their obedience to God.

106. *called (it) a lie*: i.e. rejected the warning of imminent judgment (cf. Q3.137; 6.11, 148; 16.36).

107. *Do the people of the towns...*: this seems to be a warning to present-day people, but it is not clear who they are or what towns are being referred to.

108. *you*: the Prophet.

109. *stories*: or 'news.'

110. *the clear signs*: or 'the clear proofs,' 'the indisputable evidence.'

103–137 The story of Moses and Pharaoh

111. *did evil to them*: lit. 'to it;' i.e. they rejected the miracles (or 'signs') performed by Moses.

a messenger from the Lord of the worlds. **105** (There is) an obligation on (me) that[112] I do not say about God (anything) but the truth. I have brought you a clear sign from your Lord, so send forth the Sons of Israel with me.' **106** He said, 'If you have come with a sign, bring it, if you are one of the truthful.' **107** So he cast (down) his staff, and suddenly it became a real snake. **108** And he drew forth his hand, and suddenly it became white to the onlookers.[113] **109** The assembly of the people of Pharaoh said, 'Surely this man is a skilled magician indeed. **110** He wants to expel you from your land.[114] So what do you command?' **111** They said, 'Put him and his brother[115] off (for a while), and send out searchers into the cities **112** to bring you every skilled magician.'

113 And the magicians came to Pharaoh, (and) said, 'Surely for us (there will be) a reward indeed, if we are the victors.' **114** He said, 'Yes, and surely you will indeed be among the ones brought near.'[116] **115** They said, 'Moses! Are you going to cast (first), or are we to be the ones who cast?' **116** He said, 'Cast!' So when they cast, they bewitched the eyes of the people, and terrified them, and produced a great (feat of) magic.[117] **117** And We inspired Moses: 'Cast (down) your staff!,' and suddenly it swallowed up what they were falsely contriving.[118] **118** So the truth came to pass,[119] and what they were doing was invalidated. **119** They were overcome there, and turned back disgraced.[120] **120** And the magicians were cast (down) in prostration. **121** They said, 'We believe in the Lord of the worlds, **122** the Lord of Moses and Aaron.' **123** Pharaoh said, 'You have believed in Him before I gave you permission. Surely this is indeed a scheme which you have schemed in the city to expel its people from it. But soon you will know! **124** I shall indeed cut off your hands and your feet on opposite sides, (and) then I shall indeed crucify you – all (of you)!' **125** They said, 'Surely we are going to return to our Lord. **126** You are not taking vengeance on us (for any other reason) than that we believed in the signs of our Lord when they came to us. Our Lord, pour out on us patience, and take us[121] as ones who have submitted.'[122]

127 The assembly of the people of Pharaoh said, 'Will you leave Moses and his people to foment corruption on the earth and to forsake you and your gods?' He said, 'We shall kill their sons and keep their women alive.[123] Surely we shall be supreme over them!' **128** Moses said to his people, 'Seek help from God and be patient. Surely the earth (belongs) to God. He causes whomever He pleases of His servants to inherit it. The outcome (belongs) to the ones who guard (themselves).' **129** They said, 'We have suffered harm before you came to us and after you came to us.' He said, 'It may be that your Lord will destroy your enemy and make you successors on the earth, and then see how you will act.'

130 Certainly We seized the house of Pharaoh with years (of famine),[124] and scarcity of fruits, so that

112. *(There is) an obligation on (me) that*: or '(I am) approved on the condition that.'

113. *he cast (down) his staff...he drew forth his hand...*: cf. Q20.17-23; 26.30-37; 28.29-32; and the account at Exodus 4.1-8 (according to Exodus 7.8-10, it was Aaron who cast his staff before Pharaoh).

114. *land*: lit. 'earth.'

115. *his brother*: Aaron (Ar. *Hārūn*).

116. *the ones brought near*: i.e. 'among Pharaoh's close circle of advisers' (Ar. *al-muqarrabūn* is a designation of special privilege at the royal court); cf. Q26.42.

117. *a great (feat of) magic*: their staffs became snakes (cf. Exodus 7.12).

118. *swallowed up what they were falsely contriving*: cf. Exodus 7.12, where Aaron's staff accomplishes this feat.

119. *came to pass*: lit. 'fell.'

120. *They were overcome...turned back disgraced*: referring to Pharaoh and his assembly.

121. *take us*: in death.

122. *as ones who have submitted*: or 'as Muslims.'

123. *kill their sons and keep their women alive*: cf. Pharaoh's order to kill all Hebrew boys but spare the girls (Exodus 1.15-16, 22).

124. *years (of famine)*: cf. the 'seven lean years' of Genesis 41.53-57 (though this occurred earlier, in the time of

they might take heed.[125] **131** But when good came to them, they said, 'This (belongs) to us,' but if evil smote them, they attributed it to the evil omen of Moses and those with him. Is it not a fact that their evil omen was with God?[126] But most of them did not know (it). **132** And they said, 'Whatever kind of sign you[127] bring us, to bewitch us by means of it, we are not going to believe in you.' **133** So We sent on them the flood, and the locusts, and the lice, and the frogs, and the blood, as distinct signs.[128] But they became arrogant and were a sinful people. **134** When the wrath fell upon them, they said, 'Moses! Call on your Lord for us by whatever covenant He has made with you. If indeed you remove this wrath from us, we shall indeed believe in you, and send forth the Sons of Israel with you.' **135** But when We removed the wrath from them, until a time they reached (later), suddenly they broke (their promise). **136** So We took vengeance on them and drowned them in the sea,[129] because they called Our signs a lie and were oblivious of them. **137** And We caused the people who were weak to inherit the land We had blessed[130] – the east (parts) and the west (parts) of it – and the best word of your Lord was fulfilled for the Sons of Israel, because they were patient. And We destroyed what Pharaoh and his people had been making and what they had been building.[131]

138 We crossed the sea with the Sons of Israel, and they came upon a people devoted to their idols. They said, 'Moses! Make for us a god like the gods they have.' He said, 'Surely you are an ignorant people. **139** Surely these – what they (are engaged) in (will be) destroyed, and what they are doing is worthless.'[132] **140** He said, 'Shall I seek a god for you other than God, when He has favored you over the worlds?'[133]

141 (Remember) when[134] We rescued you from the house of Pharaoh. They were inflicting on you the evil punishment, killing your sons and sparing your women. In that was a great test from your Lord. **142** And We appointed for Moses (a period of) thirty night(s), and We completed them with ten (more), so the meeting with his Lord was completed in forty night(s).[135] And Moses said to his brother Aaron, 'Be my successor[136] among my people, and set (things) right, and do not follow the way of the fomenters of corruption.' **143** And when Moses came to Our meeting, and his Lord spoke to him,[137] he said, 'My Lord, show me (Yourself), so that I may look at You.' He said, 'You will not see Me,[138] but look at the mountain. If it remains in its place, you will see Me.' But when his Lord revealed His splendor to the mountain, He shattered it, and Moses fell down thunderstruck. And when he recovered, he said, 'Glory to You! I turn to You (in repentance), and I am the first of the believers.' **144** He said, 'Moses! I have chosen you over

---

Joseph, not Moses).

125. *take heed*: i.e. heed the admonition of famine in the land.

126. *their evil omen was with God*: referring to their fate assigned by God (see Q17.13; cf. Q27.47).

127. *you*: Moses.

128. *as distinct signs*: cf. the 'ten plagues' described at Exodus 7-12 (though a 'flood' is not one of them).

129. *drowned them in the sea*: cf. Exodus 14.21-31.

130. *the land We had blessed*: the Holy Land (Palestine); see Q5.21; cf. Q17.1; 21.71, 81; 34.18.

131. *what they had been building*: lit. 'what they had been trellising' or 'terracing' (the pyramids?).

138–157 Moses and the Sons of Israel

132. *worthless*: or 'a lie.'

133. *favored you over the worlds*: or 'preferred you over all peoples;' the distinctiveness of Israel's election is recognized (see e.g. Q2.47, 122; 3.33; 6.86; 44.32; 45.16).

134. *(Remember) when...*: a stock narrative formula; the Arabic particle *idh* often marks the beginning of a story, and means something like 'Once...,' or 'There was a time when...,' or 'Remember when....'

135. *forty night(s)*: Moses spent forty days and forty nights on the mountain of God, according to Exodus 24.18.

136. *my successor*: or 'ruler in my place' (cf. Q2.30n., of Adam).

137. *his Lord spoke to him*: see Q4.164, 'God spoke to Moses directly' (cf. Q19.52; 42.51n.).

138. *You will not see Me*: cf. Exodus 33.18-23.

the people for My messages and for My word. So take what I have given you, and be one of the thankful.'
145 And We wrote for him on the Tablets[139] an admonition of everything, and a distinct setting forth of everything:[140] 'So hold it fast,[141] and command your people to take the best of it. I shall show you the home of the wicked.
146 I shall turn away from My signs those who are arrogant on the earth without any right. Even if they see every sign, they will not believe in it. And if they see the right way, they will not take it as a way, but if they see the way of error, they will take it as a way. That (is) because they called Our signs a lie and were oblivious of them.
147 Those who have called Our signs a lie, and (also) the meeting of the Hereafter – their deeds come to nothing. Will they be repaid (for anything) except for what they have done?'

148 And the people of Moses, after he (was gone), made a calf[142] out of their ornaments[143] – a (mere) image[144] of it (having) a mooing sound. Did they not see that it could not speak to them or guide them to a way? (Yet) they made it and became evildoers.
149 But when they stumbled[145] and saw that they had gone astray, they said, 'If indeed our Lord does not have compassion on us, and does not forgive us, we shall indeed be among the losers.'
150 When Moses returned to his people, in anger (and) grief, he said, 'Evil is what you have done as my successors, after I (left you). Have you sought to hurry[146] the command of your Lord?'[147] And he cast (down) the Tablets, and seized his brother's head, dragging him toward himself. He said,[148] 'Son of my mother! Surely the people thought me weak, and nearly killed me. So do not let (my) enemies gloat over me, and do not place me among the people who are evildoers.'
151 He said, 'My Lord, forgive me and my brother, and cause us to enter into Your mercy, (for) You are the most compassionate of the compassionate.'
152 Surely those who made the calf – anger from their Lord will reach them, and humiliation in this present life. In this way We repay the forgers (of lies).
153 But those who do evil deeds, (and) then turn (in repentance) after that, and believe – surely after that your Lord is indeed forgiving, compassionate.

154 When the anger of Moses abated, he took (up) the Tablets, and in their inscription (there was) a guidance and mercy for those who fear their Lord.
155 And Moses chose his people – seventy men[149] – for Our meeting. So when the earthquake seized them, he said, 'My Lord, if You had pleased, You could have destroyed them before, and me (as well). Will You destroy us for what the foolish among us have done? It is only Your test by which You lead astray whomever You please and guide whomever You please. You are our ally, so forgive us and have compassion on us, (for) You are the best of forgivers.
156 And prescribe[150] for us good in this world and in the Hereafter. Surely we have turned[151] to You.' He said, 'My punishment – I smite with it whomever I please, but My mercy comprehends everything.

139. *We wrote for him on the Tablets*: see Q7.150, 154 below (cf. Exodus 24.12; 31.18; 32.15-20; 34.1-7, 28-32). The same word is used in reference to the Qur'ān (Q85.21-22), as well as the wooden 'boards' of Noah's ark (Q54.13).

140. *a distinct setting forth of everything*: cf. Q7.52 above.

141. *hold it fast*: lit. 'take it with force' (cf. Q7.171 below; Q2.63, 93; 19.12; 43.43).

142. *made a calf*: lit. 'took a calf;' for a parallel version of this story, see Q20.83-98; cf. the story of the 'golden calf' at Exodus 32.1-35.

143. *ornaments*: or 'jewelry.'

144. *image*: lit. 'body.'

145. *when they stumbled*: lit. 'when there was a falling on their hands;' usually interpreted as 'when they repented.'

146. *hurry*: the verb (Ar. *'ajila*) is a pun on the word for 'calf' (*'ijl*).

147. *command of your Lord*: here referring to judgment (cf. Q2.109; 4.47; 5.52; 10.24; 16.1, 33).

148. *He said*: Aaron addresses Moses here; then Moses prays.

149. *seventy men*: 'seventy elders,' according to Exodus 24.1, 9; cf. Numbers 11.16-23.

150. *prescribe*: lit. 'write.'

151. *we have turned*: or perhaps 'we have become Jews' (punning on Yahūd).

I shall prescribe it for the ones who guard (themselves), and give the alms, and those who – they believe in Our signs – **157** those who follow the messenger, the prophet of the common people,[152] whom they find written in their Torah and Gospel.[153] He will command them what is right and forbid them what is wrong, and he will permit them good things and forbid them bad things, and he will deliver them of their burden and the chains that were on them.[154] Those who believe in him, and support him and help him, and follow the light which has been sent down with him,[155] those – they are the ones who will prosper.'

158 Say: 'People! Surely I am the messenger of God to you – all (of you)[156] – (the messenger of) the One to whom (belongs) the kingdom of the heavens and the earth. (There is) no god but Him. He gives life and causes death. So believe in God and His messenger, the prophet of the common people,[157] who believes in God and His words, (and) follow him, so that you may be (rightly) guided.'

159 Among the people of Moses (there was) a community which guided by the truth, and by means of
it acted fairly. **160** We divided them (into) twelve tribes as communities, and We inspired Moses, when his people asked him for water: 'Strike the rock with your staff,' and (there) gushed forth from it twelve springs[158] – each tribe knew its drinking place – and We overshadowed them (with) the cloud, and We sent down on them the manna and the quails:[159] 'Eat from the good things which We have provided you.' They did not do Us evil, but they did themselves evil.

161 (Remember) when it was said to them, 'Inhabit this town and eat of it wherever you please, and say: "Ḥiṭṭa,"[160]and enter the gate in prostration. We shall forgive you your sins and increase the doers of good.' **162** But those of them who did evil exchanged a word other than that which had been spoken to them. So We sent down on them wrath from the sky, because of the evil they were doing.

163 Ask them[161] them about the town which was near the sea, when they transgressed in (the matter of) the sabbath, when their fish came to them on the day of their sabbath, (swimming) right to the shore.[162] But on the day when they did not observe the sabbath, they did not come to them. In this way

152. *the prophet of the common people*: or 'the gentile prophet' (Ar. *al-nabī al-ummī*, here and in the next verse). Ar. *ummī* means something like 'gentile' in the sense of those who do not have a written scripture, and thus refers to the 'gentile Arabs' (see n. on Q2.78; cf. Q3.20, 75; 62.2). That is, instead of sending the Arabs a missionary from the Jews or Christians ('those who already had a Book'), God chose to send them a prophet from among themselves. Accordingly, *ummī* may be similar in meaning to *ḥanīf* (see n. on Q2.135). Traditional scholars interpret *ummī* as 'illiterate,' and claim that Muḥammad could not read or write (further emphasizing the miraculous character of the Qur'ān).

153. *whom they find written in their Torah and Gospel*: i.e. predictions of the Prophet's coming in the Jewish and Christian scriptures (see e.g. Deuteronomy 18.15, 18; John 14.16; 15.26; 16.7).

154. *deliver them of their burden and the chains...*: perhaps a reference to the many commandments and prohibitions of the Torah, especially as later elaborated in rabbinic Judaism (but cf. Q94.2-3).

155. *the light which has been sent down with him*: referring to the Qur'ān (cf. Q64.8).

158 Call to believe in the Prophet

156. *all (of you)*: i.e. Jews and Christians, and perhaps all humanity (cf. Q34.28; 36.70).

157. *the prophet of the common people*: see n. on Q7.157 above.

159–171 Moses and the Sons of Israel (continued)

158. *Strike the rock...*: see Q2.60; cf. Exodus 17.1-7; Numbers 20.2-13.

159. *the cloud...the manna and the quails*: referring to God's appearance to the Israelites in the 'pillar of cloud' (see e.g. Exodus 13.21; 33.9-10; 40.38; Numbers 9.15; 14.14; Psalm 105.39; 1 Corinthians 10.1); and to their provision of food from heaven (see Exodus 16.1-36; Numbers 11.1-35; John 6.31; 1 Corinthians 10.3).

160. *Ḥiṭṭa*: meaning uncertain, as is the identity of the town (Jerusalem?); cf. Q2.58.

161. *Ask them*: the Prophet is to ask the Jews. The Cairo edition, reflecting the views of traditional scholars, attributes the following section (Q7.163-170) to the 'Medinan' period.

162. *right to the shore*: meaning obscure; some explain the word as meaning 'on the surface' (and thus 'visibly').

We were testing them because they were acting wickedly. **164** (Remember) when a (certain) community of them said, 'Why do you admonish a people whom God is going to destroy or punish (with) a harsh punishment?' They[163] said, '(As) an excuse to your Lord, and so that they might guard (themselves).' **165** So when they forgot what they were reminded of, We rescued those who had been forbidding evil, and We seized the evildoers with a violent punishment because they were acting wickedly. **166** So when they disdained what they had been forbidden from, We said to them, 'Become apes, skulking away!'[164]

167 (Remember) when your Lord proclaimed (that) He would indeed raise up against them – until the Day of Resurrection – those who would inflict them (with) evil punishment.[165] Surely your Lord is indeed quick in retribution, yet surely He is indeed forgiving, compassionate.

168 We divided them (into) communities on the earth, some of them righteous and some of them other than that, and We tested them with good things and bad, so that they might return. **169** And after them came successors[166] (who) inherited the Book, taking (the fleeting) goods of this lower (world) and saying, 'It will be forgiven us.' And if there comes to them goods like that (again), they will take them. Has the covenant of the Book not been taken upon them, (namely) that they should not say about God (anything) but the truth? And have they (not) studied what is in it? The Home of the Hereafter is better for the ones who guard (themselves). Will you not understand? **170** Those who hold fast the Book and observe the prayer[167] – surely We do not let the reward of those who set (things) right go to waste.

171 (Remember) when We shook the mountain above them,[168] as if it were a canopy,[169] and they thought it was going to fall on them: 'Hold fast what We have given you,[170] and remember what is in it, so that you may guard (yourselves).'

172 (Remember) when your Lord took from the sons of Adam[171] – from their loins[172] – their descendants, and made them bear witness about themselves: 'Am I not your Lord?' They said, 'Yes indeed! We bear witness.' (We did that) so that you would not say on the Day of Resurrection, 'Surely we were oblivious of this,'[173] **173** or say, 'Our fathers were idolaters[174] before (us), and we are descendants after them. Will You destroy us for what the perpetrators of falsehood did?' **174** In this way We make the signs distinct,[175] so that they will return.

---

163. *They*: the righteous among them.

164. *Become apes, skulking away*: cf. Q2.65; 5.60. Some modern translators treat this episode metaphorically ('Be *like* apes'), but the transformation of humans into animals is a widespread motif in ancient myth. Cf. e.g. the story of the Cercopians, the sinful inhabitants of the island of Pithecusa ('Island of the Apes') off the Bay of Naples, whom Jupiter turned into apes as punishment for their dishonesty (Ovid, *Metamorphoses* 14.88-100).

165. *evil punishment*: perhaps a reference to Israel's subjugation by foreign powers (Assyrians, Babylonians, Greeks, Romans, Christians, and eventually Muslims).

166. *came successors*: lit. 'successions succeeded' (cf. Q19.59).

167. *the prayer*: the ritual prayer (or *ṣalāt*).

168. *shook the mountain above them*: Mount Sinai; see n. on Q2.63, 93 (cf. the description of the theophany at Sinai at Exodus 19.16-20).

169. *canopy*: lit. 'shade.'

170. *what We have given you*: the Torah.

172–174 God's covenant with the Sons of Adam

171. *when your Lord took from the sons of Adam...*: reference obscure, but cf. Deuteronomy 29.1-30.20 (esp. 29.14-15).

172. *their loins*: lit. 'their backs.'

173. *were oblivious of this*: that God was their Lord.

174. *were idolaters*: lit. 'associated (other gods with God).'

175. *make the signs distinct*: or 'expound the verses.'

175 Recite[176] to them the story[177] of the one to whom We gave Our signs,[178] but he passed them by, and Satan followed him, and he became one of those who are in error. **176** If We had (so) pleased, We would indeed have exalted him by them,[179] but he clung to the earth and followed his (vain) desire. So his parable is like the parable of the dog: If you attack it, it lolls its tongue out, or if you leave it alone, it (still) lolls its tongue out. That is the parable of the people who called Our signs a lie. So recount the account, that they may reflect.

177 Evil is the parable of the people who called Our signs a lie, but (who only) did themselves evil. **178** Whoever God guides is the (rightly) guided one, and whoever He leads astray, those – they are the losers. **179** Certainly We have created[180] for Gehenna many of the jinn and humans: they have hearts, but they do not understand with them; they have eyes, but they do not see with them; they have ears, but they do not hear with them. Those (people) are like cattle – No! They are (even) farther astray! Those – they are the oblivious.

180 To God (belong) the best names.[181] So call on Him with them, and leave those who pervert His names. They will be repaid for what they have done.

181 Among those whom We have created is a community which guides by the truth and by means of it acts fairly. **182** But those who call Our signs a lie – We shall lead them on step by step[182] without their realizing it,[183] **183** and I shall spare them[184] – surely My plan is strong. **184** Do they not reflect? Their companion is not possessed.[185] He is only a clear warner.[186] **185** Do they not look into the kingdom of the heavens and the earth, and whatever things God has created, and that it may be that their time has already drawn near? So in what (kind of) proclamation[187] will they believe after this? **186** Whoever God leads astray has no guide. He leaves them in their insolent transgression, wandering blindly.

187 They ask you[188] about the Hour:[189] 'When is its arrival?'[190] Say: 'Knowledge of it is only with my

---

175–176 The story of the messenger who failed

176. *Recite...*: or 'Read aloud...' (addressed to the Prophet).

177. *story*: or 'news.'

178. *the one to whom We gave Our signs*: there is no agreement about the identity of this messenger.

179. *them*: the signs.

177–179 Those who reject God's signs

180. *created*: lit. 'sown.'

180 The best names

181. *the best names*: or 'the most beautiful names' (Ar. *al-asmā' al-ḥusnā*); cf. Q17.110; 20.8; 59.24. A list of ninety-nine names was eventually compiled, consisting of those mentioned in the Qur'ān as well as others. They play an important role in theology and worship.

181–186 Those who reject God's signs

182. *lead them on step by step*: or 'come upon them gradually.'

183. *without their realizing it*: lit. 'from where they do not know.'

184. *I shall spare them*: or 'prolong their time' (notice the sudden shift from first-person plur. to sing.).

185. *Their companion is not possessed*: lit. '(There are) no jinn in their companion;' for the charge of 'possession,' see Q15.6; 23.70; 34.8; 37.36; 44.14; 68.51; the same accusation is leveled against Noah (Q23.25; 54.9) and Moses (Q26.27; 51.39).

186. *warner*: for this role, see n. on Q2.119.

187. *proclamation*: or 'report' (Ar. *ḥadīth*), referring to the Qur'ān (cf. Q45.6; 68.44; 77.50).

187–188 When will the Hour strike?

188. *you*: the Prophet.

189. *the Hour*: of judgment.

190. *its arrival*: lit. 'its anchoring;' cf. Q79.42; and the similar question put to Jesus at Mark 13.3-4 par.

Lord.[191] No (one) will reveal it at its (appointed) time but He. It is heavy in the heavens and the earth,[192] (but) it will only come upon you unexpectedly.' They ask you as if you are well informed about it. Say: 'Knowledge of it is only with God, but most of the people do not know (it).' **188** Say: 'I have no power to (cause) myself benefit or harm, except for whatever God pleases. If I had knowledge of the unseen,[193] I would indeed have acquired much good, and evil would not have touched me. I am only a warner and bringer of good news[194] to a people who believe.'

189 He (it is) who created you from one person,[195] and made from him his spouse, so that he might dwell with her. And when he covered her,[196] she bore a light burden and passed on with it (unnoticed). But when she became heavy, they both called on God their Lord, 'If indeed You give us a righteous (son), we shall indeed be among the thankful.' **190** But when He gave them a righteous (son),[197] they set up[198] associates for Him in (return for) what He had given them.[199] Yet God is exalted above what they associate. **191** Do they associate (with Him) what does not create anything, since they are (themselves) created? **192** They cannot (give) them any help, nor can they (even) help themselves. **193** If you[200] call them to the guidance,[201] they will not follow you. (It is) the same for you whether you call them or you remain silent.

194 Surely those you call on instead of God are servants[202] like you. So call on them and let them respond to you, if you are truthful. **195** Do they have feet with which they walk, or do they have hands with which they grasp, or do they have eyes with which they see, or do they have ears with which they hear? Say: 'Call on your associates, (and) then plot against me and do not spare me! **196** Surely my ally is God, who has sent down the Book. He takes the righteous as allies. **197** Those you call on instead of Him cannot help you, nor can they (even) help themselves.' **198** If you[203] call them to the guidance, they do not hear. You[204] see them looking at you, but they do not see.

199 Take the excess,[205] and command what is right, and turn away from the ignorant. **200** If any provocation from Satan provokes you, take refuge with God. Surely He is hearing, knowing. **201** Surely the ones

---

191. *Knowledge of it is only with my Lord*: cf. Q33.63; 41.47; 43.85; 46.23; 67.26; and Mark 13.32 par.
192. *It is heavy...*: perhaps meaning that it is 'imminent' or will be 'momentous.'
193. *the unseen*: here referring to 'the future' (see n. on Q2.3), and a reminder that prophets do not predict the future.
194. *warner...bringer of good news*: for these roles, see n. on Q2.119.

189–198 The creation of humanity and origin of idolatry

195. *one person*: Adam.
196. *when he covered her*: i.e. 'when he had sex with her.'
197. *a righteous (son)*: Adam and Eve's first son was Cain, followed by his brother Abel (see Genesis 4.1-2); neither is mentioned by name in the Qur'ān.
198. *set up*: lit. 'made.'
199. *...associates for Him in (return for) what He had given them*: i.e. they attributed the birth of their son to other gods instead of (or in addition to) God.
200. *you*: plur.
201. *the guidance*: one of the most frequent terms (Ar. *al-hudā*) for revelation in general, and the Qur'ān in particular (cf. Q7.52, 154 above).
202. *servants*: i.e. their 'gods' are created beings like them (see esp. Q4.172; 21.26; 43.19).
203. *you*: plur.
204. *you*: or 'one' (a sudden switch from plur. to sing.).

199–206 Advice for the Prophet

205. *excess*: or 'abundance,' perhaps referring to contributions (cf. Q2.219b), but the meaning is obscure.

who guard (themselves), when a circler[206] from Satan touches them, remember,[207] and suddenly they see (clearly). **202** But their brothers increase them in error, (and) then they do not stop.[208]

203 When you do not bring them a sign,[209] they say, 'If only you would choose (to do) it.' Say: 'I only follow what I am inspired (with) from my Lord. This[210] is evidence from your Lord, and a guidance and mercy for a people who believe.' **204** When the Qur'ān is recited,[211] listen to it and remain silent, so that you[212] may receive compassion.

205 Remember your Lord within yourself, in humility and in fear, and without loud words, in the mornings and the evenings.[213] Do not be one of the oblivious. **206** Surely those who are with your Lord[214] are not too proud to serve Him. They glorify Him and prostrate themselves before Him.

206. *circler*: or 'visitor,' but the meaning is obscure (cf. Q68.19).

207. *remember*: i.e. remind themselves of God.

208. *But their brothers increase them...*: the meaning of this sentence is obscure (cf. Q2.15).

209. *sign*: here meaning a 'miracle,' such as was given to Moses and other prophets.

210. *This*: the Qur'ān.

211. *recited*: or 'read aloud;' here 'the Qur'ān' comes close to its present meaning as the name of the Muslim scripture (cf. Q9.111; see n. on Q2.185).

212. *you*: plur.

213. *Remember your Lord...*: prayer may be performed in silence (cf. Q6.63; 7.55 above; 17.110); only two times are mentioned, morning and evening (cf. Q3.41; 6.52; 13.15; 18.28; 24.36; 33.42; 49.9; 76.25).

214. *those who are with your Lord*: the angels.

8 The Spoils ❁ Al-Anfāl

In the Name of God, the Merciful, the Compassionate

1 They ask you[1] about the spoils.[2] Say:[3] 'The spoils (belong) to God and the messenger.[4] So guard (yourselves) against God, and set right what is between you.[5] Obey God and His messenger, if you are believers.'

2 Only those are believers who, when God is mentioned, their hearts become afraid, and when His signs are recited[6] to them, it increases them in belief. They put their trust in their Lord. **3** Those who observe the prayer,[7] and contribute[8] from what We have provided them, **4** those – they are the true believers. For them (there are) ranks (of honor) with their Lord, and forgiveness and generous provision.

5 – As your Lord brought you[9] forth from your house with the truth, when a group of the believers were indeed unwilling, **6** disputing with you about the truth after it had become clear, as if they were being driven to death with their eyes wide open.[10]

7 (Remember) when[11] God was promising you[12] that one of the two contingents[13] would be yours, and you were wanting the unarmed one to be yours, but God wished to verify the truth by His words, and to cut off the last remnant of the disbelievers, **8** so that He might verify the truth and falsify the false,[14] even though the sinners disliked (it). **9** (Remember) when you were calling on your Lord for help, and He responded

---

Q8: Much of thus sūra is connected with victory in battle. It is traditionally assigned to the 'Medinan' period, shortly after the battle of Badr (624 CE/2 AH), the first encounter between Muslim forces and their Meccan opponents. The two different directives about the distribution of 'spoils' (Q8.1, 41) may indicate that some parts of Q8 belong to different times.

1 Spoils belong to God and the Messenger

1. *you*: the Prophet.
2. *the spoils*: Ar. *anfāl* is usually understood to mean 'spoils' of war, but its precise meaning is uncertain (cf. Q8.41, 69 below).
3. *Say*: on this form of address, see n. on Q2.80.
4. *the messenger*: for this important title, see n. on Q2.87.
5. *set right what is between you*: or 'act uprightly among yourselves.'

2–4 True believers

6. *signs are recited*: or 'verses are read aloud' (see n. on Q2.39).
7. *the prayer*: the ritual prayer (or *ṣalāt*).
8. *contribute*: lit. 'spend' (for those in need or for the cause).

5–6 Some unwilling to fight

9. *you*: the Prophet (vv. 5-6 may have originally followed v. 1; vv. 2-4 appear to be a later insertion).
10. *with their eyes wide open*: lit. 'while they looked on.'

7–14 Help comes from God

11. *(Remember) when...*: the Arabic particle *idh* serves as a common introduction to a narrative or a section, and often means something like 'Once...,' or 'There was a time when...,' or 'Remember when....'
12. *you*: plur.
13. *the two contingents*: according to tradition, an unarmed Meccan caravan returning from Syria and an armed force sent out from Mecca to protect it.
14. *verify the truth...falsify the false*: referring to God's promise to overthrow the disbelievers.

to you: 'I am going to increase you with a thousand angels[15] following behind.' **10** God did it only as good news, and that your hearts might be satisfied by it. Help (comes) only from God. Surely God is mighty, wise.

11 (Remember) when He covered you[16] with slumber as a security from Him, and sent down on you water from the sky, so that He might purify you by means of it, and take away from you the abomination of Satan,[17] and that he might strengthen your hearts and make firm (your) feet by means of it. **12** When your[18] Lord inspired the angels: 'I am with you,[19] so make firm those who believe. I shall cast dread into the hearts of those who disbelieve. So strike above (their) necks, and strike (off) all their fingers!' **13** That was because they broke with God and His messenger, and whoever breaks with God and His messenger – surely God is harsh in retribution. **14** 'That is for you! So taste it! And (know) that the punishment of the Fire[20] is for the disbelievers.'

15 You who believe! When you encounter those who disbelieve advancing (for battle), do not turn (your) backs to them. **16** Whoever turns his back to them on that day – unless turning aside to fight or to join (another) cohort – he has incurred the anger of God. His refuge will be Gehenna[21] – and it is an evil destination!

17 You[22] did not kill them, but God killed them, and you did not throw when you threw,[23] but God threw, and (He did that) in order to test the believers (with) a good test from Himself. Surely God is hearing, knowing. **18** That is for you! (Know) that God weakens the plot of the disbelievers. **19** If you[24] ask for a victory,[25] the victory has already come to you.[26] And if you stop, it will be better for you. But if you return, We shall return (too), and your cohort will be of no use to you, even if it should be numerous. (Know) that God is with the believers.

20 You who believe! Obey God and His messenger, and do not turn away from him[27] when you hear (him). **21** Do not be like those who say, 'We hear,' when they do not hear. **22** Surely the worst of creatures in the sight of God are the deaf (and) the speechless – those which do not understand.[28] **23** If God had known any good in them, He would indeed have made them hear. But (even) if He had made them hear, they would indeed have turned away in aversion.

---

15. *a thousand angels*: cf. Q3.124 ('three thousand angels'); for these beings and their various roles, see n. on Q2.30.
16. *you*: plur.
17. *abomination of Satan*: reading 'abomination' (Ar. *rijs*) instead of 'wrath' (*rijz*); perhaps meaning 'idolatry' (see Q22.30). For the figure of Satan, see n. on Q2.36.
18. *your*: sing.
19. *you*: plur.
20. *the Fire*: Ar. *al-nār* is the most common of the various designations for Hell.

15–16 Do not retreat in battle

21. *Gehenna*: another name for Hell (see n. on Q2.206).

17–19 God fought the battle

22. *You*: plur.
23. *...when you threw*: reference uncertain; tradition says that Muḥammad threw a handful of gravel at the enemy, whereupon it fled.
24. *you*: the disbelievers.
25. *ask for a victory*: or 'seek an opening.'
26. *victory has already come to you*: reference uncertain; it may mean that the disbelievers had their chance for victory (at Badr?), but lost.

20–29 Appeal to believers

27. *him*: or 'Him.'
28. *...which do not understand*: a derisive comparison, likening disbelievers to senseless animals (cf. Q8.55 below).

24 You who believe! Respond to God and to the messenger, when he[29] calls you to what gives you life. Know that God stands between a person and his (own) heart,[30] and that to Him you will be gathered. **25** Guard (yourselves) against trouble,[31] which will indeed smite not just the evildoers among you, and know that God is harsh in retribution.

26 Remember when you were few (and) weak on the earth, (and) you feared that the people might snatch you away, and He gave you refuge, and supported you with His help, and provided you with good things, so that you might be thankful. **27** You who believe! Do not betray God and the messenger, and do not betray your pledges when you know (better). **28** Know that your wealth and your children are a test,[32] and that God – with Him (there is) a great reward. **29** You who believe! If you guard (yourselves) against God, He will grant[33] deliverance[34] for you, and absolve you of your evil deeds, and forgive you. God is full of great favor.

30 (Remember) when[35] those who disbelieved were scheming against you,[36] to confine you, or kill you, or expel you. They were scheming but God was scheming (too), and God is the best of schemers. **31** When Our signs are recited[37] to them, they say, 'We have already heard (this). If we wished, we could indeed say (something) like this. This is nothing but old tales.'[38] **32** And (remember) when they said, 'God! If this is the truth from You, rain down on us stones from the sky or bring us a painful punishment.'[39] **33** But God was not one to punish them while you[40] were among them, and God was not one to punish them while they were asking for forgiveness. **34** But what (excuse) have they (now) that God should not punish them, when they are keeping (people) from (going to) the Sacred Mosque,[41] and they are not its (true) allies?[42] Its only allies are the ones who guard (themselves),[43] but most of them do not know (it). **35** Their prayer at the House[44] is nothing but whistling and clapping of hands. So taste the punishment for what you disbelieve!

36 Surely those who disbelieve spend their wealth to keep (people) from the way of God – and they will (continue to) spend it. Then it will be a (cause of) regret for them,[45] (and) then they will be overcome. Those who disbelieve will be gathered into Gehenna, **37** so that God may separate the bad from the good, and place the bad one on top of the other, and so pile them all up, and place them in Gehenna. Those – they are the

---

29. *he*: or 'He.'
30. *heart*: here, as often, the heart is spoken of as synonymous with mind.
31. *trouble*: or 'tribulation' (Ar. *fitna* has a range of meanings), though the reference is uncertain (cf. Q8.39, 73 below).
32. *test*: or 'trial,' 'temptation' (Ar. *fitna*).
33. *grant*: lit. 'make.'
34. *deliverance*: see n. on Q2.53; cf. Q8.41 below (the 'Day of Deliverance').

30–40 Opposition in the past

35. *(Remember) when...*: the Cairo edition, reflecting the views of traditional scholars, attributes the following seven verses (Q8.30-36) to the 'Meccan' period.
36. *you*: the Prophet.
37. *signs are recited*: or 'verses are read aloud.'
38. *old tales*: or 'tales of the ancients;' a contemptuous reference to the stories of earlier generations who were punished for disobeying their prophets (cf. Q8.38 below; see n. on Q7.59; 25.5).
39. *rain down on us stones from the sky or bring us a painful punishment*: the disbelievers dare God to punish them as he is alleged to have punished previous peoples, according to the 'old tales.'
40. *you*: the Prophet.
41. *Sacred Mosque*: traditionally identified with the Ka'ba at Mecca (see n. on Q5.95).
42. *allies*: Ar. *awliyā'* implies the obligation of mutual protection, almost in the sense of 'friends' or 'brothers.'
43. *guard (themselves)*: against evil, or God.
44. *the House*: of God; another name for the Ka'ba (see n. on Q5.95).

36–40 Further opposition possible

45. *a (cause of) regret...*: lit. 'a sighing...' (cf. Q19.39 , the 'Day of Regret').

losers. **38** Say to those who disbelieve (that) if they stop,[46] whatever is already past will be forgiven them, but if they return, the customary way of those of old has already passed away.[47] **39** Fight them[48] until (there) is no persecution[49] and the religion – all of it – (belongs) to God. If they stop – surely God sees what they do. **40** If they turn away, know that God is your Protector. Excellent is the Protector, and excellent is the Helper!

41 Know that whatever spoils you take, a fifth[50] of it (belongs) to God and to the messenger, and to family, and the orphans, and the poor, and the traveler,[51] if you believe in God and what We sent down on Our servant[52] on the Day of Deliverance,[53] the day the two forces met. God is powerful over everything.

42 (Remember) when you were on the nearer side, and they on the farther side, and the caravan[54] was below you. (Even) if you had set a time (to fight), you would indeed have failed to keep the appointment. But (the battle took place) so that God might decide the affair – it was done! – (and it took place) so that those who perished might perish on (the basis of) a clear sign, and that those who lived might live on (the basis of) a clear sign.[55] Surely God is indeed hearing, knowing.

43 (Remember) when God showed them to you[56] in your dream as (only) a few, and if had He shown them as many, you[57] would indeed have lost courage, and indeed argued about the matter. But God kept (you) safe. Surely He knows what is in the hearts.[58] **44** (Remember) when He showed them to you[59] – when you met – as few in your eyes, and He made you (appear as) few in their eyes. (This took place) so that God might decide the affair – it was done! To God all affairs are returned.

45 You who believe! When you encounter a (hostile) cohort, stand firm, and remember God often, so that you may prosper. **46** Obey God and His messenger, and do not argue, so that you lose courage and your strength fails. And be patient. Surely God is with the patient. **47** Do not be like those who went forth from their homes boastfully, and to show off to the people, and to keep (them) from the way of God. God encompasses what they do.

48 (Remember) when Satan made their deeds appear enticing to them, and said, '(There is) no one

---

46. *stop*: i.e. cease hostilities (cf. Q8.19 above).

47. *the customary way of those of old has already passed away*: meaning obscure; it may be a threat that if the disbelievers do not cease hostilities, they will suffer the same fate as those generations before them who were destroyed for their sins; or else that they will persist in their disbelief, despite having the example of the 'way' (Ar. *sunna*) God punished earlier generations (cf. Q3.137; 15.13; 18.55; 35.43; 40.85; 48.23).

48. *Fight them...*: plur. imperative; cf. Q2.193; contrast Q2.256; 10.99; 12.103; 16.37.

49. *persecution*: or 'dissension' (Ar. *fitna*); cf. Q2.193.

41 Distribution of spoils

50. *a fifth*: presumably to be handed over to the Prophet for distribution to the persons mentioned (but cf. Q8.1 above, where all spoils are to be handed over 'to God and the messenger').

51. *traveler*: lit. 'son of the way.'

52. *what We sent down on Our servant*: this may refer to the 'sending down' of the Qur'ān (cf. Q25.1); the word 'servant' (Ar. *'abd*) also means 'slave.'

53. *Day of Deliverance*: Ar. *yawm al-furqān* is usually taken as a reference to the victory at Badr (see n. on Q2.53).

42–44 God determined the outcome of the battle

54. *caravan*: traditionally, a caravan returning from Syria (see Q8.7n. above).

55. *clear sign*: or 'clear proof,' 'indisputable evidence' (i.e. of God's control over the outcome of the battle).

56. *you*: the Prophet.

57. *you*: plur.

58. *hearts*: lit. 'chests,' considered the seat of knowledge and understanding.

59. *you*: plur.

45–48 Believers must stand firm in battle

among the people to defeat you today. Surely I am your neighbor.'[60] But when the two cohorts saw each other, he turned on his heels, and said, 'Surely I am free of you, (for) surely I see what you do not see. Surely I fear God, (for) God is harsh in retribution.'

49 (Remember) when the hypocrites and those in whose hearts is a sickness were saying: 'Their religion has deceived these (people).'[61] But whoever puts his trust in God – surely God is mighty, wise. **50** If (only) you[62] could see when the angels take[63] those who have disbelieved, striking their faces and their backs, and (saying): 'Taste the punishment of the burning (Fire)! **51** That is for what your (own) hands have sent forward,[64] and (know) that God is not an evildoer to (His) servants.' **52** (It will be) like the case of the house of Pharaoh, and those who were before them: they disbelieved in the signs of God, so God seized them for their sins. Surely God is strong, harsh in retribution. **53** That is because God is not one to change the blessing with which He has blessed a people, until they change what is within themselves. (Know) that God is hearing, knowing. **54** Like the case of the house of Pharaoh, and those who were before them: they called the signs of their Lord a lie, so We destroyed them for their sins, and We drowned the house of Pharaoh. All were evildoers.

55 Surely the worst of creatures in the sight of God are those who disbelieve – and they will not believe – **56** those of them with whom you[65] have made a treaty, (and) then they break their treaty every time, and they do not guard (themselves). **57** If you come upon them in war, scatter with them those who are behind them, so that they may take heed.[66] **58** If you fear treachery from a people, toss (the treaty) back at them likewise. Surely God does not love the treacherous. **59** Do not let those who disbelieve think they have gotten away. Surely they will not escape. **60** Prepare for them whatever force and cavalry you[67] can, to terrify by this means the enemy of God and your enemy, and others besides them. You do not know them, but God knows them. Whatever you contribute[68] in the way of God will be repaid to you in full, and you will not be done evil. **61** If they incline toward peace, you[69] incline toward it (as well). Put (your) trust in God. Surely He is the Hearing, the Knowing. **62** But if they intend to deceive you – surely God is enough for you. He (it is) who supported you with His help and with the believers, **63** and He has brought their hearts together. If you had spent what is on the earth – all (of it) – you could not have brought their hearts together. But God has brought their hearts together. Surely He is mighty, wise.

64 Prophet![70] God is enough for you, and whoever follows you of the believers. **65** Prophet! Urge on the believers to the fighting. If (there) are twenty of you (who are) patient, they will overcome two hundred, and if (there) are a hundred of you, they will overcome a thousand of those who disbelieve, because they are a

---

60. *I am your neighbor*: and responsible to protect them.

49–54 The hypocrites will be punished

61. *these (people)*: the believers.
62. *you*: the Prophet, or perhaps intended generally ('one').
63. *take*: in death (see n. on Q6.61).
64. *what your (own) hands have sent forward*: i.e. their deeds, which are 'sent forward' to the Judgment.

55–63 Treatment of traitors

65. *you*: the Prophet.
66. *...that they may take heed*: the strategy is not entirely clear; perhaps the leaders are to be made an example of in order to deter their followers.
67. *you*: plur.
68. *contribute*: lit. 'spend.'
69. *you*: the Prophet.

64–71 Instructions to the Prophet about fighting

70. *Prophet*: for this important title, see n. on Q2.87.

people without understanding. **66** Now God has lightened (the task) for you,[71] and He knows that (there is) weakness in you. If (there) are a hundred of you (who are) patient, they will overcome two hundred, and if (there) are a thousand of you, they will overcome two thousand by the permission of God. God is with the patient.

67 It is not for a prophet to have captives,[72] until he has subdued[73] (the enemy) on the earth. You[74] desire (the fleeting) goods of this world, but God desires the Hereafter.[75] God is mighty, wise. **68** Were it not for a preceding Book from God,[76] a great punishment would indeed have touched you for what you took. **69** So eat from what you have taken as spoils as permitted[77] (and) good, and guard (yourselves) against God. Surely God is forgiving, compassionate.

70 Prophet! Say to the captives in your hands: 'If God knows of any good in your hearts, He will give you (something) better than what has been taken from you, and He will forgive you. Surely God is forgiving, compassionate.' **71** But if they intend to betray you, they have already betrayed God before (that). So He has given (you) power over them. God is knowing, wise.

72 Surely those who have believed and emigrated,[78] and struggled with their wealth and their lives in the way of God,[79] and those who have given refuge and help,[80] those – they are allies of each other.[81] But those who have believed and not emigrated – their protection is not (an obligation) on you[82] at all, until they emigrate. Yet if they seek your help in the (matter of) religion, (their) help is (an obligation) on you, unless (it be) against a people with whom you have a treaty. God sees what you do.

73 Those who disbelieve are allies of each other. Unless you do this,[83] (there) will be trouble[84] on the earth and great corruption. **74** But those who have believed, and emigrated, and struggled in the way of God, and those who have given refuge and help, those – they are the true believers. For them (there is) forgiveness and generous provision. **75** But those who have believed after that, and emigrated, and struggled (along) with you, they (too) belong to you. Yet those related by blood[85] are closer to one another in the Book of God.[86] Surely God has knowledge of everything.

---

71. *you*: plur.
72. *captives*: prisoners of war.
73. *subdued*: an obscure word (Ar. *athkhana*; cf. Q47.4).
74. *You*: plur.
75. *the Hereafter*: see n. on Q2.4.
76. *a preceding Book from God*: i.e. what God had decreed or written in the 'Book of God' or 'Book of Destiny' (see Q8.75 below; cf. Q10.19; 11.110; 20.129; 41.45; 42.14, 21).
77. *permitted*: Ar. *ḥalāl*.

72–75 Cutting ties with disbelievers

78. *emigrated*: from Mecca to Medina, though this is not explicitly stated in the Qur'ān.
79. *struggled...in the way of God*: i.e. supported and fought for the cause (cf. Q8.74, 75 below).
80. *refuge and help*: the believers of Medina were called 'helpers' (Ar. *anṣār*).
81. *allies of each other*: 'allies' (Ar. *awliyā'*) implies the obligation of mutual protection, almost in the sense of 'friends' or 'brothers' (but cf. Q8.75 below).
82. *you*: plur.
83. *Unless you do this*: i.e. unless the believers, too, become 'allies' of one another.
84. *trouble*: or 'discord' (Ar. *fitna*).
85. *those related by blood*: lit. 'those of the (same) wombs.'
86. *Book of God*: probably refers to the heavenly 'Record' of all things (see Q33.6; cf. e.g. Q6.38, 59; 9.36; 10.61; 11.6; 13.38; 22.70; 57.22).

9 Repentance ۞ Al-Tawba

1 A renunciation[1] from God and His messenger[2] to those of the idolaters[3] with whom you have made a treaty:[4] 2 'Move about (freely) on the earth for four months,[5] and know that you cannot escape God, and that God will disgrace the disbelievers.'

3 And a proclamation from God and His messenger to the people on the day of the great pilgrimage:[6] 'God renounces[7] the idolaters, and (so does) His messenger. If you turn (in repentance), it will be better for you, but if you turn away, know that you cannot escape God.'

Give[8] those who disbelieve news of a painful punishment, 4 except those of the idolaters with whom you have made a treaty, (and who) since then have not failed you in anything and have not supported anyone against you.[9] Fulfill their treaty with them until their term.[10] Surely God loves the ones who guard (themselves).[11]

5 Then, when the sacred months have passed,[12] kill[13] the idolaters wherever you find them, and seize them, and besiege them, and sit (in wait) for them at every place of ambush. If they turn (in repentance), and observe the prayer and give the alms,[14] let them go their way. Surely God is forgiving, compassionate.

Q9: This sūra deals with various matters connected with fighting for the cause of God. It opens with a renunciation of all treaty obligations with the 'idolaters' (Q9.1-28). This is followed by a short exhortation to fight against the 'People of the Book' (Q9.29-35). Then comes a sustained diatribe against the 'hypocrites' and others for their refusal to fight alongside the Prophet (Q9.38-106). It concludes by emphasizing again the duty to fight for the cause (Q9.119-129). Most scholars assign Q9 to the 'Medinan' period, after the break with the 'idolaters' in the closing years of the Prophet's life (631 CE/9 AH). It is the only sūra in the Cairo edition which is not introduced by the *basmala* (though the codex of Ibn Mas'ūd is said to have included it). The title comes from the reference to 'repentance' at Q9.104, but it is also known as 'The Renunciation' (*al-Barā'a*) from its first word.

1–2 Renunciation of treaties

1. *renunciation*: or 'disowning.'
2. *messenger*: for this important title, see n. on Q2.87.
3. *the idolaters*: or 'the ones who associate (other gods with God).'
4. *treaty*: or 'covenant.'
5. *four months*: i.e. all treaties with the 'idolaters' will cease to be effective after four months.

3–12 A proclamation

6. *the great pilgrimage*: probably a reference to the Ḥajj (or 'greater pilgrimage') as distinct from the 'Umra (or 'lesser pilgrimage'). This 'proclamation' may extend to Q9.28.
7. *renounces*: or 'disowns;' i.e. is no longer under obligation to.
8. *Give...*: addressed to the Prophet.
9. *except those of the idolaters...*: this proviso looks like it may have originally followed v. 1.
10. *until their term*: i.e. until the end of the period stated in the treaty.
11. *guard (themselves)*: against evil, or God.
12. *when the sacred months have passed*: according to Q9.36 (below), there are twelve months in the year, four of which are 'sacred' (traditionally, Rajab, Dhū-l-Qa'da, Dhū-l-Ḥijja, and Muḥarram).
13. *kill*: plur. imperative.
14. *observe the prayer and give the alms*: i.e. *ṣalāt*, the ritual prayer, and *zakāt*, a kind of tithe required for the benefit of the poor, as well as other purposes.

6 If one of the idolaters seeks your protection,[15] grant him protection until he hears the word of God. Then convey him to his place of safety – that is because they are a people who have no knowledge.

7 How can the idolaters have a treaty with God and with His messenger, except those with whom you have made a treaty at the Sacred Mosque?[16] So long as they go straight with you, go straight with them. Surely God loves the ones who guard (themselves). **8** How (can there be a treaty with them)? If they were to prevail over you, they would not respect any bond or agreement with you. They please you with their mouths, but their hearts[17] refuse (you). Most of them are wicked. **9** They have sold the signs[18] of God for a small price, and kept (people) from His way. Surely evil is what they have done. **10** They do not respect any bond or agreement with a believer. Those – they are the transgressors. **11** If they turn (in repentance), and observe the prayer and give the alms, (they are) your brothers in the religion. We make the signs distinct[19] for a people who know. **12** But if they break their oaths, after their treaty, and vilify your religion, fight the leaders of disbelief – surely they have no (binding) oaths – so that they stop (fighting).

13 Will you[20] not fight (against) a people who have broken their oaths,[21] and are determined to expel the messenger, and started (to attack) you the first time? Are you afraid of them? God – (it is more) right that you should fear Him, if you are believers. **14** Fight them! God will punish them by your hands, and disgrace them, and help you against them, and heal the hearts[22] of a people who believe, **15** and take away (all) rage from their hearts. God turns (in forgiveness) to whomever He pleases. God is knowing, wise.

16 Or did you think that you would be left (in peace), when God did not (yet) know those of you who have struggled,[23] and have not taken any ally other than God and His messenger and the believers? God is aware of what you do. **17** It is not for the idolaters to inhabit the mosques of God, (while) bearing witness against themselves of disbelief. Those – their deeds have come to nothing, and in the Fire[24] they will remain. **18** Only he will inhabit the mosques of God who believes in God and the Last Day, and observes the prayer and gives the alms, and does not fear (anyone) but God. It may be that those – they will be among the (rightly) guided ones.

19 Do you make the giving of water[25] to the pilgrims and the inhabiting of the Sacred Mosque like the one who believes in God and the Last Day and struggles in the way of God? They are not equal with God, and God does not guide the people who are evildoers. **20** Those who have believed, and emigrated, and struggled in the way of God with their wealth and their lives are higher in rank with God. Those – they are the triumphant. **21** Their Lord gives them good news of mercy from Himself, and approval, and (there are) Gardens[26] for them in which (there is) lasting bliss, **22** there to remain forever. Surely God – with Him is a great reward.

---

15. *your protection*: the Prophet's protection.
16. *Sacred Mosque*: traditionally identified with the Ka'ba at Mecca (see n. on Q5.95), which now appears to be in the hands of the Muslims (cf. Q9.28 below).
17. *hearts*: here, as often, the heart is spoken of as synonymous with mind.
18. *signs*: or 'verses' (see n. on Q2.39).
19. *make the signs distinct*: or 'expound the verses.'

13–24 Exhortation to resume fighting

20. *you*: plur. (throughout this section).
21. *a people who have broken their oaths*: said to refer to the renunciation of the treaty of al-Ḥudaybiya (concluded in 628 CE/6 AH).
22. *hearts*: lit. 'chests,' considered the seat of knowledge and understanding.
23. *struggled*: or 'fought' (Ar. *jāhada*); cf. Q9.19, 20, 88 below.
24. *the Fire*: Ar. *al-nār* is the most common of the various designations for Hell.
25. *the giving of water*: the provision of water to pilgrims (Ar. *siqāya*) was said to be the privilege of one of the clans of the Quraysh.
26. *Gardens*: in heaven (for this imagery, see n. on Q2.25).

23 You who believe! Do not take your fathers and your brothers as allies, if they prefer disbelief over belief.[27] Whoever among you takes them as allies, those – they are the evildoers. **24** Say:[28] 'If your fathers, and your sons, and your brothers, and your wives, and your clan, and wealth you have acquired, and (business) transaction(s) you fear (may) fall off, and dwellings you take pleasure in are dearer to you than God and His messenger, and struggling[29] in His way, then wait until God brings His command.[30] God does not guide the people who are wicked.'

25 Certainly God has helped you on many (battle)fields, and on the day of Ḥunayn,[31] when your multitude impressed you but was of no use to you at all, and the earth was too narrow for you, despite its breadth, and you turned back, retreating. **26** Then God sent down His Sakīna[32] on His messenger and on the believers, and He sent down forces you did not see,[33] and punished those who disbelieved – that was the payment of the disbelievers. **27** Then, after that, God turns (in forgiveness) to whomever He pleases. God is forgiving, compassionate.

28 You who believe! Only the idolaters are impure,[34] so let them not go near the Sacred Mosque after this, their (final) year. If you fear poverty,[35] God will enrich you from His favor, if He pleases. Surely God is knowing, wise.

29 Fight those who do not believe in God or the Last Day, and do not forbid what God and His messenger have forbidden, and do not practice the religion of truth[36] – from among those who have been given the Book[37] – until they pay tribute[38] out of hand,[39] and they are disgraced.

30 The Jews say, 'Ezra is the son of God,'[40] and the Christians[41] say, 'The Messiah[42] is the son of God.' That is their saying with their mouths. They imitate the saying of those who disbelieved before (them). (May)

---

27. *...if they prefer disbelief over belief*: religious affiliation supersedes the strongest of family ties; 'allies' (Ar. *awliyā'*) implies the obligation of mutual protection, almost in the sense of 'friends' or 'brothers.'
28. *Say*: on this form of address, see n. on Q2.80.
29. *struggling*: or 'fighting' (Ar. *jihād*).
30. *command*: some kind of divine intervention is meant, perhaps 'judgment' (cf. Q2.109; 4.47; 5.52; 7.150; 10.24; 16.1, 33).

25–27 God's help at the battle of Ḥunayn

31. *Ḥunayn*: not far from Ṭā'if, and said to refer to the battle with the Hawāzin and Thaqīf (630 CE/8 AH), shortly after the capture of Mecca.
32. *Sakīna*: or 'assurance' (see n. on Q2.248; cf. Q9.40 below; 48.4, 18, 26).
33. *forces you did not see*: angels.

28 Conclusion of the proclamation

34. *impure*: i.e. in a state of ritual defilement; Ar. *najas* ('dirt,' 'filth') occurs only here (cf. Q9.95, 125 below).
35. *If you fear poverty...*: this may mean that Mecca depended on income from pilgrims to the Ka'ba.

29–35 Fighting against the People of the Book

36. *religion of truth*: Islam (cf. Q9.33 below).
37. *from among those who have been given the Book*: i.e. Jews and Christians, but since they are described as not believing in God or the Last Day, this phrase may be a later addition and the original reference was to 'pagans.'
38. *pay tribute*: or 'render the poll tax' (Ar. *al-jizya* only occurs here); later levied on non-Muslims.
39. *out of hand*: or perhaps 'willingly,' but the meaning of this phrase is uncertain.
40. *Ezra is the son of God*: Ezra (Ar. *'Uzayr*, though the form of the name is unusual) is a major figure in the Bible, and the book which bears his name describes how he led a group of exiles out of Babylon and back to Jerusalem. Later Jewish tradition held that his knowledge of the Torah rivaled, or surpassed, that of Moses. For Ezra as the 'son of God,' see 4 Ezra 14.9.
41. *Christians*: Ar. *Naṣārā* (see n. on Q2.62).
42. *The Messiah*: the Qur'ān uses this title (Ar. *al-Masīḥ*) almost as a proper name, without any discussion of the ideas associated with it.

God fight them. How are they (so) deluded? **31** They have taken their teachers and their monks as Lords instead of God, and (also) the Messiah, son of Mary,[43] when they were only commanded to serve one God. (There is) no god but Him. Glory to Him above what they associate![44] **32** They want to extinguish the light of God with their mouths, but God refuses (to do anything) except perfect His light, even though the disbelievers dislike (it). **33** He (it is) who has sent His messenger with the guidance[45] and the religion of truth, so that He[46] may cause it to prevail over religion – all of it – even though the idolaters dislike (it).

34 You who believe! Surely many of the teachers and the monks consume the wealth of the people by means of falsehood, and keep (people) from the way of God. Those who hoard the gold and the silver, and do not spend it in the way of God[47] – give them[48] news of a painful punishment. **35** On the Day when it[49] will be heated in the Fire of Gehenna,[50] and their foreheads and their sides and their backs will be branded with it: 'This is what you hoarded for yourselves, so taste what you have hoarded!'

36 Surely the number of months with God is twelve, (written) in the Book of God[51] on the day when He created the heavens and the earth. Of them, four are sacred.[52] That is the right religion. Do not do yourselves evil during them, but fight (against) the idolaters all together,[53] as they fight you all together, and know that God is with the ones who guard (themselves). **37** The postponement[54] is an increase of disbelief by which those who disbelieve go astray. They make it profane (one) year, and make it sacred (another) year, to adjust the number (of months) God has made sacred, and to profane what God has made sacred. The evil of their deeds is made to appear enticing to them, but God does not guide the people who are disbelievers.

38 You who believe! What is (the matter) with you? When it is said to you, 'Go forth[55] in the way of God,' you slump to the earth. Are you pleased with this present life, rather than the Hereafter?[56] Yet what enjoyment (there is) of this present life is only a little (thing) in (comparison to) the Hereafter. **39** If you do not go forth, He will punish you (with) a painful punishment, and exchange a people other than you.[57]

---

43. *son of Mary*: there is no mention in the Qur'ān of Joseph, Jesus' putative father (cf. Mark 6.3).
44. *what they associate*: other gods with God; in this sense Jews and Christians can be considered 'idolaters' (see also Q4.51; 30.30-33; 42.13-14).
45. *the guidance*: one of the most frequent terms (Ar. *al-hudā*) for revelation in general, and the Qur'ān in particular (cf. Q6.127).
46. *He*: or 'he' (the Prophet).
47. *spend it in the way of God*: i.e. contribute to God's cause.
48. *give them*: sing. imperative.
49. *it*: their 'gold and silver.'
50. *Gehenna*: a name for Hell (see n. on Q2.206).

36–37 Fighting during the sacred months

51. *Book of God*: i.e. the 'Book of Destiny' by which everything was ordained at creation (cf. Q6.38, 59; 10.61; 11.6; 22.70; 57.22 etc.). The specification of twelve months excludes the use of an intercalary month every so often to make the lunar year accord with the solar year (see Q9.37 below; cf. Q10.5).
52. *four are sacred*: see n. on Q9.5 above.
53. *all together*: or 'continuously,' i.e. in all months, whether sacred or not (cf. Q9.2, 5 above).
54. *the postponement*: i.e. by means of an intercalary month, occasionally required to align the calendar with the seasons. By prohibiting an intercalary month the Islamic lunar calendar ceased to accord with the solar.

38–49 Fighting and excuses for avoiding it

55. *Go forth*: to fight (cf. Q4.71).
56. *the Hereafter*: see n. on Q2.4.
57. *exchange a people other than you*: i.e. put another people in their place.

You will not harm Him at all, (for) God is powerful over everything. **40** If you do not help him,[58] God has already helped him, when those who disbelieved expelled him, the second of two: when the two were in the cave,[59] (and) when he said to his companion, 'Do not sorrow, (for) surely God is with us.' Then God sent down His Sakīna[60] on him, and supported him with forces which you did not see, and made the word of those who disbelieved the lowest, while the word of God is the highest. God is mighty, wise.

41 Go forth, light and heavy, and struggle[61] in the way of God with your wealth and your lives. That is better for you, if (only) you knew. **42** If it were (some fleeting) gain near (at hand), and an easy journey, they would indeed have followed you,[62] but the distance is (too) far for them. (Still) they will swear by God, 'If we had been able, we would indeed have gone out with you.' (In this way) they destroy themselves. But God knows: 'Surely they are liars indeed!

43 God pardon you![63] Why did you give them permission,[64] before (it was) clear to you (who were) those who spoke the truth, and (before) you knew (who) the liars (were)? **44** Those who believe in God and the Last Day do not ask your permission,[65] so that they may struggle with their wealth and their lives. God knows the ones who guard (themselves). **45** Only those who do not believe in God and the Last Day ask your permission, and their hearts are filled with doubt, and they waver in their doubt. **46** If they had intended to go forth, they would indeed have made some preparation for it. But God disliked their going forth, so He held them back, and it was said (to them), 'Sit (at home) with the ones who sit.'[66] **47** If they had gone forth with you,[67] they would have added to you nothing but ruin, and would indeed have run around in your midst, seeking to stir up trouble[68] among you – and some of you would have listened to them. But God knows the evildoers. **48** Certainly they sought to stir up trouble before (this), and upset matters for you,[69] until the truth came and the command of God prevailed, even though they were unwilling. **49** (There is) one of them who says, 'Give me permission,[70] and do not tempt me.'[71] Is it not (a fact) that they have (already) fallen into temptation? Surely Gehenna will indeed encompass the disbelievers.

50 If some good smites you,[72] it distresses them,[73] but if some smiting smites you, they say, 'We took hold of our affair before (this),'[74] and they turn away, gloating. **51** Say: 'Nothing smites us except what God

---

58. *him*: the Prophet.
59. *...when the two were in the cave*: said to refer to the Prophet's flight from Mecca, when he and Abū Bakr took shelter in a cave near Mecca until their pursuers abandoned the chase.
60. *Sakīna*: or 'assurance' (see Q9.26n. above).
61. *struggle*: or 'fight' (cf. Q9.44, 73, 81, 86 below).
62. *you*: the Prophet.
63. *you*: the Prophet.
64. *permission*: to remain at home and not go out to fight.
65. *permission*: to be excused from fighting.
66. *the ones who sit*: lit. 'the sitters' (Ar. *al-qāʿidūn*), referring to women, children, and those unfit for fighting (cf. Q9.86 below; 4.95).
67. *you*: plur.
68. *trouble*: or 'discord' (Ar. *fitna*).
69. *you*: the Prophet.
70. *Give me permission*: to remain at home and not go out to fight.
71. *do not tempt me*: to dissension or sedition.

50–57 Diatribe against the hypocrites

72. *you*: the Prophet.
73. *them*: probably the 'hypocrites,' based on what follows.
74. *We took hold of our affair before (this)*: by remaining at home and not fighting.

has prescribed[75] for us. He is our Protector, and in God let the believers put (their) trust.' **52** Say: 'Do you wait for anything in our case except for one of the two good (rewards)?[76] But we are waiting in your case for God to smite you with punishment from Him or at our hands. (Just) wait! Surely we shall be waiting with you.'

53 Say: 'Contribute[77] willingly or unwillingly, it will not be accepted from you. Surely you are a wicked people.' **54** Nothing prevents their contributions being accepted from them, except that they have not believed in God and in His messenger, and they do not come to the prayer, except in a lazy fashion, and they do not contribute, except unwillingly.

55 Do not let their wealth and their children impress you. God only intends to punish them by means of it in this present life, and (that) they themselves should pass away while they are disbelievers. **56** They swear by God that they indeed belong to you, but they do not belong to you. They are a people who are afraid. **57** If they could find a shelter, or caves, or a place to hide, they would indeed resort to it and rush off.

58 (There is) one of them who finds fault with you[78] concerning freewill offerings.[79] Yet if they are given (a share) of it, they are pleased, but if they are not given (a share) of it, they are angry. **59** If (only) they had been pleased with what God gave them, and His messenger, and had said, 'God is enough for us. God will give us (more) of His favor, and (so will) His messenger. Surely we turn in hope to God.' **60** Freewill offerings are only for the poor and the needy, and the ones who collect it, and the ones whose hearts are united, and for the (freeing of) slaves,[80] and the (relief of) debtors, and for the way of God,[81] and the traveler.[82] (That is) an obligation from God. God is knowing, wise.

61 (There are) some of them who hurt the prophet, and say, 'He is all ears!'[83] Say: 'Good ears for you! He believes in God and believes in the believers, and (he is) a mercy for those of you who believe. But those who hurt the messenger of God – for them (there is) a painful punishment.' **62** They swear to you by God in order to please you, but God and His messenger – (it is more) right that they should please Him, if they are believers. **63** Do they not know that the one who opposes God and His messenger – surely for him (there is) the Fire of Gehenna, there to remain? That is the great humiliation!

64 The hypocrites are afraid that a sūra[84] will be sent down against them, informing them of what is in their hearts. Say: 'Go on mocking! Surely God will bring forth what you are afraid of.' **65** If indeed you ask them, they will indeed say, 'We were only bantering and jesting.' Say: 'Were you mocking God, and His signs,[85] and His messenger? **66** Do not make excuses! You have disbelieved after your believing. If We pardon (one) contingent of you, We will punish (another) contingent because they have been sinners.'

---

75. *prescribed*: lit. 'written.'
76. *the two good (rewards)*: either the reward of victory or death leading to Paradise.
77. *Contribute*: lit. 'Spend' (in support of God's cause).

58–60 Contributions

78. *you*: the Prophet.
79. *freewill offerings*: or 'voluntary contributions' (Ar. *al-ṣadaqāt*), intended for the benefit of the community (cf. Q9.60, 79, 103, 104 below).
80. *(freeeing of) slaves*: or '(ransoming of) captives.'
81. *for the way of God*: for God's cause.
82. *traveler*: lit. 'son of the way.'

61–70 Diatribe against the hypocrites (continued)

83. *He is all ears*: lit. 'He is an ear;' perhaps accusing him of spying or being gullible.
84. *sūra*: here referring to a 'unit' of revelation and not to present sūras, though there is no indication how long these 'units' were. The mention of a sūra being 'sent down' (cf. below Q9.86, 124, 127; 24.1; 47.20) is similar to the way in which terms like 'sign' (Ar. *āya*), 'book' (*kitāb*), and 'recitation' (*qur'ān*) are used (see n. on Q2.23).
85. *signs*: or 'verses.'

67 The hypocrite men and the hypocrite women are all alike.[86] They command wrong and forbid right, and they withdraw their hands.[87] They have forgotten God, so He has forgotten them. Surely the hypocrites – they are the wicked. **68** God has promised the hypocrite men and the hypocrite women, and the disbelievers, the Fire of Gehenna, there to remain. It will be enough for them. God has cursed them, and for them (there is) a lasting punishment. **69** Like those before you: they were stronger than you in power and (had) more wealth and children, and they took enjoyment in their share. You have taken enjoyment in your share, as those before you took enjoyment in their share. You have bantered as they bantered. Those – their deeds have come to nothing in this world and the Hereafter. And those – they are the losers. **70** Has no story[88] come to them of those who were before them: the people of Noah, and 'Ād, and Thamūd, and the people of Abraham, and the companions of Midian, and the overturned (cities)?[89] Their messengers brought them the clear signs.[90] God was not one to do them evil, but they did themselves evil.

71 The believing men and the believing women are allies of each other. They command right and forbid wrong, they observe the prayer and give the alms, and they obey God and His messenger. Those – God will have compassion on them. God is mighty, wise. **72** God has promised the believing men and the believing women Gardens through which rivers flow, there to remain, and good dwellings in Gardens of Eden – but the approval of God is greater. That is the great triumph!

73 Prophet! Struggle against[91] the disbelievers and the hypocrites, and be stern with them. Their refuge is Gehenna – and it is an evil destination! **74** They swear by God that they did not say (it), but certainly they have said the word of disbelief, and have disbelieved after their submission.[92] They determined (to do) what they did not attain,[93] and they took vengeance for no other reason than that God and His messenger had enriched them from His favor.[94] If they turn (in repentance) it will be better for them, but if they turn away, God will punish them (with) a painful punishment in this world and the Hereafter. They have no ally and no helper on the earth.

75 (There is) one of them who has made a covenant with God: 'If He gives us some of His favor, we shall indeed make contributions and indeed be among the righteous.' **76** But when He gave them some of His favor, they were stingy with it and turned away in aversion. **77** So He placed hypocrisy in their hearts until the Day when they meet Him, because they broke (with) God (concerning) what they promised Him, and because they have lied. **78** Do they not know that God knows their secret and their secret talk, and that God is the Knower of the unseen?[95] **79** Those who find fault with those of the believers who contribute voluntarily, and those who ridicule those (believers) who do not find (anything to offer) but their effort – God has ridiculed them, and for them (there is) a painful punishment. **80** Ask forgiveness[96] for them or do not ask forgiveness for them. (Even) if you ask forgiveness for them seventy times, God

86. *are all alike*: lit. 'some of them (are) from others.'
87. *they withdraw their hands*: i.e. they refuse to contribute to the cause.
88. *story*: or 'news.'
89. *the overturned (cities)*: perhaps the cities of Sodom and Gomorrah, associated with Lot, or else a general reference to the stories of previous peoples who were punished for their sins (cf. Q53.53; 69.9; see n. on Q7.59).
90. *the clear signs*: or 'the clear proofs,' 'the indisputable evidence.'

71–72 Rewards for believers

73–80 Diatribe against the hypocrites (continued)

91. *Struggle against*: or 'fight' (Ar. *jāhid*); cf. Q9.29 above; 66.9.
92. *after their submission*: i.e. after they had professed Islam (lit. 'after their Islam').
93. *what they did not attain*: reference obscure; said to refer to a plot to kill the Prophet.
94. *they took vengeance for no other reason than...*: to be taken in an ironic sense.
95. *the unseen*: see n. on Q2.3.
96. *Ask forgiveness...*: addressed to the Prophet.

will not forgive them. That is because they have disbelieved in God and His messenger. God does not guide the wicked.

81 The ones who stayed behind[97] gloated over their sitting (at home) behind the messenger of God, and disliked (it) that they should (have to) struggle with their wealth and their lives in the way of God. They said, 'Do not go forth in the heat.' Say: 'The Fire of Gehenna is hotter!' If (only) they understood! **82** So let them laugh a little (now) and weep a lot in payment for what they have earned. **83** If God brings you back[98] to some contingent of them, and they ask your permission to go forth, say: 'You will never go forth with me, nor will you ever fight any enemy with me. Surely you were pleased with sitting (at home) the first time, so sit with the ones who stay behind.'

84 Never pray over anyone of them who has died, nor stand over his grave. Surely they disbelieved in God and His messenger, and died while they were wicked. **85** Do not let their wealth and their children impress you. God only intends to punish them by means of it in this world, and (that) they themselves should pass away while they are disbelievers.

86 When a sūra is sent down (stating): 'Believe in God, and struggle alongside[99] His messenger,' the wealthy among them ask your permission, and say, 'Let us be with the ones who sit (at home).' **87** They are pleased to be with the ones who stay behind, and a seal is set on their hearts, and so they do not understand. **88** But the messenger and those who believe with him have struggled with their wealth and their lives. And those – for them (there are) the good things, and those – they are the ones who prosper. **89** God has prepared for them Gardens through which rivers flow, there to remain. That is the great triumph!

90 The excuse-makers among the Arabs[100] came to get permission for themselves,[101] and those who lied to God and His messenger sat (at home). A painful punishment will smite those of them who disbelieve. **91** There is no blame on the weak or on the sick or on those who find nothing to contribute, if they are true to God and His messenger. (There is) no way[102] against the doers of good – God is forgiving, compassionate – **92** nor against those (to) whom, when they came to you for you to give them mounts, you said, 'I cannot find a mount for you.' They turned away, and their eyes were full of the tears of sorrow, because they did not find anything to contribute. **93** The way[103] is only open against those who ask your permission[104] when they are rich. They are pleased to be with the ones who stay behind. God has set a seal on their hearts, but they do not know (it).

94 They will make excuses to you[105] when you return to them. Say: 'Do not make excuses, (for) we do not believe you. God has already informed us of the reports about you. God will see your deed, and (so will) His messenger. Then you will be returned to the Knower of the unseen and the seen,[106] and He will inform you about what you have done.' **95** They will swear to you by God, when you turn back to them, that you may turn away from them. Turn away from them, (for) surely they are an abomination. Their refuge is Gehenna – a payment for what they have earned. **96** They will swear to you in order that you

---

81–96 Reluctance to fight condemned

97. *The ones who stayed behind*: i.e. those who refused to fight.
98. *brings you back*: i.e. brings the Prophet back safely from the fighting.
99. *struggle alongside*: i.e. 'fight alongside.'
100. *the Arabs*: desert nomads (Ar. *al-aʿrāb*); see Q9.97-99, 101, 120 below.
101. *permission for themselves*: to be exempted from fighting.
102. *no way*: to blame or punish.
103. *The way*: to blame or punish.
104. *your permission*: to be exempted from fighting.
105. *you*: plur.
106. *the seen*: lit. 'the witnessed.'

may be pleased with them. Yet (even) if you are pleased with them, surely God will not be pleased with the people who are wicked.

97 The Arabs are (even) stronger in disbelief and hypocrisy, and more likely not to know the limits of what God has sent down on His messenger. God is knowing, wise. **98** Among the Arabs (there is) one who regards what he contributes as a fine, and waits for the wheels (of fortune to turn) against you. The wheel of evil (will turn) against them! God is hearing, knowing. **99** Among the Arabs (there is) one who believes in God and the Last Day, and takes what he contributes as a (means of) drawing near to God, and (likewise) the prayers of the messenger. Is it not a fact that it is a (means of) drawing near for them? God will cause them to enter into His mercy. God is forgiving, compassionate.

100 The foremost[107] – the first of the emigrants and the helpers, and those who have followed them in doing good – God is pleased with them and they are pleased with Him. He has prepared for them Gardens through which rivers flow, there to remain forever. That is the great triumph!

101 Some of the Arabs who (dwell) around you are hypocrites, and some of the people of the city[108] (also). They have become obstinate in (their) hypocrisy. You[109] do not know them, (but) We know them, (and) We shall punish them twice.[110] Then they will be returned to a great punishment. **102** Others have acknowledged their sins. They have mixed a righteous deed and another (that is) evil. It may be that God will turn (in forgiveness) to them. Surely God is forgiving, compassionate. **103** Take from their wealth a contribution, to cleanse them and purify them by means of it, and pray over them. Surely your prayers are a rest for them. God is hearing, knowing. **104** Do they not know that God – He accepts repentance from His servants[111] and takes (their) contributions, and that God – He is the One who turns (in forgiveness), the Compassionate? **105** Say: 'Work! God will see your deed, and (so will) His messenger and the believers, and you will be returned to the Knower of the unseen and the seen, and He will inform you about what you have done.' **106** (There are) others (who will be) deferred[112] to the command of God, (to see) whether He will punish them or turn (in forgiveness) to them. God is knowing, wise.

107 Those who have taken a mosque[113] (to cause) harm and disbelief and division among the believers, and (to provide) a place of ambush for those who fought against God and His messenger before – they will indeed swear, 'We wanted nothing but good!' But God bears witness: 'Surely they are liars indeed!' **108** Never stand in it![114] A mosque founded from the first day on the (obligation of) guarding (oneself) is indeed (more) worthy for you to stand in. In it (there are) are men who love to purify themselves, and

---

97–99 Attitudes of the Arabs

100 The foremost believers

107. *The foremost*: 'the ones who go before' or 'the ones who have precedence' (Ar. *al-sābiqūn*) are here identified as the first of the 'emigrants' (*muhājerūn*) and 'helpers' (*anṣār*); i.e. the first converts to Islam (see Q56.10-12; cf. Q23.61).

101–106 Attitudes of the Arabs (continued)

108. *the city*: Ar. *al-madīna* simply means 'the city,' but is said to be short for 'City of the Prophet' (cf. Q9.120 below; 33.60; 63.8), and identical with 'Yathrib' (Q33.13). Whether this refers to the city of 'Medina' in present-day Saudi Arabia is disputed by some modern scholars.
109. *You*: the Prophet.
110. *punish them twice*: perhaps meaning they will be disgraced and then die.
111. *servants*: the word 'servant' (Ar. *'abd*) also means 'slave.'
112. *others (who will be) deferred*: perhaps those who refuse to repent for not fighting.

107–110 A rival mosque

113. *Those who have taken a mosque...*: said to refer to the mosque at Qubā' (toward the south of Medina) built just before the expedition to Tabūk to fight the Byzantine army (630 CE/9 AH). According to tradition, the Prophet was asked to pray in it, but he excused himself and later had it destroyed.
114. *Never stand in it*: to pray (addressed to the Prophet).

God loves the ones who purify themselves. **109** So is someone who founded his building on (the obligation of) guarding (oneself) against God, and (on His) approval, better, or someone who founded his building on the brink of a crumbling precipice, (which) then collapsed with him into the Fire of Gehenna? God does not guide the people who are evildoers. **110** Their building which they have built will continue (to be a cause of) doubt in their hearts, unless their hearts are cut (to pieces). God is knowing, wise.

111 Surely God has purchased from the believers their lives and their wealth with (the price of) the Garden (in store) for them. They fight in the way of God, and they kill and are killed. (That is) a promise binding[115] on Him in the Torah, and the Gospel, and the Qur'ān.[116] Who fulfills his covenant better than God? So welcome the good news of the bargain you have made with Him. That is the great triumph! **112** The ones who turn (in repentance), the ones who serve,[117] the ones who praise, the ones who wander,[118] the ones who bow, the ones who prostrate themselves, the ones who command right, and the ones who forbid wrong, (and) the ones who keep the limits of God – give good news to the believers.[119]

113 It is not for the prophet and those who believe to ask forgiveness for the idolaters, even though they may be family,[120] after it has become clear to them that they are the companions of the Furnace.[121] **114** Abraham's asking forgiveness for his father[122] was only because of a solemn promise he had made to him.[123] But when it became clear to him that he was an enemy to God, he disowned him. Surely Abraham was indeed kind (and) forbearing. **115** God is not one to lead a people astray after He has guided them, until He makes clear to them what they should guard (themselves) against. Surely God has knowledge of everything. **116** Surely God – to Him (belongs) the kingdom of the heavens and the earth. He gives life and causes death. You have no ally and no helper other than God.

117 Certainly God has turned (in forgiveness) to the prophet, and (to) the emigrants and the helpers who followed him in the hour of hardship,[124] after the hearts of a group of them had nearly turned aside. Then He turned to them (in forgiveness). Surely He was kind (and) compassionate with them. **118** And to the three who stayed behind,[125] when the earth became narrow for them despite its breadth, and they themselves were constrained, and they thought that (there was) no shelter from God except (going) to Him, then He turned to them (in forgiveness), so that they might (also) turn (in repentance). Surely God – He is the One who turns (in forgiveness), the Compassionate.

119 You who believe! Guard (yourselves) against God, and be with the truthful. **120** It is not for the people of the city,[126] and those of the Arabs who (dwell) around them, to lag behind the messenger

---

111–112 God's bargain with the believers

115. *binding*: lit. 'true.'
116. *the Torah, and the Gospel, and the Qur'ān*: one of the clearest statements of the idea of three 'parallel scriptures' (cf. Q2.136; 3.84; 29.46-47).
117. *the ones who serve*: or 'the worshippers.'
118. *the ones who wander*: perhaps itinerancy is meant; cf. Gospel of Thomas 42, 'Jesus said, "Become wanderers."'
119. *give good news...*: addressed to the Prophet.

113–116 No prayer for idolaters

120. *even though they may be family*: religious affiliation supersedes family ties (cf. Q9.23-24 above).
121. *the Furnace*: a name for Hell (Ar. *al-jaḥīm*).
122. *Abraham's asking forgiveness for his father*: see Q14.41; 19.47; 26.86; 60.4; cf. Q71.28 (Noah).
123. *a solemn promise he had made to him*: lit. 'a promise he had promised him.'

117–118 Believers restored to favor

124. *...the hour of hardship*: said to refer to the restoration of God's favor after the expedition to Tabūk to fight the Byzantine army (630 CE/9 AH).
125. *the three who stayed behind*: said to refer to three individuals who avoided the expedition (cf. Q9.106 above).

119–129 Obligation to fight

of God, nor should they prefer their lives to his. That is because no thirst and no weariness and no emptiness[127] smites them in the way of God, nor do they make any attack[128] (that) enrages the disbelievers, nor do they take any gain[129] from an enemy, except that a righteous deed is thereby written down for them.[130] Surely God does not let the reward of the doers of good go to waste. **121** Nor do they make any contribution,[131] small or great, nor cross any wādi, except that it is written down for them, so that God may repay them (for the) best of what they have done.

122 It is not for the believers to go forth[132] all together. Why not have a contingent of every group of them go forth, so that they[133] may gain understanding in religion, and that they may warn their people when they return to them, so that they (in turn) may beware?

123 You who believe! Fight those of the disbelievers who are close to you, and let them find sternness in you, and know that God is with the ones who guard (themselves).

124 Whenever a sūra is sent down, some of them say, 'Which of you has this increased in belief?' As for those who believe, it increases them in belief, and they welcome the good news. **125** But as for those in whose hearts is a sickness, it increases them in abomination (added) to their abomination, and they die while they are disbelievers. **126** Do they not see that they are tested every year once or twice? Yet still they do not turn (in repentance), nor do they take heed.[134]

127 Whenever a sūra is sent down, some of them look at others: 'Does anyone see you?' Then they turn away. God has turned away their hearts, because they are a people who do not understand.

128 Certainly a messenger has come to you from among you. What you suffer is a mighty (weight) on him, (for he has) concern over you, (and he is) kind (and) compassionate with the believers.

129 If they turn away, say: 'God is enough for me. (There is) no god but Him. In Him have I put my trust. He is the Lord of the great throne.'

---

126. *the city*: see n. on Q9.101 above.
127. *emptiness*: perhaps 'hunger' or 'want.'
128. *make any attack*: lit. 'step any step.'
129. *take any gain*: lit. 'gain any gain.'
130. *written down for them*: in the 'record' of their deeds, or as a 'credit' to their account.
131. *make any contribution*: lit. 'spend any spending.'
132. *go forth*: to fight.
133. *they*: i.e. those who remain behind
134. *take heed*: or 'remember.'

10 Jonah ۞ Yūnus

In the Name of God, the Merciful, the Compassionate

1 Alif Lām Rā'.[1] Those are the signs[2] of the wise Book.[3]

2 Is it amazing to the people that We have inspired a man[4] from among them: 'Warn the people, and give good news to those who believe, that for them (there is) a sure footing with their Lord'? (But) the disbelievers say, 'Surely this (man) is a clear magician[5] indeed.'

3 Surely your Lord is God, who created the heavens and the earth in six days.[6] Then He sat down on the throne. He directs the (whole) affair.[7] (There is) no intercessor without His permission. That is God, your Lord, so serve Him![8] Will you not take heed?[9]
4 To Him is your return – all (of you) – the promise of God in truth! Surely He brought about the creation, (and) then He restores it, so that He may repay those who believe and do righteous deeds in justice. But those who disbelieve – for them (there is) a drink of boiling (water) and a painful punishment, because they were disbelieving.

5 He (it is) who made the sun an illumination, and the moon a light, and determined it by stations,[10] so that you might know the number of the years and the reckoning (of time). God created that only in truth.[11] He makes the signs distinct[12] for a people who know.
6 Surely in the alternation of the night and

Q10: This sūra opens with a declaration of God's creative power, which eventually leads into a condemnation of idolatry. The certainty of judgment and the authenticity of the Qur'ān are also stressed. A final section contains stories about Noah and Moses (Q10.71-103). Most scholars assign Q10 to the 'Meccan' period, though a few verses are considered to be 'Medinan.' It receives its title from the reference to 'Jonah's people' at Q10.98.

1 Signs of the Book

1. *Alif Lām Rā'*: the names of Arabic letters ', *l*, and *r*. The same letter combination occurs in a block of sūras from Q10 to Q15 (Q13 has an additional 'mīm'). Twenty-nine sūras begin with letters like these, ranging from one to five. No satisfactory explanation has been given for their occurrence. The Cairo edition varies in counting these letters as a separate verse, or as the beginning of the first verse (as here).
2. *signs*: here referring to the letters ', *l*, and *r* (for the various meanings of 'signs,' see n. on Q2.39).
3. *the wise Book*: here referring to the Qur'ān not only as a 'recited' but also 'written' scripture (see n. on Q2.2; cf. Q31.2; 36.2).

2 Prophet or magician?

4. *a man*: the Prophet.
5. *clear magician*: a variant reading has 'clear magic;' cf. Q10.76 below (of Moses).

3–6 Signs of God's power and providence

6. *in six days*: cf. Q7.54; 11.7; 25.59; 32.4; 41.9-12; 50.38; and Genesis 1.1-31.
7. *directs the (whole) affair*: or 'directs the command' (Ar. *amr*); the idea may be that God controls the universe from his throne through his *amr*, which may correspond to the rabbinic notion of the 'divine word' (Aram. *mēmrā*), or to the related Christian idea of the *logos* as the manifestation of God's word, or as God's messenger in place of God himself (see Q10.31 below; 13.2; 16.2; 32.5; 65.12).
8. *serve Him*: or 'worship Him' (plur. imperative).
9. *take heed*: or 'be reminded,' 'remember.'
10. *determined it by stations*: referring to the 'phases' of the moon (cf. Q36.39).
11. *in truth*: or 'with the truth' (cf. e.g. Q6.73; 14.19; 16.3 etc.).
12. *He makes the signs distinct*: a variant reading has 'We make the signs distinct' (cf. Q10.24 below).

the day, and (in) what God has created in the heavens and the earth, (there are) signs indeed for a people who guard (themselves).[13]

7 Surely those who do not expect to meet Us, and are satisfied with this present life and feel secure in it, and those who are oblivious of Our signs, **8** those – their refuge is the Fire[14] for what they have earned.
9 Surely those who believe and do righteous deeds – their Lord guides them for[15] their belief. Beneath them rivers flow in Gardens of Bliss.[16] **10** Their call there is: 'Glory to You, God!,' and their greeting there is: 'Peace!,'[17] and the last (part) of their call is: 'Praise (be) to God, Lord of the worlds!'[18]

11 If God were to hurry the evil[19] for the people, (as) their seeking to hurry the good,[20] their time would indeed have been completed for them. But We leave those who do not expect the meeting with Us in their insolent transgression, wandering blindly.

12 When hardship touches a person, he calls on Us,[21] (whether lying) on his side or sitting or standing.[22] But when We have removed his hardship from him, he continues on, as if he had not called on Us about the hardship (that) had touched him. In this way what the wanton do is made to appear enticing to them.

13 Certainly We destroyed the generations before you when they did evil, when their messengers[23] brought them the clear signs[24] and they would not believe. In this way We repay the people who are sinners. **14** Then, after them, We made you successors on the earth, so that We might see how you would do.

15 When Our signs are recited[25] to them as clear signs, those who do not expect the meeting with Us say, 'Bring a different Qur'ān[26] than this one, or change it.'[27] Say:[28] 'It is not for me to change it of my own accord. I only follow what I am inspired (with). Surely I fear, if I disobey my Lord, the punishment of a great Day.' **16** Say: 'If God had (so) pleased, I would not have recited it to you, nor would He have made it known to you. I had already spent a lifetime among you before it (came to me).[29] Will you not

---

13. *guard (themselves)*: against evil, or God.

7–10 Punishment and reward

14. *the Fire*: Ar. *al-nār* is the most common of the various designations for Hell.
15. *for*: or 'by.'
16. *Gardens of Bliss*: in heaven (for this imagery, see n. on Q2.25).
17. *Peace*: Ar. *salām* connotes 'submission' (*islām*) to God.
18. *Praise (be) to God, Lord of the worlds*: cf. Q1.2n.

11 Sinners are blind

19. *hurry the evil*: i.e. judgment or punishment.
20. *the good*: i.e. wealth and possessions.

12 People are ungrateful

21. *he calls on Us*: in prayer.
22. *on his side or sitting or standing*: i.e. continually.

13–14 Punishment of earlier generations a warning

23. *messengers*: for this important title, see n. on Q2.87.
24. *the clear signs*: or 'the clear proofs,' 'the indisputable evidence.'

15–17 Disbelievers mock the Qur'ān

25. *signs are recited*: or 'verses are read aloud.'
26. *Qur'ān*: or 'recitation;' here the term may be used in the sense of a 'unit' of revelation (like *āya* and *surā*), rather than of the entire Qur'ān (cf. Q10.61 below; see n. on Q2.185).
27. *change it*: or 'substitute something else.'
28. *Say*: on this form of address, see n. on Q2.80.
29. *a lifetime...before it (came to me)*: according to tradition, the Prophet was about forty when he began to receive revelations.

understand?' **17** Who is more evil than the one who forges a lie against God, or calls His signs a lie? Surely the sinners will not prosper.

18 They serve what neither harms them nor benefits them, instead of God (alone), and they say, 'These are our intercessors with God.'[30] Say: 'Will you inform God about what He does not know either in the heavens or on the earth? Glory to Him! He is exalted above what they associate.'[31] **19** The people were (once) one community, then they differed.[32] Were it not for a preceding word[33] from your Lord, it would indeed have been decided between them concerning their differences. **20** They say, 'If only a sign were sent down on him from his Lord.'[34] Say: 'The unseen[35] (belongs) only to God. (Just) wait! Surely I shall be one of those waiting with you.' **21** When We give the people a taste of mercy, after hardship has touched them, suddenly they (devise) some scheme against Our signs. Say: 'God is quicker (at devising) a scheme. Surely Our messengers[36] are writing down what you are scheming.'

22 He (it is) who enables you to travel on the shore and the sea, until, when you are on the ship, and they sail[37] with them[38] by means of a fair wind, and they gloat over it, a violent wind comes upon it[39] and the waves come at them[40] from every side, and they think they are encompassed by them. (Then) they call on God, devoting (their) religion to Him:[41] 'If indeed you rescue us from this, we shall indeed be among the thankful.' **23** Yet when He has rescued them, suddenly they become greedy on the earth without any right. People! Your envy is only against yourselves – (the fleeting) enjoyment of this present life. Then to Us is your return, and We shall inform you about what you have done.

24 A parable of this present life: (It is) is like water which We send down from the sky, and (there) mingles with it the vegetation of the earth from which the people and livestock eat, until, when the earth takes on its decoration and is adorned, and its people think that they have power over it, Our command[42] comes on it by night or by day, and We cut it down,[43] as if it had not flourished the day before. In this way We make the signs distinct[44] for a people who reflect.

18–21 The folly of idolatry

30. *intercessors with God*: this may refer to the 'pagan' belief that their deities interceded with the supreme God (cf. Q21.24; 39.43; 42.9), but it could also refer to Christian veneration of Jesus, Mary, and the saints as intercessors with God (see n. on Q39.3).
31. *what they associate*: other gods with God.
32. *the people were (once) one community...*: for this idea, see n. on Q2.213.
33. *a preceding word*: or prior decree, establishing the time judgment (cf. Q8.68; 11.110; 20.129; 41.45; 42.14, 21).
34. *If only a sign were sent down...*: i.e. they demand a miracle from the Prophet before they will believe him (see e.g. Q17.90-95; 25.7-8, 20-21, 32; cf. the similar demand for a 'sign' from Jesus at John 2.18; 6.30).
35. *the unseen*: here referring to 'the future' (see n. on Q2.3), and thus implying that a miracle may yet come.
36. *Our messengers*: the recording angels (cf. Q43.80; 82.10-12); for their various roles, see n. on Q2.30.

22–23 The uncertainty of life

37. *they sail*: lit. 'they run,' referring to the ships (a switch from sing. to plur.).
38. *them*: the people on board the ships.
39. *it*: the ship (a switch back to sing.).
40. *them*: the people on board the ships.
41. *devoting (their) religion to Him*: i.e. they regard God as the sole object of prayer at such a moment of danger.

24 A parable of the transience of life

42. *command*: here referring to judgment (cf. Q2.109; 4.47; 5.52; 7.150; 16.1, 33).
43. *cut it down*: lit. 'make it a harvest.'
44. *make the signs distinct*: or 'expound the verses' (cf. Q10.37 below).

25 God calls to the Home of peace,[45] and guides whomever He pleases to a straight path. **26** For those who have done good, (there is) the good (reward) and more (besides). Neither dust nor humiliation will cover their faces. Those are the companions of the Garden. There they will remain. **27** But those who have done evil deeds[46] – (the) payment for an evil deed is (an evil) like it – humiliation will cover them. They will have no protector from God. (It will be) as if their faces were covered (with) pieces of the darkness of night. Those are the companions of the Fire. There they will remain.

28 On the Day when We shall gather them all together, then We shall say to those who associated:[47] '(Take) your place, you and your associates!' Then We shall separate them, and their associates will say, 'You were not serving us.[48] **29** God is sufficient as a witness between us and you that we were indeed oblivious of your service.' **30** There every person will stand trial (for) what he has done, and they will be returned to God, their true Protector, and (then) what they forged will abandon them.[49]

31 Say: 'Who provides for you from the sky and the earth? Or who has power over hearing and sight? Who brings forth the living from the dead, and brings forth the dead from the living, and who directs the (whole) affair?' Then they will say, 'God.'[50] So say: 'Will you not guard (yourselves)?' **32** That is God, your true Lord. And what (is there) after the truth except straying (from it)? How (is it that) you are turned away? **33** In this way the word of your Lord has proved true[51] against those who acted wickedly: 'They will not believe.' **34** Say: '(Is there) any of your associates[52] who (can) bring about the creation, (and) then restore it?' Say: 'God – He brings about the creation, (and) then He restores it. How are you (so) deluded?' **35** Say: '(Is there) any of your associates who (can) guide to the truth?' Say: 'God – He guides to the truth. Is He who guides to the truth more worthy to be followed, or he who does not guide unless he is guided? What is (the matter) with you? How do you judge?' **36** Most of them only follow conjecture,[53] (and) surely conjecture is of no use at all against the truth. Surely God is aware of what they do.

37 This Qur'ān[54] is not the kind (of Book) that it could have been forged apart from God. (It is) a confirmation of what was before it,[55] and a distinct setting forth of the Book[56] – (there is) no doubt about it[57] – from

---

25–27 Rewards and punishments

45. *peace*: Ar. *salām* connotes 'submission' (*islām*) to God (cf. Q6.127).
46. *done evil deeds*: lit. 'earned the evil deeds.'

28–30 A judgment scene

47. *those who associated*: other gods with God.
48. *serving us*: or 'worshiping us.'
49. *abandon them*: lit. 'go astray from them' (a pun).

31–36 Proofs of monotheism

50. *'God'*: their answer makes explicit their belief in God as the supreme deity (cf. Q29.61, 63; 31.25; 39.38; 43.87).
51. *the word...has proved true*: or 'the sentence (of condemnation)...has been passed.'
52. *your associates*: the other gods.
53. *conjecture*: or 'opinion,' as opposed to 'revealed (i.e. certain) knowledge.'

37–44 The Qur'ān could only be produced by God

54. *This Qur'ān*: or perhaps 'this recitation,' since the expression (Ar. *hādhā al-qur'ān*) is sometimes used only in reference to a part of the Qur'ān (cf. Q6.19; 10.61 below; 13.31; 72.1; see n. on Q2.185). Otherwise, 'this Qur'ān' may come close to its present meaning as the name of the Muslim scripture (cf. Q9.111), and perhaps imply the existence of 'other Qur'āns' (cf. Q39.27-28).
55. *a confirmation of what was before it*: i.e. the Qur'ān 'confirms' the Torah and Gospel.
56. *a distinct setting forth of the Book*: cf. Q6.114, 154; 7.52, 145; 11.1; 12.111; 41.3, 44. Here 'the Book' may refer to the heavenly archetype or source of all scripture. According to this view, the Qur'ān, like the Torah and the Gospel, is only a portion of this all encompassing 'mother of the Book' (see Q13.39; 43.4; cf. Q56.78, 'hidden Book;' 85.22, 'guarded Tablet'). Alternatively, it may refer to 'the Book' previously revealed.
57. *no doubt about it*: or 'no doubt in it' (cf. Q2.2; 32.2).

the Lord of the worlds. **38** Or do they say, 'He[58] has forged it'? Say: 'Then bring a sūra like it,[59] and call on anyone you can, other than God, if you are truthful.' **39** No! They have called a lie what they cannot encompass in (their) knowledge of it, and when the interpretation of it has not (yet) come to them. Those who were before them called (it) a lie (too), and see how the end was for the evildoers!

40 (There is) one of them[60] who believes in it,[61] and (there is) one of them who does not believe in it, but your Lord knows the ones who foment corruption.[62] **41** If they call you[63] a liar, say: 'To me my deed, and to you your deed. You are free of what I do, and I am free of what you do.' **42** (There is) one of them who listens to you, but can you make the deaf hear, when they do not understand? **43** (There is) one of them who looks to you, but can you guide the blind, when they do not see? **44** Surely God does not do the people any evil at all, but the people do themselves evil.

45 On the Day when He gathers them, (it will seem) as if they had remained (in the grave) only for an hour of the day, (and) they will recognize each other. Lost (are) those who called the meeting with God[64] a lie, and were not (rightly) guided. **46** Whether We show you some of that which We promise them, or take you,[65] to Us is their return. Then God is a witness over what they do. **47** For every community (there is) a messenger. When their messenger comes, it will be decided between them in justice[66] – and they will not be done evil.

48 They say, 'When (will) this promise[67] (come to pass), if you[68] are truthful?' **49** Say: 'I do not have power to (cause) myself harm or benefit – except whatever God pleases. For every community (there is) a time.[69] When their time comes, they will not delay (it) by an hour, nor will they advance (it by an hour).' **50** Say: 'Do you see? If His punishment comes to you by night or by day, what (part) of it would the sinners seek to hurry? **51** When it falls, will you believe in it? Now? When you had been seeking to hurry it?'[70] **52** Then it will be said to those who have done evil: 'Taste the punishment of eternity! Are you being repaid (for anything) except for what you have earned?'

53 They ask you to inform them: 'Is it true?' Say: 'Yes, by my Lord! Surely it is true indeed! You will not escape (it).' **54** If each person who has done evil had all that is on the earth, he would indeed (try to) ransom (himself) with it. They will be full of secret regret when they see the punishment. It will be decided between them in justice – and they will not be done evil. **55** Is it not a fact that to God (belongs) whatever

---

58. *He*: the Prophet.
59. *bring a sūra like it*: or 'bring a scripture like it.' The failure of the Prophet's contemporaries to take up this challenge (cf. Q2.23; 11.13; 28.49; 52.34) was later seen as proof that it was impossible, and the Qur'ān's 'inimitability' (referred to as the *i'jāz al-qur'ān*) would be taken as proof of its miraculous nature and divine origin (see n. on Q2.23).
60. *them*: it is not clear to whom 'them' refers (also in vv. 42 and 43).
61. *it*: the Qur'ān, or possibly 'him' (the Prophet or God).
62. *...who foment corruption*: the Cairo edition, reflecting the views of traditional scholars, attributes this verse to the 'Medinan' period. It seems to imply that the Qur'ān has now been fully revealed.
63. *you*: the Prophet.

45–56 Judgment certain

64. *the meeting with God*: on the Day of Judgment.
65. *take you*: i.e. take the Prophet in death, before the disbelievers are punished (cf. Q13.40; 40.77).
66. *it will be decided between them in justice*: i.e. between the messenger with his followers and the disbelievers.
67. *promise*: or 'threat' of punishment (cf. Q21.38; 27.71; 34.29; 36.48; 67.25).
68. *you*: plur.
69. *time*: or 'term' (Ar. *ajal*), which is predetermined and cannot be changed (cf. Q7.34; 16.61; 34.29-30).
70. *...seeking to hurry it*: a sarcastic response to the disbelievers' equally sarcastic demand to 'bring us what you threaten.'

is in the heavens and the earth? Is it not a fact that the promise of God is true? But most of them do not know (it). **56** He gives life and causes death, and to Him you will be returned.

57 People! An admonition has come to you from your Lord, and a healing for what is in the hearts,[71] and a guidance[72] and mercy for the believers. **58** Say: 'In the favor of God and in His mercy – let them gloat over that, (for) it is better than what they accumulate.' **59** Say: 'Have you seen what God has sent down for you from (His) provision, yet you have made some of it forbidden[73] and (some) permitted?'[74] Say: 'Has God given permission to you, or do you forge (lies) against God?' **60** What will they think who forge lies against God on the Day of Resurrection? Surely God is indeed full of favor to the people, but most of them are not thankful (for it).

61 You[75] are not (engaged) in any matter, nor do you recite any recitation of it,[76] nor do you[77] do any deed, except (that) We are witnesses over you when you are busy with it. Not (even) the weight of a speck on the earth or in the sky escapes from your Lord, nor (is there anything) smaller than that or greater, except (that it is recorded) in a clear Book.[78] **62** Is it not a fact that the allies of God[79] – (there will be) no fear on them, nor will they sorrow? **63** Those who believe and guard (themselves) – **64** for them (there is) good news in this present life and in the Hereafter.[80] No one can change the words of God. That is the great triumph! **65** Do not let their speech cause you[81] sorrow. Surely honor (belongs) to God altogether. He is the Hearing, the Knowing.

66 Is it not a fact that to God (belongs) whoever is in the heavens and whoever is on the earth? They follow – those who call on associates[82] other than God – they only follow conjecture and they only guess. **67** He (it is) who made the night for you to rest in and the day to see. Surely in that are signs indeed for a people who hear.

68 They say,[83] 'God has taken a son.'[84] Glory to Him! He is the wealthy One.[85] To Him (belongs) whatever is in the heavens and whatever is on the earth. You have no authority for this (claim). Do you say about God what you do not know? **69** Say: 'Surely those who forge lies against God will not prosper.'

57–65 God's goodness and knowledge

71. *hearts*: lit. 'chests,' considered the seat of knowledge and understanding.
72. *guidance*: one of the most frequent terms (Ar. *hudā*) for revelation in general, and the Qur'ān in particular.
73. *some of it forbidden*: see e.g. Q6.138.
74. *permitted*: Ar. *ḥalāl*.
75. *You*: the Prophet.
76. *any recitation of it*: lit. 'any *qur'ān* of it;' here the word denotes a single passage or 'unit' of revelation (like *āya* and *surā*), but of unspecified length (cf. Q13.31; 72.1; see n. on Q2.185).
77. *you*: switch to plur.
78. *a clear Book*: i.e. the 'Book of God' or heavenly 'Record' of all things (see n. on Q6.59).
79. *allies of God*: 'allies' (Ar. *awliyā'*) implies the obligation of mutual protection, almost in the sense of 'friends' or 'brothers' (cf. Q62.6; contrast Q4.76).
80. *the Hereafter*: see n. on Q2.4.
81. *you*: the Prophet.

66–67 Existence of other Gods is mere opinion

82. *associates*: the other gods.

68–70 God has no son

83. *They say*: the Christians, though this claim always remains anonymous.
84. *son*: or 'child' (Ar. *walad*), but referring to Christian claims about Jesus as God's son (cf. Q2.116; 4.171; 19.88-92; 21.26; 25.2).
85. *the wealthy One*: i.e. God has no need of anyone or anything.

70 A (little) enjoyment in this world, then to Us is their return. Then We (shall) make them taste the harsh punishment for what they have disbelieved.

71 Recite[86] to them the story of Noah:[87] when he said to his people, 'My people! If my stay (here) and my reminding (you) by the signs of God are hard[88] on you, yet in God have I put my trust. So put together your plan,[89] (you) and your associates.[90] Then do not let your plan (be a cause of) distress for you. Then decide about me and do not spare me. **72** If you turn away, (know that) I have not asked you for any reward. My reward (depends) only on God, and I have been commanded to be one of those who submit.'[91]
73 But they called him a liar, so We rescued him and those who were with him in the ship,[92] and We made them successors, and We drowned those who called Our signs a lie. See how the end was for the ones who were warned!

74 Then, after him, We raised up messengers for their people, and they brought them the clear signs. But they would not believe in what they had called a lie before. In this way We set a seal on the hearts[93] of the transgressors.

75 Then, after them, We raised up Moses and Aaron for Pharaoh and his assembly with Our signs, but they became arrogant and were a sinful people. **76** When the truth came to them from Us, they said, 'Surely this is clear magic indeed.' **77** Moses said, 'Do you say (this) about the truth, when it has come to you? Is this magic? Yet magicians do not prosper.' **78** They said, 'Have you come to us in order to turn us away from what we found our fathers doing, and (in order that) you two (might) have greatness on the earth? We do not believe in you two.' **79** And Pharaoh said, 'Bring me every skilled magician.' **80** When the magicians came, Moses said to them, 'Cast (down) what you are going to cast.'[94] **81** Then, when they had cast, Moses said, 'What you have brought is magic. Surely God will invalidate it. Surely God does not set right any deed of the fomenters of corruption. **82** God verifies the truth by His words, even though the sinners dislike (it).' **83** So no one believed in Moses, except for the descendants of his people, out of fear that Pharaoh and their assembly would persecute them. Surely Pharaoh was indeed haughty on the earth. Surely he was indeed one of the wanton.

84 Moses said, 'My people! If you believe in God, put your trust in Him, if you have submitted.'[95] **85** They said, 'In God we have put our trust. Our Lord, do not make us an (object of) persecution[96] for the people who are evildoers, **86** but rescue us by Your mercy from the people who are disbelievers.' **87** And We inspired Moses and his brother: 'Establish[97] houses for your people in Egypt, and make[98] your houses a direction

---

71–73 The story of Noah

86. *Recite...*: or 'Read aloud...' (addressed to the Prophet).
87. *story of Noah*: or 'news of Noah' (see n. on Q7.59).
88. *hard*: lit. 'great.'
89. *your plan*: lit. 'your affair.'
90. *your associates*: i.e. the other gods they have 'associated' with God.
91. *those who submit*: or 'the Muslims.'
92. *the ship*: Noah's 'ark' (cf. Q7.64; 11.37; and Genesis 7.11-16); according to Q66.10, Noah's wife perished.

74 Other messengers

93. *hearts*: here, as often, the heart is spoken of as synonymous with mind.

75–89 The story of Moses and Pharaoh

94. *Cast (down)...*: their staffs, which turned into snakes (see e.g. Q7.114-118; cf. Exodus 7.12).
95. *have submitted*: or 'have become Muslims.'
96. *an (object of) persecution*: or 'a temptation' (Ar. *fitna*); cf. Q60.5 (said by Abraham and his people).
97. *Establish*: dual imperative.
98. *make*: plur. imperative.

(of prayer),[99] and observe the prayer,[100] and give[101] good news to the believers.' **88** Moses said, 'Our Lord, surely You have given Pharaoh and his assembly splendor and wealth in this present life, Our Lord, so that they might lead (people) astray from Your way. Our Lord, obliterate their wealth[102] and harden their hearts, so that they do not believe until they see the painful punishment.' **89** He said, 'The request of both of you has been answered. So both of you go straight, and do not follow the way of those who do not know.'

90 And We crossed the sea with the Sons of Israel, and Pharaoh and his forces followed them (out of) envy and enmity, until, when the drowning overtook him, he[103] said, 'I believe that (there is) no god but the One in whom the Sons of Israel believe. I am one of those who submit.'[104] **91** 'Now? When you had disobeyed before and were one of the fomenters of corruption? **92** Today We rescue you with your body, so that you may be a sign for those who succeed you.[105] Yet surely many of the people are indeed oblivious of Our signs.' **93** Certainly We settled the Sons of Israel in a sure settlement and provided them with good things. They did not (begin to) differ until (after) the knowledge had come to them. Surely your Lord will decide between them on the Day of Resurrection concerning their differences.

94 If you[106] are in doubt about what We have sent down to you, ask those who have been reciting the Book before you.[107] The truth has come to you from your Lord, so do not be one of the doubters. **95** And do not be one of those who call the signs of God a lie, or you will be one of the losers. **96** Surely those against whom the word of your Lord has proved true[108] will not believe, **97** even though every sign comes to them, until they see the painful punishment. **98** Why was there no town which believed, and its belief benefited it, except the people of Jonah?[109] When they believed, We removed from them the punishment of disgrace in this present life and gave them enjoyment (of life) for a time. **99** If your Lord had (so) pleased, whoever was on the earth would indeed have believed – all of them together. Will you compel the people until they become believers? **100** It is not for any person to believe, except by the permission of God. He places abomination on those who do not understand.

101 Say: 'See what is in the heavens and the earth!' But signs and warnings are of no use to a people who do not believe. **102** Do they expect (anything) but the same as the days of those who passed away before them? Say: '(Just) wait! Surely I shall be one of those waiting with you.' **103** Then We rescue Our messengers and those who believe. In this way – (it is) an obligation on Us – We shall rescue the believers.

---

99. *a direction (of prayer)*: an obscure feature of the story; perhaps a reference to 'synagogues' or 'prayer houses,' and possibly intended as a precedent for the adoption of the Ka'ba as the 'direction' (Ar. *qibla*) of prayer (see Q2.142-152).

100. *observe the prayer*: plur. imperative; referring to the ritual prayer (or *ṣalāt*).

101. *give*: sing. imperative.

102. *obliterate their wealth*: perhaps an allusion to the despoiling of the Egyptians by the Israelites (Exodus 3.21-22; 11.2-3; 12.35-36).

90–93 The exodus and settlement of the Sons of Israel

103. *he*: Pharaoh.

104. *those who submit*: or 'the Muslims.'

105. *Today We rescue you...*: Pharaoh's unusual 'escape' reflects later Jewish lore that he repented and was saved.

94–100 Assurance to the Prophet

106. *you*: the Prophet; the Cairo edition attributes the following three verses to the 'Medinan' period.

107. *those who have been reciting the Book before you*: or 'reading the Book...;' referring to Jews and/or Christians.

108. *the word...has proved true*: or 'the sentence (of condemnation)...has been passed' (cf. Q10.33 above).

109. *except the people of Jonah*: all other peoples mentioned in the Qur'ān were punished for their disobedience (see n. on Q7.59). Jonah was sent to the inhabitants of Nineveh (according to Jonah 1.1-2), an ancient city of Assyria on the eastern bank of the Tigris River.

101–103 Signs and warnings futile

104 Say: 'People! If you are in doubt about my religion, (know that) I do not serve those whom you serve instead of God, but I serve God, the One who takes you.[110] I have been commanded to be one of the believers.' **105** And: 'Set your face to the religion (as) a Ḥanīf,[111] and do not be one of the idolaters.[112] **106** Do not call on what can neither benefit nor harm you, instead of God (alone). If you do, surely then you will be one of the evildoers. **107** If God touches you with any harm, (there is) no one to remove it but Him, and if He intends for you any good, (there is) no one to turn back His favor. He smites with it whomever He pleases of His servants.[113] He is the Forgiving, the Compassionate.'

108 Say: 'People! The truth has come to you from your Lord. Whoever is (rightly) guided, is guided only for himself,[114] and whoever goes astray, goes astray only against himself. I am not a guardian over you.'

109 Follow what you[115] are inspired (with), and be patient until God judges, (for) He is the best of judges.

104–107 The Prophet's religion

110. *takes you*: in death.

111. *(as) a Ḥanīf*: or perhaps '(though you are) a Gentile,' like Abraham (see n. on Q2.135; cf. Q30.30).

112. *the idolaters*: or 'the ones who associate (other gods with God).'

113. *servants*: the word 'servants,' which also means 'slaves,' is used here in the sense of 'all people.'

108 The truth has come

114. *for himself*: i.e. for his own benefit.

109 Final exhortation

115. *you*: the Prophet.

11 Hūd ❁ Hūd

In the Name of God, the Merciful, the Compassionate

1 Alif Lām Rā'.[1] A Book[2] – its verses have been clearly composed[3] (and) then made distinct[4] – (sent down)
from One (who is) wise, aware.

2 'Do not serve[5] (anyone) but God! Surely I am a warner and bringer of good news[6] to you from Him.'
3 And: 'Ask forgiveness from your Lord, then turn to Him (in repentance). He will give you good enjoyment (of life) for an appointed time,[7] and give His favor to everyone (deserving) of favor. If you turn
away – surely I fear for you the punishment of a great Day. **4** To God is your return. He is powerful over
everything.'

5 Is it not a fact that they cover their hearts to hide from Him?[8] Is it not (a fact) that (even) when they
cover themselves with their clothing, He knows what they keep secret and what they speak aloud?
Surely He knows what is in the hearts.[9] **6** (There is) not a creature on the earth but its provision
(depends) on God. He knows its dwelling place and its storage place. Everything is (recorded) in a clear
Book.[10] **7** He (it is) who created the heavens and the earth in six days[11] – and His throne was upon the
water[12] – that He might test you (to see) which of you is best in deed.

If indeed you[13] say, 'Surely you will be raised up after death,' those who disbelieve will indeed say, 'This is
nothing but clear magic.' **8** If indeed We postpone the punishment from them until a set period (of time),
they will indeed say, 'What is holding it back?' Is it not (a fact) that on the Day when it comes to them, it

---

Q11: This sūra is made up almost entirely of stories about the following messengers: Noah, Hūd, Ṣāliḥ, Abraham, Lot, Shu'ayb, and Moses. Most scholars assign Q11 to the 'Meccan' period.

1 A Book from God

1. *Alif Lām Rā'*: the names of Arabic letters ', *l*, and *r*. The same letter combination occurs in a block of sūras from Q10 to Q15 (Q13 has an additional 'mīm'). Twenty-nine sūras begin with letters like these, ranging from one to five. No satisfactory explanation has been given for their occurrence. The Cairo edition varies in counting these letters as a separate verse, or as the beginning of the first verse (as here).
2. *Book*: here referring to the Qur'ān not only as a 'recited' but also 'written' scripture (see n. on Q2.2).
3. *clearly composed*: for this idea, cf. Q3.7; 22.52; 47.20.
4. *made distinct*: or 'expounded' (cf. Q6.114; 154; 7.52, 145; 12.111; 41.3, 44).

2–4 The Messenger and the message

5. *Do not serve...*: or 'Do not worship...;' cf. what Noah says at Q11.25-26 below; and 41.14; 46.21.
6. *warner...bringer of good news*: for these roles, see n. on Q2.119.
7. *an appointed time*: or 'term' (Ar. *ajal*), i.e. the precise date of a person's death is predetermined.

5–7a God's knowledge and power

8. *cover their hearts...*: lit. 'fold their chests;' since the chest was considered to be the site of thinking and knowledge, they hoped to conceal their thoughts from God by covering them up.
9. *hearts*: lit. 'chests.'
10. *a clear Book*: i.e. the 'Book of God' or heavenly 'Record' of all things (see n. on Q6.59).
11. *in six days*: cf. Q7.54; 10.3; 25.59; 32.4; 41.9-12; 50.38; and Genesis 1.1-31.
12. *upon the water*: i.e. the waters above the 'dome' of the sky (cf. Genesis 1.6-8; Exodus 24.10; Ezekiel 1.22-28).

7b–11 Capriciousness of disbelievers

13. *you*: the Prophet.

will not be diverted from them, and what they were mocking will overwhelm them? **9** If indeed We give a person a taste of mercy from Us, (and) then We withdraw it from him, surely he is indeed despairing (and) ungrateful.[14] **10** But if indeed We give him a taste of blessing, after hardship has touched him, he will indeed say, 'The evils have gone from me.' Surely he is indeed gloating (and) boastful **11** – except those who are patient and do righteous deeds. Those – for them (there is) forgiveness and a great reward.

12 Perhaps you are leaving out[15] part of what you are inspired (with), and your heart[16] is weighed down by it, because they say, 'If only a treasure were sent down on him or an angel came with him.' You are only a warner. God is guardian over everything. **13** Or do they say, 'He has forged it'? Say:[17] 'Then bring ten sūras forged like it,[18] and call on whomever you can,[19] other than God, if you are truthful.' **14** If they do not respond to you,[20] know that it has been sent down with the knowledge of God, and that (there is) no god but Him. So (will) you submit?[21] **15** Whoever desires this present life and its (passing) splendor – We shall pay them in full for their deeds in it, and they will not be shortchanged in it. **16** Those are the ones who – for them (there is) nothing in the Hereafter[22] but the Fire.[23] What they have done will come to nothing there. What they have done will be in vain.

17 Is the one who (stands) on a clear sign[24] from his Lord, and recites it[25] as a witness from Him, and before it[26] was the Book of Moses[27] as a model[28] and mercy [...]?[29] Those believe in it,[30] but whoever disbelieves in it from the factions[31] – the Fire is his appointed place. So do not be in doubt about it.[32] Surely it is the truth from your Lord, but most of the people do not believe.

---

14. *ungrateful*: Ar. *kafūr*, punning on *kāfir*, 'disbeliever.'

12–16 Encouragement to the Prophet

15. *Perhaps you are leaving out*: i.e. leaving unspoken or undone; the Cairo edition, reflecting the views of traditional scholars, attributes this verse to the 'Medinan' period.
16. *heart*: lit. 'chest,' considered the seat of knowledge and understanding.
17. *Say*: on this form of address, see n. on Q2.80.
18. *bring ten sūras forged like it*: the failure of the Prophet's contemporaries to take up this challenge (cf. Q2.23; 10.38; 28.49; 52.34) was later seen as proof that it was impossible, and the Qur'ān's 'inimitability' (referred to as the *i'jāz al-qur'ān*) would be taken as proof of its miraculous nature and divine origin. The word 'sūra' refers here to a 'unit' of revelation, and not to present sūras, though there is no indication how long these 'units' were (see n. on Q2.23). The mention of 'ten,' however, is curious.
19. *call on whomever you can*: i.e. other gods.
20. *you*: plur.
21. *submit*: or 'become Muslims.'
22. *the Hereafter*: see n. on Q2.4.
23. *the Fire*: Ar. *al-nār* is the most common of the various designations for Hell.

17 The Prophet's authority

24. *clear sign*: or 'clear proof,' 'indisputable evidence;' the Cairo edition attributes this verse to the 'Medinan' period.
25. *recites it*: or 'reads it aloud' (i.e. the Qur'ān).
26. *before it*: or 'before him.'
27. *Book of Moses*: the Torah.
28. *model*: Ar. *imām* (cf. Q46.12).
29. *[...]*: something appears to be missing here; perhaps originally a contrast was drawn between the Prophet's authority (namely, the Qur'ān and, before it, the Torah) and that of his (Jewish?) opponents (cf. Q46.12).
30. *it*: the Qur'ān.
31. *the factions*: or 'the sectarians' (Ar. *al-aḥzāb*), probably referring to Jews and Christians (see e.g. Q13.36; 23.53).
32. *it*: the Qur'ān (addressed to the Prophet).

18 Who is more evil than the one who forges a lie against God? Those will be presented before their Lord, and the witnesses[33] will say, 'These are those who lied against their Lord.' Is it not (a fact) that the curse of God is on the evildoers, **19** who keep (people) from the way of God and desire (to make) it crooked, and they are disbelievers in the Hereafter? **20** Those – they cannot escape (Him) on the earth, and they have no allies other than God. The punishment will be doubled for them. They could not hear and did not see. **21** Those are the ones who have lost their (own) selves, and what they forged has abandoned them.[34] **22** (There is) no doubt that they will be the worst losers in the Hereafter. **23** Surely those who believe, and do righteous deeds, and humble themselves to their Lord – those are the companions of the Garden.[35] There they will remain. **24** The parable of the two groups is like the blind and the deaf, and the sighted and the hearing. Are they equal in comparison?[36] Will you not take heed?[37]

25 Certainly We sent Noah to his people:[38] 'I am a clear warner for you. **26** Do not serve[39] (anyone) but God! Surely I fear for you the punishment of a painful Day.' **27** The assembly of those who disbelieved of his people said, 'We do not see you as (anything) but human being like us, and we do not see following you (any) but the worst (and) most gullible of us. We do not see in you any superiority[40] over us. No! We think you are liars.' **28** He said, 'My people! Do you see? If I (stand) on a clear sign from my Lord, and He has given me mercy from Himself, but it has been obscured for you, shall we compel you (to accept) it when you are unwilling? **29** My people! I do not ask you for any money for it. My reward (depends) only on God. I am not going to drive away those who believe. Surely they are going to meet their Lord, but I see that you are an ignorant people. **30** My people! Who would help me against God if I drove them away?[41] Will you not take heed? **31** I do not say to you, "I possess the storehouses of God," nor do I know the unseen.[42] And I do not say, "I am an angel," nor do I say to those your eyes look down on, "God will not give them any good." God knows what is in them. Surely then I would indeed be one of the evildoers.' **32** They said, 'Noah! You have disputed with us, and disputed (too) much with us. Bring us what you promise us,[43] if you are one of the truthful.' **33** He said, 'Only God will bring it to you, if He (so) pleases, and you will not escape. **34** My advice will not benefit you – (even) if I wish to advise you – if God wishes to make you err. He is your Lord, and to Him you will be returned.'

35 Or do they say, 'He has forged it'?[44] Say: 'If I have forged it, my sin is on me, but I am free of the sins you commit.'

18–24 The two groups

33. *the witnesses*: probably the angels (for their various roles, see n. on Q2.30).
34. *abandoned them*: lit. 'gone astray from them' (a pun).
35. *Garden*: in heaven (for this imagery, see n. on Q2.25).
36. *in comparison*: lit. 'as a parable.'
37. *take heed*: or 'be reminded,' 'remember.'

25–49 The story of Noah and his people

38. *We sent Noah to his people*: here begins a series of seven 'punishment stories' (Q11.25-109; see nn. on Q7.59; 15.87). For the story of Noah which follows, cf. the versions at Q7.59-64; 10.71-73; 23.23-30; 26.105-120; and Genesis 6.5-10.1.
39. *serve*: or worship.
40. *superiority*: lit. 'favor.'
41. *Who would help me against God...*: i.e. God would punish Noah if he abandoned his followers.
42. *the unseen*: here referring to 'the future' (see n. on Q2.3), and a reminder that prophets do not predict it.
43. *what you promise us*: i.e. the threat of punishment.
44. *Or do they say, 'He...*: this verse appears to refer to the Prophet (not Noah), and seems out of place here; it may have originally stood in the context of Q11.13-14 above.

36 And Noah was inspired:[45] 'None of your people will believe, except for the one who has (already) believed, so do not be distressed by what they have done. **37** Build the ship[46] under Our eyes and Our inspiration, and do not address Me concerning those who have done evil. Surely they are going to be drowned.' **38** And he was building the ship, and whenever the assembly of his people passed by him, they ridiculed him. He said, 'If you ridicule us, surely we shall ridicule you as you ridicule. **39** Soon you will know (on) whom punishment will come, disgracing him, and on whom a lasting punishment will descend.' **40** – Until, when Our command came and the oven boiled,[47] We said, 'Load into it two of every kind, a pair, and your family – except for the one against whom the word has (already) gone forth[48] – and whoever has believed.' But only a few had believed with him. **41** And he said, 'Sail in it![49] In the name of God (is) its running and its anchoring. Surely my Lord is indeed forgiving, compassionate.' **42** It ran with them in (the midst of) wave(s) like mountains, and Noah called out to his son, since he was in a place apart, 'My son! Sail with us and do not be with the disbelievers!' **43** He said, 'I shall take refuge on a mountain (that) will protect me from the water.' He[50] said, '(There is) no protector today from the command of God,[51] except for the one on whom He has compassion.' And the waves came between them, and he was among the drowned.[52]

44 And it was said: 'Earth! Swallow your water! And sky! Stop!' And the waters subsided, and the command was accomplished,[53] and it[54] came to rest on al-Jūdī.[55] And it was said: 'Away with the people who were evildoers!' **45** And Noah called out to his Lord, and said, 'My Lord, surely my son is one of my family, and surely Your promise is the truth, and You are the most just of judges.' **46** He said, 'Noah! Surely he is not one of your family. Surely it is an unrighteous deed.[56] So do not ask Me about what you have no knowledge of. Surely I admonish you not to be one of the ignorant.' **47** He said, 'My Lord, surely I take refuge with You for asking You about what I have no knowledge of, and unless You forgive me and have compassion on me, I shall be one of the losers.' **48** It was said, 'Noah! Go down[57] with peace from Us, and blessings on you and on the communities of those who are with you. But (to other) communities We shall give enjoyment (of life), (and) then a painful punishment from Us will touch them.' **49** That is one of the stories[58] of the unseen.[59] We inspired you[60] (with) it. You did not know it, (neither) you nor your

45. *Noah was inspired*: lit. 'it was inspired to Noah' (cf. Q23.27).
46. *the ship*: Noah's 'ark' (cf. Q7.64; 10.73; and Genesis 7.11-16).
47. *the oven boiled*: cf. Q23.27; the waters of the flood were 'boiling,' according to Jewish tradition.
48. *except for the one against whom the word has (already) gone forth*: or '...against whom sentence has already been passed;' referring to one of Noah's sons, see Q11.42-43 below (a unique feature of this version of the story).
49. *Sail in it*: lit. 'Ride in it.'
50. *He*: Noah.
51. *command of God*: here referring to God's judgment (cf. Q2.109; 4.47; 5.52; 7.150; 10.24; 16.1, 33).
52. *he was among the drowned*: according to Q66.10, Noah's wife also perished.
53. *the command was accomplished*: or 'the affair was finished.'
54. *it*: the ship.
55. *al-Jūdī*: traditionally identified with a mountain in Mesopotamia (near Mosul), but al-Jūdī may have been the name of a mountain in Arabia, where the people of Noah, like those of 'Ād and Thamūd, were thought to have lived. Cf. Genesis 8.4, 'The ark came to rest on the mountains of Ararat.'
56. *it is an unrighteous deed*: i.e. Noah's intercession for his disbelieving son is (lit.) 'a deed other than righteous,' even though it was on behalf of a member of his own family. Religious affiliation supersedes family ties (see e.g. Q9.23-24).
57. *Go down*: either 'disembark' from the ship or 'descend' the mountain.
58. *stories*: or 'news' (cf. Q11.100, 120 below).
59. *the unseen*: here referring to 'the distant past' (see n. on Q2.3; cf. Q3.44 [Mary]; 12.102 [Joseph]).
60. *you*: the Prophet.

people, before (this). So be patient. Surely the outcome (belongs) to the ones who guard (themselves).[61]

50 And to 'Ād (We sent) their brother Hūd.[62] He said, 'My people! Serve God! You have no god other than Him. You are nothing but forgers (of lies). **51** My people! I do not ask you for any reward for it. My reward (depends) only on the One who created me. Will you not understand?' **52** And: 'My people! Ask forgiveness from your Lord, (and) then turn to Him (in repentance). He will send the sky (down) on you in abundance (of rain), and increase you in strength upon your strength. Do not turn away as sinners.' **53** They said, 'Hūd! You have not brought us any clear sign, and we are not going to abandon our gods on your saying, (for) we do not believe in you. **54** We (can) only say (that) one of our gods has seized you with evil.' He said, 'Surely I call God to witness, and you bear witness (too), that I am free of what you associate,[63] **55** other than Him. So plot against me, all of you, (and) then do not spare me. **56** Surely I have put my trust in God, my Lord and your Lord. (There is) no creature He does not seize by its hair.[64] Surely my Lord is on a straight path. **57** If you turn away, I have delivered to you what I was sent to you with, and my Lord will make another people succeed you, and you will not harm Him at all. Surely my Lord is a watcher over everything.' **58** And when Our command came, We rescued Hūd, and those who believed with him, by a mercy from Us, and We rescued them from a stern punishment. **59** That was 'Ād: they denied the signs of their Lord, and disobeyed His messengers,[65] and followed the command of every stubborn tyrant. **60** And they were followed in this world (by) a curse, and on the Day of Resurrection: 'Is it not a fact that 'Ād disbelieved their Lord? Is it not, "Away with 'Ād, the people of Hūd"?'

61 And to Thamūd (We sent) their brother Ṣāliḥ.[66] He said, 'My people! Serve God! You have no god other than Him. He produced you from the earth and settled you in it. So ask forgiveness from Him, (and) then turn to Him (in repentance). Surely my Lord is near (and) responsive.' **62** They said, 'Ṣāliḥ! You were among us as someone in whom hope was placed before. Do you forbid us to serve what our fathers have served? Surely we are in grave doubt indeed about what you call us to.' **63** He said, 'My people! Do you see? If I (stand) on a clear sign from my Lord, and He has given me mercy from Himself, who would help me against God if I disobeyed Him? You would only increase my loss. **64** My people! This is the she-camel of God,[67] a sign for you. Let her graze on God's earth, and do not touch her with evil, or a punishment near (at hand) will seize you.' **65** But they wounded her,[68] and he said, 'Enjoy (yourselves) in your home(s) for three days – that is a promise not to be denied.' **66** And when Our command came, We rescued Ṣāliḥ, and those who believed with him, by a mercy from Us, and from the disgrace of that day. Surely your Lord – He is the Strong, the Mighty. **67** And the cry[69] seized those who did evil, and morning found them leveled in their homes. **68** (It was) as if they had not lived in prosperity there. 'Is it not a fact that Thamūd disbelieved their Lord? Is it not, "Away with Thamūd"?'

---

61. *guard (themselves)*: against evil, or God.

50–60 The story of Hūd and the people of 'Ād

62. *Hūd*: for the story that follows, cf. the versions at Q7.65-72; 26.123-140.
63. *what you associate*: other gods with God.
64. *by its hair*: lit. 'by its forelock.'
65. *messengers*: for this important title, see n. on Q2.87.

61–68 The story of Ṣāliḥ and the people of Thamūd

66. *Ṣāliḥ*: for the story that follows, cf. the versions at Q7.73-79; 26.141-158; 27.45-53. The people of Thamūd were inhabitants of ancient Arabia, and are mentioned in an inscription of the Assyrian king Sargon II (c. 715 BCE), as well as in the writings of Ariston of Chios, Ptolemy, and Pliny the Elder.
67. *she-camel of God*: see n. on Q7.73.
68. *wounded her*: or perhaps 'killed her.'
69. *the cry*: or 'the shout' (Q54.31); cf. Q7.78 ('the earthquake'); Q41.17; 51.44 ('a thunderbolt').

69 Certainly Our messengers[70] brought Abraham the good news. They said, 'Peace!' He said, 'Peace!,' and did not delay in bringing a roasted calf. **70** When he saw their hands not reaching for it,[71] he became suspicious of them and began to feel fear of them.[72] They said, 'Do not fear! Surely we have been sent to the people of Lot.' **71** His wife[73] was standing (there), and she laughed.[74] And so We gave her the good news of Isaac, and after Isaac, Jacob.[75] **72** She said, 'Woe is me! Shall I give birth when I am an old woman and my husband here is an old man? Surely this is an amazing thing indeed!' **73** They said, 'Are you surprised by the command of God? The mercy of God and His blessings (be) upon you, People of the House![76] Surely He is indeed praiseworthy, glorious.' **74** When the fright had left Abraham and the good news had come to him, he was disputing with Us concerning the people of Lot.[77] **75** Surely Abraham was indeed tolerant, kind, (and) turning (in repentance). **76** 'Abraham! Turn away from this! Surely it has come – the command of your Lord. Surely they – a punishment is coming upon them which cannot be turned back.'

77 And when Our messengers[78] came to Lot, he became distressed about them, and felt powerless (to protect) them, and he said, 'This is a hard day.' **78** His people came to him, rushing to him,[79] (for) they had been in the habit of doing evil deeds before (this). He said, 'My people! These are my daughters, they are purer for you.[80] So guard (yourselves) against God, and do not disgrace me concerning my guests. Is (there) no one among you of right mind?' **79** They said, 'Certainly you know that we have no right to your daughters, and surely you know indeed what we want.' **80** He said, 'If only I had the strength for you, or could take refuge in a strong supporter!' **81** They[81] said, 'Lot! Surely we are messengers of your Lord. They will not reach you. So journey with your family in a part of the night,[82] and let none of you turn around, except your wife, (for) surely what is about to smite them is going to smite her. Surely their appointment is the morning. Is the morning not near?' **82** So when Our command came, We turned it upside down,[83] and rained on it stones of baked clay, one after another, **83** marked in the presence of

---

69–76 The story of Abraham and the messengers

70. *Our messengers*: here referring to angels (see Q22.75); for the story that follows, cf. the versions at Q15.51-77; 51.24-37 ('guests of Abraham'); and Genesis 18.1-33 ('three men,' later called 'angels' at Genesis 19.1, 15).
71. *not reaching for it*: angels do not eat human food (see Q21.8; cf. Judges 13.15-16; Tobit 12.19; contrast Genesis 18.8); that is the mark of human messengers (see Q5.75 [Jesus and Mary]; 21.8; 23.33; 25.7 [the Prophet], 20).
72. *he became suspicious of them...*: to refuse food became a sign of hostility.
73. *his wife*: Abraham's wife was Sarah, though she is not named in the Qur'ān.
74. *and she laughed*: her laughter appears to be in response to what the angels have just said; cf. Genesis 18.12, where Sarah's laughter was in response to the announcement that she would conceive in old age.
75. *and after Isaac, Jacob*: notice that Ishmael is not mention here (cf. Q6.84; 19.49; 21.72; 38.45). In other passages, however, emphasis is placed on Ishmael as Abraham's son (see e.g. Q2.125, 127; 4.163; 14.39).
76. *People of the House*: a reference either to the household of Abraham or perhaps to the Ka'ba (see n. on Q5.95; cf. Q33.33).
77. *disputing with Us concerning the people of Lot*: i.e. about whether it would be just to punish the innocent with the guilty, according to Genesis 18.23-32.

77–83 The story of Lot and his people

78. *Our messengers*: the same angels who visited Abraham; for the story that follows, cf. the versions at Q15.57-74; 26.160-173; and Genesis 19.1-29.
79. *rushing to him*: because they wanted to have sex with Lot's 'visitors.'
80. *they are purer for you*: to hand over his 'guests' (the angels) would have been shameful (cf. Genesis 19.8), so Lot offers his daughters instead.
81. *They*: the angels.
82. *journey with your family in a part of the night*: cf. the similar descriptions of the famous 'night journey' (Q17.1) and of Moses' departure from Egypt (Q20.77; 26.52; 44.23) .
83. *turned it upside down*: lit. 'made its upside its downside;' Lot's city was Sodom, according to Genesis 19.1.

your Lord.[84] It[85] is not far from the evildoers.

84 And to Midian (We sent) their brother Shu'ayb.[86] He said, 'My people! Serve God! You have no god other than Him. Do not diminish the measure or the scale. Surely I see you in prosperity, but surely I fear for you the punishment of an overwhelming day. **85** My people! Fill up the measure and the scale in justice, and do not shortchange the people of their wealth,[87] and do not act wickedly on the earth, fomenting corruption. **86** A remnant of God[88] is better for you, if you are believers. I am not a watcher over you.' **87** They said, 'Shu'ayb! Does your prayer command you that we should abandon what our fathers have served, or that (we should abandon) doing what we please with our wealth? Surely you – you indeed are the tolerant (and) right-minded one.' **88** He said, 'My people! Have you considered?[89] If I (stand) on a clear sign from my Lord, and He has provided me with good provision from Himself [...].[90] I do not wish to go behind your backs to (do) what I forbid you from. I only wish to set (things) right, as much as I am able, but my success is only with God. In Him I have put my trust, and to Him I turn (in repentance). **89** My people! Do not let my defiance (of you) provoke you to sin, or something will smite you similar to what smote the people of Noah, or the people of Hūd, or the people of Ṣāliḥ. And the people of Lot are not far from you.[91] **90** Ask forgiveness from your Lord, (and) then turn to Him (in repentance). Surely my Lord is compassionate, loving.'

91 They said, 'Shu'ayb! We do not understand much of what you say. Surely we indeed see you as weak among us. But (for) your gang (of followers)[92] we would indeed have stoned you, (for) you are not mighty against us.' **92** He said, 'My people! Is my gang (of followers) mightier against you than God? Have you taken Him (as something to cast) behind you? Surely my Lord encompasses what you do. **93** My people! Do as you are able. Surely I am going to do (what I can). Soon you will know the one (on) whom punishment will come, disgracing him, and the one who is a liar. (Just) watch! Surely I am watching with you.' **94** And when Our command came, We rescued Shu'ayb, and those who believed with him, by a mercy from Us. And the cry[93] seized those who did evil, and morning found them leveled in their homes. **95** (It was) as if they had not lived there. 'Is it not away with Midian, (just) as Thamūd was done away with?'

96 Certainly We sent Moses with Our signs and clear authority **97** to Pharaoh and his assembly, but they followed the command of Pharaoh, when the command of Pharaoh was not right-minded. **98** He will precede his people on the Day of Resurrection, and lead them to the Fire. Evil is the place (to which they

---

84. *marked in the presence of your Lord*: said to refer to special markings, or that each had inscribed on it the name of the person it would kill (cf. Q51.34).
85. *It*: either Lot's city or such a punishment (see n. on Q11.89 below).

84–95 The story of Shu'ayb and the people of Midian

86. *Shu'ayb*: for the story that follows, cf. the versions at Q7.85-93; 26.176-189 (sent to the people of 'the Grove').
87. *Fill up..., and do not shortchange...*: a distinctive feature of the story of Shu'ayb and Midian (Q7.85; cf. Q26.181-183).
88. *A remnant of God*: reference obscure; perhaps a 'lasting reward' is meant, in contrast to the 'fleeting wealth' of the world, or it may refer to a 'remnant of the righteous.'
89. *considered*: lit. 'seen.'
90. *[...]*: there is a lacuna here, which can be restored on the basis of the parallel at Q11.63 above ('who would help me against God if I disobeyed Him?').
91. *the people of Lot are not far from you*: Sodom was thought to be in the region of the Dead Sea. This implies that the location of the addressees ('you') was far from the vicinity of present-day Mecca (see Q37.137; cf. Q11.83 above; 30.3n.; 46.27n.).
92. *your gang (of followers)*: usually taken to mean 'your tribe' or 'your family,' which would have felt bound to avenge Shu'ayb; but there is something contemptuous in the Arabic word *rahṭ*.
93. *the cry*: or 'the shout;' cf. Q7.91; 29.37 ('the earthquake').

96–99 The story of Moses and Pharaoh

are) led![94] **99** They were followed in this (world by) a curse, and on the Day of Resurrection – evil is the gift (they will be) given!

100 That is from the stories of the towns (which) We recount to you.[95] Some of them are (still) standing and some (are already) cut down.[96] **101** Yet We did not do them evil, but they did themselves evil. Their gods, on whom they called instead of God, were of no use to them at all, when the command of your Lord came, and they only added to their ruin. **102** Such was the seizing of your Lord, when He seized the towns while they were doing evil. Surely His seizing was painful (and) harsh. **103** Surely in that is a sign indeed for whoever fears the punishment of the Hereafter. That is a Day to which the people will be gathered, and that is a Day (that will be) witnessed. **104** We postpone it only for a set time.[97] **105** (When that) Day comes, no one will speak, except by His permission. Some of them will be miserable, and some happy. **106** As for those who are miserable, (they will be) in the Fire, where (there will be) a moaning and panting for them,[98] **107** remaining there as long as the heavens and the earth endure, except as your Lord pleases. Surely your Lord accomplishes whatever He pleases. **108** But as for those who are happy, (they will be) in the Garden, there to remain as long as the heavens and earth endure, except as your Lord pleases – an unceasing gift. **109** Do not be in doubt about what these (people)[99] serve: they only serve as their fathers served before (them). Surely We shall indeed pay them their portion in full, undiminished.

110 Certainly We gave Moses the Book, and then differences arose about it. Were it not for a preceding word[100] from your Lord, it would indeed have been decided between them.[101] Surely they are in grave doubt indeed about it.[102] **111** Surely each (of them) – when your Lord will indeed pay them in full for their deeds. Surely He is aware of what they do.

112 So go straight, as you[103] have been commanded, (you) and those who have turned (in repentance) with you. Do not transgress insolently,[104] (for) surely He sees what you do. **113** Do not incline[105] toward those who do evil, or the Fire will touch you – you have no allies other than God – (and) then you will not be helped. **114** And observe the prayer[106] at the two ends of the day[107] and at the approach of the night.[108]

---

94. *Evil is the place (to which they are) led*: playing on the image of a 'herder' (Pharaoh) leading his 'herd' (people) to water (the Fire).

100–109 Conclusion to the stories of previous messengers

95. *you*: the Prophet.
96. *cut down*: lit. 'a harvest.'
97. *a set time*: or 'term' (Ar. *ajal*), i.e. the time of judgment is predetermined and cannot be changed.
98. *a moaning and panting for them*: a graphic expression of the Fire's lust to possess them (cf. Q21.100; 25.12; 67.7).
99. *these (people)*: the disbelievers.

110–111 Disagreement about the Book of Moses

100. *a preceding word*: or prior decree, establishing the time of judgment (cf. Q8.68; 10.19; 20.129; 41.45; 42.14, 21).
101. *them*: referring to the Jews (and possibly the Christians).
102. *it*: the Torah, or perhaps the Qur'ān (cf. Q11.62 above; 14.9; 41.45; 42.14).

112–123 Encouragement to the Prophet

103. *you*: the Prophet.
104. *Do not transgress*: plur. imperative.
105. *Do not incline*: plur. imperative.
106. *observe the prayer*: addressed to the Prophet; the Cairo edition attributes this verse to the 'Medinan' period.
107. *two ends of the day*: sunrise and sunset.
108. *approach of the night*: or perhaps 'early evening.'

Surely good (deeds) take away evil (ones). That is a reminder to the mindful.[109] **115** And be patient.[110] Surely God does not let the reward of the doers of good go to waste.

116 If only there had been a remnant of men, among the generations before you, to forbid the (fomenting of) corruption on the earth – aside from a few of those whom We rescued among them. But those who did evil pursued what luxury they were given to delight in, and became sinners. **117** Yet your Lord was not one to destroy the towns in an evil manner, while its people were setting (things) right. **118** If your Lord had (so) pleased, He would indeed have made the people one community,[111] but they will continue to differ, **119** except for the one on whom your Lord has compassion, and for that (purpose) He created them. But the word of your Lord is fulfilled: 'I shall indeed fill Gehenna[112] with jinn[113] and people – all (of them)!'[114]

120 Everything We recount to you[115] from the stories of the messengers (is) what We make firm your heart with, and by this means the truth has come to you, and an admonition, and a reminder to the believers. **121** Say to those who do not believe: 'Do as you are able. Surely we are going to do (what we can).' **122** And: '(Just) wait! Surely we (too) are waiting.'

123 To God (belongs) the unseen[116] in the heavens and the earth, and to Him the affair – all of it – will be returned. So serve Him and put your trust in Him![117] Your[118] Lord is not oblivious of what you[119] do.

109. *a reminder to the mindful*: see n. on Q3.58.
110. *be patient*: addressed to the Prophet.
111. *one community*: for this idea, see n. on Q2.213.
112. *Gehenna*: a name for Hell (see n. on Q2.206).
113. *jinn*: for these beings, see n. on Q6.100.
114. *...jinn and people – all (of them)*: cf. Q7.18; 32.13; 38.85.
115. *Everything We recount to you*: the Prophet; referring to the set of stories related above (Q11.25-100).
116. *the unseen*: here referring to 'the future' (see n. on Q2.3).
117. *serve Him...trust in Him*: addressed to the Prophet.
118. *Your*: sing.
119. *you*: plur.

12 Joseph ۞ Yūsuf

In the Name of God, the Merciful, the Compassionate

1 Alif Lām Rā'.[1] Those are the signs[2] of the clear Book.[3] **2** Surely We have sent it down as an Arabic Qur'ān,[4] so that you[5] may understand.

3 We shall recount to you[6] the best of accounts in what We have inspired you (with of) this Qur'ān,[7] though before it[8] you were indeed one of the oblivious.[9]

4 (Remember) when[10] Joseph[11] said to his father, 'My father! Surely I saw eleven stars, and the sun and the moon.[12] I saw them prostrating themselves before me.' **5** He said, 'My son! Do not recount your vision to your brothers or they will hatch a plot against you.[13] Surely Satan[14] is a clear enemy to humankind.

Q12: This sūra is devoted almost entirely to the story of Joseph, beloved son of Jacob. While there are many parallels between the Qur'ānic version and the account in Genesis 37-50, there are also some striking differences. In contrast to his biblical counterpart, Jacob is a prophet who is not tricked into thinking Joseph was killed. The Qur'ānic Jacob is also clairvoyant, even though he cannot physically see, and in the end miraculously receives his sight when Joseph's shirt is laid over his face. With the exception of a few verses, Q12 is assigned by most scholars to the 'Meccan' period.

1–2 An Arabic Qur'ān

1. *Alif Lām Rā'*: the names of Arabic letters ', *l*, and *r*. The same letter combination occurs in a block of sūras from Q10 to Q15 (Q13 has an additional 'mīm'). Twenty-nine sūras begin with letters like these, ranging from one to five. No satisfactory explanation has been given for their occurrence. The Cairo edition varies in counting these letters as a separate verse, or as the beginning of the first verse (as here).
2. *signs*: here referring to the letters ', *l*, and *r* (for the various meanings of 'signs,' see n. on Q2.39).
3. *the clear Book*: or 'the Book that makes (things) clear;' referring to the Qur'ān not only as a 'recited' but also 'written' scripture (see n. on Q2.2).
4. *an Arabic Qur'ān*: perhaps meaning that it is a translation into Arabic of the heavenly archetype or 'mother of the Book' (cf. Q13.37; 16.103; 20.113; 39.28; 41.3; 42.7; 43.3; 46.12). The specification 'Arabic Qur'ān' (Ar. *qur'ān 'arabiyya*) may imply the existence of 'Qur'āns' (as it were) in other languages, but it is probably an answer to some objection, perhaps that Hebrew was thought to be the exclusive language of revelation.
5. *you*: plur.

3 Introduction to the story of Joseph

6. *you*: the Prophet.
7. *this Qur'ān*: or perhaps 'this recitation,' since the expression (Ar. *hādhā al-qur'ān*) may be used here only in reference to the story of Joseph, not to the Qur'ān as a whole (cf. Q10.61; 13.31; 72.1; and see n. on Q2.185).
8. *before it*: i.e. before the revelation of the story.
9. *one of the oblivious*: i.e. the Prophet had no prior knowledge of the story of Joseph (see Q12.102 below; cf. Q11.49; 42.52). The Cairo edition, reflecting the views of traditional scholars, attributes these first three verses of Q12 to the 'Medinan' period.

4–6 Joseph's dream

10. *(Remember) when...*: a stock narrative formula; the Arabic particle *idh* often marks the beginning of a story, and means something like 'Once...,' or 'There was a time when...,' or 'Remember when....'
11. *Joseph*: apart from the story here, Joseph is mentioned only two other times in the Qur'ān (Q6.84; 40.34).
12. *I saw eleven stars...*: cf. Genesis 37.9.
13. *hatch a plot against you*: lit. 'plot against you a plot.'
14. *Satan*: for this figure, see n. on Q2.36.

6 In this way your Lord will choose you, and teach you about the interpretation of dreams,[15] and complete His blessing on you and on the house of Jacob, as He completed it before on your fathers, Abraham and Isaac. Surely your Lord is knowing, wise.'

7 Certainly in (the story of) Joseph and his brothers (there) are signs for the ones who ask.[16]

8 (Remember) when they said, 'Joseph and his brother[17] are indeed dearer to our father than we, (even) though we are a (large) group. Surely our father is indeed clearly astray.[18] **9** Kill Joseph, or cast him (into some other) land,[19] so that your father's favor will be exclusively for you,[20] and after that you will be a righteous people.' **10** A speaker among them said,[21] 'Do not kill Joseph, but cast him to the bottom of the well, (and) some caravan will pick him up – if you are going to do (anything).'[22]

11 They said, 'Our father! Why do you not trust us with Joseph? Surely we shall indeed look after him.[23]
12 Send him out with us tomorrow to enjoy (himself) and jest. Surely we shall indeed watch over him.'
13 He said, 'Surely I – it sorrows me indeed that you should take him away – I fear that the wolf may eat him while you are oblivious of him.' **14** They said, 'If indeed the wolf eats him, when we are (so large) a group, surely then we (would be) losers indeed.'

15 When they had taken him away, and agreed to put him in the bottom of the well, We inspired him:[24] 'You will indeed inform them about this affair (of theirs), though they will not realize (who you are).'
16 And they came to their father in the evening, weeping. **17** They said, 'Our father! Surely we went off racing (one another), and we left Joseph (behind) with our things, and the wolf ate him. But you will not believe us, even though we are truthful.' **18** And they brought his shirt with fake blood on it. He said, 'No! You have only contrived a story for yourselves. Patience is becoming (for me),[25] and God is the One to be sought for help against what you allege.'

19 A caravan came, and they sent their water-drawer, and he let down his bucket. He said, 'Good news! This is a young boy (here).' And they hid him as merchandise, but God knew what they were doing.
20 And they sold him for a small price, a number of dirhams,[26] (for) they had no interest in him. **21** The one who bought him,[27] (being) from Egypt, said to his wife, 'Make his dwelling place honorable. It may be that he will benefit us, or we may adopt him as a son.'[28] In this way We established Joseph in the land, and (this took place) in order that We might teach him about the interpretation of dreams. God is in control

15. *dreams*: lit. 'sayings' or 'tales' (Ar. *aḥādīth*), but the context favors 'dreams' (cf. Q12.21, 101 below).

7–22 Joseph and his brothers

16. *...signs for the ones who ask*: the Cairo edition attributes this verse to the 'Medinan' period.
17. *his brother*: i.e. his full brother (Benjamin); see Q12.63 below.
18. *clearly astray*: lit. 'in clear straying.'
19. *land*: lit. 'earth.'
20. *your father's favor will be exclusively for you*: i.e. there will be no rivals for his favor (lit. 'face').
21. *A speaker among them said*: Reuben, according to Genesis 37.21-22.
22. *...if you are going to do (anything)*: thus they would avoid direct responsibility in the event of Joseph's death.
23. *look after him*: lit. 'be trusty advisers for him.'
24. *him*: Joseph.
25. *Patience is becoming (for me)*: because he knows they are lying; contrast Jacob's grief-stricken behavior at Genesis 37.33-35.
26. *dirhams*: cf. Genesis 37.25-36: Joseph's brothers sold him to Midianite traders for 'twenty pieces of silver' (later the Midianites sold Joseph to Potiphar in Egypt). The dirham was a unit of currency (cf. Gk. *drachmē*), smaller than a dīnār (Q3.75). These are the only references to coinage in the Qur'ān (Q18.19 may refer to 'paper money').
27. *The one who bought him*: unnamed here, but called 'Potiphar, one of Pharaoh's officials, the captain of the guard,' according to Genesis 37.36.
28. *It may be that he will benefit us...*: the same words are spoken about Moses by the wife of Pharaoh (Q28.9).

of His affair, but most of the people do not know (it). **22** When he reached his maturity, We gave him judgment[29] and knowledge. In this way We repay the doers of good.

23 She,[30] in whose house he was, tried to seduce him. She closed the doors and said, 'Come here, you!' He said, 'God's refuge! Surely he is my lord,[31] and he has given me a good dwelling place. Surely the evil-doers do not prosper.' **24** Certainly she was obsessed with him, and he would have been obsessed with her, if (it had) not (been) that he saw a proof of his Lord.[32] (It happened) in this way in order that We might turn evil and immorality away from him. Surely he was one of Our devoted servants.[33] **25** They both raced to the door, and she tore his shirt from behind. They both met her husband[34] at the door. She said, 'What penalty[35] (is there) for (someone) who intended (to do) evil to your family, except that he should be imprisoned or (suffer) a painful punishment?' **26** He[36] said, 'She tried to seduce me!' (Just then) a witness of her household bore witness: 'If his shirt is torn from the front, she has been truthful, and he is one of the liars. **27** But if his shirt is torn from behind, she has lied, and he is one of the truthful.' **28** So when he[37] saw his shirt torn from behind, he said, 'Surely it is a plot of you women! Surely your plot is grave.[38] **29** Joseph, turn away from this. And you (woman), ask forgiveness for your sin. Surely you are one of the sinners!'[39]

30 Some women in the city said, 'The wife of that mighty one[40] has been trying to seduce her young man.[41] He has affected her deeply (with) love. Surely we see (that) she is indeed clearly astray.' **31** When she heard their cunning (gossip), she sent for them, and prepared a banquet for them, and gave each one of them a knife. Then she said (to Joseph), 'Come forth to (wait on) them.' When they saw him, they admired him, and cut their hands, and said, 'God preserve (us)! This is no (mere) mortal. This is nothing but a splendid angel!' **32** She said, 'That is the one you blamed me about. I certainly did try to seduce him, but he defended himself, and (now) if he does not do what I command him, he will indeed be imprisoned, and become one of the disgraced.' **33** He[42] said, 'My Lord, prison is preferable to me than what they invite me to. But unless You turn their plot away from me, I shall give in to them, and I shall become one of the ignorant.' **34** Then his Lord responded to him, and turned their plot away from him. Surely He – He is the Hearing, the Knowing.

35 Then it became apparent to them,[43] after they had seen the signs,[44] (that) they should imprison him for a time. **36** And two young men entered the prison with him. One of them said, 'Surely I saw myself

29. *judgment*: or 'wisdom' (see n. on Q3.79).

23–34 Joseph and the wife of the Egyptian

30. *She*: the wife of the Egyptian remains nameless in the Qur'ān (as in Genesis), though later tradition calls her Zulaykha.
31. *he is my lord*: referring to the Egyptian, Joseph's master.
32. *a proof of his Lord*: reference obscure; one tradition says he saw the angel Gabriel.
33. *servants*: the word 'servant' (Ar. *'abd*) also means 'slave.'
34. *her husband*: Ar. her *sayyid*.
35. *penalty*: lit. 'payment.'
36. *He*: Joseph.
37. *he*: the Egyptian, the woman's husband.
38. *grave*: lit. 'great.'
39. *Joseph, turn away...*: contrast Potiphar's reaction at Genesis 39.19-20.
40. *mighty one*: Joseph's master.
41. *her young man*: Joseph.
42. *He*: Joseph.

35–42 Joseph imprisoned

43. *them*: the men of the city.
44. *the signs*: probably the 'signs' that Joseph posed a threat to their women.

(in a dream) pressing wine,' and the other said, 'Surely I saw myself (in a dream) carrying bread on my head, from which the birds were eating. Inform us about its interpretation. Surely we see you are one of the doers of good.' **37** He said, 'Before any food comes to either of you for provision, I shall inform each of you about its interpretation before it comes to you.[45] That is part of what my Lord has taught me. Surely I have forsaken the creed of a people (who) do not believe in God and (who) are disbelievers in the Hereafter,[46] **38** and I have followed the creed of my fathers, Abraham, and Isaac, and Jacob.[47] (It) was not for us to associate anything with God.[48] That is part of the favor of God to us and to the people, but most of the people are not thankful (for it). **39** My two companions of the prison! Are various Lords better, or God, the One, the Supreme? **40** Instead of Him, you only serve names which you have named,[49] you and your fathers. God has not sent down any authority for it. Judgment (belongs) only to God. He has commanded you not to serve (anyone) but Him. That is the right religion, but most of the people do not know (it). **41** My two companions of the prison! As for one of you, he will give his lord wine to drink, and as for the other, he will be crucified, and birds will eat from his head. The matter about which you two asked for a pronouncement has been decided.' **42** He said to the one of them he thought would be released, 'Mention me[50] in the presence of your lord.' But Satan made him forget to mention (him)[51] to his lord. So he[52] remained in the prison for several years.

43 The king[53] said, 'Surely I saw (in a dream) seven fat cows, (and) seven lean ones are eating them, and seven green ears (of corn) and others dry. Assembly! Make a pronouncement to me about my vision, if you can interpret visions.' **44** They said, 'A jumble of dreams. We know nothing of the interpretation of dreams.' **45** But the one who had been released (from prison) said – (for) he remembered after a period (of time) – 'I shall inform you about its interpretation. So send me.'

46 'Joseph, you truthful man! Make a pronouncement to us about the seven fat cows (and) seven lean ones eating them, and the seven green ears (of corn) and others dry, in order that I may return to the people, so that they will know.' **47** He said, 'You will sow for seven years as usual, but what you harvest leave in its ear, except a little from which you may eat. **48** Then, after that, will come seven hard (years), (which will) eat up what you stored up for them, (all) except a little of what you preserved.[54]
49 Then, after that, will come a year in which the people will have rain, and in which they will press.'[55]

50 The king said, 'Bring him to me!' But when the messenger came to him, he[56] said, 'Return to your lord and ask him, "What (about the) case of the women who cut their hands?" Surely my Lord knew of

---

45. *Before any food comes...*: a difficult construction, but the general sense seems to be that Joseph will interpret their dreams before their next meal arrives (and of course before their dreams come to pass).
46. *the Hereafter*: see n. on Q2.4.
47. *the creed of my fathers...*: cf. Q2.130-135.
48. *associate anything with God*: i.e. associate other gods with God.
49. *names which you have named*: referring to their false gods (cf. Q7.71; 53.23).
50. *Mention me*: or 'Remember me.'
51. *forgot to mention (him)*: lit. ' forgot the mention' or 'the reminder' (notice the double entendre; cf. Q58.19).
52. *he*: Joseph.

43–49 Joseph interprets the king's dream

53. *the king*: i.e. the 'pharaoh' of Egypt, though he is not referred to as such here. In the Qur'ān 'Pharaoh' is understood to be the proper name of the Egyptian ruler who opposed Moses.
54. *preserved*: lit. 'sent forward.'
55. *press*: i.e. press out wine and oil.

50–57 Joseph's release from prison and elevation in Egypt

56. *he*: Joseph.

their plot.' **51** He[57] said, 'What is this business of yours, when you tried to seduce Joseph?' They[58] said, 'God preserve (us)! We know no evil against him.' The wife of the mighty one said, 'Now the truth has come to light. I tried to seduce him, but surely he is indeed one of the truthful.' **52** 'That (is) so that he[59] may know that I[60] did not betray him in secret, and that God does not guide the plot of the treacherous. **53** Yet I do not pronounce myself innocent, (for) surely the self is indeed an instigator of evil, except as my Lord has compassion. Surely my Lord is forgiving, compassionate.'

54 The king said, 'Bring him to me! I want him for myself.' So when he spoke to him, he said, 'Surely this day you are secure with us (and) trustworthy.' **55** He said, 'Set me over the storehouses of the land. Surely I am a skilled overseer.' **56** In this way We established Joseph in the land. He settled in it wherever he pleased. We smite whomever We please with Our mercy, and We do not let the reward of the doers of good go to waste. **57** But the reward of the Hereafter is indeed better for those who believe and guard (themselves).[61]

58 The brothers of Joseph came, and they entered upon him. He recognized them, but they did not know him. **59** When he had supplied them with their supplies, he said, 'Bring me a brother of yours from your father. Do you not see that I fill up the measure, and that I am the best of hosts? **60** But if you do not bring him to me, (there will be) no measure for you with me, and you will not come near me.' **61** They said, 'We shall solicit[62] his father for him. Surely we shall indeed do (so).' **62** He said to his young men, 'Put their merchandise[63] (back) in their packs, so that they will recognize it when they turn back to their family, (and) so that they will return (here).'

63 When they returned to their father, they said, 'Our father! The measure was refused us,[64] so send our brother[65] (back) with us, (and) we shall get the measure. Surely we shall indeed watch over him.'[66] **64** He said, 'Shall I trust you with him as I trusted you with his brother before? God is the best Watcher,[67] and He (is) the most compassionate of the compassionate.' **65** When they opened their belongings, they found their merchandise returned to them. They said, 'Our father, what (more) do we desire? This is our merchandise returned to us. We shall supply (food for) our family, and watch over our brother, and get an extra measure of a camel(-load). That is an easy measure.' **66** He said, 'I shall not send him with you until you give me a promise from God that you will indeed bring him (back) to me, unless you are surrounded.'[68] When they had given him their pledge, he said, 'God is guardian over what we say.' **67** And he said, 'My sons! Do not enter by one gate, but enter by different gates.[69] I am of no use to you at all against God. Judgment (belongs) only to God. In Him have I put my trust, and in Him let the trusting put their trust.'

---

57. *He*: the king.
58. *They*: the women.
59. *he*: the woman's husband (this and the following verse are spoken by Joseph).
60. *I*: Joseph.
61. *guard (themselves)*: against evil, or God.

58–69 Joseph's brothers come to Egypt

62. *solicit*: the same verb is used of the attempt to 'seduce' Joseph (see e.g. Q12.23 above).
63. *their merchandise*: i.e. what they had brought with them to barter for corn.
64. *was refused us*: i.e. future supplies of corn were denied.
65. *our brother*: i.e. Joseph's full brother (Benjamin, according to Genesis 42.36).
66. *watch over him*: just what they had said about Joseph at the beginning of the story (Q12.12 above).
67. *Watcher*: or 'Overseer,' 'Keeper;' precisely what the brothers had promised, but failed, to be (Q12.12, 63 above).
68. *surrounded*: perhaps by an enemy, but the meaning is obscure.
69. *...enter by different gates*: the reason for this precaution is obscure (cf. the following verse).

68 When they had entered in the way their father commanded them – it was of no use to them at all against God, but (it was only) a need in Jacob himself which he satisfied.[70] Surely he was indeed full of knowledge because of what We had taught him, but most of the people do not know (it). **69** And when they entered upon Joseph, he took his brother to himself and said, 'Surely I am your brother, so do not be distressed at what they have done.'

70 When he had supplied them with their supplies, he put the drinking cup in the pack of his brother. Then a crier cried out, 'Caravan! Surely you are thieves indeed!' **71** They said as they approached them, 'What is it you are missing?' **72** They said, 'We are missing the king's cup. To the one who brings it a camel-load (will be given). I guarantee it.' **73** They said, 'By God! Certainly you know (that) we did not come to foment corruption on the earth. We are not thieves.' **74** They said, 'What will the penalty for it be, if you are liars?' **75** They said, 'The penalty for it (will be): the one in whose pack it is found, he (will be) liable for it. In this way we repay the evildoers.' **76** So he[71] began with their packs before (searching) his brother's pack, (and) then he brought it out of his brother's pack. In this way We plotted for (the sake of) Joseph. He was not one to take his brother, in (accord with) the religion of the king, unless God had (so) pleased. We raise in rank whomever We please, and above everyone who has knowledge is the One who knows.

77 They[72] said, 'If he steals, a brother of his has stolen before.'[73] But Joseph kept it secret within himself and did not reveal it to them. He said, 'You are (in) a bad situation. God knows what you are alleging.' **78** They said, 'Great one! Surely he has a father (who is) very old, so take one of us (in) his place. Surely we see (that) you are one of the doers of good.' **79** He said, 'God's refuge! That we should take (anyone) except (the one) in whose possession we found our things! Surely then we (would be) evildoers indeed.' **80** So when they had given up hope of (moving) him, they withdrew in private conversation. The eldest of them said, 'Do you not know that your father has already taken you under a promise from God? And (that) before that you neglected (to keep your promise) concerning Joseph? I shall not leave the land until my father gives me permission or (until) God judges for me.[74] He is the best of judges. **81** Return to your father and say, "Our father! Surely your son has stolen. We bear witness only about what we know. We were not observers of the unseen. **82** Ask (the people of) the town where we were, and (those in) the caravan in which we have come. Surely we are truthful indeed."'

83 He[75] said, 'No! You have only contrived a story for yourselves. Patience is becoming (for me). It may be that God will bring them all to me. Surely He – He is the Knowing, the Wise.' **84** He turned away from them and said, 'My sorrow for Joseph!' And his eyes became white from the grief,[76] and he choked back his sadness. **85** They said, 'By God! You will never stop mentioning Joseph until you are frail or are on the verge of death.'[77] **86** He said, 'I only complain (of) my anguish and my grief to God, (for) I know from God what you do not know.[78] **87** My sons! Go and search out news of Joseph and his brother, and do not despair of the comfort of God. Surely everyone has hope of the comfort of God, except for the people who are disbelievers.'

---

70. *a need in Jacob himself...*: perhaps his lack of trust in God, but the meaning is obscure.

70–87 Joseph tricks his brothers

71. *he*: Joseph.
72. *They*: Joseph's brothers.
73. *a brother of his has stolen before*: the brothers compound their misdeeds by now maligning Joseph.
74. *judges for me*: or 'decides in my favor.'
75. *He*: Jacob; the brothers have now returned to their father (cf. Jacob's identical retort at Q12.18 above).
76. *his eyes became white...*: i.e. Jacob became blind.
77. *on the verge of death*: lit. 'one of the perishing.'
78. *I know from God what you do not know*: i.e. Jacob 'knows' that Joseph is still alive (see Q12.96 below).

88 When they entered upon him,[79] they said, 'Great one! Hardship[80] has touched us and our house, and
we have brought merchandise of little value. Fill up the measure for us and be charitable to us. Surely
God rewards the charitable.' **89** He said, 'Do you know what you did with Joseph and his brother, when
you were ignorant?' **90** They said, 'Are you indeed Joseph?' He said, 'I am Joseph, and this is my brother.
God has bestowed favor on us. Surely the one who guards (himself) and is patient – surely God does not
let the reward of the doers of good go to waste.' **91** They said, 'By God! Certainly God has preferred you
over us, and we have been sinners indeed.' **92** He said, '(There is) no reproach on you today. God will
forgive you, (for) He is the most compassionate of the compassionate. **93** Go with this shirt of mine and
cast it on my father's face. He will regain (his) sight. And (then) bring me your family all together.'

94 When the caravan set forth, their father said, 'Surely I do indeed perceive the scent of Joseph, though
you may think me senile.' **95** They said, 'By God! Surely you are indeed in your (same) old error.'[81]
96 So when the bringer of good news came (to him), he cast it[82] on his face and (his) sight returned.
He said, 'Did I not say to you, "Surely I know from God what you do not know"?' **97** They said, 'Our
father! Ask forgiveness for us for our sins. Surely we have been sinners.' **98** He said, 'I shall ask my Lord
for forgiveness for you. Surely He – He is the Forgiving, the Compassionate.'

99 When they entered upon Joseph, he took his parents to himself and said, 'Enter Egypt, if God pleases,
secure.' **100** He raised his parents on the throne, and they (all) fell down before him in prostration. And
he said, 'My father! This is the interpretation of my vision from before. My Lord has made it (come)
true. He has been good to me, when He brought me out of the prison, and when He brought you out of
the desert, after Satan had caused strife between me and my brothers. Surely my Lord is astute to whatever He pleases. Surely He – He is the Knowing, the Wise. **101** My Lord, you have given me some of the
kingdom, and taught me some of the interpretation of dreams. Creator of the heavens and the earth,
You are my ally in this world and the Hereafter. Take me[83] as one who has submitted,[84] and join me with
the righteous.'

102 That is one of the stories[85] of the unseen.[86] We inspired you[87] (with) it. You were not with them when
they agreed on their plan and were scheming. **103** Most of the people are not going to believe, even if
you are eager (for that). **104** You do not ask them for any reward for it. It is nothing but a reminder[88]
to the worlds.[89] **105** How many a sign in the heavens and the earth do they pass by! Yet they turn away
from it. **106** Most of them do not believe in God, unless they associate.[90] **107** Do they feel secure that a
covering of God's punishment will not come upon them, or that the Hour[91] will not come upon them

88–101 Jacob and his family come to Egypt

79. *him*: Joseph.
80. *Hardship*: i.e. famine.
81. *error*: lit. 'straying.'
82. *it*: Joseph's shirt.
83. *Take me*: in death.
84. *as one who has submitted*: or 'as a Muslim.'

102–108 Conclusion to the story of Joseph

84. *stories*: or 'news.'
86. *the unseen*: here referring to 'the distant past' (see n. on Q2.3; cf. Q3.44 [Mary]; 11.49 [Noah]).
87. *you*: the Prophet.
88. *reminder*: referring either to the story of Joseph in particular or to the Qur'ān in general (cf. Q12.3 above; see n. on Q3.58).
89. *to the worlds*: or 'to all peoples.'
90. *unless they associate*: other gods with God.
91. *the Hour*: of judgment (cf. Q43.66; 47.18).

unexpectedly, when they do not realize (it)? **108** Say: 'This is my way. I call (you) to God on (the basis of) evidence – I and whoever follows me. Glory to God! I am not one of the idolaters.'[92]

109 We have not sent (anyone) before you[93] except men whom We inspired from the people of the towns. Have they not traveled on the earth and seen how the end was for those who were before them?[94] The Home of the Hereafter is indeed better for those who guard (themselves). Do you not understand? **110** – Until, when the messengers[95] had given up hope, and thought that they had been called liars,[96] Our help came to them, and those whom We pleased were rescued. But Our violence was not turned back from the people who were sinners. **111** Certainly in their accounts[97] (there is) a lesson for those with understanding.

It[98] is not a forged proclamation,[99] but a confirmation of what was before it,[100] and a distinct setting forth of everything,[101] and a guidance[102] and mercy for a people who believe.

---

92. *the idolaters*: or 'the ones who associate (other gods with God).'

109–111A Punishment of earlier generations a warning

92. *you*: the Prophet.

94. *Have they not traveled on the earth and seen...*: a reference to previous peoples who were punished for their disbelief (see n. on Q7.59). The remains of their destroyed cities were believed to be still visible.

95. *messengers*: for this important title, see n. on Q2.87.

96. *thought that they had been called liars*: or 'thought that they had spoken falsely.'

97. *in their accounts*: referring to the stories of punishment.

111B The Qur'ān not a forgery

97. *It*: antecedent unclear, but 'it' probably refers to the Qur'ān (thus the close of this sūra parallels its opening).

99. *proclamation*: or 'report' (Ar. *ḥadīth*).

100. *what was before it*: the Torah and Gospel.

101. *a distinct setting forth of everything*: for this idea, cf. Q6.114, 154; 7.52, 145; 10.37; 11.1; 41.3, 44.

102. *guidance*: one of the most frequent terms (Ar. *hudā*) for revelation in general, and the Qur'ān in particular.

13 The Thunder ✽ Al-Ra'd

In the Name of God, the Merciful, the Compassionate

1 Alif Lām Mīm Rā'.[1] Those are the signs[2] of the Book.[3] What has been sent down to you[4] from your Lord is the truth, but most of the people do not believe.

2 (It is) God who raised up the heavens without pillars that you (can) see. Then He mounted the throne, and subjected the sun and the moon, each one running (its course) for an appointed time.[5] He directs the (whole) affair.[6] He makes the signs distinct,[7] so that you[8] may be certain of the meeting with your Lord.[9]
3 He (it is) who stretched out the earth, and placed on it firm mountains and rivers.[10] And of all the fruits He has placed on it two in pairs.[11] He covers the day with the night. Surely in that are signs indeed for a people who reflect. 4 On the earth (there are) parts neighboring (each other), and gardens of grapes, and (fields of) crops, and palm trees, (growing in) bunches and singly, (all) watered with one water. Yet We favor some of it over others in fruit. Surely in that are signs indeed for a people who understand.

5 If you[12] are amazed, their saying is amazing: 'When we have turned to dust, shall we indeed (return) in a new creation?'[13] Those are the ones who have disbelieved in their Lord, and those – the chains will

---

Q13: This sūra is an assemblage of short passages touching on a variety of topics, including God's power and providence, rewards and punishments, and encouragement to the Prophet. While most traditional scholars assign Q13 to the 'Medinan' period, modern scholars tend to place it in the late 'Meccan' period. It takes its name from 'the thunder' which praises God at Q13.13.

1 Signs of the Book

1. *Alif Lām Mīm Rā'*: the names of Arabic letters ', *l*, *m*, and *r*. With the exception of an additional 'mīm,' the same letter combination occurs in a block of sūras from Q10 to Q15. Twenty-nine sūras begin with letters like these, ranging from one to five. No satisfactory explanation has been given for their occurrence. The Cairo edition varies in counting these letters as a separate verse, or as the beginning of the first verse (as here).
2. *signs*: here referring to the letters ', *l*, *m*, and *r* (for the various meanings of 'signs,' see n. on Q2.39).
3. *the Book*: here referring to the Qur'ān not only as a 'recited' but also 'written' scripture (see n. on Q2.2).
4. *you*: the Prophet.

2–4 Signs of God's power and providence

5. *an appointed time*: or 'term' (Ar. *ajal*), which is predetermined and cannot be changed.
6. *directs the (whole) affair*: or 'directs the command' (Ar. *amr*); the idea may be that God controls the universe from his throne through his *amr*, which may correspond to the rabbinic notion of the 'divine word' (Aram. *mēmrā*), or to the related Christian idea of the *logos* as the manifestation of God's word, or as God's messenger in place of God himself (see e.g. Q10.3, 31; 16.2; 32.5; 65.12).
7. *makes the signs distinct*: here referring to the 'signs' of God's cosmic power.
8. *you*: plur.
9. *meeting with your Lord*: on the Day of Judgment.
10. *placed on it firm mountains and rivers*: to keep the earth from moving (cf. Q15.19; 16.15; 21.31; 31.10; 50.7).
11. *two in pairs*: or 'two kinds,' but the meaning is obscure (cf. Q36.36; 43.12; 51.49).

5–6 Disbelievers reject the resurrection

12. *you*: the Prophet.
13. *(return) in a new creation*: i.e. they are baffled at the idea of resurrection of the dead.

be on their necks – those are the companions of the Fire.[14] There they will remain. **6** They seek to hurry you with the evil before the good,[15] though the examples (of punishment) have already happened before them.[16] Surely your Lord is indeed full of forgiveness for the people, despite their evildoing, yet surely your Lord is (also) indeed harsh in retribution.

7 Those who disbelieve say, 'If only a sign were sent down on him from his Lord.'[17] You are only a warner,[18] and for every people (there is) a guide.

8 God knows what every female bears, and (in) what (way) the womb shrinks and (in) what (way) it swells. Everything with Him has (its) measure. **9** (He is) the Knower of the unseen and the seen,[19] the Great, the Exalted. **10** (It is) the same (for) any of you who keeps (his) saying secret or who makes it public, and (for) anyone who hides in the night or goes about in the day. **11** For him[20] (there is) a following,[21] before him and behind him, who watch over him by the command of God. Surely God does not change what is in a people, until they change what is in themselves. And when God wishes evil for a people, (there is) no turning (it) back for them. They have no ally other than Him.

12 He (it is) who shows you the lightning – in fear and desire[22] – and He produces the clouds heavy (with rain). **13** The thunder glorifies (Him) with His praise, and the angels (too) out of awe of Him. He sends the thunderbolts, and smites with it whomever He pleases. Yet they dispute about God, when He is mighty in power. **14** The true call[23] (is) to Him, and those whom they call on instead of Him do not respond to them at all. (They are) only like someone stretching out his hands toward water, so that it may reach his mouth, but it does not reach it. The call of the disbelievers only goes astray. **15** Whatever is in the heavens and the earth prostrates itself before God, willingly or unwillingly, and (so do) their shadows in the morning and the evenings.[24]

16 Say:[25] 'Who is Lord of the heavens and the earth?' Say: 'God.' Say: 'Have you taken allies[26] other than Him? They do not have power to (cause) themselves benefit or harm.' Say: 'Are the blind and the sighted equal, or are the darkness and the light equal? Or have they set up[27] associates for God who have created a creation like His, so that the creation is (all) alike to them?' Say: 'God is the Creator of everything. He is the One, the Supreme.'

---

14. *the Fire*: Ar. *al-nār* is the most common of the various designations for Hell.
15. *the evil before the good*: i.e. they dare the Prophet to bring God's punishment on them first, before any rewards.
16. *examples...before them*: i.e. before their time; a reference to previous peoples who were punished for rejecting their messengers (see n. on Q7.59).

7 Demand for a sign

17. *If only a sign were sent down...*: i.e. they demand a 'miracle' as proof of the Prophet's legitimacy (cf. Q13.27, 31 below); see the lists of their demands at Q17.90-95; 25.7-8, 20-21, 32 (cf. the similar demand for a 'sign' from Jesus at John 2.18; 6.30).
18. *only a warner*: for this role, see n. on Q2.119; cf. Q13.38 below (no messenger 'brings a sign,' unless God permits).

8–17 Signs of God's power and providence

19. *the seen*: lit. 'the witnessed.'
20. *For him*: i.e. for each person.
21. *a following*: of recording angels (for these beings and their various roles, see n. on Q2.30).
22. *in fear and desire*: i.e. fear of the storm, but desire for rain (cf. Q30.24).
23. *call*: or 'petition,' 'plea.'
24. *...in the morning and the evenings*: i.e. long shadows in the morning and evening appear to be 'bowing down.'
25. *Say*: on this form of address, see n. on Q2.80.
26. *allies*: Ar. *awliyā'* implies the obligation of mutual protection, almost in the sense of 'friends' or 'brothers.'
27. *set up*: lit. 'made.'

17 He sends down water from the sky, and the wādis flow, (each) in its measure, and the torrent carries a rising (layer of) froth (on top), like the froth that arises from what they heat in the fire,[28] seeking some ornament or utensil. In this way God strikes (a parable of) the true and the false. As for the froth, it becomes worthless, but as for what benefits the people, it remains on the earth. In this way God strikes parables.

18 For those who respond to their Lord (there is) the good (reward), but those who do not respond to Him – (even) if they had what is on the earth – all (of it) – and as much again, they would indeed (try to) ransom (themselves) with it. Those – for them (there is) the evil reckoning. Their refuge is Gehenna[29] – it is an evil bed!

19 Is the one who knows that what has been sent down to you[30] from your Lord is the truth, like the one who is blind? Only those with understanding take heed:[31] **20** those who fulfill the covenant of God and do not break the compact, **21** and who join together what God has commanded to be joined with it, and fear their Lord, and are afraid of the evil reckoning, **22** and who are patient in seeking the face of their Lord,[32] and observe the prayer,[33] and contribute[34] from what We have provided them, in secret and in open, and avert evil by means of the good. Those – for them (there is) the outcome of the Home: **23** Gardens of Eden[35] which they (will) enter, and (also) those who were righteous among their fathers, and their wives, and their descendants. The angels (will) come in to them from every gate: **24** 'Peace (be) upon you because you were patient! Excellent is the outcome of the Home!'

25 But those who break the covenant of God, after its ratification, and sever what God has commanded to be joined, and foment corruption on the earth, those – for them (there is) the curse, and for them (there is) the evil Home. **26** God extends (His) provision to whomever He pleases, and restricts (it). They gloat over this present life, but this present life is nothing but a (fleeting) enjoyment in (comparison to) the Hereafter.[36]

27 Those who disbelieve say, 'If only a sign were sent down on him[37] from his Lord?' Say: 'Surely God leads astray whomever He pleases and guides to Himself whoever turns (to Him).' **28** Those who believe and whose hearts[38] are secure in the remembrance of God – surely hearts are secure in the remembrance of God – **29** those who believe and do righteous deeds – for them (there is) happiness and a good (place of) return.

30 In this way We have sent you[39] among a community – before it (other) communities have already passed away[40] – in order that you might recite[41] to them what We have inspired you (with). Yet they

---

28. *what they heat in the fire*: i.e. in metalworking.

18 Reward and punishment

29. *Gehenna*: a name for Hell (see n. on Q2.206).

19–29 Believers and disbelievers not alike

30. *you*: the Prophet.
31. *take heed*: or 'remember.'
32. *seeking the face of their Lord*: i.e. desiring God's favor.
33. *the prayer*: the ritual prayer (or *ṣalāt*).
34. *contribute*: lit. 'spend' (for those in need or for the cause).
35. *Gardens of Eden*: in heaven (for this imagery, see n. on Q2.25).
36. *the Hereafter*: see n. on Q2.4.
37. *him*: the Prophet (cf. Q13.7 above).
38. *hearts*: here, as often, the heart is spoken of as synonymous with mind.

30–32 Encouragement to the Prophet

39. *you*: the Prophet.
40. *before it...(other) communities have already passed away*: a reference to previous peoples who were punished for their disbelief (see n. on Q7.59; cf. Q13.6 above).
41. *recite*: or 'read aloud.'

disbelieve in the Merciful.[42] Say: 'He is my Lord – (there is) no god but Him. In Him I have put my trust, and to Him is my turning (in repentance).' **31** If (only there were) a Qur'ān[43] by which the mountains were moved, or by which the earth were split open, or by which the dead were spoken to.[44] No! The affair (belongs) to God altogether. Have those who believe no hope that, if God (so) pleased, He would indeed guide all the people?[45] (As for) those who disbelieve, a striking[46] will continue to smite them for what they have done, or it will descend near their home(s), until the promise of God comes.[47] Surely God will not break the appointment. **32** Certainly messengers[48] have been mocked before you, but I spared those who disbelieved. Then I seized them – and how was my retribution?

33 Is He who stands over every person for what he has earned[49] [...]?[50] They have set up associates for God. Say: 'Name them! Or will you inform Him about what He does not know on the earth, or about what is said openly?' No! Their scheming is made to appear enticing to those who disbelieve, and they are kept from the way. Whoever God leads astray has no guide. **34** For them (there is) punishment in this present life, yet the punishment of the Hereafter is indeed harder. They have no defender against God.

35 A parable of the Garden[51] which is promised to the ones who guard (themselves):[52] through it rivers flow, its fruit is unending, and (also) its shade. That is the outcome for the ones who guard (themselves), but the outcome for the disbelievers is the Fire.

36 Those to whom We have given the Book rejoice in what has been sent down to you,[53] though some among the factions[54] reject part of it. Say: 'I am only commanded to serve God, and not to associate (anything) with Him. To Him do I call (you), and to Him is my return.'

37 In this way We have sent it down as an Arabic judgment.[55] If indeed you[56] follow their (vain) desires,

---

42. *the Merciful*: Ar. *al-raḥmān* is used here as a proper name for God. It seems to have caused confusion or objections among some, who found it either unfamiliar or unacceptable (cf. Q17.110; 21.36; see n. on Q25.60).
43. *Qur'ān*: here in the sense of a separate 'Recitation' (see n. on Q2.185).
44. *...by which the dead were spoken to*: the wish is for a 'recitation' possessing the power to effect such miracles (cf. the demand for a 'sign' at Q13.7, 27 above). The point, however, is that even if there were such a 'recitation,' they would still not believe.
45. *guide all the people*: for this idea, see n. on Q2.213.
46. *a striking*: i.e. divine punishment (cf. Q69.4; 101.1-5).
47. *...until the promise of God comes*: here the threat of punishment is temporal rather than eschatological, and the sense seems to be that disaster has always been the fate of those who rejected their messengers, and that this will also hold true for the Prophet's audience (cf. Q69.4; contrast Q101.1-3).
48. *messengers*: for this important title, see n. on Q2.87.

33–34 Punishment for disbelievers

49. *for what he has earned*: i.e. rewards or punishments for what each has done.
50. *[...]*: there appears to be a lacuna here.

35 The Garden or the Fire

51. *Garden*: in heaven (for this imagery, see n. on Q2.25).
52. *guard (themselves)*: against evil, or God.

36–43 Encouragement to the Prophet

53. *Those whom we have given the Book rejoice...*: referring to those Jews and Christians who also believed in the revelation given to the Prophet. Here 'the Book' seems to be used as a generic term for revelation, rather than as a reference to any individual book (see n. on Q2.2).
54. *the factions*: or 'the sectarians' (Ar. *al-aḥzāb*), referring to those Jews and Christians who refused to accept the Prophet's revelation.
55. *an Arabic judgment*: another designation for the Qur'ān (see n. on Q12.2, 'an Arabic Qur'ān;' cf. Q3.79n.).
56. *you*: the Prophet.

after what has come to you of the knowledge,[57] you will have no ally and no defender against God.
38 Certainly We sent messengers before you, and gave them wives and descendants, but it was not for
any messenger to bring a sign,[58] except by the permission of God. For every (period of) time (there is) a
written decree.[59] **39** God blots out whatever he pleases, and He confirms (whatever He pleases).[60] With
Him is the mother of the Book.[61]

40 Whether We let you see part of what We promise them, or We take you,[62] only (dependent) on you is
the delivery (of the message). (Dependent) on Us is the reckoning. **41** Do they not see that We come to
the land,[63] pushing back its borders?[64] God judges, (and there is) no revision of His judgment. He is quick
at the reckoning.

42 Those who were before them schemed, but the scheme (belongs) to God altogether. He knows what
every person earns, and soon the disbelievers will know to whom the outcome of the Home (belongs).
43 Those who disbelieve say, 'You are not an envoy.'[65] Say: 'God is sufficient as a witness between me and
you, and (so is) whoever has knowledge of the Book.'

---

57. *of the knowledge*: has either a partitive or an epexegetical meaning (elucidating the preceding 'what').
58. *sign*: or 'miracle;' this answers the question posed by the Prophet's opponents at Q13.7, 27 above.
59. *written decree*: lit. 'book;' it may mean that every age has its revealed 'Book,' or that the time of judgment for every age is fixed as a 'written decree' (cf. Q15.4; see n. on Q6.59).
60. *God blots out...confirms...*: this implies that some revision has been made in the text of the Qur'ān and other 'scriptures' (cf. Q2.106n.; 16.101n.; 22.52n.), or else that God can make changes in the 'Book of God' or 'Book of Destiny' (see previous n.).
61. *mother of the Book*: Ar. *umm al-kitāb* is usually taken as a reference to the heavenly original or archetype of all revelation. According to this view, the Qur'ān, like the Torah and the Gospel, is only a portion of this all encompassing 'Book' (see Q3.7; 43.4; cf. Q56.78, 'hidden Book;' 85.22, 'guarded Tablet'). Here, however, the 'mother of the Book' may refer to the 'Book of God' or 'Book of Destiny' by which everything is ordained (see e.g. Q6.38, 59; 9.36; 10.61; 11.6; 22.70; 57.22).
62. *take you*: in death, i.e. before the Prophet sees the disbelievers punished.
63. *land*: lit. 'earth.'
64. *pushing back its borders*: meaning obscure; perhaps a reference to the military successes of the Prophet and his followers (cf. Q21.44).
65. *envoy*: lit. 'one who is sent' (Ar. *mursal*), a word roughly equivalent to 'messenger' (*rasūl*). If this denial comes from the Jews, then the reference to 'the Book' in the following sentence may be to the Torah, which was supposed to have predicted the coming of the Prophet (see Deuteronomy 18.18).

14 Abraham ✿ Ibrāhīm

In the Name of God, the Merciful, the Compassionate

1 Alif Lām Rā'.[1] A Book[2] – We have sent it down to you,[3] so that you may bring the people out of the darkness to the light, by the permission of their Lord, to the path of the Mighty, the Praiseworthy. **2** God who – to Him (belongs) whatever is in the heavens and whatever is on the earth. Woe to the disbelievers because of a harsh punishment! **3** Those who love this present life more than the Hereafter,[4] and keep (people) from the way of God, and desire (to make) it crooked – those are far astray![5]

4 We have not sent any messenger[6] except in the language of his people,[7] so that he might make (things) clear to them. Then God leads astray whomever He pleases and guides whomever He pleases. He is the Mighty, the Wise.

5 Certainly We sent Moses with Our signs:[8] 'Bring your people out of the darkness to the light,[9] and remind them of the days of God.'[10] Surely in that are signs indeed for every patient (and) thankful one.

6 (Remember) when[11] Moses said to his people, 'Remember the blessing of God on you, when He rescued you from the house of Pharaoh. They were inflicting on you the evil punishment, and slaughtering your

---

Q14: This sūra, like the previous one, is an assemblage of short passages touching on a variety of topics, including a brief recounting of the stories of Moses and other messengers, human ingratitude for God's blessings, and the prayer of Abraham, from which it receives its title. Q14 is assigned by most scholars to the late 'Meccan' period, though a few verses are considered 'Medinan.'

1–3 A Book from God

1. *Alif Lām Rā'*: the names of Arabic letters ', *l*, and *r*. The same letter combination occurs in a block of sūras from Q10 to Q15 (Q13 has an additional 'mīm'). Twenty-nine sūras begin with letters like these, ranging from one to five. No satisfactory explanation has been given for their occurrence. The Cairo edition varies in counting these letters as a separate verse, or as the beginning of the first verse (as here).
2. *Book*: here referring to the Qur'ān not only as a 'recited' but also 'written' scripture (see n. on Q2.2)
3. *you*: the Prophet.
4. *the Hereafter*: see n. on Q2.4.
5. *far astray*: lit. 'in far straying.'

4 Messengers speak the language of their people

6. *messenger*: for this important title, see n. on Q2.87.
7. *in the language of his people*: this is consistent with the idea that the revelation to the Prophet constitutes 'an Arabic Qur'ān' (see n. on Q12.2; cf. 13.37); but it may also be an answer to some objection, perhaps that Hebrew was thought to be the exclusive language of revelation.

5 The mission of Moses

8. *signs*: referring to the miraculous 'signs' accompanying the deliverance from Pharaoh (see n. on Q2.39).
9. *Bring your people out…*: the missions of Moses and the Prophet are identically described (cf. Q14.1 above).
10. *days of God*: may refer to the times of God's intervention, or when he fought for them (only here and at Q45.14, to the Prophet).

6–8 Moses appeals to his people

11. *(Remember) when…*: a stock narrative formula; the Arabic particle *idh* often marks the beginning of a story, and means something like 'Once…,' or 'There was a time when…,' or 'Remember when….'

sons and sparing your women.[12] In that was a great test from your Lord.' **7** And (remember) when your Lord proclaimed, 'If indeed you are thankful, I shall indeed give you more, but if indeed you are ungrateful, surely My punishment is harsh indeed.' **8** And Moses said, '(Even) if you disbelieve, you and whoever is on the earth all together – surely God is indeed wealthy, praiseworthy.'

9 Has no story[13] come to you[14] of those who were before you: the people of Noah, 'Ād, Thamūd, and those who (came) after them? No one knows them but God. Their messengers brought them the clear signs,[15] but they put their hands in their mouths,[16] and said, 'Surely We disbelieve in what you are sent with, and surely we are in grave doubt indeed about what you call us to.'[17] **10** Their messengers said, '(Is there any) doubt about God, Creator of the heavens and the earth? He calls you so that He may forgive you of your sins and spare you for an appointed time.'[18] They said, 'You are nothing but human beings like us. You want to keep us from what our fathers have served.[19] Bring us some clear authority (for this).' **11** Their messengers said to them, 'We are nothing but human beings like you, but God bestows favor on whomever He pleases of His servants.[20] It is not for us to bring you any authority, except by the permission of God. In God let the believers put their trust. **12** Why should we not put our trust in God, when He has guided us to our ways. Indeed we shall patiently endure whatever harm you do us. In God let the trusting put their trust.' **13** Those who had disbelieved said to their messengers, 'We shall indeed expel you from our land,[21] or (else) you will return to our creed.' Then their Lord inspired them: 'We shall indeed destroy the evildoers **14** and cause you to inhabit the land after them.[22] That is for whoever fears My position[23] and fears My promise.'[24]

15 They asked for victory,[25] and every stubborn tyrant despaired. **16** Behind him is Gehenna,[26] and he is given a drink of filthy water.[27] **17** He gulps it but can hardly swallow it. Death comes upon him from every side, yet he does not die, and behind him is a stern punishment.

18 A parable of those who disbelieve in their Lord: their deeds are like ashes, on which the wind blows

---

12. *slaughtering your sons and sparing your women*: cf. Pharaoh's order to kill all Hebrew boys but spare the girls (Exodus 1.15-16, 22).

9–17 Previous messengers

13. *story*: or 'news;' referring to the stories of previous peoples who were punished for disobeying their messengers (see n. on Q7.59).
14. *you*: plur.; it is not clear whether Moses continues to address his people here.
15. *the clear signs*: or 'the clear proofs,' 'the indisputable evidence.'
16. *they put their hands in their mouths*: lit. 'returned their hands...;' apparently a gesture of contempt or anger.
17. *what you call us to*: revelation (cf. Q11.62, 110; 41.45; 42.14).
18. *an appointed time*: or 'term' (Ar. *ajal*), i.e. the precise date of a person's death is predetermined.
19. *served*: or 'worshipped.'
20. *servants*: the word 'servants,' which also means 'slaves,' is used here in the sense of 'all people.'
21. *land*: lit. 'earth.'
22. *cause you to inhabit the land after them*: see n. on Q14.45 below.
23. *My position*: or perhaps 'My judgment seat' (cf. Q55.46; 79.40).
24. *promise*: or 'threat' of punishment (cf. Q50.45).
25. *They asked for victory*: lit. 'an opening;' the antecedent is unclear, but 'they' presumably refers to 'the messengers' (cf. Q7.89; 26.118; 32.28-29; 48.1).
26. *Gehenna*: a name for Hell (see n. on Q2.206); it is not clear whether the expression (Ar. *min warā'ihī*) is to be understood in a spatial sense ('Behind him') or temporal sense ('Afterwards for him').
27. *filthy water*: meaning uncertain; said to be what oozes from a wound.

18 Parable of the disbelievers

strongly on a stormy day. They have no power over anything of what they have earned.[28] That is straying far.[29]

19 Do you[30] not see that God created the heavens and the earth in truth?[31] If He (so) pleases, He will do away with you and bring a new creation. **20** That is no great matter for God.

21 They will come forth to God all together, and the weak will say to those who were arrogant, 'Surely we were your followers, so are you going relieve us (now) of any of the punishment of God?' They will say, 'If God had guided us, we would indeed have guided you. (It is) the same for us whether we become distressed or are patient. (There is) no place of escape for us.' **22** And Satan[32] will say, when the matter is decided, 'Surely God promised you a true promise, and I (too) promised you, (but) then I broke (my promise) to you. I had no authority over you, except that I called you and you responded to me. So do not blame me, but blame yourselves. I am not going to help you, nor are you going to help me. Surely I disbelieved in your associating me (with God) before.'[33] Surely the evildoers – for them (there is) a painful punishment. **23** But those who believe and do righteous deeds – they are made to enter Gardens[34] through which rivers flow, there to remain by the permission of their Lord. Their greeting there is: 'Peace!'[35]

24 Do you[36] not see how God has struck a parable?[37] A good word is like a good tree. Its root is firm and its branch (reaches) to the sky, **25** giving its fruit every season by the permission of its Lord. God strikes parables for the people so that they may take heed.[38] **26** But the parable of a bad word is like a bad tree, uprooted from the earth, without any support for it. **27** God makes firm those who believe by the firm word in this present life and in the Hereafter. But God leads astray the evildoers. God does whatever He pleases.

28 Do you[39] not see those who have exchanged the blessing of God for disbelief, and caused their people to descend to the home of ruin – **29** Gehenna – where they will burn? It is an evil dwelling place! **30** They have set up[40] rivals[41] to God in order to lead (people) astray from His way. Say: 'Enjoy (yourselves)! Surely your destination is to the Fire!'[42]

---

28. *what they have earned*: i.e. 'what they have done' (cf. Q14.51 below).
29. *straying far*: from the truth.

19–20 The Creator does as He pleases

30. *you*: sing., but here an impersonal expression ('Does no one see...?').
31. *in truth*: or 'with the truth.'

21–23 A judgment scene

32. *Satan*: for this figure, see n. on Q2.36.
33. *your associating me (with God) before*: implying that their worship of 'other gods' was in reality the worship of Satan (cf. Q6.100; 34.40-42; 37.158-159; contrast Q53.23n.)
34. *Gardens*: in heaven (for this imagery, see n. on Q2.25).
35. *Peace*: Ar. *salām* connotes 'submission' (*islām*) to God.

24–27 Parable of the good and bad trees

36. *you*: sing., but here an impersonal expression.
37. *a parable*: for what follows, cf. Psalm 1.1-6.
38. *take heed*: or 'be reminded,' 'remember.'

28–30 Fate of disbelievers

39. *you*: sing., but here an impersonal expression. The Cairo edition, reflecting the views of traditional scholars, attributes this and the following verse to the 'Medinan' period.
40. *set up*: lit. 'made.'
41. *rivals*: or 'equals' (Ar. *andād*), i.e. other gods alleged to be equal with God.
42. *the Fire*: Ar. *al-nār* is the most common of the various designations for Hell.

31 Say to My servants who believe (that) they should observe the prayer,[43] and contribute[44] from what We have provided them, in secret and in open, before a Day comes when (there will be) no bargaining and no friendship.

32 (It is) God who created the heavens and the earth, and sent down water from the sky, and brought forth fruits by means of it as a provision for you. And He subjected the ship to you, to run on the sea by
His command, and subjected the rivers to you. **33** And He subjected the sun and the moon to you, both
being constant (in their courses), and subjected the night and the day to you. **34** He has given you some
of all that you have asked Him for. If you (try to) number God's blessing, you will not (be able to) count it. Surely the human is indeed an evildoer (and) ungrateful![45]

35 (Remember) when Abraham said, 'My Lord, make this land secure,[46] and keep me and my sons away
from serving the idols.[47] **36** My Lord, surely they[48] have led many of the people astray. Whoever follows me, surely he belongs to me,[49] and whoever disobeys me[50] – surely You are forgiving, compassionate.
37 Our Lord, I have settled some of my descendants[51] in a wādi without any cultivation, near your Sacred House,[52] Our Lord, in order that they may observe the prayer.[53] So cause the hearts of some of the people to yearn toward them, and provide them with fruits, so that they may be thankful. **38** Our Lord,
You know what we hide and what we speak aloud. Nothing is hidden from God (either) on the earth or
in the sky. **39** Praise (be)[54] to God, who has granted me Ishmael and Isaac in (my) old age. Surely my Lord
is indeed the Hearer of the call.[55] **40** My Lord, make me observant of the prayer, and (also) some of my
descendants, our Lord, and accept my call. **41** Our Lord, forgive me, and my parents,[56] and the believers, on the Day when the reckoning takes place.'

42 Do not think[57] (that) God is oblivious of what the evildoers do. He is only sparing them for a Day when
(their) eyes will stare, **43** (as they go) rushing with their heads raised up, unable to turn back their gaze,
and their hearts empty. **44** Warn the people (of) a Day when the punishment will come to them, and those who have done evil will say, 'Our Lord, spare us for a time near (at hand)![58] We shall respond to

---

31 Prayer and alms required of believers

43. *the prayer*: the ritual prayer (or *ṣalāt*).
44. *contribute*: lit. 'spend' (for those in need or for the cause).

32–34 Signs of God's power and providence

45. *ungrateful*: or 'disbelieving' (perhaps a pun).

35–41 Abraham's prayer

46. *make this land secure*: said to refer to the sacred area (or *ḥaram*) of Mecca, where bloodshed was forbidden (cf. Q2.126).
47. *serving the idols*: or 'worshipping the idols.'
48. *they*: the idols.
49. *belongs to me*: lit. 'is of me;' the 'children of Abraham' are related by religion rather than blood.
50. *disobeys me*: i.e. rejects Abraham's belief in God alone.
51. *some of my descendants*: Ishmael and his descendents are said to have settled near Mecca.
52. *Sacred House*: the Ka'ba (see Q5.97).
53. *the prayer*: the ritual prayer (or *ṣalāt*).
54. *(be)*: or '(belongs).'
55. *the call*: or 'the petition,' 'the plea.'
56. *and my parents*: here Abraham's parents seem to be included among the believers (see Q19.47; 26.86; 60.4; cf. Q71.28 [Noah]); otherwise prayer for disbelievers is forbidden (see Q9.113-114).

42–51 Punishment certain

57. *Do not think*: addressed to the Prophet, or perhaps intended generally ('Let no one think...').
58. *spare us for a time near (at hand)*: i.e. until death comes in its natural course (in other words, 'Let us live a little longer').

Your call and follow the messengers.' 'Did you not swear before that (there would be) no end for you?[59] **45** You dwell in the (same) dwelling places as those who did themselves evil,[60] and it became clear to you how We dealt with them, and (how) We struck parables for you.[61] **46** They schemed their scheme, but their scheme was known to God, even though their scheme was (such as) to remove the mountains by it.'

47 Do not think[62] (that) God is going to break His promise to His messengers. Surely God is mighty, a taker of vengeance. **48** On the Day when the earth will be changed (into something) other (than) the earth, and the heavens (as well), and they will go forth to God, the One, the Supreme, **49** and you will see[63] the sinners on that Day bound together in chains, **50** their clothing (made) of pitch, and the Fire will cover their faces, **51** so that God may repay everyone for what he has earned. Surely God is quick at the reckoning.

52 This is a delivery[64] for the people, and (it is delivered) so that they may be warned by means of it, and that they may know that He is one God, and that those with understanding may take heed.[65]

---

59. *no end for you*: i.e. they swore they would not suffer the same fate as other disobedient peoples before them.
60. *You dwell in the (same) dwelling places...*: this implies that the different peoples of the 'punishment stories' were thought to inhabit successively the same geographical region (see Q14.14 above; cf. Q20.128; 21.11; 32.26).
61. *(how) We struck parables for you*: i.e. how God had made examples of earlier generations.
62. *Do not think*: addressed to the Prophet, or perhaps intended generally ('Let no one think...').
63. *you will see*: addressed to the Prophet, or perhaps intended generally ('one will see...').

52 Conclusion

64. *This is a delivery*: referring to the Qur'ān, either in whole or in part (cf. Q3.20).
65. *take heed*: or 'remember.'

15 Al-Ḥijr ❁ Al-Ḥijr

In the Name of God, the Merciful, the Compassionate

1 Alif Lām Rā'.[1] Those are the signs[2] of the Book and a clear Qur'ān.[3]

2 Perhaps those who disbelieve (will) wish, if they had submitted[4] [...].[5] **3** Leave them[6] (to) eat and enjoy
(themselves), and (let their) hope divert them. Soon they will know! **4** We have not destroyed any town
without its having a known decree.[7] **5** No community precedes its time,[8] nor do they delay (it).

6 They have said: 'You on whom the Reminder[9] has been sent down! Surely you are possessed[10] indeed!
7 Why do you not bring the angels to us,[11] if you are one of the truthful?' **8** We only send down the angels
with the truth,[12] and then they will not be spared. **9** Surely We have sent down the Reminder, and surely
We are indeed its Watchers.[13] **10** Certainly We sent (messengers) before you among the parties of old,
11 yet not one messenger came to them whom they did not mock. **12** In this way We put it into the
hearts[14] of the sinners – **13** they do not believe in it,[15] though the customary way of those of old has

---

Q15: This sūra, assigned by most scholars to the 'Meccan' period, contains accounts of the rebellion of Iblīs (Q15.28-48) and the angels' visits to Abraham and Lot (Q15.49-77). Two short stories of punishment follow: the people of 'the Grove' and the inhabitants of 'al-Ḥijr' (Q15.78-84). Q15 concludes with a series of admonitions to the Prophet.

1 Signs of the Book

1. *Alif Lām Rā'*: the names of Arabic letters ', *l*, and *r*. The same letter combination occurs in a block of sūras from Q10 to Q15 (Q13 has an additional 'mīm'). Twenty-nine sūras begin with letters like these, ranging from one to five. No satisfactory explanation has been given for their occurrence. The Cairo edition varies in counting these letters as a separate verse, or as the beginning of the first verse (as here).
2. *signs*: here referring to the letters ', *l*, and *r* (for the various meanings of 'signs,' see n. on Q2.39).
3. *a clear Qur'ān*: or 'a Qur'ān that makes (things) clear.' Here the Qur'ān is described as an actual 'Book' (see nn. on Q2.2, 185).

2–5 Punishment certain

4. *if they had submitted*: or 'if they had become Muslims.'
5. *[...]*: there appears to be a lacuna here; it may be that the disbelievers will, when faced with punishment, wish they had become Muslims.
6. *Leave them...*: the Prophet is to leave them as they are, since their punishment will come in due time.
7. *decree*: lit. 'book;' the meaning is that every town is punished at the time decreed or written in the 'Book of God' or 'Book of Destiny' (see n. on Q6.59).
8. *time*: or 'term' (Ar. *ajal*); i.e. the time of punishment is predetermined and cannot be changed (cf. Q7.34; 10.49; 23.43).

6–15 Messengers always ridiculed

9. *the Reminder*: referring to the Qur'ān (see n. on Q3.58).
10. *possessed*: or 'jinn-struck' (Ar. *majnūn*); i.e. they accuse the Prophet of being possessed by jinn (see n. on Q7.184).
11. *bring the angels to us*: cf. the similar charge at Q17.92; 25.7 (for the angels and their various roles, see n. on Q2.30).
12. *with the truth*: or 'in truth,' but with the implication of 'judgment' (i.e. when the angels come, they will execute God's judgment and the disbelievers will not be spared).
13. *Watchers*: or 'overseers,' 'keepers.'
14. *hearts*: here, as often, the heart is spoken of as synonymous with mind.
15. *they do not believe in it*: or perhaps 'cannot believe in it' (the Reminder); for this idea, cf. Q2.6-7; 4.155; and Isaiah 6.9-10; Mark 4.11-12.

already passed away.[16] **14** (Even) if We opened on them a gate of the sky,[17] and they[18] were going up through it continually, **15** they would (still) indeed say, 'Our sight is bewildered! No! We are a bewitched people!'[19]

16 Certainly We have made constellations[20] in the sky, and made it appear enticing for the onlookers, **17** and protected it from every accursed satan[21] **18** – except any who (may) steal in to overhear,[22] then a clear flame pursues him.[23] **19** And the earth – We stretched it out, and cast on it firm mountains,[24] and caused everything (that is) weighed to sprout in it. **20** We have made for you a means of living on it, and (for those creatures) for which you are not providers.[25] **21** The storehouses of everything are only with Us, and We send it down only in a known measure. **22** We send the fertilizing winds, and We send down water from the sky and give it to you to drink. You are not the storekeepers of it. **23** Surely We – We indeed give life and cause death, and We are the inheritors. **24** Certainly We know the ones who press forward among you, and certainly We know the ones who lag behind.[26] **25** Surely your Lord – He will gather them. Surely He is wise, knowing.

26 Certainly We created the human from dry clay,[27] from molded mud, **27** and the (ancestor of the) jinn, We created him before (that) from scorching fire.[28]

28 (Remember) when[29] your Lord said to the angels: 'Surely I am going to create a human being from dry clay, from molded mud. **29** When I have fashioned him, and breathed some of My spirit into him,[30] fall down before him in prostration.' **30** So the angels prostrated themselves – all of them together **31** – except Iblīs.[31] He refused to be with the ones who prostrated themselves. **32** He[32] said, 'Iblīs! What is (the matter) with you that you are not with the ones who prostrated themselves?' **33** He[33] said, 'I am not (one) to

16. *...though the customary way of those of old has already passed away*: i.e. they will persist in their sin despite having the example of the 'way' (Ar. *sunna*) God punished earlier generations (cf. Q3.137; 8.38; 18.55; 35.43; 40.85; 48.23).
17. *sky*: or 'heaven.'
18. *they*: could refer either to the disbelievers or the angels (probably the latter).
19. *a bewitched people*: i.e. instead of recognizing the truth, they will claim they have been tricked by magic.

16–25 Signs of God's power and providence

20. *constellations*: lit. 'towers' (i.e. the signs of the zodiac).
21. *accursed satan*: or 'stoned satan' (see n. on Q2.14).
22. *steal in to overhear*: lit. 'steal the hearing;' i.e. they try to find out what is being planned in the heavenly council (cf. Q37.6-10; 72.8-9).
23. *a clear flame pursues him*: the angels drive away such 'eavesdroppers' by hurling shooting stars at them (cf. Q37.9-10; 67.5; 72.8-9).
24. *cast on it firm mountains*: to keep the earth from moving (cf. Q13.3; 16.15; 21.31; 31.10).
25. *for which you are not providers*: i.e. wild animals, which are provided with their own means of survival.
26. *the ones who press forward...lag behind*: or perhaps 'the ones who have gone before...and who (will) come later.'

26–27 The creation of humans and jinn

27. *from dry clay*: likened to 'potter's clay' at Q55.14; cf. Q6.2; 7.12; 17.61; 23.12; 32.7; 38.71, 76; 'from dust,' according to Q3.59; 18.37; 22.5; 30.20; 35.11; 40.67; 'from water,' according to Q21.30; 24.45; 25.54.
28. *scorching fire*: cf. Q55.15; for the jinn, see n. on Q6.100.

28–48 The story of Iblīs

29. *(Remember) when...*: a stock narrative formula; the Arabic particle *idh* often marks the beginning of a story, and means something like 'Once...,' or 'There was a time when...,' or 'Remember when....' For the story that follows, cf. the version at Q38.71-85.
30. *breathed some of My spirit into him*: cf. Q38.72; and Genesis 2.7.
31. *except Iblīs*: for this figure, see n. on Q2.34.
32. *He*: God.
33. *He*: Iblīs.

prostrate myself before a human being whom you have created from dry clay, from molded mud.'[34] **34** He
said, 'Get out of here![35] Surely you are accursed![36] **35** Surely the curse (is going to remain) on you until the
Day of Judgment.' **36** He said, 'My Lord, spare me until the Day when they are raised up.' **37** He said, 'Surely
you are one of the spared **38** – until the Day of the known time.'[37] **39** He said, 'My Lord, because You have
made me err, I shall indeed make (things) appear enticing to them on the earth, and I shall indeed make
them err – all (of them) **40** – except for Your devoted servants[38] among them.' **41** He[39] said, 'This is the
straight path (incumbent) on Me. **42** Surely My servants – you will not have any authority over them, except
for whoever follows you of the ones who are in error. **43** Surely Gehenna[40] is indeed their appointed place –
all (of them). **44** It has seven gates: to each gate a part of them is assigned. **45** (But) surely the ones who guard
(themselves)[41] will be in (the midst of) gardens and springs: **46** "Enter it in peace, secure!" **47** We shall strip
away whatever rancor is in their hearts.[42] (As) brothers (they will recline) on couches, facing each other.
48 No weariness will touch them there, nor will they be expelled from it.'

49 Inform My servants that I am the Forgiving, the Compassionate, **50** and that My punishment is the
painful punishment. **51** And inform them about the guests of Abraham:[43] **52** when they entered upon
him, and said, 'Peace!,' he said, 'Surely we are afraid of you.' **53** They said, 'Do not be afraid. Surely we
give you good news of a knowing boy.'[44] **54** He said, 'Do you give me good news, even though old age has
touched me? What good news do you give me?' **55** They said, 'We give you good news in truth, so do not
be one of the despairing.' **56** He said, 'Who despairs of the mercy of his Lord, except for the ones who go
astray?' **57** He said, 'What is your business, you envoys?'[45] **58** They said, 'Surely we have been sent to a
people who are sinners, **59** except for the house(hold) of Lot. Surely we shall indeed rescue them – all (of
them) **60** – except his wife. We have determined that she indeed (will be) one of those who stay behind.'

61 When the envoys came to the house(hold) of Lot, **62** he said, 'Surely you are a people unknown (to me).'[46]
63 They said, 'No! We have brought you what they were in doubt about.[47] **64** We have brought you the
truth.[48] Surely we are truthful indeed. **65** So journey with your family in a part of the night,[49] but you follow behind them. Let none of you turn around, but proceed where you are commanded.' **66** We decreed for

34. *I am not (one) to prostrate...*: because of his superior 'fiery' nature (cf. Q7.12; 17.61; 38.76).
35. *here*: lit. 'it;' the heavenly Garden or Paradise.
36. *accursed*: or 'stoned.'
37. *the known time*: or 'the appointed time' (i.e. the time of judgment decreed by God; cf. Q15.4-5, 21 above).
38. *servants*: the word 'servant' (Ar. *'abd*) also means 'slave.'
39. *He*: God.
40. *Gehenna*: a name for Hell (see n. on Q2.206).
41. *guard (themselves)*: against evil, or God.
42. *hearts*: lit. 'chests,' considered the seat of emotion as well as knowledge.

49–60 The story of Abraham and his guests

43. *guests of Abraham*: the angels who visited Abraham on their way to destroy Lot's city (see n. on Q11.69); for the story that follows, cf. the versions at Q11.69-76; 51.24-37; and Genesis 18.1-33.
44. *knowing boy*: or perhaps 'cunning boy' (Isaac); cf. Q51.28.
45. *envoys*: a designation roughly equivalent to 'messengers,' and here used of the angels.

61–77 The story of Lot and his people

46. *a people unknown (to me)*: and therefore a potential threat; for the story that follows; cf. the versions at Q11.77-83; 26.160-173; and Genesis 19.1-29.
47. *what they were in doubt about*: the threat of judgment and destruction which Lot's people doubted.
48. *truth*: perhaps in the sense of 'judgment' (cf. Q15.8 above).
49. *So journey with your family in a part of the night*: cf. the similar descriptions of the famous 'night journey' (Q17.1) and of Moses' departure from Egypt (Q20.77; 26.52; 44.23).

him that command, that the last remnant of these (people) would be cut off in the morning. **67** The people of the city[50] came welcoming the good news.[51] **68** He said, 'Surely these are my guests, so do not shame me. **69** Guard (yourselves) against God, and do not disgrace me.' **70** They said, 'Did we not forbid you from the worlds?'[52] **71** He said, 'These are my daughters, if you would do (it).'[53] **72** By your life![54] Surely they were wandering blindly in their drunkenness. **73** So the cry[55] seized them at sunrise. **74** We turned (the city) upside down and rained on them stones of baked clay. **75** Surely in that are signs indeed for the discerning. **76** Surely it is indeed on a (path)way (which still) exists.[56] **77** Surely in that is a sign indeed for the believers.

78 The people of the Grove[57] were evildoers indeed, **79** so We took vengeance on them. Surely both of them[58] are indeed in a clear record.[59]

80 Certainly the people of al-Ḥijr[60] called the envoys liars. **81** We gave them Our signs, but they turned away from it. **82** They carved secure houses out of the mountains, **83** but the cry seized them in the morning. **84** What they had earned[61] was of no use to them.

85 We did not create the heavens and the earth, and whatever is between them, except in truth.[62] Surely the Hour[63] is coming indeed, so excuse (them) gracefully.[64] **86** Surely your Lord – He is the Creator, the Knowing.

87 Certainly We have given you[65] seven of the oft-repeated (stories),[66] and the great Qur'ān.

88 Do not yearn after[67] what We have given classes of them to enjoy,[68] and do not sorrow over them, but

---

50. *the city*: Lot's city was Sodom, according to Genesis 19.1.
51. *welcoming the good news*: because they were interested in having sex with Lot's 'visitors.'
52. *forbid you from the worlds*: meaning obscure; cf. the different versions of their statement at Q7.82; 11.79.
53. *...if you would do (it)*: i.e. have sex with them; to hand over his 'guests' (the angels) would have been shameful, so Lot offers his daughters instead (cf. Genesis 19.8).
54. *By your life*: God swears by the Prophet.
55. *the cry*: cf. Q11.67 (Thamūd), 94 (Midian).
56. *...(which still) exists*: i.e. the remains of the destroyed city were still visible.

78–84 Stories of the Grove and al-Ḥijr

57. *people of the Grove*: or 'companions of the Thicket' (Ar. *al-ayka*); this may be an alternative name for the people of Midian, since both have the same messenger, Shu'ayb (Q26.176-189; cf. Q38.13; 50.14).
58. *both of them*: referring to the peoples of Lot and the Grove.
59. *record*: lit. 'leader' or 'model' (Ar. *imām*), but probably referring to the 'record' of their deeds which will make clear their sin (cf. Q17.71; 36.12).
60. *people of al-Ḥijr*: otherwise unknown, but they may correspond to the people of Thamūd (cf. the references to their 'carving out' houses at Q7.74; 26.149, with 15.82 below).
61. *what they had earned*: their wealth and possessions.

85–86 Judgment is certain

62. *in truth*: or 'with the truth,' but here almost meaning 'for the purpose of judgment,' as the following words indicate (cf. Q30.8; 44.39; 46.3).
63. *the Hour*: of judgment, which appears imminent (cf. Q20.15; 22.7; 40.59).
64. *excuse (them) gracefully*: the Prophet is to forgive what the disbelievers have done to him.

87–99 Encouragement to the Prophet

65. *you*: the Prophet.
66. *the oft-repeated (stories)*: or 'the repetitions.' The meaning of this word (Ar. *al-mathānī*) is uncertain (both here and at Q39.23), but it probably refers to the stories of previous peoples who were punished for rejecting their messengers. Although the peoples vary, the seven main ones are: the peoples of 'Ād, Thamūd, and Midian, and the peoples of Noah, Abraham, Lot, and Moses (see n. on Q7.59).
67. *Do not yearn after*: lit. 'Do not extend your eyes toward' (addressed to the Prophet).
68. *what We have given classes of them to enjoy*: probably wealth, but the word 'classes' (Ar. *azwāj*) may mean 'pairs'

lower your wing[69] to the believers, **89** and say: 'Surely I am the clear warner.'[70]

90 – As We have sent (it) down on the dividers,[71] **91** those who have cut the Qur'ān (into) parts.[72]
92 By your Lord![73] We shall indeed question them all **93** about what they have done.

94 Break forth with what you are commanded, and turn away from the idolaters.[74] **95** Surely We are
sufficient for you (against) the mockers, **96** who set up[75] another god with God. Soon they will know!
97 Certainly We know that you – your heart[76] is distressed by what they say. **98** Glorify your Lord with
praise, and be one of those who prostrate themselves, **99** and serve your Lord, until the certainty[77]
comes to you.

---

or 'couples,' in which case 'what We have given them' would refer to sons.

69. *lower your wing*: i.e. 'take under your protection' or 'treat with kindness.'
70. *the clear warner*: or 'the warner who makes (things) clear;' for this role, see n. on Q2.119.
71. *the dividers*: reference obscure; perhaps the Jews and Christians who have 'divided up' the scriptures by accepting some parts of the revelation and rejecting other parts (cf. Q23.53; 30.32; and see following n.). This section (Q15.90-93) may have originally followed Q15.87.
72. *those who have cut the Qur'ān (into) parts*: meaning obscure (lit. 'who have made the Qur'ān parts'); perhaps Muslims who accepted some parts of the Qur'ān but rejected other parts; or it may just be another way of referring to the 'dividing up' of the scriptures on the part of Jews and Christians. If so, the meaning of 'the Qur'ān' here would have the sense of 'the totality of revelation' (see n. on Q2.185).
73. *By your Lord*: for God's unusual 'swearing by himself,' cf. Q4.65; 16.56, 63; 19.68; 70.40; and Hebrews 6.13 (Genesis 22.16); but perhaps it is the angels who are speaking here.
74. *the idolaters*: or 'the ones who associate (other gods with God).'
75. *set up*: lit. 'make.'
76. *heart*: lit. 'chest,' considered the seat of knowledge and understanding.
77. *the certainty*: referring to death or judgment (cf. Q74.46-47; 102.5, 7).

16 The Bee ✽ Al-Naḥl

In the Name of God, the Merciful, the Compassionate

1 The command of God has come![1] Do not seek to hurry it.[2] Glory to Him! He is exalted above what they associate.[3]

2 He sends down the angels[4] with the spirit of His command[5] on whomever He pleases of His servants:[6] 'Give warning that (there is) no god but Me, so guard (yourselves) against Me!'

3 He created the heavens and the earth in truth.[7] He is exalted above what they associate. **4** He created
the human from a drop,[8] and suddenly he (becomes) a clear adversary. **5** And the cattle[9] – He created
them for you. (There is) warmth in them and (other) benefits, and from them you eat. **6** And (there is)
beauty in them for you, when you bring them in and when you lead them out. **7** They carry your loads to
a land you would (otherwise) not reach without exhausting yourselves. Surely your Lord is indeed kind,
compassionate. **8** (He also created) horses and mules and donkeys for you to ride, and for display. And
He creates what you do not know. **9** (It is incumbent) on God (to set the) direction of the way, yet (there
is) deviation from it. If He had (so) pleased, He would indeed have guided you all.[10]

10 He (it is) who sends down water from the sky. From it you have (something to) drink, and from it
vegetation (grows) on which you pasture (livestock). **11** By means of it He causes the crops to grow for

---

Q16: This sūra treats a variety of topics and themes. In general it extols God's creative power and condemns the foolishness of idolatry. It takes its title from the reference to the bees (Q16.68-69), which are 'inspired' by God and only one of many signs of his providence. A later section (Q16.98-105) sheds important light on the recitation and revelation of the Qur'ān. While most scholars assign Q16 to the late 'Meccan' period, some contend that it is an amalgam of materials from various periods. Some traditional scholars consider only the first part 'Meccan,' and assign the latter part (Q16.106-128) to Medina. The Cairo edition considers it late 'Meccan,' except for the final three verses.

1 Judgment imminent

1. *The command of God has come*: God's 'command' often refers to judgment (cf. Q2.109; 4.47; 5.52; 7.150; 10.24; 16.33 below).
2. *Do not seek to hurry it*: plur. imperative; probably intended ironically, since judgment is at hand (cf. Q6.57-58; 13.6; 10.50; 22.47; 26.205; 29.53-54; 37.176).
3. *what they associate*: other gods with God.

2 Spirit of revelation

4. *angels*: for these beings and their various roles, see n. on Q2.30.
5. *with the spirit of His command*: or 'with the spirit from His command' (Ar. *bil-rūḥi min amrihī*). This seems to indicate the mode of revelation as much as the fact of it. The mysterious being called 'the spirit' (cf. below Q16.102, 'the holy spirit;' 26.193, 'the trustworthy spirit') appears to be the bearer of revelation in the company of the angels (cf. Q97.4). Some interpreters identify 'the spirit' with Gabriel (see n. on Q2.97). God's 'command' (Ar. *amr*) may correspond to the rabbinic notion of the 'divine word' (Aram. *mēmrā*), or to the related Christian idea of the *logos* as the manifestation of God's word, or as God's messenger in place of God himself (cf. Q17.85; 40.15; 42.52).
6. *servants*: the word 'servant' (Ar. *'abd*) also means 'slave.'

3–18 Signs of God's power and providence

7. *in truth*: or 'with the truth.'
8. *a drop*: of semen.
9. *cattle*: or 'livestock' in general.
10. *guided you all*: for this idea, see n. on Q2.213; cf. Q10.19; 11.118.

you, and (also) olives, and date palms, and grapes, and all (kinds of) fruit. Surely in that is a sign[11] indeed for a people who reflect. **12** He subjected the night and the day for you, and the sun and the moon, and the stars (are) subjected by His command. Surely in that are signs indeed for a people who understand. **13** And whatever He has scattered[12] for you on the earth (with) its various colors – surely in that is a sign indeed for a people who take heed.[13] **14** He (it is) who subjected the sea, so that you may eat fresh fish[14] from it, and bring out of it an ornament[15] which you wear, and you[16] see the ship cutting through it, and (it is) so that you[17] may seek some of His favor,[18] and that you may be thankful. **15** And He cast on the earth firm mountains, so that it does not sway with you (on it),[19] and rivers and (path)ways, that you may guide yourselves, **16** and landmarks (too). And by the stars they guide (themselves). **17** Is the One who creates like the one who does not create? Will you not take heed? **18** If you (try to) number God's blessing, you will not (be able to) count it. Surely God is indeed forgiving, compassionate.

19 God knows what you keep secret and what you speak aloud. **20** Those they call on instead of God do not create anything, since they are (themselves) created. **21** (They are) dead, not alive, and they do not realize when they will be raised.[20] **22** Your God is one God. Those who do not believe in the Hereafter[21] – their hearts[22] are defiant, and they are arrogant. **23** (There is) no doubt that God knows what they keep secret and what they speak aloud. Surely He does not love the arrogant.

24 When it is said to them, 'What has your Lord sent down?,' they say, 'Old tales!'[23] **25** – that they may bear their own burdens fully on the Day of Resurrection, and (also) some of the burdens of those whom they led astray without (their) realizing (it). Evil is what they will bear! **26** Those who were before them schemed, but God came (against) their building from the foundations,[24] and the roof fell down on them from above them, and the punishment came upon them from where they did not realize (it would). **27** Then on the Day of Resurrection He will disgrace them, and say, 'Where are My associates[25] for whose sake you broke away?'[26] Those who were given the knowledge[27] will say, 'Surely today disgrace and evil are on the

---

11. *sign*: of God's power and providence (see n. on Q2.39).
12. *scattered*: as a sower scatters seed, but here referring to the creation of animals and plants.
13. *take heed*: or 'are reminded,' 'remember.'
14. *fish*: lit. 'flesh,' 'meat.'
15. *ornament*: such as pearls and coral (see Q55.22).
16. *you*: sudden switch to sing. ('and one sees...').
17. *you*: switch back to plur.
18. *seek some of His favor*: i.e. seek to make a livelihood.
19. *so that it does not sway...*: i.e. the earth would move if it were not held in place by mountains.

19–23 God knows all

20. *they do not realize when they will be raised*: i.e. their gods do not know when the disbelievers will be raised.
21. *the Hereafter*: see n. on Q2.4.
22. *their hearts*: here, as often, the heart is spoken of as synonymous with mind.

24–29 A judgment scene: disbelievers

23. *Old tales*: or 'Tales of the ancients;' a contemptuous reference to the stories of earlier generations who were punished for disobeying their prophets (see n. on Q7.59; cf. Q25.5).
24. *came (against) their building from the foundations*: perhaps an allusion to the story of the 'tower of Babel' (Genesis 11.1-9), or to the 'tower' Pharaoh intended to build (Q28.38).
25. *My associates*: or 'My partners;' i.e. the gods of the disbelievers (cf. Q6.22-24; 10.28-30).
26. *for whose sake you broke away*: i.e. they opposed the messenger on behalf of their so-called gods.
27. *Those who were given the knowledge*: i.e. the believers, who comment on the coming judgment of the disbelievers.

disbelievers, **28** those who – the angels take them[28] (while they are doing) themselves evil.' They[29] will offer peace:[30] 'We were not doing anything evil.' 'Yes indeed (you were)! Surely God is aware of what you have done. **29** So enter the gates of Gehenna,[31] there to remain. Evil indeed is the dwelling place of the arrogant!'

30 And it is said to those who guard (themselves),[32] 'What has your Lord sent down?' They say, 'Good!' For those who do good in this world (there is) good, but the Home of the Hereafter is indeed better. Excellent indeed is the Home of the ones who guard (themselves) **31** – Gardens of Eden,[33] which they will enter, through which rivers flow, where they will have whatever they please. In this way God repays the ones who guard (themselves), **32** those who – the angels take them (while they are doing) good. They will say, 'Peace (be) upon you! Enter the Garden for what you have done.'

33 Do they[34] expect (anything) but the angels to come to them, or the command[35] of your Lord to come? So did those who were before them. God did not do them evil, but they did themselves evil. **34** So the evils of what they had done smote them, and what they were mocking[36] overwhelmed them.

35 The idolaters[37] say, 'If God had (so) pleased, we would not have served[38] anything other than Him, neither we nor our fathers, and we would not have forbidden anything other than Him.'[39] So did those who were before them. (Does anything depend) on the messengers except the clear delivery (of the message)? **36** Certainly We have raised up in every community a messenger (saying): 'Serve God and avoid al-Ṭāghūt!'[40] (There were) some of them whom God guided, and some whose going astray was deserved.[41] Travel the earth and see how the end was for the ones who called (it) a lie.[42] **37** If you[43] are eager for their guidance – surely God does not guide those whom He leads astray. They will have no helpers.

38 They have sworn by God the most solemn of their oaths: 'God will not raise up anyone who dies!' Yes indeed! (It is) a promise (binding) on Him in truth, but most of the people do not know (it). **39** (They will

28. *take them*: in death (see n. on Q6.61).
29. *They*: the disbelievers.
30. *offer peace*: lit. 'cast the peace' (Ar. *al-salām*), a distinctive Muslim greeting, with the implication of submission (*islām*) to God (cf. Q16.87 below).
31. *Gehenna*: a name for Hell (see n. on Q2.206).

30–32 A judgment scene: believers

32. *guard (themselves)*: against evil, or God.
33. *Gardens of Eden*: in heaven (for this imagery, see n. on Q2.25).

33–34 Disbelievers only harm themselves

34. *they...*: the disbelievers (these two verses appear to be dislocated, and may have originally followed Q16.23).
35. *command*: here referring to judgment (cf. Q2.109; 4.47; 5.52; 7.150; 10.24; 16.1 above).
36. *what they were mocking*: the threat of judgment and destruction.

35–37 Idolaters have no excuse

37. *the idolaters*: or 'those who associate (other gods with God).'
38. *served*: or 'worshipped.'
39. *forbidden anything other than Him*: i.e. they would not have forbidden anything apart from what He had forbidden (cf. Q6.138-139, 148-150; 10.48-60).
40. *al-Ṭāghūt*: perhaps '(other) gods' or 'idols' (cf. Q2.256; 39.17), but sometimes taken as a proper name (see Q4.60, 76, where it appears to be another name for Satan). It may be related to the word for 'gods' in Ethiop. (*ṭāʿōt*).
41. *whose going astray was deserved*: or 'who were rightly destined to go astray' (cf. Q7.30)
42. *...who called (it) a lie*: i.e. who rejected the warning of imminent judgment; the remains of their destroyed cities were believed to be still visible (cf. Q3.137; 6.11, 148; 43.25; see n. on Q7.59).
43. *you*: the Prophet.

38–40 Resurrection certain

be raised) so that He may make clear their differences to them, and so that those who disbelieved may know that they were liars. **40** Our only word to a thing, when We intend it, is that We say to it, 'Be!'[44] and it is.

41 Those who emigrate[45] in (the way of) God, after they have been done evil – We shall indeed give them a good settlement in this world, but the reward of the Hereafter is indeed greater, if (only) they knew. **42** (They are) those who are patient and put their trust in their Lord.

43 We have not sent (anyone) before you[46] except men whom We inspired – just ask the People of the Reminder,[47] if you do not know (it) – **44** with the clear signs[48] and the scriptures,[49] and We have sent down to you the Reminder,[50] so that you may make clear to the people what has been sent down to them,[51] and that they will reflect.

45 Do those who have schemed evils feel secure that God will not cause the earth to swallow them, or that the punishment will not come upon them from where they do not realize? **46** Or that He will not seize them in their comings and goings, and they will not be able to escape? **47** Or that He will not seize them with a (sudden) fright? Surely your Lord is indeed kind, compassionate.

48 Do they not see anything of what God has created? (How) its shadows revolve from the right and the left, prostrating themselves before God, and they are humble? **49** Whatever is in the heavens and whatever is on the earth prostrates itself before God – every living creature and the angels (too) – and they are not arrogant. **50** They fear their Lord above them, and they do what they are commanded.

51 God has said: 'Do not take two gods.[52] He is only one God. So Me – fear Me (alone)!' **52** To Him (belongs) whatever is in the heavens and the earth, and to Him (belongs) the religion forever. Will you guard (yourselves) against (anyone) other than God? **53** Whatever blessing you have is from God. Then when hardship touches you, (it is) to Him you cry out. **54** Then when He removes the hardship from you, suddenly a group of you associates with their Lord,[53] **55** to show ingratitude for what We have given them. Enjoy (yourselves)! Soon you will know!

---

44. *Be!*: God's creative word (Ar. *kun*); cf. Q2.117; 3.47 (to Mary), 59 (of Jesus and Adam); 6.73; 19.35; 36.82; 40.68.

41–42 Rewards for the emigrants

45. *Those who emigrate*: from Mecca to Medina, though this is not explicitly stated in the Qur'ān.

43–44 Messengers and their Books

46. *you*: the Prophet.
47. *People of the Reminder*: i.e. Jews and Christians, who already had 'scriptures' or a 'Book;' on the analogy of 'people of the Book' (cf. Q21.7)
48. *the clear signs*: or 'the clear proofs,' 'the indisputable evidence.'
49. *the scriptures*: Ar. *al-zubur*; cf. Q3.184; 23.53; 26.196; 35.25; 54.43, 52 (where it seems to refer to the 'Book of Destiny').
50. *the Reminder*: referring to the Qur'ān (see n. on Q3.58).
51. *make clear to the people what has been sent down to them*: perhaps implying that one of the purposes of the Qur'ān is to make possible the proper interpretation of previous Books (cf. the Christian claim that the 'Old Testament' can only be understood in light of the New Testament).

45–47 False sense of security

48–50 All creation fears God

51–55 God is one

52. *Do not take two gods*: plur. imperative; the dual 'two gods' is curious, but it probably refers to the Christian attribution of divinity to Jesus and exaltation of Mary (see Q5.72-75, 116; cf. Q4.171).
53. *associates with their Lord*: i.e. associates other gods with God.

56 They assign[54] to what they do not know a portion of what We have provided them.[55] By God![56] Surely you will indeed be questioned about what you have forged. **57** And they assign daughters to God[57] – glory to Him! – and to themselves (they assign) what they desire.[58] **58** When one of them is given news of a female (child), his face turns dark and he chokes back his disappointment. **59** He hides himself from the people because of the evil of what he has been given news about. Should he keep it in humiliation or bury it in the dust?[59] Is it not evil what they judge? **60** An evil parable[60] (is fitting) for those who do not believe in the Hereafter, but (only) the highest parable (is fitting) for God. He is the Mighty, the Wise.

61 If God were to take the people to task for their evildoing, He would not leave on it[61] any living creature. But He is sparing them until an appointed time.[62] When their time comes, they will not delay (it) by an hour, nor will they advance (it by an hour). **62** They assign to God what they (themselves) dislike,[63] and their tongues allege the lie that the best is for them.[64] (There is) no doubt that the Fire (is fitting) for them, and that they (will) be rushed (into it).

63 By God! Certainly We sent messengers to communities before you,[65] but Satan[66] made their deeds appear enticing to them. So he is their ally today, and for them (there is) a painful punishment. **64** We have not sent down on you the Book,[67] except for you to make clear their differences[68] to them, and (We have sent it down) as a guidance[69] and mercy for a people who believe.

65 (It is) God (who) sends down water from the sky, and by means of it gives the earth life after its death. Surely in that is a sign indeed for a people who hear. **66** And surely in the cattle[70] is a lesson indeed for you: We give you to drink from what is in their bellies – between excretions and blood – pure milk, pleasant tasting to the drinkers. **67** And from the fruits of the date palms and the grapes, from which you take an intoxicating drink[71] and a good provision – surely in that is a sign indeed for a people who understand.

56–64 Idolatry and infanticide condemned

54. *assign*: lit. 'make.'
55. *...a portion of what We have provided them*: i.e. they offer to others what God alone has given them (cf. Q6.136).
56. *By God*: for God's unusual 'swearing by himself,' cf. Q4.65; 15.92; 16.63; 19.68; 70.40; and Hebrews 6.13 (Genesis 22.16); but perhaps it is the angels who are speaking here.
57. *they assign daughters to God*: for the belief that the angels were 'daughters of God,' see Q17.40; 37.149-153; 43.19; 53.27; cf. Q53.19-23.
58. *what they desire*: i.e. sons, regarded as preferable to daughters, as the following verses make clear (cf. Q52.39; 53.21-22).
59. *bury it in the dust*: referring to the practice of female infanticide (see Q81.8-9; cf. Q6.137, 140, 151; 17.31; 60.12).
60. *parable*: or 'comparison.'
61. *it*: the earth.
62. *an appointed time*: or 'term' (Ar. *ajal*), i.e. the precise date of judgment is predetermined and cannot be changed.
63. *what they (themselves) dislike*: i.e. daughters.
64. *the best is for them*: i.e. sons.
65. *you*: the Prophet.
66. *Satan*: for this figure, see n. on Q2.36.
67. *the Book*: the Qur'ān.
68. *their differences*: this probably refers to conflicts between Jews and Christians (cf. Q16.43-44 above).
69. *guidance*: one of the most frequent terms (Ar. *hudā*) for revelation in general, and the Qur'ān in particular.

65–74 Signs of God's power and providence

70. *cattle*: or 'livestock' in general.
71. *an intoxicating drink*: Ar. *sakar* occurs only here, but the other words derived from it are all connected to drunkenness (see Q4.43; 15.72; 22.2; 50.19).

68 And your Lord inspired the bee:[72] 'Make hives[73] among the mountains, and among the trees, and among what they construct. **69** Then eat from all the fruits, and follow the ways of your Lord subserviently.'[74] (There) comes forth from their bellies[75] a drink of various colors,[76] in which (there is) healing for the people. Surely in that is a sign indeed for a people who reflect.

70 (It is) God (who) creates you. Then He will take you.[77] But among you (there is) one who is reduced to the worst (stage) of life,[78] so that he knows nothing after (having had) knowledge. Surely God is knowing, powerful.

71 God has favored some of you over others in the (matter of) provision, but those who have been favored do not give over their provision to what their right (hands) own,[79] so (that) they are (all) equal in that respect.[80] Is it the blessing of God they deny? **72** God has given you wives from yourselves, and from your wives He has given you sons and grandsons, and He has provided you with good things. Do they believe in falsehood,[81] and do they disbelieve in the blessing of God? **73** Do they serve, instead of God, what has no power to provide anything for them from the heavens or the earth, nor are they able (to do anything)? **74** Do not strike any parables for God.[82] Surely God knows and you do not know.

75 God strikes a parable: a slave (who is) owned – he has no power over anything – and (another) whom We have provided with a good provision from Us, and he contributes[83] from it in secret and in public. Are they equal? Praise (be)[84] to God! No! But most of them do not know (it).

76 God strikes a parable: two men, one of them cannot speak – he has no power over anything, and he is a burden on his master[85] – wherever he directs him, he does not bring (back anything) good. Is he equal to the one who commands justice and is himself on a straight path?

77 To God (belongs) the unseen[86] of the heavens and the earth, and the affair of the Hour[87] is only like a blink of the eye, or it is nearer.[88] Surely God is powerful over everything.

---

72. *inspired the bee*: the technical term 'to inspire' (Ar. *awḥā*) is here used of God's assigning the bees their special tasks (cf. Q41.12).
73. *Make hives*: lit. 'Take houses.'
74. *subserviently*: or '(which are made) subservient (to you);' cf. Q36.72; 67.15.
75. *their bellies*: lit. 'its bellies.'
76. *a drink of various colors*: honey.
77. *take you*: in death.
78. *the worst (stage) of life*: old age.
79. *what their right (hands) own*: slaves.
80. *in that respect*: lit. 'in it;' the point seems to be that just as a master does not treat his slaves alike, so God does not treat his servants alike.
81. *falsehood*: lit. 'the falsehood' (i.e. the existence of false gods).
82. *Do not strike any parables for God*: i.e. do not make any comparisons for an incomparable God (cf. Q36.78), probably in the sense of 'associating other gods with God.'

75–76 Two parables

83. *contributes*: lit. 'spends' (for those in need or for the cause).
84. *(be)*: or '(belongs).'
85. *master*: or 'protector.'

77 The Hour

86. *the unseen*: here referring to 'the future' (see n. on Q2.3).
87. *affair of the Hour*: or 'command of the Hour' (i.e. judgment; cf. Q16.33 above).
88. *a blink of the eye, or...nearer*: stressing the imminence of judgment (see Q54.50; cf. 1 Corinthians 15.52).

78 (It is) God (who) brought you forth from the bellies of your mothers – you did not know a thing – and made for you hearing and sight and hearts,[89] so that you may be thankful. **79** Do they not see the birds, subjected[90] in the midst of the sky? No one holds them (up) but God. Surely in that are signs indeed for a people who believe.

80 God has made (a place of) rest for you from your houses, and made houses for you from the skins of the livestock, which you find light (to carry) on the day of your departure and on the day of your encampment. And from their wool and their fur and their hair (He has made for you) furnishings and enjoyment for a time.

81 God has made (places of) shade for you from what He has created, and made (places of) cover for you from the mountains, and made clothing for you to guard you from the heat, and clothing to guard you from your (own) violence. In this way He completes His blessing on you, so that you will submit. **82** If they turn away – only (dependent) on you[91] is the clear delivery (of the message). **83** They recognize the blessing of God, (and) then they reject it. Most of them are ungrateful.[92]

84 On the Day when We raise up a witness from every community, then no permission (to speak) will be given to those who have disbelieved, nor will they be allowed to make amends. **85** When those who have done evil see the punishment, it will not be lightened for them, nor will they be spared.

86 When those who were idolaters see their associates,[93] they will say, 'Our Lord, these are our associates, on whom we used to call instead of You.' But they[94] will cast (back) at them the word: 'Surely you are liars indeed!'
87 And they[95] will offer peace[96] to God on that Day, and (then) what they have forged will abandon them.[97]

88 Those who disbelieve and keep (people) from the way of God – We shall increase them in punishment upon punishment because they were fomenting corruption.

89 On the Day when We raise up in every community a witness against them from among them, and bring you as a witness against these (people) [...].[98] We have sent down on you the Book as an explanation for everything, and as a guidance and mercy, and as good news for those who submit.[99]

90 Surely God commands justice and good, and giving to family, and He forbids immorality, and wrong, and envy. He admonishes you so that you may take heed.

91 Fulfill the covenant of God, when you have made a covenant, and do not break (your) oaths after their confirmation, when you have made God a guarantor over you. Surely God is aware of what you do.

78–83 Signs of God's power and providence

89. *hearts*: i.e. minds.
90. *subjected*: by God for the benefit of humans (cf. Q16.12 above).
91. *you*: the Prophet.
92. *ungrateful*: or 'disbelievers' (perhaps a pun).

84–89 Judgment scenes

93. *their associates*: i.e. their gods (whom the idolaters 'associated' with God).
94. *they*: their gods.
95. *they*: the disbelievers.
96. *offer peace*: lit. 'cast the peace' (Ar. *al-salām*), a distinctive Muslim greeting, with the implication of submission (*islām*) to God (cf. Q16.28 above).
97. *abandon them*: lit. 'go astray from them' (a pun).
98. *bring you as a witness against these (people) [...]*: the Prophet will testify against his own people, as other messengers will testify against their peoples (cf. Q16.84 above); but there appears to be a lacuna here.
99. *those who submit*: or 'the Muslims.'

90 God commands justice

91–97 Oaths and covenants

92 Do not be like the one who unraveled her yarn, after (it was) firmly spun,[100] (into) broken strands, (by) taking your oaths as a (means of) deception between you, because (one) community is more numerous than (another) community.[101] God is only testing you by means of it. He will indeed make clear to you your differences on the Day of Resurrection. **93** If God had (so) pleased, He would indeed have made you one community,[102] but He leads astray whomever He pleases and guides whomever He pleases. You will indeed be questioned about what you have done.

94 Do not take your oaths as a (means of) deception between you, so that a foot should slip after its standing firm, and you taste evil for having kept (people) from the way of God, and (there be) for you a great punishment. **95** Do not sell the covenant of God for a small price. Surely what is with God is better for you, if (only) you knew. **96** What is with you fails, but what is with God lasts, and We shall indeed pay those who are patient their reward for the best of what they have done. **97** Whoever does righteousness – whether male or female – and he is a believer – We shall indeed give him a good life, and We shall indeed pay them their reward for the best of what they have done.

98 When you recite the Qur'ān,[103] take refuge with God from the accursed Satan.[104] **99** Surely he has no authority over those who believe and put their trust in their Lord. **100** His authority is only over those who take him as an ally, and those who associate (other gods) with Him.

101 When We exchange a verse in place of (another) verse[105] – and God knows what He sends down – they say, 'You are only a forger!' No! But most of them do not know (anything).

102 Say:[106] 'The holy spirit[107] has brought it down[108] from your Lord in truth,[109] to make firm those who believe, and as a guidance and good news for those who submit.'[110] **103** Certainly We know that they say, 'Only a human being teaches him.'[111] The language of the one to whom they perversely allude is foreign,

100. *firmly spun*: lit. 'strong;' the simile looks like it refers to an actual person (an allusion to Penelope[?] in Homer's *Odyssey*), but it may just be proverbial.

101. *...because (one) community is more numerous than (another) community*: meaning obscure.

102. *one community*: for this idea, see n. on Q2.213.

98–100 Recitation of the Qur'ān

103. *When you recite the Qur'ān*: this seems to refer to an actual edition of the Qur'ān in the Prophet's possession, which he is commanded to 'recite' or 'read aloud' (cf. Q17.45; 27.91-92)

104. *take refuge...from the accursed Satan*: referring to the possibility that Satan might insert words into the revelation (see Q22.52n.).

101 Alterations in the Qur'ān

105. *When We exchange a verse...*: this is usually understood as referring to cases where one verse has been 'abrogated' by another (see n. on Q2.106; cf. Q13.39; 22.52).

102–105 Revelation of the Qur'ān

106. *Say*: on this form of address, see n. on Q2.80.

107. *The holy spirit*: or 'spirit of holiness' (Ar. *rūḥ al-qudus*); for 'the spirit' as the bearer of revelation, see n. on Q16.2 above; cf. Q26.193 ('the trustworthy spirit'); 40.15; 42.52 ('spirit of Our command').

108. *brought it down*: the Qur'ān (cf. Q2.97, Gabriel 'brought it down').

109. *in truth*: or 'with the truth.'

110. *those who submit*: or 'the Muslims.'

111. *Only a human being teaches him*: cf. Q25.4-5: 'He has forged it, and other people have helped him with it. (...) He has written it down, and it is dictated to him morning and evening.' Later tradition supplies various names (e.g. of Christian or Jewish slaves) for the person alleged to have helped the Prophet produce the Qur'ān. This verse insists that the person in question could not have helped with the 'clear' Arabic of the Qur'ān, since he was a 'foreigner' (Ar. *a'jamī*); cf. Q26.195, 198-199; 41.44.

but this language is clear Arabic.[112] **104** Surely those who do not believe in the signs[113] of God – God will not guide them, and for them (there is) a painful punishment. **105** Only they forge lies who do not believe in the signs of God. Those – they are the liars!

106 Whoever disbelieves in God after having believed – except for someone who is compelled, yet his heart is (still) secure in belief – and whoever expands his heart[114] in disbelief – on them is anger from God, and for them (there is) a great punishment. **107** That is because they loved this present life over the Hereafter, and because God does not guide the disbelievers. **108** Those – God has set a seal on their hearts and their hearing and their sight.[115] And those – they are the oblivious. **109** (There is) no doubt that in the Hereafter they (will be) the losers.

110 Then surely your Lord – to those who emigrated after having been persecuted,[116] (and) then struggled and were patient – surely your Lord after that is indeed forgiving, compassionate, **111** on the Day when each person will come disputing on his own behalf, and each person will be paid in full for what he has done – and they will not be done evil.

112 God strikes a parable: a town was secure (and) at rest, its provision coming to it in abundance from every place, but it was ungrateful for the blessings of God. So God caused it to wear[117] the clothing of hunger and fear for what they[118] had been doing. **113** Certainly a messenger had come to them from among them, but they called him a liar. So the punishment seized them while they were doing evil.

114 Eat from what God has provided you as permitted[119] (and) good, and be thankful for the blessing of God, if it is Him you serve. **115** He has only forbidden you: the dead (animal),[120] and the blood,[121] and swine's flesh,[122] and what has been dedicated to (a god) other than God.'[123] But whoever is forced (by necessity),[124] not desiring or (deliberately) transgressing – surely God is forgiving, compassionate. **116** (As) for what your tongues (may) allege, do not speak the (following) lie: 'This is permitted but that is forbidden,' so that you forge lies against God. Surely those who forge lies against God – they will not prosper. **117** A little enjoyment (of life), and (then) for them (there is) a painful punishment.

118 To those who are Jews,[125] We have forbidden what We recounted to you before.[126] We did not do

---

112. *this language is clear Arabic*: or 'this language is Arabic, making (things) clear.'

113. *signs*: here probably 'verses' (see n. on Q2.39).

106–109 Punishment for apostasy

114. *expands his heart*: lit. 'expands his chest' (i.e. 'opens his mind').

115. *God has set a seal...*: for this idea, see Q2.6-7; 4.155; cf. Isaiah 6.9-10; Mark 4.11-12.

110–111 Rewards for the emigrants

116. *persecuted*: or 'tested.'

112–113 A parable of disbelief

117. *wear*: lit. 'taste.'

118. *they*: the town's inhabitants.

114–119 Regulations concerning food

119. *permitted*: Ar. *ḥalāl*.

120. *the dead (animal)*: i.e. 'carrion;' cf. Leviticus 17.15.

121. *the blood*: cf. Genesis 9.4; Leviticus 17.10-12; Acts 15.29.

122. *swine's flesh*: cf. Leviticus 11.7; Deuteronomy 14.8.

123. *dedicated to (a god) other than God*: i.e. what has been sacrificed or dedicated to 'other gods' (see Q2.173; 5.3; 6.145; cf. Acts 15.29; 1 Corinthians 8.1-13; 10.23-30).

124. *forced (by necessity)*: i.e. compelled to eat something forbidden.

125. *those who are Jews*: lit. 'those who have judaized,' or follow Jewish law, punning on the name Yahūd.

126. *what We recounted to you before*: see Q6.146; the additional food restrictions of the Jews are regarded as a

them evil, but they did themselves evil. **119** Then surely your Lord – to those who have done evil in ignorance, (and) then repented and set (things) right – surely your Lord after that is indeed forgiving, compassionate.

120 Surely Abraham was a community[127] obedient before God – a Ḥanīf[128] – yet he was not one of the idolaters. **121** (He was) thankful for His blessings. He[129] chose him and guided him to a straight path. **122** We[130] gave him good in this world, and surely in the Hereafter he will indeed be among the righteous. **123** Then We inspired you:[131] 'Follow the creed of Abraham the Ḥanīf.[132] He was not one of the idolaters.'

124 The sabbath was only made for those who differed concerning it. Surely on the Day of Resurrection your Lord will judge between them concerning their differences.

125 Call to the way of your Lord with wisdom and good admonition, and dispute with them by means of what is better.[133] Surely your Lord – He knows who goes astray from His way, and He knows the ones who are (rightly) guided.

126 If you[134] take retribution, take it in the same way as retribution was taken against you.[135] But if indeed you are patient – it is indeed better for the ones who are patient. **127** And you[136] be patient (too). Yet your patience (comes) only with (the help of) God. Do not sorrow over them, and do not be in distress because of what they are scheming. **128** Surely God is with those who guard (themselves), and those who do good.

---

punishment (Q3.93; 6.146; 62.5).

120–123 Abraham the Ḥanīf

127. *Abraham was a community*: the use of the word *umma* here is unusual at first sight, but cf. Genesis 18.18, 'Abraham will surely become a great and powerful nation' (Hebr. *goy*). That is, Abraham was, strictly speaking, 'a Gentile' (see the following n.). See also Q2.134, 141, where Abraham and his immediate descendants are described as a 'community' unto themselves, prior to and distinct from Jews and Christians.
128. *a Ḥanīf*: or perhaps 'a Gentile' (see n. on Q2.135; cf. Q16.123 below).
129. *He*: God.
130. *We*: notice the sudden shift to first-person plur.
131. *you*: the Prophet.
132. *Follow the creed of Abraham the Ḥanīf*: or 'Follow the religion of Abraham the Gentile' (cf. Q10.105; 30.30).

124 The sabbath

125 Exhortation to the Prophet

133. *by means of what is better*: or 'in the best way' (cf. Q29.46).

126–128 Patience better than vengeance

134. *you*: plur.; the Cairo edition attributes the final three verses of Q16 to the 'Medinan' period.
135. *take retribution...in the same way...*: i.e. according to the *lex talionis* ('an eye for an eye'); see Q2.178-179; 5.45.
136. *you*: the Prophet.

17 The Journey ۞ Al-Isrā'

In the Name of God, the Merciful, the Compassionate

1 Glory to the One who sent His servant on a journey by night[1] from the Sacred Mosque[2] to the Distant Mosque,[3] whose surroundings We have blessed, so that We might show him some of Our signs.[4] Surely He – He is the Hearing, the Seeing.

2 We gave Moses the Book,[5] and made it a guidance[6] for the Sons of Israel: 'Do not take any guardian other than Me!' **3** (They were) descendants of those whom We carried with Noah.[7] Surely he was a thankful servant. **4** And We decreed for the Sons of Israel in the Book: 'You will indeed foment corruption on the earth twice, and you will indeed rise to a great height.'[8] **5** When the first promise came (to pass), We raised against you servants of Ours,[9] men of harsh violence, and they invaded (your) homes, and it was a promise fulfilled. **6** Then We returned to you (another) chance against them, and increased you with wealth and sons, and made you more numerous. **7** 'If you do good, you do good for yourselves, but if you do evil, (it is likewise) for yourselves.' When the second promise came (to pass), (We raised against

---

Q17: This sūra opens with the famous and tantalizingly brief report of a 'night journey.' A variety of topics then follow, including a series of commandments resembling the Decalogue in form and content (Q17.22-39a), as well as passages dealing with the nature and purpose of the Qur'ān. The Prophet's role as the 'messenger' is emphasized, and disbelievers are chastised for their objection that he is merely a 'human being' who does not perform any miracles. Q17 is assigned by most scholars to the 'Meccan' period, though some traditional authorities consider parts of it to be 'Medinan' (e.g. Q17.73-80). This sūra is also known as the 'Sons of Israel' from the references to the Banū Isrā'īl at its beginning and end.

1 The Night Journey

1. *sent His servant on a journey by night*: the 'servant' (or 'slave,' Ar. *'abd*) is traditionally identified with the Prophet, but it may refer to Moses, who is mentioned in the verse immediately following; cf. the similar descriptions of Moses' departure from Egypt (Q20.77; 26.52; 44.23); and Lot's departure from Sodom (Q11.81; 15.65).
2. *Sacred Mosque*: traditionally identified with the Ka'ba at Mecca (see n. on Q5.95).
3. *Distant Mosque*: or 'Farthest Mosque;' there is much debate about the identity of the *masjid al-aqṣā*, because its exact location is not specified. It is traditionally identified with the site of the mosque now in the temple area at Jerusalem, near the Dome of the Rock, though the city of Jerusalem is not mentioned by name in the Qur'ān. Cf. the miraculous 'transport-stories' of the prophet Ezekiel, who was taken by the spirit from Babylon to Jerusalem (Ezekiel 3.10-15; 8.3; 11.1; 43.1-5; cf. 1 Kings 18.12 [Elijah]; Bel and the Dragon 1.33-36 [Habakkuk]). According to tradition, after reaching the 'Distant Mosque' the Prophet ascended into heaven.
4. *signs*: here referring to revelation in general (see n. on Q2.39).

2–8 Sons of Israel

5. *the Book*: the Torah.
6. *guidance*: one of the most frequent terms (Ar. *hudā*) for revelation in general, and the Qur'ān in particular, but here applied to the Torah of Moses.
7. *carried with Noah*: in the ark.
8. *great height*: or 'great haughtiness;' the 'Book' in which this decree is said to occur is probably the 'Book of God' or 'Book of Destiny' (see n. on Q6.59; cf. Q17.58 below), rather than being a prophecy in the Torah.
9. *We raised against you servants of Ours...*: this could refer to the conquest of Jerusalem in 587 BCE by the Babylonians, or to the conquests of Jerusalem by the Romans in 70 and 135 CE, but the reference to '(another) turn' in the following verse makes the former more likely (unless this refers to some future event).

you servants of Ours) to cause you distress,[10] and to enter the Temple[11] as they entered it the first time, and to destroy completely what they had conquered. **8** It may be that your Lord will have compassion on you. But if you return, We shall return,[12] and We have made Gehenna[13] a prison for the disbelievers.

9 Surely this Qur'ān[14] guides to that which is more upright, and gives good news to the believers who do righteous deeds, that for them (there is) a great reward, **10** and that those who do not believe in the Hereafter[15] – We have prepared for them a painful punishment. **11** But the human calls[16] for evil (as if) calling for good, (for) the human is (always) hasty.

12 We have made the night and the day as two signs: We have blotted out the sign of the night and made the sign of the day to (let you) see, so that you may seek some favor from your Lord,[17] and that you may know the number of the years and the reckoning (of time). Everything – We have made it distinct.

13 And every human – We have fastened his fate[18] to him on his neck, and We shall bring forth a book[19] for him on the Day of Resurrection, which he will find unrolled.[20] **14** 'Read your book! You are sufficient today as a reckoner against yourself.'

15 Whoever is (rightly) guided, is guided only for himself,[21] and whoever goes astray, goes astray only against himself. No one bearing a burden bears the burden of another.[22] We never punish until We have sent a messenger.[23]

16 When We wish to destroy a town, We (first) command its affluent ones, and they act wickedly in it, so that the word against it is proved true,[24] and We destroy it completely. **17** How many generations have We destroyed after Noah![25] Your Lord is sufficient (as One who) is aware of (and) sees the sins of His servants.

---

10. *cause you distress*: lit. 'sadden your faces.'
11. *the Temple*: lit. 'the mosque' (Ar. *al-masjid*); this probably refers to the Roman conquest of Jerusalem in 70 or 135 CE, if the statement is understood as indicating something that happened in the past. But the verbs may be taken as referring to the future; in which case it would refer to a destruction yet to come.
12. *But if you return, We shall return*: i.e. if they return to doing evil, God will return to punish them.
13. *Gehenna*: a name for Hell (see n. on Q2.206).

9–11 The Qur'ān as guidance

14. *this Qur'ān*: or perhaps 'this recitation,' since the expression (Ar. *hādhā al-qur'ān*) is sometimes used only in reference to a part of the Qur'ān (cf. Q6.19; 10.61; 13.31; 72.1; see n. on Q2.185). Otherwise, 'this Qur'ān' may come close to its present meaning as the name of the Muslim scripture (cf. Q9.111), and perhaps imply the existence of 'other Qur'āns' (cf. Q39.27-28).
15. *the Hereafter*: see n. on Q2.4.
16. *calls*: i.e. prays.

12 Two signs of God's power and providence

17. *seek some favor from your Lord*: i.e. seek to make a livelihood.

13–21 Rationale for rewards and punishments

18. *his fate*: lit. 'his bird (of omen),' referring to the fate assigned to each person (cf. Q7.131; 27.47).
19. *a book*: i.e. the 'record' of a person's deeds (see Q17.71 below; 69.19, 25; 84.7, 10; cf. Q18.49; 23.62).
20. *unrolled*: or 'spread open;' this may mean that the 'book' was imagined to be in the form of a scroll rather than a codex (cf. Q52.3; 74.52; 81.10).
21. *for himself*: i.e. for his own benefit.
22. *No one...bears the burden of another*: i.e. judgment falls on individuals, whom neither family nor friends can help (an implicit rejection of the Christian doctrine of 'vicarious atonement' and 'intercession' by the saints); cf. Q6.164; 35.18; 39.7; 53.38.
23. *messenger*: for this important title, see n. on Q2.87.
24. *the word against it is proved true*: or 'the sentence against it is passed' (cf. Q10.33).
25. *How many generations have We destroyed...*: a reference to the punishment of earlier generations who disobeyed

18 Whoever desires this hasty[26] (world) – We hasten to (give) him in it whatever We please to whomever
We wish. Then We have made Gehenna for him, (where) he will burn, condemned (and) rejected. **19** But
whoever desires the Hereafter and strives with effort for it,[27] and he is a believer, those – their striving
will be thanked. **20** Each one We increase – these and those – with some gift of your Lord. The gift of your
Lord is not limited. **21** See how We have favored some of them over others. Yet the Hereafter is indeed
greater in ranks (of honor) and greater in favor.

22 Do not set up[28] another god with God, or you will sit down condemned (and) forsaken.

23 Your Lord has decreed that you do not serve any but Him, and (that you do) good to your parents,
whether one or both of them reaches old age with you. Do not say to them, 'Uff,'[29] and do not repulse
them, **24** but speak to them an honorable word. And conduct yourself humbly toward them[30] out of
mercy, and say: 'My Lord, have compassion on both of them, as they brought me up (when I was) small.'
25 Your Lord knows what is in you. If you are righteous, surely He is forgiving to those who regularly
turn (to Him in repentance).

26 Give the family member his due, and the poor and the traveler,[31] but do not squander (your wealth)
wastefully.[32] **27** Surely the squanderers are brothers of the satans,[33] and Satan[34] is ungrateful to his Lord.
28 But if you turn away from them, seeking a mercy from your Lord that you expect,[35] speak to them a
gentle word. **29** Do not keep your hand chained to your neck,[36] nor extend it all the way, or you will sit
down blamed (and) impoverished. **30** Surely your Lord extends (His) provision to whomever He pleases,
and restricts (it). Surely He is aware of His servants (and) sees (them).

31 Do not kill your children for fear of poverty. We will provide for them and for you. Surely their killing
is a great sin.

32 Do not go near adultery.[37] Surely it is an immoral act and evil as a way.

33 Do not kill the person whom God has forbidden (to be killed),[38] except by right.[39] Whoever is killed

---

their messengers, beginning with the people of Noah (see n. on Q7.59).

26. *hasty*: i.e. fleeting or transient (punning on the following verb).
27. *strives with effort for it*: lit. 'strives for it (with) its striving.'

22–39a Commandments and prohibitions

28. *Do not set up...*: lit. 'Do not make...;' although the following commandments alternate between the second-person sing. and plur., they are intended generally (cf. Exodus 20.2-17; Deuteronomy 5.6-21).
29. *Uff*: an expression of disrespect (cf. Q21.67; 46.17).
30. *conduct yourself humbly toward them*: lit. 'lower to them the wing of humility.'
31. *traveler*: lit. 'son of the way.'
32. *...wastefully*: the Cairo edition, reflecting the views of traditional scholars, attributes this verse to the 'Medinan' period.
33. *satans*: or 'demons' (Ar. *shayāṭīn*); individually assigned to incite people to evil (see Q19.83; 43.36; cf. Q23.97; 41.25).
34. *Satan*: for this figure, see n. on Q2.36.
35. *But if you turn away from them...*: i.e. if present circumstances prevent one from helping them, though one expects to be in a position to help in the future.
36. *Do not keep your hand chained to your neck*: i.e. do not be ungenerous or miserly.
37. *adultery*: or 'fornication' (Ar. *zinā'* applies to all unlawful sexual activity). The Cairo edition attributes Q17.32-33 to the 'Medinan' period.
38. *forbidden (to be killed)*: i.e. made sacrosanct or inviolable (Ar. *ḥarām*).
39. *except by right*: i.e. for just cause.

in an evil manner – We have given authority to his ally,[40] but he should not be excessive in the killing,[41] (for) surely he has been helped.[42]

34 Do not go near the property of the orphan, except to improve it,[43] until he reaches his maturity.

Fulfill the covenant.[44] Surely you are responsible for a covenant.[45]

35 Fill up the measure when you measure, and weigh with the straight balance. That is better and fairer in interpretation.

36 Do not pursue what you have no knowledge of.[46] Surely the hearing and the sight and the heart[47] – all those you are responsible for.[48]

37 Do not walk on the earth in jubilation. Surely you will not plumb the depths of[49] the earth, nor reach the mountains in height.

38 All that – the evil of it – is hateful in the sight of your Lord. **39** That is some of the wisdom your Lord has inspired you[50] (with).

Do not set up another god with God, or you will be cast into Gehenna, blamed (and) rejected. **40** Has your Lord distinguished you with sons and taken (for Himself) females from the angels?[51] Surely you speak a dreadful word indeed! **41** Certainly We have varied (the signs) in this Qur'ān,[52] so that they may take heed,[53] but it only increases them in aversion (to it). **42** Say:[54] 'If there were (other) gods with Him, as they say, they[55] would indeed have sought a way to the Holder of the throne.'[56] **43** Glory to Him! He is exalted a great height above what they say. **44** The seven heavens and the earth, and whatever is in them, glorify Him, and (there is) nothing that does not glorify (Him) with His praise, but you[57] do not understand their glorifying. Surely He is forbearing, forgiving.

---

40. *his ally*: i.e. someone with whom he shared the obligation of mutual protection (Ar. *walī*), and who has the right to avenge the killing according to the *lex talionis* ('an eye for an eye,' see Q2.178-179; 5.45).
41. *not be excessive in the killing*: i.e. not exceed the limit of 'a life for a life.'
42. *he has been helped*: probably referring to the one who exacts vengeance, since he now has a religious warrant for retaliation, but it may refer to the victim (or his heir) who would have legal recourse in the event that retaliation is 'excessive.'
43. *except to improve it*: lit. 'except with what is better' (cf. Q4.2, 10; 6.152).
44. *covenant*: or perhaps 'contract,' 'promise.' It is not clear whether this is a general command or pertains specifically to the matter of the property of orphans.
45. *you are responsible for a covenant* : lit. 'the covenant will be asked (about).'
46. *what you have no knowledge of*: perhaps referring to vain speculations or simply being a busybody.
47. *heart*: here, as often, the heart is spoken of as synonymous with mind.
48. *you are responsible for*: lit. 'will be asked (about).'
49. *plumb the depths of*: lit. 'dig a hole in.'
50. *you*: the Prophet.

39b–44 Arguments against idolatry

51. *females from the angels*: for the belief that the angels were 'daughters of God,' see Q16.57; 37.149-153; 43.19; 53.27 (for the angels and their various roles, see n. on Q2.30).
52. *this Qur'ān*: see n. on Q17.9 above.
53. *take heed*: or 'be reminded,' 'remember.'
54. *Say*: on this form of address, see n. on Q2.80.
55. *they*: i.e. the other gods.
56. *sought a way to the Holder of the throne*: i.e. the other gods would have risen up to usurp God's throne (cf. Q23.91).
57. *you*: plur.

45 When you recite the Qur'ān,[58] We place between you and those who do not believe in the Hereafter an obscuring veil. **46** And We make coverings over their hearts, so that they do not understand it,[59] and a heaviness in their ears. When you mention your Lord alone[60] in the Qur'ān, they turn their backs in aversion (to it). **47** We know what they listen to when they listen to you, and when they (are in) secret talk, when the evildoers say, 'You are only following a man (who is) bewitched.'[61] **48** See how they strike parables for you![62] But they have gone astray and cannot (find) a way.

49 They say, 'When we have become bones and fragments, shall we indeed be raised up as a new creation?' **50** Say: 'Become stones or iron, **51** or something greater still in your estimation!'[63] And then they will say, 'Who will restore us?' Say: '(He) who created you the first time.' And then they will shake their heads at you, and say, 'When will it be?' Say: 'It may be that it is near **52** – the Day when He will call you, and you will respond with His praise, and you will think that you remained (in the grave) only for a little (while).'

53 Say[64] to My servants (that) they should say that which is best. Surely Satan provokes discord among them. Surely Satan is a clear enemy to humankind. **54** Your Lord knows about you.[65] If He pleases, He will have compassion on you, or if He pleases, He will punish you. We have not sent you[66] as a guardian over them. **55** Your Lord knows whatever is in the heavens and the earth. Certainly We have favored some of the prophets over others,[67] and We gave David (the) Psalms.[68]

56 Say: 'Call on those whom you have claimed (as gods) instead of Him. They have no power (to) remove hardship from you, nor (to) change (it).' **57** Those whom they call on seek access to their Lord,[69] whichever of them (may be) nearest, and they hope for His mercy and fear His punishment. Surely the punishment of your Lord is something to beware of.

58 (There is) no town that We are not going to destroy before the Day of Resurrection, or are not going to punish (with a) harsh punishment. That is written in the Book.[70]

45–48 Disbelievers reject the Qur'ān

58. *When you recite the Qur'ān*: this seems to refer to an actual edition of the Qur'ān in the Prophet's possession, which he is commanded to 'recite' or 'read aloud' (cf. Q16.98; 27.91-92).
59. *so that they do not understand it*: i.e. the Qur'ān; for this idea, see Q2.6-7; 4.155; cf. Isaiah 6.9-10; Mark 4.11-12.
60. *your Lord alone*: thereby denying the existence of other gods (cf. Q39.45; 40.12).
61. *bewitched*: i.e. a victim of magic or under a magic spell (cf. Q25.8; the same accusation is laid against Moses at Q17.101 below).
62. *strike parables for you*: i.e. make comparisons about the Prophet.

49–52 Disbelievers reject the resurrection

63. *or something greater still in your estimation*: lit. 'or a creation of what is great in your chests;' i.e. they will be raised up no matter how heavy or large a thing they might imagine turning themselves into.

53–55 Believers must be conciliatory

64. *Say*: the Prophet is addressed.
65. *you*: plur.
66. *you*: the Prophet.
67. *favored some of the prophets over others*: or 'preferred some of the prophets over others.' Not all prophets are equal (nor all messengers, Q2.253n.). The most celebrated is Moses, who is mentioned by name more frequently than any other prophet in the Qur'ān (for the important title 'prophet,' see n. on Q2.87).
68. *Psalms*: or perhaps simply a 'scripture' or 'book' (Ar. *zabūr* [sing.]); cf. Q4.163; 21.105 (quoting Psalm 37.29); for the plur. *al-zubur*, see n. on Q3.184.

56–57 Angels are powerless

69. *...seek access to their Lord*: this indicates that they worshipped or prayed to angels (cf. Q17.40 above). The Cairo edition attributes this verse to the 'Medinan' period.

58 Punishment certain

70. *the Book*: i.e. the 'Book of God' or 'Book of Destiny' by which everything is ordained (see n. on Q6.59; cf. Q17.4 above).

59 Nothing prevented Us from sending the signs, except that those of old called them a lie.[71] We gave Thamūd the she-camel as a visible (sign), but they did her evil.[72] We send the signs only to frighten.

60 (Remember) when[73] We said to you,[74] 'Surely your Lord encompasses the people,'[75] and We made the vision which We showed you[76] only a test[77] for the people, and (also) the cursed tree in the Qur'ān.[78] We frighten them, but it only increases them in great(er) insolent transgression.

61 (Remember) when We said to the angels, 'Prostrate yourselves before Adam,'[79] and they prostrated themselves, except Iblīs.[80] He said, 'Shall I prostrate myself before one whom You have created (from) clay?'[81] **62** He[82] said, 'Do You see this (creature) whom You have honored above me? If indeed You spare me until the Day of Resurrection, I shall indeed root out his descendants, except for a few.' **63** He[83] said, 'Go, and any of them who follows you! Surely Gehenna will be your[84] payment – an ample payment! **64** Scare any of them you can with your voice, and assemble against them with your cavalry and your infantry, and associate with them in (their) wealth and children, and make promises to them.' Yet Satan[85] does not promise them (anything) but deception. **65** 'Surely My servants – you will have no authority over them.' Your Lord is sufficient as a guardian.

66 Your Lord (it is) who drives the ship on the sea for you, so that you may seek some of His favor.[86] Surely He is compassionate with you. **67** When hardship touches you on the sea, (all those) whom you call on abandon (you),[87] except Him, but when He has delivered you (safely) to the shore, you turn away. The human is ungrateful.[88] **68** Do you feel secure that He will not cause the shore to swallow you, or

---

59–60 Why the Prophet performed no miracles

71. *...those of old called them a lie*: a reference to previous peoples who disobeyed their messengers and rejected their miracles (see n. on Q7.59). This is one explanation why the Prophet performed no 'sign' (cf. Q21.5-6).
72. *but they did her evil*: for the story alluded to here, see Q7.73-79; 11.61-68.
73. *(Remember) when...*: a stock narrative formula; the Arabic particle *idh* serves as a common introduction to a narrative or a section, and often means something like 'Once...,' or 'There was a time when...,' or 'Remember when....'
74. *you*: the Prophet.
75. *your Lord encompasses the people*: this saying does not occur in the Qur'ān, but cf. Q85.20.
76. *the vision which We showed you*: sometimes taken as referring to the 'night journey' (Q17.1 above) or to the visions of Q53.1-18 and 81.15-24 (cf. Q8.43-44); but it may refer, like the preceding saying, to something not mentioned elsewhere in the Qur'ān.
77. *test*: or 'trial,' 'temptation' (Ar. *fitna*).
78. *the cursed tree...*: probably referring to the tree in Hell called 'Zaqqūm' (see Q37.62; 44.43; 56.52).

61–65 The story of Iblīs

79. *Prostrate yourselves before Adam*: for the story that follows, cf. the versions at Q2.34-39; 7.10-18; 15.28-48; 20.115-123; and Genesis 2.4-3.24. The prostration of the angels before Adam is not a part of the Genesis account, but was a prominent theme in Christian tradition (see e.g. Hebrews 1.6; Life of Adam and Eve 12.1-16.1; Cave of Treasures 2.22-25).
80. *except Iblīs*: for this figure, see n. on Q2.34.
81. *(from) clay*: cf. Q6.2; 7.12; 15.26; 23.12; 32.7; 38.71, 76; 'from dust,' according to Q3.59; 18.37; 22.5; 30.20; 35.11; 40.67; 'from water,' according to Q21.30; 24.45; 25.54.
82. *He*: Iblīs.
83. *He*: God.
84. *your*: plur. (i.e. Iblīs and his followers).
85. *Satan*: note the switch in name; this sentence, which appears to interrupt the quotation, may be a later gloss.

66–69 Human ingratitude for God's goodness

86. *seek some of His favor*: i.e. seek to make a livelihood.
87. *abandon (you)*: lit. 'go astray' (a pun).
88. *ungrateful*: Ar. *kafūr*, punning on *kāfir*, 'disbeliever.'

send a sandstorm[89] against you? Then you will find no guardian for yourselves. **69** Or do you feel secure that He will not send you back into it[90] a second time, and send a hurricane against you, and drown you because you were ungrateful? Then you will find no attendant (to help) you with it against Us.

70 Certainly We have honored the sons of Adam, and carried them on the shore and the sea, and provided them with good things, and favored them greatly over many of those whom We have created.

71 On the Day when We shall call all people with their record,[91] whoever is given his book[92] in his right (hand) – those will read their book, and they will not be done evil in the slightest.[93] **72** Whoever is blind in this (world will be) blind in the Hereafter, and farther astray (from the) way.

73 Surely they almost tempted you[94] away from what We inspired you (with), so that you might forge against Us (something) other than it,[95] and then they would indeed have taken you as a friend. **74** And had We not made you (stand) firm, you would almost have been disposed toward them a little. **75** Then We would have made you taste the double of life and the double of death, (and) then you would have found no helper for yourself against Us. **76** They almost scared you from the land,[96] so that they might expel you from it, but then they would not have remained (there) after you, except for a little (while). **77** (That was Our) customary way (concerning) those of Our messengers whom We sent before you,[97] and you will find no change in Our customary way.

78 Observe the prayer[98] at the setting of the sun until the darkness of the night, and (deliver) a recitation[99] at the dawn – surely a recitation at the dawn is witnessed. **79** And a part of the night – keep watch[100] in it as a gift for you. It may be that your Lord will raise you up to a praised position.[101] **80** And say: 'My Lord, cause me to enter a truthful entrance, and cause me to exit a truthful exit,[102] and grant me authority from Yourself (to) help (me).' **81** And say: 'The truth has come and falsehood has passed away. Surely falsehood is (bound) to pass away.'

82 What We send down of the Qur'ān[103] is a healing and mercy for the believers, but it only increases the

---

89. *sandstorm*: cf. Q29.40; 54.34; 67.17.
90. *it*: the sea.

70 Sons of Adam preferred above all creation

71–72 All will be held accountable

91. *record*: lit. 'leader' or 'model' (Ar. *imām*), but probably referring to the 'record' of their deeds (cf. Q15.79; 36.12).
92. *his book*: i.e. the 'record' of a person's deeds (see n. on Q6.59; cf. Q17.13 above).
93. *in the slightest*: lit. 'a fiber on a date seed.'

73–77 The Prophet is tempted to compromise

94. *they almost tempted you*: the Prophet; the Cairo edition attributes this section (Q17.73-80) to the 'Medinan' period.
95. *...(something) other than it*: i.e. something other than the Qur'ān.
96. *land*: lit. 'earth.'
97. *(That was Our) customary way...*: i.e. had the Prophet's contemporaries succeeded in expelling him, they would have been destroyed in short order, just as earlier generations were destroyed for rejecting their messengers.

78–81 The Prophet to observe the prayer

98. *Observe the prayer*: the ritual prayer (or *ṣalāt*).
99. *(deliver) a recitation*: lit. 'a qur'ān;' perhaps a reading of a part of it.
100. *keep watch*: or 'awaken for prayer' (Ar. *tahajjud*); cf. Q25.64; 73.1-6, 20.
101. *a praised position*: the word 'praised' (Ar. *maḥmūd*) may be a pun on the name 'Muḥammad' ('praised one').
102. *a truthful entrance...exit*: meaning obscure.

82–84 The Qur'ān a healing and mercy

103. *What We send down of the Qur'ān*: here 'the Qur'ān' appears to refer to something in God's possession, which is larger than what has been 'sent down' (cf. Q43.2-4).

evildoers in loss. **83** When We bless a person, he turns away and distances himself, but when evil touches him, he is in despair. **84** Say: 'Each does according to his own disposition, but your Lord knows who is best guided (as to the) way.'

85 They ask you[104] about the spirit. Say: 'The spirit (comes) from the command of my Lord.[105] You[106] have only been given a little knowledge (of it).'

86 If We (so) pleased, We could indeed take away what We have inspired you[107] (with). Then you would find no guardian for yourself against Us concerning it, **87** except as a mercy from your Lord. Surely His favor toward you is great.

88 Say: 'If indeed humankind and the jinn[108] joined together to produce something like this Qur'ān,[109] they would not produce anything like it, even if they were supporters of each other.' **89** Certainly We have varied (the signs) for the people in this Qur'ān by means of every (kind of) parable, yet most of the people refuse (everything) but disbelief.[110]

90 They say,[111] 'We shall not believe you until you cause a spring to gush forth for us from the earth,
91 or (until) you have a garden of date palms and grapes, and cause rivers to gush forth abundantly in the midst of it, **92** or (until) you make the sky fall on us in fragments, as you have claimed,[112] or (until) you bring God and the angels before (us), **93** or (until) you have a decorative house, or (until) you ascend into the sky.[113] And we shall not believe in your ascent until you bring down on us a book, so that we may read it.' Say: 'Glory to my Lord! Am I anything but a human being, a messenger?'[114]

94 What prevented the people from believing when the guidance came to them, except that they said,

---

85 The spirit

104. *you*: the Prophet.

105. *The spirit (comes) from the command of my Lord*: or 'The spirit (is) part of my Lord's affair' (Ar. *al-rūḥu min amri rabbī*). Here God's 'command' (Ar. *amr*) may correspond to the rabbinic notion of the 'divine word' (Aram. *mēmrā*), or to the related Christian idea of the *logos* as the manifestation of God's word, or as God's messenger in place of God himself (cf. Q16.2; 40.15; 42.52). The mysterious being called 'the spirit' (cf. Q16.102, 'the holy spirit;' 26.193, 'the trustworthy spirit') appears to be the bearer of revelation in the company of the angels (cf. Q97.4). Some interpreters identify 'the spirit' with Gabriel (see n. on Q2.97).

106. *You*: plur.

86–87 Inspiration could be withdrawn from the Prophet

107. *you*: the Prophet.

88–89 The Qur'ān's inimitability

108. *jinn*: for these beings, see n. on Q6.100.

109. *this Qur'ān*: unless 'this Qur'ān' (Ar. *hādhā al-qur'ān*) refers only to what has preceded, it comes close to its present meaning as the name of the Muslim scripture (cf. Q9.111; see n. on Q2.185).

110. *disbelief*: or 'ingratitude' (perhaps a pun).

90–93 Challenges to the Prophet

111. *They say...*: taken at face value, the following demands reflect a relatively coherent set of religious expectations or 'tests' that could be applied to religious claims (cf. the set of challenges at Q25.7-8, 20-21, 32). In general, the Prophet's contemporaries expected the messenger to be a 'miracle worker' or 'divine man.'

112. *as you have claimed*: probably an allusion to the threat of punishment 'raining down' on them or the 'sky falling' on them (cf. Q26.187; 34.9); but it may also be a challenge to produce a 'rain miracle' (cf. Q30.48).

113. *the sky*: or 'heaven.'

114. *a human being, a messenger*: the Prophet's claim to authority rests in part on his fulfillment of their last challenge to 'bring down a book,' though no ascension is mentioned in the Qur'ān (with the possible exception of Q17.1; cf. Q53.13-18). Later tradition would yield a complex '*mi'rāj*-literature' which would also become a frequent subject of Islamic art.

94–99 Objection to a human messenger

'Has God sent a human being as a messenger?' **95** Say: 'If there were angels walking contentedly on the earth,[115] We would indeed have sent down on them an angel from the sky as a messenger.' **96** Say: 'God is sufficient as a witness between me and you. Surely He is aware of His servants (and) sees (them).' **97** Whoever God guides is the (rightly) guided one, and whoever He leads astray – you will not find for them any allies other than Him. We shall gather them on the Day of Resurrection on their faces – without sight, or speech, or hearing. Their refuge is Gehenna – whenever it dies down We increase (for) them a blazing (Fire). **98** That is their payment because they disbelieved in Our signs, and said, 'When we have become bones and fragments, shall we indeed be raised up as a new creation?' **99** Do they not see that God, who created the heavens and the earth, is able to create their equivalent? He has appointed a time[116] for them – (there is) no doubt about it – yet the evildoers refuse (everything) but disbelief.[117]

100 Say: '(Even) if you possessed the storehouses of my Lord's mercy, you would (still) hold back (out of) a fear (of) spending (it).[118] Humankind is stingy.'

101 Certainly We gave Moses nine clear signs[119] – (just) ask the Sons of Israel. (Remember) when he came to them, and Pharaoh said to him, 'Moses! Surely I think you are bewitched indeed.'[120] **102** He said, 'Certainly you know that no one has sent down these (signs) as clear proofs except the Lord of the heavens and the earth. Pharaoh! Surely I think you are doomed indeed.' **103** He[121] wanted to scare them from the land,[122] but We drowned him and those who were with him – all (of them). **104** After that We said to the Sons of Israel, 'Inhabit the land, and when the promise of the Hereafter comes, We shall bring you (all together) as a mob.'[123]

105 With the truth[124] We have sent it down, and with the truth it has come down, and We have sent you only as a bringer of good news and a warner.[125] **106** (It is) a Qur'ān – We have divided it,[126] so that you may recite it[127] to the people at intervals,[128] and We have sent it down once and for all.[129] **107** Say:

---

115. *angels...on the earth*: i.e. if angels inhabited the earth instead of humans.

116. *time*: or 'term' (Ar. *ajal*), which is predetermined and cannot be changed.

117. *disbelief*: or 'ingratitude.'

100 Humanity lacks generosity

118. *(of) spending (it)*: i.e. of exhausting it.

101–104 The nine signs of Moses

119. *nine clear signs*: Moses performed more miracles than any other prophet in the Qur'ān (see e.g. Q7.130-137; 20.17-24, 47, 56; 27.12-14 etc.), but the reference to 'nine signs' is mentioned only here and at Q27.12, though they are not specified (cf. Q28.32, 'two proofs'). There may have once been a passage listing them (see Q20.17-24). According to Exodus 7-12, God brought 'ten plagues' against Egypt to convince Pharaoh to release the Israelites.

120. *bewitched*: cf. the same accusation laid against the Prophet at Q17.47 above; 25.8.

121. *He*: Pharaoh.

122. *land*: lit. 'earth.'

123. *bring you...as a mob*: for judgment.

105–109 The Qur'ān is true

124. *With the truth*: or 'In truth,' 'Truly.'

125. *bringer of good news...warner*: for these roles, see n. on Q2.119.

126. *We have divided it*: or 'We have made it distinct' (Ar. *faraqnāhu*); this may refer to some division or partition of the text for reading or recitation; cf. Q44.4, 'every wise command was divided out' or 'made distinct' (*yufraqu*).

127. *recite it*: or 'read it aloud.'

128. *at intervals*: or perhaps 'slowly' (cf. Q20.114; 25.32).

129. *once and for all*: or 'all at once' (lit. 'We have sent it down [with] a sending down'). The verbal noun 'a sending down' (Ar. *tanzīlan*) is usually understood to mean 'gradually' or 'in stages,' consistent with the traditional view that the Qur'ān was 'sent down' or revealed at intervals over a period of some twenty years. But that

'Believe in it, or do not believe. Surely those who were given the knowledge before it[130] – when it is recited to them, they fall down on their chins in prostration, **108** and say, "Glory to our Lord! Surely our Lord's promise has been fulfilled indeed." **109** They fall down on their chins weeping, and it increases them in humility.'

110 Say: 'Call on God or call on the Merciful[131] – whichever you call on, to Him (belong) the best names.'[132] And do not be loud in your prayer, nor silent in it, but seek a way between that.[133]

111 Say: 'Praise (be)[134] to God, who has not taken a son,[135] nor has He any associate[136] in the kingdom, nor has He any (need of) an ally (to protect Him) from disgrace.' Magnify Him (with all) magnificence.

---

meaning is open to question. The word *tanzīlan* is used as a cognate accusative to give added emphasis to the main verb, 'We have sent it down' (*anzalnāhu*). The declaration that 'We have sent it down once and for all' is thus an emphatic response to the disbelievers' challenge (at Q17.93 above) to 'send down a book' from heaven. A similar expression occurs at Q76.23 (cf. Q25.25, where it is used of the 'sending down' of all the angels on the Last Day). Some interpreters claim, partly on the basis of this verse (and Q25.32), that it was the Qur'ān's 'serial mode' of revelation which distinguished it from the revelation of the Torah, but it is not certain that is being affirmed here. In fact there are other passages which indicate that the Qur'ān was 'sent down' or revealed all at once (see Q2.89; 3.3, 7; 4.105; 5.48; 6.92; 8.41; 16.64; 26.193-194; 28.86; 44.3; 46.12, 30; 97.1; cf. Q2.185, 'The month of Ramaḍān, in which the Qur'ān was sent down'). There were similarly conflicting views within Judaism about the revelation of the Torah. According to the Babylonian Talmud (Gittin 60a), some thought the Torah had been 'transmitted scroll by scroll,' others that it had been 'transmitted entire.'

130. *those who were given the knowledge before it*: i.e. Jews and Christians, in their scriptures.

110–111 Prayer to God or to the Merciful is the same

131. *the Merciful*: Ar. *al-raḥmān* is used here as a proper name for God. It seems to have caused confusion or objections among some, who found it either unfamiliar or unacceptable (cf. Q13.30; 21.36). This verse seems to be an attempt to resolve the problem (see n. on Q25.60).

132. *the best names*: or 'the most beautiful names' (Ar. *al-asmā' al-ḥusnā*); cf. Q7.180; 20.8; 59.24. A list of ninety-nine names was eventually compiled, consisting of those mentioned in the Qur'ān as well as others. They play an important role in theology and worship.

133. *And do not be loud in your prayer...*: addressed to the Prophet.

134. *(be)*: or '(belongs).'

135. *son*: or 'child' (Ar. *walad*), but referring to Christian claims about Jesus as God's son (cf. Q17.40 above).

136. *associate*: 'partner' or 'equal.'

18 The Cave ۞ Al-Kahf

In the Name of God, the Merciful, the Compassionate

1 Praise (be)[1] to God, who has sent down on His servant[2] the Book![3] He has not made in it any crookedness. **2** (He has made it) right: to warn of harsh violence from Himself, and to give good news to the
believers who do righteous deeds, that for them (there is) a good reward **3** in which they will remain
forever, **4** and to warn those who have said, 'God has taken a son.'[4] **5** They have no knowledge about it,
nor (did) their fathers. Monstrous is the word (that) comes out of their mouths! They say nothing but a
lie. **6** Perhaps you[5] are going to destroy yourself[6] by following after them,[7] if they do not believe in this
proclamation.[8] **7** Surely We have made what is on the earth a splendor for it, so that We may test them
(to see) which of them is best in deed. **8** And surely We shall make what is on it barren soil.

9 Or did you[9] think that the companions of the cave[10] and al-Raqīm[11] were an amazing thing among
Our signs?[12] **10** (Remember) when[13] the young men took refuge in the cave, and said, 'Our Lord, grant
us mercy from Yourself, and furnish the right (course) for us in our situation.' **11** So We sealed up their
ears[14] in the cave for a number of years, **12** and then We raised them up (again), so that We might know
which of the two factions[15] would better count (the length of) time (they had) remained (there).

Q18: This sūra is distinctive for being composed almost entirely of stories. The three main ones are: the 'Men of the Cave' (Q18.9-26), Moses and the servant (18.60-82), and Dhū-l-Qarnayn, a figure usually identified with Alexander the Great (18.83-98). Q18 is assigned by most scholars to the 'Meccan' period, though some traditional authorities assign the story of Dhū-l-Qarnayn to the 'Medinan' period (including the Cairo edition).

1–8 The purpose of the Qur'ān

1. *(be)*: or '(belongs).'
2. *His servant*: the Prophet; the word 'servant' (Ar. *'abd*) also means 'slave.'
3. *the Book*: here referring to the Qur'ān not only as a 'recited' but also 'written' scripture (see n. on Q2.2).
4. *son*: or 'child' (Ar. *walad*), but referring to Christian claims about Jesus as God's son.
5. *you*: the Prophet.
6. *destroy yourself*: with grief or anguish (cf. Q26.3).
7. *by following after them*: lit. 'on their footsteps.'
8. *proclamation*: or 'story' (Ar. *ḥadīth*), referring either to the Qur'ān or to the following story about the 'Men of the Cave.'

9–26 The Story of the Men of the Cave

9. *you*: the Prophet.
10. *companions of the cave*: usually identified with the 'Seven Sleepers of Ephesus.' According to Christian legend, they were young men who hid in a cave to avoid the persecution of the Roman emperor Decius (c. 250 CE), and there fell asleep for many years. The legend first appears in Syriac Christian sources of the 6th century CE.
11. *al-Raqīm*: reference uncertain; it may be a place name (of the mountain or nearby city), the name of a document or inscription, the name of the men's dog, or perhaps a garbled reference to the emperor Decius.
12. *signs*: or 'verses' (see n. Q2.39).
13. *(Remember) when...*: a stock narrative formula; the Arabic particle *idh* often marks the beginning of a story, and means something like 'Once...,' or 'There was a time when...,' or 'Remember when....'
14. *sealed up their ears*: lit. 'struck on their ears;' usually taken to mean 'put to sleep.' If taken literally, however, it might mean that an actual number or date was 'stamped' on their ears.
15. *two factions*: i.e. of the young men in the cave (see Q18.19 below).

13 We shall recount to you their story[16] in truth:[17] Surely they were young men who believed in their Lord, and We increased them in guidance. **14** We strengthened their hearts, when they stood up and said, 'Our Lord is the Lord of the heavens and the earth. We do not call on any god other than Him. Certainly we would then have spoken an outrageous thing. **15** These people of ours have taken gods other than Him. If only they would bring some clear authority concerning them! Who is more evil than the one who forges a lie against God? **16** When you have withdrawn from them and what they serve instead of God, take refuge in the cave. Your Lord will display some of His mercy to you, and will furnish some relief for you in your situation.'

17 And you (would) see[18] the sun when it rose, inclining from their cave toward the right, and when it set, passing them by on the left, while they were in the open part of it. That was one of the signs of God. Whoever God guides is the (rightly) guided one, and whoever He leads astray – you will not find for him an ally guiding (him). **18** And you (would) think them awake, even though they were asleep, and We were turning them (now) to the right and (now) to the left, while their dog[19] (lay) stretched out (with) its front paws at the door (of the cave). If you (had) observed them, you would indeed have turned away from them in flight, and indeed been filled (with) dread because of them.

19 So We raised them up (again) that they might ask questions among themselves. A speaker among them said, 'How long have you remained (here)?' Some[20] said, 'We have (only) remained (here) a day, or part of a day.' Others[21] said, 'Your Lord knows how long you have remained (here). So send one of you with this paper (money)[22] of yours to the city,[23] and let him see which (part) of it (has the) purest food, and let him bring you a supply of it. But let him be astute, and let no one realize (who) you (are).
20 Surely they – if they become aware of you – they will stone you, or make you return to their creed, and then you will never prosper.' **21** So We caused (the people of the city) to stumble upon them, in order that they might know that the promise of God is true, and that the Hour – (there is) no doubt about it.[24]

When they[25] argued among themselves about their situation, they said, 'Build over them a building. Their Lord knows about them.' Those who prevailed over their situation said, 'We shall indeed take (to building) a place of worship[26] over them.'

22 Some[27] say, '(There were) three, the fourth of them was their dog.' But others[28] say, '(There were) five, the sixth of them was their dog' – guessing about what is unknown.[29] Still others[30] say, '(There were)

16. *story*: or 'news.'
17. *in truth*: the full version of the story now follows, in contrast to the preceding summary of it.
18. *And you (would) see...*: or perhaps 'And one (would) see....'
19. *their dog*: which kept guard at the mouth of the cave; there is no parallel to this in the Christian version of the story.
20. *Some*: lit. 'They.'
21. *Others*: lit. 'They.'
22. *paper (money)*: lit. 'leaf' or 'sheet;' it is usually taken in the sense of 'money,' but it may have some symbolic meaning in keeping with the parabolic nature of the story (e.g. a 'record' of their deeds).
23. *the city*: Ar. *al-madīna*; Ephesus, according to the Christian version of the story.
24. *promise of God...the Hour...*: i.e. the story is also a parable of resurrection and judgment.
25. *they*: the people of the city.
26. *place of worship*: or 'mosque' (Ar. *masjid*).
27. *Some*: lit. 'They.'
28. *others*: lit. 'they.'
29. *guessing about what is unknown*: lit. 'casting stones at the unseen.'
30. *Still others*: lit. 'They.'

seven, the eighth of them was their dog.' Say:[31] 'My Lord knows about their number. No one knows (about) them except a few.' So do not dispute about them, except (on) an obvious point, and do not ask for a pronouncement about them from any of them.[32] **23** And do not say of anything, 'Surely I am going to do that tomorrow,' **24** except (with the proviso): 'If God pleases.'[33] And remember[34] your Lord, when you forget, and say, 'It may be that my Lord will guide me to something nearer the right (way) than this.'

25 They remained in their cave for three hundred years and (some) add nine (more). **26** Say: 'God knows about how long they remained (there). To Him (belongs) the unseen[35] of the heavens and the earth. How well He sees and hears! They have no ally other than Him, and He does not associate anyone in His judgment.'

27 Recite[36] what you have been inspired (with) of the Book of your Lord.[37] No one can change His words, and you will find no refuge other than Him. **28** Be patient within yourself with those who call on their Lord in the morning and the evening, desiring His face,[38] and do not let your eyes turn away from them, desiring the (passing) splendor of this present life. Do not obey (anyone) whose heart[39] We have made oblivious of Our remembrance, and (who only) follows his desire and whose concern is (only) excess.[40]

29 Say: 'The truth is from your Lord. Whoever pleases, let him believe, and whoever pleases, let him disbelieve.' Surely We have prepared a Fire[41] for the evildoers – its walls will encompass them. If they call for help, they will be helped with water like molten metal (which) will scald their faces. Evil is the drink and evil the resting place! **30** Surely those who believe and do righteous deeds – surely We do not allow the reward of anyone who does a good deed to go to waste. **31** Those – for them (there are) Gardens of Eden[42] through which rivers flow. There they will be adorned with bracelets of gold, and they will wear green clothes of silk and brocade, reclining there on couches. Excellent is the reward, and good the resting place!

32 Strike for them a parable of two men: We made for one of them two gardens of grapes, and surrounded both with date palms, and placed between them (a field of) crops. **33** Each of the two gardens produced its fruit and did not fail in any way. And We caused a river to gush forth between them. **34** And he had fruit.[43] So he said to his companion, while he was talking with him, 'I am greater than you in wealth, and mightier in family.'[44] **35** And he entered his garden, doing himself evil, (for) he said, 'I do

---

31. *Say*: on this form of address, see n. on Q2.80.
32. *So do not dispute...do not ask for a pronouncement...*: the Prophet is not to get into arguments over the story with Christians (presumably), or to ask them for information about it.
33. *If God pleases*: cf. Q18.39 below; 68.17-18; and James 4.13-15.
34. *remember*: or 'make mention of,' 'call to mind.'
35. *the unseen*: here perhaps referring to the distant past (see n. on Q2.3).

27–31 Encouragement to the Prophet

36. *Recite...*: or 'Read aloud...' (addressed to the Prophet).
37. *of the Book of your Lord*: or 'from the Book of your Lord' (cf. Q29.45); this may refer to the heavenly archetype or source of all scripture. According to this view, the Qur'ān, like the Torah and the Gospel, is only a portion of this all encompassing 'mother of the Book' (see Q13.39; 43.4; cf. Q56.78, 'hidden Book;' 85.22, 'guarded Tablet').
38. *desiring His face*: i.e. seeking God's favor; cf. Psalms 24.3-6; 27.7-9; 105.4; 2 Chronicles 7.14.
39. *heart*: here, as often, the heart is spoken of as synonymous with mind.
40. *...(only) excess*: the Cairo edition, reflecting the views of traditional scholars, attributes this verse to the 'Medinan' period.
41. *Fire*: Ar. *nār* is the most common of the various designations for Hell.
42. *Gardens of Eden*: in heaven (for this imagery, see n. on Q2.25).

32–44 Parable of the two men

43. *he had fruit*: or 'he had wealth' (depending on how the word is vocalized).
44. *family*: lit 'band (of men),' but probably in the sense of 'having sons' (see Q18.39, 46 below; cf. Q74.12-13).

not think that this will ever perish, **36** nor do I think the Hour[45] is coming. If indeed I am returned to my Lord, I shall indeed find a better (place of) return than this.' **37** His companion said to him, while he was talking with him, 'Do you disbelieve in Him who created you from dust,[46] then from a drop,[47] (and) then fashioned you as a man? **38** But as for us, He is God, my Lord, and I do not associate anyone with my Lord. **39** Why did you not say, when you entered your garden, "What God pleases," (for there is) no power except in God? If you see me as inferior to you in wealth and children, **40** it may be that my Lord will give me (something) better than your garden, and send on it[48] a reckoning from the sky, so that it becomes slippery soil, **41** or its water sinks (into the earth), so that you will not be able to find it.' **42** And (all) his fruit was overwhelmed, and in the morning he began wringing his hands over what he had spent on it, (for) it had collapsed on its trellises, and he said, 'I wish I had not associated anyone with my Lord!' **43** But there was no cohort to help him, other than God, and he was helpless. **44** In such a case protection (belongs only) to God, the True One. He is best in reward, and best in final outcome.

45 Strike for them a parable of this present life: (It is) like water which We send down from the sky, and the vegetation of the earth mingles with it, and it becomes stubble[49] which the winds scatter. God is powerful over everything. **46** Wealth and sons are the (passing) splendor of this present life, but the things that endure – righteous deeds – are better in reward with your Lord, and better in hope.

47 On the Day when We shall cause the mountains to move, and you see[50] the earth coming forth,[51] and We gather them[52] so that We do not leave any of them behind, **48** and they are presented before your Lord in lines: 'Certainly you have come to Us as We created you the first time.[53] Yet you claimed that We had not set an appointment for you!'[54] **49** And the Book[55] will be laid down, and you will see the sinners apprehensive because of what is in it, and they will say, 'Woe to us! What (kind of) Book is this? It omits nothing small or great, but it has counted it?' And they will find what they have done presented (to them), and your Lord will not do anyone evil.

50 (Remember) when We said to the angels:[56] 'Prostrate yourselves before Adam,'[57] and they prostrated

45. *the Hour*: of judgment.

46. *from dust*: see Q3.59; 22.5; 30.20; 35.11; 40.67 (cf. Genesis 2.7, 'from the dust of the ground'); 'from clay,' according to Q6.2; 7.12; 15.26; 17.61; 23.12; 32.7; 38.71, 76; 55.14; 'from water,' according to Q21.30; 24.45; 25.54.

47. *a drop*: of semen.

48. *it*: i.e. the rich man's garden.

45–46 Parable of the rain and plants

49. *it becomes stubble*: i.e. the plants become so much dried up and broken stuff (the subject should be 'they,' referring to 'plants'). The point of the parable is the ephemeral character of the things of this world.

47–49 A judgment scene

50. *you see*: since 'you' is sing. here (and at Q18.49), this may indicate that the Prophet would witness these events in his lifetime (i.e. that 'the Day' is imminent); but it may be a general reference (i.e. 'one will see...').

51. *the earth coming forth*: perhaps the earth 'steps forward' to be plainly seen, but the meaning is obscure.

52. *them*: humankind.

53. *as we created you the first time*: i.e. naked.

54. *Yet you claimed...*: i.e. they had denied the coming Judgment.

55. *the Book*: the heavenly 'Record' or 'Account' of the deeds of humankind (see e.g. Q23.62; cf. Q17.13, 71; 69.19, 25; 84.7, 10, where each person is given an individual 'book' containing a record of his deeds).

50–51 Idolatry is worship of Iblīs and the jinn

56. *angels*: for these beings and their various roles, see n. on Q2.30.

57. *Prostrate yourselves before Adam*: the prostration of the angels before Adam is not a part of the Genesis account, but was a prominent theme in Christian tradition (see e.g. Hebrews 1.6; Life of Adam and Eve 12.1-16.1; Cave of Treasures 2.22-25).

themselves, except Iblīs.[58] He was one of the jinn,[59] and acted wickedly (against) the command of his Lord. Do you take him and his descendants as allies instead of Me, when they are your enemy? Evil is the exchange for the evildoers! **51** I did not make them witnesses of the creation of the heavens and the earth, nor of the creation of themselves. I am not one to take those who lead (others) astray (for) support.

52 On the Day when He will say, 'Call those who you claimed were My associates,' they will call them, but they will not respond to them – (for) We have set between them a place of destruction.[60] **53** The sinners will see the Fire and think that they are about to fall into it, but they will find no escape from it.

54 Certainly We have varied (the signs) for the people in this Qur'ān[61] by means of every (kind of) parable, yet the people remain contentious for the most part. **55** Nothing prevented the people from believing, when the guidance[62] came to them, and from asking forgiveness from their Lord, except that the customary way of those of old should come upon them, or the punishment come upon them head on.[63]
56 We send the envoys[64] only as bringers of good news and warners,[65] but those who disbelieve dispute by means of falsehood in order to refute the truth with it. They have taken My signs[66] and what they were warned about in mockery. **57** Who is more evil than the one who, having been reminded by the signs of his Lord, turns away from them, and forgets what his hands have sent forward?[67] Surely We have made coverings over their hearts,[68] so that they do not understand it,[69] and a heaviness in their ears. Even if you[70] call them to the guidance, they will never be guided. **58** Yet your Lord is the Forgiving, the One full of mercy. If He were to take them to task for what they have earned,[71] He would indeed hurry the punishment for them. Yet for them (there is) an appointment[72] from which they will find no escape. **59** Those towns[73] – We destroyed them when they did evil, and We set an appointment for their destruction.

---

58. *except Iblīs*: for this figure, see n. on Q2.34.
59. *He was one of the jinn*: this is the only passage identifying Iblīs as one of the jinn (see n. on Q6.100; cf. Q38.85).

52–53 A JUDGMENT SCENE

60. *a place of destruction*: meaning obscure.

54–59 DISBELIEF AND ITS CONSEQUENCES

61. *this Qur'ān*: or perhaps 'this recitation,' since the expression (Ar. *hādhā al-qur'ān*) is sometimes used only in reference to a part of the Qur'ān (cf. Q6.19; 10.61; 13.31; 72.1; see n. on Q2.185). Otherwise, 'this Qur'ān' may come close to its present meaning as the name of the Muslim scripture (cf. Q9.111), and perhaps imply the existence of 'other Qur'āns' (cf. Q39.27-28).
62. *the guidance*: one of the most frequent terms (Ar. *al-hudā*) for revelation in general, and the Qur'ān in particular.
63. *...except that the customary way of those of old should come upon them, or the punishment come upon them...*: i.e. the people will persist in their disbelief until they experience for themselves the 'way' (Ar. *sunna*) God punished earlier generations for their disbelief, but then it will be too late (cf. Q3.137; 8.38; 15.13; 35.43; 40.85; 48.23).
64. *the envoys*: lit. 'the ones who are sent' (Ar. *al-mursalūn*), a designation roughly equivalent to 'messengers' (*rusul*).
65. *bringers of good news...warners*: for these roles, see n. on Q2.119.
66. *signs*: or 'verses.'
67. *what his hands have sent forward*: i.e. his deeds, which are 'sent forward' to the Judgment.
68. *hearts*: here, as often, the heart is spoken of as synonymous with mind.
69. *so that they do not understand it*: the Qur'ān; for this idea, see Q2.6-7; 4.155; cf. Isaiah 6.9-10; Mark 4.11-12.
70. *you*: the Prophet.
71. *for what they have earned*: i.e. for the sins they have committed.
72. *an appointment*: the Day of Judgment.
73. *Those towns*: i.e. the cities of previous peoples who were punished for disobeying their prophets (see n. on Q7.59).

60 (Remember) when Moses[74] said to his young man, 'I shall not give up until I reach the junction of the two seas,[75] or (else) I shall go on for a long time.' **61** When they reached the junction of them, they forgot their fish, (for) it had taken its way into the sea, swimming off. **62** So when they had passed beyond (that place), he said to his young man, 'Bring us our morning meal. We have indeed become weary from this journey of ours.' **63** He[76] said, 'Did you see when we took refuge at the rock?[77] Surely I forgot the fish – none other than Satan[78] made me forget to remember it – and it took its way into the sea – an amazing thing!' **64** He[79] said, 'That is what we were seeking!'[80] So they returned, retracing their footsteps. **65** And they found a servant,[81] one of Our servants to whom We had given mercy from Us, and whom We had taught knowledge from Us. **66** Moses said to him, 'Shall I follow you on (the condition) that you teach me some of what you have been taught (of) right (knowledge)?' **67** He said, 'Surely you will not be able (to have) patience with me. **68** How could you have patience for what you cannot encompass in (your) awareness of it?' **69** He said, 'You will find me, if God pleases, patient, and I shall not disobey you in any command.' **70** He said, 'If you follow (me), do not ask me about anything, until I mention it to you.'

71 So they both[82] set out (and continued on) until, when they sailed[83] in the ship, he[84] made a hole in it. He[85] said, 'Have you made a hole in it in order to drown its passengers? You have indeed done a dreadful thing!' **72** He said, 'Did I not say, "Surely you will not be able (to have) patience with me?"' **73** He said, 'Do not take me to task for what I forgot, and do not burden me (with) hardship in my affair.' **74** So they both set out (and continued on) until, when they met a young boy, he killed him. He said, 'Have you killed an innocent person, other than (in retaliation) for a person? Certainly you have done a terrible thing!' **75** He said, 'Did I not say to you, "Surely you will not be able (to have) patience with me?"' **76** He said, 'If I ask you about anything after this, do not keep me as a companion. You have had enough excuses from me.' **77** So they both set out (and continued on) until, when they came to the people of a town, they asked its people for food, but they refused to offer them hospitality. They both found in it a wall on the verge of collapse, and he[86] set it up. He[87] said, 'If you had wished, you could indeed have taken a

---

60–82 The story of Moses and the servant of God

74. *(Remember) when Moses...*: the following story is strikingly different from all other accounts of Moses in the Qur'ān; nor is there any reference to it in the biblical book of Exodus. Various features of the story have parallels in the *Epic of Gilgamesh*, the *Alexander Romance*, and the Jewish legend of Elijah and rabbi Joshua ben Levi.
75. *junction of the two seas*: i.e. at the end of the world, where the waters of heaven and earth were thought to meet.
76. *He*: the young man.
77. *the rock*: reference obscure; but based on the context it may have been the marker for the 'spring of immortality,' or the 'waters of life,' located near the confluence of the two seas. By contact with these waters the fish they had been carrying (for food) came to life, and then escaped into the sea.
78. *Satan*: for this figure, see n. on Q2.36.
79. *He*: Moses.
80. *That is what we were seeking*: Moses now realizes that the water in which the fish came to life was the 'spring of immortality,' for which he had been searching all along.
81. *a servant*: this mysterious figure remains unnamed, though a majority of commentators call him al-Khaḍr (or al-Khiḍr), 'the green man,' but other possibilities have been suggested (e.g. the prophet Elijah, or Utnapishtim in the *Epic of Gilgamesh*).
82. *they both*: i.e. Moses and the mysterious servant; the 'young man' of the previous episode receives no further mention.
83. *sailed*: lit. 'rode.'
84. *he*: the mysterious servant.
85. *He*: Moses.
86. *he*: the servant.
87. *He*: Moses.

reward for that.' **78** He said, 'This is the parting between me and you. (Now) I shall inform you about the interpretation of what you were not able (to have) patience with. **79** As for the ship, it belonged to poor people working on the sea, and I wanted to damage it, (because) behind them (there) was a king seizing every ship by force. **80** As for the young boy, his parents were believers, and we feared that he would burden them both (with) insolent transgression and disbelief. **81** We wanted their Lord to give to them both in exchange (one) better than him in purity, and closer (to them) in affection. **82** As for the wall, it belonged to two orphan boys in the city, and underneath it was a treasure belonging to them both, (for) their father had been a righteous man. Your Lord wanted them both to reach their maturity, and bring forth their treasure as a mercy from your Lord. I did not do it on my (own) command. That is the interpretation (of) what you were not able (to have) patience with.'

83 They ask you[88] about Dhū-l-Qarnayn.[89] Say: 'I shall recite to you a remembrance[90] of him. **84** Surely We established him on the earth and gave him a way of access[91] to everything. **85** He followed (one such) way of access **86** until, when he reached the setting of the sun, he found it setting in a muddy spring, and he found next to it a people. We said, "Dhū-l-Qarnayn! Either punish (them) or do them (some) good." **87** He said, "As for the one who does evil, we shall punish him. Then he will be returned to his Lord, and He will punish him (with) a terrible punishment. **88** But as for the one who believes, and does righteousness, for him (there is) the good payment, and we shall speak to him something easy from our command."

89 Then he followed (another) way of access **90** until, when he reached the rising (place) of the sun,[92] he found it rising on a people for whom We had not provided any shelter from it. **91** So (it was), but We had already encompassed what his situation was in (our) awareness. **92** Then he followed (another) way of access **93** until, when he arrived (at the place) between the two barriers, he found on this side of them a people hardly able to understand (his) speech. **94** They said, "Dhū-l-Qarnayn! Surely Yajūj and Majūj[93] are fomenting corruption on the earth. Shall we pay tribute to you on (the condition) that you construct a barrier between us and them?" **95** He said, "What my Lord has established me with is better.[94] Help me with a force, (and) I shall construct a rampart between you and them. **96** Bring me blocks of iron!" – Until, when he had made level (the gap) between the two cliffs, he said, "Blow!" – Until, when he had made it a fire, he said, "Bring me (blocks of brass)! I will pour molten brass over it." **97** So they[95] were not able to surmount it, nor were they able (to make) a hole in it. **98** He said, "This is a mercy from my Lord. But when the promise of my Lord comes,[96] He will shatter it. The promise of my Lord is true."'

83–98 The story of Dhū-l-Qarnayn

88. *you*: the Prophet.
89. *Dhū-l-Qarnayn*: lit. 'He of the two horns,' and usually identified with Alexander the Great (d. 323 BCE), whose widely circulating image on coins depicted him in the guise of the two-horned god Zeus-Ammon. The Cairo edition attributes the following story (Q18.83-101) to the 'Medinan' period.
90. *remembrance*: or 'reminder' (see n. on Q3.58).
91. *way of access*: lit. 'rope.'
92. *the rising (place) of the sun*: Dhū-l-Qarnayn travels from west to east, or from one end of the earth to the other.
93. *Yajūj and Majūj*: probably 'Gog and Magog' (cf. Ezekiel 38.2-3). They are variously understood as men, supernatural beings, peoples, or lands. In the *Alexander Romance*, Alexander visited a northern land devastated by incursions from barbarian peoples, including Gog and Magog. There he fortified the land by constructing the 'Gates of Alexander,' an immense wall between two mountains that will stop the invaders until the end of days. According to Q21.95-97, Yajūj and Majūj will be released shortly before the Day of Judgment (cf. Q18.98 below).
94. *What my Lord has established me with is better*: i.e. better than any tribute they might pay him.
95. *they*: Yajūj and Majūj.
96. *when the promise of my Lord comes*: on the Last Day.

99 We shall leave some of them on that Day crashing into each other,[97] and there will be a blast on the trumpet,[98] and We shall gather them all together. **100** We shall present Gehenna[99] on that Day to the disbelievers, **101** whose eyes were covered from My remembrance[100] and (who) were not capable (of) hearing. **102** Do those who disbelieve think that they can take My servants as allies instead of Me? Surely We have prepared Gehenna as a reception for the disbelievers.

103 Say: 'Shall We inform you about the worst losers in (regard to their) deeds? **104** (They are) those whose striving goes astray in this present life, even though they think that they are doing good in (regard to their) work. **105** Those – (they are) those who disbelieve in the signs of their Lord and in the meeting with Him.[101] So their deeds have come to nothing. We shall not assign any weight to them on the Day of Resurrection. **106** That is their payment – Gehenna – because they disbelieved and took My signs and My messengers in mockery. **107** (But) surely those who believe and do righteous deeds – for them (there will be) Gardens of Paradise[102] as a reception, **108** there to remain. They will not desire any removal from there.'

109 Say: 'If the sea were ink for the words of my Lord, the sea would indeed give out before the words of my Lord would give out, even if We brought (another sea) like it as an extension.'[103]

110 Say: 'I am only a human being like you. I am inspired[104] that your God is one God. So whoever expects the meeting with his Lord, let him do righteous deeds and not associate anyone in the service[105] of his Lord.'

99–102 A JUDGMENT SCENE

97. *crashing into each other*: i.e. like waves; a depiction of the turmoil and confusion accompanying the arrival of the Last Day.

98. *a blast on the trumpet*: the Last Day will be announced by the blast of a trumpet (e.g. Q6.73; 20.102; 39.68 [a double blast]; 69.13; 74.8; 78.18; cf. Matthew 24.31; 1 Corinthians 15.52; 1 Thessalonians 4.16).

99. *Gehenna*: a name for Hell (see n. on Q2.206).

100. *My remembrance*: or 'My Reminder,' referring to the Qur'ān.

103–108 PUNISHMENT AND REWARD

101. *the meeting with Him*: on the Day of Judgment.

102. *Paradise*: the word (Ar. *firdaus*) occurs only here and at Q23.11. In the Hebrew Bible *pardes* (a transliteration of a Persian word) occurs in its original meaning of 'park' or 'garden' (see Song of Songs 4.13; Ecclesiastes 2.5; Nehemiah 2.8), but in later Judaism the word came to be associated with the Garden of Eden. The Septuagint employs the Greek word *paradeisos* of Eden (e.g. Genesis 2.8) and of Eden restored (e.g. Ezekiel 28.13; 36.35). The same word is used in the New Testament to refer to 'heaven' (see Luke 23.43; 2 Corinthians 12.4; Revelation 2.7).

109 OCEANS OF REVELATION

103. *If the sea were ink...*: clearly implies that the revelation is being written down (cf. Q31.27; 68.1; 96.4-5).

110 THE PROPHET ONLY HUMAN

104. *I am inspired*: or 'I have received inspiration.'

105. *service*: or 'worship.'

19 Mary ✿ Maryam

In the Name of God, the Merciful, the Compassionate

1 Kāf Hā' Yā' 'Ayn Ṣād.[1]

2 A remembrance[2] of the mercy of your Lord (to) His servant[3] Zachariah:[4] **3** When he called on his Lord in secret, **4** he said, 'My Lord, surely I – (my) bones have become weak within me, and (my) head is aflame (with) white (hair), but I have not been disappointed in calling on You (before), my Lord. **5** Surely I fear (who) the heirs (will be) after me, (for) my wife cannot conceive.[5] So grant me from Yourself an heir,[6] **6** (who) will inherit from me and inherit from the house of Jacob, and make him, my Lord, pleasing.'

7 'Zachariah! Surely We[7] give you good news of a boy. His name (will be) John. We have not given (this) name to anyone before.'[8] **8** He said, 'My Lord, how shall I have a boy, when my wife cannot conceive and I have already reached extreme old age?' **9** He said,[9] 'So (it will be)! Your Lord has said,[10] "It is easy for Me, seeing that I created you before, when you were nothing."' **10** He said, 'My Lord, give me[11] a sign.' He said, 'Your sign is that you will not speak[12] to the people for three days[13] exactly.' **11** So he came out to his people from the place of prayer[14] and inspired them:[15] 'Glorify (Him) morning and evening.'

Q19: This sūra begins with a series of stories about earlier prophets. The longest of these is the story of Mary and Jesus (Q19.16-36), from which Q19 receives its title. The remainder of the sūra explains the role of angels, responds to objections about the resurrection, and pronounces judgment on disbelievers. Most scholars assign Q19 to the 'Meccan' period.

1 Letters

1. *Kāf Hā' Yā' 'Ayn Ṣād*: the names of the Arabic letters *k, h, y, '*, and *ṣ*, a combination unique to Q19. Twenty-nine sūras begin with letters like these, ranging from one to five. No satisfactory explanation has been given for their occurrence. The Cairo edition varies in counting these letters as a separate verse (as here), or as the beginning of the first verse.

2–15 The story of Zachariah and John the Baptist

2. *remembrance*: or 'reminder' (see n. on Q3.58).
3. *servant*: the word 'servant' (Ar. *'abd*) also means 'slave.'
4. *Zachariah*: for the story that follows, cf. Q3.37-41; and Luke 1.5-25.
5. *my wife cannot conceive*: Zachariah's wife was Elizabeth, according to Luke 1.5.
6. *heir*: lit. 'ally' (Ar. *walī* implies the obligation of mutual protection).
7. *We...*: it is not clear whether God and/or the angels are speaking.
8. *We have not given (this) name to anyone before*: lit. 'We have not made for him a name from before;' cf. Luke 1.61, 'None of your relatives has this name.'
9. *He said...*: notice the sudden switch from first-person plur. to third-person sing.
10. *So (it will be)! Your Lord has said*: or 'Thus your Lord says' (cf. Q3.40); the same response given to Mary (Q19.21 below) and to Abraham's wife (Q51.30).
11. *give me*: lit. 'make for me.'
12. *you will not speak*: cf. Luke 1.20, '...unable to speak until the day these things occur.'
13. *days*: lit. 'nights.'
14. *the place of prayer*: or 'the prayer niche' (Ar. *al-miḥrāb*) of a mosque, but here it refers to the temple in Jerusalem (cf. Q3.37, 39), where Zachariah served as a priest, according to Luke 1.21-23.
15. *inspired them*: this is the only instance in which a human being is the subject of the technical term 'to inspire'

12 'John! Hold fast the Book!'[16] And We gave him the judgment[17] as a child, **13** and grace from Us, and purity.[18] He was one who guarded (himself)[19] **14** and was dutiful to his parents. He was not a tyrant (or) disobedient. **15** Peace (be) upon him the day he was born, and the day he dies, and the day he is raised up alive.

16 And remember in the Book[20] Mary:[21] When she withdrew from her family to an eastern place,
17 and took a veil[22] apart from them, We sent to her Our spirit,[23] and it took for her the form of a human
being exactly.[24] **18** She said, 'Surely I take refuge with the Merciful[25] from you, if you are one who guards
(yourself).' **19** He said, 'I am only a messenger[26] of your Lord (sent) to grant you a boy (who is) pure.'
20 She said, 'How can I have a boy, when no human being has touched me, nor am I a prostitute?'
21 He said, 'So (it will be)! Your Lord has said:[27] "It is easy for Me. And (it is) to make him a sign to the
people and a mercy from Us. It is a thing decreed."'

22 So she conceived him, and withdrew with him to a place far away. **23** The pains of childbirth drove
her to the trunk of the date palm.[28] She said, 'I wish I had died before (this) and was completely forgotten!' **24** And then he[29] called out to her from beneath her, 'Do not sorrow! Your Lord has made a stream
beneath you. **25** Shake the trunk of the date palm toward you, and it will drop on you fresh ripe (dates).
26 Eat and drink and be comforted.[30] If you see any human being, say: "Surely I have vowed a fast to the

---

(Ar. *awḥā*); cf. Q3.41.

16. *Hold fast the Book*: lit. 'Take the Book with force;' unless John was given a special book, this probably refers to the Torah. The same command occurs elsewhere only in reference to the revelation to Moses (Q2.63, 93; 7.145, 171). John's name occurs in a list of Abraham's descendants who were given 'the Book, the judgment, and the prophetic office' (see Q6.84-90).
17. *the judgment*: or 'the wisdom' (see n. on Q3.79).
18. *purity*: or 'alms' (Ar. *zakāt*); cf. below Q19.31 (Jesus), 55 (Ishmael).
19. *guarded (himself)*: against evil, or God.

16–36 The story of Mary and Jesus

20. *remember in the Book*: or 'mention in the Book' (Ar. *udhkur fi-l-kitāb*); the same formula occurs again at Q19.41 (Abraham), 51 (Moses), 54 (Ishmael), and 56 (Idrīs), but only here in the Qur'ān (cf. the formula 'And remember...' in Q38, used to introduce the stories of David [Q38.17], Job [41], Abraham, Isaac, and Jacob [45], and Ishmael, Elisha, and Dhū-l-Kifl [48]). The formula may be intended to 'remind' the audience of a particular story 'in the Book' (i.e. in the 'Torah' or 'Gospel'), or it may indicate that the Prophet had (or was thought to have) been instructed to undertake the production of a 'Book' (i.e. the Qur'ān in written form).
21. *Mary*: the only woman referred to by name in the Qur'ān. Though she is not considered a 'prophet,' she is listed among them at Q21.91, and God addresses her as a 'messenger' at Q23.51. For the story that follows, cf. the version at Q3.42-51; and Matthew 1.18-25; Luke 1.26-38; and the Proto-Gospel of James 12.
22. *took a veil*: Ar. *ḥijāb*; Mary is said to have served as a seamstress for the 'curtain' in the Jerusalem temple (see the Proto-Gospel of James 10), but the expression is simply metaphorical for 'hid herself' (cf. Q83.15).
23. *We sent to her Our spirit*: cf. Q21.91; 66.12 ('We breathed into her some of Our spirit'). The 'spirit' is traditionally identified with Gabriel, though this is not explicitly stated. Gabriel appears in the infancy narratives of both the Gospel of Luke (1.19, 26) and the Proto-Gospel of James (11.1-3; 12.2), where Mary is impregnated by the 'holy spirit' and 'power' of God. In the Gospel of Matthew (1.18-25) Jesus' conception is likewise said to occur 'through the holy spirit,' though the angel who announces this is unidentified.
24. *exactly*: the word may have an aesthetic or moral connotation ('well-formed' or 'upright').
25. *the Merciful*: Ar. *al-raḥmān* is used throughout Q19 as a proper name for God (see n. on Q25.60).
26. *only a messenger*: cf. Q3.144 (Muḥammad); 4.171; 5.75 (Jesus).
27. *So (it will be)! Your Lord has said*: or 'Thus your Lord says' (cf. Q3.47); the same response given to Zachariah (Q19.9 above) and to Abraham's wife (Q51.30).
28. *date palm*: for this and other features of the story, see the Gospel of Ps.-Matthew 20.
29. *he*: the infant Jesus, who speaks miraculously here as he does later at Q19.30-33 (cf. the Gospel of Ps.-Matthew 20).
30. *be comforted*: lit. 'cool (your) eye.'

Merciful, and so I shall not speak to any human today."'

27 Then she brought him to her people, carrying him. They said, 'Mary! Certainly you have brought something strange. **28** Sister of Aaron![31] Your father was not a bad man, nor was your mother a prostitute.' **29** But she referred (them) to him.[32] They said, 'How shall we speak to one who is in the cradle, a (mere) child?' **30** He said, 'Surely I am a servant of God. He has given me the Book[33] and made me a prophet.[34] **31** He has made me blessed wherever I am, and He has charged me with the prayer and the alms[35] as long as I live, **32** and (to be) respectful to my mother. He has not made me a tyrant (or) miserable. **33** Peace (be) upon me the day I was born, and the day I die,[36] and the day I am raised up alive.'

34 That was Jesus, son of Mary[37] – a statement of the truth[38] about which[39] they are in doubt. **35** It is not for God to take any son.[40] Glory to Him! When He decrees something, He simply says to it, 'Be!'[41] and it is. **36** 'Surely God is my Lord and your Lord, so serve Him![42] This is a straight path.'[43]

37 But the factions[44] differed among themselves. So woe to those who disbelieve on account of (their) witnessing a great Day! **38** How well they will hear on it! How well they will see on the Day when they come to Us! But the evildoers today are clearly astray.[45] **39** Warn them of the Day of Regret,[46] when the matter will be decided while they are (still) oblivious and disbelieving. **40** Surely We shall inherit the earth, and whoever is on it, and to Us they will be returned.

41 And remember in the Book Abraham: Surely he was a man of truth, a prophet. **42** When he said to his father, 'My father! Why do you serve what does not hear and does not see, and is of no use to you at all? **43** My father! Surely some knowledge has come to me that has not come to you. So follow me, and I shall guide you to an even path. **44** My father! Do not serve Satan![47] Surely Satan is disobedient to the Merciful. **45** My father! I fear that punishment from the Merciful will touch you, and you become an ally of Satan.'[48]

---

31. *Sister of Aaron*: there may be confusion here with Miriam, daughter of Amram and sister of Aaron and Moses (see n. on Q3.33; 66.12). Both Mary and Miriam would be 'Maryam' in Arabic.
32. *she referred (them) to him*: i.e. Mary advises them to consult with the infant Jesus (cf. Q3.46).
33. *the Book*: the Gospel (Ar. *Injīl*); see e.g. Q3.48; 5.110.
34. *prophet*: for this important title, see n. on Q2.87.
35. *the prayer and the alms*: *ṣalāt* (the ritual prayer) and *zakāt* (a kind of tithe); cf. below Q19.55 (Ishmael).
36. *and the day I die*: there are conflicting reports of Jesus' fate in the Qur'ān (cf. Q3.55; 4.157-158; 5.117).
37. *son of Mary*: there is no mention in the Qur'ān of Joseph, Jesus' putative father (cf. Mark 6.3).
38. *statement of the truth*: or 'word of truth,' so possibly referring to Jesus (cf. Q3.45, 'a word from Him;' 4.171, 'His word').
39. *about which*: or 'about whom.'
40. *son*: or 'child' (Ar. *walad*), but referring to Christian claims about Jesus as God's son (see Q19.88-92 below).
41. *Be!*: God's creative word (Ar. *kun*); cf. Q2.117; 3.47 (to Mary), 59 (of Jesus and Adam); 6.73; 16.40; 36.82; 40.68.
42. *serve Him*: or 'worship Him.'
43. *Surely God is...a straight path*: it is not clear whether Jesus is speaking or the Prophet.

37–40 Warning to those who dispute about Jesus

44. *the factions*: or 'the sectarians' (Ar. *al-aḥzāb*), referring to Jews and Christians in general, but perhaps also to Christian 'sectarians' and their contradictory views of Jesus (cf. Q43.65).
45. *clearly astray*: lit. 'in clear straying.'
46. *Day of Regret*: or 'Day of Sighing' (addressed to the Prophet).

41–50 Abraham, Isaac, and Jacob

47. *Satan*: for this figure, see n. on Q2.36.
48. *ally of Satan*: Ar. *walī* implies the obligation of mutual protection, almost in the sense of 'friend' or 'brother.'

46 He said, 'Do you forsake my gods, Abraham?[49] If indeed you do not stop, I shall indeed stone you. So leave me[50] for a long time!' **47** He said, 'Peace (be) upon you! I shall ask forgiveness for you from my Lord.[51] Surely He has been gracious to me. **48** I shall withdraw from you and what you call on instead of God, and I shall call on my Lord. It may be that I shall not be disappointed in calling on my Lord.' **49** So when he had withdrawn from them and what they were serving instead of God, We granted him Isaac and Jacob,[52] and each one We made a prophet. **50** We granted them some of Our mercy, and We assigned to them[53] a true (and) high reputation.[54]

51 And remember in the Book Moses: Surely he was devoted, and he was a messenger, a prophet.[55] **52** We called him from the right side of the mountain,[56] and We brought him near in conversation.[57] **53** And We granted him some of Our mercy: his brother Aaron, a prophet.

54 And remember in the Book Ishmael: Surely he was true to the promise, and he was a messenger, a prophet. **55** He commanded his people with the prayer and the alms, and he was pleasing before his Lord.

56 And remember in the Book Idrīs:[58] Surely he was a man of truth, a prophet. **57** We raised him up to a high place.[59]

58 Those were the ones[60] whom God has blessed among the prophets from the descendants of Adam, and from those We carried with Noah,[61] and from the descendants of Abraham and Israel,[62] and from those whom We have guided and chosen. When the signs[63] of the Merciful were recited to them, they fell down in prostration and weeping. **59** But after them came successors[64] (who) neglected[65] the prayer and

---

49. *Do you forsake...*: or 'Do you flee from...' (from the same root as Hijra).
50. *leave me*: or 'flee from me' (see previous n.).
51. *I shall ask forgiveness for you...*: see Q14.41; 26.86; 60.4 (cf. Q71.28, Noah); otherwise prayer for disbelievers is forbidden (see Q9.113-114).
52. *Isaac and Jacob*: Ishmael is mentioned only later at Q19.54, with no apparent connection to Abraham (cf. Q6.84-86; 11.71; 21.72-85; 38.45-48). In other passages, however, emphasis is placed on Ishmael as Abraham's son (see e.g. Q2.125, 127; 4.163; 14.39).
53. *assigned to them*: lit. 'made for them.'
54. *reputation*: lit. 'tongue' (i.e. being well spoken of); cf. Q26.84 (of Abraham).

51–53 Moses and Aaron

55. *a messenger, a prophet*: for these important titles, see n. on Q2.87.
56. *from the right side of the mountain*: i.e. Mount Sinai (Q23.20; 95.2); according to Q28.44, the 'right side' is the 'western side' (cf. Deuteronomy 33.2).
57. *brought him near in conversation*: see Q4.164, 'God spoke to Moses directly' (cf. Q7.143; 42.51n.).

54–55 Ishmael

56–57 Idrīs

58. *Idrīs*: mentioned only here and at Q21.85, where he is linked with Ishmael and Dhū-l-Kifl. Though sometimes identified with Enoch, who 'walked with God, and he was not, for God took him' (Genesis 5.24), he is probably Ezra (derived from 'Esdras,' the Greek form of the name), who was also taken up to heaven, like Enoch and Elijah (see 4 Ezra 14.7-9).
59. *a high place*: heaven.

58–63 God's special prophets

60. *Those were the ones...*: the Cairo edition, reflecting the views of traditional scholars, attributes this verse to the 'Medinan' period.
61. *carried with Noah*: in the ark.
62. *Israel*: here designating the patriarch Jacob/Israel (cf. Q3.93).
63. *signs*: or 'verses.'
64. *came successors*: lit. 'successions succeeded' (cf. Q7.169).
65. *neglected*: or 'corrupted' (lit. 'wasted').

followed (their own) desires. Soon they will meet error **60** – except for the one who turns (in repentance), and believes, and does righteousness.[66] Those will enter the Garden, and they will not be done evil at all **61** – Gardens of Eden,[67] which the Merciful has promised to His servants in the unseen.[68] Surely He – His promise will come to pass. **62** There they will not hear any frivolous talk, only 'Peace!'[69] And there they will have their provision morning and evening. **63** That is the Garden which We give as an inheritance to those of Our servants who guard (themselves).

64 'We[70] only come down by the command[71] of your Lord. To Him (belongs) whatever is before us and whatever is behind us, and whatever is between that. Your Lord is not forgetful **65** – Lord of the heavens and the earth, and whatever is between them. So serve Him and be patient in His service! Do you[72] know (another) name for Him?'[73]

66 The human says, 'When I am dead, shall I indeed be brought forth alive?' **67** Does the human not remember that We created him before, when he was nothing? **68** By your Lord![74] We shall indeed gather them together, and (also) the satans.[75] Then We shall indeed bring them around Gehenna[76] (on) bended knees. **69** Then We shall indeed draw out from each party those of them (who are) most (in) rebellion against the Merciful. **70** Then indeed We shall know those who most deserve burning with it. **71** (There is) not one of you (who is) not coming to it[77] – (that) is for your Lord an inevitability decreed. **72** Then We shall rescue the ones who guarded (themselves), and leave the evildoers in it (on) bended knees.

73 When Our signs[78] are recited to them as clear signs,[79] those who disbelieve say to those who believe, 'Which of the two groups is better in status and better as a cohort?' **74** But how many a generation We have destroyed before them![80] They were better in wealth and outward appearance. **75** Say:[81] 'Whoever is astray, let the Merciful prolong his life[82] until, when they see what they are promised – either the

66. *does righteousness*: or 'acts uprightly.'
67. *the Garden...Gardens of Eden*: in heaven (for this imagery, see n. on Q2.25).
68. *in the unseen*: or 'in the future' (see n. on Q2.3).
69. *Peace*: Ar. *salām* connotes 'submission' (*islām*) to God.

64–65 The function of the angels

70. *We...*: the angels are speaking in these two verses.
71. *by the command*: or 'with the affair' (see nn. on Q16.1-2).
72. *you*: the Prophet, or perhaps intended generally ('one').
73. *(another) name for Him*: i.e. other than the title 'Lord.'

66–72 Resurrection certain

74. *By your Lord*: for God's unusual 'swearing by himself,' cf. Q4.65; 15.92; 16.56, 63; 70.40; and Hebrews 6.13 (Genesis 22.16); but perhaps it is the angels who are speaking here.
75. *satans*: or 'demons' (Ar. *shayāṭīn*); individually assigned to incite people to evil (see Q19.83 below; 43.36; cf. Q23.97; 41.25).
76. *Gehenna*: a name for Hell (see n. on Q2.206).
77. *not one of you (who is) not coming to it*: apparently even believers will be brought to Hell, until a separation is made between the righteous and the wicked. The Cairo edition attributes this verse to the 'Medinan' period.

73–87 Punishment for disbelief and idolatry

78. *signs*: or 'verses.'
79. *clear signs*: or 'clear proofs,' 'indisputable evidence.'
80. *how many a generation We have destroyed before them*: a reference to previous peoples who were punished for their sins (cf. Q19.98 below; see n. on Q7.59).
81. *Say*: on this form of address, see n. on Q2.80.
82. *prolong his life*: lit. 'extend for him an extension.'

punishment or the Hour[83] – they will know who is worse in position and weaker in forces.' **76** But God will increase in guidance those who are guided. And the things that endure – righteous deeds – are better with your Lord, and better in return.

77 Have you[84] seen the one who disbelieves in Our signs, and says, 'I shall indeed be given wealth and children'? **78** Has he looked into the unseen,[85] or has he taken a covenant with the Merciful? **79** By no means! We shall write down what he says, and We shall increase the punishment for him. **80** We shall inherit from him what he says,[86] and he will come to Us alone.

81 They have taken gods other than God, so that they[87] might be a (source of) honor for them. **82** By no means! They will deny[88] their service, and they will be opposed to them. **83** Do you[89] not see that We have sent the satans against the disbelievers to incite them.[90] **84** So do not be in a hurry with them. We are only counting for them a (certain) number (of years).[91] **85** On the Day when We shall gather to the Merciful the ones who guarded (themselves) like a delegation, **86** and drive the sinners into Gehenna like a herd, **87** they will have no power of intercession, except for the one who has made a covenant with the Merciful.

88 They say,[92] 'The Merciful has taken a son.'[93] **89** Certainly you have put forth something abhorrent! **90** The heavens are nearly torn apart because of it, and the earth split open, and the mountains collapse in pieces **91** – that they should attribute[94] to the Merciful a son, **92** when it is not fitting for the Merciful to take a son.

93 (There is) no one in the heavens and the earth who comes to the Merciful except as a servant. **94** Certainly He has counted them and numbered them exactly.[95] **95** Each one of them will come to Him on the Day of Resurrection alone. **96** Surely those who believe and do righteous deeds – to them the Merciful will show[96] (His) love.

97 Surely We have made it[97] easy in your language,[98] so that you may give good news by means of it to the ones who guard (themselves), and warn by means of it a contentious people. **98** But how many a generation We have destroyed before them! Do you see a single one of them, or hear (even) a whisper of them?

---

83. *the Hour*: of judgment.
84. *you*: the Prophet, or perhaps intended generally ('one').
85. *the unseen*: or 'the future.'
86. *what he says*: i.e. the wealth and children of which he spoke, and which will be left behind at death.
87. *they*: i.e. their gods.
88. *They will deny*: i.e. their gods will deny (lit. 'disbelieve').
89. *you*: the Prophet.
90. *to incite them*: lit. 'to incite them an incitement;' i.e. instigate them to even greater sin (cf. Q7.27; 23.97; 41.25; 43.36).
91. *counting...a (certain) number (of years)*: i.e. the time of judgment has already been determined.

88–96 God has no son

92. *They say*: the Christians, though this claim always remains anonymous.
93. *son*: or 'child' (Ar. *walad*), but referring to Christian claims about Jesus as God's son (cf. Q2.116; 4.171; 10.68; 21.26; 25.2).
94. *attribute*: lit. 'call.'
95. *numbered them exactly*: lit. 'numbered them (with or by) a number.'
96. *show*: lit. 'make' (cf. Q11.90; 85.14).

97–98 Final words to the Prophet

97. *it*: the Qur'ān.
98. *your language*: lit. 'your tongue' (Arabic).

20 Ṭā' Hā' ۞ Ṭā' Hā'

In the Name of God, the Merciful, the Compassionate

1 Ṭā' Hā'.[1] **2** We have not sent down the Qur'ān on you for you to be miserable, **3** but as a reminder[2] to the one who fears **4** – as a sending down from the One who created the earth and the high heavens. **5** The Merciful[3] is mounted upon the throne. **6** To Him (belongs) whatever is in the heavens and whatever is on the earth, and whatever is between them, and whatever is beneath the ground.[4] **7** If you[5] speak the word[6] publicly, surely He knows the secret and (what is even) more hidden.[7] **8** God – (there is) no god but Him. To Him (belong) the best names.[8]

9 Has the story of Moses[9] come to you?[10] **10** When he saw a fire, he said to his family, 'Stay (here). Surely I perceive a fire. Perhaps I shall bring you a flaming torch from it, or I shall find at the fire guidance.'[11] **11** But when he came to it, he was called: 'Moses! **12** Surely I am your Lord, so take off your shoes. Surely you are in the holy wādi of Ṭuwā.[12] **13** I have chosen you, so listen to what is inspired. **14** Surely I am God – (there is) no god but Me. So serve Me, and observe the prayer for My remembrance! **15** Surely the Hour is coming[13] – I almost hide it, so that every person may be repaid for what he strives after.[14] **16** So do not

---

Q20: This sūra, assigned by most scholars to the 'Meccan' period, is devoted almost entirely to the story of Moses (Q20.9-101). It features accounts of his early life, call to be a messenger, struggles with Pharaoh, exodus from Egypt, and finally the episode of 'the calf.' Q20 concludes with sections on the 'Last Day' and the 'covenant with Adam.' It receives its title from the two letters with which it begins.

1–8 Purpose of the Qur'ān

1. *Ṭā' Hā'*: the names of Arabic letters *ṭ* and *h*, a combination unique to Q20. Twenty-nine sūras begin with letters like these, ranging from one to five. No satisfactory explanation has been given for their occurrence. The Cairo edition varies in counting these letters as a separate verse (as here), or as the beginning of the first verse.
2. *reminder*: or 'remembrance' (see n. on Q3.58).
3. *the Merciful*: Ar. *al-raḥmān* is used here and at the end of this sūra as a proper name for God (see n. on Q25.60).
4. *beneath the ground*: perhaps meaning 'the lowest depths' or 'the watery abyss' (Ar. *al-tharā* occurs only here).
5. *you*: the Prophet.
6. *the word*: perhaps concerning the coming judgment, or else a reference to the Prophet's proclamation in general.
7. *the secret and (what is even) more hidden*: reference obscure; perhaps the 'secret time' of the Last Day (cf. Q20.15 below), or the Prophet's 'inner thoughts' (cf. Q2.33).
8. *the best names*: or 'the most beautiful names' (Ar. *al-asmā' al-ḥusnā*); cf. Q7.180; 17.110; 59.24. A list of ninety-nine names was eventually compiled, consisting of those mentioned in the Qur'ān as well as others. They play an important role in theology and worship.

9–36 The story of Moses: his call and mission

9. *story of Moses*: or 'report about Moses' (Ar. *ḥadīth Mūsā*); for the story that follows, cf. the versions at Q27.7-14; 28.29-35; and the account of Moses' call at Exodus 3-4.
10. *you*: sing., but probably intended generally.
11. *guidance*: one of the most frequent terms (Ar. *hudā*) for revelation in general, and the Qur'ān in particular.
12. *holy wādi of Ṭuwā*: reference obscure; it is mentioned only here and at Q79.16; cf. Q28.30.
13. *the Hour is coming*: for judgment.
14. *I almost hide it, so that...*: meaning that 'the coming Hour' is not widely known, so that people will receive what they really deserve.

let anyone who does not believe in it, and who (only) follows his (own) desire, keep you from it,[15] or you will be brought to ruin.'

17 'What is that in your right (hand), Moses?' **18** He said, 'It is my staff. I lean on it, and I bring down leaves with it to (feed) my sheep, and I have other uses for it.' **19** He said, 'Cast it (down), Moses!' **20** So he cast it, and suddenly it became a slithering snake. **21** He said, 'Take hold of it, and do not fear. We shall restore it to its former state. **22** Now draw your hand to your side.[16] It will come out white, unharmed – another sign.[17] **23** (We have done this) to show you one of Our greatest signs.'

24 'Go to Pharaoh! Surely he has transgressed insolently.' **25** He said, 'My Lord, expand my heart[18] for me, **26** and make my task[19] easy for me. **27** Untie the knot from my tongue,[20] **28** so that they may understand my words. **29** And appoint[21] an assistant for me from my family: **30** Aaron, my brother. **31** Strengthen me through him, **32** and associate him in my task, **33** so that we may glorify You often, **34** and remember You often. **35** Surely you see us.' **36** He said, 'You are granted your request, Moses.'

37 'Certainly We bestowed favor on you another time, **38** when We inspired your mother (with) what was inspired:[22] **39** "Cast him into the ark,[23] and cast it into the sea,[24] and let the sea throw it up on the shore, and an enemy to Me and an enemy to him will take him." But I cast love on you from Me, and (I did this) so that you might be brought up[25] under My eye. **40** When your sister went out, she said, "Shall I direct you[26] to (someone) who will take charge of him?" And We returned you to your mother, so that she might be comforted[27] and not sorrow. And (then) you killed a man,[28] and We rescued you from that distress, and We tested you thoroughly. So you remained for (some) years with the people of Midian,[29] (and) then you came (here),[30] according to a decree, Moses.'

41 'I have brought you up[31] for Myself. **42** Go, you and your brother, with My signs, and do not be lax in My remembrance. **43** Go, both of you, to Pharaoh. Surely he has transgressed insolently. **44** But speak to him a soft word. Perhaps he may take heed or fear.' **45** They said, 'Our Lord, surely we are afraid that he may

---

15. *keep you from it*: i.e. from believing that 'the Hour is coming.'
16. *draw your hand to your side*: meaning obscure (lit. 'fold your wing to yourself'); perhaps 'put your hand under your arm,' or 'into your cloak' (cf. Q28.32 for the same expression).
17. *another sign*: or 'miracle' (cf. Exodus 4.6).
18. *expand my heart*: or 'open my mind' (lit. 'chest'); cf. Q6.125; 94.1 (of the Prophet).
19. *task*: or 'command.'
20. *Untie the knot from my tongue*: see Q43.52; Moses was 'slow of speech and slow of tongue,' according to Exodus 4.10; 6.12, 30.
21. *appoint*: lit. 'make.'

37–40 Moses' childhood and early life

22. *We inspired your mother (with) what was inspired*: for the story that follows, cf. the version at Q28.7-14; and Exodus 2.1-10.
23. *ark*: or 'chest' (Ar. *tābūt*), the same word as the 'ark' or 'chest' containing God's Sakīna at Q2.248; see the parallel version of this story at Q28.7-13; and cf. Exodus 2.1-10 (which uses the same word for Moses' 'ark' as Noah's).
24. *sea*: the Nile river, according to Exodus 2.3-5.
25. *brought up*: lit. 'built' or 'constructed.'
26. *you*: the household of Pharaoh who had picked up Moses, according to Q28.8 (cf. Exodus 2.7).
27. *that she might be comforted*: lit. 'that her eye might be cooled.'
28. *killed a man*: see Q28.14-17; cf. Exodus 2.11-15.
29. *people of Midian*: to whom the messenger Shu'ayb was sent (see e.g. Q7.85; 11.84; cf. Exodus 2.15).
30. *(here)*: i.e. the 'wādi of Ṭuwā' (see Q20.12 above).

41–48 Moses and Aaron sent to Pharaoh

31. *brought you up*: lit. 'built you.'

act rashly against us, or that he may transgress insolently.' **46** He said, 'Do not be afraid! Surely I am with both of you. I hear and I see. **47** So go to him, both of you, and say: "We are two messengers[32] of your Lord, so send forth the Sons of Israel with us, and do not punish them. We have brought you a sign from your Lord. Peace (be) upon anyone who follows the guidance! **48** Surely we have been inspired[33] that the punishment (will fall) on anyone who calls (it) a lie and turns away."'

49 He[34] said, 'And who is your Lord, Moses?' **50** He said, 'Our Lord is the One who gave everything its creation, (and) then guided (it).' **51** He said, 'What (about the) case of the former generations?' **52** He said, 'The knowledge of it is with my Lord in a Book.[35] My Lord does not go astray, nor does He forget. **53** (It is He) who made the earth as a cradle for you, and put (path)ways in it for you, and sent down water from the sky. And by means of it We[36] brought forth pairs of various (kinds of) vegetation. **54** Eat (of it) and pasture your livestock (on it). Surely in that are signs indeed for those with reason. **55** We created you from it,[37] and into it We shall return you, and from it We shall bring you forth another time.'

56 Certainly We showed him[38] Our signs, all of them,[39] but he called (them) a lie and refused. **57** He said, 'Have you come to bring us forth from our land[40] by your magic, Moses?[41] **58** We shall indeed bring you magic like it. So set an appointment between us and you – We shall not break it, nor will you – at a fair place.' **59** He[42] said, 'Your appointment is on the Day of Splendor.[43] Let the people be gathered at morning light.'

60 So Pharaoh turned away, and put together his plot. Then he came (again).[44] **61** Moses said to them, 'Woe to you! Do not forge a lie against God, or He will destroy you with a punishment. Whoever forges (a lie) has failed.' **62** So they disputed their situation among themselves, but they kept their talk secret. **63** They said, 'Surely these two magicians want to expel you from your land[45] by their magic, and to do away with your exemplary way (of life). **64** So put together your plot, (and) then line up. He who has the upper hand today will indeed prosper.' **65** They said, 'Moses! Are you going to cast or shall we be first to cast?' **66** He said, 'No! You cast (first)!' And suddenly their ropes and their staffs seemed to him to be moving[46] as a result of their magic. **67** So Moses felt fear within himself. **68** We said to him, 'Do not be afraid! Surely you will be the superior one. **69** Cast (down) what is in your right (hand),[47] and it will swallow up what they have made. What they have done is only a magician's trick, and the magician does not prosper, (no matter) where he comes.'

---

32. *messengers*: for this important title, see n. on Q2.87.
33. *we have been inspired*: or 'we have received inspiration.'

49–76 Moses' struggle with Pharaoh

34. *He*: Pharaoh; the scene suddenly shifts from Moses' audience with God at Ṭuwā to Pharaoh's court.
35. *a Book*: i.e. the 'Book of God' or the heavenly 'Record' of all things (see n. on Q6.59).
36. *We*: notice the sudden shift from third- to first-person discourse.
37. *from it*: from the earth.
38. *him*: Pharaoh; for this first audience with Pharaoh, which is only summarized here, see the version at Q7.103-112; and cf. Exodus 5.1-6.1.
39. *all of them*: lit. 'all of it.'
40. *land*: lit. 'earth.'
41. *Have you come to bring us forth...*: there is no motive for this question by Pharaoh, unless he has misunderstood Moses' prior statement about the resurrection ('We shall bring you forth another time') at Q20.55.
42. *He*: Moses.
43. *Day of Splendor*: perhaps some festival, but the reference is obscure.
44. *he came (again)*: for the episode that follows, cf. Q7.113-126; and Exodus 7.8-13.
45. *land*: lit. 'earth.'
46. *moving*: like snakes; for the additional 'ropes,' see Q26.44; cf. Exodus 7.11-12.
47. *what is in your right (hand)*: Moses' staff; according to Exodus 7.8-10, it was Aaron who cast his staff before Pharaoh.

70 And the magicians were cast (down) in prostration. They said, 'We believe in the Lord of Aaron and Moses.' **71** He[48] said, 'Have you believed in him[49] before I gave you permission? Surely he indeed is your master,[50] the (very) one who taught you magic? I shall indeed cut off your hands and your feet on opposite sides, and I shall indeed crucify you on the trunks of date palms, and you will indeed know which of us is harsher in punishment, and more lasting.' **72** They said, 'We shall not prefer you over the clear signs[51] which have come to us, nor (over) Him who created us. So decree whatever you are going to decree. You can only decree for this present life. **73** Surely we have believed in our Lord, so that He may forgive us our sins and the magic you forced us to (practice). God is better and more lasting.'

74 Surely the one who comes to his Lord as a sinner, surely for him (there is) Gehenna,[52] where he will neither die nor live. **75** But whoever comes to Him as a believer, (and) he has done righteous deeds, those – for them (there are) the highest ranks: **76** Gardens of Eden,[53] through which rivers flow, there to remain. That is the payment for the one who purifies himself.

77 Certainly We inspired Moses: 'Journey with My servants,[54] and strike for them a dry passage in the sea, without fear of being overtaken[55] or being afraid.' **78** So Pharaoh followed them with his forces, but (there) covered them of the sea what covered them.[56] **79** Pharaoh led his people astray and did not guide (them).

80 Sons of Israel! We have rescued you from your enemy, and made a covenant with you at the right side of the mountain,[57] and sent down on you the manna and the quails: **81** 'Eat from the good things which We have provided you, but do not transgress insolently in that, or My anger will descend on you. Whoever My anger falls on has perished. **82** Yet surely I am indeed forgiving to whoever turns (in repentance) and believes, and does righteousness, (and) then is (rightly) guided.'

83 'What has made you hurry (ahead) of your people, Moses?' **84** He said, 'They are close on my footsteps, but I have hurried (ahead) to you, my Lord, in order that You might be pleased.' **85** He[58] said, 'Surely We have tempted[59] your people after you (left them), and al-Sāmirī[60] has led them astray.' **86** So Moses returned to his people, angry (and) sorrowful. He said, 'My people! Did your Lord not promise you a good promise? Did (the time of) the covenant last too long for you, or did you wish that the anger of your Lord would descend on you, and so you broke (your) appointment with me?' **87** They said,

48. *He*: Pharaoh.
49. *him*: probably Moses; or 'Him' (God).
50. *master*: lit. 'great one.'
51. *the clear signs*: or 'the clear proofs,' 'the indisputable evidence,' referring to the miracle performed by Moses.
52. *Gehenna*: a name for Hell (see n. on Q2.206).
53. *Gardens of Eden*: in heaven (for this imagery, see n. on Q2.25).

77–79 The exodus from Egypt

54. *Journey with My servants*: cf. Q26.52; 44.23 ('by night').
55. *overtaken*: by Pharaoh.
56. *(there) covered them...what covered them*: for this expression, cf. Q53.16, 54.

80–82 The covenant with the Sons of Israel

57. *at the right side of the mountain*: i.e. Mount Sinai (Q23.20; 95.2); according to Q28.44, the 'right side' is the 'western side' (cf. Deuteronomy 33.2).

83–98 The episode of the Calf

58. *He*: God.
59. *tempted*: or 'tested.'
60. *al-Sāmirī*: perhaps 'the Samaritan,' but the meaning is uncertain. Many traditions in the Bible reflect Judean opposition to the northern kingdom of 'Israel' or 'Samaria.' The prophet Hosea denounced the inhabitants of 'Samaria' for their idolatrous worship of an image of a 'calf' (Hosea 8.5-6; 10.5). Animosity toward Samaritans continued in post-biblical literature as well.

'We did not break (our) appointment with you by our (own) will, but we were loaded with burdens of the ornaments of the people,[61] and we cast them (down),[62] and so did al-Sāmirī.' **88** Then he brought forth for them a calf,[63] a (mere) image[64] of it (having) a mooing sound, and they[65] said, 'This is your god, and the god of Moses, though he has forgotten.' **89** Did they not see that it did not return a word to them, and had no power to (cause) them harm or benefit? **90** Certainly Aaron had said to them before, 'My people! You are only being tempted by it. Surely your Lord is the Merciful, so follow me and obey my command!' **91** They said, 'We shall continue (to be) devoted to it until Moses returns to us.'

92 He[66] said, 'Aaron! What prevented you, when you saw them going astray, **93** from following me? Did you disobey my command?' **94** He said, 'Son of my mother! Do not seize (me) by my beard or by my head! Surely I was afraid that you would say, "You have caused a division among the Sons of Israel, and you have not respected my word."' **95** He[67] said, 'What was this business of yours, al-Sāmirī?' **96** He said, 'I saw what they did not see, and I took a handful (of dust) from the footprint of the messenger, and I tossed it. In this way my mind contrived (it) for me.' **97** He[68] said, 'Go! Surely it is yours in this life to say, "Do not touch (me)!" And surely for you (there is) an appointment[69] – you will not break it. Look at your god which you remained devoted to! We shall indeed burn it (and) then scatter it as dust[70] in the sea. **98** Your only god is God – (there is) no god but Him – who comprehends everything in knowledge.'

99 In this way We recount to you[71] some of the stories[72] of what has already gone before, and We have given you a reminder from Us. **100** Whoever turns away from it, surely he will bear a burden on the Day of Resurrection. **101** [...][73] there to remain, and evil (will be the) load for them on the Day of Resurrection.

102 On the Day when there is a blast on the trumpet[74] – and We shall gather the sinners on that Day blue[75] – **103** they will murmur among themselves: 'You have remained (in the grave) only for ten (days).' **104** We know what they will say, when the best of them in way (of life) will say, 'You have remained only for a day.'

105 They ask you[76] about the mountains. Say:[77] 'My Lord will scatter them as dust, **106** and He will leave

---

61. *ornaments of the people*: probably the spoils they had taken from the Egyptians (see Q10.88n.).
62. *cast them (down)*: into a fire for melting.
63. *a calf*: for a parallel version of this story, see Q7.148-153; cf. the story of the 'golden calf' at Exodus 32.1-35.
64. *image*: lit. 'body.'
65. *they*: perhaps the text should be emended to read 'he' (i.e. al-Sāmirī).
66. *He*: Moses.
67. *He*: Moses.
68. *He*: Moses.
69. *an appointment*: the Day of Judgment.
70. *scatter it as dust*: lit. 'scatter it a scattering' (also Q20.105 below).

99–101 Conclusion to the story of Moses

71. *you*: the Prophet.
72. *stories*: or 'news.'
73. *[...]*: there appears to be a lacuna here.

102–112 Events of the Last Day

74. *a blast on the trumpet*: the Last Day will be announced by the blast of a trumpet (e.g. Q6.73; 18.99; 39.68 [a double blast]; 69.13; 74.8; 78.18; cf. Matthew 24.31; 1 Corinthians 15.52; 1 Thessalonians 4.16).
75. *blue*: Ar. *zurq* is usually taken as a reference to the color of their eyes, and as equivalent to 'blind,' but the meaning is obscure.
76. *you*: the Prophet.
77. *Say*: on this form of address, see n. on Q2.80.

it a barren plain **107** in which you[78] will not see any crookedness or curve.'

108 On that Day they will follow the Caller,[79] in whom (there is) no crookedness, and voices will be hushed before the Merciful, so that you[80] will hear nothing but a faint murmur. **109** On that Day intercession will not be of any benefit, except for the one to whom the Merciful gives permission, and whose word He approves. **110** He knows what is before them and what is behind them, but they do not encompass Him in knowledge. **111** Faces will be humbled before the Living, the Everlasting. Whoever carries (a load of) evildoing will have failed, **112** but whoever does any righteous deeds – and he is a believer – he will not fear (any) evil or dispossession.

113 In this way We have sent it down as an Arabic Qur'ān,[81] and We have varied some of the promise(s)[82] in it, so that they may guard (themselves),[83] or so that it may arouse in them a reminder.[84] **114** Exalted is God, the true King![85] Do not be in a hurry with the Qur'ān,[86] before its inspiration is completed to you, but say: 'My Lord, increase me in knowledge.'

115 Certainly We made a covenant with Adam before, but he forgot, and We found in him no determination. **116** (Remember) when We said to the angels,[87] 'Prostrate yourselves before Adam,'[88] and they prostrated themselves, except Iblīs.[89] He refused. **117** And We said, 'Adam! Surely this is an enemy to you and to your wife. Do not let him expel you both from the Garden, and you become miserable. **118** Surely it is yours not to hunger there or go naked, **119** nor to thirst there or be exposed to the sun.' **120** But Satan whispered to him.[90] He said, 'Adam! Shall I direct you to the Tree of Immortality,[91] and (to) a kingdom that does not decay?' **121** So they both ate from it, and their shameful parts became apparent to them,[92] and they both began fastening on themselves some leaves of the Garden, and Adam disobeyed his Lord and erred. **122** Then his Lord chose him, and turned to him (in forgiveness),[93] and guided (him).

---

78. *you*: or 'one.'
79. *the Caller*: summoning people to judgment (cf. Q30.25; 54.6).
80. *you*: the Prophet, or perhaps intended generally.

113–114 An Arabic Qur'ān

81. *an Arabic Qur'ān*: perhaps meaning that it is a translation into Arabic of the heavenly archetype or 'mother of the Book' (cf. Q12.2; 13.37; 16.103; 39.28; 41.3; 42.7; 43.3; 46.12). The specification 'Arabic Qur'ān' (Ar. *qur'ān 'arabiyya*) may imply the existence of 'Qur'āns' (as it were) in other languages, but it is probably an answer to some objection, perhaps that Hebrew was thought to be the exclusive language of revelation.
82. *promise(s)*: or 'threat(s)' (of punishment).
83. *guard (themselves)*: against evil, or God.
84. *reminder*: or 'remembrance.'
85. *the true King*: or 'the King, the Truth.'
86. *Do not be in a hurry with the Qur'ān*: either in reciting or collecting it (see Q75.16-19; cf. Q17.106).

115–127 The covenant with Adam

87. *angels*: for these beings and their various roles, see n. on Q2.30.
88. *Prostrate yourselves before Adam*: for the story that follows, cf. the versions at Q2.34-39; 7.19-25; and Genesis 2.4-3.24. The prostration of the angels before Adam is not a part of the Genesis account, but was a prominent theme in Christian tradition (see e.g. Hebrews 1.6; Life of Adam and Eve 12.1-16.1; Cave of Treasures 2.22-25).
89. *except Iblīs*: for this figure, see n. on Q2.34.
90. *Satan whispered to him*: here Satan 'whispers' to Adam alone; cf. Q2.36; 7.20-22, where both Adam and his wife are tempted; and Genesis 3.1-24, for the story of the temptation of Eve.
91. *Tree of Immortality*: only mentioned here (cf. Q2.35; 7.19-22 ['this tree']; and Genesis 2.9; 3.22-23 ['Tree of Life']).
92. *their shameful parts became apparent to them*: i.e. they realized that they were naked.
93. *turned to him (in forgiveness)*: Adam's sin is forgiven; the Christian doctrine of 'original sin' is as foreign to the Qur'ān as it is to the Jewish Bible (or Old Testament).

123 He said, 'Go down from it,[94] both of you together, some of you an enemy to others.[95] If any guidance
comes to you from Me, whoever follows My guidance will not go astray, nor become miserable. **124** But
whoever turns away from My reminder,[96] surely for him (there will be) a life of deprivation, and We
shall gather him blind on the Day of Resurrection.' **125** He will say, 'My Lord, why have you gathered me
blind, when I had sight before?' **126** He will say, 'So (it is). Our signs came to you, but you forgot them,
so today you are forgotten.' **127** In this way We repay anyone who acts wantonly and does not believe in
the signs of his Lord. Yet the punishment of the Hereafter[97] is indeed harsher and more lasting.

128 Is it not a guide for them how many generations We destroyed before them, (seeing that) they walk
in (the midst of) their dwelling places?[98] Surely in that are signs indeed for those with reason. **129** Were it
not for a preceding word from your Lord, it would indeed be close at hand – but (there is) a time appointed
(for punishment).[99] **130** So be patient with what they say,[100] and glorify your Lord with praise before the
rising of the sun, and before its setting, and during the hours of the night, and glorify (Him) at the ends of
the day, so that you may find satisfaction. **131** Do not yearn after[101] what We have given classes of them
to enjoy[102] – the flower of this present life – that We may test them by means of it. The provision of your
Lord is better and more lasting.[103] **132** Command your family (to observe) the prayer, and be patient in it.
We do not ask you for provision.[104] We provide for you, and the outcome (is) for the guarding (of yourself).

133 They say, 'If only he would bring us a sign from his Lord.'[105] Has there not come to them a clear sign[106]
(of) what was in the former pages?[107] **134** If We had destroyed them with a punishment before him,[108]
they would indeed have said, 'Our Lord, if only you had sent us a messenger, so that we might have followed your signs before we were humiliated and disgraced?' **135** Say: 'Each one is waiting, so you wait
(too), and then you will know who are the followers of the even path, and who is (rightly) guided.'

---

94. *Go down from it*: i.e. from the heavenly Garden to earth.
95. *some of you an enemy to others*: 'you' is plur. here, and probably refers to humanity in general, whereas the preceding imperative was dual (referring to Adam and his wife).
96. *My reminder*: or 'remembrance of Me.'
97. *the Hereafter*: see n. on Q2.4.

128–132 Exhortation to the Prophet

98. *they walk in (the midst of) their dwelling places*: for this idea, see n. on Q14.45.
99. *...a time appointed (for punishment)*: i.e. punishment would have occurred already, if it had not been for a previous decree which determined the 'time' or 'term' (Ar. *ajal*) for it (cf. Q8.68; 10.19; 11.110; 41.45; 42.14, 21).
100. *So be patient...*: addressed to the Prophet.
101. *Do not yearn after*: lit. 'Do not stretch your eyes toward.'
102. *what We have given classes of them to enjoy*: probably wealth, but the word 'classes' (Ar. *azwāj*) may mean 'pairs' or 'couples,' in which case 'what We have given them' would refer to sons.
103. *...more lasting*: the Cairo edition, reflecting the views of traditional scholars, attributes the preceding two verses (Q20.130-131) to the 'Medinan' period.
104. *We do not ask you for provision*: God does not demand sacrifices 'for food,' as other gods do (cf. Q6.14; 22.37; 51.57).

133–135 Demand for a sign

105. *a sign from his Lord*: i.e. they demand a miracle as proof of the Prophet's legitimacy; see the lists of their demands at Q17.90-95 and 25.7-8, 20-21, 32 (cf. the similar demand for a 'sign' from Jesus at John 2.18; 6.30).
106. *clear sign*: or 'clear proof,' 'indisputable evidence.'
107. *the former pages*: or 'the first scriptures' (Ar. *al-ṣuḥuf al-ūlā*); the word 'pages' (lit. 'leaves' or 'sheets,' Ar. *ṣuḥuf*) occurs several times in connection with the Qur'ān (Q80.13), the revelation to Abraham and Moses (Q53.36-37; 87.18-19), and perhaps the heavenly archetype (Q98.2-3). The word is also used for the 'record' of a person's deeds (Q74.52; 81.10). Here 'the former pages' may mean something like 'the previous scriptures' of the Jews (and perhaps Christians), written either on 'papyrus' (Q6.7, 91) or 'parchment' (Q52.3).
108. *before him*: i.e. before the coming of the Prophet, predicted in 'the former pages.'

21 The Prophets ✵ Al-Anbiyā

In the Name of God, the Merciful, the Compassionate

1 Their reckoning has drawn near to the people, while they are turning away oblivious. **2** No new reminder[1] comes to them from their Lord, without their listening to it while they jest, **3** their hearts diverted.[2] Those who do evil keep their talk secret: 'Is this (anything) but a human being like you?[3] Will you surrender to magic when you see (it)?' **4** Say:[4] 'My Lord knows the words (spoken) in the sky and the earth. He is the Hearing, the Knowing.' **5** 'No!' they say, '(It is) a jumble of dreams! No! He has forged it![5] No! He is a poet![6] Let him bring us a sign,[7] as the ones of old were sent (with signs).' **6** Not one town which We destroyed before them believed.[8] Will they believe?

7 We have not sent (anyone) before you[9] except men whom We inspired – just ask the People of the Reminder,[10] if you do not know (it) – **8** nor did We give them a body not eating food,[11] nor were they immortal. **9** But We were true to them in the promise, so We rescued them and whomever We pleased, and We destroyed the wanton. **10** Certainly We have sent down to you[12] a Book in which (there is) your reminder. Will you not understand?

Q21: This sūra, assigned by most scholars to the 'Meccan' period, begins with a warning of approaching judgment and condemns idolatry in the face of God's power and providence. Its second half is comprised of a series of stories about earlier 'prophets' (Q21.48-91), from which Q21 receives its title. Many of these prophets have counterparts among biblical figures.

1–6 Judgment is near

1. *reminder*: or 'remembrance' (see n. on Q3.58), here referring to a part of the revelation.
2. *their hearts diverted*: here, as often, the heart is spoken of as synonymous with mind.
3. *Is this (anything) but a human being like you*: i.e. they expected the prophet to be a 'divine man' (the same was said of previous messengers; see e.g. Q11.27 [Noah]; 26.154 [Thamūd] etc.).
4. *Say*: following the alternative reading 'Say' (Ar. *qul*) instead of 'He said' (*qāla*), which seems unlikely here (and at Q21.112 below). On this form of address, see n. on Q2.80.
5. *forged it*: the Qur'ān (cf. Q25.4).
6. *a poet*: the traditional translation of a word (Ar. *shā'ir*) which etymologically means 'one who is aware' or 'one who perceives,' and originally was probably closer to 'diviner' or 'soothsayer' (cf. Q52.29-30, where there seems to be little difference between 'oracle giver,' 'madman,' and 'poet'). 'Poets' are criticized in the Qur'ān (Q26.224-226) and were thought to be inspired by jinn (Q37.36). Here the Prophet's opponents appear to share that negative view, for their calling him 'a poet' is meant derisively. Elsewhere it is explicitly denied that he was one (Q69.41; cf. Q36.69; 52.30).
7. *sign*: or 'miracle' (for the various meanings of this term, see n. on Q2.39).
8. *Not one town...*: a reference to previous peoples who disobeyed their messengers and rejected their miracles (see n. on Q7.59; cf. Q21.11-15 below). This is one explanation why the Prophet performed no 'sign' (cf. Q17.59).

7–10 Messengers are human

9. *you*: the Prophet.
10. *People of the Reminder*: i.e. Jews and Christians, on the analogy of 'People of the Book' (cf. Q16.43; 21.24 below).
11. *nor did We give them a body not eating food*: cf. Q5.75 (Jesus and Mary); 23.33; 25.7 (the Prophet), 20; contrast Q11.70 (the angels).
12. *you*: plur.

11 How many a town (which) was doing evil have We smashed, and produced another people after it! **12** And when they sensed Our violence, suddenly they began fleeing from it. **13** 'Do not flee, but return to what luxury you were given to delight in, and (to) your dwellings, so that you may be questioned.' **14** They said, 'Woe to us! Surely we have been evildoers.' **15** This cry of theirs did not stop until We cut them down[13] (and) snuffed (them) out.

16 We did not create the sky and the earth, and whatever is between them, in jest. **17** If We wanted to choose a diversion, We would indeed have chosen it from Ourselves, if We were going to do (anything). **18** No! We hurl the truth against falsehood, and it breaks its head, and suddenly it passes away. Woe to you for what you allege![14]

19 To Him (belongs) whoever is in the heavens and the earth, and those who are in His presence are not (too) proud for His service,[15] nor do they grow weary (of it). **20** They glorify (Him) night and day – they do not cease.

21 Or have they taken gods from the earth? Do they raise (the dead)?[16] **22** If there were any gods in the two of them[17] other than God, the two would indeed go to ruin.[18] So glory to God, Lord of the throne, above what they allege![19] **23** He will not be questioned about what He does, but they will be questioned. **24** Or have they taken gods other than Him? Say: 'Bring your proof! This is a Reminder[20] (for)[21] those who are with me, and a Reminder (for)[22] those who were before me.' But most of them do not know the truth, so they turn away. **25** We have not sent any messenger[23] before you except that We inspired him: '(There is) no god but Me, so serve Me!'

26 They say,[24] 'The Merciful[25] has taken a son.'[26] Glory to Him! No! (They are) honored servants.[27] **27** They do not precede Him in speech, but they act on His command. **28** He knows what is before them and what is behind them, and they do not intercede, except for the one whom He approves, and they are apprehensive because of fear of Him. **29** Whoever of them says, 'Surely I am a god instead of Him,' We repay that one with Gehenna.[28] In this way We repay the evildoers.

11–15 Punishment of earlier generations a warning

13. *cut them down*: lit. 'made them a harvest.'

16–18 Creation is no game

14. *what you allege*: the existence of other gods.

19–20 The angels serve God

15. *service*: or 'worship.'

21–25 One God, not many

16. *Or have they taken gods...*: perhaps referring to humans elevated to divine rank; but the meaning is obscure.
17. *the two of them*: the dual refers to 'the heavens and the earth' (cf. Q21.30 below).
18. *the two would...go to ruin*: i.e. the heavens and the earth would be ruined by the conflict among rival gods.
19. *what they allege*: the existence of other gods.
20. *This is a Reminder*: referring to the Qur'ān.
21. *(for)*: or '(proclaimed by).'
22. *(for)*: or '(proclaimed by).'
23. *messenger*: for this important title, see n. on Q2.87.

26–29 God has no son

24. *They say*: the Christians, though this claim always remains anonymous.
25. *the Merciful*: Ar. *al-raḥmān* is used here as a proper name for God (cf. Q21.36, 42, 112 below; see n. on Q25.60).
26. *son*: or 'child' (Ar. *walad*), but referring to Christian claims about Jesus as God's son (cf. Q2.116; 4.171; 10.68; 19.88-92; 25.2).
27. *honored servants*: this may include Jesus, Mary, and the saints, as well as the angels (see e.g. Q4.172; 7.194; 19.93; 43.19); the word 'servant' (Ar. *'abd*) also means 'slave.'
28. *Gehenna*: a name for Hell (see n. on Q2.206).

30 Do those who disbelieve not see that the heavens and the earth were (once) a solid mass, and We split the two of them apart, and We made every living thing from water?[29] Will they not believe? **31** We have placed on the earth firm mountains, so that it does not sway with them (on it),[30] and placed in it passes (to serve) as (path)ways, so that they might be guided. **32** And We have made the sky as a guarded roof.[31] Yet they (still) turn away from its signs. **33** He (it is) who created the night and the day, and the sun and the moon, each floating in (its own) orbit.

34 We have not granted[32] immortality to any human being before you.[33] If you die, will they live forever? **35** Every person will taste death. We try you[34] with evil and good as a test,[35] and to Us you will be returned. **36** When those who disbelieve see you,[36] they take you only in mockery: 'Is this the one who makes mention[37] of your gods?' Yet they (become) disbelievers at any mention[38] of the Merciful. **37** The human was created out of haste.[39] I shall show you[40] My signs,[41] so do not ask Me to hasten (them). **38** But they say, 'When (will) this promise[42] (come to pass), if you[43] are truthful?' **39** If (only) those who disbelieved knew the time when they will not be able to hold off the Fire[44] from their faces and from their backs, nor will they be helped! **40** No! It[45] will come upon them unexpectedly and confound them, and they will not be able to turn it back, nor will they be spared. **41** Certainly messengers have been mocked before you,[46] but those of them who ridiculed (were) overwhelmed (by) what they were mocking.[47]

42 Say: 'Who will guard you in the night and the day from the Merciful?' No! They (still) turn away from (any) reminder[48] of their Lord. **43** Or do they have gods other than Us to protect them? They are not able to help themselves, nor will they have any companions (to shield them) from Us. **44** No! We gave these

---

30–33 Signs of God's power and providence

29. *...made every living thing from water*: this account of creation is without parallel in the Qur'ān (cf. Q24.45; 25.54), but reflects a scenario similar to what is described in Genesis 1, especially the description of the 'watery chaotic mass' prior to the creation of the heavens and the earth (Genesis 1.1-2), which is carried out through a process of separation or 'splitting apart' (Genesis 1.3-19).
30. *so that it does not sway...*: i.e. the earth would move if it were not held in place by mountains.
31. *a guarded roof*: i.e. the sky acts as a barrier against any (e.g. 'satans') who might try to ascend to heaven to find out what is being planned there (cf. Q15.16-18; 37.6-10; 72.8-9).

34–41 Objections to the Prophet refuted

32. *granted*: lit. 'made.'
33. *you*: the Prophet.
34. *you*: plur.
35. *test*: or 'trial,' 'temptation' (Ar. *fitna*).
36. *you*: the Prophet.
37. *makes mention*: or 'reminds,' 'remembers.'
38. *mention*: or 'reminder,' 'remembrance.'
39. *out of haste*: for this idea, cf. Q17.11.
40. *you*: plur.
41. *signs*: here referring to God's punishment of the disbelievers.
42. *promise*: or 'threat' of punishment (cf. Q10.48; 27.71; 34.29; 36.48; 67.25).
43. *you*: plur.
44. *the Fire*: Ar. *al-nār* is the most common of the various designations for Hell.
45. *It*: punishment.
46. *you*: the Prophet.
47. *what they were mocking*: the threat of judgment and punishment (cf. Q6.10).

42–47 Other Gods powerless

48. *reminder*: or 'remembrance,' 'mention.'

(people) and their fathers enjoyment (of life), until life had lasted a long time for them. Do they not see that We come to the land,[49] pushing back its borders?[50] Are they the victors? **45** Say: 'I warn you only by means of inspiration.' But the deaf do not hear the call when they are warned. **46** If indeed a whiff of the punishment of your Lord should touch them, they would indeed say, 'Woe to us! Surely we – we have been evildoers.' **47** We shall lay down the scales of justice for the Day of Resurrection, and no one will be done any evil. (Even) if there is (only) the weight of a mustard seed, We shall produce it, and We are sufficient as reckoners.

48 Certainly We gave Moses and Aaron the Deliverance,[51] and a light, and a reminder to the ones who guard (themselves),[52] **49** who fear their Lord in the unseen,[53] and they are apprehensive of the Hour.[54]
50 And this is a blessed Reminder.[55] We have sent it down. Will you reject it?

51 Certainly We gave Abraham his right (path) before (them), (for) We knew him. **52** (Remember) when[56]
he said to his father and his people: 'What are these images which you are devoted to?' **53** They said,
'We found our fathers serving them.'[57] **54** He said, 'Certainly you and your fathers were clearly astray.'[58]
55 They said, 'Have you brought us the truth, or are you one of those who jest?' **56** He said, 'No! Your
Lord – Lord of the heavens and the earth – is the One who created them, and I am one of the witnesses
to this. **57** By God! I shall indeed plot (to destroy) your idols after you have turned away, withdrawing.'[59]
58 So he broke them into pieces,[60] (all) except a big one they had, so that they would return to it.
59 They said, 'Who has done this with our gods? Surely he is indeed one of the evildoers.' **60** They said,
'We heard a young man mentioning them – he is called Abraham.' **61** They said, 'Bring him before the
eyes of the people, so that they may bear witness.' **62** They said, 'Have you done this with our gods,
Abraham?' **63** He said, 'No! This big one of them did it. Just ask them, if they are able to speak.' **64** And
they turned to each other, and said, 'Surely you – you are the evildoers.' **65** Then they became utterly
confused:[61] 'Certainly you know (that) these do not speak.' **66** He said, 'Do you serve what does not
benefit you at all, or harm you, instead of God (alone)? **67** Uff[62] to you and to what you serve instead
of God! Will you not understand?' **68** They said, 'Burn him, and help your gods, if you are going to do
(anything).' **69** We said, 'Fire! Be coolness and peace for Abraham!' **70** They intended a plot against him,

---

49. *land*: lit. 'earth.'
50. *pushing back its borders*: meaning obscure; perhaps a reference to military successes of the Prophet and his followers (cf. Q13.41).

48–50 Moses and Aaron

51. *the Deliverance*: here another name for the Torah (see n. on Q2.53; cf. Q3.3-4; 25.1).
52. *guard (themselves)*: against evil, or God.
53. *in the unseen*: or 'in secret' (see n. on Q2.3).
54. *the Hour*: of judgment.
55. *this is a blessed Reminder*: referring to the Qur'ān.

51–71 The story of Abraham

56. *(Remember) when...*: a stock narrative formula; the Arabic particle *idh* often marks the beginning of a story, and means something like 'Once...,' or 'There was a time when...,' or 'Remember when....' For the story that follows, cf. the version at Q6.74-83.
57. *serving them*: or 'worshipping them.'
58. *clearly astray*: lit. 'in clear straying.'
59. *I shall indeed plot...*: the context requires that this be understood as spoken by Abraham to himself.
60. *broke them into pieces*: lit. 'made them pieces' (cf. Q37.91-93). Though not mentioned in Genesis, Abraham's destruction of the 'idols' was a popular theme in later Jewish tradition (see e.g. Jubilees 12.12-14).
61. *became utterly confused*: lit. 'were turned on their heads.'
62. *Uff*: an expression of disrespect (cf. Q17.23; 46.17).

but We made them the worst losers, **71** and We rescued him, and Lot, (and brought them) to the land[63] which We have blessed for the worlds.[64]

72 And We granted him Isaac, and Jacob[65] as a gift, and each (of them) We made righteous. **73** And We made them leaders[66] (who) guide (others) by Our command, and We inspired them (with) the doing of good deeds, and the observance of the prayer and the giving of the alms,[67] and they served Us.

74 And Lot – We gave him judgment[68] and knowledge, and we rescued him from the town[69] which was doing bad things. Surely they were an evil people (and) wicked. **75** And We caused him to enter Our mercy. Surely He was one of the righteous.

76 And Noah[70] – when he called out before (that), and We responded to him, and rescued him and his family from great distress. **77** We helped him against the people who called Our signs a lie. Surely they were an evil people, and so We drowned them – all (of them)!

78 And David and Solomon – when they rendered judgment concerning the field, when the people's sheep had grazed in it – We were witnesses to their judgment.[71] **79** We caused Solomon to understand it,[72] and to each We gave judgment and knowledge. (Along) with David We subjected the mountains and the birds to glorify (Us)[73] – We were the doers (of it). **80** We taught him the making of clothing to protect you from your (own) violence.[74] Are you thankful? **81** And to Solomon (We subjected) the wind,[75] blowing strongly at his command to the land[76] which We have blessed[77] – We have knowledge of everything. **82** And among the satans,[78] (there were) those who dived for him and did other work besides – We were watching over them.

---

63. *land*: lit. 'earth.'
64. *which We have blessed for the worlds*: or 'for all peoples' (i.e. the Holy Land or Palestine).

72–73 Isaac and Jacob

65. *Isaac, and Jacob*: Ishmael is mentioned only later at Q21.85, with no apparent connection to Abraham (cf. Q6.84-86; 11.71; 19.49; 38.45-48). In other passages, however, emphasis is placed on Ishmael as Abraham's son (see e.g. Q2.125, 127; 4.163; 14.39).
66. *leaders*: or 'models,' a term later used for the leader (Ar. *imām*) of a religious community (cf. Q2.124, Abraham).
67. *observance of the prayer...giving of the alms*: i.e. *ṣalāt*, the ritual prayer, and *zakāt*, a kind of tithe required for the benefit of the poor, as well as other purposes.

74–75 Lot

68. *judgment*: or 'wisdom' (see n. on Q3.79; cf. Q21.79 below).
69. *town*: Lot's city was Sodom, according to Genesis 19.1.

76–77 Noah

70. *Noah*: for the story of Noah, see e.g. Q7.59-64; 11.25-34; 23.23-30; 26.105-120.

78–82 David and Solomon

71. *We were witnesses to their judgment*: according to tradition, David decreed that sheep which had strayed and eaten a crop of corn should be forfeited to the owner of the corn, but Solomon argued that the owner should only receive the produce of the sheep until the field was restored.
72. *it*: antecedent uncertain; perhaps a reference to the episode of 'the sheep.'
73. *...to glorify (Us)*: i.e. the mountains and birds were to praise God, as did David in the Psalms (cf. Q34.10; 38.18-19; and Psalms 104, 148).
74. *clothing to protect you...*: i.e. protective armor.
75. *the wind*: meaning obscure (cf. Q34.12); according to tradition the wind is said to have carried Solomon's throne.
76. *land*: lit. 'earth.'
77. *which We have blessed*: Palestine (cf. Q21.71 above).
78. *satans*: or 'demons' (Ar. *shayāṭīn*); but here some of them are placed under the authority of Solomon (see also Q38.37; cf. Q34.12-13, where it is said that 'the jinn' worked for him).

83 And Job – when he called on his Lord, 'Surely hardship has touched me, and You are the most compassionate of the compassionate.' **84** We responded to him, and removed what hardship was upon him, and We gave him his family, and as much again, as a mercy from Us, and a reminder to the ones who serve.[79]

85 And Ishmael, and Idrīs,[80] and Dhū-l-Kifl[81] – each one was among the patient. **86** And We caused them to enter Our mercy. Surely they were among the righteous.

87 And Dhū-l-Nūn[82] – when he went away angry, and thought that We had no power over him, but he called out in the darkness: '(There is) no god but You. Glory to You! Surely I – I have been one of the evil-doers.' **88** We responded to him and rescued him from (his) distress. In this way We rescue the believers.

89 And Zachariah – when he called out to his Lord: 'My Lord, do not leave me alone,[83] when You are the best of inheritors.' **90** We responded to him, and granted him John,[84] and set his wife right for him.[85] Surely they were quick in the (doing of) good deeds, and they used to call on Us in hope and fear, and humble (themselves) before Us.

91 And she[86] who guarded her private part – We breathed into her some of Our spirit,[87] and made her and her son a sign to the worlds:[88] **92** 'Surely this community of yours is one community, and I am your Lord. So serve Me!' **93** But they cut up their affair among them.[89] (Yet) all (of them) will return to Us. **94** Whoever does any righteous deeds – and he is a believer – (there will be) no ingratitude[90] for his striving. Surely We are writing (them) down for him.

95 (There is) a ban on any town which We have destroyed: they[91] shall not return **96** until, when Yajūj

---

83–84 Job

79. *the ones who serve*: or 'the worshippers.'

85–86 Ishmael, Idrīs, and Dhū-l-Kifl

80. *Idrīs*: mentioned only here and at Q19.56, where he is likewise linked with Ishmael. Though sometimes identified with Enoch, who 'walked with God, and he was not, for God took him' (Genesis 5.24), he is probably Ezra (derived from 'Esdras,' the Greek form of the name), who was also taken up to heaven, like Enoch and Elijah (see 4 Ezra 14.7-9).

81. *Dhū-l-Kifl*: some commentators suggest the prophet Ezekiel, others Elijah (cf. Q38.48, where he is listed with Ishmael and Elisha).

87–88 Dhū-l-Nūn

82. *Dhū-l-Nun*: probably Jonah (lit. 'he of the fish'); cf. Q37.139-148; 68.48-50.

89–90 Zachariah

83. *alone*: i.e. childless.

84. *John*: the Baptist (see the stories at Q3.37-41; 19.2-15).

85. *set his wife right for him*: i.e. made her capable of conceiving a child.

91–94 Mary

86. *She*: Mary, the only woman referred to by name in the Qur'ān. Although she is not considered a 'prophet,' she is listed among them here, and God addresses her as a 'messenger' at Q23.51.

87. *We breathed into her some of Our spirit*: see Q66.12 (cf. Q4.171, God 'cast into Mary...a spirit from Him;' 19.17, 'We sent to her Our spirit'); otherwise this is said only of Adam (Q15.29; 38.72; cf. Q32.9).

88. *to the worlds*: or 'to all peoples.'

89. *cut up their affair among them*: i.e. they separated into different religious communities, Jews and Christians.

90. *ingratitude*: or 'denial' (on God's part); cf. Q4.124; 19.60; 20.112.

95–100 A destroyed city restored at the end of days

91. *they*: the town's inhabitants.

and Majūj[92] are opened,[93] and they come swooping down[94] from every height, **97** and the true promise draws near,[95] and suddenly (there) it (is)![96] The eyes of those who disbelieved (will be) staring (and they will say): 'Woe to us! We were oblivious of this. No! We were evildoers.' **98** 'Surely you, and what you were serving instead of God, are coals for Gehenna – you will go down to it.' **99** If these had been gods, they would not have gone down to it, but everyone (of them) will remain in it. **100** In it (there is) a moaning for them,[97] and in it they do not hear (anything else).

101 Surely those for whom the best (reward) has gone forth from Us – those will be (kept) far from it.[98] **102** They will not hear (even) a slight sound of it, and they will remain in what they themselves desired. **103** The great terror will not cause them sorrow, and the angels will meet them: 'This is your Day which you were promised.'

104 On the Day when We shall roll up the sky like the rolling up of a scroll for the writings:[99] as We brought about the first creation, (so) We shall restore it – (it is) a promise (binding) on Us. Surely We shall do (it)! **105** Certainly We have written in the Psalms,[100] after the Reminder:[101] 'The earth – My righteous servants will inherit it.'[102] **106** Surely in this (there is) a delivery[103] indeed for a people who serve.

107 We have sent you[104] only as a mercy to the worlds.[105] **108** Say: 'I am only inspired[106] that your God is one God. Are you going to submit?'[107] **109** If they turn away, say: 'I have proclaimed to all of you equally, but I do not know whether what you are promised is near or far.[108] **110** Surely He knows what is spoken publicly and He knows what you conceal. **111** I do not know. Perhaps it[109] is a test for you, and enjoyment

---

92. *Yajūj and Majūj*: probably 'Gog and Magog' (cf. Ezekiel 38.2-3). They are variously understood as men, supernatural beings, peoples, or lands. Here they will be released shortly before the Day of Judgment. According to Q18.94-98, Dhū-l-Qarnayn (probably Alexander the Great) constructed an immense wall between two mountains to keep them at bay until the end of days. The *Alexander Romance* refers to this barrier as the 'Gates of Alexander.'
93. *are opened*: meaning that 'Yajūj and Majūj' are probably best understood as the 'Gates of Alexander.'
94. *they come swooping down*: 'they' probably refers to the resurrected inhabitants of the destroyed cities ('they' in the previous verse, cf. Q36.51), rather than to Yajūj and Majūj (since the dual is not used).
95. *the true promise draws near*: judgment (cf. Q21.1 above).
96. *suddenly (there) it (is)*: i.e. the destroyed city, now restored for judgment.
97. *a moaning for them*: a graphic expression of Gehenna's lust to possess them (cf. Q11.106; 25.12; 67.7).

101–103 The righteous will not suffer

98. *it*: Gehenna.

104–106 The righteous will inherit the restored earth

99. *like the rolling up of a scroll for the writings*: a difficult construction, but the word (Ar. *sijill*) is usually taken here as meaning a scroll or book (cf. Q39.67; and for a similar image, see Revelation 6.14, 'And the sky vanished like a scroll being rolled up' [cf. Isaiah 34.4]).
100. *the Psalms*: or perhaps simply 'the scripture' or 'the book' (Ar. *al-zabūr* [sing.]); cf. Q4.163; 17.55 (for the plur. *al-zubur*, see n. on Q3.184).
101. *the Reminder*: here referring to the Torah.
102. *The earth – My righteous servants will inherit it*: cf. Psalm 37.9, 11, 29, 34; Matthew 5.5.
103. *delivery*: of the message.

107–112 The Prophet sent as a mercy for all people

104. *you*: the Prophet.
105. *to the worlds*: or 'to all peoples.'
106. *I am only inspired*: or 'I have only received inspiration.'
107. *Are you going to submit*: or 'Will you become Muslims?'
108. *whether what you are promised is near or far*: i.e. whether judgment is imminent or not.
109. *it*: the apparent delay of judgment.

(of life) for a time.' **112** Say:[110] 'My Lord, judge in truth![111] Our Lord is the Merciful – the One to be sought for help against what you allege.'[112]

110. *Say*: following the alternative reading 'Say' (Ar. *qul*) instead of 'He said' (*qāla*), which seems unlikely here (and at Q21.4 above).

111. *in truth*: or 'with the truth.'

112. *what you allege*: the existence of other gods.

22 The Pilgrimage ✵ Al-Ḥajj

In the Name of God, the Merciful, the Compassionate

1 People! Guard (yourselves) against your Lord! Surely the earthquake of the Hour[1] is a great thing.
2 On the Day when you[2] see it, every nursing woman will forget what she has nursed, and every
pregnant female will deliver her burden, and you[3] will see the people drunk when they are not drunk
– but the punishment of God is harsh! 3 Yet among the people (there is) one who disputes about God
without any knowledge, and follows every rebellious satan.[4] 4 It is written about him: 'He who takes him
as an ally[5] – he will lead him astray and guide him to the punishment of the blazing (Fire).'

5 People! If you are in doubt about the raising up – surely We created you from dust,[6] then from a drop,[7] then from a clot, (and) then from a lump, formed and unformed,[8] so that We may make (it) clear to you. We establish in the wombs what We please[9] for an appointed time, then We bring you forth as a child, (and) then (We provide for you) so that you may reach your maturity. Among you (there is) one who is taken,[10] and among you (there is) one who is reduced to the worst (stage) of life,[11] so that he knows nothing after (having had) knowledge. And you[12] see the earth withered,[13] but when We send down water on it, it stirs and swells, and grows (plants) of every beautiful kind. 6 That is because God – He is the Truth,
and because He gives the dead life, and because He is powerful over everything, 7 and because the Hour is
coming – (there is) no doubt about it – and because God will raise up those who are in the graves.

Q22: This sūra takes its title from the reference to the Ḥajj, the pilgrimage originally established by Abraham (Q22.26-38). In addition to dealing with matters connected with the pilgrimage, it condemns those who deny believers access to the 'Sacred Mosque,' and concludes with an address to the believers, urging them to remain steadfast to the religion of Abraham. While some traditional scholars assign Q22 to the 'Medinan' period, others consider it a 'Meccan' sūra. Many modern scholars consider Q22 to be a composite of 'Meccan' and 'Medinan' elements. The Cairo edition assigns it to the 'Medinan' period.

1–4 The Last Day

1. *the Hour*: of judgment.
2. *you*: plur.
3. *you*: the Prophet, or perhaps intended generally ('one').
4. *every rebellious satan*: 'satans' (Ar. *shayāṭīn*) are individually assigned to incite people to evil (see Q19.83; 43.36; cf. Q7.27; 23.97; 41.25).
5. *takes him as an ally*: or 'guardian;' Ar. *walī* implies the obligation of mutual protection, almost in the sense of 'friend' or 'brother.'

5–7 Resurrection certain

6. *from dust*: see Q3.59; 18.37; 30.20; 35.11; 40.67 (cf. Genesis 2.7, 'from the dust of the ground'); 'from clay,' according to Q6.2; 7.12; 15.26; 17.61; 23.12; 32.7; 38.71, 76; 55.14; 'from water,' according to Q21.30; 24.45; 25.54.
7. *a drop*: of semen.
8. *formed and unformed*: precise meaning uncertain, but obviously an attempt to describe prenatal development.
9. *what We please*: i.e. male or female.
10. *taken*: in death.
11. *worst (stage) of life*: old age.
12. *you*: or 'one.'
13. *withered*: or 'lifeless,' but the exact meaning is uncertain.

8 Yet among the people (there is) one who disputes about God without any knowledge or guidance[14] or illuminating Book, **9** (who) turns away in scorn[15] to lead (people) astray from the way of God. For him (there is) disgrace in this world, and on the Day of Resurrection We shall make him taste the punishment of the burning (Fire): **10** 'That is for what your (own) hands have sent forward, and (know) that God is not an evildoer to (His) servants.'[16] **11** Among the people (there is also) one who serves[17] God sitting on the fence.[18] If some good smites him, he is satisfied with it, but if some trouble[19] smites him, he is overturned[20] (by it). He loses this world and the Hereafter.[21] That – it is the clearest loss! **12** Instead of God, he calls on what does not harm him, and what does not benefit him. That – it is straying the farthest!
13 He calls indeed on one whose harm is nearer than his benefit. Evil indeed is the protector, and evil indeed the friend!

14 Surely God will cause those who believe and do righteous deeds to enter Gardens[22] through which rivers flow. Surely God does whatever He wills. **15** Whoever thinks that God will not help him in this world and the Hereafter, let him stretch a rope to the sky. Then let him cut (it), and see whether his scheme will take away what enrages (him).[23] **16** In this way We have sent it[24] down as signs[25] – clear signs[26] – and because God guides whomever He wills.

17 Surely those who believe, and those who are Jews,[27] and the Sabians,[28] and the Christians,[29] and the Magians,[30] and the idolaters[31] – surely God will distinguish between them on the Day of Resurrection. Surely God is a witness over everything. **18** Do you[32] not see that God – whoever is in the heavens and whoever is on the earth prostrates before Him, and (so do) the sun, and the moon, and the stars, and the mountains, and the trees, and the animals, and many of the people? But (there are) many for whom the punishment is justified, and whomever God humiliates, (there is) no one to honor him. Surely God does whatever He pleases.

8–13 Still there is disbelief

14. *guidance*: one of the most frequent terms (Ar. *hudā*) for revelation in general, and the Qur'ān in particular.
15. *turns away in scorn*: or 'turns a cold shoulder' (lit. 'turns his side').
16. *servants*: the word 'servant' (Ar. *'abd*) also means 'slave.'
17. *serves*: or 'worships.'
18. *sitting on the fence*: lit. 'on an edge.'
19. *trouble*: or 'trial,' 'temptation' (Ar. *fitna*).
20. *overturned*: lit. 'turned on his face.'
21. *the Hereafter*: see n. on Q2.4.

14–16 Belief and disbelief contrasted

22. *Gardens*: in heaven (for this imagery, see n. on Q2.25; cf. Q22.56 below, 'Gardens of Bliss').
23. *stretch a rope to the sky...take away what enrages (him)*: the meaning of this verse is obscure.
24. *it*: the Qur'ān.
25. *signs*: or 'verses' (see n. on Q2.39).
26. *clear signs*: or 'clear proofs,' 'indisputable evidence.'

17–18 Religious communities distinguished

27. *those who are Jews*: lit. 'those who have judaized,' or follow Jewish law, punning on the name Yahūd.
28. *Sabians*: see n. on Q2.62.
29. *Christians*: see n. on Q2.62
30. *Magians*: i.e. Zoroastrians (Ar. *Majūs*), only mentioned here; cf. Matthew 2.1, 7, 16 ('Magi').
31. *the idolaters*: or 'those who associate (other gods with God).'
32. *you*: the Prophet, or perhaps intended generally ('one').

19 These two disputants dispute about their Lord.[33] But those who disbelieve – clothes of fire have been cut for them, and boiling (water) will be poured (on them) from above their heads, **20** by which what is in their bellies and (their) skins will be melted. **21** And for them (there are) hooked rods[34] of iron. **22** Whenever they want to come out of it,[35] because of (their) agony, they will be sent back into it, and: 'Taste the punishment of the burning (Fire)!' **23** Surely God will cause those who believe and do righteous deeds to enter Gardens through which rivers flow. There they will be adorned with bracelets of gold and (with) pearls, and there their clothes (will be of) silk. **24** They have been guided to good speech, and they have been guided to the path of the Praiseworthy.

25 Surely those who disbelieve and keep (people) from the way of God and the Sacred Mosque,[36] which We have made for the people equally – the resident there and the visitor – and whoever intends to pervert it in an evil manner – We shall make him taste a painful punishment.

26 (Remember) when[37] We settled the place of the House[38] for Abraham: 'Do not associate anything with Me, but purify My House for the ones who go around (it),[39] and the ones who stand,[40] and the ones who bow, (and) the ones who prostrate themselves. **27** And proclaim the pilgrimage[41] among the people. Let them come to you[42] on foot and on every lean animal.[43] They will come from every remote mountain pass, **28** so that they may witness things of benefit to them, and mention[44] the name of God, on (certain) specified days, over whatever animal of the livestock He has provided them: "Eat from them, and feed the wretched poor." **29** Then let them bring an end to their ritual state,[45] and fulfill their vows, and go around the ancient House.'

30 That (is the rule). Whoever respects the sacred things[46] of God – it will be better for him with his Lord. Permitted to you (to eat) are the livestock, except for what is recited to you.[47] Avoid the abomination of

---

19–24 Fate of believers and disbelievers contrasted

33. *These two disputants...*: reference uncertain; perhaps the two examples mentioned above at Q22.3-4, 8-9.
34. *hooked rods*: this word is usually explained as a crooked stick used to control animals.
35. *it*: the Fire.

25 Punishment for those who deny access to the Sacred Mosque

36. *Sacred Mosque*: traditionally identified with the Ka'ba at Mecca (see n. on Q5.95).

26–29 Abraham proclaims the pilgrimage

37. *(Remember) when...*: a stock narrative formula; the Arabic particle *idh* often marks the beginning of a story, and means something like 'Once...,' or 'There was a time when...,' or 'Remember when....' For the story that follows, cf. Q2.124-129.
38. *House*: the Ka'ba (cf. Q5.97).
39. *the ones who go around (it)*: i.e. who circumambulate the Ka'ba (cf. Q2.125).
40. *stand*: to pray.
41. *the pilgrimage*: the Ḥajj; see further Q2.196-203; 3.97; and cf. Exodus 23.14-17; 34.18-24, for Israel's three annual pilgrimages [Hebr. *ḥag*] to God's sanctuary). The detailed regulations pertaining to the Ḥajj are not recorded in the Qur'ān.
42. *you*: Abraham.
43. *lean animal*: i.e. an animal worn down by a long journey.
44. *mention*: or 'remember.'
45. *ritual state*: meaning uncertain, but the word is taken to refer to the state of ritual sanctity (*iḥrām*) adopted for the central part of the pilgrimage period.

30–33 Regulations concerning the pilgrimage

46. *sacred things*: or 'prohibited things;' given the context it may refer to forbidden foods.
47. *except for what is recited to you*: i.e. what is forbidden in the Qur'ān (cf. Q2.173; 5.3; 16.115).

the idols, and avoid the speaking of falsehood, **31** (being) Ḥanīfs[48] before God, not associating (anything) with Him. Whoever associates (anything) with God – (it is) as if he has fallen from the sky, and the birds snatched him away, or (as if) the wind has swept him away to some far off place.

32 That (is the rule). Whoever respects the symbols[49] of God – surely that (comes) from the guarding of (your) hearts.[50] **33** (There are) benefits for you in this up to an appointed time. Then their lawful place[51] is to the ancient House.

34 For every community We have appointed[52] a ritual: that they should mention[53] the name of God over whatever animal of the livestock He has provided them. Your God is one God, so submit to Him. And give good news[54] to the humble, **35** those who, when God is mentioned, their hearts become afraid, and the ones who are patient with whatever smites them, and the ones who observe the prayer,[55] and contribute[56] from what We have provided them. **36** The (sacrificial) animals – We have appointed them for you among the symbols of God: there is good for you in them. So mention the name of God over them, (as they stand) in lines. Then when their sides fall (to the ground),[57] eat from them, and feed the needy and the beggar. In this way We have subjected them to you, so that you may be thankful. **37** Its flesh will not reach God, nor its blood,[58] but the guarding (of yourselves) will reach Him from you.[59] In this way He has subjected them to you, so that you may magnify God because He has guided you. Give good news to the doers of good. **38** Surely God will repel (evil) from those who believe. Surely God does not love any traitor (or) ungrateful one.[60]

39 Permission is given to those who fight[61] because they have been done evil – and surely God is indeed able to help them – **40** those who have been expelled from their homes without any right, only because they said, 'Our Lord is God.' But if God had not repelled some of the people by the means of others, many monasteries, and churches, and synagogues, and mosques, in which the name of God is mentioned often, would indeed have been destroyed. God will indeed help the one who helps Him – surely God is indeed strong, mighty – **41** those who, if We establish them on the earth, observe the prayer and give the alms,[62]

---

48. *Ḥanīfs*: or perhaps 'Gentiles,' like Abraham (see n. on Q2.135; cf. Q98.5).
49. *symbols*: meaning uncertain (Ar. *sha'ā'ir*); it may refer Ṣafā and Marwa, two hills near the Ka'ba in Mecca (cf. Q2.158), or to cult-symbols or rituals in general (cf. Q22.36 below).
50. *guarding of (your) hearts*: against evil; here, as often, the heart is spoken of as synonymous with mind.
51. *lawful place*: for sacrifice (cf. Q2.196; 48.25)

34–38 Sacrifice of animals

52. *appointed*: lit. 'made' (cf. Q22.67 below).
53. *mention*: or 'remember.'
54. *give good news*: addressed to the Prophet (also at Q22.37 below); the preceding imperative ('submit') is plur.
55. *the prayer*: the ritual prayer (or *ṣalāt*).
56. *contribute*: lit. 'spend.'
57. *fall (to the ground)*: i.e. when they are dead.
58. *Its flesh will not reach God...*: i.e. though the animal is ritually slaughtered, it is not sacrificed 'to feed God,' in contrast to most sacrificial systems in the ancient world, including that of the Bible (cf. Q6.14; 20.132; 51.57).
59. *the guarding (of yourselves) will reach Him...*: i.e. righteous conduct is the true sacrifice (cf. Hosea 6.6, 'For I desire mercy, not sacrifice, and acknowledgment of God rather than burnt offerings;' also quoted by Jesus at Matthew 9.13).
60. *ungrateful one*: Ar. *kafūr*, punning on *kāfir*, 'disbeliever.'

39–41 Fighting against disbelievers permitted

61. *fight*: or, with the change of a single vowel, 'are fought against' (Ar. *yuqātilūna* or *yuqātalūna*). While some scholars prefer the latter reading, context favors the former.
62. *observe the prayer and give the alms*: i.e. *ṣalāt*, the ritual prayer, and *zakāt*, a kind of tithe required for the benefit

and command right and forbid wrong. To God (belongs) the outcome of all affairs.

42 If they call you[63] a liar, the people of Noah called (him) a liar before you, and (so did) 'Ād, and Thamūd, **43** and the people of Abraham, and the people of Lot, **44** and the companions of Midian, and Moses[64] was called a liar (too). I spared the disbelievers, then I seized them, and how was My loathing (of them)! **45** How many a town have We destroyed while it was doing evil, so it is (now) collapsed on its supports! (How many) an abandoned well and well-built palace! **46** Have they not traveled on the earth?[65] Do they have hearts to understand with or ears to hear with? Surely it is not the sight (which) is blind, but the hearts which are within the chests are blind. **47** They seek to hurry you with the punishment.[66] God will not break His promise. Surely a day with your Lord is like a thousand years of what you count.[67] **48** How many a town have I have spared while it was doing evil! Then I seized it. To Me is the (final) destination. **49** Say:[68] 'People! I am only a clear warner[69] for you.' **50** Those who believe and do righteous deeds – for them (there is) forgiveness and generous provision. **51** But those who strive against Our signs to obstruct (them) – those are the companions of the Furnace.[70]

52 We have not sent any messenger or any prophet[71] before you, except that, when he began to wish,[72] Satan cast (something)[73] into his wishful thinking. But God cancels[74] what Satan casts, (and) then God clearly composes[75] His verses – surely God is knowing, wise – **53** so that He may make what Satan casts a test[76] for those in whose hearts is a sickness, and whose hearts are hardened – and surely the evildoers are indeed in extreme defiance[77] – **54** and so that those who have been given the knowledge may know that it is the truth from your Lord, and may believe in it, and so that their hearts may be humble before

---

of the poor, as well as other purposes.

42–51 Punishment of earlier generations a warning

63. *you*: the Prophet.
64. *people of Noah...'Ād...Thamūd...people of Abraham...Lot...Midian...Moses*: alluding to the stories of previous peoples who were punished for rejecting their messengers (see n. on Q7.59). For the seven listed here, see n. on Q15.87.
65. *Have they not traveled on the earth*: the remains of their destroyed cities were believed to be still visible.
66. *seek to hurry you with the punishment*: i.e. they (sarcastically) dare the Prophet to stop threatening them with imminent punishment and make it happen.
67. *a day...like a thousand years of what you count*: cf. Psalm 90.4, 'for a thousand years in your sight are like a day;' and 2 Peter 3.8, 'with the Lord one day is like a thousand years.'
68. *Say*: on this form of address, see n. on Q2.80.
69. *warner*: for this role, see n. on Q2.119.
70. *the Furnace*: a name for Hell (Ar. *al-jaḥīm*).

52–54 Satanic verses

71. *messenger...prophet*: for these important titles, see n. on Q2.87.
72. *wish*: or 'long,' 'desire.'
73. *Satan cast (something)*: just as God 'casts' genuine revelation (see e.g. Q28.86; 40.15; 77.5); elsewhere Satan 'whispers' (see Q7.20; 20.120; 114.4-5).
74. *cancels*: or 'will cancel;' the verb occurs only here and at Q2.106 (cf. Q13.39; 16.101). This passage claims that there has been 'Satanic' tampering with the revelations to previous messengers, as well as perhaps in the Qur'ān. Though no examples are given, one strand of tradition holds that it applies to verses originally proclaimed as following Q53.19-20 (see n.), but later removed on the ground that they had been falsely inserted by Satan. Those verses permitted intercession to 'pagan' goddesses, and were said to have come to the Prophet while he was 'earnestly desiring' to find some way of making his religion acceptable to his fellow Meccans. Like so much of the tradition, however, the story is probably a fiction invented to explain an otherwise puzzling text.
75. *clearly composes*: or 'will clearly compose;' for this idea, cf. Q3.7; 11.1; 47.20.
76. *test*: or 'trial,' 'temptation' (Ar. *fitna*).
77. *extreme defiance*: or 'wide schism.'

Him. Surely God is indeed guiding those who believe to a straight path.

55 Those who disbelieve will continue (to be) in doubt about it,[78] until the Hour comes upon them unexpectedly, or the punishment of a barren Day comes upon them. **56** The kingdom on that Day (will belong) to God. He will judge between them. Those who believe and do righteous deeds (will be) in Gardens of Bliss, **57** but those who disbelieve and call Our signs a lie – for them (there will be) a humiliating punishment.

58 Those who have emigrated[79] in the way of God, (and) then were killed or died, God will indeed provide them (with) a good provision. Surely God – He indeed is the best of providers. **59** He will indeed cause them to enter by an entrance with which they will be pleased. Surely God is indeed knowing, forbearing. **60** That (will be so). And whoever takes retribution with the same retribution he suffered, (and) then is sought out[80] – God will indeed help him. Surely God is indeed pardoning, forgiving.

61 That is because God causes the night to pass into the day, and causes the day to pass into the night, and because God is hearing, seeing. **62** That is because God – He is the Truth, and because what they call on instead of Him, that is the falsehood, and because God is the Most High, the Great. **63** Do you[81] not see that God sends down water from the sky, (and) then the earth becomes green? God is astute, aware. **64** To Him (belongs) whatever is in the heavens and whatever is on the earth. Surely God – He indeed is the wealthy One,[82] the Praiseworthy. **65** Do you[83] not see that God has subjected to you[84] whatever is on the earth, and the ship that runs on the sea by His command, and He (that) holds up the sky so that it does not fall upon the earth, except by His permission? Surely God is indeed kind (and) compassionate with the people. **66** He (it is) who gave you life, then He causes you to die, (and) then He will give you life (again). Surely the human is ungrateful[85] indeed.

67 For every community we have appointed a ritual which they practice. So let them not argue with you[86] about the matter, but call (them) to your Lord. Surely you are indeed on a straight guidance. **68** If they dispute with you, say: 'God knows what you do. **69** God will judge between you on the Day of Resurrection concerning your differences.' **70** Do you[87] not know that God knows whatever is in the sky and the earth? Surely that is in a Book.[88] Surely that is easy for God.

71 Instead of God, they serve what He has not sent down any authority for, and what they have no knowledge of. The evildoers will have no helper. **72** When Our signs are recited[89] to them as clear signs,

---

55–57 The Day of Judgment

78. *it*: usually taken as referring to the Qur'ān, but in light of what follows it may refer to judgment.

58–60 The emigrants

79. *Those who have emigrated*: from Mecca to Medina, though this is not explicitly stated in the Qur'ān.
80. *(and) then is sought out*: because the original aggressor does not accept the justice of retaliation.

61–66 Signs of God's power and providence

81. *you*: or 'one.'
82. *the wealthy One*: i.e. God has no need of anyone or anything.
83. *you*: or 'one.'
84. *you*: plur.
85. *ungrateful*: Ar. *kafūr*, punning on *kāfir*, 'disbeliever.'

67–70 Differences in religious practice

86. *you*: the Prophet.
87. *you*: the Prophet, or perhaps intended generally ('one').
88. *a Book*: i.e. the 'Book of God' or the heavenly 'Record' of all things (see n. on Q6.59).

71–72 Fate of disbelievers

89. *signs are recited*: or 'verses are read aloud.'

you[90] recognize defiance in the faces of those who disbelieve – they all but attack those who recite Our signs to them. Say: 'Shall I inform you about (something) worse than that? The Fire![91] God has promised it to those who disbelieve – and it is an evil destination!'

73 People! A parable is struck, so listen to it. Surely those you call on instead of God will not create a fly, even if they joined together for it. And if a fly were to snatch anything away from them, they would not (be able to) rescue it from it. Weak is the seeker and the sought (alike)! **74** They have not measured God (with) the measure due Him. Surely God is indeed strong, mighty.

75 God chooses messengers from the angels[92] and from the people. Surely God is hearing, seeing. **76** He knows what is before them and what is behind them. To God all affairs are returned.

77 You who believe! Bow and prostrate yourselves, and serve your Lord, and do good, so that you may prosper. **78** And struggle[93] for God with the struggling due Him. He has chosen you, and has not placed any difficulty on you in the (matter of) religion: the creed of your father Abraham. He named you Muslims, (both) before and in this,[94] so that the messenger might be a witness against you, and that you might be witnesses against the people.[95] So observe the prayer and give the alms, and hold fast to God. He is your Protector. Excellent is the Protector, and excellent is the Helper!

---

90. *you*: the Prophet.

91. *the Fire*: Ar. *al-nār* is the most common of the various designations for Hell.

73–74 False Gods are powerless

75–76 God chooses his messengers

92. *angels*: for these beings and their various roles, see n. on Q2.30.

77–78 Encouragement to believers

93. *struggle*: or 'fight.'

94. *(both) before and in this*: referring to the time of Abraham and the present (or perhaps 'in this Qur'ān'); in other words, 'Muslim' is not a new name.

95. *against the people*: or 'against all humankind.'

23 The Believers ۞ Al-Mu'minūn

In the Name of God, the Merciful, the Compassionate

1 The believers have prospered **2** who are humble in their prayers, **3** and who turn away from frivolous
talk, **4** and who give the alms,[1] **5** and who guard their private parts, **6** except from their wives or what
their right (hands) own[2] – surely then they are not (to be) blamed, **7** but whoever seeks beyond that, those
– they are the transgressors – **8** and those who keep their pledges and their promise(s),[3] **9** and who guard
their prayers. **10** Those – they are the inheritors **11** who will inherit Paradise.[4] There they will remain.

12 Certainly We created the human from an extract of clay.[5] **13** Then We made him a drop[6] in a secure
dwelling place,[7] **14** then We made a clot (from) the drop, then We made a lump (from) the clot, then We
made bones (from) the lump, then We clothed the bones (with) flesh, (and) then We (re)produced him
as another creature. So blessed (be) God, the best of creators! **15** Then, after that, you will indeed die,
16 (and) then surely on the Day of Resurrection you will be raised up.

17 Certainly We created above you seven orbits,[8] and We were not oblivious of the creation. **18** We send
down water from the sky in (due) measure, and cause it to settle in the earth – and surely We are able
indeed to take it away. **19** By means of it We produce gardens of date palms and grapes for you, in which
(there are) many fruits for you, and from which you eat, **20** and a tree[9] (which) comes forth from Mount
Sinai[10] (which) bears oil and seasoning[11] for eaters. **21** Surely in the cattle[12] is a lesson indeed for you:

Q23: This sūra opens with an enumeration of the virtues of believers. It then extols the signs of God's power and providence, relates accounts of previous messengers, and emphasizes the certainty of resurrection and judgment. Most scholars assign Q23 to the 'Meccan' period.

1–11 Virtues of the believers

1. *the alms*: i.e. *zakāt*, a kind of tithe required for the benefit of the poor, as well as other purposes.
2. *what their right (hands) own*: i.e. female slaves (cf. Q4.3, 24).
3. *promise(s)*: or 'contract(s).'
4. *Paradise*: the word (Ar. *firdaus*) occurs only here and at Q18.105. In the Hebrew Bible *pardes* (a transliteration of a Persian word) occurs in its original meaning of 'park' or 'garden' (see Song of Songs 4.13; Ecclesiastes 2.5; Nehemiah 2.8), but in later Judaism the word came to be associated with the Garden of Eden. The Septuagint employs the Greek word *paradeisos* both of Eden (e.g. Genesis 2.8) and of Eden restored (e.g. Ezekiel 28.13; 36.35). The same word is used in the New Testament to refer to 'heaven' (see Luke 23.43; 2 Corinthians 12.4; Revelation 2.7).

12–16 God's power and providence: signs of life

5. *an extract of clay*: meaning uncertain; 'extract' probably referred to semen originally (cf. Q32.8), and 'of clay' was added later (perhaps for the sake of rhyme).
6. *a drop*: of semen.
7. *dwelling place*: the womb; what follows is a description of prenatal development.

17–22 God's power and providence: signs of nature

8. *seven orbits*: lit. 'roads,' referring to the courses of the seven heavens.
9. *a tree*: the olive, but the reference is obscure (there may be some confusion with the Mount of Olives).
10. *Mount Sinai*: mentioned by name only here and at Q95.2.
11. *seasoning*: meaning uncertain.
12. *cattle*: or 'livestock' in general.

We give you to drink from what is in their bellies,[13] and in them (there are) many benefits for you, and from them you eat. **22** On them, and on the ship (as well), you are carried.

23 Certainly We sent Noah[14] to his people, and he said, 'My people! Serve God! You have no god other than Him. Will you not guard (yourselves)?'[15] **24** But the assembly of those who disbelieved among his people said, 'This is nothing but a human being like you. He wants to gain superiority over you. If God had (so) pleased, He would indeed have sent down angels.[16] We have not heard of this among our fathers of old. **25** He is nothing but a man possessed.[17] Wait on him for a time.'[18] **26** He said, 'My Lord, help me, because they are calling me a liar.' **27** So We inspired him: 'Build the ship[19] under Our eyes and Our inspiration, and when Our command comes and the oven boils,[20] put into it two of every kind, a pair, and your family – except for him against whom the word has (already) gone forth.[21] Do not address Me concerning those who have done evil. Surely they are going to be drowned! **28** When you have boarded the ship – you and (those) who are with you – say: "Praise (be)[22] to God, who has rescued us from the people who were evildoers!" **29** And say: "My Lord, bring me to land (at) a blessed landing place, (for) You are the best of those who bring to land."'[23] **30** Surely in that are signs indeed. Surely We have been testing (people) indeed.

31 Then, after them, We produced another generation,[24] **32** and We sent among them a messenger[25] from among them: 'Serve God! You have no god other than Him. Will you not guard (yourselves)?' **33** But the assembly of his people, those who disbelieved and called the meeting of the Hereafter[26] a lie, even though We had given them luxury in this present life, said, 'This is nothing but a human being like you. He eats from what you eat from, and drinks from what you drink.[27] **34** If indeed you obey a human being like you, surely then you will be the losers indeed. **35** Does he promise you that when you are dead, and become dust and bones, that you will be brought forth?[28] **36** Away! Away with what you are promised! **37** There is nothing but our present life. We die, and we live, and we are not going to be raised up. **38** He is nothing but a man who has forged a lie against God. We are not believers in him.' **39** He said, 'My Lord, help me, because they are calling me a liar.' **40** He[29] said, 'In a little (while) they will indeed be

---

13. *what is in their bellies*: milk.

23–30 The story of Noah

14. *Noah*: for the story that follows, cf. the versions at Q7.59-64; 10.71-73; 11.25-34; 26.105-120; and Genesis 6.5-10.1.
15. *guard (yourselves)*: against evil, or God.
16. *angels*: for these beings and their various roles, see n. on Q2.30.
17. *possessed*: by the jinn (lit. '[there are] jinn in him' [Ar. *bi-hi jinna*]); cf. below Q23.70 (the Prophet); and see n. on Q7.184.
18. *Wait on him for a time*: i.e. wait to see what happens to him.
19. *the ship*: Noah's ark.
20. *the oven boils*: cf. Q11.40; the waters of the flood were 'boiling,' according to Jewish tradition.
21. *except for (him) against whom...*: a son of Noah who perished in the flood (see Q11.42-43).
22. *(be)*: or '(belongs).'
23. *bring me to land...*: lit. 'send me down...;' this verb (and the different forms of it which follow) is the same one used for the 'sending down' of angels, of revelation in general, and of the Qur'ān in particular.

31–41 An unnamed messenger

24. *another generation*: probably the people of Thamūd, but see below Q23.41n.
25. *messenger*: for this important title, see n. on Q2.87.
26. *the Hereafter*: see n. on Q2.4.
27. *He eats...and drinks*: cf. Q5.75 (Jesus and Mary); 21.8; 25.7 (the Prophet), 20; contrast Q11.70.
28. *brought forth*: from the grave.
29. *He*: God.

full of regret.' **41** Then the cry[30] seized them in truth,[31] and We turned them into ruins. Away with the people who are evildoers!

42 Then, after them, We produced other generations. **43** No community precedes its time,[32] nor do they delay (it). **44** Then We sent Our messengers in succession: whenever its messenger came to a community, they called him a liar. So We caused some of them to follow others, and We turned them (into) stories.[33] Away with a people who do not believe!

45 Then We sent Moses and his brother Aaron, with Our signs[34] and clear authority, **46** to Pharaoh and his assembly, but they became arrogant and were a haughty people. **47** They said, 'Shall we believe in two human beings like us, when their people are serving us?' **48** So they called them both liars, and were among the destroyed.

49 Certainly We gave Moses the Book, so that they might be (rightly) guided. **50** And We made the son of Mary[35] and his mother a sign, and We gave them both refuge on high ground, (where there was) a hollow (as) a dwelling place and a flowing spring:[36] **51** 'Messengers![37] Eat from the good things,[38] and do righteousness! Surely I am aware of what you do. **52** Surely this community of yours is one community, and I am your Lord. So guard (yourselves) against Me!' **53** But they[39] cut their affair (in two) between them (over the) scriptures,[40] each faction gloating over what was with them.[41] **54** Leave them in their flood (of confusion) for a time.[42] **55** Do they think that in increasing them with wealth and children **56** We are quick to do them good? No! But they do not realize (it).[43]

57 Surely those who – they are apprehensive on account of fear of their Lord, **58** and those who – they believe in the signs of their Lord, **59** and those who – they do not associate (anything) with their Lord, **60** and those who give what they give, while their hearts are afraid because they are going to return to their Lord – **61** (it is) those who are quick in the (doing of) good deeds, and they are foremost in them.[44]

---

30. *the cry*: or 'the shout' (cf. Q11.67; 54.31, Thamūd; 11.94, Midian; 15.73, people of Lot; 15.83, people of al-Ḥijr).
31. *in truth*: or 'with the truth,' implying 'with judgment.'

42–44 Other messengers

32. *time*: or 'term' (Ar. *ajal*); i.e. the time of punishment is predetermined and cannot be changed (cf. Q15.5).
33. *stories*: i.e. accounts or reports (Ar. *aḥādīth*) of punishment (see n. on Q7.59).

45–48 Moses and Aaron

34. *signs*: referring to Moses' 'miracles' (see n. on Q2.39).

49–56 Jesus and Mary

35. *son of Mary*: Jesus; there is no mention in the Qur'ān of Joseph, Jesus' putative father (cf. Mark 6.3).
36. *a flowing spring*: cf. Q19.24.
37. *Messengers*: notice the plur.; Mary too is addressed as a 'messenger' (cf. Q21.91, where she is mentioned in a long list of 'prophets').
38. *Eat from the good things*: perhaps an allusion to Jesus' abrogation of Jewish food restrictions.
39. *they*: Jews and Christians.
40. *scriptures*: Ar. *zubur* (cf. Q3.184n.).
41. *each faction gloating over what was with them*: the Jews in the Torah, the Christians in the Gospel (cf. Q30.32).
42. *Leave them...*: referring to Jews and Christians (addressed to the Prophet).
43. *they do not realize (it)*: that these 'blessings' are really intended to lead them astray (for this idea, see e.g. Q3.10, 14, 116).

57–61 Believers are quick to do good

44. *they are foremost in them*: see Q9.100; 56.10-12.

62 We do not burden anyone beyond his capacity,[45] and with Us is a Book[46] (which) speaks in truth – and they will not be done evil. **63** No! But their hearts[47] are in a flood (of confusion) about this, and they have deeds other than that, which they (will continue to) do[48] **64** – until, when We seize their affluent ones with the punishment, suddenly they cry out. **65** 'Do not cry out today! Surely you will receive no help from Us. **66** My signs[49] were recited to you, but you turned on your heels, **67** being arrogant toward it,[50] (and) forsaking (one who was) conversing by night.'[51]

68 Have they not contemplated the word? Or did (there) come to them what did not come to their fathers of old? **69** Or did they not recognize their messenger,[52] and so rejected him? **70** Or do they say, 'He is possessed'?[53] No! He brought them the truth, but most of them were averse to the truth. **71** If the truth had followed their desires, the heavens and the earth and whatever is in them would indeed have been corrupted. No! We brought them their Reminder,[54] but they turned away from their Reminder. **72** Or do you ask them for payment? Yet the payment of your Lord is better, and He is the best of providers. **73** Surely you indeed call them to a straight path, **74** and surely those who do not believe in the Hereafter are indeed deviating from the path. **75** Even if We had compassion on them, and removed whatever hardship they had, they would indeed persist in their insolent transgression, wandering blindly. **76** Certainly We have seized them with the punishment (already),[55] but they did not submit themselves to their Lord, nor were they humble. **77** – Until, when We open a gate of harsh punishment on them, suddenly they are in despair about it.

78 He (it is) who has produced for you hearing and sight and hearts[56] – little thanks you show! **79** He (it is) who has scattered[57] you on the earth, and to Him you will be gathered. **80** He (it is) who gives life and causes death, and to Him (belongs) the alternation of the night and the day. Will you not understand? **81** No! They said just what those of old said. **82** They said, 'When we are dead, and turned to dust and bones, shall we indeed be raised up? **83** We have been promised this before – we and our fathers. This is nothing but old tales.'[58]

62–77 God's dealings with disbelievers

45. *beyond his capacity*: God does not impose any duty on humans which they are not able to perform (cf. 1 Corinthians 10.13).
46. *a Book*: i.e. the heavenly 'Record' or 'Account' of the deeds of humankind (see e.g. Q18.49; cf. Q17.13, 71; 69.19, 25; 84.7, 10, where each person is given an individual 'book' containing a record of his deeds).
47. *their hearts*: i.e. the disbelievers' hearts (here spoken of as synonymous with 'their minds').
48. *they have deeds other than that, which they (will continue to) do*: i.e. they fail to do the 'good deeds' just mentioned (Q23.57-61), and will go on doing 'other (evil) deeds,' unaware that these are being 'recorded.'
49. *signs*: or 'verses.'
50. *toward it*: the Qur'ān, implied by 'My signs/verses,' or perhaps 'toward him' (the Prophet).
51. *forsaking (one who was) conversing by night*: referring to the Prophet (cf. Q25.5), or possibly 'forsaking (him like) a Samaritan' (cf. Q20.85).
52. *messenger*: the Prophet.
53. *He is possessed*: lit. '(There are) jinn in him' (cf. above Q23.25, Noah).
54. *their Reminder*: referring to the Qur'ān (see n. on Q3.58).
55. *We have seized them with the punishment (already)*: reference obscure.

78–83 Signs of God's power and providence

56. *hearts*: minds.
57. *scattered*: as a sower scatters seed.
58. *old tales*: or 'tales of the ancients;' a contemptuous reference to the stories of earlier generations who were punished for disobeying their prophets (see n. on Q7.59; cf. Q25.5).

84 Say:[59] 'To whom (does) the earth and whatever is on it (belong), if you know?' **85** They will say, 'To God.'[60] Say: 'Will you not take heed?'[61] **86** Say: 'Who is Lord of the seven heavens, and Lord of the great throne?' **87** They will say, 'To God.'[62] Say: 'Will you not guard (yourselves)?' **88** Say: 'Who is (it) in whose hand is the kingdom of everything, (who) protects and needs no protection, if you know?' **89** They will say, 'To God.' Say: 'How are you (so) bewitched?' **90** No! We have brought them the truth. Surely they are liars indeed! **91** God has not taken a son,[63] nor is there any (other) god with Him. Then each god would indeed have gone off with what he had created, and some of them would indeed have exalted (themselves) over others. Glory to God above what they allege! **92** (He is the) Knower of the unseen and the seen.[64] He is exalted above what they associate.

93 Say: 'My Lord, if You show me what they are promised,[65] **94** my Lord, do not place me among the people who are evildoers.' **95** Surely We are able indeed to show you what We promise them. **96** Repel the evil with that which is better. We know what they allege. **97** And say: 'My Lord, I take refuge with You from the incitements[66] of the satans,[67] **98** and I take refuge with You, my Lord, from their being present with me.'

99 – Until, when death comes to one of them, he says, 'My Lord, send me back, **100** so that I may do righteousness concerning what I left (undone).' By no means! Surely it is (only) a word which he says. Behind them is a barrier,[68] until the Day when they will be raised up.

101 When there is a blast on the trumpet,[69] (there will be) no (claims of) kinship among them on that Day, nor will they ask each other questions. **102** Whoever's scales are heavy,[70] those – they are the ones who prosper, **103** but whoever's scales are light, those are the ones who have lost their (own) selves – remaining in Gehenna.[71] **104** The Fire[72] will scorch their faces, while they grimace in it. **105** 'Were My signs not recited[73] to you, and did you not call them a lie?' **106** They will say, 'Our Lord, our miserableness overcame us, and we were a people in error. **107** Our Lord, bring us out of it! Then if we return

---

84–92 God is One

59. *Say*: on this form of address, see n. on Q2.80.
60. *They will say, 'To God'*: cf. Q23.87, 89 below; this indicates that the people addressed believed in a supreme deity of this name (cf. also Q23.38 above).
61. *take heed*: or 'remember,' 'be reminded.'
62. *To God*: the preposition is in Arabic (here and in the following verse).
63. *son*: or 'child' (Ar. *walad*), but probably referring to Christian claims about Jesus as God's son (cf. Q2.116; 4.171; 10.68; 19.88-92; 21.26; 25.2).
64. *the seen*: lit. 'the witnessed.'

93–98 The Prophet's prayer

65. *if You show me what they are promised*: i.e. if the Prophet should live to see their punishment.
66. *incitements*: or 'promptings,' 'suggestions.'
67. *satans*: or 'demons' (Ar. *shayāṭīn*); individually assigned to incite people to evil (see Q19.83; 43.36; cf. Q41.25).

99–100 Deathbed repentance

68. *a barrier*: separating the dead from the living (Ar. *barzakh*). In later Islamic thought it became a kind of purgatory for the period between death and resurrection.

101–115 The Last Day, Resurrection, and Judgment

69. *a blast on the trumpet*: the Last Day will be announced by the blast of a trumpet (e.g. Q6.73; 18.99; 20.102; 39.68 [a double blast]; 69.13; 74.8; 78.18; cf. Matthew 24.31; 1 Corinthians 15.52; 1 Thessalonians 4.16).
70. *scales are heavy*: good deeds are 'heavier' than bad deeds (see Q18.105).
71. *Gehenna*: a name for Hell (see n. on Q2.206).
72. *the Fire*: Ar. *al-nār* is the most common of the various designations for Hell.
73. *Were My signs not recited*: or 'Were My verses not read aloud.'

(to evil), surely we shall be evildoers.' **108** He will say, 'Skulk away into it, and do not speak to Me! **109** Surely there was a group of My servants (who) said, "Our Lord, we believe, so forgive us, and have compassion on us, (for) You are the best of the compassionate." **110** But you took them (in) ridicule, until they made you forget My remembrance,[74] and you were laughing at them. **111** Surely I have repaid them today for their patience. Surely they – they are the triumphant!' **112** He will say, 'How long did you remain in the earth, (by) number of years?' **113** They will say, 'We remained a day, or part of a day. Ask those who keep count.' **114** He will say, 'You remained only a little (while) – if only you knew! **115** Did you think that We created you in vain, and that you would not be returned to Us?'

116 Exalted is God, the true King![75] (There is) no god but Him, Lord of the honorable throne. **117** Whoever calls on another god with God – for which he has no proof – his reckoning is with his Lord. Surely he will not prosper, (nor will) the disbelievers. **118** Say: 'My Lord, forgive and have compassion, (for) You are the best of the compassionate.'

74. *My remembrance*: or 'My Reminder,' referring to the Qur'ān.

116–118 God alone is King

75. *the true King*: or 'the King, the Truth.'

24 The Light ❁ Al-Nūr

In the Name of God, the Merciful, the Compassionate

1 A sūra[1] – We have sent it down and made it obligatory, and We have sent down in it clear signs,[2] so that you[3] may take heed.[4]

2 The adulterous woman and the adulterous man[5] – flog[6] each one of them a hundred lashes,[7] and let no pity for the two of them affect[8] you concerning the religion[9] of God, if you believe in God and the Last Day. And let a group of the believers witness their punishment. **3** The adulterous man shall marry no one but an adulterous woman or an idolatrous woman,[10] and the adulterous woman – no one shall marry her but an adulterous man or an idolatrous man. That is forbidden to the believers.

4 Those who hurl (accusations)[11] against women of reputation,[12] (and) then do not bring four witnesses, flog them eighty lashes, and do not accept their testimony ever (again). Those – they are the wicked, **5** except for those who turn (in repentance) after that and set (things) right. Surely God is forgiving, compassionate. **6** Those who hurl (accusations) against their wives, and have no witnesses except themselves, the testimony of such a person shall be to bear witness four times 'by God,' that he is indeed one of the truthful, **7** and the fifth time, that the curse of God (be) upon him if he is one of the liars.[13]

Q24: This sūra, which almost all scholars assign to the 'Medinan' period, takes its title from the reference to God as 'the light of the heavens and the earth' (Q24.35). It is comprised for the most part of regulations governing the household, including appropriate dress, conduct, and sexual behavior.

1 A sūra from God

1. *sūra*: usually refers to a 'unit' of revelation, but here it comes close to its present meaning. The mention of a sūra being 'sent down' (e.g. Q9.64, 86, 124, 127; 47.20) is similar to the way in which terms like 'sign' or 'verse' (Ar. *āya*), 'book' (*kitāb*), and 'recitation' (*qur'ān*) are also used (see n. on Q2.23).
2. *clear signs*: here 'signs' refers to 'verses' (see n. on Q2.39).
3. *you*: plur.
4. *take heed*: or 'remember,' 'be reminded.'

2–3 Punishment for unlawful sexual activity

5. *adulterous woman...man*: or 'sexually promiscuous woman (Ar. *al-zāniya*)...man (*al-zānī*),' since *zinā'* refers to all illicit sexual activity. This verse is usually understood as referring to 'fornication,' since the penalty for adultery is stoning in later legal tradition, but not in the Qur'ān.
6. *flog*: plur. imperative.
7. *a hundred lashes*: some traditions report that there was once a verse in the Qur'ān which prescribed stoning for adultery, but that may be a later invention to minimize the difference between the Qur'ān and the Torah on this point. Stoning is the penalty for adultery at Deuteronomy 22.23-24 (cf. John 8.3-11); death is prescribed at Leviticus 20.10. Cf. the punishment for sexual immorality at Q4.15, which is usually said to be abrogated by the present verse, since it is traditionally thought to have been revealed later.
8. *affect*: lit. 'seize.'
9. *religion*: or 'judgment,' since the word for 'religion' is a homonym of 'judgment' (Ar. *dīn*).
10. *idolatrous woman*: lit. a woman who 'associates (other gods with God).'

4–10 Punishment for false accusations

11. *hurl (accusations)*: of sexual immorality.
12. *women of reputation*: i.e. either married women or young women of good family.
13. *curse of God (be) upon him...*: cf. Q3.61.

8 And it shall avert the punishment from her that she bear witness four times 'by God,' that he is indeed
one of the liars, **9** and the fifth time, that the anger of God (be) upon her if he is one of the truthful.[14]
10 And if (it were) not (for the) favor of God on you, and His mercy, and that God turns (in forgiveness),
wise [...].[15]

11 Surely those who brought the lie[16] are a group of you.[17] Do not think[18] it a bad (thing) for you – No! It
is good for you! Each one of them will bear what sin he has earned, and the one who took upon himself
the greater part of it[19] – for him (there will be) a great punishment. **12** Why, when you heard it, did the
believing men and the believing women not think better of themselves, and say, 'This is a clear lie'?
13 Why did they not bring four witnesses concerning it? Since they did not bring the witnesses, they
are liars in the sight of God. **14** If (it were) not (for the) favor of God on you, and His mercy, in this world
and the Hereafter,[20] a great punishment would have touched you for what you spread about. **15** When
you were receiving it with your tongues, and speaking with your mouths what you had no knowledge
of, and thought it was a trivial (thing), when with God it was a mighty (thing) – **16** why, when you
heard it, did you not say, 'It is not for us to speak about this. Glory to You! This is a great slander'?
17 God admonishes you from ever returning to such a thing (again), if you are believers. **18** God makes
clear to you the signs.[21] God is knowing, wise. **19** Surely those who love (allegations of) immorality[22] to
circulate among those who believe – for them (there is) a painful punishment in this world and the Hereafter. God knows, and you do not know. **20** If (it were) not (for the) favor of God on you, and His mercy,
and that God is kind, compassionate [...].[23]

21 You who believe! Do not follow the footsteps of Satan.[24] Whoever follows the footsteps of Satan – surely he commands (what is) immoral and wrong. If (it were) not (for the) favor of God on you, and His mercy, not one of you would ever have been pure. God purifies whomever He pleases. God is hearing, knowing.

22 Let not those of you who possess favor and abundance swear against giving (support) to family, and the poor, and the ones who emigrate in the way of God, but let them pardon and excuse (them). Would you not like God to forgive you? God is forgiving, compassionate.

---

14. *...if he is one of the truthful*: cf. the elaborate ritual for wives suspected of adultery at Numbers 5.11-31.
15. *[...]*: there appears to be a lacuna here, and it is not certain whether this verse belongs with the preceding section or with what follows (cf. Q24.20 below).

11–20 The 'affair of the lie'

16. *the lie*: also translated 'the slander' (Ar. *al-ifk*); the reference is obscure, but it is said to allude to an incident involving 'Ā'isha, youngest wife of the Prophet, whom he had taken with him on an expedition in 627 CE/6 AH. At the last stop on the way home 'Ā'isha got left behind, but eventually came back to Medina riding the camel of a handsome young man. When allegations of misconduct on 'Ā'isha's part were spread about, she withdrew to her parents' house until at length the Prophet received a revelation (said to be Q24.11-20) declaring 'Ā'isha innocent.
17. *a group of you*: said to refer to the Prophet's enemies.
18. *Do not think*: plur. imperative.
19. *the one who took...the greater part of it*: i.e. the person chiefly responsible.
20. *the Hereafter*: see n. on Q2.4.
21. *signs*: or 'verses.'
22. *immorality*: or 'indecency' (Ar. *fāḥisha*), of a sexual nature.
23. *[...]*: there appears to be a lacuna here, and it is not clear whether this verse belongs with the preceding section or with what follows.

21 Shun immorality

24. *Satan*: for this figure, see n. on Q2.36.

22 Give to family, the poor, and the emigrants

23 Surely those who hurl (accusations) against chaste women – the oblivious[25] (but) believing women – are accursed in this world and the Hereafter. For them (there is) a great punishment. **24** On the Day when their tongues, and their hands, and their feet will bear witness against them about what they have done, **25** on that Day God will pay them their just due[26] in full, and they will know that God – He is the clear Truth.[27]

26 The bad women for the bad men, and the bad men for the bad women. And the good women for the good men, and the good men for the good women – those are (to be declared) innocent of what they say.[28] For them (there is) forgiveness and generous provision.

27 You who believe! Do not enter houses other than your (own) houses, until you ask permission and greet its inhabitants. That is better for you, so that you may take heed. **28** But if you do not find anyone inside, do not enter it until permission is given to you. If it is said to you, 'Go away,' go away. It is purer for you. God is aware of what you do. **29** (There is) no blame on you that you enter uninhabited houses, where (there is) enjoyment for you.[29] God knows what you reveal and what you conceal.

30 Say to the believing men (that) they (should) lower their sight and guard their private parts. That is purer for them. Surely God is aware of what they do. **31** And say to the believing women (that) they (should) lower their sight and guard their private parts, and not show their charms,[30] except for what (normally) appears of them. And let them draw[31] their head coverings over their breasts, and not show their charms, except to their husbands, or their fathers, or their husbands' fathers, or their sons, or their husbands' sons, or their brothers, or their brothers' sons, or their sisters' sons, or their women, or what their right (hands) own,[32] or such men as attend (them who) have no (sexual) desire, or children (who are) not (yet) aware of women's nakedness. And let them not stamp their feet to make known what they hide of their charms.[33] Turn to God (in repentance) – all (of you) – believers, so that you may prosper.

32 Marry off the unmarried among you, and (also) the righteous among your male slaves and your female slaves. If they are poor, God will enrich them from His favor. God is embracing, knowing. **33** Let those who do not find (the means for) marriage abstain,[34] until God enriches them from His favor. Those who seek the writ,[35] among what your right hands own, write (it) for them, if you know any good in them, and give them some of the wealth of God which He has given you. And do not force your young women into prostitution, if they wish (to live in) chastity, so that you may seek (the fleeting) goods of

---

23–25 Slander condemned

25. *oblivious*: i.e. either 'unaware' of the accusation or 'careless' about getting into compromising situations.
26. *their just due*: or perhaps 'the judgment (Ar. *dīn*) which they are due' (cf. Q69.1), but the meaning is uncertain.
27. *the clear Truth*: or 'the Truth who makes (things) clear' (cf. Q22.6, 62; 31.30).

26 Like should marry like

28. *innocent of what they say*: i.e. innocent of whatever 'bad people' may say about them.

27–29 Privacy to be respected

29. *...where (there is) enjoyment for you*: reference obscure; said to refer to inns, shops, etc.

30–31 Modest behaviour encouraged

30. *charms*: or 'ornaments,' perhaps a euphemism for breasts.
31. *draw*: lit. 'strike' or 'stamp' (cf. Q33.59).
32. *what their right (hands) own*: slaves.
33. *let them not stamp their feet...*: probably refers to walking in a sexually suggestive fashion (i.e. 'strutting' in such a way to make their 'charms' stand out).

32–33 Marriage recommended

34. *abstain*: i.e. remain abstinent.
35. *the writ*: lit. 'the book;' usually said to be a 'manumission contract' or written declaration by the slave owner to liberate a slave on condition of receiving a certain sum of money, but it may refer to a marriage contract.

this present life. Whoever forces them – surely God is forgiving (and) compassionate (to them) after their being forced.

34 Certainly We have sent down to you[36] signs that make (things) clear,[37] and an example[38] of those who passed away before you,[39] and an admonition for those who guard (themselves).[40]

35 God (is the) light[41] of the heavens and the earth. The parable of His light is like a niche in which (there is) a lamp, the lamp in a glass, the glass like a brilliant star, lit from a blessed tree, an olive (tree) that is neither (of the) East nor (of the) West, whose oil almost shines, even though no fire has touched it – Light upon light, God guides to His light whomever He pleases, and God strikes parables for the people, and God has knowledge of everything[42] – **36** in houses (which) God has permitted to be raised up and in which (He has permitted) His Name to be remembered. Glorifying Him there, in the mornings and the evenings, **37** are men (whom) neither a (business) transaction nor bargaining diverts from the remembrance of God, or (from) observing the prayer and giving the alms.[43] They fear a Day on which the hearts and the sight will be overturned, **38** so that God may repay them (for the) best of what they have done, and increase them from His favor. God provides for whomever He pleases without reckoning.

39 But those who disbelieve – their deeds are like a mirage in a desert which the thirsty man thinks (to be) water, until, when he comes to it, he finds it (to be) nothing, but he finds God beside him, and then He pays him his account in full. God is quick at the reckoning. **40** Or (he[44] is) like the darkness in a deep sea – a wave covers him, above which is (another) wave, above which is a cloud – darkness upon darkness. When he puts out his hand, he can hardly see it. The one to whom God does not give light has no light (at all).

41 Do you[45] not see that God – whatever is in the heavens and the earth glorifies Him, and (so do) the birds spreading (their wings in flight)? Each one knows its prayer and its glorifying, and God is aware of what they do. **42** To God (belongs) the kingdom of the heavens and the earth. To God is the (final) destination. **43** Do you not see that God drives the clouds, then gathers them, then makes them (into) a mass, and then you see the rain come forth from the midst of it? He sends down mountains (of them)[46] from the sky, in which (there is) hail, and He smites whomever He pleases with it, and turns it away from whomever He pleases. The flash of His lightning almost takes away the sight. **44** God alternates the night and the day. Surely in that is a lesson indeed for those who have sight. **45** God has created every

---

34 Clear signs

36. *you*: plur.
37. *signs...*: or 'verses....'
38. *example*: or 'parable' (cf. Q43.8).
39. *those who passed away before you*: a reference to the stories of previous peoples who were punished for their disbelief (see n. on Q7.59).
40. *guard (themselves)*: against evil, or God.

35–38 Parable of God's light

41. *God (is the) light...*: known as the 'light verse' (*āyat al-nūr*), this passage has received various mystical interpretations. It may be based on a description of the lighted altar of a Christian church; cf. John 8.12; 9.39.
42. *Light upon light...has knowledge of everything*: v. 35b is probably a later addition, since the rhyme scheme suggests that vv. 36-37 originally followed v. 35a.
43. *observing the prayer and giving the alms*: i.e. *ṣalāt*, the ritual prayer, and *zakāt*, a kind of tithe.

39–40 Parables of disbelief

44. *(he)*: the disbeliever.

41–46 Signs of God's power and providence

45. *you*: or 'one.'
46. *mountains (of them)*: i.e. mountains of clouds.

living creature from water.[47] (There are) some of them who walk on their bellies, and some of them who walk on two feet, and some of them who walk on four. God creates whatever He pleases. Surely God is powerful over everything. **46** Certainly We have sent down signs that make (things) clear.[48] God guides whomever He pleases to a straight path.

47 They say, 'We believe in God and the messenger,[49] and we obey.' Then, after that, a group of them turns away.[50] Those are not with the believers. **48** When they are called to God and His messenger, so that he may judge between them,[51] suddenly a group of them turns away. **49** But if (they think) the truth is on their side, they come to him readily. **50** (Is there) a sickness in their hearts,[52] or do they doubt, or do they fear that God will be unjust to them, and His messenger (too)? No! Those – they are the evil-doers. **51** The only saying of the believers, when they are called to God and His messenger so that he may judge between them, is that they say, 'We hear and obey.' Those – they are the ones who prosper. **52** Whoever obeys God and His messenger, and fears God, and guards (himself) against Him, those – they are the triumphant. **53** They have sworn by God the most solemn of their oaths: if you command them, they will indeed go forth. Say:[53] 'Do not swear! Honorable obedience (is sufficient). Surely God is aware of what you do.' **54** Say: 'Obey God and obey the messenger! If you turn away, (there is) only on him what is laid on him, and (only) on you what is laid on you. But if you obey him, you will be (rightly) guided. Nothing (depends) on the messenger except the clear delivery (of the message).'

55 God has promised those of you who believe and do righteous deeds that He will indeed make them successors on the earth,[54] (even) as He made those who were before them successors, and (that) He will indeed establish their religion for them – that which He has approved for them – and (that) He will indeed give them security in exchange for their former fear: 'They will serve Me,[55] not associating anything with Me. Whoever disbelieves after that, those – they are the wicked.' **56** Observe the prayer and give the alms, and obey the messenger, so that you may receive compassion. **57** Do not think (that) those who disbelieve are able to escape (God) on the earth. Their refuge is the Fire[56] – and it is indeed an evil destination!

58 You who believe! Let those whom your right (hands) own,[57] and those of you who have not reached the (age of) puberty, ask permission of you at three times (of the day)[58] – before the dawn prayer, and

---

47. *from water*: see Q21.30; 25.54; 'from dust,' according to Q3.59; 18.37; 22.5; 30.20; 35.11; 40.67; 'from clay,' according to Q6.2; 7.12; 15.26; 17.61; 23.12; 32.7; 38.71, 76; 55.14.

48. *signs...*: or 'verses....'

47–54 Obey God and the Messenger

49. *messenger*: for this important title, see n. on Q2.87.
50. *a group of them turns away*: probably referring to the 'hypocrites' (cf. Q24.50 below).
51. *that he may judge between them*: disputes were to be referred to the Prophet (see e.g. Q4.59-70).
52. *hearts*: here, as often, the heart is spoken of as synonymous with mind.
53. *Say*: on this form of address, see n. on Q2.80.

55–57 God's promise to the believers

54. *successors on the earth*: i.e. successors of previous generations, or perhaps 'rulers' (see e.g. Q6.133, 165; 7.69, 74; 27.62).
55. *serve Me*: or 'worship Me.'
56. *the Fire*: Ar. *al-nār* is the most common of the various designations for Hell.

58–60 Household etiquette

57. *those whom your right (hands) own*: slaves.
58. *ask permission of you at three times (of the day)*: i.e. some members of the household were required to ask permission at certain times of the day before entering a room, so as to guard against inadvertently seeing the householder naked. At other times no such permission was required.

when you lay down your clothes at the noon hour, and after the evening prayer – the three (times) of
nakedness for you. But beyond those (times there is) no blame on you or on them in going about among
each other. In this way God makes clear to you the signs. God is knowing, wise. **59** When your children reach the (age of) puberty, let them ask permission (before entering), as those before them asked
permission. In this way God makes clear to you His signs. God is knowing, wise. **60** And your women who
are past childbearing and have no hope of marriage, (there is) no blame on them that they lay down
their clothes, (as long as there is) no flaunting of (their) charms. But that they abstain is better for them.
God is hearing, knowing.

61 There is no blame on the blind, and no blame on the disabled, and no blame on the sick, nor on yourselves, that you eat at your houses, or your fathers' houses, or your mothers' houses, or your brothers' houses, or your sisters' houses, or your paternal uncles' houses, or your paternal aunts' houses, or your maternal uncles' houses, or your maternal aunts' houses, or (at houses) of which you possess the keys, or (at the house) of your friend. There is no blame on you that you eat together or in separate groups. When you enter (these) houses, greet one another (with) a greeting from God, blessed (and) good. In this way God makes clear to you the signs, so that you may understand.

62 Only those are believers who believe in God and His messenger, and who, when they are with him on some common matter, do not go away until they ask his permission. Surely those who ask your permission – those are the ones who believe in God and His messenger. When they ask your permission for some affair of theirs, give permission to whomever you please of them, and ask forgiveness for them from God. Surely God is forgiving, compassionate.

63 Do not make the messenger's calling of you like the calling of some of you to others. God already knows those of you who slip away secretly. Let those who go against his command beware, or trouble will smite them, or a painful punishment will smite them.

64 Is it not a fact that to God (belongs) whatever is in the heavens and the earth? He already knows what you are up to, and on the Day when they will be returned to Him, He will inform them about what they have done. God has knowledge of everything.

---

61 Eating in each other's houses

62 Asking the Messenger's permission

63 Heeding the Messenger's call

64 God knows all

25 The Deliverance ۞ Al-Furqān

In the Name of God, the Merciful, the Compassionate

1 Blessed (be) the One who sent down the Deliverance[1] on His servant,[2] so that he may be a warner[3] to the worlds[4] **2** – the One who – to Him (belongs) the kingdom of the heavens and the earth. He has not taken a son,[5] nor has He any associate in the kingdom. He created everything and decreed it exactly.[6]
3 Yet they have taken gods other than Him. They[7] do not create anything, since they are (themselves) created, and do not have power to (cause) themselves harm or benefit, and do not have power over death or life or raising up.[8]

4 Those who disbelieve say, 'This is nothing but a lie! He has forged it, and other people have helped him with it.'[9] So they have come to evil and falsehood. **5** And they say, 'Old tales![10] He has written it down,[11] and it is dictated to him morning and evening.' **6** Say:[12] 'He has sent it down – He who knows the secret in the heavens and earth. Surely He is forgiving, compassionate.'

7 They say,[13] 'What is wrong with this messenger?[14] He eats food and walks about in the markets.[15] If only

---

Q25: This sūra begins by responding to the disbelievers' rejection of the messenger and his message, and then warns them by way of examples of earlier generations who were punished for similar disbelief. The second half of the sūra is largely devoted to the signs of God's power and providence discernible in the natural world. It concludes with a description of the characteristic qualities of God's servants. Most scholars assign Q25 to the 'Meccan' period.

1–3 God is One

1. *the Deliverance*: another name for the Qur'ān (see n. on Q2.53; cf. Q21.48, where it is used in reference to the Torah).
2. *His servant*: the Prophet; the word 'servant' (Ar. *'abd*) also means 'slave.'
3. *warner*: for this role, see n. on Q2.119.
4. *to the worlds*: or 'to all peoples.'
5. *son*: or 'child' (Ar. *walad*), but probably referring to Christian claims about Jesus as God's son (cf. Q2.116; 4.171; 10.68; 19.88-92; 21.26).
6. *decreed it exactly*: lit. 'decreed it (according to its) decree,' emphasizing God's design and control of the universe (cf. Q6.96; 36.38; 41.12).
7. *They*: the 'other gods.'
8. *raising up*: or 'resurrection.'

4–6 Disbelievers reject the Qur'ān

9. *other people have helped him with it*: i.e. with the Qur'ān (cf. Q16.103, 'Only a human being teaches him').
10. *Old tales*: or 'Tales of the ancients;' a contemptuous reference to the stories of previous peoples who were punished for disobeying their prophets (see n. on Q7.59).
11. *He has written it down*: notice the reference to the Prophet's literacy, though tradition holds that he could not read or write.
12. *Say*: on this form of address, see n. on Q2.80.

7–10 Disbelievers reject the Messenger

13. *They say*: for the objections that follow, cf. Q25.20-21, 32 below, and the set of demands at Q17.90-96. Taken at face value, they may reflect some of the religious expectations of the time. In general, 'they' expected the messenger to be a 'miracle worker' or 'divine man.'
14. *messenger*: for this important title, see n. on Q2.87.
15. *He eats food...*: proof of his humanity (see Q25.20 below; cf. Q5.75 [Jesus and Mary]; 21.8; 23.33; contrast Q11.70).

an angel were sent down to him to be a warner with him, **8** or a treasure were cast (down) to him, or he had a garden from which to eat.' The evildoers say, 'You are only following a man (who is) bewitched.'[16] **9** See how they strike parables for you![17] But they have gone astray and cannot (find) a way. **10** Blessed is He who, if He pleases, will give you[18] (what is) better than that – Gardens[19] through which rivers flow – and He will give you palaces.

11 No! They have called the Hour[20] a lie – and We have prepared a blazing (Fire) for whoever calls the Hour a lie. **12** When it sees them from a place far off, they will hear its raging and moaning.[21] **13** When they are cast into a narrow part of it, bound in chains, they will call out there (for) destruction.[22] **14** 'Do not call out today (for) one destruction, but call out (for) many destruction(s)!' **15** Say: 'Is that better, or the Garden of Eternity which is promised to the ones who guard (themselves)?[23] It is their payment and (final) destination.' **16** Remaining there, they will have whatever they please. It is a promise (binding) on your Lord, (something) to be asked for.

17 On the Day when He will gather them and what they serve instead of God, He will say, 'Did you[24] lead astray these servants of Mine, or did they (themselves) go astray from the way?' **18** They will say, 'Glory to You! It was not fitting for us to take any allies other than You, but You gave them and their fathers enjoyment (of life), until they forgot the Reminder[25] and became a ruined people.' **19** 'So they have called you a liar in what you say,[26] and you are incapable of turning (it) aside or (finding any) help. Whoever among you does evil – We shall make him taste a great punishment.'

20 We have not sent any of the envoys[27] before you, except that they indeed ate food and walked about in the markets.[28] We have made some of you a test[29] for others: 'Will you be patient?' Your Lord is seeing. **21** Those who do not expect to meet Us say, 'If only the angels were sent down on us, or we saw our Lord.' Certainly they have become arrogant within themselves and behaved with great disdain.

22 On the Day when they see the angels,[30] (there will be) no good news that Day for the sinners, and they will say, 'An absolute ban!'[31] **23** We shall press forward to whatever deeds they have done, and make

16. *bewitched*: i.e. a victim of magic or under a magic spell (cf. Q17.47).
17. *strike parables for you*: i.e. make comparisons about the Prophet.
18. *give you*: lit. 'make for you' (sing.).
19. *Gardens*: in heaven (for this imagery, see n. on Q2.25).

11–16 Disbelievers punished

20. *the Hour*: of judgment.
21. *its raging and moaning*: a graphic expression of the Fire's lust to possess them (cf. Q11.106; 21.100; 67.7).
22. *call out there (for) destruction*: i.e. they will beg for death to escape the torment.
23. *guard (themselves)*: against evil, or God.

17–19 A judgment scene

24. *you*: i.e. the 'other gods.'
25. *the Reminder*: here referring to the scriptures of the Jews and Christians (cf. Q25.29 below; see n. on Q3.58).
26. *So they have called you a liar in what you say*: i.e. their own gods will denounce the disbelievers as liars.

20–21 Disbelievers demand to see angels and God

27. *the envoys*: lit. 'the ones who are sent' (Ar. *al-mursalūn*), a designation roughly equivalent to 'messengers' (*rusul*).
28. *they indeed ate food...*: i.e. they were human (see n. on Q25.7 above).
29. *test*: or 'trial,' 'temptation' (Ar. *fitna*).

22–29 A judgment scene

30. *On the Day when they see the angels*: there is some irony here: when the disbelievers do finally see the angels, the news will not be good.
31. *An absolute ban*: the meaning of this exclamation is obscure, nor is it clear who is speaking (the sinners or the angels). It may refer to the 'barrier' separating the dead from the living (Q23.100) or to the 'partition' or 'wall'

them scattered dust. **24** The companions of the Garden on that Day (will be in) a better dwelling place and a finer resting place. **25** On the Day when the sky is split open,[32] (along) with the clouds, and the angels are sent down all at once,[33] **26** the true kingdom that Day (will belong) to the Merciful, and it will be a hard Day for the disbelievers. **27** On the Day when the evildoer bites down on both his hands, he will say, 'Would that I had taken a way with the messenger! **28** Woe to me! Would that I had not taken So-and-so as a friend! **29** Certainly he led me astray from the Reminder, after it came to me. Satan[34] is the betrayer of humankind.'

30 The messenger said, 'My Lord! Surely my people have taken this Qur'ān[35] (as a thing to be) shunned.' **31** In this way We have assigned to every prophet[36] an enemy from the sinners.[37] Yet your Lord is sufficient as a guide and helper. **32** Those who disbelieve say, 'If only the Qur'ān were sent down on him all of one piece.'[38] (It has been sent down)[39] in this way,[40] so that We may make firm your heart[41] by means of it.[42] We have arranged it very carefully.[43] **33** They do not bring you any parable,[44] except (that) We have (already) brought you the truth, and (something) better in exposition.[45] **34** Those who are going to be gathered to Gehenna[46] on their faces – those will be worse in position and farther astray (from the) way.

(Q7.46; 57.13) separating the saved from the lost (cf. the 'barrier' separating the two seas at Q25.53 below).

32. *sky is split open*: cf. Q55.37; 69.16; 84.1.

33. *all at once*: or 'once and for all' (lit. 'sent down [with] a sending down' [Ar. *nuzzila anzīlan*]). This is an emphatic response to the disbelievers' question about why no angels had been 'sent down' (Q25.7, 21 above). On the Last Day they will come all at once.

34. *Satan*: for this figure, see n. on Q2.36.

30–34 Disbelievers shun the Qur'ān

35. *this Qur'ān*: or perhaps 'this recitation,' since the expression (Ar. *hādhā al-qur'ān*) is sometimes used only in reference to a part of the Qur'ān (cf. Q6.19; 10.61; 13.31; 72.1; see n. on Q2.185). Otherwise, 'this Qur'ān' may come close to its present meaning as the name of the Muslim scripture (cf. Q9.111), and perhaps imply the existence of 'other Qur'āns' (cf. Q39.27-28).

36. *assigned to every prophet*: lit. 'made for every prophet;' for this important title, see n. on Q2.87.

37. *from the sinners*: cf. Q6.112, from 'satans of the people and the jinn.'

38. *all of one piece*: Ar. *jumlatan wāḥidatan*, though what is meant is not precisely clear. Are the disbelievers challenging the Qur'ān's gradual revelation 'in stages,' or are they demanding to see an actual book or the 'heavenly book' the Prophet claimed to possess (cf. Q4.153; 6.7)? Their question is usually taken as a reference to the Qur'ān's 'serial mode' of revelation (i.e. 'gradually' or 'in stages'), which later interpreters claimed was what distinguished it from the revelation of the Torah (see e.g. Q7.144-145, 150, 154, 171, though the expression 'all of one piece' is never used of the Torah's revelation). According to the Babylonian Talmud (Gittin 60a), some thought the Torah had been 'transmitted scroll by scroll,' others that it had been 'transmitted entire.'

39. *(It has been sent down)...*: or '(We allow them to speak)...,' but something like this has to be supplied.

40. *in this way*: or 'thus' (Ar. *kadhālika*). This is usually understood as implying a 'serial mode' of revelation, consistent with the traditional view that the Qur'ān was 'sent down' or revealed at intervals over a period of some twenty years. But that is not explicitly stated here (see n. on Q17.106), and the meaning of this adverb depends on what is supplied parenthetically at the beginning of the sentence.

41. *heart*: here, as often, the heart is spoken of as synonymous with mind.

42. *by means of it*: i.e. by means of the Qur'ān.

43. *arranged it very carefully*: lit. 'arranged it (by/in) an arranging' (Ar. *rattalnāhu tartīlan*); possibly referring to elocution or to the arrangement of verses (cf. Q73.4), though it is usually understood as a reference to the Qur'ān's 'serial mode' of revelation.

44. *parable*: probably referring to the negative 'comparisons' the disbelievers made about the Prophet, especially their likening of him to a 'bewitched man' (see Q25.8-9 above).

45. *exposition*: or 'interpretation' (Ar. *tafsīr*), the only occurrence of this word in the Qur'ān.

46. *Gehenna*: a name for Hell (see n. on Q2.206).

35 Certainly We gave Moses the Book, and appointed[47] his brother Aaron as an assistant with him.
36 We said, 'Both of you go to the people who have called Our signs a lie.' We destroyed them completely.
37 And the people of Noah – when they called the messengers[48] liars – We drowned them, and made
them a sign for the people. We have prepared for the evildoers a painful punishment. **38** And 'Ād, and
Thamūd, and the companions of al-Rass,[49] and many generations between that. **39** Each – We struck
parables for it, and each We destroyed completely. **40** Certainly they[50] have come upon the town which
was rained on by an evil rain.[51] Have they not seen it? No! They do not expect any raising up.[52]

41 When they see you, they take you only in mockery: 'Is this the one whom God has raised up as a
messenger? **42** He would indeed have led us astray from our gods, had we not been patient toward
them.' Soon they will know, when they see the punishment, who is farther astray (from the) way.
43 Do you[53] see the one who takes his own desire as his god? Will you be a guardian over him? **44** Or do
you think that most of them hear or understand? They are just like cattle – No! They are (even) farther
astray (from the) way!

45 Have you[54] not regarded your Lord, how He has stretched out the shadow?[55] If He had (so) pleased,
He would indeed have made it stand still. Then We made the sun a guide for it,[56] **46** (and) then We drew
it to Us gradually.[57] **47** He (it is) who has made the night as a covering for you, and made sleep as a rest,
and He has made the day as a raising up. **48** He (it is) who has sent the winds as good news before His
mercy,[58] and We have sent down pure water from the sky, **49** so that We might give some barren[59] land
life by means of it, and give it as a drink to some of what We have created – livestock and many people.
50 Certainly We have varied it[60] among them so that they might take heed,[61] yet most of the people
refuse (everything) but disbelief.[62] **51** If We had (so) pleased, We would indeed have raised up a warner
in every town. **52** So do not obey the disbelievers,[63] but struggle mightily against them by means of it.[64]

53 He (it is) who has let loose the two seas, this one sweet and fresh, and this (other) one salty (and)

35–40 Punishment of earlier generations a warning

47. *appointed*: lit. 'made.'
48. *messengers*: the use of the plur. here is curious.
49. *companions of al-Rass*: reference obscure; they are mentioned only here and at Q50.12.
50. *they*: the disbelievers.
51. *rained on by an evil rain*: perhaps Sodom, the city of Lot (cf. Q15.74-77).
52. *raising up*: or 'resurrection.'

41–44 Disbelievers ridicule the Prophet

53. *you*: the Prophet.

45–62 Signs of God's power and providence

54. *you...*: the Prophet, or perhaps intended generally ('one').
55. *stretched out the shadow*: referring to the lengthening of shadows as the day moves toward evening.
56. *a guide for it*: i.e. the sun 'directs' or 'steers' the shadows over the course of the day. (Notice the shifting back and forth between third-person sing. and first-person plur. in this section.)
57. *drew it to Us gradually*: lit. 'drew it to Us an easy drawing;' i.e. caused the shadows to gradually shorten.
58. *before His mercy*: i.e. before the coming of rain.
59. *barren*: lit. 'dead.'
60. *it*: referring to rain as a 'sign' of God's power and providence.
61. *take heed*: or 'remember,' 'be reminded.'
62. *disbelief*: or 'ingratitude' (a pun).
63. *do not obey the disbelievers*: addressed to the Prophet.
64. *by means of it*: i.e. by means of the Qur'ān.

bitter, and placed between them a barrier, and an absolute ban.[65] **54** He (it is) who created a human being from water,[66] and made him related by blood and by marriage, (for) Your Lord is powerful. **55** Yet they serve what neither benefits them nor harms them, instead of God (alone). The disbeliever (always) allies himself against his Lord.[67] **56** We have sent you only as a bringer of good news and a warner.[68] **57** Say: 'I do not ask you for any reward for it, except for whoever pleases to take a way to his Lord.' **58** Put your trust in the Living One who does not die, and glorify (Him) with His praise. He is sufficient (as One who) is aware of the sins of His servants, **59** who created the heavens and the earth, and whatever is between them, in six days.[69] Then He mounted the throne (as) the Merciful. Ask anyone (who is) aware about Him! **60** But when it is said to them, 'Prostrate yourselves before the Merciful,' they say, 'What is the Merciful?[70] Shall we prostrate ourselves before what you command us?' And it (only) increases them in aversion (to Him). **61** Blessed is He who has made constellations[71] in the sky, and has made a lamp in it, and an illuminating moon. **62** He (it is) who has made the night and the day a succession – for anyone who wishes to take heed or wishes to be thankful.

63 The servants of the Merciful are those who walk humbly on the earth, and when the ignorant address them, say: 'Peace!'[72] **64** (They are) those who spend the night prostrating themselves and standing before their Lord, **65** and those who say, 'Our Lord, turn away from us the punishment of Gehenna. Surely its punishment is torment! **66** Surely it is an evil dwelling and resting place!' **67** And (they are) those who, when they contribute,[73] are neither wanton nor stingy, but right between that, **68** and those[74] who do not call on another god with God, and do not kill the person whom God has forbidden (to be killed),[75] except by right,[76] and do not commit adultery – whoever does that will meet (his) penalty. **69** The punishment will be doubled for him on the Day of Resurrection, and he will remain in it humiliated, **70** except for the one who turns (in repentance), and believes, and does a righteous deed – and those, God will change their evil deeds (into) good ones, (for) God is forgiving, compassionate. **71** Whoever turns (in repentance) and does righteousness, surely he turns to God in complete repentance. **72** (They are) those who do not bear false witness, and, when they pass by any frivolous talk, they pass by with dignity, **73** and those who, when they are reminded by the signs of their Lord, do not fall down over it, deaf and

---

65. *an absolute ban*: preventing the two seas from mingling (the same phrase used at Q25.22 above); cf. Q27.61; 35.12; 55.19-20.
66. *from water*: see Q21.30; 24.45; 'from dust,' according to Q3.59; 18.37; 22.5; 30.20; 35.11; 40.67; 'from clay,' according to Q6.2; 7.12; 15.26; 17.61; 23.12; 32.7; 38.71, 76; 55.14.
67. *The disbeliever (always) allies himself against his Lord*: lit. 'The disbeliever is a supporter against his Lord.'
68. *bringer of good news...warner*: for these roles, see n. on Q2.119.
69. *in six days*: cf. Q10.3; 11.7; 32.4; 41.9-12; 50.38; and Genesis 1.1-31.
70. *What is the Merciful*: the Prophet's choice of the name 'al-Raḥmān' to designate his 'Lord' caused confusion or objections among some, who found it either unfamiliar or unacceptable (cf. Q13.30; 21.36). They seem to have regarded 'the Merciful' as a separate god from the God worshipped at the Ka'ba. Q17.110 may be an attempt to address the problem, and eventually what was once a proper name would be reduced to one of the epithets (and characteristics) of God. As a proper name, 'the Merciful' occurs more than fifty times in those sūras assigned to the 'second Meccan' period by modern scholars.
71. *constellations*: lit. 'towers;' i.e. the signs of the zodiac.

63–76 Servants of the Merciful

72. *Peace*: Ar. *salām* connotes 'submission' (*islām*) to God.
73. *contribute*: lit. 'spend' (for those in need or for the cause).
74. *and those...*: the Cairo edition, reflecting the views of traditional scholars, attributes the following three verses to the 'Medinan' period.
75. *forbidden (to be killed)*: i.e. made sacrosanct or inviolable.
76. *except by right*: i.e. for just cause.

blind,[77] **74** and those who say, 'Our Lord, grant us comfort (to our) eyes from our wives and descendants, and make us a model[78] for the ones who guard (themselves).' **75** Those will be repaid with the exalted room[79] because they were patient, and there they will meet a greeting and 'Peace!'[80] **76** There they will dwell – it is good as a dwelling and resting place.

77 Say: 'My Lord would not care about you,[81] if it were not for your prayer.[82] But you have called (it) a lie, so it will be close at hand.'

77. *do not fall down over it, deaf and blind*: like the disbelievers do.
78. *model*: or 'leader' (Ar. *imām*), a term later used for the leader of a religious community (cf. Q2.124, Abraham).
79. *the exalted room*: or 'the upper room;' referring to heaven (cf. Q29.58; 39.20).
80. *Peace*: Ar. *salām* connotes 'submission' (*islām*) to God.

77 A FINAL WARNING

81. *My Lord would not care about you...*: the meaning of this final verse is obscure (cf. Q20.129; 26.6); it may be dislocated from its original context.
82. *your prayer*: lit. 'your calling' (plur.).

26 The Poets ۞ Al-Shu'arā'

In the Name of God, the Merciful, the Compassionate

1 Ṭā' Sīn Mīm.[1] **2** Those are the signs[2] of the clear Book.[3]

3 Perhaps you are going to destroy yourself[4] because they do not believe. **4** If We (so) please, We shall send down on them a sign from the sky, and their necks will stay bowed before it. **5** But no new reminder[5] comes to them from the Merciful without their turning away from it. **6** They have called (it) a lie, so the story[6] of what they were mocking[7] will come to them.[8] **7** Do they not look at the earth – how many (things) of every excellent kind We have caused to grow in it? **8** Surely in that is a sign indeed, but most of them are not believers. **9** Surely your Lord – He indeed is the Mighty, the Compassionate.

10 (Remember) when[9] your Lord called to Moses: 'Go to a people who are evildoers, **11** the people of Pharaoh. Will they not guard (themselves)?'[10] **12** He said, 'My Lord, surely I fear that they will call me a liar, **13** and my heart[11] will be distressed, and my tongue will not work.[12] So send for Aaron. **14** And they (also) have a crime against me,[13] and I fear they will kill me.' **15** He said, 'By no means! Go, both of you, with Our signs. Surely We shall be with you, hearing (everything). **16** So come, both of you, to Pharaoh, and

---

Q26: This sūra is made up almost entirely of stories about the following messengers: Moses, Abraham, Noah, Hūd, Ṣāliḥ, Lot, and Shu'ayb, all linked together by a recurring refrain (Q26.8-9). Most scholars assign Q26 to the 'Meccan' period, though some traditional scholars hold that a few verses near the end are 'Medinan.' It receives its title from the dismissive reference to 'the poets' at Q26.224-225.

1–2 Signs of the Book

1. *Ṭā' Sīn Mīm*: the names of Arabic letters *ṭ*, *s*, and *m*. The same letter combination occurs again in Q28 (Q27 has *ṭ* and *s*). Twenty-nine sūras begin with letters like these, ranging from one to five. No satisfactory explanation has been given for their occurrence. The Cairo edition varies in counting these letters as a separate verse (as here), or as the beginning of the first verse.
2. *signs*: here referring to the letters *ṭ*, *s*, and *m* (for the various meanings of 'signs,' see n. on Q2.39).
3. *the clear Book*: or 'the Book that makes (things) clear;' referring to the Qur'ān not only as a 'recited' but also 'written' scripture (see n. on Q2.2).

3–9 The obstinacy of disbelievers

4. *destroy yourself*: with grief or anguish (cf. Q18.6).
5. *reminder*: here referring to a part of the revelation (see n. on Q3.58).
6. *story*: or 'news.'
7. *what they were mocking*: the threat of judgment and punishment.
8. *will come to them*: this makes it appear that the end is near (cf. Q6.5).

10–51 The story of Moses and Pharaoh

9. *(Remember) when...*: a stock narrative formula; the Arabic particle *idh* often marks the beginning of a story, and means something like 'Once....' or 'There was a time when....' or 'Remember when....' Here begins a series of seven 'punishment stories' (Q26.10-191; see nn. on Q7.59; 15.87). For the story of Moses that follows, cf. e.g. the version at Q7.103-137.
10. *guard (themselves)*: against evil, or God.
11. *heart*: lit. 'chest,' considered the seat of knowledge and understanding.
12. *my tongue will not work*: lit. 'will not go forth' (cf. Q20.27); Moses was 'slow of speech and slow of tongue,' according to Exodus 4.10 (cf. 6.12, 30).
13. *a crime against me*: Moses had killed an Egyptian (Q28.14-17; cf. Exodus 2.11-15).

say: "Surely we are the messenger[14] of the Lord of the worlds.[15] **17** Send forth the Sons of Israel with us."'

18 He[16] said, 'Did we not bring you up among us as a child, and did you not remain among us for some years of your life? **19** Yet you did the deed you did, and were one of the ungrateful.' **20** He[17] said, 'I did it when I was one of those who had gone astray, **21** and I fled from you when I became afraid of you. But my Lord granted me judgment,[18] and made me one of the envoys.[19] **22** And that is a blessing you bestow on me, that you have enslaved the Sons of Israel.'[20]

23 Pharaoh said, 'What is the Lord of the worlds?' **24** He said, 'The Lord of the heavens and the earth, and whatever is between them, if you (would) be certain.' He[21] said to those who were around him, **25** 'Do you not hear?' **26** He[22] said, 'Your Lord and the Lord of your fathers of old.' **27** He said, 'Surely your messenger who has been sent to you is possessed[23] indeed.' **28** He said, 'The Lord of the East and the West, and whatever is between them, if you (would) understand.' **29** He said, 'If indeed you take a god other than me, I shall indeed make you one of the imprisoned.' **30** He said, 'Even if I brought you something clear?' **31** He said, 'Bring it, if you are one of the truthful.' **32** So he cast (down) his staff, and suddenly it became a real snake, **33** and he drew forth his hand, and suddenly it became white to the onlookers.[24] **34** He said to the assembly around him, 'Surely this is a skilled magician indeed. **35** He wants to expel you from your land[25] by his magic. So what do you command?' **36** They said, 'Put him and his brother off (for a while), and send out searchers into the cities **37** to bring you every skilled magician.' **38** So the magicians were gathered together for the meeting on a day made known. **39** And it was said to the people, 'Will you (too) gather together?' **40** 'Perhaps we will follow the magicians, if they are the victors.'[26]

41 When the magicians came, they said to Pharaoh, '(Will there) surely (be) for us a reward indeed, if we are the victors?' **42** He said, 'Yes, and surely then you will indeed be among the ones brought near.'[27] **43** Moses said to them, 'Cast (down) what you are going to cast.' **44** So they cast their ropes and their staffs,[28] and said, 'By the honor of Pharaoh! Surely we shall be the victors indeed.' **45** And then Moses cast his staff, and suddenly it swallowed up what they were falsely contriving.[29] **46** And the magicians were cast (down) in prostration. **47** They said, 'We believe in the Lord of the worlds, **48** the Lord of Moses

14. *messenger*: sing. (for this important title, see n. on Q2.87).
15. *Lord of the worlds*: for this title, see n. on Q1.2; cf. Q26.23-28 below.
16. *He*: Pharaoh; what follows (Q26.18-22) may be a later addition, since it interrupts the connection between Q26.15-17 and 23.
17. *He*: Moses.
18. *judgment*: or 'wisdom' (see n. on Q3.79).
19. *the envoys*: lit. 'the ones who are sent' (Ar. *al-mursalūn*), a designation roughly equivalent to 'messengers' (*rusul*).
20. *And that is a blessing...*: the meaning of this verse is obscure; 'that' is usually taken as a reference to Moses' upbringing in Egypt. This verse would make better sense if it were placed between vv. 15 and 16 above.
21. *He*: Pharaoh.
22. *He*: Moses.
23. *possessed*: or 'jinn-struck' (Ar. *majnūn*); cf. Q51.39; the same accusation is leveled at Noah and the Prophet (see n. on Q7.184).
24. *he cast (down) his staff...and he drew forth his hand...*: cf. Q7.106-112; 20.17-23; 28.29-32; and the account in Exodus 4.1-8 (according to Exodus 7.8-10, it was Aaron who cast his staff before Pharaoh).
25. *land*: lit. 'earth.'
26. *Perhaps we will follow...*: the response of the people to the preceding question.
27. *the ones brought near*: i.e. among Pharaoh's close circle of advisers (Ar. *al-muqarrabūn* is a designation of special privilege in the royal court).
28. *their ropes and their staffs*: for the additional 'ropes,' see Q20.66; cf. Exodus 7.11-12.
29. *swallowed up what they were falsely contriving*: cf. Exodus 7.12, where Aaron's staff accomplishes this feat.

and Aaron.' **49** He[30] said, 'You have believed in him[31] before I gave you permission. Surely he is indeed your master,[32] the (very) one who taught you magic. But soon indeed you will know! I shall indeed cut off your hands and your feet on opposite sides, and I shall indeed crucify you – all (of you)!' **50** They said, 'No harm![33] Surely we are going to return to our Lord. **51** Surely we are eager that our Lord should forgive us our sins, because we are the first of the believers.'

52 And We inspired Moses: 'Journey with My servants. Surely you will be followed.'[34] **53** So Pharaoh sent out searchers into the cities: **54** 'Surely these (people) are indeed a small band, **55** and surely they are indeed enraging us, **56** but surely we are indeed all vigilant.' **57** So We brought them forth from gardens and springs, **58** and treasures and an honorable place. **59** So (it was), and We caused the Sons of Israel to inherit them.[35] **60** So they followed them at sunrise, **61** and when the two forces saw each other, the companions of Moses said, 'Surely we are indeed overtaken!' **62** He said, 'By no means! Surely my Lord is with me. He will guide me.' **63** And so We inspired Moses: 'Strike the sea with your staff!' And it parted, and each part was like a great mountain. **64** We brought the others[36] near to that place, **65** and We rescued Moses and those who were with him – all (of them). **66** Then We drowned the others. **67** Surely in that is a sign indeed, but most of them do not believe. **68** Surely your Lord – He indeed is the Mighty, the Compassionate.

69 Recite[37] to them the story[38] of Abraham: **70** When he said to his father and his people, 'What do you serve?'[39] **71** They said, 'We serve idols, and continue (to be) devoted to them.' **72** He said, 'Do they hear you when you call, **73** or do they benefit you or harm (you)?' **74** They said, 'No! But we found our fathers doing so.' **75** He said, 'Do you see what you have been serving, **76** you and your fathers who preceded (you)? **77** Surely they are an enemy to me – except the Lord of the worlds, **78** who created me, and He guides me, **79** and who – He gives me food and gives me drink, **80** and when I am sick, He heals me. **81** He (it is) who causes me to die, (and) then gives me life, **82** and who – I am eager that He should forgive me my sin on the Day of Judgment. **83** My Lord, grant me judgment,[40] and join me with the righteous, **84** and assign to me[41] a good reputation[42] among later (generations). **85** Make me one of the inheritors of the Garden of Bliss.[43] **86** And forgive my father,[44] (for) surely he is one of those who have gone astray.

30. *He*: Pharaoh.
31. *him*: probably Moses; or 'Him' (God).
32. *master*: lit. 'great one' (referring to Moses).
33. *No harm*: cf. Q20.70-73.

52–68 The exodus from Egypt

34. *Journey with My servants...*: for the story of the exodus that follows, cf. the version at Q44.23-33 ('by night'); and Exodus 14.1-31.
35. *inherit them*: perhaps a reference to the despoiling of the Egyptians by the Israelites (Exodus 3.21-22; 11.2-3; 12.35-36).
36. *the others*: Pharaoh and his army.

69–104 The story of Abraham and his people

37. *Recite...*: or 'Read aloud...;' for the story that follows, cf. e.g. the version at Q6.74-84.
38. *story*: or 'news.'
39. *serve*: or 'worship.'
40. *judgment*: or 'wisdom.'
41. *assign to me*: lit. 'make for me.'
42. *reputation*: lit. 'tongue' (i.e. being well spoken of); cf. Q19.50 (of Abraham, Isaac, and Jacob).
43. *Garden of Bliss*: in heaven (for this imagery, see n. on Q2.25).
44. *forgive my father*: see Q14.41; 19.47; 60.4; cf. Q71.28 (Noah); otherwise prayer for disbelievers is forbidden, see Q9.113-114.

87 Do not disgrace me on the Day when they are raised up, **88** the Day when neither wealth nor children will benefit (them), **89** except for the one who comes to God with a sound heart.[45] **90** The Garden will be brought near for the ones who guard themselves, **91** and the Furnace[46] will come forth for the ones who are in error. **92** And it will be said to them, "Where is what you were serving **93** instead of God? (Can) they defend you or defend themselves?" **94** And then they will be tossed into it – they and the ones who are in error[47] – **95** and the forces of Iblīs[48] – all (of them). **96** They will say, as they are disputing there, **97** "By God! We were indeed far astray, **98** when we made you[49] equal with the Lord of the worlds. **99** (It was) only the sinners who led us astray. **100** (Now) we have no intercessors, **101** and no true friend. **102** If only we had (another) turn, and (could) be among the believers!'" **103** Surely in that is a sign indeed, but most of them do not believe. **104** Surely your Lord – He indeed is the Mighty, the Compassionate.

105 The people of Noah[50] called the envoys liars: **106** When their brother Noah said to them, 'Will you not guard (yourselves)? **107** Surely I am a trustworthy messenger for you, **108** so guard (yourselves) against God and obey me. **109** I do not ask you for any reward for it. My reward (depends) only on the Lord of the worlds. **110** Guard (yourselves) against God and obey me.' **111** They said, 'Shall we believe you, when (only) the worst (people) follow you?' **112** He said, 'What do I know about what they have done? **113** Their reckoning is only with my Lord, if (only) you realized (it). **114** I am not going to drive away the believers. **115** I am only a clear warner.' **116** They said, 'If indeed you do not stop, Noah, you will indeed be one of the stoned.' **117** He said, 'My Lord, surely my people have called me a liar, **118** so disclose (the truth) decisively between me and them,[51] and rescue me and those of the believers who are with me.' **119** So We rescued him, and those who were with him, in the loaded ship.[52] **120** Then, after that, We drowned the rest. **121** Surely in that is a sign indeed, but most of them do not believe. **122** Surely your Lord – He indeed is the Mighty, the Compassionate.

123 'Ād called the envoys liars: **124** When their brother Hūd[53] said to them, 'Will you not guard (yourselves)? **125** Surely I am a trustworthy messenger for you, **126** so guard (yourselves) against God and obey me. **127** I do not ask you for any reward for it. My reward (depends) only on the Lord of the worlds. **128** Do you build a sign on every high place in vain,[54] **129** and take strongholds in the hope that you may remain there?[55] **130** And when you attack (someone), do you attack like tyrants? **131** Guard (yourselves) against God and obey me. **132** Guard (yourselves) against the One who has increased you with what you know. **133** He has increased you with livestock and sons, **134** and gardens and fountains. **135** Surely I fear for you the punishment of a great day.' **136** They said, '(It is) the same for us whether you admonish (us) or are not one of the admonishers. **137** This is nothing but the creation of those of old.[56] **138** We are not going to be punished.' **139** So they called him a liar, and We destroyed them. Surely in

45. *heart*: here, as often, the heart is spoken of as synonymous with mind.
46. *the Furnace*: a name for Hell (Ar. *al-jaḥīm*).
47. *they and the ones who are in error*: i.e. both the disbelievers and their gods.
48. *Iblīs*: for this figure, see n. on Q2.34.
49. *you*: their gods.

105–122 The story of Noah and his people

50. *Noah*: for the story that follows, cf. the versions at Q7.59-64; 10.71-73; 11.25-49; 23.23-30; and Genesis 6.5-10.1.
51. *disclose (the truth) decisively...*: cf. Q7.89 (Shu'ayb); 34.26; 48.1 (the Prophet).
52. *the loaded ship*: Noah's 'ark.'

123–140 The story of Hūd and the people of 'Ād

53. *Hūd*: for the story that follows, cf. the versions at Q7.65-72; 11.50-60.
54. *build a sign...in vain*: reference obscure.
55. *take strongholds...that you may remain there*: reference obscure.
56. *nothing but the creation of those of old*: i.e. they dismiss Hūd's warning as merely an old tale.

that is a sign indeed, but most of them do not believe. **140** Surely your Lord – He indeed is the Mighty, the Compassionate.

141 Thamūd called the envoys liars: **142** When their brother Ṣāliḥ[57] said to them, 'Will you not guard (yourselves)? **143** Surely I am a trustworthy messenger for you, **144** so guard (yourselves) against God and obey me. **145** I do not ask you for any reward for it. My reward (depends) only on the Lord of the worlds. **146** Will you be left secure in what is here, **147** in gardens and springs, **148** and (fields of) crops and date palms (with) its slender sheath? **149** Will you (continue to) carve houses out of the mountains with skill? **150** Guard (yourselves) against God and obey me. **151** Do not obey the command of the wanton, **152** those who foment corruption on the earth and do not set (things) right.' **153** They said, 'You are only one of the bewitched.[58] **154** You are nothing but a human being like us. Bring (us) a sign, if you are one of the truthful.' **155** He said, 'This is a she-camel:[59] to her a drink and to you a drink, on a day made known. **156** Do not touch her with evil, or the punishment of a great day will seize you.' **157** But they wounded her,[60] and morning found them full of regret, **158** and the punishment seized them. Surely in that is a sign indeed, but most of them do not believe. **159** Surely your Lord – He indeed is the Mighty, the Compassionate.

160 The people of Lot called the envoys liars: **161** When their brother Lot[61] said to them, 'Will you not guard (yourselves)? **162** Surely I am a trustworthy messenger for you, **163** so guard (yourselves) against God and obey me. **164** I do not ask you for any reward for it. My reward (depends) only on the Lord of the worlds. **165** Do you approach the males of all peoples,[62] **166** and leave your wives whom your Lord created for you? Yes! You are a people who transgress!' **167** They said, 'If indeed you do not stop, Lot, you will indeed be one of the expelled.' **168** He said, 'Surely I am one of those who despise what you do. **169** My Lord, rescue me and my family from what they do.' **170** So We rescued him and his family – all (of them) – **171** except for an old woman[63] among those who stayed behind. **172** Then We destroyed the others. **173** We rained down on them a rain,[64] and evil was the rain on those who had been warned! **174** Surely in that is a sign indeed, but most of them do not believe. **175** Surely your Lord – He indeed is the Mighty, the Compassionate.

176 The people of the Grove[65] called the envoys liars: **177** When Shu'ayb[66] said to them, 'Will you not guard (yourselves)? **178** I am a trustworthy messenger for you, **179** so guard (yourselves) against God and obey me. **180** I do not ask you for any reward for it. My reward (depends) only on the Lord of the worlds. **181** Fill up the measure, and do not be cheaters, **182** and weigh with the even scale, **183** and do not

---

141–159 The story of Ṣāliḥ and the people of Thamūd

57. *Ṣāliḥ*: for the story that follows, cf. the versions at Q7.73-79; 11.61-68; 27.45-53. The people of Thamūd were inhabitants of ancient Arabia, and are mentioned in an inscription of the Assyrian king Sargon II (c. 715 BCE), as well as in the writings of Ariston of Chios, Ptolemy, and Pliny the Elder.
58. *bewitched*: i.e. a victim of magic or under a magic spell
59. *she-camel*: see n. on Q7.73.
60. *wounded her*: or perhaps 'killed her.'

160–175 The story of Lot and his people

61. *Lot*: for the story that follows, cf. the versions at Q11.77-83; 15.57-74; and Genesis 19.1-29.
62. *of all peoples*: lit. 'of the worlds.'
63. *an old woman*: Lot's wife, cf. Q27.57; 66.10.
64. *rained down on them a rain*: of stones of baked clay, according to Q11.82; 15.74.

176–191 The story of Shu'ayb and the people of the Grove

65. *people of the Grove*: or 'companions of the Thicket' (Ar. *al-ayka*); this may be an alternative name for the people of Midian, since both have the same messenger, Shu'ayb (cf. Q15.78-79; 38.13; 50.14).
66. *Shu'ayb*: for the story that follows, cf. the versions at Q7.84-93; 11.84-95.

shortchange the people of their wealth,[67] and do not act wickedly on the earth, fomenting corruption.
184 Guard (yourselves) against the One who created you and the multitudes of old.' **185** They said, 'You
are only one of the bewitched. **186** You are nothing but a human being like us. Surely we think (that)
you are indeed one of the liars. **187** Make fragments of the sky fall on us,[68] if you are one of the truthful.' **188** He said, 'My Lord knows what you are doing.' **189** But they called him a liar, and the punishment of the Day of Shadow seized them. Surely it was the punishment of a great day. **190** Surely in that
is a sign indeed, but most of them do not believe. **191** Surely your Lord – He indeed is the Mighty, the
Compassionate.

192 Surely it[69] is indeed a sending down from the Lord of the worlds. **193** The trustworthy spirit[70] has
brought it down **194** on your heart, so that you may be one of the warners,[71] **195** in a clear Arabic
language.[72] **196** Surely it is indeed in the scriptures of those of old.[73] **197** Was it not a sign for them
that it was known to the learned of the Sons of Israel?[74] **198** If We had sent it down on one of the
foreigners,[75] **199** and he had recited it[76] to them, they would not have believed in it. **200** In this way We
put it into the hearts of the sinners. **201** They will not believe in it until they see the painful punishment,
202 and it will come upon them unexpectedly, when they do not realize (it), **203** and they will say, 'Are we
going to be spared?' **204** Do they seek to hurry Our punishment? **205** Have you considered?[77] If We give
them enjoyment (of life) for (some) years, **206** (and) then what they were promised comes upon them,
207 what use will the enjoyment they were given be to them? **208** We have not destroyed any town
without its having warners **209** as a reminder. We have not been evildoers.

210 The satans[78] have not brought it down. **211** It is not fitting for them (to do), nor are they able (to).
212 Surely they are removed indeed from the hearing (of it). **213** Do not call on another god (along) with
God, or you[79] will be one of the punished. **214** Warn your clan, **215** and lower your wing[80] to whoever
follows you of the believers. **216** If they disobey you, say: 'I am free of what you do.' **217** Put your trust
in the Mighty, the Compassionate, **218** who sees you when you stand,[81] **219** and when you turn about

---

67. *Fill up... and do not shortchange...*: a distinctive feature of the story of Shu'ayb (cf. Q7.85; 11.85).
68. *make fragments of the sky fall on us*: perhaps an allusion to the threat of punishment 'raining down' on them, or the 'sky falling' on them (cf. Q17.92; 34.9).

192–209 The Qur'ān is authentic

69. *it*: the Qur'ān.
70. *the trustworthy spirit*: cf. Q16.2, 102 ('the holy spirit'); 40.15; 42.52 ('spirit of Our command'). Some interpreters identify 'the spirit' with Gabriel (see n. on Q2.97).
71. *warners*: for this role, see n. on Q2.119.
72. *in a clear Arabic language*: or 'in an Arabic language, making (things) clear.'
73. *in the scriptures of those of old*: this may refer to the predictions in previous 'scriptures' (Ar. *zubur*) of the coming of the Prophet, or it may mean that the content of the Qur'ān and previous scriptures was understood to be essentially the same.
74. *Was it not a sign...*: the Cairo edition, reflecting the views of traditional scholars, attributes this verse to the 'Medinan' period.
75. *foreigners*: i.e. non-Arabic speakers (cf. Q16.103; 41.44).
76. *recited it*: or 'read it aloud.'
77. *considered*: lit. 'seen;' addressed to the Prophet, or perhaps intended generally ('one').

210–220 Not satanic

78. *satans*: or 'demons' (Ar. *shayāṭīn*); individually assigned to incite people to evil (see Q19.83; 43.36; cf. Q7.27; 23.97; 41.25).
79. *you*: the Prophet.
80. *lower your wing*: i.e. 'take under your protection' or 'treat with kindness.'
81. *stand*: to pray.

among the ones who prostrate themselves. **220** Surely He – He is the Hearing, the Knowing.

221 Shall I inform you[82] on whom the satans come down? **222** They come down on every liar (and) sinner. **223** They listen attentively,[83] but most of them are liars. **224** And the poets[84] – the ones who are in error follow them. **225** Do you[85] not see that they wander in every wādi, **226** and that they say[86] what they do not do? **227** – except for those who believe, and do righteous deeds, and remember God often, and defend themselves after they have suffered evil. Those who have done evil will come to know what a complete overturning they will suffer.

221–227 Liars and poets

82. *you*: plur.
83. *They listen attentively*: lit. 'They cast (their) hearing;' i.e. in hopes of hearing some piece of genuine revelation.
84. *poets*: thought to be inspired by jinn (Q37.36; see n. on Q21.5); the Prophet was dismissed as one by his skeptics (see Q21.5; 69.41; cf. Q52.30). The Cairo edition, reflecting the views of traditional scholars, attributes the final four verses to the 'Medinan' period.
85. *you*: the Prophet, or perhaps intended generally ('one').
86. *say*: in their poetry.

27 The Ant ۞ Al-Naml

In the Name of God, the Merciful, the Compassionate

1 Ṭā' Sīn.[1] Those are the signs[2] of the Qur'ān[3] and a clear Book,[4] **2** a guidance[5] and good news for the believers, **3** who observe the prayer and give the alms,[6] and they are certain of the Hereafter.[7] **4** Those who do not believe in the Hereafter – We have made their deeds appear enticing to them, and they wander blindly. **5** Those are the ones for whom (there is) an evil punishment, and in the Hereafter they will be the worst losers. **6** Surely you[8] have indeed received the Qur'ān from One (who is) wise, knowing.

7 (Remember) when[9] Moses said to his family: 'Surely I perceive a fire. I shall bring you some news of it, or I shall bring you a flame – a torch – so that you may warm yourselves.' **8** But when he came to it, he was called: 'Blessed is He who is in the fire, and whoever is around it. Glory to God, Lord of the worlds![10]
9 Moses! Surely I am God, the Mighty, the Wise.' **10** And: 'Cast (down) your staff!' When he saw it wiggling as if it were a snake, he turned around, retreating, and did not look back. 'Moses! Do not fear! Surely in My presence the envoys[11] do not fear **11** – except for the one who has done evil, (and) then has exchanged good after evil – surely I am forgiving, compassionate. **12** Put your hand inside your cloak.[12] It will come out white, unharmed – (these are two) among nine signs[13] for Pharaoh and his people. Surely

---

Q27: This sūra opens with a reference to the Qur'ān as 'guidance and good news' for the believers and closes with a description of the Day of Judgment. It recounts the stories of previous messengers, including one about Solomon and the Queen of Sheba. God's power and uniqueness are also emphasized. Most scholars assign Q27 to the 'Meccan' period. It receives its title from 'the ant' who speaks in the story of Solomon (Q27.18).

1–6 The Qur'ān, believers and disbelievers

1. *Ṭā' Sīn*: the names of Arabic letters *ṭ* and *s*, a combination unique to Q27 (Q26 and Q28 have an additional 'mīm'). Twenty-nine sūras begin with letters like these, ranging from one to five. No satisfactory explanation has been given for their occurrence. The Cairo edition varies in counting these letters as a separate verse, or as the beginning of the first verse (as here).
2. *signs*: here referring to the letters *ṭ* and *s* (for the various meanings of 'signs,' see n. on Q2.39).
3. *the Qur'ān*: here 'the Qur'ān' comes close to its present meaning as the name of the Muslim scripture (cf. Q9.111; see n. on Q2.185).
4. *a clear Book*: or 'a Book that makes (things) clear;' referring to the Qur'ān not only as a 'recited' but also 'written' scripture (see n. on Q2.2).
5. *guidance*: one of the most frequent terms (Ar. *hudā*) for revelation in general, and the Qur'ān in particular.
6. *observe the prayer and give the alms*: i.e. *ṣalāt*, the ritual prayer, and *zakāt*, a kind of tithe required for the benefit of the poor, as well as other purposes.
7. *the Hereafter*: see n. on Q2.4.
8. *you*: the Prophet.

7–14 The call of Moses

9. *(Remember) when...*: a stock narrative formula; the Arabic particle *idh* often marks the beginning of a story, and means something like 'Once...,' or 'There was a time when...,' or 'Remember when....' For the story that follows, cf. the versions at Q20.9-36; 28.29-35; and the account of Moses' call at Exodus 3-4.
10. *Lord of the worlds*: for this title, see n. on Q1.2.
11. *the envoys*: lit. 'the ones who are sent' (Ar. *al-mursalūn*), a designation roughly equivalent to 'messengers' (*rusul*).
12. *inside your cloak*: lit. 'into your chest' (cf. Exodus 4.6-8).
13. *nine signs*: Moses performed more miracles than any other prophet in the Qur'ān (see e.g. Q7.130-137; 20.17-

they are a wicked people.' **13** But when Our signs came to them visibly, they said, 'This is clear magic.' **14** They denied them, even though they were convinced of them in themselves, out of evil and haughtiness. See how the end was for the fomenters of corruption!

15 Certainly We gave David and Solomon knowledge, and they said, 'Praise (be)[14] to God, who has favored us over many of His believing servants!' **16** Solomon inherited (it)[15] from David, and said, 'People! We have been taught the speech of birds, and we have been given (some) of everything.[16] Surely this – it indeed is clear favor.' **17** Gathered before Solomon were his forces – jinn,[17] and men, and birds – and they were arranged (in rows) **18** – until, when they came upon the Wādi of the Ants,[18] an ant said, 'Ants! Enter your dwellings, or Solomon and his forces will crush you without realizing (it).' **19** But he[19] smiled, laughing at its words, and said, 'My Lord, (so) dispose me that I may be thankful for your blessing with which You have blessed me and my parents, and that I may do righteousness (that) pleases You, and cause me to enter, by Your mercy, among your righteous servants.'

20 He[20] reviewed the birds, and said, 'Why do I not see the hudhud?[21] Or is it one of the absent? **21** I shall indeed punish it severely, or slaughter it, or it will bring me a clear authority.'[22] **22** But it[23] did not stay (away) for long, and said, 'I have encompassed what you have not encompassed, and I have brought you reliable news from (the people of) Sheba.[24] **23** Surely I found a woman ruling over them, and she has been given (some) of everything, and she has a great throne. **24** I found her and her people prostrating themselves before the sun instead of God. Satan[25] has made their deeds appear enticing to them, and he has kept them from the way, and they are not (rightly) guided. **25** (He did this) so that they would not prostrate themselves before God, who brings forth what is hidden in the heavens and the earth. He knows what you hide and what you speak aloud. **26** God – (there is) no god but Him, Lord of the great throne.' **27** He[26] said, 'We shall see whether you have spoken the truth or are one of the liars. **28** Go with this letter[27] of mine, and cast it (down) to them. Then turn away from them and see what they return.'

29 She[28] said, 'Assembly! Surely an honorable letter has been cast (down) to me. **30** Surely it is from

---

24, 47, 56 etc.), but the reference to 'nine signs' is mentioned only here and at Q17.101, though they are not specified. There may have once been a passage listing them (see Q20.17-24). According to Exodus 7-12, God brought 'ten plagues' against Egypt to convince Pharaoh to release the Israelites.

15–44 The story of Solomon and the Queen of Sheba

14. *(be)*: or '(belongs).'
15. *(it)*: knowledge, or perhaps the kingdom.
16. *(some) of everything*: cf. 1 Kings 4.29-34; 10.23, for Solomon's unparalleled wealth and wisdom.
17. *jinn*: cf. Q34.12-13, where the jinn are said to have worked for Solomon ('satans,' according to Q21.82).
18. *Wādi of the Ants*: cf. Proverbs 6.6-8 (a book thought to be written by Solomon), where the ant is used as an example against laziness.
19. *he*: Solomon.
20. *He*: Solomon.
21. *the hudhud*: or 'hoopoe,' a colorful bird found across Afro-Eurasia, and notable for its distinctive crown of feathers.
22. *a clear authority*: i.e. an excuse for its absence.
23. *it*: the hudhud.
24. *Sheba*: Ar. *Sabā'*; cf. the story of the Queen of Sheba's visit to Solomon at 1 Kings 10.1-13.
25. *Satan*: for this figure, see n. on Q2.36.
26. *He*: Solomon.
27. *letter*: lit. 'book' or 'writing' (Ar. *kitāb*).
28. *She*: the Queen of Sheba.

Solomon, and surely it (reads): "In the Name of God, the Merciful, the Compassionate.[29] **31** Do not exalt yourselves over me,[30] but come to me in surrender."'[31] **32** She said, 'Assembly! Make a pronouncement to me about my affair. I do not decide any affair until you bear me witness.' **33** They said, 'We are full of strength and full of harsh violence, but the affair (belongs) to you. See what you will command.' **34** She said, 'Surely kings, when they enter a town, corrupt it, and make the upper class[32] of its people the lowest, and that is what they[33] will do. **35** Surely I am going to send a gift to them, and see what the envoys bring back.'

36 When he[34] came to Solomon, he[35] said, 'Would you increase me with wealth, when what God has given me is better than what He has given you? No! (It is) you (who) gloat over your own gift.[36] **37** Return to them! We shall indeed come upon them with forces which they have no power to face, and we shall indeed expel them from there in humiliation, and they will be disgraced.' **38** He said, 'Assembly! Which of you will bring me her throne before they come to me in surrender?' **39** A crafty one[37] of the jinn said, 'I shall bring it to you before you (can) rise from your place. Surely I have strength for it (and am) trustworthy.' **40** One who had knowledge of the Book said, 'I will bring it to you in the wink of an eye.'[38] So when he[39] saw it set before him, he said, 'This is from the favor of my Lord to test me (to see) whether I am thankful or ungrateful. Whoever is thankful is thankful only for his own good, and whoever is ungrateful – surely my Lord is wealthy,[40] generous.' **41** He said, 'Disguise her throne for her. We shall see whether she is (rightly) guided or is one of those who are not (rightly) guided.' **42** So when she came, it was said, 'Is your throne like this?' She said, 'It seems like it.' 'And we[41] had been given the knowledge before her, and were in surrender, **43** but what she served,[42] instead of God, kept her back. Surely she was from a disbelieving people.' **44** It was said to her, 'Enter the palace.' When she saw it, she thought it was a pool (of water), and she uncovered her legs. He[43] said, 'Surely it is a polished palace of crystal.' She said, 'My Lord, surely I have done myself evil. I surrender[44] with Solomon to God, Lord of the worlds.'

45 Certainly We sent to Thamūd their brother Ṣāliḥ:[45] 'Serve God!' And suddenly they were two groups[46]

---

29. *In the Name of God...*: the *basmala* (see n. on Q1.1).
30. *over me*: or 'against me.'
31. *in surrender*: or 'in submission,' punning on the name 'Muslims' (cf. Q27.42, 44 below).
32. *upper class*: lit. 'great ones.'
33. *they*: Solomon and his people.
34. *he*: the Queen's envoy.
35. *he*: Solomon.
36. *...gloat over your own gift*: i.e. Solomon refuses their gift as a self-serving display of their own wealth.
37. *crafty one*: or 'powerful one' (Ar. *'ifrīt*), but the precise meaning is uncertain. Some interpreters take this to be an especially wicked class of jinn.
38. *in the wink of an eye*: lit. 'before your glance returns to you.'
39. *he*: Solomon.
40. *wealthy*: i.e. God has no need of anyone or anything (cf. Q31.12).
41. *And we...*: what follows is apparently spoken by some members of the Queen's entourage, who claim to have been 'in surrender' (i.e. 'Muslims') all along.
42. *served*: or 'worshipped.'
43. *He*: Solomon.
44. *surrender*: or 'become a Muslim' (what Solomon had demanded in his letter to her).

45–53 The story of Ṣāliḥ and the people of Thamūd

45. *Ṣāliḥ*: for the story that follows, cf. the versions at Q7.73-79; 11.61-68; 26.141-158. The people of Thamūd were inhabitants of ancient Arabia, and are mentioned in an inscription of the Assyrian king Sargon II (c. 715 BCE), as well as in the writings of Ariston of Chios, Ptolemy, and Pliny the Elder.
46. *two groups*: i.e. believers and disbelievers.

disputing each other. **46** He said, 'My people! Why do you seek to hurry the evil before the good? Why do you not ask forgiveness from God, so that you may receive compassion?' **47** They said, 'We have an evil omen about you and those who are with you.' He said, 'Your evil omen is with God.[47] But you are a people being tested!' **48** In the city (there) was a group of nine persons who were fomenting corruption on the earth, and not setting (things) right. **49** They said, 'Swear to each other by God, "We shall indeed attack him and his family by night." Then we shall indeed say to his ally,[48] "We were not witnesses of the destruction of his family" and "Surely we are truthful indeed."' **50** They schemed a scheme, but We (too) schemed a scheme, though they did not realize (it). **51** See how the end of their scheme was: We destroyed them and their people – all (of them)! **52** Those are their houses, collapsed because of the evil they did. Surely in that is a sign indeed for a people who know. **53** And We rescued those who believed and guarded (themselves).[49]

54 And Lot,[50] when he said to his people: 'Do you commit immorality with your eyes open? **55** Do you indeed approach men with lust instead of women? But you are an ignorant people!' **56** The only response of his people was that they said, 'Expel the house(hold) of Lot from your town, (for) surely they are men who keep themselves clean.'[51] **57** So We rescued him and his family, except for his wife. We decreed that she (would be) one of those who stayed behind. **58** And We rained down on them a rain.[52] Evil was the rain on those who had been warned!

59 Say:[53] 'Praise (be) to God, and peace (be) upon His servants whom He has chosen!' Is God better, or what they associate?[54] **60** Or (is He not better) who created the heavens and earth, and sent down water from the sky for you, and then by means of it We cause orchards to grow, full of beauty, whose trees you could never grow? (Is there any other) god with God? No! But they are a people who equate (others to Him). **61** Or (is He not better) who made the earth a dwelling place, and placed rivers in the midst of it, and made firm mountains for it, and placed a partition between the two seas?[55] (Is there any other) god with God? No! But most of them do not know (it). **62** Or (is He not better) who responds to the distressed (person) when he calls on Him and removes the evil, and establishes you as successors on the earth?[56] (Is there any other) god with God? Little do you take heed![57] **63** Or (is He not better) who guides you in the darkness of the shore and the sea, and who sends the winds as good news before His mercy?[58] (Is there any other) god with God? God is exalted above what they associate! **64** Or (is He not better) who brings about the creation, (and) then restores it, and who provides for you from the sky and the earth? (Is there any other) god with God? Say: 'Bring your proof, if you are truthful.'

---

47. *Your evil omen is with God*: referring to their fate assigned by God (see Q17.13; cf. Q7.131).
48. *his ally*: i.e. someone with whom Ṣāliḥ shared the obligation of mutual protection (Ar. *walī*), and who would be responsible for exacting revenge.
49. *guarded (themselves)*: against evil, or God.

54–58 The story of Lot and his people

50. *Lot*: for this version of the story, cf. Q7.80-84.
51. *who keep themselves clean*: or 'who hold themselves to be clean' (said in derision).
52. *a rain*: of stones of baked clay, according to Q11.82; 15.74.

59–64 God's uniqueness

53. *Say*: on this form of address, see n. on Q2.80.
54. *what they associate*: other gods with God.
55. *a partition between the two seas*: cf. Q25.53; 35.12; 55.19-20.
56. *successors on the earth*: i.e. successors of previous generations, or perhaps 'rulers' (see e.g. Q6.133, 165; 7.69, 74; 24.55).
57. *take heed*: or 'remember.'
58. *before His mercy*: i.e. before the coming of rain.

65 Say: 'No one in the heavens or the earth knows the unseen[59] except God. They do not realize when they will be raised up. **66** No! Their knowledge is confused concerning the Hereafter. No! They are in doubt about it. No! They are blind to it.'

67 Those who disbelieve say, 'When we have become dust, and our fathers (too), shall we indeed be brought forth?[60] **68** Certainly we have been promised this before, we and our fathers. This is nothing but old tales.'[61] **69** Say: 'Travel the earth and see how the end was for the sinners.'[62] **70** Do not sorrow over them, nor be in distress because of what they are scheming.

71 They say, 'When (will) this promise[63] (come to pass), if you[64] are truthful?' **72** Say: 'It may be that part of what you seek to hurry is bearing down on you (now).' **73** Surely your Lord is indeed full of favor to the people, but most of them are not thankful (for it). **74** Surely your Lord indeed knows what their hearts[65] conceal and what they speak aloud. **75** (There is) nothing hidden in the sky or the earth, except (that it is recorded) in a clear Book.[66]

76 Surely this Qur'ān[67] recounts to the Sons of Israel most of their differences,[68] **77** and surely it is indeed a guidance and mercy to the believers. **78** Surely your Lord will decide between them by His judgment. He is the Mighty, the Knowing. **79** Put your trust in God, (for) surely you[69] (stand) on the clear truth.
80 Surely you cannot make the dead to hear, nor can you make the deaf to hear the call, when they turn away, withdrawing. **81** Nor can you guide the blind out of their straying. You cannot make (anyone) hear, except the one who believes in Our signs, and so they submit.[70]

82 When the word[71] falls upon them, We shall bring forth for them a creature from the earth,[72] (which) will speak to them: 'The people were not certain of Our signs.' **83** On the Day when We shall gather from every community a crowd of those who have called Our signs a lie, and they are arranged (in rows)
84 – until, when they come, He will say, 'Did you call My signs a lie, when you did not encompass them in knowledge, or what (it was) you were doing?' **85** And the word will fall upon them because of the evil

---

65–66 God alone knows the future

59. *the unseen*: here referring to 'the future' (see n. on Q2.3).

67–75 Disbelievers reject the resurrection

60. *brought forth*: from the grave.
61. *old tales*: or 'tales of the ancients;' a contemptuous reference to the stories of previous peoples who were punished for disobeying their prophets (see n. on Q7.59; cf. Q25.5).
62. *Travel the earth and see...*: the remains of their destroyed cities were believed to be still visible (cf. Q3.137).
63. *promise*: or 'threat' of punishment (cf. Q10.48; 21.38; 34.29; 36.48; 67.25).
64. *you*: plur.
65. *hearts*: lit. 'chests,' considered the seat of knowledge and understanding.
66. *a clear Book*: i.e. the 'Book of God' or the heavenly 'Record' of all things (see n. on Q6.59).

76–81 The Qur'ān clarifies disputes among the Sons of Israel

67. *this Qur'ān*: or perhaps 'this recitation,' since the expression (Ar. *hādhā al-qur'ān*) is sometimes used only in reference to a part of the Qur'ān (cf. Q6.19; 10.61; 13.31; 72.1; and see n. on Q2.185). Otherwise, 'this Qur'ān' may come close to its present meaning as the name of the Muslim scripture (cf. Q9.111), and perhaps imply the existence of 'other Qur'āns' (cf. Q39.27-28).
68. *most of their differences*: probably referring to disputes between Jews and Christians (cf. Q5.48-49).
69. *you*: the Prophet.
70. *submit*: or 'become Muslims.'

82–90 Two judgment scenes

71. *the word*: or 'the sentence' (of judgment); cf. Q27.85 below.
72. *creature from the earth*: mentioned only here; cf. the satanic 'beast from the sea' in Revelation 13 (based on the 'four beasts' of Daniel 7), though here it delivers God's message.

they have done, and they will not speak.

86 Do they not see that We made the night for them to rest in, and the day to see? Surely in that are signs indeed for a people who believe. **87** On the Day when there is a blast on the trumpet,[73] and whoever is in the heavens and whoever is on the earth will be terrified, except for whomever God pleases, and all will come to Him humbled, **88** and you[74] see the mountains, supposedly solid, yet passing by (as) the clouds pass by – (such is) the work of God who has perfected everything. Surely He is aware of what you do. **89** (On that Day) whoever brings a good (deed) will have a better one than it, and they will be secure from the terror of that Day. **90** But whoever brings an evil (deed), they will be cast down face first into the Fire:[75] 'Are you repaid (for anything) except for what you have done?'

91 'I have only been commanded to serve the Lord of this land,[76] who has made it sacred. To Him everything (belongs). And I have been commanded to be one of those who submit,[77] **92** and to recite[78] the Qur'ān. Whoever is (rightly) guided is guided only for himself,[79] and whoever goes astray [...].'[80] Say: 'I am only one of the warners.'[81] **93** And say: 'Praise (be)[82] to God! He will show you His signs and you will recognize them. Your Lord is not oblivious of what you do.'

---

73. *a blast on the trumpet*: the Last Day will be announced by the blast of a trumpet (e.g. Q6.73; 18.99; 20.102; 39.68 [a double blast]; 69.13; 74.8; 78.18; cf. Matthew 24.31; 1 Corinthians 15.52; 1 Thessalonians 4.16).
74. *you*: the Prophet, or perhaps intended generally ('one').
75. *the Fire*: Ar. *al-nār* is the most common of the various designations for Hell.

91–93 The Prophet's mission

76. *this land*: said to refer to the sacred area (or *ḥaram*) of Mecca (cf. Q2.126).
77. *those who submit*: or 'the Muslims.'
78. *recite*: or 'read aloud.'
79. *for himself*: i.e. for his own benefit.
80. *[...]*: this sentence is incomplete, either inadvertently or for effect.
81. *warners*: for this role, see n. on Q2.119.
82. *(be)*: or '(belongs).'

28 The Story ۞ Al-Qaṣaṣ

In the Name of God, the Merciful, the Compassionate

1 Ṭā' Sīn Mīm.[1] **2** Those are the signs[2] of the clear Book.[3]

3 We recite to you[4] some of the story[5] of Moses and Pharaoh in truth, for a people who believe:
4 Surely Pharaoh had exalted himself on the earth, and divided its people (into) parties, weakening one contingent of them (by) slaughtering their sons and sparing their women.[6] Surely he was one of the fomenters of corruption. **5** But We wanted to bestow favor on those who were weak on the earth, and make them leaders,[7] and make them the inheritors, **6** and to establish them on the earth, and show Pharaoh and Haman,[8] and their forces, what they had to beware of from them.

7 We inspired Moses' mother:[9] 'Nurse him, and when you fear for him, cast him into the sea,[10] but do not fear and do not sorrow. Surely We are going to return him to you, and make him one of the envoys.'[11]
8 And the house of Pharaoh picked him up, so that he might be an enemy to them and a (cause of) sorrow. Surely Pharaoh and Haman, and their forces, were sinners. **9** The wife of Pharaoh said, '(He is) a comfort[12] to me and to you. Do not kill him! It may be that he will benefit us, or we may adopt him as a son.'[13]

Q28: This sūra is devoted almost entirely to the story of Moses, featuring accounts of his childhood and early life, his call to be a messenger, and finally his struggles with Pharaoh (with a later addendum on the story of Qārūn /Korah). It concludes with three scenes of judgment and a final word of encouragement to the Prophet. Most scholars assign Q28 to the late 'Meccan' period, though some traditional scholars hold that a few verses were revealed at Medina, and one during the Hijra. It receives its title from 'the story' Moses recounts at Q28.25.

1–2 Signs of the Book

1. *Ṭā' Sīn Mīm*: the names of Arabic letters *ṭ*, *s*, and *m*. The same letter combination occurs again in Q26 (Q27 has *ṭ* and *s*). Twenty-nine sūras begin with letters like these, ranging from one to five. No satisfactory explanation has been given for their occurrence. The Cairo edition varies in counting these letters as a separate verse (as here), or as the beginning of the first verse.
2. *signs*: here referring to the letters *ṭ*, *s*, and *m* (for the various meanings of 'signs,' see n. on Q2.39).
3. *the clear Book*: or 'the Book that makes (things) clear;' referring to the Qur'ān not only as a 'recited' but also 'written' scripture (see n. on Q2.2).

3–6 The story of Moses: Introduction

4. *you*: plur.
5. *story*: or 'news.'
6. *slaughtering their sons and sparing their women*: cf. Pharaoh's order to kill all Hebrew boys but spare the girls (Exodus 1.15-16, 22).
7. *leaders*: or 'models,' a term later used for the leader (Ar. *imām*) of a religious community (cf. Q21.73; 32.24).
8. *Haman*: an official of Pharaoh's court (also at Q40.24, 36); cf. Haman in the biblical book of Esther (3.1-6; 7.6-10), who was likewise an antagonist of the Jews, but an adviser to the Persian king Ahasuerus (Xerxes).

7–14 Moses' childhood and early life

9. *We inspired Moses' mother...*: for the story that follows, cf. the version at Q20.37-40; and Exodus 2.1-10.
10. *sea*: the Nile river, according to Exodus 2.3-5.
11. *the envoys*: lit. 'the ones who are sent' (Ar. *al-mursalūn*), a designation roughly equivalent to 'messengers' (*rusul*).
12. *a comfort*: lit. 'a cooling of the eye.'
13. *It may be that he will benefit us...*: the same words spoken by the Egyptian ('Potipher') about Joseph (Q12.21).

But they did not realize (what they were doing). **10** The next day the heart of Moses' mother was empty.[14] She would almost have betrayed him, if We had not strengthened her heart, so that she might be one of the believers. **11** She said to his sister, 'Follow him.' So she watched him on the sly,[15] though they did not realize (it). **12** Before (this) We had forbidden any wet nurses for him, so she said, 'Shall I direct you to the people of a household who will take charge of him for you, and look after him?'[16] **13** And We returned him to his mother, so that she might be comforted[17] and not sorrow, and that she might know that the promise of God is true. But most of them do not know (it). **14** When he reached his maturity and established (himself), We gave him judgment[18] and knowledge. In this way We reward the doers of good.

15 He entered the city at a time when its people were oblivious, and in it he found two men fighting: the one of his (own) party,[19] and the other of his enemies. The one who was of his (own) party called him for help against the one who was of his enemies. So Moses struck him, and finished him off.[20] He said, 'This is the work of Satan.[21] Surely he is a clear enemy (who) leads (people) astray.' **16** He said, 'My Lord, surely I have done myself evil. Forgive me!' So God forgave him. Surely He – He is the Forgiving, the Compassionate. **17** He said, 'My Lord, because of the blessing with which You have blessed me, I shall not be a supporter of the sinners.'

18 The next day he was in the city, afraid (and) watchful, when suddenly the one who had sought his help the day before cried out to him for help (again). Moses said to him, 'Surely you are in error indeed!' **19** But when he was about to attack the one who was an enemy to them both, he said, 'Moses! Do you intend to kill me as you killed (that) person yesterday? You only want to be a tyrant on the earth, and you do not want to be one of those who set (things) right.' **20** And (just then) a man came running from the farthest part of the city.[22] He said, 'Moses! Surely the assembly is taking counsel about you, to kill you. So get out! Surely I am one of your trusty advisers.' **21** So he went forth from it, afraid (and) watchful. He said, 'My Lord, rescue me from the people who are evildoers.'

22 When he turned his face toward Midian,[23] he said, 'It may be that my Lord will guide me to the right way.' **23** And when he came to the water of Midian, he found by it a community of the people watering (their flocks), and besides them he found two women driving off their flocks. He said, 'What is the matter with you two?' They said, 'We may not water (our flocks) until the shepherds drive off (their flocks), and our father is very old.'[24] **24** So he watered (their flocks) for them. Then he turned aside to the shade, and said, 'My Lord, surely I am in need of whatever good You may send down to me.' **25** Then one of the two women came to him, walking shyly. She said, 'My father calls you, so that he may pay you a reward for your watering (our flocks) for us.' When he had come to him and recounted the story to him, he said, 'Do not fear! You have escaped from the people who are evildoers.' **26** One of the two women said, 'My father! Hire him, (for) surely the best man whom you can hire is the strong (and) the trustworthy one.'

---

14. *heart...was empty*: i.e. devoid of understanding (here, as often, the heart is spoken of as synonymous with mind).
15. *on the sly*: lit. 'from a side.'
16. *look after him*: lit. 'be trusty advisers for him.'
17. *that she might be comforted*: lit. 'that her eye might be cooled.'
18. *judgment*: or 'wisdom' (see n. on Q3.79).

15–28 Moses as a young man

19. *party*: i.e. people.
20. *finished him off*: i.e. killed him (cf. Exodus 2.11-15).
21. *Satan*: for this figure, see n. on Q2.36.
22. *a man came running...*: cf. Q36.20.
23. *Midian*: the people to whom the messenger Shu'ayb was sent (see e.g. Q7.85; 11.84; cf. Exodus 2.15); at this point the story of Moses begins to run parallel to that of Jacob, Rachel, and Leah (Genesis 29.1-30).
24. *our father is very old*: and therefore unable to help them.

27 He said, 'Surely I wish to marry you to one of these two daughters of mine, on (the condition) that you hire yourself to me for eight years. But if you complete ten, that will be of your own accord, (for) I am not about to make it a hardship for you. You will find me, if God pleases, one of the righteous.' **28** He said, 'That is between me and you. No matter which of the two terms I fulfill, (let there be) no enmity against me. God is guardian over what we say.'

29 When Moses[25] had fulfilled the term and traveled with his family, he perceived a fire on the side of the mountain.[26] He said to his family, 'Stay (here). Surely I perceive a fire. Perhaps I shall bring you some news of it, or some wood from the fire, so that you may warm yourselves.' **30** But when he came to it, he was called out to from the right side of the wādi,[27] in the blessed hollow, from the tree: 'Moses! Surely I am God, Lord of the worlds.'[28] **31** And: 'Cast (down) your staff!' And when he saw it wiggling as if it were a snake, he turned around, retreating, and did not look back. 'Moses! Come forward and do not fear! Surely you are one of the secure. **32** Put your hand into your cloak.[29] It will come out white, unharmed. Now draw your hand to your side from fear.[30] Those are two proofs from your Lord for Pharaoh and his assembly. Surely they are a wicked people.' **33** He said, 'My Lord, surely I have killed one of them, and I fear that they will kill me. **34** My brother Aaron – he is more eloquent than me in speech.[31] Send him with me as a support (who) will confirm me. Surely I fear that they will call me a liar.' **35** He said, 'We shall strengthen your arm by means of your brother, and give authority to both of you, so that they will be no match for you because of Our signs.[32] You two, and whoever follows you, will be the victors.'

36 When Moses brought them Our clear signs,[33] they said, 'This is nothing but a magic trick. We have not heard of this among our fathers of old.' **37** But Moses said, 'My Lord knows who brings the guidance from Him, and to whom the final Home (belongs). Surely the evildoers will not prosper.' **38** Pharaoh said, 'Assembly! I know of no other god for you than me. So light a fire for me, Haman, on the clay,[34] and make a tower for me, so that I may look at the god of Moses.[35] Surely I think he is indeed one of the liars.' **39** He and his forces became arrogant on the earth without any right, and thought that they would not be returned to Us. **40** So We seized him and his forces, and tossed them into the sea. See how the end was for the evildoers! **41** We made them leaders[36] (who) call (others) to the Fire,[37] and on the Day of Resurrection they will not be helped. **42** We pursued them in this world with a curse, and on the Day of

---

29–35 The call of Moses

25. *When Moses...*: for the story that follows, cf. the versions at Q20.9-36; 27.7-14; and the account of Moses' call at Exodus 3-4.
26. *the mountain*: i.e. Mount Sinai (Q23.20; 95.2).
27. *from the right side of the wādi*: cf. Q20.12; 79.16 ('the holy wādi of Ṭuwā'); the 'right side' is further specified as the 'western side' at Q28.44 below.
28. *Lord of the worlds*: for this title, see n. on Q1.2.
29. *into your cloak*: lit. 'into your chest' (cf. Exodus 4.6-8).
30. *draw your hand to your side from fear*: meaning obscure; lit. 'fold your wing to yourself from fear' (cf. Q20.22).
31. *speech*: lit. 'tongue;' cf. Q20.27; 43.52; Moses was 'slow of speech and slow of tongue,' according to Exodus 4.10 (cf. 6.12, 30).
32. *signs*: or 'miracles' (see n. on Q2.39).

36–42 Moses' struggle with Pharaoh

33. *Our clear signs*: cf. Q17.101, 'nine clear signs;' 27.12, 'nine signs.'
34. *light a fire...on the clay*: to bake bricks.
35. *a tower...look at the god of Moses*: the idea is similar to the one behind the building of the tower of Babel at Genesis 11.4.
36. *leaders*: or 'models,' a term later used for the leader (Ar. *imām*) of a religious community.
37. *the Fire*: Ar. *al-nār* is the most common of the various designations for Hell.

Resurrection they will be among the scorned.[38]

43 Certainly We gave Moses the Book, after We had destroyed the former generations, as evidence for the people, and a guidance[39] and mercy, so that they might take heed.[40] **44** You[41] were not on the western side[42] when We decreed the command to Moses, nor were you among the witnesses. **45** But We produced (other) generations, and life was prolonged for them. You were not dwelling among the people of Midian, reciting to them Our signs, when We were sending (messengers). **46** You were not on the side of the mountain when We called out (to Moses), but (you were sent) as a mercy from your Lord, so that you might warn a people to whom no warner[43] had come before you, so that they might take heed.[44] **47** If (it were) not that a smiting might smite them for what their hands have sent forward,[45] and (that) they might say, 'Our Lord, why did You not send a messenger[46] to us, so that we might have followed Your signs, and (so) been among the believers [...]?'[47] **48** Yet when the truth did come to them from Us, they said, 'If only he were given the same as what Moses was given.'[48] Did they not disbelieve in what was given to Moses before? They said, 'Two magic (tricks) supporting each other,' and they said, 'Surely we are disbelievers in all (of it).' **49** Say:[49] 'Bring a Book from God that is a better guide than these two[50] – I shall follow it, if you are truthful.' **50** If they do not respond to you, know that they are only following their (vain) desires. And who is farther astray than the one who follows his desire without guidance from God? Surely God does not guide the people who are evildoers. **51** Certainly We have caused the word[51] to reach them, so that they may take heed.[52]

52 Those[53] to whom We gave the Book[54] before it[55] – they believe in it. **53** When it is recited to them, they say, 'We believe in it. Surely it is the truth from our Lord. Surely we were Muslims before it.'[56]

---

38. *We seized him...We made them...We pursued them...*: these three verses appear to be three alternative endings to the story.

43–51 Confirmation of the story of Moses

39. *guidance*: one of the most frequent terms (Ar. *hudā*) for revelation in general, and the Qur'ān in particular.
40. *take heed*: or 'remember,' 'be reminded.'
41. *You*: the Prophet.
42. *western side*: of the wādi (Q28.30 above), or the mountain (Q19.52).
43. *warner*: for this role, see n. on Q2.119.
44. *a people to whom no warner had come before you...*: this implies that the Prophet's contemporaries were thought to be a different 'people' than those of Abraham's time (cf. Q32.3; 34.44; 36.6).
45. *what their hands have sent forward*: i.e. their deeds, which are 'sent forward' to the Judgment.
46. *messenger*: for this important title: see n. on Q2.87.
47. *[...]*: there appears to be a lacuna in the text here.
48. *If only he were given the same as what Moses was given*: i.e. why is the Qur'ān different than the Torah?
49. *Say*: on this form of address, see n. on Q2.80.
50. *these two*: i.e. the Torah and Qur'ān (cf. Q2.23; 10.38; 11.13; 52.34).
51. *the word*: probably referring to the Qur'ān.
52. *take heed*: or 'remember,' 'be reminded.'

52–55 People of the Book believe

53. *Those...*: i.e. Jews and Christians. The Cairo edition, reflecting the views of traditional scholars, attributes the following four verses to the 'Medinan' period.
54. *the Book*: here probably used as a generic term for the totality of revelation, rather than as a reference to any individual book (see n. on Q2.2).
55. *before it*: i.e. before the Qur'ān was given.
56. *we were Muslims before it*: or 'we had submitted before it (was given);' believers in previous revelations (Jews and Christians) could be considered 'Muslims,' since the revelations were thought to be essentially the same

54 Those – they will be given their reward twice over for what they have endured. They avert evil by means of the good, and contribute[57] from what We have provided them. **55** When they hear any frivolous talk, they turn away from it, and say, 'To us our deeds and to you your deeds.[58] Peace (be) upon you! We do not seek out the ignorant.'

56 Surely you[59] will not guide whomever you like, but God guides whomever He pleases, and knows the ones who are (rightly) guided. **57** They say,[60] 'If we follow the guidance with you, we shall be snatched from our land.'[61] Have We not established a secure sanctuary[62] for them, where fruits of every kind are brought as a provision from Us? But most of them do not know (it). **58** How many a town have We destroyed (which) boasted of its means of livelihood! Those are their dwelling places (which remain) uninhabited after them, except for a few. We became the inheritors! **59** Yet your Lord was not one to destroy the towns until He had sent a messenger into their mother (city),[63] reciting Our signs to them. We would not have destroyed the towns unless their people had been evildoers.

60 Whatever thing you have been given is (only) an enjoyment of this present life, and its (passing) splendor, but what is with God is better and more lasting. Will you not understand? **61** Is the one whom We have promised a good promise, and (who) receives it, like the one whom We have given the enjoyment of this present life, (and) then on the Day of Resurrection will be one of those brought forward (to the punishment)?

62 On the Day when He will call them, and say, 'Where are My associates[64] whom you used to claim (as gods)?,' **63** those[65] against whom the word has proved true[66] will say, 'Our Lord, these are those whom we made err. We made them err as we had erred. We disown (them) before You. They were not serving us.'[67] **64** And it will be said, 'Call your associates!' And they will call them, but they will not respond to them, and they will see the punishment. If only they had been guided!

65 On the Day when He will call them, and say, 'What response did you give the envoys?' **66** The news will be dark for them on that Day, nor will they ask each other questions. **67** But as for the one who turns (in repentance), and believes, and does righteousness, it may be that he will be one of those who prosper.

68 Your Lord creates whatever He pleases, and chooses (whomever He pleases) – the choice is not

---

(cf. e.g. Q3.52; 5.44, 111).

57. *contribute*: lit. 'spend' (for those in need or for the cause).

58. *To us our deeds and to you your deeds*: or 'We have our deeds and you have your deeds' (see Q2.139-141; 42.15; cf. Q109.6).

56–59 Danger of not following the Prophet

59. *you*: the Prophet.

60. *They say*: the Prophet's contemporaries.

61. *land*: lit. 'earth.'

62. *a secure sanctuary*: said to designate the sacred area (or *ḥaram*) of Mecca, where bloodshed was forbidden (cf. Q2.126).

63. *their mother (city)*: or 'their metropolis,' but the reference is obscure (cf. Q6.92).

60–61 Future life better than the present

62–67 Two judgment scenes

64. *My associates*: the other gods they had worshipped (cf. Q28.74-75 below; 6.22-24; 10.28-30).

65. *those*: the other gods.

66. *against whom the word has proved true*: this may refer to the fulfilment of the threat to 'fill Hell with jinn and people' (Q7.18; 11.119), and thus imply that the 'other gods' were regarded as jinn (cf. Q2.14); but the phrase may simply mean 'those against whom the sentence (of condemnation) has been passed.'

67. *serving us*: or 'worshipping us.'

68–73 Signs of God's power and providence

theirs. Glory to God! He is exalted above what they associate. **69** Your Lord knows what their hearts[68] conceal and what they speak aloud. **70** He is God – (there is) no god but Him. To Him (be)[69] praise, at the first and at the last![70] To Him (belongs) the judgment, and to Him you will be returned.

71 Say: 'Have you considered?[71] If God makes the night continuous for you until the Day of Resurrection, what god other than God will bring you light? Will you not hear?' **72** Say: 'Have you considered? If God makes the day continuous for you until the Day of Resurrection, what god other than God will bring you night to rest in? Will you not see? **73** But out of His mercy He has made the night and the day for you, so that you may rest in it, and that you may seek some of His favor,[72] and that you may be thankful.'

74 On the Day when He will call them, and say, 'Where are My associates whom you used to claim (as gods)?' **75** We shall draw out a witness from every community, and say, 'Bring your proof!' And then they will know that the truth (belongs) to God, and what they have forged will abandon them.[73]

76 Surely Qārūn[74] was one of the people of Moses, and acted oppressively toward them. We had given him treasures, the keys of which would indeed have been a burden for a group (of men) endowed with strength. (Remember) when his people said to him, 'Do not gloat! Surely God does not love those who gloat. **77** But seek the Home of the Hereafter[75] by means of what God has given you, and do not forget your portion of this world. Do good, as God has done good to you, and do not seek to foment corruption on the earth. Surely God does not love the fomenters of corruption.' **78** He said, 'I have been given it[76] only because of the knowledge (that is) in me.' Did he not know that God had destroyed those of the generations before him who were stronger than him and had accumulated more? The sinners will not be questioned about their sins.[77] **79** So he went forth to his people in his splendor. Those who desired this present life said, 'Would that we had the same as what has been given to Qārūn! Surely he is indeed the possessor of great good luck.' **80** But those to whom knowledge had been given said, 'Woe to you! The reward of God is better for the one who believes and does righteousness. But no one will obtain it[78] except the patient.' **81** So We caused the earth to swallow him and his home, and he had no cohort to help him, other than God, and he was not one of those who could help themselves. **82** In the morning those who had longed (to be in) his place the day before were saying, 'Woe (to Qārūn)! Surely God extends (His) provision to whomever He pleases of His servants, and restricts (it). If God had not bestowed favor on us, He would indeed have caused (the earth) to swallow us (too). Woe to him! The disbelievers will not prosper.'

83 That is the Home of the Hereafter: We assign[79] it to those who do not desire haughtiness on the earth,

---

68. *hearts*: lit. 'chests,' considered the seat of knowledge and understanding.
69. *(be)*: or '(belongs).'
70. *at the first and at the last*: or 'in this world and in the Hereafter.'
71. *considered*: lit. 'seen' (and the following v.).
72. *seek some of His favor*: i.e. seek to make a livelihood.

74–75 A judgment scene

73. *abandon them*: lit. 'go astray from them' (a pun).

76–82 The story of Qārūn

74. *Qārūn*: elsewhere an associate of Pharaoh and Haman (Q29.39; 40.23-25); but for the story here, cf. the rebellion of Korah in Numbers 16 (his great wealth is also mentioned in later Jewish tradition).
75. *Home of the Hereafter*: see n. on Q2.4.
76. *It*: his extraordinary wealth.
77. *sinners will not be questioned about their sins*: because God will inform them about what they have done.
78. *it*: 'it'(fem.) does not agree with its apparent antecedent 'reward' (masc.); perhaps the idea has shifted to something like 'the Home (fem.) of the Hereafter.'

83–84 The Home of the Hereafter

79. *assign*: lit. 'make.'

nor corruption. The outcome (belongs) to the ones who guard (themselves).[80] **84** Whoever brings a good (deed) will have a better one than it, and whoever brings an evil (deed) – those who have done evil deeds will only be repaid for what they have done.

85 Surely He who made the Qur'ān obligatory for you[81] will indeed return you to (your) home.[82] Say: 'My Lord knows who brings the guidance, and who is clearly astray.'[83] **86** You did not expect that the Book would be cast (down) to you,[84] except as a mercy from your Lord. So do not be a supporter of the disbelievers. **87** Let them not keep you from the signs[85] of God, after they have been sent down to you, but call (people) to your Lord, and do not be one of the idolaters.[86] **88** Do not call on another god (along) with God. (There is) no god but Him. Everything perishes except His face.[87] To Him (belongs) the judgment, and to Him you will be returned.

---

80. *guard (themselves)*: against evil, or God.

85–88 Encouragement to the Prophet

81. *made the Qur'ān obligatory for you*: i.e. for the Prophet; here 'the Qur'ān' comes close to its present meaning as the name of the Muslim scripture (cf. Q9.111; see n. on Q2.185).
82. *(your) home*: lit. 'a place of return;' most interpret this either as a reference to the future life or as prediction of the Prophet's return to Mecca, but neither alternative is certain. The Cairo edition, reflecting the views of some traditional scholars, holds that this verse was revealed at Juḥfah during the Hijra to Medina.
83. *clearly astray*: lit. 'in clear straying.'
84. *the Book would be cast (down) to you*: cf. Q40.15 ('the spirit of His command'); 77.5 ('a reminder').
85. *signs*: or 'verses.'
86. *the idolaters*: or 'the ones who associate (other gods with God).'
87. *His face*: i.e. God's favor.

29 The Spider ❁ Al-ʿAnkabūt

In the Name of God, the Merciful, the Compassionate

1 Alif Lām Mīm.[1]

2 Do the people think that they will be left (in such a position) that they (can) say, 'We believe,' but (that) they will not be tested? **3** Certainly We tested those who were before them, and God will indeed know those who are truthful, and He will indeed know the liars. **4** Or do those who do evil deeds think that they will escape Us? Evil is what they judge! **5** Whoever expects the meeting with God – surely the time[2] of God is coming indeed! He is the Hearing, the Knowing. **6** Whoever struggles, struggles only for himself. Surely God is indeed wealthy beyond the worlds. **7** Those who believe and do righteous deeds – We shall indeed absolve them of their evil deeds, and indeed repay them (for the) best of what they have done.

8 We have charged each person (to do) good to his parents, but if they both struggle with you[3] – to make you associate with Me what you have no knowledge of – do not obey them. To Me is your[4] return, and I shall inform you about what you have done. **9** Those who believe and do righteous deeds – We shall indeed cause them to enter among the righteous.

10 Among the people (there is) one who says, 'We believe in God,' but when he is hurt in (the way of) God, he takes[5] the persecution[6] of the people as the punishment of God. But if indeed help comes to you[7] from your Lord, they indeed say, 'Surely we were with you.' Does God not know what is in the hearts of all?[8] **11** God indeed knows those who believe, and He indeed knows the hypocrites.[9]

12 Those who disbelieve say to those who believe, 'Follow our way, and let us bear your sins.' Yet they cannot bear a single one of their own sins. Surely they are liars indeed! **13** But they will indeed bear their

---

Q29: This sūra begins by exhorting believers to remain steadfast in the face of opposition, and then recounts the stories of seven previous messengers. It also describes the nature of 'the Book' revealed to the Prophet and its relationship to the previous scriptures of the 'People of the Book.' Most scholars, traditional as well as modern, think Q29 is a composite of materials from the late 'Meccan' and early 'Medinan' periods. The Cairo edition lists it as the penultimate 'Meccan' sūra. It takes its title from the parable of 'the spider' (Q29.41).

1 Letters

1. *Alif Lām Mīm*: the names of Arabic letters ', *l*, and *m*. The same letter combination occurs in a block of sūras from Q29 to Q32, as well as at the beginning of Q2, Q3, and Q7 (which has an additional 'ṣād'). Twenty-nine sūras begin with letters like these, ranging from one to five. No satisfactory explanation has been given for their occurrence. The Cairo edition varies in counting these letters as a separate verse (as here), or as the beginning of the first verse.

2–13 Believers will be tested

2. *time*: or 'term' (Ar. *ajal*), which is predetermined and cannot be changed.
3. *you*: sing., but probably intended generally.
4. *your*: plur.
5. *takes*: lit. 'makes.'
6. *persecution*: or 'trial,' 'tribulation' (Ar. *fitna*).
7. *you*: sing., but probably intended generally.
8. *hearts of all*: lit. 'chests of the worlds;' the chest was considered the seat of knowledge.
9. *...He indeed knows the hypocrites*: the Cairo edition, reflecting the views of traditional scholars, attributes vv. 2-11 to the 'Medinan' period.

burdens, and (other) burdens[10] with their burdens, and on the Day of Resurrection they will indeed be questioned about what they have forged.

14 Certainly We sent Noah[11] to his people, and he stayed among them a thousand years, minus fifty years,[12] and then the flood seized them while they were doing evil. **15** But We rescued him and (his) companions on the ship,[13] and made it a miracle for all peoples.[14]

16 And Abraham, when he said to his people: 'Serve God, and guard (yourselves) against Him. That is better for you, if (only) you knew. **17** Instead of God, you only serve idols, and you create a lie. Surely those whom you serve, instead of God, do not possess any provision for you. Seek (your) provision from God, and serve Him, and be thankful to Him – to Him you will be returned. **18** But if you call (it) a lie, (know that) communities called (it) a lie before you. Nothing (depends) on the messenger[15] except the clear delivery (of the message).'

19 Do they not see[16] how God brings about the creation, (and) then restores it? Surely that is easy for God. **20** Say:[17] 'Travel the earth and see how He brought about the creation. Then God produces the latter growth.[18] Surely God is powerful over everything. **21** He punishes whomever He pleases and has compassion on whomever He pleases – and to Him you will be turned. **22** You cannot escape (Him) either on the earth or in the sky, and you have no ally and no helper other than God.' **23** Those who disbelieve in the signs of God and the meeting with Him – those have no hope of My mercy, and those – for them (there is) a painful punishment.

24 But the only response of his people[19] was that they said, 'Kill him, or burn him!' And then God rescued him from the fire. Surely in that are signs indeed for a people who believe. **25** And he said, 'Instead of God, you have only taken idols (in a bond of) friendship among you in this present life. Then on the Day of Resurrection some of you will deny[20] others, and some will curse others, and your refuge will be the Fire,[21] and you will have no helpers.' **26** Lot believed in him, and said, 'I am going to flee[22] to my Lord. Surely He – He is the Mighty, the Wise.' **27** And We granted him Isaac and Jacob,[23] and We placed among his descendants the prophetic office and the Book.[24] We gave him his reward in this world, and in the Hereafter[25] he will indeed be among the righteous.

---

10. *(other) burdens*: perhaps for having led others astray.

14–15 The story of Noah and his people

11. *We sent Noah...*: here begins another series of seven 'punishment stories' (Q29.14-40; see nn. on Q7.59; 15.87).
12. *a thousand years, minus fifty years*: cf. Genesis 9.29, 'All the days of Noah were nine hundred fifty years.'
13. *the ship*: Noah's 'ark.'
14. *a miracle for all peoples*: lit. 'a sign for the worlds' (for the various meanings of 'sign,' see n. on Q2.39).

16–27 The story of Abraham and his people

15. *messenger*: for this important title, see n. on Q2.87.
16. *Do they not see...*: this paragraph (Q29.19-23) interrupts the story, and looks like a later addition.
17. *Say*: on this form of address, see n. on Q2.80.
18. *...the latter growth*: referring to the death and revival of vegetation (a frequent metaphor of resurrection).
19. *his people*: i.e. Abraham's people; the story now resumes.
20. *deny*: lit. 'disbelieve.'
21. *the Fire*: Ar. *al-nār* is the most common of the various designations for Hell.
22. *I am going to flee*: or 'I am going to emigrate.'
23. *Isaac and Jacob*: notice that Ishmael is not mentioned here (cf. Q6.84; 11.71; 19.49; 21.72; 38.45). In other passages, however, emphasis is placed on Ishmael as Abraham's son (see e.g. Q2.125, 127; 4.163; 14.39).
24. *the Book*: the Torah (cf. Q3.79; 6.89; 45.16; 57.26).
25. *the Hereafter*: see n. on Q2.4.

28 And Lot,[26] when he said to his people: 'Surely you commit (such) immorality (as) no one in all the worlds has committed before you. **29** Do you indeed approach men, and cut off the way,[27] and commit wrong in your meeting?' But the only response of his people was that they said, 'Bring us the punishment of God, if you are one of the truthful.' **30** He said, 'My Lord, help me against the people who foment corruption.' **31** When Our messengers[28] brought Abraham the good news, they said, 'Surely we are going to destroy the people of this town,[29] (for) its people are evildoers.' **32** He said, 'Surely Lot is in it.' They said, 'We know who is in it. We shall indeed rescue him and his family, except his wife. She will be one of those who stay behind.' **33** When Our messengers came to Lot, he became distressed about them, and felt powerless (to protect) them, but they said, 'Do not fear and do not sorrow. Surely we are going to rescue you and your family, except your wife. She will be one of those who stay behind. **34** Surely We are going to send down wrath from the sky[30] on the people of this town, because they have acted wickedly.' **35** Certainly We have left some of it[31] as a clear sign for a people who understand.

36 And to Midian (We sent) their brother Shu'ayb.[32] He said, 'My people! Serve God and expect the Last Day. Do not act wickedly on the earth, fomenting corruption.' **37** But they called him a liar, so the earthquake[33] seized them, and morning found them leveled in their home(s).

38 And 'Ād and Thamūd[34] – it is clear to you from their dwellings. Satan made their deeds appear enticing to them, and kept them from the way, though they saw (it) clearly.

39 And Qārūn,[35] and Pharaoh, and Haman[36] – certainly Moses brought them the clear signs, but they became arrogant on the earth. Yet they did not outrun (Us).[37] **40** We seized each one for his sin. We sent a sandstorm against one of them, and another of them was seized by the cry, and We caused the earth to swallow (yet) another of them, and We drowned (still) another of them. Yet God was not one to do them evil, but they did themselves evil.

41 The parable of those who take allies other than God is like the parable of the spider: it takes a house, but surely the house of the spider is indeed the most feeble of houses – if (only) they knew. **42** Surely God knows whatever they call on instead of Him. He is the Mighty, the Wise. **43** Those parables – We strike them for the people, but no one understands them except the ones who know. **44** God created the

---

28–35 The story of Lot and his people

26. *Lot*: for the story that follows, cf. the versions at Q11.77-83; 15.57-74; 26.160-173; and Genesis 19.1-29.
27. *cut off the way*: of having children.
28. *Our messengers*: here referring to 'angels;' cf. e.g. Q51.24-36; and the story at Genesis 18.16-21.
29. *this town*: Lot's city was Sodom, according to Genesis 19.1.
30. *wrath from the sky*: stones of baked clay, according to Q11.82; 15.74.
31. *some of it*: i.e. the remains of Lot's city, which was thought to be in the region of the Dead Sea.

36–37 The story of Shu'ayb and the people of Midian

32. *Shu'ayb*: for a fuller version of the story, see e.g. Q7.85-93.
33. *earthquake*: cf. Q7.91; 11.94 ('the cry').

38 The story of the peoples of 'Ād and Thamūd

34. *'Ād and Thamūd*: to whom the messengers Hūd and Ṣāliḥ were sent, respectively; see e.g. Q7.65-72, 73-79.

39–40 The story Moses and Pharaoh, Qārūn, and Haman

35. *Qārūn*: here an associate of Pharaoh and Haman (and at Q40.24), but cf. the story at Q28.76-82, where he is one of Moses' people (the biblical 'Korah' of Numbers 16).
36. *Haman*: an official of Pharaoh's court (and at Q28.6; 40.24); cf. Haman in the biblical book of Esther (3.1-6; 7.6-10), who was likewise an antagonist of the Jews, but an adviser to the Persian king Ahasuerus (Xerxes).
37. *they did not outrun (Us)*: cf. Q56.60; 70.41.

41–44 Parable of the spider

heavens and the earth in truth.[38] Surely in that is a sign indeed for the believers.

45 Recite[39] what you have been inspired (with) of the Book,[40] and observe the prayer.[41] Surely the prayer forbids immorality and wrong, yet the remembrance of God is indeed greater. God is aware of what you do. **46** Do not dispute[42] with the People of the Book except with what is better[43] – except for those of them who do evil.[44] And say:[45] 'We believe in what has been sent down to us, and what has been sent down to you.[46] Our God and your God is one, and to Him we submit.'[47] **47** In this way We have sent down the Book to you.[48] Those to whom We have given the Book believe in it,[49] and among these (people)[50] (there are) some who believe in it. No one denies Our signs but the disbelievers.

48 You were not accustomed to read from any book before it, or to write it with your right (hand),[51] (for) then the perpetrators of falsehood would indeed have had (reason to) doubt (you). **49** No! It[52] is clear signs[53] in the hearts[54] of those who have been given knowledge. No one denies Our signs but the evildoers.

50 They say, 'If only signs were sent down on him from his Lord.'[55] Say: 'The signs are only with God. I am only a clear warner.'[56] **51** Is it not sufficient for them that We have sent down on you the Book to be recited[57] to them? Surely in that is a mercy indeed, and a reminder to a people who believe. **52** Say: 'God is sufficient as a witness between me and you.' He knows whatever is in the heavens and the earth. Those who believe in falsehood[58] and disbelieve in God, those – they are the losers.

---

38. *in truth*: or 'with the truth.'

45–47 Three parallel scriptures

39. *Recite...*: or 'Read aloud...' (addressed to the Prophet).
40. *of the Book*: or 'from the Book;' this may refer to the heavenly archetype or source of all scripture. According to this view, the Qur'ān, like the Torah and the Gospel, is only a portion of this all encompassing 'mother of the Book' (see Q13.39; 43.4; cf. Q56.78, 'hidden Book;' 85.22, 'guarded Tablet').
41. *observe the prayer*: the ritual prayer (or *ṣalāt*).
42. *Do not dispute...*: plur. imperative, addressed to the believers.
43. *except with what is better*: or 'except in the best way.'
44. *except for those of them who do evil*: this proviso may be a later insertion (cf. Q16.125).
45. *say*: plur. imperative, addressed to the believers (see Q2.136; cf. Q3.84; 112.1).
46. *We believe...*: a recognition of all three 'scriptures' as coming from God (see Q9.111; cf. Q2.136; 3.84; 42.15).
47. *submit*: or 'are Muslims.'
48. *In this way We have sent down the Book to you*: i.e. the Qur'ān has been 'sent down' to the Prophet, just as the Torah and Gospel were sent down to Moses and Jesus (cf. e.g. Q3.3).
49. *Those to whom We have given the Book believe in it*: referring to Jews and Christians who recognize the Qur'ān.
50. *these (people)*: the Prophet's contemporaries; said to refer to the Meccans.

48–49 The Prophet was not a scribe

51. *not accustomed to read...or to write...*: i.e. the Prophet was not a reader or writer of books, prior to the Qur'ān.
52. *It*: the Qur'ān.
53. *signs*: or 'verses.'
54. *hearts*: lit. 'chests.'

50–52 Demand for signs

55. *If only signs...*: i.e. they demand 'miracles' as proof of the Prophet's legitimacy; see the lists of their demands at Q17.90-95; 25.7-8, 20-21, 32 (cf. the similar demand for a 'sign' from Jesus at John 2.18; 6.30)
56. *warner*: for this role, see n. on Q2.119.
57. *recited*: or 'read aloud' (implying that the Qur'ān is the Prophet's 'miracle').
58. *falsehood*: i.e. false gods.

53 They seek to hurry you with the punishment.[59] If it were not for an appointed time,[60] the punishment would indeed have come upon them (already). Yet it will indeed come upon them unexpectedly, when they do not realize (it). **54** They seek to hurry you with the punishment. Surely Gehenna[61] will indeed encompass the disbelievers. **55** On the Day when the punishment will cover them – from above them and from beneath their feet – (then) He will say, 'Taste what you have done!'

56 My servants who believe! Surely My earth is wide, so serve Me![62] **57** Every person will taste death, then to Us you will be returned. **58** Those who have believed and done righteous deeds – We shall indeed settle them in exalted rooms of the Garden,[63] through which rivers flow, there to remain. Excellent is the reward of the doers,[64] **59** who are patient and trust in their Lord.

60 How many a creature (there is which) does not carry its own provision, yet God provides for it and for you.[65] He is the Hearing, the Knowing. **61** If indeed you ask them, 'Who created the heavens and the earth, and subjected the sun and the moon?,' they will indeed say, 'God.'[66] How then are they (so) deluded? **62** God extends (His) provision to whomever He pleases of His servants, and restricts (it) from him (whom He pleases). God has knowledge of everything. **63** If indeed you ask them, 'Who sends down water from the sky, and by means of it gives the earth life after its death?,' they will indeed say, 'God.' Say: 'Praise (be)[67] to God!' But most of them do not understand.

64 This present life is nothing but jest and diversion.[68] Surely the Home of the Hereafter – it is life indeed, if (only) they knew. **65** When they sail[69] in the ship, they call on God, devoting (their) religion to Him.[70] But when He brings them safely to the shore, suddenly they associate (other gods with Him). **66** Let them be ungrateful for what We have given them, and enjoy (themselves). Soon they will know! **67** Do they not see that We established a secure sanctuary[71] (for them), while all around them the people are plundered?[72] Do they believe in falsehood,[73] but disbelieve in the blessing of God?

68 Who is more evil than the one who forges a lie against God, or calls the truth a lie when it comes to him? Is there not in Gehenna a dwelling place for the disbelievers? **69** But those who struggle for Us,[74] We shall indeed guide them in Our ways. Surely God is indeed with the doers of good.

53–55 Demand to bring the punishment

59. *They seek to hurry you with the punishment*: i.e. they (sarcastically) dare the Prophet to make it happen.
60. *an appointed time*: or 'term' (Ar. *ajal*), i.e. the time of judgment is predetermined and cannot be changed.
61. *Gehenna*: a name for Hell (see n. on Q2.206).

56–59 Reward for righteousness

62. *My earth is wide, so serve Me*: some interpreters take this as a call to 'emigrate' to Medina.
63. *exalted rooms of the Garden*: in heaven (for this imagery, see n. on Q2.25; cf. Q25.75; 39.20).
64. *the doers*: of righteous deeds.

60–67 Disbelievers inconsistent and ungrateful

65. *God provides for it and for you*: cf. the similar saying of Jesus at Matthew 6.26; Luke 12.24.
66. *'God'*: their answer makes explicit their belief in God as the supreme deity (cf. Q29.63 below; 10.31; 31.25; 39.38; 43.87).
67. *(be)*: or '(belongs).'
68. *jest and diversion*: i.e. trivial in comparison with the Hereafter.
69. *sail*: lit. 'ride.'
70. *devoting (their) religion to Him*: i.e. they regard God as the sole object of prayer at such a moment of danger.
71. *a secure sanctuary*: said to designate the sacred area (or *ḥaram*) of Mecca, where bloodshed was forbidden (cf. Q2.126).
72. *plundered*: or 'snatched away' (cf. Q28.57).
73. *falsehood*: i.e. false gods.

68–69 Believers and disbelievers

74. *for Us*: lit. 'in Us.'

30 The Romans ✵ Al-Rūm

In the Name of God, the Merciful, the Compassionate

1 Alif Lām Mīm.[1]

2 The Romans[2] have been conquered[3] **3** in the nearest (part) of the land,[4] but after their conquering, they will conquer[5] **4** in a few years. The affair (belongs) to God before and after, and on that day the believers will gloat **5** over the help of God. He helps whomever He pleases. He is the Mighty, the Compassionate.

6 The promise of God! God will not break His promise, but most of the people do not know (it). **7** They perceive (only) what is obvious in this present life, but they are oblivious of the Hereafter.[6] **8** Do they not reflect within themselves?[7] God did not create the heavens and the earth, and whatever is between them, except in truth[8] and (for) an appointed time.[9] Yet surely many of the people are indeed disbelievers in the meeting with their Lord. **9** Have they not traveled on the earth and seen how the end was for those who

---

Q30: This sūra opens with a reference to a military defeat of the Byzantine empire, which is followed by a prophecy of their ultimate victory over the Sassanid Persians. It then extols the signs of God's power in the natural world as evidence of his benevolence and ability to raise the dead. Most scholars assign Q30 to the late 'Meccan' period.

1 Letters

1. *Alif Lām Mīm*: the names of Arabic letters ', *l*, and *m*. The same letter combination occurs in a block of sūras from Q29 to Q32, as well as at the beginning of Q2, Q3, and Q7 (which has an additional 'ṣād'). Twenty-nine sūras begin with letters like these, ranging from one to five. No satisfactory explanation has been given for their occurrence. The Cairo edition varies in counting these letters as a separate verse (as here), or as the beginning of the first verse.

2–5 The Romans

2. *The Romans*: Ar. *al-Rūm* designates the Byzantine (or eastern Roman) empire, whose inhabitants spoke Greek but called themselves 'Romans' (Gk. *Rōmaioi*). They are mentioned only here in the Qur'ān.
3. *have been conquered*: this may refer to the Byzantine loss of Damascus (613 CE) or Jerusalem (614 CE) to the Sassanid Persian empire, or more generally to some victory in the Persian advance against the Byzantines either before or after these events (611-616 CE). However, an early variant reading reverses the passive form of the verb in v. 2 and the active form in v. 3. If adopted, the passage would then read: 'The Romans have conquered..., but...they will be conquered.' This would transform the passage into a prophecy of the Muslim conquest of Byzantine Syria and Palestine (636-638 CE). Although this is an early reading, it is not generally accepted, nor does it remove the difficulty of specifying the particular event referred to in v. 2.
4. *nearest (part) of the land*: lit. 'nearest (part) of the earth;' if the Byzantine loss of Damascus or Jerusalem is in view, this would likely refer to the Byzantine frontier in Syria-Palestine, and imply that the location from which it was spoken was far from the vicinity of present-day Mecca (cf. Q11.83, 89n.; 37.137n.; 46.27n.).
5. *will conquer*: the Byzantine recovery began under the emperor Heraclius with his decisive victory over the Persians at Nineveh (627 CE), though there were earlier successes in Asia Minor (622-625 CE).

6–19 Judgment and Resurrection certain

6. *the Hereafter*: see n. on Q2.4.
7. *within themselves*: or 'about themselves.'
8. *in truth*: or 'with the truth,' but here almost meaning 'for the purpose of judgment,' as the following words indicate (cf. Q15.85; 44.39; 46.3).
9. *(for) an appointed time*: or 'term' (Ar. *ajal*), i.e. the heavens and earth will cease to exist at the time set for Judgment Day (cf. Q46.3).

were before them?[10] They were stronger than them in power, and they ploughed the earth and populated it more than they have populated it. Their messengers[11] brought them the clear signs.[12] God was not one to do them evil, but they did themselves evil. **10** Then the end of those who had done evil was evil, because they had called the signs[13] of God a lie and mocked them.

11 God brings about the creation, then restores it, (and) then to Him you[14] will be returned. **12** On the Day when the Hour[15] strikes, the sinners will despair. **13** They will not have any intercessors among their associates,[16] but they (will come to) disbelieve in their associates. **14** On the Day when the Hour strikes, on that Day they will be separated. **15** As for those who have believed and done righteous deeds, they will be made happy in a meadow.[17] **16** But as for those who have disbelieved, and called Our signs a lie, and the meeting of the Hereafter, those will be brought forward to the punishment. **17** So glory to God, when you come to evening and when you come to morning.[18] **18** Praise (be)[19] to Him in the heavens and the earth – and at night and when you appear (in the day)![20] **19** He brings forth the living from the dead, and brings forth the dead from the living. He gives the earth life after its death, and in this way you (too) will be brought forth.[21]

20 (One) of His signs is that He created you from dust,[22] and now you are human beings spreading (far and wide). **21** (Another) of His signs is that He created spouses for you from yourselves, so that you may live with them, and He has established[23] love and mercy between you. Surely in that are signs indeed for a people who reflect. **22** (Another) of His signs is the creation of the heavens and the earth, and the variety of your languages and colors. Surely in that are signs indeed for those who know. **23** (Another) of His signs is your sleeping by night and day, and your seeking some of His favor.[24] Surely in that are signs indeed for a people who hear. **24** (Another) of His signs (is that) He shows you lightning – in fear and desire[25] – and He sends down water from the sky, and by means of it gives the earth life after its death. Surely in that are signs indeed for a people who understand. **25** (Another) of His signs is that the sky and the earth stand (fast) by His command. Then, when He calls you out of the earth once and for all,[26] suddenly you will come forth. **26** To Him (belongs) whoever is in the heavens and the earth: all are

10. *Have they not traveled on the earth and seen...*: a reference to previous peoples who were punished for their disbelief (see n. on Q7.59). The remains of their destroyed cities were believed to be still visible (see Q30.42 below).
11. *messengers*: for this important title, see n. on Q2.87.
12. *the clear signs*: or 'the clear proofs,' 'the indisputable evidence.'
13. *signs*: here referring to 'verses' or perhaps to revelation in general (see n. on Q2.39).
14. *you*: plur.; a variant reading has 'they.'
15. *the Hour*: of judgment.
16. *their associates*: i.e. the gods they 'associated' with God.
17. *meadow*: cf. Q42.22, 'meadows of the Gardens.'
18. *So glory...*: the Cairo edition, reflecting traditional scholarship, attributes this verse to the 'Medinan' period.
19. *(be)*: or '(belongs).'
20. *and at night and when you appear (in the day)*: this phrase appears misplaced, and would fit better after v. 17; but taken together vv.17-18 mention four of the five times of prayer.
21. *brought forth*: from the grave.

20–27 Signs of God's power and providence

22. *from dust*: see Q3.59; 18.37; 22.5; 35.11; 40.67 (cf. Genesis 2.7, 'from the dust of the ground'); 'from clay,' according to Q6.2; 7.12; 15.26; 17.61; 23.12; 32.7; 38.71, 76; 55.14; 'from water,' according to Q21.30; 24.45; 25.54.
23. *established*: lit. 'made.'
24. *seeking some of His favor*: i.e. seeking to make a livelihood.
25. *in fear and desire*: i.e. fear of the storm, but desire for rain (cf. Q13.12).
26. *calls you...once and for all*: lit. 'calls you...a call' (i.e. at the resurrection).

obedient before Him. **27** He (it is) who brings about the creation, then restores it – it is easy for Him. (Only) the highest parable[27] in the heavens and the earth (is fitting) for Him. He is the Mighty, the Wise.

28 He has struck a parable for you from yourselves: Among what your right (hands) own,[28] do you have associates in what We have provided you with, so that you are (all) equal in that respect[29] – (you) fearing them as you fear each other? In this way We make the signs distinct[30] for a people who understand.

29 No! Those who do evil follow their own (vain) desires without any knowledge. So who will guide those whom God has led astray? They have no helpers. **30** Set your face[31] to the religion (as) a Ḥanīf[32] – the creation of God[33] for which He created humankind. (There is) no change in the creation of God. That is the right religion, but most of the people do not know (it) – **31** turning to Him (in repentance). Guard (yourself) against Him,[34] and observe the prayer,[35] and do not be one of the idolaters,[36] **32** one of those who have divided up their religion[37] and become parties, each faction gloating over what was with them.[38] **33** When hardship touches the people, they call on their Lord, turning to Him (in repentance). Then, when He gives them a taste of mercy from Himself, suddenly a group of them associates (other gods) with their Lord. **34** Let them be ungrateful for what We have given them: 'Enjoy (yourselves)! Soon you will know!' **35** Or have We sent down any authority on them (for this), and does it speak about what they associate with Him?

36 When We give the people a taste of mercy, they gloat over it, but if some evil smites them because of what their (own) hands have sent forward,[39] suddenly they despair. **37** Do they not see that God extends (His) provision to whomever He pleases, and restricts (it)? Surely in that are signs indeed for a people who believe.

38 Give the family its due, and the poor, and the traveler[40] – that is better for those who desire the face of God,[41] and those – they are the ones who prosper. **39** Whatever you give in usury, in order that it may increase on the wealth of the people, does not increase with God, but what you give in alms,[42] desiring the face of God – those are the ones who gain double.[43]

---

27. *parable*: or 'comparison.'

28 Parable of a slave

28. *what your right (hands) own*: slaves.
29. *in that respect*: lit. 'in it;' the point seems to be that just as a master does not treat his slaves alike, so God does not treat his servants alike (cf. Q16.71).
30. *make the signs distinct*: or 'expound the verses.'

29–45 Establish right religion

31. *Set your face...*: addressed to the Prophet, or perhaps intended generally.
32. *(as) a Ḥanīf*: or perhaps '(though you are) a Gentile,' like Abraham (see n. on Q2.135; cf. Q10.105).
33. *the creation of God*: i.e. the 'original form' (Ar. *fiṭra*) of religion which God created for humanity to follow, and which the Prophet re-establishes.
34. *Guard (yourself)...*: this and following imperatives are plur.
35. *the prayer*: the ritual prayer (or *ṣalāt*).
36. *the idolaters*: or 'the ones who associate (other gods with God).'
37. *those who have divided up their religion*: i.e. Jews and Christians, who are here the ones considered 'idolaters' (see also Q4.51; 9.30-33; 42.13-14).
38. *each faction gloating over what was with them*: the Jews in the Torah, the Christians in the Gospel (cf. Q23.53).
39. *what their (own) hands have sent forward*: i.e. their deeds, which are 'sent forward' to the Judgment.
40. *traveler*: lit. 'son of the way.'
41. *the face of God*: i.e. God's favor.
42. *alms*: or *zakāt*, a kind of tithe required for the benefit of the poor, as well as other purposes.
43. *gain double*: for this idea, see e.g. Q2.245 ('lend to God a good loan'); cf. Proverbs 19.17.

40 (It is) God who created you, then provided for you, then causes you to die, (and) then gives you life. (Are there) any of your associates who (can) do any of that? Glory to Him! He is exalted above what they associate. **41** Corruption has appeared on the shore and the sea because of what the hands of the people have earned,[44] so that He may give them a taste of what they have done, that they may return. **42** Say:[45] 'Travel the earth and see how the end was for those who were before (you).[46] Most of them were idolaters.'

43 Set your face to the right religion,[47] before a Day comes from God which cannot be turned back.[48] On that Day they will be divided: **44** whoever disbelieves – his disbelief (will be) on him,[49] but whoever does righteousness – they are smoothing (the way) for themselves, **45** so that He may repay from His favor those who believe and do righteous deeds. Surely He does not love the disbelievers.

46 (One) of His signs is that He sends the winds as bringers of good news, so that He may give you a taste of His mercy, and that the ship may run by His command, and that you may seek some of His favor,[50] and that you may be thankful. **47** Certainly We sent messengers to their people before you,[51] and they brought them the clear signs.[52] Then We took vengeance on those who sinned, but it was an obligation on Us (to) help the believers. **48** (It is) God who sends the winds, and it stirs up a cloud, and He spreads it in the sky as He pleases, and breaks it into fragments, and you see the rain coming forth from the midst of it. When He smites with it whomever He pleases of His servants, suddenly they welcome the good news, **49** though before (this), before it was sent down on them, they were in despair. **50** Observe the traces[53] of the mercy of God, how He gives the earth life after its death. Surely that One will indeed give the dead life. He is powerful over everything. **51** If indeed We send a wind, and they see it growing yellow,[54] they indeed remain disbelievers after that. **52** You[55] cannot make the dead to hear, nor can you make the deaf to hear the call when they turn away, withdrawing. **53** You cannot guide the blind out of their straying, nor can you make (anyone) hear, except for those who believe in Our signs, and so they submit.[56] **54** (It is) God who created you[57] from weakness, then after weakness He made strength, (and) then after strength He made weakness and grey hair. He creates whatever He pleases. He is the Knowing, the Powerful.

55 On the Day when the Hour strikes, the sinners will swear they remained (in the grave) only for an hour – that is how deluded they were[58] – **56** but those who have been given knowledge and belief will say (to them), 'You have remained in the Book of God[59] until the Day of Raising Up, and this is the Day of

---

44. *because of what the hands of the people have earned*: i.e. as a result of the sins they have committed.
45. *Say*: on this form of address, see n. on Q2.80.
46. *Travel the earth and see...*: see n. on Q30.9 above.
47. *Set your face...*: addressed to the Prophet, or perhaps intended generally.
48. *before a Day comes from God which cannot be turned back*: or 'before a Day comes on which (there will be) no turning back from God' (cf. Q42.47).
49. *on him*: i.e. to his own loss.

46–54 Signs of God's power and providence

50. *seek some of His favor*: i.e. seek to make a livelihood.
51. *you*: the Prophet.
52. *the clear signs*: or 'the clear proofs,' 'the indisputable evidence.'
53. *traces*: lit. 'footsteps' or 'tracks.'
54. *see it growing yellow*: i.e. the vegetation withering as a result of a hot, dry wind.
55. *You*: the Prophet.
56. *submit*: or 'become Muslims.'
57. *you*: plur.

55–57 A judgment scene

58. *that is how deluded they were*: or 'so perverted were they.'
59. *Book of God*: here referring to the 'Book of Destiny' by which everything is ordained (see n. on Q6.59).

Raising Up, but you did not know (it).' **57** On that Day their excuses will not benefit those who have done evil, nor will they be allowed to make amends.

58 Certainly We have struck for the people every (kind of) parable in this Qur'ān.[60] But if indeed you[61] bring them a sign,[62] those who disbelieve will indeed say, 'You[63] are nothing but perpetrators of falsehood.' **59** In this way God sets a seal on the hearts of those who do not know. **60** So be patient![64] Surely the promise of God is true. And (let) not those who are uncertain unsettle you.

58–60 The Prophet to remain steadfast

60. *this Qur'ān*: or perhaps 'this recitation,' since the expression (Ar. *hādhā al-qur'ān*) is sometimes used only in reference to a part of the Qur'ān (cf. Q6.19; 10.61; 13.31; 72.1; see n. on Q2.185). Otherwise, 'this Qur'ān' may come close to its present meaning as the name of the Muslim scripture (cf. Q9.111), and perhaps imply the existence of 'other Qur'āns' (cf. Q39.27-28).
61. *you*: the Prophet.
62. *sign*: or 'miracle.'
63. *You*: plur.
64. *be patient*: addressed to the Prophet.

31 Luqmān ❁ Luqmān

In the Name of God, the Merciful, the Compassionate

1 Alif Lām Mīm.[1] **2** Those are the signs[2] of the wise Book,[3] **3** a guidance[4] and mercy for the doers of good,
4 who observe the prayer and give the alms,[5] and they are certain of the Hereafter.[6] **5** Those (depend)
on guidance from their Lord, and those – they are the ones who prosper. **6** But among the people (there
is) one who buys a diverting tale[7] to lead (others) astray from the way of God without any knowledge,
and to take it in mockery.[8] Those – for them (there is) a humiliating punishment. **7** When Our signs[9] are
recited to him, he turns away arrogantly, as if he had not heard them, as if (there were) a heaviness in
his ears. So give him news of a painful punishment! **8** Surely those who believe and do righteous deeds –
for them (there are) Gardens of Bliss,[10] **9** there to remain. The promise of God in truth! He is the Mighty,
the Wise.

10 He created the heavens without any pillars you (can) see, and He cast on the earth firm mountains,
so that it does not sway with you (on it),[11] and He scattered[12] on it all (kinds of) creatures. And We
sent down water from the sky, and caused (things) of every excellent kind to grow in it. **11** This is the
creation of God. Show me what those (whom you worship) instead of Him have created. No! The
evildoers are clearly astray.[13]

Q31: This sūra takes its title from the story of Luqmān, a sage who presents his son with a succinct version of his wisdom (Q31.12-19). Among its diverse themes, it extols the signs of God's power and providence, and warns disbelievers of the certainty of judgment. Most scholars assign Q31 to the 'Meccan' period, though they recognize some verses as 'Medinan.'

1–9 The Book, a source of guidance and object of ridicule

1. *Alif Lām Mīm*: the names of Arabic letters ', *l*, and *m*. The same letter combination occurs in a block of sūras from Q29 to Q32, as well as at the beginning of Q2, Q3, and Q7 (which has an additional 'ṣād'). Twenty-nine sūras begin with letters like these, ranging from one to five. No satisfactory explanation has been given for their occurrence. The Cairo edition varies in counting these letters as a separate verse (as here), or as the beginning of the first verse.
2. *signs*: here referring to the letters ', *l*, and *m* (for the various meanings of 'signs,' see n. on Q2.39).
3. *the wise Book*: referring to the Qur'ān not only as a 'recited' but also 'written' scripture (see n. on Q2.2; cf. Q10.1; 36.2).
4. *guidance*: one of the most frequent terms (Ar. *hudā*) for revelation in general, and the Qur'ān in particular.
5. *observe the prayer and give the alms*: i.e. *ṣalāt*, the ritual prayer, and *zakāt*, a kind of tithe required for the benefit of the poor, as well as other purposes.
6. *the Hereafter*: see n. on Q2.4.
7. *a diverting tale*: Ar. *ḥadīth*; reference obscure (perhaps forged scripture?).
8. *take it in mockery*: referring to the Qur'ān.
9. *signs*: or 'verses.'
10. *Gardens of Bliss*: in heaven (for this imagery, see n. on Q2.25).

10–11 Signs of God's power and providence

11. *so that it does not sway...*: i.e. the earth would move if it were not held in place by mountains (cf. Q16.15; 21.31).
12. *scattered*: as a sower scatters seed.
13. *clearly astray*: lit. 'in clear straying.'

12 Certainly We gave Luqmān[14] wisdom: 'Be thankful to God. Whoever is thankful is thankful only for
himself, and whoever is ungrateful – surely God is wealthy,[15] praiseworthy.'

13 (Remember) when Luqmān said to his son, when he was admonishing him, 'My son! Do not associate
(anything) with God. Surely the association (of anything) with God is a great evil indeed.'

14 We have charged[16] the human concerning his parents – his mother bore him in weakness upon weakness, and his weaning took two years – 'Be thankful to Me and to your parents. To Me is the (final)
destination.' **15** But if they both struggle with you[17] – to make you associate with Me what you have no
knowledge of – do not obey them. Keep rightful company with them in this world, but follow the way of
the one who turns to Me (in repentance). Then to Me is your[18] return, and I shall inform you about what
you have done.'

16 'My son![19] Surely it – if it should be (only) the weight of a mustard seed, and it should be in a rock, or
in the heavens, or on the earth, God will bring it forth.[20] Surely God is astute, aware. **17** My son! Observe
the prayer, and command right and forbid wrong. Bear patiently whatever smites you – surely that is
one of the determining factors in (all) affairs. **18** Do not turn your cheek to the people,[21] and do not walk
on the earth in jubilation. Surely God does not love anyone who is arrogant (and) boastful. **19** Be modest
in your walking, and lower your voice. Surely the most hateful of voices is the voice of donkeys.'

20 Do you[22] not see that God has subjected to you whatever is in the heavens and whatever is on the
earth, and has lavished on you His blessings, both outwardly and inwardly? But among the people (there
is) one who disputes about God without any knowledge or guidance or illuminating Book. **21** When it is
said to them, 'Follow what God has sent down,' they say, 'No! We will follow what we found our fathers
doing.' Even if Satan[23] were calling them to the punishment of the blazing (Fire)? **22** Whoever submits
his face to God, being a doer of good, has grasped the firmest handle. To God (belongs) the outcome of
all affairs. **23** Whoever disbelieves – do not let his disbelief cause you[24] sorrow. To Us is their return, and
We shall inform them about what they have done. Surely God knows what is in the hearts.[25] **24** We give
them enjoyment (of life) for a little (while), then We force them to a stern punishment. **25** If indeed you
ask them, 'Who created the heavens and the earth?,' they will indeed say, 'God.'[26] Say:[27] 'Praise (be)[28] to
God!' But most of them do not know (it). **26** To God (belongs) whatever is in the heavens and the earth.

12–19 Luqmān's advice to his son

14. *Luqmān*: said to be a sage of Arabian legend, but mentioned only here in the Qur'ān. Later tradition credited him with a collection of proverbs and fables similar to those associated with Aesop.
15. *wealthy*: i.e. God has no need of anyone or anything (cf. Q27.40).
16. *We have charged...*: the following two verses interrupt the story of Luqmān, and look like a later addition.
17. *you*: sing., but intended generally.
18. *your*: plur.
19. *My son*: Luqmān's discourse to his son now resumes.
20. *God will bring it forth*: i.e. every deed will be brought to light, no matter how insignificant (cf. Q21.47).
21. *Do not turn your cheek to the people*: i.e. 'Do not be disdainful of people.'

20–26 Disbelievers ungrateful and stubborn

22. *you*: plur.
23. *Satan*: for this figure, see n. on Q2.36.
24. *you*: the Prophet.
25. *hearts*: lit. 'chests,' considered the seat of knowledge and understanding.
26. *'God'*: their answer makes explicit their belief in God as the supreme deity (cf. Q10.31; 29.61, 63; 39.38; 43.87).
27. *Say*: on this form of address, see n. on Q2.80.
28. *(be)*: or '(belongs).'

Surely God – He is the wealthy One, the Praiseworthy.

27 Even if all the trees on the earth were pens, and the sea (were ink)[29] – (and) extending it (were) seven seas after it – the words of God would (still) not give out. God is mighty, wise.

28 Your creation and your raising up are only as (that of) a single person. God is hearing, seeing.

29 Do you[30] not see that God causes the night to pass into the day, and causes the day to pass into the night, and has subjected the sun and the moon, each one running (its course) for an appointed time,[31] and that God is aware of what you do? **30** That is because God – He is the Truth, and what they call on instead of Him – that is the falsehood, and because God is the Most High, the Great. **31** Do you not see that the ship runs on the sea by the blessing of God, so that He may show you some of His signs? Surely in that are signs indeed for every patient (and) thankful one. **32** And when wave(s) cover them like shadows, they call on God, devoting (their) religion to Him.[32] But when He has brought them safely to the shore, some of them become lax.[33] No one denies Our signs except every traitor (and) ungrateful one.[34]

33 People! Guard (yourselves) against your Lord, and fear a Day when no father will offer any compensation for his son, and no son will offer any compensation for his father.[35] Surely the promise of God is true, so do not let this present life deceive you, and do not let the Deceiver[36] deceive you about God.
34 Surely God – with Him is the knowledge of the Hour.[37] He sends down the rain, and He knows what is in the wombs, but no person knows what he will earn tomorrow, and no person knows in what (place on) earth he will die. Surely God is knowing, aware.

---

27 Oceans of revelation

29. *and the sea (were ink)*: the words 'were ink' must have fallen out, but can be restored on the basis of the parallel passage at Q18.109. Both clearly imply that the revelation is being written down (cf. Q68.1; 96.4-5). The Cairo edition, reflecting the views of traditional scholars, attributes this and the two following verses (Q31.27-29) to the 'Medinan' period.

28 Creation and resurrection inseparable

29–32 Signs of God's power and providence

30. *you*: sing., but intended generally.
31. *an appointed time*: or 'term' (Ar. *ajal*), which is predetermined and cannot be changed.
32. *devoting (their) religion to Him*: i.e. they regard God as the sole object of prayer at such a moment of danger.
33. *become lax*: the meaning is disputed, but it must imply some kind of falling away (cf. the parallel passage at Q29.65, '...suddenly they associate').
34. *ungrateful one*: Ar. *kafūr*, punning on *kāfir*, 'disbeliever.'

33–34 Judgment certain

35. *no father will offer any compensation...*: judgment falls on individuals, whom neither family nor friends can help (an implicit rejection of the Christian doctrine of 'vicarious atonement' and 'intercession' by the saints); cf. Q2.48, 123.
36. *the Deceiver*: Satan (Q4.120; 17.64).
37. *the Hour*: of judgment.

32 The Prostration ✿ Al-Sajda

In the Name of God, the Merciful, the Compassionate

1 Alif Lām Mīm.[1] **2** The sending down of the Book[2] – (there is) no doubt about it[3] – (is) from the Lord of the worlds.[4] **3** Or do they say, 'He has forged it'? No! It is the truth from your Lord, so that you may warn a people to whom no warner has come before you,[5] so that they may be (rightly) guided.

4 (It is) God who created the heavens and the earth, and whatever is between them, in six days.[6] Then He mounted the throne. You have no ally and no intercessor other than Him. Will you not take heed?[7] **5** He directs the (whole) affair[8] from the sky to the earth; then it will go up to Him in a day, the measure of which is a thousand years of what you count.[9] **6** That One is the Knower of the unseen and the seen,[10] the Mighty, the Compassionate, **7** who made well everything He created. He brought about the creation of the human from clay,[11] **8** then He made his progeny from an extract of despicable water,[12] **9** then

---

Q32: This sūra opens with a pronouncement about the truth of the Qur'ān. It then extols God's power as creator and defends the resurrection against the objection of disbelievers, whose fate is contrasted with the ultimate vindication of believers. With the exception of a few verses, most scholars assign Q32 to the 'Meccan' period. It takes its title from the 'prostration' of believers in worship (Q32.15).

1–3 The Book and the warner

1. *Alif Lām Mīm*: the names of Arabic letters ', *l*, and *m*. The same letter combination occurs in a block of sūras from Q29 to Q32, as well as at the beginning of Q2, Q3, and Q7 (which has an additional 'ṣād'). Twenty-nine sūras begin with letters like these, ranging from one to five. No satisfactory explanation has been given for their occurrence. The Cairo edition varies in counting these letters as a separate verse (as here), or as the beginning of the first verse.
2. *The sending down of the Book*: here referring to the Qur'ān not only as a 'recited' but also 'written' scripture (see n. on Q2.2; cf. the similar openings at Q39.1; 40.2; 41.2; 45.2; 46.2).
3. *no doubt about it*: or 'no doubt in it' (cf. Q2.2; 10.37).
4. *Lord of the worlds*: for this title, see n. on Q1.2.
5. *a people to whom no warner has come before you*: this implies that the Prophet's contemporaries were thought to be a different 'people' than those of Abraham's time (cf. Q28.46; 34.44; 36.6); for the role of 'warner,' see n. on Q2.119.

4–9 God's power as creator

6. *in six days*: cf. Q7.54; 10.3; 11.7; 25.59; 41.9-12; 50.38; and Genesis 1.1-31.
7. *take heed*: or 'be reminded,' 'remember.'
8. *directs the (whole) affair*: or 'directs the command' (Ar. *amr*); the idea may be that God controls the universe from his throne through his *amr*, which may correspond to the rabbinic notion of the 'divine word' (Aram. *mēmrā*), or to the related Christian idea of the *logos* as the manifestation of God's word, or as God's messenger in place of God himself (see e.g. Q10.3, 31; 13.2; 16.2; 65.12).
9. *...a thousand years of what you count*: everything will return to God, but his reckoning of time is not the same as that of humans (see Q22.47; 70.4; cf. Psalm 90.4, 'for a thousand years in your sight are like a day;' and 2 Peter 3.8, '...with the Lord one day is like a thousand years....').
10. *the seen*: lit. 'the witnessed.'
11. *from clay*: see Q6.2; 7.12; 15.26; 17.61; 23.12; 38.71, 76; 55.14; 'from dust,' according to Q3.59; 18.37; 22.5; 30.20; 35.11; 40.67; 'from water,' according to Q21.30; 24.45; 25.54.
12. *despicable water*: semen (cf. Q77.20).

He fashioned him and breathed into him some of His spirit,[13] and made for you hearing and sight and hearts.[14] Little thanks you show!

10 They say, 'When we have gotten lost[15] in the earth, shall we indeed (return) in a new creation?' Yes! But they are disbelievers in the meeting with their Lord. **11** Say:[16] 'The angel of death,[17] who is put in charge of you, will take you, (and) then you will be returned to your Lord.' **12** If (only) you[18] (could) see when the sinners are hanging their heads before their Lord: 'Our Lord, (now) we have seen and heard, so let us return (and) we shall do righteousness. Surely (now) we are certain.' **13** 'If We had (so) pleased, We would indeed have given every person his guidance. But My word has proved true: "I shall indeed fill Gehenna[19] with jinn[20] and people – all (of them)!"[21] **14** So taste (the punishment) because you have forgotten the meeting of this Day of yours. Surely We have forgotten you! Taste the punishment of eternity for what you have done!'

15 Only those believe in Our signs who, when they are reminded of them, fall down in prostration and glorify their Lord with praise. They are not arrogant. **16** They forsake their beds[22] (during the night) to call on their Lord in fear and eagerness, and they contribute[23] from what We have provided them. **17** No one knows what comfort[24] is hidden (away) for them in payment for what they have done. **18** So is the one who believes like the one who is wicked? They are not equal! **19** As for those who believe and do righteous deeds, for them (there are) Gardens of the Refuge,[25] as a reception for what they have done. **20** But as for those who act wickedly, their refuge is the Fire.[26] Whenever they want to come out of it, they will be sent back into it, and it will be said to them: 'Taste the punishment of the Fire which you called a lie!' **21** And We shall indeed make them taste the nearer punishment,[27] before the greater punishment, so that they may return. **22** Who is more evil than the one who is reminded of[28] the signs of his Lord, (and) then turns away from them? Surely We are going to take vengeance on the sinners.

23 Certainly We gave Moses the Book – so do not be in doubt of meeting Him[29] – and We made it a

---

13. *breathed into him some of His spirit*: this probably refers to Adam in particular (cf. Q15.29; 38.72).
14. *hearts*: here, as often, the heart is spoken of as synonymous with mind or understanding.

10–14 Disbelievers reject the resurrection

15. *gotten lost*: lit. 'gone astray' (a pun).
16. *Say*: on this form of address, see n. on Q2.80.
17. *angel of death*: see n. on Q6.61 (for the various roles of angels, see n. on Q2.30).
18. *you*: the Prophet, or perhaps intended generally ('one').
19. *Gehenna*: a name for Hell (see n. on Q2.206).
20. *jinn*: for these beings, see n. on Q6.100.
21. *...all (of them)*: for the declaration of this 'word,' see Q7.18; 11.119; 38.85.

15–22 Rewards and punishments

22. *They forsake their beds*: lit. 'Their sides withdraw from (their) beds,' i.e. for the night-prayer. The Cairo edition, reflecting the views of traditional scholars, attributes the following five verses (Q32.16-20) to the 'Medinan' period.
23. *contribute*: lit. 'spend.'
24. *comfort*: lit. 'cooling of the eyes;' for this idea, cf. 1 Corinthians 2.9 (drawing on Isaiah 64.4).
25. *Gardens of the Refuge*: in heaven (for this imagery, see n. on Q2.25; cf. Q53.15).
26. *the Fire*: Ar. *al-nār* is the most common of the various designations for Hell.
27. *the nearer punishment*: i.e. punishment in this world (cf. Q52.47).
28. *of*: or 'by.'

23–25 The Book of Moses and the Sons of Israel

29. *so do not be in doubt of meeting Him*: addressed to the Prophet(?), but it seems out of place here (cf. Q6.154).

guidance for the Sons of Israel. **24** And We appointed[30] from among them leaders[31] (who) guide (others) by Our command, when they were patient and were certain of Our signs. **25** Surely your Lord – He will distinguish between them on the Day of Resurrection concerning their differences.

26 Is it not a guide for them how many generations We have destroyed before them, (seeing that) they walk in (the midst of) their dwelling places?[32] Surely in that are signs indeed. Will they not hear? **27** Do they not see that We drive water to the barren earth, and bring forth crops by means of it, from which their livestock and they themselves eat? Will they not see? **28** They say, 'When will the victory[33] take place, if you are truthful?' **29** Say: 'On the Day of Victory,[34] their belief will not benefit those who disbelieve, nor will they be spared.' **30** So turn away from them, and wait. Surely they (too) are waiting.

30. *appointed*: lit. 'made.'

31. *leaders*: or 'models,' a term later used for the leader (Ar. *imām*) of a religious community (cf. Q21.73; 28.5).

26–30 Vindication of believers

32. *they walk in (the midst of) their dwelling places*: this implies that the different peoples of the 'punishment stories' were thought to inhabit successively the same geographical region (cf. Q14.14, 45; 20.128; 21.11).

33. *victory*: lit. 'opening.'

34. *Day of Victory*: elsewhere it seems to refer to a historical event (see Q8.19, the victory at Badr [?]; 48.1, 110.1, the conquest of Mecca [?]), but here it seems to refer to imminent Judgment.

33 The Factions ✿ Al-Aḥzāb

In the Name of God, the Merciful, the Compassionate

1 Prophet![1] Guard (yourself) against God, and do not obey the disbelievers and the hypocrites. Surely God is knowing, wise. **2** Follow what you are inspired (with) from your Lord. Surely God is aware of what you do. **3** Put your trust in God, (for) God is sufficient as a guardian.

4 God has not placed two hearts inside anyone.[2] He has not made your wives whom you declare to be as your mothers' backs[3] your (real) mothers, nor has He made your adopted sons your (real) sons. That is what you say with your mouths, but God speaks the truth and guides (you) to the (right) way. **5** Call them by (the names of) their (real) fathers: that is more just in the sight of God. If you do not know their (real) fathers, (regard them) as your brothers in religion, and your clients. There is no blame on you in any mistakes you have made, but only in what your hearts have intended. God is forgiving, compassionate.

6 The prophet is closer to the believers than they are to themselves,[4] and his wives are their mothers, but those related by blood[5] are closer to one another in the Book of God[6] than the believers and the emigrants – but you should do right by your allies.[7] That is written in the Book.

7 (Remember) when We took a covenant with the prophets[8] – and from you,[9] and from Noah, and Abraham, and Moses, and Jesus, son of Mary[10] – We took a firm covenant with them, **8** so that He might question the truthful about their truthfulness. He has prepared a painful punishment for the disbelievers.

9 You who believe! Remember the blessing of God on you, when the forces came upon you, and We sent

---

Q33: Most scholars assign this sūra to the 'Medinan' period, based on an event to which it is said to refer: the siege of Medina (627 CE/5 AH) by 'factions' of Meccans and allied tribes (Q33.9-27). This assault is also referred to as the 'Day of the Trench,' from the strategy the Prophet is said to have adopted to defend the city. The rest of Q33 deals with the Prophet's marriage to a woman formerly married to his adopted son, as well as with other matters concerning his wives.

1–3 The Prophet to remain steadfast

1. *Prophet*: for this important title, see n. on Q2.87.

4–6 Kinship reckoned according to nature

2. *two hearts inside anyone*: i.e. the same person cannot be two different people. The point relates to the redefinition of relationships which follows. (Here, as often, the heart is spoken of as synonymous with mind.)
3. *declare to be as your mothers' backs*: said to be a pre-Islamic (or 'pagan') formula for ending a marriage. It was not a divorce in the modern sense, since the woman continued to live where she was, but she was forbidden to marry anyone else (cf. Q58.1-4).
4. *than they are to themselves*: i.e. he is closer than they are to one another.
5. *those related by blood*: lit. 'those of the (same) wombs.'
6. *Book of God*: probably refers to the heavenly 'Record' of all things (cf. Q8.75; see n. on Q6.59), as does the reference to the following 'Book' (cf. Q17.58).
7. *allies*: Ar. *awliyā'* implies the obligation of mutual protection, almost in the sense of 'friends' or 'brothers.'

7–8 The covenant of the prophets

8. *covenant with the prophets*: see Q3.81, where the terms of the covenant are specified.
9. *from you*: the Prophet (this may be a later addition to the list).
10. *son of Mary*: there is no mention in the Qur'ān of Joseph, Jesus' putative father (cf. Mark 6.3).

9–27 The siege of Yathrib

against them a wind, and (also) forces which you did not see.[11] God sees what you do. **10** When they came upon you from above you and from below you, and when (your) sight turned aside and (your) hearts reached (your) throats, and you were thinking about God (all kinds of) thoughts, **11** there and then the believers were tested and severely shaken. **12** And when the hypocrites, and those in whose hearts is a sickness, said, 'God and His messenger have promised us nothing but deception.' **13** And when a group of them said, 'People of Yathrib![12] (There is) no dwelling place for you (here), so return!' And (another) contingent of them was asking permission of the prophet, saying, 'Surely our houses are vulnerable' – yet they were not vulnerable, they only wished to flee. **14** If an entrance had been made against them from that side,[13] (and) then they had been asked (to join in) the troublemaking,[14] they would indeed have done it, and scarcely have hesitated with it. **15** Certainly they had made a covenant with God before (this), that they would not turn their backs, and a covenant with God is (something) to be responsible for.[15] **16** Say:[16] 'Flight will not benefit you. If you flee from death or killing, you will only enjoy (life) a little (while).' **17** Say: 'Who is the one who will protect you against God, if He intends evil for you, or intends mercy for you?' They will not find for themselves any ally or helper other than God.

18 God knows those of you who are a hindrance, and those who say to their brothers, 'Come to us,' but who seldom come out to the battle, **19** (in their) greed toward you.[17] When fear comes (upon them), you[18] see them looking at you, their eyes rolling around like one who faints at the point of death. But when fear departs, they sting you[19] with (their) sharp tongues (in their) greed for the good (that has come to you).[20] Those – they have not believed. God has made their deeds worthless. That is easy for God. **20** They think (that) the factions have not gone away. If the factions come (again), they will wish that they were living in the desert[21] among the Arabs, asking for news of you. Yet (even) if they were among you, they would seldom fight. **21** Certainly the messenger of God has been a good example for you – for the one who hopes in God and the Last Day, and remembers God often.

22 When the believers saw the factions, they said, 'This is what God and His messenger promised us, and God and His messenger were truthful.' It only increased them in belief and submission. **23** Among the believers are men who have been truthful to the covenant which they made with God: some of them have fulfilled their vow,[22] and some of them are (still) waiting (to do so). They have not changed in the least, **24** so that God may repay the truthful for their truthfulness, and punish the hypocrites, if He (so) pleases, or turn to them (in forgiveness). Surely God is forgiving, compassionate. **25** God turned back those who disbelieved[23] in their rage, and they did not attain any advantage. God was sufficient for the believers in the fighting. Surely God is strong, mighty. **26** He brought down from their fortifications

11. *forces which you did not see*: angels.
12. *Yathrib*: the name occurs only here in the Qur'ān; tradition identifies it with 'Medina' or the 'City of the Prophet' (Ar. *Madīnat al-Nabī*). Whether this refers to the city of 'Medina' in present-day Saudi Arabia is disputed by some modern scholars.
13. *from that side*: presumably the side on which their houses stood.
14. *troublemaking*: or 'mischief' (Ar. *fitna*).
15. *responsible for*: lit. 'asked about' (cf. Q17.34).
16. *Say*: on this form of address, see n. on Q2.80.
17. *you*: plur.
18. *you*: the Prophet.
19. *you*: plur.
20. *greed for the good (that has come to you)*: perhaps a reference to spoils.
21. *in the desert*: i.e. in the safety of the desert.
22. *fulfilled their vow*: by dying in battle.
23. *turned back those who disbelieved*: said to refer to the Meccans who laid siege to Medina.

those of the People of the Book who supported them,[24] and cast dread into their hearts. You[25] killed a group (of them), and took captive (another) group. **27** And He caused you to inherit their land,[26] their homes, and their wealth, and a land you had not set foot on.[27] God is powerful over everything.

28 Prophet! Say to your wives: 'If you desire this present life and its (passing) splendor, come! I shall make provision for you, and release you gracefully. **29** But if you desire God and His messenger, and the Home of the Hereafter – surely God has prepared a great reward for the doers of good among you.'
30 Wives of the prophet! Whoever among you commits clear immorality,[28] for her the punishment will be doubled. That is easy for God. **31** But whoever among you is obedient to God and His messenger, and does righteousness – We shall give her her reward twice over. We have prepared a generous provision for her. **32** Wives of the prophet! You are not like any of the (other) women. If you guard (yourselves),[29] do not be beguiling in (your) speech, or he in whose heart is a sickness will become lustful, but speak in a rightful fashion. **33** Stay in your houses, and do not flaunt (yourselves) with the flaunting of the former ignorance,[30] but observe the prayer and give the alms,[31] and obey God and His messenger. God only wishes to take away the abomination[32] from you, People of the House,[33] and to purify you completely. **34** Remember[34] what is recited in your houses of the signs[35] of God and the wisdom. Surely God is astute, aware.

35 Surely the submitting men and the submitting women,[36] the believing men and the believing women, the obedient men and the obedient women, the truthful men and the truthful women, the patient men and the patient women, the humble men and the humble women, the charitable men and the charitable women,[37] the fasting men and the fasting women, the men who guard their private parts and the women who guard (them), the men who remember God often and the women who remember (Him) – for them God has prepared forgiveness and a great reward.

36 It is not for a believing man or a believing woman, when God and His messenger have decided a matter, to have the choice in their matter. Whoever disobeys God and His messenger has very clearly gone astray.[38]

---

24. *People of the Book who supported them*: said to refer to a Jewish tribe (the Banū Qurayẓa) which colluded with the enemy during the siege, and afterwards were besieged by the Muslims until they surrendered.
25. *You*: plur.
26. *land*: lit. 'earth.'
27. *a land you had not set foot on*: reference obscure.

28–34 Wives of the Prophet

28. *immorality*: or 'indecency' (Ar. *fāḥisha*), of a sexual nature.
29. *guard (yourselves)*: against evil, or God.
30. *the former ignorance*: i.e. the pre-Islamic period of ignorance about God (Ar. *al-jāhiliyya al-ūlā*).
31. *observe the prayer and give the alms*: i.e. *ṣalāt*, the ritual prayer, and *zakāt*, a kind of tithe required for the benefit of the poor, as well as other purposes.
32. *the abomination*: of 'paganism'(?).
33. *People of the House*: referring to the household of the Prophet, or perhaps to the Muslim community as the 'People of the Ka'ba,' God's 'House' (cf. Q11.73).
34. *Remember*: or 'Take heed of.'
35. *signs*: here 'verses' (see n. on Q2.39).

35 Believers have their reward

36. *submitting men...women*: or 'Muslim men...women.'
37. *charitable men...women*: those who make 'voluntary contributions' or 'freewill offerings' (Ar. *al-ṣadaqāt*) for the benefit of the community.

36 Obey God and the Messenger

38. *has very clearly gone astray*: lit. 'has gone astray (with) a clear straying.'

37 (Remember) when you[39] said to the one whom God had blessed,[40] and whom you had blessed: 'Keep your wife to yourself, and guard (yourself) against God,' and you hid within yourself what God was going to reveal,[41] and feared the people, when God had a better right that you feared Him. So when Zayd had gotten what he needed from her,[42] We married her to you, so that there should not be any blame on the believers concerning the wives of their adopted sons, when they have gotten what they needed from them. The command of God was (to be) fulfilled. **38** There is no blame on the prophet concerning what God has made obligatory for him. (That was) the customary way of God concerning those who passed away before – and the command of God is a determined decree – **39** who were delivering the messages of God, and fearing Him, and not fearing anyone but Him. God is sufficient as a reckoner.

40 Muḥammad[43] is not the father of any of your men,[44] but the messenger of God and the seal of the prophets.[45] God has knowledge of everything.

41 You who believe! Remember God often, **42** and glorify Him morning and evening. **43** He (it is) who prays over you, and His angels (do too),[46] to bring you out of the darkness to the light. He is compassionate with the believers. **44** On the Day when they meet Him, their greeting will be: 'Peace!'[47] He has prepared a generous reward for them.

45 Prophet! Surely We have sent you as a witness, and as a bringer of good news and a warner,[48]
46 and as one calling to God, by His permission, and as an illuminating lamp. **47** Give good news to the believers that they have great favor[49] from God. **48** Do not obey the disbelievers and the hypocrites. Ignore their hurt but put your trust in God. God is sufficient as a guardian.

49 You who believe! When you marry believing women (and) then divorce them before you touch them, you have no waiting period[50] to count for them. So make provision for them, and release them gracefully.

50 Prophet! Surely We have made lawful for you your wives to whom you have granted their marriage gifts,[51] and what your right (hand) owns from what God has given you,[52] and the daughters of your

---

37–39 The Prophet's marriage

39. *you*: the Prophet.
40. *the one whom God had blessed*: said to be the Prophet's adopted son, Zayd ibn-Ḥāritha.
41. *what God was going to reveal*: said to refer to the Prophet's love for Zayd's wife (Zaynab), or thought of marrying her.
42. *had gotten what he needed from her*: or 'had completed the necessary (steps for divorce).'

40 Muḥammad the seal of the prophets

43. *Muḥammad*: for this name, see n. on Q3.144.
44. *not the father of any...*: Zayd may have been called his son, but Q33.4 (above) established that adoption did not create a blood-relationship. Hence the Prophet's marriage was legal.
45. *seal of the prophets*: traditionally interpreted as the 'last of the prophets' or 'the final prophet,' but it may have eschatological significance. For Paul's 'seal of apostleship,' see 1 Corinthians 9.2.

41–48 Encouragement to the believers and the Prophet

46. *and His angels (do too)*: the angels join with God in praying for the believers (cf. Q33.56 below; 40.7; for these beings and their various roles, see n. on Q2.30).
47. *Peace*: Ar. *salām* connotes 'submission' (*islām*) to God.
48. *bringer of good news...warner*: for these roles, see n. on Q2.119; cf. Q48.8.
49. *great favor*: or 'superior merit.'

49 Divorce before a marriage is consummated

50. *no waiting period*: i.e. no *'idda*, as required for women whose marriages had been consummated (see Q2.226-228).

50–52 The Prophet's special marriage privileges

51. *their marriage gifts*: lit. 'their rewards,' probably referring to the payment of a 'dower' for support in the event a wife should survive her husband's death (see Q4.24-25).
52. *what your right (hand) owns...*: i.e. slave women taken as spoils.

paternal uncles and paternal aunts, your maternal uncles and maternal aunts, who have emigrated with you, and any believing woman, if she gives herself to the prophet, and if the prophet wishes to take her in marriage. (That is) exclusively for you, apart from the believers – We know what We have made obligatory for them concerning their wives and what their right (hands) own – so that there may be no blame on you. God is forgiving, compassionate.
51 You may put off whomever you please of them, and you may take to yourself whomever you please.[53] And whomever you desire of those you have set aside, (there is) no blame on you (if you take her again). That is more appropriate, so that they may be comforted[54] and not sorrow, and (that) they may be pleased with what you give them – all of them. God knows what is in your hearts. God is knowing, forbearing.
52 Beyond (that) women are not permitted to you, nor (is it permitted to you) to take (other) wives in exchange for them, even though their beauty pleases you, except for what your right (hand) owns. God is watching over everything.

53 You who believe! Do not enter the houses of the prophet[55] to (attend) a meal without waiting (until it) is ready, unless permission is given to you. But when you are invited, enter, and when you have eaten, disperse, and do not linger for conversation. Surely that is hurtful to the prophet, and he is ashamed[56] of you, but God is not ashamed of the truth. When you ask them for anything,[57] ask them from behind a veil.[58] That is purer for your hearts and their hearts. It is not for you to hurt the messenger of God, nor to marry his wives after him – ever. Surely that is a great (offense) in the sight of God.
54 Whether you reveal a thing or hide it, surely God has knowledge of everything.

55 (There is) no blame on them[59] concerning their fathers,[60] or their sons, or their brothers, or their brothers' sons, or their sisters' sons, or their women, or what their right (hands) own. But guard (yourselves) against God. Surely God is a witness over everything.

56 Surely God and His angels pray for the prophet. You who believe! You pray for him (too), and greet him (with a worthy) greeting.
57 Surely those who hurt God and His messenger – God has cursed them in this world and the Hereafter, and has prepared a humiliating punishment for them.
58 Those who hurt believing men and believing women – other than what they have earned – they will indeed bear (the burden of) slander and clear sin.

59 Prophet! Say to your wives, and your daughters, and the believing women, to draw some of their outer clothes over themselves. That is more appropriate for their being recognized and not hurt. God is forgiving, compassionate.

60 If indeed the hypocrites do not stop – and those in whose hearts is a sickness, and those who cause

---

53. *put off...take to yourself whomever you please*: i.e. he was free to make conjugal rounds as he pleased.
54. *that they may be comforted*: lit. 'that their eyes may be cooled.'

53–54 Respect due to the Prophet and his wives

55. *houses of the prophet*: reference obscure; it is said that each of the Prophet's wives had her own house or 'private room' (cf. Q49.4).
56. *ashamed*: lit. 'shy.'
57. *When you ask them for anything*: i.e. when believers ask the Prophet's wives for anything.
58. *veil*: i.e. a 'curtain' or 'screen' (Ar. *ḥijāb*), for reasons of etiquette.

55 Relatives of the Prophet's wives excepted

59. *them*: the Prophet's wives.
60. *concerning their fathers...*: i.e. in receiving visits from members of their households.

56–58 Respect due to the Prophet

59 Precaution for women against being insulted

60–62 Punishment for hypocrites

commotion in the city[61] – We shall indeed incite you[62] against them, (and) then they will not be your neighbors there, except for a little (while). **61** (They will be) accursed! Wherever they are found, they will be seized and completely killed. **62** (That was) the customary way of God concerning those who have passed away before, and you will find no change in the customary way of God.[63]

63 The people ask you about the Hour.[64] Say: 'Knowledge of it is only with God.[65] What will make you[66] know? Perhaps the Hour is near.' **64** Surely God has cursed the disbelievers, and prepared for them a blazing (Fire), **65** there to remain forever. They will not find any ally or helper. **66** On the Day when their faces will be turned about in the Fire,[67] they will say, 'Oh, would that we had obeyed God, and obeyed the messenger!' **67** And they will say, 'Our Lord, surely we obeyed our men of honor and our great men, and so they led us astray from the way. **68** Our Lord, give them a double (share) of the punishment, and curse them with a great curse!'

69 You who believe! Do not be like those who hurt Moses,[68] but God cleared him of what they said, and he was eminent in the sight of God.[69] **70** You who believe! Guard (yourselves) against God, and speak a direct word. **71** He will set right your deeds for you, and forgive you your sins. Whoever obeys God and His messenger has attained a great triumph.

72 Surely We offered the trust[70] to the heavens and the earth, and the mountains, but they refused to bear it, and were afraid of it, and (instead) the human bore it. Surely he has become an evildoer (and) ignorant. **73** (It is) so that God might punish the hypocrite men and the hypocrite women (alike), and the idolatrous men and the idolatrous women alike,[71] and so that God might turn (in forgiveness) to the believing men and the believing women (alike). God is forgiving, compassionate.

---

61. *the city*: said to be 'Medina' (see n. on Q9.101).
62. *you*: the Prophet.
63. *the customary way of God*: lit. 'the *sunna* of God' (for this idea, cf. Q48.23; and see n. on Q8.38).

63–68 Punishment for disbelievers

64. *the Hour*: of judgment.
65. *Knowledge of it is only with God*: cf. Q7.187; 41.47; 43.85; 46.23; 67.26; and Mark 13.32 par.
66. *you*: sing., but intended generally.
67. *the Fire*: Ar. *al-nār* is the most common of the various designations for Hell.

69–71 Believers must not insult the Prophet

68. *those who hurt Moses*: lit. 'harmed Moses;' alluding to the complaint of Miriam and Aaron against Moses at Numbers 12.1-15 (cf. Q61.5).
69. *eminent in the sight of God*: cf. Q3.45 (of Jesus).

72–73 Humans are bearers of 'the trust'

70. *We offered the trust*: said to refer to moral responsibility, but the reference is obscure (cf. Q59.21).
71. *idolatrous men...women*: lit. men and women who 'associate (other gods with God).'

34 Sheba ۞ Sabā’

In the Name of God, the Merciful, the Compassionate

1 Praise (be)[1] to God – to Him (belongs) whatever is in the heavens and whatever is on the earth – and to Him (be)[2] praise in the Hereafter![3] He is the Wise, the Aware. **2** He knows what penetrates into the earth and what comes forth from it, and what comes down from the sky and what goes up into it. He is the Compassionate, the Forgiving.

3 Those who disbelieve say, 'The Hour[4] will not come upon us.' Say:[5] 'Yes indeed! By my Lord! It will indeed come to you! (He is the) Knower of the unseen.[6] Not (even) the weight of a speck in the heavens and the earth escapes from Him, nor (is there anything) smaller than that or greater, except (that it is recorded) in a clear Book[7] **4** – so that He may repay those who believe and do righteous deeds.' Those – for them (there is) forgiveness and generous provision. **5** But those who strive against Our signs[8] to obstruct (them), those – for them (there is) a punishment of painful wrath. **6** But those who have been given the knowledge see (that) what has been sent down to you[9] from your Lord is the truth, and (that) it guides to the path of the Mighty, the Praiseworthy.

7 Those who disbelieve say, 'Shall we direct you to a man who will inform you (that) when you have been completely torn to pieces, you will indeed (return) in a new creation? **8** Has he forged a lie against God, or is he possessed?'[10] No! Those who do not believe in the Hereafter are in punishment and far astray.
9 Do they not look to what is before them and what is behind them of the sky and the earth? If We (so) please, We could cause the earth to swallow them, or make fragments of the sky fall on them. Surely in that is a sign indeed for every servant who turns (in repentance).[11]

10 Certainly We gave David favor from Us: 'You mountains! Return (praises) with him, and you birds

---

Q34: The main subject of this sūra is the certainty of judgment and resurrection. It receives its title from the story of the people of Sheba (Q34.15-21). Most scholars assign Q34 to the 'Meccan' period.

1–2 Praise to God

1. *(be)*: or '(belongs).'
2. *(be)*: or '(belongs).'
3. *the Hereafter*: see n. on Q2.4.

3–6 Disbelievers doubt the Judgment

4. *The Hour*: of judgment.
5. *Say*: on this form of address, see n. on Q2.80.
6. *the unseen*: or 'the future' (see n. on Q2.3).
7. *a clear Book*: i.e. the 'Book of God' or the heavenly 'Record' of all things (see n. on Q6.59).
8. *signs*: or 'verses' (see n. on Q2.39).
9. *you*: the Prophet; the Cairo edition, reflecting the views of some traditional scholars, assigns this verse to the 'Medinan' period.

7–9 Disbelievers reject the resurrection

10. *possessed*: by the jinn (lit. '[are there] jinn in him?' [Ar. *bi-hi jinna*]); cf. Q34.46 below; and see n. on Q7.184.
11. *for every servant who turns (in repentance)*: the word 'servant' (Ar. *'abd*), which also means 'slave,' is used here in the sense of 'every person' (cf. Q50.8).

10–14 David and Solomon

(too)!'[12] And We made iron malleable for him: **11** 'Make full (coats of armor), and measure (well) in the sewing (of them).' And: 'Do righteousness,[13] (for) surely I see what you do.' **12** And to Solomon (We subjected) the wind, its morning was a month's (journey), and its evening was a month's (journey), and We made a spring of molten brass to flow for him. And among the jinn, (there were) those who worked for him[14] by the permission of his Lord. Whoever of them turns aside from Our command – We shall make him taste the punishment of the blazing (Fire). **13** They made for him whatever he pleased: places of prayer,[15] and statues, and basins like cisterns, and fixed cooking pots. 'House of David! Work in thankfulness, (for) few of My servants are thankful!' **14** And when We decreed death for him, nothing indicated his death to them except a creature of the earth devouring his staff.[16] When he fell down, it became clear to the jinn that, if they had known the unseen, they would not have remained in the humiliating punishment.[17]

15 Certainly for Sheba[18] there was a sign in their dwelling place – two gardens, on the right and left: 'Eat from the provision of your Lord, and be thankful to Him. A good land and a forgiving Lord.' **16** But they turned away, so We sent on them the flood of 'Arim,[19] and We replaced for them their two gardens (with) two gardens producing bitter fruit, and tamarisks, and a few lote trees. **17** We repaid them that because they disbelieved. We do not repay (anyone) but the ungrateful?[20] **18** We set between them and the towns which We have blessed[21] (other) towns (which are still) visible, and We measured out the traveling (distance) between them: 'Travel among them by night and day in security!' **19** But they said, 'Our Lord, lengthen (the distance) between our journeys.'[22] They did themselves evil, so We made them legendary,[23] and We tore them completely to pieces. Surely in that are signs indeed for every patient (and) thankful one. **20** Certainly Iblīs confirmed his conjecture about them,[24] and they followed him, except for a group of the believers. **21** But he had no authority over them, except that We might know the one who believed in the Hereafter from the one who was in doubt about it. Your Lord is a watcher over everything.

---

12. *You mountains...you birds (too)*: i.e. the mountains and birds were to praise God, as did David in the Psalms (cf. Q21.79; 38.18-19; and Psalms 104, 148).
13. *Do righteousness*: or 'act uprightly' (this and the preceding imperatives are plur.).
14. *jinn...who worked for him*: cf. Q21.82; 38.37 ('satans').
15. *places of prayer*: or 'prayer niches' (of mosques), but here it probably refers to the building of Solomon's temple in Jerusalem.
16. *nothing indicated his death to them...*: reference obscure; according to tradition, after Solomon's death his body remained standing or seated on his throne, propped up by his staff, while the jinn went on working on the temple unaware that Solomon had died. The fact of his death was finally revealed by a worm (or ants) gnawing away at his staff, but by then the temple had been finished.
17. *if they had known the unseen...*: i.e. if the jinn had known that Solomon was dead, they would not have continued their demeaning labor.

15–21 The people of Sheba

18. *Sheba*: a people ruled by a queen (see Q27.22-44); the following story resembles other 'punishment stories' (see n. on Q7.59).
19. *the flood of 'Arim*: or 'the flood of the dam.' Some scholars take this to refer to the bursting of the dam of Ma'rib in Yemen, and the beginning of a period of economic decline in south Arabia (c. 451-542 CE).
20. *ungrateful*: Ar. *kafūr*, punning on *kāfir*, 'disbeliever.'
21. *towns which We have blessed*: in the Holy Land or Palestine.
22. *lengthen (the distance) between our journeys*: meaning obscure.
23. *legendary*: lit. 'stories' or 'accounts' (Ar. *aḥādīth*); i.e. the people of Sheba entered into the annals of those peoples who were punished for their disbelief.
24. *his conjecture about them*: or 'his opinion of them,' see e.g. Q7.16-17; for the figure of Iblīs, see n. on Q2.34.

22 Say: 'Call on those whom you claim (as gods) instead of God! They do not possess (even) the weight of a speck in the heavens or on the earth. They have no partnership in (the creation of) either of them,[25] nor has He any support from them.' **23** Intercession will be of no benefit with Him, except for the one to whom He gives permission – until, when terror is removed from their hearts, they say, 'What did your Lord say?,' and they say, 'The truth. He is the Most High, the Great.' **24** Say: 'Who provides for you from the heavens and the earth?' Say: 'God. Surely (either) we or you (stand) indeed on guidance,[26] or (are) clearly astray.'[27]

25 Say: 'You will not be questioned about what sins we have committed, nor shall we be questioned about what you do.'

26 Say: 'Our Lord will gather us together, (and) then disclose the truth between us,[28] (for) He is the Discloser, the Knowing.'

27 Say: 'Show me those whom you have joined with Him as associates. By no means (can you do so)! No! He (alone) is God, the Mighty, the Wise.'

28 We have sent you only as a bringer of good news and a warner[29] to the people all together.[30] But most of the people do not know (it).

29 They say, 'When (will) this promise[31] (come to pass), if you[32] are truthful?' **30** Say: 'For you (there is) the appointment of a Day. You will not delay it by an hour, nor will you advance (it by an hour).'

31 Those who disbelieve say, 'We will not believe in this Qur'ān,[33] nor in that which was before it.'[34] If (only) you[35] could see when the evildoers are made to stand before their Lord, (how) some of them hurl the blame[36] at others. Those who were weak will say to those who were arrogant, 'If not for you, we would have been believers.' **32** Those who were arrogant will say to those who were weak, 'Did we keep you from the guidance after it had come to you? No! You (yourselves) were sinners.' **33** Those who were weak will say to those who were arrogant, 'No! (It was your) scheming by night and day, when you commanded us to disbelieve[37] in God and to set up[38] rivals[39] to Him.' They will be full of secret regret

---

22–24 Idolaters challenged

25. *no partnership...*: lit. 'no association...' (cf. Q35.40; 46.4); the following 'from them' refers to their gods.
26. *guidance*: one of the most frequent terms (Ar. *hudā*) for revelation in general, and the Qur'ān in particular.
27. *clearly astray*: lit. 'in clear straying.'

25 Each judged according to his deeds

26 God will decide

28. *disclose the truth...*: lit. 'open the truth...;' see Q48.1; cf. Q7.89 (Shu'ayb); 26.118 (Noah).

27 Idolaters challenged

28 The Prophet's mission

29. *bringer of good news...warner*: for these roles, see n. on Q2.119.
30. *to the people all together*: or perhaps 'to all humankind' (cf. Q7.158; 36.70).

29–30 Judgment ridiculed

31. *promise*: or 'threat' of punishment (cf. Q10.48; 21.38; 27.71; 36.48; 67.25).
32. *you*: plur.

31–33 A judgment scene

33. *this Qur'ān*: here close to its present meaning as the name of the Muslim scripture (cf. Q9.111; see n. on Q2.185).
34. *that which was before it*: the previous 'scriptures' of Jews and Christians.
35. *you*: the Prophet, or perhaps intended generally ('one').
36. *the blame*: lit. 'the word.'
37. *disbelieve*: or 'be ungrateful' (perhaps a pun).
38. *set up*: lit. 'made.'
39. *rivals*: or 'equals' (Ar. *andād*), i.e. other gods alleged to be equal with God.

when they see the punishment. We shall put chains on the necks of those who disbelieved. Will they be repaid (for anything) except for what they have done?

34 We have not sent any warner to a town, except that its affluent ones said, 'Surely we are disbelievers in what you are sent with.' **35** And they (also) said, 'We (have) more wealth and children, and we shall not be punished.' **36** Say: 'Surely my Lord extends (His) provision to whomever He pleases, and restricts (it), but most of the people do not know (it).' **37** Neither your wealth nor your children are the things which bring you near to Us in intimacy, except for whoever believes and does righteousness. And those – for them (there is) a double payment[40] for what they have done, and they will be secure in exalted rooms. **38** But those who strive against Our signs to obstruct (them) – those will be brought forward to the punishment. **39** Say: 'Surely my Lord extends (His) provision to whomever He pleases of His servants, and restricts (it) from him (whom He pleases). Whatever thing you contribute,[41] He will replace it, (for) He is the best of providers.'

40 On the Day when He gathers them all together, He will say to the angels,[42] '(Was it) you these were serving?'[43] **41** They will say, 'Glory to You! You are our ally, not they. No! They used to serve the jinn[44] – most of them believed in them.' **42** 'So today none of you has power to (cause) another benefit or harm.' And We shall say to those who did evil, 'Taste the punishment of the Fire[45] which you called a lie.'

43 When Our clear signs[46] are recited to them, they say, 'This is only a man who wants to keep you from what your fathers have served.' And they say, 'This[47] is nothing but a forged lie.' Those who disbelieve say to the truth, when it comes to them, 'This is nothing but clear magic' **44** – though We have not given them any Books to study, nor have We sent to them any warner before you.[48] **45** Those who were before them (also) called (it) a lie, though they have not reached (even) a tenth of what We gave them.[49] They (too) called My messengers[50] liars, and how was My loathing (of them)!

46 Say: 'I give you only one admonition, (namely) that you stand before God, in pairs or singly, (and) then reflect: (there are) not any jinn in your companion.[51] He is only a warner for you in the face of a harsh punishment.' **47** Say: 'I have not asked you for any reward, but it was (only) for your own sake. My reward (depends) only on God. He is a witness over everything.' **48** Say: 'My Lord hurls the truth[52] –

34–39 Judgment on the rich and powerful

40. *a double payment*: lit. 'payment of the double.'
41. *contribute*: lit. 'spend,' for the cause.

40–42 Worship of the jinn

42. *angels*: for these beings and their various roles, see n. on Q2.30.
43. *serving*: or 'worshipping.'
44. *They used to serve the jinn*: sometimes the Qur'ān regards the gods of the disbelievers as angels or (as here) jinn (see Q6.100n.), but at other times it declares them to be non-existent or 'mere names' (e.g. Q53.23).
45. *the Fire*: Ar. *al-nār* is the most common of the various designations for Hell.

43–45 Objections of disbelievers

46. *clear signs*: or 'signs as proof,' 'signs as indisputable evidence' (see n. on Q2.39).
47. *This*: i.e. the Qur'ān.
48. *not given them any Books...nor...sent to them any warner before you*: this implies that the Prophet's contemporaries were thought to be a different 'people' than those of Abraham's time (cf. Q28.46; 32.3; 36.6).
49. *they have not reached (even) a tenth of what We gave them*: i.e. the Prophet's contemporaries do not have a tenth of the material wealth or religious advantages of earlier generations.
50. *messengers*: for this important title, see n. on Q2.87.

46–50 The Prophet responds

51. *not any jinn in your companion*: a denial that the Prophet is possessed (cf. Q34.8 above).
52. *hurls the truth*: against falsehood (cf. Q21.18).

Knower of the unseen.' **49** Say: 'The truth has come! Falsehood (can) neither bring (anything) about, nor restore (it).' **50** Say: 'If I go astray, I go astray only against myself,[53] but if I am guided, it is by what my Lord inspires me (with). Surely He is hearing (and) near.'

51 If (only) you[54] could see when they are terrified and (there is) no escape, and they are seized from a place nearby, **52** and say, 'We believe in it (now).'[55] Yet how will they reach (it)[56] from a place far away, **53** when they disbelieved in it[57] before? They conjecture about the unseen from a place far away. **54** But (a barrier) has been set between them and what they desire, as was done with their parties before.[58] Surely they (too) were in grave doubt indeed (about it).[59]

---

53. *against myself*: i.e. to my own loss.

51–54 A JUDGMENT SCENE

54. *you*: the Prophet, or perhaps intended generally ('one').
55. *We believe in it (now)*: i.e. judgment and punishment.
56. *(it)*: probably knowledge or belief.
57. *it*: judgment.
58. *their parties before*: i.e. earlier generations of disbelievers like them (cf. Q54.51).
59. *in grave doubt indeed (about it)*: cf. Q11.62, 110; 14.9.

35 Creator ❁ Fāṭir

In the Name of God, the Merciful, the Compassionate

1 Praise (be)[1] to God, Creator of the heavens and the earth, (who) makes the angels messengers[2] having two, and three, and four wings.[3] He adds to the creation whatever He pleases. Surely God is powerful over everything. **2** Whatever mercy God opens to the people, (there is) no withholder of it, and whatever (mercy) He withholds, (there is) no sender of it after that. He is the Mighty, the Wise.

3 People! Remember the blessing of God on you. (Is there) any creator other than God, (who) provides for you from the sky and the earth? (There is) no god but Him. How are you (so) deluded? **4** If they call you[4] a liar, (know that) messengers have been called liars before you. To God all affairs are returned.

5 People! Surely the promise of God is true, so (do) not let this present life deceive you, and (do) not let the Deceiver[5] deceive you about God. **6** Surely Satan[6] is an enemy to you, so take him as an enemy. He only calls his faction so that they may be among the companions of the blazing (Fire). **7** Those who disbelieve – for them (there is) a harsh punishment, but those who believe and do righteous deeds – for them (there is) forgiveness and a great reward.

8 Is the one whose evil deed is made to appear enticing to him, and he perceives it as good, (like the one who is rightly guided)?[7] Surely God leads astray whomever He pleases and guides whomever He pleases. So do not exhaust yourself[8] in regrets over them. Surely God is aware of what they do.

9 (It is) God who sends the winds, and it stirs up a cloud, and We drive it to some barren[9] land, and by means of it give the earth life after its death. So (too) is the raising up.[10] **10** Whoever desires honor – honor (belongs) to God altogether. To Him good words ascend, and the righteous deed – He raises it. But those who scheme evil deeds – for them (there is) a harsh punishment, and their scheming – it will be in vain.

Q35: The first part of this sūra is in the form of an address to the people, setting forth the claims of God (Q35.1-17). It then shifts to address the Prophet, consoling him with the reminder that previous messengers also faced rejection (Q35.18-26). It concludes with the different fates awaiting believers and disbelievers. Most scholars assign Q35 to the 'Meccan' period, though some modern scholars contend that much of the second half is 'Medinan.' It takes its title from the reference to God as 'creator' in the opening verse, but is also called 'the angels' (*al-Malā'ika*) from another word in the first verse.

1–17 Signs of God's power and providence

1. *(be)*: or '(belongs).'
2. *makes the angels messengers*: for the angels and their various roles, see n. on Q2.30.
3. *two, and three, and four wings*: cf. Psalm 104.4; Isaiah 6.2; Ezekiel 1.6.
4. *you*: the Prophet.
5. *the Deceiver*: Satan (cf. Q4.120; 17.64).
6. *Satan*: for this figure, see n. on Q2.36.
7. *(like the one who is rightly guided)*: something like this must be supplied to complete the sentence (cf. Q47.14).
8. *do not exhaust yourself*: lit. 'do not let your self go out' (addressed to the Prophet).
9. *barren*: lit. 'dead.'
10. *the raising up*: or 'the resurrection.'

11 God created you from dust,[11] then from a drop,[12] (and) then He made you pairs. No female conceives or delivers, except with His knowledge, and no one grows old who grows old, or is diminished in his life, except (it) is in a Book.[13] Surely that is easy for God.

12 The two seas are not alike: this one is sweet, fresh, good to drink, and this (other) one is salty (and) bitter. Yet from each you[14] eat fresh fish,[15] and bring out of it an ornament[16] which you wear, and you[17] see the ship cutting through it, so that you[18] may seek some of His favor,[19] and that you may be thankful. **13** He causes the night to pass into the day, and causes the day to pass into the night, and He has subjected the sun and the moon, each one running (its course) for an appointed time.[20] That is God, your Lord – to Him (belongs) the kingdom, and those you call on, instead of Him, do not possess even the skin of a date seed. **14** If you call on them, they do not hear your calling, and (even) if they heard, they would not respond to you. On the Day of Resurrection they will deny[21] your association.[22] No one (can) inform you[23] like One who is aware.

15 People! You are the ones in need of God, and God – He is the wealthy One,[24] the Praiseworthy. **16** If He (so) pleases, He will do away with you and bring a new creation. **17** That is no great matter for God.

18 No one bearing a burden bears the burden of another.[25] If one heavy-burdened calls for his load (to be carried), nothing of it will be carried, even though he be a family member. You[26] warn only those who fear their Lord in the unseen,[27] and (who) observe the prayer.[28] Whoever purifies himself, only purifies (himself) for (the sake of) his own self. To God is the (final) destination. **19** The blind and the sighted are not equal, **20** nor are the darkness and the light, **21** nor the shade and the heat. **22** The living and the dead are not equal. Surely God causes whomever He pleases to hear. You will not cause those who are in the graves to hear **23** – you are only a warner. **24** Surely We have sent you with the truth,[29] as a bringer of good news and a warner.[30] (There has) not (been) any community except that a warner has passed away

---

11. *from dust*: see Q3.59; 18.37; 22.5; 30.20; 40.67 (cf. Genesis 2.7, 'from the dust of the ground'); 'from clay,' according to Q6.2; 7.12; 15.26; 17.61; 23.12; 32.7; 38.71, 76; 55.14; 'from water,' according to Q21.30; 24.45; 25.54.
12. *a drop*: of semen.
13. *a Book*: i.e. the 'Book of God' or 'Book of Destiny' by which everything is ordained (see n. on Q6.59).
14. *you*: plur.
15. *fish*: lit. 'flesh,' 'meat.'
16. *ornament*: pearls and coral (see Q55.22).
17. *you*: switch to sing., but intended generally.
18. *you*: switch back to plur.
19. *seek some of His favor*: i.e. seek to make a livelihood.
20. *an appointed time*: or 'term' (Ar. *ajal*), which is predetermined and cannot be changed.
21. *deny*: lit. 'disbelieve.'
22. *your association*: of them with God.
23. *you*: switch to sing., but intended generally.
24. *the wealthy One*: i.e. God has no need of anyone or anything.

18–26 Encouragement to the Prophet

25. *No one...bears the burden of another*: i.e. judgment falls on individuals, whom neither family nor friends can help (an implicit rejection of the Christian doctrine of 'vicarious atonement' and 'intercession' by the saints); cf. Q6.164; 17.15; 39.7; 53.38.
26. *You*: the Prophet.
27. *in the unseen*: or 'in secret' (see n. on Q2.3).
28. *the prayer*: the ritual prayer (or *ṣalāt*).
29. *with the truth*: or 'in truth,' 'truly.'
30. *bringer of good news...warner*: for these roles, see n. on Q2.119.

in it.[31] **25** If they call you a liar, (know that) those who were before them called (their messengers) liars. Their messengers[32] brought them the clear signs,[33] and the scriptures,[34] and the illuminating Book.[35] **26** Then I seized those who disbelieved, and how was My loathing (of them)!

27 Do you[36] not see that God sends down water from the sky, and by means of it We bring forth fruits of various colors? And in the mountains (there are) streaks (of) white and red – their colors are diverse – and (of) deep black. **28** And among people and (wild) animals and livestock – their colors are diverse as well. Only those of His servants[37] who have knowledge fear God. Surely God is mighty, forgiving.

29 Surely those who recite the Book of God,[38] and observe the prayer, and contribute[39] from what We have provided them, in secret and in open, hope for a transaction – it will not be in vain – **30** so that He may pay them their rewards in full, and increase them from His favor. Surely He is forgiving, thankful.

31 What We have inspired you[40] (with) of the Book[41] – it is the truth, confirming what was before it.[42] Surely God is indeed aware of His servants (and) sees (them). **32** Then We caused those of Our servants whom We chose to inherit the Book. Some of them do themselves evil, and some of them are moderate, and some of them are foremost in good deeds,[43] by the permission of God. That is the great favor![44]

33 Gardens of Eden[45] – they will enter them. There they will be adorned with bracelets of gold and (with) pearls, and there their clothes (will be of) silk. **34** And they will say, 'Praise (be)[46] to God, who has taken away all sorrow from us! Surely our Lord is indeed forgiving, thankful, **35** who out of His favor has settled us in a lasting Home. No fatigue will touch us here, and no weariness will touch us here.'

36 But those who disbelieve – for them (there is) the fire of Gehenna.[47] (Death) is not decreed for them, and so they do not die, nor will any of its punishment be lightened for them. In this way We repay every ungrateful one.[48] **37** There they will cry out, 'Our Lord, bring us out! We will do righteousness instead of what we used to do.' 'Did We not give you a long life, enough of it for the one who would take heed

---

31. *a warner has passed away in it*: or 'there was a warner in it in the past.'
32. *messengers*: for this important title, see n. on Q2.87.
33. *the clear signs*: or 'the clear proofs,' 'the indisputable evidence.'
34. *the scriptures*: Ar. *al-zubur*; cf. Q3.184; 16.44; 23.53; 26.196; 54.43, 52 (where it seems to refer to the 'Book of Destiny').
35. *the illuminating Book*: it is not clear what this 'Book' refers to (the same sequence occurs at Q3.184; cf. Q22.8; 31.20).

27–28 Differences in nature and in people

36. *you*: sing., but probably intended generally ('one').
37. *servants*: the word 'servants,' which also means 'slaves,' is used here in the sense of 'all people' (cf. Q35.45 below).

29–40 Rewards and punishments

38. *Book of God*: here referring to the Qur'ān (see n. on Q2.2).
39. *contribute*: lit. 'spend' (i.e. for those in need or for the cause).
40. *you*: the Prophet.
41. *of the Book*: either the Qur'ān or the heavenly archetype, depending on whether 'of' has a partitive or an epexegetical meaning (elucidating the preceding 'what').
42. *confirming what was before it*: the Qur'ān 'confirms' the Torah and Gospel (see e.g. Q2.97; 3.3; 5.48; 46.30).
43. *foremost in good deeds*: see Q9.100; 56.10-12.
44. *great favor*: or 'superior merit.'
45. *Gardens of Eden*: in heaven (for this imagery, see n. on Q2.25).
46. *(be)*: or '(belongs).'
47. *Gehenna*: a name for Hell (see n. on Q2.206).
48. *ungrateful one*: Ar. *kafūr*, punning on *kāfir*, 'disbeliever.'

to take heed? The warner came to you, so taste (the punishment)! The evildoers will have no helper.'

38 Surely God knows the unseen (things)[49] of the heavens and the earth. Surely He knows what is in the hearts.[50] **39** He (it is) who made you successors on the earth.[51] Whoever disbelieves, his disbelief (will be) on him. Their disbelief only increases the disbelievers in hatred in the sight of their Lord. Their disbelief only increases the disbelievers in loss. **40** Say:[52] 'Have you seen your associates whom you call on instead of God? Show me what part of the earth they have created. Or do they have any partnership in (the creation of) the heavens?' Or have We given them a Book,[53] so that they (stand) on a clear sign[54] from it? No! The evildoers promise each other nothing but deception.

41 Surely God holds the heavens and the earth, or they would move. If indeed they moved, no one would hold them after Him. Surely He is forbearing, forgiving. **42** They have sworn by God the most solemn of their oaths: if a warner comes to them, they will be more (rightly) guided than one of the (other) communities. But when a warner came to them, it only increased them in aversion (to it), **43** (and) in arrogance on the earth, and in scheming evil. Yet evil scheming only overwhelms its own people.[55] Do they expect anything but the customary way of those of old?[56] You will find no change in the customary way of God. You will find no change in the customary way of God.[57] **44** Have they not traveled on the earth and seen how the end was for those who were before them, though they were stronger than them in power?[58] But God is not one that anything should escape Him in the heavens or on the earth. Surely He is knowing, powerful. **45** If God were to take the people to task for what they have earned,[59] He would not leave on it[60] any living creature. But He is sparing them until an appointed time.[61] When their time comes – surely God sees His servants.

---

49. *unseen (things)*: or 'secrets' (see n. on Q2.3).
50. *hearts*: lit. 'chests,' considered the seat of knowledge and understanding.
51. *successors on the earth*: i.e. successors of previous generations, or perhaps 'rulers' (see e.g. Q6.133, 165; 7.69, 74; 24.55; 27.62).
52. *Say*: on this form of address, see n. on Q2.80.
53. *a Book*: the idolaters have no 'Book' on which to base their belief in other gods (cf. Q43.21; 46.4).
54. *clear sign*: or 'clear proof,' 'indisputable evidence.'

41–45 Disbelievers stubborn

55. *its own people*: i.e. the people who practice it.
56. *the customary way of those of old*: i.e. the way (Ar. *sunna*) God punished earlier generations for their disbelief (cf. Q3.137; 15.13; 18.55; 40.85; 48.23).
57. *...the customary way of God*: the repetition of this phrase is either for effect, or else the result of scribal error (dittography).
58. *Have they not traveled on the earth and seen...*: the remains of their destroyed cities were believed to be still visible.
59. *for what they have earned*: i.e. for the sins they have committed.
60. *it*: the earth.
61. *an appointed time*: or 'term' (Ar. *ajal*), i.e. the precise date of judgment is predetermined and cannot be changed.

36 Yā' Sīn ❁ Yā' Sīn

In the Name of God, the Merciful, the Compassionate

1 Yā' Sīn.[1]

2 By the wise Qur'ān![2] **3** Surely you[3] are indeed one of the envoys,[4] **4** on a straight path, **5** a sending down[5] of the Mighty, the Compassionate, **6** so that you may warn a people. Their fathers have not been warned, and so they are oblivious.[6]

7 Certainly the word has proved true[7] against most of them: 'They will not believe.' **8** Surely We have placed chains on their necks, and it (reaches up) to the chin, and so they (are forced to) hold their heads up. **9** We have made a barrier before them and a barrier behind them, and We have covered them, and so they do not see. **10** (It is) the same for them whether you warn them or you do not warn them. They will not believe. **11** You warn only the one who follows the Reminder[8] and fears the Merciful in the unseen.[9] So give him the good news of forgiveness and a generous reward. **12** Surely We – We give the dead life and We write down what they have sent forward and their traces.[10] And everything – We have counted it up in a clear record.[11]

Q36: This sūra begins with an affirmation of the Prophet's mission. It then relates a parable about a 'disbelieving city,' enumerates the signs of God's power and providence, and describes the different fates awaiting believers and disbelievers. Most scholars assign Q36 to the 'Meccan' period. It receives its title from the two letters with which it begins.

1 Letters

1. *Yā' Sīn*: the names of the Arabic letters *y* and *s*, a combination unique to Q36. Twenty-nine sūras begin with letters like these, ranging from one to five. No satisfactory explanation has been given for their occurrence. The Cairo edition varies in counting these letters as a separate verse (as here), or as the beginning of the first verse.

2–6 The Prophet's mission

2. *By the wise Qur'ān*: i.e. 'I swear by...;' see Q38.1; 50.1; cf. Q10.1; 31.2 ('the wise Book'); 3.58 ('the wise Reminder'); here 'the Qur'ān' comes close to its present meaning as the name of the Muslim scripture (cf. Q9.111; see n. on Q2.185).
3. *you*: the Prophet.
4. *the envoys*: lit. 'the ones who are sent' (Ar. *al-mursalūn*), a designation roughly equivalent to 'messengers' (*rusul*).
5. *a sending down*: perhaps referring to the Prophet himself, or the 'straight path' (cf. Q26.192).
6. *Their fathers have not been warned...*: this implies that the Prophet's contemporaries were thought to be a different 'people' than those of Abraham's time (cf. Q28.46; 32.3; 34.44).

7–12 Disbelievers doomed

7. *the word has proved true...*: or 'the sentence (of condemnation) has been passed...' (cf. Q10.33; 36.70 below).
8. *the Reminder*: referring to the Qur'ān (see n. on Q3.58).
9. *in the unseen*: or 'in secret' (see n. on Q2.3).
10. *their traces*: lit. 'their footsteps' or 'tracks;' i.e. a written 'Record' is kept of their deeds and of the traces they have left behind (see following n.; cf. Q40.21, 82).
11. *record*: lit. 'leader' or 'model' (Ar. *imām*), but probably referring to the 'record' of their deeds (cf. Q15.79; 17.71).

13 Strike a parable for them:[12] the companions of the town, when the envoys came to it.[13] **14** When We sent two men to them, and they called them liars, We reinforced (them) with a third. They said, 'Surely we are envoys to you.' **15** They said, 'You are nothing but human beings like us. The Merciful has not sent down anything. You are only lying.' **16** They said, 'Our Lord knows that we are indeed envoys to you. **17** Nothing (depends) on us except the clear delivery (of the message).' **18** They said, 'Surely we have an evil omen about you. If indeed you do not stop, we shall indeed stone you, and a painful punishment from us will indeed touch you.' **19** They said, 'Your evil omen refers to yourselves. If you had taken heed – No! You are a wanton people!' **20** (Just then) a man came running from the farthest part of the city.[14] He said, 'My people! Follow the envoys! **21** Follow those who do not ask you for any reward, and (who) are (rightly) guided. **22** Why should I not serve Him who created me? You will (all) be returned to Him. **23** Shall I take (other) gods instead of Him? If the Merciful intends any harm for me, their intercession will be of no use to me at all, nor will they save me. **24** Surely then I would indeed be far astray. **25** Surely I believe in your Lord, so listen to me!'[15] **26** It was said, 'Enter the Garden!' He said, 'Would that my people knew **27** that my Lord has forgiven me, and made me one of the honored.' **28** We did not send down on his people after him any force from the sky, nor are We (in the habit of) sending down (such a force). **29** It was only a single cry,[16] and suddenly they were snuffed out. **30** Alas for the servants![17] Not one messenger comes to them whom they do not mock. **31** Do they not see how many generations We destroyed before them, (and) that they[18] do not return to them? **32** But every one of them will be brought forward before Us.

33 A sign[19] for them is the dead earth: We give it life, and bring forth grain from it, and from it they eat. **34** And We have placed in it gardens of date palms and grapes, and We have caused springs to gush forth in it, **35** so that they may eat from its fruit and what their hands have made. Will they not be thankful? **36** Glory to the One who created pairs of all that the earth grows, and of themselves,[20] and of what they do not know.

37 A sign for them is the night: We strip the day from it, and suddenly they are in darkness. **38** And the sun: it runs to a dwelling place (appointed) for it. That is the decree of the Mighty, the Knowing. **39** And the moon: We have determined it by stations,[21] until it returns like an old palm branch.[22] **40** It is not fitting for the sun to overtake the moon, nor does the night outrun the day, but each floats in (its own) orbit.

13–32 Parable of the disbelieving city

12. *Strike a parable...*: addressed to the Prophet.
13. *the town...the envoys...*: neither are identified in keeping with the story's character as a parable.
14. *a man came running...*: cf. Q28.20.
15. *Surely I believe in your Lord, so listen to me*: it is not clear whether the first part of this statement is addressed to the envoys, and the second part to the people of the city, or whether all of it is spoken to the people of the city (in which case 'your Lord' would refer to the 'Lord' of the people of the city, i.e. 'the Merciful'). However that may be, the reader must assume that the 'third man' was then put to death.
16. *a single cry*: or 'shout' (see Q36.49, 53 below; cf. Q11.67); the parable turns out to be yet another story of a city punished for its disbelief (see n. on Q7.59).
17. *Alas for the servants*: the word 'servants,' which also means 'slaves,' is used here in the sense of 'all people'.
18. *they*: referring to the people destroyed for their disbelief.

33–44 Signs of God's power and providence

19. *sign*: for the various meanings of this term, see n. on Q2.39.
20. *of themselves*: of humans.
21. *determined it by stations*: referring to the 'phases' of the moon (cf. Q10.5).
22. *like an old palm branch*: the return of the crescent moon is compared to the curve of an old palm branch.

41 A sign for them is that We carried their descendants in the loaded ship,[23] **42** and We have created for
them (ships) like it (in) which they sail.[24] **43** If We (so) please, We drown them, and then (there is) no cry
(for help) for them, nor are they saved, **44** except as a mercy from Us, and enjoyment (of life) for a time.

45 When it is said to them, 'Guard (yourselves) against what is before you and what is behind you, so that
you may receive compassion'[25] – **46** yet not a sign comes to them from the signs of their Lord without
their turning away from it. **47** When it is said to them, 'Contribute[26] from what God has provided you,'
those who disbelieve say to those who believe, 'Shall we feed one whom, if God (so) pleased, He would
have fed? You are only far astray!'[27]

48 They say, 'When (will) this promise[28] (come to pass), if you[29] are truthful?' **49** They are only waiting
for a single cry[30] – it will seize them while they are (still) disputing, **50** and then they will not be able to
make a bequest, nor will they return to their (own) families.

51 There will be a blast on the trumpet,[31] and suddenly they will come swooping down[32] from the graves
to their Lord. **52** They will say, 'Alas for us! Who has raised us up from our sleeping place? This is what the
Merciful promised, and the envoys were truthful.' **53** It was only a single cry, and suddenly they are all
brought forward before Us. **54** 'Today no one will be done evil at all, nor will you be repaid (for anything)
except what you have done.' **55** Surely the companions of the Garden today are busy rejoicing **56** – they
and their spouses – reclining on couches in (places of) shade. **57** There they have fruit, and they have
whatever they call for. **58** 'Peace!' – a word (of greeting) from a compassionate Lord. **59** 'But separate
(yourselves) today, you sinners! **60** Did I not make a covenant with you, sons of Adam, that you should not
serve Satan[33] – surely he is a clear enemy to you – **61** and that you should serve Me? This is a straight path.
62 Certainly he has led astray many multitudes of you. Did you not understand? **63** This is Gehenna,[34]
which you were promised. **64** Burn in it today for what you disbelieved!'

65 Today We will set a seal on their mouths, but their hands will speak to Us, and their feet will bear
witness about what they have earned.[35] **66** If We (so) pleased, We would indeed have obliterated their
eyes, and they would race to the path, but how could they see? **67** And if We (so) pleased, We would
indeed have transformed them where they were, and they could not go on, nor could they return.
68 (To) whomever We grant a long life, We reverse him in (his) constitution.[36] Do they not understand?

---

23. *the loaded ship*: Noah's 'ark' (see Q26.119).
24. *sail*: lit. 'ride.'

45–50 Disbelievers stubborn

25. *...so that you may receive compassion*: the Cairo edition, reflecting the views of traditional scholars, attributes this verse to the 'Medinan' period.
26. *Contribute*: lit. 'spend.'
27. *far astray*: lit. 'in far straying;' the disbelievers mock one of the Prophet's turns of phrase.
28. *promise*: or 'threat' of punishment (cf. Q10.48; 21.38; 27.71; 34.29; 67.25).
29. *you*: plur.
30. *a single cry*: or 'shout,' of impending doom (see Q36.53 below; cf. Q38.15; 50.42).

51–68 The different fates of believers and disbelievers

31. *a blast on the trumpet*: the Last Day will be announced by the blast of a trumpet (e.g. Q6.73; 18.99; 20.102; 39.68 [a double blast]; 69.13; 74.8; 78.18; cf. Matthew 24.31; 1 Corinthians 15.52; 1 Thessalonians 4.16).
32. *they will come swooping down*: cf. Q21.96.
33. *Satan*: for this figure, see n. on Q2.36.
34. *Gehenna*: a name for Hell (see n. on Q2.206).
35. *their hands...and their feet...*: i.e. the disbelievers' hands and feet will report the sins they have committed.
36. *We reverse him in (his) constitution*: i.e. make him weak instead of strong.

69 We have not taught him the (art of) poetry, nor is it fitting for him.[37] It is nothing but a Reminder and
a clear Qur'ān,[38] **70** so that he may warn whoever is living, and that the word may be proved true against
the disbelievers.[39]

71 Do they not see that We created for them – from what Our hands have made – livestock, and (that)
they are their masters? **72** We have made them subservient to them, and some of them they ride,
and some they eat. **73** And they have (other) benefits in them, and drinks. Will they not be thankful?
74 But they have taken (other) gods, instead of God, so that they might be helped. **75** (But) they cannot
help them, (for) they will be brought forward before them as a group.[40] **76** So do not let their saying[41]
cause you[42] sorrow. Surely We know what they keep secret and what they speak aloud.

77 Does the human not see that We created him from a drop?[43] Yet suddenly he is a clear adversary.[44]
78 He has struck a parable for Us[45] and forgotten (the fact of) his creation.[46] He says, 'Who will give the
bones life when they are decayed?' **79** Say:[47] 'He will give them life who produced them the first time. He
has knowledge of all creation, **80** who has made fire for you from the green tree – and so you (too) light
a fire from it.' **81** Is not the One who created the heavens and the earth able to create their equivalent?
Yes indeed! He is the Creator, the Knowing. **82** His only command, when He intends something, is to say
to it, 'Be!'[48] and it is. **83** Glory to the One in whose His hand is the kingdom of everything! To Him you
will be returned.

69–70 The Prophet not a poet

37. *nor is it fitting for him*: see n. on Q21.5.
38. *a clear Qur'ān*: or 'a Qur'ān that makes (things) clear.'
39. *the word may be proved true...*: or 'the sentence (of condemnation) may be passed...' (cf. Q36.7 above).

71–76 Signs of God's power and providence

40. *(for) they will be brought forward before them as a group*: probably that their gods will be brought before God for judgment, just as the disbelievers will, or else that their gods will be brought before them to condemn or disown them.
41. *their saying*: i.e. what the disbelievers say.
42. *you*: the Prophet.

77–83 Resurrection defended

43. *a drop*: of semen.
44. *a clear adversary*: i.e. he openly disputes the revelation in general, and the possibility of resurrection in particular.
45. *He has struck a parable for Us*: i.e. made comparisons for an incomparable God (cf. Q16.74), probably in the sense of 'associating other gods with God.'
46. *forgotten...his creation*: i.e. his status as a creature.
47. *Say*: on this form of address, see n. on Q2.80.
48. *Be!*: God's creative word (Ar. *kun*); cf. Q2.117; 3.47 (to Mary), 59 (of Jesus and Adam); 6.73; 16.40; 19.35; 40.68.

37 The Ones Who Line Up ۞ Al-Ṣāffāt

In the Name of God, the Merciful, the Compassionate

1 By the ones who line up in lines,[1] **2** and the shouters of a shout,[2] **3** and the reciters of a reminder![3] **4** Surely your God is one, **5** Lord of the heavens and the earth, and of whatever is between them, and Lord of the Easts.[4]

6 Surely We have made the sky of this world[5] appear enticing by means of the splendor of the stars, **7** and (We have made them) a (means of) protection from every rebelling satan.[6] **8** They do not listen to the exalted Assembly,[7] **9** but they are pelted from every side, driven off – for them (there is) punishment forever – **10** except for the one who snatches a word,[8] and then a piercing flame[9] pursues him. **11** So ask them for a pronouncement:[10] 'Are they a stronger creation, or those (others) whom We have created?'[11] Surely We created them from sticky clay.[12]

12 But you[13] are amazed when they ridicule, **13** and, when they are reminded, do not take heed, **14** and, when they see a sign,[14] ridicule, **15** and say, 'This is nothing but clear magic. **16** When we are dead, and turned to dust and bones, shall we indeed be raised up? **17** And our fathers of old (too)?' **18** Say: 'Yes, and you will be humbled.' **19** (For) it will only be a single shout, and suddenly they will see, **20** and

---

Q37: This sūra opens with an emphatic declaration of the unity and creative power of God. Next come sections on the resurrection and the different fates awaiting believers and disbelievers, followed by stories of previous messengers from Noah to Jonah. It concludes with a refutation of the worship of angels as 'daughters of God.' Most scholars assign Q37 to the 'Meccan' period. Its title may refer to the angels standing in assembly around the divine throne.

1–5 God is one

1. *By the ones who line up in lines*: i.e. 'I swear by...;' this may refer to the angels standing in assembly around the divine throne (Q37.165-166 below; 78.38; 89.22), or their lining up sinners for punishment (Q18.48). For sūras that begin with oaths like these, see Q51.1-4; 77.1-6; 79.1-5; 100.1-5.
2. *the shouters of a shout*: may refer to the angels' role in heralding the Last Day (see Q37.19 below; 79.13).
3. *the reciters of a reminder*: may refer to the angels as agents of revelation (see Q16.2; 97.4).
4. *the Easts*: or 'the risings' (Ar. *al-mashāriq*), the plur. may refer to the different points at which the sun and stars rise in the East, depending on the season of the year.

6–11 God's creative power

5. *the sky of this world*: i.e. the lowest of the seven heavens (cf. Q41.12).
6. *...protection from every rebelling satan*: shooting stars were thought to be stones hurled to drive off demons and prevent them from 'eavesdropping' on the heavenly council (see Q37.9-10 below; cf. Q15.16-18; 72.8-9).
7. *exalted Assembly*: i.e. the heavenly council.
8. *snatches a word*: lit. 'snatches a snatch,' i.e. some piece of heavenly information or wisdom.
9. *a piercing flame*: i.e. a shooting star.
10. *So ask them for a pronouncement*: the Prophet is to ask the disbelievers.
11. *those (others) whom We have created*: referring to the heavenly bodies (cf. Q40.57; 79.27).
12. *from sticky clay*: cf. Q6.2; 7.12; 15.26; 17.61; 23.12; 32.7; 38.71, 76; 55.14; 'from dust,' according to Q3.59; 18.37; 22.5; 30.20; 35.11; 40.67; 'from water,' according to Q21.30; 24.45; 25.54.

12–34 The Day of Decision: a judgment scene

13. *you*: the Prophet.
14. *sign*: or 'miracle' (see n. on Q2.39).

say, 'Woe to us! This is the Day of Judgment.' **21** 'This is the Day of Decision,[15] which you called a lie. **22** Gather those who have done evil,[16] and their wives, and what they used to serve,[17] **23** instead of God, and guide them to the path of the Furnace.[18] **24** And stop them (there), (for) they are to be questioned: **25** "What is (the matter) with you (that) you do you not help each other?" **26** No! Today they are resigned.' **27** Some of them will approach others asking each other questions. **28** They will say,[19] 'Surely you used to come to us from the right (side).'[20] **29** They will say,[21] 'No! You were not believers. **30** We had no authority over you. No! You were a people who transgressed insolently. **31** So the word of our Lord has proved true against us.[22] Surely we are indeed tasting (it). **32** We made you err (because) we were in error.' **33** Surely on that Day they will be partners in the punishment.[23] **34** Surely in this way We deal with the sinners,

35 Surely they – when it was said to them, '(There is) no god but God,' they became arrogant, **36** and said, 'Are we to abandon our gods for a possessed poet?'[24] **37** 'No! He has brought the truth and confirmed the envoys.[25] **38** Surely you will indeed taste the painful punishment, **39** and you will not be repaid (for anything) except what you have done.'

40 – Except for the devoted servants[26] of God. **41** Those – for them (there will be) a known provision **42** (of) fruits,[27] and they will be honored **43** in Gardens of Bliss,[28] **44** on couches, facing each other, **45** (and) a cup[29] from a flowing spring will be passed around among them – **46** white,[30] delicious to the drinkers, **47** (there is) no ill effect in it, nor do they become drunk from it. **48** With them (there will be maidens) restraining (their) glances, wide-eyed, **49** as if they were hidden eggs.[31]

50 Some of them[32] will approach others asking each other questions. **51** One of them will say, 'Surely I had a comrade, **52** who used to say, "Are you indeed one of the confirmers?[33] **53** When we are dead, and turned to dust and bones, shall we indeed be judged?"' **54** (Another) will say, 'Are you looking (down)?'

---

15. *Day of Decision*: or 'Day of Distinguishing,' i.e. between the righteous and the wicked (cf. Q44.40; 77.13-14; 78.17). The reader must assume that what follows is spoken by God at the Judgment.
16. *Gather those who have done evil...*: addressed to the angels.
17. *what they used to serve*: i.e. their gods.
18. *the Furnace*: a name for Hell (Ar. *al-jaḥīm*).
19. *They will say*: the disbelievers address their gods who had led them astray.
20. *from the right (side)*: i.e. from the favored side.
21. *They will say*: their gods now respond to them.
22. *the word...has proved true against us*: or 'the sentence (of condemnation)...has been passed against us.'
23. *partners in the punishment*: or 'associates in the punishment,' punning on their having 'associated' other gods with God (cf. Q43.39).

35–39 The Prophet will be vindicated

24. *a possessed poet*: or 'a jinn-struck (Ar. *majnūn*) poet' (see nn. on Q7.184; 21.5).
25. *the envoys*: lit. 'the ones who are sent' (Ar. *al-mursalūn*), a designation roughly equivalent to 'messengers' (*rusul*).

40–61 The delights of Paradise

26. *servants*: the word 'servant' (Ar. *'abd*) also means 'slave.'
27. *a known provision (of) fruits*: see Q2.25.
28. *Gardens of Bliss*: in heaven (for this imagery, see n. on Q2.25).
29. *a cup*: of wine.
30. *white*: probably meaning 'clear.'
31. *hidden eggs*: or 'cherished eggs' (cf. Q56.23, 'hidden pearls').
32. *Some of them*: the inhabitants of Paradise.
33. *one of the confirmers*: i.e. one who accepted the truth of the resurrection.

55 So he looks (down) and sees him in the midst of the Furnace. **56** He will say, 'By God! You nearly brought me to ruin. **57** Were it not for the blessing of my Lord, I (too) would have been one of those brought forward (to the punishment). **58** So do we not die, **59** except for our first death, and are we not punished? **60** Surely this – it indeed is the great triumph! **61** Let the workers work for something like this!'

62 Is that better as a reception, or the tree of al-Zaqqūm?[34] **63** Surely We have made it a test for the evil-doers. **64** It is a tree which comes forth from the root of the Furnace. **65** Its fruits are like the heads of the satans, **66** and they eat from it, and fill their bellies from it. **67** Then on (top of) it they have a drink of boiling (water). **68** Then their return is to the Furnace.

69 Surely they found their fathers astray, **70** and they run in their footsteps. **71** Certainly most of those of old went astray before them, **72** even though We sent warners[35] among them. **73** See how the end was for those who were warned **74** – except for the devoted servants of God.

75 Certainly Noah[36] called on Us, and excellent indeed were the responders! **76** We rescued him and his family from great distress, **77** and We made his descendants – they were the survivors. **78** We left (this blessing) upon him among the later (generations): **79** 'Peace (be) upon Noah among all peoples!'[37] **80** In this way We repay the doers of good. **81** Surely he was one of Our believing servants. **82** Then We drowned the others.[38]

83 Surely Abraham was indeed of his party:[39] **84** When he came to his Lord with a sound heart,[40] **85** when he said to his father and his people, 'What do you serve? **86** (Is it) a lie – gods other than God – you desire? **87** What do you think about the Lord of the worlds?'[41] **88** And he took a look at the stars,[42] **89** and said, 'Surely I am sick.'[43] **90** So they[44] turned away from him, withdrawing. **91** But he turned to their gods, and said, 'Do you not eat? **92** What is (the matter) with you (that) you do not speak?' **93** So he turned on them, striking (them) with the right (hand).[45] **94** Then they[46] came running to him. **95** He said, 'Do you serve what you carve, **96** when God created you and what you make?' **97** They said, 'Build a building for him, and cast him into the blazing (Fire)!' **98** They intended a plot against him, but We brought them down.[47]

62–68 The agonies of Hell

34. *tree of al-Zaqqūm*: a tree in Hell (see Q44.43; 56.52; cf. Q17.60).

69–74 Introduction to the stories of previous messengers

35. *warners*: for this role, see n. on Q2.119.

75–82 Noah

36. *Noah*: here begins another series of 'punishment stories' (Q37.75-148; see n. on Q7.59).
37. *among all peoples*: lit. 'in the worlds.'
38. *Then We drowned the others*: this verse seems out of place and may have followed v. 77 originally.

83–98 The story of Abraham

39. *his party*: i.e. Noah's 'party.'
40. *heart*: here, as often, the heart is spoken of as synonymous with mind.
41. *Lord of the worlds*: for this title, see n. on Q1.2.
42. *took a look at the stars*: cf. Q6.76-78 (a star, moon, and sun); and Genesis 15.5; Jubilees 12.16-17; Apocalypse of Abraham 7.8-10.
43. *I am sick*: i.e. disgusted by their worship of the creation instead of the creator.
44. *they*: Abraham's people.
45. *...striking (them) with the right (hand)*: cf. Q21.57-58; though not mentioned in Genesis, Abraham's destruction of the 'idols' became a popular theme in later Jewish tradition (see e.g. Jubilees 12.12-14).
46. *they*: the people.
47. *brought them down*: lit. 'made them the lowest.'

99–111 Abraham willing to sacrifice his son

99 He said, 'Surely I am going to my Lord. He will guide me. **100** My Lord, grant me one of the righteous.'
101 So We gave him the good news of a forbearing boy.[48] **102** When he had reached the (age of) running
with him, he said, 'My son! Surely I saw in a dream that I am going to sacrifice you.[49] So look, what do
you think?' He said, 'My father! Do what you are commanded. You will find me, if God pleases, one of
the patient.' **103** When they both had submitted,[50] and he had laid him face down,[51] **104** We called out to
him, 'Abraham! **105** Now you have confirmed the vision. Surely in this way We repay the doers of good.
106 Surely this – it indeed was the clear test.' **107** And We ransomed him with a great sacrifice,[52] **108** and
left (this blessing) on him among the later (generations): **109** 'Peace (be) upon Abraham!' **110** In this way
We repay the doers of good. **111** Surely he was one of Our believing servants.

112 And We gave him the good news of Isaac, a prophet, one of the righteous. **113** We blessed him and
Isaac, and some of their descendants are doers of good, and some clearly do themselves evil.

114 Certainly We bestowed favor on Moses and Aaron, **115** and We rescued them and their people from
the great distress. **116** We helped them, and they were the victors. **117** We gave them both the clear
Book,[53] **118** and guided them to the straight path, **119** and left (this blessing) on both of them among the
later (generations): **120** 'Peace (be) upon Moses and Aaron!' **121** In this way We repay the doers of good.
122 Surely they were two of Our believing servants.

123 Surely Elijah[54] was indeed one of the envoys: **124** When he said to his people, 'Will you not guard
(yourselves)?[55] **125** Do you call on Baal,[56] and abandon the best of creators **126** – God – your Lord and the
Lord of your fathers of old?' **127** Yet they called him a liar. Surely they will indeed be brought forward
(to the punishment) **128** – except for the devoted servants of God. **129** And We left (this blessing) on him
among the later (generations): **130** 'Peace (be) upon Elijah!'[57] **131** In this way We repay the doers of good.
132 Surely he was one of Our believing servants.

133 Surely Lot was indeed one of the envoys: **134** When We rescued him and his family – all (of them) –
135 except for an old woman[58] among those who stayed behind. **136** Then We destroyed the others.
137 Surely you indeed pass near them in the morning **138** and in the night.[59] Will you not understand?

---

48. *a forbearing boy*: said be Ishmael, since Isaac is mentioned only after this (Q37.112 below).
49. *sacrifice you*: lit. 'slaughter you;' cf. the story of the sacrifice of Isaac at Genesis 22.1-19.
50. *both had submitted*: to God's command.
51. *face down*: lit. 'to the forehead;' in keeping with their 'submission,' Abraham 'prostrates' his son.
52. *sacrifice*: lit. 'slaughter;' cf. Genesis 22.13 (a ram).

112–113 Abraham and Isaac

114–122 Moses and Aaron

53. *the clear Book*: or 'the Book that makes (things) clear;' referring to the Torah.

123–132 Elijah

54. *Elijah*: mentioned only here and at Q6.85. The form of the name (Ar. *Ilyās*) is in accord with Christian usage (Gk. *Elias*) rather than Jewish (Hebr. *Elijah*). The early codex (Ar. *muṣḥaf*) of Ibn Mas'ūd is reported to have read 'Idrīs' for 'Ilyās.'
55. *guard (yourselves)*: against evil, or God.
56. *Baal*: this name (Ar. *Ba'l*) was originally a title ('Lord') applied to a variety of semitic gods; here it refers to the contest between Elijah and the prophets of Baal at 1 Kings 18.17-21.
57. *Elijah*: here *Ilyāsīn* (the ending '-īn' added for the sake of rhyme).

133–138 Lot

58. *an old woman*: Lot's wife, see Q27.57; 66.10; cf. the story at Genesis 19.1-29.
59. *you indeed pass near them...*: Lot's city (Sodom) was thought to be in the region of the Dead Sea. This implies that the location from which this was spoken was far from the vicinity of present-day Mecca (see Q11.89; cf. Q30.3n.; 46.27n.).

139 Surely Jonah[60] was indeed one of the envoys: **140** When he ran away to the loaded ship, **141** and cast lots, but was one of the losers.[61] **142** So the fish swallowed him, seeing that he was to blame. **143** Were it not that he was one of those who glorified (God), **144** he would indeed have remained in its belly until the Day when they are raised up. **145** But We tossed him on the desert (shore)[62] while he was (still) sick,[63] **146** and We caused a gourd tree[64] to grow over him. **147** We sent him to a hundred thousand, or more,[65] **148** and they believed. So We gave them enjoyment (of life) for a time.

149 Ask them for a pronouncement:[66] 'Does your[67] Lord have daughters while they have sons? **150** Or did We create the angels female[68] while they were witnesses?' **151** Is it not a fact that out of their own lie they indeed say, **152** 'God has begotten'?[69] Surely they are liars indeed! **153** Has He chosen daughters over sons? **154** What is (the matter) with you? How do you judge?[70] **155** Will you not take heed?[71] **156** Or do you have any clear authority? **157** Bring your Book, if you are truthful.

158 They have fabricated[72] an affiliation between Him and the jinn.[73] Yet certainly the jinn know that they[74] will indeed be brought forward (to the punishment) **159** – glory to God above what they allege! – **160** except for the devoted servants of God.

161 Surely you and what you serve – **162** you will not tempt (anyone to rebellion) against Him, **163** except for the one who is (destined) to burn in the Furnace. **164** (There is) not one of us[75] who does not have an assigned position.[76] **165** Surely we – we indeed are the ones who line up,[77] **166** and surely we – we indeed are the ones who glorify (God).

139–148 Jonah

60. *Jonah*: only here is his story related at any length (cf. Q68.48-49; and the biblical book which bears his name). The form of the name (Ar. *Yūnus*) reflects Christian usage rather than Jewish.
61. *the losers*: lit. 'the refuted,' i.e. the lot fell against him and he was thrown overboard.
62. *desert (shore)*: since the story jumps immediately to the incident of the 'gourd tree,' perhaps only the 'desert' or 'wilderness' is meant (cf. Q68.49).
63. *(still) sick*: from being inside the fish.
64. *gourd tree*: lit. 'tree of gourd,' but the meaning 'of gourd' (Ar. *min yaqṭīnin*) is uncertain. The meaning of Hebr. *qiqayon* (castor bean plant?) at Jonah 4.6 is equally unclear.
65. *a hundred thousand, or more*: Jonah was sent to 'the great city' of Nineveh, according to Jonah 1.2; 3.2. Jonah is the only prophet in the Qur'ān who was sent to a city whose inhabitants were not destroyed.

149–166 God has no offspring or partner

66. *Ask them for a pronouncement*: the Prophet is to ask the disbelievers.
67. *your*: sing.
68. *the angels female*: for the belief that the angels were 'daughters of God,' see Q16.57; 17.40; 43.19; 53.27 (for the angels and their various roles, see n. on Q2.30).
69. *begotten*: i.e. fathered children (cf. Q112.3).
70. *How do you judge?*: or 'How you judge!'
71. *take heed*: or 'remember,' 'be reminded.'
72. *fabricated*: lit. 'made.'
73. *an affiliation between Him and the jinn*: sometimes the Qur'ān regards the gods of the disbelievers as angels or jinn (see Q6.100n.), but at other times it declares them to be non-existent or 'mere names' (e.g. Q53.23).
74. *they*: i.e. those who have 'fabricated an affiliation between God and the jinn.'
75. *us*: i.e. the angels, who are speaking here.
76. *assigned position*: or 'known place.'
77. *the ones who line up*: cf. Q37.1n. (above), though here the participle is masc., not fem.

167 If they were to say, **168** 'If (only) we had a reminder[78] from those of old, **169** we would indeed have been the devoted servants of God.' **170** Yet they have disbelieved in it.[79] Soon they will know! **171** Certainly Our word has (already) gone forth to Our servants, the envoys. **172** Surely they – they indeed are the ones who will be helped. **173** Surely Our army – they indeed are the victors. **174** So turn away from them for a time,[80] **175** and observe them. Soon they will observe![81] **176** Do they seek to hurry Our punishment? **177** When it comes down in their (own) courtyard, (how) evil the morning will be for those who were warned! **178** So turn from away them for a time, **179** and observe (them). Soon they will observe!

180 Glory to your Lord, Lord of honor, above what they allege! **181** Peace (be) upon the envoys, **182** and praise (be)[82] to God, Lord of the worlds!

167–179 Let them be

78. *reminder*: here referring to a written revelation (see n. on Q3.58).

79. *it*: the Qur'ān.

80. *turn away from them...*: the Prophet is to turn away from the disbelievers for a time.

81. *they will observe*: their own punishment.

180–182 Concluding doxology

82. *(be)*: or '(belongs).'

38 Ṣād ✿ Ṣād

In the Name of God, the Merciful, the Compassionate

1 Ṣād.[1] By the Qur'ān,[2] containing the Reminder![3] **2** – No! Those who disbelieve are in false pride and defiance.[4] **3** How many a generation We have destroyed before them![5] They (all) called out, but there was no time for escape. **4** Yet they are amazed that a warner[6] has come to them from among them. The disbelievers say, 'This (man) is a magician, a liar! **5** Has he made the gods (into) one god? Surely this is an amazing thing indeed.' **6** The assembly of them set out (saying): 'Walk (away), and remain steadfast to[7] your gods. Surely this is a thing to be desired indeed. **7** We have not heard of this in the last religion.[8] This is only a fabrication. **8** Has the Reminder been sent down on him (alone) among us?' No! They are in doubt about My Reminder! No! They have not yet tasted My punishment! **9** Or do they have the storehouses of the mercy of your Lord, the Mighty, the Giver? **10** Or do they have the kingdom of the heavens and the earth, and whatever is between them? Let them ascend on the ropes.[9] **11** An army of the factions will be routed there. **12** Before them the people of Noah called (it) a lie, and 'Ād, and Pharaoh, he of the stakes,[10] **13** and Thamūd, and the people of Lot, and the people of the Grove[11] – those were the factions. **14** Each of them called the messengers[12] liars, and My retribution was justified. **15** What do these (people) expect but a single cry,[13] for which (there will be) no delay.[14]

Q38: The first part of this sūra describes the defiance of the Prophet's contemporaries. Next come stories of David, Solomon, Job, and several others. It then describes the different fates awaiting believers and disbelievers, before concluding with the story of Iblīs. Most scholars assign Q38 to the 'Meccan' period. It takes its title from the letter with which it begins.

1–15 Disbelievers defy the Prophet

1. *Ṣād*: the name of the Arabic letter *ṣ* (unique to Q38). Twenty-nine sūras begin with a letter (or letters) like this, ranging from one to five. No satisfactory explanation has been given for their occurrence. The Cairo edition varies in counting these letters as a separate verse, or as the beginning of the first verse (as here).
2. *By the Qur'ān*: i.e. 'I swear by…;' cf. Q50.1; here 'the Qur'ān' comes close to its present meaning as the name of the Muslim scripture (cf. Q9.111; see n. on Q2.185).
3. *the Reminder*: referring to the message or revelation (cf. Q38.8 below; see n. on Q3.58). The complement of this oath is omitted (cf. Q50.1; 89.1-4).
4. *defiance*: or 'disobedience,' 'schism.'
5. *How many a generation We have destroyed before them*: a reference to previous peoples who were punished for their sins (see n. on Q7.59).
6. *warner*: for this role, see n. on Q2.119.
7. *remain steadfast to*: lit. 'be patient over.'
8. *in the last religion*: perhaps 'in any religion before this' or 'in the religion of our forefathers,' but the meaning is obscure.
9. *ascend on the ropes*: i.e. into heaven (cf. Q40.36-37; 52.38, 'a ladder').
10. *he of the stakes*: meaning obscure; perhaps a reference to the remains of his monumental buildings (cf. Q7.137; 89.10).
11. *people of the Grove*: or 'companions of the Thicket' (Ar. *al-ayka*); this may be an alternative name for the people of Midian, since both have the same messenger, Shu'ayb (Q26.176-189; cf. Q15.78-79; 50.14).
12. *messengers*: for this important title, see n. on Q2.87.
13. *a single cry*: or 'shout,' of impending doom (cf. Q36.49, 53; 50.42)
14. *delay*: or 'recovery.'

16 They say, 'Our Lord, hurry our share[15] to us before the Day of Reckoning!' **17** Bear with what they say, and remember Our servant[16] David, (who was) endowed with strength.[17] Surely he turned regularly (in repentance). **18** Surely We subjected the mountains (along) with him to glorify (Us) in the evening and at sunrise, **19** and the birds (too),[18] gathered together, all regularly turning to Him (in praise).[19] **20** We strengthened his kingdom, and gave him wisdom and a decisive word.[20]

21 Has the story[21] of the dispute come to you?[22] When they climbed over the wall of the place of prayer,[23] **22** when they entered upon David, and he was terrified of them, but they said, 'Do not fear! (We are) two disputants:[24] one of us has acted oppressively toward the other. So judge between us in truth,[25] and do not be unjust, and guide us to the right path. **23** Surely this (man) is my brother. He has ninety-nine ewes, and I have (only) one ewe. He said, "Give her into my charge," and he overcame me in the argument.'[26] **24** He said,[27] 'Certainly he has done you evil in asking for your ewe (in addition) to his ewes. Surely many (business) partners indeed act oppressively toward one another, except those who believe and do righteous deeds – but few they are.' And David guessed that We had (somehow) tested him,[28] so he asked his Lord for forgiveness, and fell down, bowing, and turned (in repentance). **25** So We forgave him that. Surely he has intimacy indeed with Us and a good (place of) return.

26 'David! Surely We have made you a ruler on the earth,[29] so judge among the people in truth, and do not follow (vain) desire, or it will lead you astray from the way of God. Surely those who go astray from the way of God – for them (there is) a harsh punishment, because they have forgotten the Day of Reckoning.' **27** We did not create the sky and the earth, and whatever is between them, without purpose. That is the conjecture[30] of those who disbelieve. So woe to those who disbelieve on account of the Fire![31] **28** Or shall We treat[32] those who believe and do righteous deeds the same as the ones who foment corruption on the earth? Or shall We treat the ones who guard (themselves)[33] the same as the depraved?

16–28 The story of David and the dispute

15. *hurry our share*: of worldly or material goods, but spoken in derision.
16. *servant*: the word 'servant' (Ar. *'abd*) also means 'slave.'
17. *(who was) endowed with strength*: lit. 'he of the hands.'
18. *mountains (along) with him to glorify (Us)...and the birds (too)*: i.e. the mountains and birds were to praise God, as did David in the Psalms (cf. Q21.79; 34.10; and Psalms 104, 148).
19. *all regularly turning to Him (in praise)*: or 'all joining with him (in praising God).'
20. *a decisive word*: or 'a distinct (way of) speaking;' perhaps an allusion to the style of the Psalms (but cf. Q86.13).
21. *story*: or 'news.'
22. *you*: sing., but probably intended generally; for the story that follows, cf. 2 Samuel 12.1-15.
23. *the place of prayer*: or 'the prayer niche' (Ar. *al-miḥrāb*) of a mosque, but here it must refer David's palace in Jerusalem, since the temple had not yet been built (but notice the anachronism at 2 Samuel 12.20).
24. *two disputants*: said to be two angels; but cf. Nathan's parable to David at 2 Samuel 12.1-6.
25. *in truth*: or 'with the truth.'
26. *overcame me in the argument*: or 'was haughty with me in (his) speech.'
27. *He said*: David now decides the dispute.
28. *We had (somehow) tested him*: for having taken Bathsheba, the wife of Uriah, to add to his many wives (cf. 2 Samuel 12.7-15).
29. *ruler on the earth*: the basic meaning of Ar. *khalīfa* is 'successor,' but 'ruler' is preferable here. The word is used individually only of David and Adam (see n. on Q2.30).
30. *conjecture*: or 'opinion,' as opposed to 'revealed (i.e. certain) knowledge.'
31. *the Fire*: Ar. *al-nār* is the most common of the various designations for Hell.
32. *treat*: lit. 'make.'
33. *guard (themselves)*: against evil, or God.

29 A blessed Book[34] – We have sent it down to you,[35] so that those with understanding may contemplate its verses[36] and take heed.[37]

30 To David We granted Solomon – an excellent servant he was! Surely he turned regularly (in repentance). **31** When the standing horses were presented before him in the evening, **32** he said, 'Surely I have loved the love of good (things) more than the remembrance of my Lord, until the sun[38] has (now) been hidden by the veil.[39] **33** Return them to me!'[40] Then he began to stroke their legs and necks.[41] **34** Certainly We tested Solomon, and placed[42] on his throne a (mere) image.[43] Then he turned (in repentance). **35** He said, 'My Lord, forgive me, and grant me a kingdom (such as) will not be fitting for anyone after me (to have).[44] Surely You – You are the Giver.' **36** So We subjected the wind to him, to blow gently at his command wherever he decided, **37** and (also) the satans, every builder and diver, **38** and others (as well) bound in chains:[45] **39** 'This is Our gift, so bestow or withhold without reckoning.' **40** Surely he had intimacy indeed with Us, and a good (place of) return.

41 And remember Our servant Job: When he called out to his Lord, 'Surely I – Satan[46] has touched me with weariness and punishment.' **42** 'Stamp with your foot! This (will become) a cool (place for) washing and a drink.'[47] **43** And We granted him his household, and their equivalent with them,[48] as a mercy from Us, and a reminder to those with understanding. **44** 'And take in your hand a bunch, and strike with it, and do not break your oath.'[49] Surely We found him patient – an excellent servant he was! Surely he turned regularly (in repentance).

45 And remember Our servants Abraham, and Isaac, and Jacob: endowed with strength and vision.[50]

---

29 A BLESSED BOOK

34. *a blessed Book*: the Qur'ān.
35. *you*: the Prophet.
36. *verses*: or 'signs' (see n. on Q2.39).
37. *take heed*: or 'remember,' 'be reminded.'

30–40 THE STORY OF SOLOMON AND THE HORSES

38. *the sun*: lit. 'she,' but probably referring to 'the sun' (Ar. *al-shams* is fem.).
39. *veil*: of night.
40. *Return them to me*: the meaning of this episode is obscure. It is said that in admiring his horses, Solomon missed the evening prayer, and having realized this ordered the horses to be brought back and slaughtered in sacrifice.
41. *stroke their legs and necks*: some commentators add 'with a sword,' implying the beginning of the slaughter, but there is no evidence for this in the text. Rather it appears that after calling for the horses to be returned, Solomon again became enamored of their beauty and once again forgot his religious obligation.
42. *placed*: lit. 'cast.'
43. *image*: lit. 'body.' According to Jewish legend, Solomon was punished in the following way for allowing one of his wives to worship an idol: after getting hold of Solomon's signet, a demon turned himself into the likeness of Solomon and occupied his throne for forty days, while Solomon was turned into a beggar.
44. *grant me a kingdom...*: cf. Solomon's prayer and God's response at 1 Kings 3.5-14 (3.13b, '...no other king will compare with you').
45. *So we subjected the wind...the satans...and others...*: cf. Q21.81-82; 34.12-13 ('jinn' instead of 'satans').

41–44 THE STORY OF JOB

46. *Satan*: for this figure, see n. on Q2.36.
47. *This (will become)...*: i.e. when Job stamped his foot, a place for washing and drinking miraculously appeared.
48. *and their equivalent with them*: cf. Job 42.10, 'the Lord gave Job twice as much as he had before.'
49. *...and do not break your oath*: reference obscure; it is said that Job had sworn to give his wife a hundred lashes for having blasphemed, but failed to fulfill his oath.

45–47 ABRAHAM, ISAAC, AND JACOB

50. *endowed with strength and vision*: lit. 'they of the hands and sight.'

46 Surely We purified them with a pure (thought): remembrance of the Home.[51] **47** Surely with Us they are indeed among the chosen, the good.

48 And remember Our servants Ishmael, Elisha,[52] and Dhū-l-Kifl:[53] each (of them) was one of the good.

49 This is a Reminder.[54] Surely for the ones who guard (themselves) (there is) indeed a good (place of) return: **50** Gardens of Eden, (where) the gates are open for them, **51** where they recline, (and) where they call for abundant fruit and drink. **52** With them (are maidens) restraining (their) glances, (all) of the same age. **53** 'This is what you were promised for the Day of Reckoning. **54** Surely this is indeed Our provision – (there is) no end to it. **55** (All) this!'

But surely for the insolent transgressors (there is) indeed an evil (place of) return: **56** Gehenna,[55] (where) they will burn – it is an evil bed! **57** (All) this! So make them taste it – boiling (water) and rotten (food),[56] **58** and other (torments) of (this) kind in pairs. **59** 'This is a crowd rushing in with you[57] – for them (there is) no welcoming. Surely they will burn in the Fire.' **60** They say, 'No! It is you for whom (there is) no welcoming. You sent it forward for us,[58] and it is an evil resting place!' **61** They say, 'Our Lord, whoever sent this forward for us, give him a double punishment in the Fire!' **62** And they say, 'What is (the matter) with us (that) we do not see men (here)[59] whom we used to count among the evil? **63** Did we take them in ridicule? Or has (our) sight turned aside from them?' **64** Surely that is true indeed – the disputing of the companions of the Fire.

65 Say:[60] 'I am only a warner. (There is) no god but God, the One, the Supreme, **66** Lord of the heavens and the earth, and whatever is between them, the Mighty, the Forgiver.'

67 Say: 'It is a great story[61] **68** from which you turn away. **69** I had no knowledge of the exalted Assembly when they disputed. **70** I am only inspired[62] that I am a clear warner.' **71** (Remember) when your Lord said to the angels:[63] 'Surely I am going to create a human being from clay.[64] **72** When I have fashioned

51. *the Home*: in heaven; for this idea, cf. Hebrews 11.8-10.

48 Ishmael, Elisha, and Dhū-l-Kifl

52. *Elisha*: Ar. *Alyasa'* or *al-Yasa'* (mentioned only here and at Q6.86).
53. *Dhū-l-Kifl*: some commentators suggest the prophet Ezekiel, others Elijah (cf. Q21.85, where he is listed with Ishmael and Idrīs).

49–55a The delights of Paradise

54. *This is a Reminder*: antecedent unclear, but probably referring to the Qur'ān in its entirety (cf. Q21.24, 50).

55b–64 The agonies of Hell

55. *Gehenna*: a name for Hell (see n. on Q2.206).
56. *rotten (food)*: meaning uncertain.
57. *This is a crowd...*: usually understood as spoken by God to those who led the disbelievers astray, but it is more likely said by these same leaders to one another. The disbelievers then reply in the next verse.
58. *you sent it forward for us*: i.e. the disbelievers accuse their leaders of 'sending forward' their deeds, which have brought them to this punishment.
59. *we do not see men (here)...*: the reference (here and in the next verse) is to the Prophet's followers.

65–66 The Prophet only a warner

60. *Say*: on this form of address, see n. on Q2.80.

67–85 The story of Iblīs

61. *story*: or 'news,' referring to the story about Iblīs which follows.
62. *I am only inspired*: or 'I have only received inspiration.'
63. *When your Lord said to the angels*: for the story that follows, cf. the version at Q15.28-43.
64. *from clay*: see Q6.2; 7.12; 15.26; 17.61; 23.12; 32.7; 55.14; 'from dust,' according to Q3.59; 18.37; 22.5; 30.20; 35.11; 40.67; 'from water,' according to Q21.30; 24.45; 25.54.

him, and breathed some of My spirit into him,[65] fall down before him in prostration.' **73** So the angels prostrated themselves – all of them together **74** – except Iblīs.[66] He became arrogant, and was one of the disbelievers. **75** He[67] said, 'Iblīs! What prevented you from prostrating yourself before what I created with My two hands?[68] Have you become arrogant, or are you one of the exalted?'[69] **76** He[70] said, 'I am better than him.[71] You created me from fire, but You created him from clay.' **77** He said, 'Get out of here![72] Surely you are accursed![73] **78** Surely My curse (is going to remain) on you until the Day of Judgment.' **79** He said, 'My Lord, spare me until the Day when they are raised up.' **80** He said, 'Surely you are one of the spared **81** – until the Day of the known time.'[74] **82** He said, 'Then, by Your honor, I shall indeed make them err – all (of them) **83** – except for Your devoted servants among them.' **84** He[75] said, '(This is) the truth, and the truth I say: **85** I shall indeed fill Gehenna with you[76] and those of them who follow you – all (of you)!'[77]

86 Say: 'I do not ask you for any reward for it, nor am I one of the pretenders.[78] **87** It[79] is nothing but a reminder to the worlds.[80] **88** You will indeed know its story[81] after a time.'

---

65. *breathed some of My spirit into him*: cf. Q15.29; and Genesis 2.7.
66. *except Iblīs*: for this figure, see n. on Q2.34.
67. *He*: God.
68. *with My two hands*: cf. Genesis 2.7.
69. *one of the exalted*: i.e. one of the angels.
70. *He*: Iblīs.
71. *him*: Adam.
72. *here*: lit. 'it' (the heavenly Garden or Paradise).
73. *accursed*: or 'stoned.'
74. *the known time*: or 'the appointed time' (i.e. the time of judgment decreed by God).
75. *He*: God.
76. *you*: Iblīs.
77. *I shall indeed fill Gehenna with you and those who follow you...*: cf. Q7.18; elsewhere God swears to 'fill Gehenna with jinn and people' (Q11.119; 32.13).

86–88 The Prophet asks no reward

78. *the pretenders*: or 'the imposters' (lit. 'the ones who take things upon themselves').
79. *It*: the Qur'ān.
80. *to the worlds*: or 'to all peoples.'
81. *story*: or 'news,' of judgment and punishment (cf. e.g. Q6.5; 26.6).

39 The Companies ۞ Al-Zumar

In the Name of God, the Merciful, the Compassionate

1 The sending down of the Book is from God, the Mighty, the Wise.[1] **2** Surely We have sent down to you[2]
the Book with the truth.[3] So serve[4] God, devoting (your) religion to Him.[5]

3 Is it not (a fact) that pure religion is for God (alone)? But those who take allies instead of Him – 'We only
serve them so that they may bring us near to God in intimacy'[6] – surely God will judge between them
concerning their differences. Surely God does not guide anyone who is a liar (or) ungrateful. **4** If God
wanted to take a son,[7] He would indeed have chosen whatever He pleased from what He created. Glory
to Him! He is God, the One, the Supreme.

5 He created the heavens and the earth in truth.[8] He wraps the night around the day, and wraps the
day around the night, and He has subjected the sun and the moon, each running (its course) for an
appointed time.[9] Is He not the Mighty, the Forgiver? **6** He created you from one person,[10] (and) then made
from him his wife, and He sent down to you four kinds of livestock.[11] He creates you in the bellies of your
mothers, creation after creation, in three darknesses.[12] That is God, your Lord. To Him (belongs) the
kingdom. (There is) no god but Him. How (is it that) you are turned away?[13] **7** If you are ungrateful[14]

Q39: This sūra opens with a statement of the unity and creative power of God. The contrasting fates of believers and disbelievers occupy much of the remainder of the sūra. It concludes with a vivid description of Judgment Day. Most scholars assign Q39 to the 'Meccan' period, though some traditional scholars attribute a few verses to the 'Medinan' period. Its title comes from the reference to believers and disbelievers entering the Garden and Gehenna in 'companies' (Q39.71, 73).

1–2 A Book from God

1. *The sending down of the Book...*: here referring to the Qur'ān not only as a 'recited' but also 'written' scripture (see n. on Q2.2; cf. the similar openings at Q32.2; 40.2; 41.2; 45.2; 46.2).
2. *you*: the Prophet.
3. *with the truth*: or 'in truth,' 'truly.'
4. *serve*: or 'worship.'
5. *devoting (your) religion to Him*: i.e. serving God alone (addressed to the Prophet).

3–4 God is one

6. *...near to God in intimacy*: here the statement refers to Christian veneration of Jesus, Mary, and the saints as intercessors with God (see the following verse and Q39.43-44 below; cf. Q3.64, 79; 5.76, 116; 9.31; 10.18; 43.86). The people of 'Ād are said to have believed the same thing about their gods at Q46.28.
7. *son*: or 'child' (Ar. *walad*), but referring to Christian claims about Jesus as God's son.

5–7 Signs of God's power and providence

8. *in truth*: or 'with the truth.'
9. *an appointed time*: or 'term' (Ar. *ajal*), which is predetermined and cannot be changed.
10. *one person*: Adam.
11. *four kinds of livestock*: lit. 'eight pairs of the cattle;' referring to sheep, goats, camels, and oxen (see Q6.143-144).
12. *creation after creation, in three darknesses*: meaning obscure, but obviously an attempt to describe the stages of prenatal development (cf. Q22.5; 23.13-14).
13. *turned away*: from the one God.
14. *are ungrateful*: or 'disbelieve' (perhaps a pun).

– surely God is wealthy (enough) without you. Yet He does not approve ingratitude[15] in His servants.[16] If you are thankful, He approves it in you. No one bearing a burden bears the burden of another.[17] Then to your Lord is your return, and He will inform you about what you have done. Surely he knows what is in the hearts.[18]

8 When hardship touches a person, he calls on his Lord,[19] turning to Him (in repentance). Then, when He bestows blessing on him from Himself, he forgets what he was calling to Him for before, and sets up[20] rivals[21] to God to lead (people) astray from His way. Say:[22] 'Enjoy (life) in your disbelief for a little. Surely you will be one of the companions of the Fire.'[23] **9** Or is he who is obedient in the hours of the night, prostrating himself and standing, bewaring the Hereafter[24] and hoping for the mercy of his Lord [...]?[25] Say: 'Are those who know and those who do not know equal?' Only those with understanding take heed.[26]

10 Say: 'My servants who believe! Guard (yourselves) against your Lord. For those who do good in this present world, (there is) good, and God's earth is wide. Surely the patient will be paid their reward in full without reckoning.' **11** Say: 'I have been commanded to serve God, devoting (my) religion to Him, **12** and I have been commanded to be the first of those who submit.'[27] **13** Say: 'Surely I fear, if I disobey my Lord, the punishment of a great Day.' **14** Say: 'I serve God, devoting my religion to Him. **15** So serve whatever you please instead of Him.' Say: 'Surely the losers are those who lose themselves and their families on the Day of Resurrection. Is that not – it is the clearest loss! **16** For them (there are) shadows of fire above them, and shadows (of fire) below them.[28] That is what God frightens His servants with: "My servants! Guard (yourselves) against Me!"'

17 Those who avoid al-Ṭāghūt[29] – for fear that they serve it[30] – and turn to God (in repentance) – for them (there is) good news. So give good news to My servants, **18** those who listen to the word and follow the best of it. Those are the ones whom God has guided, and those – they are those with understanding. **19** So is the one against whom the word of punishment is proved true[31] – will you[32] save the one who is (already) in the Fire? **20** But those who guard (themselves) against their Lord – for them (there will be)

15. *ingratitude*: or 'disbelief' (again, perhaps a pun).
16. *servants*: the word 'servants,' which also means 'slaves,' is used here in the sense of 'all people.'
17. *No one...bears the burden of another*: i.e. judgment falls on individuals, whom neither family nor friends can help (an implicit rejection of the Christian doctrine of 'vicarious atonement' and 'intercession' by the saints); cf. Q6.164; 17.15; 35.18; 53.38.
18. *hearts*: lit. 'chests,' considered the seat of knowledge and understanding.

8–20 Faithfulness and its reward

19. *calls on his Lord*: in prayer.
20. *sets up*: lit. 'makes.'
21. *rivals*: or 'equals' (Ar. *andād*), i.e. other gods alleged to be equal with God.
22. *Say*: on this form of address, see n. on Q2.80.
23. *the Fire*: Ar. *al-nār* is the most common of the various designations for Hell.
24. *the Hereafter*: see n. on Q2.4.
25. *[...]?*: the reader must supply 'like the one who does not do these things.'
26. *take heed*: or 'remember.'
27. *those who submit*: or 'the Muslims.'
28. *shadows of fire above them...below them*: the point is clear, even if the imagery is obscure (cf. Q7.41; 29.55).
29. *al-Ṭāghūt*: perhaps '(other) gods' or 'idols' (cf. Q16.36), but sometimes taken as a proper name (see Q4.60, 76, where it appears to be another name for Satan). It may be related to the word for 'gods' in Ethiop. (*ṭā'ōt*).
30. *it*: lit. 'her' (cf. Q4.60, 'it'/'him').
31. *the word of punishment is proved true*: or 'the sentence of punishment is passed.'
32. *you*: the Prophet.

exalted rooms, above which exalted rooms are built, (and) below which rivers flow – the promise of God! God will not break the appointment.

21 Do you[33] not see that God has sent down water from the sky, and put it into the earth as springs, (and) then by means of it He brings forth crops of various colors, (and) then they wither,[34] and you see them turning yellow, (and) then He makes them broken debris? Surely in that is a reminder indeed to those with understanding.

22 Is the one whose heart God has expanded[35] to Islam,[36] and so he (depends) on a light from his Lord [...]?[37] Woe to those whose hearts are hardened against the remembrance of God! Those are clearly astray.[38]

23 God has sent down the best proclamation[39] – a Book, resembling (itself),[40] oft-repeating.[41] The skins of those who fear their Lord shiver from it. Then their skins and their hearts soften to the remembrance of God. That is the guidance[42] of God. He guides by means of it whomever He pleases, but whoever God leads astray has no guide.

24 Is he who guards (himself) with his face[43] against the evil of the punishment on the Day of Resurrection [...]?[44] But it will be said to the evildoers, 'Taste what you have earned!' **25** Those who were before them called (it) a lie, and the punishment came upon them from where they did not realize (it would). **26** So God made them taste disgrace in this present life, but the punishment of the Hereafter is indeed greater, if (only) they knew.

27 Certainly We have struck in this Qur'ān[45] every (kind of) parable for the people, so that they may take heed[46] **28** – an Arabic Qur'ān,[47] without any crookedness, so that they may guard (themselves).

---

21 Signs of God's power and providence

33. *you*: or 'one.'
34. *wither*: the usual translation, but the verb means 'heave.'

22 Believers and disbelievers contrasted

35. *whose heart God has expanded*: i.e. whose mind God has opened (lit. 'whose chest God has expanded'); cf. Q20.25 (of Moses); 94.1 (of the Prophet).
36. *Islam*: lit. 'the submission' or 'the surrender' to God (Ar. *al-Islām*).
37. *[...]?*: the reader must supply 'like the hard-hearted.'
38. *clearly astray*: lit. 'in clear straying.'

23 The Book as guidance

39. *proclamation*: or 'report' (Ar. *ḥadīth*), referring to the Qur'ān.
40. *resembling (itself)*: lit. 'alike' (Ar. *mutashābih*), i.e. consistent with itself, or perhaps with other revealed Books.
41. *oft-repeating*: probably a reference to 'the oft-repeated' (Ar. *al-mathānī*) stories of previous peoples who were punished for their sins (see n. on Q15.87). It could also be said of those stories that they 'resemble each other.'
42. *guidance*: one of the most frequent terms (Ar. *hudā*) for revelation in general, and the Qur'ān in particular.

24–26 Believers and disbelievers contrasted

43. *with his face*: or 'by his face' (perhaps a pleonasm for 'himself').
44. *[...]?*: usually taken as referring to disbelievers, but the expression 'guards (himself)...against the evil' suggests that it refers to believers (cf. Q13.21). Once again the reader must supply 'like the one who does not guard (himself).'

27–29 A parable against serving many gods

45. *this Qur'ān*: the expression 'this Qur'ān' (Ar. *hādhā al-qur'ān*) comes close to its present meaning as the name of the Muslim scripture (cf. Q9.111; see n. on Q2.185).
46. *take heed*: or 'remember,' 'be reminded.'
47. *an Arabic Qur'ān*: perhaps meaning that it is a translation into Arabic of the heavenly archetype or 'mother of the Book' (cf. Q12.2; 13.37; 16.103; 20.113; 41.3; 42.7; 43.3; 46.12). The specification 'Arabic Qur'ān' (Ar. *qur'ān*

29 God has struck a parable: a man concerning whom partners are quarreling, and a man belonging to one man.[48] Are they both equal in comparison?[49] Praise (be)[50] to God! No! But most of them do not know (it).

30 Surely you[51] are mortal, and surely they are mortal, **31** and surely on the Day of Resurrection you[52] will dispute in the presence of your Lord. **32** Who is more evil than the one who lies against God, and calls the truth a lie when it comes to him? Is there not a dwelling place in Gehenna[53] for the disbelievers? **33** But the one who brings the truth and confirms it, those – they are the ones who guard (themselves). **34** They will have whatever they please with their Lord. That is the payment of the doers of good **35** – so that God may absolve them of the worst of what they have done, and pay them their reward for the best of what they have done. **36** Is God not sufficient for His servant,[54] when they frighten you with (gods) other than Him? Whoever God leads astray has no guide, **37** but whoever God guides – no one (will) lead him astray. Is God not mighty, a taker of vengeance?

38 If indeed you[55] ask them, 'Who created the heavens and the earth?,' they will indeed say, 'God.'[56] Say: 'Do you see what you call on instead of God?[57] If God intends any harm for me, will they[58] be removers of His harm? Or if He intends any mercy for me, will they[59] be withholders of His mercy?' Say: 'God is enough for me. In Him the trusting put their trust.' **39** Say: 'My people! Do as you are able. Surely I am going to do (what I can). Soon you will know **40** on whom punishment will come, disgracing him. On him a lasting punishment will descend.'

41 Surely We have sent down on you[60] the Book for the people with the truth.[61] Whoever is (rightly) guided, is guided only for himself,[62] and whoever goes astray, goes astray only against himself. You are not a guardian over them.

42 God takes the self at the time of its death, and that which has not died in its sleep,[63] and He retains the

---

'arabiyya) may imply the existence of 'Qur'āns' (as it were) in other languages, but it is probably an answer to some objection, perhaps that Hebrew was thought to be the exclusive language of revelation.

48. *a man...a man...*: the contrast is between a slave owned by several masters, and one owned by a single master; the phrase 'belonging to one man' (Ar. *salaman li-rajulin*) evokes 'submission' (*islām*) to one God.
49. *in comparison*: lit. 'as a parable;' cf. Matthew 6.24, 'No man can serve two masters.'
50. *(be)*: or '(belongs).'

30–37 God will judge

51. *you*: the Prophet.
52. *you*: plur.
53. *Gehenna*: a name for Hell (see n. on Q2.206).
54. *His servant*: the Prophet.

38–40 Trust in God alone

55. *you*: the Prophet.
56. *'God'*: their answer makes explicit their belief in God as the supreme deity (cf. Q10.31; 29.61, 63; 31.25; 43.87).
57. *what you call on...*: their gods, who are powerless against God.
58. *they*: fem. (the 'daughters of God'?)
59. *they*: fem.

41 Each is responsible to accept or reject the revelation

60. *you*: the Prophet.
61. *with the truth*: or 'in truth,' 'truly.'
62. *for himself*: i.e. to his own benefit.

42 God causes death

63. *in its sleep*: an individual's 'self' or 'soul' goes to God during sleep, but then returns to normal 'waking' life until its appointed time to die (cf. Q6.60).

one for whom He has decreed death, but sends back the other until an appointed time.[64] Surely in that are signs[65] indeed for a people who reflect.

43 Or have they taken intercessors[66] instead of God? Say: 'Even if they possess nothing and do not understand?' **44** Say: 'Intercession (belongs) to God altogether.[67] To Him (belongs) the kingdom of the heavens and the earth. Then to Him you will be returned.'

45 When God is mentioned alone,[68] the hearts of those who do not believe in the Hereafter shrink, but when those (gods) are mentioned instead of Him, suddenly they welcome the good news. **46** Say: 'God! Creator of the heavens and the earth, Knower of the unseen and the seen, You will judge between your servants concerning their differences.' **47** (Even) if those who have done evil had what is on the earth – all (of it) – and as much again, they would indeed (try to) ransom (themselves) with it from the evil of the punishment on the Day of Resurrection. But what they were not counting on will become apparent to them from God, **48** and the evils of what they have earned will become apparent to them, and what they were mocking will overwhelm them.

49 When hardship touches a person, he calls on Us. Then, when We bestow blessing on him from Us, he says, 'I have only been given it because of knowledge.'[69] No! It is a test,[70] but most of them do not know (it). **50** Those who were before them said it (too), but what they earned[71] was of no use to them, **51** and the evils of what they earned smote them. And those of these (people)[72] who have done evil – the evils of what they have earned will smite them (too), and they will not be able to escape. **52** Do they[73] not know that God extends (His) provision to whomever He pleases, and restricts (it)? Surely in that are signs indeed for a people who believe.

53 Say: 'My servants who have acted wantonly against themselves![74] Do not despair of the mercy of God. Surely God forgives sins – all (of them). Surely He – He is the Forgiving, the Compassionate. **54** Turn to your Lord (in repentance), and submit to Him, before the punishment comes upon you, (for) then you will not be helped. **55** Follow the best of what has been sent down to you from your Lord, before the punishment comes upon you unexpectedly, when you do not realize (it)' **56** – in case anyone (should) say, 'Alas for me, in regard to what I neglected concerning God, for I was indeed one of the scoffers!' **57** Or say, 'If only God had guided me, I would indeed have been one of those who guard (themselves)!' **58** Or say, when he sees the punishment, 'If only I had (another) turn, and (could) be one of the doers of good!' **59** 'Yes indeed! My signs did come to you,[75] but you called them a lie, and were arrogant, and were

---

64. *an appointed time*: or 'term' (Ar. *ajal*), i.e. the precise date of a person's death is predetermined by God.
65. *signs*: of God's power (see n. on Q2.39).

43–44 Intercession belongs to God

66. *intercessors*: see n. on Q39.3 above; cf. Q10.18; 21.24; 42.9.
67. *Intercession (belongs) to God altogether*: i.e. only God can give permission to intercede with him.

45–48 God will judge

68. *God is mentioned alone*: thereby denying the existence of other gods (cf. Q17.46; 40.12).

49–52 Adversity and prosperity a test

69. *because of knowledge*: i.e. he wrongly supposes that it was his own wisdom which merited his success (cf. Q28.78).
70. *test*: or 'trial,' 'temptation' (Ar. *fitna*); for this idea, see e.g. Q7.168; 21.35.
71. *what they earned*: i.e. their deeds.
72. *these (people)*: the Prophet's contemporaries; said to refer to the Meccans.
73. *Do they...*: the Cairo edition, reflecting the views of traditional scholars, attributes the following three verses (Q39.52-54) to the 'Medinan' period.

53–59 Call for repentance

74. *acted wantonly against themselves*: i.e. by abandoning all restraint, they only sinned against themselves.
75. *you*: sing.; this is God's reply to the preceding expressions of a disbeliever's regret at the Judgment.

one of the disbelievers.'

60 On the Day of Resurrection you[76] will see those who lied against God, their faces blackened. Is there not a dwelling place in Gehenna for the arrogant? **61** But God will rescue those who guarded (themselves) in their (place of) safety. Evil will not touch them, nor will they sorrow. **62** God is the Creator of everything. He is guardian over everything. **63** To Him (belong) the keys[77] of the heavens and the earth. Those who disbelieve in the signs of God, those – they are the losers.

64 Say: 'Do you command me to serve (anyone) other than God, you ignorant ones?' **65** You have been inspired,[78] and those who were before you: 'If indeed you associate,[79] your deed(s) will indeed come to nothing, and you will indeed be one of the losers.' **66** No! Serve God, and be one of the thankful.

67 They have not measured God (with) due measure, when the entire earth will be His handful on the Day of Resurrection, and the heavens will be rolled up in His right (hand).[80] Glory to Him! He is exalted above what they associate. **68** There will be a blast on the trumpet,[81] and whoever is in the heavens and whoever is on the earth will be thunderstruck, except for those whom God pleases. Then there will be another blast on it, and suddenly they will stand up,[82] looking around. **69** And the earth will shine with the light of its Lord, and the Book[83] will be laid down, and the prophets and witnesses[84] will be brought, and it will be decided between them in truth[85] – and they will not be done evil. **70** Each one will be paid in full for what he has done, (for) He knows what they do.

71 Those who disbelieved will be driven in companies into Gehenna, until, when they have come to it, its gates will be opened, and its keepers will say to them: 'Did messengers not come to you from among you, reciting to you the signs[86] of your Lord and warning you about the meeting of this Day of yours?' They will say, 'Yes indeed! But the word of punishment has proved true against the disbelievers.' **72** It will be said, 'Enter the gates of Gehenna, there to remain.' Evil is the dwelling place of the arrogant!

73 But those who guarded (themselves) against their Lord will be driven in companies into the Garden, until, when they have come to it, and its gates will be opened, and its keepers will say to them: 'Peace (be) upon you! You have been good, so enter it, to remain (there).' **74** They will say, 'Praise (be)[87] to God, who has fulfilled His promise to us, and has caused us to inherit the earth! We (may) settle in the Garden

---

60–63 God will judge

76. *you*: the Prophet, or perhaps intended generally ('one').
77. *keys*: or 'storehouses.'

64–66 The Prophet to serve God alone

78. *You have been inspired*: or 'You have received inspiration' (referring to the Prophet).
79. *if you associate*: other gods with God.

67–75 A judgment scene

80. *the heavens will be rolled up...*: like a scroll; cf. Q21.104 (for a similar image, see Revelation 6.14, 'And the sky vanished like a scroll being rolled up' [alluding to Isaiah 34.4]).
81. *a blast on the trumpet*: the Last Day will be announced by the blast of a trumpet (e.g. Q6.73; 18.99; 20.102; 69.13; 74.8; 78.18; cf. Matthew 24.31; 1 Corinthians 15.52; 1 Thessalonians 4.16); here there is a 'double blast.'
82. *stand up*: i.e. the dead will be raised.
83. *the Book*: the heavenly 'Record' or 'Account' of the deeds of humankind (see Q23.62; cf. Q17.13, 71; 69.19, 25; 84.7, 10, where each person is given an individual 'book' containing a record of his deeds).
84. *witnesses*: probably the angels (for their various roles, see n. on Q2.30).
85. *it will be decided between them in truth*: i.e. between the prophets with their followers and the disbelievers (cf. Q10.47).
86. *signs*: or 'verses.'
87. *(be)*: or '(belongs).'

wherever we please.'[88] Excellent is the reward of the doers![89]

75 And you[90] will see the angels completely surrounding the throne, glorifying their Lord with praise.
It will be decided between them in truth,[91] and it will be said, 'Praise (be)[92] to God, Lord of the worlds!'[93]

---

88. *...We (may) settle...wherever we please*: this makes it appear that the Garden is on earth, not in heaven (cf. Q12.56, for a similar expression used of Joseph in Egypt).
89. *the doers*: of righteous deeds (cf. Q29.58-59).
90. *you*: the Prophet, or perhaps intended generally ('one').
91. *It will be decided between them in truth*: if this is not a recapitulation of Q39.69 (above), it would indicate that the angels too will be judged.
92. *(be)*: or '(belongs).'
93. *Lord of the worlds*: for this title, see n. on Q1.2.

40 Forgiver ✿ Ghāfir

In the Name of God, the Merciful, the Compassionate

1 Ḥā' Mīm.[1]

2 The sending down of the Book is from God, the Mighty, the Knowing,[2] **3** Forgiver of sin and Accepter of repentance, harsh in retribution, full of forbearance. (There is) no god but Him. To Him is the (final) destination.

4 No one disputes about the signs[3] of God, except those who disbelieve. Do not let their comings and goings in the lands deceive you.[4] **5** The people of Noah before them (also) called (it) a lie, and the factions after them,[5] and each community was determined to seize its messenger,[6] and disputed by means of falsehood to refute the truth. So I seized them – and how was My retribution? **6** In this way the word of your Lord has proved true against those who disbelieve: 'They are the companions of the Fire.'[7]

7 Those who bear the throne, and those around it,[8] glorify their Lord with praise, and believe in Him, and they ask forgiveness for those who believe:[9] 'Our Lord, You comprehend everything in mercy and knowledge, so forgive those who turn (in repentance) and follow Your way. Guard them against the punishment of the Furnace,[10] **8** Our Lord, and cause them to enter the Gardens of Eden,[11] which You

---

Q40: This is the first of a group of seven sūras known as the 'Ḥawāmīm,' from the two letters (Ḥā' Mīm) with which they all begin. It consists mainly of the story of Moses, with a number of features which distinguish it from other versions of his story in the Qur'ān. Most scholars assign Q40 to the 'Meccan' period, though some traditional scholars attribute a couple of verses to the 'Medinan' period. It takes its name from one of the divine epithets in its opening verses, but it is also known as *al-Mu'min*, from 'the believer' in the house of Pharaoh who tried to dissuade his people from opposing Moses (Q40.28-45).

1 Letters

1. *Ḥā' Mīm*: the names of Arabic letters *ḥ* and *m*. The same letter combination occurs in a block of sūras from Q40 to Q46 (Q42 has an additional ', *s*, and *q*). Twenty-nine sūras begin with letters like these, ranging from one to five. No satisfactory explanation has been given for their occurrence. The Cairo edition varies in counting these letters as a separate verse (as here), or as the beginning of the first verse.

2–3 A Book from God

2. *The sending down of the Book...*: here referring to the Qur'ān not only as a 'recited' but also 'written' scripture (see n. on Q2.2; cf. the similar openings at Q32.2; 39.1; 41.2; 45.2; 46.2).

4–6 Disbelievers warned

3. *signs*: or 'verses' (see n. on Q2.39).
4. *you*: the Prophet (cf. Q3.196).
5. *the factions after them*: referring to the generations or 'communities' after Noah (see Q40.30-31 below; cf. Q38.11-13).
6. *messenger*: for this important title, see n. on Q2.87.
7. *the Fire*: Ar. *al-nār* is the most common of the various designations for Hell.

7–9 The angels intercede for believers

8. *Those who bear the throne, and those around it*: the angels (for their various roles, see n. on Q2.30).
9. *they ask forgiveness for those who believe*: the idea of the angels offering intercessory prayer for the forgiveness of believers is unusual (cf. Q33.43; 42.5).
10. *the Furnace*: a name for Hell (Ar. *al-jaḥīm*).
11. *Gardens of Eden*: in heaven (for this imagery, see n. on Q2.25).

have promised them – and anyone who was righteous among their fathers, and their wives, and their descendants. Surely You – You are the Mighty, the Wise. **9** And guard them against evil deeds. Whoever You guard against evil deeds on that Day, You have had compassion on him. That is the great triumph!'

10 Surely those who disbelieved will be called to: 'God's hatred is indeed greater than your hatred of one another, when you were called to belief and you disbelieved.' **11** They will say, 'Our Lord, You have caused us to die twice, and You have given us life twice.[12] (Now) we confess our sins. (Is there) any way to get out?' **12** That is because, when God was called on alone,[13] you disbelieved, but if (another) was associated with Him, you believed. Judgment (belongs) to God, the Most High, the Great.

13 He (it is) who shows you His signs, and sends down provision for you from the sky, but no one takes heed[14] except the one who turns (in repentance). **14** So call on God,[15] devoting (your) religion to Him,[16] (even) though the disbelievers dislike (it).

15 Exalter of ranks,[17] Holder of the throne, He casts the spirit of His command[18] on whomever He pleases of His servants,[19] to warn of the Day of Meeting. **16** On the Day when they go forth, nothing of theirs will be hidden from God. 'To whom (belongs) the kingdom today?' 'To God, the One, the Supreme! **17** Today each person will be repaid for what he has earned.[20] (There will be) no evil (done) today. Surely God is quick at the reckoning.'

18 Warn them[21] of the Day of the Impending,[22] when (their) hearts will be in (their) throats, choking (them). The evildoers will not have any loyal friend or intercessor (who) will be obeyed. **19** He knows the treachery of the eyes and what the hearts[23] hide. **20** God will decide in truth, while those they call on instead of Him will not decide at all. Surely God – He is the Hearing, the Seeing.

21 Have they not traveled on the earth and seen how the end was for those who were before them?[24]

10–12 A judgment scene

12. *die twice...life twice*: for this idea, see Q2.28.
13. *when God was called on alone*: thereby denying the existence of other gods (cf. Q17.46; 39.45).

13–14 Call on God alone

14. *takes heed*: or 'remembers.'
15. *So call on God*: plur. imperative.
16. *devoting (your) religion to Him*: i.e. serving God alone.

15–20 God will judge

17. *Exalter of ranks*: i.e. it is God who has the power to confer rank.
18. *He casts the spirit of His command*: or 'He casts the spirit from His command' (Ar. *al-rūḥa min amrihī*), referring to the prophetic spirit or spirit of revelation. This seems to indicate the mode of revelation as much as the fact of it (cf. Q16.2, 102; 26.193; 97.4). Some interpreters identify 'the spirit' with Gabriel (see n. on Q2.97). God's 'command' (Ar. *amr*) may correspond to the rabbinic notion of the 'divine word' (Aram. *mēmrā*), or to the related Christian idea of the *logos* as the manifestation of God's word, or as God's messenger in place of God himself (cf. Q16.2; 17.85; 42.52).
19. *servants*: the word 'servant' (Ar. *'abd*) also means 'slave.'
20. *for what he has earned*: i.e. for what he has done, whether good or evil.
21. *Warn them*: addressed to the Prophet.
22. *Day of the Impending*: 'the Impending' is fem., so it cannot agree with 'Day' (cf. Q53.57, 'the impending [Hour?] is impending'); in any case it suggests that the end was thought to be near (see Q40.70, 77 below; cf. e.g. Q6.5; 26.6).
23. *hearts*: lit. 'chests,' considered the seat of knowledge and understanding.

21–22 Punishment of earlier generations a warning

24. *Have they not traveled on the earth and seen...*: a reference to previous peoples who were punished for their disbelief (see n. on Q7.59; cf. Q40.82 below). The remains of their destroyed cities were believed to be still visible.

They were stronger than them in power, and in the traces[25] (they left behind) on the earth. Yet God seized them in their sins, and they had no defender against God. **22** That was because they – (when) their messengers came to them with the clear signs[26] – they disbelieved. So God seized them. Surely He is strong, harsh in retribution.

23 Certainly We sent Moses with Our signs and clear authority **24** to Pharaoh, and Haman,[27] and Qārūn,[28] but they said, 'A magician, a liar!'[29] **25** When he brought them the truth from Us, they said, 'Kill the sons of those who believe with him, and keep their women alive.'[30] Yet the plot of the disbelievers always goes astray. **26** Pharaoh said, 'Let me kill Moses, and let him call on his Lord. Surely I fear that he will change your religion, or that he will cause corruption to appear on the earth.' **27** Moses said, 'I take refuge with my Lord and your Lord from every arrogant one (who) does not believe in the Day of Reckoning.'

28 A (certain) man, a believer from the house of Pharaoh, (who) concealed his belief,[31] said, 'Will you kill a man because he says, "My Lord is God," when he has brought you the clear signs from your Lord? If he is a liar, his lie is on him, but if he is truthful, some of what he promises you will smite you. Surely God does not guide anyone who is wanton (and) a liar. **29** My people! Today the kingdom (belongs) to you (who) prevail on the earth, but who will help us against the violence of God, if it comes upon us?'

Pharaoh said, 'I only show you what I see, and I only guide you to the right way.' **30** But the one who believed said, 'My people! Surely I fear for you something like the Day of the Factions,[32] **31** like the case of the people of Noah, and 'Ād, and Thamūd, and those who (came) after them. Yet God does not intend any evil to (His) servants. **32** My people! Surely I fear for you the Day of Calling,[33] **33** the Day when you will turn back, retreating, having no protector from God. Whoever God leads astray has no guide.
34 Certainly Joseph brought you the clear signs before, but you did not stop doubting about what he brought you, until, when he perished, you said, "God will never raise up a messenger after him." In this way God leads astray anyone who is wanton (and) a doubter.'

35 Those who dispute[34] about the signs of God, without any authority having come to them[35] – (that) is a very hateful thing in the sight of God and those who believe. In this way God sets a seal on the heart of every arrogant tyrant.

36 Pharaoh said, 'Haman! Build a tower for me,[36] so that I may reach the ropes,[37] **37** the ropes of the heavens,

---

25. *traces*: lit. 'footsteps' or 'tracks.'
26. *the clear signs*: or 'the clear proofs,' 'the indisputable evidence.'

23–50 The story of Moses and Pharaoh

27. *Haman*: an official of Pharaoh's court (also at Q28.6); cf. Haman in the biblical book of Esther (3.1-6; 7.6-10), who was likewise an antagonist of the Jews, but an adviser to the Persian king Ahasuerus (Xerxes).
28. *Qārūn*: here an associate of Pharaoh and Haman (also at Q29.39), but cf. the story at Q28.76-82, where he is one of Moses' people (the biblical 'Korah' of Numbers 16).
29. *magician...liar*: cf. Q38.4 (of the Prophet).
30. *Kill the sons..., and keep their women alive*: cf. Pharaoh's order to kill all Hebrew boys but spare the girls (Exodus 1.15-16, 22).
31. *a (certain) man...*: a distinctive feature of this version of the story of Moses and Pharaoh.
32. *Day of the Factions*: i.e. the judgment (in history) of earlier generations (see n. on Q40.5 above; cf. Q40.21).
33. *Day of Calling*: perhaps when God summons them to judgment, or when believers and disbelievers call out to each other (cf. Q7.44, 50; 57.14).
34. *Those who dispute...*: since this parenthesis interrupts the flow of the story, it may be a later addition.
35. *without any authority...*: i.e. they oppose the signs without any divinely authorized alternative.
36. *Build a tower for me*: i.e. a tower that will reach up to heaven (cf. Q28.38); the idea is similar to the one behind the building of the tower of Babel (Genesis 11.4).
37. *reach the ropes*: i.e. ascend into heaven (cf. Q38.10; 52.38, 'a ladder').

and look upon the god of Moses. Surely I think he is a liar indeed.' In this way the evil of his deed was made to appear enticing to Pharaoh, and he was kept from the way. But the plot of Pharaoh only (came) to ruin.

38 Certainly the one who believed said, 'My people! Follow me, and I shall guide you to the right way. **39** My people! Surely this present life is enjoyment, but surely the Hereafter[38] – it is the permanent Home. **40** Whoever does an evil deed will only be repaid the equal of it, but whoever does a righteous deed, whether male or female – and is a believer – those will enter the Garden, where they will be provided for without reckoning. **41** My people! Why is it that I call you to salvation, but you call me to the Fire.[39] **42** You call me to disbelieve in God, and to associate with Him what I have no knowledge of, but I call you to the Mighty, the Forgiving. **43** (There is) no doubt that what you call me to has no calling to[40] in this world or in the Hereafter, and that our return is to God, and that the wanton – they will be the companions of the Fire. **44** You will remember what I say to you, and (now) I commit my affair to God. Surely God sees His servants.' **45** So God guarded him against the evils of what they devised, and the evil punishment overwhelmed the house of Pharaoh. **46** The Fire – they will be presented to it morning and evening. On the Day when the Hour[41] strikes: 'Cause the house of Pharaoh to enter[42] the harshest punishment!'[43]

47 When they argue with each other in the Fire, and the weak say to those who were arrogant: 'Surely we were your followers, so are you going relieve us (now) of any portion of the Fire?' **48** Those who were arrogant will say, 'Surely we are all in it. Surely God has already rendered judgment among (His) servants.' **49** Those who are in the Fire will say to the keepers of Gehenna, 'Call on your Lord to lighten for us one day of the punishment!' **50** They will say, 'Did your messengers not bring you the clear signs?' They will say, 'Yes indeed!' They will say, 'Then call!' But the call of the disbelievers only goes astray.

51 Surely We do indeed help Our messengers and those who believe, (both) in this present life and on the Day when the witnesses[44] arise **52** – the Day when their excuse will not benefit the evildoers. For them (there will be) the curse, and for them (there will be) the evil home. **53** Certainly We gave Moses the guidance, and caused the Sons of Israel to inherit the Book, **54** as a guidance and reminder to those with understanding. **55** So be patient![45] Surely the promise of God is true. Ask forgiveness for your sin, and glorify your Lord with praise in the evening and the morning.

56 Surely those who[46] dispute about the signs of God, without any authority having come to them – they have their minds set only on greatness,[47] but they will not reach it. So take refuge in God![48] Surely He – He is the Hearing, the Seeing. **57** Indeed the creation of the heavens and earth is greater than the creation of the people, but most of the people do not know (it).

---

38. *the Hereafter*: see n. on Q2.4.
39. *you call me to the Fire*: i.e. if he were to follow their religion, he would be condemned to Hell (cf. Q2.221; 28.41).
40. *has no calling to*: i.e. hears no prayer.
41. *the Hour*: of judgment.
42. *Cause...to enter*: addressed to, or spoken by, the angels (cf. Q40.8 above).
43. *the evil punishment...the Fire...the harshest punishment*: this seems to refer to three distinct times of punishment: the first is temporal (occurring in history, as is typical of the 'punishment stories'), the next two are eschatological, one occurring after death but before Judgment, the other after the Judgment or the 'Hour').

51–55 God helps his messengers and their followers

44. *the witnesses*: probably the angels.
45. *be patient*: addressed to the Prophet (as are the following two imperatives).

56–68 Signs of God's power and providence

46. *Surely those who...*: the Cairo edition, reflecting the views of traditional scholars, attributes this verse and the next to the 'Medinan' period.
47. *they have their minds set only on greatness*: lit. '(there is) nothing in their chests but greatness.'
48. *take refuge...*: addressed to the Prophet.

58 The blind and the sighted are not equal, nor are those who believe and do deeds of righteousness and the evildoer. Little do you take heed![49] **59** Surely the Hour is coming indeed – (there is) no doubt about it – but most of the people do not believe. **60** Your Lord has said, 'Call on Me! I shall respond to you.[50] Surely those who are too proud to serve Me[51] will enter Gehenna humbled.'

61 (It is) God who made the night for you to rest in, and the day to see. Surely God is indeed full of favor to the people, but most of the people are not thankful (for it). **62** That is God, your Lord, Creator of everything. (There is) no god but Him. How are you (so) deluded? **63** In this way those who denied the signs of God were (also) deluded. **64** (It is) God who made the earth a dwelling place for you, and the sky a dome.[52] He fashioned you, and made your forms well, and provided you with good things. That is God, your Lord. Blessed (be) God, Lord of the worlds![53] **65** He is the Living One. (There is) no god but Him. Call on Him, devoting (your) religion to Him. Praise (be)[54] to God, Lord of the worlds!

66 Say: 'I am forbidden to serve those whom you call on, instead of God, when the clear signs[55] have come to me from my Lord, and I am commanded to submit to the Lord of the worlds.' **67** He (it is) who created you from dust,[56] then from a drop,[57] then from a clot, then He brings you forth as children, then (He provides for you) so that you may reach your maturity, then that you may become old men – though among you (there is) one who is taken before (this) – and that you may reach an appointed time,[58] and that you may understand. **68** He (it is) who gives life and causes death, and when He decrees something, He simply says to it, 'Be!'[59] and it is.

69 Do you[60] not see those who dispute about the signs of God? How they are turned away? **70** – Those who call the Book a lie and what We sent Our messengers with? Soon they will know! **71** – When (there are) chains on their necks, and they are dragged (by) chains **72** into the boiling (water), (and) then they are poured into the Fire. **73** Then it will be said to them, 'Where is what you used to associate,[61] **74** instead of God?' They will say, 'They have abandoned us.[62] No! We were not calling on anything before!'[63] In this way God leads the disbelievers astray. **75** 'That is because you gloated on the earth without any right, and because you were jubilant.[64] **76** Enter the gates of Gehenna, there to remain.' Evil is the dwelling place of the arrogant!

---

49. *take heed*: or 'remember.'
50. *Call on Me...*: cf. Psalm 91.15.
51. *serve Me*: or 'worship Me.'
52. *dome*: lit. 'something erected (overhead);' cf. Q2.22.
53. *Lord of the worlds*: for this title, see n. on Q1.2.
54. *(be)*: or '(belongs).'
55. *the clear signs*: or 'the clear proofs,' 'the indisputable evidence.'
56. *from dust*: see Q3.59; 18.37; 22.5; 30.20; 35.11 (cf. Genesis 2.7, 'from the dust of the ground'); 'from clay,' according to Q6.2; 7.12; 15.26; 17.61; 23.12; 32.7; 38.71, 76; 55.14; 'from water,' according to Q21.30; 24.45; 25.54.
57. *a drop*: of semen.
58. *an appointed time*: or 'term' (Ar. *ajal*), i.e. the precise date of a person's death is predetermined.
59. *Be!*: God's creative word (Ar. *kun*); cf. Q2.117; 3.47 (to Mary), 59 (of Jesus and Adam); 6.73; 16.40; 19.35; 36.82.

69–76 A judgment scene

60. *you*: the Prophet, or perhaps intended generally ('one').
61. *what you used to associate*: other gods with God.
62. *abandoned us*: lit. 'gone astray from us' (a pun).
63. *We were not calling on anything before*: i.e. the gods they prayed to turned out to be non-existent; though elsewhere their gods are said to be jinn (e.g. Q6.100; 34.40-42; 37.158-159), here their existence is denied altogether (see Q53.23n.).
64. *gloated...were jubilant*: see Q17.37; 31.18.

77 So be patient![65] Surely the promise of God is true. Whether We show you some of that which We promise them, or take you,[66] to Us they will be returned. **78** Certainly We sent messengers before you: some of whom We have recounted to you, and some of whom We have not recounted to you. But it was not for any messenger to bring a sign,[67] except by the permission of God. When the command of God comes, it will be decided in truth, and the perpetrators of falsehood will lose.

79 (It is) God who made the livestock for you, for you to ride some of them and some of them to eat **80** – and (there are other) benefits for you in them – and for you to reach any place you set your mind on,[68] and on them, and on the ship (as well), you are carried. **81** He shows you His signs – so which of the signs of God do you reject?

82 Have they not traveled on the earth and seen how the end was for those who were before them? They were more numerous than them, and stronger in power, and in the traces[69] (they left behind) on the earth. Yet what they earned[70] was of no use to them. **83** When their messengers brought them the clear signs, they gloated over what knowledge they (already) had, and what they were mocking overwhelmed them.[71] **84** Then, when they saw Our violence, they said, 'We believe in God alone, and we disbelieve in what we were associating (with Him).' **85** But their belief did not benefit them when they saw Our violence – the customary way of God,[72] which has already occurred in the past concerning His servants[73] – and then the disbelievers were lost.

77–78 Encouragement to the Prophet

65. *be patient*: addressed to the Prophet.
66. *take you*: i.e. take the Prophet in death, before the disbelievers are punished (cf. Q10.46; 13.40).
67. *sign*: or 'miracle,' confirming the truth of his message.

79–81 Signs of God's power and providence

68. *any place you set your mind on*: lit. 'a need in your chests.'

82–85 Punishment of earlier generations a warning

69. *traces*: lit. 'footsteps' or 'tracks.'
70. *what they earned*: i.e. the deeds they accomplished.
71. *what they were mocking...*: the threat of judgment and punishment.
72. *the customary way of God...*: i.e. the way (Ar. *sunna*) God punished earlier generations for their disbelief (cf. Q3.137; 15.13; 18.55; 35.43; 48.23).
73. *servants*: the word 'servants' is used here in the sense of 'people generally.'

41 Made Distinct ❁ Fuṣṣilat

In the Name of God, the Merciful, the Compassionate

1 Ḥā Mīm.[1]

2 A sending down from the Merciful, the Compassionate.[2] **3** A Book – its verses[3] made distinct[4] – an Arabic Qur'ān[5] for a people who know.

4 (He is) a bringer of good news and a warner.[6] But most of them have turned away, and they do not hear.
5 They say, 'Our hearts are covered[7] from what you call us to, and (there is) a heaviness in our ears, and between us and you (there is) a veil. So do (as you are able). Surely we are going to do (what we can).'[8]
6 Say:[9] 'I am only a human being like you. I am inspired[10] that your God is one God. So go straight with Him, and ask forgiveness from Him. But woe to the idolaters,[11] **7** who do not give the alms,[12] and (who) are disbelievers in the Hereafter![13] **8** Surely those who believe and do righteous deeds – for them (there is) a reward without end.'

Q41: This sūra opens with a declaration of the 'sending down' of the Qur'ān. It extols God as creator and pronounces judgment on those who refuse to recognize the signs of his power and providence. Most scholars assign Q41 to the 'Meccan' period. Its title comes from a word used to describe the Qur'ān (Q41.3, 44), though it is also known as 'The Prostration' (the same title as Q32).

1 Letters

1. *Ḥā Mīm*: the names of Arabic letters *ḥ* and *m*. The same letter combination occurs in a block of sūras from Q40 to Q46 (Q42 has an additional ', *s*, and *q*). Twenty-nine sūras begin with letters like these, ranging from one to five. No satisfactory explanation has been given for their occurrence. The Cairo edition varies in counting these letters as a separate verse (as here), or as the beginning of the first verse.

2–3 An Arabic Qur'ān

2. *A sending down...*: cf. the similar openings at Q32.2; 39.1; 40.2; 45.2; 46.2.
3. *verses*: or 'signs' (see n. on Q2.39).
4. *made distinct*: or 'expounded'; for this idea, see Q41.44 below; cf. Q6.114, 154; 7.52, 145; 10.37; 11.1; 12.111; 17.12).
5. *an Arabic Qur'ān*: perhaps meaning that it is a translation into Arabic of the heavenly archetype or 'mother of the Book' (cf. Q12.2; 13.37; 16.103; 20.113; 39.28; 42.7; 43.3; 46.12). The specification 'Arabic Qur'ān' (Ar. *qur'ān 'arabiyya*) may imply the existence of 'Qur'āns' (as it were) in other languages, but it is probably an answer to some objection, perhaps that Hebrew was thought to be the exclusive language of revelation.

4–8 The Messenger and the message

6. *bringer of good news...warner*: referring to the Prophet, not the Qur'ān (for these roles, see n. on Q2.119).
7. *Our hearts are covered*: lit. 'Our hearts are in coverings' (cf. Q6.25; 17.46; 18.57); here, as often, the heart is spoken of as synonymous with mind.
8. *They say...*: the disbelievers ridicule the Prophet by mimicking one of his own turns of phrase (cf. Q6.25; 17.45-46; 36.9; and Q6.135; 11.93; 39.39).
9. *Say*: on this form of address, see n. on Q2.80.
10. *I am inspired*: or 'I have received inspiration.'
11. *the idolaters*: or 'the ones who associate (other gods with God).'
12. *alms*: i.e. *zakāt*, a kind of tithe required for the benefit of the poor, as well as other purposes.
13. *the Hereafter*: see n. on Q2.4.

9 Say: 'Do you indeed disbelieve in the One who created the earth in two days,[14] and do you set up[15] rivals[16] to Him? That is the Lord of the worlds.[17] **10** He placed on it firm mountains (towering) above it, and blessed it, and decreed for it its (various) foods in four days,[18] equal to the ones who ask.[19] **11** Then He mounted (upward) to the sky, while it was (still) smoke,[20] and said to it and to the earth, "Come, both of you, willingly or unwillingly!"[21] They both said, "We come willingly." **12** He finished[22] them (as) seven heavens in two days, and inspired each heaven (with) its affair.[23] And We[24] adorned the sky of this world[25] with lamps, and (made them) a protection.[26] That is the decree of the Mighty, the Knowing.'

13 If they turn away, say: 'I warn you of a thunderbolt like the thunderbolt of 'Ād and Thamūd.'[27] **14** When the messengers[28] came to them from before them and from behind them[29] (saying): 'Do not serve (anyone) but God,' they said, 'If our Lord had (so) pleased, He would indeed have sent down angels. Surely we are disbelievers in what you are sent with.' **15** As for 'Ād, they became arrogant on the earth without any right, and said, 'Who is stronger than us in power?' Did they not see that God, who created them, was stronger than them in power? They denied Our signs. **16** So We sent a furious wind against them in the days of calamity, so that We might make them taste the punishment of disgrace in this present life. But the punishment of the Hereafter is indeed more disgraceful, and they will not be helped. **17** As for Thamūd, We guided them, but they preferred blindness over the guidance.[30] So the thunderbolt of the punishment of humiliation took them for what they had earned.[31] **18** But We rescued those who believed and guarded (themselves).[32]

19 On the Day when the enemies of God are gathered to the Fire,[33] and they are arranged (in rows)

9–12 Signs of God's power and providence

14. *in two days*: cf. the creation of the earth on 'the third day' at Genesis 1.9-13.
15. *set up*: lit. 'make.'
16. *rivals*: or 'equals' (Ar. *andād*), i.e. other gods alleged to be equal with God.
17. *Lord of the worlds*: for this title, see n. on Q1.2.
18. *(various) foods in four days*: cf. the creation of vegetation on 'the third day' (Genesis 1.11-13), and the creation of sea and land animals on 'the fifth and sixth days' (Genesis 1.20-25).
19. *equal to the ones who ask*: meaning obscure; the phrase is usually taken to refer to the provision of food as being free to all who seek it, but it may be that it refers to the fact of creation being equally open to all who inquire.
20. *smoke*: meaning obscure (cf. the 'darkness' at Genesis 1.2, and the 'mist' at Genesis 2.6).
21. *willingly or unwillingly*: cf. Q3.83; 13.15.
22. *finished*: or 'decreed.'
23. *inspired each heaven (with) its affair*: the technical term 'to inspire' (Ar. *awḥā*) is here used of God's assigning to each of the seven heavens its special task (cf. Q16.68).
24. *And We...*: notice the sudden shift from third- to first-person discourse.
25. *the sky of this world*: i.e. the lowest of the seven heavens (cf. Q37.6).
26. *a protection*: from demons (see n. on Q37.7).

13–18 The example of 'Ād and Thamūd

27. *'Ād and Thamūd*: for the stories of these two peoples, see e.g. Q7.65-72, 73-79.
28. *messengers*: for this important title, see n. on Q2.87.
29. *from before them...behind them*: perhaps to be understood temporally, i.e. 'when the messengers came to various peoples before and after 'Ād and Thamūd.'
30. *the guidance*: one of the most frequent terms (Ar. *al-hudā*) for revelation in general, and the Qur'ān in particular.
31. *what they had earned*: i.e. their deeds.
32. *guarded (themselves)*: against evil, or God.

19–23 A judgment scene

33. *the Fire*: Ar. *al-nār* is the most common of the various designations for Hell.

20 – until, when they have come to it, their hearing and their sight and their skins will bear witness against them about what they have done, **21** and they will say to their skins, 'Why did you bear witness against us?' They will say, 'God, who gave speech to everything, has given us speech. He created you the first time, and to Him you are (now) returned. **22** You did not protect[34] yourselves against your hearing and your sight and your skins bearing witness against you. You thought that God would not know much of what you had done. **23** And that – the thought you thought about your Lord – has brought you to ruin. (Now) you are among the losers.'

24 If they persist,[35] the Fire will be a dwelling place for them, and if they ask to make amends, they will not be among the ones allowed to make amends.[36] **25** We have allotted to them comrades,[37] and they have made what is before them and behind them appear enticing to them. The word about the communities of jinn and humankind (which) have passed away before them has proved true against them (as well).[38] Surely they were losers.

26 Those who disbelieve say, 'Do not listen to this Qur'ān,[39] but talk frivolously about it, so that you may overcome (them).' **27** We shall indeed make those who disbelieve taste a harsh punishment, and We shall indeed repay them for the worst of what they have done. **28** That is the payment of the enemies of God – the Fire – where they will have the Home of Eternity as payment for their having denied Our signs.

29 Those who disbelieve (will) say, 'Our Lord, show us those of the jinn and humankind who led us astray. We shall place them beneath our feet, so that they may be among the lowest.' **30** Surely those who have said, 'Our Lord is God,' (and) then have gone straight – the angels will come down on them (saying): 'Do not fear, and do not sorrow, but welcome the good news of the Garden[40] which you were promised. **31** We are your allies[41] in this present life and in the Hereafter, where you will have whatever you desire, whatever you call for **32** – a reception from One forgiving, compassionate.'

33 Who is better in speech than the one who calls (people) to God, and does righteousness, and says, 'Surely I am one of those who submit'?[42] **34** The good deed and the evil deed are not equal. Repel (evil) with that which is better,[43] and suddenly the one with whom (there was) enmity between you and him (will behave) as if he were an ally.[44] **35** Yet no one will receive it[45] except those who are patient, and no one will receive it except one who possesses great good luck.[46] **36** If any provocation from Satan

---

34. *protect*: lit. 'cover.'

24–25 Disbelievers stubborn

35. *If they persist*: lit. 'are patient,' referring to the disbelievers' stubborn refusal to believe.
36. *if they ask to make amends...*: for this idea, see Q16.84; 30.57; 45.35.
37. *comrades*: the 'satans' (cf. Q43.36-38).
38. *The word...has proved true...*: cf. Q11.119, 'I shall indeed fill Gehenna with jinn and people' (for the jinn, see n. on Q6.100).

26–28 Disbelievers mock the Qur'ān

39. *this Qur'ān*: here 'this Qur'ān' comes close to its present meaning as the name of the Muslim scripture (cf. Q9.111; see n. on Q2.185).

29–32 A judgment scene

40. *Garden*: in heaven (for this imagery, see n. on Q2.25).
41. *allies*: Ar. *awliyā'* implies the obligation of mutual protection, almost in the sense of 'friends' or 'brothers.'

33–36 Advice for the Prophet

41. *those who submit*: or 'the Muslims.'
43. *Repel (evil)...*: addressed to the Prophet (cf. Q23.96).
44. *as if he were an ally*: i.e. as if he were a 'friend' or 'brother.'
45. *it*: antecedent unclear; perhaps divine favor in general (or did this verse originally follow v. 32?).
46. *great good luck*: cf. Q28.79.

provokes you, take refuge with God. Surely He – He is the Hearing, the Knowing.

37 Among His signs are the night and the day, and the sun and the moon. Do not prostrate yourselves before the sun or before the moon, but prostrate yourselves before God, who created them, if you serve Him. **38** If they are (too) proud,[47] those who are in the presence of your Lord glorify Him by night and day, and do not become tired.[48] **39** (Another) of His signs is that you[49] see the earth barren,[50] (and) then, when We send down water on it, it stirs and swells. Surely the One who gives it life is indeed the giver of life to the dead. Surely He is powerful over everything. **40** Surely those who pervert Our signs are not hidden from Us. Is the one who is cast into the Fire better, or the one who comes (out) secure on the Day of Resurrection? Do whatever you please. Surely He sees what you do.

41 Surely those who disbelieve in the Reminder[51] when it comes to them – surely it is a mighty Book indeed! **42** Falsehood does not come to it, (either) from before it or from behind it. (It is) a sending down from One wise, praiseworthy. **43** Nothing is said to you[52] except what has already been said to the messengers before you. Surely your Lord is indeed full of forgiveness, but (also) full of painful retribution. **44** If We had made it a foreign Qur'ān,[53] they would indeed have said, 'Why are its signs not made distinct?[54] Foreign and Arabic?'[55] Say: 'It is a guidance and healing for those who believe, but those who do not believe – (there is) a heaviness in their ears, and for them it[56] is a blindness. Those – (it is as if) they are being called from a place far away.'[57]

45 Certainly We gave Moses the Book, and then differences arose about it. Were it not for a preceding word[58] from your Lord, it would indeed have been decided between them.[59] Surely they are in grave doubt indeed about it.[60]

46 Whoever does righteousness, it is for himself,[61] and whoever does evil, it is (likewise) against himself. Your Lord is not an evildoer to (His) servants.

47 Knowledge of the Hour is reserved for Him.[62] No fruit comes forth from its sheath, and no female

---

37–40 Signs of God's power and providence

46. *If they are (too) proud*: i.e. if the disbelievers are too proud to bow down before God.
48. *those who are in the presence of your Lord glorify...*: referring to the angels (cf. Q21.19-20).
49. *you*: sing., but probably intended generally.
50. *barren*: lit. 'humbled,' i.e. with its vegetation withered (cf. Q22.5).

41–44 The Prophet's revelation is identical to previous messengers

50. *the Reminder*: referring to the Qur'ān (see n. on Q3.58).
52. *Nothing is said to you...*: thus affirming that the revelation to the Prophet was identical to that of previous messengers.
53. *a foreign Qur'ān*: i.e. non-Arabic (cf. Q16.103; 26.195, 198-199).
54. *Why are its signs not made distinct*: or 'Why are its verses not expounded' (see Q41.3 above).
55. *Foreign and Arabic?*: or 'Is this a foreign (Book with) an Arab?'
56. *it*: the Qur'ān.
57. *called from a place far away*: i.e. they cannot hear or understand what is being said.

45 Disagreement about the Book of Moses

57. *a preceding word*: or prior decree, establishing the time of judgment (cf. Q8.68; 10.19; 11.110; 20.129; 42.14, 21).
59. *them*: referring to the Jews (and possibly Christians).
60. *it*: the Torah, or perhaps the Qur'ān (cf. Q11.110; 14.9; 42.14).

46 Each is responsible

60. *for himself*: i.e. for his own benefit.

47–48 A judgment scene

61. *Knowledge of the Hour is reserved for Him*: cf. Q7.187; 33.63; 43.85; 46.23; 67.26; and Mark 13.32 par.

conceives or delivers, except with His knowledge. On the Day when He will call to them, 'Where are My associates?,'[63] they will say, 'We proclaim to You: (there is) no witness among us.'[64] **48** What they called on before will abandon them,[65] and they will know (that there is) no place of escape for them.

49 The human does not tire of calling for good,[66] but if evil touches him, he is in despair (and) downcast. **50** If indeed We give him a taste of mercy from Us, after hardship has touched him, he will indeed say, 'This is mine! I do not think the Hour[67] is coming. If indeed I am returned to my Lord, surely I shall have the best (reward) indeed with Him.' We shall indeed inform those who disbelieve about what they have done, and indeed make them taste a stern punishment. **51** When We bless a person, he turns away and distances himself, but when evil touches them, he is full of long prayers.[68]

52 Say: 'Do you see? If it[69] is from God, and you disbelieve in it – who is farther astray than the one who is in extreme defiance?'[70]

53 We shall show them Our signs in the skies[71] and in themselves,[72] until it becomes clear to them that it[73] is the truth. Is it not sufficient in (regard to) your Lord that He is a witness over everything? **54** Is it not a fact that they are in doubt about the meeting with their Lord? Is it not a fact that He encompasses everything?

---

63. *My associates*: the other gods (cf. Q6.22-24; 10.28-30).
64. *no witness among us*: i.e. their ploy will be to refuse to testify against themselves about their worship of other gods.
65. *abandon them*: lit. 'go astray from them' (a pun).

49–51 People are ungrateful

65. *calling for good*: i.e. praying for wealth and possessions.
67. *the Hour*: of judgment.
68. *long prayers*: lit. 'a wide calling.'

52 Disbelief a serious matter

68. *it*: the Qur'ān.
70. *extreme defiance*: or 'wide schism.'

53–54 Encouragement to the Prophet

70. *skies*: lit. 'horizons;' said to refer (prophetically) to future Muslim victories in various lands, but it probably refers to the familiar theme of the signs of God's power and providence as manifested in the sky (see e.g. Q51.20-23).
72. *and in themselves*: probably referring to signs of God's power and providence as manifested in the creation and reproduction of humans (see e.g. Q45.3-4; 51.20-23).
73. *it*: the Qur'ān, or perhaps resurrection and judgment.

42 Consultation ۞ Al-Shūrā

In the Name of God, the Merciful, the Compassionate

1 Ḥā Mīm. **2** ʿAyn Sīn Qāf.[1]

3 In this way He inspires you,[2] and those who were before you[3] – God, the Mighty, the Wise. **4** To Him (belongs) whatever is in the heavens and whatever is on the earth. He is the Most High, the Almighty. **5** The heavens are nearly torn apart from above, when the angels glorify their Lord with praise,[4] and ask forgiveness for those on the earth.[5] Is it not a fact that God – He is the Forgiving, the Compassionate? **6** Those who have taken allies[6] other than Him – God is watcher over them. You are not a guardian over them.

7 In this way We have inspired you[7] (with) an Arabic Qur'ān,[8] so that you may warn the Mother of Towns[9] and those around it, and so that you may warn of the Day of Gathering – (there is) no doubt about it – (one) group in the Garden,[10] and (another) group in the blazing (Fire). **8** If God had (so) pleased, He would indeed will have made them one community.[11] But He causes whomever He pleases to enter into His mercy. The evildoers will have no ally and no helper.

Q42: This sūra opens by extolling the power and majesty of God and stresses the purpose of the Qur'ān as a warning. Next comes a declaration of the unity of religion in the face of religious differences. The contrasting fates of believers and disbelievers occupy much of the remainder of the sūra. The conclusion is noteworthy for the light it sheds on different modes of revelation. Most scholars assign Q42 to the 'Meccan' period, though some traditional scholars attribute several verses to the 'Medinan' period. It takes its title from the reference to the believers' 'consultation' among themselves at Q42.38.

1–2 Letters

1. *Ḥā Mīm ʿAyn Sīn Qāf*: the names of Arabic letters *ḥ*, *m*, *ʿ*, *s*, and *q*. Apart from the last three letters (unique to this sūra), the same letter combination occurs in a block of sūras from Q40 to Q46. Twenty-nine sūras begin with letters like these, ranging from one to five. No satisfactory explanation has been given for their occurrence. The Cairo edition varies in counting these letters as a separate verse (here two verses), or as the beginning of the first verse.

3–6 God's majesty

2. *you*: the Prophet.
3. *those who were before you*: previous messengers (cf. Q4.163-164).
4. *The heavens are nearly torn apart...*: i.e. from the sound of the angels glorifying God (cf. Q7.206; 39.75; 40.7).
5. *ask forgiveness for those on the earth*: the idea of the angels offering intercessory prayer for the forgiveness of believers is unusual (cf. Q33.43; 40.7).
6. *allies*: here referring to 'other gods' (Ar. *awliyā'* implies the obligation of mutual protection, almost in the sense of 'friends' or 'brothers').

7–8 Purpose of the Qur'ān

7. *you*: the Prophet.
8. *an Arabic Qur'ān*: perhaps meaning that it is a translation into Arabic of the heavenly archetype or 'mother of the Book' (cf. Q12.2; 13.37; 16.103; 20.113; 39.28; 41.3; 43.3; 46.12). The specification 'Arabic Qur'ān' (Ar. *qur'ān ʿarabiyya*) may imply the existence of 'Qur'āns' (as it were) in other languages, but it is probably an answer to some objection, perhaps that Hebrew was thought to be the exclusive language of revelation.
9. *Mother of Towns*: Ar. *umm al-qurā* is said to refer to Mecca (cf. Q6.92).
10. *Garden*: in heaven (for this imagery, see n. on Q2.25).
11. *one community*: for this idea, see n. on Q2.213.

9 Or have they taken allies other than Him? God – He is the (true) Ally. He gives the dead life. He is powerful over everything. **10** Whatever you differ about, judgment of it (belongs) to God. That is God, my Lord. In Him I have put my trust, and to Him I turn (in repentance). **11** (He is) the Creator of the heavens and the earth. He has made pairs for you from yourselves, and pairs (also) from the livestock. He scatters you by this means.[12] There is nothing like Him. He is the Hearing, the Seeing. **12** To Him (belong) the keys[13] of the heavens and the earth. He extends (His) provision to whomever He pleases, and restricts (it). Surely He has knowledge of everything.

13 He has instituted for you[14] from the religion what He charged Noah with, and that which We have inspired you[15] (with), and what We charged Abraham, and Moses, and Jesus with: 'Observe the religion, and do not become divided in it.'[16] What you[17] call them to is hard[18] on the idolaters.[19] God chooses for Himself[20] whomever He pleases, and He guides to Himself whoever turns (to Him in repentance). **14** They did not become divided until after the knowledge had come to them,[21] (because of) envy among themselves.[22] Were it not for a preceding word[23] from your Lord, until an appointed time,[24] it would indeed have been decided between them.[25] Surely those who inherited the Book after them[26] are in grave doubt indeed about it.[27] **15** So call (them) to that,[28] and go straight as you have been commanded, and do not follow their (vain) desires, but say: 'I believe in whatever Book God has sent down,[29] and I have been commanded to act fairly among you. God is our Lord and your Lord. To us our deeds and to you your deeds.[30] (There is) no argument between us and you. God will gather us together. To Him is the (final) destination.'

9–12 Signs of God's power and providence

12. *scatters you...*: as a sower scatters seed.
13. *keys*: or 'storehouses.'

13–15 The unity of religion

14. *you*: plur.
15. *you*: the Prophet. (Notice the sudden shift from third-person to first-person discourse.)
16. *do not become divided in it*: i.e. do not divide the one, true religion into different 'factions' or 'sects' (see Q3.105; cf. Q19.37).
17. *you*: the Prophet.
18. *hard*: lit. 'great.'
19. *the idolaters*: or 'the ones who associate (other gods with God).'
20. *for Himself*: or 'for it' (i.e. the religion).
21. *until after the knowledge had come to them*: i.e. differences arose only after the revelation was given (see Q2.213).
22. *envy among themselves*: referring to Jews and Christians (and their disputes); here they are the ones considered 'idolaters' (see also Q4.51; 9.30-33; 30.30-33).
23. *a preceding word*: or prior decree, establishing the time of judgment (cf. Q8.68; 10.19; 11.110; 20.129; 41.45; 42.21 below).
24. *an appointed time*: or 'term' (Ar. *ajal*), which is predetermined and cannot be changed.
25. *them*: Jews and Christians.
26. *those who inherited the Book after them*: i.e. Jews and Christians of the Prophet's day.
27. *it*: the Torah, or perhaps the Qur'ān (cf. Q11.110; 14.9; 41.45).
28. *So call (them) to that*: either to their own scriptures or the Qur'ān, or perhaps to the 'unity of religion' (the Prophet is addressed).
29. *I believe in whatever Book God has sent down*: an unqualified endorsement of previous scriptures (cf. Q2.136; 3.84; 29.46), though this would later be modified by some in light of the (non-Qur'ānic) assertion that the 'Books' actually in the hands of Jews and Christians had been subjected to wholesale 'corruption' (Ar. *taḥrīf*); see e.g. Q2.75, 79.
30. *To us our deeds and to you your deeds*: or 'We have our deeds and you have your deeds' (see Q2.139-141; 28.55; cf. Q109.6).

16 Those who (still) argue about God, after whatever response has been made to Him[31] – their argument is refuted in the sight of their Lord. Anger (will fall) on them, and for them (there will be) a harsh punishment. **17** (It is) God who has sent down the Book with the truth,[32] and (also) the scale.[33] What will make you[34] know? Perhaps the Hour[35] is near. **18** Those who do not believe in it seek to hurry it, but those who believe in it are apprehensive about it, and know that it is the truth. Is it not a fact that those who are in doubt about the Hour are far astray?[36]

19 God is astute with His servants,[37] providing for whomever He pleases. He is the Strong, the Mighty.

20 Whoever desires the harvest of the Hereafter[38] – We shall give him increase in his harvest, and whoever desires the harvest of this world – We shall give him some of it, but he will not have any portion in the Hereafter. **21** Or do they have associates[39] who have instituted for them from the religion what God has not given permission for? Were it not for a decisive word,[40] it would indeed have been decided between them. Surely the evildoers – for them (there is) a painful punishment. **22** You[41] will see the evildoers apprehensive about what they have earned,[42] when it[43] falls on them, while those who believe and do righteous deeds are in meadows of the Gardens. They will have whatever they please in the presence of their Lord. That is the great favor![44]

23 That is the good news[45] which God gives to His servants who believe and do righteous deeds. Say:[46] 'I do not ask you for any reward for it, except love for family.'[47] Whoever acquires a good (deed) – We shall increase the good for him in it. Surely God is forgiving, thankful.

24 Or do they say, 'He has forged a lie against God?' If God pleases, He will set a seal on your heart,[48] and God will blot out falsehood and verify the truth by His words.[49] Surely He knows what is in the hearts.[50]

16–18 Encouragement to the Prophet

31. *after whatever response has been made to Him*: i.e. after some profession of faith has been made.
32. *with the truth*: or 'in truth,' 'truly.'
33. *the scale*: said to refer to the laws laid down in the Qur'ān, but probably symbolic of divine justice in general (cf. Q55.7-9; 57.25).
34. *you*: sing., but probably intended generally.
35. *the Hour*: of judgment.
36. *far astray*: lit. 'in far straying.'

19–26 Fate of believers and disbelievers

37. *servants*: the word 'servants,' which also means 'slaves,' is used here in the sense of 'all people.'
38. *the Hereafter*: see n. on Q2.4.
39. *associates*: i.e. their gods.
40. *a decisive word*: i.e. 'sparing them' until the appointed time of judgment (see Q42.14 above; cf. Matthew 13.24-30).
41. *You*: the Prophet.
42. *what they have earned*: i.e. the sins they have committed.
43. *it*: punishment.
44. *great favor*: or 'superior merit.'
45. *That is the good news...*: the Cairo edition, reflecting the views of traditional scholars, attributes vv. 23-25 and v. 27 to the 'Medinan' period.
46. *Say*: on this form of address, see n. on Q2.80.
47. *except love for family*: i.e. good treatment for his family.
48. *your heart*: the Prophet's heart (here, as often, the heart is spoken of as synonymous with mind).
49. *...verify the truth by His words*: i.e. if the Prophet were speaking falsely, God would cease using him as a messenger and establish the truth otherwise.
50. *hearts*: lit. 'chests,' considered the seat of knowledge and understanding.

25 He (it is) who accepts repentance from His servants and pardons evil deeds. He knows what you do.

26 He responds to those who believe and do righteous deeds, and gives them increase from His favor. But the disbelievers – for them (there is) a harsh punishment.

27 If God were to extend (His) provision to His servants, they would indeed act oppressively on the earth, but He sends down in measure whatever He pleases. Surely He is aware of His servants (and) sees (them).

28 He (it is) who sends down the rain after they have despaired, and displays His mercy. He is the Ally, the Praiseworthy.

29 Among His signs are the creation of the heavens and the earth, and the creatures He has scattered[51] in
both of them. He has power over gathering them[52] whenever He pleases. **30** Whatever smiting may smite
you is because of what your (own) hands have earned – yet He pardons much. **31** You cannot escape
(Him) on the earth, and you have no ally and no helper other than God.

32 Among His signs are the (ships) running on the sea, like landmarks. **33** If He pleases, He stills the
wind and they remain motionless on its surface. Surely in that are signs indeed for every patient (and)
thankful one. **34** Or He wrecks them[53] for what they[54] have earned – yet He pardons much – **35** and (it is
so that)[55] He may know those who dispute about Our signs. For them (there is) no place of escape.

36 Whatever things you have been given are (only) the enjoyment of this present life, but what
is with God is better and more lasting for those who believe and put their trust in their Lord
37 – and (also for) those who avoid great sins and immoral deeds,[56] and when they are angry, they forgive,
38 and those who respond to their Lord and observe the prayer,[57] and their affair (is a matter of)
consultation among themselves, and they contribute[58] from what We have provided them, **39** and those
who, when envy smites them, defend themselves (against it). **40** (The) payment for an evil deed is an evil
like it, but whoever pardons and sets (things) right – his reward (depends) on God.[59] Surely He does not
love the evildoers. **41** Whoever indeed defends himself after he has suffered evil, those – against them
(there is) no way.[60] **42** The way is only open against those who do the people evil, and act oppressively
on the earth without any right. Those – for them (there is) a painful punishment. **43** But whoever indeed
is patient and forgives – surely that indeed is one of the determining factors in (all) affairs.

44 Whoever God leads astray has no ally after Him, and you[61] will see the evildoers, when they see the
punishment, saying, '(Is there) any way to return?' **45** You will see them presented to it,[62] humbled by
the disgrace, looking with furtive glance(s). And those who believe will say, 'Surely the losers are those
who have lost their (own) selves and their families on the Day of Resurrection.' Is it not a fact that the
evildoers (will remain) in lasting punishment? **46** They will have no allies to help them, other than God,

---

27–35 Signs of God's power and providence

51. *scattered*: as a sower scatters seed.
52. *gathering them*: at the resurrection (cf. Q42.7 above; 64.9).
53. *them*: the ships.
54. *they*: those on board.
55. *and (it is so that)...*: the grammatical connection with what precedes is problematic.

36–46 Fate of believers and disbelievers

56. *immoral deeds*: lit. 'the immoralities' (Ar. *al-fawāḥisha*), usually of a sexual nature.
57. *the prayer*: the ritual prayer (or *ṣalāt*).
58. *contribute*: lit. 'spend.'
59. *his reward (depends) on God*: i.e. God is responsible for rewarding him.
60. *no way*: i.e. to blame or inflict punishment.
61. *you*: sing., but perhaps intended generally ('one').
62. *it*: probably referring to 'the Fire,' since the pronoun is fem. (cf. Q40.46).

and whoever God leads astray has no way.[63]

47 Respond to your Lord, before a Day comes from God which cannot be turned back.[64] You will not have any shelter on that Day, nor any denial (of what you have done). **48** If they turn away – We have not sent you[65] as a watcher over them. Nothing (depends) on you except the delivery (of the message). Surely We – when We give a person a taste of mercy from Us, he gloats about it, but if some evil smites them because of what their (own) hands have sent forward[66] – surely the human is ungrateful.[67]

49 To God (belongs) the kingdom of the heavens and the earth. He creates whatever He pleases. He grants females to whomever He pleases, and He grants males to whomever He pleases,[68] **50** or He pairs them males and females. He makes barren whomever He pleases. Surely He is knowing, powerful.

51 It is not (fitting) for any human being that God should speak to him,[69] except (by) inspiration,[70] or from behind a veil,[71] or (that) He should send a messenger[72] and he inspire by His permission whatever He pleases. Surely He is most high, wise. **52** In this way We have inspired you[73] (with) a spirit of Our command.[74] You did not know what the Book was, nor (what) belief (was), but We have made it a light[75] by means of which We guide whomever We please of Our servants. Surely you will guide (people) to a straight path, **53** the path of God, the One to whom (belongs) whatever is in the heavens and whatever is on the earth. Is it not a fact that all affairs are returned to God?

---

63. *...has no way*: it is not clear whether the quotation should have ended here, instead of two sentences earlier.

47–48 Call to repent

64. *before a Day comes from God which cannot be turned back*: or 'before a Day comes on which (there will be) no turning back from God' (cf. Q30.43).
65. *you*: the Prophet.
66. *what their (own) hands have sent forward*: i.e. their deeds, which are 'sent forward' to the Judgment.
67. *ungrateful*: Ar. *kafūr*, punning on *kāfir*, 'disbeliever.'

49–50 God's is the kingdom and the power

68. *females...males...*: i.e. daughters and sons.

51–53 Modes of revelation

69. *It is not (fitting) for any human being that God should speak to him*: Moses seems to have enjoyed special status in this regard, for he received an unmediated revelation (see Q4.164: 'God spoke to Moses directly;' cf. Q7.143; 19.52).
70. *except (by) inspiration*: Ar. *waḥy*, referring to one mode of revelation; the following phrases indicate others.
71. *from behind a veil*: i.e. hearing words without seeing anything (perhaps for reasons of etiquette; cf. Q33.53).
72. *messenger*: here probably referring to an angel.
73. *you*: the Prophet (notice the sudden shift from third- to first-person discourse).
74. *a spirit of Our command*: or 'a spirit from Our command' (Ar. *rūḥan min amrinā*). This seems to indicate the mode of revelation as much as the fact of it. The mysterious being called 'the spirit' (cf. Q16.102, 'the holy spirit;' 26.193, 'the trustworthy spirit') appears to be the bearer of revelation (in the company of the angels, cf. Q16.2; 97.4). Some interpreters identify 'the spirit' with Gabriel (see n. on Q2.97). God's 'command' (Ar. *amr*) may correspond to the rabbinic notion of the 'divine word' (Aram. *mēmrā*), or to the related Christian idea of the *logos* as the manifestation of God's word, or as God's messenger in place of God himself (cf. Q16.2; 17.85; 40.15).
75. *made it a light*: referring to the Qur'ān (cf. Q5.15).

43 Decoration ❁ Al-Zukhruf

In the Name of God, the Merciful, the Compassionate

1 Ḥā Mīm.[1]

2 By the clear Book![2] **3** Surely We have made it an Arabic Qur'ān,[3] so that you[4] may understand.
4 And surely it is in the mother of the Book,[5] with Us, most high indeed, wise.[6]

5 Shall We strike the Reminder[7] away from you, on the excuse that you have been a wanton people?
6 How many prophets[8] have We sent among those of old! **7** Yet not one prophet came to them whom they did not ridicule.
8 So We destroyed (those peoples who were) stronger than them[9] in power, and the example[10] of those of old has passed away.[11]

9 If indeed you[12] ask them, 'Who created the heavens and the earth?,' they will indeed say, 'The Mighty, the Knowing created them.'[13]
10 (It is He) who made the earth as a cradle for you, and made (path)ways

---

Q43: This sūra condemns the folly of idolatry (especially the idea that God has 'daughters'), and warns of the dangers of persistent disbelief. It goes on to recount the stories of Moses and Jesus, and concludes with a vivid scene of judgment. Most scholars assign Q43 to the 'Meccan' period. It takes its name from the 'decoration' referred to at Q43.35.

1 Letters

1. *Ḥā Mīm*: the names of Arabic letters *ḥ* and *m*. The same letter combination occurs in a block of sūras from Q40 to Q46 (Q42 has an additional ', *s*, and *q*). Twenty-nine sūras begin with letters like these, ranging from one to five. No satisfactory explanation has been given for their occurrence. The Cairo edition varies in counting these letters as a separate verse (as here), or as the beginning of the first verse.

2–4 An Arabic Qur'ān

2. *the clear Book*: or 'the Book that makes (things) clear;' referring to the Qur'ān not only as a 'recited' but also 'written' scripture (see n. on Q2.2).
3. *an Arabic Qur'ān*: perhaps meaning that it is a translation into Arabic of the heavenly archetype or 'mother of the Book' (cf. Q12.2; 13.37; 16.103; 20.113; 39.28; 41.3; 42.7; 46.12). The specification 'Arabic Qur'ān' (Ar. *qur'ān 'arabiyya*) may imply the existence of 'Qur'āns' (as it were) in other languages, but it is probably an answer to some objection, perhaps that Hebrew was thought to be the exclusive language of revelation.
4. *you*: plur.
5. *mother of the Book*: Ar. *umm al-kitāb* is usually taken as a reference to the heavenly original or archetype of all revelation. According to this view, the Qur'ān, like the Torah and the Gospel, is only a portion of this all encompassing 'Book' (see Q3.7; 13.39; cf. Q56.78, 'hidden Book;' 85.22, 'guarded Tablet').
6. *most high...wise*: often used of God, but here predicated of the heavenly Book (see n. on Q36.2).

5–8 Punishment of past generations a warning

7. *the Reminder*: the Qur'ān (see n. on Q3.58).
8. *prophets*: for this important title, see n. on Q2.87.
9. *them*: the disbelievers.
10. *example*: or 'parable' (cf. Q24.34).
11. *...has passed away*: i.e. into history; a reference to the stories of previous peoples who received 'exemplary' punishment for rejecting the prophets sent to them (cf. Q43.56 below; see n. on Q7.59).

9–15 Disbelievers are inconsistent

12. *you*: the Prophet.
13. *The Mighty, the Knowing created them*: their answer makes explicit their belief in God as the supreme deity (see Q43.87 below; cf. Q29.61, 63; 31.25; 39.38).

in it for you, so that you might be guided, **11** and (it is He) who sends down water from the sky in measure – and by means of it We give some barren[14] land life, and in this way you (too) will be brought forth[15] – **12** and (it is He) who created the pairs,[16] all of them,[17] and made for you what you ride on from the ship(s) and the livestock, **13** so that you may mount their backs, (and) then remember the blessing of your Lord when you are mounted upon them, and say, 'Glory to the One who has subjected this to us, when we (ourselves) were not fit for it. **14** Surely we are indeed going to return to our Lord.' **15** Yet they assign to Him[18] a part of His (own) servants.[19] Surely the human is clearly ungrateful[20] indeed.

16 Or has He taken (for Himself) daughters[21] from what He creates, and singled you out with sons? **17** When one of them is given news of what he has struck as a parable for the Merciful,[22] his face turns dark and he chokes back his disappointment. **18** 'One who is brought up in luxury,[23] and he is not clear in the (time of) dispute?'[24] **19** Yet they have made the angels – those who are themselves servants of the Merciful – females. Did they witness their creation? Their testimony will be written down, and they will be questioned. **20** They say, 'If the Merciful had (so) pleased, we would not have served them.'[25] They have no knowledge about that; they are only guessing. **21** Or have We given them a Book[26] before it,[27] and do they hold fast to it? **22** No! They say, 'Surely we found our fathers (set) on a community,[28] and surely we are guided in their footsteps.' **23** In this way We have not sent any warner[29] before you to a town, except that its affluent ones said, 'Surely we found our fathers (set) on a community, and surely we are following in their footsteps.' **24** He said,[30] 'Even if I bring you better guidance[31] than what you found your fathers (set) on?' They said, 'Surely we are disbelievers in what you

---

14. *barren*: lit. 'dead' (notice the sudden shift from third- to first-person discourse, and then back again).
15. *brought forth*: from the grave.
16. *the pairs*: of different species (cf. Q36.36; 51.49).
17. *all of them*: lit. 'all of it.'
18. *assign to Him*: lit. 'make for Him.'
19. *a part of His (own) servants*: here referring to the angels, which they worship in addition to God (a topic addressed in the following section).
20. *ungrateful*: Ar. *kafūr*, punning on *kāfir*, 'disbeliever.'

16–25 God does not have daughters

21. *daughters*: for the belief that the angels were 'daughters of God,' see Q16.57; 17.40; 37.149-153; 53.27 (for the angels and their various roles, see n. on Q2.30).
22. *news of what he has struck as a parable for the Merciful*: i.e. news of the birth of a daughter, which is what he had 'likened to God' as offspring (cf. Q16.60). 'The Merciful' (Ar. *al-raḥmān*) is used throughout this sūra as a proper name for God (see n. on Q25.60).
23. *in luxury*: lit. 'among the ornaments.'
24. *...in the (time of) dispute?*: meaning obscure; nor is it clear whether this question is posed by the man in exasperation after the announcement of the birth of his daughter, or whether it is spoken by God in reference to his alleged 'daughters.' In any case the general point seems to be that a daughter is simply not as good as a son, whether for a human or divine father.
25. *served them*: or 'worshipped them.'
26. *a Book*: the idolators have no 'Book' on which to base their belief that the angels were God's 'daughters' (cf. Q35.40; 46.4).
27. *it*: the Qur'ān.
28. *(set) on a community*: the idea being that a 'community' (Ar. *umma*) is constituted by its 'religion' (*dīn*).
29. *warner*: for this role, see n. on Q2.119.
30. *He said*: not the Prophet, but one of the former prophets (another reading has 'Say,' but that does not fit here).
31. *guidance*: one of the most frequent terms (Ar. *hudā*) for revelation in general, and the Qur'ān in particular.

are sent with.' **25** So We took vengeance on them. See how the end was for the ones who called (it) a lie![32]

26 (Remember) when Abraham said to his father and his people, 'Surely I am free of what you serve, **27** except for the One who created me. Surely He will guide me.' **28** And he made it a lasting word among his descendants,[33] so that they might return.

29 No! I gave these (people) and their fathers enjoyment (of life), until the truth came to them, and (also) a clear messenger.[34] **30** But when the truth came to them, they said, 'This is magic. Surely we are disbelievers in it.'

31 They said, 'If only this Qur'ān[35] had been sent down on some great man of the two towns.'[36] **32** Do they distribute the mercy of your Lord?[37] We have distributed their livelihood among them in this present life, and raised some of them above others in rank, so that some of them may take others in slavery. But the mercy of your Lord is better than what they accumulate. **33** If it were not that humankind would be one community,[38] We would indeed have made for those who disbelieve in the Merciful roofs of silver for their houses, and stairways on which to ascend, **34** and doors for their houses, and couches on which to recline, **35** and (all manner of) decoration. Yet all that is but the enjoyment of this present life – the Hereafter with your Lord is for the ones who guard (themselves).[39]

36 Whoever turns away from the Reminder[40] of the Merciful – We allot to him a satan,[41] and he becomes his comrade. **37** Surely they indeed keep them from the way,[42] even though they think that they are (rightly) guided, **38** until, when he comes to Us,[43] he says, 'Would that (there were) between me and you the distance of the two Easts!'[44] And:[45] 'Evil is the comrade! **39** It will not benefit you today – since you have done evil – that you are partners in the punishment.'[46]

---

32. *...who called (it) a lie*: i.e. who rejected the warning of imminent judgment; the remains of their destroyed cities were believed to be still visible (cf. Q3.137; 6.11, 148; 16.36).

26–28 The example of Abraham

33. *a lasting word among his descendants*: cf. what Abraham says to his sons at Q2.132.

29–30 The Prophet rejected

34. *a clear messenger*: or 'a messenger making (things) clear,' referring to the Prophet (cf. Q21.44; 28.48; for the important title 'messenger,' see n. on Q2.87).

31–35 God chooses whom He pleases

35. *this Qur'ān*: here 'this Qur'ān' comes close to its present meaning as the name of the Muslim scripture (cf. Q9.111; see n. on Q2.185).
36. *the two towns*: reference obscure; said to be Mecca and Ṭā'if.
37. *Do they distribute the mercy of your Lord*: i.e. 'Must God act as they see fit?'
38. *one community*: of disbelievers.
39. *guard (themselves)*: against evil, or God. The idea here is twofold: first, that God is not bound to choose a messenger of wealth and social position (since wealth has no ultimate value), and second, that God would have bestowed untold wealth on humankind, if it would not have resulted in all people being disbelievers.

36–39 The danger of persistent disbelief

40. *Reminder*: or 'remembrance.'
41. *a satan*: 'satans' (Ar. *shayāṭīn*) are individually assigned to incite people to evil (see Q19.83; cf. Q7.27; 23.97; 41.25).
42. *they indeed keep them from the way*: i.e. the satans prevent disbelievers from following the 'straight path.'
43. *when he comes to Us*: at the Judgment.
44. *the distance of the two Easts*: explained by the commentators as 'the distance between East and West;' spoken by the disbeliever to his satan.
45. *And*: what follows is spoken by God to all of them.
46. *partners in the punishment*: or 'associates in the punishment,' punning on their having 'associated' other gods with God (cf. Q37.33).

40 Can you[47] make the deaf to hear, or can you guide the blind and the one who is clearly astray?[48] **41** Whether We take you away[49] – surely We are going to take vengeance on them – **42** or show you what We have promised them – surely We are powerful over them. **43** So hold fast to what you are inspired (with). Surely you are on a straight path. **44** Surely it[50] is a reminder indeed to you and to your people. Soon you will (all) be questioned. **45** Ask those of Our messengers whom We sent before you: Did We appoint any other gods than the Merciful to be served?

46 Certainly We sent Moses with Our signs[51] to Pharaoh and his assembly. He said, 'Surely I am a messenger of the Lord of the worlds.'[52] **47** But when he brought them Our signs, suddenly they began to laugh at them, **48** even though every sign We showed them was greater than the one before it.[53] We seized them with the punishment, so that they might return. **49** They said, 'Magician! Call on your Lord for us by whatever covenant He has made with you, (and) surely we shall indeed be (rightly) guided.' **50** But when We removed the punishment from them, immediately they broke (their promise). **51** Pharaoh called out among his people: 'My people! Is the kingdom of Egypt not mine, and these rivers (which) flow beneath me? Do you not see? **52** Am I not better than this (man), who is despicable and scarcely makes (things) clear?[54] **53** If only bracelets of gold were cast (down) on him or the accompanying angels came with him.'[55] **54** So he unsettled his people,[56] and they obeyed him. Surely they were a wicked people. **55** When they had angered Us, We took vengeance on them and drowned them – all (of them)! **56** We made them a thing of the past, and an example[57] for the later (generations).

57 When the son of Mary[58] is cited as an example,[59] suddenly your people keep (others) from it,[60] **58** and they say, 'Are our gods better, or is he?' They only cite him to you as a (matter of) dispute. Yes! They are a contentious people. **59** He was only a servant whom We blessed, and We made him an example for the Sons of Israel. **60** If We (so) pleased, We could indeed make angels out of you to be successors on the earth.

40–45 Encouragement to the Prophet

47. *you*: the Prophet.
48. *clearly astray*: lit. 'in clear straying.'
49. *take you away*: in death.
50. *it*: the Qur'ān.

46–56 The story of Moses and Pharaoh

51. *signs*: here referring to the miracles of Moses (for the various meanings of this term, see n. on Q2.39).
52. *Lord of the worlds*: for this title, see n. on Q1.2.
53. *greater than the one before it*: lit. 'greater than its sister (sign);' Moses performed more miracles than any other prophet in the Qur'ān (see e.g. Q17.101; 27.12). The reference here is to the 'plagues of Egypt' (see Q7.133; cf. Exodus 7-12).
54. *scarcely makes (things) clear*: a reference to Moses' speech impediment (see Q20.27; cf. Exodus 4.10; 6.12, 30).
55. *bracelets of gold...angels came with him*: cf. the similar challenges laid before the Prophet by his contemporaries (Q6.8; 11.12; 25.8).
56. *unsettled his people*: the exact sense is not clear, but it probably means 'led them astray' (cf. Q30.60). The Cairo edition, reflecting the views of traditional scholars, attributes this verse to the 'Medinan' period.
57. *example*: or 'parable.'

57–65 Objections to the story of Jesus

58. *son of Mary*: Jesus; there is no mention in the Qur'ān of Joseph, Jesus' putative father (cf. Mark 6.3).
59. *cited as an example*: lit. 'struck as a parable.'
60. *it*: or 'him' (Jesus).

61 Surely it is indeed knowledge for the Hour,[61] so do not be in doubt about it,[62] but follow me.[63] This is a straight path. **62** Do not let Satan[64] keep you[65] from (it). Surely he is a clear enemy to you.

63 When Jesus brought the clear signs,[66] he said, 'I have brought you the wisdom, and (I have done so) to make clear to you some of your differences. Guard (yourselves) against God and obey me. **64** Surely God – He is my Lord and your Lord, so serve Him! This is a straight path.' **65** But the factions[67] differed among themselves. Woe to those who have done evil because of the punishment of a painful Day!

66 Are they[68] looking for anything but the Hour – that it should come upon them unexpectedly, when they do not realize (it)? **67** Friends on that Day – some of them will be enemies to others, except for the ones who guard (themselves). **68** 'My servants! (There is) no fear on you today, nor will you sorrow **69** – those (of you) who believed in Our signs and submitted.[69] **70** Enter the Garden,[70] you and your wives, you will be made happy!' **71** Plates and cups of gold will be passed around among them, and there (they will have) whatever they desire and their eyes delight in. And: 'There you will remain.' **72** And: 'That is the Garden which you have been given as an inheritance for what you have done. **73** There you have many fruits from which you will eat.'

74 Surely the evildoers will remain in the punishment of Gehenna.[71] **75** It will not subside for them, and there they will be in despair. **76** We did not do them evil, but they themselves were the evildoers. **77** They will call out, 'Master![72] Let your Lord finish us off!' He will say, 'Surely you will remain. **78** Certainly we brought you the truth, but most of you were averse to the truth.'

79 Or have they woven some plot? We (too) are weaving (a plot). **80** Or do they think that We do not hear their secret and their secret talk? Yes indeed! Our messengers[73] are present with them writing (it) down.
81 Say:[74] 'If the Merciful had a son,[75] I (would be) the first of the ones who served (him).[76] **82** Glory to the Lord of the heavens and the earth, Lord of the throne, above what they allege!' **83** So leave them! Let

---

61. *it is indeed knowledge for the Hour*: 'it' probably refers to the Qur'ān; however, if the passage is read continuously, the pronoun 'it' could refer to Jesus (whose second coming was later thought to be one of the signs of 'the Hour'). Hence the variant reading and interpretation: 'He [Jesus] is indeed a mark [reading *'alam* for *'ilm*, 'knowledge'] for the Hour' (cf. Q4.159).
62. *it*: the Hour (of judgment).
63. *me*: the Prophet, or 'Me' (God), but the former is more likely.
64. *Satan*: for this figure, see n. on Q2.36.
65. *you*: plur.
66. *the clear signs*: or 'the clear proofs,' 'the indisputable evidence' (Ar. *al-bayyināt*); referring to Jesus' miracles (see Q5.110).
67. *the factions*: or 'the sectarians' (Ar. *al-aḥzāb*), referring to Jews and Christians in general, but perhaps also to Christian 'sectarians' and their contradictory views of Jesus (cf. Q19.37).

66–78 A judgment scene

68. *they*: the disbelievers (cf. Q12.107; 47.18).
69. *...and submitted*: or 'and were Muslims' (this verse may be a later gloss).
70. *Garden*: in heaven (for this imagery, see n. on Q2.25).
71. *Gehenna*: another name for Hell (see n. on Q2.206).
72. *Master*: or 'Mālik' (said to be the name of the chief angel-guard of Hell).

79–80 Nothing is hidden from God

73. *Our messengers*: the recording angels (cf. Q10.21; 82.10-12).

81–89 God has no son

74. *Say*: on this form of address, see n. on Q2.80.
75. *son*: or 'child' (Ar. *walad*), but referring to Christian claims about Jesus as God's son.
76. *first of the ones who served (him)*: or 'first among (his) worshippers.'

them banter and jest, until they meet their Day which they are promised. **84** He (it is) who is God in the sky and God on the earth. He is the Wise, the Knowing. **85** Blessed (be) the One who – to Him (belongs) the kingdom of the heavens and the earth, and whatever is between them. With Him is the knowledge of the Hour,[77] and to Him you will be returned. **86** Those whom they call on instead of Him have no power of intercession, except for the one who has borne witness to the truth – and they know (this). **87** If indeed you[78] ask them, 'Who created them?,'[79] they will indeed say, 'God.'[80] How are they (so) deluded? **88** And his saying:[81] 'My Lord! Surely these are a people who do not believe.' **89** So excuse them, and say: 'Peace!'[82] Soon they will know!

77. *With Him is the knowledge of the Hour*: cf. Q7.187; 33.63; 41.47; 46.23; 67.26; and Mark 13.2 par.
78. *you*: the Prophet.
79. *them*: i.e. the heavens and the earth (see Q43.9 above).
80. *'God'*: their answer makes explicit their belief in God as the supreme deity (cf. Q10.31; 29.61, 63; 31.25; 39.38).
81. *his saying*: the Prophet's.
82. *Peace*: Ar. *salām* connotes 'submission' (*islām*) to God.

44 The Smoke ۞ Al-Dukhān

In the Name of God, the Merciful, the Compassionate

1 Ḥā Mīm.[1]

2 By the clear Book![2] **3** Surely We sent it down on a blessed night[3] – surely We were warning[4] – **4** during
which[5] every wise command[6] was divided out,[7] **5** as a command from Us – surely We were sending[8] –
6 as a mercy from your Lord. Surely He – He is the Hearing, the Knowing, **7** Lord of the heavens and the
earth, and whatever is between them, if you (would) be certain. **8** (There is) no god but Him. He gives life
and causes death – your Lord and the Lord of your fathers of old.

9 No! They are in doubt (while) they jest. **10** So watch[9] for the Day when the sky will bring a visible
smoke[10] **11** covering the people: 'This is a painful punishment! **12** Our Lord, remove the punishment

---

Q44: This sūra opens with a declaration of the 'sending down' of the Qur'ān, followed by a warning that punishment is coming. It recounts the story of Pharaoh and the Sons of Israel, defends the idea of resurrection, and concludes with a description of the rewards and punishments awaiting the righteous and wicked. Most scholars assign Q44 to the 'Meccan' period. It takes its title from the reference to the appearance of a heavenly 'smoke' which will be a sign of the Last Day (Q44.10).

1 Letters

1. *Ḥā Mīm*: the names of Arabic letters *ḥ* and *m*. The same letter combination occurs in a block of sūras from Q40 to Q46 (Q42 has an additional ', *s*, and *q*). Twenty-nine sūras begin with letters like these, ranging from one to five. No satisfactory explanation has been given for their occurrence. The Cairo edition varies in counting these letters as a separate verse (as here), or as the beginning of the first verse.

2–8 A Book from God

2. *the clear Book*: or 'the Book that makes (things) clear;' referring to the Qur'ān not only as a 'recited' but also 'written' scripture (see n. on Q2.2).
3. *We sent it down on a blessed night*: cf. Q97.1, 'We sent it down on the Night of the Decree.' This reflects a different understanding than the traditional one, according to which the Qur'ān was 'sent down' or revealed at intervals over a period of some twenty years. Some interpreters understand this verse as referring to the descent of the Qur'ān from the highest to the lowest of the seven heavens, whence it was revealed to Muḥammad as occasion required. But there are other passages, like this one, which indicate that the Qur'ān was 'sent down' or revealed all at once (see Q2.89; 3.3, 7; 4.105; 5.48; 6.92; 8.41; 16.64; 17.106; 26.193-194; 28.86; 46.12, 30; 76.23; 97.1; cf. Q2.185, 'The month of Ramaḍān, in which the Qur'ān was sent down'). There were similarly conflicting views within Judaism about the revelation of the Torah. According to the Babylonian Talmud (Gittin 60a), some thought the Torah had been 'transmitted scroll by scroll,' others that it had been 'transmitted entire.'
4. *surely We were warning*: or 'surely We were warners.'
5. *during which*: lit. 'in it' (i.e. the 'blessed night').
6. *every wise command*: or 'every wise matter' (cf. Q97.4).
7. *was divided out*: or 'was made distinct' (Ar. *yufraqu*); cf. Q17.106, 'We have divided it' (*faraqnāhu*). There may also be an allusion here to the revelation of the Qur'ān as 'deliverance' (*furqān*), see e.g. Q2.185; 3.4; 25.1; cf. Q2.53; 21.48; but the meaning of this verse remains obscure.
8. *surely We were sending*: or 'surely We were senders.'

9–16 Punishment is coming

9. *So watch*: addressed to the Prophet (cf. Q44.59 below).
10. *a visible smoke*: probably refers to one of the signs of the Last Day (cf. Joel 2.30-31; Acts 2.19-20).

from us! Surely We are believers.' **13** How will the reminder be for them,[11] when a clear messenger has already come to them? **14** Then they turned away from him, and said, '(He is) tutored,[12] (he is) possessed!'[13] **15** 'Surely We are going to remove the punishment a little, (but) surely you are going to revert!'[14] **16** On the Day when We attack with the great attack, surely We are going to take vengeance.

17 Certainly before them We tested the people of Pharaoh, when an honorable messenger[15] came to them: **18** 'Deliver to me the servants of God![16] Surely I am a trustworthy messenger for you.' **19** And: 'Do not exalt yourselves against God! Surely I bring you clear authority. **20** Surely I take refuge with my Lord and your Lord, for fear that you stone me.[17] **21** If you do not believe me, withdraw from me!' **22** So he called on his Lord: 'These are a sinful people.' **23** And: 'Journey with My servants by night. Surely you will be followed.[18] **24** And leave the sea parted, (for) surely they are a force (to be) drowned.' **25** How many gardens and springs they[19] left (behind), **26** and (fields of) crops, and an honorable place, **27** and prosperity in which they used to rejoice. **28** So (it was), and We caused another people to inherit them.[20] **29** Neither the sky nor the earth wept for them, nor were they spared. **30** Certainly We rescued the Sons of Israel from the humiliating punishment, **31** (and) from Pharaoh. Surely he was haughty, one of the wanton. **32** Certainly We chose them, on (the basis of) knowledge, over the worlds,[21] **33** and gave them signs[22] in which (there was) a clear test.[23]

34 Surely these (people)[24] indeed say, **35** 'There is nothing but our first death. We are not going to be raised. **36** Bring (back) our fathers, if you[25] are truthful!' **37** Are they better, or the people of Tubba',[26] and those who were before them? We destroyed them. Surely they were sinners. **38** We did not create the heavens and earth, and whatever is between them, in jest. **39** We created them only in truth,[27] but most

---

11. *How will the reminder be for them*: i.e. what use will it be then? (cf. Q89.23).
12. *tutored*: cf. Q16.103; 25.4-5.
13. *possessed*: or 'jinn-struck' (Ar. *majnūn*); i.e. they accuse the Prophet of being possessed by jinn (see n. on Q7.184).
14. *going to revert*: return to their sinful ways (cf. Q7.135; 43.50); vv. 13-14 are best read as spoken by God as an aside, v. 15 as spoken directly to the disbelievers, and v. 16 as an aside again.

17–33 The story of Pharaoh and the Sons of Israel

15. *honorable messenger*: Moses, though he is not mentioned by name (for this important title, see n. on Q2.87; cf. Q69.40, the Prophet; 81.19, the Prophet [or Gabriel?]).
16. *servants of God*: i.e. the Sons of Israel; the word 'servant' (Ar. *'abd*) also means 'slave.'
17. *for fear that you stone me*: cf. Exodus 8.26.
18. *Journey with My servants...*: for the story that follows, cf. version at Q26.52-68; and Exodus 14.1-31.
19. *they*: the Egyptians.
20. *inherit them*: perhaps a reference to the despoiling of the Egyptians by the Israelites (Exodus 3.21-22; 11.2-3; 12.35-36).
21. *chose them...over the worlds*: or 'chose them...over all peoples;' the distinctiveness of Israel's election is recognized (see Q2.47, 122; 3.33; 6.86; 7.140; 45.16).
22. *signs*: probably referring to revelation in general (for the various meanings of this term, see n. on Q2.39).
23. *clear test*: used in reference to Abraham's readiness to obey God's command to sacrifice his son (see Q37.106; cf. 2.124); but whereas Abraham 'passed' his test, the implication here is that the Sons of Israel failed theirs.

34–42 Disbelievers reject the resurrection

24. *these (people)*: the disbelievers.
25. *you*: plur.
26. *Tubba'*: the title of the kings of the Ḥimyarites of South Arabia (Yemen); mentioned only here and at Q50.14.
27. *in truth*: or 'with the truth,' but here almost meaning 'for the purpose of judgment,' as the following verse indicates (cf. Q15.85; 30.8; 46.3).

of them do not know (it). **40** Surely the Day of Decision[28] is their meeting – all (of them) – **41** a Day when a protector will be of no use at all as a protector,[29] and they will not be helped **42** – except for the one on whom God has compassion. Surely He – He is the Mighty, the Compassionate.

43 Surely the tree of al-Zaqqūm[30] **44** is the food of the sinner, **45** like molten metal boiling in the belly, **46** as hot (water) boils. **47** 'Seize him[31] and drag him into the midst of the Furnace.[32] **48** Then pour over his head from the punishment of hot (water)!' **49** 'Taste (it)! Surely you are the mighty, the honorable![33] **50** Surely this is what you doubted about.'

51 Surely the ones who guard (themselves)[34] are in a secure place, **52** in (the midst of) gardens and springs, **53** wearing clothes of silk and brocade, facing each other. **54** So (it is), and We shall marry them to (maidens) with dark, wide eyes. **55** There they will call for every (kind of) fruit, secure. **56** There they will not taste death, except the first death,[35] and He will guard them against the punishment of the Furnace. **57** Favor[36] from your Lord! That is the great triumph!

58 Surely We have made it[37] easy in your language,[38] so that they may take heed.[39] **59** So watch! Surely they (too) are watching.

---

28. *Day of Decision*: or 'Day of Distinguishing,' i.e. between the righteous and the wicked (cf. Q37.21; 77.13-14; 78.17).
29. *when a protector will be of no use at all...*: cf. Noah's words at Q11.43.

43–50 Punishment of the wicked

30. *tree of al-Zaqqūm*: a tree in Hell (see Q37.62; 56.52; cf. Q17.60).
31. *Seize him...*: spoken by God to the angels.
32. *the Furnace*: a name for Hell (Ar. *al-jaḥīm*).
33. *Taste (it)! Surely you are the mighty, the honorable*: spoken by the angels in sarcastic derision.

51–57 Reward of the righteous

34. *guard (themselves)*: against evil, or God.
35. *There they will not taste death, except the first death*: for this idea, cf. Revelation 2.11.
36. *Favor*: or 'Merit.'

58–59 Final words to the Prophet

37. *it*: the Qur'ān.
38. *in your language*: lit. 'in your tongue' (Arabic).
39. *take heed*: or 'be reminded,' 'remember.'

45 The Kneeling ۞ Al-Jāthiya

In the Name of God, the Merciful, the Compassionate

1 Ḥā Mīm.[1]

2 The sending down of the Book is from God, the Mighty, the Wise.[2]

3 Surely in the heavens and the earth (there are) signs indeed for the believers. **4** And in your creation,
and what He scatters[3] of the creatures, (there are) signs for a people who are certain. **5** And (in the)
alternation of the night and the day, and what God sends down from the sky of (His) provision, and by
means of it gives the earth life after its death, and (in the) changing of the winds, (there are) signs for a
people who understand. **6** Those are the signs of God.[4] We recite them to you[5] in truth. In what (kind of)
proclamation[6] – after God and His signs – will they believe?

7 Woe to every liar (and) sinner! **8** He hears the signs of God recited to him, (but) then persists in being
arrogant, as if he had not heard them. Give him the news of a painful punishment. **9** When he comes to
know any of Our signs, he takes them in mockery. Those – for them (there is) a humiliating punishment.
10 Behind them is Gehenna,[7] and what they have earned will be of no use to them at all, nor those whom
they have taken as allies[8] instead of God. For them (there is) a great punishment. **11** This is guidance,[9]
but those who disbelieve in the signs of their Lord – for them (there is) a punishment of painful wrath.

12 (It is) God who has subjected the sea to you, so that the ship may run on it by His command, and so

---

Q45: This sūra opens with a declaration of the 'sending down' of the Qur'ān and an enumeration of the signs of God's power and providence in nature. The Prophet is then urged to follow God's path independently of the 'Sons of Israel.' The sūra concludes with a judgment scene, at which each community will be found 'kneeling' (Q45.28). Most scholars assign Q45 to the late 'Meccan' period, though some traditional scholars consider one verse to be 'Medinan.'

1 Letters

1. *Ḥā Mīm*: the names of Arabic letters *ḥ* and *m*. The same letter combination occurs in a block of sūras from Q40 to Q46 (Q42 has an additional ', *s*, and *q*). Twenty-nine sūras begin with letters like these, ranging from one to five. No satisfactory explanation has been given for their occurrence. The Cairo edition varies in counting these letters as a separate verse (as here), or as the beginning of the first verse.

2 A Book from God

2. *The sending down of the Book...*: here referring to the Qur'ān not only as a 'recited' but also 'written' scripture (see n. on Q2.2; cf. the similar openings at Q32.2; 39.1; 40.2; 41.2; 46.2).

3–13 Signs of God's power and providence

3. *scatters*: as a sower scatters seed.
4. *signs of God*: i.e. the order of nature indicates the existence of a powerful and beneficent creator (cf. Q45.35 below; for the various meanings of 'signs,' see n. on Q2.39).
5. *you*: the Prophet.
6. *proclamation*: or 'report' (Ar. *ḥadīth*).
7. *Gehenna*: a name for Hell (see n. on Q2.206); it is not clear whether the expression *min warā'ihim* is to be understood in a spatial ('behind them') or temporal sense ('afterwards for them').
8. *those whom they have taken as allies*: here referring to their gods (Ar. *awliyā'* implies the obligation of mutual protection, almost in the sense of 'friends' or 'brothers').
9. *guidance*: one of the most frequent terms (Ar. *hudā*) for revelation in general, and the Qur'ān in particular.

that you may seek some of His favor,[10] and that you may be thankful. **13** And He has subjected to you whatever is in the heavens and whatever is on the earth – all (of it is) from Him. Surely in that are signs indeed for a people who reflect.

14 Say to those who believe to forgive those who do not expect the days of God,[11] so that He may repay a people for what they have earned. **15** Whoever does righteousness, it is for himself,[12] and whoever does evil, it is (likewise) against himself – then to your Lord you will be returned.

16 Certainly We gave the Sons of Israel the Book, and the judgment,[13] and the prophetic office. We provided them with good things and favored them over the worlds.[14] **17** And We gave them clear signs[15] of the matter.[16] They did not differ until after the knowledge had come to them,[17] (because of) envy among themselves.[18] Surely your Lord will decide between them on the Day of Resurrection concerning their differences. **18** Then We placed you on a pathway[19] of the matter.[20] So follow it, and do not follow the (vain) desires of those who do not know. **19** Surely they will be of no use to you at all against God. Surely the evildoers are allies of each other, but God is the Ally of the ones who guard (themselves).[21]

20 This[22] is evidence for the people, and a guidance and mercy for a people who are certain. **21** Or do those who commit[23] evil deeds think that We shall treat them as those who believe and do righteous deeds – alike in their life and their death? Evil is what they judge! **22** God created the heavens and the earth in truth,[24] and so that each person may be paid for what he has earned – and they will not be done evil. **23** Have you[25] seen the one who has taken his (vain) desire as his god? God has led him astray on

---

10. *seek some of His favor*: i.e. seek to make a livelihood.

14–15 The Days of God

11. *days of God*: may refer to the times of God's intervention, or when he fought for them (only here and at Q14.5, to Moses). This verse is said to refer to the expedition against the Banū Muṣṭaliq (627 CE/6 AH), and for that reason the Cairo edition attributes it to the 'Medinan' period.
12. *for himself*: i.e. to his own benefit.

16–19 The Sons of Israel have one path, the Prophet another

13. *the judgment*: or 'the wisdom' (see n. on Q3.79; cf. Q6.89; 29.27; 57.26).
14. *favored them over the worlds*: or 'preferred them over all peoples;' the distinctiveness of Israel's election is recognized (see Q2.47, 122; 3.33; 6.86; 7.140; 44.32).
15. *clear signs*: or 'clear proofs,' 'indisputable evidence.'
16. *of the matter*: or 'from the command' (Ar. *mina l-amri*). Most commentators take *amr* here as almost equivalent to 'religion' (i.e. 'We gave them clear signs of the religion;' cf. Q45.18 below), but it may correspond to the rabbinic notion of the 'divine word' (Aram. *mēmrā*), or to the related Christian idea of the *logos* as the manifestation of God's word, or as God's messenger in place of God himself (cf. Q16.2; 17.85; 40.15; 42.52).
17. *...after the knowledge had come to them*: i.e. differences arose only after the revelation was given (see Q2.213).
18. *envy among themselves*: referring to Jews and Christians, and their disputes (cf. Q2.213, 253; 3.19; 5.14; 42.14).
19. *pathway*: Ar. *sharīʿa*, but its later meaning as 'law' is not entirely appropriate here; instead the sense is that God has revealed to the Prophet an independent 'pathway' to truth (cf. Q5.48).
20. *of the matter*: or 'from the command' (see n. on Q45.17 above).
21. *guard (themselves)*: against evil, or God.

20–26 Resurrection and Judgment certain

22. *This*: the Qur'ān (cf. Q7.203).
23. *commit*: lit. 'earn' (cf. Q6.60).
24. *in truth*: or 'with the truth,' but here almost meaning 'for the purpose of judgment,' as the latter part of the verse indicates (cf. Q15.85; 30.8; 46.3).
25. *you*: the Prophet, or perhaps intended generally ('one').

(the basis of) knowledge,[26] and set a seal on his hearing and his heart,[27] and made a covering on his sight. Who will guide him after God? Will you[28] not take heed?[29] **24** But they say, 'There is nothing but our present life. We die, and we live, and nothing destroys us but time.' They have no knowledge about that. They only conjecture. **25** When Our signs[30] are recited to them as clear signs, their only argument is that they say, 'Bring (back) our fathers, if you[31] are truthful!' **26** Say:[32] 'God gives you life, then causes you to die, (and) then He gathers you to the Day of Resurrection – (there is) no doubt about it. But most of the people do not know (it).'

27 To God (belongs) the kingdom of the heavens and the earth. On the Day when the Hour[33] strikes, on that Day the perpetrators of falsehood will lose. **28** You[34] will see each community kneeling,[35] each community called to its Book:[36] 'Today you will be repaid for what you have done. **29** This is Our Book – it speaks about you in truth. Surely We have been copying down what you were doing.' **30** As for those who have believed and done righteous deeds, their Lord will cause them to enter into His mercy. That is the clear triumph! **31** But as for those who have disbelieved: 'Were My signs not recited to you? Yet you became arrogant and were a sinful people. **32** And when it was said, "Surely the promise of God is true, and the Hour – (there is) no doubt about it," you said, "We do not know what the Hour is. We think (it is) only conjecture, and we are not certain."' **33** The evils of what they have done will become apparent to them, and what they were mocking will overwhelm them. **34** And it will be said, 'Today We forget you, as you forgot the meeting of this Day of yours. Your refuge is the Fire,[37] and you have no helpers. **35** That is because you took the signs of God in mockery, and this present life deluded you.' So today they will not be brought forth from it, nor will they be allowed to make amends.

36 Praise (be)[38] to God, Lord of the heavens and Lord of the earth, Lord of the worlds![39] **37** To Him (belongs) the greatness in the heavens and the earth. He is the Mighty, the Wise.

---

26. *on (the basis of) knowledge*: perhaps meaning 'purposely' on God's part, or implying some knowledge of revelation on the part of the person referred to (cf. Q2.7; 30.29).
27. *heart*: here, as often, the heart is spoken of as synonymous with mind.
28. *you*: plur.
29. *take heed*: or 'be reminded,' 'remember.'
30. *signs*: or 'verses' (see n. on Q2.39).
31. *you*: plur.
32. *Say*: on this form of address, see n. on Q2.80.

27–35 A JUDGMENT SCENE

33. *the Hour*: of judgment.
34. *You*: the Prophet, or perhaps intended generally ('one').
35. *kneeling*: cf. Q19.68-72.
36. *called to its Book*: to the 'Record' of its deeds, as the following verse indicates (cf. e.g. Q17.71; 18.49; 36.69; 50.4).
37. *the Fire*: Ar. *al-nār* is the most common of the various designations for Hell.

36–37 CONCLUDING DOXOLOGY

38. *(be)*: or '(belongs).'
39. *Lord of the worlds*: for this title, see n. on Q1.2.

46 The Sand Dunes ۞ Al-Aḥqāf

In the Name of God, the Merciful, the Compassionate

1 Ḥā Mīm.[1]

2 The sending down of the Book is from God, the Mighty, the Wise.[2]

3 We did not create the heavens and the earth, and whatever is between them, except in truth[3] and (for)
an appointed time,[4] but those who disbelieve are turning away from what they are warned of. 4 Say:[5] 'Do
you see what you call on instead of God? Show me what (part) of the earth they have created. Or do they
have any partnership in (the creation of) the heavens? Bring me any Book before this (one) or any trace
of knowledge,[6] if you are truthful.' 5 Who is farther astray than the one who, instead of God, calls on those
who will not respond to him until the Day of Resurrection, while they[7] are (otherwise) oblivious of their
calling? 6 When the people are gathered, they[8] will be enemies to them, and will deny[9] their service.[10]

7 When Our signs[11] are recited to them as clear signs,[12] those who disbelieve say to the truth, when it

---

Q46: This is the last of a group of seven sūras known as the 'Ḥawāmīm,' from the two letters (Ḥā' Mīm) with which they all begin. It opens with a declaration of the 'sending down' of the Qur'ān, and then condemns the folly of idolatry in the face of God's power and providence. The Prophet is set forth as a typical messenger whose 'Book' confirms the 'Book of Moses.' Next comes the story of the punishment of the people of 'Ād, followed by one about a band of jinn who came to believe after listening to the Qur'ān. A conclusion stresses the certainty of resurrection and judgment. Most scholars assign Q46 to the 'Meccan' period, though some consider a few verses to be 'Medinan.' The title refers to 'the sand dunes' where the 'Ād were destroyed (Q46.21).

1 Letters

1. *Ḥā Mīm*: the names of Arabic letters *ḥ* and *m*. The same letter combination occurs in a block of sūras from Q40 to Q46 (Q42 has an additional ', *s*, and *q*). Twenty-nine sūras begin with letters like these, ranging from one to five. No satisfactory explanation has been given for their occurrence. The Cairo edition varies in counting these letters as a separate verse (as here), or as the beginning of the first verse.

2 A Book from God

2. *The sending down of the Book...*: here referring to the Qur'ān not only as a 'recited' but also 'written' scripture (see n. on Q2.2; cf. the similar openings at Q32.2; 39.1; 40.2; 41.2; 45.2).

3–6 The folly of idolatry

3. *in truth*: or 'with the truth,' but here almost meaning 'for the purpose of judgment,' as the latter part of the verse indicates (cf. Q15.85; 30.8; 44.39).
4. *(for) an appointed time*: or 'term' (Ar. *ajal*), i.e. the heavens and earth will come to an end before Judgment Day (cf. Q30.8).
5. *Say*: on this form of address, see n. on Q2.80.
6. *any book...knowledge*: the idolators have no 'Book' or revelation on which to base their belief in other gods (cf. Q35.40; 43.21).
7. *they*: their gods.
8. *they*: their gods.
9. *will deny*: i.e. their gods will deny (lit. 'disbelieve').
10. *service*: or 'worship' (cf. Q10.28-29; 19.82).

7–8 Rejection of the message

11. *signs*: or 'verses' (see n. on Q2.39).
12. *clear signs*: or 'clear proofs,' 'indisputable evidence.'

has come to them, 'This is clear magic.' **8** Or do they say, 'He has forged it'? Say: 'If I have forged it, you (would) have no power at all to (help) me against God. He knows what you are busy with. He is sufficient as a witness between me and you. He is the Forgiving, the Compassionate.'

9 Say: 'I am not the first of the messengers,[13] and I do not know what will be done with me or with you. I only follow what I am inspired (with).[14] I am only a clear warner.'[15]

10 Say:[16] 'Do you see? If it[17] is from God, and you disbelieve in it, and a witness from the Sons of Israel has borne witness to (a Book) like it,[18] and believed, and you become arrogant – surely God does not guide the people who are evildoers.' **11** Those who disbelieve say to those who believe, 'If it had been something good, they would not have gotten to it before us' – even when they are not guided by it. And they say, 'This is an old lie!' **12** Yet before it was the Book of Moses as a model[19] and mercy; and this is a Book confirming (it)[20] in the Arabic language, to warn those who do evil, and as good news for the doers of good. **13** Surely those who say, 'Our Lord is God,' (and) then go straight – (there will be) no fear on them, nor will they sorrow. **14** Those are the companions of the Garden,[21] there to remain – a payment for what they have done.

15 We have charged each person (to do) good to his parents – his mother bore him with difficulty, and she delivered him with difficulty – his bearing and his weaning are thirty months[22] – until, when he reaches his maturity, and reaches forty years, he says, 'My Lord, (so) dispose me that I may be thankful for your blessing with which You have blessed me and my parents, and that I may do righteousness pleasing to You, and do right by me concerning my descendants. Surely I turn to You (in repentance), and surely I am one of those who submit.'[23] **16** Those are the ones from whom We shall accept the best of what they have done, and We shall pass over their evil deeds. (They will be) among the companions of the Garden – the promise of truth which they were promised. **17** But the one who says to his parents, 'Uff[24] to both of you! Do you promise me that I shall be brought forth,[25] when generations have already passed away before me?,' while both of them[26] call on God for help: 'Woe to you! Believe! Surely the promise of God is true!,' and he says, 'This is nothing but old tales'[27] – **18** those are the ones against whom the word has proved true about the communities of jinn and humankind (which) have already passed

---

9 The Prophet a typical messenger

13. *I am not the first of the messengers*: or 'I am not an innovation among the messengers.'
14. *what I am inspired (with)*: or 'what inspiration I have received.'
15. *warner*: for this role, see n. on Q2.119.

10–14 The Prophet's Book like Moses' Book

16. *Say…*: the Cairo edition, reflecting the views of traditional scholars, attributes this verse to the 'Medinan' period.
17. *it*: the Qur'ān.
18. *a witness…has borne witness…*: the 'witness' probably refers to Moses (cf. Q11.17; and Deuteronomy 18.18).
19. *model*: Ar. *imām* (cf. Q11.17).
20. *a Book confirming (it)*: i.e. 'confirming' the Torah of Moses (cf. Q46.30 below; see n. on Q3.3).
21. *Garden*: in heaven (for this imagery, see n. on Q2.25).

15–18 Kindness to parents

22. *thirty months*: cf. Q31.14 ('two years'). The Cairo edition, reflecting the views of traditional scholars, attributes this verse to the 'Medinan' period. Some traditional scholars consider the entire passage (Q46.15-18) 'Medinan.'
23. *those who submit*: or 'the Muslims.'
24. *Uff*: an expression of disrespect (cf. Q17.23; 21.67).
25. *brought forth*: i.e. from the grave.
26. *both of them*: i.e. his parents.
27. *old tales*: or 'tales of the ancients;' a contemptuous reference to the stories of earlier generations who were punished for disobeying their prophets (see n. on Q7.59; cf. Q25.5).

away before them.[28] Surely they were losers.

19 For each (there are) ranks,[29] according to what they have done, and so that He may pay them in full
for their deeds – and they will not be done evil. **20** On the Day when those who disbelieve are presented
to the Fire: 'You squandered your good things in your present life, and enjoyed them.[30] So today you will
be paid the punishment of humiliation because you became arrogant on the earth without any right, and
because you have acted wickedly.'

21 Remember the brother of 'Ād:[31] When he warned his people at the sand dunes[32] – and warners had
already passed away before him and after him – (saying): 'Do not serve (anyone) but God! Surely I fear
for you the punishment of a great Day.' **22** They said, 'Have you come to defraud us of our gods? Bring
us what you promise us,[33] if you are one of the truthful.' **23** He said, 'The knowledge (of it) is only with
God.[34] I deliver to you what I was sent with, but I see you are an ignorant people.' **24** When they saw it as
a cloud approaching their wādis, they said, 'This is a cloud (which) is going to give us rain.' 'No! It is what
you were seeking to hurry – a wind in which (there is) a painful punishment, **25** destroying everything
by the command of its Lord.' And morning found them not to be seen, except for their dwelling places.
In this way We repay the people who are sinners. **26** Certainly We had established them with what We
have not established you,[35] and We gave them hearing and sight and hearts.[36] Yet their hearing and their
sight and their hearts were of no use to them at all, since they denied the signs of God, and what they
were mocking overwhelmed them. **27** Certainly We destroyed the towns around you,[37] and varied the
signs so that they[38] might return. **28** Why did they not help them – those gods whom they had taken,
instead of God, as a (means of) drawing near (to Him)?[39] No! They abandoned them.[40] That[41] was their lie
and what they had forged.

29 (Remember) when[42] We turned a band of jinn[43] to you to listen to the Qur'ān: When they were in its

---

28. *the word has proved true...*: cf. Q11.119, 'I shall indeed fill Gehenna with jinn and people' (for the jinn, see n. on Q6.100).

19–20 Each judged according to his deeds

29. *ranks*: or 'degrees,' of honor and dishonour, or rewards and punishments.
30. *...and enjoyed them*: for this idea, cf. Luke 16.25.

21–28 The story of the people of 'Ād

31. *the brother of 'Ād*: Hūd, who was sent to the people of 'Ād; for the story that follows, cf. the versions at Q7.65-72; 11.50-60; 26.123-140.
32. *at the sand dunes*: or, if this is a place name, 'at the Sand Dunes;' but the reference is obscure.
33. *what you promise us*: or 'what you threaten us with' (i.e. punishment), spoken in derision.
34. *knowledge (of it) is only with God*: for this idea, cf. Q33.63; 41.47; 43.85; 67.26; and Mark 13.32 par.
35. *you*: the disbelievers.
36. *hearts*: minds.
37. *We destroyed the towns around you*: i.e. around the disbelievers; since there were no such towns in the vicinity of Mecca, this would imply that the addressees ('you') were situated elsewhere (cf. Q11.83, 89n.; 30.3n.; 37.137n.).
38. *they*: the inhabitants of the towns.
39. *as a (means of) drawing near (to Him)*: i.e. as intercessors with God (cf. Q39.3).
40. *abandoned them*: lit. 'went astray from them' (a pun).
41. *That*: i.e. the idea their gods were intermediaries between them and God.

29–32 Jinn hear the Qur'ān and believe

42. *(Remember) when...*: a stock narrative formula; the Arabic particle *idh* often marks the beginning of a story, and means something like 'Once...,' or 'There was a time when...,' or 'Remember when....' For the story that follows, cf. the version at Q72.1-14.
43. *a band of jinn*: for the jinn, see n. on Q6.100.

presence, they said, 'Be silent!' And when it was finished, they turned back to their people as warners. **30** They said, 'Our people! Surely We have heard a Book (which) has been sent down after Moses, confirming what was before it,[44] guiding to the truth and to a straight road. **31** Our people! Respond to the caller of God, and believe in Him. He will forgive you some of your sins, and protect you from a painful punishment. **32** Whoever does not respond to the caller of God – there is no escaping (Him) on the earth, and he has no allies other than Him. Those are clearly astray.'[45]

33 Do they not see that God, who created the heavens and earth, and was not tired out by their creation, is able to give the dead life? Yes indeed! Surely He is powerful over everything. **34** On the Day when those who disbelieve are presented to the Fire:[46] 'Is this not the truth?' They will say, 'Yes indeed! By our Lord!' He will say, 'Taste the punishment for what you have disbelieved.'

35 Be patient,[47] as the messengers of firm resolve were (also) patient. Do not seek to hurry it for them. On the Day when they see what they are promised, (it will seem) as if they had remained (in the grave) for only an hour of the day. A delivery! Will any be destroyed but the people who are wicked?

---

44. *confirming what was before it*: the Qur'ān 'confirms' the Torah and Gospel (see e.g. Q2.97; 3.3; 5.48; 35.31).

45. *clearly astray*: lit. 'in clear straying.'

33–35 Resurrection and Judgment certain

46. *the Fire*: Ar. *al-nār* is the most common of the various designations for Hell.

47. *Be patient...*: addressed to the Prophet. The Cairo edition, reflecting the views of traditional scholars, attributes this verse to the 'Medinan' period.

47 Muḥammad ۞ Muḥammad

In the Name of God, the Merciful, the Compassionate

1 Those who disbelieve and keep (people) from the way of God – He will lead their deeds astray.[1] **2** But those who believe and do righteous deeds, and believe in what has been sent down on Muḥammad[2] – and it is the truth from their Lord – He will absolve them of their evil deeds, and set their case right. **3** That is because those who disbelieve follow falsehood, and because those who believe follow the truth from their Lord. In this way God strikes parables for the people.[3]

4 When you[4] meet those who disbelieve, (let there be) a striking of the necks, until, when you have subdued them,[5] bind (them) securely,[6] and then either (set them free) as a favor or by ransom, until the war lays down its burdens. That (is the rule). If God had (so) pleased, He would indeed have defended Himself against them,[7] but (He allows fighting) so that He may test some of you by means of others. Those who are killed[8] in the way of God – He will not lead their deeds astray. **5** He will guide them and set their case right, **6** and He will cause them to enter the Garden[9] – He has made it known to them.

7 You who believe! If you help God, He will help you, and make firm your feet. **8** But those who disbelieve – (there will be) downfall for them, and He will lead their deeds astray. **9** That is because they disliked what God sent down, and so He has made their deeds worthless. **10** Have they not traveled on the earth and seen how the end was for those who were before them? God destroyed them. The disbelievers have examples of it.[10] **11** That is because God is the Protector of those who believe, and because the disbelievers have no protector.

12 Surely God will cause those who believe and do righteous deeds to enter Gardens through which rivers flow. But those who disbelieve – they take their enjoyment and eat as the cattle eat. The Fire[11] will be their dwelling place.

Q47: Much of this sūra is concerned with matters of war. It is assigned to the 'Medinan' period by most scholars, traditionally about the time of the battle of Badr (624 CE/2 AH). Q47 receives its title from the rare mention of Muḥammad's name (Q47.2).

1–3 God's dealings with believers and disbelievers

1. *lead their deeds astray*: i.e. cause their deeds to be lost (cf. Q47.4, 8 below).
2. *Muḥammad*: for this name, see n. on Q3.144.
3. *strikes parables for the people*: or 'shows the people what they are like.'

4–14 Fight the disbelievers

4. *you*: plur.
5. *subdued them*: an obscure word (Ar. *athkhana*; cf. Q8.67).
6. *bind (them) securely*: i.e. take the rest as prisoners.
7. *defended Himself against them*: i.e. God could have punished the disbelievers directly, not through human agents.
8. *are killed*: a variant reading has 'fight.'
9. *Garden*: in heaven (for this imagery, see n. on Q2.25).
10. *The disbelievers have examples of it*: a reference to previous peoples who were punished for their disbelief (see n. on Q7.59; cf. Q47.13 below). The remains of their destroyed cities were believed to be still visible.
11. *The Fire*: Ar. *al-nār* is the most common of the various designations for Hell.

13 How many a town[12] We have destroyed that was stronger in power than your town which expelled you![13] And there was no helper for them. **14** Is the one who (stands) on a clear sign[14] from his Lord like the one who – the evil of his deeds is made to appear enticing to him, and they follow their (vain) desires?

15 A parable of the Garden which is promised to the ones who guard (themselves):[15] In it (there are) rivers of water without pollution, and rivers of milk – its taste does not change – and rivers of wine – delicious to the drinkers – and rivers of purified honey. In it (there is) every (kind of) fruit for them, and forgiveness from their Lord. (Are they) like those who remain in the Fire? They are given boiling water to drink, and it cuts their insides (to pieces).

16 (There are) some of them who listen to you,[16] until, when they go forth from your presence, they say to those who have been given knowledge,[17] 'What did he say just now?' Those are the ones on whose hearts[18] God has set a seal, and they follow their (vain) desires. **17** But those who are (rightly) guided – He increases them in guidance, and gives them their (sense of) guarding (themselves). **18** So are they[19] looking for anything but the Hour[20] – that it will come upon them unexpectedly? The conditions for it have already come, and when it comes upon them, how will they have their reminder?[21] **19** Know that[22] He – (there is) no god but God. Ask forgiveness for your sin, and for the believing men and the believing women. God knows your[23] comings and goings, and your dwelling place.

20 Those who believe say, 'If only a sūra were sent down.'[24] But when a clearly composed[25] sūra is sent down, and fighting is mentioned in it, you see those in whose hearts is a sickness[26] looking at you with the look of one who faints at the point of death. Woe to them! **21** Obedience and rightful words (are called for)! When the matter is determined, and if they are true to God, it will indeed be better for them. **22** Is it possible, if you turned away, that you would foment corruption on the earth, and sever your family ties?[27] **23** Those are the ones whom God has cursed, and made them deaf, and blinded their sight. **24** Do they not contemplate the Qur'ān,[28] or (are there) locks on their hearts? **25** Surely those who have

12. *How many a town...*: the Cairo edition, reflecting the views of traditional scholars, assigns this verse to the time of the Prophet's flight to Medina, when he is said to have looked back toward Mecca in tears.
13. *you*: the Prophet.
14. *clear sign*: or 'clear proof,' 'indisputable evidence.'

15 The delights of Paradise and agony of Hell

15. *guard (themselves)*: against evil, or God.

16–19 Advice for the Prophet

16. *you*: the Prophet.
17. *those who have been given knowledge*: i.e. the believers (cf. e.g. Q16.27).
18. *hearts*: here, as often, the heart is spoken of as synonymous with mind.
19. *they*: the disbelievers (cf. Q12.107; 43.66).
20. *the Hour*: of judgment.
21. *their reminder*: or 'their warning' of punishment (see n. on Q3.58).
22. *Know that...*: addressed to the Prophet.
23. *your*: plur.

20–38 Reluctance to fight condemned

24. *If only a sūra were sent down*: i.e. a sūra (or 'unit' of revelation) that authorized fighting (see n. on Q2.23). Their question implies that a distinction may have been made between the Qur'ān and what the Prophet said.
25. *clearly composed*: for this idea, cf. Q3.7; 11.1; 22.52.
26. *those in whose hearts is a sickness*: a reference to the 'hypocrites.'
27. *sever your family ties*: lit. 'your wombs;' i.e. cause bloodshed within the community (cf. Q2.27; 13.25).
28. *the Qur'ān*: here close to its present meaning as the name of the Muslim scripture (cf. Q9.111; see n. on Q2.185).

turned their backs, after the guidance[29] has become clear to them – (it was) Satan[30] (who) contrived (it) for them, but He has spared them.[31] **26** That is because they said to those who disliked what God had sent down, 'We will obey you in part of the matter' – but God knows their secrets. **27** How (will it be) when the angels take them,[32] striking their faces and their backs? **28** That is because they have followed what angers God, and have disliked His approval, so He has made their deeds worthless.

29 Or do those in whose hearts is a sickness think that God will not bring to light their malice? **30** If We had (so) pleased, We would indeed have shown them to you,[33] and you would indeed know them by their marks – indeed you do know them by their devious speech. God knows your deeds, **31** and We shall indeed test you, until We know those of you who struggle and those who are patient, and We shall test the reports about you. **32** Surely those who disbelieve, and keep (people) from the way of God, and break with the messenger, after the guidance has become clear to them – they will not harm God at all, and He will make their deeds worthless.

33 You who believe! Obey God, and obey the messenger, and do not invalidate your (own) deeds. **34** Surely those who disbelieve and keep (people) from the way of God, (and) then die while they are disbelievers – God will not forgive them. **35** Do not grow weak and call for peace, when you are the prevailing (force), and God is with you, and will not deprive you of your deeds. **36** This present life is nothing but jest and diversion,[34] but if you believe and guard (yourselves), He will give you your rewards and not ask you for your wealth. **37** If He asks you for it, and presses you, you are stingy, and He brings to light your malice. **38** There you are! These (people)! You are called on to contribute[35] in the way of God, and (there are) some of you who are stingy. Whoever is stingy is stingy only to himself. God is the wealthy One,[36] and you are the poor (ones). If you turn away, He will exchange a people other than you.[37] Then they will not be like you.

---

29. *the guidance*: one of the most frequent terms (Ar. *al-hudā*) for revelation in general, and the Qur'ān in particular.
30. *Satan*: for this figure, see n. on Q2.36.
31. *He has spared them*: i.e. God has granted them a reprieve for a time (the pronoun must refer to God, not Satan).
32. *take them*: in death (see n. on Q6.61; for the various roles of the angels, see n. on Q2.30).
33. *you*: the Prophet.
34. *jest and diversion*: i.e. trivial in comparison with the Hereafter.
35. *contribute*: lit. 'spend.'
36. *the wealthy One*: i.e. God has no need of anyone or anything.
37. *exchange a people other than you*: i.e. put another people in their place.

48 The Victory ❁ Al-Fatḥ

In the Name of God, the Merciful, the Compassionate

1 Surely We have given you a clear victory,[1] **2** so that[2] God may forgive you what is past of your sin and what is (still) to come,[3] and complete His blessing on you, and guide you to a straight path, **3** and that God may help you with a mighty help. **4** He (it is) who sent down the Sakīna[4] into the hearts[5] of the believers, so that they might add belief to their belief – to God (belong) the forces of the heavens and the earth, and God is knowing, wise – **5** and that He may cause the believing men and the believing women to enter Gardens[6] through which rivers flow, there to remain, and absolve them of their evil deeds – that is the great triumph in the sight of God! – **6** and that He may punish the hypocrite men and the hypocrite women alike, and the idolatrous men and the idolatrous women[7] alike, and the ones who think evil thoughts about God. The wheel of evil (will turn) against them. God is angry with them, and has cursed them, and has prepared Gehenna[8] for them – and it is an evil destination! **7** To God (belong) the forces of the heavens and the earth. God is mighty, wise.

8 Surely We have sent you[9] as a witness, and as a bringer of good news and a warner,[10] **9** so that you[11] may believe in God and His messenger,[12] and support him, and respect him, and that you may glorify Him morning and evening. **10** Surely those who swear allegiance to you[13] swear allegiance to God – the hand of God is over their hands. So whoever breaks (his oath), only breaks it against himself, but whoever fulfils what he has covenanted with God – He will give him a great reward.

Q48: This sūra is assigned to the 'Medinan' period, traditionally about the time of the expedition to al-Ḥudaybiya (628 CE/6 AH). The Prophet is said to have had a dream in which he saw himself performing pilgrimage to Mecca. But when he and his followers actually approached the city, the Meccans blocked his way, and he stopped at al-Ḥudaybiya on the edge of the sacred territory of Mecca. Eventually a treaty with the Meccans was signed, by which the Muslims agreed to withdraw for that year. Q48 takes its title from the 'victory' mentioned in the opening verse.

1–10 Assurance to the Prophet

1. *We have given you a clear victory*: lit. 'We have opened for you a clear opening;' addressed to the Prophet and usually taken as a proleptic reference to the conquest of Mecca in 630 CE/8 AH; but it could refer to some otherwise unknown event (see Q48.18-19, 27 below; 8.19; 32.28-29; 57.10; 61.13; 110.1; cf. Q7.89, Shuʿayb; 26.118, Noah).
2. *so that...*: the connection with what follows v. 1 is not immediately apparent.
3. *God may forgive you...your sin...*: cf. Q47.19.
4. *the Sakīna*: or 'the assurance' (see n. on Q2.248; cf. Q48.18, 26 below).
5. *hearts*: here, as often, the heart is spoken of as synonymous with mind.
6. *Gardens*: in heaven (for this imagery, see n. on Q2.25).
7. *idolatrous men...women*: lit. men and women who 'associate (other gods with God).'
8. *Gehenna*: a name for Hell (see n. on Q2.206).
9. *you*: the Prophet.
10. *bringer of good news...warner*: for these roles, see n. on Q2.119; cf. Q33.45.
11. *you*: plur.
12. *messenger*: for this important title, see n. on Q2.87.
13. *you*: the Prophet (cf. Q48.18 below).

11 Those of the Arabs[14] who stayed behind[15] will say to you, 'Our wealth and our families kept us busy, so ask forgiveness for us.' They say with their tongues what is not in their hearts. Say:[16] 'Who has any power for you against God, whether He intends harm for you or intends benefit for you?[17] No! God is aware of what you do. **12** No! You thought that the messenger and the believers would never return to their families, and that was made to appear enticing in your hearts,[18] and you thought evil thoughts, and became a ruined people.' **13** Whoever does not believe in God and His messenger – surely We have prepared for the disbelievers a blazing (Fire). **14** To God (belongs) the kingdom of the heavens and the earth. He forgives whomever he pleases and punishes whomever He pleases. God is forgiving, compassionate.

15 The ones who stayed behind will say, when you[19] set out to take spoils, 'Let us follow you.' They want to change the word of God. Say: 'You will not follow us. So God has said before.'[20] They will say, 'No! You are jealous of us.' No! They have not understood, except for a little. **16** Say to those of the Arabs who stayed behind: 'You will be called to (fight) a people of harsh violence.[21] You will fight them or they will surrender.[22] If you obey, God will give you a good reward, but if you turn away, as you turned away before,[23] He will punish you with a painful punishment.' **17** There is no blame on the blind, and no blame on the disabled, and no blame on the sick.[24] Whoever obeys God and His messenger – He will cause him to enter Gardens through which rivers flow; but whoever turns away – He will punish him with a painful punishment.

18 Certainly God was pleased with the believers when they were swearing allegiance to you[25] under the tree,[26] and He knew what was in their hearts. So He sent down the Sakīna[27] on them, and rewarded them with a near victory,[28] **19** and many spoils to take. God is mighty, wise. **20** And God has promised you[29] many (more) spoils to take, and He has hurried this for you, and has restrained the hands of the people from you. (This happened) so that it might be a sign to the believers, and guide you to a straight path. **21** The other (spoils) which you were not able (to take), God has already encompassed them. God is powerful over everything.

22 If those who disbelieve fight you,[30] they will indeed turn their backs, (and) then they will not find any ally or any helper. **23** (That was) the customary way of God (concerning) those who have passed away before,

---

11–17 Reluctance to fight condemned

14. *the Arabs*: desert nomads (Ar. *al-a'rāb*); for what follows, cf. Q9.90, 97-99, 101, 120.
15. *who stayed behind*: from military campaign (see Q48.12, 15 below).
16. *Say*: on this form of address, see n. on Q2.80.
17. *...whether He intends harm...benefit for you*: i.e. God's will cannot be resisted.
18. *that was made to appear enticing...*: i.e. the Arabs would have been delighted if the Prophet and his followers had been killed.
19. *you*: plur.
20. *So God has said before*: see Q9.83.
21. *a people of harsh violence*: reference obscure (cf. Q17.5; 27.33).
22. *surrender*: or 'become Muslims' (Ar. *yuslimūn*).
23. *as you turned away before*: reference obscure.
24. *no blame on the blind...disabled...sick*: i.e. for not fighting.

18–21 Spoils taken and more spoils promised

25. *you*: the Prophet.
26. *under the tree*: said to refer to the oath of allegiance made at al-Ḥudaybiya, which came to be known as 'the pledge under the tree.'
27. *Sakīna*: or 'assurance' (cf. Q48.4 above, 26 below).
28. *victory*: lit. 'opening' (cf. Q48.27 below; 61.13).
29. *you*: plur.

22–26 Conflict with Mecca

30. *you*: plur.

and you will find no change in the customary way of God.[31] **24** He (it is) who restrained their hands from you, and your hands from them, in the heart[32] of Mecca,[33] after He gave you victory over them[34] – God sees what you do. **25** They are those who disbelieved, and kept you from the Sacred Mosque,[35] and (also) the offering, (which was) prevented from reaching its lawful place.[36] If not for (certain) believing men and believing women, whom you did not know, or you would have trampled them, and guilt smitten you without (your) realizing (it) because of them – so that God may cause to enter into His mercy whomever He pleases – if they had been separated out (clearly), We would indeed have punished those among them who disbelieved with a painful punishment.[37] **26** When those who disbelieved fostered[38] a fury in their hearts – the fury of the (time of) ignorance[39] – God sent down His Sakīna[40] on His messenger and on the believers, and fastened to them the word of guarding (themselves).[41] They have more right to it and are worthy of it. God has knowledge of everything.

27 Certainly God has spoken the truth in the vision to His messenger: 'You[42] will indeed enter the Sacred Mosque, if God pleases, in security, your heads shaved, your hair cut short, not fearing.'[43] He knew what you did not know, and besides that produced a near victory.[44] **28** He (it is) who has sent His messenger with the guidance[45] and the religion of truth, so that He[46] may cause it to prevail over religion – all of it. God is sufficient as a witness.

29 Muḥammad[47] is the messenger of God. Those who are with him are harsh against the disbelievers, (but) compassionate among themselves. You see them bowing and prostrating themselves, seeking favor from God and approval. Their marks on their faces are the trace of prostration. That is their image in the Torah,[48] and their image in the Gospel[49] is like a seed (that) puts forth its shoot, and strengthens it, and it becomes stout and stands straight on its stalk, pleasing the sowers – so that He may enrage the disbelievers by means of them. God has promised those of them who believe and do righteous deeds forgiveness and a great reward.

---

31. *the customary way of God*: lit. 'the *sunna* of God;' for this idea, cf. Q33.62; and see n. on Q8.38.
32. *heart*: lit. 'belly.'
33. *Mecca*: Ar. *Makka* occurs only here (cf. 'Becca' at Q3.96); whether this refers to the city in present-day Saudi Arabia is disputed by some modern scholars.
34. *after He gave you victory over them*: it is not certain what victory is being referred to here.
35. *Sacred Mosque*: traditionally identified with the Ka'ba at Mecca (see n. on Q5.95).
36. *lawful place*: for sacrifice (cf. Q2.196; 22.33).
37. *If not for (certain) believing men...*: a difficult construction but the general sense is clear: If a violent conquest of Mecca had occurred, some believers residing there would have been injured because they were unknown to the Prophet, and as a result he and his fighters would have unwittingly incurred guilt. Otherwise God would have allowed the conquest.
38. *fostered*: lit. 'made.'
39. *the (time of) ignorance*: i.e. the pre-Islamic period of ignorance about God (Ar. *al-jāhiliyya*).
40. *Sakīna*: or 'assurance' (cf. Q48.4, 18 above).
41. *the word of guarding (themselves)*: against evil, or God; contrast 'the word of disbelief' (Q9.74).

27–29 Muḥammad and his followers will receive their reward

42. *You*: plur.
43. *your heads shaved, your hair cut*: marks of the pilgrim (cf. Q2.196).
44. *produced a near victory*: lit. 'made a near opening.'
45. *the guidance*: one of the most frequent terms (Ar. *al-hudā*) for revelation in general, and the Qur'ān in particular
46. *He*: God, or 'he' (the Prophet).
47. *Muḥammad*: for this name, see n. on Q3.144.
48. *their image in the Torah*: cf. Deuteronomy 6.8; 11.18, God's words are 'as an emblem on your forehead.'
49. *their image in the Gospel*: for what follows, cf. Mark 4.26-29, 30-32 par. (the scattered and mustard seed parables).

49 The Private Rooms ✵ Al-Ḥujurāt

In the Name of God, the Merciful, the Compassionate

1 You who believe! Do not be forward[1] before God and His messenger,[2] but guard (yourselves) against God. Surely God is hearing, knowing. **2** You who believe! Do not raise your voices above the voice of the prophet, and do not be loud in (your) speech to him, like the loudness of some of you to others, or your deeds will come to nothing without your realizing (it). **3** Surely those who lower their voices in the presence of the messenger of God, those are the ones whose hearts God has tested for the guarding (of themselves). For them (there is) forgiveness and a great reward. **4** Surely those who call out to you[3] from behind the private rooms[4] – most of them do not understand. **5** If they were patient, until you come out to them, it would indeed be better for them. Yet God is forgiving, compassionate.

6 You who believe! If a wicked person brings you some (piece of) news, be discerning,[5] or you will smite a people in ignorance, and then become regretful over what you have done. **7** Know that the messenger of God is among you. If he obeyed you in much of the affair, you would indeed be in distress. But God has made belief dear to you, and made it appear enticing in your hearts,[6] and made disbelief and wickedness and disobedience hateful to you. Those – they are the right-minded. **8** Favor from God and a blessing! God is knowing, wise.

9 If two contingents of the believers fight, set (things) right between them, and if one of them oppresses the other, fight the one which oppresses until it returns to the command of God.[7] If it returns, set (things) right between them with justice, and act fairly. Surely God loves the ones who act fairly. **10** Only the believers are brothers,[8] so set (things) right between your two brothers, and guard (yourselves) against God, so that you may receive mercy.

11 You who believe! Do not let one people ridicule (another) people who may be better than them, or women (ridicule other) women who may be better than them. Do not find fault with each other, or insult each other with nicknames. A bad name is wickedness after belief. Whoever does not turn (in repentance), those – they are the evildoers.

Q49: This sūra is assigned to the 'Medinan' period, traditionally about a year or two before the Prophet's death. It deals with the conduct of his followers in their interactions with him and each other, and it concludes with criticism of the bedouin Arabs. Q49 takes its name from a word which is said to refer to the private living quarters of the Prophet's wives.

1–5 Believers must act respectfully toward the Prophet

1. *Do not be forward*: or perhaps 'do not send forward (proposals).'
2. *messenger*: for this title, and 'prophet' in the next verse, see n. on Q2.87.
3. *you*: the Prophet.
4. *from behind the private rooms*: i.e. while he is in the living quarters of his wives (each wife is said to have had a separate room; cf. Q33.53).

6–8 Believers must be discerning

5. *be discerning*: or 'verify (it);' cf. Q4.94.
6. *hearts*: here, as often, the heart is spoken of as synonymous with mind.

9–13 Relations among believers

7. *the command of God*: or 'the affair of God;' perhaps meaning 'the precepts of God's religion.'
8. *Only the believers are brothers*: i.e. by religion rather than blood (cf. Q3.103; 9.11; 33.5).

12 You who believe! Avoid too much conjecture,[9] (for) surely some conjecture is a sin. Do not pry or go behind each other's back. Would any of you like to eat the flesh of his dead brother? You would hate it![10] Guard (yourselves) against God. Surely God turns (in forgiveness), compassionate.

13 People! Surely We have created you from a male and a female,[11] and made you different peoples[12] and tribes, so that you may recognize one another. Surely the most honorable among you in the sight of God is the one among you who guards (himself) most. Surely God is knowing, aware.

14 The Arabs[13] say, 'We believe.' Say:[14] 'You do not believe. Rather say, "We submit,"[15] (for) belief has not yet entered your hearts. But if you obey God and His messenger, He will not deprive you of your deeds at all.[16] Surely God is forgiving, compassionate. **15** The believers are only those who believe in God and His messenger, (and) then have not doubted but struggled[17] with their wealth and their lives in the way of God. Those – they are the truthful.'

16 Say: 'Will you teach God about your religion, when God knows whatever is in the heavens and whatever is on the earth? God has knowledge of everything.'

17 (They think) they bestow a favor on you in that they have submitted![18] Say: 'Do not bestow your submission[19] on me as a favor! No! God bestows a favor on you, in that He has guided you to belief, if you are truthful. **18** Surely God knows the unseen (things)[20] of the heavens and the earth. God sees what you do.'

---

9. *conjecture*: or 'opinion,' as opposed to 'revealed (i.e. certain) knowledge.'
10. *You would hate it*: so how much more should you not defame (or 'backbite') your brother in religion while he is alive.
11. *a male and a female*: Adam and Eve.
12. *different peoples*: lit. 'branches.'

14–18 Diatribe against the Arabs

13. *the Arabs*: desert nomads (Ar. *al-a'rāb*); cf. Q9.97-99; 48.11, 16.
14. *Say*: on this form of address, see n. on Q2.80.
15. *We submit*: Ar. *aslamnā* can also mean 'we have become Muslims,' which would imply a distinction between 'believers' and 'Muslims.' For that reason, some commentators claim that here the word *aslamnā* is equivalent to 'we have sought peace by submission' (Ar. *iṣtaslamnā*).
16. *...He will not deprive you of your deeds at all*: i.e. even if they are not believers, their obedience will secure their deeds at the Judgment.
17. *struggled*: or 'fought.'
18. *have submitted*: or 'become Muslims.'
19. *your submission*: or 'your Islam.'
20. *unseen (things)*: or 'secrets' (see n. on Q2.3).

50 Qāf ❁ Qāf

In the Name of God, the Merciful, the Compassionate

1 Qāf.[1] By the glorious Qur'ān![2] **2** – No! They are amazed that a warner[3] has come to them from among
them, and the disbelievers say, 'This is an amazing thing! **3** When we are dead, and turned to dust [...]?[4]
That is a far return!' **4** We know what the earth takes away from them,[5] and with Us is a Book (that is)
keeping watch.[6] **5** No! They called the truth a lie when it came to them, and they are in a confused state.
6 Do they not look at the sky above them, how We have built it, and adorned it, and it has no cracks?
7 And the earth – We stretched it out, and cast on it firm mountains,[7] and caused every beautiful kind
(of plant) to grow on it, **8** as evidence and a reminder[8] to every servant[9] who turns (in repentance).
9 And We sent down blessed water from the sky, and caused gardens to grow by means of it, and grain
for harvest, **10** and tall date palms with bunches (of fruit), **11** as a provision for the servants, and We give
a barren[10] land life by means of it. In this way the coming forth (will take place).[11]

12 Before them the people of Noah called (it)[12] a lie, and the people of al-Rass,[13] and Thamūd, **13** and 'Ād,
and Pharaoh, and the brothers of Lot, **14** and the people of the Grove,[14] and the people of Tubba'[15] – each

---

Q50: This sūra opens by defending the resurrection through an appeal to the signs of God's power and providence. It stresses the certainty of death and judgment, and then concludes with some words of advice for the Prophet. Most scholars assign Q50 to the 'Meccan' period. It takes its title from the letter with which it begins.

1–11 Disbelievers reject the resurrection

1. *Qāf*: the name of the Arabic letter *q* (unique to Q50). Twenty-nine sūras begin with a letter (or letters) like this, ranging from one to five. No satisfactory explanation has been given for their occurrence. The Cairo edition varies in counting these letters as a separate verse, or as the beginning of the first verse (as here).
2. *Qur'ān*: here close to its present meaning as the name of the Muslim scripture (cf. Q50.45 below; see n. on Q2.185). The complement of this oath is omitted (cf. Q38.1; 89.1-4).
3. *warner*: for this role, see n. on Q2.119.
4. *[...]*: the reader must supply something like, 'shall we really be raised up?' (see e.g. Q37.12-17); i.e. they are baffled at the idea of resurrection of the dead.
5. *what the earth takes away from them*: i.e. how their bodies decompose in the grave.
6. *a Book...keeping watch*: referring to the heavenly 'Record' or 'Account' of their deeds (see e.g. Q18.49; 23.62; cf. Q17.13, 71; 69.19, 25; 84.7, 10, where each person is given an individual 'book' containing a record of his deeds).
7. *cast on it firm mountains*: to keep the earth from moving (cf. Q13.3; 15.19; 16.15; 21.31; 31.10).
8. *reminder*: the word is often used of revelation in general, and the Qur'ān in particular, but here it refers to the signs of God's power and providence (cf. Q50.45 below; see n. on Q3.58).
9. *every servant*: the word 'servant' (Ar. *'abd*), which also means 'slave,' is used here in the sense of 'every person' (cf. Q50.11, 29 below; 34.9).
10. *barren*: lit. 'dead.'
11. *the coming forth...*: from the grave (i.e. resurrection from the dead).

12–14 Previous examples of disbelief

12. *(it)*: refers to the threat of punishment, rather than the resurrection.
13. *people of al-Rass*: reference obscure (only here and at Q25.38).
14. *people of the Grove*: or 'companions of the Thicket' (Ar. *al-ayka*); this may be an alternative name for the people of Midian, since both have the same messenger, Shu'ayb (Q26.176-189; cf. Q15.78-79; 38.13).
15. *Tubba'*: the title of the kings of the Ḥimyarites of South Arabia (Yemen); mentioned only here and at Q44.37.

(of them) called the messengers[16] liars, and My promise[17] was proved true.

15 Were We tired out by the first creation? No! They are in doubt about a new creation. **16** Certainly We created the human, and We know what his own self whispers within him, (for) We are closer to him than (his) jugular vein. **17** When the two meeters[18] meet together, (one) seated on the right, and (one) on the left, **18** he does not utter a word without (there being) a watcher ready beside him.[19] **19** The daze of death comes in truth: 'That is what you were trying to avoid!'

20 There will be a blast on the trumpet:[20] 'That is the Day of Promise.'[21] **21** Each person will come, (and) with him a driver and a witness.[22] **22** 'Certainly you were oblivious of this, so We have removed your covering,[23] and today your sight is sharp.' **23** His comrade[24] will say, 'This is what I have ready.' **24** '(You two),[25] cast into Gehenna[26] every stubborn disbeliever, **25** preventer of the good, transgressor, doubter, **26** who set up[27] another god with God. Cast him into the harsh punishment.' **27** His (other) comrade[28] will say, 'Our Lord, I did not make him transgress insolently, but he was far astray.'[29] **28** He[30] will say, 'Do not dispute in My presence, when I have already sent forth the promise[31] to you. **29** The word[32] is not going to change with Me. I am not an evildoer to (My) servants.' **30** On the Day when We say to Gehenna, 'Are you filled?,' and it says, 'Are there any more (to come)?,' **31** and the Garden[33] is brought near for the ones who guard (themselves) – (it is) not far: **32** 'This is what you were promised. (It is) for everyone who turns (in repentance and) keeps watch[34] **33** – whoever fears the Merciful in the unseen,[35] and brings a heart turning (in repentance). **34** Enter it in peace!' That is the Day of Eternity. **35** There they will have whatever they please, and with Us (there is still) more.

---

16. *messengers*: for this important title, see n. on Q2.87.
17. *promise*: or 'threat' (of punishment); cf. Q50.28, 45 below.

15–19 Death and resurrection certain

18. *the two meeters*: two angels of death (see Q50.21, 24 below; cf. Q6.61n.).
19. *a watcher ready beside him*: to write down what he says.

20–35 A judgment scene

20. *a blast on the trumpet*: the Last Day will be announced by the blast of a trumpet (e.g. Q6.73; 18.99; 20.102; 39.68 [a double blast]; 69.13; 74.8; 78.18; cf. Matthew 24.31; 1 Corinthians 15.52; 1 Thessalonians 4.16).
21. *Day of Promise*: or 'Day of Threat' (cf. Q85.2).
22. *a driver and a witness*: the former 'herds' him before the tribunal, while the latter 'testifies' to his good and bad deeds.
23. *covering*: probably meaning his 'veil of ignorance' (see e.g. Q17.45-46; cf. Q2.88).
24. *his comrade*: the 'recording angel,' or the 'witness,' who now presents a record of the man's deeds.
25. *(You two)*: the verb is dual here (and in the following verse), and probably refers to the two angels of death, or to the angelic 'driver' and 'witness.' God is the speaker.
26. *Gehenna*: a name for Hell (see n. on Q2.206).
27. *set up*: lit. 'made.'
28. *His (other) comrade*: the 'satan' who had been assigned to him in life (see Q41.25; cf. Q4.38; 43.36).
29. *far astray*: lit. 'in far straying.'
30. *He*: God.
31. *promise*: or 'threat' (of punishment); i.e. God had already warned them.
32. *word*: or 'sentence' (of judgment).
33. *Garden*: in heaven (for this imagery, see n. on Q2.25).
34. *keeps watch*: i.e. observes God's commands.
35. *in the unseen*: or 'in secret' (see n. on Q2.3).

36 How many a generation We have destroyed before them![36] They were stronger than them[37] in power, and they searched about in the lands – was there any place of escape? **37** Surely in that is a reminder indeed to whoever has a heart[38] or listens attentively,[39] and he is a witness.

38 Certainly We[40] created the heavens and the earth, and whatever is between them, in six days.[41] No weariness touched Us in (doing) that. **39** Be patient with what they say, and glorify your Lord with praise before the rising of the sun, and before its setting. **40** And glorify Him during part of the night, and at the ends of the prostration.[42] **41** And listen for the Day when the caller will call from a place nearby. **42** The Day when they hear the cry[43] in truth – that is the Day of Coming Forth.[44] **43** Surely We – We give life and cause death, and to Us is the (final) destination.

44 On the Day when the earth is split open from them, (and they come forth from the graves) rushing – that is an easy gathering for Us. **45** We know what they say. You[45] are not a tyrant over them. So remind, by means of the Qur'ān,[46] anyone who fears My promise.[47]

36–37 Punishment of earlier generations a warning

36. *How many a generation We have destroyed before them*: a reference to previous peoples who were punished for their sins (cf. Q50.12-14 above; see n. on Q7.59).
37. *them*: the disbelievers.
38. *heart*: here, as often, the heart is spoken of as synonymous with mind.
39. *listens attentively*: lit. 'casts (his) hearing.'

38–45 Advice for the Prophet

40. *Certainly We...*: the Cairo edition, reflecting the views of traditional scholars, assigns this verse to the 'Medinan' period.
41. *in six days*: cf. Q7.54; 10.3; 11.7; 25.59; 32.4; 41.9-12; and Genesis 1.1-31.
42. *at the ends of the prostration*: meaning obscure (lit. '[at the] backs of the prostration').
43. *the cry*: or 'the shout,' of impending doom (cf. Q36.49, 53; 38.15).
44. *Day of Coming Forth*: i.e. the Day of Resurrection (cf. Q50.11 above).
45. *You*: the Prophet.
46. *So remind...*: i.e. admonish or warn them by the Qur'ān (cf. Q6.70; 51.55; 52.29; 87.9; 88.21).
47. *promise*: or 'threat' of punishment (cf. Q50.28 above).

51 The Scatterers ✵ Al-Dhāriyāt

In the Name of God, the Merciful, the Compassionate

1 By the scatterers (with their) scattering,[1] **2** and the bearers (with their) burden,[2] **3** and the runners
(with their) effortlessness, **4** and the distributors (with their) affair![3] **5** Surely what you[4] are promised[5] is
true indeed! **6** Surely the Judgment is indeed going to fall!

7 By the sky with all its tracks![6] **8** Surely you differ indeed in what you say![7] **9** Whoever is deluded about
it is (really) deluded. **10** May the guessers[8] perish, **11** those who are in a flood (of confusion),[9] heedless.
12 They ask, 'When is the Day of Judgment?' **13** The Day when they will be tried over the Fire:[10] **14** 'Taste
your trial! This is what you were seeking to hurry.'

15 Surely the ones who guard (themselves)[11] will be in (the midst of) gardens and springs, **16** taking
whatever their Lord has given them. Surely before (this) they were doers of good. **17** Little of the night
would they sleep, **18** and in the mornings they would ask for forgiveness, **19** and in their wealth (there
was) a due (portion) for the beggar and the outcast.

20 In the earth (there are) signs[12] for the ones who are certain, **21** and (also) in yourselves.[13] Do you not
see? **22** And in the sky is your provision[14] and what you are promised.[15] **23** By the Lord of the sky and the

---

Q51: This sūra opens with a series of vivid affirmations of the certainty and imminence of the Day of Judgment. Next comes the story of Abraham and his guests, followed by briefer reports of the punishment of Pharaoh and the peoples of 'Ād, Thamūd, and Noah. A final section extols God's power and providence. Most scholars assign Q51 to the 'Meccan' period. It takes its name from a word in the opening verse.

1–19 Judgment certain and imminent

1. *By the scatterers (with their) scattering...*: i.e. 'I swear by...;' the first four verses contain fem. plur. participles, which may refer to the angels or possibly to the winds of an approaching storm (cf. Q18.45) as a metaphor for the arrival of Judgment Day, but all four clauses are so cryptic that their precise meaning can only be guessed at. For sūras that begin with oaths by female entities like these, see Q37.1-3; 77.1-6; 79.1-5; 100.1-5.
2. *the bearers (with their) burden*: winds bringing clouds heavy with rain (?) or perhaps women giving birth (?).
3. *the distributors (with their) affair*: or 'the distributors (of God's) command' (Ar. *amr*).
4. *you*: plur.
5. *what you are promised*: or 'what you are threatened with' (i.e. punishment); vv. 5-6 break the rhyme of the preceding oaths.
6. *tracks*: i.e. the courses which the heavenly bodies follow.
7. *differ indeed in what you say*: about the coming Judgment.
8. *the guessers*: those who follow 'mere opinion' rather than 'revealed (i.e. certain) knowledge' (cf. Q6.116, 148; 10.66; 43.20).
9. *a flood (of confusion)*: cf. Q23.54, 63.
10. *the Fire*: Ar. *al-nār* is the most common of the various designations for Hell.
11. *guard (themselves)*: against evil, or God.

20–23 Signs of God's power and providence

12. *signs*: for the various meanings of 'signs,' see n. on Q2.39.
13. *and (also) in yourselves*: probably referring to the creation and reproduction of humans (cf. Q41.53; 45.4).
14. *your provision*: i.e. rain as a source of sustenance.
15. *what you are promised*: the coming judgment.

earth! Surely it[16] is true indeed – (even) as what you (are able to) speak.[17]

24 Has the story[18] come to you[19] of the honored guests of Abraham?[20] **25** When they entered upon him, and said, 'Peace!,' he said, 'Peace! (You are) a people unknown (to me).' **26** So he turned to his family and brought a fattened calf, **27** and he placed it near them. He said, 'Will you not eat?' **28** And he began to feel a fear of them.[21] They said, 'Do not fear!' And they gave him good news of a knowing boy.[22] **29** And then his wife came forward in a loud voice, and struck her face, and said, 'An old woman, barren!' **30** They said, 'So (it will be)! Your Lord has said.[23] Surely He – He is the Wise, the Knowing.' **31** He[24] said, 'What is your business, you envoys?'[25] **32** They said, 'Surely we have been sent to a sinful people,[26] **33** to send (down) on them stones of clay, **34** marked by your Lord for the wanton.'[27] **35** We (would have) brought out any of the believers who were in it,[28] **36** but We found in it only one house of those who had submitted.[29] **37** And We left in it a sign for those who fear the painful punishment.

38 And (there is also a sign)[30] in Moses: when We sent him to Pharaoh with clear authority. **39** But he turned away with his supporter(s), and said, 'A magician or a man possessed!'[31] **40** So We seized him and his forces, and tossed them into the sea, (for) he was to blame.

41 And (there is also a sign) in 'Ād: when We sent upon them the desolating[32] wind. **42** It left nothing it came upon, but made it like decayed (ruins). **43** And (there is also a sign) in Thamūd: when it was said to them, 'Enjoy (yourselves) for a time!' **44** But they disdained the command of their Lord,[33] and the thunderbolt took them while they were looking on, **45** and they were not able to stand, nor were they helped. **46** And the people of Noah before (them) – surely they were a wicked people.

---

16. *it*: judgment.
17. *(even) as what you (are able to) speak*: i.e. it is as certain as the fact that they can speak.

24–37 The story of Abraham and his guests

18. *story*: or 'report' (Ar. *ḥadīth*).
19. *you*: the Prophet, or perhaps intended generally ('one').
20. *the honored guests of Abraham*: the angels who visited Abraham on their way to destroy Lot's city (see n. on Q11.69); for the story that follows, cf. the versions at Q11.69-76; 15.51-77; and Genesis 18.1-33.
21. *feel a fear of them*: to refuse food was a sign of hostility, but angels do not eat (cf. Q11.70).
22. *knowing boy*: or perhaps 'cunning boy' (Isaac); cf. Q11.71.
23. *So (it will be)! Your Lord has said*: or 'Thus your Lord says;' the same response given to Zachariah about the birth of John (Q19.9; cf. Q3.40), and to Mary about the birth of Jesus (Q19.21; cf. Q3.47).
24. *He*: Abraham.
25. *envoys*: a designation roughly equivalent to 'messengers,' and here used of the 'angels.'
26. *a sinful people*: i.e. the people of Lot (cf. Q11.74; and Genesis 19.1-29).
27. *marked by your Lord...*: meaning obscure, but said to refer to special markings, or that each had inscribed on it the name of the person it would kill (cf. Q11.83).
28. *it*: Lot's city (Sodom, according to Genesis 19.1).
29. *those who had submitted*: or 'the Muslims' (referring the household of Lot).

38–40 Moses and Pharaoh

30. *(there is also a sign)*: consistent with the construction of the previous verse.
31. *possessed*: or 'jinn-struck' (Ar. *majnūn*); cf. Q26.27; the same accusation is leveled at Noah and the Prophet (see n. on Q7.184; 51.52 below).

41–46 The peoples of 'Ād, Thamūd, and Noah

32. *desolating*: lit. 'barren.'
33. *the command of their Lord*: not to harm the she-camel (see e.g. Q7.73-79).

47 The sky – We built it with (Our own) hands, and surely We were (its) extenders[34] indeed. **48** And the earth – We spread it out. Excellent were the smoothers![35] **49** And We created pairs of everything, so that you might take heed.[36] **50** So flee to God! Surely I am a clear warner[37] for you from Him. **51** And do not set up[38] another god with God. Surely I am a clear warner for you from Him.

52 (Even) so, not a messenger came to those who were before them, except they said, 'A magician or a man possessed!'[39] **53** Have they bequeathed it to each other?[40] No! They are a people who transgress insolently. **54** So turn away from them, (for) you[41] are not to be blamed, **55** but remind (them).[42] Surely the Reminder will benefit the believers.

56 I did not create the jinn and humankind except to serve Me.[43] **57** I do not desire any provision from them, nor do I desire that they should feed Me.[44] **58** Surely God – He is the Provider, One full of power, the Firm.

59 Surely for the ones who do evil (there will be) a portion like the portion of their companions.[45] Let them not seek to hurry Me! **60** Woe to those who disbelieve on account of their Day which they are promised!

47–50 Signs of God's power and providence

34. *extenders*: or 'wideners.'
35. *We spread it out. Excellent were the smoothers*: the imagery is that of laying out a bed (cf. Q20.53; 78.6).
36. *take heed*: or 'be reminded,' 'remember.'
37. *warner*: for this role, see n. on Q2.119.
38. *set up*: lit. 'make.'

52–55 Previous messengers rejected

39. *magician...possessed*: cf. Q51.39 above.
40. *Have they bequeathed it to each other?*: the question is intended sarcastically.
41. *you*: the Prophet.
42. *remind (them)*: i.e. admonish or warn them by the Qur'ān, 'the Reminder' (cf. Q6.70; 50.45; 52.29; 87.9; 88.21).

56–58 Jinn and humans created to serve God

43. *serve Me*: or 'worship Me.'
44. *nor do I desire that they should feed Me*: God does not require sacrifices 'for food,' as other gods do (cf. Q6.14; 20.132; 22.37).

59–60 Disbelievers will be punished

45. *companions*: in evildoing, referring to those of earlier generations.

52 The Mountain ۞ Al-Ṭūr

In the Name of God, the Merciful, the Compassionate

1 By the mountain[1] **2** and a Book written **3** on parchment unrolled![2] **4** By the inhabited House![3] **5** By the roof raised up[4] **6** and the sea surging! **7** Surely the punishment of your Lord is indeed going to fall! **8** (There is) no one to repel it.[5]

9 On the Day when the sky will shake, **10** and the mountains fly away, **11** woe that Day to the ones who called (it) a lie, **12** who – they were playing around in (their) banter. **13** On the Day when they will be shoved forcefully[6] into the fire of Gehenna:[7] **14** 'This is the Fire[8] which you called a lie! **15** Is this magic or do you not see? **16** Burn in it! Bear it patiently or do not bear it patiently – (it is) the same for you. You are only being repaid for what you have done.'

17 Surely the ones who guard (themselves)[9] will be in Gardens[10] and bliss, **18** rejoicing in what their Lord has given them, and (because) their Lord has guarded them against the punishment of the Furnace.[11] **19** 'Eat and drink with satisfaction, (in return) for what you have done.' **20** (There they will be) reclining on couches lined up, and We shall marry them to (maidens) with dark, wide eyes. **21** (For) those who believe, and whose descendants followed them in belief, We shall join their descendants with them, and We shall not deprive them of any of their deeds. Each person (is held) in pledge for what he has earned.[12] **22** We shall increase them with fruits and meat of whatever (kind) they desire. **23** There they will pass (around) a cup[13] to each other in which there is no frivolous or sinful talk, **24** and among them will circulate boys of their own, as if they were hidden pearls.[14] **25** Some of them will approach others asking

---

Q52: This sūra opens with a series of affirmations of the certainty and imminence of the Day of Judgment. This is followed by a description of the delights awaiting the righteous in Paradise. The latter half of the sūra is an unrelenting diatribe against the disbelievers. Most scholars consider Q52 a fairly early 'Meccan' sūra. It takes its title from the reference to Mount Sinai in the opening verse.

1–16 Judgment certain and imminent

1. *the mountain*: probably Mount Sinai (cf. Q95.2); if so, then the following reference to the 'Book' would be the Torah given to Moses there.
2. *on parchment unrolled*: i.e. in the form of a scroll rather than a codex (cf. Q17.13; 74.52; 81.10), and written on 'parchment' (Ar. *raqq*) rather than papyrus (cf. Q6.7, 91).
3. *the inhabited House*: said to refer to the Ka'ba, 'inhabited' by pilgrims (cf. Q9.17-19; see n. on Q5.95).
4. *the roof raised up*: the sky (see e.g. Q21.32; 55.7; 79.28; 88.18).
5. *Surely the punishment...no one to repel it*: vv. 7-8 break the rhyme of the preceding oaths.
6. *shoved forcefully*: lit. 'shoved (with) a shove.'
7. *Gehenna*: a name for Hell (see n. on Q2.206).
8. *the Fire*: Ar. *al-nār* is the most common of the various designations for Hell.

17–28 The delights of Paradise

9. *guard (themselves)*: against evil, or God.
10. *Gardens*: in heaven (for this imagery, see n. on Q2.25).
11. *the Furnace*: another name for Hell (Ar. *al-jaḥīm*).
12. *for what he has earned*: i.e. for his deeds.
13. *cup*: of wine (cf. Q37.45-47; 56.19).
14. *hidden pearls*: or 'cherished pearls' (cf. Q76.19, 'scattered pearls').

each other questions. **26** They will say, 'Surely we were fearful among our family before,[15] **27** but God has bestowed favor on us, and guarded us against the punishment of the scorching (Fire).[16] **28** Surely we used to call on Him before. Surely He – He is the Beneficent, the Compassionate.'

29 So remind (them)![17] By the blessing of your Lord, you are neither an oracle-giver[18] nor possessed.[19]
30 Or do they say, 'A poet,[20] for whom we await the uncertainty of Fate'?[21] **31** Say:[22] '(Just) wait! Surely I shall be one of those waiting with you.' **32** Or do their minds command them (to do) this, or are they a people who transgress insolently? **33** Or do they say, 'He has invented it?'[23] No! They do not believe.
34 Let them bring a proclamation like it,[24] if they are truthful. **35** Or were they created out of nothing?[25] Or were they the creators? **36** Or did they create the heavens and the earth? No! They are not certain.
37 Or are the storehouses of your Lord with them, or are they the record-keepers? **38** Or do they have a ladder[26] on which they (can) listen? Then let their listener bring clear authority. **39** Or does He have daughters while you have sons?[27] **40** Or do you ask them for a reward,[28] so that they are burdened with debt? **41** Or is the unseen in their keeping, so that they are writing it down?[29] **42** Or do they intend a plot? Then those who disbelieve will be the ones plotted against. **43** Or do they have a god other than God? Glory to God above what they associate! **44** Even if they see fragments of the sky falling,[30] they will say, 'A heap of clouds!' **45** So leave them, until they meet their Day on which they will be thunderstruck
46 – the Day when their plot will be of no use to them at all, and they will not be helped. **47** Surely for those who do evil (there is) a punishment before that,[31] but most of them do not know (it).

48 Be patient for the judgment of your Lord. Surely you are in Our sight. Glorify your Lord with praise when you arise,[32] **49** and glorify Him during part of the night, and (at) the setting of the stars.[33]

---

15. *fearful among our family before*: i.e. fearful of the coming Judgment.
16. *the scorching (Fire)*: presumably another name for Hell, see Q52.18 above (but cf. Q15.27; 56.42).

29–47 Diatribe against the disbelievers

17. *So remind (them)*: i.e. 'admonish' or 'warn (them);' addressed to the Prophet (cf. Q6.70; 50.45; 51.55; 87.9; 88.21).
18. *oracle-giver*: or 'diviner' (Ar. *kāhin*), a religious entrepreneur who was paid to give inspired answers to all sorts of questions (only here and at Q69.42).
19. *possessed*: or 'jinn-struck' (Ar. *majnūn*); see n. on Q7.184.
20. *poet*: see n. on Q21.5.
21. *we await the uncertainty of Fate*: i.e. for some future calamity to befall the Prophet.
22. *Say*: on this form of address, see n. on Q2.80.
23. *it*: the Qur'ān.
24. *bring a proclamation like it*: the failure of the Prophet's contemporaries to take up this challenge (cf. Q2.23; 10.38, 11.13; 28.49) was later seen as proof that it was impossible, and the Qur'ān's 'inimitability' (referred to as the *i'jāz al-qur'ān*) would be taken as proof of its miraculous nature and divine origin. The word 'proclamation' (or 'report,' Ar. *ḥadīth*) may either refer to some 'unit' of revelation or to the Qur'ān in its entirety (cf. Q28.49).
25. *out of nothing*: or 'for no purpose' (lit. 'without anything').
26. *a ladder*: to ascend into heaven, and so listen in on what is said in the divine council.
27. *...daughters...sons*: referring to the belief that the angels were 'daughters of God,' and reflecting the cultural preference of sons over daughters (see Q16.57; 17.40; 37.149-154; 43.19; 53.21-22).
28. *reward*: for delivering messages from God.
29. *is the unseen in their keeping...*: i.e. 'do they know the future...' (cf. Q68.47; see n. on Q2.3).
30. *fragments of the sky falling*: see Q17.92; 26.187; 34.9; cf. Q30.48.
31. *punishment before that*: i.e. punishment in this world (cf. Q32.21).

48–49 Final word to the Prophet

32. *when you arise*: cf. Q50.39-40.
33. *setting...*: lit. 'withdrawing...' (before dawn?).

53 The Star ۞ Al-Najm

In the Name of God, the Merciful, the Compassionate

1 By the star when it falls![1] **2** Your companion[2] has not gone astray, nor has he erred, **3** nor does he
speak on a whim.[3] **4** It[4] is nothing but an inspiration inspired.[5] **5** One harsh in power has taught him[6]
6 – One full of strength![7] He stood poised,[8] **7** while He was at the highest horizon, **8** then He drew near and
came down. **9** He was two bow-lengths tall, or nearly.[9] **10** And so He inspired His servant (with) what He
inspired.[10] **11** His heart did not lie about what it saw.[11] **12** Will you dispute with him about what he sees?[12]

13 Certainly he saw Him at a second descent,[13] **14** by the Lote Tree of the Boundary, **15** near which is the
Garden of the Refuge,[14] **16** when (there) covered the Lote Tree what covered (it).[15] **17** His sight did not
turn aside, nor did it transgress. **18** Certainly he saw one of the greatest signs of his Lord.[16]

Q53: This sūra opens with the reports of two 'visions.' These are followed by a section rejecting the idea that angels are the 'daughters of God.' The sūra concludes with a summary of the contents of 'the scrolls of Moses and Abraham.' Most scholars assign Q53 to the 'Meccan' period, though some attribute a few verses to 'Medina.' It takes its title from 'the star' mentioned in the opening verse.

1–18 Two visions

1. *By the star...*: i.e. 'I swear by the star...,' usually taken to be Sirius (see Q53.49 below); cf. the oaths at Q56.75; 81.15-16.
2. *Your companion*: the Prophet (cf. Q34.46; 81.22).
3. *on a whim*: or 'out of (vain) desire.'
4. *It*: the Qur'ān.
5. *an inspiration inspired*: Ar. *waḥy yūḥā* (cf. Q35.31).
6. *him*: or 'it' (cf. Q55.1-2, 'The Merciful has taught the Qur'ān').
7. *One harsh in power...One full of strength*: this figure is usually identified as the angel Gabriel, though it is said that some of the companions of the Prophet (e.g. Ibn 'Abbās) believed it was God whom the Prophet saw. Since similar epithets are applied to God elsewhere (e.g. Q4.84; 8.52; 40.22; 51.58), and since the following reference 'to His servant' (v. 10) can only mean 'to God's servant,' this and the vision which follows (vv. 13-18) are probably theophanies. Cf. the vision at Q81.15-25, which appears to be an allusion to (or variant recension of) this account.
8. *He stood poised*: or perhaps 'He mounted (upward);' cf. Q2.29; 41.11.
9. *two bow-lengths tall, or nearly*: or 'two bow-lengths away, or nearer.'
10. *He inspired His servant (with) what He inspired*: referring to the Prophet as God's 'servant' or 'slave;' cf. a similar expression at Q20.38 (Moses' mother).
11. *His heart did not lie about what it saw*: i.e. the Prophet's mind (lit. 'the heart') did not falsely represent what it perceived. It is noteworthy that neither this vision, nor the one following, reports any words being spoken; each is without explicit content (contrast Q96.1-5).
12. *Will you dispute with him about what he sees*: or 'Do you dispute with it [i.e. his heart] about what it sees.'
13. *at a second descent*: or 'at another descent.'
14. *Lote Tree of the Boundary...Garden of the Refuge*: mentioned only here in the Qur'ān. Traditionally, the 'Garden of the Refuge' is taken to refer to heaven (Q32.19 has the plur. 'Gardens of the Refuge'), and the 'Lote Tree of the Boundary' (Ar. *sidrat al-muntahā*) is said to be a celestial tree marking the boundary between heaven and earth. But it may be that both refer to terrestrial places, in keeping with this vision as another 'descent' of God. Compare the theophany to Moses at the 'tree' (Q28.29-35) in 'the holy wādi of Ṭuwā' (Q20.12; 79.16).
15. *(there) covered...what covered (it)*: meaning obscure; for the same expression, see Q53.54 below; cf. Q20.78.
16. *one of the greatest signs of his Lord*: cf. the description of the theophany to Moses at Q20.23.

19 Have you seen al-Lāt, and al-'Uzzā, **20** and Manāt, the third, the other?[17] **21** Do you have male (offspring) while He has female? **22** Then that (would be) an unfair division![18] **23** They are only names which you have named,[19] you and your fathers. God has not sent down any authority for it. They only follow conjecture[20] and whatever they themselves desire – when certainly the guidance[21] has come to them from their Lord. **24** Or will a person have whatever he longs for? **25** To God (belongs) the last and the first.[22]

26 How many an angel there is in the heavens whose intercession is of no use at all, until God gives permission to whomever He pleases and approves. **27** Surely those who do not believe in the Hereafter[23] indeed name the angels with the names of females. **28** But they have no knowledge about it. They only follow conjecture, and surely conjecture is of no use at all against the truth. **29** So turn away[24] from the one who turns away from Our reminder[25] and desires nothing but this present life. **30** That is the extent of their knowledge. Surely your Lord – He knows who goes astray from His way, and He knows who is (rightly) guided. **31** To God (belongs) whatever is in the heavens and whatever is on the earth, so that He may repay those who do evil for what they have done, and repay those who do good with the best (reward).

32 Those who[26] avoid great sins and immoral deeds,[27] except for inadvertent ones[28] – surely your Lord is embracing in forgiveness. He knows about you, when He produced you from the earth, and when you were (still) embryos in the bellies of your mothers. So do not claim purity for yourselves. He knows the one who guards (himself).[29]

33 Do you[30] see the one who turns away, **34** and gives little, and (then) grudgingly? **35** Is knowledge of the unseen[31] in his keeping, and so he sees (it)? **36** Or has he not been informed about what is in the

---

19–25 The pagan goddesses

17. *al-Lāt...al-'Uzzā...Manāt...*: said to be 'goddesses' connected with three shrines in the region of Mecca, but they are probably angels, as the following section (Q53.26-31) makes clear. One strand of tradition holds that when the Prophet first recited these verses, he was 'earnestly desiring' to find some way of making his religion acceptable to his fellow Meccans, and failed to notice when Satan 'whispered' two (or three) verses permitting intercession with God through these goddesses (cf. Q22.52-53). Later, when the Prophet realized this (or Gabriel drew his attention to it), he received the revelation as it now stands in the Qur'ān. Like so much of the tradition, however, this story is probably a fiction invented to explain an otherwise puzzling text.
18. *an unfair division*: referring to the belief that these 'goddesses' were 'daughters of God,' and reflecting the cultural preference of sons over daughters (cf. Q16.57; 17.40; 37.149-154; 43.19-20; 52.39).
19. *only names which you have named*: the most extreme criticism of 'paganism' in the Qur'ān, denying the existence of other gods altogether (cf. Q7.71; 12.40); elsewhere the gods are said to be 'jinn' (Q6.100; 34.40-42; 37.158-159).
20. *conjecture*: or 'opinion,' as opposed to 'revealed (i.e. certain) knowledge.'
21. *the guidance*: one of the most frequent terms (Ar. *al-hudā*) for revelation in general, and the Qur'ān in particular.
22. *the last and the first*: or 'the Hereafter and the former (life);' cf. Q79.25; 92.13.

26–31 Angels not female

23. *the Hereafter*: see n. on Q2.4.
24. *So turn away...*: addressed to the Prophet.
25. *Our reminder*: or 'Our Reminder,' referring to the Qur'ān (see n. on Q3.58).

32 God knows all

26. *Those who...*: the Cairo edition, reflecting the views of traditional scholars, attributes this verse to the 'Medinan' period.
27. *immoral deeds*: lit. 'the immoralities' (Ar. *al-fawāḥisha*), usually of a sexual nature.
28. *except for inadvertent ones*: meaning obscure.
29. *guards (himself)*: against evil, or God.

33–55 The scrolls of Moses and Abraham

30. *you*: the Prophet.
31. *the unseen*: here referring to 'the future' (see n. on Q2.3).

pages of Moses **37** and Abraham,[32] who paid (his debt) in full?[33] **38** – That no one bearing a burden bears the burden of another;[34] **39** and that a person will receive only what he (himself) strives for; **40** and that his striving will be seen, **41** (and) then he will be paid for it with the fullest payment; **42** and that to your Lord is the (ultimate) goal;[35] **43** and that He causes laughter and causes weeping; **44** and that He causes death and gives life; **45** and that He created pairs, the male and the female, **46** from a drop,[36] when it is emitted; **47** and that the second growth (depends) on Him;[37] **48** and that He enriches (people) and gives wealth; **49** and that He is the Lord of Sirius;[38] **50** and that He destroyed 'Ād of old, **51** and Thamūd – He did not spare (them) **52** – or the people of Noah before (them) – surely they were – they (were) evil and insolent transgressor(s) – **53** and the overturned (cities) He overthrew,[39] **54** when (there) covered them what covered (them).[40] **55** So which of the blessings of your Lord will you[41] dispute?

56 This (man) is a warner,[42] of the warners of old. **57** The impending (Hour) is impending![43] **58** (There is) no one to remove it, other than God. **59** Are you amazed at this proclamation?[44] **60** And do you laugh and not weep, **61** while you amuse yourselves? **62** Prostrate yourselves before God and serve (Him)![45]

---

32. *the pages of Moses and Abraham*: the word 'pages' (lit. 'leaves' or 'sheets,' Ar. *ṣuḥuf*) occurs several times in connection with the Qur'ān (Q80.13), the revelation to Abraham and Moses (Q87.18-19; cf. Q20.133, 'the former pages'), and perhaps the heavenly archetype (Q98.2-3). The word is also used for the 'record' of a person's deeds (Q74.52; 81.10). Here it seems that 'the *ṣuḥuf* of Moses and Abraham' implies something like 'books' or 'scriptures.' Since Abraham was a prophet, it would not be surprising that he too was thought to have received a written revelation or 'book.' See e.g. the 2nd-century CE Jewish-Christian apocalypse known as the Testament of Abraham, in which the patriarch is taken on a 'heavenly tour' by the archangel Michael.
33. *paid (his debt) in full*: an allusion to Abraham's willingness to obey God's command to sacrifice his son (Q37.101-106).
34. *no one...bears the burden of another*: i.e. judgment falls on individuals, whom neither family nor friends can help (an implicit rejection of the Christian doctrine of 'vicarious atonement' and 'intercession' by the saints); cf. Q6.164; 17.15; 35.18; 39.7.
35. *the (ultimate) goal*: or 'the boundary' (cf. Q53.14 above; 79.44).
36. *a drop*: of semen.
37. *the second growth (depends) on Him*: i.e. to give life a second time at the resurrection (cf. Q29.20; 36.79; 56.60-62).
38. *Lord of Sirius*: the star Sirius (Ar. *al-Shi'rā*; cf. Gk. *Seirios*), which the Meccans were said to have worshipped.
39. *the overturned (cities) He overthrew*: perhaps the cities of Sodom and Gomorrah, associated with Lot, or else a general reference to the stories of previous peoples who were punished for their sins (cf. Q9.70; 69.9; see n. on Q7.59).
40. *(there) covered them what covered (them)*: probably a reference to the 'rain of stones' which fell on Lot's city (Q11.82; 15.74; 51.32-33; cf. the same expression for the destruction of Pharaoh and his forces at Q20.78).
41. *your...you*: sing. (cf. the refrain of Q55).

56–62 Judgment imminent

42. *This (man) is a warner*: referring to the Prophet (for this role, see n. on Q2.119).
43. *The impending (Hour) is impending*: this suggests that the end was thought to be near (see Q40.18, 'Day of the Impending;' cf. e.g. Q6.5; 26.6; 40.70, 77).
44. *proclamation*: or 'report' (Ar. *ḥadīth*).
45. *serve (Him)*: or 'worship (Him).'

54 The Moon ۞ Al-Qamar

In the Name of God, the Merciful, the Compassionate

1 The Hour[1] has drawn near, and the moon has been split open![2] **2** Yet if they see a sign,[3] they turn away, and say, 'Non-stop magic!' **3** They call (it) a lie, and follow their (own vain) desires, yet everything is set.[4] **4** Certainly enough of the story[5] has come to them to act as a deterrent – **5** far-reaching wisdom (it is) – but warnings are of no use. **6** So turn away from them.[6] On the Day when the Caller[7] will call to a terrible thing: **7** with sight downcast, they will come forth from the graves as if they were locusts spreading, **8** rushing to the Caller. The disbelievers will say, 'This is a hard day!'

9 The people of Noah called (it) a lie before them, and they called Our servant[8] a liar, and said, 'A man possessed!'[9] He was deterred **10** and called on his Lord: 'I am overcome. Help (me)!' **11** So We opened the gates of the sky with water pouring (down), **12** and made the earth gush forth with springs, and the water met for a purpose already decreed.[10] **13** We carried him on a vessel of planks and nails, **14** running before Our eyes – a payment for the one who was disbelieved. **15** Certainly We left it as a sign,[11] yet (is there) anyone who takes heed?[12] **16** How were My punishment and My warnings?

17 Certainly We have made the Qur'ān[13] easy for remembrance,[14] yet (is there) anyone who takes heed?

Q54: This sūra is made up almost entirely of stories about earlier generations which were destroyed for their disobedience, all linked together by a recurring refrain which ends with the question, 'Is there anyone who takes heed?' Fittingly, both the beginning and the end warn that judgment is near. Most scholars assign Q54 to the 'Meccan' period, though some attribute a few verses to 'Medina.' It takes its title from the opening reference to the moon being split open, a sign that the end is at hand.

1–8 Judgment imminent

1. *the Hour*: of judgment.
2. *the moon has been split open*: usually celestial phenomena of this sort are future signs of the Last Day (e.g. Q25.25; 55.37; 69.16; 84.1), but this one is said to have already occurred.
3. *sign*: or 'miracle' (for the various meanings of this term, see n. on Q2.39).
4. *set*: i.e. 'fixed' or 'predetermined' (cf. Q54.38 below).
5. *story*: or 'news,' referring to the Qur'ān (in which the following 'punishment stories' are found).
6. *turn away from them*: addressed to the Prophet.
7. *the Caller*: summoning people to judgment (cf. Q20.108; 30.25).

9–17 The people of Noah

8. *Our servant*: Noah (see e.g. Q7.59-64); the word 'servant' (Ar. *'abd*) also means 'slave.'
9. *possessed*: or 'jinn-struck' (Ar. *majnūn*); see n. on Q7.184.
10. *for a purpose already decreed*: the flood.
11. *left it as a sign*: referring to the story, or perhaps the 'ark' itself.
12. *takes heed*: or 'remembers.'
13. *the Qur'ān*: here 'the Qur'ān' comes close to its present meaning as the name of the Muslim scripture (cf. Q9.111; see n. on Q2.185).
14. *for remembrance*: or 'for reminder,' 'for admonition' (cf. Q19.97; 44.58; see n. on Q3.58).

18 'Ād[15] called (it) a lie. How were My punishment and My warnings? **19** Surely We sent a furious wind
against them on a day of the non-stop calamity. **20** It snatched the people away as if they were trunks of
uprooted date palms. **21** How were My punishment and My warnings?

22 Certainly We have made the Qur'ān easy for remembrance, yet (is there) anyone who takes heed?

23 Thamūd[16] called the warnings a lie, **24** and said, 'Shall we follow a single human being from among
us? Surely then we would indeed be astray and raving mad. **25** Has the Reminder been cast (down) on
him (alone) among us? No! He is an impudent liar.' **26** 'Tomorrow they will know who the impudent liar
is! **27** We are sending the she-camel as a test[17] for them, so watch them and be patient.[18] **28** And inform
them that the water is to be divided between them,[19] each drink is to be brought (in turn).' **29** But they
called their companion, and he took (a sword) and wounded (her).[20] **30** How were My punishment and
My warnings? **31** Surely We sent against them a single cry,[21] and they were like the rubble (used by) the
fence maker.

32 Certainly We have made the Qur'ān easy for remembrance, yet (is there) anyone who takes heed?

33 The people of Lot called the warnings a lie. **34** Surely We sent a sandstorm[22] against them, except
for the house(hold) of Lot. We rescued them at dawn **35** – a blessing from Us. In this way We repay the
one who is thankful. **36** Certainly he had warned them of Our attack, and they disputed the warnings.
37 Certainly they solicited him for his guest(s),[23] but We obliterated their eyes: 'Taste My punishment
and My warnings!' **38** Certainly in the morning a set punishment[24] came upon them: **39** 'Taste My punishment and My warnings!'

40 Certainly We have made the Qur'ān easy for remembrance, yet (is there) anyone who takes heed?

41 Certainly the warnings came to the house of Pharaoh. **42** They called Our signs a lie – all of it – so We
seized them with the seizing of a mighty, powerful (One).

43 Are your disbelievers[25] better than those? Or do you have an exemption in the scriptures?[26]

44 Or do they say,[27] 'We shall all be victorious'? **45** They will be routed and turn their back! **46** Yes! The

---

18–22 The people of 'Ād

15. *'Ād*: to whom the messenger Hūd was sent (see e.g. Q7.65-72)

23–32 The people of Thamūd

16. *Thamūd*: to whom the messenger Ṣāliḥ was sent (see e.g. Q7.73-79).
17. *test*: or 'trial,' 'temptation' (Ar. *fitna*).
18. *so watch them...*: addressed to Ṣāliḥ.
19. *divided between them*: i.e. between the people and the she-camel (cf. Q26.155).
20. *wounded (her)*: or perhaps 'killed (her).'
21. *a single cry*: or 'shout' (Q11.67); cf. Q7.78 ('the earthquake'); 41.17; 51.44 ('a thunderbolt').

33–40 The people of Lot

22. *sandstorm*: a feature only mentioned here as part of the story of Lot (cf. Q17.68; 29.40; 67.17).
23. *his guest(s)*: the angels who had been sent to destroy Lot's city (Q11.78; 15.67-69).
24. *set punishment*: i.e. a 'fixed' or 'predetermined punishment.'

41–42 The people of Pharaoh

43–55 Warning to disbelievers

25. *your disbelievers*: the Prophet's contemporaries.
26. *exemption in the scriptures*: or 'immunity in the scriptures;' here 'scriptures' (Ar. *al-zubur*) must refer to the heavenly 'Record' of human deeds, rather than to previously revealed Books (see Q54.52 below; and n. on Q3.184).
27. *Or do they say...*: the Cairo edition, reflecting the views of traditional scholars, attributes the following three verses to the 'Medinan' period.

Hour is their appointed time, and the Hour is grievous and bitter.

47 Surely the sinners are astray and raving mad! **48** On the Day when they are dragged on their faces into the Fire:[28] 'Taste the effect[29] of Saqar!'[30] **49** Surely We have created everything in measure, **50** and Our command[31] is but a single (act), like a blink of the eye.[32] **51** Certainly We have destroyed your parties (before),[33] yet (is there) anyone who takes heed?

52 Everything they have done is in the scriptures,[34] **53** and every small and great (deed) is inscribed. **54** Surely the ones who guard (themselves)[35] will be in (the midst of) gardens and a river, **55** in a sure seat in the presence of a powerful King.

28. *the Fire*: Ar. *al-nār* is the most common of the various designations for Hell.
29. *effect*: lit. 'touch.'
30. *Saqar*: said to be a name for Hell (only here and at Q74.26-27, 42).
31. *Our command*: here referring to judgment (cf. Q2.109; 4.47; 5.52; 7.150; 10.24; 16.1, 33).
32. *like a blink of the eye*: stressing the suddenness of judgment (see Q16.77; cf. 1 Corinthians 15.52).
33. *your parties (before)*: referring to the peoples previously mentioned (and likewise implying a temporal rather than eschatological punishment).
34. *in the scriptures*: see n. on Q54.43 above.
35. *guard (themselves)*: against evil, or God.

55 The Merciful ۞ Al-Raḥmān

In the Name of God, the Merciful, the Compassionate

1 The Merciful **2** has taught the Qur'ān.[1] **3** He created the human. **4** He taught him the explanation.[2] **5** The sun and the moon (move) in predictable paths,[3] **6** and the star and the tree prostrate themselves.[4] **7** The sky – He raised it, and He laid down the scale[5] **8** – do not transgress insolently concerning the scale, **9** but establish the weight in justice, and do not cheat concerning the scale. **10** And the earth – He laid it down for all living creatures. **11** On it (there are) fruit, and date palms with sheaths, **12** and grain with its husk, and fragrant herbs. **13** Which of the blessings of your Lord will you two call a lie?[6]

14 He created the human from clay like pottery,[7] **15** and He created the jinn from a mixture of fire.[8] **16** Which of the blessings of your Lord will you two call a lie?

17 Lord of the two Easts, Lord of the two Wests.[9] **18** Which of the blessings of your Lord will you two call a lie?

19 He let loose the two seas (which) meet.[10] **20** Between them (there is) a barrier (which) they do not seek (to cross). **21** Which of the blessings of your Lord will you two call a lie?

22 Pearl and coral come forth from both of them. **23** Which of the blessings of your Lord will you two call a lie?

24 His are the (ships) running, raised up on the sea like landmarks. **25** Which of the blessings of your Lord will you two call a lie?

Q55: The first half of this sūra recounts God's blessings; the second half describes the punishments of the wicked and rewards of the righteous. One of its distinctive features is that it addresses both humans and jinn in the form of a refrain which is repeated some thirty-one times ('Which of the blessings of your Lord will you two call a lie?'). While most modern scholars assign Q55 to the 'Meccan' period, the Cairo edition, reflecting the views of traditional scholars, assigns it to the 'Medinan' period. It receives its title from the opening reference to God as 'the Merciful.'

1–32 God's blessings

1. *The Merciful has taught the Qur'ān*: cf. Q53.5; 96.4-5; here 'the Qur'ān' comes close to its present meaning as the name of the Muslim scripture (cf. Q9.111; see n. on Q2.185).
2. *the explanation*: referring to the Qur'ān (cf. Q3.138; 75.19), rather than to 'speech' as it is usually taken.
3. *in predictable paths*: lit. 'in a reckoning' (cf. Q6.96; 10.5; 36.38-40).
4. *the star and the tree prostrate themselves*: for this idea, cf. Q22.18.
5. *laid down the scale*: probably symbolic of divine justice in general (see Q42.17; 57.25, 'sent down' by God; cf. Q21.47, 'scales of justice' laid down for the Day of Resurrection).
6. *Which of the blessings of your Lord will you two call a lie*: dual pronouns ('your' and 'you') are used in this refrain, and are usually taken to refer to humans and jinn (on the basis of Q55.33 below, where they are addressed directly).
7. *from clay like pottery*: see Q6.2; 7.12; 15.26; 17.61; 23.12; 32.7; 38.71, 76; 'from dust,' according to Q3.59; 18.37; 22.5; 30.20; 35.11; 40.67; 'from water,' according to Q21.30; 24.45; 25.54.
8. *mixture of fire*: also said to mean 'smokeless fire' (cf. Q15.27); for the jinn, see n. on Q6.100.
9. *two Easts...two Wests*: said to refer to the points of sunrise and sunset at the winter and summer solstices; but the dual may be used simply for the purpose of rhyme (cf. Q26.28).
10. *the two seas (which) meet*: fresh and salt water seas (see Q25.53; 27.61; 35.12; cf. Q18.60).

26 All who are on it[11] pass away, **27** but the face of your Lord remains, full of splendor and honor. **28** Which of the blessings of your Lord will you two call a lie?

29 (All) who are in the heavens and the earth make requests of Him. Every day He (is engaged) in some task. **30** Which of the blessings of your Lord will you two call a lie?

31 Soon We shall be free (to attend) to you, you two burdens![12] **32** Which of the blessings of your Lord will you two call a lie?

33 Assembly of jinn and humankind! If you are able to pass beyond the confines of the heavens and the earth,[13] pass! You will not pass beyond (them) except by authority. **34** Which of the blessings of your Lord will you two call a lie?

35 A flame of fire and a furious wind[14] will be sent against you, and you will not (be able to) defend yourselves. **36** Which of the blessings of your Lord will you two call a lie?

37 When the sky is split open[15] and turns red like oil – **38** Which of the blessings of your Lord will you two call a lie?

39 – on that Day neither human nor jinn will be questioned about his sin.[16] **40** Which of the blessings of your Lord will you two call a lie?

41 The sinners will be known by their mark, and they will be seized by the hair[17] and the feet. **42** Which of the blessings of your Lord will you two call a lie?

43 This is Gehenna[18] which the sinners called a lie. **44** They will go around between it and hot, boiling (water).[19] **45** Which of the blessings of your Lord will you two call a lie?

46 But for the one who fears the position of his Lord,[20] (there are) two gardens[21] – **47** Which of the blessings of your Lord will you two call a lie?

48 – with branches – **49** Which of the blessings of your Lord will you two call a lie?

50 – in both (there are) two flowing springs – **51** Which of the blessings of your Lord will you two call a lie?

52 – in both (there are) two of every (kind of) fruit – **53** Which of the blessings of your Lord will you two call a lie?

54 – (they are) reclining on couches lined with brocade, and fresh fruit of both gardens is near (at hand) – **55** Which of the blessings of your Lord will you two call a lie?

---

11. *it*: the earth.
12. *you two burdens*: referring to humans and jinn, perhaps with a view to judgment.

33–45 Punishment of the sinners: Gehenna

13. *pass beyond the confines...*: i.e. to escape the reach of God (cf. Q29.22).
14. *furious wind*: or 'smoke,' but meaning uncertain.
15. *sky is split open*: cf. Q25.25; 69.16; 84.1.
16. *neither...will be questioned about his sin*: because the nature of their sin will be evident from 'their mark' (see Q55.41 below).
17. *by the hair*: lit. 'by the forelocks.'
18. *Gehenna*: a name for Hell (see n. on Q2.206).
19. *They will go around...*: v. 44 follows awkwardly on v. 43 and both may be corrupt. The early codex (Ar. *muṣḥaf*) of Ibn Mas'ūd is reported to have read: 'This is Gehenna which you two called a lie. You will burn in it, neither dying in it nor living.'

46–78 Reward of the righteous: Two gardens

20. *the position of his Lord*: or perhaps 'the judgment seat of his Lord' (cf. Q14.14; 79.40).
21. *two gardens*: in addition to a sing. 'Garden,' the plur. 'Gardens' occurs frequently in the Qur'ān's eschatology, but the reference here to 'two gardens' remains obscure. Perhaps one was for humans and the other for jinn.

56 – in them[22] (there are maidens) restraining (their) glances – no man or jinn has had sex with them
before them – **57** Which of the blessings of your Lord will you two call a lie?

58 – as if they were rubies and coral – **59** Which of the blessings of your Lord will you two call a lie?

60 Is the payment for good anything but the good? **61** Which of the blessings of your Lord will you two
call a lie?

62 And besides these two (there are another) two gardens[23] – **63** Which of the blessings of your Lord will
you two call a lie?

64 – deep green – **65** Which of the blessings of your Lord will you two call a lie?

66 – in both (there are) two springs gushing forth – **67** Which of the blessings of your Lord will you two
call a lie?

68 – in both (there are) fruit, and date palms, and pomegranates – **69** Which of the blessings of your Lord
will you two call a lie?

70 – in them[24] (there are) good and beautiful (maidens) – **71** Which of the blessings of your Lord will you
two call a lie?

72 – dark-eyed (maidens), confined in tents – **73** Which of the blessings of your Lord will you two call a
lie?

74 – no man or jinn has had sex with them before them – **75** Which of the blessings of your Lord will you
two call a lie?

76 – (they are) reclining on green cushions and beautiful carpets – **77** Which of the blessings of your
Lord will you two call a lie?

78 Blessed (be) the name of your Lord, full of splendor and honor.

---

22. *in them*: the gardens, but the pronoun is now plur. not dual.

23. *And besides these two (there are another) two gardens*: the existence of a second pair of gardens is noteworthy, but it is not clear how they (or their inhabitants) differ from the previous two. These two descriptions are probably variant recensions which have somehow become attached.

24. *in them*: the gardens, once again the pronoun switches from dual to plur.

56 The Falling ✿ Al-Wāqiʿa

In the Name of God, the Merciful, the Compassionate.

1 When the falling falls[1] **2** – at its falling (there) will be no calling (it) a lie – **3** bringing low, raising high, **4** when the earth is violently shaken, **5** and the mountains utterly crumble, **6** and become scattered dust, **7** and you become three classes: **8** the companions on the right – what are the companions on the right?[2] **9** And the companions on the left – what are the companions on the left?[3] **10** And the foremost.[4]

The foremost **11** – those are the ones brought near,[5] **12** in Gardens of Bliss[6] – **13** a host from the ones of old, **14** but few from the later (generations) – **15** on well-woven couches, **16** reclining on them, facing each other. **17** Boys of eternal youth will circulate among them, **18** with cups and pitchers, and a cup[7] from a flowing spring **19** – they do not suffer any headache from it, nor do they become drunk – **20** and with fruit of their own choosing, **21** and the meat of birds of their own desiring, **22** and (maidens) with dark, wide eyes **23** like hidden pearls[8] **24** – a reward for what they have done. **25** There they will not hear any frivolous or sinful talk, **26** only the saying, 'Peace! Peace!'[9]

27 The companions on the right – what are the companions of the right? **28** (They will be) in (the midst of) thornless lote trees, **29** and acacia trees one after another, **30** and extensive shade, **31** and flowing water, **32** and many fruits **33** – unlimited, unforbidden – **34** and raised couches. **35** Surely We produced them[10] specially, **36** and made them virgins, **37** amorous, (all) of the same age, **38** for the companions on

---

Q56: This sūra opens with a vivid description of the Last Day, when people will be divided into three classes – 'the foremost' and 'the companions on the right and left' – whose rewards and punishments are then described. The second half of the sūra extols God's power and providence, and praises the Qur'ān. Most scholars assign Q56 to the early 'Meccan' period, though some attribute a few verses to 'Medina.' It takes its title from the 'falling' of Judgment referred to in the opening verse.

1–10a The arrival of Judgment Day

1. *When the falling falls*: referring to the 'event' of judgment (cf. Q69.15).
2. *companions on the right*: the believers.
3. *companions on the left*: the disbelievers.
4. *the foremost*: or 'the ones who go before' or 'the ones who have precedence' (Ar. *al-sābiqūn*). They are identified at Q9.100 as 'the first of the emigrants' (*al-muhājerūn*) and the helpers' (*al-anṣār*), and those who have followed them in doing good' (cf. Q23.61); i.e. the first converts to Islam. However, the early codices (Ar. *maṣāḥif*) of Ibn Mas'ūd and Ubayy are said to have contained a passage here identifying 'Alī and his descendants as 'the foremost.'

10b–26 The foremost

5. *the ones brought near*: a designation of special privilege (Ar. *al-muqarrabūn*), elsewhere used of the angels (Q4.172n.; cf. 40.7) and Jesus (Q3.45). Some translators add 'to God' or 'to the throne (of God),' though these words are not present in Arabic. But something like this may be assumed (here and at Q56.88 below), since *al-muqarrabūn* is also used in reference to those given special access to the throne in Pharaoh's court (Q7.114; 26.42).
6. *Gardens of Bliss*: in heaven (for this imagery, see n. on Q2.25; cf. Q56.89 below, sing. 'Garden of Bliss').
7. *a cup*: of wine.
8. *hidden pearls*: or 'cherished pearls' (cf. Q37.49, 'hidden eggs').
9. *Peace! Peace!*: Ar. *salām* connotes 'submission' (*islām*) to God.

27–40 The companions on the right

10. *them*: the pronoun is fem. plur., and refers to 'maidens' created specially for 'those on the right' (like the 'dark- wide-eyed maidens' enjoyed by 'the foremost').

the right. **39** A host from the ones of old, **40** and a host from the later (generations).[11]

41 The companions on the left – what are the companions on the left? **42** (They will be) in (the midst of) scorching (fire) and boiling (water), **43** and a shadow of black smoke, **44** neither cool nor kind. **45** Surely before (this) they were affluent, **46** and persisted in the great refusal,[12] **47** and used to say, 'When we are dead, and turned to dust and bones, shall we indeed be raised up? **48** And our fathers of old (too)?' **49** Say:[13] 'Surely those of old and the later (generations) **50** will indeed be gathered to the meeting of a known Day. **51** Then surely you – you who have gone astray and called (it) a lie! – **52** will indeed eat from the tree of Zaqqūm,[14] **53** and fill your bellies from it, **54** and drink on (top of) it from boiling water, **55** drinking like the thirsty (camel) drinks.' **56** This will be their reception on the Day of Judgment.

57 We created you.[15] Why will you not affirm (it)? **58** Do you see what you emit?[16] **59** Do you create it, or are We the Creators? **60** We have decreed death (to be) among you – We are not (to be) outrun – **61** so that We may exchange the likes of you,[17] and (re)produce you in what you do not know.[18] **62** Certainly you have known the first growth. Why will you not take heed?[19] **63** Do you see what you cultivate? **64** Do you (yourselves) sow it, or are We the Sowers?[20] **65** If We (so) pleased, We could indeed make it broken debris, and you would be left rejoicing,[21] **66** 'Surely we have incurred debt indeed! **67** No! We have been robbed!'[22] **68** Do you see the water which you drink? **69** Do you send it down from the clouds, or are We the Ones who send (it) down? **70** If We (so) pleased, We could make it bitter. Why are you not thankful? **71** Do you see the fire which you ignite? **72** Do you produce the timber for it,[23] or are We the Ones who produce (it)? **73** We have made it a reminder and a provision for the desert dwellers. **74** So glorify the name of your Lord, the Almighty.[24]

75 I swear by[25] the fallings of the stars **76** – surely it is a great oath indeed, if (only) you[26] knew – **77** surely it is an honorable Qur'ān indeed, **78** in a hidden Book![27] **79** No one touches it but the purified. **80** (It is) a

---

11. *and a host from the later (generations)*: apart from this, it is not clear how the 'companions on the right' differ from 'the foremost' (their rewards are nearly identical).

41–56 The companions on the left

12. *refusal*: to believe.
13. *Say*: on this form of address, see n. on Q2.80.
14. *tree of Zaqqūm*: a tree in Hell (see Q37.62; 44.43; cf. Q17.60).

57–74 Signs of God's power and providence

15. *you*: plur.
16. *what you emit*: or 'ejaculate' (cf. Q53.46; 75.37).
17. *exchange the likes of you*: i.e. substitute another people for them.
18. *in what you do not know*: i.e. 'in a form or fashion which you do not understand' (at the resurrection).
19. *take heed*: or 'be reminded,' 'remember.'
20. *the Sowers*: in the sense of bringing about the growth of the seed.
21. *rejoicing*: intended ironically or sarcastically.
22. *We have been robbed*: of their labors.
23. *timber for it*: lit. 'its tree.'
24. *So glorify...*: sing. imperative.

75–80 The honorable Qur'ān

25. *I swear by...*: for God's swearing by things, cf. Q69.38-39; 75.1, 2; 81.15-18; 84.16-18; 90.1, 3.
26. *you*: plur.
27. *in a hidden Book*: or 'in a cherished Book;' usually taken as a reference to the heavenly original or archetype of all revelation. According to this view, the Qur'ān, like the Torah and the Gospel, is only a portion of this all encompassing 'Book' (see Q13.39; 43.4; cf. Q85.22, 'guarded Tablet'). But it may refer to the Qur'ān 'in (the form) of a cherished Book.' Notice the verse immediately following: 'No one touches it but the purified.'

sending down from the Lord of the worlds.[28]

81 Do you[29] hold this proclamation[30] in disdain, **82** and do you make it your living to call (it) a lie? **83** Why
not, when the life of the dying man leaps into his throat, **84** and you are looking on **85** – though We are
nearer to him than you, only you do not see (Us) – **86** why, if you are not (to be) judged, **87** do you not
return it,[31] if you are truthful? **88** If he[32] is one of those brought near,[33] **89** (there will be) comfort, and
fragrance, and a Garden of Bliss. **90** And if he is one of the companions on the right: **91** 'Peace (be) to you,
from the companions on the right!' **92** But if he is one of those who called (it) a lie (and) went astray,
93 (there will be) a reception of boiling (water) **94** and burning in a Furnace.[34] **95** Surely this – it indeed
is the certain truth.[35] **96** So glorify the name of your Lord, the Almighty.[36]

---

28. *Lord of the worlds*: for this title, see n. on Q1.2.

81–96 Judgment certain

29. *you*: plur.; the Cairo edition attributes this verse and the next to the 'Medinan' period.
30. *proclamation*: or 'report' (Ar. *ḥadīth*).
31. *return it*: i.e. give the dying man his life back.
32. *he*: the dying man.
33. *those brought near*: see n. on Q56.11 above.
34. *Furnace*: a name for Hell (Ar. *jaḥīm*).
35. *the certain truth*: or 'the truth of the certainty' (i.e. the truth about what happens at death).
36. *So glorify...*: sing. imperative.

57 Iron ۞ Al-Ḥadīd

In the Name of God, the Merciful, the Compassionate

1 Whatever is in the heavens and the earth glorifies God. He is the Mighty, the Wise. **2** To Him (belongs) the kingdom of the heavens and the earth. He gives life and causes death. He is powerful over everything. **3** He is the First and the Last,[1] the Outer and the Inner.[2] He has knowledge of everything. **4** He (it is) who created the heavens and the earth in six days.[3] Then He mounted the throne. He knows what penetrates into the earth, and what comes forth from it, and what comes down from the sky, and what goes up into it. He is with you wherever you are. God sees what you do. **5** To Him (belongs) the kingdom of the heavens and the earth, and to God (all) matters are returned. **6** He causes the night to pass into the day, and causes the day to pass into the night. He knows what is in the hearts.[4]

7 Believe in God and His messenger,[5] and contribute[6] from what He has made you inheritors in.[7] Those of you who believe and contribute – for them (there will be) a great reward. **8** What is (the matter) with you that you do not believe in God, when the messenger calls you to believe in your Lord, and He has already taken a covenant with you, if you are believers? **9** He (it is) who sends down on His servant[8] clear signs,[9] so that He[10] may bring you forth from the darkness to the light. Surely God is indeed kind (and) compassionate with you.

10 What is (the matter) with you that you do not contribute in the way of God, when the inheritance of the heavens and the earth (belongs) to God? The one among you who contributed and fought before the victory[11] is not equal.[12] They are higher in rank than those who contributed and fought after that. Yet to each God has promised the good (reward).[13] God is aware of what you do. **11** Who is the one who

---

Q57: This sūra opens by extolling the glory of God, and then appeals for belief and contributions in support of the cause. It describes the different fates awaiting the 'hypocrites' and believers, and concludes with a reference to the previous messengers Abraham, Noah, and Jesus. Most scholars assign Q57 to the 'Medinan' period. It receives its title from the mention of 'iron,' which God has sent down along with 'the Book' and 'the scale' (Q57.25).

1–6 The glory of God

1. *the First and the Last*: for this idea, cf. Isaiah 44.6; 48.12; Revelation 1.8, 17; 22.13.
2. *the Outer and the Inner*: or 'the Apparent and the Hidden.'
3. *in six days*: cf. Q7.54; 10.3; 11.7; 25.59; 32.4; 41.9-12; and Genesis 1.1-31.
4. *hearts*: lit. 'chests,' considered the seat of knowledge and understanding.

7–11 Appeal for belief and contributions

5. *messenger*: for this important title, see n. on Q2.87.
6. *contribute*: lit. 'spend' (in support of God's cause).
7. *inheritors in*: lit. 'successors in,' perhaps referring to spoils (cf. Q6.165).
8. *His servant*: the Prophet; the word 'servant' (Ar. *'abd*) also means 'slave.'
9. *clear signs*: or 'signs as proof' (for the various meanings of 'signs,' see n. on Q2.39).
10. *He*: or 'he' (the Prophet).
11. *the victory*: lit. 'the opening;' said to refer to the conquest of Mecca (see Q32.28-29; 48.1).
12. *is not equal*: i.e. such a person is superior to one who did not fight or contribute (cf. Q4.95-96).
13. *the good (reward)*: the future life.

will lend to God a good loan,[14] and He will double it for him? For him (there will be) a generous reward.

12 On the Day when you[15] see the believing men and the believing women: their light will run before them, and at their right (hands):[16] 'Good news for you today! Gardens[17] through which rivers flow, there to remain. That is the great triumph!'

13 On the Day when the hypocrite men and the hypocrite women will say to those who believed: 'Wait for us! Let us borrow your light!'[18] It will be said, 'Turn back and search for a light!' And a wall with a door will be set up[19] between them: on the inside of it (there is) mercy, and on the outside of it – facing (it) – (there is) the punishment.[20] **14** They[21] will call out to them: 'Were we not with you?' They will say, 'Yes, indeed! But you tempted yourselves, and you waited[22] and doubted, and wishful thinking deceived you, until the command of God came,[23] and the Deceiver[24] deceived you about God. **15** So today no ransom will be accepted from you, nor from those who have disbelieved. Your refuge is the Fire[25] – it is your protector – and it is an evil destination!'

16 Is it not time for those who believe that their hearts become humble before the Reminder of God, and (before) what has come down of the truth,[26] and (that) they not be like those to whom the Book was given before,[27] and for whom the time lasted too long, so that their hearts became hard, and many of them were wicked?[28] **17** Know that God gives the earth life after its death. We have made clear to you[29] the signs, so that you may understand.

18 Surely the charitable men and the charitable women,[30] and (those who) have lent to God a good loan – it will be doubled for them, and for them (there will be) a generous reward. **19** Those who believe in God and His messengers, those – they are the truthful and the martyrs[31] in the sight of their Lord – they have their reward and their light. But those who disbelieve and call Our signs[32] a lie – those are the

14. *lend to God a good loan*: by contributing to or 'investing in' God's cause (cf. Q2.245; 5.12; 30.39; 64.17; 73.20).

12–15 A JUDGMENT SCENE: THE FATE OF BELIEVERS AND HYPOCRITES

15. *you*: the Prophet, or perhaps intended generally ('one').
16. *at their right (hands)*: or 'in their right (hands),' perhaps referring to some document they hold.
17. *Gardens*: in heaven (for this imagery, see n. on Q2.25).
18. *Let us borrow your light*: cf. the parable of the ten maidens and their lamps at Matthew 25.1-13.
19. *set up*: lit. 'struck.'
20. *on the inside...on the outside...*: i.e. on the inside, there is mercy for the believers, and on the outside, punishment for the hypocrites.
21. *They*: the hypocrites.
22. *you waited*: for some misfortune to overtake the Prophet and the Muslims (cf. Q4.141).
23. *the command of God came*: referring to judgment (cf. Q2.109; 4.47; 5.52; 7.150; 10.24; 16.1, 33).
24. *the Deceiver*: Satan (Q4.120; 17.64).
25. *the Fire*: Ar. *al-nār* is the most common of the various designations for Hell.

16–24 REWARDS FOR BELIEVING AND CONTRIBUTING

26. *the Reminder of God...what has come down...*: referring to the Qur'ān.
27. *those to whom the Book was given before*: referring to the Sons of Israel.
28. *for whom the time lasted too long...*: probably an allusion to the time leading up to Israel's worship of 'the calf' (see Q20.83-91).
29. *you*: plur.
30. *charitable men...women*: i.e. those who make 'voluntary contributions' or 'freewill offerings' (Ar. *al-ṣadaqāt*) for the benefit of the community.
31. *martyrs*: or 'witnesses.'
32. *signs*: or 'verses.'

companions of the Furnace.[33]

20 Know that this present life is nothing but jest and diversion, and a (passing) splendor, and a (cause for) boasting among you, and a rivalry in wealth and children. (It is) like rain: the vegetation it produces pleases the disbelievers, (but) then it withers[34] and you see it turning yellow, (and) then it becomes broken debris. In the Hereafter (there is) a harsh punishment, **21** and forgiveness from God and approval. But this present life is nothing but the enjoyment of deception.

Race toward forgiveness from your Lord, and a Garden – its width is like the width of the sky and the earth – prepared for those who believe in God and His messengers. That is the favor of God. He gives it to whomever He pleases. God is full of great favor. **22** No smiting smites in the earth or among yourselves, except that it was in a Book before We brought it about[35] – surely that is easy for God – **23** so that you may not grieve over what eludes you, nor gloat about what has come to you. God does not love anyone who is arrogant (and) boastful, **24** (nor) those who are stingy and command the people to be stingy. Whoever turns away – surely God – He is the wealthy One,[36] the Praiseworthy.

25 Certainly We sent Our messengers with the clear signs,[37] and We sent down with them the Book and the scale,[38] so that the people might uphold justice. And We sent down iron – in which (there is) harsh violence, but (also) benefits for the people – and (We did so) in order that God might know who would help Him and His messengers in the unseen.[39] Surely God is strong, mighty.

26 Certainly We sent Noah and Abraham,[40] and We placed among his descendants the prophetic office and the Book.[41] Yet (there is only the occasional) one of them who is (rightly) guided, but many of them are wicked. **27** Then in their footsteps We followed up with Our messengers, and We followed up with Jesus, son of Mary,[42] and gave him the Gospel, and placed in the hearts of those who followed him kindness and mercy. But monasticism – they originated it.[43] We did not prescribe it[44] for them. (It) only (arose out of their) seeking the approval of God. Yet they did not observe it as it should have been observed. So We gave those of them who believed their reward, but many of them were wicked.

28 You who believe! Guard (yourselves) against God and believe in His messenger! He will give you a double portion of His mercy, and will make a light for you by means of which you will walk, and He will forgive you – God is forgiving, compassionate – **29** so that the People of the Book may know that they have no power over any of the favor of God, and that favor is in the hand of God. He gives it to whomever He pleases. God is full of great favor.

---

33. *the Furnace*: a name for Hell (Ar. *al-jaḥīm*).
34. *withers*: the usual translation, but the verb means 'heave.'
35. *in a Book before We brought it about*: referring to the 'Book of God' or 'Book of Destiny' by which everything is ordained (see n. on Q6.59).
36. *the wealthy One*: i.e. God has no need of anyone or anything.

25–27 Messengers and their followers

37. *the clear signs*: or 'the clear proofs,' 'the indisputable evidence.'
38. *the scale*: symbolic of divine justice in general (cf. Q42.17; 55.7-9).
39. *in the unseen*: or 'in the future' (see n. on Q2.3).
40. *We sent Noah and Abraham...*: the absence of Moses' name is noteworthy here.
41. *the Book*: the Torah (cf. Q3.79; 6.89; 29.27; 45.16).
42. *son of Mary*: there is no mention in the Qur'ān of Joseph, Jesus' putative father (cf. Mark 6.3).
43. *they originated it*: i.e. monasticism is a Christian 'innovation' or 'invention.'
44. *prescribe it*: lit. 'write it.'

28–29 Final exhortation to believers

58 The Disputer ✿ Al-Mujādila

In the Name of God, the Merciful, the Compassionate

1 God has heard the words of the woman who disputes with you about her husband,[1] and (who) complains to God, and God hears the discussion of the two of you. Surely God is hearing, seeing. **2** Those of you who declare their wives to be as their mothers' backs[2] – they are not their mothers. Their mothers are only those who gave them birth. Surely they indeed say a wrong word and a falsehood. Yet surely God is indeed pardoning (and) forgiving. **3** Those who declare their wives to be as their mothers' backs, (and) then return to what they have said,[3] (the penalty is) the setting free of a slave before the two of them touch each other.[4] That is what you are admonished. God is aware of what you do. **4** Whoever does not find (the means to do that), (the penalty is) a fast for two months consecutively, before the two of them touch each other. And whoever is not able (to do that), (the penalty is) the feeding of sixty poor persons. That is so that you may believe in God and His messenger.[5] Those are the limits (set by) God – and for the disbelievers (there will be) a painful punishment.

5 Surely those who oppose God and His messenger have been disgraced, as those before them were disgraced. We have already sent down clear signs[6] – and for the disbelievers (there will be) a humiliating punishment, **6** on the Day when God will raise them up – all (of them) – and inform them about what they have done. God has counted it up,[7] though they have forgotten it. God is a witness over everything.

7 Do you[8] not see that God knows whatever is in the heavens and whatever is on the earth? There is no secret talk of three men but He is the fourth of them, nor of five men but He is the sixth of them, nor less than that, nor more, but He is with them wherever they may be. Then on the Day of Resurrection He will

---

Q58: This sūra takes its title from a woman who 'disputed' her husband's attempt to end their marriage by means of a pre-Islamic formula. The case concludes by stipulating the penalty for anyone who continues to use such a formula in the future. The rest of the sūra is a warning that those who conspire against the Prophet, or otherwise oppose him, will suffer defeat both in this world and the next. Most scholars assign Q58 to the 'Medinan' period.

1–4 A pagan formula penalized

1. *the woman who disputes...*: reference obscure, but it is said to refer to a certain Khawla, daughter of Tha'laba, whose husband had ended their marriage by declaring, 'Be to me as my mother's back.' When she appealed to the Prophet, he initially said the dissolution of the marriage was valid. But she continued to press the matter with God, with the following result.
2. *declare their wives to be as their mothers' backs*: said to be a pre-Islamic formula for ending a marriage (cf. Q33.4). It was not a divorce in the modern sense, since the woman continued to live where she was, but she was forbidden to marry anyone else.
3. *return to what they have said*: i.e. 'continue to repeat this formula in the future,' though the usual translation is 'retract what they have said' (but see Q58.8 below; cf. Q6.28).
4. *...before the two of them touch each other*: since the formula ('Be to me as my mother's back') would technically make any further sexual contact between the pair incestuous.
5. *messenger*: for this important title, see n. on Q2.87.

5–6 Opposition to God's messenger futile

6. *clear signs*: or 'signs as proof' (for the various meanings of 'signs,' see n. on Q2.39).
7. *counted it up*: i.e. recorded what they have done (cf. Q36.12).

7–10 Nothing escapes God's notice

8. *you*: the Prophet, or perhaps intended generally ('one').

inform them about what they have done. Surely God has knowledge of everything.

8 Do you[9] not see those who were forbidden from secret talk, (and) then return to what they were forbidden, and converse secretly in sin and enmity and disobedience to the messenger? And when they come to you, they greet you with what God does not greet you with, and they say within themselves, 'If only God would punish us for what we say.' Gehenna[10] will be enough for them, where they will burn – and it is an evil destination!

9 You who believe! When you converse secretly, do not converse in sin and enmity and disobedience to the messenger, but converse in piety and the guarding (of yourselves). Guard (yourselves) against God, to whom you will be gathered. **10** Secret talk is only from Satan,[11] so that he may cause those who believe to grieve. But he will not harm them at all, except by the permission of God. In God let the believers put their trust.

11 You who believe! When it is said to you 'Make room in the assemblies,' make room! God will make room for you. And when it is said, 'Rise up,' rise up![12] God will raise in rank those of you who have believed and those who have been given knowledge. God is aware of what you do.

12 You who believe! When you converse privately with the messenger, send forward a freewill offering[13] before your private talk. That is better for you and purer. If you do not find (the means to do so) – God is forgiving, compassionate. **13** Are you afraid to send forward freewill offerings before your private talk? When you do not (do so), and God has turned to you (in forgiveness), observe the prayer and give the alms,[14] and obey God and His messenger. God is aware of what you do.

14 Do you[15] not see those who have taken as allies a people with whom God is angry?[16] They are neither of you nor of them. They swear upon lies – and they know (it). **15** God has prepared a harsh punishment for them. Surely they – evil indeed is what they have done! **16** They have taken their oaths as a cover, and kept (people) from the way of God. For them (there will be) a humiliating punishment. **17** Neither their wealth nor their children will be of any use against God. Those are the companions of the Fire.[17] There they will remain. **18** On the Day when God will raise them up – all (of them) – they will swear to Him as they swear to you, and think they (are standing) on something. Is it not a fact that they – they are the liars? **19** Satan has prevailed over them, and made them forget the Reminder of God.[18] Those are the faction of Satan. Is it not a fact that the faction of Satan – they are the losers? **20** Surely those who oppose God and His messenger – they will be among the most humiliated. **21** God has written, 'I shall

---

9. *you*: sing., but probably intended generally.
10. *Gehenna*: a name for Hell (see n. on Q2.206).
11. *Satan*: for this figure, see n. on Q2.36.

11 Conduct in the Messenger's assemblies

12. *rise up*: perhaps for prayer, or it may mean 'move closer;' in any case it is not clear what the purpose of these 'assemblies' was (Ar. *majālis* occurs only here; a variant reading has the sing. 'assembly').

12–13 Private conversations with the Messenger

13. *freewill offering*: or 'voluntary contribution' (Ar. *ṣadaqa*).
14. *observe the prayer and give the alms*: i.e. *ṣalāt*, the ritual prayer, and *zakāt*, a kind of tithe required for the benefit of the poor, as well as other purposes.

14–21 Opponents will be defeated

15. *you*: the Prophet, or perhaps intended generally.
16. *those who have taken as allies a people...*: some interpreters claim this refers to the hypocrites and their alliance with the Jews; others that the reference is to the hypocrites who allied themselves with the 'rival mosque' mentioned at Q9.107-110; but their precise identity remains uncertain (cf. Q60.13).
17. *the Fire*: Ar. *al-nār* is the most common of the various designations for Hell.
18. *Reminder of God*: referring to the Qur'ān (see n. on Q3.58).

indeed conquer – I and My messengers!' Surely God is strong, mighty.

22 You[19] will not find a people who believe in God and the Last Day loving anyone who opposes God and His messenger, even if they were their fathers, or their sons, or their brothers, or their clan.[20] Those – He has written belief[21] on their hearts,[22] and supported them with a spirit from Him,[23] and will cause them to enter Gardens through which rivers flow, there to remain. God is pleased with them, and they are pleased with Him. Those are the faction of God. Is it not a fact that the faction of God – they are the ones who prosper?

---

22 No relations with opponents

19. *You*: sing., but intended generally.
20. *even if they were their fathers, or their sons...*: religious affiliation now supersedes family ties (cf. Q9.23-24).
21. *belief*: or 'the Faith' (cf. Q49.7).
22. *written...on their hearts*: cf. Jeremiah 31.33; Psalm 40.8; 2 Corinthians 3.3; Hebrews 8.10; 10.16 (here, as often, the heart is spoken of as synonymous with mind).
23. *supported them with a spirit from Him*: otherwise only said of Jesus (Q2.87, 253; 5.110).

59 The Gathering ❁ Al-Ḥashr

In the Name of God, the Merciful, the Compassionate

1 Whatever is in the heavens and whatever is on the earth glorifies God. He is the Mighty, the Wise.

2 He (it is) who expelled those of the People of the Book[1] who disbelieved from their homes for the first gathering.[2] You[3] did not think that they would go forth, and they thought that their strongholds would defend them against God. But God came upon them from where they were not expecting, and cast dread into their hearts. They destroyed their houses with their (own) hands[4] and the hands of the believers. Learn a lesson, you who have sight! **3** If God had not prescribed[5] exile for them, He would indeed have punished them in this world[6] – and for them (there is) the punishment of the Fire[7] in the Hereafter.[8] **4** That is because they opposed God and His messenger. Whoever opposes God – surely God is harsh in retribution.

5 Whatever palm trees you cut down, or left standing on their roots[9] – (it was) was by the permission of God, and (it was) so that He might disgrace the wicked. **6** What God has given to His messenger[10] (as spoils) from them – you did not spur on any horse or camel for it,[11] but God gives authority to His messengers over whomever He pleases. God is powerful over everything. **7** What God has given to His messenger (as spoils) from the people of the towns (belongs) to God and to the messenger, and to family, and the orphans, and the poor, and the traveler,[12] so that it does not (just) circulate among the wealthy of you. Whatever (spoils) the messenger gives you, take it, and whatever he forbids you, stop (asking for it). Guard (yourselves) against God! Surely God is harsh in retribution.

8 (Spoils belong) to the poor emigrants,[13] who were expelled from their homes and their wealth,

---

Q59: Most of this sūra is said to refer to the expulsion of the Banū Naḍīr (a Jewish tribe) from Medina (625 CE/4 AH). It receives its title from 'the gathering' of them for exile (Q59.2).

1 The glory of God

2–4 Expulsion of the People of the Book

1. *People of the Book*: used of both Jews and Christians, but here it is said to refer to the Jews of Medina.
2. *the first gathering*: i.e. for exile, probably contrasted with the 'second gathering' for judgment on the Last Day (the various forms of the word are used most often in this eschatological sense; see e.g. Q50.44).
3. *You*: plur., referring to the believers throughout this section.
4. *They destroyed their houses with their (own) hands*: according to tradition, after they had surrendered and agreed to leave Medina, the Jews tore down the beams of their houses to carry away with them.
5. *prescribed*: lit. 'written.'
6. *punished them in this world*: i.e. killed them.
7. *the Fire*: Ar. *al-nār* is the most common of the various designations for Hell.
8. *the Hereafter*: see n. on Q2.4.

5–10 Distribution of spoils

9. *Whatever palm trees you cut down...*: according to tradition, the Naḍīr are said to have surrendered when they saw the Muslims cutting down their palm trees.
10. *messenger*: for this important title, see n. on Q2.87.
11. *you did not spur on any horse or camel for it*: i.e. the spoils were not taken as a result of fighting.
12. *traveler*: lit. 'son of the way.'
13. *the poor emigrants*: said to refer to those who had emigrated from Mecca to Medina, though this is not explicitly stated in the Qur'ān.

seeking favor from God and approval, and helping God and His messenger. Those – they are the truthful.
9 And those who settled in 'the home'[14] and in belief[15] before them, they love whoever emigrates to
them, and do not find in their hearts[16] any need for what they have been given, but prefer (emigrants)
above themselves, even though there is poverty among them. Whoever is guarded against his own
greed, those – they are the ones who prosper. **10** Those who came after them[17] say, 'Our Lord, forgive us
and our brothers, who preceded us in belief, and do not place any rancor in our hearts toward those who
believe. Our Lord, surely You are kind (and) compassionate.'

11 Do you[18] not see those who have played the hypocrite? They say to their brothers who disbelieve
among the People of the Book, 'If indeed you[19] are expelled, we shall indeed go forth with you, and
we shall never obey anyone concerning you. And if you are fought against, we shall indeed help you.'
God bears witness: 'Surely they are liars indeed!' **12** If indeed they are expelled, they will not go forth
with them, and if indeed they are fought against, they will not help them. And if indeed they do help
them, they will indeed turn their backs. Then they will not be helped. **13** Indeed you[20] (strike) greater
fear in their hearts[21] than God. That is because they are a people who do not understand. **14** They will
not fight against you all together, except in fortified towns or from behind walls. Their violence among
themselves is (so) harsh, you (might) think them all (united) together, but their hearts are divided.
That is because they are a people who have no sense. **15** (They are) like those who shortly before them
tasted the consequence of their action[22] – for them (there is) a painful punishment. **16** (They are) like
Satan,[23] when he said to the human, 'Disbelieve!,' and when he[24] disbelieved, he[25] said, 'Surely I am free
of you. Surely I fear God, Lord of the worlds.'[26] **17** So the end of both of them is: they will both be in the
Fire, (and) there they both will remain. That is the payment of the evildoers.

18 You who believe! Guard (yourselves) against God, and let each person look to what he sends forward
for tomorrow.[27] Guard (yourselves) against God! Surely God is aware of what you do. **19** Do not be like
those who forgot God, and He caused them to forget their own selves. Those – they are the wicked.
20 The companions of the Fire and the companions of the Garden[28] are not equal. The companions of

---

14. *'the home'*: said to be a reference to Medina, so that what follows would refer to 'the helpers' (i.e. the Muslims of Medina who welcomed the emigrants).
15. *belief*: or 'the Faith.'
16. *hearts*: lit. 'chests,' considered the seat of knowledge and understanding.
17. *Those who came after them*: presumably later emigrants from Mecca.

11–17 Hypocrites are cowards

18. *you*: the Prophet, or perhaps intended generally ('one').
19. *you*: plur.
20. *you*: the believers.
21. *hearts*: lit. 'chests.'
22. *those who shortly before them...*: obscure; said to refer either to another Jewish group or to the Meccans killed at the battle of Badr.
23. *Satan*: for this figure, see n. on Q2.36.
24. *he*: the human.
25. *he*: Satan.
26. *Lord of the worlds*: for this title, see n. on Q1.2.

18–21 Exhortation to fear God

27. *for tomorrow*: i.e. for the Day of Judgment.
28. *Garden*: in heaven (for this imagery, see n. on Q2.25).

the Garden – they are the triumphant. **21** If We had sent down this Qur'ān[29] on a mountain, you[30] would indeed have seen it humbled (and) split apart out of the fear of God. These parables – We strike them for the people so that they will reflect.

22 He is God, the One who – (there is) no god but Him – is the Knower of the unseen and the seen.[31] He is the Merciful, the Compassionate.

23 He is God, the One who – (there is) no god but Him – is the King, the Holy One,[32] the Peace, the Faithful, the Preserver,[33] the Mighty, the Sole Ruler,[34] the Magnificent. Glory to God above what they associate![35]

24 He is God – the Creator, the Maker, the Fashioner. To Him (belong) the best names.[36] Whatever is in the heavens and the earth glorifies Him. He is the Mighty, the Wise.

---

29. *this Qur'ān*: here 'this Qur'ān' comes close to its present meaning as the name of the Muslim scripture (cf. Q9.111; see n. on Q2.185).
30. *you*: sing., but intended generally.

22–24 The glory of God

31. *the seen*: lit. 'the witnessed.'
32. *the King, the Holy One*: or 'the holy King.'
33. *the Preserver*: meaning uncertain (cf. Q5.48).
34. *the Sole Ruler*: lit. 'the Tyrant.'
35. *what they associate*: other gods with God.
36. *the best names*: or 'the most beautiful names' (Ar. *al-asmā' al-ḥusnā*); cf. Q7.180; 17.110; 20.8. A list of ninety-nine names was eventually compiled, consisting of those mentioned in the Qur'ān as well as others. They play an important role in theology and worship.

60 The Examined Woman ❁ Al-Mumtaḥana

In the Name of God, the Merciful, the Compassionate

1 You who believe! Do not take My enemy and your enemy as allies.[1] Do you offer them friendship[2] when
they have disbelieved in the truth which has come to you, expelling the messenger and you because you
believe in God your Lord? If you have gone forth to struggle[3] in My way and to seek My approval, do
you keep secret (your) friendship for them? I know what you hide and what you speak aloud. Whoever
of you does that has gone astray from the right way. **2** If they come upon you, they will be enemies to
you, and will stretch out their hands and their tongues with evil against you, and want you to disbelieve.
3 Neither your family ties[4] nor your children will benefit you on the Day of Resurrection. He will distinguish between you. God sees what you do.

4 There was a good example for you in Abraham, and those who were with him, when they said to their people, 'Surely we are free of you and what you serve instead of God. We repudiate you,[5] and between us and you
enmity has shown itself, and hatred forever, until you believe in God alone' – except for Abraham's saying to
his father: 'I shall indeed ask forgiveness for you, but I have no power from God to (benefit) you at all'[6] – 'Our
Lord, in You we put our trust, to You we turn (in repentance), and to You is the (final) destination. **5** Our
Lord, do make us an (object of) persecution[7] for those who disbelieve, but forgive us, Our Lord. Surely You
– You are the Mighty, the Wise.' **6** Certainly there was a good example for you in them – for whoever hopes
in God and the Last Day. But whoever turns away – surely God – He is the wealthy One,[8] the Praiseworthy.

7 It may be that God will (yet) establish[9] friendship between you and those of them with whom you are

---

Q60: This sūra warns believers about secret alliances with the enemy. According to tradition it was revealed after a believer in Medina had secretly sent a letter to warn his family in Mecca of impending attack. The letter was intercepted and the man reprimanded. It also gives instructions on how to 'examine' women who leave their husbands behind in Mecca to join the believers in Medina, and what to do about the wives of believers in Medina who run off to Mecca. Most scholars assign Q60 to the late 'Medinan' period, sometime between the treaty of al-Ḥudaybiya (628 CE/6 AH) and the conquest of Mecca (630 CE/8 AH).

1–3 Treatment of enemies

1. *Do not take My enemy and your enemy as allies*: 'allies' (Ar. *awliyā'*) implies the obligation of mutual protection, almost in the sense of 'friends' or 'brothers.' (The fragmented structure of this long first verse makes it difficult to construe, but the general meaning is clear.)
2. *offer them friendship*: lit. 'cast before them with (your) affection.'
3. *struggle*: or 'fight.'
4. *your family ties*: lit. 'your wombs;' i.e. blood-relatives.

4–6 The example of Abraham

5. *repudiate you*: lit. 'disbelieve in you.'
6. *I shall indeed ask forgiveness for you...*: see Q14.41; 19.47; 26.86 (cf. Q71.28, Noah); otherwise prayer for disbelievers is forbidden (see Q9.113-114). This clause looks like a later addition, since it interrupts what is said by Abraham and his followers.
7. *an (object of) persecution*: or 'a temptation' (Ar. *fitna*); cf. Q10.85 (said by the people of Moses).
8. *the wealthy One*: i.e. God has no need of anyone or anything.

7–9 Reconciliation still possible

9. *establish*: lit. 'make.'

on hostile terms. God is powerful, and God is forgiving, compassionate. **8** God does not forbid you from those who have not fought you in the (matter of) religion, and have not expelled you from your homes, that you should do good and act fairly toward them. Surely God loves the ones who act fairly. **9** God only forbids you from those who have fought you in the (matter of) religion, and have expelled you from your homes, and have supported your expulsion, that you should take them as allies. Whoever takes them as allies, those – they are the evildoers.

10 You who believe! When believing women come to you as emigrants, examine them[10] – God knows their belief – and if you know them to be believers, do not return them to the disbelievers. They are not permitted to them,[11] nor are they are permitted to them.[12] Give them what they have spent.[13] (There is) no blame on you if marry them, when you have given them their marriage gifts.[14] Do not hold to ties with disbelieving women,[15] but ask (back) what you have spent, and let them ask (back)[16] what they have spent. That is the judgment of God. He judges between you, and God is knowing, wise. **11** If any of your wives escape from you to the disbelievers, and you take retribution,[17] give those whose wives have gone off the equivalent of what they have spent. Guard (yourselves) against God, in whom you believe.

12 Prophet![18] When believing women come to you, swearing allegiance to you on (the condition) that they will not associate anything with God, and will not steal, and will not commit adultery, and will not kill their children, and will not bring a slander they have forged between their hands and their feet,[19] and will not disobey you in anything right, accept their oath of allegiance, and ask forgiveness for them from God. Surely God is forgiving, compassionate.

13 You who believe! Do not take as allies a people with whom God is angry.[20] They have despaired[21] of the Hereafter,[22] even as the disbelievers have despaired of the companions of the graves.

10–11 Treatment of women refugees and runaway wives

10. *examine them*: to see if they are really believers.
11. *They...them*: the believing women...the disbelievers.
12. *they...them*: the disbelievers...the believing women.
13. *Give them what they have spent*: i.e. what the disbelievers paid as a dowry when they married the women.
14. *their marriage gifts*: lit. 'their rewards' (see e.g. Q4.24).
15. *Do not hold to ties with disbelieving women*: i.e. disbelieving wives are to be divorced.
16. *let them ask (back)*: referring to the disbelieving husbands of believing women.
17. *and you take retribution*: not for the runaway bride, but in general (i.e. 'if you gain spoils, give...').

12 Treatment of women adherents

18. *Prophet*: for this important title, see n. on Q2.87.
19. *a slander they have forged between their hands and their feet*: usually said to refer to a false allegation of paternity, but it may simply refer to slander in general.

13 Treatment of other enemies

20. *a people with whom God is angry*: see n. on Q58.14.
21. *have despaired*: or 'have no hope.'
22. *the Hereafter*: see n. on Q2.4.

61 The Lines ✿ Al-Ṣaff

In the Name of God, the Merciful, the Compassionate

1 Whatever is in the heavens and whatever is on the earth glorifies God. He is the Mighty, the Wise.

2 You who believe! Why do you say what you do not do?[1] **3** It is very hateful in the sight of God that you say what you do not do. **4** God loves those who fight in His way, (drawn up) in lines (for battle) as if they were a solid building.

5 (Remember) when[2] Moses said to his people, 'My people! Why do you hurt me,[3] when you already know that I am the messenger[4] of God to you?' Then, when they turned aside, God caused their hearts[5] to turn aside, (for) God does not guide the people who are wicked. **6** And (remember) when Jesus, son of Mary,[6] said, 'Sons of Israel! Surely I am the messenger of God to you, confirming what was before me of the Torah,[7] and bringing good news of a messenger who will come after me,[8] whose name will be Aḥmad.'[9] Then, when he[10] brought them the clear signs,[11] they said, 'This is clear magic.' **7** Who is more evil than the one who forges lies against God, when he is called to Islam?[12] God does not guide the people who are evildoers. **8** They want to extinguish the light of God with their mouths, but God will perfect His light, even though the disbelievers dislike (it). **9** He (it is) who has sent His messenger with the

---

Q61: This sūra consists of several short passages. Notable among them is a section on the Sons of Israel's opposition to Moses, Jesus, and finally the Prophet, whose coming (under the name of 'Aḥmad') Jesus is said to have predicted. Most scholars assign Q61 to the 'Medinan' period. It takes its title from the reference to troops drawn up in battle 'lines' (Q61.4).

1 The glory of God

2–4 Do what you say

1. *Why do you say what you do not do*: said to refer to the believers who had agreed to fight but then fled at the battle of Uḥud (625 CE/3 AH).

5–9 Opposition from the Sons of Israel

2. *(Remember) when...*: a stock narrative formula; the Arabic particle *idh* often marks the beginning of a story, and means something like 'Once...,' or 'There was a time when...,' or 'Remember when....'
3. *hurt me*: see n. on Q33.69; cf. Q9.61; 33.48.
4. *messenger*: for this important title, see n. on Q2.87.
5. *hearts*: here, as often, the heart is spoken of as synonymous with mind.
6. *son of Mary*: there is no mention in the Qur'ān of Joseph, Jesus' putative father (cf. Mark 6.3).
7. *of the Torah*: has either a partitive or an epexegetical meaning (elucidating the preceding 'what').
8. *a messenger who will come after me*: see Jesus' predictions at John 14.16, 26; 15.26; 16.7 (cf. 1 John 2.1), referring to the coming of one called the 'Paraclete' (Gk. *paraklētos*), interpreted variously as the 'advocate,' 'helper,' or 'comforter.'
9. *whose name will be Aḥmad*: or 'whose name [Muḥammad] will be more praised.' Like 'Muḥammad,' it could be read as an adjective and taken as an epithet, not a proper name.
10. *he*: probably Jesus, but sometimes taken as referring to the Prophet, the predicted messenger.
11. *the clear signs*: or 'the clear proofs,' 'the indisputable evidence,' probably referring to Jesus' miracles (see e.g. Q5.110). If the preceding 'he' refers to the Prophet, then the 'clear signs' would refer to otherwise unspecified miracles (but cf. Q4.174).
12. *Islam*: lit. 'the submission' or 'the surrender' to God (Ar. *al-Islām*).

guidance[13] and the religion of truth, so that He[14] may cause it to prevail over religion – all of it – even though the idolaters[15] dislike (it).

10 You who believe! Shall I direct you to a transaction that will rescue you from a painful punishment? **11** You (should) believe in God and His messenger, and struggle in the way of God with your wealth and your lives – that is better for you, if (only) you knew. **12** He will forgive you your sins, and cause you to enter Gardens through which rivers flow,[16] and good dwelling places in Gardens of Eden – that is the great triumph! – **13** and another thing which you love: help from God and a victory[17] near (at hand). Give good news to the believers![18]

14 You who believe! Be the helpers of God,[19] as Jesus, son of Mary, said to the disciples,[20] 'Who will be my helpers to God?'[21] The disciples said, 'We will be the helpers of God.' One contingent of the Sons of Israel believed, and (another) contingent disbelieved. So We supported those who believed against their enemy, and they were the ones who prevailed.

---

13. *the guidance*: one of the most frequent terms (Ar. *al-hudā*) for revelation in general, and the Qur'ān in particular.
14. *He*: or 'he' (the Prophet).
15. *the idolaters*: or 'the ones who associate (other gods with God).'

10–13 Believers to struggle for God's cause

16. *Gardens...*: in heaven (for this imagery, see n. on Q2.25).
17. *victory*: lit. 'opening' (cf. Q48.18, 27; see nn. on Q32.29; 48.1).
18. *Give good news...*: addressed to the Prophet.

14 Believers to help God

19. *helpers of God*: this eventually became the name (Ar. *anṣār*) of the believers among the people of Medina.
20. *the disciples*: or 'the apostles' (Ar. *al-ḥawārīyūn*), a word used only of Jesus' followers (cf. Q3.52; 5.111-112).
21. *Who will be my helpers...*: see Q3.52; 'helpers' (Ar. *anṣār*) is a pun on the name for 'Christians' (Ar. *Naṣārā*).

62 The Assembly ❁ Al-Jumuʿa

In the Name of God, the Merciful, the Compassionate

1 Whatever is in the heavens and whatever is on the earth glorifies God, the King, the Holy One,[1] the Mighty, the Wise.

2 He (it is) who has raised up among the common people[2] a messenger[3] from among them, to recite His signs[4] to them, and to purify them,[5] and to teach them the Book and the wisdom, though before (this) they were indeed clearly astray[6] **3** – and others of them who have not (yet) joined them.[7] He is the Mighty, the Wise. **4** That is the favor of God. He gives (it) to whomever He pleases. God is full of great favor.

5 Those who have been loaded down with the Torah, (and) then have not carried it, are like a donkey carrying books.[8] Evil is the parable[9] of the people who have called the signs of God a lie. God does not guide the people who are evildoers. **6** Say:[10] 'You who are Jews![11] If you claim that you are the allies of God to the exclusion of the people,[12] wish for death, if you are truthful.'[13] **7** But they will never wish for it because of what their (own) hands have sent forward.[14] God knows the evildoers. **8** Say: 'Surely the death from which you flee – surely it will meet you. Then you will be returned to the Knower of the unseen and the seen,[15] and He will inform you about what you have done.'

9 You who believe! When the call to prayer is made on the day of assembly,[16] hurry to the remembrance

---

Q62: This sūra consists of several short passages. The Prophet is identified as a 'native' messenger, Jewish exceptionalism is criticized, and prayer is established on Friday, the 'day of assembly,' from which Q62 receives its title. Most scholars assign Q62 to the 'Medinan' period.

1 The glory of God

1. *the King, the Holy One*: or 'the holy King.'

2–4 The Prophet sent to those without a Book

2. *common people*: or 'native people,' i.e. the Arabs, or those without a written scripture (see nn. on Q2.78; 3.20).
3. *messenger*: for this important title, see n. on Q2.87.
4. *signs*: or 'verses' (see n. on Q2.39).
5. *purify them*: or perhaps 'appoint *zakāt* for them' (cf. Q2.129, 151; 3.164).
6. *clearly astray*: lit. 'in clear straying.'
7. *and others of them...*: i.e. others of the 'common people' or the Arabs; this may be a later addition (cf. Q3.164).

5–8 Diatribe against Jewish exceptionalism

8. *like a donkey carrying books*: the donkey is not benefited no matter how many books it carries.
9. *parable*: or 'comparison.'
10. *Say*: on this form of address, see n. on Q2.80.
11. *You who are Jews*: lit. 'You who have judaized,' or follow Jewish law, punning on the name Yahūd.
12. *to the exclusion of the people*: a sarcastic allusion to the idea of Israel as God's 'chosen people' (cf. Q2.94).
13. *wish for death...*: i.e. if they are certain of heaven, they should long for death, since heaven is better than life (cf. Q2.94-95).
14. *what their (own) hands have sent forward*: i.e. their misdeeds, which will be awaiting them at the Judgment.
15. *the seen*: lit. 'the witnessed.'

9–11 Worship on Friday

16. *day of assembly*: Friday.

of God, and leave business aside. That is better for you, if (only) you knew. **10** Then, when the prayer is finished, disperse on the earth and seek some favor from God,[17] and remember God often, so that you may prosper. **11** But when they see (the chance of) some (business) transaction or diversion, they rush off to it, and leave you[18] standing. Say: 'What is with God is better than any diversion or transaction. God is the best of providers.'

17. *seek some favor from God*: i.e. seek to make a livelihood.
18. *you*: the Prophet.

63 The Hypocrites ✵ Al-Munāfiqūn

In the Name of God, the Merciful, the Compassionate

1 When the hypocrites come to you, they say, 'We bear witness that you are indeed the messenger[1] of God.' God knows that you are indeed His messenger, and God bears witness: 'Surely the hypocrites are liars indeed!' **2** They have taken their oaths as a cover, and have kept (people) from the way of God. Surely they – evil is what they have done. **3** That is because they believed, (and) then they disbelieved. So a seal was set on their hearts,[2] and they do not understand. **4** When you see them, their bodies please you,[3] but when they speak, you hear their speech as if they were planks of wood propped up.[4] They think every cry is against them. They are the enemy, so beware of them. God fight them! How deluded they are! **5** When it is said to them, 'Come, the messenger of God will ask forgiveness for you,' they shake their heads, and you see them turning aside, and they become arrogant. **6** (It is) the same for to them whether you ask forgiveness for them or you do not ask forgiveness for them: God will not forgive them. Surely God does not guide the people who are wicked. **7** They are those who say, 'Do not contribute to[5] those who are with the messenger of God until they disperse,'[6] when the storehouses of the heavens and the earth (belong) to God. But the hypocrites do not understand (this). **8** They say, 'If indeed we return to the city,[7] the mightier in it will indeed expel the lowlier,'[8] when all honor (belongs) to God, and to His messenger, and to the believers. But the hypocrites do not know (this).

9 You who believe! Do not let your wealth or your children divert you from the remembrance of God. Whoever does that, those – they are the losers. **10** Contribute from what We have provided you, before death comes upon one of you, and he says, 'My Lord, if only You would spare me for a time near (at hand),[9] so that I might make a freewill offering,[10] and become one of the righteous.' **11** But God will not spare anyone when his time comes.[11] God is aware of what you do.

Q63: This sūra is comprised of two passages, one describing the 'hypocrites' (whence its title), and the other admonishing the believers. Most scholars assign Q63 to the 'Medinan' period.

1–8 Description of the hypocrites

1. *you are...the messenger*: for this important title, see n. on Q2.87.
2. *hearts*: here, as often, the heart is spoken of as synonymous with mind.
3. *their bodies please you*: referring to the outward impression they make.
4. *planks of wood propped up*: to reinforce a wall (?), and thus perhaps a metaphor of their resistance to the message.
5. *contribute to*: lit. 'spend on.'
6. *until they disperse*: or 'until they leave;' i.e. the hypocrites hope to induce the believers to leave the city with a promise of contributions afterwards.
7. *the city*: said to be 'Medina' (see n. on Q9.101).
8. *the mightier...the lowlier*: i.e. the hypocrites boast that they will expel the Prophet and his followers from the city.

9–11 Believers urged to contribute

9. *spare me for a time near (at hand)*: i.e. until death comes in its natural course (in other words, 'Let me live a little longer').
10. *freewill offering*: or 'voluntary contribution' (Ar. *ṣadaqa*) to benefit the community (cf. Q9.60).
11. *when his time comes*: a person's 'time' or 'term' (Ar. *ajal*) is predetermined and cannot be changed.

64 Mutual Defrauding ۞ Al-Taghābun

In the Name of God, the Merciful, the Compassionate

1 Whatever is in the heavens and whatever is on the earth glorifies God. To Him (belongs) the kingdom, and to Him (belongs) the praise. He is powerful over everything. **2** He (it is) who created you. One of you is a disbeliever, and one of you a believer. God sees what you do. **3** He created the heavens and the earth in truth.[1] He fashioned you, and made your forms well. To Him is the (final) destination. **4** He knows whatever is in the heavens and the earth. He knows what you keep secret and what you speak aloud. God knows what is in the hearts.[2]

5 Has the story[3] not come to you[4] of those who disbelieved before,[5] and tasted the consequence of their action, and for whom (there was) a painful punishment? **6** That was because their messengers[6] brought them the clear signs,[7] and they said, 'Will a human being guide us?' So they disbelieved and turned away, but God had no need (of them). God is wealthy,[8] praiseworthy.

7 Those who disbelieve claim that they will not be raised up. Say:[9] 'Yes indeed! By my Lord! You will indeed be raised up, (and) then you will indeed be informed about what you have done. That is easy for God.' **8** So believe in God and His messenger, and the light which We have sent down.[10] God is aware of what you do. **9** On the Day when He will gather you for the Day of Gathering – that will be the Day of Mutual Defrauding.[11] Whoever believes in God and does righteousness – He will absolve him of his evil deeds, and cause him to enter Gardens through which rivers flow,[12] there to remain forever. That is the great triumph! **10** But those who disbelieved and called Our signs[13] a lie – those are the companions of

---

Q64: This sūra extols the glory, power, and knowledge of God, and then describes the different fates awaiting believers and disbelievers. It concludes by encouraging believers to remain steadfast and contribute to the cause. Most scholars assign Q64 to the 'Medinan' period (including the Cairo edition), though some traditional scholars consider it 'Meccan.' It receives its title from a word whose exact significance is uncertain (Q64.9).

1–4 The glory, power, and knowledge of God

1. *in truth*: or 'with the truth.'
2. *hearts*: lit. 'chests,' considered the seat of knowledge and understanding.

5–6 Punishment of earlier generations a warning

3. *story*: or 'news.'
4. *you*: plur.
5. *those who disbelieved before*: previous peoples who were punished for rejecting their messengers (see n. on Q7.59).
6. *messengers*: for this important title, see n. on Q2.87.
7. *the clear signs*: or 'the clear proofs,' 'the indisputable evidence.'
8. *wealthy*: i.e. God has no need of anyone or anything.

7–10 Fate of believers and disbelievers

9. *Say*: on this form of address, see n. on Q2.80.
10. *the light which We have sent down*: referring to the Qur'ān (cf. Q7.157).
11. *Day of Mutual Defrauding*: the idea may be that the tables have now been turned, and the believers will get the better of disbelievers, but the exact meaning remains obscure.
12. *Gardens...*: in heaven (for this imagery, see n. on Q2.25).
13. *signs*: or 'verses' (see n. on Q2.39).

the Fire,[14] there to remain – and it is an evil destination!

11 No smiting smites,[15] except by the permission of God. Whoever believes in God – He will guide his heart. God has knowledge of everything. **12** Obey God and obey the messenger! If you turn away – only (dependent) on Our messenger is the clear delivery (of the message). **13** God – (there is) no god but Him. In God let the believers put their trust.

14 You who believe! Surely among your wives and your children (there is) an enemy to you. So beware of them.[16] If you pardon and excuse and forgive – surely God is forgiving, compassionate. **15** Surely your wealth and your children are a trial, but God – with Him (there is) a great reward. **16** Guard (yourselves) against God as much as you are able, and hear and obey, and contribute! (That is) better for yourselves. Whoever is guarded against his own greed, those – they are the ones who prosper. **17** If you lend to God a good loan,[17] He will double it for you, and will forgive you. God is thankful, forbearing, **18** Knower of the unseen and the seen,[18] the Mighty, the Wise.

14. *the Fire*: Ar. *al-nār* is the most common of the various designations for Hell.

11–18 Trials and temptations of believers

15. *No smiting smites*: i.e. no misfortune happens (cf. Q57.22).
16. *(there is) an enemy to you...*: usually taken to mean that family can be a distraction, but the following mention of pardon suggests something more specific.
17. *lend to God a good loan*: by contributing to or 'investing in' God's cause (cf. Q2.245; 5.12; 30.39; 57.11; 73.20).
18. *the seen*: lit. 'the witnessed.'

65 Divorce ۞ Al-Ṭalāq

In the Name of God, the Merciful, the Compassionate

1 Prophet![1] When you divorce women,[2] divorce them when they have reached (the end of) their waiting period.[3] Count the waiting period, and guard (yourselves) against God your Lord. Do not expel them from their houses, nor let them leave, unless they commit clear immorality.[4] Those are the limits (set by) God. Whoever transgresses the limits (set by) God has done himself evil. You[5] do not know, perhaps after that God may bring about a new situation.[6] **2** When they reach their term, either retain them rightfully, or part from them rightfully. Call in two of your just men as witnesses, and conduct the witnessing (as if) before God. That is what anyone who believes in God and the Last Day is admonished. Whoever guards (himself) against God – He will make a way out for him, **3** and will provide for him from where he was not expecting. Whoever puts his trust in God – He will be enough for him. Surely God attains his purpose. God has appointed[7] a measure for everything.

4 (As for) those of your women who have no hope of (further) menstruation: if you[8] are in doubt, their waiting period is three months,[9] and (also for) those who have not (yet) menstruated. (As for) those who are pregnant, their term (is) when they deliver what they bear. Whoever guards (himself) against God – He will bring about some relief for him from His command. **5** That is the command of God, which He has sent down to you.[10] Whoever guards (himself) against God – He will absolve him of his evil deeds, and make his reward great.

6 Let them[11] reside where you are residing, according to your means, and do not treat them harshly, so that you cause distress for them. If they are pregnant, support them until they deliver what they bear. If they nurse (the child) for you, give them their payment, and consult together rightfully. But if you encounter difficulties, another woman will nurse (the child) for him. **7** Let a man of means spend out of his means, and whoever is limited in provision, let him spend out of what God has given him. God does

---

Q65: As its title indicates, this sūra is mostly comprised of regulations concerning divorce (similar to those found at Q2.226-232). It also alludes briefly to the punishment of previous cities and mentions the future reward of believers, before concluding with a striking reference to the creation of the 'seven heavens.' Most scholars assign Q65 to the 'Medinan' period.

1–7 Regulations about divorce

1. *Prophet*: for this important title, see n. on Q2.87.
2. *When you divorce...*: plur. (i.e. 'When you believers divorce...').
3. *reached (the end of) their waiting period*: i.e. the prescribed period of waiting (Ar. *'idda*) for a divorced woman, during which she may not remarry (see Q2.228).
4. *immorality*: or 'indecency' (Ar. *fāḥisha*), of a sexual nature.
5. *You*: sing., but probably intended generally.
6. *bring about a new situation*: i.e. there may be some change of mind during the waiting period, leading to a possible reconciliation.
7. *appointed*: lit. 'made.'
8. *you*: plur.
9. *three months*: cf. the three menstrual periods prescribed at Q2.228.
10. *you*: plur.
11. *Let them...*: the women during their waiting period.

not burden anyone except (according to) what He has given him. God will bring about[12] some ease after hardship.

8 How many a town disdained the command of its Lord and His messengers, and We made a harsh reckoning with it, and punished it with a terrible punishment. **9** So it tasted the consequence of its action, and the result of its action was loss. **10** God prepared a harsh punishment for them. Guard (yourselves) against God, those (of you) with understanding!

(You) who believe! God has sent down to you a reminder[13] **11** – a messenger[14] reciting over you the signs of God that make (things) clear,[15] so that He[16] may bring those who believe and do righteous deeds out of the darkness to the light. Whoever believes in God and does righteousness – He will cause him to enter Gardens through which rivers flow,[17] there to remain forever. God has made good provision for him.

12 (It is) God who created seven heavens, and of the earth a similar (number) to them.[18] The command descends between them,[19] so that you may know that God is powerful over everything, and that God encompasses everything in knowledge.

12. *bring about*: lit. 'make.'

8–10a Punishment of earlier generations a warning

10b–11 Fate of believers

13. *reminder*: though this term is often used of the Qur'ān, here it designates the Prophet himself (cf. Q88.21; see n. on Q3.58).
14. *messenger*: for this important title, see n. on Q2.87.
15. *signs...that make (things) clear*: or 'verses...that make (things) clear' (see n. on Q2.39; cf. Q24.34, 46).
16. *He*: or 'he' (the Prophet).
17. *Gardens...*: in heaven (for this imagery, see n. on Q2.25).

12 Seven heavens and seven earths

18. *a similar (number) to them*: unless this phrase simply means 'their counterpart,' the idea seems to be that 'seven earths' were also created, corresponding to the seven heavens.
19. *The command descends between them*: or 'in the midst of them,' but the imagery is tantalizingly obscure. God's 'command' (Ar. *amr*) often refers to judgment (see Q65.8 above; cf. Q2.109; 4.47; 5.52; 7.150; 10.24; 16.1, 33), but here its 'descent' or intervention may refer to revelation in general, or possibly to God's 'Word,' by which he carried out the creation and oversees the running of it (see e.g. Q10.3, 31; 13.2; 32.4-5).

66 The Forbidding ✵ Al-Taḥrīm

In the Name of God, the Merciful, the Compassionate

1 Prophet![1] Why do you forbid what God has permitted to you, seeking the approval of your wives?[2] God is forgiving, compassionate. **2** God has already specified (what is) obligatory for you[3] in the absolution of your oaths.[4] God is your Protector. He is the Knowing, the Wise.

3 When the prophet confided a (certain) story[5] to one of his wives, and when she informed (another) about it and God disclosed it to him, he made known part of it, and avoided a part.[6] And when he informed her about it, she said, 'Who informed you of this?' He said, 'The Knowing (and) the Aware informed me.' **4** If both of you[7] turn to God (in repentance), both your hearts[8] are (well) inclined, but if both of you support each other against him,[9] surely God – He is his Protector, and Gabriel[10] (too), and the righteous among the believers, and beyond that the angels[11] are (his) supporters. **5** It may be that, if he divorces you,[12] his Lord will give him in exchange better wives than you – women who have submitted,[13] believing, obedient, repentant, worshipping, fasting – (both) previously married and virgins.

Q66: The first half of this sūra deals with an incident between the Prophet and his wives, though the exact circumstances remain obscure. It concludes by giving famous examples from the past of both believing and disbelieving women. Most scholars assign Q66 to the 'Medinan' period.

1–5 The Prophet and his wives

1. *Prophet*: for this important title, see n. on Q2.87.
2. *Why do you forbid..., seeking the approval of your wives*: reference obscure; it is said to be connected with an oath the Prophet had taken to abstain from conjugal relations, after he was found by Ḥafṣa, one of his wives, with a slave girl (Mary the Copt) on a day that 'belonged' to Ḥafṣa (or 'Ā'isha), according to the Prophet's custom of assigning a day to each wife. Another story has it that the Prophet swore an oath to abstain from honey, after one of his wives had given him a dish which he particularly liked, but which three other wives (falsely) said made him smell. Like so much of the tradition, however, these stories are probably fictions invented to explain an otherwise puzzling text.
3. *you*: plur.
4. *absolution of your oaths*: 'absolution' (Ar. *taḥilla*) of an oath involved not only annulment but 'atonement' (already specified at Q5.89).
5. *a (certain) story*: or 'report' (Ar. *ḥadīth*); the Prophet is said to have told Ḥafṣa some secret in order to placate her (in some versions, that he would be succeeded by Abū Bakr ['Ā'isha's father] and 'Umar [Ḥafṣa's father]), whereupon Ḥafṣa revealed the secret to 'Ā'isha.
6. *avoided a part*: the Prophet is said to have withheld the name of his informant.
7. *both of you*: the dual is taken to refer to Ḥafṣa and 'Ā'isha.
8. *hearts*: here, as often, the heart is spoken of as synonymous with mind.
9. *him*: the Prophet.
10. *Gabriel*: mentioned three times by name in the Qur'ān (see n. on Q2.97); here he is clearly distinguished from the angels.
11. *angels*: for these beings and their various roles, see n. on Q2.30.
12. *you*: plur., not dual (addressed to all the Prophet's wives?).
13. *who have submitted*: or 'are Muslims.'

6 You who believe! Guard yourselves and your families against a Fire[14] – its fuel is people and stones[15] – over which are angels, stern (and) harsh. They do not disobey God in what He commands them, but they do what they are commanded. **7** 'You who disbelieve![16] Do not make excuses today, you are only being repaid for what you have done.'

8 You who believe! Turn to God in sincere repentance. It may be that your Lord will absolve you of your evil deeds, and cause you to enter Gardens[17] through which rivers flow. On the Day when God will not disgrace the prophet or those who believe with him: their light will run before them, and at their right (hands) [...],[18] and they will say, 'Our Lord, perfect our light for us, and forgive us. Surely You are powerful over everything.'

9 Prophet! Struggle against[19] the disbelievers and the hypocrites, and be stern with them. Their refuge is Gehenna – and it is an evil destination!

10 God has struck a parable for those who disbelieve: the wife of Noah[20] and the wife of Lot. They were under two of Our righteous servants,[21] but they both betrayed them. Neither of them was of any use at all to either of them against God,[22] when it was said, 'Enter the Fire, both of you, with the ones who enter!'

11 And God has struck a parable for those who believe: the wife of Pharaoh,[23] when she said, 'My Lord, build a house in the Garden for me in Your presence, and rescue me from Pharaoh and his deed(s), and rescue me from the people who are evildoers.' **12** And Mary, daughter of 'Imrān,[24] who guarded her private part: We breathed into it[25] some of Our spirit, and she affirmed the words of her Lord[26] and His Books,[27] and became one of the obedient.

6–7 Admonition to believers

14. *Fire*: Ar. *nār* is the most common of the various designations for Hell.
15. *stones*: reference obscure; perhaps 'brimstone' or 'stone idols' is meant (cf. Q2.24).
16. *You who disbelieve*: understood as spoken by the angels as they ready disbelievers for the Fire.

8 Reward for repentance

17. *Gardens*: in heaven (for this imagery, see n. on Q2.25).
18. *at their right (hands) [...]*: or 'in their right (hands) [...];' there is a lacuna here, but it can be restored on the basis of the parallel at Q57.12: 'Good news for you today!'

9 Struggle against disbelievers and hypocrites

19. *Struggle against...*: or 'Fight against...' (cf. Q9.73).

10–12 Examples of believing and disbelieving women

20. *wife of Noah*: the following reference to her betrayal of Noah is a novel feature (according to Q11.40, one of Noah's sons was left behind); cf. the wife of Job (Q38.44).
21. *servants*: the word 'servant' (Ar. *'abd*) also means 'slave.'
22. *Neither...was of any use at all to either of them...*: i.e. Noah and Lot were unable to help their wives against the judgment of God.
23. *wife of Pharaoh*: for her surprisingly positive portrayal, cf. Q28.9.
24. *Mary, daughter of 'Imrān*: see Q3.35-37; cf. Q19.28.
25. *into it*: i.e. her private part, though Ar. *fīhi* could refer to Jesus ('into him'). The variant reading 'into her' (*fīhā*) is also possible (see Q21.91; cf. Q4.171, God 'cast into Mary...a spirit from Him;' 19.17, 'We sent to her Our spirit'); otherwise this is said only of Adam (Q15.29; 38.72; cf. Q32.9).
26. *affirmed the words of her Lord*: for this idea, cf. Luke 1.38, 45.
27. *Books*: the Torah and Gospel (a variant reading has sing. 'Book').

67 The Kingdom ۞ Al-Mulk

In the Name of God, the Merciful, the Compassionate

1 Blessed (be) He in whose hand is the kingdom – He is powerful over everything – **2** who created death and life to test which of you is best in deed – He is the Mighty, the Forgiving – **3** who created seven heavens in stories (one upon another).[1] You[2] do not see any mistake in the creation of the Merciful. Cast your sight again! Do you see any fissure?[3] **4** Then cast your sight again and again! Your sight will come crawling back to you, worn out.

5 Certainly We adorned the lower heaven with lamps, and made them missiles for the satans[4] – and We have prepared for them the punishment of the blazing (Fire). **6** For those who disbelieve in their Lord (there is) the punishment of Gehenna[5] – and it is an evil homecoming! **7** When they are cast into it, they will hear its panting,[6] as it boils up **8** (and) nearly bursts apart from rage. Whenever a crowd is cast into it, its keepers will ask them, 'Did a warner[7] not come to you?' **9** They will say, 'Yes indeed! A warner did come to us, but we called (him) a liar, and said, "God has not sent down anything. You are simply terribly astray."'[8] **10** And they will say, 'If (only) we had heard or understood, we would not have been among the companions of the blazing (Fire).' **11** And so they confess their sin. Away with the companions of the blazing (Fire)! **12** Surely those who fear their Lord in the unseen[9] – for them (there is) forgiveness and a great reward.

13 Keep your word secret or speak it publicly – surely He knows what is in (your) hearts.[10] **14** Does the One who created not know, when He is the Astute, the Aware? **15** He (it is) who made the earth subservient to you. So walk about in its regions, and eat from His provision, but to Him is the raising up.[11]

16 Do you feel secure that the One who is in the sky[12] will not cause the earth to swallow you, and then suddenly it shakes? **17** Or do you feel secure that the One who is in the sky will not send a sandstorm

---

Q67: This sūra consists mostly of short passages, many of which revolve around the theme of God's power. It concludes with a series of individual pronouncements. Most scholars assign Q67 to the 'Meccan' period.

1–4 God the creator

1. *in stories...*: see Q71.15; cf. Q41.12; 65.12; 84.19.
2. *You*: the Prophet, or perhaps intended generally ('one').
3. *fissure*: cf. Q50.6.

5–12 Punishments and rewards

4. *missiles for the satans*: shooting stars ('lamps') were thought to be stones hurled to drive off demons and prevent them from 'eavesdropping' on the heavenly council (see Q15.16-18; 37.9-10; 72.8-9).
5. *Gehenna*: another name for Hell (see n. on Q2.206).
6. *its panting*: a graphic expression of the Fire's lust to possess them (cf. Q11.106; 21.100; 25.12).
7. *warner*: for this role, see n. on Q2.119.
8. *terribly astray*: lit. 'in great straying' (cf. Q36.47).
9. *in the unseen*: or 'in secret' (see n. on Q2.3).

13–22 God's knowledge and power

10. *hearts*: lit. 'chests,' considered the seat of knowledge and understanding.
11. *the raising up*: or 'the resurrection.'
12. *sky*: or 'heaven.'

against you, and then you will know how My warning is? **18** Certainly those who were before them called (it) a lie, and how was My loathing (of them)?

19 Do they not see the birds above them, spreading (their wings), and they fold (them)? No one holds them (up) but the Merciful. Surely He sees everything. **20** Or who is this who will be a (fighting) force for you to help you, other than the Merciful? The disbelievers are only in delusion. **21** Or who is this who will provide for you, if He withholds His provision? No! But they persist in (their) disdain and aversion. **22** Is the one who walks bent over on his face[13] better guided, or the one who walks upright on a straight path?

23 Say:[14] 'He (it is) who produced you, and made for you hearing and sight and hearts[15] – little thanks you show!'

24 Say: 'He (it is) who scattered[16] you on the earth, and to Him you will be gathered.'

25 They say, 'When (will) this promise[17] (come to pass), if you[18] are truthful?' **26** Say: 'The knowledge (of it) is only with God.[19] I am only a clear warner.'

27 When they see it near at hand, the faces of those who disbelieve will become sad, and it will be said, 'This is what you have been calling for.'

28 Say: 'Have you considered?[20] If God destroys me and whoever is with me, or has compassion on us, who will protect the disbelievers from a painful punishment?'

29 Say: 'He is the Merciful. We believe in Him, and in Him we put our trust. Soon you will know who it is (who is) clearly astray.'[21]

30 Say: 'Have you considered? If one morning your water should sink (into the ground), who would bring you flowing water?'

---

13. *walks bent over on his face*: i.e. like an animal.

23–30 A series of declarations

14. *Say*: on this form of address, see n. on Q2.80.
15. *hearts*: minds.
16. *scattered*: as a sower scatters seed.
17. *promise*: or 'threat' of punishment (cf. Q10.48; 21.38; 27.71; 34.29; 36.48).
18. *you*: plur.
19. *knowledge (of it) is only with God*: cf. Q7.187; 33.63; 41.47; 43.85; 46.23; and Mark 13.32 par.
20. *considered*: lit. 'seen.'
21. *clearly astray*: lit. 'in clear straying.'

68 The Pen ۞ Al-Qalam

In the Name of God, the Merciful, the Compassionate

1 Nūn.[1]

By the pen and what they write![2] **2** You are not, by the blessing of your Lord, possessed.[3] **3** Surely for you (there is) indeed a reward without end, **4** (for) surely you (are) indeed on a great undertaking.[4] **5** So you will see, and they will see, **6** which of you is the troubled one.[5] **7** Surely your Lord – He knows who goes astray from His way, and He knows the ones who are (rightly) guided. **8** So do not obey the ones who call (it) a lie. **9** They wish that you would compromise, and then they would compromise.

10 And do not obey[6] any despicable swearer, **11** a slanderer (who) trades in gossip, **12** a hinderer of the good, a transgressor (and) sinner, **13** crude, and besides all that, a bastard,[7] **14** (just) because he has wealth and sons. **15** When Our signs[8] are recited to him, he says, 'Old tales!'[9] **16** We shall brand him on the snout!

17 Surely We have tested them[10] as We tested the owners of the garden,[11] when they swore they would

---

Q68: This sūra opens with a denial that the Prophet is 'possessed,' before turning to denounce one of his opponents directly. Next comes a parable warning against arrogant self-satisfaction, followed by a section on eschatological rewards and punishments, and a concluding exhortation to the Prophet. Most traditional scholars regard Q68 as a very early 'Meccan' sūra, though some attribute sections of it to 'Medina.' Most modern scholars would place it in the middle 'Meccan' period, with additions from the later 'Meccan' and 'Medinan' periods. It receives its title from the opening reference to 'the pen.'

1a Letter

1. *Nūn*: the name of the Arabic letter *n* (unique to Q68). Twenty-nine sūras begin with a letter (or letters) like this, ranging from one to five. No satisfactory explanation has been given for their occurrence. The Cairo edition varies in counting these letters as a separate verse, or as the beginning of the first verse (as here).

1b–9 The Prophet is not possessed

2. *By the pen and what they write*: i.e. 'I swear by…;' this may simply refer to the art of writing in general, but it is usually understood to designate the heavenly 'Mother of the Book,' or the 'Book of Destiny' by which everything is ordained, or the 'Record' of human deeds kept by the recording angels (cf. Q96.3-5).
3. *possessed*: or 'jinn-struck' (Ar. *majnūn*); cf. Q68.51 below; see n. on Q7.184.
4. *undertaking*: or 'custom,' 'practice;' though the usual translation is 'you are of great (moral) character.'
5. *which of you is the troubled one*: i.e. the one really disturbed by jinn.

10–16 A despised opponent

6. *And do not obey…*: some scholars take this short passage as a typical example of *hijā'*, a satiric genre of poetry or poetic lampooning.
7. *bastard*: or perhaps 'low born;' usually taken to mean 'adopted from an ignoble family,' and said to refer to al-Walīd ibn al-Mughīra, a steadfast opponent of the Prophet (cf. Q74.11-26); but it may simply be a depiction of a typical disbeliever.
8. *signs*: or 'verses' (see n. on Q2.39).
9. *Old tales*: or 'Tales of the ancients;' a contemptuous reference to the stories of earlier generations who were punished for disobeying their prophets (see n. on Q7.59; cf. Q25.5).

17–33 Parable of the ruined garden

10. *Surely We have tested them…*: the Cairo edition, reflecting the views of traditional scholars, attributes the following parable to the 'Medinan' period.
11. *owners of the garden*: this description usually designates the 'companions of the Garden;' but it is probably to

indeed harvest it in the morning, **18** but did not make exception.[12] **19** And so a circler[13] from your Lord went around it while they were sleeping, **20** and in the morning it was as if it had been harvested. **21** They called to each other in the morning: **22** 'Go out early to your field, if you are going to harvest (it).' **23** So they set out, murmuring among themselves: **24** 'No poor person will enter it today in your presence.' **25** They went out early, able to (their) task. **26** But when they saw it, they said, 'Surely we have gone astray indeed![14] **27** No! We have been robbed!'[15] **28** The most moderate one of them said, 'Did I not say to you, "Why do you not glorify (God)?"' **29** They said, 'Glory to our Lord! Surely we have been evildoers!' **30** So some of them approached others blaming each other. **31** They said, 'Woe to us! Surely we have been insolent transgressors! **32** It may be that our Lord will give us a better one[16] in exchange for it. Surely we turn in hope to our Lord.' **33** Such was the punishment. Yet the punishment of the Hereafter[17] is indeed greater, if (only) they knew.

34 Surely for the ones who guard (themselves)[18] (there will be) Gardens of Bliss[19] with their Lord. **35** Shall We treat[20] those who submit[21] like the sinners? **36** What is (the matter) with you? How do you judge? **37** Or do you have a Book which you study? **38** Surely you (would) have in it whatever indeed you choose! **39** Or do you have guarantees[22] from Us, reaching to the Day of Resurrection? Surely you (would) have whatever indeed you judge![23] **40** Ask them which of them will guarantee that. **41** Or do they have associates?[24] Let them bring their associates, if they are truthful. **42** On the Day when the leg will be bared,[25] and they will be called to (make) prostration, but are unable: **43** their sight will be downcast, and humiliation will cover them, because they had been called to (make) prostration[26] when they were able.[27]

44 So leave Me[28] (to deal with) anyone who calls this proclamation[29] a lie. We shall lead them on step by step[30]

---

be understood as a typical parable or example story (cf. e.g. Q3.117; 18.32-44).

12. *did not make exception*: i.e. did not qualify what they intended to do with the phrase, 'if God pleases' (see Q18.24; cf. James 4.13-15).
13. *circler*: or 'visitor,' probably an angel (cf. Q7.201).
14. *we have gone astray*: i.e. they think have come to the wrong garden (but they speak more wisely than they know).
15. *We have been robbed*: i.e. of their labors (more double entendre).
16. *a better one*: a better garden/Garden.
17. *the Hereafter*: see n. on Q2.4.

34–43 Rewards and punishments

18. *guard (themselves)*: against evil, or God.
19. *Gardens of Bliss*: in heaven (for this imagery, see n. on Q2.25).
20. *treat*: lit. 'make.'
21. *those who submit*: or 'the Muslims.'
22. *guarantees*: lit. 'oaths,' guaranteeing their safety.
23. *whatever indeed you judge*: i.e. whatever you decide.
24. *associates*: i.e. other gods which they 'associate' with God.
25. *when the leg will be bared*: a poetic metaphor for the outbreak of war; here referring to Judgment Day.
26. *prostration*: to God in worship.
27. *able*: lit. 'sound;' i.e. when they could bow in submission but did not.

44–47 God will punish the disbelievers

28. *So leave Me...*: addressed to the Prophet.
29. *proclamation*: or 'report' (Ar. *ḥadīth*), referring to the Qur'ān, either in whole or in part.
30. *lead them on step by step*: or 'come upon them gradually.'

without their realizing it.[31] **45** And I shall spare them[32] – surely My plan is strong.

46 Or do you ask them for a reward,[33] so that they are burdened with debt? **47** Or is the unseen in their keeping, and so they are writing (it) down?[34]

48 Be patient[35] for the judgment of your Lord, and do not be like the companion of the fish,[36] when he called out, choked with distress. **49** If a blessing from his Lord had not reached him, he would indeed have been tossed on the desert (shore),[37] condemned. **50** But his Lord chose him, and made him one of the righteous.

51 Surely those who disbelieve almost indeed make you stumble with their look, when they hear the Reminder.[38] They say, 'Surely he is possessed indeed!'[39] **52** Yet it is nothing but a reminder to the worlds.[40]

---

31. *without their realizing it*: lit. 'from where they do not know.'
32. *spare them*: or 'give them a reprieve.'
33. *reward*: for delivering messages from God.
34. *is the unseen in their keeping...*: i.e. 'do they know the future...' (cf. Q52.41; see n. on Q2.3).

48–52 The Prophet to remain steadfast

35. *Be patient...*: the Cairo edition, reflecting the views of traditional scholars, attributes the following three verses to the 'Medinan' period.
36. *companion of the fish*: probably Jonah (cf. Q21.87-88; 37.139-148).
37. *desert (shore)*: perhaps only the 'desert' or 'wilderness' is meant (cf. Q37.145).
38. *the Reminder*: the Qur'ān (see n. on Q3.58).
39. *possessed*: or 'jinn-struck' (see Q68.2 above).
40. *to the worlds*: or 'to all peoples.'

69 The Payment Due ❁ Al-Ḥāqqa

In the Name of God, the Merciful, the Compassionate

1 The payment due![1] **2** What is the payment due? **3** And what will make you[2] know what the payment due is? **4** Thamūd and 'Ād[3] called the striking[4] a lie. **5** As for Thamūd, they were destroyed by the outbreak.[5] **6** And as for 'Ād, they were destroyed by a furious, violent wind,[6] **7** which He forced on them for seven nights and eight days consecutively,[7] and during which you[8] (could) see the people lying flat, as if they were the trunks of collapsed date palms. **8** Do you[9] see any remnant of them (now)? **9** And Pharaoh (too) – and those who were before him,[10] and the overturned (cities)[11] – committed sin,[12] **10** and they disobeyed the messenger[13] of their Lord, so He seized them with a surpassing seizing. **11** Surely We – when the waters overflowed[14] – We carried you[15] in the running (ship),[16] **12** so that We might make it a reminder to you, and (that) an attentive ear might attend to it.

13 When a single blast is blown on the trumpet,[17] **14** and the earth and the mountains are lifted up and shattered with a single shattering, **15** on that Day the falling will fall,[18] **16** and the sky will be split

---

Q69: This sūra begins with a reference to several previous peoples who dismissed the threat of impending punishment and were destroyed. It then describes the terror of the Last Day and Judgment, and concludes with God affirming the truth of the Qur'ān. Most scholars assign Q69 to the 'Meccan' period. Its title comes from its first word.

1–12 Destruction of disbelieving peoples

1. *The payment due*: lit. 'that which is due' or 'owed,' probably referring to judgment (cf. Q24.25); notice the similar type of opening at Q101.1-3 ('the Striking').
2. *you*: sing., but intended generally (for this phrase, cf. Q74.27; 77.14; 82.17-18; 83.8; 86.2; 90.12; 97.2; 101.3; 104.5).
3. *Thamūd and 'Ād*: for the story of these peoples, see e.g. Q7.65-72, 73-79.
4. *the striking*: see Q101.1-5 (eschatological); cf. Q13.31 (temporal).
5. *by the outbreak*: lit. 'by that which transgresses insolently' (Ar. *bil-ṭāghiya* [a flood? (cf. Q69.11 below)]), but this does not correspond to the punishment described in other passages. It may be intentionally vague, or perhaps *bil-ṭāghiya* means that they were destroyed 'for their insolent transgression.'
6. *by a furious...wind*: see Q41.16; 54.19.
7. *consecutively*: or 'destructively.'
8. *you*: sing., but intended generally.
9. *you*: sing., but intended generally.
10. *those who were before him*: the people of Noah (?).
11. *the overturned (cities)*: perhaps the cities of Sodom and Gomorrah, associated with Lot, or else a general reference to the stories of previous peoples who were punished for their sins (cf. Q9.70; 53.53; see n. on Q7.59).
12. *committed sin*: lit. 'brought the sin.'
13. *messenger*: for this important title, see n. on Q2.87.
14. *overflowed*: lit. 'transgressed insolently.'
15. *you*: plur.
16. *the running (ship)*: Noah's 'ark.'

13–18 The terror of the Last Day

17. *a single blast...on the trumpet*: the Last Day will be announced by the blast of a trumpet (e.g. Q6.73; 18.99; 20.102; 39.68 [a double blast]; 74.8; 78.18; cf. Matthew 24.31; 1 Corinthians 15.52; 1 Thessalonians 4.16).
18. *the falling will fall*: referring to the 'event' of judgment (cf. Q56.1).

open,[19] (for) on that Day it[20] will be frail, **17** and the angels[21] (will stand) on its borders, and they will bear the throne of your Lord above them on that Day – eight (of them). **18** On that Day you will (all) be presented[22] – not a secret of yours will be hidden.

19 As for the one who is given his book[23] in his right (hand), he will say, 'Take (and) read my book. **20** Surely I thought that I would meet my reckoning.' **21** And he will be in a pleasing life, **22** in a Garden on high, **23** its clusters (of fruit) near (at hand). **24** 'Eat and drink with satisfaction, (in return) for what you did in days past.' **25** But as for the one who is given his book in his left (hand), he will say, 'Would that I had not been given my book, **26** and not known what my reckoning is! **27** Would that it had been the end![24] **28** My wealth is of no use to me. **29** My authority has perished from me.' **30** 'Seize him and bind him! **31** Then burn him in the Furnace,[25] **32** (and) then put him in a chain of seventy cubits. **33** Surely he never believed in God, the Almighty, **34** nor did he ever urge the feeding of the poor. **35** So today he has no friend here, **36** nor any food except refuse,[26] **37** which only the sinners eat.'

38 I swear by[27] what you[28] see **39** and what you do not see! **40** Surely it[29] is indeed the word[30] of an honorable messenger.[31] **41** It is not the word of a poet[32] – little do you believe! **42** Nor (is it) the word of an oracle-giver[33] – little do you take heed! **43** (It is) a sending down from the Lord of the worlds.[34] **44** If he had forged any (false) words against Us, **45** We would indeed have seized him by the right (hand). **46** Then We would indeed have cut his (main) artery, **47** and not one of you could have defended him from it. **48** Surely it is a reminder[35] indeed to the ones who guard (themselves).[36] **49** Yet surely We indeed know that some of you are calling (it) a lie. **50** Surely it will be a (cause of) regret indeed to the disbelievers.[37] **51** Yet surely it is the certain truth[38] indeed. **52** So glorify the name of your Lord, the Almighty.[39]

---

19. *sky will be split open*: cf. Q25.25; 55.37; 84.1.
20. *it*: the sky.
21. *angels*: for these beings and their various roles, see n. on Q2.30.
22. *presented*: before God for judgment.

19–37 A judgment scene

23. *his book*: the record of his deeds (cf. Q17.71).
24. *Would that it had been the end*: i.e. that death had been the end.
25. *the Furnace*: a name for Hell (Ar. *al-jaḥīm*).
26. *refuse*: the precise meaning is obscure (cf. Q38.57; 78.25).

38–52 The truth of the Qur'ān

26. *I swear by...*: for God's swearing by things, cf. Q56.75; 75.1, 2; 81.15-18; 84.16-18; 90.1, 3.
28. *you*: plur.
29. *it*: the Qur'ān (throughout this final passage).
30. *word*: or 'speech' (i.e. way of speaking); cf. Q81.19; 86.13.
31. *honorable messenger*: the Prophet (see Q81.19, the Prophet [or Gabriel?]; cf. Q44.17, Moses).
32. *poet*: see n. on Q21.5.
33. *oracle-giver*: or 'diviner' (Ar. *kāhin*), a religious entrepreneur who was paid to give inspired answers to all sorts of questions (only here and at Q52.29).
34. *Lord of the worlds*: for this title, see n. on Q1.2.
35. *it is a reminder*: the Qur'ān (see n. on Q3.58).
36. *guard (themselves)*: against evil, or God.
37. *a (cause of) regret...*: lit. 'a sighing' (cf. Q19.39, the 'Day of Regret').
38. *the certain truth*: or 'the truth of the certainty' (i.e. the truth about what happens at death).
39. *So glorify...*: sing. imperative.

70 The Stairways ۞ Al-Maʿārij

In the Name of God, the Merciful, the Compassionate

1 A questioner questioned[1] about the punishment going to fall **2** – the disbelievers have no one to repel it! – **3** from God, controller of the stairways.[2] **4** The angels[3] and the spirit[4] ascend to Him in a day, the measure of which is fifty thousand years.[5] **5** So be patient with a patience that becomes (you).[6] **6** Surely they[7] see it as far off, **7** but We see it is near **8** – the Day when the sky will be like molten metal,[8] **9** and the mountains will be like (tufts of) wool, **10** and friend will not question friend. **11** (As) they come into sight of each other, the sinner will wish that he (could) ransom (himself) from the punishment of that Day with his sons, **12** and his consort, and his brother, **13** and his family who gave him refuge, **14** and whoever is on the earth – all (of them) – (wishing that) then it might rescue him. **15** By no means! Surely (there is) a flame, **16** a scalp remover! **17** It will call the one who turned and went away, **18** and (who) accumulated and hoarded.

19 Surely the human was created anxious (for gain). **20** When misfortune touches him, (he is) complaining, **21** but when good touches him, refusing (to give), **22** except for the ones who pray **23** (and) who continue at their prayers, **24** and in whose wealth (there is) an acknowledged (portion) due **25** for the beggar and the outcast, **26** and who affirm the Day of Judgment, **27** and who are apprehensive of the punishment of their Lord **28** – surely no one feels secure (against) the punishment of their Lord – **29** and who guard their private parts, **30** except concerning their wives or what their right (hands) own[9] – surely then they are not (to be) blamed, **31** but whoever seeks beyond that, those – they are the transgressors – **32** and those who keep their pledges and their promise(s),[10] **33** and who stand by their testimonies, **34** and who guard their prayers. **35** Those will be honored in Gardens.[11]

36 What is (the matter) with those who disbelieve, rushing toward you, **37** from the right (hand) and

---

Q70: This sūra begins by responding to a question about the coming punishment. A description of those who will enter the Garden follows. It then concludes by assuring the Prophet that the punishment of his opponents is certain. Most scholars assign Q70 to the 'Meccan' period. It takes its title from the reference to the 'stairways' or 'ladders' to heaven at Q70.3.

1–18 The impending punishment

1. *A questioner questioned*: usually taken in the sense of a skeptic, who was saying in effect, 'If what you say is true, bring it on!'
2. *stairways*: or 'ladders;' i.e. the means by which the angels descend and ascend to God (cf. Genesis 28.12-13, 17).
3. *angels*: for these beings and their various roles, see n. on Q2.30.
4. *spirit*: for 'the spirit' as the bearer of revelation, see n. on Q16.2.
5. *fifty thousand years*: cf. Q22.47; 32.5.
6. *So be patient...*: cf. what Jacob says at Q12.18, 83.
7. *they*: the disbelievers.
8. *the sky will be like molten metal*: for this idea, cf. 2 Peter 3.10.

19–35 Characteristics of the righteous

9. *what their right (hands) own*: i.e. their female slaves (cf. Q4.3, 24).
10. *promise(s)*: or 'contract(s).'
11. *Gardens*: in heaven (for this imagery, see n. on Q2.25; cf. Q70.38 below, 'a Garden of Bliss').

36–44 The Prophet to ignore those who ridicule him

from the left in groups?[12] **38** Is every person among them eager to enter a Garden of Bliss? **39** By no means! Surely We have created them from what they know. **40** I swear by the Lord of the Easts and the Wests![13] Surely We are able indeed **41** to exchange (others who are) better than them – We are not (to be) outrun! **42** So leave them! Let them banter and jest, until they meet their Day which they are promised,
43 the Day when they will come forth from the graves rushing – as if they were running to some goal –
44 their sight downcast, humiliation covering them. That is the Day which they were promised.

12. *rushing toward you...*: this is usually taken to refer to the disbelievers crowding around the Prophet to ridicule him. But their 'running' to him in groups 'on the right and left' may be their deliberate parody (or an unwitting anticipation) of a 'judgment scene.' If so, this final section would connect with the skeptic's question with which Q70 began.

13. *I swear by the Lord of the Easts and the Wests*: for God's unusual 'swearing by himself,' cf. Q4.65; 15.92; 16.56, 63; 19.68; and Hebrews 6.13 (Genesis 22.16). Notice the sudden shift from first-person plur. to sing., and then back again.

71 Noah ❁ Nūḥ

In the Name of God, the Merciful, the Compassionate

1 Surely We sent Noah to his people: 'Warn your people before a painful punishment comes upon them.' **2** He said, 'My people! I am a clear warner[1] for you. **3** Serve God, and guard (yourselves) against Him, and obey me! **4** He will forgive you your sins, and spare you until an appointed time.[2] Surely the time of God, when it comes, cannot be postponed. If (only) you knew!'

5 He said, 'My Lord, surely I have called my people night and day, **6** but my calling has only increased them in flight. **7** Surely I – whenever I called them, so that You might forgive them, they put their fingers in their ears, and covered themselves with their clothes, and persisted (in disbelief), and became very arrogant. **8** Then surely I called them publicly, **9** then surely I spoke openly to them, and I confided to them in secret, **10** and I said, "Ask forgiveness from your Lord, surely He is forgiving, **11** and He will send the sky (down) on you in abundance,[3] **12** and increase you with wealth and sons, and make gardens for you, and make rivers for you. **13** What is (the matter) with you that do not expect seriousness (of purpose) on the part of God, **14** when He created you in stages?[4] **15** Do you not see how God created seven heavens in stories,[5] **16** and placed the moon in them as a light, and placed the sun (in them) as a lamp? **17** And God caused you to grow from of the earth,[6] **18** (and) then He will return you into it, and bring you forth again. **19** God has made the earth an expanse for you, **20** so that you may traverse its open (path)ways."'

21 Noah said, 'My Lord, surely they have disobeyed me, and followed one whose wealth and children increase him only in loss,[7] **22** and they have schemed a great scheme, **23** and said, "Do not forsake your gods, and do not forsake Wadd, nor Suwāʿ, nor Yaghūth, and Yaʿūq, and Nasr."[8] **24** And they have led many astray. Increase the evildoers only in going astray!'[9]

25 They were drowned on account of their sins, and forced to enter a fire,[10] and they found they had no helpers other than God. **26** Noah said, 'My Lord, do not leave any of the disbelievers as an inhabitant on the earth. **27** Surely You – if You leave them, they will lead Your servants astray, and will give birth

Q71: As its title indicates, this sūra is devoted to Noah, including details not found in other iterations of his story. Most scholars assign Q71 to the 'Meccan' period.

1–20 Noah's mission and message

1. *warner*: for this role, see n. on Q2.119.
2. *an appointed time*: or 'term' (Ar. *ajal*), which is predetermined and cannot be changed.
3. *send the sky (down) on you in abundance*: referring to rain, but here as a blessing not a punishment (cf. Q71.25 below; and Genesis 6.17; 7.4, 11-12).
4. *in stages*: see the descriptions of prenatal development at Q22.5; 23.12-14.
5. *in stories*: i.e. one upon another (see Q67.3; cf. Q41.12; 65.12; 84.19).
6. *...from the earth*: referring to the creation of Adam from 'dust.'

21–28 Noah's people reject him and are destroyed

7. *followed one whose wealth...*: reference obscure.
8. *do not forsake Wadd, nor Suwāʿ, nor Yaghūth, and Yaʿūq, and Nasr*: gods presumably worshipped in the time of Noah (mentioned only here).
9. *Increase the evildoers...*: Noah calls upon God to do this (cf. Q71.28 below).
10. *forced to enter a fire*: a novel feature of this version of the story; otherwise Ar. *nār* is the most common of the various designations for Hell.

only to depraved disbeliever(s). **28** My Lord, forgive me and my parents, and whoever enters my house believing, and the believing men and the believing women, and increase the evildoers only in destruction!'

72 The Jinn ❁ Al-Jinn

In the Name of God, the Merciful, the Compassionate

1 Say:[1] 'I am inspired[2] that a band of the jinn listened,[3] and they said, "Surely we have heard an amazing Qur'ān![4] **2** It guides to the right (course). We believe in it, and we shall not associate anyone with our Lord. **3** And (we believe) that[5] He – exalted (be) the majesty of our Lord! – He has not taken a consort or son.[6] **4** And that the foolish among us used to say an outrageous thing against God. **5** And that we had thought that humans and jinn would never say any lie against God. **6** And that individuals[7] of humankind used to take refuge with individuals of the jinn, and they increased them in depravity. **7** And that they thought as you (also) thought, that God will not raise up anyone. **8** And that we touched the sky and found it filled with harsh guards and piercing flames.[8] **9** And that we used to sit there on seats to listen (in), but whoever listens now finds a piercing flame lying in wait for him. **10** And that we do not know whether evil is intended for those who are on the earth, or whether their Lord intends right (guidance) for them. **11** And that some of us are righteous, and some of us are other than that – we are on different roads. **12** And that we (now) think that we shall not be able to escape God on the earth, and shall not escape Him by flight. **13** And that when we heard the guidance,[9] we believed in it, and whoever believes in his Lord will not fear any deprivation or depravity. **14** And that some of us have submitted,[10] and some of us are the ones who have deviated. Whoever submits, those have sought out right (guidance), **15** but as for the ones who have deviated, they have become firewood for Gehenna!"'[11]

16 And (We say) that if they[12] had gone straight on the road, We would indeed have given them water to drink in abundance, **17** so that We might test them concerning it. Whoever turns away from the

---

Q72: This sūra is said to have been revealed after the Prophet's return to Mecca from Ṭā'if (c. 621CE). On his way back some jinn are reported to have heard him reciting the Qur'ān, and came to believe. Their affirmations make up the first half of the sūra, which then concludes with a series of pronouncements by the Prophet. Most scholars assign Q72 to the 'Meccan' period.

1–15 Jinn affirm the Qur'ān

1. *Say*: on this form of address, see n. on Q2.80 (four other sūras begin with this imperative, see Q109 and Q112-114).
2. *I am inspired*: or 'I have received inspiration.'
3. *the jinn listened*: cf. Q72.14 (below), which indicates that some of the jinn were 'Muslims' (see n. on Q6.100); according to Q46.29, they went off to proclaim the message to their fellow jinn.
4. *an amazing Qur'ān*: or 'an amazing recitation,' referring to a portion of the Qur'ān.
5. *And (we believe) that...*: this repeated construction introduces a series of affirmations on the part of the jinn.
6. *son*: or 'child' (Ar. *walad*).
7. *individuals*: lit. 'men.'
8. *harsh guards and piercing flames*: angels were supposed to keep demons from the 'eavesdropping' on the heavenly council by hurling shooting stars at them (cf. Q15.17-18; 37.9-10).
9. *the guidance*: one of the most frequent terms (Ar. *al-hudā*) for revelation in general, and the Qur'ān in particular.
10. *have submitted*: or 'are Muslims.'
11. *Gehenna*: a name for Hell (see n. on Q2.206).

16–19 A warning

12. *And (We say) that if they...*: while the same construction ('And that...') continues, the speaker suddenly switches from the jinn to God (or the angels), and 'they' now refers to humans.

remembrance of his Lord – He will place him in hard punishment. **18** And that the mosques (belong) to God, so do not call on anyone (along) with God. **19** And that when the servant of God[13] stood calling on Him,[14] they[15] were almost upon him in hordes.

20 Say: 'I call only on my Lord, and I do not associate anyone with Him.'

21 Say: 'Surely I possess no power over you, either for harm or for right (guidance).'

22 Say: 'No one will protect me from God, and I shall not find any refuge other than Him. **23** (I bring) only a delivery[16] from God and His messages.' Whoever disobeys God and His messenger, surely for him (there is) the Fire of Gehenna, there to remain forever. **24** – Until, when they see what they are promised, they will know who is weaker in helper(s) and fewer in number.

25 Say: 'I do not know whether what you are promised is near, or whether my Lord will appoint[17] a (distant) time for it.[18] **26** (He is) the Knower of the unseen,[19] and He does not disclose His unseen to anyone, **27** except to a messenger whom He has approved, and then He dispatches before him and behind him (watchers) lying in wait,[20] **28** so that He may know that they have delivered the messages of their Lord. He encompasses all that is with them, and He counts everything by number.'[21]

13. *servant of God*: usually taken to be the Prophet; the word 'servant' (Ar. *'abd*) also means 'slave.'
14. *calling on Him*: in prayer.
15. *they*: usually taken to refer to the jinn.

20–28 A SERIES OF DECLARATIONS

16. *delivery*: referring to the Qur'ān, either in whole or in part (cf. Q3.20).
17. *appoint*: lit. 'make.'
18. *it*: judgment.
19. *the unseen*: here referring to 'the future' (see n. on Q2.3).
20. *(watchers) lying in wait*: i.e. angels who keep watch on the messenger to make sure he faithfully carries out his mission (cf. Q6.61; 13.11).
21. *He counts everything by number*: i.e. keeps a record or 'account book' of everything (cf. Q36.12).

73 The Enwrapped One ❁ Al-Muzzammil

In the Name of God, the Merciful, the Compassionate

1 You, enwrapped one![1] **2** Stay up through the night, except a little **3** – half of it or a little less,
4 or a little more[2] – and arrange the Qur'ān very carefully.[3] **5** Surely We shall cast upon you a heavy
word. **6** Surely the first part of the night – it is more efficacious[4] and more suitable for speaking. **7** Surely
during the day you have protracted business, **8** but remember the name of your Lord and devote
yourself to Him completely.

9 Lord of the East and the West – (there is) no god but Him, so take Him as a guardian, **10** and be patient[5]
with what they say, and forsake them gracefully.[6] **11** Leave Me (to deal with) the ones who call (it) a
lie – (those) possessors of prosperity – and let them be for a little (while). **12** Surely We have chains and
a Furnace,[7] **13** and food that chokes, and a painful punishment, **14** on the Day when the earth and the
mountains will quake, and the mountains will become a heap of shifting sand.

15 Surely We have sent to you a messenger[8] as a witness over you, as We sent to Pharaoh a messenger.[9]
16 But Pharaoh disobeyed the messenger, and We seized him harshly.[10] **17** If you disbelieve, how will you
guard (yourselves) against a Day which will turn the children grey, **18** on which the sky will be split open
and His promise comes to pass? **19** Surely this is a Reminder,[11] and whoever pleases takes a way to his Lord.

20 Surely your Lord knows that you[12] stay up nearly two-thirds of the night – or a half of it or a third

---

Q73: This sūra opens with the Prophet being urged to spend the night attending to the Qur'ān. This is followed by a warning to the people and an appeal for belief. It concludes with a modification of what was imposed at the beginning of the sūra. Most scholars assign Q73 to the 'Meccan' period, except for the long final verse which is generally agreed to be 'Medinan.' Its title comes from the opening address to the Prophet as 'the one wrapped up in his robe.'

1-8 The Prophet to attend to the Qur'ān throughout the night

1. *enwrapped one*: this is how the word is usually understood (cf. Q74.1), but 'overburdened one' may be closer to its the root meaning.
2. *half of it, or...*: this qualification (vv. 3-4a) looks like a later addition.
3. *arrange the Qur'ān very carefully*: lit. 'arrange the Qur'ān (by/in) an arranging' (Ar. *rattili...tartīlan*), possibly referring to elocution or to composition (cf. Q25.32), though it is usually taken as a reference to the formal recitation (or cantillation) of the Qur'ān.
4. *more efficacious*: or 'stronger in impression' (lit. 'stronger in step'), but the meaning is obscure.

9–14 Leave the disbelievers to God

5. *and be patient...*: the Cairo edition, reflecting the views of traditional scholars, attributes the following two verses to the 'Medinan' period.
6. *forsake them gracefully*: lit. 'flee from them with a graceful fleeing' (from the same root as Hijra).
7. *Furnace*: a name for Hell (Ar. *jaḥīm*).

15–19 A warning and appeal for belief

8. *messenger*: for this important title, see n. on Q2.87.
9. *messenger*: Moses.
10. *seized him harshly*: lit. 'seized him with a heavy seizing.'
11. *this is a Reminder*: referring to the Qur'ān (see n. on Q3.58).

20 Abrogation of night vigils

12. *you*: the Prophet. The Cairo edition, reflecting the views of traditional scholars, attributes the long final verse

of it – and (so do) a contingent of those with you. God determines the night and the day. He knows that you[13] do not count it up,[14] and He has turned to you (in forgiveness). So recite[15] what is easy (for you) of the Qur'ān. He knows that some of you are sick, and others are striking forth on the earth, seeking some of the favor of God,[16] and (still) others are fighting in the way of God. So recite what is easy (for you) of it, and observe the prayer and give the alms,[17] and lend to God a good loan.[18] Whatever good you send forward for yourselves, you will find it with God – it will be better and greater as a reward. Ask forgiveness from God. Surely God is forgiving, compassionate.

---

to the 'Medinan' period (a view also shared by most modern scholars). It is understood to cancel the command at 73.2-4 (above), though what follows is addressed generally.

13. *you*: plur. (here and throughout the rest of this section).
14. *do not count it up*: i.e. do not keep an exact record of the time.
15. *recite*: or 'read aloud' (plur. imperative).
16. *seeking some of the favor of God*: i.e. seeking to make a livelihood.
17. *observe the prayer and give the alms*: i.e. *ṣalāt*, the ritual prayer, and *zakāt*, a kind of tithe required for the benefit of the poor, as well as other purposes.
18. *lend to God a good loan*: by contributing to or 'investing in' God's cause (cf. Q2.245; 5.12; 30.39; 57.11; 64.17).

74 The Cloaked One ❁ Al-Muddaththir

In the Name of God, the Merciful, the Compassionate

1 You, cloaked one![1] **2** Arise and warn! **3** Magnify your Lord, **4** and purify your clothes, **5** and flee from the defilement![2] **6** Do not confer a favor to gain more, **7** and be patient before your Lord. **8** When there is a blast on the trumpet,[3] **9** that Day will be a hard Day **10** – far from easy on the disbelievers.

11 Leave Me (to deal with) him whom I created alone,[4] **12** and for whom I supplied[5] extensive wealth, **13** and sons as witnesses, **14** and made everything smooth for him. **15** Then he is eager that I should do more. **16** By no means! He is stubborn to Our signs.[6] **17** I shall burden him with a hard climb. **18** Surely he thought and decided – **19** so may he perish (for) how he decided! **20** Once again, may he perish (for) how he decided! **21** Then he looked, **22** then he frowned and scowled, **23** then he turned back and became arrogant, **24** and said, 'This is nothing but ordinary magic.[7] **25** This is nothing but the word[8] of a human being.' **26** I shall burn him in Saqar![9]

27 And what will make you[10] know what Saqar is? **28** It spares nothing, and leaves nothing, **29** scorching all flesh.[11] **30** Over it are nineteen.[12] **31** We have made only angels as keepers[13] of the Fire,[14] and We have

---

Q74: This sūra is a collection of diverse passages. It opens with a command to the Prophet to 'arise and warn' (which led some scholars to consider Q74 the earliest sūra in the Qur'ān). This is followed by sections dealing with an opponent, the number of angels guarding Hell, and the fate awaiting those who disregard the message. Most scholars consider Q74 an early 'Meccan' sūra. Its title comes from the opening address to the Prophet as 'the one wrapped up in his cloak.'

1–10 Arise and warn

1. *cloaked one*: the dathār was a kind of outer garment or coat (cf. Q73.1). The Prophet is said to have covered himself with his cloak when the revelation came to him.
2. *defilement*: perhaps meaning the defilement of 'idolatry' (see Q22.30; cf. Q8.11); but it may refer to the coming 'wrath' (see Q34.5; 45.11; cf. Matthew 3.7).
3. *a blast on the trumpet*: the Last Day will be announced by the blast of a trumpet (e.g. Q6.73; 20.102; 39.68 [a double blast]; 69.13; 78.18; cf. Matthew 24.31; 1 Corinthians 15.52; 1 Thessalonians 4.16).

11–26 God will deal with an opponent

4. *him whom I created alone*: said to refer to al-Walīd ibn al-Mughīra, a steadfast opponent of the Prophet (cf. Q68.10-16); but it may simply be a depiction of a typical disbeliever.
5. *supplied*: lit. 'made.'
6. *signs*: or 'verses' (see n. on Q2.39).
7. *ordinary magic*: i.e. unoriginal, derivative.
8. *word*: or 'speech' (i.e. way of speaking).
9. *Saqar*: a name for Hell, as is explained in what follows (but mentioned only here and at Q54.48).

27–31 The guards of Hell

10. *you*: sing., but intended generally (for this phrase, cf. Q69.3; 77.14; 82.17-18; 83.8; 86.2; 90.12; 97.2; 101.3; 104.5).
11. *all flesh*: or 'humankind.'
12. *nineteen*: i.e. angel guards; the number may go back to Gnostic cosmology in which the seven planets and twelve signs of the zodiac were combined. (The rest of this section, sometimes regarded as one verse [as here], or divided into four, may be a later addition to address speculation about the mysterious number 'nineteen.')
13. *keepers*: lit. 'companions.'
14. *the Fire*: Ar. *al-nār* is the most common of the various designations for Hell, here used to explain Saqar.

made their number only as a test[15] for the disbelievers, so that those who have been given the Book may be certain, and that those who believe may increase in belief, and that those who have been given the Book and those who believe may not be in doubt, and that those in whose hearts is a sickness[16] and the disbelievers may say, 'What did God intend by this as a parable?' In this way God leads astray whomever He pleases and guides whomever He pleases. No one knows the (angelic) forces of your Lord but Him. It[17] is nothing but a reminder[18] to humankind.

32 By no means! By the moon,[19] **33** and the night when it retreats, **34** and the morning when it brightens!
35 Surely it is indeed one of the greatest things **36** – a warning to humankind – **37** to whoever of you
pleases to go forward or lag behind.

38 Each person (is held) in pledge for what he has earned,[20] **39** except for the companions on the right.[21]
40 In Gardens[22] they will ask each other questions **41** about the sinners: **42** 'What put you into Saqar?'
43 They will say, 'We were not among the ones who prayed,[23] **44** and we did not feed the poor, **45** and we
bantered with the banterers, **46** and we called the Day of Judgment a lie, **47** until the certainty[24] came to
us.' **48** The intercession of the intercessors will not benefit them.

49 What is (the matter) with them, turning away from the Reminder, **50** as if they were frightened
donkeys **51** fleeing from a lion? **52** No! Each one of them wants to be given scrolls unrolled.[25] **53** By no
means! No! They do not fear the Hereafter.[26] **54** By no means! Surely it is a reminder, **55** and whoever
pleases takes heed of it. **56** But they will not take heed unless God pleases. He is worthy of guarding
(oneself) against, and worthy of (dispensing) forgiveness.

---

15. *test*: or 'trial,' 'temptation' (Ar. *fitna*).
16. *those in whose hearts is a sickness*: i.e. false believers or 'hypocrites.'
17. *It*: the Qur'ān (cf. Q74.49, 54 below).
18. *reminder*: see n. on Q3.58.

32–37 A warning

19. *By the moon...*: i.e. 'I swear by...;' for the oaths which follow, cf. Q81.15-19.

38–48 Fate of sinners

20. *for what he has earned*: i.e. for his deeds.
21. *companions on the right*: the believers (see Q56.27-40, 90-91).
22. *Gardens*: in heaven (for this imagery, see n. on Q2.25).
23. *the ones who prayed*: i.e. the ritual prayer (or *ṣalāt*).
24. *the certainty*: referring to death or judgment (cf. Q15.99; 102.5, 7).

49–56 The reminder is rejected

25. *scrolls unrolled*: or 'pages spread out;' i.e. each one wants (demands?) a revealed book for himself, or wants (dares?) to be presented with the record of his deeds, because he 'has no fear of the Hereafter' (as the following verse states). The word 'pages' (lit. 'leaves' or 'sheets,' Ar. *ṣuḥuf*) occurs several times in connection with the Qur'ān (Q80.13), the revelation to Abraham and Moses (Q53.36-37; 87.18-19; cf. Q20.133), and perhaps the heavenly archetype (Q98.2-3). It is also used for the 'record' of a person's deeds (Q81.10).
26. *the Hereafter*: see n. on Q2.4.

75 THE RESURRECTION ❁ AL-QIYĀMA

In the Name of God, the Merciful, the Compassionate

1 I swear by the Day of Resurrection![1] **2** And I swear by the accusing self![2] **3** Does the human think that We shall not gather his bones? **4** Yes indeed! We are (even) able to fashion his fingers (again). **5** Yet the human (still) wants to know what is in store for him.[3] **6** He asks, 'When is the Day of Resurrection?' **7** When the sight is dazed, **8** and the moon is eclipsed,[4] **9** and the sun and moon are brought together, **10** on that Day the human will say, 'Where is the escape?' **11** By no means! (There is) no refuge! **12** The (only) dwelling place on that Day will be to your Lord. **13** On that Day the human will be informed about what has he sent forward and kept back.[5] **14** No! The human will be a clear proof against himself,[6] **15** even though he offers[7] his excuses.

16 Do not move your tongue with it to hurry it.[8] **17** Surely on Us (depends) its collection and its recitation. **18** When We recite it,[9] follow its recitation.[10] **19** Then surely on Us (depends) its explanation.[11]

20 By no means! No! You[12] love this fleeting (world), **21** and neglect the Hereafter.[13] **22** (Some) faces that Day will be radiant, **23** looking to their Lord, **24** and (other) faces that Day will be scowling, **25** thinking that a calamity will be visited on them. **26** By no means! When it[14] reaches the collarbones, **27** and it is said, 'Who will carry (him) off?,'[15] **28** and he thinks that the parting has come, **29** when leg is tangled with leg,[16] **30** the (only) drive on that Day will be to your Lord.

Q75: This sūra is a collection of short passages, most of which revolve around the Last Day and God's power to raise the dead. Noteworthy among them is a section dealing with the Prophet's method of reciting the Qur'ān. Most scholars consider Q75 an early 'Meccan' sūra. Its title comes from the oath with which it begins.

1–15 RESURRECTION ON THE LAST DAY

1. *I swear by...*: for God's swearing by things, cf. Q56.75; 69.38-39; 81.15-18; 84.16-18; 90.1, 3.
2. *the accusing self*: meaning obscure; either the person who will blame himself for having rejected the message, or who will cast blame on others.
3. *to know what is in store for him*: translation conjectural.
4. *eclipsed*: lit. 'swallowed' (cf. Ezekiel 32.7).
5. *what he has sent forward and kept back*: i.e. all his deeds.
6. *clear proof against himself*: for this idea, cf. Q24.24; 36.65; 41.20.
7. *offers*: lit. 'casts.'

16–19 METHOD FOR RECITING THE QUR'ĀN

8. *to hurry it*: cf. Q20.114.
9. *recite it*: or 'read it aloud.'
10. *follow its recitation*: unless 'We' refers to the angels, this implies that the Prophet actually heard the Qur'ān recited (or 'dictated') by God himself.
11. *its explanation*: cf. Q55.4.

20–30 JUDGMENT CERTAIN

12. *You*: plur.
13. *the Hereafter*: see n. on Q2.3.
14. *it*: the person's 'self' as it departs at death.
15. *Who will carry (him) off*: i.e. who will take him away at death (spoken by the angels).
16. *leg is tangled with leg*: perhaps as a preparation for burial.

31 (For) he did not affirm (it),[17] nor did he pray, **32** but he called (it) a lie and turned away. **33** Then he
went to his household with an arrogant swagger. **34** Nearer to you and nearer![18] **35** Once again, nearer
to you and nearer! **36** Does the human think that he will be left to go about at will? **37** Was he not a drop
of semen emitted? **38** Then he was a clot, and He created and fashioned (him), **39** and made from it the
two sexes, the male and the female. **40** Is that One not able to give the dead life?

31–40 A DENIER REBUKED

17. *(For) he did not affirm (it)*: this verse begins abruptly, and probably did not follow the previous section originally.
18. *Nearer to you and nearer*: perhaps a threatening reference to the unavoidable approach of death or judgment ('you' is sing.).

76 The Human ۞ Al-Insān

In the Name of God, the Merciful, the Compassionate

1 Has (there) come upon the human a period of time when he was a thing not mentioned?[1] **2** Surely We created the human from a drop, a mixture[2] – We test him[3] – and We made him hearing (and) seeing. **3** Surely We guided him to the way, (to see) whether (he would be) thankful or whether (he would be) ungrateful.[4]

4 Surely We have prepared for the disbelievers chains and fetters and a blazing (Fire). **5** Surely the pious will drink from a cup containing a mixture of camphor, **6** (from) a spring at which the servants of God drink, making it gush forth abundantly.[5] **7** They fulfill (their) vows, and fear a Day – its evil is (already) in the air – **8** and they give food, despite their love for it,[6] to the poor, and the orphan, and the captive: **9** 'We feed you only for the face of God.[7] We do not desire any payment or thanks from you. **10** Surely we fear a grim (and) ominous Day from our Lord.' **11** So God has guarded them against the evil of that Day, and made them encounter radiance and happiness, **12** and repaid them for their patience with a Garden[8] and silk. **13** Reclining there on couches, **14** they do not see there any (hot) sun or bitter cold,[9] and its shades are close upon them, and its clusters (of fruit) near (at hand). **15** Vessels of silver and cups made of crystal are passed around among them **16** – crystal of silver which they have measured very exactly.[10] **17** There they are given a cup to drink, containing a mixture of ginger, **18** (from) a spring there named Salsabīl.[11] **19** And boys of eternal youth circulate among them. When you[12] see them, you

---

Q76: This sūra opens with a reference to the generation of humans, describes the rewards awaiting the righteous, and closes with an exhortation to the Prophet to remain steadfast. While most modern scholars assign Q76 to the 'Meccan' period, most traditional scholars consider it 'Medinan' (including the Cairo edition). It also goes under the name 'Time' (Ar. *al-Dahr*).

1–3 The creation of humans

1. *time when he was a thing not mentioned*: referring to the time before birth; an allusion to the familiar claim that God created humans the first time and will be able to 'recreate' them at the resurrection (cf. e.g. Q19.9, 67).
2. *a drop, a mixture*: referring to a male 'drop' of semen and the 'mingling' of it with some element within the female.
3. *We test him*: this phrase seems out of place as it stands (perhaps a scribal error), and would fit better if transferred to the middle of the following verse ('We guided him to the way, testing him, whether…').
4. *ungrateful*: Ar. *kafūr*, punning on *kāfir*, 'disbeliever' (cf. Q76.24 below).

4–22 Rewards for the righteous

5. *making it gush forth abundantly*: i.e. whenever they wish (the sentence is difficult to construe, but the general sense is clear).
6. *despite their love for it*: or 'for love of Him.'
7. *for the face of God*: i.e. to win God's favor.
8. *Garden*: in heaven (for this imagery, see n. on Q2.25).
9. *bitter cold*: meaning uncertain.
10. *crystal of silver which they have measured very exactly*: meaning uncertain; variously interpreted as implying that the righteous will receive any size cup they wish, or as much of its contents as they wish, or that its size will correspond to the deeds they have done.
11. *Salsabīl*: mentioned only here.
12. *you*: sing., but intended generally.

(would) think them scattered pearls. **20** When you see (it all), then you will see bliss and a great kingdom. **21** On them[13] are green clothes of silk and brocade, and they are adorned with bracelets of silver, and their Lord gives them a pure drink to drink. **22** 'Surely this is a payment for you, and your striving is appreciated.'

23 Surely We – We have sent down on you the Qur'ān once and for all.[14] **24** So be patient for the Judgment of your Lord, and do not obey any sinner (or) ungrateful one[15] among them. **25** But remember the name of your Lord morning and evening, **26** and part of the night, and prostrate yourself before Him, and glorify Him all night long.

27 Surely these (people) love the fleeting (world), and leave behind them a heavy Day.[16] **28** We created them and strengthened their constitution, and when We please, We shall exchange the likes of them.[17] **29** Surely this is a Reminder,[18] and whoever pleases takes a way to his Lord. **30** But you will not (so) please unless God pleases. Surely God is knowing, wise. **31** He causes whomever He pleases to enter into His mercy, but the evildoers – He has prepared a painful punishment for them.

---

13. *them*: the righteous.

23–26 The Prophet to be patient

14. *once and for all*: or 'all at once' (lit. 'We have sent down on you the Qur'ān [with] a sending down'). The verbal noun 'a sending down' (Ar. *tanzīlan*) is usually understood as meaning 'gradually' or 'in stages,' consistent with the traditional view that the Qur'ān was 'sent down' or revealed at intervals over a period of some twenty years. But that meaning is open to question. The word *tanzīlan* is used as a cognate accusative to give added emphasis to the main verb, 'We have sent down' (*nazzalnā*). A similar expression occurs at Q17.106 (cf. Q25.25, where it is used of the 'sending down' of all the angels on the Last Day). Some interpreters claim that it was the Qur'ān's 'serial mode' of revelation which distinguished it from the revelation of the Torah, but it is not certain that is being affirmed here. In fact there are other passages which indicate that the Qur'ān was 'sent down' or revealed all at once (see Q2.89; 3.3, 7; 4.105; 5.48; 6.92; 8.41; 16.64; 17.106; 26.193-194; 28.86; 44.3; 46.12, 30; 97.1; cf. Q2.185, 'The month of Ramaḍān, in which the Qur'ān was sent down'). There were similarly conflicting views within Judaism about the revelation of the Torah. According to the Babylonian Talmud (Gittin 60a), some thought the Torah had been 'transmitted scroll by scroll,' others that it had been 'transmitted entire.'
15. *ungrateful one*: or 'disbeliever' (a pun).

27–31 A warning

16. *leave behind them a heavy Day*: i.e. they disregard the Day of Judgment.
17. *exchange the likes of them*: i.e. substitute another people for them.
18. *this is a Reminder*: referring to the Qur'ān (see n. on Q3.58).

77 The Ones Sent Forth ❁ Al-Mursalāt

In the Name of God, the Merciful, the Compassionate

1 By the ones sent forth[1] in succession,[2] and the ones blasting (with their) blast! **2** By the scatterers **3** (with their) scattering, **4** and the ones splitting asunder, **5** and the ones casting a reminder,[3] **6** as an excuse or warning! **7** Surely what you are promised is indeed going to fall!

8 When the stars are obliterated, **9** and when the sky is split open, **10** and when the mountains are scattered (as dust),[4] **11** and when the messengers' time is given – **12** for what Day are these things appointed? **13** For the Day of Decision![5]

14 And what will make you[6] know what the Day of Decision is? **15** Woe that Day to the ones who call (it) a lie![7]

16 Did We not destroy those of old?[8] **17** Then We caused later (generations) to follow them. **18** In this way We deal with the sinners. **19** Woe that Day to the ones who call (it) a lie!

20 Did We not create you from despicable water, **21** and put it in a secure dwelling place[9] **22** for a known term? **23** We determined (it) – excellent were the Ones able (to do that)![10] **24** Woe that Day to the ones who call (it) a lie!

25 Did We not make the earth as a container **26** of the living and dead? **27** And did We not place on it lofty mountains, and give you fresh water to drink? **28** Woe that Day to the ones who call (it) a lie!

29 Depart to what you called a lie! **30** Depart to a three-branched shadow[11] **31** – (it affords) no sheltering (shade) and (it is of) no use against the flame. **32** Surely it shoots out sparks, (each one) the size of a

---

Q77: This sūra, unified by the theme of coming punishment, opens with a series of vivid affirmations of the certainty of judgment, and then, just as vividly, describes the signs of the Last Day. The remainder of the sūra is a series of eschatological 'woes' directed against those who deny judgment. Most scholars assign Q77 to the early or middle 'Meccan' period. It takes its name from a word in the opening verse.

1–7 Judgment certain

1. *By the ones sent forth...*: i.e. 'I swear by...;' the first five verses contain fem. plur. participles, which probably refer to the winds of an approaching storm as a metaphor for the arrival of Judgment Day, but they are so cryptic that their precise meaning can only be guessed at. For sūras that begin with oaths by female entities like these, see Q37.1-3; 51.1-4; 79.1-5; 100.1-5.
2. *succession*: meaning uncertain.
3. *casting a reminder*: cf. Q28.86; 40.15.

8–13 Signs of the Last Day

4. *scattered (as dust)*: cf. Q20.105.
5. *Day of Decision*: or 'Day of Distinguishing,' i.e. between the righteous and the wicked (cf. Q37.21; 44.40; 78.17).

14–50 Eschatological woes

6. *you*: sing., but intended generally (for this phrase, cf. Q69.3; 74.27; 82.17-18; 83.8; 86.2; 90.12; 97.2; 101.3; 104.5).
7. *Woe that Day...*: this serves as a refrain throughout the remainder of the passage.
8. *Did We not destroy those of old*: referring to earlier generations who were destroyed for rejecting their messengers (cf. Q77.38 below; see n. on Q7.59).
9. *water...a secure dwelling place*: referring to semen and the womb.
10. *the Ones able (to do that)*: unless this refers to the angels, the plur. participle refers to God himself.
11. *three-branched shadow*: reference obscure; said to be the smoke of Hell rising in three columns (cf. Q56.43-44).

castle, **33** as if it were (the color) of yellow camels. **34** Woe that Day to the ones who call (it) a lie!

35 This is a Day when they will not speak, **36** nor will it be permitted to them to make excuses.
37 Woe that Day to the ones who call (it) a lie!

38 'This is the Day of Decision. We have gathered you and those of old together. **39** If you have a plot,
plot against Me!' **40** Woe that Day to the ones who call (it) a lie!

41 Surely the ones who guard (themselves)[12] will be in (the midst of) shades and springs, **42** and fruits
of whatever (kind) they desire: **43** 'Eat and drink with satisfaction (in return) for what you have done.'
44 Surely in this way We repay the doers of good. **45** Woe that Day to the ones who call (it) a lie!

46 'Eat and enjoy (life) a little. Surely you are sinners!' **47** Woe that Day to the ones who call (it) a lie!

48 When it is said to them, 'Bow down,' they do not bow down.[13] **49** Woe that Day to the ones who call
(it) a lie!

50 In what proclamation[14] will they believe after this?

12. *guard (themselves)*: against evil, or God.

13. *When it is said...*: the Cairo edition, reflecting the views of traditional scholars, attributes this verse to the 'Medinan' period.

14. *proclamation*: or 'report' (Ar. *ḥadīth*).

78 The News ۞ Al-Naba'

In the Name of God, the Merciful, the Compassionate

1 What are they asking each other questions about? **2** About the awesome news,[1] **3** concerning which they differ. **4** By no means! Soon they will know! **5** Once again, by no means! Soon they will know!

6 Have We not made the earth as a bed, **7** and the mountains as stakes? **8** We created you in pairs, **9** and made your sleep as a rest, **10** and made the night as a covering, **11** and made the day for (your) livelihood. **12** We have built above you seven firm (heavens), **13** and made a blazing lamp.[2] **14** We have sent down water from the rainclouds, pouring forth, **15** so that by means of it We may bring forth grain and vegetation, **16** and luxuriant gardens.

17 Surely the Day of Decision[3] is an appointed time: **18** the Day when there will be a blast on the trumpet,[4] and you will come in crowds, **19** and the sky will be opened and become gates, **20** and the mountains will be moved and become a mirage. **21** Surely Gehenna[5] lies in wait **22** as a (place of) return for the insolent transgressors, **23** there to remain for ages. **24** They will not taste there any coolness or drink, **25** except for boiling (water) and rotten (food)[6] **26** – a fitting payment! **27** Surely they were not expecting a reckoning **28** when they called Our signs an utter lie. **29** But We have counted up everything in a Book.[7] **30** So: 'Taste (it)! We shall only increase you in punishment.'

31 Surely for the ones who guard (themselves)[8] (there is) a (place of) safety: **32** orchards and grapes, **33** and full-breasted (maidens), (all) of the same age, **34** and a cup full (of wine) **35** – in which they will not hear any frivolous talk, nor any lying **36** – a payment from your Lord, a gift, a reckoning!

37 Lord of the heavens and the earth, and whatever is between them, the Merciful, of whom they have no power to speak. **38** On the Day when the spirit[9] and the angels stand in lines, they will not speak, except the one to whom the Merciful has given permission, and he will say what is correct. **39** That is the true Day. Whoever pleases takes a (way of) return to his Lord. **40** Surely We have warned you of a

---

Q78: This sūra, which begins with 'the news' of impending judgment, extols the power and providence of God, and describes the events of the Last Day, including the different fates awaiting believers and disbelievers. Most scholars assign Q78 to the early or middle 'Meccan' period.

1–5 Judgment imminent

1. *awesome news*: lit. 'great news,' of judgment and punishment.

6–16 Signs of God's power and providence

2. *a blazing lamp*: the sun (cf. Q25.61; 71.16).

17–40 The Last Day

3. *Day of Decision*: or 'Day of Distinguishing,' i.e. between the righteous and the wicked (cf. Q37.21; 44.40; 77.12-13).
4. *a blast on the trumpet*: the Last Day will be announced by the blast of a trumpet (e.g. Q6.73; 18.99; 20.102; 39.68 [a double blast]; 69.13; 74.8; cf. Matthew 24.31; 1 Corinthians 15.52; 1 Thessalonians 4.16).
5. *Gehenna*: a name for Hell (see n. on Q2.206).
6. *rotten (food)*: meaning uncertain.
7. *Book*: i.e. the heavenly 'Record' or 'Account' of people's deeds (see n. on Q6.59).
8. *guard (themselves)*: against evil, or God.
9. *the spirit*: for this mysterious being, see e.g. Q16.2; 40.15; 42.52. Some interpreters identify 'the spirit' with Gabriel (see n. on Q2.97).

punishment near (at hand), on the Day when a person will see what his hands have sent forward,[10] and the disbeliever will say, 'Would that I were dust!'

10. *what his hands have sent forward*: i.e. his deeds, which are 'sent forward' to the Judgment.

79 The Snatchers ✵ Al-Nāzi'āt

In the Name of God, the Merciful, the Compassionate

1 By the ones who snatch violently![1] **2** By the ones who draw out completely! **3** By the ones who glide
smoothly, **4** and race swiftly, **5** and direct the affair![2] **6** On the Day when the (earth)quake quakes, **7** and that
which ensues follows it,[3] **8** hearts on that Day will pound, **9** their sight downcast. **10** They will say, 'Are we
indeed being turned back into (our) former state?[4] **11** When we were rotten bones?' **12** They will say, 'That
would then be a losing turn!' **13** Yet it will only be a single shout, **14** and suddenly they will be awakened.

15 Has the story of Moses[5] come to you?[6] **16** When his Lord called to him in the holy wādi of Ṭuwā:[7] **17** 'Go
to Pharaoh! Surely he has transgressed insolently. **18** And say: "Do you have (any desire) to purify yourself?" **19** And: "I would guide you to your Lord, and then perhaps you will fear (Him)."' **20** So he showed
him the great sign,[8] **21** but he called (it) a lie and disobeyed. **22** Then he turned away in haste, **23** and he
gathered (his people) and called out, **24** and said, 'I am your Lord, the Most High!' **25** So God seized him
with the punishment of the last and the first.[9] **26** Surely in that is a lesson indeed for whoever fears.

27 Are you a stronger creation or the sky?[10] He built it. **28** He raised its roof and fashioned it. **29** He
darkened its night and brought forth its morning light. **30** And the earth, after that, He spread it out.
31 He brought forth from it its water and its pasture **32** – and the mountains, He anchored it (to them)[11]
– **33** a provision for you and for your livestock.

Q79: This sūra opens with a series of affirmations which lead into a dramatic representation of sinners at the resurrection. This is followed by an abridged version of the story of Moses, as well as passages on God's providential power and the different fates awaiting the righteous and wicked. It concludes with a question: when will the Hour strike? Most scholars assign Q79 to the early or middle 'Meccan' period. It receives its title from the opening verse.

1–14 The Day of Resurrection

1. *By the ones who snatch...*: i.e. 'I swear by...;' the reference may be to angels coming to 'snatch' people at death, but this and the following fem. plur. participles are so cryptic that their precise meaning can only be guessed at. For sūras that begin with oaths by female entities like these, see Q37.1-3; 51.1-4; 77.1-6; 100.1-5.
2. *direct the affair*: or 'direct the command;' a task usually reserved for God (see Q10.3; 13.2; 32.5; 65.12).
3. *that which ensues...*: the resurrection.
4. *former state*: meaning uncertain.

15–26 The story Moses

5. *story of Moses* : or 'report about Moses' (Ar. *ḥadīth Mūsā*); for the story that follows, cf. the longer version at Q20.9-36; and Moses' call at Exodus 3-4.
6. *you*: sing., but probably intended generally.
7. *holy wādi of Ṭuwā*: reference obscure; it is mentioned only here and at Q20.12; cf. Q28.30.
8. *the great sign*: the miracle of Moses' staff turning into a snake (see Q7.106-107; 20.18-21; cf. Exodus 7.8-13).
9. *of the last and the first*: or 'in the Hereafter and in this world' (cf. Q53.25; 92.13).

27–33 Signs of God's power and providence

10. *Are you a stronger creation or the sky*: cf. Q37.11; 40.57.
11. *He anchored it (to them)*: the implication is that the earth is a disc which floats on the surface of the sea (cf. Psalms 24.2; 136.6). In order to keep it from 'pitching' or 'swaying' (see Q16.15; 21.31; 31.10), God has firmly anchored it to mountains (see Q13.3; 15.19; 16.15; 21.31; 27.61; 31.10; 41.10; 50.7; 77.27).

34 When the great overwhelming comes, **35** on the Day when a person will remember what he strove for, **36** and the Furnace[12] will come forth for all to see: **37** as for the one who transgressed insolently, **38** and preferred this present life, **39** surely the Furnace – it will be the refuge. **40** But as for the one who feared the position of his Lord,[13] and restrained himself from (vain) desire, **41** surely the Garden[14] – it will be the refuge.

42 They ask you[15] about the Hour: 'When is its arrival?'[16] **43** What do you have to do with the mention of it? **44** To your Lord is its (ultimate) goal.[17] **45** You are only a warner[18] for whoever fears it. **46** On the Day when they see it, (it will seem) as if they had remained (in the grave) for only an evening or its morning light.

34–41 Punishment and reward

12. *the Furnace*: a name for Hell (Ar. *al-jaḥīm*).
13. *the position of his Lord*: or perhaps 'the judgment seat of his Lord' (cf. Q14.14; 55.46).
14. *Garden*: in heaven (for this imagery, see n. on Q2.25).

42–46 When will the Hour strike?

15. *you*: the Prophet.
16. *its arrival*: lit. 'its anchoring;' cf. Q7.187; and the similar question put to Jesus at Mark 13.3-4 par.
17. *its (ultimate) goal*: cf. Q53.42.
18. *warner*: for this role, see n. on Q2.119.

80 He Frowned ✿ 'Abasa

In the Name of God, the Merciful, the Compassionate

1 He frowned and turned away, **2** because the blind man came to him.[1] **3** What will make you[2] know?
Perhaps he will (yet) purify himself,[3] **4** or take heed,[4] and the Reminder[5] will benefit him. **5** As for the one
who considers himself independent,[6] **6** you give your attention to him. **7** Yet it is not (dependent) on you
if he does not purify himself. **8** But as for the one who comes running to you, **9** and (who) fears (God),
10 from him you are distracted.[7]

11 By no means! Surely it is a Reminder **12** – and whoever pleases (may) take heed of it – **13** (written)
in honored pages,[8] **14** exalted (and) purified, **15** by the hands of scribes, **16** (who are) honorable (and)
dutiful.

17 May the human perish! How ungrateful[9] he is! **18** From what did He create him? **19** From a drop! He
created him, and determined him,[10] **20** then He made the way easy for him, **21** then He caused him to
die and buried him, **22** then, when He pleases, He will raise him (again). **23** By no means! He[11] has not
accomplished what He commanded him.

24 Let the human consider his food: **25** We[12] pour out water in abundance, **26** then We split open the

---

Q80: This sūra begins by admonishing the Prophet not to be concerned exclusively with the rich. Next come sections on the authority of the written message and human ingratitude for God's providential care. It concludes with a vivid scene of the Last Day. Most scholars assign Q80 to the early 'Meccan' period. Its title comes from the first word.

1–10 The Prophet admonished

1. *He frowned and turned away...*: usually taken to refer to the Prophet himself. It is said that while he was talking to some leaders of the Quraysh, a believer, who happened to be blind, interrupted him and asked for teaching, whereupon the Prophet 'frowned and turned away.' God later reproached him for this. Another possible context is that it refers to a rich man who scorned a blind man's request for a handout, and thereby revealed how ineffectual the Prophet's approach to the wealthy had been. He is now exhorted to persevere in the face of apparent failure, and admonished for neglecting those who approach him.
2. *you*: the Prophet.
3. *purify himself*: by giving alms, and thereby indicating his belief .
4. *take heed*: or 'be reminded,' 'remember.'
5. *Reminder*: referring to the Qur'ān (cf. Q80.11 below; see n. on Q3.58).
6. *considers himself independent*: or 'free of need' (i.e. wealthy).
7. *from him you are distracted*: as a result of preaching only to the rich.

11–16 The authority of the written word

8. *pages*: the word 'pages' (lit. 'leaves' or 'sheets,' Ar. *ṣuḥuf*) seems to designate the Qur'ān itself, rather than the heavenly archetype, as is usually held (cf. Q98.2-3). Elsewhere the word occurs in connection with the revelation to Abraham and Moses (Q53.36-37; 87.18-19; cf. Q20.133), as well as to the 'record' of a person's deeds (Q74.52; 81.10).

17–32 People ungrateful

9. *ungrateful*: or 'disbelieving' (perhaps a pun).
10. *determined him*: i.e. whether he would be male or female (see Q22.5; cf. Q77.20-22).
11. *He*: the human.
12. *We...*: notice the sudden shift from third- to first-person discourse.

earth in cracks,[13] **27** and We cause grain to grow in it, **28** and grapes and green plants, **29** and olives and date palms, **30** and lush orchards, **31** and fruits and herbs **32** – a provision for you and your livestock.

33 When the blast comes, **34** on the Day when a person will flee from his brother, **35** and his mother and his father, **36** and his consort and his sons, **37** each of them that Day will have some matter to keep him busy. **38** (Some) faces that Day will be shining, **39** laughing, rejoicing at the good news. **40** But (other) faces that Day – dust will be upon them, **41** (and) darkness will cover them. **42** Those – they are the disbelievers, the depraved.

---

13. *in cracks*: to allow plants to push their way up through the earth.

33–42 The Last Day

81 The Shrouding ❁ Al-Takwīr

In the Name of God, the Merciful, the Compassionate

1 When the sun is shrouded,[1] **2** and when the stars become dim,[2] **3** and when the mountains are moved, **4** and when the pregnant camels[3] are abandoned, **5** and when the wild beasts are herded together, **6** and when the seas are made to surge, **7** and when selves are paired,[4] **8** and when the buried baby girl[5] is asked **9** for what sin she was killed, **10** and when the pages are spread open,[6] **11** and when the sky is stripped off, **12** and when the Furnace[7] is set ablaze, **13** and when the Garden[8] is brought near, **14** (then each) person will know what he has presented.[9]

15 I swear by[10] the slinking (stars),[11] **16** the runners, the hiders, **17** by the night when it departs,[12] **18** by the dawn when it breathes! **19** Surely it[13] is indeed the word[14] of an honorable messenger[15] **20** – one full of power,[16] secure with the Holder of the throne, **21** one (to be) obeyed, (and) furthermore trustworthy.[17]

Q81: This sūra consists of two passages: the first is a description of events of the Last Day, the other relates a vision. Most scholars assign Q81 to the early 'Meccan' period. Its title comes from 'the shrouding' of the sun, one of the signs of the Last Day.

1–14 The Last Day

1. *shrouded*: lit. 'wrapped up' (cf. Q39.5).
2. *become dim*: or 'fall.'
3. *pregnant camels*: lit. 'tenners' or 'ten-monthers' (said to be the time when they require the most care).
4. *selves are paired*: said to refer to 'souls' being reunited with their bodies.
5. *buried baby girl*: referring to the practice of female infanticide (see Q16.58-59; cf. Q6.137, 140, 151; 17.31; 60.12).
6. *pages are spread open*: or 'scrolls are unrolled,' referring to the 'Record' of people's deeds (see n. on Q74.52).
7. *the Furnace*: a name for Hell (Ar. *al-jaḥīm*).
8. *Garden*: for this imagery, see n. on Q2.25.
9. *what he has presented*: of good and bad deeds (see Q82.5; cf. Q3.30; 18.49; 75.13).

15–29 A vision

10. *I swear by...*: for God's swearing by things, cf. Q56.75; 69.38-39; 75.1, 2; 84.16-18; 90.1, 3.
11. *the slinking (stars)*: or perhaps 'the slinking (planets),' but cf. the oaths at Q53.1 (the parallel 'vision-text'); 56.75.
12. *departs*: or 'comes on' (the meaning is disputed). The scene seems to describe the break of day, when the stars 'retreat' and 'hide,' and night 'departs.'
13. *it*: the Qur'ān (throughout this section).
14. *word*: or 'speech' (i.e. way of speaking), also at Q81.25 below; cf. Q69.40; 86.13.
15. *honorable messenger*: traditionally identified with Gabriel as the bringer of revelation, but it may to refer to the Prophet himself (see Q69.40; cf. Q44.17, Moses). Some modern scholars contend that the following two lines (vv. 20-21) were added later to make Gabriel the 'honorable messenger,' and to turn what was originally a theophany (cf. Q53.1-18) into an 'angelophany' (or vision of Gabriel).
16. *one full of power*: cf. Q53.5-6.
17. *secure...trustworthy*: cf. the similar description of Joseph in the court of the Egyptian king (Q12.54); each of the following is called a 'trustworthy messenger': Noah (Q26.107), Hūd (Q26.125), Ṣāliḥ (Q26.143), Lot (Q26.162), Shu'ayb (Q26.178), and Moses (Q44.18).

22 Your companion[18] is not possessed.[19] **23** Certainly he did see Him[20] on the clear horizon. **24** He is not grudging of the unseen.[21] **25** It is not the word of an accursed satan.[22] **26** So where will you go?[23] **27** It is nothing but a reminder to the worlds[24] **28** – to whoever of you pleases to go straight. **29** But you will not (so) please unless God pleases, the Lord of the worlds.[25]

---

18. *Your companion*: the Prophet.
19. *possessed*: or 'jinn-struck' (Ar. *majnūn*); see n. on Q7.184.
20. *Him*: God, though usually taken to refer to Gabriel. This appears to be an allusion to (or variant recension of) the theophany described at Q53.1-12 (esp. v. 7).
21. *not grudging of the unseen*: i.e. not unwilling to communicate what has been revealed to him; a variant reading has 'hold baseless opinions of' (Ar. *ẓanīn*, for *ḍanīn*); for 'the unseen,' see n. on Q2.3.
22. *accursed satan*: or 'stoned satan' (see n. on Q2.14; cf. Q69.40-42).
23. *where will you go?*: i.e. what decision will you (plur.) make?
24. *to the worlds*: or 'to all peoples.'
25. *Lord of the worlds*: for this title, see n. on Q1.2.

82 The Rending ۞ Al-Infiṭār

In the Name of God, the Merciful, the Compassionate

1 When the sky is rent, **2** and when the stars are scattered, **3** and when the seas are made to gush forth,[1] **4** and when the graves are ransacked, **5** (then each) person will know what he has sent forward and kept back.[2]

6 Human! What has deceived you about your generous Lord, **7** who created you and fashioned you and balanced you?[3] **8** He constructed you in whatever form He pleased. **9** By no means! No! You (still) call the Judgment[4] a lie. **10** Surely (there are) indeed watchers[5] over you, **11** honorable, writing. **12** They know whatever you do. **13** Surely the pious will indeed be in (a place of) bliss, **14** and surely the depraved will indeed be in a Furnace.[6] **15** They will burn in it on the Day of Judgment, **16** and from it they will not be absent.

17 What will make you[7] know what the Day of Judgment is? **18** Once again, what will make you know what the Day of Judgment is? **19** The Day when no one will have any power to (help) another. The command[8] on that Day (will belong) to God.

Q82: This sūra falls into three related parts: events of the Last Day, the certainty of Judgment, and an explanation of Judgment Day. Most scholars assign Q82 to the early 'Meccan' period. Its title comes from 'the rending' of the sky, one of the signs of the Last Day.

1–5 The Last Day

1. *seas are made to gush forth*: perhaps a reference to the fresh and salt water seas overflowing their barrier (cf. Q81.6), or to the seas giving up their dead (as do the 'graves' in the following verse).
2. *what he has sent forward and kept back*: i.e. all his deeds.

6–16 Judgment certain

3. *balanced you*: perhaps a reference to the symmetry of the human form, but the meaning is uncertain.
4. *the Judgment*: or 'the religion' (i.e. Islam); the word for 'judgment' is a homonym of 'religion' (Ar. *dīn*).
5. *watchers*: the recording angels.
6. *Furnace*: a name for Hell (Ar. *jaḥīm*).

17–19 Judgment Day explained

7. *you*: sing., but intended generally (for this phrase, cf. Q69.3; 74.27; 77.14; 83.8; 86.2; 90.12; 97.2; 101.3; 104.5).
8. *command*: referring to judgment (cf. Q2.109; 4.47; 5.52; 7.150; 10.24; 16.1, 33).

83 THE DEFRAUDERS ❁ AL-MUṬAFFIFĪN

In the Name of God, the Merciful, the Compassionate

1 Woe to the defrauders, **2** who take full measure when they measure against the people, **3** but give less when they measure for themselves or weigh for themselves. **4** Do those (people) not think that they will be raised up **5** for a great Day, **6** a Day when the people will stand before the Lord of the worlds?[1] **7** By no means! Surely the book of the depraved is indeed in Sijjīn.[2] **8** And what will make you[3] know what Sijjīn is? **9** A written book. **10** Woe that Day to the ones who call (it) a lie, **11** who call the Day of Judgment a lie! **12** No one calls it a lie except every transgressor (and) sinner. **13** When Our signs are recited to him,[4] he says, 'Old tales!'[5] **14** By no means! No! What they have earned[6] has rusted on their hearts.[7] **15** By no means! Surely on that Day they will indeed be veiled from their Lord.[8] **16** Then surely they will indeed burn in the Furnace.[9] **17** Then it will be said to them, 'This is what you called a lie.'

18 By no means! Surely the book of the pious is indeed in 'Illiyyīn.[10] **19** And what will make you know what 'Illiyyīn is? **20** A written book. **21** The ones brought near[11] bear witness to it. **22** Surely the pious will indeed be in (a place of) bliss, **23** (lying) on couches gazing about. **24** You will recognize in their faces the radiance of bliss. **25** They are given a pure, sealed wine to drink, **26** its seal is musk – for that let the seekers seek! – **27** and its mixture contains Tasnīm,[12] **28** (from) a spring at which the ones brought near drink.

29 Surely those who sinned used to laugh on account of those who believed, **30** and when they passed them by used to wink at each other. **31** And when they turned back to their people, they turned back

---

Q83: As its title suggests, this sūra opens with a denunciation of those who cheat others by giving 'short measure.' Their punishment is contrasted with the fate of the pious. Most scholars assign Q83 to the 'Meccan' period. The Cairo edition considers it the last of the 'Meccan' sūras.

1–17 THE DEFRAUDERS AND DEPRAVED

1. *Lord of the worlds*: for this title, see n. on Q1.2.
2. *Sijjīn*: may be an intensive form of the word for 'prison' (Ar. *sijn*), and thus originally a reference to Hell, but on the basis of the explanation which follows, it appears to be a book.
3. *you*: sing., but intended generally (for this phrase, cf. Q69.3; 74.27; 77.14; 82.17-18; 86.2; 90.12; 97.2; 101.3; 104.5).
4. *signs are recited to him*: or 'verses are read aloud to him' (see n. on Q2.39).
5. *Old tales*: or 'Tales of the ancients;' a contemptuous reference to the stories of earlier generations who were punished for disobeying their prophets (see n. on Q7.59; cf. Q25.5).
6. *What they have earned*: i.e. their evil deeds.
7. *rusted on their hearts*: and so dulled their perception (here, as often, the heart is spoken of as synonymous with mind).
8. *veiled from their Lord*: i.e. excluded from his presence.
9. *the Furnace*: a name for Hell (Ar. *al-jaḥīm*).

18–28 THE PIOUS

10. *'Illiyyīn*: may be connected with the root meaning 'high' (Ar. *'-l-w*); it is contrasted with Sijjīn.
11. *the ones brought near*: to God's throne (cf. Q40.7); Ar. *al-muqarrabūn* (cognate with Hebr. *kerūbīm*) is a designation of special privilege in the royal court (cf. Q7.114; 26.42). Here it appears to refer to the angels in God's heavenly 'court.' The same expression is used of Jesus (Q3.45) and of certain believers (Q56.10-12).
12. *Tasnīm*: meaning unknown.

29–36 WHO'S LAUGHING NOW?

amused, **32** and when they saw them, they said, 'Surely these (people) have gone astray indeed!'
33 Yet they had not been sent as watchers over them. **34** So today those who believed are laughing on
account of the disbelievers, **35** (as) they gaze about (lying) on couches. **36** Have the disbelievers been
rewarded for what they have done?

84 The Splitting ۞ Al-Inshiqāq

In the Name of God, the Merciful, the Compassionate

1 When the sky is split open,[1] **2** and listens to its Lord and is made fit,[2] **3** and when earth is stretched out,[3]
4 and casts forth what is in it[4] and becomes empty, **5** and listens to its Lord and is made fit, **6** you human
– surely you are laboring to your Lord laboriously and are about to meet Him.

7 As for the one who is given his book[5] in his right (hand), **8** he will receive an easy reckoning, **9** and turn
back to his family, rejoicing. **10** But as for the one who is given his book behind his back, **11** he will call
out for destruction,[6] **12** and burn in a blazing (Fire). **13** Surely he used to be among his family, rejoicing.
14 Surely he thought that he would not return.[7] **15** Yes indeed! Surely his Lord was watching him.

16 I swear by[8] the twilight, **17** by the night and what it envelops,[9] **18** by the moon when it becomes full!
19 You will indeed ride story upon story.[10]

20 What is (the matter) with them that they do not believe, **21** and when the Qur'ān[11] is recited to them,
do not prostrate themselves? **22** No! Those who disbelieve call (it) a lie. **23** Yet God knows what they
hide away.[12] **24** So give them news of a painful punishment **25** – except for those who believe and do
righteous deeds. For them (there is) a reward without end.

Q84: This sūra opens with a description of events of the Last Day which culminate in resurrection and judgment. It concludes with a warning to those who reject the Qur'ān. Most scholars assign Q84 to the early 'Meccan' period. Its title comes from 'the splitting' of the sky, one of the signs of the Last Day.

1–6 The Last Day

1. *sky is split open*: cf. Q25.25; 55.37; 69.16.
2. *made fit*: for the appearance of God (also at v. 5).
3. *stretched out*: usually a description of its creation; here it is said to refer to the leveling of the mountains at the end of days.
4. *what is in it*: the dead.

7–15 The Judgment

5. *his book*: the record of his deeds (cf. Q17.71; 69.19).
6. *call out for destruction*: i.e. wish he were destroyed, rather than having to face punishment.
7. *would not return*: to God, or perhaps 'revert' from prosperity to misfortune.

16–19 The dead will rise

8. *I swear by...*: for God's swearing by things, cf. Q56.75; 69.38-39; 75.1, 2; 81.15-18; 90.1, 3.
9. *envelops*: or 'gathers;' probably referring to the stars.
10. *...ride story upon story*: this mysterious little passage is usually taken of the various 'stages' of life, but it probably refers to those who are resurrected rising through the 'stories' of the seven heavens (cf. Q67.3; 71.15).

20–25 A warning for those who reject the Qur'ān

11. *the Qur'ān*: here close to its present meaning as the name of the Muslim scripture (cf. Q9.111; see n. on Q2.185).
12. *hide away*: or 'hoard' (in their hearts).

85 The Constellations ❁ Al-Burūj

In the Name of God, the Merciful, the Compassionate

1 By the sky full of constellations,[1] **2** by the promised Day, **3** by a witness[2] and what is witnessed! **4** May the companions of the Pit[3] perish **5** – the Fire[4] full of fuel – **6** when they are sitting over it, **7** and they (themselves) are witnesses of what they have done to the believers. **8** They took vengeance on them only because they believed in God, the Mighty, the Praiseworthy, **9** the One who – to Him (belongs) the kingdom of the heavens and the earth. God is a witness over everything.

10 Surely those who persecute the believing men and the believing women, (and) then have not turned (in repentance) – for them (there is) the punishment of Gehenna,[5] and for them (there is) the punishment of the burning (Fire). **11** Surely those who believe and do righteous deeds – for them (there are) Gardens[6] through which rivers flow. That is the great triumph!

12 Surely your Lord's attack is harsh indeed. **13** Surely He – He brings about (the creation) and restores (it). **14** He is the Forgiving, the Loving, **15** Holder of the throne, the Glorious, **16** Doer of what He intends.

17 Has the story[7] of the forces come to you,[8] **18** of Pharaoh and Thamūd?[9] **19** No! But those who disbelieve persist in calling (it) a lie. **20** Yet God surrounds them from behind.

21 Yes! It is a glorious Qur'ān,[10] **22** in a guarded Tablet.[11]

Q85: This sūra promises judgment for disbelievers and reward for believers. Most scholars assign Q85 to the early 'Meccan' period.

1–9 Denizens of the Pit

1. *constellations*: lit. 'towers' (probably the signs of the zodiac).
2. *a witness*: perhaps God.
3. *companions of the Pit*: said to refer to the followers of Dhū Nuwās, the Jewish king of Yemen, who persecuted the Christians of Najrān and is said to have martyred some of them in fire-filled trenches in 523 CE. However, it is more likely a designation for disbelievers in general; cf. the warnings about the 'men/sons of the pit' in the Dead Sea Scrolls (e.g. Damascus Document 4.12-19; 6.11-7.1; 13.14; Community Rule 10.19); and the numerous references to 'the pit' in biblical literature (e.g. Psalms 30.3; 94.13; Isaiah 14.15; 24.17; 38.18; Ezekiel 31.16; 32.23; Job 33.22; 2 Peter 2.4; Revelation 9.1-2; 11.7; 17.8; 21.1-3).
4. *the Fire*: Ar. *al-nār* is the most common of the various designations for Hell.

10–11 Punishment and reward

5. *Gehenna*: a name for Hell (see n. on Q2.206).
6. *Gardens*: in heaven (for this imagery, see n. on Q2.25).

12–16 An awesome God

17–20 Pharaoh and Thamūd

7. *story*: or 'report' (Ar. *ḥadīth*).
8. *you*: the Prophet, or perhaps intended generally.
9. *Pharaoh and Thamūd*: see e.g. Q7.73-79 (people of Thamūd), 103-17 (Pharaoh and his people).

21–22 A glorious Qur'ān

10. *a glorious Qur'ān*: cf. Q50.1; here 'Qur'ān' comes close to its present meaning as the name of the Muslim scripture (cf. Q9.111; see n. on Q2.185).
11. *in a guarded Tablet*: or 'preserved on a Tablet;' usually understood to refer to the heavenly archetype (see Q13.39; 43.4, 'mother of the Book; 56.78, 'hidden Book'), which not only contained the Qur'ān, but the other 'Books' derived from it (i.e. the 'Torah,' 'Gospel,' and 'Psalms'); cf. e.g. the 'heavenly tablet' at 1 Enoch 81.1-2. For the 'Tablets of Moses,' see n. on Q7.145.

86 The Night Visitor ✵ Al-Ṭāriq

In the Name of God, the Merciful, the Compassionate

1 By the sky and the night visitor![1] **2** And what will make you[2] know what the night visitor is? **3** The piercing star![3] **4** Over every person (there is) a watcher.[4] **5** So let the human consider: what was he created from? **6** He was created from spurting water.[5] **7** It comes forth from (a place) between the spine and the ribs. **8** Surely He is able indeed to bring him back, **9** on the Day when (all) secrets will be examined,[6] **10** and he will have no power (and) no helper.

11 By the sky full of returning (rain), **12** by the earth full of cracks![7] **13** Surely it is a decisive word[8] indeed! **14** It is no joke.

15 Surely they are hatching a plot, **16** but I[9] (too) am hatching a plot.[10] **17** So let the disbelievers be, let them be for a little (while).[11]

Q86: This sūra stresses God's power to raise the dead and the accountability of each individual before him. In conclusion the Prophet is told to leave the disbelievers alone temporarily. Most scholars assign Q86 to the 'Meccan' period. Its title comes from a word in the opening verse.

1–10 Each is accountable

1. *By the sky...*: i.e. 'I swear by....'
2. *you*: sing., but intended generally (for this phrase, cf. Q69.3; 74.27; 77.14; 82.17-18; 83.8; 90.12; 97.2; 101.3; 104.5).
3. *piercing star*: or 'shooting star' (cf. Q37.10).
4. *a watcher*: the angel assigned to record a person's deeds (see e.g. Q6.61; 10.21; 82.10-12), though some take it as a reference to God.
5. *spurting water*: semen.
6. *examined*: or 'tried.'

11–14 The message is no joke

7. *cracks*: which allow plants to push their way up through the earth (cf. Q80.25-32).
8. *a decisive word*: or 'a distinct (way of) speaking' (see Q38.20 [David]; cf. Q69.40; 81.19); referring to the message in general or the Qur'ān in particular.

15–17 Let the disbelievers be

9. *I*: God.
10. *hatching a plot*: lit. 'plotting a plot.'
11. *So let the disbelievers be...*: addressed to the Prophet (cf. Q73.11).

87 The Most High ❁ Al-Aʿlā

In the Name of God, the Merciful, the Compassionate

1 Glorify[1] the name of your Lord, the Most High, **2** who creates and fashions, **3** who determines[2] and guides, **4** who brings forth the pasture, **5** and then turns it into darkened ruins. **6** We shall make you recite,[3] and you will not forget – except whatever God pleases.[4] **7** Surely He knows what is spoken publicly and what is hidden. **8** We shall make it very easy for you.[5] **9** So remind (them),[6] if the reminder benefits. **10** He who fears[7] will take heed,[8] **11** but the most miserable will turn away from it **12** – who will burn in the great Fire.[9] **13** Then he will neither die there nor live.

14 Prosperous is he who purifies himself,[10] **15** and remembers the name of his Lord, and prays. **16** No! But you prefer this present life, **17** when the Hereafter[11] is better and more lasting. **18** Surely this is indeed in the former pages, **19** the pages of Abraham and Moses.[12]

Q87: This sūra promises the Prophet God's support in reciting the Qur'ān, and commends those who accept its message. It concludes by emphasizing the superiority of the future life over the present one. Most scholars assign Q87 to the early 'Meccan' period. Its title is one of God's epithets.

1–13 God will support the recitation

1. *Glorify...*: addressed to the Prophet.
2. *determines*: male or female.
3. *recite*: the Qur'ān.
4. *except whatever God pleases...*: vv. 6b-7 may be a later addition (notice the sudden shift from first- to third-person discourse).
5. *We shall make it very easy for you*: lit. 'We shall ease you to the ease;' referring to the recitation of the Qur'ān.
6. *So remind (them)...*: here almost meaning 'warn (them);' see n. on Q3.58; cf. Q50.45; 51.55.
7. *fears*: God, or the warning about judgment.
8. *take heed*: or 'accept the reminder.'
9. *the great Fire*: Ar. *al-nār* is the most common of the various designations for Hell.

14–19 The future life superior

10. *purifies himself*: by giving alms, and thereby indicating his belief.
11. *the Hereafter*: see n. on Q2.4.
12. *the former pages...*: or 'the first scriptures' (Ar. *al-ṣuḥuf al-ūlā*); the word 'pages' (lit. 'leaves' or 'sheets,' Ar. *ṣuḥuf*) occurs several times in connection with the Qur'ān (Q80.13), the revelation to Abraham and Moses (Q53.36-37, where the names are reversed; cf. Q20.133, 'the former pages'), and perhaps the heavenly archetype (Q98.2-3). The word is also used for the 'record' of a person's deeds (Q74.52; 81.10). Here it seems that 'the *ṣuḥuf* of Abraham and Moses' implies something like 'books' or 'scriptures.' Since Abraham was a prophet, it would not be surprising that he too was thought to have received a written revelation or 'book.' See e.g. the 2nd-century CE Jewish-Christian apocalypse known as the Testament of Abraham, in which the patriarch is taken on a 'heavenly tour' by the archangel Michael.

88 The Covering ۞ Al-Ghāshiya

In the Name of God, the Merciful, the Compassionate

1 Has the story[1] of the Covering[2] come to you?[3] **2** (Some) faces that Day will be downcast, **3** laboring,
weary. **4** They will burn in a scorching Fire. **5** They will be made to drink from a boiling spring. **6** They
will have no food except dry thorns, **7** (which) neither nourishes[4] nor satisfies hunger. **8** (Other) faces
that Day will be blessed, **9** content with their striving,[5] **10** in a Garden on high **11** – where they will hear
no frivolous talk, **12** where (there is) a flowing spring, **13** where (there are) raised couches, **14** and cups
laid down, **15** and cushions lined up, **16** and carpets spread out.

17 Will they not look at the camels,[6] how they were created, **18** and at the sky, how it was raised up,
19 and at the mountains, how they were constructed, **20** and at the earth, how it was spread flat?

21 So remind (them)![7] You are only a reminder.[8] **22** You are not a record-keeper[9] over them **23** – except
for the one who turns away and disbelieves. **24** God will punish him with the greatest punishment.
25 Surely to Us is their return. **26** Then surely on Us (depends) their reckoning.

Q88: This sūra contrasts the fates of the righteous and the wicked on the Day of Judgment. It concludes with an exhortation to the Prophet to continue in his role as a 'warner.' Most scholars assign Q88 to the early 'Meccan' period.

1–16 The Covering

1. *story*: or 'report' (Ar. *ḥadīth*).
2. *the Covering*: Judgment Day (cf. Q12.107).
3. *you*: sing., but probably intended generally.
4. *nourishes*: lit. 'fattens.'
5. *content with their striving*: i.e. with the result of their deeds.

17–20 Signs of God's power

6. *camels*: sometimes interpreted as meaning 'clouds.'

21–26 Warn them

7. *So remind (them)*: here almost meaning 'warn (them);' see n. on Q3.58; cf. Q50.45; 51.55.
8. *a reminder*: here almost meaning 'warner' (cf. Q65.10-11).
9. *record-keeper*: meaning uncertain.

89 The Dawn ✤ Al-Fajr

In the Name of God, the Merciful, the Compassionate

1 By the dawn **2** and ten nights! **3** By the even and the odd! **4** By the night when it journeys on![1]
5 (Is there) in that an oath for a person of understanding?

6 Do you[2] not see how your Lord dealt with ʿĀd,[3] **7** Iram[4] of the pillars,[5] **8** the like of which was never
created in (all) the lands, **9** and Thamūd,[6] who carved out the rock in the wādi,[7] **10** and Pharaoh, he of the
stakes,[8] **11** who (all) transgressed insolently in (their) lands, **12** and spread (too) much corruption there?
13 So your Lord poured on them a scourge of punishment. **14** Surely your Lord indeed lies in wait.[9]

15 As for the human, whenever his Lord tests him, and honors him and blesses him,[10] he says, 'My Lord
has honored me.' **16** But whenever he tests him, and restricts his provision for him, he says, 'My Lord
has humiliated me.' **17** By no means! No! You do not honor the orphan, **18** nor do you urge the feeding
of the poor, **19** yet you devour the inheritance greedily,[11] **20** and love wealth passionately.

21 By no means! When the earth is shattered with a double shattering,[12] **22** and your Lord comes, and
the angels, line after line, **23** and Gehenna[13] is brought (forth) on that Day – on that Day the human
will (finally) take heed,[14] but how will the reminder be for him?[15] **24** He will say, 'Would that I had sent

---

Q89: Following a mysterious oath, this sūra describes the punishment of earlier generations and concludes with an anticipation of final judgment. Most scholars assign Q89 to the early 'Meccan' period.

1–5 An oath

1. *By the dawn...*: i.e. 'I swear by...;' this passage is so cryptic that the reader can only guess at its meaning. The complement of the oath is also missing (cf. Q38.1; 50.1).

6–14 Punishment of earlier generations a warning

2. *you*: sing., but probably intended generally.
3. *ʿĀd*: among the many iterations of their story, see Q7.65-72.
4. *Iram*: usually taken in apposition to ʿĀd (i.e. ʿĀd, namely Iram), but sometimes read as a genitive (i.e. ʿĀd of Iram). Iram may be identical with Aram, the biblical designation for the Aramean kingdom (11th-8th cent. BCE) in southern Syria, whose capital was Damascus. It was destroyed by the Assyrians in 732 BCE.
5. *pillars*: perhaps a reference to the remains of their monumental buildings (cf. Q26.128-129).
6. *Thamūd*: for their story, see e.g. Q7.73-79.
7. *carved out the rock in the wādi*: cf. Q7.74; 26.149.
8. *he of the stakes*: meaning obscure; perhaps a reference to the remains of his monumental buildings (cf. Q7.137; 38.12).
9. *lies in wait*: to 'ambush' sinners; implying that punishment is imminent (cf. Q89.21-30 below).

15–20 Humanity's lust for wealth

10. *blesses him*: or 'confers prosperity on him.'
11. *devour the inheritance greedily*: instead of being the trustee of it (cf. Q4.2, 10).

21–30 A judgment scene

12. *a double shattering*: lit. 'a shattering, a shattering' (cf. Q69.14).
13. *Gehenna*: a name for Hell (see n. on Q2.206).
14. *take heed*: or 'remember,' 'be reminded.'
15. *how will the reminder be for him*: i.e. what use will it be then? (cf. Q44.13).

forward (righteous deeds) for my life!'[16] **25** On that Day no one will punish as He punishes, **26** and no one will bind as He binds. **27** 'You, secure one![17] **28** Return to your Lord, approving (and) approved! **29** Enter among My servants![18] **30** Enter My Garden!'[19]

16. *sent forward (righteous deeds) for my life*: which would have ensured his life in the next.
17. *You, secure one*: God now addresses the righteous person.
18. *servants*: the word 'servant' (Ar. *'abd*) also means 'slave.'
19. *Garden*: in heaven (for this imagery, see n. on Q2.25).

90 The Land ۞ Al-Balad

In the Name of God, the Merciful, the Compassionate

1 I swear by[1] this land[2] **2** – and you[3] are a lawful (resident)[4] in this land – **3** by a begetter and what he
begot![5] **4** Certainly We created the human in trouble.[6] **5** Does he think that no one has power over him?
6 He says, 'I have squandered vast wealth!'[7] **7** Does he think that no one has seen him? **8** Have We not
made two eyes for him, **9** and a tongue, and two lips? **10** And have We not guided him to the two ways?[8]
11 Yet he has not attempted the (steep) ascent.[9]

12 And what will make you[10] know what the (steep) ascent is? **13** The setting free of a slave, **14** or feeding
on a day of hunger **15** an orphan who is related, **16** or a poor person (lying) in the dust. **17** Then he has
become one of those who believe, and (who) exhort (each other) to patience, and (who) exhort (each
other) to mercy.

18 Those are the companions on the right.[11] **19** But those who disbelieve in Our signs,[12] they are the
companions on the left.[13] **20** A fire (will be) closed over them.[14]

Q90: This sūra criticizes people who take the easy path and neglect the steep ascent to virtue. Only the latter path leads to reward, while the former ends in punishment. Most scholars assign Q90 to the 'Meccan' period.

1–11 Two paths

1. *I swear by...*: for God's swearing by things, cf. Q56.75; 69.38-39; 75.1, 2; 81.15-18; 84.16-18.
2. *this land*: said to refer to the sacred area (*ḥaram*) of Mecca.
3. *you*: the Prophet.
4. *lawful (resident)*: or perhaps 'open to attack;' but the precise meaning is uncertain. (This phrase may be a later addition, as it interrupts the oath.)
5. *by a begetter and what he begot*: or 'by a father and what he fathered.'
6. *in trouble*: i.e. 'subject to trouble.'
7. *squandered vast wealth*: or 'wasted' (lit. 'destroyed'); i.e. he boasts about his ostentatious display of wealth.
8. *the two ways*: the paths of good and evil, or virtue and vice.
9. *the (steep) ascent*: or 'mountain ascent' (Ar. *'aqaba*); a metaphor for the arduous path of righteousness.

12–17 Explanation of the steep path

10. *you*: sing., but intended generally (for this phrase, cf. Q69.3; 74.27; 77.14; 82.17-18; 83.2; 86.2; 97.2; 101.3; 104.5).

18–20 Companions on the right and left

11. *companions on the right*: see Q56.8, 27-40, 90-91.
12. *signs*: or 'verses' (see n. on Q2.39).
13. *companions on the left*: see Q56.9, 41-56, 92-94.
14. *A fire (will be) closed over them*: cf. Q104.6-9.

91 The Sun ۞ Al-Shams

In the Name of God, the Merciful, the Compassionate

1 By the sun and her morning light![1] **2** By the moon when he follows her! **3** By the day when it reveals her! **4** By the night when it covers her! **5** By the sky and what[2] built it! **6** By the earth and what spread it! **7** By the self[3] and what fashioned it, **8** and instilled[4] it with its (tendency to) depravity and its (sense of) guarding (itself)![5] **9** He has prospered who purifies it, **10** and he has failed who corrupts it.

11 Thamūd[6] called (it) a lie by their insolent transgression, **12** when the most miserable (one) of them was raised up,[7] **13** and the messenger of God said to them, 'The she-camel of God and her drink!'[8] **14** But they called (him) a liar and wounded her.[9] So their Lord covered them over for their sin and leveled it.[10] **15** He was not afraid of its outcome.[11]

Q91: This sūra consists of two passages. The first is a series of contrasting oaths which culminate in the contrast between true success and failure. The second recounts the story of the people of Thamūd, who were destroyed for their evildoing. Most scholars assign Q91 to the early 'Meccan' period.

1–10 Prosperity and failure

1. *By the sun and her morning light*: i.e. 'I swear by...;' retaining the different genders helps in understanding the passage (in Arabic the sun is fem., and the moon masc.). The point of these oaths is in the contrasts (cf. Q92.1-4).
2. *what*: can only refer to God, despite the use of the impersonal pronoun.
3. *the self*: i.e. a person's 'inner self' or 'soul.'
4. *instilled*: or 'inspired' (Ar. *alhama*); the word occurs only once in the Qur'ān, but later interpreters understood *alhama* and its verbal noun *ilhām* as synonymous with the technical terms for 'inspire' (*awḥā*) and 'inspiration' (*waḥy*).
5. *guarding (itself)*: against evil, or God.

11–15 The story of Thamūd

6. *Thamūd*: for a fuller version of their story, see e.g. Q7.73-79.
7. *the most miserable (one) of them...*: usually taken to be their leader in transgression, but it probably refers to their messenger Ṣāliḥ (as the verb 'was raised up' and the following verse suggest), who was rendered 'miserable' or 'unhappy' by their rejection of him.
8. *she-camel...and her drink*: for this story, see Q26.155-156; 54.27-28.
9. *wounded her*: or perhaps 'killed her.'
10. *leveled it*: perhaps their 'city' or 'them,' but the antecedent is unclear.
11. *was not afraid of its outcome*: meaning perhaps that God had no fear of retaliation.

92 The Night ✿ Al-Layl

In the Name of God, the Merciful, the Compassionate

1 By the night[1] when it covers! **2** By the day when it reveals its splendor! **3** By what[2] created the male and the female! **4** Surely your striving is indeed (to) divided (ends). **5** As for the one who gives and guards (himself),[3] **6** and affirms[4] the best (reward), **7** We shall ease him to ease.[5] **8** But as for the one who is stingy, and considers himself independent,[6] **9** and calls the best (reward) a lie, **10** We shall ease him to hardship.[7] **11** His wealth will be of no use to him when he perishes. **12** Surely on Us (depends) the guidance[8] indeed. **13** Surely to Us indeed (belong) the last and the first.[9]

14 I have warned you of a flaming Fire.[10] **15** Only the most miserable will burn in it: **16** the one who called (it) a lie and turned away. **17** But the one who guards (himself) will avoid it: **18** the one who gives his wealth to purify himself, **19** and (confers) no blessing on anyone (expecting) to be repaid, **20** but only seeks the face of his Lord, the Most High.[11] **21** Soon indeed he will be pleased.

Q92: This sūra, like the previous one, begins with a series of contrasting oaths which culminate in the choice between the two ways of life. It concludes with the contrasting fates of the righteous and wicked. Most scholars assign Q92 to the early 'Meccan' period.

1–13 Two paths

1. *By the night...*: i.e. 'I swear by...;' the point of these oaths is in the contrast (cf. Q91.1-8).
2. *what*: can only refer to God, despite the use of the impersonal pronoun.
3. *guards (himself)*: against evil, or God.
4. *affirms*: or 'takes as true.'
5. *ease him to ease*: or 'make it very easy for him,' referring to eschatological rewards (but cf. Q87.8).
6. *considers himself independent*: or 'free of need' (i.e. wealthy).
7. *ease him to hardship*: i.e. smooth the way to punishment for him.
8. *the guidance*: one of the most frequent terms (Ar. *al-hudā*) for revelation in general, and the Qur'ān in particular.
9. *the last and the first*: or 'the Hereafter and the former (life);' cf. Q53.25; 79.25.

14–21 Warning and promise

10. *Fire*: Ar. *nār* is the most common of the various designations for Hell.
11. *only seeks the face of his Lord...*: i.e. only desires God's favor (cf. e.g. Q2.272; 13.22; 76.9).

93 The Morning Light ۞ Al-Ḍuḥā

In the Name of God, the Merciful, the Compassionate

1 By the morning light! **2** By the night when it darkens! **3** Your Lord has not forsaken you,[1] nor does He despise you. **4** The last will indeed be better for you than the first.[2] **5** Soon indeed your Lord will give to you, and you will be pleased.

6 Did He not find you an orphan[3] and give (you) refuge? **7** Did He not find you astray and guide (you)?[4] **8** Did He not find you poor and enrich (you)?

9 As for the orphan, do not oppress (him), **10** and as for the beggar, do not repulse (him), **11** and as for the blessing of your Lord, proclaim (it).

Q93: This sūra offers the Prophet reassurance and encouragement. It is noteworthy for the light it may shed on his former life. Most scholars assign Q93 to the early 'Meccan' period.

1–5 Reassurance

1. *you*: the second person sing. is used throughout Q96, and is traditionally taken to refer to the Prophet, but Q96 could also be understood as spoken by the Prophet and intended for believers generally.
2. *the last will...be better for you than the first*: or 'the Hereafter will...be better for you than the former (life).'

6–8 God's favor in the past

3. *Did He not find you an orphan...*: these three questions are traditionally understood as addressed to the Prophet by God. If so, they are as close as we get in the Qur'ān to a biographical sketch of the his early life. But again, they could also be understood as intended for believers generally.
4. *astray...guide (you)*: the words for 'astray' (Ar. *ḍālla*) and 'guided' (*hadā*) suggest that the 'error' was not simply confusion but heterodoxy or 'theological error.'

9–11 Concluding exhortation

94 The Expanding ۞ Al-Sharḥ

In the Name of God, the Merciful, the Compassionate

1 Did We not expand your heart[1] for you, **2** and deliver you of your burden,[2] **3** which had broken your back? **4** Did We not raise your reputation[3] for you? **5** Surely with hardship (there is) ease. **6** Surely with hardship (there is) ease. **7** So when you are free,[4] work on. **8** And to your Lord set (your) desire.

Q94: Like the previous sūra (with which it may be connected), this one offers the Prophet reassurance by recounting God's past favor. Most scholars assign Q94 to the early 'Meccan' period. Its title derives from a word in the opening verse.

1. *expand your heart*: or 'open your mind' (lit. 'chest,' considered the seat of knowledge and understanding); cf. Q6.125; 20.25 (of Moses). Some commentators take it as a reference to the 'opening' of the Prophet's chest by the angels in order to cleanse his heart of sin.
2. *burden*: often taken as the burden of sins committed in his earlier life (see Q93.7; cf. Q7.157).
3. *reputation*: or 'fame' (lit. 'remembrance').
4. *free*: of difficulty.

95 The Fig ۞ Al-Ṭīn

In the Name of God, the Merciful, the Compassionate

1 By the fig and the olive! **2** By Mount Sinai![1] **3** By this secure land![2] **4** Certainly We created the human in the finest state. **5** Then We return him to the lowest of the low[3] **6** – except for those who believe and do righteous deeds. For them (there is) a reward without end.[4] **7** What will call you[5] a liar after (that) in (regard to) the Judgment?[6] **8** Is God not the most just of judges?

Q95: The point of this short sūra is not entirely clear. It seems concerned to alleviate any doubt or hesitancy the Prophet may have had about proclaiming the coming Judgment. Most scholars assign Q95 to the early 'Meccan' period.

1. *By Mount Sinai*: cf. Q52.1.
2. *this secure land*: said to designate the sacred area (or *ḥaram*) of Mecca, where bloodshed was forbidden (cf. Abraham's prayer at Q2.126).
3. *the lowest of the low*: referring to the deterioration of old age or death (cf. Q16.70; 22.5; 36.68); but see following n.
4. *except for those...*: v. 6 may be a later addition (cf. Q84.25; also 41.8; 68.3), which has the effect of shifting the original reference in v. 5 from old age or death to punishment after death.
5. *you*: sing., but probably intended generally ('one'); cf. Q82.9; 107.1.
6. *the Judgment*: or 'the religion' (i.e. Islam); the word for 'judgment' is a homonym of 'religion' (Ar. *dīn*).

96 The Clot ۞ Al-ʿAlaq

In the Name of God, the Merciful, the Compassionate

1 Recite in the name of your Lord[1] who creates, **2** creates the human from a clot.[2] **3** Recite, for your Lord[3] is the Most Generous,[4] **4** who teaches by the pen,[5] **5** teaches the human what he does not know.[6]

6 By no means! Surely the human transgresses insolently indeed,[7] **7** for he considers himself independent.[8] **8** Surely to your Lord is the return.[9]

9 Have you[10] seen the one who forbids[11] **10** a servant[12] when he prays? **11** Have you seen whether he (relies) on the guidance,[13] **12** or commands the guarding (of oneself)?[14] **13** Have you seen whether he calls (it) a lie, and turns away? **14** Does he not know that God sees? **15** By no means! If indeed he does not stop, We shall indeed seize (him) by the hair[15] – **16** (his) lying, sinful hair. **17** So let him call his cohorts! **18** We shall call the guards of Hell.[16] **19** By no means! Do not obey him, but prostrate yourself and draw near.

Q96: This sūra opens with an exhortation to recite in the name of God. It is traditionally regarded as the first revelation, though this may only be an inference from the logical priority of the command to 'recite' (a word from the same root as 'Qur'ān'). The latter half of the sūra deals with opposition to Muslim worship. Q96 takes its name from a word in the second verse. It is also known as 'Recite' (Ar. *Iqra'*) from its opening command.

1–5 Recite!

1. *Recite in the name of your Lord...*: or 'Recite: In the name of your Lord....' The word 'recite' also means 'read aloud.'
2. *from a clot*: cf. the descriptions of prenatal development at Q22.5; 23.14; 40.67; 75.38.
3. *Recite, for your Lord...*: or 'Recite: And your Lord....'
4. *Most Generous*: the superlative occurs only here (cf. Q27.40; 82.6-8).
5. *teaches by the pen*: i.e. 'by Books' (the depiction of God as a 'scribe' is noteworthy). For the association of pen and ink with revelation, see Q18.109; 31.27; 68.1.
6. *what he does not know*: i.e. revealed truth in written form (see Q2.151; 4.113; 6.91; cf. Q2.239; 55.1-4).

6–8 Insolent humanity

7. *transgresses insolently indeed*: despite the fact that he is the recipient of revealed truth; the expression is also used of Pharaoh (Q20.24; 79.17; 89.10-11), the eye (Q53.17), and the flood (Q69.11).
8. *considers himself independent*: or 'free of need' (i.e. wealthy).
9. *the return*: for judgment.

9–19 An opponent threatened

10. *you*: the Prophet, or perhaps intended generally.
11. *the one who forbids*: said to be Abū Jahl, a bitter opponent of the Prophet at Mecca, but it may be a description of a typical disbeliever.
12. *a servant*: or 'slave' (Ar. *'abd*); said to be the Prophet, but the reference may be general (i.e. 'any servant of God').
13. *the guidance*: one of the most frequent terms (Ar. *al-hudā*) for revelation in general, and the Qur'ān in particular.
14. *the guarding (of oneself)*: against evil, or God.
15. *by the hair*: lit. 'by the forelock.'
16. *guards of Hell*: or 'angels of Death' (these are the usual translations, but the meaning of this word is uncertain).

97 The Decree ✵ Al-Qadr

In the Name of God, the Merciful, the Compassionate

1 Surely We sent it down on the Night of the Decree.[1] **2** And what will make you[2] know what the Night of the Decree is? **3** The Night of the Decree is better than a thousand months. **4** The angels and the spirit[3] come down during it, by the permission of their Lord, on account of every command.[4] **5** It is (a night of) peace,[5] until the rising of the dawn.

Q97: This short sūra describes the night on which the Qur'ān was sent down. Most scholars assign Q97 to the early 'Meccan' period.

1–5 Night of the Decree

1. *We sent it down on the Night of the Decree*: or 'the Night of Destiny,' though the usual translation of Ar. *laylat al-qadr* is 'Night of Power' (cf. Q44.3, 'We sent it down on a blessed night'). The references to the descent of the Qur'ān on a single night reflect a different understanding than the traditional one, according to which the Qur'ān was 'sent down' or revealed at intervals over a period of some twenty years. Some interpreters understand this verse as referring to the descent of the Qur'ān from the highest to the lowest of the seven heavens, whence it was revealed to Muḥammad as occasion required. But there are other passages, like this one, which indicate that the Qur'ān was 'sent down' or revealed all at once (see Q2.89; 3.3, 7; 4.105; 5.48; 6.92; 8.41; 16.64; 17.106; 26.193-194; 28.86; 44.3; 46.12, 30; 76.23; cf. Q2.185, 'The month of Ramaḍān, in which the Qur'ān was sent down'). There were similarly conflicting views within Judaism about the revelation of the Torah. According to the Babylonian Talmud (Gittin 60a), some thought the Torah had been 'transmitted scroll by scroll,' others that it had been 'transmitted entire.' The 'Night of the Decree,' or the 'Night of Power' as it is usually translated, is held to be one of the last ten nights of the month of Ramaḍān.
2. *you*: sing., but intended generally (for this phrase, cf. Q69.3; 74.27; 77.14; 82.17-18; 83.8; 86.2; 90.12; 101.3; 104.5).
3. *the spirit*: the mysterious being called 'the spirit' here (cf. Q16.102, 'the holy spirit;' 26.193, 'the trustworthy spirit') appears to be the bearer of revelation in the company of the angels (see n. on Q16.2). Some interpreters identify 'the spirit' with the angel Gabriel (see n. on Q2.97).
4. *on account of every command*: or 'with regard to every matter;' however, the exact sense of this phrase (Ar. *min kulli amrin*) is obscure (cf. Q44.4).
5. *peace*: Ar. *salām* connotes 'submission' (*islām*) to God.

98 The Clear Sign ✾ Al-Bayyina

In the Name of God, the Merciful, the Compassionate

1 Those who disbelieve among the People of the Book, and the idolaters,[1] were not (to be) set free until the clear sign had come to them[2] **2** – a messenger from God,[3] reciting[4] purified pages,[5] **3** in which (there are) true books.[6] **4** Those who were given the Book did not become divided until after the clear sign had come to them.[7] **5** They were commanded only to serve[8] God, devoting (their) religion to Him,[9] (being) Ḥanīfs,[10] and to observe the prayer and give the alms.[11] That is the right religion.

6 Surely those who disbelieve among the People of the Book, and the idolaters, will be in the Fire of Gehenna,[12] there to remain. Those – they are the worst of creation. **7** Surely those who believe and do righteous deeds, those – they are the best of creation. **8** Their payment is with their Lord – Gardens of Eden[13] through which rivers flow, there to remain forever. God is pleased with them, and they are pleased with Him. That is for whoever fears his Lord.

Q98: This sūra explains the cause of religious divisions, and then concludes with the fate awaiting believers and disbelievers. Most scholars assign Q98 to the 'Medinan' period. Its title is taken from the reference in the first verse to 'the clear sign' or 'clear proof' – none other than the Prophet himself.

1–5 The clear sign

1. *the idolaters*: or 'the ones who associate (other gods with God).'
2. *were not (to be) set free until the clear sign had come to them*: i.e. Jews, Christians, and pagans were not to be abandoned until they had had the opportunity to believe, once the 'the clear sign' or 'proof' had been presented to them.
3. *messenger from God*: the Prophet; here in apposition with 'the clear sign' (cf. Q11.17).
4. *reciting*: or 'reading aloud'
5. *purified pages*: the word 'pages' (lit. 'leaves' or 'sheets,' Ar. *ṣuḥuf*) may refer to the heavenly archetype or 'mother of the Book' (Q13.39; 43.4; cf. Q56.78, 'hidden Book;' 85.22, 'guarded Tablet'), but elsewhere the word occurs in connection with the Qur'ān (Q80.13), the revelation to Abraham and Moses (Q53.36-37; 87.18-19; cf. Q20.133), and the 'record' of a person's deeds (Q74.52; 81.10).
6. *true books*: or 'eternal writings.'
7. *did not become divided until after the clear sign had come to them*: for this idea, see e.g. Q3.19, 105; 6.159; 23.53; 42.13-14.
8. *serve*: or 'worship.'
9. *devoting (their) religion to Him*: i.e. serving God alone.
10. *Ḥanīfs*: or perhaps 'Gentiles' (Ar. *ḥunafā'*), like Abraham (see n. on Q2.135; cf. Q22.31).
11. *observe the prayer and give the alms*: i.e. *ṣalāt*, the ritual prayer, and *zakāt*, a kind of tithe required for the benefit of the poor, as well as other purposes.

6–8 Fate of believers and disbelievers

12. *Gehenna*: here almost synonymous with 'the Fire,' the most common of all the names for Hell (see n. on Q2.206).
13. *Gardens of Eden*: in heaven (for this imagery, see n. on Q2.25).

99 THE EARTHQUAKE ۞ AL-ZALZALA

In the Name of God, the Merciful, the Compassionate

1 When the earth is shaken with her shaking,[1] **2** and the earth brings forth her burdens,[2] **3** and a person says, 'What is (the matter) with her?'**4** On that Day she will proclaim her news, **5** because your Lord has inspired her (with it).[3] **6** On that Day the people will come forth separately to be shown their deeds. **7** Whoever has done a speck's weight of good will see it, **8** and whoever has done a speck's weight of evil will see it.

Q99: This short sūra describes 'the earthquake' on the Day of Resurrection, when the dead will come forth from the grave for judgment. While most modern scholars assign Q99 to the early 'Meccan' period, most traditional scholars consider it 'Medinan' (including the Cairo edition).

1. *shaken with her shaking*: i.e. 'utterly' or 'violently shaken;' cf. Q22.1. (The Arabic word for 'earth' is fem., and retaining the gender helps in understanding this passage.)
2. *her burdens*: the dead.
3. *inspired her...*: the technical term 'to inspire' (Ar. *awḥā*) is here used to describe God's prompting of the earth to speak on the Last Day.

100 The Runners ۞ Al-ʿĀdiyāt

In the Name of God, the Merciful, the Compassionate

1 By the runners panting,[1] **2** and the strikers of fire, **3** and the chargers at dawn, **4** when they kick up a (cloud of) dust, **5** and pierce through the midst of it all together! **6** Surely the human is indeed an ingrate to his Lord, **7** and surely he[2] is indeed a witness to that, **8** and surely he is indeed harsh in (his) love for (worldly) goods.[3] **9** Does he not know? When what is in the graves is ransacked,[4] **10** and what is in the hearts[5] is extracted **11** – surely on that Day their Lord will indeed be aware of them.

Q100: This sūra begins with a series of oaths leading up to a pronouncement decrying people's ingratitude to God and lust for wealth. The threat of resurrection and judgment serves as a stark warning. Most scholars assign Q100 to the 'Meccan' period. Its title comes from its first word.

1. *By the runners panting...*: i.e. 'I swear by...;' the first five verses contain fem. plur. participles and verbs, which are usually said to refer to warhorses, but they are so cryptic that their precise meaning can only be guessed at (see nn. 3 and 4 below). For sūras that begin with oaths by female entities like this, see Q37.1-3; 51.1-4; 77.1-6; 79.1-5.
2. *he*: or 'He' (God).
3. *harsh in (his) love for (worldly) goods*: the imagery of the opening verses may thus refer to human rapacity when it comes to acquiring wealth.
4. *ransacked*: at the resurrection (cf. Q82.4); perhaps picking up on the imagery of the opening verses.
5. *hearts*: lit. 'chests,' considered the seat of knowledge and understanding.

101 The Striking ❁ Al-Qāriʿa

In the Name of God, the Merciful, the Compassionate

1 The striking![1] **2** What is the striking? **3** And what will make you[2] know what the striking is? **4** The Day
when the people will be like scattered moths, **5** and the mountains will be like (tufts of) wool. **6** As for
the one whose scales are heavy,[3] **7** he will be in a pleasing life, **8** but as for the one whose scales are light,
9 his mother will be Hāwiya.[4] **10** And what will make you know what she is? **11** A scorching Fire!

Q101: This sūra, assigned by most scholars to the early 'Meccan' period, vividly describes an event of the Last Day called 'the striking.'

1. *The striking*: see Q69.4, where it refers to the punishment in history of the peoples of Thamūd and 'Ād; here it is clearly eschatological (cf. Q13.31).
2. *you*: sing., but intended generally (for this phrase, cf. Q69.3; 74.27; 77.14; 82.17-18; 83.8; 86.2; 90.12; 97.2; 104.5).
3. *scales are heavy*: good deeds are 'heavier' than evil deeds (see Q18.105).
4. *Hāwiya*: meaning uncertain, but the final verse explains it as another name for Hell.

102 Rivalry ❁ Al-Takāthur

In the Name of God, the Merciful, the Compassionate

1 Rivalry[1] diverts you, **2** until you visit the graves.[2] **3** By no means! Soon you will know! **4** Once again,
by no means! Soon you will know! **5** By no means! If (only) you knew (now) with the knowledge of
certainty:[3] **6** you will indeed see the Furnace.[4] **7** Once again, you will indeed see it with the eye of
certainty. **8** Then, on that Day, you will indeed be asked about (what) bliss (is).[5]

Q102: This sūra, assigned by most scholars to the early 'Meccan' period, condemns the 'rivalry' or 'competition' among people for wealth and status.

1. *Rivalry*: i.e. the competitive desire to increase one's wealth and status.
2. *visit the graves*: i.e. die.
3. *certainty*: lit. 'the certainty;' referring to death or judgment (cf. Q15.99; 74.46-47).
4. *the Furnace*: a name for Hell (Ar. *al-jaḥīm*).
5. *(what) bliss (is)*: intended with bitter sarcasm.

103 The Afternoon ۞ Al-ʿAṣr

In the Name of God, the Merciful, the Compassionate

1 By the afternoon![1] **2** Surely the human is indeed in (a state of) loss[2] **3** – except for those who believe and do righteous deeds, and exhort (each other) in truth, and exhort (each other) in patience.

Q103: This short pronouncement declares the impoverished state of human existence. The final verse may be a later addition. Most scholars assign Q103 to the early 'Meccan' period.

1. *the afternoon*: or 'the decline of the day;' an image consistent with the idea of 'loss.'
2. *in (a state of) loss*: or 'in (danger of) loss.'

104 The Slanderer ❁ Al-Humaza

In the Name of God, the Merciful, the Compassionate

1 Woe to every slanderer, fault finder, **2** who accumulates wealth and counts it over and over![1] **3** He thinks that his wealth will make him last. **4** By no means! Indeed He will be tossed into al-Ḥuṭama.[2] **5** And what will make you[3] know what al-Ḥuṭama is? **6** The Fire of God ignited, **7** which rises up to the hearts. **8** Surely it (will be) closed over them **9** in extended columns (of flame).[4]

Q104: This sūra attacks wealthy critics of the Prophet and his followers. It is assigned by most scholars to the early 'Meccan' period.

1. *counts it over and over*: i.e. hoards it for himself.
2. *al-Ḥuṭama*: meaning uncertain (the word occurs only here in the Qur'ān); it is sometimes taken as a proper name, and translated as 'the Crusher,' 'the Smasher' etc.
3. *you*: sing., but intended generally (for this phrase, cf. Q69.3; 74.27; 77.14; 82.17-18; 83.8; 86.2; 90.12; 97.2; 101.3).
4. *closed over them in extended columns (of flame)*: the image is of an arched vault supported by columns.

105 The Elephant ۞ Al-Fīl

In the Name of God, the Merciful, the Compassionate

1 Have you[1] not seen how your Lord did with the companions of the elephant?[2] **2** Did He not make their plot go astray? **3** He sent against them birds in flocks[3] **4** – (which)[4] were pelting them with stones of baked clay[5] – **5** and He made them like chewed-up husks (of straw).

Q105: This sūra, assigned by most scholars to the early 'Meccan' period, is said to refer to an attack on Mecca by Abraha, the Christian Abyssinian ruler of Yemen, sometime between 540 and 547 CE (i.e. two or three decades before the traditional date of Muḥammad's birth).

1. *you*: the Prophet, or perhaps intended generally ('one').
2. *companions of the elephant*: an elephant is said to have been part of Abraha's army.
3. *flocks*: meaning uncertain (Ar. *abābīl*).
4. *(which)*: the subject of the verb is fem. sing., though the preceding 'birds' is masc. plur.
5. *baked clay*: meaning uncertain (Ar. *sijjīl*).

106 Quraysh ❁ Quraysh

In the Name of God, the Merciful, the Compassionate

1 For the uniting[1] of Quraysh,[2] **2** for their uniting for the caravan of the winter and the summer:[3] **3** Let them serve[4] the Lord of this House,[5] **4** who has fed them on account of (their) hunger, **5** and secured them on account of (their) fear.

Q106: This sūra is an appeal to the Quraysh to worship God in gratitude for his benefits. Most scholars assign Q106 to the early 'Meccan' period. It is sometimes joined to 'The Elephant' (Q105) to produce a single sūra.

1. *uniting*: may simply mean 'for the general harmony of the Meccans,' or (if connected with the previous sūra) it may state the purpose of the defeat of the 'companions of the elephant.'
2. *Quraysh*: said to be the main tribe inhabiting Mecca, but they are only mentioned here in the entire Qur'ān.
3. *caravan of the winter and the summer*: it is said that Mecca was a trading center, and that the winter caravan went south to the Yemen and the summer caravan went north to Syria. Both claims are open to question.
4. *serve*: or 'worship.'
5. *Lord of this House*: i.e. the deity worshipped in the Ka'ba or 'Sacred House' (see n. on Q5.95).

107 Assistance ✵ Al-Mā'ūn

In the Name of God, the Merciful, the Compassionate

1 Have you[1] seen the one who calls the Judgment[2] a lie? **2** That is the one who shoves away the orphan,
3 and does not urge (people) to the feeding of the poor.

4 Woe to the ones who pray, **5** who – they are heedless of their prayers, **6** who – they (only) make a show,
7 and withhold assistance![3]

Q107: This sūra links neglect of the poor to denial of the Judgment, before turning to condemn false piety. Most scholars assign Q107 to the early 'Meccan' period. Its title comes from the last word in the final verse.

1–3 Denial of judgment the source of misconduct

1. *you*: the Prophet, or perhaps intended generally ('one').
2. *the Judgment*: or 'the religion' (i.e. Islam); the word for 'judgment' is a homonym of 'religion' (Ar. *dīn*).

4–7 False piety

3. *assistance*: Ar. *mā'ūn* occurs only once in the Qur'ān and is a word of uncertain meaning. It may be related to the word for 'refuge' in Hebrew (*mā'ōn*). It is traditionally understood as referring to almsgiving or *zakāt*, but other suggested meanings are more general (e.g. 'help,' 'comfort,' 'kindness' etc.).

108 Abundance ✿ Al-Kawthar

In the Name of God, the Merciful, the Compassionate

1 Surely We have given you[1] the abundance.[2] **2** So pray to your Lord and sacrifice.[3] **3** Surely your hater – he is the one cut off![4]

Q108: This sūra offers the Prophet encouragement after insult. Most scholars assign Q108 to the early 'Meccan' period. Its title comes from a word in the opening verse.

1. *you*: the Prophet.
2. *the abundance*: some take this as a reference to followers and wealth (see n. 4 below), others as the name of a river in Paradise. But perhaps the 'abundance of revelation' or the Qur'ān is meant.
3. *sacrifice*: this is the only occurrence in the Qur'ān of the verb 'to sacrifice' (Ar. *naḥara*), here in the form of an imperative to the Prophet (*inḥar*). Animal sacrifice was one of the rituals of the Ḥajj.
4. *the one cut off*: lit. 'the mutilated one,' or 'the one having its tail cut off' (Ar. *al-abtar*), referring to an animal. It is said to be a reply to an opponent ('your hater') who had mocked the Prophet for not having a son.

109 The Disbelievers ۞ Al-Kāfirūn

In the Name of God, the Merciful, the Compassionate

1 Say:[1] 'You disbelievers! **2** I do not serve what you serve,[2] **3** and you are not serving what I serve. **4** I am not serving what you have served, **5** and you are not serving what I serve. **6** To you your religion and to me my religion.'[3]

Q109: This sūra, which is not rhymed, declares the Prophet's complete break with the disbelievers. Most scholars assign Q109 to the early 'Meccan' period.

1. *Say*: on this form of address, see n. on Q2.80 (four other sūras begin with this imperative, see Q72 and Q112-114).
2. *serve*: or 'worship.'
3. *To you your religion and to me my religion*: or 'You have your religion and I have my religion' (cf. Q2.139-141; 28.55; 42.15).

110 HELP ۞ AL-NAṢR

In the Name of God, the Merciful, the Compassionate

1 When the help of God comes, and the victory,[1] **2** and you[2] see the people entering into the religion of God in crowds, **3** glorify your Lord with praise, and ask forgiveness from Him. Surely He turns (in forgiveness).

Q110: This sūra foresees the coming of triumph, which many interpret as a reference to the conquest of Mecca. For that reason most scholars assign Q110 to the 'Medinan' period. The Cairo edition considers it the last sūra to be revealed.

1. *the victory*: lit. 'the opening;' some take this as a reference to the conquest of Mecca (see n. on Q48.1), but at Q32.28-29 the word appears to refer to the Day of Judgment (cf. Q7.89, Shu'ayb; 26.118, Noah).
2. *you*: the Prophet.

111 The Fiber ✲ Al-Masad

In the Name of God, the Merciful, the Compassionate

1 The hands of Abū Lahab[1] have perished,[2] and he has perished. **2** His wealth and what he has earned were[3] of no use to him. **3** He will burn in a flaming Fire,[4] **4** and his wife (will be) the carrier of the firewood,[5] **5** with a rope of fiber around her neck.

Q111: This sūra is usually taken as a curse upon the Prophet's uncle, who is said to have opposed him at Mecca. For that reason most scholars assign Q111 to the 'Meccan' period. It is also named 'Lahab' (*al-Lahab*) and 'Perished' (*Tabbat*).

1. *Abū Lahab*: or 'Father of Flame;' said to refer to the Prophet's uncle, 'Abd al-'Uzzā. This is the only instance in the Qur'ān where an opponent is denounced by name. However, since it is a clearly nickname, it may be a derogatory designation for any disbeliever doomed to 'the Fire.'
2. *perished*: both verbs are translated here as statements (in accord with v. 2, which is also in the form of a statement), but they are usually taken as expressing a curse: 'May the hands of Abū Lahab perish! And may he perish!'
3. *were*: or 'will be.'
4. *flaming Fire*: lit. 'fire of flame' (whence his nickname).
5. *and his wife (will be) the carrier of the firewood*: or 'and his wife (too), the carrier of the firewood.'

112 Devotion ۞ Al-Ikhlāṣ

In the Name of God, the Merciful, the Compassionate

1 Say:[1] 'He is God. One![2] **2** God the Eternal![3] **3** He has not begotten and was not begotten,[4] **4** and He has no equal.[5] None!'

Q112: This sūra, assigned by most scholars to the early 'Meccan' period, is distinct for having as its title a word which does not occur in the sūra itself. The title alludes to the basic tenet of 'devoting one's religion to God exclusively' (see Q4.146; 7.29 etc.). The sūra is also known as 'The Unity' (*al-Tawḥīd*), from its emphasis on the oneness and uniqueness of God. Some have read it as directed against the Christian doctrine of the 'divine sonship' of Jesus; others see it as denying the 'pagan' belief that their goddesses were the 'daughters of God.' The liturgical ring of the sūra suggests that it may have been intended for repetition.

1. *Say*: on this form of address, see n. on Q2.80 (four other sūras begin with this imperative, see Q72, Q109, and Q113-114). The early codices (Ar. *maṣāḥif*) of Ibn Mas'ūd and Ubayy are said to have lacked *qul* ('say!').
2. *One*: the unusual use of Ar. *aḥad* (instead of *wāḥid*; cf. Q6.19; 12.39; 13.16; 14.48; 39.4) may recall Hebr. *eḥād* (cf. Deuteronomy 6.4: 'Hear, O Israel: The LORD our God, the LORD is One!'). Notice how the repetition of *aḥad* ('one'/'none') as the rhyme word in the first and last verse has the neat effect of en/closure.
3. *the Eternal*: the meaning of Ar. *al-ṣamad*, which occurs only here, is uncertain. It may be a cognate of Ar. *ṣamda* ('rock'); cf. the descriptions of God as 'Rock' in the Bible (e.g. Psalm 18.2).
4. *He has not begotten and was not begotten*: see Q37.152; cf. Q2.116; 6.101; 17.111; 72.3. This looks like a denial of the Nicean (325 CE) creedal formulation about Jesus, as 'the only begotten Son of God, begotten of his Father before all worlds, God of God, Light of Light, very God of very God, begotten, not made, being of one substance (Gk. *homoousios*) with the Father.'
5. *equal*: Ar. *kufuwan* ('equal,' 'peer,' 'one of equal standing') occurs only here.

113 The Daybreak ۞ Al-Falaq

In the Name of God, the Merciful, the Compassionate

1 Say:[1] 'I take refuge with the Lord of the daybreak,[2] **2** from the evil of what He has created,[3] **3** and from the evil of darkness when it looms, **4** and from the evil of the women who blow on knots,[4] **5** and from the evil of an envier when he envies.'

Q113: The final two sūras of the Qur'ān, known as the 'sūras of taking refuge,' are apotropaic formulae to ward off magic (Q113) and evil suggestions (Q114). The practice of 'taking refuge with God' is referred to often in the Qur'ān (see Q2.67; 7.200; 11.47; 12.23; 16.98; 19.18; 23.97-98; 41.36 etc.). Most scholars assign Q113 to the 'Meccan' period. Both Q113 and Q114 are reported to have been absent from the early codex (Ar. *muṣḥaf*) of Ibn Mas'ūd.

1. *Say*: on this form of address, see n. on Q2.80 (four other sūras begin with this imperative, see Q72, Q109, Q112, and Q114).
2. *daybreak*: Ar. *falaq* occurs only here (cf. Q6.96).
3. *from the evil of what He has created*: God creates evil as well as good (cf. Isaiah 45.7, for the same notion).
4. *women who blow on knots*: use of knots in magic was common, and the women (perhaps 'witches') should be understood as casting a spell.

114 The People ۞ Al-Nās

In the Name of God, the Merciful, the Compassionate

1 Say:[1] 'I take refuge with the Lord of the people,[2] **2** King of the people, **3** God[3] of the people,
4 from the evil of the whispering one,[4] the slinking one,[5] **5** who whispers in the hearts[6] of the people,
6 of the jinn and the people.'[7]

Q114: This and the preceding sūra are known as the 'sūras of taking refuge.' They are apotropaic formulae to ward off magic (Q113) and evil suggestions (Q114). The practice of 'taking refuge with God' is referred to often in the Qur'ān (see Q2.67; 7.200; 11.47; 12.23; 16.98; 19.18; 23.97-98; 41.36 etc.). Most scholars assign Q114 to the 'Meccan' period. Both Q113 and Q114 are reported to have been absent from the early codex (Ar. *muṣḥaf*) of Ibn Mas'ūd.

1. *Say*: on this form of address, see n. on Q2.80 (four other sūras begin with this imperative, see Q72, Q109, and Q112-113).
2. *the people*: or 'all humanity.'
3. *God*: here Ar. *ilāh*, not *allāh*.
4. *the whispering one*: usually taken as Satan (see Q7.20; 20.120; cf. Q22.52; 50.16).
5. *the slinking one*: or 'the stealthy one' (cf. Q81.15).
6. *hearts*: lit. 'chests,' considered the seat of knowledge and understanding.
7. *of the jinn and the people*: for the 'jinn,' see n. on Q6.100; cf. Q6.112.

Index to the Qur'ān

Aaron (*Hārūn*)

brother and assistant of Moses, 7.142; 10.75, 87; 20.29-34, 90-94; 21.48; 23.45; 25.35; 26.13; 28.34-35; 37.114-120; a prophet, 4.163; 6.84; 19.53; family of, 2.248; sister of, 19.28; Lord of, 7.122; 20.70; 26.48

Abel *see* Adam, two sons of

ablutions *see* washing

Abraham (*Ibrāhīm*)

abandons idolatry, 6.74-84; 21.51-71; 26.69-102; 29.16-25; 37.83-101; 43.26-28; 60.4; abandons his father, 9.114; 19.41-49; visited by angels, 11.69-76; 15.51-60; 29.31-32; 51.24-34; sacrifice of son, 37.102-113; religion of, a Ḥanīf and Muslim, 2.130-135; 3.67, 95; 4.125; 6.161; 16.120-123; 22.78; builds/purifies God's House, with Ishmael, 2.125-129; 3.96-97; 22.26-31; not a Jew or Christian, 2.140; 3.65-68; God took him as a friend, 4.125; community of, 2.134, 139-141; pages of, 53.36-37; 87.19; prayer of, 14.35-41 (and title); also 2.124 (an *imām*), 136, 258; 3.33, 84; 4.54, 163; 9.70; 12.6, 38; 19.58; 22.43; 33.7; 38.45; 42.13; 57.26

abrogation *see* cancelation

Abū Lahab

111.1

acacia trees

in Paradise, 56.29

'Ād

people to whom Hūd was sent, 7.65-72; 11.50-60; 26.123-40; 46.21-26; 54.18-21; 69.4-8; also 7.74; 9.70; 14.9; 22.42; 29.38; 38.12; 40.31; 41.13, 15; 50.13; 51.41-42; 53.50; 89.6-7

Adam (*Ādam*)

God made him 'ruler on earth' and taught him 'all the names,' 2.30-33; worshipped by angels, except Iblīs, 2.34; 7.11; 15.28-31 (not named); 17.61; 18.50; 20.116; 38.71-74 (not named); eats from forbidden tree and expelled from Garden, 2.35-39; 7.19-25; 20.120-124; two sons of (not named), 5.27-31; descendants of Adam ('sons of Adam'), 7.26, 27, 31, 35; 17.70; 36.60-61; God's covenant with the 'sons of Adam,' 7.172-174; creation of first human, 6.98; 7.189-193; 15.28; 39.6; also 3.33, 59; 19.58

adultery *see* sexual immorality

Aḥmad

Jesus predicts his coming, 61.6

Alexander the Great *see* Dhū-l-Qarnayn

alliances

between believers and emigrants, 8.72; between hypocrites and disbelievers, 4.138-139; renunciation of with disbelievers; 9.1-12; forbidden with disbelievers, 4.144; 9.23 (among family); Jews and Christians, 5.51; hypocrites, 4.88-89

alms

by itself, 7.156; 23.4; 41.7; alms and prayer together, 2.43, 83 (Israelites), 110, 177; 4.77, 162; 5.12 (Israelites), 55; 9.5, 11, 18, 71; 19.31 (Jesus), 55 (Ishmael); 21.73; 22.41, 78; 24.37, 56; 31.4; 33.33; 58.13; 73.20; 98.5; contrasted with usury, 2.276; 30.39; *see also* contributions

alteration of scripture
2.59, 75; 3.78; 4.46; 5.13, 41; 7.162; concealing of scripture, 2.42, 76-77, 140, 146, 159, 174; 3.71; 5.15; forging of scripture, 2.79

Alyasa' *see* Elisha

angels
winged messengers of God, 35.1; agents of revelation, 16.2; 37.3; 77.5; 97.4; glorify God, 7.206; 21.20; 37.166; 39.75; 40.7; bear his throne, 40.7; 69.17; intercede for believers, 40.7-9; not gods, but servants, 21.26-29; 37.149-150; 43.19; wrongly given fem. names, 53.27; recording angels, 6.61; 50.18; 82.10-12; 86.4; seize people at death, 7.37; 32.11; 50.17; present at Judgment, 37.165; 89.22; descend at God's command, 19.64; on the 'Night of Power,' 97.3-4; ascend to God, 70.4; worshipped Adam, 2.34; 7.11; 15.30; 17.61; 18.50; 20.116; 38.73; disbelievers want revelation from angels, 15.6-9; help believers in battle, 3.124; 8.9; guardians of Hell, 74.31; 96.18; *see also* Gabriel; Hārūt; Mārūt; spirit

animals
2.164; 5.4; 6.38 (form communities); 15.20; 22.18, 36; 25.49; 29.60; 31.10; 34.14; 35.28; 42.29; 45.4; 55.10; *see also* ants; apes; bees; birds; camels; elephant; fish; horses; hudhud; livestock; quails

anṣār *see* helpers

ants
27.18 (and title)

apes
sabbath-breakers turned into, 2.64; 5.60; 7.166

apostasy
warning against, 5.54; will not be pardoned, 4.137; punishable, 3.86-90; 9.74; 88.23-24; except under compulsion, 16.106

Arabic
'an Arabic Qur'ān,' 12.2; 20.113; 39.28; 41.3, 44; 42.7; 43.3; Qur'ān in 'clear Arabic,' 16.103; 26.195; also 13.37; 46.12

Arabs
unsatisfactory attitude of, 9.90, 97-100, 101-106; relations with the Prophet, 48.11-17; not true believers, 49.14-17; also 33.20

'Arafāt
2.198

arbitration
of disputes between husband and wife, 4.35

ark
cult object of the Israelites, 2.248; Moses cast into, 20.39; *see also* ship (Noah's)

armor
given by God, 16.81

atonement
in forgoing retaliation, 5.45; for breaking an oath, 5.89; for hunting in state of sanctity, 5.95; *see also* compensation; ransom

augury
7.131; 17.13; 27.47; 36.18

Ayyūb *see* Job

Āzar
Abraham's father, 6.74; *see also* Abraham

Baal (*Ba'l*)
false god, 37.125; *see also* Elijah

Babylon (*Bābil*)
2.102

Badr
God's help at the battle of, 3.123; also 3.13; 8.7-17, 42-44

Be!
God's creative word, 2.117; 3.47, 59; 6.73; 16.40; 19.35; 36.82; 40.68

Becca (*Bakka*)
'first House' founded at, 3.96

bees
inspired by God, 16.68 (and title)

behavior *see* social etiquette

belief (selected references)
2.3, 285; 4.136; 7.158; 9.2; 10.9; 30.56; 33.22; 42.52; 48.4; 49.7, 14; 52.21; 58.22; 59.9-10; 74.31; *see also* believers

believers (selected references)
duties and character of, 4.135; 5.8, 35; 9.71, 123; 22.77-78; 23.1-9, 57-61 (and title); 27.2-3; 32.15-16; 33.41-42; 48.29; 59.18-19; rewards of, 2.25; 5.9; 6.48; 8.1-4; 9.72, 111; 13.28-29; 22.23; 32.17; 37.40-49; 38.49-55; 44.51-57; 52.17-28; 55.46-78; 56.10-40; 57.12, 19-21; 65.11; 78.31-36; 98.8; warnings about disbelief, 3.100, 102-106; 5.57-61; 57.16; 63.9-11; 64.14-17; 66.6, 8; believers to be tested, 29.2-6; belief only by God's permission, 10.100

birds
form communities, 6.38; their ability to fly a sign, 16.79; 67.19; their praise a sign, 21.79; 24.41; 34.10; 38.19; Abraham's sacrifice of, 2.260; their language known to Solomon, part of his army, 27.16, 20; clay birds brought to life by Jesus, 3.49; 5.110; sent by God against the 'companions of the elephant,' 105.3; *see also* augury; hudhud

blood
forbidden as food, 2.173; 5.3; 6.145; 16.115; plague on Egypt, 7.133; bloodshed prohibited, 2.84; angels predict that humans will shed blood, 2.30; fake blood on Joseph's shirt, 12.18; blood relations, 8.75; 25.54; 33.6; also 16.66; 22.37

Book (selected references)
referring to the Qur'ān, 2.2; 3.3, 7; 5.48; 6.92, 155; 11.1; 12.1; 13.1; 14.1; 15.1; 18.1; 19.16, 41, 51, 54, 56; 31.1; 32.1; 40.2; 41.3; 43.2; 44.2; 45.2; 46.2; referring to the Torah, 3.48 (Jesus); 3.187 (Jews); 5.110 (Jesus); 6.154 (Moses); 13.36; 19.12 (John), 30 (Jesus); 23.49 (Moses); 29.27 (Abraham's descendants); 37.117 (Moses and Aaron); 52.2-3(?); referring to the Torah and Gospel, 3.48 (Jesus); 5.110; 19.30(?); referring to the heavenly archetype, 13.39; 43.4; 56.78(?); referring to the heavenly record of deeds, 18.49; 23.62; 69.19, 25; 84.7, 10; referring to the heavenly book of destiny, 6.38, 59; 9.36 ('Book of God'); 10.61; 11.6; 13.38; 22.70; 57.22; *see also* Gospel; pages; Psalms; Qur'ān; Tablet(s); Torah

Book, People of the
appealed to, 3.64-68; 4.171; 5.67-69, 77; warning to, 3.98-99; warning about, 2.104-110; 5.57-66; diatribe against, 3.69-85, 98-99; 4.44-57, 153-162, 171-173; 5.12-19, 59; believers among, 3.113-117, 199; 28.52-55; disbelievers among, 98.1; fighting against, 9.29-35; 33.26-27; expulsion of, 59.2-4; are

clouds
one of God's signs, 2.164; 7.57; 13.12; 24.43; 30.48; 35.9; 56.69; 78.14; overshadowed Israel, 2.57; 7.160; God will come in the shadow of, 2.210; will be split on Last Day, 25.25; mountains will appear like on Last Day, 27.88; disbelievers will mistake the falling sky for on Last Day, 52.44

commerce
by ship, 16.14; 17.66; permissible during pilgrimage, 2.198; measures to be just, 17.35; *see also* trading

Compassionate, the (*al-Raḥīm*)
attribute of God, 1.1 (and *basmala*), 3; 2.37, 54, 128, 160, 163; 7.151; 9.104, 118; 10.107; 12.64, 92, 98; 15.49; 21.83; 23.109, 118; 26.9, 68, 104, 121, 140, 159, 175, 191, 217; 27.30; 28.17; 30.5; 32.6; 34.2; 36.5; 39.53; 41.2; 42.5; 44.42; 46.8; 52.28; 59.22

compensation
for unintentional homicide, 4.92; none accepted at Judgment, 2.48, 123; 6.70; 31.33; *see also* atonement; ransom

constellations *see* stars

contributions
to God's cause, 2.195, 254, 261-262, 267, 270, 272, 274; 3.92, 180; 4.37-39; 34.39; to family, orphans, the poor etc., 2.215, 273; voluntary contributions (*ṣadaqāt*), 2.196 (in place of pilgrimage), 263, 271, 276; 4.114; 9.58-59, 60 (for the poor, slaves, debtors etc.), 79, 103-104 (as purification); 58.12 (before an audience with the Prophet); as marriage gifts to women, 4.4; *see also* alms

coral
55.22, 58

couch
earth created as a, 2.22; believers recline on in Paradise, 15.47; 18.31; 36.56; 37.44; 52.20; 55.54; 56.15, 34; 76.13; 83.23, 35; 88.13; also 43.34

covenant
with Adam, 20.115; with 'sons of Adam,' 7.172; with the prophets, 3.81; 33.7; with Israel, 2.83-85, 93; 3.187; 5.12; with Christians, 5.14

creation (selected references)
of the heavens and earth, 10.5-6; 13.2-3; 31.10-11; 41.9-12; in six days, 7.54; 10.3; 11.7; 25.59; 32.4; 41.9-12; 50.38; 57.4; of human(s), 4.1; 6.2; 7.11; 16.4; 22.5; 32.7-9; 35.11; 40.67; 76.2; 86.6-7; of humans and jinn, 15.26-27; 51.56; of animals, 16.5-8; 24.45; creation purposeful, 21.16; 30.8; *see also* God

crystal
Solomon's palace of, 27.44; cups of in Paradise, 76.15

customary way (*sunna*)
of God, 17.77; 33.38, 62; 35.43; 40.84; 48.23; of previous generations, 4.26; 8.38; 15.13; 18.55; 35.43

darkness
created by God, 6.1; God leads out of, 2.257; 5.16; 33.43; 57.9; 65.11; leaves disbelievers in, 2.17; 6.39, 122; 10.27; al-Ṭāghūt leads into, 2.257; Moses leads out of, 14.5; the Prophet leads out of, 14.1; Dhū-l-Nūn calls out in, 21.87; of Last Day, 80.41; evil of, 113.3; also 6.63, 97; 13.16; 24.40; 27.63; 35.20; 36.37; 39.6 ('three darknessess')

date palms
2.266; 6.99, 141; 13.4; 16.11, 67; 17.91; 18.32; 19.23, 25; 20.71; 23.19; 26.148; 36.34; 50.10; 54.20; 55.11, 68; 69.7; 80.29

daughters
prejudice against, 16.58-59; 43.17; ascribed to God, 16.57; 17.40; 53.21; God has none, 37.149, 153; 43.16; 52.39; *see also* children; sons

David (*Dāwūd*)
killed Jālūt (Goliath), 2.251; a prophet, given Psalms, 4.163; 17.55; given judgment and knowledge, 21.78; 27.15; mountains and birds join him praising God, 34.10; 38.17-20; story of the lamb and his repentance, 38.21-25; made a ruler, 38.26; cursed disbelieving Israelites, 5.78; given Solomon, 38.30; also 6.84; 34.13

day *see* night and day

death
occurs at a fixed time (*ajal*) by God's will, 3.145; 16.61; 39.42; angels summon at death, 4.97; 6.61, 93; 7.37; 8.50; 16.28, 32; 32.11 (angel of death); 47.27; 50.17-19; disbelievers' experience of death, 75.26-30; it will seem only a short time between death and resurrection, 20.103; 23.112-114; 46.35; also called 'the certainty' (*al-yaqīn*), 15.99; 74.46-47; reference to possible death of Muḥammad, 3.144

debts
rules for recording of, 2.282-283; relief for debtors, 9.60; also 4.11, 12; 52.39, 66; 68.46

Deliverance, the (*al-furqān*)
2.53, 185; 3.4; 8.29, 41 ('Day of Deliverance'); 21.48; 25.1 (and title)

demons *see* satans

Devil *see* Iblīs, Satan

Dhū-l-Kifl
a prophet, 21.85; 38.48

Dhū-l-Qarnayn
Alexander the Great(?), story of, 18.83-98

Dhū-l-Nūn
a prophet (Jonah) 21.87; 68.48

diatribe
against Jews and Christians, 2.111-121; against the Israelites, 5.70-71; against the Jews, 3.21-27, 181-189; 62.5-8; against the People of the Book, 3.69-85; 4.44-57, 153-162, 171-173; 5.12-19; against the Christian doctrine of the trinity, 5.72-77; against the disbelievers, 5.103-105; 6.25-32; 52.29-47; against the hypocrites, 4.138-149; 9.50-57, 61-70, 73-80; against the Arabs, 49.14-18

disbelievers (selected references)
a seal on their hearts, a covering over their sight, 2.7; 4.155; 6.25; 9.93; 10.74; 16.108; 17.46; 45.23; 47.16; associate other gods with God, 3.151; 6.1, 64, 94, 100, 136-137; 7.190; 13.16, 33; 14.30; 16.54; 29.65; 30.33, 35; 34.27; 40.12, 73-74; disrespect the Prophet, 6.25; 8.30; 15.6; 21.36; 25.5; 27.68; 37.35; 41.26; 44.14; 50.2-3; 52.30, 33; 68.51; stubborn, 2.6; 7.193; 26.5; 36.10; 50.24; 74.16; arrogant, 2.87; 4.172-173; 6.93; 7.36, 40, 75; 10.75; 14.21; 16.22; 23.66-67; 25.21; 29.39; 31.7; 34.32; 37.35; 38.2; 39.59-60; 40.26; 41.15; 45.8, 31; 46.20; 63.5; 71.7; 74.21-26; the Prophet's break with, 109.1-6 (and title); believers to fight them, 47.4; among the People of the Book, 98.1; punishment of, 3.10; 7.40-41; 14.29-30; 22.19-22, 72; 25.11-14; 27.5; 33.64; 36.64; 40.71-72, 76; 64.5-6; 67.6-11; *see also* idolaters

disciples
Jesus' followers and God's helpers, 3.52; 61.14; are 'Muslims,' 5.111; ask for a table from heaven, 5.112-115

divination arrows
forbidden, 5.3, 90

factions
referring to the people of Thamūd, Lot, and the Grove, 38.13; after Noah, 40.5; the Day of, 40.31-32 (people of Noah, 'Ād, and Thamūd); of Jews and Christians, 11.17; 13.36; 19.37; 23.53; 43.65; of the men of the cave, 18.12; of hostile disbelievers, 33.20, 22 (and title)

fasting
prescribed for believers in Ramaḍān, 2.183-185, 187; vowed by Mary, 19.26; as compensation, 4.92 (for unintended homicide); 5.89 (for breaking an oath), 95 (for hunting in state of sanctity); 58.4 (for using a forbidden formula of divorce)

fathers
disbelievers follow the errors of their fathers, 2.170; 5.104; 7.28, 173; 11.109; 21.52-53; 26.74- 76; 31.21; 34.43; 37.69-70; 43.23-24; disbelievers demand that their fathers be made alive, 45.25; disbelieving fathers to be treated as enemies, 9.23; 58.22; *see also* parents

fig
95.1 (and title)

fighting
for the cause of God, 2.190, 216-218, 244; 3.142; 4.71, 95; 5.35, 54; 8.39, 65, 72, 74; 9.12-14, 19-20, 24, 29-31, 36, 123; 22.39-40; 47.4; 49.15; 61.11; fighting in the sacred months, 2.217; 9.36; reluctance to fight, 2.246; 4.77; 9.38, 42-49, 86; 47.20; dying for the cause of God, 2.154; 3.157, 169, 195; 47.4-6; also 9.41, 73; 22.78; 66.9

fire
created by God, 36.80; humans ignite it, 56.71-72

Fire, the *see* Hell

fish
permissible to eat, 5.96; 16.14; 35.12; of Jonah, 37.142; 68.48; also 7.163; 18.61-63

flood
of Noah, 11.40-44; 23.27-29; 54.11-15; 69.11-12; plague against Egypt, 7.133; of 'Arim, 34.16

food, regulations concerning
forbidden: carrion, blood, pig, what is dedicated to another god, 2.173; 5.3 (with additions); 6.121, 145; 16.115; most foods permissible, 2.168-172; 3.93 (except what Israel/Jacob forbade); 5.1, 4 (including game caught by hunting dogs), 5 (also the food of the People of the Book), 87; 6.118-119, 142; 16.114; special food laws for the Jews, 3.93; 4.160; 6.146; 16.118; other lawful foods, 5.96 (fish); violation of food laws pardonable, 5.93; 6.119; also 6.143; 10.59; 16.116; *see also* camels, livestock, wine

forgiveness
of believers, 24.22; 42.37; of disbelievers, 45.14; better than retaliation, 42.37-43; *see also* repentance

Friday
'day of assembly' for prayer, business temporally suspended, 62.9-10

Furqān *see* Deliverance

Gabriel (*Jibrīl*)
mentioned by name, 2.97, 98 (with Michael); 66.4 (supports the Prophet)

gambling
forbidden, 2.219; 5.90

garden
parables about earthly gardens, 18.32-44; 68.17-33; *see also* Paradise

Garden(s) *see* Paradise

Garden of the Refuge
theophany near, 53.15

Gehenna (*Jahannam*) *see* Hell

God (selected references)
God's power and providence, 6.95-99; 7.54-58; 10.3-6; 13.2-4, 8-17; 14.32-34; 15.16-25; 16.3-18, 65-74, 78-83; 17.12; 21.30-33; 22.5-7, 61-66; 23.12-22, 78-83; 24.41-46; 25.45-62; 28.68-73; 29.19; 30.20-27, 46-54; 31.10-11, 29-32; 32.4-9; 35.1-17, 44; 36.33-44, 71-76; 37.6-11; 39.5-7, 21; 40.56-68, 79-81; 41.9-12, 37-40; 42.9-12, 27-35, 49; 45.3-13; 51.20-23, 47-50; 56.57-74; 78.6-16; 79.27-33; 88.17-20; knowledge, 6.59-60; 10.61; 11.5-6; 13.8-10; 22.70; 27.65; 58.7; benevolence, 2.268; 10.58-60; 35.3; 55.1-28; 80.24-32; the only deity, 16.51; 23.116-117; 27.59-64; 37.4-5; 38.65-66; 39.2-3, 64-66; 112.1-4; has the best names, 7.180; 17.110; 20.8; 59.24; has no son or daughter, 2.116; 6.101; 10.68; 17.111; 19.88-95; 37.149-157; 43.16, 81; 72.3; 112.3; determines a person's fate, 3.145; 45.26; 57.22; *see also* creation

gods *see* idols, false gods

Gog *see* Yājūj

gold
3.14, 91; 9.34; 43.53; bracelets of in Paradise, 18.31; 22.23; 35.33; plates and cups of in Paradise, 43.71

Goliath *see* Jālūt

Gospel (*Injīl*)
book given to Jesus, 3.3, 48, 65; 5.46, 47, 66, 68, 110; 9.111; 48.29; 57.27; predicts coming of the Prophet, 7.157

Gospel, People of the
5.47; *see also* Book, People of the; Reminder, People of the

grapes
2.266; 6.99; 13.4; 16.11, 67; 17.91; 18.32; 23.19; 36.34; 78.32; 80.28

greed
3.180-181; 4.37; 9.34-35; 47.38; 70.21

greetings *see* social etiquette

Grove, people of the
story of, 26.176-189 (Shu'ayb sent to them); also 15.78; 38.13; 50.14

guidance
Qur'ān as guidance, 2.2, 97, 159, 185; 3.138; 6.157; 7.52, 203; 9.33; 10.57; 12.111; 16.64, 89, 102; 17.94; 27.2, 76; 31.3; 39.23; 41.44; 45.20; 47.25, 32; 48.28; 53.23; 61.9; 72.13; 96.11; Torah and Gospel as guidance, 3.3-4; 5.44, 46; 6.91, 154; 7.154; 17.2; 28.43; 32.23; 40.53-54; God's House as guidance, 3.96; revelation in general as guidance, 2.16, 38, 120, 175, 185; 3.73; 4.115; 6.71, 84-90; 7.193; 16.37; 18.13, 55; 19.76; 20.47, 123; 22.8; 28.37, 50; 32.13; 34.24; 41.17; 43.24; 47.17; 92.12

Ḥajj *see* pilgrimage

Hāmān
associate of Pharaoh, 28.6, 8, 38; 29.39-40; 40.24, 36

Ḥanīf
Abraham, 2.135; 3.67, 95; 4.125; 6.79, 161; 16.120, 123; the Prophet, 10.105; 30.30; also (in plur.), 22.31; 98.5

Hārūn *see* Aaron

al-Ḥuṭama
name of Hell(?), 104.4

hypocrites (*munafiqūn*)
false believers, 4.61, 88, 138-145; 8.49; 9.64-68, 73; 29.11; 33.1, 12-13, 24, 48, 60, 73; 48.6; 57.13; 63.1-8 (and title); 66.9; 'those in whose hearts is a sickness,' 2.10; 5.52; 8.49; 9.125; 22.53; 33.12, 32, 60; 47.20, 29; 74.31; among the Arabs, 9.101

Iblīs
an angel who refused to worship Adam, 2.34; 7.11-18; 15.28-42; 17.61-65; 20.116-117; 38.71-85; 'one of the jinn', 18.50; also 26.95 (his forces); 34.20; *see also* Satan

Ibrāhīm *see* Abraham

idolaters (*mushrikūn*)
believe in God but 'associate' other gods with him, 6.22, 68, 136; 23.84-89; 29.61, 63, 65; 43.9-15; are in a state of ritual defilement and banned from the 'mosques of God,' 9.17; and 'Sacred Mosque,' 9.28; are like a spider, 29.41; not to be prayed for, 9.113; renunciation of treaty with, 9.1-17; command to fight against, 9.36; also 2.105, 135; 5.82; 10.28, 66; 22.17; 48.6; *see also* disbelievers

idolatry (selected references)
'association' of other gods with God unforgivable, 4.48, 116; also 3.64, 151; 4.36; 5.72; 6.151; 7.33, 190; 12.38; 13.36; 18.38, 110; 22.26, 31; 29.8; 31.13; 35.14; 39.64; 60.12; 72.2, 20

idols, false gods
are powerless, 7.191-198; 16.20-22; 25.3; 35.40; unable to intercede, 6.94; 10.18; 30.13; 39.3, 38; turn against their worshippers at Judgment, 10.28-29; 16.86; 18.52; 19.82; 29.25; 30.13; 35.14; 46.5-6; various gods named, 53.19-20; 71.23; some regarded as females, 16.57; 17.40; 37.149-155; are jinn or angels, 6.100; 34.40-41; are merely names, 7.71; 12.40; 53.23; *see also* daughters; al-Ṭāghūt

Idrīs
a prophet (probably Ezra, sometimes identified with Enoch), 19.56; 21.85

'ifrīt
a type of jinnī, 27.39

'Illiyyīn
a book(?), 83.18-19

Ilyās *see* Elijah

imām
'leader' or 'model,' 2.124 (Abraham); 9.12 (of disbelief); 21.73 (Isaac and Jacob); 25.74 (believers); 28.5 (people of Israel), 41 (Pharaoh and his forces); 32.24 (people of Israel); also 11.17; 46.12 (Book of Moses); 15.79; 17.71; 36.12 (record of a person's deeds)

'Imrān
father of Mary, 3.33-35 (and title); 66.12

incest
rules against, 4.22-23; 33.4

infanticide *see* children

Injīl *see* Gospel

inheritance
rules concerning, 4.7-9, 11-12, 19 (of women), 176; wills, 2.180-182, 240-241; 5.106-108; also 89.19; *see also* orphans

Jibrīl *see* Gabriel

al-Jibt
other gods, idols(?), 4.51

jinn
created from fire, 15.27; 55.15; created to serve God, 51.56; lead people astray, 41.29; Hell filled with jinn and humans, 6.128; 11.119; 32.13; 41.24; part of Solomon's forces, worked for him, 27.17, 39-40; 34.12-14; Iblīs one of them, 18.50; *'ifrīt* a type of, 27.39; listened to the Qur'ān and believed, 46.29-32; 72.1-19; messengers sent to them, 6.130; worshipped by humans, 6.100; also 55.33; *see also* possession; satans

Job (*Ayyūb*)
a prophet, 4.163; 6.84; his sufferings, 21.83-84; 38.41-44

John the Baptist (*Yaḥyā*)
his birth, 3.38-41; 19.2-15; 21.90; also 6.85

Jonah (*Yūnus*)
a prophet, 4.163; 6.86; his story, 37.139-148; 68.48-50; his people alone believed, 10.98 (and title); *see also* Dhū-l-Nūn

Joseph (*Yūsuf*)
his story, 12.3-108 (and title); also 6.84; 40.34

Judaism *see* Jews; Israel, Sons of; rabbis; synagogues

al-Jūdī
resting place of Noah's ark, 11.44

Judgment, Day of (also 'the Day,' 'the Last Day,' 'the Day of Resurrection,' 'the Hour' etc.)
comes suddenly, 6.31; 7.187; 12.107; 22.55; 43.66; 47.18; signs of, 20.105-108; 22.1-2; 36.53; 39.68; 50.20; 54.1; 56.1-7; 69.13-17; 73.14, 17-18; 74.8; 75.7-10; 77.8-13; 78.18-20; 79.6-7; 80.33-36; 81.1-14; 82.1-5; 84.1-6; descriptions of, 7.6-9; 11.103-108; 21.47; 75.12-15; 77.28-50; 78.38-40; 79.6-14; 80.33-42; 84.7-15; each will face it alone, 31.33; 82.19; date known only to God, 7.187; 79.42-44; God is judge, 1.4; 22.56; 40.20; *see also* intercession; scale

Judgment scenes
6.93-94, 128-135; 7.38-51; 14.21-23; 16.24-32, 84-89; 18.47-49, 52-53; 19.99-101; 25.17-19, 22-29; 27.82-90; 28.62-67, 74-75; 30.55-57; 34.31-33, 51-54; 37.12-34; 39.67-75; 40.10-12, 69-76; 41.19-23, 29-32, 47-48; 43.66-78; 45.27-35; 50.20-35; 57.12-15; 69.19-37; 89.21-30

Ka'ba
5.95, 97 ('Sacred House'); *see also* House, the; Mosque, the Sacred

khalīfa *see* successor

killing
4.29, 89, 92-93; 5.32; 6.137, 140; 9.5; 17.33; 60.12

king
God, 20.114; 23.116; 25.2; 59.23; 62.1; 114.1-2; Saul, 2.246-248; David, 2.251; of Egypt, 12.43, 50, 54, 72, 76; also 27.34

kingdom
of the heavens and earth, 2.107; 3.189; 5.17, 18, 40, 120; 6.74; 7.158, 185; 9.116; 24.42; 25.2; 38.10; 39.44; 42.49; 43.85; 45.27; 48.14; 57.2, 5; 64.1; 85.9; of God, 3.26; 6.73; 17.111; 22.56; 23.88; 25.26; 35.13; 36.83; 39.6; 40.16; 67.1 (and title); God gives it, 2.247; 3.26; of Abraham (and Israel), 2.258; 4.54; of Solomon, 2.102; 38.35; of David, 2.251; 38.20; of Egypt, 12.101; 43.51

manna
and quails 'sent down,' 2.57; 7.160; 20.80

marriage
forbidden with idolaters, 2.221; permitted with believers, and Jewish and Christian women, 5.5; marriage of widows, 2.234-235; marriage with female slaves, 4.3, 25; 23.6; 70.30; up to four wives, 4.3; sex in marriage, 2.223; rules against incest, 4.22-23; 33.4; various rules, 4.4 (dowries), 24-28, 127-129; 24.26, 32-33; 60.10-11 (of fugitives); the Prophet's wives, 33.6 ('mothers of believers'), 28-34, 50-52 (slaves as concubines), 53-55, 59; 66.3-5; *see also* divorce; women

martyrs
2.154; 3.140, 143, 169; 4.69, 72; 57.19

Mārūt
angel in Babylon, 2.102

al-Marwa
2.158

Mary (*Maryam*)
birth and upbringing, 3.35-44; announcement and birth of Jesus, 3.45-47; 19.16-33 (and title); slandered, 4.156; a messenger, 23.50-51; example of, 66.12; also 4.171; 21.91

Mary, son of
'son of Mary' (alone), 23.50; 43.57; 'Jesus, son of Mary', 2.87, 253; 3.45; 4.157, 171; 5.46, 78, 110, 112, 114; 19.34; 33.7; 57.27; 61.6, 14; 'the Messiah, son of Mary', 5.17, 72, 75; 9.31; *see also* Jesus

al-Masīḥ *see* Messiah, the

maysir *see* gambling

Mecca (*Makka*)
48.24

Medina *see* city, the

men
rank above women, 2.228; are responsible for them, 4.34; modest behavior for, 24.30; not to marry idolaters, 2.221; permitted with believers, and Jewish and Christian women, 5.5; marriage with widows, 2.234-235; marriage with female slaves, 4.3, 25; 23.6; 70.30; up to four wives permitted, 4.3; sex in marriage, 2.223; rules against incest, 4.22-23; 33.4; as witnesses, 2.283; 65.2; *see also* divorce; inheritance; marriage; menstruation; sexual immorality; women

menstruation
men not to have sex with women during, 2.222

Merciful, the (*al-Raḥmān*)
attribute of God, 1.1 (and *basmala*), 3; 2.163; 27.30; 41.2; 59.22; as a proper name of God, 13.30; 17.110; 19.18, 26, 44, 45, 58, 61, 69, 75, 78, 85, 87, 88, 91, 92, 93, 96; 20.5, 90, 108, 109; 21.26, 36, 42, 112; 25.26, 59, 60, 63; 26.5; 36.11, 15, 23, 52; 43.17, 19, 20, 33, 36, 45, 81; 50.33; 55.1 (and title); 67.3, 19, 20, 29; 78.37, 38

messengers
are human, 7.35, 63, 69; 10.2; 11.27; 12.109; 14.10-11; 16.43; 18.110; 21.3, 7; 23.24, 33-34; 26.154, 186; 36.15; or angels, 22.75; 35.1; no distinction among messengers, 2.136; 3.84; 4.150, 152; some preferred over others, 2.253; 27.15; Muḥammad is the messenger of God, 33.40; self-designation of the Prophet, 7.158; the Prophet similar to previous messengers, 4.163-165; 40.78; messengers speak the language of their people, 14.4; 19.97; 46.12; always face opposition, 15.10-11; 23.44; 46.35; 51.52; Satan tampers with their revelation, 22.52; as bringers of good news and warners, 4.165; 6.48; 18.56; their message, 16.36; 21.25; 23.23, 32; 71.1-3; perform miracles only by God's permission, 13.38; 40.78; *see also* prophets

mosques
2.114 (of God), 187; 9.17-18 (only believers permitted in, idolaters banned); 22.40; 72.18

mother of the Book (*umm al-kitāb*)
heavenly archetype of scripture, 3.7(?); 13.39; 43.4; *see also* Book

Mother of Towns (*umm al-qurā*)
6.92; 42.7

mothers
to be treated well for bearing and raising children, 31.14; 46.15; *see also* parents

mountain *see* Sinai

mountains
created by God, hold the earth in place, 13.3; 15.19; 16.15; 21.31; 31.10; 50.7

muhājirūn *see* emigrants

Muḥammad
3.144 ('only a messenger'); 33.40; 47.2 (and title); 48.29; *see also* Aḥmad; messengers; Prophet, the

mules
created by God for transport, 16.8

munāfiqūn *see* hypocrites

Muslim, Muslims (*Muslim, Muslimūn*)
meaning 'submitted' (to God), 2.128, 133, 136; 3.52, 102; 6.163; 7.126; 10.72, 84, 90; 11.14; 12.101; 15.2; 16.89, 102; 21.108; 27.31, 38, 42, 81, 91; 29.46; 30.43; 33.35; 39.12; 41.33; 43.69; 46.15; 48.16; 51.36; 66.5; 68.35; 72.14; meaning 'Muslim,' 3.64; 22.78; 28.53; *see also* believers; Islam

Naṣārā *see* Christians

Nasr
a god, 71.23

New Testament *see* Gospel

nicknames
forbidden, 49.11

night, blessed (*laylat mubārak*)
Qur'ān (sent down) on it, 44.3

night and day
created by God for rest and sight, 10.67; 17.12 ('two signs'); 25.47; 27.86; 28.73; 30.23; 40.61; 78.10-11; also 6.13, 96; 28.71-72

Night of the Decree (*laylat al-qadr*)
Qur'ān (sent down) on it, 97.1-3

Noah (*Nūḥ*)
a prophet, his story, 7.59-64; 10.71-73; 11.25-34; 23.23-30; 26.105-121; 37.75-82; 71.1-28 (and title); his people destroyed by a flood, 11.36-49; 25.37; 29.14-15; 54.9-15; his wife a disbeliever, 66.10; also 3.33-34; 4.163; 6.84; 7.69; 9.70; 11.89; 14.9; 17.3, 17; 19.58; 21.76-77; 22.42; 33.7; 40.5, 31; 42.13; 50.12; 51.46; 53.52; 57.26; 69.11-12

nudity
Adam and his wife realize they are naked, 7.20-22; 20.120-121; Satan stripped them of their clothing, 7.27; clothing 'sent down' to cover, 7.26

pen
3.44; 31.27; 68.1 (and title); 96.4

People of the Book *see* Book, People of the

persecution
2.191, 217; 8.39; 10.83, 85-86; 16.110; 29.10; 60.5; 85.10

Pharaoh (*Fir'awn*)
Moses (and Aaron) sent to, 7.103-137; 10.75-92; 11.96-97; 17.101-103; 20.24-36, 42-79; 26.10- 67; 28.30-42; 40.23-46; 43.46-56; 44.17-31; 51.38-40; 79.15-25; 'nine signs' to, 17.101; 27.12; plagues against, 7.130, 133-135; Israel rescued from 'house of Pharaoh,' 2.49-50; 7.141; 14.6; 44.30-31; orders Haman to build a tower, 28.38; 40.36-37; also 3.11; 8.52, 54; 28.3-6; 29.39; 38.12; 50.13; 54.41-42; 66.11 (wife of); 69.9; 73.15-16; 85.17-18; 89.10

pilgrimage (*ḥajj*)
regulations concerning, 2.196-203; 22.27-33 (and title); at time of new moon, 2.189; al-Ṣafā and al-Marwa included, 2.158; a duty to God, 3.97; hunting forbidden during, 5.1-2, 94-96; fishing permitted, 5.96; sacrifices, 22.33-36; *see also* 'umra

Pit, companions of the
85.4-8

poet
the Prophet accused of being one, 21.5; 37.36; 52.30; Prophet not one, 36.69; 37.37; 69.41; poets condemned, 26.224-226 (and title)

polygamy *see* marriage

polytheism *see* idolatry; idolaters; idols

pomegranates
6.99, 141; 55.68

poor, the
to be supported and fed, 2.83, 177, 215, 271, 273; 4.8, 36; 9.60; 17.26; 22.28; 24.22; 30.38; 69.34; 74.44; 76.8; 89.18; 90.12-16; 107.3; to receive their share of spoils, 8.41; 59.7, 8; also 2.184; 4.135; 5.89, 95; 24.32; 47.38; 58.4; 68.24; 93.8

possession
by jinn, an accusation leveled against every messenger, 51.52; against Noah, 23.25; 54.9; against Moses, 26.27; 51.39, against the Prophet, 15.6; 23.70; 37.36; 44.14; 68.51; denial of, 7.184; 34.8; 37.37; 52.29; 68.2; 81.22

prayer
only to God, 13.14; 40.60; who answers prayer, 2.186; 3.38; 6.41; 14.39; 19.4; 27.62; 40.60; other gods do not, 7.194; 13.14; 35.14; 46.5; toward Sacred Mosque, 2.144; times of, 2.238; 3.41; 6.52; 11.114; 13.15; 17.78; 18.28; 20.130; 24.36; 30.17; 32.15-16; 33.42; 48.9; 50.39-40; 76.25; Friday prayer, temporary cessation of business, 62.9-10; regulations concerning, 4.43; 5.6; 6.52; 17.110; 107.4-7; shortening of in dangerous situations, 2.239; 4.101-103; Israel commanded to pray, 2.43, 45, 83; 5.12; prophets commanded to pray, 14.40 (Abraham); 21.73 (Isaac and Jacob); 10.87; 20.14 (Moses); 19.21 (Jesus); 11.114; 17.78; 29.45; 73.20 (the Prophet); true believers observe prayer, 2.3, 110, 177, 277; 4.162; 5.55; 6.72, 92; 7.170; 8.3; 9.71; 13.22; 14.31; 22.35, 41, 78; 24.37, 56; 27.3; 30.31; 35.18, 29; 42.38; 98.5; marks of prostration on believers, 48.29; no prayer for idolaters, even if relatives, 9.113; prayer for hypocrites useless, 9.80; 63.5-6; deceptive prayer of hypocrites, 4.142; no funeral prayer for disbelievers, 9.84; People of the Book ridicule, 5.58; Satan hinders from, 5.91; also 31.17; 33.33; 58.13; *see also* intercession; prostration

81; 46.33; 50.15; parallel to human birth, 75.36-40 (and title); 80.18-22; period between death and, 2.259; 20.102-104; 23.112-115; 30.55-56; emptying of graves, 82.4; 84.3-4; 100.9

retaliation
regulations concerning, 2.178-179, 194; prescribed in the Torah, 5.45; not to exceed injury, 16.126; 42.40; also 22.39, 60

ritual, rituals
Abraham's request for, 2.128, performed at the pilgrimage, 200; assigned to each community, 22.34, 67; *see also* offerings; sacrifice

roads
placed in the earth by God, 16.15; 20.53; 21.31; 43.10; 71.19-20; road to Hell, 4.168-169; 37.23; separate roads of Jews, Christians, and Muslims, 5.48; jinn called to a straight road, 46.30; different roads of righteous and wicked, 72.11 (jinn), 16 (humans); 90.10; *see also* path, straight; way

Romans (*Rūm*)
30.2 (and title)

rubies
55.58

Sabā' *see* Sheba

Sabians (*Ṣābi'ūn*)
community of believers, along with Jews and Christians, 2.62; 5.69; 22.17 (also with Magians)

sabbath
Jewish day of rest, 4.154; 16.124; punishments for those who transgressed, 2.65; 4.47; 7.163

sacrifice
offered by Adam's sons, 5.27; Abraham's sacrifice of birds, 2.260; Abraham's sacrifice of his son, 37.102-107; sacrifice of cow by Moses, 2.67-71; sacrifice commanded, along with prayer, 108.2; name of God to be invoked over, 22.34, 36; God not fed by, 22.37; at the pilgrimage, 2.196; 48.25; also 3.183; *see also* offerings

al-Ṣafā
2.158

Sakīna
2.248; 9.26, 40; 48.4, 18, 26

ṣalāt *see* prayer

Ṣāliḥ
messenger sent to Thamūd, 7.73-79; 11.61-68; 26.141-158; 27.45-53; people of, 11.89

Salsabīl
a spring in Paradise, 76.18

al-Sāmirī
created golden calf, 20.85-96

Saqar
name of Hell(?), 54.48; 74.26, 42

Satan (*al-Shayṭān*)
provokes humans to evil, their enemy, 2.36, 168, 208, 268; 3.155; 4.38, 60, 117-120; 6.43, 142; 7.22, 27, 200; 8.48; 12.5; 16.63; 17.53, 64; 27.24; 28.15; 29.38; 35.6; 36.60; 41.36; 43.62; whispers in their hearts, 7.20; 20.120; 114.4-6; tampers with revelation to prophets, 22.52; false god, 4.117; also 2.275; 3.36, 175;

4.76, 83; 5.90; 6.68; 7.175; 8.11; 12.42, 100; 14.22; 16.98; 17.53; 18.63; 19.44; 24.21; 25.29; 31.21; 38.41; 47.25; 58.10, 19; 59.16; *see also* Iblīs; satans

satans (*shayāṭīn*)
lead humans astray, 6.71, 121; 7.27; 19.83; 22.3; 26.221-222; individually assigned to incite a person to evil, 19.83; 23.97; 41.25; 43.36; taught humans magic, 2.102; associated with Solomon, 2.102; 21.82; 38.37; eavesdrop on heavenly secrets, 15.17-18; 37.7-8; 67.5; believers take refuge with God from, 23.97-98; 'satans of the humans and jinn,' 6.112; false gods, 2.14; 7.27; Qur'ān not brought down by them, 26.210-211; 81.25; also 17.27; 19.68; *see also* Iblīs; jinn; Satan

Saul *see* Ṭālūt

scale
to be used justly, 6.152; 7.85 (Midian); 11.84; 55.9; established by God, 55.7-8; 57.25 ('sent down'); set up on Day of Judgment, 21.47; 55.7; 101.6, 8

scribes
2.282-283; 80.15

scriptures *see* Book

sea
ships on the sea a sign of God's providence, 2.164; 14.32; 16.14; 17.66; 22.65; 31.31; 42.32; 45.12; 55.24; God guides in darkness of land and sea, 6.63, 97 (by stars); 27.63; God brings safely to land from, 10.22; 17.67; Israelites passed through, 2.50; 7.138; 10.90; 20.77; 26.63; 44.24; seas will boil on Last Day, 81.6; 82.3; the two seas (fresh and salt), 18.60; 25.53; 27.61; 35.12; 55.19-20; if the sea were ink, there would not be enough to record God's words, 18.109; 31.27

seal of the prophets (*khāṭam al-nabiyyīn*)
title applied to Muḥammad, 33.40

semen
humans created from, 16.4; 18.37; 22.5; 23.13; 32.8; 35.11; 36.77; 40.63; 53.46; 75.37; 76.2; 77.20; 86.6

Seven Sleepers *see* cave, companions of the

sexual immorality (*zinā*)
forbidden, 17.32; 25.68; to be punished by confinement, 4.15-16; by flogging, 24.2; restrictions on marriage, 24.3, 26; four witnesses needed against women, 4.15; punishment for false accusations of, 24.4-10, 23

Sheba (*Sabā'*)
a land ruled by a queen, who eventually 'submits' to God, 27.22-44; a people punished for their ingratitude, 34.15-19 (and title)

ship
Noah's 'ark,' 7.64; 10.73; 11.37-44; 23.27; 26.119; 29.15; 36.41; 37.140; *see also* sea

Shu'ayb
messenger sent to Midian, 7.85-93; 11.84-95; 29.36-37; and to the people of the Grove, 26.176-189

signs (selected references)
as natural phenomena, 2.164; 3.190; 6.95-99; 7.57-58; 10.5-6, 101; 13.2-4; 16.65-67; 29.19-23; 30.46; 36.33-44; 41.37-40; 42.29, 32-35; 45.3-6; 50.20-21; as miracles, 3.13 (in battle), 49 (Jesus); 5.110, 114 (Jesus); 6.109-111; 7.73 (Ṣāliḥ), 130-137 (Moses); 15.73-77; 17.59, 101 (Moses); 20.17-24, 47, 56 (Moses); 27.10-13 (Moses); 29.24; 30.58; 40.78; 43.46-48 (Moses); 54.13-15; demand for, 6.37; 13.7; 21.5; as recited verses (or revelation), 2.106; 6.57; 8.2, 31; 11.17; 16.101; 24.1; 31.2, 7; 39.71; 41.3; 45.6, 25; 46.7; 47.14; 62.2; 65.11; 68.15; 83.13

Sijjīn
a book(?), 83.7-8

silk
18.31; 22.23; 35.33; 44.53; 76.12, 21

silver
3.14; 9.34; 43.33; vessels of in Paradise, 76.15; bracelets of in Paradise, 76.21

Sinai
'Mount Sinai,' 23.20; 95.2; 'the Mountain,' 2.63, 93; 4.154; 7.171; 19.52; 20.80; 28.29, 46; 52.1 (and title)

Sirius (*al-Shi'rā*)
the star, 53.49

sky
lowest of the seven heavens, 37.6; 41.12; erected by God as a 'dome,' 2.22; 40.64; as 'a guarded roof,' 21.32; 50.6; 51.47 ('built by hand'); 55.7; 79.27-28; 88.18; 91.5; held up by God, 22.65; stands fast by God's command, 30.25; nothing hidden from God in, 14.38; 21.4; 22.70; 27.75; 34.2; 57.4; God directs affairs from, 32.5; creation of purposeful, 21.16; 38.27; sends down water from, 2.22, 164; 6.6, 99; 8.11; 13.17; 14.32; 15.22; 16.10, 65; 20.53; 23.18; 25.48; 27.60; 29.63; 30.24; 31.10; 35.27; 39.21; 43.11; 78.14; a sign from, 26.4; punishment from, 2.59; 7.162; 8.32 (demand for); 29.34; 34.9; 52.44; 67.17; demand for the Prophet to make the sky fall, 17.92; 26.187; demand for the Prophet to ascend into, 17.93; demand for a Book from, 4.153; a table from, 5.112-115; promise of blessings from, 7.96; a ladder to, 6.35; told to stop for Noah, 11.44; did not weep for Pharaoh, 44.29; constellations in, 15.16; 25.61; 85.1; touched by jinn, 72.8; will be rolled up on Last Day, 21.104; will be split on Last Day, 25.25; 55.37; 69.16; 73.18; 77.9; 78.19; 82.1; 84.1; will fill with smoke on the Last Day, 44.10; will shake on Last Day, 52.9; will be like molten metal on Last Day, 70.8; will be stripped off on Last Day, 81.11; also 6.125; 15.14; 17.95; 18.40; 21.16; 22.15, 31; 29.22; 30.48; 36.28; 41.11; 43.84; 51.7; 86.1, 11; *see also* heavens

slander
4.112; 24.4, 23; 33.58

slaves
treatment of, 4.36; manumission of, 2.177; 4.92; 5.89; 9.60; 24.33(?); 58.3; marrying them off, 24.32-33; young female slaves not to be forced into prostitution, 24.33 (God will forgive them if they are)

sleep
created by God for rest, 25.47; 30.23; 78.9; a person's 'self' returns to God in sleep, 39.42; God does not sleep, 2.255; *see also* night and day

social etiquette
modesty for men and women, 24.30-31, 60; 33.59 (the Prophet's wives); walking in humility, 17.37; 25.63; proper greetings, 4.86; 6.54; 24.61; 25.63; domestic privacy respected, 24.27-28; household etiquette, 24.58-60; proper eating in other houses, 24.61; respect for the Prophet's houses, 33.53; 49.4-5; voices not raised in the Prophet's presence, 49.2-3; avoidance of private meetings, 58.8-10

Solomon (*Sulaymān*)
satans in his reign, 2.102; controls wind and satans/jinn, 21.78-82; 34.12-13; 38.36-40; understands language of birds, 27.15-21; horses of, 38.31-35; and Queen of Sheba, 27.22-44; his death, 34.14; also 4.163; 6.84

sons
desirable, 3.14; 9.24; 17.40; 18.46; 43.16; 68.14; preferable to daughters, 37.149, 153; 43.16; 52.39; adopted, 33.4, 37; God provides wealth and, 16.72; 17.6, 40; 26.133, 71.12; 74.13; wrongly ascribed to God, 6.100; God has none, 6.101; 21.26; 23.91; 25.2; *see also* Adam (sons of); children; daughters; Israel, Sons of

spider
parable of, 29.41 (and title)

spirit
God's spirit breathed into the first human, 15.29; 32.9; 38.72; into Mary, 21.91; 66.12; spirit sent to Mary, 19.17; the holy spirit supported Jesus, 2.87, 253; 5.110; Jesus is a spirit from God, 4.171; spirit sent down (from God), 16.2 (with angels); holy spirit brought down the Qur'ān, 16.102; trustworthy spirit brought down revelation, 26.192-195; 40.15; descended on the Night of the Decree, 97.4 (with angels); inspired the Prophet, 42.52; comes from God's command, 17.85; 40.15; 42.52; ascends to God, 70.4 (with angels); stands in line with angels on Last Day, 78.38; God's spirit supports believers, 58.22; *see also* angels; Gabriel

spoils
belong to God and the Prophet, 8.1 (and title); 59.6-10; a 'fifth' to be given to God, 8.41; future spoils promised, 48.15, 19-21

stars
created by God, to guide humans on land and sea, 6.97; 7.54; 16.12, 16; prostrate themselves before God, 22.18; 55.6; Abraham turned from worshipping, 6.76; 37.88-89; blotted out on Last Day, 77.8; 81.2; shooting stars chase satans away from heaven, 15.16-18; 37.6-10; 67.5; 72.8-9; constellations, 15.16; 25.61; 85.1 (and title); *see also* Sirius

submission *see* Islam

successor
God appoints Adam as, 2.30; David, 38.26; different peoples succeed others, 6.165; 7.69, 74, 129, 169; 10.14, 73; 19.59; 24.55; 27.62; 35.39; 43.60 (angels as successors)

ṣuḥuf *see* pages

Sulaymān *see* Solomon

sun
subject to God's command, 7.54; 14.33; 16.12; 29.61; 31.29; prostrates itself before God, 22.18; provides light, 10.5; 71.16; worship forbidden, 41.37; Abraham turned from worshipping, 6.78; worshipped by Queen of Sheba, 27.24; sun and its brilliance in oath, 91.1 (and title); brought together with the moon, shrouded on Last Day, 75.9; 81.1

sunna *see* customary way

sūra
opponents challenged to bring one, 2.23; 10.38; 11.13 ('ten'); also 9.64, 86, 124, 127; 24.1; 47.20

Suwā'
a god, 71.23

swearing *see* oaths

swearing allegiance
of the women, 60.12; under the tree, 48.18; *see also* covenant

synagogues
10.87(?); 22.40

table
Jesus' miracle of the, 5.112-115 (and title)

Tablet(s)
of Moses, 7.145, 150, 154; referring to the heavenly archetype (or Qur'ān written on one), 85.21-22

trumpet
announcing Last Day, 6.73; 18.99; 20.102; 23.101; 27.87; 36.51; 39.68; 50.20; 69.13; 74.8; 78.18

Tubba'
people of, 44.37; 50.14

Ṭuwā, wādi of
place of Moses' call, 20.12; 79.16; also 28.30

'umra
mentioned with the pilgrimage, 2.158, 196

usury
forbidden to Muslims, 2.275-281; 3.130; 30.39; practiced by Jews, though forbidden to, 4.161

'Uzayr *see* Ezra

al-'Uzzā
a goddess (or angel?), 53.19

victory
2.89; 3.147; 5.52; 8.19; 14.15; 32.28-29; 48.1 (and title), 18, 24, 27; 57.10; 61.13; 110.1

visions
of the Prophet, 17.60; 53.4-18; 81.22-25

Wadd
a god, 71.23

waiting period
before remarriage, 2.226, 228, 231, 234-235; 65.1, 4

washing
as preparation for prayer, 4.43; 5.6

water
all life created from, 21.30; 24.45; 25.54; God's throne upon, 11.7; sent down by God as rain, 2.22, 164; 6.6, 99; 8.11; 13.17; 14.32; 15.22; 16.10, 65; 20.53; 23.18; 25.48; 27.60; 29.63; 30.24; 31.10; 35.27; 39.21; 43.11; 78.14; giving of to pilgrims, 9.19; those in Hell will beg for, 7.50; *see also* flood; semen; washing

way (selected references)
of God, 2.190, 195, 218, 246, 261-262, 273; 3.169, 195; 4.74-76, 100; 6.153; 8.72, 74; 9.19-20; 22.58; 24.22; 47.4, 38; 49.15; 57.10; 61.11; 73.20; God guides to the, 4.137; leads astray from, 4.88, 143; 42.46; right way, 2.108; 5.12, 60, 77; 7.146; wrong way, 4.115; no middle way, 4.150; of al-Ṭāghūt, 4.76; of the workers of corruption, 7.142; disbelievers keep people from, 2.217; 5.167; 6.116; 7.45, 86; 8.36, 47; 9.9; 11.19; 14.3; 16.88; 22.8, 25; 31.6; 47.1, 32, 34; 58.16; People of the Book keep people from, 3.99; 4.44, 160; 9.34; hypocrites keep people from, 63.2; no way against the righteous, 9.91; ways of peace, 5.16; *see also* path, straight; roads

wills *see* inheritance

wind
controlled by God, one of his signs, 2.164; 7.57; 15.22; 25.48; 27.63; 30.46, 48; 35.9; 42.32; 45.5; sent by God against an enemy, 33.9; against 'Ād, 41.16; 46.24; 51.41; 54.19; 69.5; parables of 3.117; 14.18; 18.45; 22.31; Solomon's control of, 21.81; 34.12; 38.36

wine
there is sin in it (*khamr*), but also benefit, 2.219; an abomination, 5.90-91; wine (*sakar*) from dates and grapes permissible, 16.67; rivers of wine (*khamr*) in Paradise, 47.15